25th Gun Digest

Silver Anniversary Edition

ASSOCIATE EDITOR
Edward Dams

ART EDITOR
Jay Charles

TECHNICAL EDITORS
Bob Bell
John Lachuk
John Maynard
Maj. Geo. C. Nonte, Jr.
A. M. Wynne, Jr.

EUROPEAN EDITORS
Raymond Caranta
Derek Partridge

EDITORIAL ASSISTANT
Lilo Anderson

Edited by

John T. Amber

OUR COVERS

Two of Garcia-Beretta's best shotguns—the SO-5 (top) and the BL-4—decorate our front covers. The back cover shows two Garcia-F.I. rifles—the Sako Finnbear and, at left, the Vixen DeLuxe.

MEMBER OF THE
NATIONAL
SHOOTING
SPORTS
FOUNDATION
INC.

We believe you'll greatly enjoy James E. Serven's article, "Guns of the Western History Makers," which opens this big 25th edition. This excellent and well-illustrated story has earned the fifth bestowal of the Townsend Whelen Award.

In this special 25-year issue we take a nostalgic look at the past in several areas. We highly recommend these informative and entertaining pieces. "George Schoyen—Riflemaker Extraordinary" and "The Whitworth Rifle" plus "The National Rifle Club."

"Gun Proof in Spain" is the fourth segment of our continuing *History of Proof Marks*. The author, Lee Kennett, offers a wealth of material and identifying marks.

To learn more about Garcia-Beretta-Firearms International — and their numerous products—turn to page 30 for "Garcia Guns."

Published by The Gun Digest Company
Northfield, Illinois

Printed in U.S.A.

ISBN 0695-80128-7   Library of Congress Catalog Card Number 44-32588

IN THE BLACK

40th World Championships Need Shooter's Support

More than 1,500 shooters from 60 nations will compete in the 40th World Shooting Championships at Phoenix, Arizona, in October.

The United States will host national champions in Skeet, trap, handgun and rifle shooting under the rules of the International Shooting Union, the world governing body for international shooting.

More than 20 million American hunters and shooters are being asked to send checks to help host the international "super bowl" of shooting, much the same as the Olympic games depend on support from individuals and organizations.

Louis A. Benton, NRA director and chairman of the U. S. Olympic Shooting Committee, says, "We know that thousands of American shooters and gun clubs will wish to contribute funds to make the world championships a great success. Hunters and other recreational shooters have always been generous in supporting their favorite sport and we are counting on contributions from all over America to make this 40th championships the best ever held."

We strongly urge sportsmen—and everyone else—to send a check to the World Shooting Championship Fund, 1600 Rhode Island Ave., N. W., Washington, D. C. 20036.

Questions and Answers

We do our best to answer all letters received — though it may not be promptly — but many article-queries received would be unnecessary if the writer had read the book more carefully, or had looked in our Directory of the Arms Trade for a name and address.

Please address all communications to The Editors, P. O. Box Zero (0), Chicago, Ill. 60690, and a stamped envelope must be included carrying the writer's return address.

Gun Digest NBRSA Trophy

Wally Hart, Nescopeck, Pa., won the Gun Digest Trophy with a Grand Aggregate score of .3528 M.O.A. (minute of angle) in the Heavy Varmint rifle matches held at Fassett, Pa., in August of 1969. Wally's rifle was a Hart-barreled 308 (naturally), and this is the second time young Hart has won the award. Our warmest congratulations.

Franklin L. Orth, 1907-1970

The sudden death, on Jan. 4, 1970, of Franklin Lewis Orth, was a great loss to the country, his family and many friends, to the National Rifle Assn. and its million-plus members. Mr. Orth was executive vice president of the NRA. A strong conservationist always, and a dedicated fighter for the shooting sports, Mr. Orth will be sadly missed.

Ralph B. Sisk, 1894-1970

Time was, all through the 1930s, when 22 centerfire reloaders used Sisk bullets or none, save for a handful who could come by the short-supply Wotkyns-Morse bullets. Sisk made only .224″ and .228″ bullets until, in recent years, he added the 17s to his line—fine bullets they were, too, at prices most anyone could afford.

The shooting-handloading world owes an immense debt to Ralph Sisk. He died on Jan. 30, 1970.

Weatherby Trophy

The 1969 Weatherby Big Game Trophy went to C. J. (Mac) McElroy of Inglewood, Calif. From left, Governor John Love of Colorado makes presentation of the Weatherby award to McElroy with Roy E. Weatherby (right), creator of the well-known Weatherby rifles, lending a hand. McElroy became the 14th winner of the coveted award at a dinner held December 5 in Los Angeles.

The Right to Bear Arms

Bill Davidson's book of this title is well worth reading. It will acquaint you with a great array of factual matter that can be used effectively in refuting the distortions, the half-truths and the outright lies that our detractors utter. Davidson has been criticized by some pro-gun people for his advocacy in his book of an Identification Card system, but hindsight is, as always, easy. At the time the author wrote threats of outright registration of arms and even confiscation laws were real—or justly considered so— and the I.D. card system seemed the lesser evil. It may yet prove to be so.

The American Shooters Hall of Fame

No, there isn't one at this writing, but we'd like to see one in existence, wouldn't you? The concept, though, has many ramifications and problems —aspects of form and structure that we wouldn't want to set up on our own.

That's where you come in. Give us your ideas on how the Shooters Hall of Fame should be constituted. Should we go back in history for the names of illustrious shooters—rifle, handgun or shotgun—or shall only living men and women be eligible? If the former approach is made, what date should be selected as a cutoff point? Should such famed American shooters as Daniel Boone, Davy Crockett and the like be included? Or such shooters/writers as John Chapman, Ned Crossman, Dr. Hudson, Ned Roberts, et al, be included? What about famous gunmakers / gunsmiths / gun engravers? Such men as F.W. Freund, Wm. Billinghurst, Harry Pope, Adolph Niedner, and many more?

We promise to read your idea-letters carefully, to weigh your suggestions seriously, but we cannot, regretfully, promise to answer them—there'd be too many!

Col. Charles Askins will have a detailed article on the idea in our 26th edition, so let us hear from you quickly. Address all letters to The Editors, P.O. Box Zero, Chicago, Ill. 60690 (Dept. ASHF).

Townsend Whelen Award

Our $500 annual prize for the best contribution to firearms literature goes this year to Mr. James E. Serven for his superb "Guns of the Western History Makers," to be found in this 25th Silver Anniversary issue.

This is the fifth annual presentation of the Townsend Whelen Award. This prize—honoring the late and dedicated rifleman — goes to that article published which best meets the judges' criteria—originality of material, clarity of presentation, readability and lasting value.

Our hearty congratulations to old friend Jim Serven and, if we may say so, to our readers.

Arms Library Notes

We will be glad to handle orders for any of our titles—GUN DIGEST, HANDLOADER'S DIGEST, FISHERMEN'S DIGEST, GOLFER'S DIGEST, GUN DIGEST TREASURY, GUNS ILLUSTRATED, SINGLE SHOT RIFLES, CARTRIDGES OF THE WORLD and others. Send such orders to Gun Digest, 540 Frontage Rd., Northfield, Ill. 60093.

For any other books listed in our Arms Library (p. 453) do not write to us. Write to Ray Riling, 6844 Gorsten St., Philadelphia, Pa. 19119, or to Norm Flayderman, Squash Hollow RFD 2, New Milford, Conn. 06776, or to Rutgers Gun Books, 127 Raritan Ave., Highland Park, N. J. 08904.

Winchester's Model 21 double barreled
shotgun, here in gold-inlaid de luxe grade.

CONTENTS

GUNS OF THE WESTERN

by JAMES E. SERVEN

In addition to the Stars and Stripes, the flags of Spain, France, England, Russia, Mexico, the Confederacy and the short-lived Bear flag of California have been raised aloft in our American West. This is an area with a history that started well before Captain John Smith was being ransomed for "two guns and a grindstone" at Jamestown in the early 1600s, or the Pilgrims of Plymouth Colony were blasting away at turkey gobblers for their Thanksgiving dinners.

The first sound of gunfire in North America was in our Southwest when Francisco Vasquez de Coronado led a force of soldiers north from Mexico. He was in search of reported gold and other treasure, and his soldiers were armed with assorted weapons including some matchlock muskets and possibly a few wheel-lock guns. The year was 1540.

Soldiers have burned much of the gunpowder and written many pages of western history, but there were also the self-reliant Mountain Men, the hardy miners, pioneer settlers and early merchants of varied nationalities, the lawmen and the lawless. And, of course, there was the native—the Indian. For the western migration it was said that "The weak died along the way and the timid never started."

"In all the annals of the frontier and pioneer; of struggles that wrested the continent from its savage owners and made it a freehold of civilization, the rifle has been the instrument of destiny and the symbol of progress."

Augustus C. Buell

HISTORY MAKERS

The matchlock arquebus was used by Spanish soldier-explorers in the Southwest as early as 1540. Some early flintlocks (top) retained a matchlock serpentine in case the lock mechanism failed.

Rivalries among the Indian tribes made it somewhat less difficult for the white men to secure a foothold on the North American continent, but the task was not easy.

Following the explorations of Coronado, there came up from Mexico into the Southwest men with a mission like Father Eusebio Francisco Kino, "the padre on horseback," and the tireless Father Garces. In California there was Father Junipero Serra, a remarkable man among all pioneers in American history. With these pioneers of the cross came adventurous leaders like the borderlands frontiersman Juan Bautista de Anza.

Spanish endeavors in bringing Christianity to the native Indians and establishing settlements extended into the 1700s and 1800s. In this period the primary weapons were the sword, the lance and the flintlock musket. Horsemen used a short flintlock carbine often called an *escopeta*. The flintlock ignition, it will be remembered, extended well over 200 years into the 1800s and included miquelet, snaphaunce and other variations of flintlock form.

Spanish settlements at Santa Fe, Taos, Tubac and Tucson attracted the caravans of trade; and to San Diego, Monterey, Los Angeles, and Yerba Buena (San Francisco) came the sailing ships. Not only did the caravans of trade goods come up the trails from Mexico, but they eventually came overland from the Missouri. The ships of Spain, England, Russia and some other countries joined the Yankee vessels that spread their great sails and cut through the waters of the blue Pacific.

Thus there came to the Southwest and to the West Coast the stirrings of a great migration. Although the Pacific coastline was first dominated entirely by Spain, England soon had a foothold to the north of California; the Russians came across into Alaska and down into northern California; France claimed a great but little known section of the West extending from the Mississippi to the coasts of what are now the states of Oregon and Washington. In all this reaching out to extend the empires of Russia, England and the European countries, the skirmishing was light. Indian troubles attained no great proportions, and the flintlock muskets of the various nations were used primarily to harvest the game which was in great abundance.

The pace was stepped up at the end

Flintlock trade guns, usually called fusils, have in recent years been called "Northwest Guns." They were sold and traded at trading posts, and sometimes by Army sutlers from Arizona north into the Canadian West.

of the 18th century, and in 1803 France ceded to the United States its vast claim to western territory. Although up to this time a few rifles may have been brought in by traders, the smoothbore flintlock musket, or fusil, was the predominant firearm west of the Mississippi.

18th Century Arms

A favorite firearm of this pre-1800 period, and for 50 or more years thereafter, was a model we now call "The Northwest Gun." These light fusils were made with a full stock under the round smoothbore barrel; they had an unusually large trigger guard; and the flint firing lock was the bar action type. They could shoot either a ball or shot and were generally thought of as trade guns.

The pelts of the beaver and the hides of the buffalo were major items of trade with the Indians, and inasmuch as firearms could enable the redmen to devote more time to the harvesting of pelts and hides, traders took the calculated risk of putting guns in Indian hands.

Shortly after the Louisiana Purchase in early 1803 the United States began planning to send an exploring party through this vast new domain. Captain William Clark and Captain Meriwether Lewis were chosen for this arduous adventure. They started from St. Louis on May 14, 1804, leading a party of 43 men, and were destined not to see that city again until September of 1806. With Lewis and Clark went a few of the new U.S. rifles, Model of 1803, made at Harpers Ferry. These handsome brass-mounted guns, with their short half-length forestock, had round barrels with 54 caliber rifled bores; they were doubtless the first rifles carried by Americans across the continent to the west coast. Here we have a beginning of a great variety of firearms destined to serve those with a pioneering spirit whose actions were to shape our western history.

Hardy mountain men followed the path of Lewis and Clark to harvest the reported wealth in beaver pelts; in the process they served as pathfinders for the great western migration soon to follow. A Frederic Remington sketch.

Great events were in store for the first half of the 1800s, and guns were to figure importantly in almost all. The exploration of Lewis and Clark and some others had uncovered the potential of the western fur trade. In 1810 John Jacob Astor decided this alone was a basis for expanding the American empire to the Columbia River basin. Soon St. Louis became the home of the nation's principal fur companies.

The steamboat was a familiar sight on the Ohio and Mississippi rivers, and by 1820 was nosing up the Missouri, revolutionizing commerce toward the west.

Within five years the American Fur Company became a major factor in the push westward. Employed in the fur trade were great pathfinders like William Ashley, Andrew Henry, Jedediah Smith, Jim Bridger, William

The Model 1803 Harper's Ferry flintlock rifles of the 1804-1806 Lewis and Clark Expedition were probably the first American rifles to be carried across the West from the Missouri River to the Pacific Ocean.

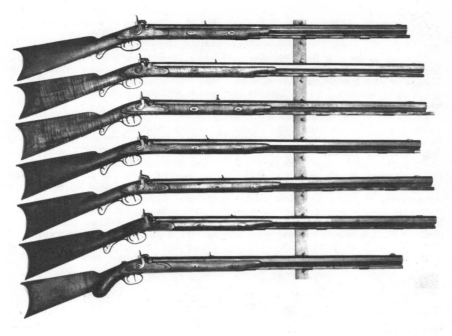

The big-bore caplock rifles made by Samuel and Jacob Hawken of St. Louis were the favorites of such mountain men as Jim Bridger and Kit Carson, and were sought by many others who ventured into the west. They were equally effective on big game and hostile Indians.

at the Montana Historical Society, and Mariano Modena's rifle may be seen at the Colorado State Museum. Many men who made western history did it with the help of a Hawken rifle. These were plain, well-made caplock guns, usually with a half stock, although some full-stock guns were made. The barrels were heavy and usually rifled to handle a ball of about 54 caliber. They were bad medicine for the grizzly bear, the buffalo, or the hostile Indian. I once had the good fortune to own a collection of seven Hawken rifles. Today a good specimen, which sold originally from $20 to $30, may bring several thousand dollars.

Contemporary with the Hawken rifles were plain caplock guns made for the Indian trade by H. E. Leman of Lancaster, Pennsylvania. These were rather short rifles with bar action locks and usually with a full stock under the octagon barrel. Indians liked to decorate them with brass-headed tacks. The largest group of these Leman Indian guns was originally in the U.S. Cartridge Company collection. While usually found in poor condition they are nevertheless valued highly by collectors.

By 1834 the old system of holding

James Bridger, one of the great guides of the early West; founder of Fort Bridger.

Sublette, James Clyman, Joe Meek, Tom Fitzpatrick and Kit Carson. All these men needed dependable guns —Jake and Sam Hawken of St. Louis were the men to provide them.

Sam Hawken joined his brother Jake at St. Louis in 1822 and their reputation for what became known as a sturdy "Mountain Rifle" spread rapidly. The name Hawken on a rifle was like the *Sterling* stamp on silver. Hawken rifles were the favorites of the bold group we call Mountain Men. Jedediah Smith carried one over his saddle when he led the first group of white men overland by the southern route, arriving at California's San Gabriel Mission in 1826. Kit Carson owned several, one now the property of Montezuma Lodge No. 1, F.&A.M., in Santa Fe, and currently on loan to the Museum of New Mexico. Another of Carson's Hawken rifles was presented to Lt. Edward F. Beale, whose heirs later gave it to Theodore Roosevelt. It is now in the collection of the Boone & Crockett Club.

Jim Bridger's Hawken Rifle

Jim Bridger's Hawken is preserved

Christopher "Kit" Carson in uniform, from photograph taken about 1863, when he held a commission in the Army.

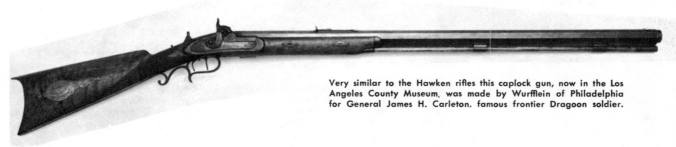

Very similar to the Hawken rifles this caplock gun, now in the Los Angeles County Museum, was made by Wurfflein of Philadelphia for General James H. Carleton, famous frontier Dragoon soldier.

GUNS OF THE WESTERN HISTORY MAKERS

a trapper trading rendezvous in the mountains gave way to private forts at strategic locations. Ambitious merchants like the Chouteaus of St. Louis established trading posts at landings on the upper Missouri, such as Westport, whence trails branched off for Fort Laramie and Fort Bridger or ran

national recognition a few years later in the hands of the Texas Rangers under John C. Hays, Samuel H. Walker and others. During the conquest of California in 1846, a few Colt revolving cylinder carbines were issued to sailors of the Pacific Squadron when these men were used as skirmishers in the attack on Los Angeles. A party of '49ers stranded in Death Valley was rescued by William Manly and John Rogers with the aid of a Colt caplock cylinder rifle.

From the early 1840s onward the Topographical Engineers of the U.S. Army began to play an important role in mapping the West and determining travel routes, selecting sites for forts and settlements, and eventually mapping the route for the transcontinental railroad. One of the first to head a government exploration of the coun-

showed up in Fremont's purchases for the first trip, the men he hired usually supplying their own. Up the Missouri at Westport a shotgun and eight rifles were purchased from the Chouteau trading post along with some shot pouches, powder horns, powder, lead and percussion caps.

Fremont's Arsenals

Before leaving Washington for his second trek in 1843 Fremont purchased from Charles Renard "one large Swiss rifle" at $40. In May 1843, he stopped in at the shop of J. & S. Hawken in St. Louis to have two brace of pistols "percussioned," a rifle barrel dressed out and a new nipple installed. From William Campbell he bought a double barrel shotgun and along the route west he purchased several guns from individuals

Lt. John Charles Fremont. Sometimes called "The Pathfinder," he made five long trips to and beyond the Rocky Mountains in the 1840s.

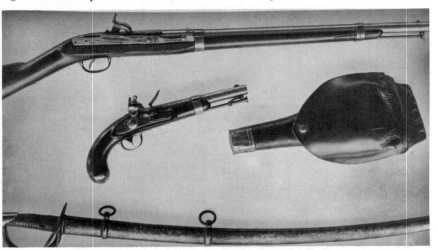

The Hall caplock carbine, the Model 1836 flintlock horse pistol and the saber were the first military weapons to travel overland in the West, carried by General Kearny's mounted infantrymen called "Dragoons."

southwest to Bent's Fort on the Arkansas.

It was via Bent's Fort that the Santa Fe Trail looped its way across Kansas and Colorado into New Mexico. This became known as the road of commerce while the Oregon Trail was the path of the home seeker; the Overland and California trails were known as the routes of the gold-seeker, mail and express; the Bozeman Trail became the bloody battleground of the fighting Sioux.

Following the Santa Fe Trail with his caravan of trade goods Josiah Gregg in 1839 probably introduced the first of many Colt repeating firearms to travel along western trails. He later wrote: "Thanks to Mr. Colt's invention I carried thirty-six charges ready loaded, which could easily fire at the rate of a dozen per minute." Gregg referred to Colt's caplock cylinder rifles and pistols made at Paterson, New Jersey, and the practice of carrying extra loaded cylinders.

The Walker Colts

These early Colt arms were to gain

try lying between the Missouri River and the Pacific slope, was a young lieutenant of the Topographical Engineers, John Charles Fremont, a very controversial figure in western history. Altogether Fremont made five trips of exploration into the West, but only three were made in behalf of the government. Of these three trips we have good accounts, and through old records deep in the archives of the General Services Administration I have learned, among other things, a lot about the firearms Fremont selected for these journeys and where he bought them.

The first Fremont government exploration proceeded only to the Rocky Mountains, but the second expedition in 1843-1844 and the journey in 1845-1846 extended through to California. Fremont's companions for the most part were voyageurs of French extraction, but he did have Kit Carson to guide him on all three trips along with Alexander Godey and a few others on whom he could fully rely, such as Charles Preuss, a German topographer. Not many guns

By the time Fremont was ready to outfit his party for his third trip, across the western plains and mountains to California, he had learned the importance of good quality firearms.

From the gun store of Joseph Cooper at New York he purchased in April, 1845, the following:

1 pair officers pistols in case, complete		$50
3 rifles with German silver mounts, patent breech, hair triggers. Percussion bar action locks @ $20.		$60
12 rifles as above with steel mounts and back action locks @ $20.		$240

With the pair of pistols and the 15 rifles, Fremont bought woolen covers for the rifles, 6 extra locks and cocks, nipples, nipple wrenches and 5000 "Best English percussion caps (probably Eley's)."

Still on the lookout for good rifles, Fremont stopped in Louisville enroute west and on May 24 purchased from Dickson & Gilmore eight half-stock caplock rifles with the patent breech, along with some powder horns and percussion caps.

Reaching St. Louis Fremont was still in a buying mood, obtaining a rifle from M. F. Safford and five rifles from Hoffman & Campbell. His most important purchase, however, was made on June 8, 1845, when he purchased the following from J.&S. Hawken:

27 rifles	@	$20	$540.00
1	"	@ 22	22.00
2	"	@ 30	60.00
Repairs			13.13

No doubt Kit Carson, long a user of Hawken rifles, had convinced Fremont that these were the best guns for what lay ahead. The Fremont party, now well armed, proceeded on its arduous and dangerous travels westward. Fremont later stated that some of the rifles he bought in 1845

important information.

A moment of decision was reached concerning the Mexican War and how the United States must react in the western territories. In May of 1846 General Stephen W. Kearny led his "Army of the West" out of Fort Leavenworth toward Mexican Santa Fe. Kearny's command was made up of 1700 mounted infantrymen known as the First Dragoons. Each trooper was armed with a Hall breechloading caplock carbine, a Model 1836 flintlock horse pistol and a heavy saber.

The Conquest of California

The progress of this army may be quickly summed up by stating that they took New Mexico with hardly a shot fired and quickly occupied that vital territory. General Kearny, leaving others to the occupation duties,

mounted Californianos and a desperate fight ensued. They eventually reached San Diego and, with a force of men from the Pacific Squadron, marched north to victories at the San Gabriel River and at Los Angeles. Fremont, in command of a force recruited in northern California, took so long on the way south that he arrived just in time for the surrender.

Sailors and marines of the Pacific Squadron were still using flintlock muskets in 1846. Some had pikes and, as has been mentioned, a group of skirmishers had Colt revolving cylinder caplock carbines.

Following closely after the first appearance of U.S. soldiers in the Southwest under General Kearny, Col. Philip St. George Cooke was ordered to build a wagon road from the Rio Grande to the Pacific Ocean. Recruit-

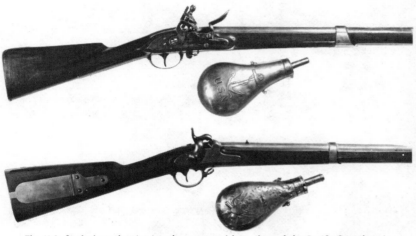

The U.S. flintlock musket (top) is the type used by sailors of the Pacific Squadron in the Mexican War. Below it, the popular Model 1841 caliber 54 "Mississippi" rifle.

One of the first artists to venture into the West, George Catlin here pictures himself shooting a buffalo with a Colt cap-and-ball pistol.

were obtained with the object of offering them as prizes for the best marksmanship, to be shot for during the journey.

On the Pacific slope, Fremont had rifles repaired by Peter Lassen and John Sutter. He purchased supplies at various places including the Leidesdorff store at Yerba Buena and the store of Henry Mellus, where, on July 2, 1846, he purchased a pair of pistols, 5 muskets, powder, lead, flints and percussion caps.

This ambitious young son-in-law of Senator Benton held various military ranks, but other than his explorations John Charles Fremont's services as a military officer and as a politican were unimpressive and controversial. He did earn a place in the history books, and guns were an inseparable part of his early career when he was known as "The Pathfinder."

The Fremont journeys into California were not altogether in the interest of topographical information. War with Mexico was threatening and California was a rich prize — Fremont's "explorations" could provide

took a detachment of about 100 men and started out for California. A short distance out of Sante Fe, Kearny met Kit Carson on the trail. Carson was returning from California to visit his family in Taos. Advised of the important nature of Kearny's mission, Carson agreed to turn around and guide the soldiers to San Diego for a rendezvous with sailors and marines of the Pacific Squadron commanded by Commodore Robert F. Stockton. At San Pascual, northeast of San Diego, the Dragoons met a force of superbly

ing a battalion comprised mostly of Mormons, who had been stranded on the way west while migrating from Illinois, Cooke's "Mormon Battalion" of about 400 men raised a lot of dust and did a creditable job. One of the conditions of their enlistment was that they could retain their arms when mustered out in California. They were armed with an assortment of weapons, mostly smoothbore muskets, but a few of the fortunate ones had Model 1841 brass-mounted caplock rifles. These excellent guns were 54 caliber

Colt revolving-cylinder repeaters were first carried down the Santa Fe Trail in 1839 by Josiah Gregg, saw service in the hands of skirmishers from the Pacific Squadron in 1846, and played an important role at Death Valley in 1849.

GUNS OF THE WESTERN HISTORY MAKERS

and are sometimes called the "Yager" or "Mississippi" rifle. They saw service in many areas of the West and were second only to the Hawken rifle in efficiency and popularity.

While all this activity was going on westward from the Missouri into the Southwest, other trails farther north felt the tread of venturesome Americans seeking a new life and land of their own.

Following Captain L.E. de Bonneville's expedition into Oregon in 1832, the missionaries Whitman and Spalding made the journey to christianize the Indians. By 1846 the dispute with England over the U.S.-Canadian border was settled, and the Hudson's Bay Company was forced to move its posts up into British Columbia. While they had been in the Oregon Territory, however, many of those "Northwest" flintlock trade guns came into the hands of Indians of that area.

With land in the Oregon Territory open to homesteading, the trail to Oregon through South Pass, Fort Bridger and Fort Hall was rutted by the passing of many wagons. In 1847 Brigham Young and his followers swung southwest from Fort Bridger, saw the great salt lake, and declared "This is the place!" While the Mormons in Utah obtained a number of Colt cap and ball pistols and other arms manufactured in the East, it was not long before their own gunsmiths were turning out weapons. Among these artisans was Jonathon Browning, father of John M. Browning, who was a greater western history-maker than John Moses Browning, whose inventions were eagerly sought and used by Winchester, Colt, and other prominent arms manufacturers!

By 1849 the stampede west got in full swing—gold had been discovered in California. Now the role of the army was complicated and greatly expanded. There were forts to build and emigrants to be protected from the Indians who were beginning to get very restive over all this traffic

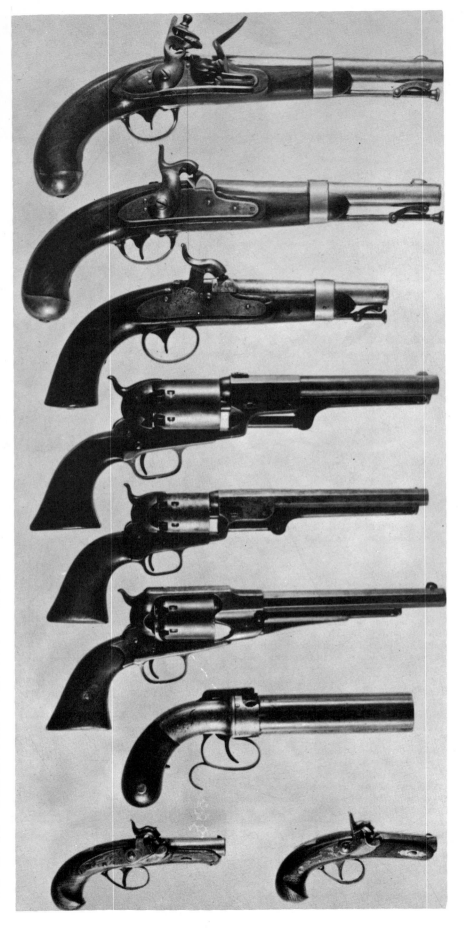

Representative of the most popular pistols used in the early West are, from top: (1) Model 1836 Army pistol; (2) Model 1842 Army pistol; (3) Model 1843 Army-Navy pistol; (4) Colt 44 Dragoon six-shooter; (5) Colt Model 1851 Navy pistol; (6) Remington Model 1858 44 Army pistol; (7) Allen '49er pepperbox pistol; (8) Pair of Pocket Deringer pistols.

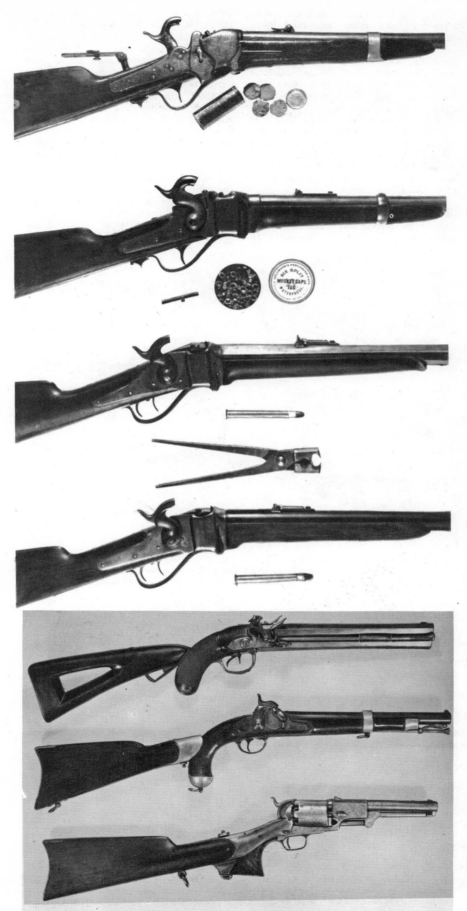

The first Sharps carbines (top) used the Maynard tape primer ignition but soldiers preferred the sure-fire percussion caps (second from top). Typical of the later guns used by buffalo hunters, the two lower Sharps rifles used metallic ammunition.

through lands which had been their private preserves for years.

Colts and Sharps

Going into the latter 1850s the horse soldiers in the West received some improved weapons. Big Colt 44 Army pistols, called the Dragoon Model, replaced the old single-shot pistols. These were caplock six-shooters weighing 4 pounds and were hard shooting weapons. Some were furnished with an attachable shoulder stock, making them into a "pistol-carbine." This experiment, along with an 1855 Model Springfield single-shot caplock pistol with attachable stock, proved unpopular; the soldiers preferred the reliable breechloading Sharps carbines, very popular throughout the West. Some were used by the Pony Express, by stagelines and others as well as by the military.

In 1858, the same year as the gold rush to Pike's Peak in Colorado, the Butterfield Overland Mail completed its first run, providing a link in transcontinental travel from coast to coast. Two years later the Pony Express started the drumming of hoof beats between St. Joseph, Missouri, and Sacramento, California.

Riders of the Pony Express preferred the Model 1851 Colt Navy pistol, a 36-caliber six-shooter, although a few carried the big 44 Dragoon Colt, 106 having been furnished by the army and 25 by citizens of Sacramento. The Colt "Navy" pistols were so named more for the naval scene engraved on their cylinder than for their use by that branch of the service. The army supplied 60 of the 54-caliber Model 1841 "Mississippi" rifles for use at the Pony Express relay stations. The riders preferred the light 52-caliber Sharps carbines when it was necessary for them to carry a shoulder arm.

When General James H. Carleton led his California Volunteers into Arizona in 1862 to drive the Confederate forces back into Texas, his men were armed with 58-caliber Springfield rifled muskets, Sharps carbines, Colt 36 Navy pistols, and sabers. Teamsters were given the big 44 Colt Dragoon six-shooters.

Life for the army became increasingly difficult as all kinds of people filtered into the West. More stagelines crisscrossed the territory, with

Borrowing the idea from European flintlock pistols, such as the stocked specimen at top, Springfield produced their 1855 Model (center) and Colt soon thereafter designed an attachable stock for their Dragoon six-shooter. Both types were given a trial in the West and abandoned in favor of the more rugged single shot carbines.

GUNS OF THE WESTERN HISTORY MAKERS

Ben Holladay emerging as "The Stagecoach King," but soon to be succeeded by Wells Fargo. By this time the Henry, the Model 1866 Winchester (both 44 rimfire caliber) and 56-52 Spencer repeating rifles had appeared. These, along with the ever-effective double barrel shotguns, were often part of the armament used by stagecoach guards "riding shotgun."

After the War between the States, pioneers like Charles Goodnight and Jesse Chisholm drove herds of cattle north to Colorado and Wyoming, and to railroad shipping points in Kansas. Not satisfied with this, in 1866 Nelson Story decided to drive a herd of 3000 cattle up to the fine grazing lands of Montana. The Sioux had other ideas. Because forts along the Bozeman Trail through Montana were undermanned no escorts were available, but Story had an ace in the hole. Somehow he had managed to obtain a number of the first Remington rolling-block 50-caliber breechloaders to be sent into the West, and when the Sioux attacked they received such a hot reception from Story and his men that they were driven off with severe losses.

It was a different story in December of 1866 when Brevet Lieutenant Colonel William J. Fetterman led a detachment of 81 men on a scouting mission near Fort Phil Kearny, a fort on the Little Piney hated by the Indians. Armed primarily with Civil War muzzle-loading rifled muskets and some Sharps carbines, Fetterman's command was surprised by 2000 Sioux and shot down to the last man. James Wheatley and Isaac Fisher had accompanied Fetterman, wishing to experiment with their new Henry 44-caliber 16-shot rimfire rifles; they were later found slumped over piles of empty cartridge cases and brutally mutilated.

The Wagon Box Fight

The tide of war swung back to favor the soldiers on August 2 of 1867. At what has become known as "The Wagon Box Fight," outside of Fort Phil Kearny, Captain James W. Powell and a detail of 31 men were attacked by a great horde of Red Cloud's Sioux warriors numbering several thousand. As in the Nelson Story battle, Captain Powell had a surprise for the Sioux. A short time

before, the command had been issued Springfield rifles converted by a "trapdoor" breech from muzzle-loaders to breechloaders of 50-70 caliber. Powell's men had plenty of copper cartridges and they poured such a rapid and withering fire into the Sioux that they were forced to withdraw with great losses.

A tragic personal note in 1867 was the shooting of John Bozeman, for whom the Bozeman Trail had been named. Bozeman was killed by a Model 1841 "Mississippi" rifle, which had somehow come into possession of a Blackfoot Indian.

Another costly repulse for the Indians near Fort C.F. Smith on the Big Horn River was further repayment for the Fetterman massacre. In

1868, at a fork of the Republican River, in what was known as "The Beecher Island Fight," fifty cavalrymen armed with breechloaders stood off 700 Cheyennes. But there was more hard fighting to come. The Indians became more desperate when, in 1869, the railroad which had cut through their hunting grounds linked East and West. With the railroad came settlements and into the settlements came hunters seeking quick money by harvesting buffalo hides.

By this time Sharps and Remington had developed strong breech-loading rifles shooting long, powerful metallic cartridges. Armed with Sharps rifles 28 buffalo hunters and a woman held off a war party of 1000 Indians at Adobe Walls. Among these men

Competing with the Sharps for the favor and brisk trade of the western hunters were, from top: John Browning's single shot rifle, forerunner of the Winchester single shot rifle; the Ballard Pacific model rifle; and the Remington rolling-block rifle.

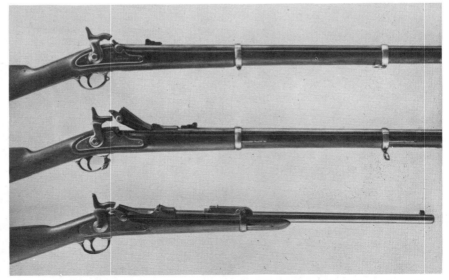

The Springfield muzzle-loading rifle at top was used by western military forces for a few years prior to issuance of such breechloaders as the 50-70 rifle (middle) and the 45-70 carbine at bottom. The breechloaders were the principal shoulder arms of the hard-fought Indian Wars.

were Billy Dixon, a famous scout, and W.B. (Bat) Masterson, later to become famous as a lawman.

The government gave tacit approval to the wanton destruction of the buffalo herds. They reasoned that the West was an area which providence had provided for an expanding population and once the Indians were deprived of their food supply they could be contained on limited reservations and easily controlled. While idealistic in conception, government ambitions were somewhat brutal in their fulfillment. Turning the empty plains into farms and ranches, converting the trails to railroads with towns and cities strung across the continent was a nice dream for the white man but the nomadic red man was not ready to give up his way of life without a final struggle. The 1870s and 1880s were to see that struggle.

The 45-70 Springfield

Although western military commanders had urgently petitioned their superiors to send them Spencer repeating rifles and carbines, very few ever were issued. The standard weapons used in the Indian Wars of the late 1870s and 1880s were the Springfield 45-70 trapdoor rifles and carbines and the Colt Single Action Army 45 revolvers. Some "44 American" and "45 Schofield" model Smith & Wesson revolvers were also used. It was with the 45-70 single-shot Springfields and Colt 45 revolvers that General Custer's command was armed when they were trapped by Sitting Bull's Sioux on the Little Big Horn and upwards of 300 brave cavalrymen gave up their lives. Custer had left his fast shooting Gatling guns back at his base camp.

On July 17, 1876, a young scout for the Fifth Cavalry had his big opportunity. In a duel with the Cheyenne Chief Yellow Hand, William F. Cody killed his adversary and promptly removed the scalp-lock, declaring it to be "the first scalp for Custer!" Cody, better known as Buffalo Bill, started out using Hawken and Mississippi rifles, Colt cap and ball pistols and, later, his favorite, a 50-70 Springfield rifle he affectionately called "Lucretia Borgia." In his later showmanship days Cody used Winchester repeating rifles, especially the Model 1873.

By the late 1870s the Indian Wars on the plains were near an end. The famous Indian fighters General Nelson A. Miles and General George Crook were in the thick of this fighting. After the plains Indians were driven onto reservations, the scene of major Indian war activity shifted to Arizona, and it was not until 1886 that the Apache reign of terror was broken by the surrender of Geronimo.

Indian hostilities were not the only dangers that plagued the West. Towns like Abilene, Dodge City, Deadwood, Panamint City and Tombstone had their share of hard characters who used their six-guns without conscience or hesitation. Stage holdups were commonplace. One shotgun-wielding California stage robber named Black Bart robbed 28 stages and sometimes left a poetic note for his victims which he signed "The Po-8." One such note read:

Brevet Major General George A. Custer.

A "Typical Trooper" of the Indian Wars. A sketch by Frederic Remington.

Below—Engraved Remington 44 caplock pistol presented to General George A. Custer prior to his fatal battle with the Sioux on the Little Big Horn. Photo courtesy John S. duMont.

GUNS
OF THE WESTERN
HISTORY MAKERS

I've labored long and hard for bread,
For honor and for riches,
But on my toes too long you've tread
You fine-haired sons of bitches.

Eventually, lawmen like the Earps, Bat Masterson, Wild Bill Hickok, John R. Hughes, Billy Breakenridge, John Slaughter, Jeff Milton and others were able to cool the ardor and restrain the activities of the lawless. For a majority of these lawmen the Colt Single Action Army revolver was a customary piece of attire. It is doubtful that any would want to have

The first repeating rifles to gain any great popularity in the West were the Henry 44 rimfire with magazine under the barrel and the 56-52 Spencer with a detachable magazine, inserted into the stock through a trap-door in buttplate.

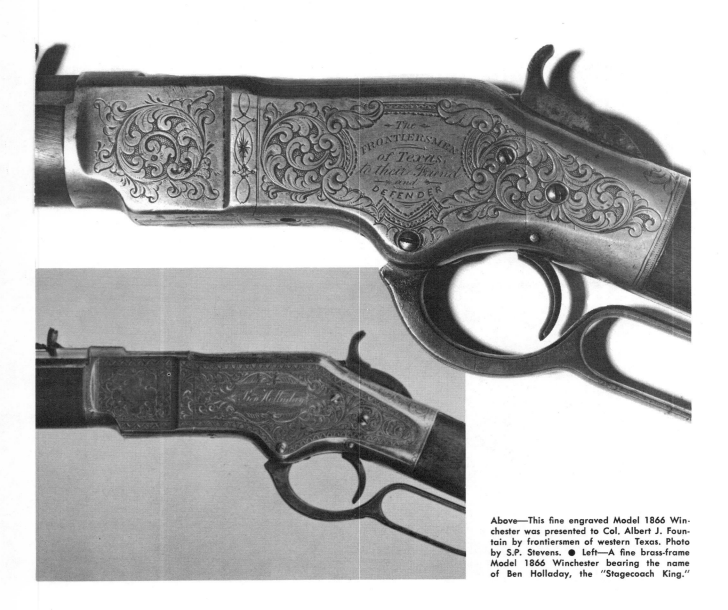

Above—This fine engraved Model 1866 Winchester was presented to Col. Albert J. Fountain by frontiersmen of western Texas. Photo by S.P. Stevens. ● Left—A fine brass-frame Model 1866 Winchester bearing the name of Ben Holladay, the "Stagecoach King."

Typical of the Colt Single Action Army revolvers used by outlaws and lawmen alike, this six-shooter in the Los Angeles County Museum was owned by Emmett Dalton of the infamous Dalton gang.

Smith & Wesson top-break revolvers were popular with some in the West, but the Colt Single Action Army model (center) predominated; it had much the same lines and grip as the popular 36-caliber Colt Navy model which preceded it (bottom).

been caught with one of those Colt models with a 16-inch barrel dramatized as the "Buntline."

Colt's Competitors

After Samuel Colt's patent ran out on his revolving cylinder principle in 1857, Remington, Smith & Wesson and a number of other manufacturers had turned to making pistols with a revolving cylinder. Some gained a degree of popularity in the West, but the Colt remained predominant. The earlier caplock pepperbox pistols, with no separate barrel and cylinder, presented the appearance of an elongated multi-bored cylinder from which the balls were directly fired. They were cheaper than most orthodox revolvers and gained some popularity in the Far West, especially among the miners.

As the metallic cartridge repeating arms gained in popularity the Spencer and Winchester became the early favorites. When Winchester's Model 1873, the first repeater to shoot centerfire reloadable cartridges, came on the market it gained great popularity. As one of the points in its favor, the cartridges were of the same calibers (except for the 45) used in Colt Single Action Army revolvers.

The progress and variety of arms after 1873 was tremendous. Fine single-shot rifles for hunting and target shooting became available along with improved repeaters. Derringers and pocket pistols in the populated areas replaced the big holster pistols, and the carrying of any sidearm went out of style.

By the 1880s prominent Easterners were looking westward to invest in the newly opened land. Among these was Theodore Roosevelt who, in 1883, purchased several ranches near Medora, Dakota Territory. Among his favorite guns while in Dakota was a 45-120 Sharps, a Model 1876 Winchester in 45-75 caliber and an ivory handled Colt Single Action Army 45.

Once the Indian hostilities had been reasonably controlled, attention was directed toward building up the settlements, extending the transportation and communication systems, and developing the land into its most profitable uses. Hunting to provide food and competitive shooting for sport kept firearms as a vital implement in every western home. The establishment of law and order in rough new settlements and self-protection in the town or in the open called for the presence of a gun.

In all this great shifting of the population from east of the Mississippi to the west, guns alone did not "Win the West." It took courage, perseverance and sweat. But the way was made possible and easier by a tool of man's ingenuity—the gun. Actually many kinds of guns gave dependable service in bringing a good way of life to this land. Here it is possible to mention only those which played the most prominent roles.

The historian Augustus C. Buell

MODEL 1873.

SPORTING RIFLE, OCTAGON BARREL, PLAIN TRIGGER.

	ROUND BARREL.	HALF OCT. BARREL.	OCTAGON BARREL.
Price,	$18.00	$19.50	$19.50
Length of Barrel,	24 inch	24 inch	24 inch
Caliber,	.44	.44	.44
Number of Shots,	15	15	15
Weight,	8¼ lbs.	8¼ lbs.	9 lbs.

SPORTING RIFLE, SHORT MAGAZINE, HALF OCTAGON BARREL, PLAIN TRIGGER.

Number of Shots, . . . 6
Price, same as full-length Magazine of corresponding style.

Shot-gun butt, same price as Rifle.   For Extras, see page 39.

Winchester's Model 1873 rifle. the first to use reloadable centerfire cartridges, outsold all other repeaters in the last quarter of the 1800s. It became a valuable tool in the hands of the western settler, the rancher and lawman.

wrote: "In all the annals of the frontier and pioneer, of struggles that wrested the continent from its savage owners and made it a freehold of civilization, the rifle has been the instrument of destiny and the symbol of progress."

If there was any way to produce an orderly society and to write the history of this nation other than by raw courage and superior weapons, that way could not be found. ●

Selected Bibliography

Bailey, L. R. (editor), *The A. B. Gray Report,* Los Angeles, 1963, Westernlore Press.

Baird, John D., *Hawken Rifles — The Mountain Man's Choice,* Pence, Ind., 1968, published by the author.

Bancroft, Hubert H., *History of Western States and Mexico,* 39 volumes, San Francisco, 1886-1890.

Bartlett, Richard A., *Great Surveys of the American West,* Norman, Okla., 1962, University of Oklahoma Press.

Bolton, Herbert Eugene, *Spanish Exploration in the Southwest,* New York, 1908, Charles Scribner's Sons; *Rim of Christendom,* New York, 1936, The Macmillan Co.

Bourke, John G., *On the Border with Crook,* New York, 1891, Scribners.

Brewerton, Douglas, B., *Overland with Kit Carson,* New York, 1930, Coward-McCann, Inc.

Browning and Gentry, *John M. Browning —American Gunmaker,* Garden City, N.Y., 1964, Doubleday & Co.

California State Archives, California State Library, Sacramento, Calif.

Clarke, Dwight L., *Stephen Watts Kearny —Soldier of the West,* Norman, Okla., 1961, University of Oklahoma Press.

Colton, Ray C., *The Civil War in the Western Territories,* Norman, Okla., 1859, University of Oklahoma Press.

Duffus, R. L., *The Santa Fe Trail,* New York, 1931, Longmans, Green and Co.

Emory, Lt. Col. W. H., *Notes of a Military Reconnaissance,* Washington, 1848, Senate Executive Document 7, 30th Congress, 1st Session.

Fremont, *Life, Exploration and Public Service of John Charles Fremont,* Boston, 1856, Ticknor and Fields.

Fremont, John Charles, *Memoirs of My Life,* Chicago, 1887, Belford, Clarke & Co.

Fuller, Claude E., *Springfield Shoulder Arms 1795-1865,* New York, 1930, Francis Bannerman Sons.

Ghent, W. J., *The Road to Oregon,* New York, 1929, Longmans, Green and Co.

Gluckman, Col. Arcadi, *U. S. Muskets, Rifles, Carbines,* Buffalo, N.Y., 1948, Otto Ulbrich Co.

Goetzmann, Wm. H., *Army Exploration in the American West,* New Haven, Conn., 1959, Yale University Press.

Goodwin, Cardinal, *John Charles Fremont —An Explanation of his Career,* Stanford University Press, 1930.

Gregg, Josiah, *Commerce of the Prairies . . .* New York, 1844, H. G. Langley, 2 vols.

Hanson, Charles E., Jr., *The Northwest Gun,* Lincoln, Nebr., 1955, Nebraska State Historical Society; *The Plains Rifle,* Harrisburg, Pa., 1960, The Stackpole Co.

Hebard and Brininstool, *The Bozeman Trail . . .* Cleveland, 1922, The Arthur H. Clark Co., 2 vols.

Hicks, Major James E., *Notes on U. S. Ordnance,* Mount Vernon, N.Y., 1940, Privately published, 2 vols.

Hunt, Aurora, *Major-General James Henry Carleton, Western Frontier Dragoon,* Glendale, Calif., 1958, Arthur H. Clark Co.

Inman and Cody, *The Great Salt Lake Trail,* New York, 1898, The Macmillan Co.

Jackson, Joseph Henry, *Bad Company,* New York, 1949, Harcourt, Brace and Co.

Laut, Agnes C., *The Overland Trail,* New York, 1929, Frederick A. Stokes Co.

Miles, Gen. Nelson A., *Serving the Republic,* New York, 1911, Harper & Bro.

National Archives, Selected records of the U. S. Accounting Office and records from the Office of the Chief of Ordnance, post returns, reports, orders, letters, House and Senate Documents, etc.

Parsons & du Mont, *Firearms in the Custer Battle,* Harrisburg, Pa., 1953, The Stackpole Co.

Prucha, Francis Paul, *Guide to the Military Posts of the United States,* Madison, Wis., 1964, The State Historical Society of Wisconsin.

Rosebush, Waldo E., *Frontier Steel—The Men and Their Weapons,* Appleton, Wis., 1958, Nelson Publishing Co.

Russell, Carl P., *Guns on the Early Frontiers,* Berkeley, Cal., 1957, University of California Press.

Sabin, Edwin L., *Kit Carson Days,* Chicago, 1914, A. C. McClurg & Co.

Schmitt, Martin F., *General George Crook —His Autobiography,* Norman, Okla., 1946, University of Oklahoma Press.

Serven, James E., *Colt Firearms,* Santa Ana, Cal., 1954, The Foundation Press.

Sharps Rifle Manufacturing Co. Records in possession of author.

Smith & Serven, *The Pony Express — The Overland Mail,* Tucson, 1968, Smoke Signal of the Westerners.

Spencer Repeating Rifle Co. Records in possession of author.

Sullivan, Maurice S., *Jedediah Smith, Trader and Trail Breaker,* New York, 1936, Press of the Pioneers, Inc.

Walsh, Richard J., *The Making of Buffalo Bill,* Indianapolis, 1928, The Bobbs-Merrill Co.

Whittaker, Frederick, *A Popular Life of Gen. George A. Custer,* New York, 1876, Sheldon & Co.

Rough Country Antelope

by BOB HAGEL

High country pronghorn pursuit is antelope hunting at its best. Up here you can stalk them as you would a Bighorn sheep — and they're every bit as hard to come up on.

WE HAD BEEN climbing the rocky sage slope for nearly half an hour, and the first pale, pink glow had just started to spread in the morning sky above the jagged peaks to the east. Far below, where the long slope of bench land drifted downward from the toe of the Lost River Range to Idaho's Pahsimeroi river, it was all but totally dark.

Down there on the antelope flats the gleam of headlights traced meandering, snake-like courses as vehicles picked their way between the dry draws, around heavy patches of sage and greasewood. These were antelope hunters, hoping somehow to find a herd in the gathering light before someone else saw them first.

As the first streaks of gold tinted the summits of the peaks above, long before there was shooting light down on the flats, the crackle of spasmodic rifle fire drifted up on the thin morning air. Perhaps some trigger-happy eager-beaver had momentarily frozen a band of pronghorn in the glare of the headlights; maybe they had been reading about the "grey ghosts of the plains." Whatever the reason, it would produce but two things: crippled or frightened antelope.

This was what we had expected, what we were ready for. As the growing light revealed details below, the twinkle of headlights was replaced by trails of dust spiraling upward as speeding vehicles twisted this way and that trying to outmaneuver herds of antelope heading for the rough country where we sat. With the number of cars, pickups and jeeps streaking across the flats, many of the antelope failed to make it but, for the most part, the herds gained the foothills. Some of them took a vigilant stand in the middle of some high mountain face where they were almost impossible to approach within rifle range. Others dissolved into the draws that twisted back into the broken, timbered lower slopes of the range, joining other small bands already feeding in the seclusion of the rough brakes.

This was the first day of the antelope season. Tomorrow there would be few antelope left on the flat benches near the floor of the valley, and those that were there would be next to impossible to approach.

As the day wore on we stayed in the rough country, above and beyond the reach of the 4-wheel-drive hunters. We sat with binoculars, sweeping the foothills and watching the antelope drift into pockets protected by rocky ridges or moving behind the cover of fir and mountain mahogany. When a little band settled down we'd glass them until we agreed there was nothing that looked good; then we'd locate another bunch.

Before the sun slid behind the ridges to the west, we'd killed a pair of bucks that were both over the 14″ mark. We'd passed up a dozen or so more that were not much smaller. If there had been any record-class heads about, we'd have had every opportunity to size them up and collect them.

Not all sections offer this kind of antelope hunting, but there is a lot more of it than many hunters realize. It may not be as scenically spectacular as the country that rises from the sage flats toward the crown of Idaho's

12,655-foot Mt. Borah, but there are often rough mountains or brakes around the perimeter of the antelope range that afford the same type of hunting.

This kind of pronghorn pursuit is hunting at its best; hunting where you can stalk them in the same manner you'd stalk Stone and Dall sheep in much of northern British Columbia, the Yukon or Alaska. Anyone who has ever hunted sheep soon finds that antelope are every bit as hard to stalk as sheep, especially in rough country. An antelope won't go into the rough stuff as far as a sheep will, nor as high, but once he's been spooked where he normally lives, down in the flat lands, you'll find him just as far-sighted, alert and hard to get on to as any ram.

Antelope in the rough stuff do have one habit that make them easier to stalk than sheep, and that is their refusal to brush up in the timber where you can't see them. Animals of the wide open spaces, they're bound to stay where they can see what is going on around them—especially after they've had a good scare! I've shot them in rough country pockets, with fairly heavy bunches of scattered timber around the edges, but they could usually see a couple of hundred yards in every direction. These were bands that hadn't been disturbed, either. In any event, if you get high enough so that you can look down into the pockets or onto the benches or wide open hillsides, you'll have no trouble spotting them. Then all you have to do is figure out how to stalk them to within rifle range. That's all!

Watch the Wind!

When stalking antelope in rough country, especially high rough country along the toe of mountain slopes where the wind whips around in unpredictable directions, don't let it get behind you. An antelope doesn't like your smell any more than a sheep, deer or elk does, and you smell pretty bad to any of them. When hunting antelope in flat country you can pretty well forget about wind direction because they depend mostly on their sight to locate danger, and on their speed to keep it at a safe distance. Most antelope country is flat or rolling, and they've already seen you before you're ready to shoot, so their winding you is of little consequence. This is especially true if the hunting is done from a car. Game laws notwithstanding, most pronghorns are killed from a vehicle or with the hunter no more than a few feet from it.

I believe that many antelope hunters are much more worried about how far the wind will drift their bullet than in whether the buck smells them or not. This attitude can easily get you into trouble in rough country.

On the last antelope hunt I made the wind gave me a bad time on the

only buck I saw that might have been worth shooting. I'd drawn my ticket for a unit that was all very rough country. In fact, bighorn sheep lived in some of the canyons that ran off into the river brakes. Higher up the ridges were open, dry and rocky, with big basins filled with sage and clumps of aspen. I'd been hunting in this country for nearly a week, looking for one of the trophy bucks that the Fish and Game boys had told me were there. I'd done it on my own hind feet, too, wearing my boots thin in 10 to 15 miles of up-and-down hunting every day. Up to then I'd seen a grand total of three antelope, two does and a lonesome little fawn. Then, late one afternoon, I found where a small band had come down off the mountain, going into the rough brakes at the edge of the sheep country.

I snooped around over the sharp little ridges until, finally, I stuck my head over a sagebrush and saw several does. They were about 175 yards

Some of the top-flight antelope cartridges that will deliver the goods in either the flatlands or in the rough country around the edges. From left—6mm Remington, 240 Weatherby; 6.5 Remington, 264 Winchester, 270 Winchester, 7mm Remington, 300 Winchester and 300 Weatherby, all magnums except the 270. Several of these are ideal for hunting where heavier game like elk may be taken on the same trip.

below me on a hat-sized flat spot on the steep sidehill. Working up until I was sitting behind the sagebrush, I waited to see if there was a buck around. Suddenly one came prancing up the hill from where several other does were feeding. Bucks were in the rut and this one's attention was divided between two girl friends, one in each bunch. He gave me little chance for a shot as he dashed from one doe to the other, and he wasn't very good anyway. At last I decided maybe I'd better take him, for this might be the last day I'd have to hunt.

On his next visit to the does he stopped, facing me, a doe tight on both sides of him. I put the crosshair

of the 240 Weatherby scope at the base of his neck, a perfect shot at that range. Then I saw a bunch of rabbit-brush twigs waving in the magnified field of the scope, right over the buck's neck and chest. I knew that the 95-gr. Nosler, traveling at just under 3400 foot seconds, might be deflected by that brush, about halfway out, and I might hit one of the does instead. They didn't know I was there so I'd just wait him out. Then, as I watched, a little puff of wind came from behind me. An old doe that had been acting as lookout threw her head in the air, blew a warning blast, and took off. The whole bunch went over the lip of the bench in a cloud of dust, and that was that.

I lost that round of rough country antelope hunting by a tiny gust of wind from the wrong direction at the right time, but that is what makes stalking all worthwhile. The moral is, the wind is there, so keep it in mind because antelope have pretty good noses and they pay strict attention to what they smell and can't see.

Indian Style

When hunting antelope in flat country, where both the hunter and the hunted can see for miles with little cover available, we are inclined to forget good stalking procedure; to see without being seen. We drive to some little rise where we can see for miles in every direction, take a good pair of binoculars or a spotting scope and glass the country so far away that if there are antelope there—even if they see us — they're seldom disturbed. Then we try to figure how to get to them for the final stalk (if any), and drive off in some other direction in a big circle and try to come within range without spooking them. In mountain hunting the same technique will buy you only disappointment.

This rough country antelope hunting is true stalking from start to finish. You don't walk the ridges and climb every high point to glass from its top. If you do that you'll stick up like a sore thumb, to be seen by every antelope anywhere in the area. Don't do it unless you've finished glassing every ridge, sidehill and basin within a mile or so, and want to study country so far away that antelope there won't see you or pay any attention to you if they do. In this kind of hunting you stay *below the skyline*. If you are traveling in the same direction the ridges run, up or down, stay below the crest, taking only an occasional peek to glass the country beyond. If you are walking the contours, as is usual with hunting rough country ,you don't just pop up on a high part of the ridge and sit

tance when you poke your head over a ridge. If you've done it right, they may not even know you are there. You may also spot them — which is more usual — far out of range, feeding or bedded on some wide slope, on the top of some ridge or bench, or down on the floor of some high basin. In any of these situations you'll be able to plan and execute your stalk in much the same manner as in hunting sheep. Always remember to keep the wind right, stay off the skyline, and, if you come up close for the shot, keep quiet—don't talk aloud. Antelope also have sensitive ears and they believe what they hear, too. If you must say something, whisper!

Rifles and Loads

There is little difference between rifle-cartridge requirements for rough country antelope hunting and those for flat country hunting. The main consideration is this — you will be packing your rifle over a lot of tough

just as much use for high power in rough country as on flat land. The higher powers will often be of more value in hill country than on the flats. Heat waves over flat land raise merry old hell with long range clear sighting when you have too much power, especially on a hot, sun-bright day. With some kind of crosshair type reticle, not coarser than medium, there is little use for more than 4x. If the antelope is so far away you can't see him fairly plainly, he's too far off to shoot at anyway. If you miss him with a good clear 4x it won't be because you can't see him well enough!

Cartridges suitable for hunting antelope in the rough stuff are much the same as those best fitted for any other kind of pronghorn shooting. They're not very big animals, few bucks dressing out at as much as 100 pounds, and they aren't hard to kill. Sure, he has his full share of vitality, and when you sprinkle bullets around the edges and start adrenalin pumping through his system, he may go a long way, but he is small and it doesn't take much of a bullet to penetrate his vital machinery. Most antelope that escape have been shot in the legs or have been wounded inadvertantly, the hunter assuming that only those which drop at the shot were hit.

Considering these things, it has always seemed to me that the prime requirements of an antelope cartridge are these: that it shoots as flat as possible, be as accurate as a good varmint cartridge, and that it uses a bullet which expands very rapidly, even at extreme ranges. Which all points to high velocity and, in most cases, fairly light bullets. The magnum cartridges make top-drawer pronghorn medicine because they fire bullets of good ballistic coefficient that shoot extremely flat from here to there and are drifted off target less by the wind along the way.

On average, the range at which antelope will be shot in rough country is not as great as it is in flat country. There is more cover and the nature of the terrain makes much closer stalking possible. However, if you have a cartridge that shoots extremely flat, so much the better; if you need the extra range you've got it, and if you don't, it doesn't matter.

Perhaps one of the finest antelope cartridges of all times is the time-tested 270 Winchester with 130-gr. bullets. The various 6mm numbers, especially the new 240 Weatherby, are all good pronghorn cartridges, as are the 6.5mm Remington and the 264 Winchester. The 7mm Remington Magnum and the various wildcats of the same configuration are outstanding for flatness and long range accuracy. Last but not least, there are the various 30-caliber cartridges ranging from the 30-06 to the 300 Weatherby. In fact, all of the Weatherby line except the 224 (which will certainly kill

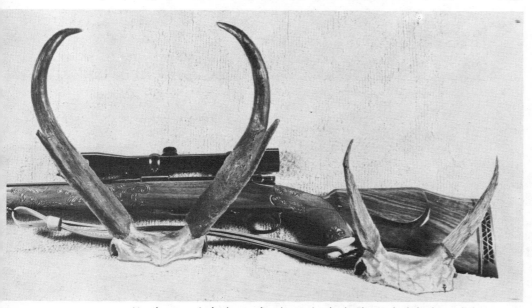

No, these aren't the horns of a doe and a buck. They're both bucks, and the skull plate at right is from an even larger buck than the one at left. The buck at left was killed in late September, while the other was killed on November 11, on a late hunt, after it had shed the outer shell of horn. Beware of these late season hunts as held in some antelope states if you are looking for a trophy.

on its top to do your glassing. When you top a ridge, no matter which way you are traveling, pick a spot where there is brush, high grass, an outcrop of rock, anything to break up the bare line of the ridge. Find something you will blend in with, something to help break up your silhouette. Then you ease up to the top very slowly, sometimes on your hands and knees or your belly, and you slip the binocular or spotting scope over the top slow and easy like. You keep moving up until you can see everything there is to see from that point. Then, and only then, do you cross the top and move on.

In this type of hunting you may find the antelope within spitting dis-

miles on your own two feet, even though some of it may be on top of a pony. Down in the flatlands, where most hunting is done from some kind of gas buggy, weight is of little consequence. Fact is, maybe the extra weight of a heavy barrel, from the standpoint of accuracy and holding qualities, will be the advantage you need to make a long shot good.

The rifle to be used in the rough stuff, especially if it is high country, should not weigh over 9 pounds complete with scope, and 8-8½ is better. A good 4x scope is as good as any, but if you like a variable and want to pack the extra weight and bulk, they're OK too. As for magnification, you'll have

antelope but is not recommended) and up to the 300, are outstanding for this kind of long range work. Certainly the big 30s are far more powerful than needed for antelope, but they do have the flat-shooting, wind-bucking, bullet-expanding accuracy required for long-range shooting at game of this size.

Most of my antelope hunting has been in rough country, and I don't recall ever killing one at over 300 honest yards. The first one was shot nearly 30 years ago with an old 30-40 Krag rifle and a 180-gr. handload. Most of those I've killed since have been taken with various 7mm cartridges, from the 7x57 to the 7mm Mashburn Super Magnum.

On average, and in most places, the pronghorn antelope always was and still is an animal of the plains and flat,

Right — In rough country antelope hunting you spot them on some distant slope, ridge or basin, then slip up behind some form of cover so they won't know you're there. It's a lot like hunting sheep. ● Below—The buck is still there so you take your time, ease the rifle up into shooting position from a good rest and put your bullet where it does the most good.

sage-covered benchlands. But many antelope hunters would be amazed if they knew how many antelope there were in the rough, broken country around the edges of the flats where they hunt. For the most part, these hunters wouldn't go after them if they did know they were there. The popular trend is to pursue them with a 4-wheel drive rig, with an occasional short hike to the top of some height of land to glass the country, then maybe a short stalk. Some of this is brought on by guides more interested in the number of hunters they can handle in a season than in the pleasure of the hunt or in the quality of the game their hunters kill. The result is that many who have hunted antelope frequently don't know there is any other way to hunt them.

Few flat land hunters realize that while they're chasing antelope until their tongues hang out a foot, trying to get a shot at just any kind of antelope, some of their more hardy kin are having the time of their lives stalking the big bucks back in the foothills.

Mountain Pronghorns

In many places antelope stay in the high, mountain country surrounding their winter range all summer. Really good bucks, too, and often alone.

Some are found at unbelievable elevations if there is such suitable habitat as high mesa country, high sage slopes and basins and long, open ridges—country that has plenty of room without too much timber. I've seen plenty of antelope in this kind of country at elevations bordering 9,000 feet. In some cases these antelope are seldom if ever hunted, Only if the season is still on after the first snows hit the high country, driving them down into the lower foothills and flats, do they feel the hunting pressure their flat land relatives are subjected to every year.

However, most antelope stalked in the foothills and rough brakes are forced there by early-season hunting pressure. Hunting in this kind of country is usually better on the second day, or thereafter, than it is on the first day. If the weather stays warm and sunny many of these antelope will stay back in the hills until a big storm pushes them down onto the valley floor again. Sometimes you can go into this rough, hill country after the first week or two of the season, after they have settled down, and get some of the finest hunting of all.

This, of course, depends on when the season opens. Where seasons open any time in September there will still be antelope back in the high country unless an unusually early snowstorm pushes them down, but they don't like snow in the rough country for some reason. When snow comes they head for the flats for the winter. Late in the season you'll find few antelope at high elevations or even in the foothills. The fact is, antelope hunting is to be avoided any time after the last week in October.

At least two antelope states have certain areas with either late seasons or where closing dates are well up into November. Nearly all of Montana's antelope seasons run until November 10, which, as we'll see later, is too damn late to hunt antelope if you are looking for horns. Idaho has for several years had two antelope areas that haven't opened until early November; in 1969 it's November 8 to 23. All of these areas, in both states, permit drawing for permits by non-resident hunters who have bought a general big game license; Montana has several areas open to non-residents via a special $35 non-resident antelope permit.

What's wrong with this setup? Two things: At least 95% of the non-resident antelope hunters anywhere are trophy hunters to some extent, and a large part of the resident hunters also look for horns to shoot at. But what a lot of antelope hunters don't know is that any time after November 1 many of the bucks are starting to shed their horns; more importantly, in an average year in most areas, nearly all horns have been dropped by November 10!

There is one disadvantage to hunting antelope in rough country: if you haven't got a pony along, you have to pack him out on your own back. But it's worth it.

Late Season Hunting

I got my first taste of this late season hunting a few years ago in Idaho when I drew for one of the late hunts. I'd known that the bucks started shedding sometime in November, but I didn't think they'd be so far along by the time the season opened on the 8th. Andy Hagel, one of the country's leading taxidermists, and, incidentally, no relation to the writer, and I wanted to make the hunt together. We couldn't get loose at the same time for an earlier season area, so the late hunt was it.

Anyway, soon after we arrived, two things were immediately obvious: the antelope were all out on the flats where there wasn't even a wrinkle in the ground for miles on end, and most of the big bucks had already lost their headgear. Many of the hunters were not aware of this because the antelope (which has true horns, not antlers), sheds only the outer shell, not the central core. These are often mistaken for horns. I'm sure we saw at least 500 antelope on that trip, but we'll never know how many were bucks. Some of the smaller bucks still had horns, but they were safe as far as we were concerned.

The first evening we located a fairish buck with horns of about 14"-14½", but it took us three days of following him around to finally get within range when he made the mistake of going down a draw to avoid us. We were there when he came out and I clobbered him as he ran flat-out across the plain. His horns were hanging on only because the hide at the the base was still stuck to them; you could turn them in almost any direction. Andy wound up killing an even larger buck that had only the cores with their new growth starting up, just so we could see what we had. To top it off, neither of these bucks were fit to eat. They were snake-poor, the meat was blue, and you could smell them a country mile away.

In the fall of 1968 I got in on the same kind of a deal in Montana, but this time I was lucky. I drew for both antelope and deer in one of the areas where both special non-resident deer and antelope permits are issued. I missed on the antelope permit, but got a deer permit, thereby saving myself $35. My son, who lives in the Big Sky country, did have an antelope permit for the same area, but could not get away until after the first of November. We hunted antelope from the brakes of the Missouri along Fort Peck Reservoir to Highway #200, and from Jordan on the east to the Musselshell river on the west. There were antelope there, although I've been in places where there were a hell of a lot more, but there were few bucks that still had their horns. He never fired a shot because the only two we saw that were big enough to be interesting, and that still had something beside the cores sticking up, were on a posted ranch.

For a state that specializes in special non-resident antelope permits, knowing full well that 95% of the antelope hunters will be looking for heads, Montana is hitting the non-resident a low blow in allowing their season to run after the bucks have lost their horns. Idaho does no better, but does not specialize in non-resident antelope permits; Idaho gives the homefolks the backhand punch.

Anyway, plan to hunt antelope as early as the season allows, and if you want some of the finest stalking offered on the American continent, try hunting them in the rough country. ●

The shooting over, Andy Hagel (Hagel's Taxidermy, Salmon, Idaho) applies steel tape to a buck killed by the author. Out of several hundred pronghorns seen on the November hunt in Idaho, this was the only buck of trophy size that still had horns.

Firearms Advertising Envelopes

Advertising covers — envelopes to you — showing guns and cartridges were in common use 50 years ago and more, but little is known about them. Here's a detailed and informative history that includes sources and prices.

by Robert F. Denny

A NOT SO surprising result of the increasing population and decreasing hunting and shooting opportunities is the large number of one-time hunters and riflemen slowly being metamorphized into collectors.

The fields and forests that used to offer an evening woodchuck hunt, or the gravel pit that witnessed many a black circle being punched out of an NRA target, are distant memories They're now too far away or have become housing developments.

Our shooting has become sporadic, relegated to the one or two times a year we visit the country. To preserve our memories of shooting we seek other fields of interest to occupy our free hours, but, given the opportunity, our leisure-time interests still center around firearms.

The collecting and study of shooting and firearms materials has mushroomed in the past 15 years. Witness the number of gunbooks available, many of them monographs on subjects thought to be of little previous interest.

Any collector of firearms or car-

tridges can attest to the increasing scarcity, and cost, of items that, a few years ago, could be bought at junk prices.

Demand has also resulted in reproductions of firearms catalogs, advertising broadsides, leaflets and calendars. The neophyte collector soon realizes that there aren't many things related to firearms that haven't been tapped. Too often, if he does think of something different or unusual, cost or space quickly deter him. Who has room for a collection of muzzle-loading cannon, or the price of three or four Pope rifles?

There is *one* field however, that has been largely overlooked. This is the collecting of firearms advertising envelopes. Compact and still relatively inexpensive, these envelopes (or covers as the philatelists call them), are most attractive and informative to the firearms historian.

Initial Acquaintance

My discovery of such mementos of the past and the collecting of them began about two years ago, the result

of a short-lived interest in philately or stamp collecting. I joined a philatelic society or two and soon my mailbox was filled with auction catalogs and lists of postal material. In one of these I saw my first firearms advertising cover, an envelope displaying the Winchester 94 and extolling its manifold virtues. Other covers pictured other firearms, hunting scenes, game animals and related material, the advertisers arms and ammunition manufacturers and gun powder companies. I discovered also that these gun cover illustrations were in full color!

In all my previous reading of gunbooks, histories of firearms makers and arms magazines I was surprised that no attention had ever been given to advertising envelopes. I had never seen this illustrated material.

Like the proverbial bloodhound, I was off on a new trail. Dozens of questions came to mind. When were advertising envelopes first used and who used them? Who printed them? Who collected them and who had them for sale? How many different

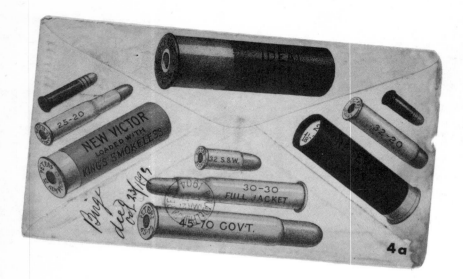

4a

5a

kinds were there? What were their current prices?

Price and Value

The prices came as a shock. After one auction I obtained a copy of the auction prices. My mail bids, guessed at in haste and with little knowledge, were low by one-fifth! Since then, however, I've purchased similar material for as little as fifty cents. At the other extreme, I've seen covers with price tags up to $11.50 and heard of some that were sold for $20 and $25. Like many other artistic and historic objects, there appear to be no accepted price standards. Through experience and inquiries, however, certain general statements about prices and pricing can be made.

Prices realized for such covers at auctions are usually somewhat higher than open-market costs. To some extent, this is caused by the excitement of auction proceedings — auction fever! More influential, however, is the generally better-quality material offered at auctions.

Average over-the-counter prices are about $4.00. Unused envelopes, that is, covers that do not indicate positive routing through a Post Office at the time of issue, usually cost about $1.00.

Prices for firearms covers in the past have been generally established by the stamp trade. The philatelist, for example, if interested in advertising covers might very well pay $5 for an illustrated cover, irrespective of the merchandise advertised. That the cover illustrates firearms is immaterial.

Dealers' prices are based primarily upon three factors: 1) scarcity, 2) condition, and 3) demand. Unfortunately, all covers displaying firearms are scarce. Auction prices also indicate that some collectors of firearms covers have rather high incomes. Covers dated in the 1880s or '90s bring higher prices than those of the early 20th century. In all instances, covers that have been through the mails and postmarked have much higher price tags than unused covers. To the philatelist, the reason is apparent. To the firearms enthusiast, however, postal usage is of little concern so long as a guarantee is obtained that the cover is a genuine original. Given two covers with identical designs, one in multicolor and the other monochrome, the colored cover would reap the highest bid.

Condition relates to the over-all neatness of the cover, the stamp, and the postmark. Clean, unripped advertising covers convey higher prices than soiled and damaged covers. Strangely enough, the postage stamp affixed to the cover, except in rare instances, does not affect cover value. It seems that stamps used for most mail at the turn of the century have little more philatelic value than the common postage stamps used to-day. Condition of the stamp and postmark however, if it distracts from the cover's over-all neatness, adversely affects price.

Demand for such covers from the rifle fraternity has been pretty light, probably because of a lack of acquaintance with them. Doubtlessly this will change. There is, however, a steady demand from our philatelic brethren, but it does not seem to increase at any fantastic rate. Prices of philatelic material have not increased as fast as coins or antique firearms.

United States stamps and covers in good or excellent condition, particularly those of the 19th and early 20th century, in spite of war, famine and depression, have always increased in dollar value at a rate comparable to or exceeding that of other investments. There is no reason to believe that firearms advertising covers will not react similarly.

Development and Usage

It is doubtful if any one factor was responsible for the development of such advertising media as the lowly envelope. The fad blossomed about 1890 and continued for a period of about 30 years.

Undoubtedly advertisers and lithographers were influenced to a great extent by the popularity of the illustrated patriotic covers that were sold by the millions during the Civil War. They may have reasoned that if people had enjoyed looking at envelopes of the then current war propaganda that they might enjoy attractive hunting scenes or a picture of a new rifle. If such works of art also included a pitch for a new product they were justified.

Firearms and gun powder were not the only products so-advertised. Tool, hardware, farm implement and carriage companies also did their best to out-advertise each other. About 1910 the automobile industry began a similar campaign. Soon tire chains and carburetors, engines and gasoline were pictured, in color, on the fronts and backs of commercial envelopes.

However, it appears that most of the firearms advertising covers were seldom seen by the buying public. As the photographs show, most envelopes were eventually sent to dealers and wholesalers. Apparently few were used for the billing of customers or personal correspondence. From the collector's point of view, perhaps, it is good that this occurred. Most individual recipients would have had little reason to preserve an envelope for the enjoyment of a future generation. It was the practice of industrial concerns in those days, however, to file both letter and envelope as records of correspondence. These were preserved until such time as the company disbanded or made an

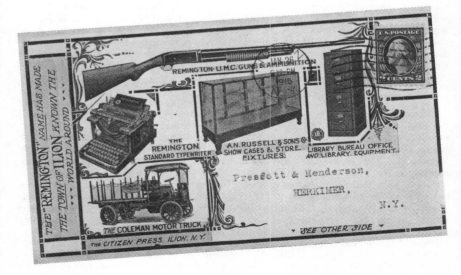

effort to clean out its files.

Such advertising was not restricted to the United States. As figs. 1 and 2 illustrate, various firearms companies with international sales issued such envelopes, appropriately printed in the proper language, to their foreign distributors. Such covers are rare today; the only two the author has seen are those illustrated.

Issuing Companies

Perhaps every firearms, gun powder and cartridge manufacturer issued envelopes to their retailers and jobbers. The list below is undoubtedly incomplete. It represents all such companies that can be accounted for through personal acquaintance with some 60 or 70 advertising covers.

Firearms: Winchester, Remington, Ithaca, Sauer, Hunter Arms Company (L. C. Smith), Stevens, Savage, Colt, Parker, Marlin and Iver Johnson.

Cartridges: Remington, UMC, U.S. Cartridge Co. and Peters.

Gun Powder: Hercules, Laflin and Rand, DuPont, Atlas, Hazard and Sycamore.

The hardware or sporting goods stores that had use of such advertising probably numbers in the hundreds or thousands since I have seldom seen two covers that originated from the same retailer.

Infinite Variety

Designs were as varied as they were tasteful. Some, as figs. 3 and 4 denote, were intended to be only artistic. Others (figs. 5 and 6) are adventurous. The hard-sell of present-day advertising is approached in figs. 7 and 8, the soft-sell in fig. 9. Occasionally humor and danger were indicated. One cover pictured a well-equipped rifleman and a brown bear high on a rocky ledge, apparently hunting each other.

Women received attention, too. Several covers show lady trapshooters or ladies afield with dog and gun. All were properly attired, of course, as befitting the sport.

Winchester and Remington, as might be expected, seem to have been the most prolific with envelopes of various designs. They certainly offered some of the most adventurous illustrations ever to pass through a postman's hands. What spirit of restlessness must have been generated in the hearts of some by the picture of a hunter on snowshoes tracking game, or the view of three elk, one with a massive head, crashing through a primitive forest.

Designs were chosen to exemplify the company's stock in trade. The J. Stevens Arms and Tool Company often pictured a target shooter, off-hand position of course, equipped with the then new Stevens-Pope target rifle. Open field scenes, bird dogs, or people engaged in trapshooting were pictured to advertise shotguns. Game birds were a favorite of gun powder companies. Other covers pic-

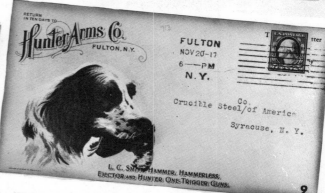

tured wild turkeys, Indians on horse-back, campfire scenes, bears, cougars, and bird dogs; all tastefully and ar-tistically crafted.

Early covers usually pictured only a finely engraved cut of a shotgun or rifle. Verbal descriptions of course, were included.

Advertising was often printed on both sides of the envelope. Figs. 4a through 6a illustrate the attempt to obtain a maximum amount of adver-tising from a minimum amount of envelope. Generally the front of the cover presented the hunting or the wild game scene, the back of the en-velope reserved for the printed mes-sage. Occasionally, smaller illustra-tions of firearms were also printed on the back in conjunction with the printed matter.

Few covers provided complete il-lustrations or pictorial matter on both sides. One cover, issued by Peters depicted a wild turkey covering half the face of the envelope while the re-verse side was illustrated with 10 different cartridges and shotshells. Both sides are in full color.

Color Covers

In the 1890s covers were most often printed in but one color. The cover in fig. 10, dated 1893, is printed in a light brown. Blue, black, orange, and red were also used, perhaps others.

As the years passed, however, mono-chrome printing evolved into bicolor and, by the early part of the 20th century, hunting and game scenes blossomed out in multicolor lithog-raphy. Soon all shades and color combinations were in use. In most instances inks were carefully chosen to picture the hunting and wild game scenes in natural color. The results exemplify the high standards of litho-graphic art attained at that time.

Colors chosen for the printed mes-sages and trademarks reflected the individual companies' taste. Winches-ter, for example, used bright red for most of its inscriptions. Observant readers will recognize that the same color is still used by this company today.

A lithographers catalog picturing samples of firearms advertising avail-able to manufacturers of rifles, pow-der and cartridges would be invalu-able to the collector. My efforts to locate such a treasure have been futile. Many dealers and philatelists and a few firearms enthusiasts know of their existence, but no one has much additional information. Perhaps this article will provide the impetus to someone to investigate the story more fully.

Sources of Supply

Quite possibly there are hoards of such firearms advertising stacked away in attics or correspondence bins of some old hardware stores. The treasures that may be found for the price of an hour's conversation and a cup of coffee could amaze the collec-

tor. Should nothing result, the time spent would be in good company.

A better source is the dealer in United States stamps and covers. Occasionally a dealer will be found who is not aware of the increasing interest in firearms advertising and, therefrom, covers may be obtained at a lower price. The number of such naïve dealers is slowly diminishing.

Members of the American Stamp Dealers Association are a good source, and can be counted on to provide fair and reasonable service. Here are some men I've dealt with:

Samuel C. Paige, 45 Bromfield St., Boston, Mass. 02108.

W. T. Pollitz, 45 Bromfield St., Boston, Mass. 02108.

Charles J. Molnar, 1246 Summit Drive, Cleveland, O. 44124.

Stanley H. Waite, 3 Washburn Terrace, Brookline 46, Mass.

Harrington's Stamp Shop, Deansboro, N. Y. 13328.

E. N. Sampson, Box 162, Hammond, N. Y. 13646.

Frank S. Landers, 155 Woodbury Rd., Huntington, L.I., N.Y.

R. H. Hess, P. O. Box 3145, Inglewood, Calif., 90304

Care and Cleaning

In the beginning, questions may arise as to the best means of storage and display or, if a somewhat soiled cover is obtained, a bit of judicious cleaning may be necessary.

The best help in both these respects will usually be from a local stamp dealer. Like some gunsmiths and sporting goods dealers, he is apt to spend as much time giving worthwhile advice on sundry matters as he does working.

The ideal arrangement is to provide protection for the cover yet make it possible to view both sides of the envelope, should advertising be so imprinted. This can be done cheaply with transparent glassine envelopes. Higher in cost are book-like cover albums similar to photo albums. Several dozen covers may be effectively stored in such albums. Each cover is encased in a slip-through acetate pocket so hinged that both sides may be examined. Whichever the choice, protection from soiled hands and careless handling is provided. The covers may be old and brittle. They are scarce and care should be taken to preserve them.

Do not mount covers with cellophane pressure tape. This otherwise useful product starts disintegrating in a few months. It will stick to and stain any paper product to which it is attached or that comes in contact with it.

Firearms covers obtained through dealers or at auction are usually quite clean but sometimes pencil marks are found on the envelopes. The collector may find these distasteful, but such markings can be effectively erased by a soft art-gum eraser. In fact, the art-gum eraser can be trusted to accomplish most, if not all, cleaning of soiled areas caused by grease or other dirt. Liquid cleaners should be avoided since they may adversely affect the envelope paper, the glue holding the cover together, or the inks used in printing.

Framing a group of firearms covers is another way to provide both protection and an ttractive display. Arranged formally or informally, perhaps with an original or a photo copy of an advertising broadside or circular, a small collection would provide a touch of color and nostalgia suitable for den or gunroom.

Collecting

To some extent, all riflemen and hunters are collectors. My armory consists of many rifles, combining the best skills and craftsmanship that modern manufacturing can produce. All shoot and shoot well. They are not antiques in any respect and, by some standards, would not be called a collection. They aren't used very often, and certainly not enough to justify their cost and care. Yet, they are among my most treasured possessions—their value being primarily intangible. Since there is more than one rifle in the rack, and since value is measured by more than mere utility, by my definition it has to be a collection.

Most collections of things aren't worth much in cash, and will hardly ever alter history. Their value is measured in other ways. It is of such stuff that museums are made, filled with wondrous things that stir the imagination and kindle strange fires. The past should be preserved. Not to escape the present, but to bring contentment for things accomplished and condition the perspective of the future. I think this applies equally to the advertising arts as well as the masterpieces of the gunsmiths.

When I think of the adventurous scenes of hunters and campfires, black bear and elk that once graced thousands of firearms advertising envelopes, it makes me wonder how many postal clerks, *circa* 1910, might have been stirred to less mundane activities after seeing dozens of these covers pass through their hands. I wonder if any one of them quit his job, bought a rifle, a box of new smokeless shells, and left for the North country. . . . I think I would have. ●

Printers and lithographers: the information below is probably of little interest to the individual wanting a few firearms covers to supplement his collection. It is, rather, oriented to the firearms advertising researcher, present or future, who wants to pursue the subject to greater depth.

These are some of the printers and lithographers that produced firearms advertising covers: The Knapp Co. Lithographers, New York; F. E. Getty (no address); "FAATZ," L. E. Stersmire (or Lestermire), New York; Bartlett and Co., New York; Dietzer-Sale Litho Co., Buffalo, N. Y.

garcia guns 1970

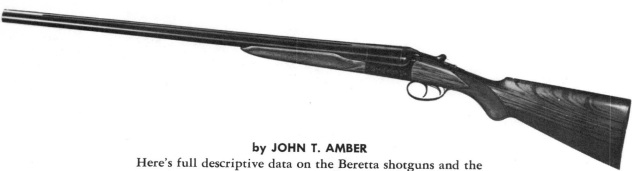

by JOHN T. AMBER

Here's full descriptive data on the Beretta shotguns and the
Sako rifles that appear on our front and back covers,
plus a rundown on the full Garcia-Beretta-FI lines in general.

Garcia Sporting Arms Corporation—which became the sole distributor of Beretta shotguns last year, and took over Firearms International more recently—furnished us with the Beretta and Sako arms pictured in full color on the front and back cover of this 25th Silver Anniversary edition of the GUN DIGEST.

One of the world's finest over-under shotguns, the Beretta Crown Grade SO-5, was selected for one of the two smoothbores shown on our front cover. The SO-5 is the top over-under shotgun in Beretta's extensive line, and everyone is a masterpiece that exhibits the combined skills and artistry of the gunsmith, the stocker and the engraver. Only the finest and fanciest-figure European walnut is used, the checkering is extra fine-line, and the most careful, painstaking attention is lavished on inletting, fitting-up and jointing to the metal. Buttstocks and fore-ends are cut from the same blank, of course, for full matching of grain flow and color. A hand-rubbed oil finish is standard, but glossy or wax finishes are optional. The standard stock on the Crown Grade is a pistol-grip type that measures 1½ inches drop at the comb nose, 2½ inches at the heel, with a 14⅛-inch pull length. However, on special order stocks can be made to the customer's specifications, and straight-hand or pistol grip as desider.

The SO-5 locks are of the fully-detachable sidelock form, of extremely simple and rugged construction. All friction surfaces are specially hardened, and all inside action parts are hard chrome-plated. Barrel locking is by means of two lugs extending from from either side of the upper barrel into mating slots in the standing breech, these locked in place by a modified Greener crossbolt system.

Barrels for the Crown Grade Berettas are made from the best barrel metal to be had—Böhler Antinit (rustless) steeel, made in Austria—and that's true of all SO-series barrels. Made normally in 26- and 28-inch length and 12 gauge only, the regular boring in improved cylinder/modified and modified/full respectively. On special order, though, barrels can be had with any choice of choking, and from 26 to 30 inches. Ventilated ribs are furnished on all SO-series guns, and all have a matted, knurled top to kill glare. SO-4 and SO-5 ribs are hand matted. Barrels may be ordered with chrome-plated bores, if desired.

Two triggers are usual on all of the SO-series over-under doubles, but selective single triggers are available. Auto ejectors are standard, as is an auto safety, but a manual safety may be ordered.

All SO Berettas carry hand-cut engraving, but the SO-5 grade we illustrate carries the finest and most lavish. The deep relief chiseling is perfectly executed and covers virtually all metal except the barrels, including screw heads, tangs, fore-end release, etc. The thumb-piece of the top-snap opening lever is filigreed (pierced) and engraved, and a superbly done gold crown is inlaid in the broad top lever.

All other SO over-unders—which start with the SO-2 (I don't' know why there isn't an SO-1!) and run through the SO-3 and SO-4—are equally well-built and offer the same functional features as does the SO-5. The essential differences are in the embellishments and visual aspects of one grade against the other—the wood quality, the engraving, the checkering and so on.

What does this luxuriousness cost?

Well, the SO-5 guns carry a catalog price of $1750, to which you'd add something for the options mentioned. Extra barrels ordered with the SO-5 are $460. The SO-2 grade lists for $950, extra barrels $365, while the SO-4 and SO-4 guns are in between. Whatever grade, a fair amount of money is involved, no question about that. Still, just about everyone of you reading this owns an automobile in one price class or another, and in a year or three you'll be buying another. You'll spend anywhere from a minimum of $2000 or so up to $5000 and more (and these figures might rise to $3000-$6000 if inflation keeps up, as it looks like doing), yet in a few short years most of those new cars will be ready for the junkyard. In the interim, more thousands of dollars will have been spent on fuel and care, heavy insurance charges, tires and the like.

Now, that doesn't happen when you buy—invest is a better and truer term—a really first class shotgun, believe me. Let's say you put $1500 or so into a fine smoothbore, and that you give it decent care over the next 5 or 10 years. At the end of that time, say 10 years or so, it's an absolute verity that your top grade double gun is going to be worth more than you paid for it, assuming that the dollar is going to continue to lose value—which is just what it has been doing for 150 years or more, notwithstanding the temporary reversals of the trend brought about by such catastrophes as our Great Depression of the 1930s.

Don't you wish—those of you who were young men or a bit beyond that in the late 1930s — that you had bought a Parker VHE or a Model 21 Winchester when both could be had at a full retail price of about $150?

A collection of Garcia's Berettas. From left: SO-4, BL-5, AL-2, TR-1 and SL-2. The GR-2 is shown on the preceding page.

That price bought either of these fine —if relatively plain—guns with fancy wood, beavertail fore-ends, single selective triggers, auto ejectors and ventilated ribs—plus a quality of workmanship and detailing hard to come by in American firearms today.

I know! That $150 or so wasn't burning a hole in many pockets in 1938-1940, but I don't imagine that a spare $1000-$1800 is much more readily to hand today. Nevertheless, these are the money mechanics I'm pointing up; how to solve 'em is where you come in.

Gee, I wish I'd had sense enough in 1939 to buy one of those Parkers at $150, or one of their GHE or DHE grades at . . .

Two brand new Berettas are on the Garcia list for 1970. These, the SO-6 and the SO-7, are side-by-side doubles that equal the top grade SO-4 and SO-5 over-unders in quality and lavishness of treatment generally, in the variety of chokes and barrel lengths offered, and in the optional constructional details and dimensions to be had on special order. We've not as familiar with these latest Berettas as we'd like to be, but Berettas in this quality and price bracket ($1360-$1820) leave little to be desired and nothing to criticize.

Beretta BL Series

The other over-under double gun on our front cover is one of Garcia's BL series, a line of high quality boxlock guns in the popular price range —a gamut these days that runs from about $200 to $500, with a few models at the top end commanding a price a bit higher.

There are 5 models in the BL group, and all of them have several features of construction in common, important aspects they all share. First there's the low profile of the BL receiver, achieved through an unusual—perhaps unique—method of hinging and barrel lockup. The hinge pins are located at a point alongside the middle of the lower barrel, not underneath as with so many other over-unders. There are no underlugs on the Beretta BL barrels, thus a considerably shorter receiver, top to bottom, is obtained. This makes for a gun easier to handle, lighter over-all, stronger and, because the mass of the receiver is around the barrels, not below them, recoil is reduced and a second shot can be got off faster.

Recoil—*felt* recoil, that is—is reduced because thrust is more directly rearwards, and lessened muzzle lift means getting back on the sights faster for that second shot.

A second common factor in all BL guns is barrel construction. Barrels, of chrome-moly steel, are processed at the Beretta factory through all steps from the raw, forged solid billet through boring, reaming and chambering to the point where they're ready for insertion into the Monobloc breeches. All machining is done on the Monobloc, none on the barrels, where the attachment of lugs, ribs, etc., requires spot heating and the attendant danger of distorsion and alteration of tensile strength. In addition, the Monobloc technique of mounting barrels results in a much stronger system.

A third feature of all BL Berettas is a clever and foolproof barrel selector system.

In many double guns, the top-tang sliding safety combines with a button or whatever to let the shooter switch from top barrel to bottom—or vice versa—and in this system it's necessary, usually, to shove the safety back to the 'Safe' position before chang-ing barrels. Not so with Beretta's BL doubles—the changeover can be made instantly, whether the safety is on 'Safe' or not. An excellent idea, and one that could well let you kill that bird that you could have failed to grass with a selector button you had to fumble with.

Mainsprings in all BL guns are of coiled type, made of the best Swedish steel; breech faces are grooved to deflect and carry gases away if a primer fails, and all BL guns show careful attention to excellent fit of wood to metal, of meticulous filing, stoning and smooth-working assembly of internal parts for perfect functioning and dependable operation.

From here on, however, the BL grades differ: BL-1 is a 2 trigger gun, made without a barrel rib, but the front trigger is hinged, a feature usually found only on guns with a much higher price tag—this lets you find the rear trigger faster, and also keeps your trigger finger from banging into the back of the front trigger when the rear trigger is touched off.

The BL-2 is like the BL-1 but has a single selective trigger, and both are available only in 12 gauge field grade, with 26", 28" or 30" barrels.

The BL-3 comes with a ventilated rib, nicely matted, a single trigger of selective type and plain extractors. Engraving on the BL-3 is of better quality and more extensive, and new this year are BL-3s in 20- and 28-gauge chambering and as Skeet guns with 2½" chambers. A 12-gauge 3" Magnum is also on the list, as are 12-gauge Skeet and trapguns. These target type BL-3s are $25 extra, but that also covers special sears, a manual safety, middle sights and straighter stocks, with Monte Carlo combs, and a trap-style recoil pad on the

BL-3 Trap Gun.

The BL-4 (the style shown on our cover) and the BL-5 are alike except for the latter offering a fully engraved, gray-finished receiver, better quality wood and finer, more extensive checkering. Both have auto ejectors, all other features of the BL-1, BL-2 and BL-3 guns mentioned, and both are available in the same wide choice of gauges listed for the BL-3.

Standard stock dimensions for all five BL 12, 20 and 28 Field and Skeet grades are: 1½"x2½"x14⅛", but trapguns have a trigger pull length of 14⅜", with drop figures of 1⅜" by 1¾". All can be had with extra sets of barrels, though differing a bit within grades as to chokes, lengths and price, of course.

Garcia-F.I.

The two rifles on our back covers are from Firearms International, an organization well and favorably known, that was recently acquired by Garcia.

The smaller rifle seen is the Sako Vixen, called by F.I. the "most accurate production rifle in the world." Well, that's a claim that takes in an awful lot of territory, but it is true that a Sako rifle, a 222 right off the shelf and without tuning, once set a world records at 100 yards in a National Bench Rest Rifle Assn. shoot—10 shots in the Light Varmint class making a target only .209" center-to-center.

Will they *all* do that well, sans tuning and whatever? I doubt it. Yet no one can deny that's a mighty nice performance, and it is indicative of what the Sako L-461 actioned rifle *can* do, and it is equally true that the L-461 action—with or without Sako barrel—has been a much-sought-after item for many years—when it could be bought! They were a scarce unit for a long time, but the supply seems to be in better shape nowadays. The Sako Vixen rifles are made in only three calibers—222, 222 Magnum and 223. The rifles come in three styles; a standard Sporter, a Heavy Barreled version, and in Carbine form, with full length or Mannlicher stock and a 20" barrel. The others use a 23½" barrel.

The other Sako pictured on our back cover is the Finnbear (L-61), made only as a half-stocked sporter and in such bigger calibers as 270, 30-06 and most of the belted magnum calibers, including the newly added 375 H&H. A rugged and well-built action, the Finnbear, and very well suited to the more potent big game loads.

The rest of the Garcia F.I. line continues pretty much intact, though there have been some product changes since a year ago. The Sako Forester bolt action and the Finnwolf lever action rifles show no change, nor does the F.N. Supreme bolt action rifle line.

Newest additions to the Garcia line are the excellent Sako rifles shown here. From top: Vixen Heavy Barrel, Forester Sporter and the Finnwolf (Finnbear, also available, is not shown).

The AYA shotgun line—a sidelock double and three boxlock side-by-sides—has been dropped, it appears, and the LaSalle auto and pump shotguns are no longer listed. The Musketeer rifles, Mauser-actioned, have been retained, and a new line of double-barreled shotguns—with outside hammers—has been added to the list. The "Overland" arms are made by Rossi in Brazil, suppliers also of the Regent Gallery Model 22 slide-action rifle and Presentation revolvers (22 LR and 38 Special), new on the F.I. list.

F.I. still carries the Gaucho, Star, Astra Cadix, Regent, Taurus and Unique handguns—revolvers and autos—but not in quite as full an array as before, thanks doubtless to the stringencies of the GCA 1968 in good part.

Other Garcia/Berettas

The AL-2 gas-operated autoloader (made in 12- and 20-gauge) has some new touches this year. Buttstock and fore-end show more checkering, in a new pattern, treatment of the now-capped pistol grip has been improved, and the fore-end offers a wider, more hand-filling form. Field guns show new de luxe engraving, with additional amounts on Skeet and trap models. Easy and virtually complete disassembly of the AL-2 permits quick cleaning and inspection, a much-ne-

glected job with some other autos. Extra barrels are readily exchanged, too, without tools or initial factory fitting.

The AL-2 offers extra safety, too—live shells can be removed from the magazine without shuffling them through the action, and a heavy, hardened steel block cams the firing pin back until the bolt is fully home.

The rest of the large Garcia-Beretta line continues in production—there's an inexpensive single-barrel folding gun in 12 or 20; another single made in 12 gauge only, the TR-1 or TR-2, and an excellent buy in a trapgun at its low $160 cost ($185 for the vent-rib TR-2); the fine Beretta GR series, a range of side-by-side doubles in 12- and 20-gauge, I consider Best Buys in their type class: the GR-4, made with single selective trigger, ventilated rib, auto ejectors and a semi-beavertail fore-end, is an especially good value.

The Beretta SL-2, a recently-introduced pump 12 bore that exhibits numerous excellent features, appears to have been taken off the Garcia list, perhaps *pro tem*.

Beretta will be delivering a single barrel trapgun before long, Dick Wolff has told me. This will be on the BL frame, their boxlock gun, and the tentative designation is the Mark II.

THE NATIONAL RIFLE CLUB

The story of an 1886 shoot between the last
of the great muzzle-loading marksmen and the
breech-loading upstarts from Walnut Hill.

Introduction and notes by John T. Amber

WE ARE particularly pleased to reprint this account of a great event in shooting history from the 1886 pages of **Forest & Stream.** It was the occasion, apparently, of the first shoulder-to-shoulder contest between the die-hard advocates of the muzzle-loading rest rifle and several noted marksmen using the newfangled breechloaders (these last had only been in use generally for some dozen years).

Mr. Murray Leyde of Painesville, Ohio, an old friend, was kind enough to send me a photo copy of the old account. In it I learned exactly how string measurements were made in that period, clearly and without question—as you will learn in your reading of the report. It had been assumed that the technique was pretty much as the anonymous correspondent has it, but here is the exact methodology outlined. Briefly, each shot in the string was measured from the intersection of the diagonal lines to the bullet hole, then the 10 measurements were simply added together.

It is difficult to compare these old string scores with today's targets—most commonly measured from center to center of the bullet holes farthest apart—unless a reproduction to a known scale of the old target is available for measuring. In the present instance we have two of them to assess.

Fletcher's first string measures 2⅝″ center to center, the string total 9⁷⁄₁₆″ as the table shows. Brown's third string measures 3⁹⁄₁₆″—almost a full inch greater than Fletcher's—but Brown's string score on his ten shots is 9¹³⁄₁₆″, or only ⅜″ worse. Fletcher's group is quite obviously a better one than Brown's, but simply reading the string measurements would not have revealed the graphic difference.

Another nice bit of source data given in this 1886 report is the quite exact load information put down for most of the contestants, to say nothing of the drawing that depicts, to scale, the variety of bullets used by 15 of the marksmen.

Further comments will appear in the text, set inside brackets.

W. Milton Farrow
From an old cut

VERNON, Vt., May 27, 1886. — A dozen sedate looking gentlemen squatted along on low stools, clad in work-a-day clothes, each looking with a pre-occupied air out through the low shutter opening of the house in which they sat. Then a lull in the blowing gale and away banged a dozen rifles with the noise and effect of small pieces of ordnance. This was the scene which greeted your correspondent on his arrival at this quiet Green Mountain hamlet yesterday morning.

It was the annual spring meet of the National Club, and the men were shooting with the old style muzzleloaders at the old-fashioned targets, and scoring according to the old mode of string measure. They were a sort of Rip Van Winkle gathering, and one felt prompted to ask where they had taken the long nap and where they had kept the weapons from

rusting all the time. The club itself had grown into one of the institutions of the country. Its record runs back long befo' de wah, and far back in the fifties and forties the charter members tell of gatherings where there was *some* shooting, plenty of rivalry and no end of a good social time. The weapons of those days were indeed massive affairs, and the printed notices of the meetings with the list of allowances which the 40-lb. barrels are to make to the 15-lb. pigmies shows what at one time were the classes of rifles in the meetings.

The club has been a progressive affair though, and now such a thing as a 40-pound barrel would be a rarity. Members recall such, but they were handicapped out of existence and nobody seems particularly sorry that they have gone. The club is rather an aggregation of atoms

than a complete entity. There are officers elected at the fall meeting. Then a programme is made up. It is always the same. Three strings of 10 shots each. Shot on two days. Each one shooting hands $5 to the secretary. This fund pays the trifling expenses of the meeting and the remainder is divided in a sweepstake fashion. Those who enter become members for the nonce and when the meeting breaks up and the shooters take courtly adieus one of another the society exists only in the secretary's note-book until the next gathering. There are no disputes, no expensive machinery, no eating up of funds in managerial waste. Simple shoot and good fellowship, what could be more truly rural, more idyllic, more sportsman-like.

The oldest member shook his head, thought a while, thought some more, and finally said that he reckoned the first steps were taken in 1854 or '55 toward making the gatherings more formal than they had been. Before that time they had met and shot, but after a surprise party fashion, nobody being quite sure when he started for the rendezvous whether he would have a solitary bit of practice or whether he would form one of a jolly company. All in all the club is a unique sort of an institution. The one great aim of its members is to secure the greatest accuracy. Such a trifling fact as the utter impracticability of lugging the arm about in any useful fashion for hunting or general target work, does not seem to bother the National members at all. Once convinced that they can gain a quarter-inch on a string of 10 shots by adding half a dozen pounds of metal to the barrel and the added weight is put on without a question.

[Ned Roberts wrote *(The Muzzle-Loading Cap Lock Rifle)* that the National Club was organized on June 16 of 1858. The first matches were held at Waltham, Mass., with the matches at Vernon, Vt., beginning in 1868, said Roberts. See his book for further data on the match rules, etc.]

This particular spring meet was to become an episode in the history of the club. Much correspondence had been indulged in with the Walnut Hill marksmen, and these capital shooters of the modern school had promised to come up Vermontward and try conclusions with their antediluvian prototypes. The old fellows were delighted with the prospect of a good lively set-to, for the spirit of fight is strong within them, and there had been so much talk on the everlasting theme of Muzzle vs. Breechloader that everybody was charmed at the prospect of having the two classes of arms brought side by side, each in the hands of enthusiastic experts and each shooting under the same weather conditions. So when the 12 o'clock train came up from the southward at yester noon, and out of it tumbled Hinman and Rabbeth, Frye, Ellsworth and Maynard, each with rifle and shooting traps, it was generally agreed that the spring meeting of 1886 was to be a big success. The chroniclers were there too, ready with pen and pencil to picture in word and line the doings of this novel rifle meet. Mr. Gould came down from Boston, that *The Rifle* might know all that occurred, and with convenient camera caught the various doings of the riflemen.

[The Walnut Hill club at Woburn, near Boston, has been a world-famous institution since 1875, the year of its incorporation. Harry Pope, Adolph Niedner, Franklin W. Mann—in addition to those mentioned in the account here—and many other shooters renowned in their day were members of Walnut Hill. ● Arthur C. Gould (1850-1903) was the editor of *The Rifle* (1885-1888), its successor *Shooting & Fishing* (1888-1906) until his death. He also wrote two excellent books, especially worth studying by those in-

Wm. V. Lowe at his machine rest in Vernon, Vermont. After a photograph.

terested in shooting lore of the past— one was *Modern American Rifles,* the other *Modern American Pistols and Revolvers.* Both were long unavailable until reprinted by Tom Samworth in the 1940s. Unfortunately, both are again out of print.

A. C. Gould, who also wrote as Ralph Greenwood, exerted a strong influence on rifle and handgun shooting in his time. He had a vast enthusiasm for shooting, he wrote well and with full knowledge of his field.]

The newcomers were greeted in the most kindly spirit. There was the range 40 rods away from that little outhouse sort of a shooting box. Across yonder bit of low-lying water-covered meadow to the face of the low hill, where a temporary fence of slab boards sufficed to hold the paper targets. Sticks here and there held all manner of streamers, for each marksman carried his own private wind signals, and stuck them up as his fancy dictated. Some used long whip-lash streamers of silk, slightly weighted at the tip. Others again preferred the bag-like bits of muslin and these stood out like great bleached bolognas. One had contrived a wee wind signal, a model on a quarter-inch scale of the big dial at Creedmoor. It was a picturesque range, but the main interest was at the firing point. Here was the house we have mentioned, about 20 ft. long; on the side facing the targets away to the westward, shutters lifted up, really opening the house side. They were low and one was compelled to stoop or sit down on the low stools if a view of the targets was desired. Pushed up against this opening ranged in line were the rests on which the muzzleloaders were placed. They were of the saw-horse pattern, securely fastened to stakes driven into the soil and so arranged that when placed upon them the gun muzzle would be about 2 ft. from the ground. Along the other side of

the shooting house was the loading table, an ordinary workbench with notches along its front edge, and here the members do the manual work of the shooting, the cleaning and swabbing, patching and loading, with all that care and deliberation which characterizes the typical muzzle-man.

Let us take our friends in order, beginning in that far away corner where a portly gentlemen whose clear eyes in a measure belie the slight tinge of gray in his hair. He is Mr. R.C. Cressy of Brattleboro, Vt. His arm is of Brockway make, with an octagonal barrel, and comes just within the 15 lbs. standard 28 in. barrel. It has a caliber of 39, with an even twist of 1 turn in 16 inches, 8 grooves. The bullet is of Brockway make, forced out cold under a 40-ton pressure into long rods, then cut off in lengths and again swaged to shape. They have a uniform composition of 1 tin to 20 lead. The powder which Mr. Cressy uses is Hazard FFg. A bullet picked up from his box weighed 338½ grains, while a powder charge weighed 84½ grains. He uses a greased paper patch laid in two pieces across the gun muzzle. Like the majority of the other weapons, his arm is slightly choke bored, a point upon which some of the marksmen lay a great deal of stress. His method of attaching the weapon to the rest is very simple. The crosspiece attached to the barrel has in it a V-shaped notch (in front), and this goes to a screw fastened in the rest top. In the rear there are the usual thumbscrews, one below lifting the rear of the piece, and one on either side giving the brass notched piece in which the barrel rests a lateral motion.

Next to Mr. Cressy sits D.A. Brown, of Boston. He has a round barrel arm made by Warner, of Syracuse. It falls within the 15 lbs. standard, has a uniform twist of rifling with one turn in 20 in., 8 grooves, of 45 caliber. The barrel is 30 in. long, and is slightly larger at the muzzle than the breech, the purpose of this disposition of weight of metal being to stiffen this outer end of the barrel and prevent in a measure the springing of the barrel. Mr. Brown uses a Warner made bullet with a hard point built up of a 1 to 1 antimony and tin composition, while the rear end of the bullet is of pure lead. The two parts are closely swaged together and the taking of the rifling by the pure lead heel is the point aimed at in this composite missile. He uses powder of the Dead Shot brand, American Powder Company make. The bullet, weighed by your correspondent, as all the other powder and bullet weights in this report were taken, showed a weight of 671 grains, while a single powder charge showed 142½ grains. In loading, Mr. Brown uses a linen shellacked and then greased, two narrow strips laid crossways of the muzzle in order that the 8 grooves might be taken uniformly. His shooting stand resembles exactly a miniature gun carriage. There are two long ways on either side on which the cross head forward rests and slides, while at the rear there are two side and bottom screws. Mr. Brown is deliberation and good nature itself. His every motion is cyphered down to a system, and it is almost amusing to see him pour the powder in and then with moistened rod at once look for it. Yet in this way he avoids that constant menace of the absent-minded muzzle marksman, a bullet in the barrel and no powder behind it.

Next in line came Farrow—W. Milton Farrow, known on every rifle range from California to Constantinople. He is now a Brattleboro resident, making rifles, and it was one of his own make that he was shooting. He had secured a rest and had elbowed his way in among the old timers. His weapon was the pigmy one of the meeting. It weighed complete but 9 lbs., had a 34 in. barrel of 32-cal. and had 7 grooves of 1 turn in 16 in. The rifling was peculiar with a ratchet cut and one on which Mr. Farrow pinned his faith. The powder charge—American Co. FF. make—weighed 45 grs. and the bullet 163½ grs. The last was a 1 to 20 composition, hot drawn. In loading, Mr. Farrow, after carefully cleaning, inserted the patched bullet, and after pushing it home with a gauged wooden rod, from the rear inserted the freshly loaded cartridge shell behind it. Mr. Farrow had all the advantages of the dead rest, the long sight and the sliding when the recoil came. He had clamped a crosspiece to his barrel near the muzzle and this enabled him to use the wooden rest he had secured.

[Farrow was probably the best rifleman of his long day—about 1878 to 1898. Not only did he win numerous matches in the U.S., he went to Europe where he literally beat everybody. He won top awards in military style shooting, as well as in offhand or schuetzen shooting. See his own book, *How I Became a Crack Shot,*

and Roberts and Waters' book, *The Breech-Loading Single-Shot Match Rifle* for details of his life and feats.]

Mr. L. Park, of Greenfield, Mass., was next in the line of closely-crowded shooters. He was the funny fellow of the company and sandwiched his shots with rallies of wit. He had come up to have a good time, and his advice to those about him on shooting topics would have filled a manual on the subject. He strongly urged a member who had missed the foot-square target to take the rifle down and introduce the weapon to the target, while his sly jokes at the men who knew it all were often keen and to the point. He had an octagonal 15 lbs. barrel, 38-cal., 1 to 16 even twist, 8 grooves. The bullets were of uniform composition, 1 tin to 20 lead, and the powder used was Hazard's FFg. The barrel was 30 in. long, and was made by Brockway. A charge taken showed 82½ grains of powder to 356 grains of lead. In loading he used paper patches; while on the rest a very complete brass cast rear device for elevating and swinging the rifle butt. The big, booming piece did not look out of place in Mr. Park's big, brawny clutch. He handled it like a toy pistol, but a puny National Guardsman would have found it a stiff burden.

Mr. F. Fenn is one of the younger members of the club. He resides at Dover Plains, N.Y., but generally manages to get up and enjoy the shoots. He uses a gun made by Phillips, of New York, and in this meeting was in very bad luck, owing, he thought to the use of some special cartridge he had made. These were of the composite type with a hard point made by putting 2 ounces of antimony in a pound of lead, while the bullet heels were of pure lead. The weapon was of 45-caliber, having 8 grooves of gain-twist rifling starting in at one turn in 72 inches and finishing with one turn in 24 inches. The barrel was 27 inches long, of octagonal form, and into it he poured Hazard's FFg powder. One charge weighed showed 128 grains, while one of the bullets turned the scale at 572 grains. A stout wooden block (plank) held the gun while the entire block was moved on its bed from (the) center pin forward by the three rear screws. It was a simple, strong, though somewhat clumsy device. A paper patch was used in loading.

[Edwin Phillips of New York City was a riflemaker of the highest attainments as well as a fine shooter. Little is known of his life or his rifles, but at least one beautiful rifle by Phillips may be seen in detail in *George Schoyen — Riflemaker Extraordinary,* by John Dutcher in this 25th GUN DIGEST. Phillips is listed in Swinney's *New York State Gunmakers* and in *American Gun Makers,* but only just.]

Mr. E.B. Stephenson followed along the line with his big muzzle-loader. It shook a small section of the State when it went off. It was a 50-caliber weapon with a 30 in. 15 lbs. octagonal barrel made by Ferris. There were 9 grooves,

necessitating in loading three paper patch slips. The rifling grooves were concentric with the bore of the barrel and had a gain twist increasing from 1 in 72 to 1 in 24 in. The bullet is worthy of special attention. It was of the composite order, with a soft heel, a soft point and a hard inner section, this gave its close grip on the rifling when the upsetting came which was particularly striven for in this make of bullet. A paper patch was used and Hazard's FFg powder. A charge taken and weighed showed 603 grains of lead and 118½ of powder. The rest device was the simplest in the house. Two bent strips on either side forward preventing any jumping up of the muzzle, while aft the barrel rested on a broad tongue, the upturned edges of which afforded place for the screws used in side adjustments.

Veteran L.C. Smith was next in the line, a patriarch among patriarchs, he knows the history of the club since its formation. He was a charter member and has never missed a meeting. He is yet full of shoot and is always deep in some experiment to settle some point in the science of rifle shooting. The consequence is that as a prize winner his name does not appear as often as it otherwise would. His gun has a 28-inch octagon barrel. To name its maker would be difficult, since it has been cut and re-cut so frequently. It is of 46-cal. with a uniform twist of 1 in 18. The bullet is of similar make to that used by Mr. Brown, and comes from the works of Warner, at Syracuse. Behind it he puts Fg powder of Hazard make. A sample charge weighed 113 grains in powder and 649 grains in bullet. He uses a cut paper patch, made in the form of a Greek cross, so that the paper is not doubled below the heel of the bullet. His rest in shooting is a very complete one with a pair of guiding ways forward, while the shifting of the trigger end is done with great throttle valve wheels. This, as many of the other guns, has the double nipple. In place of using the ordinary percussion cap, a flat primer is placed over the nipple paper (proper?), and over it a false nipple with a striking pin is screwed. This pin when struck by the falling hammer starts the primer and the charge is ignited without any loss of powder or spitting from the touch-hole.

D.S. Cox, of Neperan, Westchester Co., N.Y., has a 38-cal. gun having a 28 in. octagonal barrel, with 8 grooves and a steady twist of 1 in 16. His bullet is 1 to 20 uniform composition, and the powder FFg Hazard. The loss of one hand puts him to some disadvantage but not to any material extent, and he is always ready on time for his shot in the string. He uses stout parchment paper patch cut very narrow. His rest has a narrow iron guiding way forward, while a brass resting block, near the breech, enables quick adjustment to be made, as the cross hair lines of the telescope demand. A sample load showed 305½ grains of lead and 69 grains of powder.

Norman S. Brockway has the solemnity

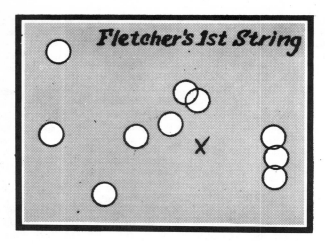

of an owl, and carries about with him the responsibilities of the whole match. He is a rifle maker at Bellows Falls, and knows all about this style of rifle. He is the secretary of the club, and seems to have a life lease on the position. He goes to work in his methodical way, not only in his official labor, but in his shooting as well. He uses one of his own make of rifles, an octagonal barrel, 28 in. long, 42-cal., with 8 grooves twisting evenly 1 in 16 inches, and the powder used is Hazard's FFg, and the patch strips are of the usual parchment paper sort. A V on the rifle cross head pushed home close on the screw projecting from the rest bed, and the rifle is ready for shooting, guided by the stout compact directing rest at the rear. One charge showed that the cold pressed bullet of 1 in 20 composition weighed 417 grains while the powder showed 99 grains.

C.F. Fletcher, of Bellows Falls, Vt., is another of the young men in the ranks. He uses a Brockway made gun and has a 38-cal. rifle with a 28 inch octagon barrel. There are six grooves of 1 in 16 twist, and the bullet is of the cold pressed type and of 1 in 20 composition. The powder is of Hazard FFg make, a charge taken weighed 339½ grains of lead with 82½ grains of powder. He uses a paper cross patch, and in loading is most careful in every movement, being specially careful about the cleaning out of the rifle before inserting a fresh charge of powder. His rest is of a simple sort, a V notch forward and a block with three screws aft completing the fixtures.

Wm. V. Lowe is a Fitchburg, Mass., citizen, and comes up to the match with what he styles a mongrel gun, that is

several makers and remakers have tried to make it better and with varying success. It has a 28-inch octagon barrel, 45-caliber with uniform-twist rifling 1 turn in 20 inches and 8 grooves. He uses a combination bullet, lead butt and hard joint, and employs Fg Hazard powder, one charge taken and weighed showed 108 grains of powder to 585½ of lead. His patch is a thin parchment paper one cut in Greek cross fashion and with an abundance of grease. His rest had a double base, the upper one on which the rifle was placed being movable at the rear and so admitting a vertical and lateral adjustment.

Outside of the shooting house the breechloader visitors from Boston were accommodated. A rest was improvised by driving two stakes in the ground, placing a cross head and then a long plank with a notched block at the end enabled the Bostonians to sit comfortably on chairs and draw their rifles carefully and exactly.

Mr. Hinman used a 35-cal. Maynard and into this he put the patched bullet and the freshly loaded shell, charged with Laflin and Rand musket powder; a sample charge of powder weighed 61½ grains, while the bullet of 1 to 20 composition weighed 258 grains.

F.J. Rabbeth had a Remington-Hepburn rifle of 38 cal. It had a round barrel and aperture front sight, as did the arms of his associates—Messrs. Hinman, Frye and Ellsworth. He had the regular 330-gr. Remington patched bullet, as shown, of 1 to 20 composition. It was loaded with Laflin and Rand powder. A sample charge showed, powder 67½ grs.; bullet 330 grs.

Mr. Frye used a Ballard 38-cal. rifle of the ordinary make. His patched bullets were the 330-gr. Remington make and the powder, Hazard's FFg, a sample charge weighing 55½ grs. in powder and 330 grs. in lead.

Mr. Ellsworth, jolly and fat, capital at off-hand work, as his Manchester score of the week preceding showed, not so good at the strange rests provided, was provided with a 30 in. long barrel Ballard of 38-cal. loaded with a homemade bullet of 1 to 30 composition. The rifle was in all respects like that of Mr. Frye, with the full Rigby barrel. The powder used was Oriental Fg and a pattern charge showed 48 grs. of powder to 293 grs. of lead.

The plan of shooting is a very simple one: On the morning of the first day each man devotes his time to fixing up his shooting stand. There is a small trunk full of tools—oil bottle, rags, ammunition and knick-knacks of every kind—to be unpacked; then the gun itself and the telescope and the rest fixture, all are unpacked, and the various parts put in place. This is no small job. Each man takes a cardboard about a foot square, tacks it upon the low fence against which the shooting is done, and then the small black patch or "budd" is banged away at until the marksman has everything down fine. He watches the flags, makes

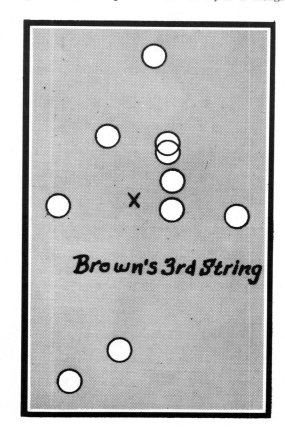

due allowance for wind, finally determines just where the aiming budd is to be placed in order to get the shots aimed about the spot where the lines drawn from opposite angles of the piece of cardboard cross in the center. So it may happen that each of a dozen men may be aiming at a dozen different points and all striving to get their shots bunched at the same point. When each man has got his piece in good working order there is a pause for luncheon, and then comes the counting string. It is shot on a time limit; that is, a timekeeper with watch in hand waits until all are loaded and then the call of "Time" is made. Five minutes elapse, and in that period of time the shot must be fired. Each rifle is in place with hammer raised; "click," and the hair triggers are set. Then in silence each waits for those flags to be a trifle less frisky; for that fishtail wind to swing about to the other side of the center before touching off. Each is, in fact, waiting for that precise wind which prevailed when he fired his last trial shot, the record of which he knew and was satisfied with. Often in a temporary lull the line of rifles will go off in a volley. While

again, some unlucky one who waited for a better chance is compelled, when he hears the voice of the timer call out "Four and three-quarters," to shoot in whatever wind may be blowing at the time. As the rifle recoils, the right hand is ready to check it; but from first to last there is no sighting beyond a glance through the telescope to see that the cross hairs have not been directed to another point.

[At this period metallic sights and telescopes lacked the precision adjustments common enough today, and "clicking over" to counteract a wind change couldn't be done. It appears to have been a better system to allow for a certain wind velocity and direction, placing the aiming budd as indicated. ● In the style of shooting described in the last paragraph above, the shooter sat facing the long axis of the rifle. He squeezed or pinched the rear of the trigger guard and the trigger between his left thumb and forefinger.]

For loading another five minutes is allowed, and there is need of it. First the muzzle end of the barrel is wiped off,

then the false muzzle is carefully fixed and linked down; then comes the pumping and the cleaning. One after another the patches are adjusted to the wiping rod and passed down. There are patches wet with saliva and others saturated with oil. Finally come the cleaner bits of rag, and then perhaps another final patch, fixed just right. Each man has his own style of swabbing out, and the expression of serious concern on the faces of some as they keep their eyes on the rafters as the stick goes up and down almost suggests that a silent prayer goes up as the stick goes down. The barrel clean, the loading is in order. The powder is poured from the flask with just such a tap and no other to the measuring tubes. Then down the funnel at the barrel mouth, and if the shooter be particularly careful he carries his method to the point of sending a stick down to see that the powder is really there, and the light stick resting on the granules gives them just the proper amount of packing. Then the patch, in some of the false muzzles, is inserted in side slits until they cross directly over the bore; or perhaps if the patch is already cut out, it is placed in

FIRST STRING

	1	2	3	4	5	6	7	8	9	10		Total
Fletcher	1 3/16	3/4	1 11/16	1 7/8	7/16	5/8	9/16	3/4	3/4	13/16		=9 7/16
Rabbeth	4	3 1/4	1 11/16	1 5/8	2 1/2	13/16	15/16	13/16	1 7/8	5/8	=18 1/8	=12 5/16
Brown	1 3/16	1/2	7/8	2	2 9/16	1/2	1/4	2 11/16	2 1/2	1/2		=13 5/16
Lowe	7/8	7/8	2 13/16	1 1/2	2 13/16	7/8	3/8	5/8	1 7/8	1 1/16		=13 11/16
Cox	2 1/2	2 3/8	1 1/8	1 7/16	2 5/16	1 1/16	1	7/8	7/8	1 1/16		=14 1/4
Brockway	3 1/2	1 5/16	1 1/4	1 13/16	1 13/16	11/16	3/16	1/2	1 3/4	2 3/8		=15 3/16
Hinman	2 1/8	2 5/16	1 13/16	2 5/8	4 1/8	2 5/8	2 1/8	1 1/4	1 5/16	4 1/4	=24 5/16	=16 15/16
Park	2 15/16	1 15/16	1 15/16	1 7/16	1 7/16	1 5/16	3/16	1 1/16	1 1/16	3 3/4		=17 1/16
Farrow	2 3/8	2 3/8	2 7/8	3 11/16	1 7/8	2 11/16	3 3/16	2 1/16	2 3/8	1 9/16	=25 1/16	=19 9/16
Ellsworth	2 3/4	3 5/8	1 3/8	2 3/4	5 3/16	1 1/8	3 7/16	4 1/2	3 1/4	4	=23	=22 15/16
Stephenson	6	4 7/8	3 1/8	1	1	1 5/8	2 13/16	1 3/4	2 5/8	3		=25 3/16

SECOND STRING

	1	2	3	4	5	6	7	8	9	10		Total
Hinman	2	3/4	2 9/16	1 5/16	1 9/16	3/4	1 1/2	3	1 7/16	1 13/16	=16 5/8	=10 1/2
Rabbeth	9/16	13/16	2 9/16	1 3/16	2 3/16	1 1/2	9/16	3 1/16	1 1/2	3 11/16	=17 7/8	=11 5/16
Park	3 7/16	7/8	15/16	9/16	3/8	1 5/8	2 1/4	11/16	11/16	15/16		=12 3/8
Brown	15/16	1 7/8	1 3/4	1 3/4	1 1/4	1/2	3/8	1/4	1 13/16	1 1/2		=12 1/2
Smith	1 7/8	2 1/16	15/16	1 3/8	1 1/2	1 13/16	2 5/8	1 11/16	3/4	1 1/2		=16 1/3
Fletcher	3/4	9/16	2 3/4	11/16	3	1 13/16	2 3/8	1 1/16	1 1/4	2 7/16		=16 11/16
Brockway	1 9/16	5/16	2 1/16	4	15/16	5/16	1 11/16	1 5/8	1 13/16	3 1/4		=17 7/16
Frye	2 1/4	3 1/2	1 3/16	2 1/8	1 7/8	2	2 1/8	3 5/8	4 1/4	3 1/2	=26 11/16	=18 11/16
Stephenson	5 11/16	3 3/8	2 3/8	2	1 1/8	3/8	15/16	13/16	1	2 1/8		=19 13/16
Ellsworth	3	1 7/8	1 1/8	3 7/16	2 1/16	2 7/8	3 3/8	4 15/16	4 3/8	3 1/16		=21 7/16
Lowe	1 1/4	2 7/8	4 9/16	3 5/16	2 1/16	3/8	15/16	1 5/8	3	3 1/4		=23 1/4
Cox	4 3/16	4 1/4	4 5/16	3 1/4	4 3/4	2	3 3/4	1 9/16	7/16	1/4		=28 3/4

THIRD STRING

	1	2	3	4	5	6	7	8	9	10		Total
Brown	2	1 9/16	1 1/16	3/8	3/8	11/16	11/16	1 9/16	3/4	3/4		=9 13/16
Fletcher	2 3/4	1 1/2	9/16	15/16	1	1 5/16	1 1/4	7/16	2 3/16	2 1/8		=14 1/16
Lowe	1 1/16	1 7/8	3/4	13/16	3/8	1/4	2 15/16	3 1/4	1 5/8	1 5/16		=14 1/4
Frye	2 15/16	2 1/16	3 3/8	2 11/16	2 5/8	3/16	1 11/16	1 7/16	1 3/16	4 1/8	=22 9/16	=15 1/8
Brockway	2	1 3/8	1 15/16	1 13/16	2 1/8	7/8	3/4	2 1/8	3/8	2 1/8		=16 1/4
Rabbeth	3 1/4	1 5/8	3 1/16	4 1/16	2 9/16	7/8	1 15/16	2 1/2	2 1/4	2	=24 1/8	=16 5/8
Park	2 7/8	1 3/8	3 1/2	5/8	3/4	2 1/16	1 7/16	7/16	1 1/16	2 9/16		=16 11/16
Hinman	3 1/8	3 5/16	1 7/8	2 5/8	1 7/16	2 3/4	1 13/16	2 1/4	2	3 1/8	=24 5/16	=16 3/4
Cressy	1 13/16	2 1/4	2 3/16	1 13/16	7/16	2 1/8	1 1/2	2 1/2	1 1/2	2 1/16		=18 3/16
Ellsworth	1 3/16	1	2	1 3/8	4 5/16	5 9/16	2 1/8	15/16	4 3/16	3 1/8	=26 3/16	=18 5/16
Smith	1 11/16	5 1/4	2 3/4	1 1/2	1	1 1/2	2 1/2	2 1/16	1 3/4	1 5/8		=21 5/8
Stephenson	7/8	1 1/2	1 9/16	4 11/16	7/16	3	2 1/4	5/8	7/8	6		=21 13/16
Farrow	2 1/16	3/4	5 3/4	3 15/16	1 3/8	6 1/4	9/16	1 13/16	4 1/4	2	=28 3/4	=22 7/8
Cox	3 1/4	3 11/16	3 3/16	2	2 3/4	4 1/16	1 1/2	1 7/8	2 1/4	1 11/16		=26 1/4

a depression cut across the top of the false muzzle. Now the bullet just given a turn in the greasy finger or perhaps wiped carefully with a oily rag and then placed upon the patch. The ball starter now comes in and assists in pressing the bullet well down into the barrel, a collar fitting over the barrel end, a piston in it whose hollow end just fits over the bullet point, and with several sharp blows from the lump of leather-bound lead at hand, the bullet, patched with exactitude, is pushed down out of sight. Then the rod comes in again, and down the bullet is propelled, now very easily, until it rests with a fixed pressure upon the top of the powder. The capping is another operation, and with gun on rest the wrench comes in, the false nipple is unscrewed, the old cap picked off with point of penknife, and when a new primer has been inserted and the nipple rescrewed, the piece is ready for the timer's call for the second shot.

Meantime a lad has patched each bullet-hole with a narrow strip of paper, a second shot comes, it may cut the patch, if so there is no dispute as might very readily arise when such close shooting is done. So on through the series of the shots consuming an hour and a half perhaps, for each man, when time is called, looks and waits for the wind to suit him, and the loading is a matter not to be slurred over by any means.

The question of a proper allowance to be made the smaller rifles was the first one considered after the Bostonians had unlimbered and prepared for work. "Make your own proposition and we will agree to it," was the generous proffer of the home guard of muzzle shooters. So the visitors thought that ten per cent for telescopic sights should be allowed, then an additional ten per cent for the fixed rest and finally three inches off the string for the difference in the weight of weapons. Under these conditions of difference the men shot, and the complete scores of the several strings will show how the handicap worked.

The first string was shot on the afternoon of the 26th. The weather was chilly, far past the point of comfort, while a wind flickering and shifting in fishtail fashion from about 12 o'clock point, made the shooting very "onsartin" indeed. The breech men soon found out where the advantages of the rest system was, for where they with eye down to peep sight were unable to catch any fluctuations of the wind, and often pulled trigger just as the gust followed the lull, the muzzle shooters sat with eyes wide open watching the streamer, and when the right second came a slight pressure of the finger on the hair trigger and off the piece of ordnance went. It will be seen that the light guns held their own, and Rabbeth, quick to catch the conditions of the difficult new range, had won a place among the three prize winners at the head of the column. Fletcher made a very creditable target indeed, especially under the conditions. The shooting over, there was a general pilgrimage to the tar-

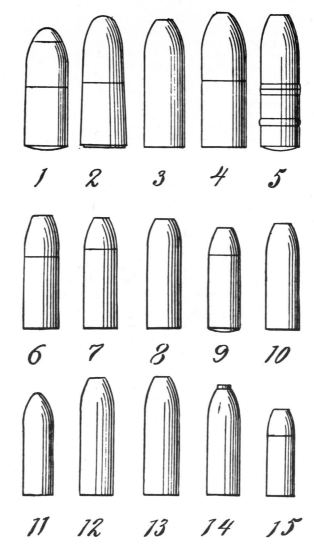

THE BULLETS—FULL SIZE

	Grains		Grains		Grains
1. Stephenson	603	6. Brockway	417	11. Hinman	258
2. Brown	671	7. Cressy	338½	12. Rabbeth	330
3. Lowe	585½	8. Park	356	13. Frye	330
4. Smith	649	9. Cox	305½	14. Ellsworth	293
5. Fenn	572	10. Fletcher	339½	15. Farrow	163½

gets, and as Secretary Brockway drew the tacks the probabilities of place were canvassed. On the back of each bit of pasteboard the shooter's name was written, so that when the scorer having thrust a pin into the exact center and having attached the measuring rod, did not know the marksmen as he read off the shots in inches, eights and sixteenths.

An evening spent in rifle chat, in talk of trajectories and deflection, of initial velocity and windage and all the other topics of interest to marksmen, and all hands retired to an early couch to sleep sound till early morn, then up for a double string. The wind had moderated in a great measure, and again the marksmen were at it bright and early to get windage before the tune was called on the first string. The breechmen had caught the bearing of things in better

shape, worked together with more harmony, and the counting up found two of them leading the score. This was somewhat of a surprise to the host club men, but they were satisfied that the score had been made in direct rivalry, and were more than pleased with the fact that the breechloaders could do so well. The target of honor in this match belongs to Mr. Hinman. It is unfortunate that the antiquated style of marking does not admit of numbering the shots, but such as the target is we present it, in full size, and remembering that it was shot at 220 yards, it is good work even from the sort of rest provided for the day.

With a sky threatening rain, there was no recess between the second and third strings of the meeting. The wind had died down some, and the strange rifle range sight was presented of men waiting for a bit more breeze to come up to waft them on the target. This was the position of those men who had sighted during the morning when the wind was fresher and could not afford to do any trial shooting in the midst of their string. There were at the finish of this string fewer men who carried off their targets rather than have their scores go upon the record. None of the breech men appear in the place of the winners, though Mr. Frye just falls without it. Mr. Farrow, who had not the 10 per cent for fixed rest deducted from his string, was not in good luck. He was busy at his perpetual experimenting, and was not in the best of form. The big Warner gun of Mr. Brown came to the front in good style, and a string of less than 10 inches was deserving of special credit when the rather tricky wind is considered. In addition to the 50, 30 and 20 per cent division to first second and third in each string there was a silver medal presented by Mr. L.C. Smith for the best aggregate string of the meeting. This went to Mr. Brown on a total of 35⅝ inches for 30 shots. Very close, even with the arm used.

The meeting, on the whole, had been a capital success; so thought the old National Rifle Club, for though it is old in years it is full of the true youthful sportsman's feeling; so thought the visitors, for they had been most kindly treated and carried away with them only the most pleasant recollections of the quiet little Vermont village just over the Massachusetts line. To our readers we present the whole story, with figures and picture. The targets are taken from the original cards. The scores are from the official record, while the weight of powder and lead where given are from the samples taken by your correspondent (and weighed by an expert in the Fairbanks Scale Co. on a Fairbanks scale.— Ed. F. and S.). There were regrets for absent ones; for Williamson, the club president, away at his home at Comack, L.I.; for Gardner of Scranton, Romer of Peekskill, Warner of Syracuse, Tyler and Col. Rice of Vermont, Wm. Wetmore of New Hampshire, D.C. Pearl of Meriden, Conn., and W.B. Farrington of Boston, while the standard conundrum was where Phillips, the gunmaker, had hidden himself in the Far West. The adieus were given, with an accompanying hope that the next meeting of the club would see a large delegation of the modern school of marksmen, those who think with your correspondent, that accuracy of the very highest degree may be secured without the accompanying discomfits of the heavy ordnance style of weapon.   W.
Forest and Stream, June 3, 1886.

SUMMARY

	1st String	2nd String	3rd String	Total
Brown	13⁵⁄₁₆	12½	9¹³⁄₁₆	35⅝
Fletcher	9⁷⁄₁₆	16¹¹⁄₁₆	14¹⁄₁₆	40³⁄₁₆
Rabbeth	12⁵⁄₁₆	11⁵⁄₁₆	16⅝	40¼
Hinman	16¹⁵⁄₁₆	10½	16¼	44³⁄₁₆
Park	17¹⁄₁₆	12⅜	16¹¹⁄₁₆	46⅛
Brockway	15³⁄₁₆	17⁷⁄₁₆	16¼	48⅞
Lowe	13¹¹⁄₁₆	23¼	14¼	51³⁄₁₆
Ellsworth	22¹⁵⁄₁₆	21⁷⁄₁₆	18⁵⁄₁₆	62¹¹⁄₁₆
Stephenson	25³⁄₁₆	19¹³⁄₁₆	21¹³⁄₁₆	66¹³⁄₁₆
Cox	14¼	28¾	26¼	69¼
Frye		18¹¹⁄₁₆	15⅛	33¹³⁄₁₆
Smith		16⅛	21⅝	37¾
Farrow	19⁹⁄₁₆		22⅞	42⁷⁄₁₆
Cressy			18³⁄₁₆	18³⁄₁₆
Fenn				

Bibliography

American Gun Makers, by Col. Arcadi Gluckman and L. D. Satterlee. The Stackpole Co., Harrisburg, Pa. 1953.
The Breech-Loading Single-Shot Match Rifle, by Major Ned Roberts and Ken Waters. D. Van Nostrand Co., Inc., Princeton, N.J. 1967.
How I Became A Crack Shot, by W. Milton Farrow, Newport, R.I. 1882.
The Modern American Pistol and Revolver, by A. C. Gould. Boston, 1888 (reprint of 2nd ed. Plantersville, So. Car. 1946).
Modern American Rifles, by A. C. Gould. Boston, 1982 (reprinted 1946, Plantersville, S.C.)
The Muzzle-Loading Cap Lock Rifle, by Ned H. Roberts. Manchester, N.H. 1944, and later eds.
New York State Gunmakers, A Partial Checklist, by Holman J. Swinney. Cooperstown, N.Y. 1951.

Detachable Aiming Points

by GUY LAUTARD

Have you ever noticed how the crosshairs of a telescopic sight can disappear in the center of the standard bullseye target? Here is what I did to gain a better aiming point and, at the same time, a record-keeping system that is among the simplest.

From a piece of white cardboard I cut a 5″ square and drew in a border 1½″ wide on all four sides. Using black water colors I painted this border an intense, flat black. Several coats were needed to give the desired color. Drying between coats was expedited by placing the 5″ square on top of the shade of a wall-hung reading lamp, which took about 5 minutes. The result is a black square (5″x5″) with a 2″x2″ white square in the center.

A hole was punched along the middle of one side of the aiming point. In use, a plain white sheet of paper is tacked up on the target frame just as would be a normal target. The aiming point is hung from a nail in the target frame at the center of the top edge of the white sheet.

I have used this aiming point with a 22 Hornet and a Lyman 6x Wolverine scope at 100 yards, but it's usable, of course with any caliber. The rifle is sighted-in to put the point of impact 6″ low at this range. After firing a group, all pertinent information is written on the white sheet of paper hung up with the aiming point. The point of aim should be marked on this sheet through a small hole punched in the center of the little white square. This allows me to keep load data and the resulting group together for future reference. The aiming point never gets shot up and can be used indefinitely.

A larger aiming point might be desirable if using a scope of lower power and/or when longer ranges are the order of the day.

Don't forget that when you go out in the field with your rifle you'll have to zero it to place the point of impact several inches higher, but having done it once you can easily switch from one elevation setting to the other thereafter if you have noted the number of clicks involved. This will instruct you, I think, in the actual click values of your scope—not all of them respond as advertised!   ●

The Israeli Army—

a history of its small arms, tactics and training.

What enabled a nation of less than three million people to defeat a foe
backed by a populace almost fifty times their number? Arms,
yes, but much more than that—Israel's secret weapon
is the fantastic spirit of her people, their firm belief that they
cannot lose a battle, much less a war.

by Dr. EUGENE SOCKUT

THE HISTORY of Israeli military small arms procurement, development, manufacture and use is directly related to the establishment and growth of the Third Jewish Commonwealth in history. In biblical times, as well as today, the land of Israel found itself surrounded by a succession of would-be conquerors. Situated at the crossroads of three continents—Europe, Asia and Africa, Israel's very geographical position made it mandatory for them to take up arms for self-defense.

Three times in the past 22 years the world witnessed events as miraculous as the biblical military victories of Joshua over the Philistines. In the Arab-Israeli Wars of 1948, 1956 and 1967, tiny Israel succeeded in vanquishing enemies whose numbers of men, quantity and quality of war materiel should have resulted in the total destruction of the Jewish State. What factors contributed to the ability of a nation of 2.5 million to defeat forces backed by populations almost 50 times its size? Tracing the small arms history of the *Yishuv,* (Hebrew name for the Jewish community of the Holy Land) best illustrates the ability of a

people to persevere against insuperable odds and emerge victorious.

1878-1904

Prior to 1874, most of the Jews living in Palestine were native born. A few traced their ancestry back to the Jewish-Roman Wars of 70 A.D., which resulted in the destruction of the Second Jewish Commonwealth, and changed the "land of milk and honey" into a desolate, eroded place—land not to be independent again until the birth of modern Israel in 1948.

During the 1870s, Jews began returning to the Holy Land, driven by their belief that the rebirth of an independent Jewish nation promised by the prophet Isaiah was at hand. Though many Jews had gone to the Holy Land throughout the exile, the first successful mass movement began at this time. This phenomenon was called Zionism, a rebirth of Zion, the Land of Israel. A gathering in of the scattered Jewish people was its goal.

The small arms of these early Zionists were representative of the period, consisting mainly of black powder muzzle-loading and cartridge guns of mixed origin, but chiefly European.

Because of incessant Bedouin Arab attacks, the pioneers constructed defense walls around their settlements which resembled the stockades of the early American pioneers. Like the early American settlers, they found it necessary to train themselves in the use of small arms. This led to the development of a defense force called *Shomrim* (watchmen), whose duty was to guard the settlement's livestock and fields. In the historical exhibition of the Hagana Museum in Tel-Aviv, there can be seen, along with ancient muzzleloaders, a "shilalee," hand carved by an old rabbi tired of being set upon by Arab ruffians as he went to prayers.

1904-1920

Spurred on by these early successes, dozens of new Jewish settlements were built in the areas of Galilee, Samaria and Judea. It soon became necessary to expand the Shomrim into a larger and better-trained force called *Hashomer.* Cartridge rifles and pistols became more prevalent though no standardization of weapons was feasible. Mauser, Luger and other pistols of 7.62 and 9mm Parabellum calibers

The Super Sherman tank carries a 105mm rifle.

were in service as well as various 25, 32 and 380 semi-automatic pistols. Large caliber revolvers of Russian and British design became common after the end of WW I.

The outbreak of World War I had found the Allies in a life and death struggle with the Central Powers. One of these was Turkey, whose empire extended throughout the Middle East. Palestine and Trans-Jordan, part of this empire, were promised to the Jewish people in exchange for their support of the Allied Powers. The Arabs, whose support was also sought, were promised the larger portions of the empire, these later to become Iraq, Syria, Lebanon, Saudi Arabia and the Persian Gulf sheikdoms. The Emir Feisal, leader of the Arabs, welcomed this arrangement between Arab, Jew and Englishman, but the honeymoon was to prove short lived.

During WW I, Jews fought in an Allied unit called the Jewish Legion. They were armed with the standard British infantry small arms of the period—the SMLE Mark I bolt action rifle, the Webley 455 top-break revolver, and the Lewis 303 machine gun. Training and tactics were de-

cidedly British. Organized by a brilliant Jewish soldier, Vladimir Jabotinsky, the Legion consisted of such units as the 1st Judean Regiment—raised in the U.S. by David Ben-Gurion, and the Third Palestine Battalion, soldiered by Jews from Palestine. These units fought under Field Marshall Allenby, and were commanded by a pro-Zionist colonel named Patterson, a regular British army officer. Arab soldiers were led by T. E. Lawrence, the famed Lawrence of Arabia, who was simultaneously pro-Zionist and pro-Arab.

After the Armistice of 1918, the British disbanded the Jewish units and confiscated their weapons. However, experience with British military methods of logistics, training and tactics was to prove invaluable in the future for the Jews of Palestine. Some British light arms were "liberated" by the returning soldiers.

1920-1936

In 1920 the region of Tel-Hai in northern Palestine saw large-scale attacks by Arab bands against Jewish settlements. In one of these battles the Jews lost Josef Trumpeldor, one

of the founders of the Jewish Legion and the only Jew ever to win a commission in the Czar of Russia's army. The need for a larger Jewish defense organization became apparent. A new group called the *Hagana* (Hebrew for "defense") replaced Hashomer. Hagana members were trained in the use of small arms and unit warfare; some of the arms were bought in Vienna. As usual after a war, these were surplus military weapons of the period—the Austrian 1907 Roth-Steyr 8mm pistol, the 1912 Steyr 9mm pistol, and the 8mm Rast-Gasser M1898 revolver. The Austrian 1888/90 8mm straight pull rifle and the Austrian Schwarzlose 8mm machine gun M07/12 were also used by the Hagana.

"Our task is not to kill, but to defend ourselves," became the motto of the Hagana. *Havalagah* (restraint) described the mood that prevailed among these settlers, who could best be described as "reluctant warriors."

In 1929 disturbances broke out once again. After a 7-year period of relative peace, Arab mobs incited by the Grand Mufti of Jerusalem attacked isolated Jewish settlements. It soon became apparent to the Hagana high

The Israeli Army

command that their forces would have to be quickly expanded to meet the new challenge. The country was then divided into 20 regional centers, each commanded by a trained officer, to furnish needed protection to the isolated settlements. Special training courses for officers were immediately instituted to enable the Haganah to cope with the new situation. Since light arms continued to be bought from many sources, ammunition supply became a nightmare. Pistols, for example, ranged from the lowly 22 rimfire to the 455. Establishment of secret underground workshops to make small arms, components and ammunition relieved this problem to a certain extent.

1936-1939

Assisted by the Fascist Powers, a full scale Arab revolt broke out in 1936. Attacks were made on British forces stationed in Palestine under the League of Nations Mandate. These forces were there, ostensibly, to help form a "Jewish National Home," but in actuality the British used the principle of divide-and-rule among the Arabs and Jews. Raids were made against British communications systems, police posts and army bases, against Jewish settlements. The British, reluctantly, were forced to rearm the Jews. Quasi-military units, called "Supernumerary Police," were immediately formed. These troops were issued such standard British military equipment as the SMLE 303 rifle, the Webley 455 revolver and the Lewis 303 MG. Meanwhile, the Hagana, which had changed its tactics from static defense to mobile offensive warfare, considered the Supernumerary Police an excellent training vehicle for future officers. One of the men the Hagana called to duty with the S.P. was young Moshe Dayan, then honeymooning in England. Meanwhile, the Hagana organized mobile field platoons, called "P.U.S.H," placing these under the command of an excellent soldier, Yitzak Sadeh. Training and active duty lasted for a period of 6 months. Many of Israel's future leaders were trained in these field units, among them Dayan and Yigal Allon (later to be Deputy Prime Minister of Israel), learning the new tactics of fluid warfare and surprise attack. A technique called "Hammer and Anvil" was developed whereby the anvil unit would ambush and engage an Arab force until the hammer group, led by Dayan, would join the conflict and crush resistance. Much information on firearms, logistics and tactics was cataloged for future use. An interesting development was a "cloth cartridge catcher" for the 9mm Hispano Suiza submachine gun. This device caught the tell-tale ejected shells.

Special Night Squads

Spring of 1938 saw a new British-led Jewish force called "Special Night Squads," commanded by a brilliant British Army intelligence officer, Orde Charles Wingate. Captain Wingate was a Bible-toting Protestant whose pro-Zionist opinions soon got him into trouble with the British Imperial Staff. The Special Night Squads attracted the brightest and bravest of the Hagana men, and daring commando raids testing new military tactics were the order of the day under Wingate.

Captain Wingate's actions and attitudes toward the Jews won him their love and respect—as well as the nickname *Hayedid* (friend). Wingate recalled the past military exploits of such Jewish generals as Joshua and Gideon. Because the topography of the

The author, flanked by two Israeli officers, holds the Uzi 9mm submachine gun of Israeli design and manufacture. A captured Egyptian T-54 tank, of Russian manufacture is in the background.

land had changed so little since biblical times, the tactics of those early Jews (sharp thrusts, mobility and carrying the battle to the enemy) were still valid. Wingate was later to find fame in masterminding the defeat of the Italians in Ethiopia during World War II. He died in the Far East after organizing and leading a group called *Chindits* or "Wingate's Raiders," who fought against the Japanese in the Burma Campaign. Today, in Israel, his name is still spoken with reverence, for Orde Charles Wingate, more than any man, helped to mould the character of the future army of Israel.

1939-1948

The Hagana Command knew that relatively few guns, spare parts, and munitions could be secretly gleaned from British Army depots, and that this small number could not meet their arms needs. Yehuda Arazi, a mysterious figure in Hagana undercover work, negotiated a secret agreement with Poland for 8mm Mauser bolt action rifles and "Browning Type" medium machine guns of good quality, plus some Radom 9mm Parabellum pistols. Luckily, the British did not believe Arab reports that large planes had landed near their villages during the night. Needed raw materials were secretly imported for the Hagana underground workshops, which were expanding into production of light mortars and hand grenades. Submachine guns such as the 9mm Sten could now be manufactured along with the ammunition needed for them. Weapons were secretly stored in cellars, holes in the ground, and in the inner walls of buildings in the expectation of the conflict that all feared would follow the end of WW II.

During May, 1939, the British issued a "White Paper" restricting Jewish immigration to Palestine. Moshe Dayan and some 42 Hagana men were imprisoned in the fortress at Acre because of their opposition to this policy. However, in 1941 the British position in the Mid-East was threatened by the pro-Nazi Vichy French governments of Syria and Lebanon. The British needed their immediate neutralization to prevent General Irwin Rommel's Afrika Corps from linking up with a feared Vichy French thrust through Palestine. Ironically, the British were again forced to use the people who they knew would and could do the job.

Jewish volunteer Commando units were asked to protect the roads and bridges leading into Palestine. Dayan and his fellow prisoners were released and assigned to this task on the northern borders of Palestine. In one engagement, Dayan was looking through his field glasses when struck by a sniper's bullet that drove one lens into his left eye, hence Dayan's famous black eye-patch. Another soldier seasoned during these battles was Yitzhak Ra-

bin, destined to command the Israeli forces during the Six-Day War of June, 1967.

The Jewish Commando units that fought in the Lebanese and Syrian operations were moulded into a new strike force called *Palmach* (short for Plugot Machatz, or Shock Platoons).

In the spring of 1942 the Palmach established a "German Department," intended to undertake missions behind the German lines. These commandos were led by two German-speaking offi-

Making their way to the recaptured Western Wall of King Solomon's Temple are, from left: Col. Narkiss, Moshe Dayan, and Gen. Rabin, hero of the Six-Day Arab-Israeli War of 1967. Dayan carries a 38 Enfield revolver.

cers, Shimon (Koch) Avidan and Israel Karmi. During the Hitler period German Jews had fled to Palestine by the tens of thousands. It was from these immigrants that the special units were formed. Armed with captured German weapons and uniforms, they gave an excellent account of themselves. A fictionalized version of their exploits was told in the Hollywood film *Tobruk*.

Toward the end of 1943, parachute units of Jewish Palestinians, who had come from countries under Nazi domi-

nation, were dropped back into Europe to help organize resistance groups behind enemy lines. At this time, some 30 thousand Palestinian Jews joined the ranks of the British Army. They fought well at El Alamein and in the campaign in the Western Desert of North Africa. Finally, in 1944, the Jews were once again allowed to form their own unit, the "Jewish Brigade Group." They saw action against German forces in the Italian Campaign.

While the battle against the Axis was raging another battle against the edicts of the British White Paper was being waged in Palestine. Jewish underground forces were divided into three groups: the Hagana, representing the majority of the population; the *Irgun Zvi-Leumi*, a large right-wing group formed by Vladimer Jabotinsky, developer of the Jewish Legion of WW I, and the smallest group, the *Lechi* (fighters for the freedom of Israel) or Stern Gang, as the British called them. During WW II, unlike the Hagana and the Irgun, the Lechi

The Israeli Army

(led by Abraham Stern) considered the British just as much the enemy as the Nazis, attacking British facilities and personnel with the same gusto the Irish Republican Army displayed during the "Irish Troubles." After the war, the Irgun and then the Hagana joined in attacks on the British in Palestine.

The small arms of these underground forces ran the gamut of weapons available around the world. As a general rule, French arms prevailed in the north because of its proximity to the Vichy French battlefields. British arms were found in the rest of Palestine. Milk cans, cut in half, then rewelded and hermetically sealed, were a favorite hiding place for arms since they could be safely placed underground. The Sten SMG was most desired because of its simplicity, portability, and the ease with which it could be broken down and hidden in the skirts of female members of the resistance groups.

1948-Israeli War of Independence

During November of 1947, the United Nations divided the country originally promised by the League of Nations to be the Jewish National Home into one Arab and one Jewish state. The Jews, desperate to resettle the survivors of the concentration camps of Europe, accepted this decree but the Arabs did not. With the departure of the British military forces in May of 1948, 8 Arab armies invaded Israel. Every able-bodied Jewish man and woman sprang to the defence, but the tremendous shortage of weapons and the chaotic mixture of calibers and types of guns made the small arms situation critical. Some Enfield 38 revolvers, 303 SMLEs, and Sten SMGs were taken from or secretly bought from departing British soldiers. Sympathetic Irish troops "lost" two tanks which the Jews found. Captured German infantry weapons, such as the MG42 LMG, Mauser rifles, Luger and Walther 9mm pistols, were brought home in bits and pieces by Jewish Palestinians who had fought with the Allies. Small numbers of light arms were brought in by plane and ship, many of them surplus American weapons collected in the U.S. by Jews and their sympathizers. Among these were Colt 45 autos, Springfield and Garand 30-06 rifles, M3s and Thompson submachine

guns. Even two B-17 bombers were flown toward the Holy Land, one never getting further than the Azores. The FBI and the U.S. government seemed to wink at these shenanigans, but the British tried to stop these arms shipments even after Israel achieved independence.

Because of the small arms shortage many ingenious Rube Goldberg shortcuts were attempted. For example, the necessary machinery for making Sten barrels was not at hand. Old rifles were cannibalized and their barrels shortened and altered to fit Israeli-made Sten guns. In time, these were replaced by barrels locally produced. Another development was the fitting of Enfield rifles with Israeli-made grenade launchers. These were humorously stamped U.S.A. (Yiddish for *Unserer Stickle Arbiet* or Our Bit of Work.

Another hastily-engineered product was the melting down of kitchen utensils into casings for hand grenades by the trapped Jewish forces in the besieged city of Jerusalem.

Because of the shortage of such essential items as mortars, cannon and bazookas, the Israelis came forth with a mortar called the *Davidka*

(Little David), designed by one David Leibovitz. These proved a godsend. Some 36 of them were fabricated from sewer pipe and steel rails, their projectiles making a tremendous noise when they landed. Though militarily ineffective they created panic among the enemy, who feared that the Jews had developed an atomic bomb! Nevertheless, effective as some of their arms were, the need for first class military hardware remained acute in the early stages of Israel's War of Independence.

The landing of large amounts of Czech-made light arms in operation *Haseda* (stork) helped ease the shortage, enabling the Israelis to open the road to Jerusalem and break the siege of that beleaguered city. These Czech arms consisted of 8mm Mauser rifles and MG34 LMGs, while another bonus was the shipment of large quantities of Polish hand grenades.

The end of Israel's War of Independence found the Israeli military in control of a mixed bag of light arms. It was felt that the 8mm Mauser rifle, the 9mm Sten and the 8mm Besa Medium MG were best suited for the young state's defence needs, so these were accepted as standard. In time,

The Davidka (Little David) mortar, the larger of two designed by David Leibovitz of Israel.

Sten guns and Mauser rifles were entirely manufactured in Israel. Large amounts of non-standard weapons remained in stock, however, and were issued to regular army troops. The British SMLE 303 rifle, a popular non-standard weapon, was issued in large numbers to regular army and border-defence settlements.

1948-1956

Israeli Prime Minister David Ben-Gurion reflected that it was more efficient from a political and military standpoint to place such elite units as the Palmach under a single unified

talion 101. By 1953 its successful exploits had had a beneficial effect on the army, and Ben-Gurion soon promoted Dayan over other senior officers to be Chief of Staff.

Now Dayan began his full reorganizational concept in earnest. He recommended that:

1. Every officer should have paratroop or commando training.
2. The army was to be primarily a combat force, with every soldier undergoing combat duties.
3. A military college in Israel was to be immediately established for officers with the rank of major

economic sanctions forced the Israelis to pull back from the Sinai, as it had in 1949. Then Great Britain threatened to intervene unless the Egyptians were given back this vast desert. Dayan, in the field with his victorious troops, helped them swallow this bitter political pill.

Uzi Submachine Gun

The 1956 Sinai Campaign established the reputation of an Israeli-designed and made 9mm Parabellum submachine gun called the "UZI" (pronounced OOO-zee). It was named after its designer, Maj. Uziel Gal, who

The smaller of the two Davidka mortars, named for the designer, David Leibovitz of Israel.

command. This was accomplished in November of 1948. Gen. Yigael Yadin, succeeding Gen. Yaakov Dori (Israel's first chief of staff) established the structure of the new army. It was to be essentially one of reservists led by a small professional nucleus. Moshe Dayan, a protege of Ben-Gurion's, and regarded as a military and organizational genius at an early stage in his career, was put in command of Israel's southern front with Egypt in 1949.

Dayan felt that the morale, training and equipment of the army needed rejuvenation, that an elite unit would act as an ideal to emulate and help to establish a spirit of competitiveness. The unit was formed and named Bat-

and above, and most officers were now to be Israeli trained.

Dayan's insistence on these three recommendations met some opposition, but in time they were all accepted as standard army policy. Experience has proven the value of his viewpoints.

In time, Arab raids and the Arab blockade of Israeli shipping in the Suez Canal and the Gulf of Aqaba triggered the outbreak of the Sinai Campaign of 1956. It was in this campaign that the new concepts of training and tactics established by Dayan proved highly successful, Israeli forces slashing across the Sinai peninsula in less than a hundred hours! But again, diplomatic pressures and the threat of

had served time in jail under the British rule in Palestine for making submachine guns for the Jewish underground. Production of the weapon began in 1951.

The Uzi has some very desirable characteristics. For example, the grip-safety acts on the sear, resembling that on the Colt 45 pistol, plus the usual trigger safety which also serves as the selector button. These help to prevent accidental discharge if the gun is dropped or jolted, features very useful for paratroopers, "tankers," or mobile infantry. It uses a grip magazine, again like the Colt 45, a convenience for night warfare, taking advantage of the "hand finds hand" concept. The grip also provides added

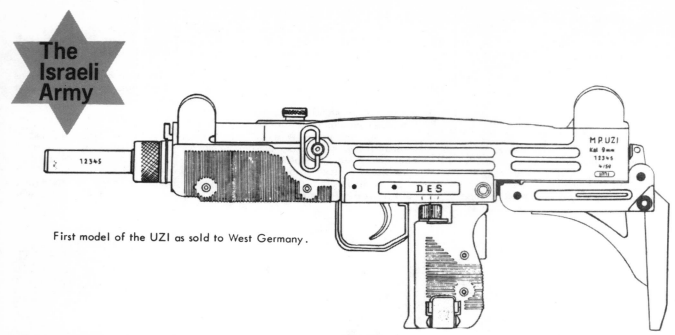

First model of the UZI as sold to West Germany.

protection for the 25, 32 or 40-round magazine since a part of the latter is surrounded by metal. The Uzi has no external moving parts when the gun goes through the firing cycle, thus reducing the chances of jams if placed against an object.

An unusual feature is the comparatively long barrel (10″) in relation to the 25.2″ over-all length of the weapon. This is achieved by machining a recess in the bolt for the barrel. Thus bolt metal surrounds the barrel on three sides, helping to hold the weapon steady, damping upward climb during full automatic fire. The extensive use of metal stampings and heat-resistant plastics insures ease of fabrication. Maintenance is relatively simple. For example, the barrel may be easily removed by unscrewing the barrel-locking nut by hand. The most widely-distributed SMG in the Western World, the Uzi is also, many experts say, one of the finest made anywhere.

The Uzi is made in Israel by IMI (Israeli Military Industries) and in Belgium (under license) by FN. Because of its many excellent characteristics it is the standard NATO submachine gun, being in service in Belgium, West Germany and the Netherlands. It has also found acceptance in South America, Africa and the Far East.

1956-1967

The post-Sinai Campaign period saw another modernization of Israeli military small arms. The 8mm Mauser 98 was relegated to a second line position, replaced by the new Belgian 7.62 NATO FN FAL assault rifle. First produced in Belgium, these were later made in Israel under contract from FN. In time most of the Mauser 98 rifles were rebarreled to the 7.62 NATO caliber. Bolt action rifles are still favored by many Israeli soldiers because of their greater accuracy.

Officially, the Italian Beretta 1951 9mm semi-auto pistol is the standard Israeli army handgun, but few are in service. Handguns are low-rated in Israeli military thinking; the Uzi SMG is portable enough to replace them, they feel. Handguns such as the 38 Enfield revolver, the 455 Webley revolver, as well as the Colt 45 auto pistol are in common use among Israeli officers. The Israeli Police seem interested in the 9mm Colt Commander.

In the 1950s Israel manufactured a few revolvers resembling the Smith and Wesson Military and Police Model. These used the rimless 9mm Parabellum cartridges in half-moon clips quite like those used in Colt and S&W 1917 revolvers chambered for the 45 ACP loads. These revolvers served to demonstrate the level of quality production that Israeli Military Industries had achieved. Most were distributed as special presentation pieces.

The Six-Day War

Once again the Arab countries surrounding Israel spoke of total war. The closing of the Gulf of Aqaba to Israeli shipping in the summer of 1967 was to be the first step in a conflict of annihilation. The capitulation of the UN forces in Sinai, because of Egyptian pressure, triggered the outbreak of hostilities, but once more the Israeli forces rolled up resistance in Egyptian Sinai. Superb training, high morale and leadership won the day for the *Zahal* (Defence Forces) of Israel. The cease-fire order some 6 days later found the Israeli army in control of the West Bank of the river Jordan, the Syrian Golan Heights with its superb Russian defences, the Gaza Strip and the wastes of the Sinai. Because of this Israeli victory the power balance in the Mid-East has shifted decidedly in favor of Israel and the West. Tremendous quantities of Russian small arms and ammunition fell into Israeli hands. The Soviet AK 54 and the Simonov 7.62mm assault carbines (both in the shorter 7.62mm Russian caliber) were now seized by the tens of thousands, plus millions of rounds of ammunition for these weapons. These weapons, along with captured Carl Gustav 9mm SMGs were soon put in service! Official policy seems to allow the use of captured small arms in those areas of Israel faced by Arab countries armed with the same weapons.

The Israeli victory of the Six-Day War proved once again that mobility and firepower are the basis for successful military campaigns. In future battles, ground support weapons must be capable of laying down a devastating screen of fire. The heavy-barreled version of the FN FAL rifle at full automatic fire is more controllable than its American M14 heavy-barreled equivalent. The Israeli rifle platoon also uses a 308 (7.62 NATO) version of the old American Browning Automatic Rifle. Its rate of fire (350-600 rpm) and its heavy weight (22 lbs.) insures accurate, controlled bursts, in full automatic fire. Another Israeli squad-support weapon is the FN type MAG general-purpose machinegun. Heavier and belt fed (the BAR type weapon uses a 20-round magazine), its faster rate of fire (750-1050 rpm) makes it suitable for use in vehicles. Its main usefulness is laying down a heavy pattern of fire so that cover is provided for half-track vehicles carrying troops or for mobile artillery and mortars. Israeli military men do not

The Piat (British designed) anti-tank gun.

favor these tripod-mounted weapons for ground use, preferring the bipod-mounted, box-magazine LMGs.

Though Israeli ordnance experts have tested the American M-16 223 assault rifle it seems unlikely that they'll change from their standard FN FAL 308. First, because the Uzi 9mm SMG is extremely useful for close-quarter work. Second, captured AK-54 and Simonov assault carbines are proving acceptable as unofficial intermediate-range weapons. Third, the M-16 is deemed more suited for jungle and house-to-house fighting than for desert warfare. Fourth, change-over cost would be prohibitive. The semi-automatic FN FAL meets the requirements of the Israeli Defence Forces for an infantry assault rifle that combines a powerful cartridge with adequate range and penetration. For more fire power, the FN FAL easily converts to full automatic.

Women In The Israeli Army

Israel is the only country in the world that drafts women into its army, not so much from manpower needs

but as a reflection of the national attitude that all citizens should serve. They no longer serve in combat units as many did in the early days of the state. The women do administrative, non-combat work, freeing the men for combat duty. Weapons training for women soldiers is mandatory, however. They are well-versed in firing the Uzi, the Mauser and the various assault rifles in service, with such training continuing throughout their National Service. Only Jewish women are subject to the draft, however, and there are exemptions for married women and those with religious scruples. Those in the latter category are rare, military service being the "in thing" among Israeli youth.

Gadna and Naham (Fighting/Pioneer Youth)

Gadna is the organization concerned with pre-military training of Israelis 16 to 18 years old. These teenagers may choose any branch of this paramilitary training they're interested in. Boys usually select sharpshooting, weapons training and gliding. Girls tend toward communications and med-

ical training. The youth of Gadna also work on forestry projects, assist new settlements, build roads, and help at archeological digs.

More advanced youths' training is provided via vocational schools, with advancement for boys to the rank of technical sergeant in general ordnance. These youngsters are then assured of this rank when they enter regular military service. Small-arms training for all Gadna youths, though, is part of their daily curriculum. When ready for regular military duty their arms familiarity is about equal to that of a rural American boy's gun knowledge and shooting ability at the turn of the century.

Nahal enables small groups of Israeli youngsters to join the army as a body and to complete their military service together. One of the chief tasks of Nahal is the combining of military service with agricultural pioneering. The establishment of new border settlements or the strengthening of those in existence is basic to this movement. Rugged commando- and parachute training is a must for this crack Military Settlement Corps. It has been

The STEN submachine gun, a British design.

The Israeli Army

proven in battle that armed and well-trained villagers can hold off superior enemy forces for a reasonable length of time. Since Israel borders are vulnerable, the Nahal network acts as a web to trap and deter attacking forces until the regular Israeli army appears.

Arms available to these border settlements run the gamut of firearms history—the village storerooms are said to be a gun collector's dream! Small arms from all over the world share equal space with modern Israeli-made arms. The Israelis believe that if a weapon is serviceable, with spare parts and ammunition available, it can be put to effective use by well-trained men.

Esprit de Corps

Israel's secret weapon is the fantastic spirit of her population. Strongly patriotic and nationalistic, Israelis "know" they cannot lose a battle, much less a war. Their motto is *Ein*

Above—Israeli soldiers on guard in the Hills of Judea. The man at left holds a captured Russian AK-54, the other a Simonov carbine. Both are chambered for the 7.62 Russian "Intermediate-sized" cartridge. Many of these weapons fell to the Israelis in the border skirmishes and wars with the Syrians and Egyptians. ● Below—An Israeli-made anti-tank rocket launcher.

Brera (no choice), and every Israeli soldier knows that he must complete the task assigned to him. There are few goldbricks and let-George-do-it types in the Israeli army.

The Israeli officer has a "follow me" attitude—their casualties during the Six-Day War were almost one-third of the dead and wounded.

After 36 months regular army service the discharged soldier automatically goes into the active reserves. Reserve privates do active duty for 30 days a year, plus one day a month. NCOs serve for 36 days a year, junior-grade officers spend 42 days annually on active duty and field-grade offcers some 58 days. Much of this time is spent training with small arms and support weapons.

Training is based on NRA-type instruction, stressing safety, use and knowledge of weapons.

On entering National Service every soldier fires complete courses of fire with the Uzi SMG, the Mauser 98 and FN FAL rifles. Ammunition is not restricted unless the supply is short. Each recruit may shoot up to 1000 rounds of ammo during his graduation from 22 rimfire rifles (as used in Gadna) to the "big bore" 308 (NATO) cartridges.

Israel's recurrent border clashes have shown that every recruit should be familiar with all of the weapons available to the infantry soldier. They are instructed in the use of medium- and heavy-barreled MGs, Uzis, Israeli 3.5″ rocket launchers, recoilless rifles, anti-tank-wire guided rockets and the new Israeli 160mm mortars, now in use by the Armored Corps. Mounted on a converted Sherman Priest tank, this super mortar combines high firepower with excellent mobility.

Today, most soldiers who go on leave take their Uzis or rifles with them because of the frequent border attacks, yet despite the tremendous number of guns in Israel, few accidents or crimes occur.

* * * * *

We have seen, in an historically brief span of time, how a group of settlers armed with antique muzzle-loaders evolved into a vigorous, modern nation, able to field what many experts describe as the "best little army in the world." It has not been by chance that this has occurred. Rather, the key to the Israeli success story lies in the ability of her people to obtain almost 100% efficiency and dedication from their military manpower and material. In many instances, armed with inferior weapons —at least on paper—Israel emerged victorious. Today, able to obtain and produce better military hardware, the Jews of Israel should be able to give an excellent account of themselves in any future conflict. ●

160mm mortar, made in Israel.

Small Arms and Light Infantry Support Weapons of the Israeli Army

Make	Cal.	Wgt./lbs.[a]	Bbl.	Over-all	Operation	Capacity	MV/fps
Beretta M-1950*	9mm	1.57	4.51	8.0	Semi-auto	8	1182
Uzi*	9mm	7.7	10.5	25.2[b] 17.9[c]	Blowback, selec. fire	25, 32 or 40	1310
Carl Gustav	9mm	9.25		31.8	Blowback, auto	36	1330
FN-FAL*	7.62 NATO	10.4	21.0	44.5	Gas, semi-auto	20	2800
AK-54	7.62 (M1943)	10.58	16.34	34.25	Gas, selec. fire	30	2329
Simonov Carbine (SKS)	7.62 (M1943)	8.8	20.47	40.16	Gas, semi-auto	10	2410
FN, Heavy Barrel	7.62 NATO	15.25	21.0	44.75	Selec. fire	20 or 30	2800
Besa Mk 1-3	7.92	47 to 53.5	29	43.5	Gas, locked	225	2650
FN-BAR	7.62 NATO	20.3	19.7	41.7	Gas, auto	20	2700
FN Type MAG	7.62 NATO	22.22	21.44	49.21	Gas, auto	Link belt	2800

*Official first line arms. [a]Loaded. [b]Metal stock. [c]Wood stock. All dimensions in inches.

Also in use, and in fair supply, are Enfield 380 revolvers, Colt M-1911-1911A1 45 Auto pistols and M98 Mauser rifles, most if not all of the last converted to shoot 7.62mm NATO ammunition.

THE NEW MANNLICHER RIFLES

by WARREN PAGE

New Steyr Mannlicher rifle in the Model M size, suitable for such cartridges as the 270, 30-06 and the like.

The new mid-lugged, low-lift 60-degree Steyr-Mannlicher action —with a mere nod to Herr Schoenauer—comes in five basic lengths, derives much of its excellence and strength from engineer Horst Wesp and a tough plastic called Makrolon. *Field & Stream's* editor wrings out several of the new rifles, both on the range and in the Austrian *gebirge* for red deer and chamois.

THE TOWN OF STEYR is located in Austria where join the Enns and the Steyr rivers, at the confluence of the greatest brown trout stream and the best water for the pike-like *huchen* in all of Europe. The people of Steyr seldom yodel on street corners, but *lederhosen* are as common as ordinary pants and wearing one of those Tyrolean-style hats rivals brandishing a beer mug as a local occupation. Steyr should be a tourist town, but it isn't, really. What Steyr is famous for is a great works, where iron and steel, swords and plow-shares, have been pounded out since the early Middle Ages, where firearms have been made for the past 105 years. It's all very well for the local Chamber of Commerce to point out that the industrial combine of Steyr-Daimler-Puch makes jillions of trucks and tractors or more jillions of motorcycles, but that gets no more tumble than do the trout in the beautiful Enns. What everybody does know is that Steyr is the home of the Mannlicher rifle.

Ferdinand Ritter von Mannlicher—the "von" indicates that he was a nobleman—has perhaps never been so glorified as Paul Mauser in the field of bolt-action rifle development, possibly because his designs were primarily produced only at Steyr and, Mannlicher being a complete patriot, chiefly for Austrian army use. His first repeating bolt action, an 11mm Austrian or .433″ is dated 1880. In that same year Mauser had about perfected the famous 1871-'84 repeater with which the Prussians overwhelmed the French. It could be argued that Mannlicher's rifle was the better, though more complex to manufacture, since in one version its magazine held 20 rounds!

As far as I know the two great designers never joined forces, but Mannlicher dreamed up as many significant ideas as did Mauser, including, for example, efficient straight-pull designs like the Model 1895 Austrian which we still see floating around. While he did not go as far into the automatic pistol field, like Mauser he ended up designing automatic rifles. Regardless of the country of usage, all of these were produced at Steyr.

But of all the military items, the model to become best known among sportsmen was the 1900 Greek Mannlicher-Schoenauer, on which engineer Schoenauer had collaborated to work up the spring-driven spool magazine, a device that has guaranteed smooth feeding for Mannlichers ever since. It is this 1900 version, with its complex multiple-piece bolt and mid-point handle, which was sporterized in carbine form, weighing only 6 pounds 9 ounces in 6.5x53 with a slim, full-length stock, with close-lying or spoon-shaped bolt handle. These packets of graceful potency earned the respect, even the love, of our fathers and their fathers before them. The light, slick, handy Mannlicher, in either rifle or

The handsome Mr. Page, grinning or leering with the better of his two stags, this one shot at over 350 meters with the 7x65 NSM held in his left mitt. Typical habitat—steep grassy slopes above timber, below that the rock and snow chamois like.

carbine form, imported into this country then as now by Stoeger, attracted scads of would-be owners.

The name Mannlicher has honestly earned its luster in sporting circles. Karamoja Bell hunted ivory with a 6.5, slew hundreds of bull elephants with it. The 6.5 carbine went with early north-country hunters like Sheldon and piled up Yukon game amazingly, the long 160-gr. bullet doing well even at mild velocities. I recall seeing my first Mannlicher-Schoenauer when I was about eleven, the prized possession of one of the oldtimers who introduced me to the outdoor world. He had never killed anything larger

than a whitetail deer with it, but from the way he handled it, he very evidently would never have swapped that carbine for an 8-cylinder Wills Ste. Claire and a pretty new wife!

The traditional Mannlicher-Schoenauer, despite its two grave drawbacks—the midway positioning of the bolt handle hardly helps repeat-shot speed and the split-bridge receiver provides major scope-mounting limitations—is still desired by tradition-minded European hunters. They now have available calibers like 7x64 and 8x60, more potent than the original 6.5x53, 7x57 and 8x56 combinations of the early 1900s. So the Steyr plant is still turn-

Left—The better of the two chamois or *gemse* I shot in Austria, the first since I was in New Zealand in 1956. I'd looked at some 100 assorted chamois and worked out a scheme to approach a bunch of 5. That involved crossing a basin, climbing half a mountain, then crawling 200 yards. The shot was made at 275 yards or so. ● When you go skipping about the high Alpine

pastures, three solid hours of climbing above your homey mountain hut, you get quite familiar with the rifle on your shoulder. It becomes an old friend or a damned clumsy nuisance, but the New SM rifle easily made the first category. The jäger carries his own rifle in a low sling, muzzle forward, totes a sizeable packsack and has a trail-up dog leashed to that rucksack.

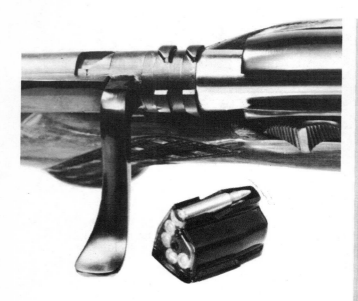

Left—Mid-bolt locking lugs of the new S-M series of rifles are 6 all told—2 rows of 3, giving 60° bolt lift. Note spoon-shaped handle, an old SDP touch, and the sliding safety. ● Rotary spool magazine (insert) is only vestige of Herr Schoenauer's old contribution to earlier M-S rifles. New spool holds one more round than do conventional-well bolt rifles, and a spare spool can be carried, eliminating loose or

belt-held cartridge boxes of standard type. Rapid reloading—if heavy fire power is your bag—is easy. ● Right—The four new S-M centerfires. From top—the short SL version, made for cartridges in the 222 class. Next, the L type, suited to 308, 243, et al. Third, the M series (30-06 and similar), last the S form, handling all magnums except the big Weatherbys. Double set triggers may be had.

ing them out, in very limited numbers. For a while, anyway.

What is really coming off the machining lines in quantity is a New Steyr-Mannlicher, and I mean new— or *neue,* as we say in Austria—New, because the design is not only new to Steyr after some 70 years but is new in its approach to several basic design problems common among sporting rifles.

Heart of the S-M

Heart and core of the New Steyr-Mannlicher—they want it called that because the design was solely conceived within the Steyr works—is a complex moulding of a synthetic developed by the Bayer people and called Makrolon. Now before you start cussing plastics consider these points. Makrolon is self-colored, so the blue-black matches the rifle's metal parts even if you manage to cut the surface. It is stable under any humidity or wetness variation, and over temperatures from a minus 150° Fahrenheit to 275° above zero, which is more than 50° above boiling. You're not about to encounter temperatures beyond either, not during this life. It will neither scratch like aluminum nor rust like steel. It is tough beyond belief. After watching an engineer pound on the table with parts made from Makrolon I tried to go him one better by whanging a steel chair leg with the one long thin-walled piece that in a New Mannlicher constitutes the trigger-guard floor section, and magazine liner-box. I hurt my hand, not the synthetic.

The same substance is used for the detachable rotary-spool magazine (modeled closely after the original Schoenauer feeding device) that slickly feeds the New Mannlicher with, in any given caliber, one more round than is usual today in commercial bolt action magazines of that caliber. Five 30-06 cartridges, for example, not four. Four fat magnums, not three.

The Makrolon element becomes heart and core of the New Steyr-Mannlicher for these reasons: 1) it permits the magazine, trigger guard and floorplate weight to be kept minimal, thus keeps gross weight down; 2) by eliminating a whole slew of complex milling/stamping operations, it permits magazine and guard parts to be made for several different lengths of rifle action (actually 5) without shoving the retail price up through the roof; 3) it makes possible a stiffer rifle since the recoil lug can be positioned so that it bears at the rear of the whole action, not under the breech end of the barrel, to keep receiver and barrel "working" as one unit. Without Makrolon, in fact, the real newness of this Mannlicher would've been impossible.

Five Action Lengths

The true novelty of this rifle lies entirely in the idea of relating action length to cartridge length. As practicing gun nuts you are presumably familiar with the fact that no American-made action is turned out in more than two lengths. One European type (the Czech-made BRNOs in the ZKK models) has been available in three lengths. As gun nuts you're all aware of certain basic facts: that a standard or 30-06-length-action, roughly an inch longer than those intended for the 308 family of rounds, is also inevitably proportionately heavier and slower to operate (where and when weight is not needed); that an action long enough to handle the 375 H&H looks pretty silly digesting a 222; that, conversely, jamming a cartridge into an action length which is marginally short for it—the 6.5 Remington or 350 Remington magnum into the M600, for example—may place ballistic limits on the round's performance by limiting the case volume. That's why you can now buy the normal-length M700 rifle in 6.5 Remington Magnum, for example.

What the people at Steyr have done is to plan 5 basic actions, all alike save in longitudinal dimensions (and also in the fatness of the magazine area, naturally) tailored for each of 5 categories of cartridge. Four of these rifles, the centerfires, are in production as this is typed; the rimfire will be along during 1970 and will in most details save length duplicate the centerfires' operating principles.

The SL series, shortest of the 4 centerfires, has been made for three years. I first tested one in 1967. Equipped with a Weaver V9 scope and weighing only 7½ pounds it shot better than most rifles hefting half again as much. Remington factory loads with Power-Lokt .224″ bullets punched clusters as tight at .769″ on the average; handloads with Sierra match bullets came up .488″ for the average of five 5-shot spreads. This is a shooting iron, believe me. Its length is strictly for the 222, 223, 222 magnum family since the SL magazine will accommodate rounds no longer than 65mm or 2⅝ inches.

The L version is one size longer, with a 76-millimeter magazine, 3 inches in our terms, and equivalent spread between the receiver bridge and the ring so the action throw is appropriate to such rounds as the 308, 243, the 22-250, and, of course, the short-coupled metrics. Longer yet is the M series, which boasts a 92.5mm magazine length and like action throw, to handle cartridges like our 30-06 and 270, the 7x64, and the 7.92x57, 7x57, or the 6.5x57 when their bullets are seated properly out, not shoved down against the primer hole as they must be through our "compact" or 722 lengths of action. The big one is called the S type. Its functioning length is indicated by the measurement on its magazine, 101 millimeters. That of course means it'll take the pony-car magnums like the 264 Winchester, 7mm Remington, the 458 Winchester and the 308 Norma. It handles the shorter Weatherby cartridges, but *not* the 460 or 378. It will digest Holland & Holland rounds (300 and 375) or others of like dimension, and of course will swallow the European blockbusters like the 8x68, 6.5x68 or 9.3x64. Only one thing bothers me about the S type. To accommodate all those elephant-jarring rounds in its magazine, it has to be a mite portly, some might say fat, around the mid-section. Otherwise it and the little SL come out of the same pasture.

Range and Field Trials

My second experience with one of the New Steyr-Mannlichers started at Steyr itself. The company's Dr. Breitenfeld drove over to Vienna to tear three of us, Pete Kuhlhof, Pete Brown, and me from the pastry shops where we were committing slow suicide on *Sachertorte* and assorted other whipped cream goodies. Out at the plant range he handed us three identical M-series sporters. Each was barreled in 7x64, each was equipped with a Helia 4x scope in a quick-detachable style of mount which, believe it or not, proved by later events to be capable of removal and return to dead zero. That range has target butts out to 1000 meters but mercifully the Steyr engineering crowd, who were anxiously wondering whether or not these American gun-scribblers could hit anything smaller than a chocolate cake, expected us to check out the rifles' zero only as far as 300. That's 330 yards, which is a fair approximation of reasonable maximum hunting range expectancy, though as it turned out later on, I had to stretch the 7x64 a mite to drop a stag, the red deer or *hirsch,* well beyond 350 meters.

Everybody hit the chocolate cake. One guy, whose name I shall refrain from mentioning, luckily had two holes cutting each other at 300 meters. He promptly quit while the was ahead. In my judgment, all three of the rifles were capable of shooting 1½ MOA (minute of angle) with factory fodder, and who needs better?

During the next few days, I really came to know my borrowed 7x64 since it was slung on my shoulder while I huffed up and down, mostly up, the assorted Alps that make up Donnersbachwald, the *revier* or hunting area jointly controlled by the Mannlicher outfit and the Semperit tire people. With it I nailed two very nice red deer, and two chamois as well, the better of which carried hooked-back horns of record-book dimensions. So I got to know that rifle even better than I did my guiding jäger, Nicholas Hochsteiner (that means high rock, and he certainly never messed around with any of the lower rock piles). If it hadn't been for that exercise in futility known as the Gun Control Act of '68 I'd somehow have sneaked that rifle home from Steyr too. It was very evidently a better rifle than the one lugged by my unnamed friend who shot the 300-meter doublet, since with it I bagged 4 head of prime game, and he only one with his!

The 7x64 or 7mm Brenneke, let me interpose, is an earlier Germanic forerunner of the 280 Remington (some say contrived as an answer to our 270), but which uses heavier bullets than either. There's a pinch of optimism mixed into the ballistic dope, perhaps, since the Torpedo-style 162-gr. bullet from the 7x64 is supposed to have 230 foot pounds more energy at 300 meters than our 165-gr. bullet from the 280 has at 300 yards, but whatever the numbers the 7x64 is a good killing cartridge. I used the 173-gr. H-Mantel Copper-Point, as put up by RWS. Far and away too much slug for a 50-55 pound chamois or even a 450 pound stag, it dropped game like a 16 pound sledge.

Then I contrived later range experience with the New Steyr-Mannlichers, two of 'em. One was a 7mm Remington Magnum (S type) with which John Olson of Stoeger had just clobbered an Ontario moose. Stuffed with Remington 175-gr. PCL loads it shot consistently at 1.75 MOA. OK for any quantity-loaded ammunition. One of the M series rifles, a 30-06 that came straight out of the box and was fitted with a scope right there on the range, hung around 1.75 inches with the 125-gr. Remington varmint load. With handloads using the 180-gr. Nosler over a rather mild dosage of DuPont 4064, 46.5 grains of it, shot very close to the magic minute of angle mark. These rifles are clearly going to deliver first rate hunting accuracy, and on the basis of my experience to date, will also hold zero well.

S-M Make-up

The Steyr-Mannlicher barrels, please note, are hammered or cold-forged over a mandrel. Steyr has been using this process on military orders for years, so they know it from muzzle to chamber. The residual outside spiral marks of the multiple hammers are left at the butt section (30mm in diameter for standard calibers, 35mm for magnums) as evidence of this. Though of conventional chrome-moly steel, the work-hardened tubes should resist erosion well. Evidently the Steyr people think they have a highly accurate barrel since I got to shoot one fancy group with an experimental 7.62 NATO target musket, meant for ISU or Olympic competition; even with iron sights it made an impressively tight cluster at 300 meters.

The action of these new rifles is itself stiff, being tubular and with minimal cutouts for magazine and ejection ports. The bolt body is round for smooth function, the bolt face is rather conventional in today's terms with a plunger ejector and a spring-supported extractor slicing through the cartridge-shrouding wall. The lockup is halfway back, with 6 lugs ahead of the bolt handle (three rows of paired lugs means a 60-degree bolt lift) to give an area of 60 square millimeters of bearing surface for standard rounds or 93mm for magnums. The safety slide is handy at the right rear, locking both firing pin and bolt handle; the firing pin shows very short travel; and the action is well gas-proofed. I had absolutely no functional problems with action or feed, will offer no opinion as to how the midpoint lockup will work with hot handloads until I can have a rifle long enough to brew up some.

We were told, over hot chocolate swimming in whipped cream, that all the centerfire models will be coming along as rifles with 23⅝-inch barrels, and the SL, L, and M types for the non-magnum rounds will also be turned out with 20-inch carbine barrels and full length or "Mannlicher" stocks. It will be interesting to see if the New Steyr-Mannlicher carbine sets people to slavering the way those old Mannlicher-Schoenauers did. The old one had a lot of romance about it. The new one is based on hard common sense.

The guy who designed it is that way. A young chap named Horst Wesp, he is the type who knows what makes a computer tick, has the gumption to throw old engineering ideas out onto the courtyard cobblestones and to try radical new approaches. He had the persuasiveness, too, to swing all of Steyr along with him, to overturn the thought habits of roughly 70 years. Without benefit of broad lapels, square-toed shoes or two bushels of hair, Horst is a modern fellow. I just want to be around when he has his first encounter with a band of U.S. rifle nuts! ●

The office buildings for the Steyr-Daimler-Puch works, largely bombed out in WW II but rebuilt. SDP manufactures a full line of diesel trucks and tractors, motorcycles of all sorts, and the Haflinger, a unique go-anywhere vehicle. The gun business represents about 10%. Note aged and decrepit gent yclept Kuhlhoff leaning on a Fiat 125S, not a Mercedes—SDP handles all the Fiats sold in Austria, not a bad racket! Dr. Breitinger, our guide-mentor, looks on.

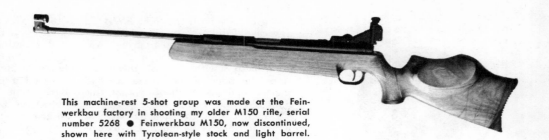

This machine-rest 5-shot group was made at the Feinwerkbau factory in shooting my older M150 rifle, serial number 5268 ● Feinwerkbau M150, now discontinued, shown here with Tyrolean-style stock and light barrel.

MATCH AIR RIFLE TEST

Five high-performance spring-air target rifles get a Test Report workout—Anschutz, Winchester and three different Feinwerkbaus.

by JOHN T. AMBER

I've had an opportunity this spring to make a side-by-side comparison of 5 different target-grade air rifles, all in 177 caliber, and all in perfect working order.

Several years ago, while in Germany, I bought one of the Model 150 Feinwerkbau air rifles in target-grade, this one with the lighter barrel, and with the Tyrolean form of buttstock —that is, the one we would normally call a schuetzen-type with a cheekpiece that lets the cheek lie snugly in position for offhand shooting. A year or so later, John Weir (then with Winchester-Western's German office), knowing of my new interest in match air rifles, obtained and sent to me another FWB 150 model, this one with the heavier barrel, and with the regular target stock—the one with the straight, high-comb line.

Toward the end of 1969 Winchester sent us one of their Model 333 match-grade air rifles, along with the proper array of target sights, etc. This is of break-down barrel type, as opposed to the solid-barrel systems of the FWB rifles, a system also used by Anschutz.

Then, early this year John Marsman of Savage sent me one of their Model 250 Anschutz 177 match rifles, and a bit later Robert Law of Air Rifle Headquarters, following a phone talk with him, shipped over to us one of the new model Feinwerkbaus, now designated the Model 300. The Model 300 shows a number of refinements over the earlier M150, but in all major essentials it's the same rifle.

Because of our extremely wet spring this year, I haven't been able to get in as much shooting with these 5 air rifles as I'd hoped, but I have done enough, I believe, to let me find out just how they perform—at least in my hands and with my aging eyes, I'll have to admit. All of this shooting was done with iron sights, of course, in that these are the only type of sights legal for organized competitive shooting, as in the Olympics or in ISU matches. I was rather surprised myself by making some fairly good groups at the standard 10-meter distance using flat top posts, but I feel more confident when I'm using aperture fronts; and I think I did do just a bit better with the apertures.

Just about all of this air rifle shooting had to be done on weekends, and I simply could not get the wind to stay still on any day. I tried to shoot when there was a minimum of wind, but invariably there was a bit of a breeze blowing, even if only of a few miles per hour. In spite of the breezes, I got 10-shot groups that were almost always in one ragged hole, but very few of them would have made possibles—the new ISU target is a tough one!

These match air rifles don't require the break-in period that lower-cost air arms do if the latter are to perform at their best. It generally takes some 1,000 rounds to get the average air rifle to operate at its smoothest and to shoot most accurately.

However, I did notice a gradual easing of functioning with four of the rifles, as you'll read later. Accuracy itself was excellent from the very beginning.

In any case, I got the best performance from my light-barreled FWB M150. I have put probably 800 to 1000 pellets through this barrel, and it did seem to me that the ease of operating the rifle, the movement or vibration when the trigger is touched off—small though it is with any of these rifles—

Anschutz Super Match pellets. Individual container holds 100 pellets, come in 500-unit cartons. Loose-pack pellets available in tins at less cost ● Winchester M333 with Match stock, barrel-locking lever, sleeved barrel.

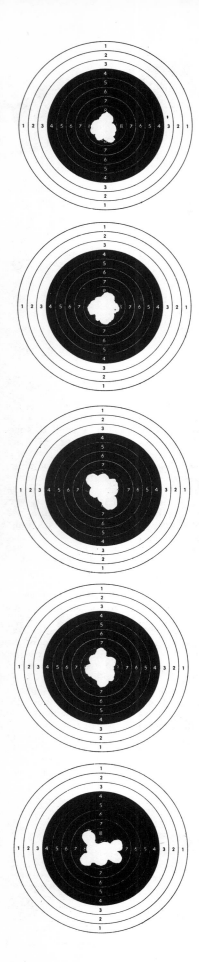

was a bit less with the light FWB. In any case, I did seem to do a bit better with it also, from group to group. Another shooter, certainly, might have done better with one of the other rifles, but none of the others has had the same break-in shooting that this light FWB has run through.

I hadn't shot the heavier-barreled FWB 150 nearly as much, but as evidence that breaking-in does help, it seemed to me that the handling and operation of this rifle was improving as I kept shooting. Group sizes ran just a hair bigger than with the light 150, though the best groups with this FWB would hardly have made 10-shot possibles—on the old target!

The new FWB M300 performed just as well as the rifles previously mentioned, but I couldn't see that it shot any particular bit better, and I would certainly tell anybody who has a 150 to keep it and use it. The changes that have been made in bringing out the M300, while doubtless worthwhile and helpful to the match shooter, do not seem to me to be absolutely necessary to fine performance. I'll readily admit that I am

others, again in my own experience. I was just a bit surprised at the excellent shooting qualities of the M333. I had thought that the break-open barrel system would not give quite as good a performance as the solid-barrel types certainly do, but I could detect no trace of difference in group to group. All of these 5 rifles, by the way, were shot during the same period—within a few hours of each other on the days when they were fired.

All of these match rifles have adjustable triggers—for weight of pull, for initial take-up and over-travel, etc. Most of them have a fair amount of initial take-up before the actual release point is reached, but I found this easy to get used to, being an old military-pull man anyway! As received, all these 5 rifles have a fair bit of trigger over-travel unless the adjustments are used to get rid of it; in this respect the Winchester M333 exhibited a trigger pull that most U.S. shooters would be more at home with—there was some initial take-up, but the trigger letoff itself was considerably crisper than with the others,

These five 10-shot targets were made at 10 meters from rest using peep sights. From the top — Feinwerkbau M150 light barrel, RWS pellets; FWB M300 with barrel sleeve, RWS pellets; FWB M150, heavy barrel. Winchester M333, H&N pellets, and the Anschutz with RWS pellets. All are shown life size on the latest ISU 10-meter target; these have a 10-ring dot of .044", the 9- and 8-rings going .240" and .436", etc. A tough target for possibles ● Sectional view of the trigger-sear mechanism found on the Feinwerkbau M300 match air rifle.

no competition match shooter—far from it—and it may well be that the serious competitive air rifle shooter could well detect and make use of the differences built into the later FWB.

There's a 2-inch shorter cocking lever, and reportedly a 15% reduction in cocking effort, but I couldn't detect the changes. The new barrel is 2¾ inches longer, resulting in a longer—and lower—sight radius and line, the new trigger offers 4 adjustments, and the stock has been redesigned via a better pistol grip, etc. I did like the new stock treatment better, especially the more vertical, closer pistol grip and the higher comb line.

These and many other aspects of the new Fainwerkbau match rifles—plus a great deal of information on numerous other air rifles — match grade and sporting—will be found in Air Rifle Headquarters' *1970-71 Full Line Catalog*. Its 48 pages are loaded with excellent data on the history, care and feeding of air guns—and it's free!

The Winchester 333 and the M250 Anschutz shot just as well as the

and the after travel of the trigger was at a minimum. I made no attempt to adjust the triggers on any of these rifles, not having time to do them all, therefore I felt that to adjust one for my personal taste would work an injustice on the others.

These match air rifles are invariably furnished with micrometer-click rear sights, fully adjustable for windage and elevation, and with detachable globe or hooded front sights that take interchangeable posts and apertures. These are excellent sights, if my limited experience with this lot of 5 rifles forms a basis for judgment, but I can say that they answered the helm in every respect whenever I wanted to move the point of impact. There is one thing to watch out for, however—disregard the markings on the elevation and windage knobs and simply move the sights in the U.S. fashion—the direction you want the shots to go—and you'll be OK. That is, clockwise for impact movement to the left, and counter clockwise for bringing the point of impact higher, and vice versa. Apparently some of these peep rear sight discs are assembled without any lubricant, and apparently tightened with a torque wrench! I had to use heavy pliers to remove a couple of them.

Target grade air rifles are now offered with an amazing variety of accessories in general, almost to the point where they have about as many gadgets available as a rimfire or centerfire match rifle. With the latest FWB sent to us by Air Rifle Hq., the kit contained the following items: 2 spacers, each about 3/8-inch thick, to lengthen the vertically-adjustable buttplate; a "clearing" lens of about 1½x for use in the globe front sight; another 1½ power magnifier, combined with an adjustable aperture and a yellow filter, that threads into the rear sight. I like this Siebert-made last item very much—I'd bought two of them years ago in Germany, and they do much for my old eyes when I'm trying to use iron sights. An extra grip cap, this in addition to the grip cap already standard on the FWB 300, which has a small shelf of sorts running around the perimeter, and which acts nicely as a hand stop.

Small combination tools are standard with all of these rifles, these for adjusting the triggers, etc., and the Anschutz is furnished with a cleaning kit as well—a pull-through, plus a couple of brushes, etc.

The 10-shot groups illustrated—one for each of the 5 rifles—were selected to show how well the rifles can shoot. Some practice groups were, of course, much worse, but when I did my part and conditions were reasonably right, the targets shown resulted. These rifles will put 10 shots into much smaller holes from a machine rest or in the hands of younger, keener-sighted shooters.

RWS, H&N and Anschutz 177 pellets were used in testing the 5 rifles. RWS and H&N pellets were packed loose in small tins and packed individually as well. The Anschutz pellets were on hand only in the latter form.

Examined under a strong glass, it seemed to me that the H&N pellets showed a trifle less uniformity from one to another in comparison with RWS pellets, but I found no difference in their shooting. True, in the loose packing a few dented or deformed pellets were found—which is guarded against in the individual packaging—but these were easily detected and not used.

Minor imperfections were visible on all pellets examined, and I could see no real difference between the loose pellets—of any brand—and the single-pellet pack. Aside from virtually all single-pack pellets being uniformly good, it has been said that the more-expensive (about twice the price) single-pellet packs carry pellets selected by trial as showing superior accuracy. I couldn't detect any difference, but mine was a relatively brief test.

Feinwerkbau M150 (now discontinued) with Match stock and heavy barrel.

This view of the 1970 M300 Feinwerkbau shows the shortened cocking lever and the adjustable buttplate lowered.

Feinwerkbau Model 300 with Match stock and heavy (sleeved) barrel. New rifle has higher comb, shorter lever, several other changes. See text for details.

Anschutz Model 250 shown is editor's older version. 1970 type has higher comb line, closer pistol grip, etc.

This Muzzle-Loading Game

R. O. (Slim) Ackerman is one of the top authorities
on the care and feeding of front loaders,
flintlock or percussion, rifle, handgun or fowling
pieces. Here's the full story—all you need
to know to become a muzzle man.

by R. O. ACKERMAN

I̲T IS INDEED appropriate that an
article covering the basics of muzzle-
loading shooting techniques should be
included in the 25th ed. GUN DIGEST
Long before the appearance of the
first practical breechloaders, individual shooters were forming their separate opinions as to the best powder
charge for a given caliber, the proper
granulation, bullet fit, etc. No self-
respecting frontiersman would have
loaded his muzzleloader the way it is
usually depicted on television — by
contrast, many black powder shooters
were a marvel of precision.

This has carried over to the present
day, when a new upsurge of interest
in muzzle-loading has made this definitely one of the fastest growing of
all shooting sports. Watch one of today's more experienced "charcoal

burners" at an important match, and
you will quickly realize that *precision*
and *uniformity* are the key words of
success in muzzle-loading shooting,
as they are in handloading metallic
cartridges.

Admittedly, there are differing
schools of thought on the technical
aspects of this sport, as with any
other. The type of person who takes
it up in the first place is a rugged
individualist, with the attributes of
patience and an inquiring mind. Demanding concentration itself, the sport
is a haven of relaxation for the professional man who needs to leave his
problems at the office or the clinic.

The author fires his favorite big-bore rifle, a 58-
caliber custom-built replica of the famous Hawken, made by Lee Paul. The load is 100 grains
of black powder behind a 505-gr. bullet.

Rare indeed is the muzzle-loading
club which does not include at least
one doctor — be he lawyer, dentist or
surgeon. Their manual dexterity finds
an additional outlet in the hand-
crafting of many shooting accessories,
a bonus hobby that's an important
and happy part of muzzle-loading
shooting.

One of the first questions asked by
the newcomer to the sport is how to
determine the powder charge for his
rifle. Herein lies one of the sport's
controversial issues, so in fairness
I'll outline the different approaches
— but first things first, ok?

Right here and now let me warn
against the unwise practice of taking Grandpappy's old "hawg rifle"
out of the attic, pouring down an
undetermined amount of aged pow-

der from the old horn or flask, stomping down a ball with the finesse of a bulldozer and letting her rip. This is funny if you read it in Mark Twain, but in real life it is more intelligent — and far safer — to have the old smoke-pole competely disassembled, cleaned up and inspected by a competent gunsmith first, and I mean one who understands and specializes in muzzleloaders! There isn't a state in the Union which doesn't have one, except possibly Hawaii.

The reason for this warning is not so much that the old relic may blow up. Much more likely is that ancient threads have rusted away, so that a drum or a nipple can fly out with injuring force.

Another strong warning — equally obvious to the initiated. After a knowledgeable gunsmith has pronounced the old rifle safe and sound (perhaps with a replaced mainspring and nipple), do *not* shoot it with anything other than the black powder for which it was designed. If you pour in the powder from a couple of today's shotgun shells you'll lose more than just the rifle. In spite of repeated warnings, people keep doing this — but only once for each person!

Powder Charges

Now then, here are some of the *original rules* for selecting the powder charge you need. You'll note that the results vary from very mild to pretty stout, the reason being that they were designed for different purposes. After these have sufficiently confused you, I'll give you a safe formula as a starting point.

Some of our hardy forefathers stipulated 3 grains of black powder for each 7 grains (avoirdupois) of the weight of the round lead ball. This gives fair medium-strength loads, but for top efficiency the cited ratio should not be the same for small calibers as for large. Another old rule was "a grain to a caliber." This is suitable for target shooting but it isn't sufficiently versatile. This means that a 45 rifle takes 45 grains of powder. The heftier rule for the longer-range "40 Rod" rifles was "1½ calibers under 40, 2 calibers over 40." (This means that a 32 would take 48 grains of powder, while a 45 would take 90 grains.)

A cardinal rule to remember at this point is that maximum power and gilt-edged accuracy seldom if ever go hand-in-hand. You should decide which you want and work for it. Actually, most experienced front-feeders either have certain rifles for competition and others for hunting, or else they work up a different load for each purpose. Not only does their powder charge vary, but some use the round ball for target and the heavier hollow-based conical "Minie bullet" for big game. My own trend has been in that

direction in recent years.

My advice to the beginner is to concentrate upon accuracy first, and leave hunting loads until he knows his rifle better. Here is a reasonable procedure with the average "patch-ball" rifle, whether it is flintlock or percussion. Use as a starting point a grain of powder to a caliber (a 40-caliber rifle would take 40 grains of black powder by weight). Then work up from this, about three grains at a time, until you find the point of maximum accuracy at normal target ranges. This will usually be found somewhere below the point of "1½ grains to a caliber," beyond which you may expect accuracy to drop off slightly.

Another thing to watch for: when the rifle report changes from a mushy boom to a sharp, businesslike crack, you should just about be at peak efficiency.

A properly loaded muzzle-loading rifle normally has a much milder recoil than a modern rifle of roughly equivalent power classification, despite the myth that they all kick like a mule. For target work, if recoil is excessive, you are beyond the point of peak efficiency and are defeating your own purpose — unless the rifle is a very light one.

A long barrel will burn a little more powder efficiently than a shorter one, but don't be too impressed. Best to pick the barrel length that suits you, and take it from there. One pioneer method of determining the correct powder charge for hunting was to gradually increase the charge while firing across an area of clean snow, until unburned grains of powder started to appear upon the snow surface. Then they would back off three or four grains, knowing that they had the load giving maximum power without wasting powder. Theoretically, peak efficiency falls off when a given amount of expanding gases are required to move unburnt powder in addition to a projectile. But this is only an exercise in interior ballistics, and negligible for practical consideration.

Balls & Patching

Black powder is made in a number of granulations, of which only the three smallest sizes concern us here. FFFFg, the finest granulation, is used only for the priming pan of a flintlock or for priming a percussion nipple to overcome or avoid a misfire. FFFg is used in all pistols of average bore size, and in rifles of small to medium caliber. FFg is preferred by many shooters for big bore rifles, and is almost universally used in muzzle-loading shotguns. The exact line of demarcation varies with the user. Some switch from FFFg to FFg when they reach 45 caliber — others not until 50 caliber or even larger.

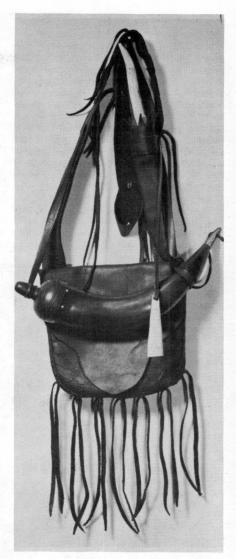

Walter Kneubuhler, a maker of excellent custom knives, offers this handsome top-grain leather hunting pouch, powder horn, patch knife and bone charger at about $53.00. Flint strikers ($5) and picks at $10 may also be ordered. A fine-looking, high quality outfit.

Ignoring extremists, the consensus would seem to average between those calibers. The difference in pressures is not great, so your choice should be governed by performance in your individual rifle, and by which one burns the cleanest.

The ball is traditionally cast of pure lead, although I consider any alloy soft enough if it can be cut with the thumbnail. A bullet mould so cheap that it will not cast a good, spherical ball with a minimal sprue surface is a poor investment. Balls may be rolled between two pieces of plate glass, if desired, to remove the sprue surfaces altogether.

Bullet patching should be of some vary tough, smooth-surfaced cloth such as denim, sailcloth, pocket drill or pillow ticking. The general rule is thicker patching for deep rifling grooves, thin material (even linen) for shallow rifling. Here again, experimentation will show what gives best results in your rifle. Wash your patching material to remove all sizing before use.

Exact ball diameter and patch thickness are not considered separately, but in conjunction with one another. One popular approach is to measure the thickness of your chosen patching cloth by closing a micrometer down firmly on it. The measurement of one thickness of cloth (in thousandths of an inch) will be the difference between the rifle bore diameter (from land to land) and the proper diameter of the ball. Example: bore diameter is .445″, patching is .008″, ball is thus .437″ diameter. By the time the patch is gathered on all sides of the ball, and overlapped in places, you need not worry about the fit being tight enough. Check this by starting a patched ball into the muzzle and then pulling it out again by the cloth. It should be tight enough so that the weave of the cloth will be impressed visibly into the lead ball. If further adjustment of this fit is desired, it can be obtained by trying different patching.

All of the foregoing tips apply equally to either flintlock or percussion rifles. The only difference is in the method of ignition. Caps for a percussion arm should be chosen for hot ignition and for fit on the nipple. The fit should be snug but the caps should seat without splitting. Be sure the nipple cone is not shorter than the cap, for this will create a cushioning effect, often causing misfires. We used to have available numbers 9, 10, 11, 12 and 13 percussion caps, plus musket or "top hat" caps. Modern nipples have become more standardized, and numbers 9 and 13 have been discontinued by most manufactures.

I find Remington No. 12 caps hotter than their others, and Alcan's GIIF is their hottest.

Before we discuss the techniques of loading, there are a couple of accessories — a powder flask with an adjustable charger and a magazine capper to dispense your caps — that can be a great convenience in the field. However, don't buy every gadget you hear of until you're familiar with all available types, and have really determined your own needs.

Loading Techniques

Prior to firing the percussion rifle, the bore, nipple and flash channel should be thoroughly degreased and left dry. This can be done with a bit of mineral spirits or other safe grease solvents, but allow plenty of time for complete evaporation before loading. Many shooters snap a cap or two on the empty rifle just before loading, to clear oil or previous-shot fouling from the nipple. Hold the muzzle several inches from some dead grass when doing this. If the grass moves,

A measured charge of black powder is poured into the muzzle.

A blow atop the "long starter" puts the patched ball about 6 inches down the bore.

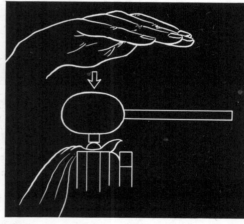

The ball, surrounded by patching, is started into the bore by a light blow on the "short starter."

The patching is now gathered and cut off at the muzzle.

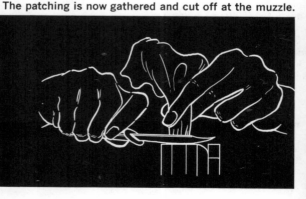

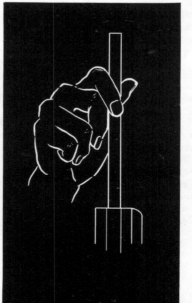

The ramrod is used to seat the ball firmly onto the powder charge.

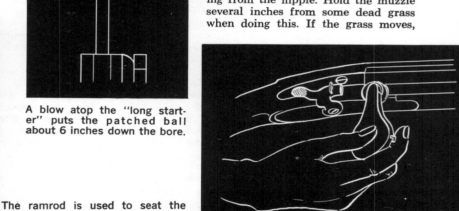

A magazine capper may be used to place a percussion cap upon the nipple.

the vent is clear.

With the hammer on safety halfcock, pour a measured charge of powder down the bore. Moisten a corner of your patching on your tongue and place it, damp side down, over the muzzle. Press in a ball, keeping the sprue surface uppermost and centered. Place the ball just below flush with the muzzle by a light blow from the hand on the handle of the "short starter" (see illustration). Gather all excess cloth up and sever it cleanly at the muzzle with a very sharp patch knife. Some shooters use one of the old straight razors for this chore. Drive the ball some 6 inches down the bore with the "long starter." Then seat the patched ball onto the powder charge with the ramrod, being sure to seat it firmly but without pounding and crushing the powder grains. If you wipe out most of the fouling with a moistened cleaning patch between shots, the ball should go down without undue effort. *Be sure you seat it all the way,* without leaving an air gap, which could be hazardous.

Now you're ready to cap the nipple and fire. It is optional, but you may wish to use one of the new nipple primers before capping. This sifts a tiny bit of FFFFg priming powder into the top opening of the nipple, giving hotter ignition and fewer misfires.

For safety's sake, if your rifle has a set trigger, you should have thoroughly learned its operation before going to the range. Some rifles fire only with their trigger set—others give

Rather than using the time-honored patch cutting for each shot, some shooters prefer to use pre-cut loading patches. These round patches may be cut by hand but a steel arch-punch of the proper diameter is a great convenience. One of your own fired patches will give you the necessary diameter needed for punched patches as well as any other method* Whichever patch type you prefer, we usually moisten them with saliva (outer side only) for target shooting, but substitute a very light coating of grease (outer side only) for hunting. This is because of the greater length of time a hunting load may remain in the bore — when saliva could cause rust. Rendered tallow was the pioneers' grease — with bear tallow vastly preferred. Tallow is still used, also equal parts of beeswax and vaseline, melted and mixed, sometimes with a little sperm oil added. A commercial product called Beare Grease is good also. The important point is to avoid overgreasing, and to keep pre-greased patches in a receptacle

Minie ball or bullet is a hollow-based cylindro-conical projectile, grooved around its circumference, instead of a round ball. The fact that it needs no patch, and is usually undersize for the bore, speeds the loading process. The Minie ball slips down the bore quite easily. Because of its rather deep hollow, the force of the burning gases expands the soft lead "skirt" of the bullet into the rifling, so that it goes in loose and comes out tight. The latest trend in Minie rifles is a form of rifling designed for good performance with the conical bullet or the round ball. A difficult compromise but it seems to work.

The Minie bullet has a higher trajectory than a round ball as its velocity is normally lower. However, what it lacks in this respect it makes up in smashing shocking power. Therefore, it is a good brush buster, and it's popular for such larger game as bear or elk.

Minie bullet moulds are made in calibers 40, 45, 54, 56, 58 and 69, with more to come. Standard loads for the 58 and 69 rifles are 60 and 70 grains of FFg respectively. These were the charges used in the rifles and rifled-muskets in Civil War days. Loads are being worked up for the other Minie

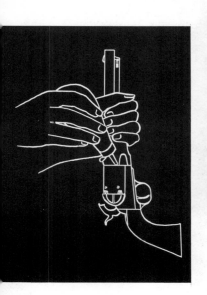  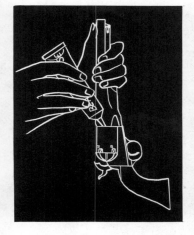 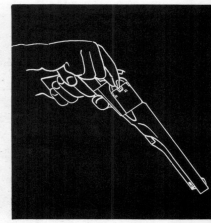

From left—A measured charge of black powder is poured into a chamber of a percussion revolver ● A ball is placed upon the charged chamber, rotated into alignment with the rammer, and seated upon the powder by means of the loading lever. Repeat with other chambers ● Grease is applied to each ball after seating, to prevent chain-fire and to soften fouling residue ● A percussion cap is pushed firmly onto each nipple, and the revolver is ready to fire.

the option of either the set "hair trigger" pull or a normal pull at your discretion. Some can be set at any time — others only in a prescribed sequence. There are also single-set triggers as well as double-set. Become familiar with all of these if feasible.

You will find a percussion rifle very pleasant to shoot. Also, once you become accustomed to a muzzleloader's tendency to be muzzle heavy, you will find that this helps to eliminate waver, and that it offers unsuspected potential accuracy.

that won't let sand and grit get on them.

The Minie Ball

The percussion rifle or carbine using the Minie ball is something else. The

*A good patch cutter can easily be made if you have access to a grinding wheel. Steel pipe of the correct—or nearly so—diameter can be bevel-ground to a sharp cutting edge. Grind at about a 30% angle to the long axis of the pipe, which may be 3"-5" long for easier handling. Use a piece of hardwood—an oak log is fine—folding the patch cloth to place several thicknesses over the end-grain of the wood. Now use a rawhide or rubber mallet on the open top end of the pipe and start cutting (a heavy steel hammer would soon batter the pipe).

sizes. In addition to the standard 460- and 505-gr. 58 Minie bullets, a heavier 570-gr. big-game bullet and a light 315-gr. semi-wadcutter are available. Counting the round ball, this gives the owner of a 58 Minie a choice of five different projectiles and a wide variety of loads.

My own favorite hunting arm is a modern copy of the famous Hawken mountain man's rifle, made by Lee Paul of 400 W. Miner St., Yreka, Calif. 96097. This excellent example of today's custom craftsmanship has a 38-inch barrel and a Harold Robbins lock, and was made in 58 percussion for the above assortment of projectiles. It has two interchangeable rear sights — a full buckhorn traditional open, plus a Redfield adjustable-aperture sight which can be slipped on for longer-range hunting. Adaptable for anything from grouse to grizzly, this is my idea of the most versatile muzzle-loading rifle a one-gun man could wish for.

This Lee Paul barrel has the combination round ball/Minie rifling mentioned earlier, the twist one turn in 60 inches. Admittedly some extra effort is called for to get it to perform well with both projectiles!

Minie projectiles are generally used with their hollow bases filled with Crisco — a cooking fat. This keeps the residue soft and, theoretically, each emerging bullet is supposed to push out the residue from the preceding shot.

Flintlock Notes

I will repeat that all of the foregoing instructions for loading patch-ball rifles, and for working up their correct powder charges, apply equally to either the percussion or the flintlock rifles. The only difference is in the method of igniting the main charge.

The flintlock is truly the traditional arm of our founding fathers. At the time the thirteen original colonies united in revolt and declared their independence, the so-called "true" flintlock had already been in use over 160 years. It was destined to continue in vogue an additional half-century before being gradually replaced by the percussion system. Actually, including various types of transitional arms, the flintlock principle's tenure was even longer than that.

Study of the accompanying photographs should clarify the operation of a flintlock. To clear up a prevailing fallacy, it is not the sharp blow of flint against steel which ignites the priming powder. Rather, it is a prolonged *scraping* action under heavy spring-pressure. The sharpest blow upon the frizzen would virtually never induce ignition if it did not have sufficient scraping "follow-through." This action of the hard, sharpened flint shaves off microscopic *rolls* of steel which, heated to incandescence, shower the priming and ignite it. Watch the steel curls produced by a metal lathe, to visualize this better. It is not surprising that a frizzen needs to be replaced, or have a new steel surface soldered on, at intervals.

The flinter is a temperamental firearm. While it requires a few extra precautions in order to be reasonably sure of ignition, this additional challenge does not deter the thousands of shooters who are discovering anew the fun of using this traditional rifle of Daniel Boone and Davey Crockett. A man who is used to the idiosyncrasies of his particular flinter will usually compete against percussion rifles without considering himself greatly handicapped.

The frizzens of some modern replica flintlocks are improperly hardened and tempered for the production of hot sparks. One cure for this is to "re-face" them with a piece shaped from a discarded power saw blade, and soldered on. Soft solder will suffice.

A touchhole which is too small can cause irritating misfires. I usually recommend drilling the touchhole out and tapping it to take one of the new threaded inserts. These simply screw into place like a headless screw, and offer three major advantages:

One, they are of stainless steel or Ampco metal, both of them resistant to the heat-erosion which ruins touchholes. Two, they have a vent like an inverted cone, placing the main charge and the priming much closer together for fast, sure ignition. Three, they may be easily removed for replacement, or to pour powder behind the ball if you forgot the powder charge while loading.

Ideally, a flint should be used which is close to the width of the frizzen face. Clamp the flint tightly, with a strip of thin leather around it to give the cock jaws a better grip. Sheet lead is also used sometimes. Be sure to install it so the entire front edge will contact the frizzen! The question of bevel-up or bevel-down can only be answered by finding if either way works better in your individual lock. Early military manuals disagree on this. The best idea is to try it one way for 15 or 20 shots—then reverse it to present a fresh edge for a few

A modern flintlock rifle (above), cocked and ready to fire. Note that pan is covered until the instant of firing ● The lock in fired position (below). As the flint strikes the steel frizzen and scrapes down its length, the priming in the pan is simultaneously uncovered to receive the incandescent sparks and transmit the flash through the touch hole ● Early French flints are amber-colored with a rounded heel. The large ones are cannon flints. The dark gray English flints are more rectangular ● Powder dispensers for flintlock pans. From left—priming horn, miniature copper flask, and a new pan-priming device with a spring-loaded valve.

more before discarding it. With practice, you can learn to resharpen a flint by lightly tapping the edge until the sides flake away at the blunt areas.

After loading the ball and before priming the pan, it pays to check the touchhole with a piano-wire pricker to be sure it is clear. Keep the muzzle pointed in a safe direction. Pour FFFFg powder in the depression of the pan only—not upon the lip of it. Do not use so much that the frizzen and pan cover will not close entirely. Using all the pan will hold is not necessarily an advantage. An amount that brings the charge level with the center of the touchhole often works well. Ignition may be a bit faster with less priming. Experiment. Wear shooting glasses and school yourself not to flinch every time that pan flashes. We all went through that—it just takes getting used to it.

Remember that if you can learn to shoot the flintlock well, you can shoot anything.

Caplock Handguns

Loading for single-shot patch-ball pistols — percussion or flintlock — is identical to that for the rifles. The one difference is in the much lighter powder charges. A good guide to proper charges may be taken from those suggested for percussion revolvers, which I'll cover next.

With very few exceptions percussion revolvers are the only arms used in this sport which are fairly stan-dardized as to calibers. The actual groove sizes of these, which were known as 31, 36 and 44 in Sam Colt's day, become the 32, 38 and 45 calibers of a later era.

Again, make sure before loading that the bore is wiped out, and that chambers and nipples are dry and clear. A powder flask with the proper size charger is almost essential here. A permissible load is all the FFFg a chamber will hold and still permit a ball to be seated. However, the usual charges for the old "cap'n'ball" are approximately 15 grains for the 31, 22 grains for the 36 and 28 for the regular 44 — the larger-framed Dragoon 44s will take 40 grains.

With the hammer on safety half-cock to let the cylinder revolve freely, pour a powder charge in one chamber. Place a ball upon it and align it under the short rammer attached to the loading lever. With the lever, seat the ball on the powder, making sure it is below flush so the cylinder may turn. Repeat the operation with the other chambers.

Next, put grease over the ball in the mouth of each chamber. The commercial product Beare Grease, with its long-nozzled tube, is ideal for this purpose. This practice will prevent multiple or "chain" fire (in which the fired chamber may ignite the ones adjacent) and keep the powder residue soft in the barrel.

Cap the nipples and you are ready to fire.

As with any single action revolver,

it is considered wise to carry the hammer on an empty chamber when wearing the gun on a hunt. A couple of drops of a black powder solvent upon the cylinder arbor (the shaft upon which it revolves) will help keep powder fouling from making the cylinder stick.

M. L. Shotguns

Percussion shotguns are really a joy to hunt with or to shoot trap, yet it is only very recently that they have started to be appreciated.

Developing a load for one is very simple. Merely remember that the *volume* of powder should equal the volume of shot, and also that the volume of the over-powder wads be equal. A good rule of thumb is this: in an average load, the depth of each of these components should be equal to its diameter (or bore size). My drawing should clarify this. Transparent pill bottles of the same inside diameter as your bore are one way you can estimate your own loads. Otherwise, here are some suggested ones — all medium loads for general use:

Gauge	Powder/grs.	Shot/ozs.
28	55	5/8
20	65	1
16	82	1
12	102	1¼
10	123	1½

I cut my over-powder wads, with an arch punch, from thick uphol-

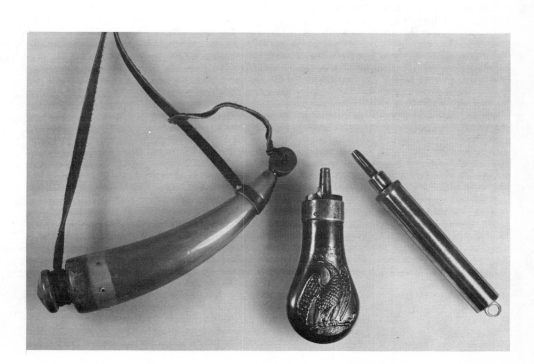

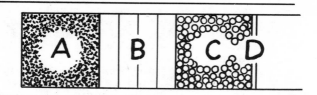

Bottom—"Hawken" style cap lock made by Cherry Corners Gun Shop, shows first class workmanship, sells for $34.50 postpaid • Musket or "top hat" cap (left), and standard rifle or pistol cap • Above— cross-section of an average percussion shotgun load. (A) powder, (B) over-powder wads, (C) shot, (D) over-shot wad. See text • Right—Lyman's .445" Minie-ball, also offered in .685", .557", .535" and .577".

sterer's felt, using whatever number of wads are necessary. My over-shot wads are punched from solid cardboard (not corrugated). Some trap-shooters moisten their felt wads very lightly with an emulsion of water and soluble oil, putting a dry wad down on the powder, hard, then the moist ones upon that. For hunting I use all dry wads, but this is optional. Over-powder wads should be rammed until the loading rod bounces — the top wad is merely pushed down to hold the shot in.

Soluble oil of one brand or another is a standard item around machine shops, used with water to cool a cut.

Care and Cleaning

There are two schools of thought about the cleaning of black powder guns. The old reliable method is with boiling hot water, which does a quick and very thorough job. If convenient to remove the barrel, place the breech end with nipple removed in a can of hot water and pump the water in and out with a snug-fitting cleaning patch until patches come out clean. The barrel will get too hot to handle without a cloth pad. Dry the bore quickly, which the heat will help. Clean other parts and oil all of them immediately inside and out, as rusting will start almost at once.

The care required to prevent rusting is the chief problem met in muzzle-loading, and the reason most shooters have turned to the special chemical solvents for black powder which are now available. These are more convenient to use. The danger here lies in not being sufficiently thorough — especially in such hard-to-reach places as the flash channel between the nipple and the bore. A clean-out screw helps here, if your rifle has one.

For everyone interested in this fast-growing sport, I strongly recommend membership in the National Muzzle Loading Rifle Association, P. O. Box 67, Friendship, Indiana 47021. For $6 a year you may participate in their many activities, be eligible to fire in national and regional matches, support their efforts to protect your legal interests and receive various other benefits. Each member receives their monthly magazine *Muzzle Blasts,* and this informative publication alone is well worth the membership dues.

If this capsule description of techniques strikes one responsive spark — why not attend a local muzzle-loading match and watch them in action? Just be careful if someone invites you to try his shootin' iron — that black powder bug is mighty contagious!

●

Front Feeder Fixin's

Cappers, chargers, short starters, nipple primers, single-set triggers, Dixon flasks, flints, touchhole inserts, etc.	Dixie Gun Works, Union City, Tenn. 38261, and others
Beare Grease, 89c tube	Caution Tool Co., Southbury, Conn. 06488
Arch punches	C. S. Osborne & Co., Harrison, N.J. 07029
Pistol powder flasks, $9.95	John Dangelzer, 3056 Frontier Ave., N.E., Albuquerque, N.M. 87106
Gunlocks	Harold W. Robbins, 653 S. Hewitt Rd., Ypsilanti, Mich. 48197
	Cherry Corners Gun Shop Rt. 1, Lodi, O. 44254
Pan priming device, $6.50	W. Morgan, 7603 Romney St., Houston, Tex. 77036

George Schoyen—from a photo made about 1900.

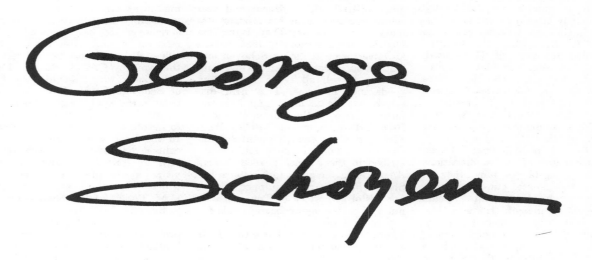

RIFLEMAKER EXTRAORDINARY

A fully detailed and thoroughly documented account of the great Denver craftsman and his long years at the bench. Profusely illustrated with numerous specimens of his superb work.

by John T. Dutcher

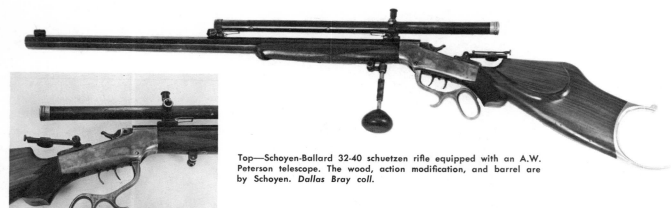

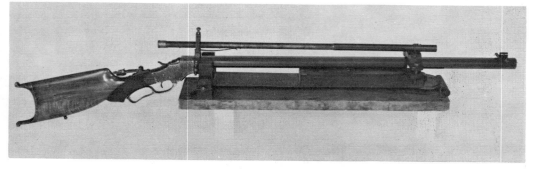

The lower portion of this Ballard receiver has been cut away to make a closer and more aesthetic pistol grip stock—a feature often found on better-grade Schoyen-Ballard rifles. Note the close inletting of wood to metal. *Dallas Bray coll.*

Top—Schoyen-Ballard 32-40 schuetzen rifle equipped with an A.W. Peterson telescope. The wood, action modification, and barrel are by Schoyen. *Dallas Bray coll.*

"FINE GUNWORK of every description," read the advertisement of George Christian Schoyen, considered to have been one of the best rifle barrelmakers of all time. Schoyen barrels were the choice of many of the best marksmen of the Schuetzen era. Noted offhand riflemen such as Dr. W.G. Hudson, Dean W. King, Jr., and C.W. Rowland, the great rest shooter, used Schoyen barrels.

Schoyen was born in Norway in 1845. He immigrated to the United States shortly after the Civil War, first settling in Chicago. Disaster struck on October 8, 1871, when the Chicago fire burned Schoyen out. Undaunted, Schoyen, his wife, and first daughter moved to Denver, Colorado. There he went to work for Carlos C. Gove, a well-known maker of percussion muzzle-loading target and sporting rifles. Gove also made under-lever conversions of the Remington rolling-block rifle; it is possible that Schoyen performed many of the modifications on these rolling blocks, plus other alterations and general gun repair.

Schoyen, who had spent 7 years learning the gunmakers' trade in Norway, proved an accomplished and prolific workman. It is no wonder, then, working in an environment such as Gove's Denver Armory, that Schoyen

should have added to his knowledge of riflemaking. Word spread quickly of the Norwegian gunsmith's talents. Before long, the gunshop in the back of Gove's Denver Armory, located on the banks of Cherry Creek at 340½ Blake Street, was filled with orders for Schoyen barrels. Most of those early barrels were fitted to Sharps, Ballard and Remington buffalo rifles, replacing the original worn barrels. Orders soon came in for target rifle barrels which were fitted to the currently popular single-shot, breech-loading actions and a few percussion rifles.

Gove and Schoyen were correspondents and disciples of William Billinghurst, of Rochester, New York, one of the better known makers of caplock muzzle-loading rifles. These three gunsmiths often followed similar lines of thought and experiment.

During 1884, Gove, who was aging and involved with political and real estate ventures, sold his Denver Armory to Schoyen and D.W. Butt. The Denver City Directory of 1885 carried an advertisement listing Schoyen and Butt as successors to Carlos Gove, and offering to sell all types of sporting goods and firearms. This firm dissolved two years later, and Schoyen formed a new partnership in 1887 with Fred A. Burgen, moving to 1420 Blake Street, next to the Elephant Corral. One product of this partnership is described in the August 1, 1888, *Sports Afield* magazine as "a fancy 40 caliber Sharps hunting rifle equipped with a fine pistol grip stock of Tunisian walnut and a Remington barrel made for big game hunter, Dr. H.A. Lemen." There is no evidence that either Butt or Burgen (sometimes spelled Bergen) were gunmakers.

As the railroads developed through the West, word of Schoyen's skill spread beyond the Rocky Mountain region, and he began getting orders for high-grade hunting rifles from many celebrities, European as well as American. Lord Lennox, Earl of Dunraven, and Col. Vivian both used and endorsed Schoyen barrels. For Lord Ogilvie, Schoyen made a fine set of double-barreled guns (one a rifle and the other a shotgun) said to have cost $250 each. William F. "Buffalo Bill" Cody and Annie Oakley had Schoyen repair their firearms, and Schoyen's grandson recalls reloading rifle ammunition with shot for them. These cartridges were undoubtedly used for aerial shooting. (God help the Indian holding the cigar in his mouth if Bill or Annie forgot they still had shot loads in their guns!). Today, Schoyen hunting arms are rarities, and in all probability they were never common.

Schoyen is best remembered for rebarreling and altering fine target rifles. He may have been directed in this area by C.W. Rowland, of Boulder, Colo., who thought very highly of Schoyen. Carlos Gove, too, was a dyed-in-the-wool target shooter, and he undoubtedly influenced Schoyen to devote his talents in this direction. In his later years, Gove used a 35-caliber muzzle-loading Schoyen-Ballard for target shooting. For many years a dispute has raged as to which was the best barrelmaker: H.M. Pope, A.O. Zischang or George Schoyen. All three were master craftsmen, and this question will probably never be resolved. L.R. Wallack, in his book, *Modern Accuracy,* quotes a letter written by Har-

Schoyen-built machine rest, with telescope, used in testing Schoyen rifles at the old Denver Rifle Club Range. The rest is fully adjustable for windage and elevation. The Stevens rifle, clamped in the V-mounts, recoils to the rear on the leaf spring below it. *George Kane coll.*

The Denver Rifle Club in 1905. George Schoyen is shown lying down at the far right side; J.P. Lower is sitting in the middle. Original photo by Dr. W. G. Hudson.

vey A. Donaldson regarding Charles W. Rowland's opinion of Schoyen barrels. "Rowland really had a warm spot in his heart for the famous Denver (Colorado) gunsmith George C. Schoyen. He told me he believed Schoyen made the finest barrels that he ever used. He said of course Pope made a good barrel, but that all of Schoyen's barrels were good, and that he never made a poor shooting barrel. I have correspondence from Rowland wherein he states that it had been necessary to return more than one barrel to Pope for additional lapping, etc., or whatever it was Pope did to it, before it performed properly."

Rowland, a famous bench rest shooter, is credited with many feats, notably the shooting of a 10-shot group measuring .725-inch—10 shots in one hole at 200 yards! To quote again from Wallack's *Modern Accuracy:* "On May 26th, 1931, Mr. Rowland completed a string of 40 consecutive shots at 100 yards with a 32-40 Schoyen rifle. The 40 shots were not all fired in one day, as a lot of time was required to get all conditions right before getting off a shot. For example, the last 10 shots fired took from 12 noon to 5:00 P.M. The day was a bit windy and the shooting was only done during lulls. Rowland's equipment was a 32-40 Schoyen rifle, breech-loaded, using a Peters shell, 9½ Remington primer (NM) 12 grains of DuPont shotgun powder and a blotter wad with 1-pound pressure. The sight used was a 20x Stevens scope. The bullet was of 200 grains, base-pour and cut-off (type), cast 1/20. A Pope machine rest was employed. The 40 consecutive shots measure ½ x ½ center to center of widest shots."

Keep in mind that Rowland was a man in his seventies when he did this shooting! This is certainly a tribute to Rowland and Schoyen as well. However, as mentioned earlier,

the discussion over who made the most accurate barrels will never end, for Rowland used a Pope 32-40 in shooting the .725-inch group which was the standard of accuracy for half a century at 200 yards.

One of Rowland's favorite rifles had a 39-caliber bore chambered for the 38-55 case. This barrel was unearthed during the excavation of a foundation for a large building near Boulder Creek, at Boulder, Colorado. Mr. Rowland was on hand and thought he heard the ring of fine steel. He called to the workmen and asked for, and was given, the old relic which he took to George Schoyen for reboring. When it was finished Schoyen said, "Yah, it is so, dat is the finest piece of steel effer I saw!" With this barrel Rowland later shot several 10-shot groups at 200 yards from a bench rest that measured ⅞-inch extreme spread.

At the offhand rifle matches, Schoyen rifles also proved to be superbly accurate. At Cheyenne, Wyoming, on May 21, 1899, Peter Bergerson equaled the world record with a Schoyen-Ballard rifle. His 32-40 was loaded with 42 grains of FFFg DuPont powder and a 216-gr. bullet muzzle-loaded. Oddly, Bergerson was also a custom barrelmaker. Today, little is known of him, although William L. Bruce, former member of the U.S. International Rifle team remembers him as being a fine gunsmith. Bergerson was competing for the first prize—a new Stevens No. 54 Schuetzen rifle—when he shot this group, narrowly defeating the runner-up, who was using a 35 caliber Schoyen-Winchester rifle.

On August 16, 1903, D.W. King, Jr., began shooting regularly each weekend at the Denver Rifle Club. His goal was the world record, then held by H.M. Pope. Early in January, 1904, he climaxed a run of 3040 consecutive shots using his Schoyen-Ballard rifle with a score of 917 out of a possible

1000. King shot 27 straight 10s (centers). He had the world record, and in doing so shot the highest average for the number of shots fired that had been attained. King manufactured early Schuetzen shooting accessories, such as a clever duplex powder measure, and gunsights, first in Denver and later in San Francisco, California. As the March, 1904, issue of *Outdoor Life* stated: "This shows the ability of Mr. King and the Schoyen rifle."

Late in 1905, Dr. Walter G. Hudson visited Denver and had Schoyen rebore his 33-caliber Remington underlever Schuetzen rifle to 38-55 at a cost of $6.00. Although this was the most economical means of attaining a Schoyen rifled barrel, it shot well, as the many records and meets that Hudson won indicate. At the American Record Match, February 22, 1910, held at Greenville, New Jersey, Hudson scored a 99 out of a possible 100. Earlier, he broke the world record with a 922 out of a possible 1000 using the same rifle.

Another Schuetzen rifleman, W.A. Kuntz, shooting offhand at 200 yards, hit a silver dollar 5 times straight with his 14½-lb. Schoyen-Ballard rifle. The list of users of Schoyen's work is endless and includes William S. Green, Tom D. East, Tom Blunt, Jim Ricker, Dr. Asquith, and J.P. Lower, the early-day Denver gun dealer.

Schoyen built both ornate and utilitarian rifles. One of J.P. Lower's sons, Joe, had Schoyen build a fine Sharps-Borchardt Schuetzen rifle with a diamond set into the engraved action. Later, the Colorado National Guard ordered fifty 22 caliber barrels that were bored off-center, so the firing pins in the Krag actions to which they were fitted could be used. If you want one of those Krags, you had better look diligently, since nearly all of them were converted back to their original calibers many years later by A.W. Peterson. Harry Pope did this job also.

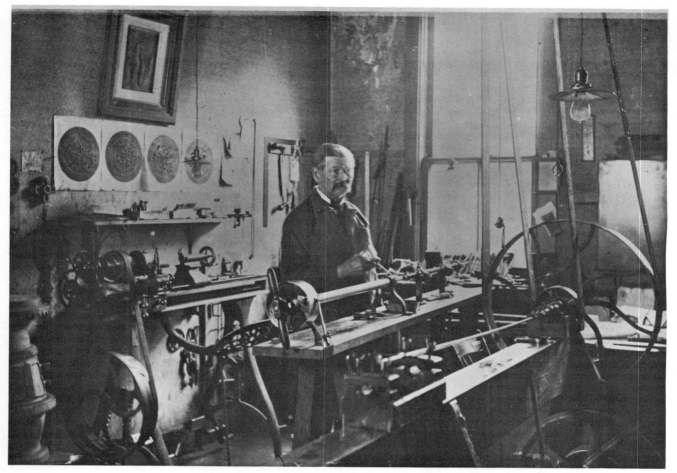

George Schoyen in his shop shortly after the turn of the century.

Schoyen's Barrels

The demand for Schoyen barrels, action modifications, custom stocks, and reloading accessories, had grown so great that by 1903 Schoyen formed another partnership. On October 1st, he was joined by Axel W. Peterson under the firm name of Schoyen and Peterson, located at 1417 Lawrence Street, Denver. A.W. Peterson had made quite a name for himself as an expert offhand rifle shot and gunsmith. He also had an inventive mind, and had recently developed one of the first rifle telescopes with internal adjustments. This partnership proved to be an advantageous combination as Peterson, who had not previously made barrels, quickly learned the skill of making the Schoyen barrel. As Peterson said of Schoyen in 1944, "His name vas on our barrels vether he made them or me. Ve both made the Schoyen barrels. He vas a very fine workman." Peterson was considered to be one of the best marksmen in the country, and traveled to many matches competing with a Schoyen-barreled Sharps-Borchardt rifle. In late 1906 Peterson scored a 98 out of a possible 100 with his muzzle-loading 38-55.

Schoyen's barrels were of the wide-groove and narrow-land type. The 22

and 25 calibers had 6 lands and grooves; the 28, 32 and 33 calibers had 7 grooves; the 38, 39, 40 and larger calibers had 9. Typically, these barrels had a right-hand twist and were generally not choked. The lands were about .03-inch wide, the grooves averaged .12-inch wide and .0025 to .003-inch deep. As Schoyen was a custom maker, deviations from the average barrel will be found. There are several larger caliber Schoyen rifles with both

6 and 8 rather than 9 grooves, and at least one rifle was made with a left-hand twist. The twist per inch varied somewhat in Schoyen's barrels. For example, Dr. John May owns a 38-55 Schoyen with one turn in 18 inches, and I have a Schoyen rifle in the same caliber with one turn in 16 inches. Until approximately 1900, these barrels were bored with a foot-operated treadle lathe and then rifled by hand. However, after Schoyen added power

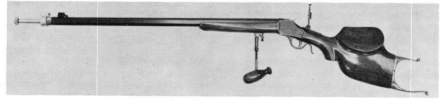

Winchester single shot rifle with Schoyen false muzzle barrel, stock, and action modifications. This perchbelly stock is the type most commonly found on Schoyen rifles. See text for details. *John Dutcher coll.*

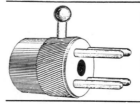

GEO. C. SCHOYEN, Gun Maker

Fine Gun Work of every description

New Rifle Barrels Made to Order. Old Barrels Bored and Re-Rifled. New and Old Barrels Fitted with False Muzzles for Target Shooting. Old barrels fitted with false muzzles have to be bored to one size larger

2326 15th Street, - - - - Denver, Colo.

A Schoyen advertisement from the November, 1902, issue of *Outdoor Life.*

Schoyen false muzzle and bullet starter, the latter commonly made of aluminum. *John Dutcher coll.*

This point-pour bullet mould is the style typically made by Schoyen. Of 32 caliber, the mould is brass lined and the sprue cutter works on the bullet nose. *Claude Roderick coll.*

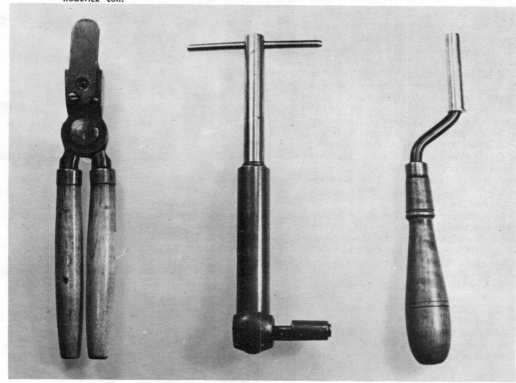

Schoyen bullet mould, bullet lubricating pump, and bullet breech-seating tool. Mould from *Claude Roderick coll.*, pump and seating tool from *John Dutcher coll.*

GEO. C. SCHOYEN   DENVER. COLO.

The mark of a master.

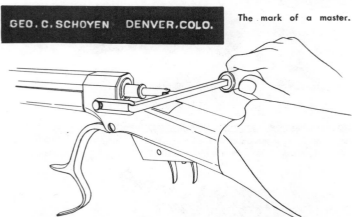

One method of breech-seating a bullet in the bore's throat and a Schoyen-made side-anchored lever. Drawing by John Dutcher.

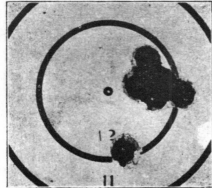

Ten shots at 200 yards, fired in April, 1903, by C.W. Rowland of Boulder, Colo. He used a Schoyen 32-40 rifle owned by John Barter of Boulder. As the July, 1903, *Outdoor Life* said: "It is rumored that Mr. Barter is now sitting up nights guarding his treasure, as there are a number of rifle cranks in Boulder."

equipment, he still continued to rifle his fine barrels by hand. Col. Frank H. Mayer, the old buffalo hunter, recalled that in the late 1890s he lost a quart of "Old Monogram" betting Dean King and Old Man Gilbert that they could not kick out a bore of 30 inches in two hours on Schoyen's treadle lathe. It is said that normally it took Schoyen nearly two days to make a complete rifle barrel. For a more detailed description on rifling these barrels, see L.L. Baker's article.

Schoyen shimmed the cutting head of his rifling machine with cigarette paper and made very light cuts. This operation was repeated until the desired bore dimensions were reached. He did little lapping or polishing, and occasionally when a barrel turns up that has been fired very little, slight traces of tool cuts are found in them. Most of these barrels were made of soft steel, and they'll polish up nicely with a little shooting. Each Schoyen barrel of 32 caliber or larger size was tested and guaranteed to shoot a 2½-inch or smaller 10-shot group at 200 yards. Schoyen, or one of his assistants, would ride the Denver & Intermountain Railroad to the Denver Rifle Club grounds at Golden, and test these barrels in an adjustable machine rest that he had built. This rest includes a telescope sight of Schoyen's manufacture.

In a recent survey of 67 different Schoyen rifles, nearly one-half of them were chambered for the 32-40 cartridge, 12 were made for the 38-55 and 8 for the 22 rimfire. The rest—many of them single specimens—were comprised of the following calibers: 40-70 Sharps straight, 33-40, 25-21, 28-30, 39-55, 40-70 Ballard, 25 rimfire, and 32- and 45-caliber caplock rifles. Undoubtedly, this is only a partial list. One third of these rifles were equipped with false muzzles and bullet starters of several styles. The false muzzle generally had 4 aligning pins. A few were equipped with locking levers made to fit lugs attached to the side of the barrel. One rifle has turned up with a 2-piece false muzzle. A few rifles were made for paper-patched bullets. Most barrels are octagonal, but part-octagon and round barrels are also found. Schoyen applied a rich chestnut-brown finish to many of his barrels. A formula for what is said to be this finish is found in Ned Roberts' book, *The Muzzle-loading Cap Lock Rifle*. His charge for "re-blacking" a rifle barrel was $1.50. An interesting copy of Schoyen & Peterson's price list reveals figures that will make you weep, my friends! However, as an old friend and single shot rifle fan, J.V.K. Wagar, has pointed out: "While prices were low in those years, so were wages."

Schoyen Tools

To assist the riflemen, Schoyen, together with Peterson, designed a full

The fine rifle seen here shows to good advantage the craftsmanship of Edwin Phillips, gunmaker in New York City circa 1860-1890. The oval gold plate set into the cheekpiece reads: Presented by the/HELVETIA RIFLE CLUB OF NEW YORK/to the/Third Union Shooting Festival/New York, July, 1868 in 5 lines. The schuetzen match in question was held near Jones Beach on Long Island—later to become the famous Creedmoor range. The various matches took a week to complete, and gross income was $30,000! Re-entry match fee was a nickel, but to compete in the American Match cost $10—a handsome sum in 1868.

All of the metal is fully and beautifully engraved—including the heavy steel buttplate, which is also silver inlaid—to patterns found in the L.D. Nimschke pattern book published by John J. Malloy.

When this Phillips rifle was made it had, most probably, a barrel of at least 45 caliber, perhaps even larger. At some time in the past, perhaps in the 1880s or so, George Schoyen fitted the muzzle-loading barrel now on the rifle. He matched the original engraving (or someone did) that shows on the breech flats to a quite good degree, but a close look reveals that the later work is not by Nimschke.

The caliber is 32-40, in effect, for the tools that came with the rifle—mould, false muzzle, piston starter, and so on—are identical with those that Schoyen furnished with his breech-loading offhand or bench rifles.

The 5 visible flats of the breech are engraved, the three flats of the breech and barrel being inlaid with gold lines. The back-action lockplate, the hammer, the steel buttplate, the barrel muzzle and both tangs are also engraved. On the left side of the action Columbia is seen seated, surrounded by a group of flags, while a golden-eyed fish is shown locked in combat with a snake.

The extension of the standing breech is marked L.D.N. over ENG.—For L. D. Nimschke, the engraver.

This Phillips-Schoyen rifle weighs 17 pounds without its false muzzle, but including the nearly 31-inch unmarked telescope sight. The barrel without false muzzle is 31¾-inch long. A steel cross-foot is attached to the underside of the barrel for rest shooting.

The name EMIL BERGER is engraved into a silver inlay on the left side of the buttplate. Berger was, presumably, the winner of the rifle of the 1868 shoot, but I've been unable to trace him. The cased rifle came to me from Iowa—the home state of many schuetzen shooters for many decades—and there was a family of marksmen named Berg in that area. Perhaps there was a connection.

line of loading tools and accessories: at least two styles of re- and decappers, both single- and duplex-cavity powder measures, bullet lubricating pumps made in two sizes (both of which had interchangeable dies), buttplates, palm rests, bullet moulds, custom buttstocks, and fore-ends. He also did repair work of all kinds and complete refinishing. Schoyen built many specialized tools, one of which was a grease-gun-type lubricating pump that ejected thin, uniform strips of olio lubricant from which Mr. Rowland made wads for his meticulous shooting.

Typically, the Schoyen mould is a brass-lined Ideal or Winchester mould altered to a point cut-off type, and casting a tapered bullet similar to the Pope. A few hand-made moulds were made in different styles. Mr. Schoyen's grandson has a beautifully crafted example, a double-cavity type with a point sprue cutter.

The custom buttstocks and fore-ends found on Schoyen rifles were generally made by A.W. Peterson or Henry Simmons; occasionally Schoyen did stock work also. Simmons worked for Schoyen prior to Peterson's entering the business, and stayed on during the partnership doing general gun repair.

Often the buttstocks are of the large perch-belly type, well-adapted to off-hand shooting, though not always understood by today's riflemen and collectors. "Too large, too ungainly looking," or "It's ugly" are comments often heard. But they have a purpose. The large high cheekrest was fitted to hold the shooter's cheek, while the deep perch-belly lower part was designed to rest on the shooter's chest muscles, giving him maximum support of the rifle. They were not made to look at, but to use and, given time, one finds they have a purposeful beauty of their own. Each was made to the individual shooter's specifications. Of course, as Schoyen and Peterson's brochure stated: "We also make other shapes to order." A number of rifles have turned up with stocks that don't have the common characteristics attributed to Schoyen and Peterson, namely—shape, checkering styles and workmanship. For example, I've examined several with stocks by O.A. Bremer. These were custom rifles, so, I'm sure many other deviations and combinations of several gunsmiths' work will turn up from time to time. In examining Schuetzens, one will find a few "improved" home-horror-and-multilation type alterations that have been perpetrated on these rifles through the years. Such frustrating examples should not be blamed on the original gunsmith. It's all part of the game and should be expected if you have a fondness for this type of rifle.

Schoyen's inventive abilities are found in the fine double-set trigger modifications that are occasionally

George Schoyen in 1912. The poster on the wall behind Schoyen advertises a Schuetzenfest held in Frankfurt, Germany that same year.

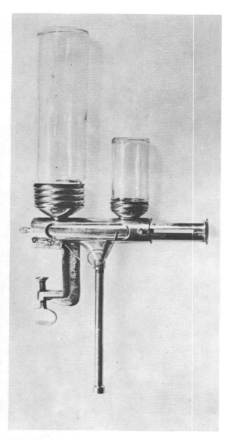

The Schoyen-Peterson duplex powder measure sold for $5.00. The smaller jar held the priming charge, while the larger jar metered the main charge of black powder. *Claude Roderick coll.*

seen on his rifles in addition to a clever barrel take-down system for the Ballard and other single shot actions. A taper pin is fitted through the action immediately below the barrel shank area. This pin passes through a groove milled in the bottom of the barrel shank. By tapping the small end of the pin, it is easily removed; and the barrel, which has coarse, easy threads, is screwed out by hand. When the pin is in place, the barrel is as tight as one could desire. A more refined version of this take-down system has a small button fitted to the left side of the action, it is pressed to dis-

engage the barrel, then screwed out in the same manner as described above. This taper pin sometimes serves a dual purpose. It may also be used as an anchor pin to attach a lever type breech-seating tool that assists in pushing bullets into the barrel's throat. It is believed that Schoyen was the first to develop the side-anchored breech-seating tool.

Schoyen, along with Peterson, built many of the machines and tools they used, including a lathe. Being frugal Scandinavians, they used the old forge that Carlos Gove brought across the Great Plains from Iowa in 1860. This

forge was still in use until the closing of the Peterson Gun Shop, shortly after World War II.

In the survey above of 67 Schoyen rifles, nearly half have Ballard actions, followed in order of numbers, by the Winchester Hi-Wall, Stevens 44 and 44½, and Sharps-Borchardt. A few Sharps side-hammer, Remington rolling block, Remington Hepburn, and two Remington-Schuetzen (underlever) actions are also found, along with several percussion-lock rifles. It is not believed that Schoyen produced caplock rifles in their entirety, but altered those made by other makers. If one were to describe the typical Schoyen rifle, as taken from the survey, it would be a 32-40 caliber offhand target rifle built on a double-set-trigger Ballard action, equipped with a full octagon No. 4 weight barrel. It may or may not be equipped with a false muzzle, and bullet starter. The barrel finish would be brown and the action case-hardened in color. It would have one of the large perch-belly Schuetzen buttstocks so typical of Schoyen's work. It would weigh between 13 and 14 pounds and, most importantly, it would be extremely accurate.

Yes, I know many are not that way —I own several without the above mentioned characteristics—but what

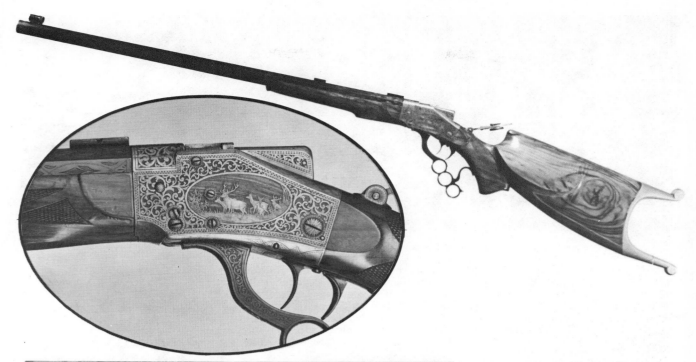

Fancy Schoyen Sharps-Borchardt 38-55 Schuetzen rifle. This rifle has Schoyen's triggers, barrel, finger lever and wood work. The close-up shows the excellent and unusual engraving, which covers the receiver, barrel breech flats, lever, etc. Rather oddly, the scroll work is less well done than the animal figure—the detailing and anatomy of these is superb. All of this engraving lies well above the background.

The Denver Rifle Club Team, winner of the Coors Championship Cup, July, 1898. Rear row, from left—D.W. King, J.A. Ricker and George C. Schoyen. Front row, from left—O.E. Adamson, Harry Willis and A.W. Peterson. Adamson holds a Maynard rifle, Willis a Remington-Hepburn, while Peterson's rifle is a Sharp-Borchardt with panelled receiver. Regrettably, the other rifles can't be seen.

I've described is the type found most frequently in the survey.

What kind of a man was this master craftsman? Schoyen is said to have been of average size, with brown hair and blue eyes, who dressed neatly in a suit and tie, even while at work making those fine rifle barrels. He is known to have had the happy faculty for making and keeping friends. A lady I talked with recently recalls Schoyen as a good family man who raised 5 daughters with the help of his Australian wife, whom he met in Chicago. She calls him "the kindest man I ever knew." He enjoyed his grandchildren, who spent much time in the shop and took turns helping Grandpa work his kick-operated treadle lathe. He also sent them out to look for old discarded shoes which, it is claimed, were used as charred leather in color-pack hardening rifle actions. A grandson, George Kane, has a diminutive Schuetzen rifle built on a Remington No. 2 action, which his grandfather built for George when he was a small boy. Schoyen was an officer in the Pioneer Rifle Club, a member of the Denver Rifle Club, and a member of the Sons of Colorado. In earlier years he was considered a consistent rifle shot, and as late as 1898 he was a member of the Denver Rifle

Henry Simmons (left) and George Schoyen, in the back ground, at his rifling machine. Photo taken in the 1890s.

Club team that won the Colorado State Championship. The Schoyen gun shop is remembered as a popular meeting place for gun enthusiasts of the day, and was often used for meetings of the Colorado Rifle Association.

By 1915, Mr. Schoyen and one of his sons-in-law had acquired a ranch south of Ralston Creek, near Golden, Colorado. Schoyen, who worked hard to attain the American dream, was thinking of retiring—but not completely. Although 70 years old, he was still capable of putting in a day's work, and there were so many old customers who insisted on a genuine Schoyen barrel. He decided to dissolve the partnership with A.W. Peterson and move his shop to the Ralston Creek ranch. But time had taken its toll, and Schoyen never made the move. He died on Saturday, January 23, 1916, at the County Hospital, shortly after midnight. He had suffered a stroke Friday morning while making a 22 caliber barrel.

The *Rocky Mountain News* carried word of Schoyen's death. In that story, J.P. Lower, the famous Denver outfitter during the frontier days, said of Schoyen: "That man was an artist, an artist. He was the best gunmaker in the country. You couldn't beat him anywhere. And a fine man, too. A fine gunmaker and a fine man was George Schoyen." ●

One of two styles of re-de cappers made by the firm of Schoyen & Peterson. *John Dutcher coll.*

RIFLE BARRELS

New muzzle loading barrels with loading outfit **$25.00**

Outfit consists of false muzzle, bullet starter, special bullet mould to run from point, lubricating pump, and ramrod.

Old barrels bored, re-rifled, and fitted with false muzzle, with loading outfit complete, same as new barrels, **$20.00**

Bore and re-rifle muzzle loading barrels **$10.00**

If new bullet moulds are necessary, they will be extra.

New breech loading barrels. **$12.00**

Bore and re-rifle old breech loading barrels **$6.00**

We do not re-bore repeating rifles.

We will fit your sights, extractor and forearm to our new barrels, but if new ones are required they will be extra.

Our barrels are fully guaranteed for accuracy, quality and workmanship. A 32-calibre and larger sizes, will make 2½ inch group or better at 200 yards from machine rest if weather and conditions are right.

We consider a 30 inch barrel, 32-calibre or larger, the best, but will furnish 32 inch at the same price. For smaller calibres we think 28 inch the best.

Barrels smaller than 32-calibre and over 28 inches long, $2.00 extra.

Weight of No. 4 barrels is about 7½ to 8 pounds; heavier barrels will be $1.00 a pound extra.

Special bullet mould to run from point **$3.50**
Lubricating pump **2.50**
Extra disc .... **.75**
Palm rests, our own make **3.50**
Finger grips fitted to levers same as on our make of rifles
Polishing and case hardening actions **3.00**
Re-black rifle barrel **1.50**
Re-black double barrel **3.00**
Re-stocking shot guns and rifles according to shape and quality of wood used .... **$6.00 to $25.00**
Forearms for rifles from $1.50 to $5.00
PRICES NET

In ordering stocks give length from forward trigger to center of butt plate, and drop from level top of barrel to top of butt plate and comb.

We also make a specialty of rifle stocks of our own design, that are made to order to fit the person and allowing the shooter to stand and hold in a perfectly natural position.

The records that have been made with our special target rifles speak for themselves.

Read it and weep! An early Schoyen & Peterson price list.

Bibliography

Books
Ripley's *Believe It or Not*.
Roberts, Major Ned and Kenneth L. Waters. *The Breech Loading Single Shot Match Rifle*. Princeton, N. J., 1967.
Wallack, L. R. *Modern Accuracy*. New York, N. Y., 1950.

Periodicals
"A Good Combination," *The Sporting Goods Dealer*, IX, No. 2 (November, 1903), 47.
Baker, Leighton L. "How Peterson Barrels Were Made," *The American Rifleman*, CVIII, No. 8 (August, 1960), 26.
Beise, Charles J. "Rifleman Extraordinary," *Western Sportsman*, IV, Nos. 2 and 3 (December, 1940 and January, 1941).
Denver City Directories, 1884 through 1916.
Leopold, E. A. "The Schoyen Rifle," *Shooting and Fishing* (November 14, 1901).
Outdoor Life (November, 1902).
——————— (July, 1903), 492.
——————— (December, 1903), 870.
——————— (March, 1904), 188.
——————— XVII-XVIII (April, 1906), 407.
——————— (January, 1907), 98.
Rocky Mountain News (January 24, 1916).
Sports Afield (August 1, 1888).
Tedmon, Allyn. "That Man Peterson," *The American Rifleman*, XCII, No. 1 (January, 1944), 22.
"The American Record Match," *Arms and The Man*, XLVII, No. 22 (February, 1910), 460.
The Denver Post (January 24, 1916).
"The Genesis of the American Rifle," *The American Rifleman*, LXXXIV, No. 3 (March, 1936), 12.
"Trap and Target," *Outdoor Life* (June, 1899 and February, 1900).

Other Sources
Personal interviews with William L. Bruce, Norman Ghen, Mr. and Mrs. George Kane, Mrs. Minne Kirk, Floyd Redding.

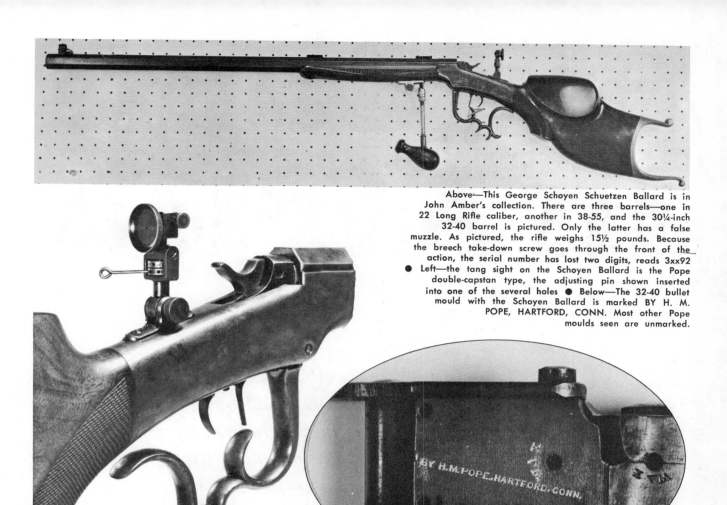

Above—This George Schoyen Schuetzen Ballard is in John Amber's collection. There are three barrels—one in 22 Long Rifle caliber, another in 38-55, and the 30¼-inch 32-40 barrel is pictured. Only the latter has a false muzzle. As pictured, the rifle weighs 15½ pounds. Because the breech take-down screw goes through the front of the action, the serial number has lost two digits, reads 3xx92 ● Left—the tang sight on the Schoyen Ballard is the Pope double-capstan type, the adjusting pin shown inserted into one of the several holes ● Below—The 32-40 bullet mould with the Schoyen Ballard is marked BY H. M. POPE, HARTFORD, CONN. Most other Pope moulds seen are unmarked.

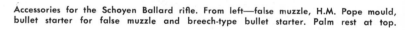

Accessories for the Schoyen Ballard rifle. From left—false muzzle, H.M. Pope mould, bullet starter for false muzzle and breech-type bullet starter. Palm rest at top.

Big Game in Africa

The wild land of Zambia is a silent place, teeming with animals and birds—buffalo and elephant in the thousands, dozens of other species, including the elusive kudu and the magnificent sable. We had a good hunt.

by JOHN T. AMBER

JOHN," Dick Wolff asked me, "are you getting excited about the hunt?"

Dick and I were sitting in Alitalia's plush lounge at Kennedy International on a balmy evening in late September of 1969. We had about an hour to kill before our airplane took off for Rome—where we'd spend a couple of days before boarding another Alitalia jet for Zambia and our big hunt. We'd registered our guns and various imported items—cameras and binoculars—at U.S. Customs, and at the moment we were relaxed, taking it easy with a draft of usquebaugh while we waited—I think it was our second flagon.

Dick—who's a vice-president of Garcia Corporation—and I had been planning this African hunt for almost a year. We're old friends, and we'd burned up the wires getting every detail squared away—or so we thought —and here we were, zero hour approaching.

"Aren't you getting excited, John," Wolff asked me again, a big grin beaming at me over his glass.

I spoke calmly, deadpan. "What's there to get balled up about? Sure, it's your first safari and my first one in Zambia, and we'll have a good chance of coming back with twelve or fifteen trophy racks, but what of it? We'll get a shot at lion, leopard, Cape buffalo, elephant, kudu, sable, hartebeest, wildebeest, eland, bushbuck, waterbuck, reedbuck, warthog and impala, but we can't get a rhino ticket, dammit, and there aren't any giraffes there, either! Why get excited, Dick?"

I was kidding, and Dick knew it. I was keyed up, trying to imagine what Zambia would be like and, like Dick, I was looking forward, even, to the long Alitalia flight to Lusaka, some 11 hours deep into South Central Africa from Rome itself.

I'll skip lightly over the smooth passage to Rome—aside from having to tell you that both of us gorged our-

Just born! This baby oribi stands about a foot high, is fully furred and its eyes open. We nearly ran over it at daybreak one morning—still very wet, the umbilical still attached to the placenta.

selves on Iranian golden caviar and Soviet vodka during the small hours over the Atlantic—and our short stay in the Eternal City. Not that we didn't contrive a few hours in the sun on the Via Veneto, sipping Campari and watching the girls go by.

Our guns almost gave us a problem on leaving Rome, but with the welcome and highly efficient help of several Alitalia people, we took off late in the evening with our arms and ammo stashed in the crews' quarters, not in the baggage hold.

We spent one day in Lusaka, getting things squared away and changing into our hunting clothes. Lusaka

is at some 4000 feet, and the day was pleasantly cool. We shopped for a few last-minute items, but we decided to buy no fly or bug dope—we'd been told by Zambia Safaris' people that we'd have no insect problems at all during our hunt, but that in any case the camps would have bug killers on hand. We were to learn the hard way how wrong they were, on all counts!

The next morning—not very bright nor very early—we took off in a Cessna for our first camp, Zambesi No. 1. Much lower than Lusaka, the heat blasted us as we left the plane, at a small bush landing strip. A few minutes later Johnny Uys (pronounced

Ace) appeared in a Land Rover to drive us the several miles to camp. Johnny, who was to be my professional hunter for the next week, was a mine of information about Zambia and all its flora and fauna, and a hell of a nice guy as well. He'd been with the Northern Rhodesia (now Zambia) game department for nearly 20 years, so he knew the country intimately.

On the Zambesi

The Zambesi camp was an excellent one, and after a good dinner under a thatched roof, Dick and I hit the hay, anxious for the first day afield. Dick

Dick Wolff's elephant carried ivory of 73-75 pounds, was shot with his 375 H&H Magnum.

My biggest buffalo, the horns running 43 inches at widest point. The 250-gr. Hornady solid was used as a first round on all buffalo, dropped them where they stood.

was to hunt with Frank MacMasters, a bright young fellow who'd come from Australia not long before, but who knew this area well. Dick and I were to hunt separately, of course, so we weren't together except early in the morning—we were up about 5:00 A.M. or so—and at dinner usually.

For the next week we covered a lot of territory, traveling 35 miles or so —in both directions—to reach better game country. We were the last hunters in the area for the season, except for one other party that followed us, and game was scarce except for buffalo and elephant—we saw thousands

of each, literally. Numerous other parties had preceded us—this was October—and the game had been hard hunted; those we did see were quite spooky, for the most part.

I had told Uys that I was most interested in finding a record kudu, but we never found any with good horns —nor did Dick. Kudu are a wary animal, indeed, living and moving in the thickest of bush. Johnny and I probably stalked a dozen or so heads through the bush—seeing only their legs usually, the stuff was so thick— only to have them detect us one way or another before we'd ever get a

chance for a shot.

It wasn't so funny at the time—at least not for me—but one morning we ran into some excitement. Driving up toward Zambesi 2, Johnny and I saw a herd of some 25 elephant crossing our rude trail about a hundred yards ahead. We slowed down a bit to let them get clear—they were strung out in twos and threes. As we crossed their trail, only a few yards from the last couple of big cows, both brutes turned and started to chase us!

We speeded up a bit, though the rough up-and-down track and the trees prevented much of that; the elephant kept after us at a brisk run, trumpeting and squealing. Johnny Uys was laughing, and I was trying to get a picture despite the jolting and bottoming of the Land Rover as we'd hit a gulley. After we'd gone several hundred yards, the cows still padding after us, Uys told me to hold on as he swung the car into a tight 180 and braked it to a halt. The elephant stopped dead—I got a picture of sorts —which Johnny had known they would. I didn't know that!

We quickly turned around, back onto our track, and I'll be damned if those cows didn't follow us again for another 200 yards or so before deciding to quit.

I wonder if our dark grey Land Rover looked like a big bull to those females?

As I've said, my chief desire was to snag a fine kudu at the Zambesi camp —there were no sable here, another species I wanted more than I did a cat or anything else except a Cape buffalo.

One day, having put up a leopard bait, we'd carefully and silently re-

This sable antelope has 47-inch horns, was shot with the Champlin 338.

turned to it. Nothing was on it—nor had there been—and as we crept away, still moving softly, we spied a small band of kudu in a rocky glen, some dozen animals. There were three bulls, and it would have been an easy shot, but none went over 45-46 inches—and that's a small kudu, really. We turned away, not a shot fired—an error I was to regret! I never had another chance at kudu—not that we didn't see other smaller ones—during the rest of the trip!

More than that, Dick and I had not been told, unfortunately, that the Zambesi area would be our best bet by far for kudu and elephant, that we'd be lucky indeed to find either in any number anywhere else. We might have gone about things a little differently, especially as far as kudu were concerned, for we neither of us ever saw one after leaving Zambesi No. 1.

I imagine Johnny Uys and I followed up and stalked a couple of dozen elephant and about that many buffalo. In spite of using a pair of 7x glasses (Bushnells, by the way, that came through beautifully, even though they got a lot of banging about), it isn't possible to determine if a rack or set of tusks is worth taking or not if you're some distance away. We had to get close and we did—often within 50 yards or so of both buff and elephant.

On the last day at Zambesi Dick shot a good elephant, the ivory running 73-75 pounds—he made the stalk at dusk, almost too late to shoot, but his 375 H&H did the trick. The best elephant I saw would have made maybe 45 pounds, certainly no more, and I didn't want one that size. I was looking for a particular type of buffalo, one whose horns would be dropping deeply down, making a frame, as it were, for his head. This is a scarce type, and I failed to find one at Zambesi despite looking over scores close up and seeing others in the many hundreds. I didn't loose a round at elephant or buffalo for those reasons, and also because none of the normal type buff were very long in the horns either—nothing over 40 inches extreme spread.

A fair number of baits had been put up for lion and leopard at Zambesi, but we had no luck—nothing ever showed, certainly not in the early morning when we'd move silently in on the baits.

Lost Lion

I had one chance at a fairly good lion, as we were coming down off a low mountain, but I muffed it. The lion was lying under the edge of a great heavy boulder, in deep shadow. We had been walking along a trail high on the slope, looking down over a vast burned-over forest for kudu, hopefully, when one of the boys spotted the lion, some hundred yards or so below us, with the same kind of

This buffalo was the nearest I could find to the deep-dropping horn type I'd hoped to locate.

burnt trees and brush between us. I'll be damned if I could make out that lion, peer as I could, until it ran out and into a bottom thicket, then through that and up the far slope, never pausing.

My fault entirely, of course—after the lion had moved, it was obvious that it would have been an easy shot.

Dick and I both did well on plains game during the Zambesi stay—record or near-record wildebeest, hartebeest, impala, reedbuck, warthog, zebra, bushbuck and the like. That was only small pay for failing to find good kudu, but that's how it goes now and again. We did have a fine camp, good food and drink—if only the fridge had made ice cubes—good guides and company.

True, the heat was intense during mid-day—110-115 degrees F. in the shade, and my one small tube of 6-12 bug dope was soon gone. The mosqui-

Dick Wolff killed this good red-maned lion with his 300 H&H Magnum.

tos were prevalent in droves, not to mention the tsetse flies. We were all a mess of welts that itched in no small way, including the natives. Don't let anyone tell you that the blacks are not bothered by insects—they gladly used the 6-12 too!

Zambia is good hunting country, no question, but I'd suggest that a hunt be made in the June-August period, and that plenty of insect repellant be taken along. Don't expect to find any in the smaller towns or villages; we couldn't. On an earlier-season hunt the game will be more plentiful, too, less wild, than it will be toward the end of the season, when the rains come.

Our next camp—which was to be our last one, and where we stayed for 18 days—was called Sichyfula, not far from a village called Mulobezi, and nearly astride one line of a narrow-gauge railway that terminates at Livingstone to the south. We flew there one morning, the camp rising a few thousand feet over Zambesi's elevation. The weather was a big improvement.

Again we found that game was scarce in the Sichyfula area, which was a very different kind of country. Here there'd be vast open grassy plains, the forest itself frequently more open. Thick stuff, too, but in patches. Because game had been heavily hunted, we again had to drive 25-30 miles each morning to reach better (read "less hunted") country, and we finally moved as far out as Mulobezi, near where another camp was sited. Zambia Safaris had no hunters there at the time, otherwise we couldn't have encroached. That kind of mileage doesn't read like much, I know, but much of that travel was over rough, near-trackless terrain, and we'd take up to a couple of hours to make the run—there and back, each way.

We soon learned that Sichyfula was where we'd find sable, more buffalo and plains animals, but no elephant and leopard. We had reports of a few scattered elephant, but we never saw any. My new hunter, Francois Coupé—a Belgian from the Congo and a very entertaining guy—and I followed the tracks of four bull tuskers one day, on foot, for about 6 hours—through the thickest damned stuff ever—but we didn't catch up with them.

Several more lion and leopard baits were hung for Dick and me, and Dick at long last found a very good lion on one and killed it. The mane was of good growth and reddish in color. I never found one, though I did see several prides of females and cubs or, occasionally, young maneless males alone or in pairs.

Buffalo!

Our chief hunting here was for sable, of course, especially after we'd

A young Zambia Game Guard, who was most helpful in finding sable and buffalo.

A quite good bush buck.

found out that there just weren't any leopards in the area. The big black beauties were scarce, though—we saw perhaps no more than a dozen sable during our 18 days at Sichyfula—so we hunted whatever the day offered of whatever we hadn't taken. There weren't many species unshot on our licenses by this time, so we found ourselves stalking buffalo a lot of the time —and there were thousands to be seen. Dick eventually found some buffalo to his liking and took the legal two permitted on our tickets, both close to 40 inches. My case was something else! Francois, one day, was handed a wire—delivered by special messenger from Livingstone—that he should provide "...3 or 4 buffalo..." to a game guards' camp to let them celebrate the 3-day "Uhuru" or liberation holiday properly. They were without fresh meat, some 30 men, women and children. I had already taken a buffalo with fair-only horns at Zambesi, and I'd looked at dozens of others in this Sichyfula country, none with those droopy horns I wanted. Now, however, and in a good cause, I could shoot five more—and legally.

I did just that in the next two days, not that I zeroed in on just any buff. I was still looking for a good one, and one of the five turned out not too bad; the horns dipped down pretty well, with each going 37 inches along the curl. Another, of less bend, went 43 inches wide. No, that's not much of a buffalo, but what could I do?

These 6 buffalo were put down using my Champlin 338 (reported on in detail in our "Sporting Arms of the World" elsewhere in this edition) with Hornady 250-gr. solids for the first shots. I held into the shoulder point as these buffalo faced me—none over 50-60 yards away—and all but one went down to stay down where they'd been standing. The other ran off for some 35 yards before falling, never to rise. Finishing shots were made with Nosler 210-gr. or 250-gr. bullets from close up, of course. The Hornady solids performed very well indeed, and though I had a 458 Ruger Single Shot along, for elephant primarily, I wouldn't hesitate to use the Champlin 338 with the Hornady solids on tuskers. Only one solid was recovered—the bullet had passed out the buff's flank on the earlier animal, and there was no way to dig for the four killed on order. Those beasts were loaded without being touched into a big trunk and hauled away.

Sable Antelope

Dick, now hunting with Harry Lee Wingfield—a Britisher living in Livingstone, and with whom I was also out for several days—had killed a 43-inch sable about midway of our stay at Sichyfula, but I didn't get a chance for a shot until a few days before the end of the safari. Francois and I had,

My wildebeest was shot with a Nosler 160-gr. bullet, the rifle a Remington 700 in their 7mm Magnum.

That sable's horns went 47 inches—a pretty good one. My last good trophy of the whole 28-day hunt, and taken almost by accident! If we'd been a few minutes earlier or later . . . .

All in all, we'd had a good hunt—minor irritations aside—but Dick and I were disappointed that we never got to make the third camp at Mumbwa—where leopard were supposed to live in profusion, or so it was said! A TV crew filming an American Sportsman segment had taken Mumbwa camp over, using up a lot of Zambia Safaris' manpower in the process, obviating our going there.

Zambia Battery

I brought three rifles to Africa—the superbly done custom Champlin 338 I've mentioned (which several professional hunters wanted to buy, until they heard the price), a Remington M700 in 7mm Magnum and the 458 Single Shot Ruger.

I used the Remington on all of the plains animals except zebra, my one and only load for it the 160-gr. Nosler ahead of 69 grains of Norma 205 powder and Remington 9½ primers. This load gave excellent accuracy, about 1½ minute of angle at worst out to 250-300 yards, and some long shots were made in Zambia on the thin-skinned stuff. No failures, either,

Dick Wolff took his wildebeest with the 300 H&H Magnum.

that day, seen a few sable but they were either a long way off, running or not worth shooting. I was getting a little uneasy by this time—after all, I hadn't found a good kudu, and time was about running out.

We left the bush track in the Land Rover, coming out on to the good road that ran alongside the railway line, and we were soon traveling at a good clip. Our intention was to drive quickly for several miles, then re-enter the bush where another track emerged.

We hadn't been driving for over 10 minutes when one of the boys—sitting on the roof for a better view—banged the top to let us know he'd seen something. There, a couple of hundred yards down the road, off in the thin forest to our right, stood a big sable, his black-brown coat gleaming in the morning sunlight. Francois, this time, did not come to a screeching halt but slowed down smoothly, stopping the car some couple of hundred yards beyond where the sable stood feeding.

We were out of the car instantly, several trees now between us and the sable. In a moment we were over the rails and into the bush, stopping about 150 yards from the sable, now turning slowly in our direction. I held the Remington 7mm Magnum on the center of his chest, a little high, and at the shot he collapsed—the one 160-gr. Nosler bullet was enough.

The rocky gorge where I might have shot a lion, but didn't. That's Johnny Uys, a South African, and my guide on the Zambesi.

to kill or put down for keeps—not that I didn't miss a time or two.

The Champlin 338 was used with three bullets—250-gr. Hornady solids, 250-gr. Noslers and 210-gr. Noslers. The former two, using 76 grains of Norma 205, printed an inch under the 210-gr. Noslers, and I had no trouble connecting with any of the three. The 210 Noslers, with 80 grains of N205, were used on zebra, the wildebeest and hartebeest, the shots at all three being 175-250 yards off, and I wanted the greater energy the 210s would give over the 160-gr. Noslers.

The Hornady 250-gr. solids, as I've said, worked to perfection on buffalo —the 458 couldn't have done any better, I'm sure. The one bullet recovered (see photograph) was undeformed in any way except for a dimple in the nose, doubtless made when it struck hard bone. It could go back into the case and be shot again!

I had only Winchester factory loads along for the Ruger 458—which was shot only in practice, and not (wince!) much of that. On the other hand, only the handloads mentioned were taken along for the Champlin and the. Ruger.

The Remington 700 carried a Redfield 1-4x variable in Redfield mounts, while the Champlin rifle wore another Redfield, this one a 2-7x variable but in Conetrol Custum rings and bases. The Ruger 458 was also scoped, the glass a 1.5-4 Bushnell in Ruger rings, of course. None of these scopes gave me anything to fret about—just keeping the lenses clean was the chief chore.

Dick had with him two rifles and a 20-bore Beretta double. His 300 H&H, a custom job, was on an FN Mauser action; the 375 H&H a de luxe Sako. He had a speck of trouble keeping the 300 in zero for a brief time, but it soon settled down. Dick used the 300 on most of the Zambia plains game, reserving

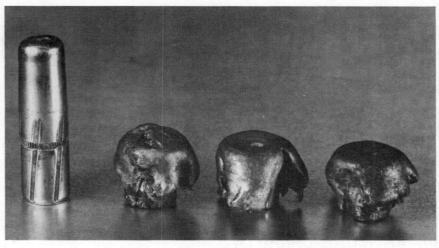

At left, the 250-gr. Hornady solid recovered from a buffalo's shoulder, the only deformation a dimple in the nose and the marks of rifling. The three recovered soft points, 210-gr. Noslers, were shot in the Champlin 338 on plains game. Average retained weight is 148 grains. Good performances, both.

the 375 for elephant and buffalo. Dick missed a few shots, too, mostly because of the 300 wandering off zero.

Dick used handloads only in the 300 —60 grains of 4350 and a prototype Finnish bullet (that takes nerve, huh?) called the Hammerhead. He told me that it went right on through most animals, leaving an exit hole about two times the caliber size, but that it did kill the game, so . . .

In the 375 he used factory loads only, Winchester 300-gr. solids and Silver Tips, and I know that these performed excellently for him.

Dick used Lyman scopes on both rifles—a 2½x on the 375, a 4x on the 300, and I can't recall that either gave him any problems.

One animal Dick lost was a hell of a big eland—and all mature eland are pretty impressive in size—that he dearly wanted. I'd taken an eland in Uganda on an earlier trip, and I

didn't want another—I'd regretted killing that big bovine the moment I'd shot it, but it was the last firing on that trip, and the big brute was running well over a broad plain, which made it a little more sporting.

Dick and the Beretta BL-4 20-gauge accounted for a goodly number of guinea fowl and other birds— which helped vary the game-flesh menu nicely. There's a tremendous amount of bird life in Zambia, with the guineas all over the place. In the areas where we hunted, at least, there were no native settlements of any kind, barring widely-scattered game guard camps. One is literally alone out in the bush, completely alone, and pollution of the land, the water and air just doesn't happen. Where we traveled the country is rugged and rolling, most of it, streams are far apart and often empty of water in the dry season.   ●

These are the cows that came trumpeting after our Land Rover.

The French Model 1950 9mm Auto Pistol

A history of the design and development of France's official sidearm, with detailed notes on its performance, care, cleaning and faults.

by RAYMOND CARANTA

THE LOCKWORK and general design of this current French service pistol are the development of a basic patent assigned on March 3, 1934 to Charles Petter, engineer at the "Societe Alsacienne de Constructions Mecaniques," better known as the "S.A.C.M." for its trade mark, stamped on the receiver of the French service handguns directly manufactured by them.

In 1935, this design was adopted by French Ordnance under the nomenclature "Pistolet Modele 1935A." This first Petter production model fired a special straightcase 7.65mm Long (.32) cartridge developing a muzzle energy of 250 ft. lb.

This gun featured an 8-shot magazine, the non-protruding barrel mounted on two swinging links instead of one, as in the current Model of 1950.

A simpler design with a 0.2″ shorter barrel mounted on a single link was also adopted for arming troops and non-commissioned officers under the name "Pistolet Modele 1935S." The gun fired the same 7.65mm Long ammunition.

In 1937 the basic Petter patent covering the "Modele 1935A" was bought by the Swiss "Schweizerische Industrie Gesellschaft" company, known also as the "Societe Industrielle Suisse" or, more commonly, as "SIG."

SIG made the French service design first in 7.65mm Long and in 7.65mm (.30) Parabellum, at that time the Swiss Ordnance or official caliber. Later the gun was also produced in 9mm Parabellum and considerably modified up to its present Swiss and Danish service versions.

After adoption of the 1935A and 1935S pistols, the French government put them into production in the M.A.S. and M.A.C. arsenals, with S.A.C.M. still manufacturing them for the French services as a commercial supplier.

When the 1939 war with Germany broke out, the stock of these pistols was not large. The French army relied mainly on the WW-I Star and Ruby .32 A.C.P. 10-shot automatics, with the French air force using the .32 A.C.P. Browning Model 1910 7-shot pistols. The "Gendarmerie Nationale" and "Corps de la Garde Mobile" (French Constabulary Corps) were armed with the sturdy 8mm Model 1892 revolver. Spanish copies of Smith & Wesson and Colt swing-out revolvers chambered for the 8mm French service cartridge and obsolete solid-frame 11mm revolvers of the 1873 and 1874 models were the lot of those reservists who could not find better handguns.

During the German occupation, the 1935A and S pistols continued to be manufactured for the Wehrmacht, and some were issued to Marshal Petain's "Armee de l'Armistice" up to November 11, 1942, when the Germans invaded the "Free Zone."

The 1935A and S pistols were also issued to the pro-German French "Milice" organization created by Joseph Darnand, and to the German G.M.R. forces fighting against the F.F.I. (Forces Françaises de l'Interieur) and the F.T.P.F. (Franc-tireurs et Partisans Francais) or "Maquis."

At the beginning of 1944, when ultimate victory of the Allies had become obvious, many G.M.R. officers who had joined that organization mostly to avoid deportation into Germany turned their coats and surrendered their arms to the French Resistance. Some of the guns so seized by Charles Tillon's F.T.P.F. went to Italian anti-Fascist guerillas on the other side of the Alps where, according to Italian sources, a 7.65mm Long French M.A.S. 38 submachine gun was used to kill Mussolini in 1945. After the war many P-08 (Lugers) and P-38 (Walthers) handguns seized

from the Germans were issued to the French armed forces, mostly to the "Gendarmerie Nationale," which is still using some of them.

By 1950, when the French Army was reorganized in terms of its WW II experience, and in line with NATO requirements, the "Manufacture Nationale d'Armes de Guerre de Saint Etienne" or, more simply, the M.A.S., designed a new pistol (still based on the 1934 Petter patents) firing the 9mm Parabellum cartridge, calling it the "Pistolet de 9mm Modele 1950." It was intended for use by all French armed forces as a replacement for the models then in general use.

The M.A.S. factory then became involved in the manufacture of military rifles and machine guns, so production of the 9mm M1950 pistol was assigned to its subsidiary, the "Manufacture Nationale d'Armes de Châtellerault," which is still making them today.

Evaluation of the M1950 Pistol

The following notes are based on French service records covering over 2000 pistols in 15 years of use; on the opinions of several gunsmiths, both commercial and military, and of French civilian and military shooters. The author's personal M1950 has fired some 2500 rounds since 1958 with no malfunctions except a chronic loosening of stock-plate screws—a common problem with all these pistols.

Military use The M1950 has been the official handgun of the French army since 1950, and is also used by the French "Compagnies Republicaines de Securite," the "Gendarmerie Nationale" and some African and Eastern military organizations.

Its very rugged and efficient low-cost military design withstands the most severe abuses. The slide is of solid construction as in the Browning Hi-Power. The recoil spring and guide form a single unit which can be removed when the pistols are not in service to render them inoperative in case of theft. The Petter system hammer mechanism is removable as a block for cleaning and inspection. Slide play is not excessive for a military model. All components are readily accessible for cleaning and complete disassembly may be easily carried out by semi-skilled personnel. Magazine design is particularly sturdy and is not sensitive to impact blows. The firing pin and extractor are not removable by hand as in the Colt government 45 auto, but this appears relatively unimportant in view of the low failure rates reported in service. As an example, in the firing of 320,000 rounds of French service ammunition in 2100 pistols, there were *no* firing-pin failures, and only 5 extractor breakages were recorded. It should be noted here that this gun, contrary to some blow-back automatics, does not function without its extractor.

Personal defense As a personal defense weapon, the M1950 is particularly dependable, and it's also well-suited to the outdoorsman's use because of its tremendous ruggedness and reliability. This pistol is very compact and pleasant to shoot in view of its medium weight. The 9th-shot magazine gives it an advantage in fire-power over competitive 8-shot models, but thereby lengthens the grip a full ½-inch. This impairs concealment if the gun has to be carried in a shoulder holster. The slide stop and magazine-release stud are well-located, and magazine attachment is very positive. A loading indicator permits seeing or "feeling" whether a cartridge is chambered, and there is an efficient magazine safety also.

Main defects Stock-plate screws loosening every 30 shots. The manufacturer unsuccessfully tried to remedy this by fitting the stock-plate screws with lock-washers. An alternate procedure is the use of Loctite. Substitution of screws threading into receiver

bushings, as in the Colt 45, has been suggested to the manufacturer.

When the slide is operated in a hurry, as in quick-draw under service regulations—which prohibit carrying the gun with a cartridge in the chamber—the shooter is apt to find the safety lever on "Safe." This constitutes a major defect for a personal defense handgun. From the manufacturer's standpoint, the soundest solution to this problem would be simply to eliminate the thumb safety (as was done in the Soviet Tokarev), the thumb safety being useless, even dangerous, under actual service conditions. As it is now, its only justification is that it interposes a positive steel block between the hammer and the firing pin in dry firing, but this hardly balances the tricky lottery it represents in quick-draw. For the civilian user, or for the military man who is the actual owner of his gun, it is strongly suggested that the thumb safety be locked in firing position by

Right and left side views of the M1950 French service pistol.

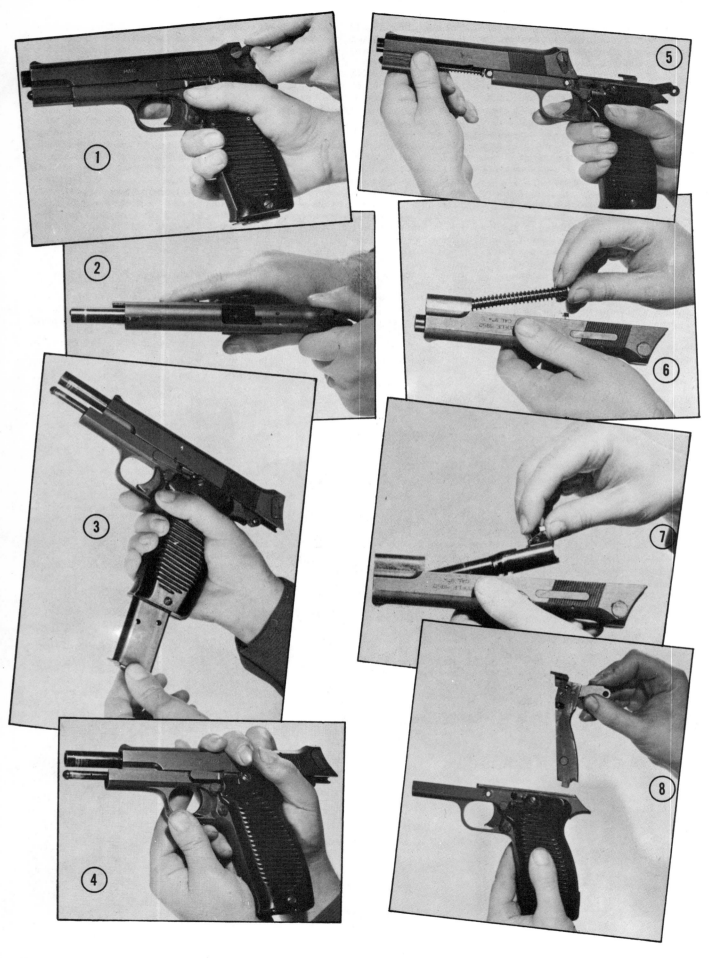

the installation of a stud in the safety recess, behind the lever.

The M1950's sights are not very good. The serrated front sight is difficult to see when aiming under poor light conditions, and there are no adjustments for windage or elevation; this adds to the general ruggedness of the gun, perhaps, but makes the selection of a specimen shooting "straight" a critical problem for the commercial buyer of this pistol.

In Government services, this condition is usually overcome by interchanging slides and barrels until the shooter and the gun shoot the same way, since serial numbers are marked on the right side of the receiver only.

The rear end of the receiver does not afford sufficient protection to the shooting hand, which may be pinched by the hammer when the latter is cocked by the recoiling slide. The manufacturer could improve this condition by lengthening the receiver tang about 0.1".

When shooting a long series of such ultra-powerful submachine gun ammunition as the German black steel-core 9mm Parabellum or the Italian Super-

is removed, unusually good access to the inside of the magazine well is provided from the rear opening.

Corrosion protection The gun is completely coated with a greyish phosphate finish similar to that on military issue Colt pistols—commonly called Parkerizing. This coating is hardly attractive, but it is glare proof and it affords a very efficient protection against corrosion.

Workmanship As a military arm built along strictly functional concepts, the workmanship is very good both on external and internal surfaces. Some tool marks appear on several surfaces, but are partly hidden by the dull phosphate coating. Front strap and back strap are plain but the rough finish provided by the protecting coating affords a good hand grip.

Sights Fixed 1/10" wide U-shaped rear sight and fixed 1/10" serrated ramp style front sight. On aiming, part of the slide upper surface appears under the front sight, which is detrimental to accuracy. The front sight height and rear sight notch depth should be changed. Such a modifica-

Model 1950 French Service Pistol

Technical Data, Operation and Functioning

Construction The Model 1950 MAC consists of 7 main components:

Receiver	Barrel
Hammer mechanism	Slide
Magazine	Recoil-spring unit
Slide stop	

The steel receiver, including the removable hammer mechanism, weighs 17½ oz. It houses the magazine and carries the magazine-release stud, the slide stop and the trigger mechanism; the latter consists of a pivoting trigger and pin, trigger bar, magazine safety, disconnector and magazine-safety coil spring.

The removable hammer mechanism consists of a housing inserted in the rear receiver well, hammer, sear, sear spring, hammer strut, mainspring and mainspring stop. The hammer and sear are pin-mounted.

The ejector is machined at the top of the hammer block housing.

The conventional sheet metal single-row magazine is 13/16" wide by .470" thick. There are 8 counting holes on both sides, a magazine-catch notch and a machined hole for the magazine-safety lever on the opposite side; a zig-zag magazine spring, a stamped sheet-metal magazine follower, a detachable floorplate and a floorplate catch. The empty magazine weighs 2.7 oz.

The slide stop consists of a pin fastening the swinging barrel to the receiver through the barrel-link lower hole, and of an external lever which locks the slide in open position when pulled back on an empty magazine.

The 9mm barrel of 4.3" is rifled for 3.58" with four grooves, L.H. twist. Two transverse ribs are machined in the upper area of the barrel-breech reinforcement, these locking into corresponding slide slots. The barrel also has a lug under the chamber, slotted to receive the pin-mounted swinging link.

The steel slide carries the loading indicator, the extractor, the firing pin, the firing-pin spring, and the thumb-safety with related retaining pins. The firing pin is *not* of the floating or flying type and protrudes into the bolt recess when pressed from the rear until flush with the thumb-safety flat side. Weight of the slide assembly is 9.9 oz.

The recoil spring unit consists of the coiled recoil spring with guide, spacer and riveted end fitting.

Operation When a loaded magazine is inserted into the grip the left side magazine cut raises the magazine safety lever under spring pressure, bringing the trigger bar in line with the sear located in the hammer block. To load the gun, the slide is pulled back as far as it will go and then released; it then closes under recoil-spring action, chambering the top cartridge held in the magazine.

Takedown Instructions

1—Put the gun on "Safe" by raising the slide thumb safety lever ● 2—Pull back slide as far as it will go ● 3—Remove magazine by pressing the release stud located aft of trigger guard ● 4—While holding slide firmly with right hand, push slide-stop pin from right side of receiver with left forefinger and lift out slide stop ● 5—Still holding slide with right hand, draw it forward out of the receiver guides with left hand ● 6—Holding slide assembly upside down, pull recoil-spring unit towards the muzzle and lift it out of engagement ● 7—Remove barrel from slide as shown ● 8—Remove hammer mechanism from the top ● Complete disassembly is not recommended except by gunsmiths or ordnance men.

Fiocchi cartridges in this M1950, the loading indicator and firing pin may be blown out; the latter failure is more serious since the shooter's face may be injured and the gun made unserviceable; in some extreme cases, the steel receiver shoulder that takes the slide impact at the end of the recoil stroke may be slightly battered. Certainly this condition is not met when firing French service ammunition or standard commercial cartridges. Accordingly, select an even sturdier handgun, such as the Polish Radom or the Ruger Blackhawk Convertible, if experimental leads, hot custom ammo or military loads are to be shot.

Lock-work construction Efficient, very simple single-action lock-work. With Petter construction, the hammer mechanism (consisting of housing, hammer, sear, sear music wire, hammer strut, coiled mainspring, mainspring stop and two sturdy 0.125" diameter pins) is removable by hand in routine maintenance as a single unit. Upon removal of the hammer unit, sear engagement can be easily checked through two side windows, and all components of the unit may be readily inspected and oiled from the front opening of the hammer unit. When the hammer unit

tion would not affect interchangeability.

Handling The M1950 is very compact and handles well, thus providing good combat efficiency. The grip is long enough for the biggest hands but its angle is rather too square to the barrel axis. The two black plastic ribbed plates fill the hand well but are more slippery under perspiration or oily conditions than are checkered ones. Trigger finger position is very good, but the 0.27" wide plain trigger is a little undersized for big hands. On the author's specimen, trigger slack at the lower end of the trigger measured 1/8". The trigger pull shows creep that varies from specimen to specimen, as in all military guns.

Safety travel is 90°. When loaded, this pistol is decidedly muzzle light.

Ruggedness Parts breakage is extremely rare in normal operation, when firing service or commercial ammunition. Beware of special submachine gun cartridges.

Accuracy Variable from excellent to poor. Excellent on the author's specimen after trying several barrel and slide combinations. Normally, groups corresponding to the "good" class are to be expected with this gun.

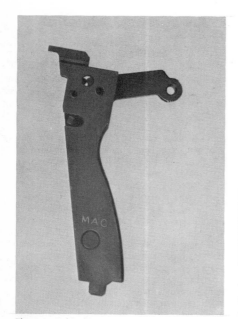

The removable hammer mechanism of the Model 1950 pistol. Note sear engagement visible through round side window, and sear lever.

The gun is now ready to fire. The hammer is cocked; the sear is engaged in the hammer full-cock notch, and the mainspring is compressed against its stop. The disconnector upper arm is engaged in the rear notch machined in the slide's left wall, the firing pin is retracted by its spring and the barrel is locked in its upper position, its locking ribs engaged in the slide slots, and the barrel link is vertical. The loading indicator is raised, since a cartridge is chambered, and the extractor hook lies in the cartridge head groove.

When the trigger is pressed against the trigger return-spring action, the trigger bar engages the sear's left-side lever. This takes up the trigger slack inherent to most automatic pistol designs.

This trigger slack, measured at the trigger's lower end of my pistol, amounts to ⅛". This displacement is limited rearwards by the magazine-release stud, which acts as a trigger stop. Under the trigger bar action, the sear pivots counterclockwise and releases the hammer which, driven by the mainspring, strikes the firing pin, compressing the firing pin spring, and fires the cartridge.

Now gas pressure forces the case head against the bolt recess, the slide is driven rearwards along with the barrel, still locked by its upper ribs. The recoil spring is now slightly compressed. When the slide begins its rearward stroke, the disconnector is cammed out of its notch in the slide wall and, through its lower arm, forces the trigger bar down out of sear engagement until the slide is closed, thus preventing accidental hammer release if the gun is not fully locked.

After about 0.2" of rearward slide travel, the barrel is unlocked by the action of its swinging link pivoting about the slide-stop pin, which draws

it downward, disengaging the barrel locking ribs from the slide slots. Gas pressure has now dropped to an acceptable level and the slide alone completes its rearward stroke, ejecting the empty case and cocking the hammer.

Then the slide, driven by the recoil spring, on its return stroke forces the next cartridge out of the magazine, pushes it over the receiver feeding ramp, and chambers it, the extractor hook snapping into the extractor cannelure of the case.

The cartridge is chambered with the barrel still in its lower position. Next, the locking step occurs during the last 0.2" of the slide return stroke, and the disconnector is again engaged in its

Loaded chamber indicator is shown by arrow.

rear slide-wall notch. This allows the trigger bar to line up with the sear lever, and the gun is ready to be fired if the trigger is pulled.

When the last shot has been fired and the slide is at the end of its backward stroke, the slide-stop lever is pushed up by the magazine follower step, locking the slide in open position by engaging the first notch machined in the left slide wall.

To release the slide, the slide-stop lever is pushed down. If the slide has to be closed on a loaded magazine, it may be released by drawing it slightly to the rear and letting it return to battery under the recoil-spring pressure.

M1950 Markings

Right side of slide, in front of ejection port: MODELE 1950/CAL 9MM in two lines.

Right side of receiver, under the slide marking: The serial number.

Right side of receiver, under stock-plate: Boxed manufacturing-arsenal name, such as MAC.

Left side of slide, above the slide stop notch, and on left side of hammer mechanism: MAC.

MAC stands for "Manufacture d'Armes de Châtellerault," MAS for "Manufacture d'Armes de Saint Etienne." ●

Technical Data
French Service Pistol Model 1950

Caliber:	9mm Parabellum	Empty wgt.: 34 oz. approx.
Over-all:	7.7"	Trigger pull: 6 to 9 lb. average.
Barrel:	4.3"	Sight radius: 6"
Height:	5.5"	Rear sight: 1/10" wide, deep U-form.
Thickness:	1.2"	Safeties: Thumb safety—solid block between rebounding hammer and firing pin. Magazine safety.
Magazine capacity: 9 rounds		
Slide stop: Left side of receiver, above trigger guard.		Thumb safety site: Left rear of slide. Raise to put on "safe."

The M1950 auto pistol has a steel receiver. Operation is short-recoil type, lock-up like the Colt 45 auto. The rear sight is machined into the slide metal, and is partly covered when the hammer is lowered. The external-hammer group is readily removable. The magazine release catch is on the left side of the receiver; the magazine is a single-row type, phosphate coated, the floorplate removable and marked "1950."

Caution: When the loading indicator (arrow) is raised, a cartridge is chambered in the barrel. Remove the magazine by pressing the magazine release stud aft of trigger guard on L.H. side of receiver. Operate the slide to clear the chamber.

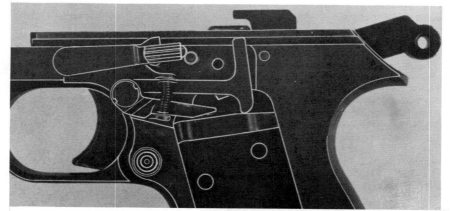

Trigger mechanism of the French M1950 service pistol. See text for details.

Some 100 years ago the idea of choke boring was invented — or discovered. Now we seem to have gone full circle, rediscovering the advantages of the true cylinder barrel, the . . .

un choke!

by ROGER BARLOW

PERHAPS reintroduces would be a more appropriate word, for up to about 100 years ago all scatterguns were *un*choked—that is, bored true cylinder. In 1866 an English gunmaker, William Pape of Newcastle, patented a system of barrel boring for which, in 1875, he was awarded a prize as the undoubted inventor of choke boring; in those years about half the world's gunmakers were laying claim to that honor.

On our side of the Atlantic, at about this same period, an Illinois duck hunter named Fred Kimble stumbled upon much the same method of tightening patterns but made no effort to patent his discovery; apparently being quite satisfied to merely have a gun of his own which enabled him to outshoot all the other mid-western professional duck shooters.

Although in England it was Pape who held a patent, it was W. W. Greener, of Birmingham, who actually developed this new system of barrel boring and promoted it enthusiastically and effectively. It is interesting to note that despite (perhaps because of) a fellow English gunmaker's well-founded claim to this invention, Greener credited the Americans (not just Kimble) with the development. Both Greener and Fred Kimble extended the effective range of their guns through increased pattern density, achieved by very slightly reducing the bore diameter of a barrel near its muzzle. Kimble used this constriction for only about an inch, Greener using a much longer and a more gradually tapered section. (The famed Parker guns were also made with a choke having a long taper). The maximum constriction found to be effective was only .030- to .040-inch. Many gunmakers got into difficulties trying to use a greater degree of muzzle constriction; they usually ended up with worse patterns than were delivered by a well-made unchoked gun.

Another method of achieving tighter patterns in this period was to bore the barrel as a true cylinder to the muzzle and then, starting back about an inch, bore the barrel out a few thousandths for a distance of around 3 inches. This "recess" or "jug" choke system was especially popular at that time for it could be easily applied to existing cylinder bored barrels of guns already in use. In 1872 a Mr. R.M. Faburn, an American, patented an expanding bit for cutting this type of choke; he sold these tools—with the right to use them as well for cutting such chokes—to gun dealers and gunsmiths all over the country. It is not clear whether or not he actually had a patent on this specific *type* of choke or only on the tool. In any event it was also quite popular in England for a time. I know that it worked very well indeed, for three of my old Damascus barreled hammer guns, made in the 1860s, were later choked by

this method, and all throw superb full choke patterns.

As Greener's choke bored guns excelled at one "Gun Trial" after another and Fred Kimble clobbered his opposition in various shooting matches, shooters in both England and America were soon standing in line to get guns of this type or to have existing ones adapted to the new boring. After all, their old cylinder bored guns might be putting only 90 to 130 #7 pellets into a 30-inch circle at 40 yards while some of the new choke bored guns could put up to 225 into the same area. Most shooters probably figured that the killing range of the shotgun had been doubled!

So what is Franchi up to now, offering cylinder bored guns in 1970 after all these years? Isn't this a step backward? Aren't choked guns more effective, harder hitting, farther ranging; better in every way?

Shooters of 100 years ago (as today) were all too eager to believe that if only their scatterguns had *less scatter* they'd come home with more in their game bags. They quite forgot (and still forget) that even if the effective killing range of a shotgun is extended appreciably, the shooter can only take advantage of this by also extending his effective *hitting* range by the same distance. Brother, there, as Shakespeare said, is the rub! Choke boring did indeed extend the certain killing range of a 12 or 16 gauge shotgun from about 35-42 yards to perhaps 55-60 yards, but it had done nothing to make it one damn bit easier to connect with birds at that distance.

At 20-25 yards, this zooming ringneck (illus. at left) is a perfect target for the fast-handling cylinder-bored Franchi O-U. Perhaps our older 8-lb. plus shotguns were so heavy, badly balanced and slow-handling that they had to be heavily choked—the bird was almost out of range before the shooter could get his gun mounted! Certainly a genuine upland gun is so lively that the hunter will be on his bird 5 to 10 yards sooner—and so can use the more open boring.

Those early choke-bore enthusiasts of the 1870s soon found their new guns very much of a mixed blessing when they discovered that it was actually more difficult to hit birds at *any range* with those smaller and tighter patterns; and that when they did center a pheasant at the normal range of about 30 yards it was all too often unfit for the table.

Now Mr. Pape, the gunmaker who actually had a patent on this new boring, had not proceeded to do much about it for the simple reason that he considered a gun delivering those smaller, tighter patterns to be *unsuitable for field use!*

Early Cylinder Bore Performance

Because the English seem to have

a comprehensive literature dealing with all of their sports, we know far more about how they came to terms with the choke bore than we do about this matter here in the U.S.

For example, we know that one of England's greatest game shots, Lord Walsingham, shot only with cylinder guns all his life; killing several hundred thousand birds over the years and bagging just over 1000 driven grouse in *one day* in 1888 while shooting with 4 such guns! Lord Ripon, another noted English shooter of this

period, did use choke bored guns when their use would be a genuine advantage (and he was a good enough shot to not be handicapped by the tight pattern) but in 1894 he had a Purdey built which had the right barrel bored cylinder, the left half-choke. This gun was so well liked that two years later he ordered another to the same specification.

More to the point, this very practical choice of boring was used by a great many English shooters after the initial infatuation with full choke boring wore off.

Before this logical use of the best aspects of both choke and open boring was adopted, the arguments pro and con were waged furiously in the shooting press of the day. The late Sir Ralph Payne-Gallwey was a shooter who used both types of guns, as needs dictated, and conducted much research himself into various aspects of shooting and the killing of game birds. Here are a few of his comments in those early days of choke boring when W.W. Greener was touting his tight patterns everywhere. "In the case of 99 out of 100 shooters I find that the chokes have more disadvantages than the reverse." And, ". . . even a first class shot when using a full choke has to aim more accurately at game at moderate distances than would be required of him were he using a cylinder, and whether for the

sake of occasional long brilliant shots, that not seldom entice a man into a habit of random shooting, it is worth-while to carry a gun that is not so easy to kill with at an ordinary range is more than doubtful." This Victorian circumlocution may require a couple of trips through that paragraph to make certain one fully understands just what is being said, but old Sir Ralph was right—as our own duck shooters prove to this day—that the guy lucky enough to once kill a bird at 60-70 yards goes on trying to do so, wounding hundreds for every one he bags and driving birds out of gunshot range of more conservative shooters.

Payne-Gallwey goes on in more specific language: "I have seen shooters, good shots too, purposely armed with full chokes blazing away at rocketing (high) pheasants, said to be too high for cylinders, and have heard them on missing say, 'That bird was too high for even my full choke,' and I have on that same occasion seen a man, certainly a first class shot, stand well behind and pull down bird after bird as dead as need be after they had been feathered by the guns in front, his gun being nothing but an ordinary cylinder making a pattern, as I afterwards tested myself, of 130 at 40 yards." In this instance even good shots were missing difficult 40 yard birds, or rather catching them with only the very edges of their full choke patterns, whereas a man with a gun throwing a broader, though thinner, pattern was *killing* the same birds.

However, it appears to me that virtually all American guns made after the successful development of choke boring were sold with a maximum of choke. Many were advertised to ". . . insure good shooting at 60-70 yards," or ". . . will kill game at 80-100 yards . . . ." It is quite common to find our old guns with both barrels full choked but I've never yet found one bored

cylinder and full or cylinder and half-choke, though some catalogs list a model as being choked only in the left barrel. Maybe no one ever ordered such a gun! I suppose this largely stemmed from the fact that most U.S. shotgunners were primarily duck hunters, and so born optimists—convinced that any duck they could *see* could be killed, if only they had a tight enough choke! I don't know what our southern quail shooters did 75 or 80 years ago; they *must* have ordered their Parkers or L.C. Smiths with at

This Franchi 20-gauge Falconet was also used by Barlow on quail. Not especially light for a 20, being built on the standard 12-gauge frame, but with so much of its weight lying between the shooter's hands, it is exceptionally lively and well balanced. Marked Cyl-Imp Cyl (and as having 3" chambers) the cylinder barrel measured a mere .0021" tighter at the muzzle over the bore diameter stamped on by the proof house. All 12-gauge Falconets stamped Cylinder seen or tried by the writer have around 2 thousandths constriction, though the spread of the shot charge is the same as that of guns having absolutely no constriction or choke. However, as IC barrels generally have 7-10 thousandths constriction, anything like less thna ¼ that amount is not going to have much effect on tightening the pattern. If it did the principle of choke boring would have been discovered long before it was, for many a barrel must have been bored with some .002" difference, one way or the other, between the bore diameter and the muzzle, simply by accident.

least one barrel with open boring. Of course a good many southern gentlemen got their light and handy "bird" shooting doubles from English makers, many of whom were, as a matter of course, still building open bored guns.

Bob Nichols, in one of his books, writes that, when a boy in the midwest, at about the turn of the century, he had the use of a Damascus barreled Spencer repeater which was the *only* cylinder bored shotgun in the entire area.

Now, 100 years after our overly enthusiastic and almost universal adoption of the full choke, we are far less of a nation of duck and goose shooters and becoming much more devoted to hunting upland game. Therefore, it is high time to have another look at the type of shotgun boring our grandfathers so precipitously gave up.

In the first place virtually all upland game—quail, ruffed grouse, pheasants, woodcock, even doves — are usually *now* killed at 20-35 yards. Does it make sense to carry a gun bored to produce a killing pattern at 50-60 yards when the opportunity or necessity to make such a shot is less than 1 in 10—and when the odds that we have the skill to *make* such a shot may be anywhere from that figure to 1 in 100? Of course it doesn't. It is even quite likely that the *average* duck shooter would bag more birds if he would give up his full choke barrels, stop attempting those impossible 60-70 yard shots, and use improved cylinder and/or half-choke barrels—setting an absolute limit of 50 yards for all shots. For that matter, a lot of ducks are decoyed into easy cylinder bore range.

But as many upland bird shooters are already using guns bored improved cylinder, why should we consider an even more open boring? Can there be any real advantage to us in the use of true cylinder barrels? Especially when that eminent authority on the shotgun, Major Sir Gerald Burrard, writing about 1931, condemned the true cylinder for use much beyond 30 yards because of erratic patterns.

For one thing, improved cylinder barrels are now throwing tighter patterns than they used to (when Major Burrard was writing) for the simple reason that our modern *shotshells* are themselves delivering more dense patterns, reaching half-choke percentages in some instances.

Also it appears that even a slight amount of choke tended to minimize the inherent weaknesses and defects of those early Nitro shells with their felt over-powder wads, card over-shot wads, roll crimp, erratic primer flame and with powder which was excessively sensitive to wad and crimp pressure — besides being too rapid burning. (This partly accounts for the continued popularity of black powder for many years after the advent of smokeless powders of various types; its low pressure and more uniform combustion, regardless of wad pressure and strength of turn-over crimp, delivered more even and consistent patterns—with or without choke).

But today's shotshells, having more progressive and uniform burning powders, more consistent primers, with plastic O-P wads and shot cups, plus a folded crimp, should deliver deadly broad patterns from those true cyl-inder barrels which once were blamed for blown, cartwheel and uneven patterns. Perhaps *now* we can take full advantage of several of the benefits to be derived from the use of this once-universal boring.

Although the Franchi cylinder bored guns are a comparatively recent entry on the U.S. market, (I did my first shooting with them in the fall of 1969), I have been shooting with En-glish-made black powder hammer guns of the 1860s (both pinfire and center-fire types) for several years. During this time I've been carrying on a volu-minous correspondence on the subject with a highly knowledgeable and dedi-cated English shooter, David Baker; comparing notes on powders, loadings, patterns and our field experiences with a wide variety of cylinder guns.

Patterns from 28 gauge Wiggins & Elliott pinfire, a 20 gauge Joseph Lang pinfire, a 12 gauge Purdey pinfire and a 12 gauge Purdey centerfire were—all cylinder bored—in every case sur-prisingly good, some exceptional, when using black powder shells of my own making; these used Alcan plastic O-P wads and most were made with folded crimp closure. However, in some in-stances high base-wads did not leave enough space for the bulky black pow-der, for those thicker plastic O-P wads and for a folded crimp so I used those frangible Federal O-S wads which were never roll crimped; usu-ally being held in place with a bit of Elmer's Glue. Yet these shells, too, produced outstandingly good patterns and put a lot of quail on our table.

However, those were low pressure black powder loads. What about mod-ern factory loads?

Shooting the Franchi TC

My first shooting with such shells in a modern true cylinder gun was with a Franchi Falconet over-under 12 gauge when the dove season opened last fall. The very first day out with this double, bored cylinder and im-proved cylinder, I bagged more doves than I had ever done before with more tightly choked guns, and I continued to come home each day with more birds than is usual for me. It seems to me that this is about the best pos-sible test of such an open bored gun. I'm convinced that because of their small size and because they are usu-ally seen against the sky, most shoot-ers believe that many doves are 40-50 yards off when they shoot and so re-quire a considerable amount of choke, if the pattern is to be dense enough. Yet these birds rarely fly as high as the trees surrounding a field, and these rarely reach 25 yards in height, so that, allowing for the angle at which we shoot, 33-38 yards is about the longest shot we *have* to attempt. The judging of distance against the sky is always tricky, but it's even more so with doves because of the speed with which they usually appear—seemingly out of nowhere. But they just aren't as far away as we usually think them to be. Carrying the Franchi, I one day walked up, in a field of cut corn, a pair of doves which seemed to me well out of range of anything but a

Diameter of Spread
(covered by the main body of the charge at listed ranges)

Choke	20 yards	30 yards	40 yards
Cylinder	32 inches	44 inches	58 inches
Imp. Cyl.	26 inches	38 inches	51 inches
Modified	21 inches	32 inches	45 inches
Full	16 inches	27 inches	40 inches

Above figures supplied by a leading shotshell manufacturer.

Although an IC choke is virtually the universal choice for quail hunting it delivers far too dense patterns at the range most quail are killed. Certainly between 18-25 yards any quail caught by the center of this 1⅛-7½ pattern at 25 yards is going to be mangled—20 pellets being consider-ably more than enough! Compare this with pattern #2.

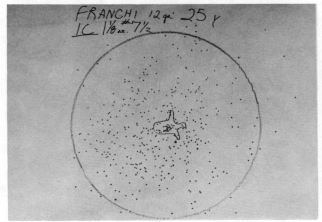

This typical true cylinder pattern (1⅛-8) clearly shows the useful-ness of such open boring, for at this same 25-yard distance a quail is not likely to receive more than half a dozen pellets, even if centered, while even at the edges of a 30-inch circle the pat-tern is still effective—far more so than with an IC choked barrel. This will appreciably improve one's chance of scoring a kill.

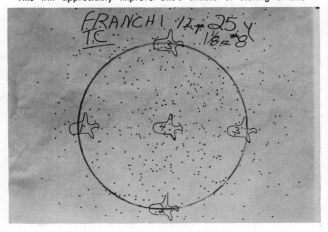

full choked gun when they took flight. Yet, much to my surprise, both fell to that open bored Franchi. The actual distance to the two dead birds was 36 and 41 yards; deduct about 2 yards for momentum after being hit and we have 34 yards for the bird hit with the cylinder barrel and about 39 yards for the other, the improved cylinder barrel. True, long shots at such small targets, yet at least 10 yards less than I had first guessed, despite seeing them against the hillside and not the sky. When I shot I simply did not believe that there would be a killing pattern, even if the birds were centered. It was a graphic illustration that cylinder and improved cylinder patterns should not be underestimated. The more so, too, because most doves fly at only 10 to 15 yards elevation, so most shots are likely to be in the 20-30 yard bracket.

A few days later when I got around to patterning that Franchi Falconet 12 gauge it was clear enough why I was hitting more doves than usual (broad patterns) and why those swung on at what seemed like a considerable distance were being killed (adequate pattern density). I was shooting Remington Skeet loads with #9 shot and W-W Trap loads with #8 shot; both, of course, are easy-shooting 1⅛-ounce loadings.

So much for doves. We all agree that most quail are grassed at genuinely short range—between 20 and 30 yards — so theoretically a cylinder bored gun should be hard to beat. So

it proved in practice, for I scored a double with that Franchi on the first covey rise of the season; that isn't the usual thing with me, for I'm far more used to missing those first two birds than hitting them. But that open bored 12 and the slightly lighter 20 gauge Falconet (also bored Cyl/IC) performed well for me all season. There were even a couple of memorable over-30 yard crossing shots with the 12 gauge cylinder barrel which I'm sure I'd have missed with a narrower pattern.

Should a quail hunter find that he is, for whatever reason, having to take shots at such ranges that he fears his cylinder patterns are getting rather thin with that popular loading of 7½ shot, he can increase the pattern density simply by going to a smaller size shot rather than to a more tightly choked barrel. Penetration, even with #9 shot will still be adequate at 38-40 yards—and that's a longer shot at quail than most of us ever expect to make. Or have to make. Heck, against most backgrounds it's almost impossible to *see* a quail at 40 yards, much less hit him!

In any case, there is little profit in being prepared with a pattern dense enough for certain kills at long range if 90% of one's birds (of whatever breed) will be taken at close range; therefore being filled with so much shot that they will hardly be worth carrying home.

Although my old hammer guns are bored cylinder in both barrels, I rare-

ly feel the need for a tighter second barrel when hunting most upland game under normal circumstances. Yet if I were to select a modern double for the same shooting I would unquestionably have the second barrel slightly choked—to give me a pattern effective out to 45-47 yards for the occasional long shot, yet still not deliver too dense a pattern at 30 yards. This is the great virtue of a double gun, especially one with double triggers—instant choice of pattern density through different choke, different load, or both.

I know that a great many shooters claim that their birds shot at 30 yards with a half- or full-choked gun are not badly shot up. If they aren't it is only because they are merely being caught with the very edges of those patterns. If they accomplish this on *purpose* I certainly admire their shooting, but if it is accidental one suspects that they would be better off with a broader pattern of reduced over-all density.

If it is somewhat foolish to use tightly choked guns on birds at around 30 yards, it is even more foolish to stretch a true cylinder barrel to 45 yards or so, often wounding game which escapes to a slow death or becomes food for predators.

With our superb modern shotshells the true cylinder barrel definitely exceeds the 30-yard range with which Major Burrard once credited it—but by only 5 to 10 additional yards, depending upon the combination of gun,

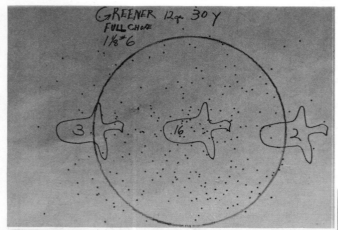

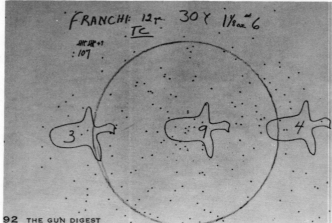

Left—A full choke barrel puts 16 pellets (often more) into a pheasant-size bird at 30 yards when it is centered, but only 2 or 3 pellets if the bird is at the edge of the 30-inch circle. Note how much more useful is the pattern at lower left . . .

. . . where even a well-centered bird is not going to be filled with too many shot while a bird way at the edges of a 30-inch circle is likely to receive more pellets than with a FC gun (pheasant size outlines).

Below—An over 100-year-old Joseph Lang pinfire 20 gauge shooting ⅞/6s delivers a fine grouse pattern at 30 yards with its *true* cylinder barrel.

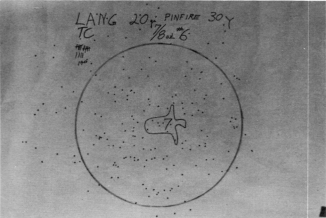

game and load. Useful as it is for most upland game hunters, on most birds, under most conditions, the true cylinder barrel, nevertheless, is *not* for genuinely long range shooting. Indeed, anything beyond 40 honest yards is long range work for the scattergun—and the scatter*gunner*.

But let me say it once again—the vast majority of shots at quail, grouse, woodcock, pheasants and even doves are offered at relatively close range, 18 to 35 yards. True cylinder range!

Pattern Density Over-Emphasized

Even this matter of pattern density can stand some rethinking. Trap, Skeet and live pigeon shooters are only interested in smashing their targets, they aren't going to eat 'em! It is quite a different matter with us bird hunters. It is to our advantage to bring our targets to bag with the least possible damage. So how many pellets are needed for certain kills? In 1910 an English doctor, H. Hammond-Smith, with exceptional experience based upon the examination of vast numbers of shot-killed game birds, said that 5 pellets were required for a certain kill. Major Burrard felt that this was an excessive number for all but the largest birds; in his view, 3 pellets were sufficient for birds of one to two pounds in weight and 2 pellets were enough for birds *under* one pound. A look at some of the Franchi test patterns with bird outlines should set doubts at rest on the matter of cylinder patterns being adequate at all normal distances game birds are taken.

I've never been an enthusiastic booster for magnum shotshells, being of the opinion that if one *misses* a bird it doesn't matter how many pellets you miss it with, but if one *is* on target anything from ¾- to 1¼-ounces of shot is quite sufficient for most upland game at reasonable range. Even if we stretch our full choke patterns to 60 yards with magnum loads, there are indeed very few of us ordinary shooters capable of laying that full choke pattern over a bird at such a distance.

Much better, in my view, is to use some additional pellets to extend the broader patterns of a true cylinder and improved cylinder gun to 45 and 50 yards. This is certainly going to put more birds in the roaster for most of us than trying for 60-70 yard targets with a heavy choke. Have you ever actually measured off 60 or 70 yards and looked at a bird at that distance? Believe me, it can be an experience which will lead you to reconsider previous ideas of the range at which one can expect to kill birds.

My English shooting friend and I agree that most shooters of average skill will benefit from a cumulative effect of the greatest value through the use of cylinder guns; because it *is* easier to bring down game with these broader shot patterns we quickly develop increased confidence in our gun and in ourselves; therefore we tend to truly *become* better shots. The other side of this coin is the experience of missing the first couple of birds of the day—and then not being able to score a hit no matter how easy the shot! Nothing succeeds like success because nothing gives a shooter confidence in his shooting than does the making of a successful shot. For this reason alone such open bored guns as those which Franchi are now offering are to be highly recommended for most shooters. This is certainly the ideal boring for the beginning shooter (for all the above reasons) and also for any experienced shooter who may be less successful in the field than he feels he should be.

It should be borne in mind that true cylinder boring does *not* produce patterns as broad as a barn door—capable of downing an entire covey of quail at 25 yards, even though the gun is merely pointed in their general direction! Indeed, the spread of the main portion of the shot charge with a true cylinder barrel is generally considered to be only about 6 inches wider than with an improved cylinder and only about 14 inches greater than a full choke at 25-30 yards. (However, my own patterns do indicate a slightly larger effective spread for the TC barrel than do the textbooks).

It should be mentioned that such features as short handy barrels, light weight and good lively balance are all vital factors in the over-all specifications we would set down in an effort to arrive at the ideal gun for hunting quail, grouse, woodcock, most pheasants and even doves. The various Franchi models I used to research this article have all of these highly desirable characteristics—plus the option of cylinder barrels.

So, Hail Franchi! Re-inventors of the *un*choke! ●

Below—With the Franchi O-U the first shot at a grouse would usually be taken with the cylinder barrel at fairly close range, the IC barrel used for the longer shot. Yet even so a grouse killing pattern can be achieved at 40 yards with the cylinder barrel by using a load like the Federal International Trap load of 1¼/7½s. It would also be deadly for pheasants. Right—We've removed the 30" circle from this pattern test to let you see how much farther, and how densely, the pellets are distributed outside the 30" diameter. Shot at 30 yards, the load was 1⅛/9s from a *true* cylinder 12-bore Franchi.

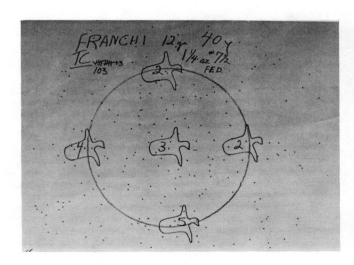

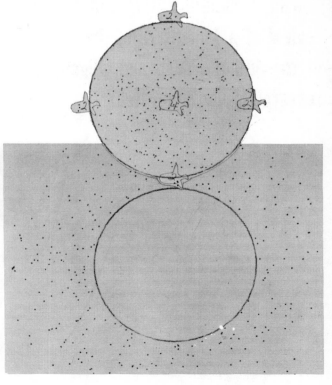

THE WHITWORTH

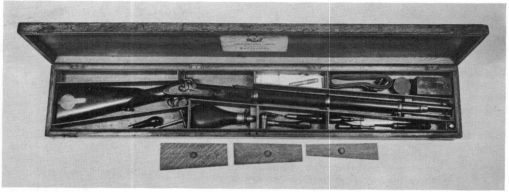

Fig. 1. Military Match Rifle, cased in oak and complete. The first commercially available Whitworth, which appeared in 1859, this is the pattern given as prizes by the National Rifle Association of Great Britain in 1860, 1861 and 1862. This type was also given as a prize by many Volunteer units and civic organizations during those years. Note that the case is unlined. The round capbox, the lock and breech design, the smooth-headed ramrod and stock design are characteristic of this model. *Courtesy E. J. Burton.*

The first comprehensive and critical review of a famous rifle, the result of the author's deep and diligent research. Fully illustrated.

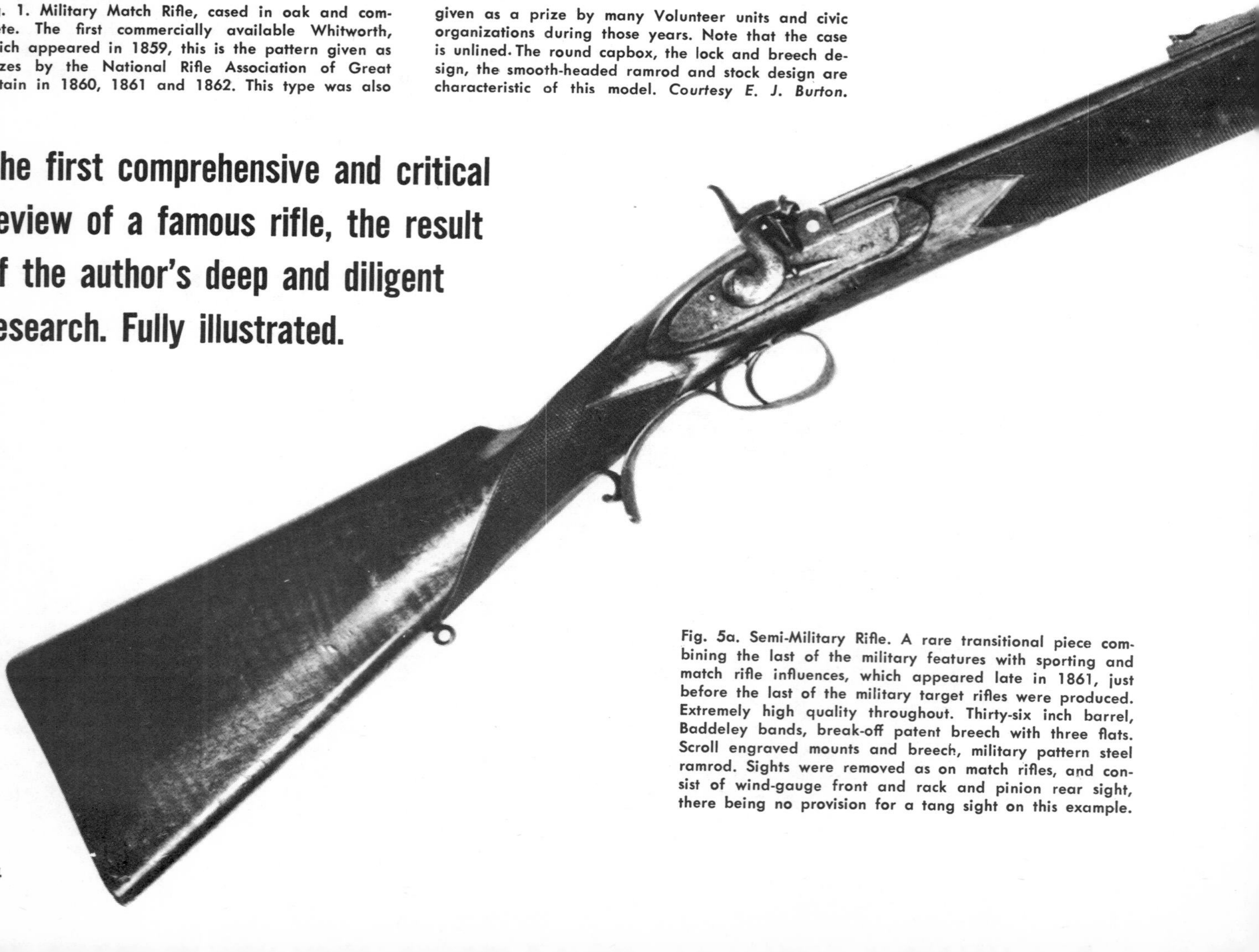

Fig. 5a. Semi-Military Rifle. A rare transitional piece combining the last of the military features with sporting and match rifle influences, which appeared late in 1861, just before the last of the military target rifles were produced. Extremely high quality throughout. Thirty-six inch barrel, Baddeley bands, break-off patent breech with three flats. Scroll engraved mounts and breech, military pattern steel ramrod. Sights were removed as on match rifles, and consist of wind-gauge front and rack and pinion rear sight, there being no provision for a tang sight on this example.

by DeWITT BAILEY II

RIFLE

a great milestone in rifle history

Fig. 2. Military Match Rifle, a reverse view of fig. 1, with contents displayed. Implements are, from left—cap tin, sling, punch for pushing bullet from mould, combination tool, German-silver topped leather covered flask, Whitworth patent cartridge, conical mould and base plug, lock brush, hammer face cleaner, nipple cleaner, screwdriver, torque bar, oil bottle, japanned tin for holding wads and other small pieces. *Courtesy E. J. Burton.*

JOSEPH WHITWORTH began his career as a toolmaker in Manchester in 1833. He died in January, 1887, with a world-wide reputation as the most eminent producer and designer of precision machine tools. The standards set by his machines are still current today. His standardization of screw threads, dating from the 1840s, still stands.

Problems with the production and performance of the Pattern 1853 Enfield rifle musket, the absence of standardization of tools and gauges, the problem of supply in the face of the Crimean War and its extraordinary demands, led the British government to call upon Whitworth in 1854 to suggest remedies to existing difficulties. Whitworth's exhibits at the Great Exhibition of 1851 had won his international acclaim, and as the nation's most outstanding engineer and machine tool manufacturer it was natural that he should be selected to investigate the standardization and mass-production possibilites of the Enfield works.

In 1854 Joseph Whitworth was not well acquainted with the manufacture of small arms, and in order to familiarize himself with the processes and practices involved he visited most of England's leading gunmakers. His basic conclusion from these visits was that gunmakers proceeded upon little if any actual proven theories, but rather from hit-and-miss experiments and methods learned during their apprenticeships. From this it followed that there was no rational explanation for the irregularities in the performance of the Pattern 1853 Enfield; before Whitworth would undertake to criticize this particular weapon he felt it necessary to establish in his own mind just what the perfect form of rifled small arm should be. From the experiments he conducted to find the answer to this question came the Whitworth rifle and the heavy ordnance so well known, at least in name, to arms collectors today.

It appeared to Whitworth that both the caliber and barrel dimensions of the Pattern 1953 Enfield had been chosen by arbitrary and unscientific methods. It was obvious to him as well that the problems encountered in its performance were due to inaccuracies in the interior of the barrels, possibly even in their basic construction. Whitworth explained his views to the government and offered, if the government would pay his expenses, to conduct a series of tests to determine the best form of small arm for military service. He refused to accept any salary for his work.

In the early stages of his work, Whitworth experimented with a wide variety of rifling twists, calibers, barrel lengths and metals, reaching such extremes as a 20-inch barrel with a twist of one turn in one inch. Whitworth had apparently not examined any other than the standard Enfield 577-caliber barrels, but had seen a polygonally-rifled barrel designed by Isabard Brunel and constructed by Westley Richards. Richards and Whitworth worked closely together during the early stages of Whitworth's work, and much of Whitworth's knowledge of

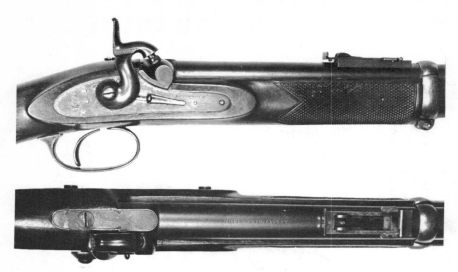

Fig. 3. Military Target Rifle, breech closeup. Note the Enfield style snail, with underside over-hanging lockplate, Whitworth trademark on tail of plate, sliding safety bolt and typical WHITWORTH marking above bolt. The rear sight is an early pattern before the rack-and-pinion type was adopted; many of this model are found refitted with a rack-and-pinion sight of an early type. Hammer, trigger guard and trigger, checkering pattern and form of breech (note patent breech but absence of hook breech) are typical of this model. *Courtesy E.J. Burton.*

the firearms trade must have been gained from Westley Richards. It was not until the end of 1856 that Whitworth appears to have settled on a design for his rifle; its first official tests came in April, 1857. From this time onwards, the now-familiar hexagonal bore, with a twist of one turn in 20 inches, seems to have been the standard in Whitworth rifles. The tests of 1857 and 1858 proved the far superior accuracy of Whitworth's system against that of the 577 Enfield (which were rifled with three lands and grooves having a twist of one turn in 78 inches, with the depth of rifling gradually decreasing from the breech to the muzzle), but as accuracy was but one of the criteria to be considered in the acceptance of any system for military use, the basic issues were far from solved. Such questions as fouling, tendency to miss-fire, ease of handling, manufacture of ammunition suitable for military conditions, costs of manufacturing—all seemed to create some doubts in the minds of the investigating committee members. In addition, a small-bore Enfield had performed very nearly as well as the Whitworth rifle, and there was some question whether Whitworth's system might be the only answer.

The Crimean War had been weathered, the national emergency was over, and thoughts of economy were again uppermost in the minds of the government. By 1859 the whole project had been narrowed down to two basic problems. First, would other manufacturers be able to produce the standard of precision required to manufacture Whitworth rifles in some future emergency, if they were to be produced on a large scale? Secondly, Whitworth still asked £10 per rifle for 1,000 or 1,200 rifles, while the Pattern

1853 rifle musket cost £3.5.1 from contractors or £1.19.8 from Enfield ($48.00 for the Whitworth as against $15.44 and $8.48 for the Pattern 1853 Enfield). Economy won the day and the question of Whitworth vs. Enfield was dropped. It was at this point that Whitworth turned his energies to heavy ordnance rifled upon his hexagonal principle. During the next 5 years a nationwide controversy developed as to the comparative merits of the Whitworth and Armstrong systems. During the Civil War the Confederacy purchased a number of Whitworth field guns and naval cannons in breech-loading and muzzle-loading styles; the Confederate ironclad ram *Stonewall* was armed with two of Whitworth's heavy naval guns.

Concurrently with the military experiments being conducted on behalf of the government, an increased interest in rifle shooting was developing among civilians, culminating in what was termed the "Volunteer Movement." The political friction between England and France present in the 1850s had increased after the conclusion of the Crimean War (in which the two countries had been allied) largely because of the expansionist tendencies of Napoleon III, and the discovery that the Orsini bomb plot against Napoleon had been planned and developed in England. The always invasion-conscious British public, egged on by a ubiquitous and inflammatory press, increasingly clamored for protective measures against possible French invasion.

In 1859 the parliamentary act authorizing the raising and equipping of volunteer corps to fight on English soil, in case of invasion—which had been passed in the Napoleonic Wars period—was regenerated. A rapid rise

in the number of rifle companies throughout England resulted. As of January 1st, 1860, one hundred per cent of such troops would be equipped at government expense if the necessary conditions were met. It soon became obvious that a national organization devoted to the development of accurate rifle shooting was highly desirable, and the National Rifle Association of Great Britain came into being in November, 1859. The first meeting was held at the beginning of July, 1860.

First Whitworths

At this meeting Queen Victoria fired the opening shot with a Whitworth rifle mounted on a rest. For the next 8 years the Whitworth rifle, in various models, was always among the top contenders for honors at British rifle matches.

Aside from the rifles themselves, the initiative of Joseph Whitworth in creating a superbly accurate rifle (for its time) spurred other gunmakers and inventors into action. The result was a profusion of rifling systems, mostly based on the basic Whitworth principles of a 451-caliber bore with a twist of one turn in 20 inches, firing a 530-gr. bullet. The fact that a number of these systems ultimately succeeded in out-shooting the Whitworth in competition does not detract from the significance of Whitworth's contribution in establishing the basic knowledge, and in taking the first positive steps towards a formerly unthought of degree of both range and accuracy in military and civilian marksmanship.

In the spring of 1860 experimental rifles were again ordered from Whitworth, but the trials were not actually held until mid-1861. Further trials were held in 1862, and both proved beyond any doubt the superiority of "small bore" (.451" as opposed to .577") weapons so far as accuracy was concerned. Other small bore rifles were tested during these trials, but Whitworth's proved the best of the lot. The Ordnance Select Committee, in charge of the trials, had stressed the importance of putting the rifles into the hands of troops to determine their performance under field conditions. It was with this factor in mind that 1,000 rifles were ordered in May, 1862. As these rifles gave no initial indications of the problems which later developed, a further 8,000 rifles of a slightly different pattern were ordered in 1863. These were issued on a trial basis to a number of British Army units in England and on foreign duty. Despite the official adoption of the Snider breech-loading system in 1865, many of these Whitworth muzzleloaders were still in the hands of troops as late as 1867. Whitworth rifles continued to be used in the firing for the Queen's Prize at Wimbledon through 1870.

To bring his rifling system to the

broader attention of the general shooting public, Whitworth entered the commercial market in mid-1859, hoping that success among sportsmen and Volunteers would induce the government to take up the matter of his rifles again. The advent of the National Rifle Association was a Godsend to Whitworth insofar as his civilian market was concerned, for the majority of the prize rifles awarded at N.R.A. meetings for the remainder of the muzzle-loading era were Whitworths.

In 1860 a retailing company known as the Whitworth Rifle Company set up offices at 51, Sackville Street, Manchester. Shortly after receiving the order for 1,000 rifles in May, 1862 (it turned out that only a part of these rifles were produced by Whitworth, aside from the barrels), the firm name was changed to the Manchester Ordnance & Rifle Company, an obvious indication that Whitworth was now actively engaged in the production of cannon. By 1865 the addresses of the Manchester Ordnance & Rifle Company and Joseph Whitworth & Company are combined, indicating that the market in both rifles and heavy ordnance was sufficiently diminished that the operation could be combined under one roof. There is, in fact, considerable doubt that the small arms made with Whitworth's rifling were actually fabricated at any Whitworth works. The barrels were probably the only part of the rifles actually made by the Whitworth firm. In the case of the Pattern 1863 Short Rifles Whitworth made but 1,803 of the 8,203 barrels supplied.

The Various Models

The rapid rise of the Volunteer movement and Whitworth's desire to keep his rifling system before the eyes of military men brought about the introduction of what was to become the most common of non-military Whitworths—the *military target rifle*. The earliest form of this rifle made its appearance in the summer of 1859, but it would seem that by the time of the formation of the National Rifle Association, and its first meeting in July of 1860, certain modifications and improvements had taken place to produce the rifle in its best-known form (figs. 1, 2 and 3). This is the rifle used in most small bore competitions at Wimbledon, and the rifle which was presented to Queen's Prize winners and numerous runners-up, as well as for other competitions. Many were presented by various organizations, both civil and military, to members of Volunteer units who had won local or regional competitions. Whitworth thus received a large measure of "free" advertising through the Kingdom.

In basic outline the military target rifle resembles the Pattern 1853 Enfield, but the refinements are legion

and the contours more elegant. Some early examples have 33-inch barrels, presumably to conform more closely to the Pattern 1860 Short Rifle, then the standard issue for rifle companies and for sergeants of line regiments. Three barrel bands of normal Enfield clamping pattern hold the barrel to the full length forearm. The steel ramrod is similar to the Enfield, having a slotted head but lacking the concentric rings of the Enfield. Most rifles have a patent breech, but there is no false breech; the tang screw must be removed to take the barrel from the stock. The patent breech is recessed on the left in the manner of contemporary sporting arms, but the tang and snail closely resemble the Enfield; the snail slightly overhangs the lockplate, and generally has borderline engraving (fig. 3). The lockplate is of Enfield pattern but smaller, and the hammer is a compromise between the heavy military and lighter sporting patterns, generally having Enfield-pattern border engraving. There is a sliding safety bolt forward of the hammer, and two lock screws hold the lock to the stock; Enfield pattern screw cups support the screws on the left of the stock.

The stock is of dark walnut, some examples having fine contrasting colors. It is fitted with steel furniture throughout, consisting of a forearm

cap of Enfield pattern, trigger guard similar to the Enfield, round capbox, and Enfield-pattern buttplate. Sling swivels are mounted on the upper barrel band and through the rear of the trigger guard strap. The wrist and forearm are checkered, the diamonds large and coarse compared to later models, but quite typical of contemporary Volunteer rifles. The furniture, excepting the color case-hardened capbox, is heat-blued.

The sights of the military target rifle present something of a confusing study to the arms collector. As they went from the works the sights were relatively plain, but because they were the "first of the breed" they later underwent, in many cases, considerable alteration at the hands of not only gunsmith and individual owners, but from the Whitworth firm itself. The original rear sight consisted of a long leaf with platinum-lined notch and slide, graduated to 4° on the left side and 1,000 yards on the right side, both on the bottom of the leaf. There were a number of minor variations in the sight bed; some were virtually flat, or with very slight elevators on either side, while others have one or two distinct steps to the elevators. The front sight was a windage-adjustable blade, a small screw in the center of the front face of the sight base allowing for adjustment.

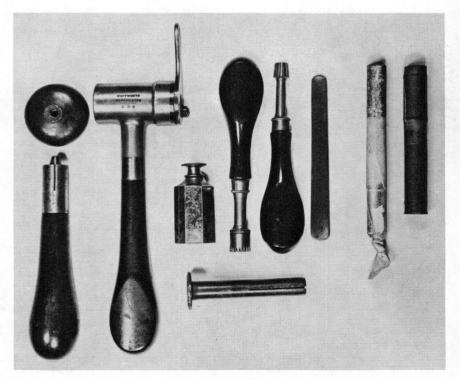

Fig. 4. Typical Whitworth accessories found with military target rifles. Left to right—wooden knob (above) screws onto steel ramrod to aid in loading; base plug for conical bronze one-piece bullet mould; bullet mould with typical Whitworth markings; octagonal steel oil bottle; nipple cleaner; hammer face cleaner; torque bar which fits through slot in head of rod to give a better grip when cleaning or extracting a ball; military Whitworth cartridge; Whitworth's Patent "trap door" cartridge, with military load of 70 grains of black powder and a 530-gr. bullet. Horizontal item at bottom center is hollow bore protector, used when loading and cleaning. *Courtesy E.J. Burton.*

The great popularity of the Whitworth rifle and its extensive use at N.R.A. meetings led shortly to a refinement of the sighting equipment, and a hooded front sight with pin-ball post replacing the earlier blade. The famous "rack & pinion" rear sight so often seen on Whitworth rifles was patented by Whitworth and Hulse on August 2, 1861, along with a hooded front sight and a combination tool. Whether the sights were actually being produced before the patent was taken out is questionable, but by 1862 the Whitworth Rifle Company was notifying dealers that they would re-equip any of their rifles with the new "Patent Sights," re-finish the barrel,

Fig. 5. Early Sporting Rifle with spur guard and 30" barrel. "Cape" rear sight, windage-adjustable "Express" front sights are typical, as are stock, lock and breech design. First appearing in 1860, these rifles were offered in light- and heavyweight (one pound difference) models, and were made in limited numbers through the muzzle-loading period. They retailed for £35 cased complete with accessories. Courtesy K. T. Brown.

Fig. 6. Whitworth Match Rifle, caliber 451, 36" barrel with "Rigby flats" at breech. Patent breech, hook breech. Whitworth's patent wind gauge front sight, rack-and-pinion rear barrel sight and Vernier tang sight. Completely typical of this model, and the forerunner of the familiar "Creedmoor" match rifles of the 1870s. This type of rifle (which came cased and complete) represents the zenith of Whitworth rifle production as regards precision shooting in all its particulars, although by the time this model appeared in 1862 Whitworth's rifling system was already being seriously challenged by those of Alexander Henry, William Metford and the Rigbys. Courtesy H. Taylor.

and shoot the barrel with the new sights, for £3,10.0 ($16.80 in 1860 dollars). A large number of the military target rifles are found with this new set of sights, which were fitted at the Whitworth works (or at the works of some gunmakers hired by Whitworth to do the work) in 1862. The first form of hooded windgauge front sight did not have interchangeable discs, but was fitted with the pin-ball post only. The rack & pinion rear sight went

through a number of variations in construction, all rather minor and of purely technical interest, but the military target rifles were fitted with the first type, which is slightly more square in appearance and wider than the suceeding types.

The third variation in the sighting equipment of the military target rifle was the fitting of a tang sight. Originally this did not form a part of the sighting equipment, but with the introduction of finer sights on Whitworth rifles, there apparently arose a desire on the part of owners of earlier rifles to have this refinement. In view of the complete lack of uniformity in the sight bases which were used to accomplish this end, it is believed that the rifles were taken to various gunmakers who ordered the sight stems from Whitworth and fitted them with their own base design (or that of the owner if he were technically inclined). These variously took the form of extended flat planes made of wood; of extensions of the tang strap which were dovetailed to receive the small base and stem, and windage adjustable by means of a drift and mallet; and various designs of bases being

let into the wood directly.

As with most English tang sights, the Whitworth sight base had no tension spring; the stem was held upright by a small stud on its bottom and by increasing the tension of the pivot screw.

Many of this model were furnished cased (figs. 1, 2 and 4). Some of these exhibit a wide variety of implements of which only a certain number can be considered standard. Such standard equipment would include a leather-covered, German-silver topped powder flask, bronze bullet mould for a cylindro-conoidal 530-gr. paper-patched bullet, powder charger for 70 or 85 grains, hammer-face and nipple cleaners, combination tool, octagonal steel oil bottle, leather sling, a tin of caps, a wooden handled rod for pushing bullets out of the mould, instructions for loading and cleaning the rifle, jags and mops for barrel cleaning, grease wads (generally hexagonal in form), and a wooden knob with threaded brass center which screwed onto the end of the ramrod to aid in loading, spare platinum-lined nipples and a screwdriver. Items which may be considered as optional in Whitworth cased sets of this and other models would include a bullet swage, a lock brush, packets of hexagonal bullets, a brass muzzle protector for use in loading; a torque bar which fitted through the slotted head of the ramrod to aid in cleaning the barrel, removing bullets when they had been seated without powder, "bad" loads, and so forth; powder chargers which screw on the end of the ramrod to place the entire charge in the breech, patch paper, patent cartridges, mainspring vise, a ball puller and a tompion or muzzle stopper. Sporting and purely target models also included loading rods and short starters, and a double-ended rod having at one end a Whitworth hexagonal scraper and at the other a brass charger to breech-position the entire powder charge.

The military target rifle sold for £20 ($96 in 1860 dollars) or £25 ($120 in 1860 dollars) cased complete. The cases were of oak, with varnished finish in natural color, and were unlined (figs. 1 and 2).

Concurrently with the introduction of the military target rifle, Withworth made his bid for the deer-stalking market with the introduction of a Sporting Rifle in the summer of 1859. They appear to have enjoyed but limited sale right through to 1866, judging from a study of serial numbers and markings. Despite the relatively long period of production—so far as Whitworth rifles are concerned—these sporting rifles are among the rarest of Whitworths (aside from the experimental models), since Whitworth production seems to have been very largely taken up with military and semi-military style rifles. This emphasis is, of course, quite natural, since it was the military authorities that

Whitworth was primarily interested in impressing.

Whitworth's sporting rifles were very similar to the usual British sporting rifles of the mid-19th century except that they were made only with full round barrels rather than the normal octagon type. They are fitted with a hook or break-off breech, a patent breech design internally, and the snail has a platinum plug. The barrels are blued, the patent breech color case-hardened. The early sporters have 30" barrels, while later rifles have varying lengths down to 28½ inches; 30 inches appears to have been the standard. Another feature typical of the early sporting rifles is the use of a spur trigger guard (fig. 5) rather than a pistol grip stock; the latter feature is found on a few of the later sporting rifles. The furniture, of blued steel, is of typical shotgun pattern, and finally engraved with scroll work and animals. The round capbox is typical. Stocks were of highly polished fine-grained walnut often showing beautiful color contrasts.

The sights of the sporting rifle as they left the works consisted of a long bead "express" front sight which was windage adjustable, and a "Cape" style leaf rear sight having separate leaves folding into the base for 100 and 200 yards, plus a long leaf, with a slide hinged forward of the short leaves, for 300, 400 and 500 yards.

Sporting rifles appear to have been sold only as complete cased sets, as there is no provision for a ramrod on the production model. This item was included in the set and carried by the gentleman-sportsman's keeper or bearer. The rifles were offered in "heavy" and "light" weights, 7½ and 6½ pounds respectively. A complete

cased outfit consisting of the rifle, "mahogany case, with leather covering . . . bullet mould, powder flask, 300 rounds of ammunition and a full set of apparatus," sold for £35 ($168 in 1860 U.S. dollars) in either weight.

The continuing growth in popularity of rifle shooting, and the expanding program of the National Rifle Association encouraged Whitworth to further refine and upgrade the appearance of his military target rifles, and the result was the semi-military rifle (fig. 5a), combination of military and sporting features, designed for long range target shooting.

These were first marketed in the late fall of 1861; they appear from the first to have been but a transitional piece. In terms of serial numbers these rifles occur for a brief period just prior to the appearance of the military target rifles with 36" barrels and Baddeley bands. They ceased to be produced about the time the Match Rifle was introduced in the spring of 1862. In point of sales, however, it appears that the supply of military target rifles continued to be sold concurrently with the semi-military rifle. All of the latter type thus far noted are highly finished arms, all having at least some scroll and floral engraving on the locks and mounts, and very fine checkering. Although obviously intended as presentation-grade weapons, only a very few of them carry inscriptions or plaques.

The barrel of the semi-military rifle, 36 inches long rather than the 33 inches of the earlier model, is fitted with a sporting pattern breech having three "Rigby" flats and a hook breech. The side of the snail has a platinum plug, and the left side of the patent breech is recessed deeply as on other

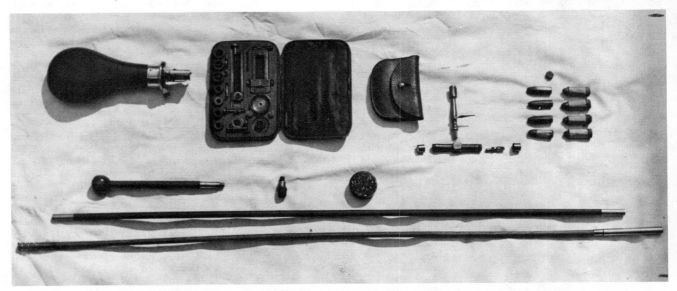

Fig. 7. Whitworth Match Rifle accessories. From left—Patent-top leather covered flask calibrated for two brands of powder; sight case holding wind gauge front, rack-and-pinion rear, and Vernier tang sights, with 8 interchangeable front sight discs, sight-adjusting key, two peep cups (one missing); wallet for small spare parts; combination tool, disassembled; Whitworth hexagonal bullets in various stages from naked to fully cased with wads attached; short starter; hexagonal bore mop; cap tin; loading-cleaning rod; double-ended rod with Whitworth hexagonal scraper on left and charger for placing powder in breech of barrel on right. *Courtesy H. Taylor.*

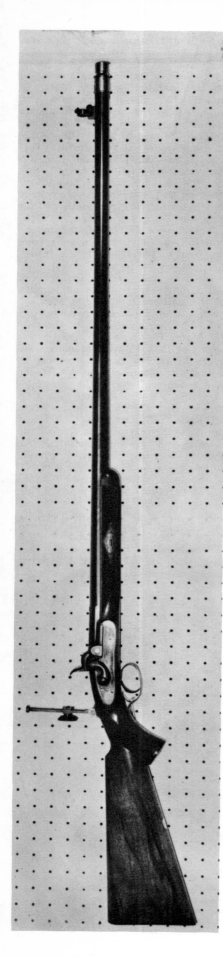

high-grade sporting arms of the period. The barrel is held to the full length stock with three barrel bands of the type patented by Major J.F.L. Baddeley, R.A., on May 10th, 1861. These bands have smooth outer contours with the screw heads recessed into the band to avoid catching on clothing. The military form of steel ramrod is retained, but of the usual Enfield pattern having both a slotted head and concentric rings, reduced in size to fit 45 caliber. The stock tip remains of the Enfield pattern, but here the military features of the rifle end; the remainder are of a sporting design.

The lock of the semi-military rifle is of the same pattern as the sporting rifle (fig. 5a), but the engraving is not quite as lavish on most examples known. The sliding safety bolt is forward of the hammer, and there is only one lock screw, having a plain circular cup supporting it on the left side of the stock. The tumbler is detented, and rifle rather than musket nipples are used. Those examples known bear the mark WITHWORTH RIFLE CO MANCHESTER on the lower edge of the plate.

The stock is of fine-grained walnut with a lighter color and better contrast than previous models, with a highly polished oil-varnish finish. The checkering is of fine quality and execution. The fore-end is longer between the lock and lover barrel band and displays a greater expanse of checkering. The furniture is heat-blued throughout and, excepting the stock tip, is of the type found on sporting rifles of the period. The trigger guard has a long checkered spur which acts as a pistol grip, the forward finial being in the form of a round pineapple. The buttplate has a short ornamental top tang, but the two screws securing it to the stock are both on the face of the plate. The capbox is omitted on this model, as on the majority of 36-inch barreled military target rifles.

The sights of this model are virtually identical with those of the match rifle which succeeded it, except that not all semi-military rifles are fitted for tang sights. The front sight, of the Whitworth patent variety, was furnished with at least 8 interchangeable discs of varying types. It was adjustable for windage, a thumb screw entering from the right side. One variation has the discs removable by the use of another thumb screw, while the other makes use of a square key fitting into a flush screw. The windage adjustment screw is also found in these two styles. The rear sight is of rack and pinion style. When a tang sight is present it is of the standard type found on the match rifle (fig. 6).

Judging from the serial numbers there were probably less than 100 of the semi-military rifles produced before Whitworth, in the spring of 1862, abandoned the military style with the introduction of his match rifle. The style of this rifle is what is generally known in the United States as a "Creedmoor" rifle, as it is identical in profile to the Rigby rifles used by the Irish teams at the International Matches held at Creedmoor, New York, beginning in 1874.

The match rifle has a 36-inch full round barrel, with the same patent breech design and lock as on the semi-military rifle (fig. 6). There is no provision for a ramrod, and the barrel is held to the half-stock by a single wedge or key surrounded by oval

Fig. 8. Probably made in the mid- or late 1860s, the 36" round barrel having the three barrel flats usually found on Rigby target rifles. The center or top flat is engraved METFORD'S PATENT 948. GEORGE GIBBS, 29, CORN STREET, BRISTOL. is engraved ahead of the Metford markings, on the top center of the barrel. The case-colored lockplate is marked GEORGE GIBBS also. The nipple boss carries a platinum plug. ● The Gibbs serial number, 9764, appears on the trigger guard rear tang. ● The Vernier tang sight is calibrated to 4 degrees, in increments of 10 minutes, with **Rad. 37.8** (for the distance between this sight and the front sight) hand engraved on a strip of platinum inlaid into one side of the staff. The front sight is adjustable for windage, takes various discs. ● The hard rubber grip cap is fluted in a sunburst design, the hard rubber buttplate grooved crosswise. The fore-end tip is of buffalo horn. ● The muzzle has a small pin at its top to take the bayonet-locking slot of the 1¾" long false muzzle. The false muzzle, not common on British match rifles, is rifled with 5 lands, these about ⅔ the width of the grooves, right hand twist of about one in 30". This is not Metford's celebrated segmental rifling, but rather his first patented system. It looks much like modern rifling—aside from land width. ● The rifle weighs an even 9 lbs. without false muzzle. John Amber's coll.

steel escutcheons on both sides of the stock. The stock tip is of black horn, as is the grip cap. There is no capbox. The stock is of full pistol grip type, with finely checkered wrist and fore-end. There is an initial plate set into the stock to the rear of the pistol grip. The wood used on match rifles is dark and straight-grained, as was typical on target arms to avoid possible warping.

The sights (fig. 7) consist of the Whitworth patent windgauge front sight, on many rifles the rack and pinion rear barrel sight, and the Whitworth Vernier tang sight. A rear barrel sight is not present on all rifles of this model.

Match rifles were furnished fully cased with loading and cleaning accessories and ammunition. Figs. 6 and 7 show an unusually complete outfit in superb condition. It should be noted that such articles as powder flasks and combination tools and, in fact, all accessories save the bullet moulds (which were not included in target outfits since extruded bullets were considered necessary to first-class accuracy at long range), were not made by Whitworths but were purchased from various contractors in such implements. The great majority are very similar to one another and it is obvious that these tools were purchased in quantity batches, and that the same contractors were patronized for succeeding purchases; it is not correct, however, to expect one set of implements to be identical to those in another similar cased set. Target Rifles are the only sets in which packets of patched hexagonal bullets should be considered standard rather than optional equipment.

Fig. 8 shows a fine match rifle made by one of Whitworth's chief rivals in the later period. The Gibbs-Metford rifle pictured is described in detail in the caption accompanying it.

At this point in the chronological examination of the various Whitworth models we turn from the best quality target rifle and revert to an issue military rifle: the *Pattern 1862 Whitworth Rifle.* It was for this rifle that an order of 1,000 stand was placed in May, 1862, but from existing examples it is clear that Whitworth did not manufacture anything close to the total numbers, he may not even have supplied all of the barrels. This rifle is, in fact, correctly termed an *Enfield-Whitworth,* as they were set up at the Royal Small Arms Factory at Enfield Lock. There are, however, a number of examples known with commercial markings, (fig. 9) which differ from the issue piece in minor aspects.

The *Pattern 1862 Whitworth* has a 36-inch iron barrel of the usual 451-caliber and rifling characteristics, the barrel being secured by three Baddeley-pattern barrel bands. As it was made at Enfield, all parts are interchangeable, and in addition all parts excepting the ramrod, stock tip and two forward barrel bands will interchange with the *Pattern 1860 Short Rifle* (so far as lock and furniture are concerned). The Pattern 1862 was intended to conform as closely as possible to the issue *Pattern 1853 Rifle Musket,* and the barrel takes the same bayonet. The front sight is of similar design, while the rear sight is basically similar but adapted for the use of either cylindrical or hexagonal bullets, the latter graduations extending for another 100 yards.

These rifles apparently met with considerable approval upon being issued to various regiments, and it was decided to equip a larger number of troops with the small bore rifle for extensive trials. The result was the *Pattern 1863 Whitworth Short Rifle.* It was decided to use steel rather than iron for the barrels of this model, and in order to keep the weight within limits the barrel length was reduced to 33 inches, thus making it officially a "Short Rifle" even though it was fitted with three barrel bands rather than the normal two. The sword bayonet fastens to the upper barrel band rather than to a standard on the barrel, as it was considered too difficult to weld a sword bar to a steel barrel. This same welding problem caused the snail to be made integral with the barrel, rather than separately as was the normal practice when using iron barrels.

The *Pattern 1863 Whitworth Short Rifle* (fig. 10) is again an "Enfield-Whitworth" even though Whitworth actually finished up 100 of these rifles at Manchester. The steel barrels were obtained from four different contractors, including Whitworth, who supplied 1,497 barrels which bore normal Whitworth serial numbers beneath the barrel as well as the date of setting up. The rear sight differed from that of the *Pattern 1862 Withworth* in having the elevators inside the sight leaf rather than outside; the graduations for conical and hexagonal bullets were unchanged. It will be remembered that, in 1859, Whitworth had quoted a figure of £10 per rifle; the Enfield cost was just over £2.10.0—or $48 as opposed to $12 in 1860 U.S. dollars. Over 8,200 of this model were produced, of which something over 1,700 appear to have been issued for trials initially. Presumably there were

Fig. 9. Pattern 1862 Whitworth military rifle, a prototype made at Manchester with commercial markings and non-standard trigger guard. The issue model, of which 1,000 were made at Enfield, has normal Enfield trigger guard and lock markings. Standard Enfield pattern ramrod. 36" barrel with three Baddeley barrel bands. Tower of London collection, British Crown copyright.

Fig. 10. Pattern 1863 Short Rifle and sword bayonet. 33" barrel, to Baddeley barrel bands and special pin-fastened upper band with bayonet lug on right side. Lock is marked ENFIELD, the stock also. Note special "H" and "C" rear sight, and over-all close resemblance to standard Enfield rifle. Courtesy E.J. Burton.

additional issues for replacement purposes.

Militarily speaking this Whitworth rifle was never a success, primarily because of prejudice against the small-bore system, dissatisfaction with certain mechanical wrinkles in the first groups of rifles issued, and the imminent change-over to a breech-loading rifle. The oft-repeated stories about fouling problems and loading difficulties are not borne out by the official reports on the trials of these rifles. Aside from obviously prejudiced exceptions the rifles were highly praised on these points from such unlikely areas as India and South Africa. It does not appear that hexagonal ammunition was ever issued in quantity with the military rifles, and in general the troops got on well with them. However, their marksmanship does not appear to have markedly improved over that obtaining with the 577 Enfields, which is rather surprising.

The Confederate Whitworth

The actual *extent* to which Whitworth rifles were used by Confederate troops during the Civil War is still conjectural, but examination of those rifles known to have been used or at least owned by Confederate personnel, and consideration of their serial numbers, has led to the conclusion that (with the possible exception of some individual pieces brought through the blockade by private persons), the Whitworth rifles used by Confederate troops were all of one basic type as shown in fig. 11. The only significant variation is the absence of checkering on one or two examples. Typical features of the type are a 33-inch barrel, two Enfield pattern barrel bands, iron mounts of the military

target rifle pattern, an Enfield type lock with no safety bolt, and a hammer very close to actual Enfield form; open sights, with a blade front being windage adjustable, and a stock which extends to within a short distance of the muzzle, giving the rifle a "snub-nosed" appearance. The presence of a Davidson telescope on the rifle would indicate a relatively late arrival in the Confederacy, since Davidson did not patent his mounting until December 19th, 1862. Many of this type, which is actually a cheap variation of the military target rifle, bear the mark *2nd Quality* on the trigger guard strap. There is no provision for a bayonet.

A most interesting Confederate Whitworth is illustrated in figure 12. Cook & Brother managed to escape from New Orleans before that city fell to Farragut's fleet on April 26th, 1862, and continued in business at Athens, Georgia. The fact that this rifle bears the New Orleans address would indicate that it was produced and purchased prior to the fall of New Orleans to Federal forces; this, coupled with the high serial number for the Confederate type (C575) indicates that most of the Whitworth rifles used by the Confederates were manufactured prior to the spring of 1862—which coincides neatly with already established serial ranges and dates. The rifle itself is typical of the type, but it lacks the checkering found on the majority of this pattern.

Later Production

Taken as a whole, civilian Whitworth rifle production tapered off sharply after 1862; while a steady trickle of match rifles and sporting rifles appears to have been turned out during the period 1862-1865, the major part of Whitworth's efforts during this period seems to have been devoted to the production of heavy ordnance, government trials of his rifling system in both ordnance and small arms, and his machine-tool business. Small arms production as such seems to have been secondary to those other considerations. It is, however, during this later period that some of the most interesting of Whitworth's rifles, including the 30-caliber sporting rifle, 568-caliber semi-military rifle, and double-barreled sporting rifle were made, all on a very limited basis which might reasonably be called—with the possible exception of the double barreled rifles —experimental production.

The single barreled sporting rifles produced in this later period generally have full pistol grip stocks, as opposed to the earlier rifles with spur trigger guards, and some of the later rifles lack capboxes.

The double-barreled sporting rifles generally have barrels varying from 24 inches to 28 inches, the majority being about 26 inches long. The barrel group is one piece of steel, into which both bores have been drilled, a feature which Whitworth patented in June, 1857. The half-length stocks have a full pistol grip, two pipes for the ramrod, no capbox, and a black horn cap on the pistol grip. The low bead express front sights have windage adjustment, while the rear sights use a series of flip-up leaves for 100 to 500 yards. The locks have sliding safety bolts forward of the hammers.

ing period proceeded on a regular chronological basis. Having commenced with the number 1, the initial series continued through to 1,000, and then re-commenced with a letter prefix and proceeded through a series of these prefixes as follows:

1—1000 : first production, 1857 through mid-1860.

B1—B999 : mid-1860 through late 1861.

C1—C999 : late 1861 through mid-1862. If gaps exist it will be in this series.

D1—D999 : spring 1862 to early 1863.

E1—E999 : early 1863 into mid-1864, primarily Pattern 1863 Military Rifles.

F1—F700 : mid-1864 through 1865; after F700 some breechloaders appear in regular numerical order. BSA-marked rifles also occur in this series.

Although there are still some unanswered questions regarding the connections between the Whitworth firm

but as most of these include a date on the lockplate, the problem is greatly simplified. There are some individual instances, however, where the date is misleadingly late for the rest of the rifle. Lockplates on these early rifles generally bear the mark WHITWORTH PATENT, plus the serial number and Birmingham proof marks. The lockplate is marked, forward of the hammer and above the safety bolt, WITHWORTH 1860 in two lines, or simply WHITWORTH. To the rear of the hammer appears the Whitworth crest (a crowned wheatsheaf), a W sometimes appearing beneath the wheatsheaf. The great majority of locks used on Whitworth rifles, even some of the plain military rifles, were made by Joseph Brazier of Wolverhampton; this is shown in some form generally on the inside of the lockplate. This may be his initials—*JB* or *IB*—to the most elaborate form noted so far: *JOSEPH BRAZIER ASHES*, the latter word being the name of Brazier's works.

Fig. 11. A Confederate Whitworth with 33″ barrel. Except for the Davidson telescope, in typical side mount, the rifle seems a standard Confederate Whitworth in all features. Some are without checkering. Note snub-nosed appearance, two Enfield barrel bands, and early-pattern adjustable open sights. Enfield-pattern lock. *Courtesy Tennessee State Museum.*

Whitworth Production and Serial Numbers

If it is accepted that there are no significant gaps in the indicated serial number ranges of Whitworth rifles, the total number produced with commercial markings would be about 5,000 of all styles, including the early rifles and BSA-marked rifles with Whitworth-serialed barrels, but excluding the greater part of 1,000 *Pattern 1862 Military Rifles* and all but 1,600 of the 8,200 *Pattern 1863 Short Rifles*; both of these were assembled at Enfield and bear Enfield marks. If these last are included, a grand total of approximately 13,400 Whitworth muzzle loading rifles were produced from all sources. Those rifles produced under license from Whitworth by such makers as Bissell, Beasley Brothers, and McCririck—which did purport to be honest imitations of Whitworth's rifling—are not included, and would increase the total somewhat.

From a study of existing rifles and fragmentary records, it appears that the serial numbering of Whitworth rifles from their first production in 1857 through the end of the muzzle-loading era and into the breech-load-

and the Birmingham Small Arms Company, it is clear that Whitworth offered to supply the gun trade with their barrels, in either finished or semi-finished state, the latter being rifled only. In 1866 B.S.A. had used Whitworth barrels on their rifles for the N.R.A. and other standard Short Rifle patterns are known with B.S.A. markings and Whitworth serial-numbered barrels; in addition several match rifles of Whitworth profile and rifling have been reported with B.S.A. markings. It is obvious that B.S.A. purchased a batch of barrels from Whitworth in various states of completion and applied them to a small group of rifles of the several popular styles, in the 1865-66 period.

Whitworth Markings

With the conspicuous exception of those experimental rifles made throughout the entire production period of Whitworth muzzle-loading rifles, a study of the markings on the rifles relates directly to the serial numbers, and makes the assignment of a production date relatively easy. The early Whitworth rifles, made prior to 1860, bear a variety of non-standard marks,

At the very end of the production period for military target rifles (during which time the "Second Quality" rifles of this type were being made), the lock markings change to WHITWORTH RIFLE Co. MANCHESTER, with the Whitworth crest behind the hammer. This mark continues in use, along with the WHITWORTH PATENT marking on the breech of the barrel, through the period of the semi-military rifle and the early production of the match rifle.

Shortly before the conclusion of the C-prefix serial number range, the lock marks change to MANCHESTER ORDNANCE & RIFLE Co.; and this marking continues through the D- and E- or F-prefix serial ranges, being found almost entirely on Pattern 1862 and 1863 military rifles, and on match rifles. The WHITWORTH PATENT mark on the breech of the barrel is retained, as is the Whitworth crest to the rear of the hammer, with and without the W beneath.

The Pattern 1862 Rifle and the Pattern 1863 Short Rifles made at Enfield bear standard Enfield markings for the period; the date is

The long Vernier-system folding tang sight is engraved on the rear of the staff, T. MURCOTT GUNMAKER (on one side), with 68 HAYMARKET LONDON N° 509 on the other.

The picture of the muzzle area shows the deep chamfering of the hexagonal rifling and the form of the slotted steel ramrod.

The 33" barrel is full round, shows double Birmingham proof marks, the serial number 937, and is marked WHITWORTH PATENT at the top rear.

The walnut stock shows good figure, and is coarsely checkered at wrist and ahead of the lockplate. Weight of the Whitworth rifle shown is 9½ pounds. John Amber's collection.

This 451 caliber Whitworth rifle was probably made in mid-1860 in view of the style of markings on the lockplate—WHITWORTH RIFLE C° MANCHESTER—and the serial number 937, without letter prefix, on the barrel. The rear barrel sight is of the Vernier type (double pinions and pinion bar are missing); the front sight dove-tail base once held a globe or hooded sight container with windage control knob, these also gone. These sights were added later, perhaps, by Whitworth, using the style patented by Whitworth and Hulse in late 1861. The right side of the rear barrel sight base is marked WHITWORTH/RIFLE Co. PATENT, while the top of the folding leaf is graduated on the right side 1 through 12 for 100 to 1200 yards; the left side is marked 10, 20, 30 and 40 for minutes of angle.

stamped over ENFIELD forward of the hammer, and a crowned *VR* on the tail of the lockplate. The barrel breeches of both military models bear the mark WHITWORTH PATENT. Where the barrels were supplied by the Whitworth firm a normal D-, E- or F- prefix serial number will appear on the underside of the barrel, generally accompanied by a figure such as 6/63, indicating that the rifle was set up in June, 1863.

In the later production period there was considerable mixing of markings, particularly on sights and sight parts. It is not uncommon that a rifle bearing MANCHESTER ORDNANCE & RIFLE CO. markings on the lock will have WHITWORTH RIFLE Co. on the sight base of the rear barrel sight and the stem of the Vernier tang sight. Similarly, a few rifles bearing THE WHITWORTH COMPANY LIMITED on the lockplate will have MANCHESTER ORDNANCE & RIFLE CO. on the above-mentioned sight parts.

In the final production period of Whitworth muzzle-loading rifles, the lock and barrel markings change almost entirely. The Whitworth crest is the only hold-over from previous patterns. The lock markings in the very high E-prefix serial range and throughout the F-prefix range read THE WHITWORTH COMPANY LIMITED, while the markings on the barrel are changed to WHITWORTH MANCHESTER in a circle or oval form. Some of the very last Whitworth muzzleloaders have J. WHITWORTH & Co. Manchester on the lockplate. As this was the firm name of Whitworth's machine tool business, this would seem to indicate nearly the end of Whitworth's production of firearms. An early breech-loading double rifle by Whitworth is marked in a similar manner, with the trade label of the case reading "JOSEPH WHITWORTH & COMPANY Patentees and Manufacturers of WHITWORTH RIFLED ORDNANCE, SMALL ARMS & SPORTING GUNS. General Machine and Tool Manufacturers. Works, Chorlton Street, Manchester, London Office, 28, Pall Mall, S.W." This rifle follows closely upon the serial number of the last muzzleloaders, and there is no evidence at present known to prove that production of breechloaders was long continued.

Whitworth's essay into the field of small arms seems never to have gone beyond the scientific and theoretical stage in his own mind. Commercially speaking very little was done by Whitworth to advance the sales of his rifles. Contemporary literature on the topic is noticeable by its scarcity, advertising nil. The success of this rifling system and the presentation of so many of his earlier rifles as prizes went far towards advertising, but quite clearly the rifles themselves were

only a vehicle for his system, and a bid for government work. It is curious that while Whitworth's reputation for the introduction of standardization in mechanical and industrial processes is so great, his rifles were no better in construction than any other eminent gunmaker of the time: the parts will not interchange in any respect. Some sights will, by pure luck, fit more than one rifle, but lock parts and furniture all exhibit minor variations to a degree precluding interchangeability. Those military rifles made at Enfield upon Whitworth's system will, of course, interchange to conform to government standard, as will other Enfield rifles

Fig. 12. Confederate-marked Whitworth, possibly unique. Made for Cook & Brother before they evacuated New Orleans in April, 1862. The crowned wheatsheaf on the lockplate's tail is a Whitworth trademark. *Courtesy Weller & Dufty Ltd.*

made after 1858. All major parts appear to have been obtained through the gun trade, Whitworth manufacturing the barrels only (even this point remains controversial), and the rifles were set up at one point following the normal procedures of the time. Although Whitworth took out several patents dealing with small arms and their appurtenances between 1854 and 1865, very few of the items covered appear to have been produced or used. Even implements peculiar to Whitworth rifles (such as the patent combination tool and hexagonal wad punches appear to have been made in lots by more than one contractor, and there are consequently very few accessories which can positively be labelled as "Whitworth tools," as will be noted in the illustrations.

The place of the Whitworth rifle in the history of rifled longarms and ballistic history is of paramount importance. Sir Joseph Whitworth (he was made a baronet in 1869), through analytical study which had never before been applied to the science of firearms design, demonstrated what could be done with elongated projectiles and precision machining; so well did he succeed in his efforts that he spurred the entire British gun trade into a period of experimental production the likes of which had not been previously witnessed. As a result of the standards for accuracy set by Whitworth's rifles, other gunmakers tried system after system—there were at least two dozen, all primarily variations of the basic Whitworth system of 45-caliber barrels with a twist of one turn in 20 inches and polygonal rifling—to equal or excel the Whitworth. This led to the ultimate development of such systems as those of William Metford and Alexander Henry, which led the world not only in civilian shooting but in military marksmanship and long range accuracy well into the 20th century. ●

The writer wishes to express his sincere gratitude to Dr. C. H. Roads for permission to use certain facts and figures concerning the experimental and military Whitworth rifles, contained in his superb volume, *The British Soldier's Firearm, 1850-1864*, and to those gentlemen who kindly furnished photographs of rifles in their collections.

Sporting Arms of the

More and more our domestic gunmakers—old and new —are importing from some foreign shore one or more products that comprise their line. We report here on firearms and related arms made in the United States and made abroad, in both instances covering the new and the imported—plus accessory items.

by JOHN T. AMBER and the Technical Editors

IN SPITE OF the problems confronting every segment of the arms field—manufacturers, importers, jobbers/dealers and consumers—because of the iniquitous Gun Control Act of 1968 and its tangled skein of rulings, counter-rulings and regional departures from Washington decisions, the National Sporting Goods Association show this year was one of the best ever—if not *the* best meeting yet!

Held at Navy Pier in Chicago again, there was heavy buying on all sides even though money had become more costly, retail patronage was threatening to slow down, and inflation continued. Perhaps, even, the specter of rising prices at all levels may have accounted in part for the surge of orders.

Certainly the GCA/1968 has made its impact on the world of guns and shooting—a dire effect in many instances. Far fewer arms are being imported, many of them unable to meet the point system set up by the ATFD. Domestic gunmakers did not display the usual broad array of new arms at the NSGA show—not that there weren't numerous new members, which we'll get to shortly.

Interest in air rifle and pistol shooting seems to be growing, perhaps on its undeniable merits alone, maybe in part because air arms don't come under GCA rules. For the same reason, black powder replica guns are moving better, and many new models are being offered or soon will be, though it must be noted that the recent threat of legal restrictions on powder sales—both black and smokeless—arising because of the bombing

this spring, may deal a death blow to black powder shooting.

Handloading continues to grow— a number of new tools and accessories were shown—but the same restrictions on "explosives," if enacted, may well put a damper on this activity.

We'll now offer some brief notes on those new rifles, shotguns and related products not covered elsewhere in this section or in this issue—you'll find a Test Fire Report on Remington's 25-06 and 5mm rimfire cartridges in this edition, by Russ Carpenter, in which he also tells about two new Brownings — their Single Barrel trapgun and their BL-22, a lever action, tubular magazine rifle.

In this section you'll also see my own coverage of our sample 25-06 Remington and its surprisingly excellent accuracy; an account of the new Champlin rifle in 338 Magnum and its performance record in Africa last year. You'll also see copy here on Interarms' revised and lightened Mark X actions/rifles; latest information from Replica Arms Co., on their latest percussion rifles, plus a report on the Shell Shrinker (solid steel "shells" bored and rifled to shoot 22 rimfires and other ammo in shotguns), and a piece on the Contra-Jet, a recoil-reducing muzzle attachment I've had installed on a Model 70 Winchester in 338 caliber.

We're also reviewing the new Jackson Hole 3-barrel (or more) rifle outfits in this issue of the GUN DIGEST. Elsewhere in this book there's a full and detailed report by Bob Hagel on the Sharps Rifle company's near-copies of the old Sharps-Borchadts,

and how two of them did for Bob on deer and elk.

There is another article, well-illustrated and full of good information, on the growing air rifle field, which we're running in this edition, the author Ladd Fanta.   (J.T.A.)

Hunting in the 1970s

THE HUNTING outlook for the 1970s is bright in spite of the crepe-hanging of some forecasters. There will be some lean times (there always have been), but there are good days ahead for the hunters willing to work at it.

In any decade, hunting depends on two things: abundance of game, and abundance of hunting opportunity. There's no doubt in our minds about the first point. Projecting what we know about wildlife conservation, and certain social and land-use trends, we are strongly optimistic.

In our forests, such game as wild turkey and deer is in good supply and likely to remain so. During the 1970s, a growing part of forest management on both public and private lands will be outdoor recreation of all kinds, and hunting will have a big piece of the action. We predict that deer hunting will continue to be good during this decade. Wild turkey range will continue to expand, and there will be more spring gobbler seasons. Elk and mule deer will hold up well, and continue to be the mainstays of western hunting.

Abundance of such farm game as pheasants, quail and rabbits depends entirely on farm economics and clean-farming. All-out crop production usu-

World

- Atlas
- Benet Arms
- Century
- Challanger
- Champlin
- Colt-Sharps
- Daly
- Flaig
- Golden Age Arms
- H&R
- High Standard
- Hy-Score
- Interarms
- Intercontinental
- Ithaca
- J-K Imports
- LAD
- Mossberg
- Navy Arms
- Numrich
- Plainfield
- Premier
- Ranger
- Remington
- Replica
- Richland
- Sanderson's
- Santa Barbara
- Savage
- Smith & Wesson
- Spesco
- Sturm, Ruger & Co.
- Thompson/Center
- Universal
- Weatherby
- Winchester

- plus gun gear from Avtron,, Jim Baiar, Butts Trap, Canjar, Chronograph Specialists, Contra-Jet, N. B. Fashingbauer, Jerry Fisher, Dale Goens, Hal Hartley, Outers Labs, Harry Owen, Shell Shrinker, Shooter's Screwdrivers, Singlepoint, Harold Waller, Yankee Hoist

ally means all-in game production. But in spite of our rising population, this probably will not occur in the 1970s. Our technology is producing more food on less land, and agricultural experts are recommending that marginal farmlands be shifted to other uses. Best of all, the farm economists feel that land retirement should be on a long-term basis rather than year-to-year. This would have a huge effect on all farm game—and give long-range game management programs a chance to pay dividends.

The 1960s was a decade of strong ups and downs for waterfowl, but generally ended on a high note. Waterfowl will continue to fluctuate in the 1970s, but we predict harvestable surpluses of ducks and geese for many years to come. There is growing support for wetlands conservation and the multimillion-dollar Federal wetlands program and other efforts should begin to tell. The rising tide of citizen-interest is having increased effect. Ducks Unlimited, for example, collected over one million dollars for the first time in 1966. Only three years later, the group doubled that amount and collected over two million dollars for wetlands management in Canada.

Dove populations are good, and fit in with suburban patterns of land use. We predict wide increases in dove hunting, and enough birds to meet the demand.

There'll be plenty of game to hunt during the 1970s, but chances to hunt will depend on the hunter. He must make those chances himself, rather than wait for them to come along or depend on a state game agency to provide them. He should be prepared to hunt some game species less and other species more, and be willing to change his customs as the times demand.

All hunting will have a higher price tag during the 1970s. Most landowners will come to regard fish, wildlife and outdoor recreation as cash crops.

We can expect a steady increase of good shooting preserves in heavily populated regions. This is a healthy trend that increases competition and quality, and can give the hunter more and better shooting at reasonable cost.

All species of game will be more closely regulated by game management units and zones. We can expect to see more species of predators classed as game animals.

The general public will demand high ethical standards of hunters during this decade, and if the hunter cannot keep his house in order, lawmakers may try to do it for him. The greatest single threat to the sport of hunting in the 1970s will not be lack of game, but the slob hunter who is so offensive to the public, the landowner, and to the ethical sportsman.

Everything considered, we are entering the 1970s with good supplies of all major wildlife species. Our conservation programs are working, and wildlife management has become a biological science instead of just a political football.

Best of all, the sportsman isn't facing his problems alone. At long last, the man on the street is becoming conscious of his environment and is beginning to realize what hunters and fishermen have known for years: that the best parts of our world are the easiest to lose. **John Madson and Ed Kozicky.**

40th World Shooting Championship Matches

If you haven't got any special plans for your next good deed, the NRA, the National Shooting Sports Foundation and the GUN DIGEST ask that you direct it toward the 40th World Shooting Championships that will be held in Phoenix, Arizona, October 14-26 of 1970.

The championships, which will be governed by the rules of the International Shooting Union, have not been held in the United States since 1923. There's a strong obligation on the U.S. to make a good showing, both as competitor and host.

America's 20 million hunters and shooters are being asked to support the United States' role as host nation by contributing whatever they can to the NRA World Shooting Championship Fund.

In 1962 at Cairo, Egypt, and in 1966 at Wiesbaden, West Germany, the World Championships received substantial monetary and other support from the governments of the host nations. *Similar assistance will not be coming from the United States government in 1970.*

To preserve America's prestige in national and international shooting, the entire shooting fraternity is rallying to support the championships.

Send your contribution to: NRA World Shooting Championship Fund, 1600 Rhode Island Ave., Washington, D.C. 20036.

Above—Hopkins & Allen muzzleloader from Challanger ● Left—Challanger's lever action 22 rimfire ● Charles Daly LTD field grade shotgun.

Atlas Arms

Atlas Arms has moved out of Chicago. The new shop is in Niles, Ill., the full address to be found in our Directory. This is another instance, the second one recently, of legitimate business being forced out of the city of Chicago because of its stringent and stupid gun laws. George Pearsall, who operated a reputable and successful gun repair shop here for many years, was also impelled to move out of the corporate limits of Chicago. Perhaps this was the way it was meant to work— if you can't put them out of business one way, make it so tough for them that they'll have to get out.

Atlas Arms continues to import the truly fine Perazzi shotguns, and the company is in a particularly favorable position to handle orders calling for special stock dimensions, weights, barrel borings, etc. Steve Polemus, the head of Atlas, can also furnish the interchangeable Perazzi trigger systems, these at $75 - $100, and buttstocks either off the shelf or to order at $85 - $150, the exact price depending on wood quality, checkering, etc.

A new shotgun, an Italian-made boxlock over-under patterned after the famed Boss shotguns of England, comes with double ventilated ribs, a modern feature that claybird shooters seem to like. No, not one rib on top of another, but one in normal fashion riding the top barrel, the other one positioned between the two barrels, the idea being to dissipate heat waves better, to avert distortion that might arise from firing the lower barrel repeatedly.

This new Atlas Supreme model comes with a non-selective single trigger, automatic ejectors and in 12 gauge only. A field grade is standard at $550, the receiver handsomely case-hardened in color and engraved. Prices run to $625 for better engraving, silver-finished receiver, etc. Skeet and trap versions are available also, and stock dimensions, chokes and barrel lengths can be specially ordered with the usual several months delay.

Benet Arms

Benet Arms Co., Inc., operated by my old friend and associate, Bill Edwards, is importing the Beretta BM-69, a gas-operated semi-auto rifle in military styling. Chambered for the 7.62mm NATO (308 Winchester) cartridge, the BM-69 has a 20″ barrel, including flash hider and muzzle brake. The standard detachable magazine holds 20 rounds, may be blocked for less capacity in the hunting field.

Genuine walnut buttstock and handguard are gloss finished, and there's a trap in the rubber buttplate.

Garand-type sights are fitted front and rear, calibrated for the standard NATO service cartridge, but adjustable, of course. Sling swivels permit either side- or bottom carry, and a bipod (optional at extra cost) may be fitted.

The Beretta BM-69 lists at $239, with extra magazines available for $9.95 each.

Edwards has told us he will be resuming importation of the German-made HEGE over-under shotgun as well as bringing in various Zoli and Bernardelli smoothbores (both Italian, of course) in the near future. If these makes are of interest to you, write to Benet Arms for details and prices.

Century Arms, well-known distributors now and in the past of surplus arms as well as purveyors of new imported and U.S.-made arms, have a new double-barrel 410 at a remarkably low price! This folding gun, side-lever opened, has twin external hammers, takes 3″ Magnum 410 shells, and weighs only 4¾ lbs. Stocked in genuine walnut, this scant-28″ barreled double gun sells for only $54.50.

Challanger

Challanger—best known, probably, for their extensive gun case line, and other cases—took over distribution of all Hopkins & Allen muzzle-loading firearms in 1969. In July of that year, the firm offered a new Minuteman, a de luxe full-stocked rifle with engraved patchbox, 36- or 45 caliber, and made in flint- or caplock form for $249.95. The Standard grade Minuteman rifle is $179.50 for either type.

Now Challanger has a new single shot lever-action 22 rifle, available in standard 22 rimfire ($28.95 or $33.95) or in 22 WMR at $33.95 or $38.95, the latter price for the Deluxe models. The lever is of short-stroke type, the external center hammer won't fire unless fully cocked, nor will it fire even then if accidentally released unless the trigger is held back. Ejection is automatic on this 18-inch barreled rifle.

Charles Daly

Charles Daly, Inc., is showing new light-weight versions of their Venture and Field grades for 1970. The LTD (Light Daly), through slimming the buttstock and fore-end, runs under 7 lbs., but the metal hasn't been touched, so there's no strength loss. Both, says Howard Walzer, are hand-fitted and hand-engraved—like other C.D. over-unders. LTD Ventures start at $350.

LTD Ventures are ready in new models, too—with single selective trigger and auto ejectors, they're $320, while a new Venture Trap gun— same features plus a recoil pad and Monte Carlo stock—is $319.

A new broader vent rib (⅜″ wide) is now standard on Superior and Diamond models (from $370), while the Flat Top Superior trap model (with ½-inch wide vent rib) may now be had with a 32-inch barrel; 12 gauge only, of course.

The Charles Daly Selexor device— which allows auto ejection or simple extraction at the shooter's option—is available on Superior grade trap and Skeet Dalys, but still in rather short supply. These start at $415.

Multi-gauge insert barrels—which are *full length* tubes, can now be had for Daly guns in owner's hands as well as on initial order (as before).

A Champlin Champion

SHOWN HERE is the 338 Champlin rifle built to my specifications by Clayton Nelson of the Enid, Oklahoma company—a superbly done rifle that served me well in Zambia in a late-season hunt there in 1969.

The octagon-topped receiver is complemented by a full octagon barrel 24 inches long, the front sight on a long, tapered ramp. The scope is a 1-4x Redfield variable—which I found a highly satisfactory and useful power range on the big stuff I shot. The reticle is Redfield's 4-Plex type — thickish crosswires at the outer edges, thin section at the center, which I also liked generally. On one or two occasions in thick brush I did think that the 4P-CCH reticle—similar to the 4-Plex but with wider-crosshair at the center, would have shown up a bit better.

The Redfield scope bases have been specially milled on the bottom to fit the octagon top receiver, which also drops the scope optical center down a bit.

All metal except the bolt body has been given a soft, matte-finish blue, including the Niedner-type checkered grip cap, the octagon-styled floorplate and the smoothly-thinned trigger guard. The bolt knob is very nicely checkered.

As the photographs should reveal, the fine-line, borderless checkering is handsomely done indeed. The fore-end pattern runs quite long—some 9 inches—and is without a division or a break from top to top of either side. The pistol grip checkering, equally well done, also runs all-but-completely around the handle.

The walnut in the stock was well-chosen for a rifle of hefty recoil—straight grained through the barrel and action area, but with a full-fancy figure in the butt. The cheekpiece is gracefully formed and excellently executed. Please note that there is no Monte Carlo comb line to mar the trim and flowing lines of the rifle.

The length of pull is a hair over 14 inches, just right for me normally when dressed for cold-weather hunting. However, with my 35-inch-sleeve arms and long neck, I was wishing in Africa for another half-inch or so—on two or three occasions, having to get into awkward shooting position by force of circumstances, I got banged in the right eyebrow!

The 338 Champlin rifle performs excellently, too. My early trials at 100 yards bench rest was with a minimum of factory loads because I knew I would be using handloads in Zambia. Five-shot groups with Winchester 200- and 250-gr. Power Points and Silver Tips ran about 2½ inches or so on

average, one flier in most groups enlarging the string.

However, after some initial working up of my handloads—all with the particular bullets I meant to use in Africa—I got groups of 5 that rarely went over 2 inches, most of them going 1¼-1½ inches, a few just under an inch. The final load with both Hornady 250-gr. solids and Nosler 250-gr. soft points was 76.0 grains of Norma's 205 powder. Both of these loads printed to the same point of impact at 100 and 200 yards. For the 210-gr. Noslers—which I used on some soft-skinned animals and as a finishing shot on buffalo, sable and the like—79.9 grains of Norma's 205 put their impact just a fraction lower than the 250-gr. bullets group center.

A perfect combination, and one that never let me down in the field. Every species hit with any of these three bullets went down immediately or within seconds—not that I didn't miss a few times!

As pictured the 338 Champlin weighs just 9 pounds, not too heavy in view of the fairly stiff recoil felt on firing 250-gr. bullets loaded for maximum power.

All in all, a most excellent rifle, and one of the best I've owned out of many fine—and not so fine—sporting rifles.

J.T.A.

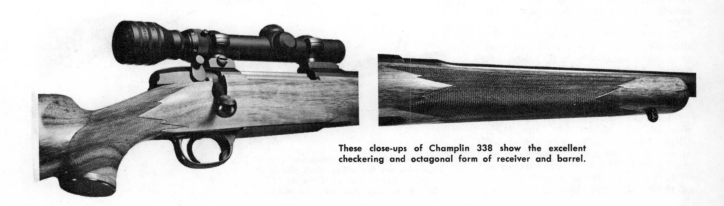

These close-ups of Champlin 338 show the excellent checkering and octagonal form of receiver and barrel.

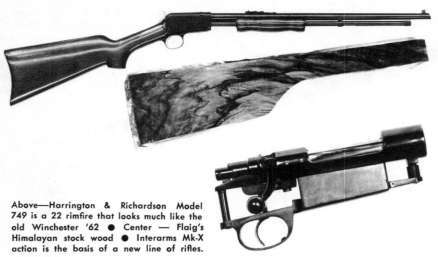

Above—Harrington & Richardson Model 749 is a 22 rimfire that looks much like the old Winchester '62 ● Center — Flaig's Himalayan stock wood ● Interarms Mk-X action is the basis of a new line of rifles.

Flaig's

While this old and highly respected firm has nothing new in firearms for 1970, it does have a batch of ultra-fine stock wood coming in (found in the Himalayan Range of northern India), as our illustration shows. Isn't that rich coloration? These "Rare and Very Rare" blanks are priced at $100-$150, and worth it!

Golden Age Arms Co.

Most black powder shooters—at least those who have been at it for a while—are probably familiar with the products of this busy little firm, but for you who only have just started on muzzleloaders, send $1 for their thick (100 pages) catalog, to Jim Johnston, the owner.

It's stuffed with stuff for the muzzle stuffer—barrels, locks, wood and metal items on all that's needed to build your own rifle or pistol; shooting accessories and gadgetry; complete rifles and handguns as well; camp gear, tomahawks, powder horns —you name it.

Harrington & Richardson

Several new things have been added to the H&R wide line for 1970, among them two brand new firearms. One of these is the Model 404, an imported side-by-side double gun model in 12, 20 and 410. This is a conventional top-lever dropping-barrel double, with top-tang safety and double triggers. It's priced just under $100.

The other new firearm is a light slide-action rifle, the Model 749, and chambered to handle 22 S, L and LR ammo interchangeably. This lightweight takedown rifle mimics the old Winchester '62 pumpgun, visible hammer and all. $79.95 is the price.

This year there is a left-hand version of the Model 360, the H&R Ultra Automatic, their gas-operated autoloading rifle that's chambered for the 243 and 308 Winchester cartridges.

H&R is also offering a variant form of their Ultra Sidekick 22 revolver,

this one to be called the Model 940. For better information on this 9-shooter see George Nonte's "Handguns 1970" elsewhere in this issue.

Several new calibers and gauges have been added to existing models of H&R's guns this year—the Models 301 and 330 now include the 7mm Remington Magnum and the 300 Winchester Magnum. The Model 158 "Topper" shotgun can now be had in 16 gauge with a 28" modified choke barrel, while the Model 198 is available with a 28" 410 and 20-gauge barrel.

H&R's Model 317 Ultra Wildcat, the only factory 17-caliber rifle offered today, is now furnished with a brass cleaning rod, brush and tips at no extra charge. The M317 can also be ordered with the special Ultragon rifling at $12.50 extra.

High Standard

A new version of the Flite-King Executive, a 12-gauge slide action trapgun, features a custom-finished stock by Reinhart Fajen, a Monte Carlo design in quality walnut, with good checkering at pistol grip and foreend. Dimensions of the new Fajen stock are 1⅜"x1⅜" along the Monte Carlo, with a 2⅛" drop at heel, and a trigger pull of 14⅜". This new stock

is also available on High Standard's Supermatic autoloader at just under $275. The Fajen-stocked Flite-King is $229.95.

The rest of the extensive High Standard line of shotguns is unchanged.

Interarms Mark X Rifles

Interarms has modified the Mark 10 rifle being imported from Yugoslavia. The new version is lighter, refined in many details and will sell for about $160 with a plain trigger. Fully adjustable triggers are available as an option, however, the extra cost under $10, we understand.

I'm looking forward to renewing acquaintance with this imported rifle in view of the several improvements. I hunted in Yugoslavia with one of the earliest specimens, in 30-06 caliber, and it could have been a bit lighter. Otherwise, it performed excellently, no problems of any kind. Later, testing it at the bench, I found accuracy with factory ammo and handloaded rounds fully acceptable. Groups ran an average 1½ inches at 100 yards with commercial loads, better than that with selected home-brewed cartridges.   (J.T.A.)

Intercontinental Arms

This Los Angeles company—longtime importers of replica and other firearms, both long guns and short— has two new items for 1970. A new rolling block rifle comes in 222, 22-250, 243 and 45-70 (other calibers later), the 25" round barrel tapped for scope bases. The checkered straight-grip stock is of genuine walnut, the metal parts are blued except for the color case-hardened breechblock, hammer and trigger. The guard is in polished solid brass. The complete rifle (no sights) is $147.50, and actions only are offered at $48.75.

A semi-auto rifle, in 22 LR and looking much like an M16, is also available—it has a 15-shot magazine, a 20" barrel (including flash reducer), is stocked in strong plastic and weighs about 6¾ lbs. $125 complete, extra mags at $3.50 each.

Two new offerings from Intercontinental Arms are the rolling block rifle in various calibers (top) and the AP-15, in 22 LR, that resembles the M-16.

Ithaca's new Model 51 autoloader in Skeet grade.

Mario Beschi Olympic Trap EL from J-K Imports.

Ithaca

The big news at Ithaca this year is a new Featherlight shotgun, the Model 51 gas-operated autoloader that's made in 12 gauge only, at least for now. As it happens, this highly interesting modern shotgun was designed and developed by a very old friend and ex-Chicagoan, Jim Tollinger. Over the many years I've known Jimmy he invented and produced—entirely by hand—a number of highly novel and interesting firearms, so I know something of his truly outstanding ability in this field. Not only is Tollinger a prolific idea man, I believe him to be as fine a gun craftsman as it is possible to be—his workmanship is superb.

The new Model 51 uses an extraordinarily simple gas system. Aside from the reciprocating fore-and-aft motions of the breechblock, the only moving part is the hardened and ground steel piston that operates the ejection and loading mechanism. The rotating bolt has three locking lugs, thus there are ample locking surfaces for high strength and safety, with the bolt rotating to the top so that dirt and debris can't be caught and trapped in the breech area.

High velocity and low-intensity loads can be used in the Model 51 without any adjustment, and the action will take high power thrust and impact without any strain.

The barrels are forged from solid steel bars, and they're completely interchangeable without any fitting whatsoever.

Barrels are available in 26″ (IC or Skeet), 28″ (F,M or Skeet) and 30″ in Full only. All are 2¾″ chambered, and weights runs about 7½ pounds.

The standard field grade Model 51 is very nicely stocked in genuine walnut, the capped pistol grip and full fore-end carrying ample checkering. Field gun stock dimensions are 14″x1⅝″x2½″, the Skeet having the same dimensions. Price for the standard field grade gun is about $165, or $195 with a ventilated rib.

The Skeet and trap guns carry vent ribs as standard equipment, and are priced at $199.95 and $197.95 respectively. Dimensions of the trapgun stock are a bit different at 14¼″x 1½″x1⅞″.

The rest of the Ithaca line for 1970 remains pretty much the same.

Prices have risen a little in some instances, but other Ithaca models hold the line.

A new offering is a cased set for the Skeet shooter, this consisting of an SKB over-under buttstock with one fore-end and three pairs of barrels—20, 28 and 410. This set is available as the M600 outfit at $595, or as the M700 set at $795.

Ithaca has a new Perazzi to offer, this one a single barrel trapgun at $795. Full details on this are lacking at the moment, but the fact that it's made by the dynamic Brescian gunmaker speaks for itself—it's got to be top quality.

J-K Imports

How anyone these days—inflation being what it is—can offer a truly custom made over-under shotgun for $177? I don't know, but J-K says it can. Some 90 days' delay, naturally, but for that low price you may have chokes and barrel lengths of your choice; a stock to your specifications in any type—pistol grip or straight—and in good French walnut hand checkered. This won't be a fancy gun, of course, but a vent rib is standard on this Greener-type crossbolt boxlock, bores are chrome-plated, and a stock through-bolt locks the buttstock solidly to the receiver. Made in 12 gauge only, this Mario Beschi double is without auto ejectors or single trigger, and the safety is manual—whaddaya want for less than $180?

OK, for $475 you can have all the goodies in the Mario Beschi "Olympic Trap" model over-under, the stock, the chokes and barrels lengths to your own ideas, plus the following features: two vent ribs, one between the barrels, the top one extra wide; single selective trigger, auto ejectors; top quality hand engraving covering the receiver; choice French walnut, de luxe hand checkered, and a semi-beavertail fore-end; gold-plated trigger, special coil mainsprings — and more! On special order, a large gold eagle and your initials in gold will be inlaid, but you'll have to write for a quotation on these extras.

All of this sounds like a great buy —in either case—and we regret that so far we haven't handled and shot one of these guns.

J-K is also importing numerous leather accessories for the shotgunner —in addition to several other smoothbores made by Beschi in Italy, these ranging from about $180 to $365, the last figure for a *genuine* sidelock side-by-side double made to your order!

Write for J-K's list of guns, leg-o-mutton cases, trunk-type shotshell boxes of leather or wood frames (under $30), shell belts, etc.

National Sportsman's Club

Wayne K. Tiller, newly-appointed President of the National Sportsman's Club, located in Dallas, Texas, outlined a progressive course of action for the club.

"Big game hunting is a big business in North America, and we are going to give big game hunters the unified voice they deserve," said Tiller.

The club, he went on, will help the hunter be a better sportsman, help the sportsman be a better hunter, and fight to preserve and improve big game hunting in North America.

It won't be just another association shadow-boxing behind legal red tape, Tiller said; the Club is geared to fight openly for or against legislation on both state and national levels, expose state and federal programs that threaten the future of big game hunting, and support game management based on facts rather than politics.

The young Club will help hunters find good hunting areas, help them obtain permits and licenses, and check qualifications of guides and outfitters. Many hunters have had bad luck with inexperienced guides, but some good guides have been unjustly maligned by hunters who are not sportsmen. The club will take an active role in helping hunters and guides have a better understanding of the other's viewpoint and work together toward better hunting.

Club membership dues are basically $8 per year, but 3 or more can join as a group for $7 each, if applications are submitted together. This includes receipt of the monthly magazine, *National Sportsman Digest*. Wives of members may join for $4, with all advantages of membership except a copy of the magazine.

For more information write: National Sportsman's Club, P.O. Box 2003, Dallas, Tex. 75221.

Jackson Hole Rifles

The Jackson Hole Rifle Corporation, located in the town of that name in northwestern Wyoming, is offering an unusual bolt action rifle outfit—readily interchangeable barrels are the big feature, and the system used to let these barrels be exchanged is a novel one, indeed.

The whole concept of this interchangeable barrel development is the brainchild of a young gunsmith named James Quinney, who has patents pending on the design.

The "standard" setup includes three barrels (others can be added at any time, as long as the head diameter and type is the same as on the original set), and the cased group we received for test and appraisal consisted of a 30-06 barrel, a 243 and a 22-250 barrel. As you'll see from the illustrations, ours is the de luxe, engraved Presentation grade, but other outfits are also offered, identical otherwise except for variation in wood quality, checking and the like.

The Sportsman, at $575 for any three barrels (wildcats $75 extra), has selected American walnut in a choice of three stock styles—the rollover comb type, the classic form or in Special Sporter type. The Custom Grade carries fancier wood, skip-line checkering, and lists at $825 in standard calibers, $875 for magnums (extra barrels $50). The one we have, the Presentation Grade, offers the customer his choice of woods and stock styles at $1000 in standard caliber, $1200 for Magnum cartridges. Engraving can be had to order as well.

Our sample has the rollover-comb style of buttstock, but I'll have to say that the metal engraving is rather on the coarse side, though nicely planned and executed.

A Redfield 2x-7x variable was on the receiver of the J.H. rifle when we got it—the action is a Spanish-made Mauser, fitted with an adjustable trigger system.

Removing the barrel and putting on another is quickly done—the stock is removed, the next step being to rotate the scope tube and lift it off.

Then the combination spanner-screwdriver is used to rotate the threaded sleeve and unlock it. The sleeve can then be turned off with the finger, and the barrel unscrewed, also easily done using only the hand.

Another barrel is then threaded into the action, seated firmly with a wrist snap, then followed by turning the sleeve home snugly with the spanner. Replacing the scope and the stock completes the job.

I don't see why the spanner couldn't be redesigned making it an L-shaped affair—so that the barrels could be removed and inserted without taking the scope off.

First Trials

The Jackson Hole rifle outfit, as delivered to me, was fitted with the 22-250 barrel. I had assumed that it was ready to go, an assumption I should not have made! My first efforts resulted in a shambles at the target. That is, after using two or three shots to get on via the Sweany collimator, I wound up with five Norma loads going into 5 inches! This seemed unreasonable even though there was a bit of wind blowing. The wind was steady, the light was bright and the target sharp and clear. I then checked the scope mounting screws and the guard screws and found them all loose to one degree or another. I turned in the guard screws a full turn and a half. Having done this, I again assumed that the shooting would improve, but at this point the trigger gave out. On closing the bolt, the firing pin would go forward, and only after fiddling with the trigger would it stay cocked. The trigger had initially exhibited a very considerable degree of creep and now, when it did fire, the pull felt long and draggy.

Taking the rifle into the shop, I removed the stock and found that the forward attachment screw of the trigger system was loose. Having no tools handy to adjust the trigger (small open-end wrenches are needed), I did nothing but tighten the attachment screw. Cocking the bolt

repeatedly when out of the wood showed no problems at all—it stayed cocked every time, and the pull was without creep. The letoff was about 4-5 pounds, but reasonably crisp. I then discovered the barrel sleeve was not drawn up tightly; in fact, it could be rotated to unthread with the fingers. In addition, the barrel itself was not up fully snug. I then tightened the barrel according to the maker's instructions, and tightened the sleeve using the spanner supplied with the rifle. It was by this time too dark to do any further shooting.

The second trial of the rifle proved to be not much better than the first as far as group size went—about 5 inches with the Norma 55-gr. cartridges. The trigger went bad again, letting the firing pin go forward on cocking, so I took the action down once more and experimented with the trigger adjustments, having got a ¼-inch wrench in the meantime. I tightened everything that I could find and the pull at the moment is crisp and at 2 pounds exactly, according to my scale.

In removing the stock from the barrel and action several times, I noticed a considerable degree of rocking motion when the guard screws are tightened down. Releasing the tightened rear guard screw lets the action assembly spring upward a quite fair amount.

Another thing noted while shooting is the stiff bolt lift effort on extraction, considerably more so than lifting the bolt with the trigger pulled and no cartridge having been fired. The base of the cases exhibit burnishing or polishing.

The third trial of the J.H. rifle took place on March 21, still shooting the 22-250 barrel, and with the same Redfield 2x-7x scope in position.

Shooting started at about 3 o'clock and the weather was very good—no wind at all and a high, bright overcast. I shot the remainder of the Norma 55-gr. soft point stuff, 6 rounds, into a group of 1⁷⁄₁₆". Then another remaining 6 rounds of some Rem-

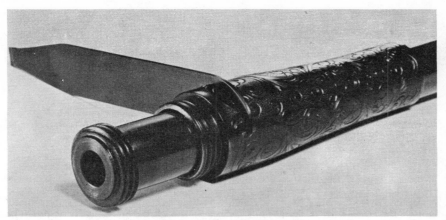

A close-up of the tapered sleeve—in this example engraved to match the receiver—shows the combination tool attached.

ington 55-gr. hollow point ammo went into 3″.

As noted earlier, bolt lift after firing was heavy. That happened with Norma ammo, and I'd been attributing this to some fault in the mechanism. However, when I used the Remington ammo, bolt lift was about normal. A little stiff, but nothing quite like it had been with the Norma cartridges.

A careful examination of the extractor and the face of each barrel revealed the cause of the heavy bolt lift. The face of the extractor—the top of the hook—bears against that part of the barrel breech that protrudes through the receiver-ring flange. A bright spot on the breech face of the barrel revealed this, more noticeably on the 30-06 barrel than on the others. A stoning of the extractor hook will cure this, I'm sure, or the barrel breech face could be taken down just enough to clear. Headspace would not be affected, of course.

I then used up 25 rounds of Remington 55-gr. Power-Lokt loads, and the first three 5-shot groups did quite well considering what I had been getting—1³⁄₁₆″, 1⁵⁄₁₆″ and 1¹⁄₈″ for the best string. The last 10 shots, all in one group, opened things up, the diameter going 1⅝″.

The next day I tried out the 30-06 barrel.

30-06 Barrel Tested

The weather was still clear and bright, a light overcast once more and a very light wind out of the northeast.

After getting sighted in, I shot Speer/DWM 150-gr. soft point loads, and some Dominion 180-gr. cartridges loaded with their Sabre Tip bullets. Groups ran about 1½″ to under 2″ for 5 shots, but the shots were strung out vertically.

Dean Lincoln (owner-operator of Custom Ammo & Gunsmithing in Moab, Utah) had sent me some samples of his cartridges, among them 20 rounds of 30-06 loaded with 150-gr. soft points that looked like Speer bullets.

I used the 10 remaining loads in the J. H. 30-06 barrel, but again I got strong verticals, especially with the first group of 5. There wasn't a half-inch, left to right, but the group was just under 1¾″ high! The second group was a bit more round, but was still a long vertical, 1″ by 1¾″.

That same lot of 30-06 ammo from Dean Lincoln had—in a Winchester 70 sporter—put two 5-shot strings into just over an inch, and both groups fully round in form.

I believe that the rocking condition I've mentioned existing in the action bedding may well account for the vertical grouping I've been getting with the J.H. rifle and the 30-06 ammo.

The same sort of grouping happened with the 243 barrel, so I'll make that test report brief—six 5-shot targets averaged just under 1½ inches, ammo used being Remington and Winchester 100-gr. in soft point form. Groups were again vertical, but lateral measurement alone went close to an inch.

During the numerous times that the barrels were removed and replaced, we found that the point of impact with a given barrel did not vary much from shot to shot with the *same* barrel —perhaps a ¼-inch on average, though the 30-06 barrel was hard to judge because of the up-and-down stringing of the shots.

On the other hand, the point of impact changed quite a bit when going from one barrel to another without resetting the scope. Then POI changes amounted to as much as 6″-8″, depending on which barrel and which ammo were used.

A bother, certainly, but the number of clicks or divisions made to re-zero can be recorded, and the groups will go back to the right place or near enough so that only a small adjustment is needed for dead zero.

All in all, a good and useful idea, this barrel interchangeability—though as you've seen, not without a few minor problems as of now. Quinney has promised that these things will be handled and corrected promptly, and it must be remembered that our test outfit was one of the first production samples.

In any case, Jackson Hole rifles carry a lifetime guarantee against defects in workmanship and materials, and I'm sure Quinney intends to honor this 100%.   (J.T.A.)

The component pieces that make up the Jackson Hole 3-barrel rifle package. Each barrel threads into the action with a snap of the wrist, then the inside-outside tapered sleeve locks the barrel tightly to the receiver ring, using the same inside threads. The special spanner/screwdriver furnished is at top right.

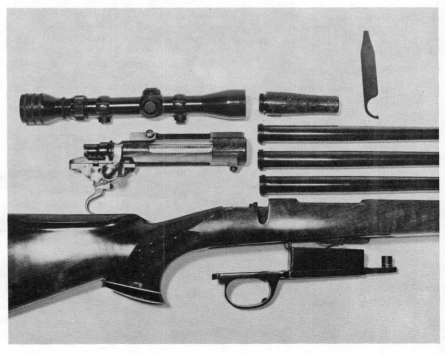

Mossberg Model 500APR, a 50th anniversary offering. Insert shows their C-Lect-Choke.

L.A. Distr.

Additions to the Erma pistol line are covered elsewhere in this edition, but here are some notes on what's new with L.A.

Also new with L.A. is a Western-type 22 lever action that is a very close copy of the Winchester M94. Straight stock, band-held fore-end and a full-length magazine tell how it looks, and the price is just under $70.

Another light 22 rifle, also German-made, is a new LA pump or slide action at $69.95.

There's a new Lames O-U this year, a 12-bore trapgun that features two ventilated ribs, the usual top one and the other lying between the 30″ or 32″ barrels. Single selective trigger, auto ejectors and a full beavertail fore-end are standard, as is a good amount of checkering. Extra sets of barrels, even in 20 gauge, can be ordered when the gun is bought, but with the usual delay on delivery for such extras. All of this for just under $400, including an engraved receiver, good European walnut, etc.

Extra pairs of barrels, including extra fore-ends, can now be had for the Lames O-U guns in 12 or 20 gauge, and in standard models and in their double vent-rib shotguns. They must be ordered when the gun is bought, these extra barrel sets are priced at $150 and $200 respectively. The rest of the LA line continues pretty much unchanged.

Mossberg

Four new 22 rifles have been added to the Mossberg line for 1970, plus additional grades being offered in the Model 500 pump shotguns, and two new calibers added to the Model 800 bolt action centerfire rifles.

The Model 432 is a new 22 rimfire autoloading carbine that looks slim, trim and attractive. The buttstock is straight gripped with a Monte Carlo comb, the fore-end is band-held at the front, and there's a full-length magazine carried under the 22″ barrel.

The Model 430, with the same autoloading action as the M432, is a pistol-gripped 24″ barreled rifle, with a matching fore-end, not held by a band. Pistol grip and fore-end are checkered in a neat multi-point pattern.

Both of these new rifles are chambered for the 22 Long Rifle cartridge, both have a top-mounted safety, open sights and the receiver grooved for scope mounting. The breech bolt stays open on the last shot, and weights run between 6 and 6¼ lbs. $54.95 for the Western-style carbine, $5 more for the M430.

Mossberg's popular 340/640 bolt action 22 rimfire rifles are available this year in Mannlicher-length stock form. The 640M Model clip-magazine is offered in a 20″ barreled Winchester Magnum Rimfire, the 18½ barreled 340M handling standard 22 S, L or LR cartridge.

The full-length stock on these two new Model 640 rifles are 99% identical—checkered pistol grips, checkered fore-ends, whiteline buttplates, a sling and sling swivels on both, and similar fore-end metal caps. Open sights are standard on each, but the 640M has a pistol grip cap to match the buttplate, and a heavy-duty receiver with Damascened or engine-turned bolt, with double extractors fitted. The 640M is $64.95, the 340M $10 less.

Two Model 500 pump shotgun variants are listed this year. Both are in Pigeon Grade with the gold-filled, roll engraving of Mossberg's Anniversary models. Both have vent ribs, recoil pads, well-checkered capped pistol grips and extension fore-ends. The 500APR is a field gun with a 28″ or 30″ barrel, while the 500APKR is identical except for having a 26″ barrel with Mossberg's C-Lect-Choke device.

The 500APTR is the new Pigeon Grade trapgun with 30″ barrel in full choke, and a Monte Carlo stock of typical trapgun dimensions. A lot of gun for the money, these—the 500-APR is $139, the APKR/APTR guns going for $145.

Two magnum calibers are now available in Mossberg's 800 rifle series. The 6.5mm and the 350, both Remington Magnums, are chambered in all but two of the 800 rifles—the Mannlicher-stocked carbine and the 800V, the target/varmint version.

I'm glad to see that the original bolt handle on these 800-series rifles has been improved. Better looking—to my eye, anyway—bolt handles and knobs are found on the Super Grade and on the V/T rifles, with the contoured bolt handle standard on the other three types, the Standard rifle, the Mannlicher-stocked carbine and 800 SM or standard version that Mossberg now offers with a Mossberg scope in 2.5x, 6x, 8x or 3x-9x variable. These scoped rifles offer a saving of around $7 or so over the rifle and scope priced separately.

Jack Boone, Mossberg's Vice President of Sales, sent me a Model 800-AM recently, this one being the Mannlicher-styled carbine in 308 caliber. It came through with a 4x32 Mossberg scope all set up for mounting, and despite the lousy weekend

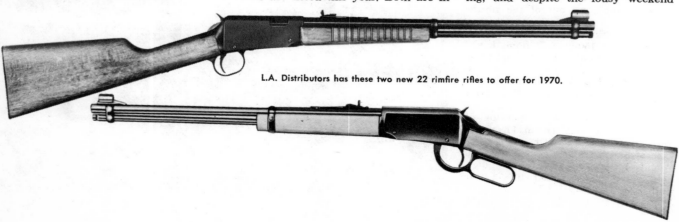

L.A. Distributors has these two new 22 rimfire rifles to offer for 1970.

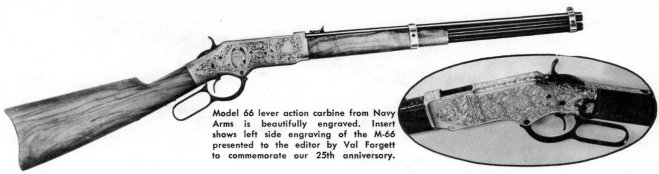

Model 66 lever action carbine from Navy Arms is beautifully engraved. Insert shows left side engraving of the M-66 presented to the editor by Val Forgett to commemorate our 25th anniversary.

weather we've had for a couple of months, I've managed to get in a fair amount of shooting with it, at least with factory ammo. While I can't do my best with a 4x scope, the results at 100 yards have been pretty good. Several brands of 308 cartridges, in 150- and 180-gr. bullet weights, have given me a broad average for some 90 rounds of less than 2 inches. One lot of Norma 150-gr. stuff and another batch of Remington 180-gr. ammo has shot with fair consistency into just over 1" except when I yanked one—1⅛"/1¼" for these two brands and weights. To give me a better chance, I later pulled the 4x Mossberg scope and installed a 10x Leupold M8 with their tapered reticle and put some handloads through the rifle. The load that performed best was 42.5/4320 and the 165-gr. Sierra bullet, with W-W 120 primers. 5 groups of these averaged just over .75", the smallest one running .68" and the biggest one 1".

I have to say that I was rather surprised at this performance, which seems pretty good to me, from a fairly light, short-barreled rifle. I think I'll see what a Varmint Grade 800 will do now in the same 308 caliber.

Navy Arms/Service Armament

Val Forgett has a new 1970 spring edition of his Navy Arms color-catalog now ready for delivery. New accessories and guns have been added, among them a single shot 357 Magnum Rolling Block pistol, a Brown Bess musket and carbine, a Harper's Ferry pistol and a brass-barreled blunderbuss. Numerous accessories are shown, and full instructions on the loading, care and maintenance of replica firearms is included. 50¢ postpaid from Navy Arms.

Pictured on these pages is a close-up of the special de luxe Navy Arms Company "Yellow Boy", a close copy of the famed 1866 Winchester. Chambered in 38 Special caliber, the solid-brass frame, tangs and buttplate are fully engraved in deep relief; the barrel, lever and hammer are softly blued. Buttstock and fore-end were made from one piece of ultra-fancy Italian walnut.

This special 66 replica was made up for presentation to your editor, in observance of our 25th birthday, and is so-inscribed. A really handsome rifle that I'm proud to add to my collection.

These Navy Arms Model 66 carbines are also made in 22 LR caliber, and any of them may be ordered plain or engraved in three styles—Type A engraving is $150. Type B is $250 and Type C (as on the carbine illustrated) is $500. These costs are in addition to the base price of $120.

In addition to those new replica arms mentioned above that appear in the 1970 Navy Arms catalog, there are several other additions to Forgett's already extensive line. Here is a brief word or two on them:

Among the handguns are two target-sighted versions of Colt 1860 caplock revolvers, one in 44 caliber, the other a 36, and both with extension top straps that carry adjustable sights. The top strap also helps strengthen these otherwise open-top six-shooters.

A new Walker 44 replica is now being offered by Navy Arms, this massive revolver weighing 4½ pounds with its 9" barrel. There are, as well, the full array of Colt Dragoon models—1st, 2nd and 3rd (all of these at $175 each), plus a Baby Dragoon replica at $125.

Still among hand arms, Forgett lists an 1806 Harper's Ferry, a flintlock single shot pistol: a percussion cap version of their older flintlock Kentucky pistol, both single shots of course, and either at $80 each, $25 extra for engraving and carved wood. There is also a near-copy of the 1855 Harper's Ferry single shot caplock pistol, a very nice looking copy of a target-grade Remington Rolling Block pistol, this one in 357 Magnum caliber and, lastly, a good copy of the Colt Wells Fargo 31-caliber pistol, plain at $75 or engraved and gold-banded at $125.

Navy Arms long guns that we haven't commented on previously are: the Buffalo Hunter, a 58-caliber single shot halfstock version of the Zouave rifle which Forgett has carried for years; the Blunderbuss mentioned above and the Brown Bess flintlock muskets and carbines in 70 caliber that were mentioned briefly last year. These handsome replicas are now available in kit form as well as in fully-finished guns. The kits are said to be 80% finished, and sell for $150 each. The fully assembled and finished muskets and carbines are priced at $250 for either. A matching Brown Bess bayonet of authentic design is $10 extra.

Under the Service Armament Company all of the British Webley firearms are available, including a Webley/Greener trapgun, a single shot 12-bore mounted on a Martini under-lever action. Stocked with Monte Carlo buttstock and a broad beavertail fore-end, the 32" or 34" barrel (optional) carries a high ventilated rib. Hand-checkered and hand-finished throughout, these are priced at $250.

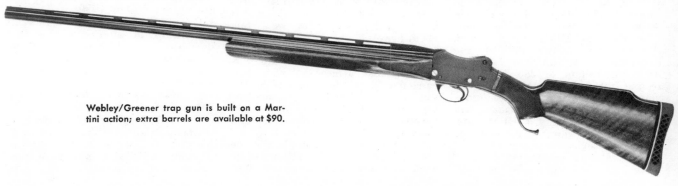

Webley/Greener trap gun is built on a Martini action; extra barrels are available at $90.

Top—Replica Arms' new Kentucky fullstock rifle, caliber 45, sells for under $150 ● Replica Arms' new Plainsman 38-caliber percussion rifle in Cecil Brooks style.

Numrich Arms

Got an old Stevens 1915 Favorite or a Model 418 rifle propping the barn door open? Numrich now has an exact copy of the original 22 rimfire barrel that's easy to install. $15.75 postpaid, and a new center position extractor sells for $2.75.

Numrich offers a rich and varied assortment of this and that, items primarily intended for the muzzle-loading fan or the restorer of old cartridge rifles, but there's a goodly number of more modern things, too. Powder horns and flasks; 45-70, 50-70, 58 and other caliber barrels in finished state or otherwise; Kentucky rifle kits, flint or caplock, with extra barrels for each version, attractively priced, and there's another kit that'll revive the old Remington rolling block rifles—new 28″ ½-octagon barrel, caliber 45-70; real walnut buttstock and fore-end, with steel crescent buttplate and screws; front and rear open sights, all for $49.50. Three of these RB kits are available, each designed for a particular form of action—two Remingtons and one Spanish-Remington.

Write to Numrich for their latest catalog.

Plainfield Machine

Well known for a variety of carbines offered that derive from the U.S. 30 M1 in style and operation (30- and 223 calibers, military in style or in sporter form) Plainfield now offers the PMC/Hill submachine gun, a novel and highly simplified true automatic hand arm that feeds its 9mm Parabellum or 380 ACP cartridges from a horizontal trough. Usable as a single shot, in short bursts or full out, the 30-round magazine can be expended at a 400 RPM rate. Ejection is downward, through the grip, so the sight line is never blocked —even with a silencer added. A silencer! The PMC/Hill SMG is available only to law enforcement people, of course.

Both calibers have 8″ barrels, but the 380 auto version is 16″ over-all, the 9mm Parabellum 20½″.

Premier Shotguns

Double barreled guns only comprise this firm's list—ranging from $110-$150 approximately for their Regent in 10, 12, 16, 20, 28 and 410, regular or magnum to about $118 for the 22-inch barreled hammerless Brush King (12 and 20) to $460 for the made-to-your-order Presentation, a de luxe gun with gold and silver inlays and high grade engraving. Several other models are also available—at in-between prices—and Ed Paul will be delighted to send you a descriptive brochure for the asking.

Ranger Arms A Mannlicher (full length) stock is now ready on the Texas Magnum in left- or right hand types. Laminated stocks, too, if wanted.

Replica Arms Co.

Replica Arms offers the greatest variety of reproduction firearms available today—virtually all early percussion Colts revolvers are on the company's list, and I've just learned that new ones are being added this year— long guns as well as handguns, and it is the percussion rifles we'll talk about here.

Ken Phelps, who heads Replica Arms, told me in a phone talk this morning that a new halfstock percussion rifle will be available by the time you read this. Made in Italy, the first shipment will be of 38 caliber, barrels will be 37 inches long, and these first examples will be fully engraved, rather than the plain grade coming along later. The latter will be about $250, the engraved types $319.95 and, some time later in 1970 the same rifle will be offered in 45 caliber. These larger bores are intended for the muzzle-loading hunting fans and, as most of you probably know, several states require that percussion rifles used for taking game must be a minimum 45 caliber.

Next on the Replica Arms long gun list—and probably to be available this year—is a fullstock percussion rifle, this one in 45 caliber and with a 37 inch barrel. It will be stocked in genuine walnut, and the design has been done by Cecil Brooks, well-known for the superb flintlock and percussion rifles he has created for presentation by the NRA at several annual meetings in the recent past. First examples of this fullstock muzzleloader will be in standard or plain grade, and will retail at just under $150.

Replica Arms has just completed an attractive and colorful brochure that describes and prices just about every one of the numerous reproductions they offer, and it's yours for the asking.

Richland Arms has at least one new item this year, the M844, a 12-gauge Spanish-made O-U with single non-selective trigger and simple extractors. 26″, 28″ and 30″ barrels, the usual choke choices, vent rib and non-auto safety. About $190.

Gunsmiths will welcome a new kit for cutting or altering chokes that uses spiral-fluted reamers. These smooth-cutting tools are said to make after-polishing unnecessary, or kept to a minimum—the parallel planes of the choke are kept parallel to the bore.

12- and 20-gauge kits include 8 reamers, 3 bore bushing guides, a 2-piece rod and head plus handle. They're furnished in protective wood cases. Write for prices.

Newest of Remington's cartridges are the 25-06 (left, actual size), and the 5mm rimfire, shown twice life-size.

New Remingtons

Remington's 25-06

In spite of the fact that the new Remington 25-06 rifle came in almost a month ago, today (Sunday, April 26, 1970) was the first opportunity to shoot the new rifle on the range. Not by virtue of having any factory 25-06 ammunition, either, inasmuch as the factory ammo has not arrived as of last Saturday, at least. Whether we ought to blame this on the Gun Control Act 1968 and its attendant problems, or on the fact that Remington may not have this 25-06 ammunition in adequate supply or something, I don't know. Whatever the cause, I was able to shoot the 25-06 today because a set of Fred Huntington's 25-06 dies did come along, and I soon got around to necking down a batch of Dominion 30-06 brass. As a matter of fact, I had worked up some ten 25-06 cases two days ago with the aid of a set of unusual dies that Ellwood Epps, of Canada, sent to us for a trial. I won't elaborate on these Epps dies at this point, because you'll find a paragraph or two describing their unusual qualities in another section in this same edition.

With the 25-06 cases made with the Epps dies, I used a moderate charge of 4895, 41.5 grains, to fireform those cases, but with the Dominion brass I put in 45.0/4895 as a trial load, coupled with 87-gr. Norma soft point bullets and two other bullets that I discovered in rummaging through one of my bullet cabinets—one of these was the 25-20 soft point bullet of 86-gr. weight, the other was another 25-20 bullet of the same weight, but of solid-nose form—both quite old. Both flat-point types, of course, in view of their intended use years ago in a 25-20 tubular magazine repeating rifle.

The weather was hardly ideal—the sun was in and out of the clouds, there was a fresh, gusty breeze running from the south, south-west about 10-12 miles per hour. I did try to shoot between gusts, but I don't suppose I

was entirely successful, even though the groups did not do too badly.

I was using a 3x-9x Redfield variable on the rifle, the mounts the recently-designed Bushnell types that use single studs front and rear.

Several 5-shot groups with the 87-gr. Normas went into an average of 1¾₆", though one of them ran close to 1⅜". The soft point 25-20 bullets did almost exactly the same grouping as far as size is concerned, but the 25-20 solids, in 86-gr. weight as I've said, did very badly indeed—five of these went into 2¼", while another five did just under 2½". I suppose this performance of these quite old bullets is not awfully surprising, but it may well be that the load isn't ideally balanced for those bullets, either.

This test shooting of the 25-06 used up only 45 rounds of ammunition, the two types of 25-20 bullets included, so not much in the way of conclusions can be drawn, but in view of the Norma bullets in two groups printing sev-

eral shots into a tight cluster leaves me to think that this particular 700 Remington BDL rifle is going to show some excellent accuracy with future testing.

25-06 Remington—Second Test

Sunday, May 3, 1970. Today, as I was about to give the new Remington 25-06 another trial run, Jack O'Connor phoned to tell me—among other things—that his like rifle was shooting very well indeed. Five-shot groups at 100 yards, Jack said, had been consistently at an inch or under, this with Remington factory loads. "This (25-06) Remington 700 rifle has shot more accurately for me than any other I can remember," Jack went on, but he also added that chronograph tests he'd made at Speer's labs had not borne out the factory velocity claims. Instead of the 3500 foot seconds advertised, Speer's results showed an average for 10 shots of 3265 at the muzzle —3210 instrumental.

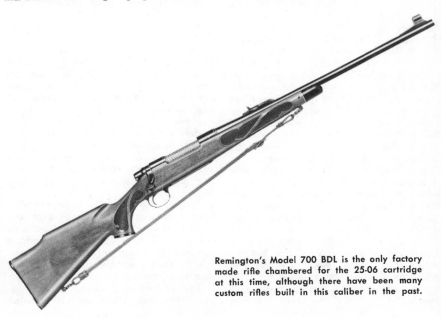

Remington's Model 700 BDL is the only factory made rifle chambered for the 25-06 cartridge at this time, although there have been many custom rifles built in this caliber in the past.

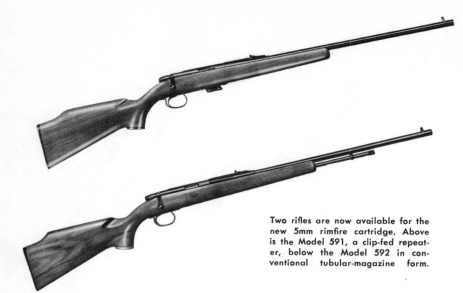

Two rifles are now available for the new 5mm rimfire cartridge. Above is the Model 591, a clip-fed repeater, below the Model 592 in conventional tubular-magazine form.

He'd broken down a few factory rounds, Jack said, and the powder charge appeared to be—or looks like —DuPont 4350, some 54 grains of it. (No, fellows, that is *not* a recommended load as such, though that weight of 4350 with an 87-gr. bullet is a listed one.)

Jack hadn't concocted any handloads—he'd loaned his RCBS 25-06 dies to someone, and that was the last of those!

About 6:30 P.M., the wind having died down, I put up some targets at my 100-yard backstop, and sat down to shoot. Since my first tests of the 25-06 I had selected a small batch of Dominion cases for uniform wall thickness, trimmed 'em to uniform length and seated Alcan 210-size primers. Neck sized for only ⅛", I'd put the same load I'd used previously—45/4895—into the cases, and then seated both Norma and very old (like 25 years!) Sierra 87-gr. bullets.

The first 5 Normas went in ²⁷⁄₃₂", the next 5s into ⅞" and 1¹⁄₁₆", the last one showing 4 holes measuring ½" on centers. With that nice performance (still using the Redfield 3x-9x in Bushnell mounts), I was pretty hopeful—and confident—that the Sierra 87-gr. bullets would do even better. It wasn't to be—for some reason (stale bullets?), I got one or two fliers with every 5-shot group and I fired four strings of 5 each. Two groups of Sierras had 3 or 4 bullets into ½-inch or slightly less, but the fliers I got ruined the picture—the average of four 5-shot runs with the old Sierras was 1³⁄₁₆".

I hadn't done any 25-caliber shooting for many years, so my stockpile of bullets in that size was and is minuscule — one box each of the two loads mentioned! I've ordered some fresh Sierra 87-gr. 25-caliber bullets, which I'm hopeful won't give me the off-shots this old lot produced.

As every varmint hunter knows, you don't get any sighting shots in the field, and for that reason I was pleased to see that my Remington 700 BDL put the first bullet right into the group center from a semi-oiled barrel, no less! I'd lightly greased the 25-06 barrel after my initial shooting with it, and before opening fire today I put a dry patch through the barrel, doing no more than removing excess grease.

Russ Carpenter, who's handling the Testfire Review section for this 25th ed., also found his sample Remington 25-06 to be a tack driver, he said in a recent phone talk. At that time he'd shot only factory loads, and these had shot into MOA figures or nearly so. His full report on the 25-06 will include handloads, however, so look there to see what results he got.

1970 Remington Components Catalog

Remington's 1970 Ammunition Components catalog is now available to all reloaders.

A particularly useful feature of it for both dealers and reloaders is the special color coding given all component items that are subject to the dealer record-keeping requirement of the amended Gun Control Act of 1968.

Under the amended law, dealers must keep records on all components suitable for use in *handgun* ammunition. Because many dealers and shooters have been confused as to just which components are in this category, Remington uses color coding in the new catalog to let dealers know positively which Remington items are and are not subject to record keeping.

The ATFD has also indicated that record keeping is *not required* on propellant powders and primers suitable for use in both long gun and handgun ammunition if the buyer declares positively that they are for use in long gun ammunition only.

The new catalog, virtually an all-in-one reference, lists all Remington components available for shotshell and centerfire rifle and pistol ammunition—centerfire bullets in 112 different caliber, weight and design combinations; 74 different centerfire cases, primed or unprimed; primers for centerfire and shotshell rounds; primed shotshell cases; "Power Piston" wads for all gauges and types of loads; plus Remington-made lead and nickel shot. Each Remington primer listing carries a notation of the case for which it is designed, and each centerfire bullet is illustrated, actual size.

Want one of the new 1970 Components catalogs? See your dealer or write Dept. GTP, Remington Arms Co., Bridgeport, Conn. 06602.

Remington 5mm Rifle

The first trials of the Remington 5mm rifle, my sample being one of the M592 tubular magazine types, took place on a raw, chilly day in mid-April, and a gusty wind of about 10 miles an hour or more didn't add to the tightness of the groups or the pleasure in the shooting.

For those reasons, I was particularly pleased at the performance of the new rifle and ammunition, several groups averaging about 1¼" for 5 shots at 100 yards. I had mounted a new Weaver variable scope, the V22 in 2x-6x, onto the grooved receiver of the Remington rifle, and I had to go to old-fashioned bore-sighting to get on the paper—my Alley collimating outfit doesn't include a 5mm spud, but I managed nevertheless to get on the 100-yard target pretty quickly— some 3 or 4 shots was all that it took.

I consider that this particular 5mm Remington rifle shoots quite well in view of the conditions prevailing when I shot it, and more particularly because of a trigger pull that runs just 9½ pounds! I feel rather sure that if this rifle had a nice, light letoff, say about 3 pounds, and carried a scope of higher power and light-gathering qualities, that I could do rather better than those 1¼" or so groups that were shot. Wishful thinking, maybe, but as soon as the opportunity offers, I'm going to try just this.

There is no ready adjustability of the triggers on the Remington Model 592, (or on its stable mate, the clip repeater M591) but I'm going to see if a bit of careful and judicious stoning of the trigger/sear engagement won't be of some help; certainly it will be relatively easy to put on a scope of some 10 power, perhaps even more.

I also want to do some further shooting and chronographing to check the mid-range trajectory over 100 and 150 yards. I have a hunch—for no really good reason, I suppose—that these mid-range heights are going to be a bit less than the factory figures indicate. I may not get this additional shooting done in time for this edition, but I'm going to try.　　J.T.A.

Left—Savage Anniversary Model 1895 rifle
● The new M-170 in 30-30 makes a good extra gun, should serve the deer hunter well.

Savage Arms

To help celebrate its 75th anniversary Savage has the Model 1895 Commemorative, which looks surprisingly like the original 1895 at first glance, even though it's made up on a modern 99 Savage barrel and action. The 1895 was, of course, the direct predecessor of the Model 1899, and it's basically the same gun these 25 years later. The genuine walnut stock is straight gripped, the fore-end tip is in schnabel form—as was the original—there's a solid brass "rifle buttplate," while the lever and cartridge carrier are brass-plated. The receiver is decorated and gold-filled, both sides, and a golden-colored relief-cut medallion of the Savage trademark is let into the right side of the stock. The Anniversary 1895 Savage will be made in limited numbers and only in 1970. You may need an early order to get one—ours has not reached us yet!

To celebrate the 1970 end of their 75th birthday, Savage has a brand new rifle—a pump- or slide-action type in 30-30 caliber that's called the Model 170. Designed for both the beginning deer hunter and for the oldtimer who wants another rifle for rough weather (or as a "loaner"), the M170 has a Monte Carlo buttstock, an extension-type fore-end with finger grooves, and open sights as standard. In that shape it sells for only $99.75, but it also comes tapped for scope bases—if you order the M170 with Savage's 1½-4x variable scope, the

rifle is $37.25 extra, whereas the same glass and mount sells for $52.50 as a separate package.

There's been no chance to try either the 1895 or the 170 rifles, but they looked and felt good at the NSGA show.

The 20-gauge Savage 440 and 330 over-under shotguns, long awaited, are here—or soon will be. The 440, 12 or 20, now with single selective trigger, sells for $237.50, the 330 for only $199.50, 12 or 20. The de luxe 444, by the way, carrying a $289.50 price tag, has SST, auto ejectors and a semi-beavertail fore-end.

Savage's Safety Key Lock, introduced in 1969, is now offered on the 63-K at $32.50-$35.50—that's Savage's full-length-stocked bolt action 22 rimfire. You lock the trigger with a key, and it won't fire until it's unlocked. Don't lose the key!

John Marsman, Savage's chief PRO, says that several Anschutz rifles (Models 1413, 1411, 1407 (once the 1408) 64 and 250) have been improved in several areas, including stock dimensions, barrel weights and checkering patterns. I liked the shooting of the Anschutz 177 match air gun so much that I bought one.

Savage has also taken over U.S. marketing of Eley rifle and pistol match ammo—84% of all smallbore rifle shooters in the 1968 Olympics used Eley Tenex 22 LR cartridges, accounting for the gold medal and the next 11 places. Eley 22 rimfires, made in England by IMI, cover the field, literally—Tenex, as indicated; Pistol

Match, 22 LR caliber; Short Pistol Match, 22 shorts, and 22 LR Pistol, a practice type. Good stuff, obviously, and with an explicit guarantee of "no flyers" when shooting Eley Tenex loads, the $2.20 price for a box of 50 won't find many competition shooters objecting too loudly.

The "new" 25-06 cartridge can be used in the Savage 110-C and CL bolt action rifles, we've just learned—they're ready for immediate delivery. Stainless steel 24-inch barrel, a Savage top feeature, fully adjustable trigger, their unique ejector clip, etc., make up the 110C-CL rifles in 25-06.

A 12-gauge barrel for rifled slugs has also been added to the Savage line. Made for the Model 30 slide action shotgun, the new 22-inch barrel carries a folding-leaf rear sight (on the barrel) and a gold bead front, sells for $27.25. The Savage M30—12 or 20 —costs $111.75.

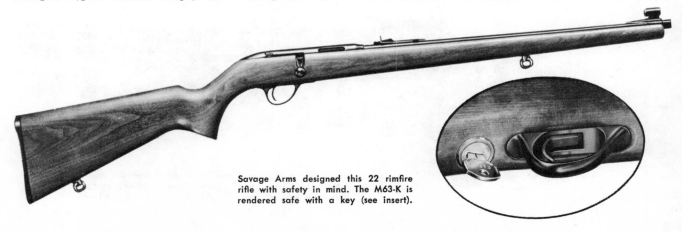

Savage Arms designed this 22 rimfire rifle with safety in mind. The M63-K is rendered safe with a key (see insert).

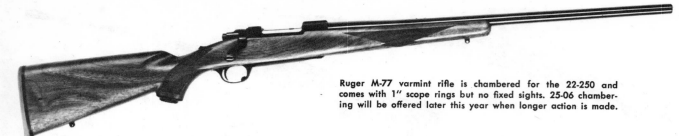

Ruger M-77 varmint rifle is chambered for the 22-250 and comes with 1" scope rings but no fixed sights. 25-06 chambering will be offered later this year when longer action is made.

Sturm, Ruger & Co.

A new varmint-type version of the Ruger Model 77 bolt action rifle was announced in May of this year. At the moment the only chambering is in 22-250, but later in 1970 the ·25-06 cartridge will be offered in the long-awaited long-action M77 rifle.

The M77V—identical in its basic features with the popular M77 hunting rifle—has a 24-inch heavy barrel, tapped for target scope bases (no iron sights fitted or furnished), and it's shipped with a pair of Ruger 1-inch scope rings at the regular price —$160.

One of the M77V rifles is on the way to us for trial, but it'll arrive too late for a published appraisal in this issue.

Just before going to press I had a long talk with Bill Ruger and Ed Nolan, Bill's general manager at Southport, and here's what I learned about upcoming new products, some of which will be available in one form or another this year.

The long-awaited longer-action Model 77 bolt action centerfire Ruger rifle should be available shortly after you read this, that is, about August 1st or so. The new version of the M77 will be exactly like the current model, I understand, aside from the lengthening of the receiver, bolt body, etc., to handle longer cartridges. The new variant will be chambered for just four cartridges initially—25-06, 270, 30-06 and 7mm Remington Magnum. Obviously this same longer action will handle the other shorter magnums, the 338 Winchester, et al, but how soon the new M77 may be available in these calibers I don't know.

I do feel sure that thousands of sportsmen are anxious to get one of the new Rugers for their favorite cartridge or cartridges, and certainly there is no denying that the 270 and the 30-06 are still prime choices among hunters, both here and abroad, with the 7mm Magnum attracting new customers all the time. How well the 25-06 will sell is anybody's guess at this time, but I have a feeling that it is going to move well for Remington and Ruger.

I suppose it is no great secret that Bill Ruger has had an over-under shotgun on the agenda for quite some time. Certainly it has been on the drawing boards for a couple of years or so. Now, at more or less long last, I can tell you that these new super-posed doubles will be visible, to say the least, before the end of 1970. I don't insist that production guns will be ready by that time, or that you can go in and grab one off the shelf, but prototypes will be ready late this year. I'm looking forward to having one of these here for trial and appraisal before long, though too late for a detailed report in this 25th edition. However, knowing something about Bill Ruger's insistence always on superb quality and equally satisfactory performance, I'm completely sure that the new over-under smoothbore will be in every respect a top quality firearm.

New Ruger Revolvers

I also learned from my talks with Ruger and Nolan that a new version of the Super Blackhawk will be ready some time this year also. While this is not the place to talk about handguns, the information has reached me too late to find a place in our Pistol and Revolver Review section (to be found elsewhere in this book), so I will point out that the new revolver will be chambered for the 45 Colt cartridge, with an extra cylinder being available in 45 ACP caliber, and that two barrel lengths will be available—4⅝ and 7½ inches. These will have adjustable sights, of course, and will look generally like the current Super Blackhawks offered in 30 Carbine caliber.

Bill Ruger has another handgun idea that he has been working on intermittently for several years. I suppose this revolver could have been brought to production quite a while ago, but other projects took precedence over the last few years, and only now has it been decided to complete and perfect the new design.

What is this new and mysterious revolver? A caplock six-shooter, no less, nominal caliber 44, but not to be confused with modern 44 bore and groove dimensions. This new percussion revolver that Ruger will introduce has barrel and chamber dimensions that spring from the days when a 44, so-called, was in reality a 45—that is, groove dimensions were about .451-.454, and those are the figures that will apply to the new Ruger caplock.

I've seen prototypes of these handsome six-shooters, but I'm afraid I won't be able to show you an illustration. They are prototypes, Bill Ruger points out, and he doesn't want anything but a production revolver to be pictured. We have not had an opportunity to shoot one of these new percussion handguns so far, but one of the several prototypes has been promised for delivery within a month or so, and I'll report on performance if deadline times permit—though I'm afraid they won't.

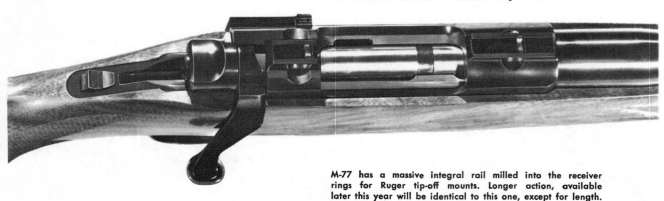

M-77 has a massive integral rail milled into the receiver rings for Ruger tip-off mounts. Longer action, available later this year will be identical to this one, except for length.

Thompson/Center's two new muzzleloaders (left) in flintlock and caplock form ● Universal will import the Mauser 66 bolt action rifle in 4 calibers.

Sanderson's Fine Arms

Robert F. Sanderson, owner-operator of the one company that's done more, doubtless, to bring shotgunners something different—and worthwhile, in our opinion—wrote a letter recently on his 1970 activities that I'll print here, in part:

"We continue to specialize in magnum doubles, lightweight bird guns, hammer doubles, and percussion long guns—from England, Belgium, Italy, France and Iberia.

"The 10-gauge magnum Neumann is now $395 for the extractor model, up a mere $95 from its early 1950 price. Our 10-gauge Spanish 32" single barrel is $59.95. Light Belgian ejector bird guns from $345, English from $495. Classic straight grip with sliver fore-end, straight grip with beavertail, sliver with pistol grip, or beavertail with pistol grip. We have 12-bore guns from 6 lbs. Conventional doubles from $129.50.

"The 28-bore continues to enthuse the upland shooter because of its light weight, easy handling, and effective shot load of ⅞ to 1 oz. Our heavier guns have been very satisfactory with the 3"/28 (up to 1⅛ oz.), which allows proper wadding.

"Our R&D program continues but we've waited to introduce the 4" 10 bore, 3" 24 bore, or 3" 16 bore until interstate trade stabilizes. If shotshell laws stay relaxed we expect to step up promotion of the 2" 12, the 24 and 32 gauge, etc."

Santa Barbara

Well-known for the 98 Mauser actions and barreled actions (Star barrels, generally, from Federal Firearms Co. of Oakdale, Penna.), SBA is also marketing a full line of Claro walnut stock blanks. 99% fitted, these run from plain grades at about $30 to AAA quality at some $60, with a few Presentation grades available now and then.

A complete stock of Mauser 98 parts is kept on hand, including adjustable triggers, and hinged guards (steel or alloy).

Smith & Wesson

The Husqvarna-made centerfire bolt action rifles imported by S&W, while not new as such, are now being manufactured with the latest version of the Mauser action produced by Husqvarna.

In general, the new action is smoother looking and more streamlined, but it is the internal design changes that make it worthy of comment. The old hook extractor has been abandoned in favor of the modern short type, with the ejector built into the bolt face now. The cartridge case is better supported as well, and the new bolt sleeve is constructed to deflect gases better in case of a pierced primer or the like. The new trigger system is adjustable without taking the rifle down, a nice feature, and the safety position permits very low scope mounting. The safety is virtually noiseless in operation. The floorplate release button is still retained in the front of the trigger guard, the bolt retains the normal twin lugs at the front end, of course, with the root of the bolt handle forming a safety lug as normally.

Spesco

This is a new import house, located in Atlanta, Ga. The starting line-up includes over-under shotguns in 12- and 20-gauge, a single-barrel break-open shotgun (12, 20 and 410) at under $35, side-by-side double smoothbores, same gauges, and a variety of replica and near-replica firearms, both cartridge and caplock, long arms and handguns. A catalog is available, I believe.

Thompson/Center Arms

Well known for their single shot pistols with readily interchangeable barrels—and the numerous chamberings offered—T/C has entered the longarm field with a new rifle.

Rather surprisingly, this will be a muzzle-loading rifle, to be available about August, 1970, in flintlock or caplock form. This black powder rifle, the T/C Hawken, will be *made* by

T/C—it's not an import—with a 28-inch blued octagon barrel in 45, 50 and 58 caliber. The genuine walnut stock will carry solid brass furniture, including a patchbox; there's a fully adjustable double-set trigger, and the weight will run about 8½ lbs. $175 for either, flint or percussion.

We've had no chance to shoot one of these, but the prototype handled at the NSGA show looked and felt very good indeed.

Universal

This Florida organization has several new things in the line this year we understand, but full specifications and prices have not been made available to us. There is a new break-open single barrel shotgun, with typical center hammer, and there's a hammerless top-snap double smoothbore, this one with pistol grip stock and semi-beavertail fore-end. The extent of the gauges and chokes available is unknown to us, but offered in 12 gauge, certainly, and perhaps 20 as well.

Universal is also importing the Mauser 66 bolt action rifles, the one with ready interchangeability of barrels, and these are available in 30-06, 308, 270 and 243, all at about $270. A cased outfit is also stocked, the case holding the rifle taken down, 3 barrels, a scope and mount, etc.

Weatherby, Inc. Roy has several intriguing things for 1970, among 'em the Regency O-U 12 bore that's been a longish time coming. $595 for this one, with the same gun in 20 gauge ere long, and with Weatherby pump and auto shotguns scheduled for later. Roy's got a new centerfire rifle, too, called the Vanguard—a bolt action that's less costly than his Mark V rifles yet has all of their mechanical aspects. Made in 243, 308, 30-06, 264, 7mm Remington and 300 Winchester Magnum, the Vanguard lists at about $200. The new Weatherby rifle scopes and his Sightmaster, a zoom spotter, are reported on in Bob Bell's "Scope and Mounts Review," in this issue, as are all the other new optical items.

Winchester Lone Star commemorative pair (left) and the Cowboy commemmorative carbine.

Winchester

Winchester has several new and interesting items in the longgun field for 1970-71, including new shotshells, too.

Two new commemoratives are at the dealers now—the Cowboy Carbine and the Lone Star Rifle and Carbine. The Cowboy model—which was authorized by the National Cowboy Hall of Fame—is made on the old reliable 94 action, as have been earlier Winchester commemorative arms, with the receiver, upper and lower tangs, lever and barrel bands finished in bright nickel plate. The curved, carbine-style buttplate is of stainless steel. The right side of the receiver shows an engraved lariat, the left side a bronco rider and the legend, "Brave Land . . . Bold Men." Made in 30-30 only, the American walnut buttstock (with matching fore-end) has a Cowboy Commemorative Medallion embedded in the right side, while a similar inscription is inscribed on the 20-inch round barrel. This handsome carbine sells for $125, and a matched pair, with consecutive serial numbers, is $275.

The Lone Star models gleam with bright gold plating on receiver, tangs, lever, fore-end cap and magazine-tube cap. Made with semi-pistol grip stocks and levers curved to match, the Lone Stars make a handsome and appealing picture, A gold colored medallion is inlet into the right side of the buttstock, which carries an old-style crescent buttplate of solid brass.

The left side of the receiver, star-studded around the border, carries a big Lone Star between the dates "1845 . . . 1970," while the upper tang is inscribed "Under Six Flags."

Both Lone Star carbine and rifle are $140 each, while $305 will buy a matched set combining the two.

The sale of these Lone Star commemoratives, which will be made in limited numbers, will provide a money contribution to Game Conservation International—otherwise known as Game Coin—for use in conservation research and to make game more plentiful in Texas.

Winchester has also announced a new version of the Model 70 rifle, designed for competition shooting at the highest level. Called the International Army Match rifle, the new target arm has a heavy 24″ barrel, and a new design of match-type stock in which the barrel and action is glass bedded. The buttplate assembly is adjustable vertically and the trigger pull may be easily adjusted from the outside.

At 11 pounds the new M70 match rifle is hardly a lightweight, but this should make it a better performer. Chambered for the 308 Winchester only, the new rifle lists at $385.

There's a new version of the Model 1200 trapgun available now—the difference lies in the new field grade stock, with Monte Carlo comb, this combination being offered at $159.95 in standard walnut. The same type of stock, but with semi-fancy wood, sells for about $205 with the Monte Carlo comb or at $195 without that feature.

The Model 1400 Mk II auto shotgun has gone the same route, offering the trap and Skeet shooter a lower price by virtue of the new field grade stock and fore-end, as on the M1200. The new field-grade stocked M1400 with Monte Carlo comb is available at just under $200 in a trap gun, against a former $224.95. The new M1400 Skeet gun with field-grade stocks, 12 or 20 gauge, lists at $189.95 against its counterpart with semi-fancy walnut going for $214.95.

Winchester has also introduced new 410 plastic Skeet loads, these in 2½″ length of course, and like the rest of Winchester's plastic shotshells, the new 410s offer all of the advantages of the compression-formed plastic shell body developed by W-W in 1964.

This unit construction, which eliminates the conventional separate base wad, offers far better gas-sealing properties. The new 410s are said to give patterns that are 10% or so denser than other 410s show, and they're also a much better bet for the handloader—he ought to get twice as many loads, perhaps, out of these new W-W 410 cases than he does with some others.

That's about the line-up for Winchester-Western this year, aside from some 38 Special loads that won't be covered in this department, and some 12 gauge 2¾″ Magnum Buckshot loads, these carrying 20 No. 1 pellets.

Winchester Hunting Guides

Four of these highly informative booklets are now available. They're described as "A pocket guide on hunting information, season licenses, and best game prospects for the entire country." They are indeed all of that, and there's one for the West, the South, the North-East and Mid-America, compiled by such well-known outdoor writers as Grits Gresham, Pete Kuhlhoff, John Gartner and Pete Czura.

These 55-page reports—which indicate generally good hunting for the fall of 1970—are available to our readers as long as the supply lasts. Write to the Winchester News Bureau, 460 Park Ave., New York, N. Y. 10022.

At the time of going to press, the companies that follow have indicated no noteworthy changes in their lines or announced any new models:

Galef, Europa, Marlin, Tradewinds, Dan Wesson, American Import, and various others.

The Model 70 International Army Match rifle is chambered only for the 308 round.

Hal Hartley
Master of Maple

The two over-unders seen here were restocked by Hartley for Mr. Sol Levine of Columbus, Nebr., a collector of fine long arms. Both were made by Joseph Winkler in Germany, and the very beautiful engraving and gold inlay work was done by the Austrian artist Albin Obiltschnig. Hartley's wood work is equally excellent, and fully complements the metalsmithing and engraving.

In this case, Hartley did not use the hard maple he likes so well but a fine piece of walnut, which was felt to be more appropriate in the circumstances.

Gun Buyers—Shop Early!

Contrary to much popular belief, it's still a relatively simple matter for law-abiding citizens to buy a rifle or shotgun in this country.

In most states, the prospective buyer need only supply the dealer with a few items of personal information which the latter records. A few states have adopted firearms identification (ID) card laws, which authorize purchase of a firearm. Out-of-state purchases of long guns in bordering states are equally simple, *provided* the state in which the buyer lives has passed a law sanctioning such transactions.

What's the problem? Many gun owners and prospective buyers got an earful prior to passage of the Gun Control Act of 1968—things like registration of every gun and licensing of each owner. Neither of these restrictions came about. What has happened is that we have become so emotionally involved that some dealers are not ordering enough guns to cover customer requirements. So, if you try to buy a gun three days before a scheduled hunt the cupboard may be bare!

Lock That Trigger

That's the motto of the people who make the Cesco Gun Trigger Lock—and it's a good one. Their trigger-guard locks are now in use in the many thousands, in the home and in many gunshops, where they guard against unauthorized handling or use, not to mention theft.

Now Cesco has a new item using the same good lock—their PM500 unit is a handgun lock attached to a metal plate (all vinyl coated to protect the gun) which can be attached to a wall via two wood screws. These are 3.95 or, including a wood wall-shelf-and-base 12" or 16" long, $10.95.

For rifles or shotguns, another new Central Specialties (Cesco) product is the WM100. Two heavy gauge steel holders, felt-lined and mounted with concealed screws, lock the gun firmly in position. The lock element is then hidden by the decorative plate. $7.95 each.

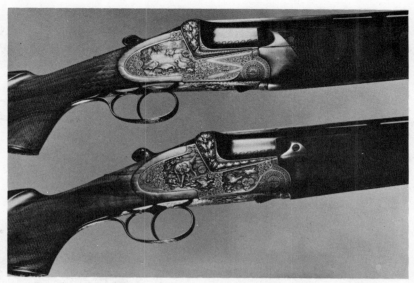

Close-up of the right side of the Winkler guns pictured full length on these pages. The superb engraving is in high relief.

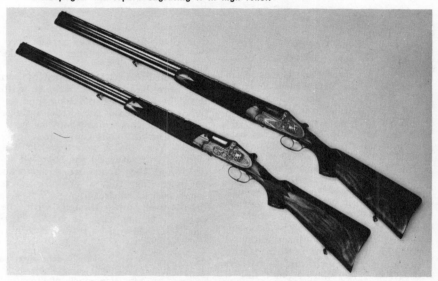

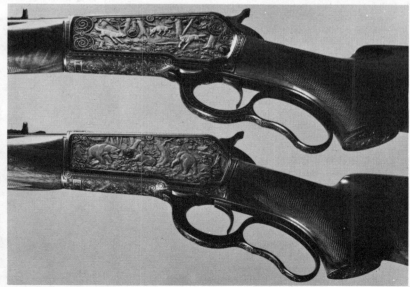

More of Albin Obiltschnig's superb artistry in metal and Hal Hartley's masterful stocking. The rifles are a matched pair of Winchester Model 71s in de luxe grade.

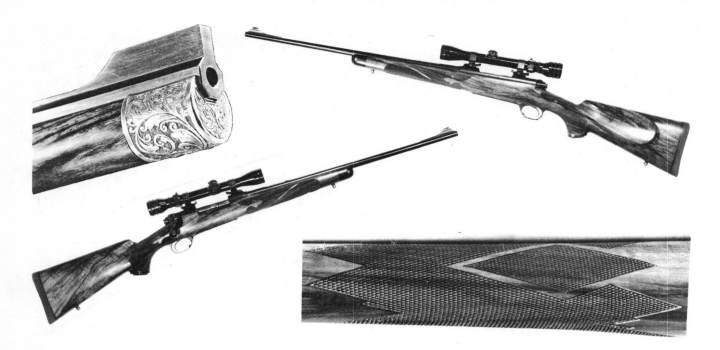

Dale Goens
Artist in Wood

In the display of Dale Goens' work appearing on our inside back cover we didn't have space to show the fore-end tip of the Mannlicher-stocked rifle in detail, so here it is on this page. As with the buttplate and the grip cap, the fore-end tip is of sterling, with E. C. Prudhomme's engraving.

Our close-up on these pages of the fore-end checkering will, we hope, give you a better idea of the high excellence of the job done on this full-length stock. The checkering pattern runs all the way around the fore-end —broken only by the inset diamond seen. This multi-point pattern carries 24 points to the inch, and is borderless. Need I say that I can't find a bobble anywhere!

This full-stocked rifle is chambered for the 264 Winchester Magnum, and is one of a pair of rifles that an old friend and hunting partner and I planned years ago.

That planning was done when the 264 was new, so you know how long ago it was. Were we to select a caliber now, it would probably be the 7mm Remington Magnum for its greater versatility as far as bullet weights are concerned.

Lou Ostendorp and I made drawings for mould patterns, these to be used in casting two each—in solid silver—of buttplates, trigger guards, grip and fore-end caps. The rifles were to be made with blind magazines (no floorplates) but that wasn't feasible, it seems, with the FN Mauser actions we used. The actions and the silver castings were sent to Germany. I'd visited Kurt Jäger's shop in Mainz, and found his work to be excellent. He had several engravers available, so he was instructed to complete the

two rifles—fit the Böhler barrels, have the steel and silver engraved, make stocks, etc.

I'm fairly sure that many of you will have had some experience with the delays, excuses and long-time deliveries that some gunsmiths indulge in. Some of this waiting may be justified, certainly, but how about six years! Yes, that's how long it was before Jäger returned the barreled actions and the silverware—no stocks, no engraving, the silver still in its rough casting state!

All's well now, though, with the work in Goens' capable hands. The rifle described will be returned to him for some final metal work (front sight made, polishing, etc.), and the second rifle will be completed then also. Norm Fashingbauer will do his soft-sheen rust blueing on both rifles and, we hope, they'll be ready for the fall hunting season.

We show another Goens rifle in this section, a Model 70 Winchester in 270 caliber made for a prominent western sportsman who prefers anonymity. A handsome and graceful rifle, isn't it? The proportioning is perfect, the cheekpiece cut and located just right, the curvature, dimension and hang of the pistol grip exactly correct.

(J.T.A.)

Seven beautifully done silver carvings from the deft hands of Sid Bell, all available as tie clips or tie tacks, etc. Bell offers a very wide variety of silver work, artistically done and moderately priced.

N. B. Fashingbauer

Norm Fashingbauer restocked and blued these two Parkers, duplicating to a very close degree the checkering pattern of the originals. The top gun is an SAA grade, the other one a BHE Parker. Fine jobs, both, as our reproduction of the photographs will show —we trust.

Mr. Fashingbauer is well and favorably known for the superb rust blue jobs he does in the old fashioned style, but as is evident he also does top quality stock work, nor is his craftsmanship limited to shotguns. His rifle work is equally excellent.

Consult our Directory pages for the location of firms or individuals mentioned.

Jerry Fisher

A fine classic-styled 1903 Springfield rifle in 30-06 that exemplifies the excellent stock work done by Mr. Fisher. Unfortunately, the photo reproduction seen here can't do justice to the metal or the handsome wood.

The barreled action is probably over 40 years old, for the barrel was fitted by the late Adolph Niedner, while the bolt handle, bolt sleeve, floorplate, guard and steel buttplate were fully engraved and game animals inlaid in gold by the late Rudolph Kornbrath. Mr. Fisher—who included a steel grip cap and an ebony fore-end tip on this beautiful piece of French walnut—says the rifle must be seen for full appreciation. I can easily believe it. Note the bolt sleeve sight, a Howe-Whelen job of long ago.

Harold Waller

The rifle pictured here is a 458 Winchester Magnum on a Mauser action that Hal built for me in 1969 for my hunt in Zambia. Hal had sent the rifle to me before it was fully finished —I'd wanted to get some pictures and try it out on the range—and I was a bit late in returning it, I found out! Waller couldn't get it completed in time, unfortunately, so it has not seen Africa so far.

The view of the whole stock seen here shows the rifle without checkering, and you'll note that the pistol grip drops a little too much. You can also see that the wood is handsomely figured in the butt section, but the grain runs fairly simply—and properly upward—in the fore-end. The close-ups show the top-notch checkering that Hal did, and his alteration of the comb nose and the grip profile for the better. All in all, a fine rifle indeed, and it shoots well. I'm a 50-yards-or-less man with a 458, and at that range it puts 'em all under two inches, with open sights.

Rifle and Shotgun Gear

Contra-Jet Muzzle Brake

I had intended for some time to get one of Dave Tanabe's Contra-Jet air brakes installed on one of my rifles, having examined the device itself and seen how well-made it was, and that its design is decidedly ingenious.

I was further impressed by a tough test that H. P. White Labs had made with a Contra-Jet. They reported in these terms: "It seems to us that the measure of the performance of a muzzle brake lies in its ability primarily to reduce recoil, secondarily to reduce flash, all without impairing accuracy or increasing noise level. In this regard, we consider the Contra-Jet brake to be quite effective."

White Labs found—in their tests of a lightweight Model 70 Winchester in 308 caliber—that recoil energy was reduced 37.5%, that sound levels with and without the Contra-Jet remained quite the same, and that accuracy (with the rifle and ammo tested, and at 100 yards in a machine rest) was improved considerably. Flash at the muzzle was much lessened, and muzzle velocity showed a slight increase, again with the particular components tested.

A few weeks ago I sent a new Model 70 Winchester in 338 caliber to the Sight Shop in Tacoma, Wash., for installation of a Contra-Jet. I'd wanted to be sure the fitting was properly done, and John Lawson's Sight Shop is highly recommended by Tanabe.

A few days ago the 338 came back, along with a full report on test firings made with and without the Contra-Jet installed. There's too much data at hand to let me put it all down, but here's the gist of it: 75 grains of 4350 and 200-gr. Hornady bullets (used in all tests) gave 3034 average MV in the unaltered 24" barrel. With the Contra-Jet fitted to an overall length of 26⁵⁄₁₆", MV increased very slightly. The 338 barrel, next cut to 21¾" and fired without the Contra-Jet, gave 2953 fps. Again attaching the unit, for a final over-all barrel length of 24⅛", got a 2954 average on the Oehler chronograph.

So, with that load and in that rifle, velocity loss was some 85 fps—a relatively minor difference, and one that may well change when I get round to chronographing other loads.

I've now shot the Contra-Jet equipped 338 twenty times and, if my memory of its plain-barrel shooting isn't faulty, I found the felt recoil softened to a very good degree with the 250-gr. handloads I used. I can definitely say that the recoil effect is quite a bit easier on my shoulder than it is with my Champlin 338 and the exact same loads—and shot at the same sitting—but the Champlin is

a good ½-lb. lighter, and has no muzzle brake. Muzzle flash is also clearly reduced; I fired a few shots from each rifle at dusk, and the flame pouring out of the Champlin was much brighter.

Muzzle noise? I can't tell you because I'm not going to shoot a 338 without ear muffs—my hearing is bad enough as it is! It seemed to be about equal with both rifles, in any case.

Further tests, for accuracy and velocity, will be made and reported on here if time permits, but at the moment I'm convinced that the Contra-Jet does its chief job very well indeed—and that's reduction of felt recoil. (J.T.A.)

Scrimshaw by Barringer

Scrimshawing, an art practiced many years ago by sailors and soldiers notably, consisted of decorating powder horns, bits of bone and ivory and the like, by cutting these objects with a sharp awl or knife. Sailing ships were commonly done, as were forts, trails and roads, etc. Some of this work was so-so, some showed a high degree of artistry.

Milt Barringer (18042 Murray Hill Rd., Detroit, Mich. 48235) has revived this ancient art form, and I wish we could show you the great variety of objects he works on—from brooches, cufflinks and earrings to knife handles, walrus tusks and powder horns—but we've space for only the one photograph. However, in it you'll see four examples of Barringer's fine hand.

Prices start attractively at $3-4 for tie tacks, pins, etc., run up to $40 and more for whale-tooth knife handles, and you can buy a big cribbage-board

for $200 and up, this last made from a whole walrus or elephant tusk.

These scrimshaw pieces make novel and desirable gifts. Write Barringer for prices and information.

Gravermeister

Here is a tool that I was skeptical about for some time. I'd seen other "engraving machines" that worked well enough for lettering and the like on essentially flat surfaces, but I hadn't realized that the Gravermeister was a quite different development.

Imagine an electric powered (115 VAC) small jack-hammer or impact tool that delivers 800-1200 strokes a minute, precisely controlled by the operator. Add an assortment of engraving tools—onglette, square, matting punches, et al—and a great deal of the heavy labor necessary in traditional engraving is virtually eliminated.

No, the Gravermeister won't make an instant artist or craftsman out of the beginner—that takes long study and determined application—but it will relieve much of the hand work, for novice and master, heretofore associated and unavoidable with chasing and cutting metal, especially steels.

The Gravermeister sells for $385 with three engraving tools, and a $6 kit brings 4 other cutters. Power is controlled by a foot pedal, leaving both hands free to control the work piece.

Outers Labs

For a while there the 17-caliber shooter had to clean his rifle with home-made or custom rods and brushes, but no more. Late last year Outers introduced a complete line of 17-caliber cleaning tools—rods, brass and bristle brushes, with one-piece and jointed rods offered as well. We've been using them since that time, and they're excellent products.

Shooter's Screwdrivers

For a year or so I've been seeing *Argosy's* Pete Kuhlhoff at various affairs—writer/editor seminars, NRA meeting, the NSGA shows—and he'd shown me more than once a cased screwdriver kit that was at once compact and complete. Seventeen different blades or bits—regular, hex and Phillips—plus a small but rugged ratchet handle, an extension and a screwdriver handle, are furnished in a high quality steel case for $14.95.

As I say, Pete showed me this attractive and highly useful outfit about 6 times, and he said he'd get a kit to us in time for a trial and report—but it hasn't reached us so far! All I've had were those tantalizingly brief peeks and briefer handling. Nevertheless, this Shooter's Screwdriver kit is, I could easily see, of professional design and quality. The regular-form bits are designed for use on specific guns, please note, and range from very thin types to beefy ones for big screws. Other sizes in hex and Phillips

Shell Shrinkers

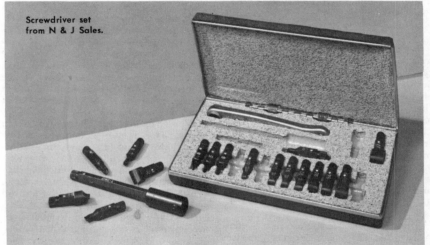

Screwdriver set from N & J Sales.

bits are available separately as well as other kits at $8.75 and $12.50.

Made of tough chrome-moly steel and properly hardened, these bits are non-tapered, truly parallel, so that full blade-to-slot contact is made. Correctly handled, they won't jump the slot or damage it, and they're interchanged in a moment.

For complete information write to N&J Sales, Northford, Conn. 06472—and tell 'em Pete Kuhlhoff sent you!

Shell Shrinkers

Made for use in 12, 16 and 20 gauge guns, the Shell Shrinker is made of the finest steel, chambered and rifled for 22 rimfires. In standard form they're just 2½ inches long, and they're usable in any shotgun—though admittedly a bit handier in single- and double-barreled break opens.

The rifled bore is offset from center —both front and rear—enough to let a certerfire firing pin hit the rim of a 22 rimfire round.

The Shell Shrinker can be inserted into the shotgun bore in any position, yet there'll be no trouble in firing unless the shotgun is so worn or altered that its own firing pin is out of normal position. However, much test shooting has shown that the Shell Shrinker seems to do better generally if the offset bore is placed at the top or bottom of the chamber.

Still, it's best to experiment a bit as we did with our sample Shell Shrinker to determine which orientation is best—we found that both group size and point of impact could be altered and bettered, by making a few trial shots with the SS unit in varying positions. Only a dozen or so shots are required.

The Shell Shrinker has been found very useful in checking shotguns to determine just where the shot pattern is hitting, but it's also a useful device for small game and pest shooting. To achieve the same point of impact each time the SS is removed and replaced,

just remember its position in the shot barrel—or make a small zero mark at the edges of both shotgun chamber and SS bore.

On special order similar Shell Shrinkers can be had chambered for 38/357 or 44 Spl./44 Magnum loads, in which case the SS bores are centrally located, of course. No, the bullets of these won't hit the bore of the shotgun!

22 rimfire shotshells don't work very well in rifled arms, so there is also a smoothbored SS available for 22 shotshells that do much better in a shotgun because the long bore travel and the choke of the latter offer better shot control.

All of these Shell Shrinkers are available at small extra cost in a 5-inch length for use in break-open guns.

Standard length Shell Shrinkers for 22s are $12.50 each, the 5-inch lengths $14.95. Centerfire models are $14.95 in standard length, $19.95 in the 5-inch type.

The maker, of course, makes no claim for precision accuracy with the 22 rimfire-bored Shell Shrinker, nor did we get that kind of shooting, either. We tested only the 12 and 20 gauge devices (no 16 being available), and with only shotgun sights in use we had 5-shot 5 or 6-inch strings at 30 yards. Then, with a 1½x scope mounted on a slug-type 12 bore pump, we got the same size groups at 50-55 yards, though with some ammo they were bigger. Groups back at 30 yards, with the scope, dropped to 2-3 inches. With a higher power glass—admittedly not a normal thing on shotguns, and certainly not usual on any but deer slug smoothbores—groups would have been better, of course.

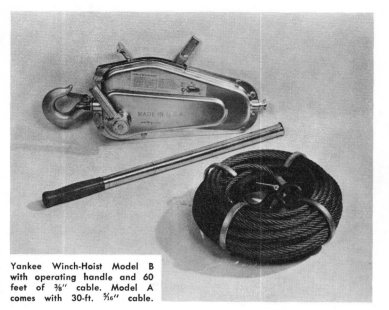

Yankee Winch-Hoist Model B with operating handle and 60 feet of ⅜" cable. Model A comes with 30-ft. ⁵⁄₁₆" cable.

Nevertheless, we feel the Shell Shrinker can be a useful, worthwhile item to throw into the kit or pocket—especially if some practice is done with it—for the occasion in the field when a shot might be wanted at a nearby varmint or the like. (J.T.A.)

Harry Owen

Harry Owen (Box 774, Sunnyvale, Cal. 94088) has a line of adapters made by Lothar Walther in Germany. Originally made only to fire 22 LRs in 222 Remington rifles, the line now includes many other calibers. The adapters are particularly useful for short-range target practice and for taking small game without all the blast, destruction and expense of full power loads. They're also useful for your wilderness survival kit. They occupy very little space, and their smaller cartridges means less survival-ammo weight to carry. There's nothing so discouraging as seeing a grouse or rabbit explode when hit with a 30-06 or the like at 50 feet when you needed that meat for supper. Here's the list:

To shoot 22 LR and 22 WMR: 221, 222 and 222 Mag., 223, 22-250, 22 Sav. HP, 220 Swift and 5.6x57mm.

To shoot 30 Carbine: 30-30, 308, 30-06 and 300 Win. Mag.

To shoot 22 Hornet: 22-250, 5.6x 57mm and 220 Swift.

All the adapters have been improved for '71, and all are $9.50 each, postpaid.

Walther adapters for shooting 22 LR or 22 LMR ammo in the 45 Gov't

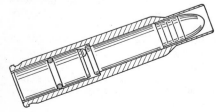

Auto or in pistols chambered for the 9mm Luger round include a 22 rimfire barrel and an auxiliary chamber. Price $32 for either.

Yankee Winch-Hoist

We've been giving some tough tests to a new winch—the push-pull lever type—that uses the draw-vise (or Chinese finger trick) principle. Two pair of forged steel jaws grip the cable, then releasing and grabbing as the lever is worked back and forth. Cable movement can be closely controlled, from a fraction of an inch to 9 feet a minute, depending on the load involved. Three shear pins protect the winch against over-load breakdown and make it safe—if a shear pin does let go, the load is held firmly regardless.

Two versions are made. The Model A is rated at ¾-ton capacity, comes with 30 feet of ⁵⁄₁₆" cable on a reel, while the Model B is a 1½-ton unit, comes with 60 feet of ⅜" reeled cable.

My first test with a Model B Winch-Hoist involved a heavy-duty pickup and a boulder about 4 feet wide—it was perhaps a lot wider than that below the ground where it was embedded. I'd wanted to get that big granite rock out of there for some time.

We braced the truck's wheels, attached the ⅜-inch cable to a chain around the boulder, and started winching. The result? We moved the 4000-lb. truck a foot sideways but the rock held firm! But so did the Yankee winch—that heavy strain had no effect at all.

An excellent tool—well made and sturdy—that many sportsmen/campers will welcome. It's light (17 lbs.), and thereby portable, and it'll pull, lift or lower in any direction.

Write to Wm. Greeley, Yankee Mechanics, Inc., Newport, N.H. 03773 for details and prices.

Thomas F. White—His Horn

We've done our best, but I don't think any photograph could give a clear idea of how well-done, how colorful and warm this beautiful horn is. The scrimshawing is so close in feeling and execution to 18th century work of this type that it will be hard to distinguish—some 50 years hence —between White's outstanding effort shown here and the handiwork of some 200 years ago.

White made this horn for John Bivins, Jr.—a man who makes a few remarkably fine Pennsylvania flintlock rifles. Depending on the extent of coverage and the layout, White's horns bring some $50, $100 or $250. White looks upon the horn pictured as being his finest effort—at least thus far—so you can guess at its price! In my opinion, a truly magnificent piece of art—and worth every penny that Bivins paid. I'm envious!

Williams Gun Sight

Several new products for 1970 have been announced by the Davison (Mich.) firm—all of them covered in the new *1970 Products Catalog*, a 28-page booklet that's free on request.

A new line of rifle scopes are now offered by Williams, from a straight 4x to 1.5-4.5x, 2-6x and 3-9x variables. These are covered in more detail in Bob Bell's department, elsewhere in this edition—as are the Williams new "Sight Thru" scope mounts, whose purpose we'll leave you to guess at for now!

What could be more fitting for a fancy grade shotgun than a genuine cultured pearl front sight? Williams now has 'em—⁹⁄₆₄ diameter—in two thread sizes, ³⁄₅₆ and ⁶⁄₄₈. The soft sheen of real pearl is ideal for poor light conditions—no glare, the target quickly caught, etc. Easily installed, of course, they're $3.95.

PRACTICAL PISTOL SHOOTING

the state of the art in 1970

A two-fisted shooting technique that develops skilled, combat-effective handgunners. Yet it's been long derided and condemned by the Establishment—military, police and civilian—with little or no justification.

by JEFF COOPER

The author demonstrates the standard Weaver hold, suitable for some 80% of combat pistol problems.

IN OUR AMAZEMENT at the scientific marvels of the modern age we sometimes overlook the fact that improvement in human capacity has almost paralleled the development of the machine. Particularly since WW II, the records of athletic achievement have been broken so frequently that we might wonder if our ancestors were really trying. Abstract barriers like the four-minute-mile have been shown to be illusory, and we are led to the conclusion that the potential of the human body, directed by the coordinating genius of the human mind, is practically limitless. In no field of endeavor is this more evident than in pistol shooting, where the events of the past 20 years have completely revolutionized the technique of the handgun, and have effectively altered the nature of the tool—in the hands of those who have followed and understood developments. Specifically, modern techniques

have changed the pistol from an emergency, last-ditch, arm's length, inconclusive instrument into a very serious weapon, demonstrably superior, in trained hands, to many of the long arms that were thought to have superseded it. We are now able to pose simulated combat problems for the pistol which cannot be handled as well with rifle, shotgun, or submachine gun. This would not have been thought possible in 1940, yet it is accomplished with weapons designed near the turn of the century. It is a human, not a mechanical, achievement.

The reasons for this lie in the abandonment of two traditional concepts: first, the separation of marksmanship standards from efficient weaponcraft; and second, the organizational system of training.

The traditional definition of a good pistol shot has always been based upon the ability to perform an unrealistic

task. Today, if one were to ask the president of the International Shooting Union to name the world's greatest shot he would name a man who almost certainly would stand no chance at all in what the pistol pioneers call a "serious" pistol contest. His ability to fire a two-inch group from offhand at 50 meters in 20 minutes with a 22 free pistol would be useful, but it would not be enough, because he would need the additional skill to dominate a major-caliber, fight-stopping instrument and he would need to dominate it quickly. As long as sidearm competition remains unrelated to the primary purpose of the sidearm, which is self-defense, mastery of such competition proves only that the champion can perform a difficult exercise in nerve control, not that he is adequately armed when carrying a pistol.

Similarly, if one were to ask a conventional NRA pistol shooter what con-

Above—At the Air Force Academy—Cooper illustrates the left-hand position from a barricade. ● Right—The author demonstrates the two-hand kneeling stance with the 45 auto.

stitutes excellent pistol shooting, he would probably suggest a score of 2600 on a three-weapon aggregate, which, while no mean feat, is only indirectly related to the tactical proficiency which can and should be "the object of the exercise."

An obvious proof of the foregoing is the very existence of the target pistol, as opposed to the duty pistol. If there is any difference at all between the two it is evidence that the task of the target pistol is not the same as that of the duty pistol. Such difference would suggest that the target pistol is thus not "for real."

The result of this tradition has been the practical elimination of the pistol as anything but a toy, and a total lack of motivation for the achievement of realistic handgun skill. Since there has been no reward or recognition for serious handgun ability—apart from per-

sonal satisfaction—such ability did not appear prior to the new era.

The second big reason for the retardation of real pistol ability has been the organizational concept of training. Serious weapon training is conducted almost exclusively by the military and police services, and they have special problems. In general, any organizational marksmanship program is designed to bring a specific percentage of trainees up to a minimal standard of proficiency in the shortest practicable space of time, using the least number of rounds per man. Any course of fire used for such training must be quite simple, not to say primitive, and it must be possible for even an uninterested novice to post about a 70% score on it. Such courses become standard, and high scores on them become evidence of a degree of mastery which does not really reflect the potential of

the marksman.

Consider the "Practical Pistol Course," originated by the Federal Bureau of Investigation and now used in various versions by practically all U.S. police agencies. This is a fairly easy course of fire, designed for 100% qualification at a score of 65%. A good shot, with a bit of time and motivation, soon learns to shoot it "clean"—at least most of the time. Therefore, when a contest is held, some method must be used to rank a considerable number of perfect scores among themselves. With traditional disregard of realism this is normally done by placing a small "X-ring" in the center of the target to reward the tightest group, which, considering the ranges used in the course in relation to the Bureau's own statistical analysis of actual ranges in actual gunfights, is the wrong thing to reward. Tagging an adversary exactly on the

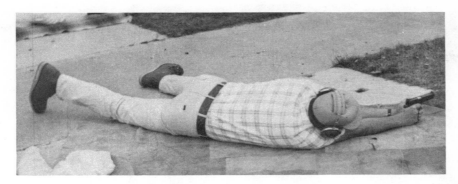

Left—Ray Chapman, combat champion, shows his own "roll-over prone" position, designed to relieve strain on the waist muscles ● Below—Bill MacMillan shooting the improved Police Pistol Course. Either hand may be used as long as feet remain in shooting box, insuring proper coverage.

wishbone is an excellent way to save your life, but not if he tags you first. The man who can place all his hits in the inner zone of a man-size target (either the 5-ring or the 10-ring, depending on who prints the target), in half the time allowed, is a more efficient policeman than the man who prints all Xs in the full allowance—and they are not likely to be the same man. If, on the other hand, the time allowance on the course is cut in half (as has been done with good success by private organizations), the novice trainee can probably not shoot it at all—hence the unrealistic X-ring.

If, then, we understand how practical pistol skill has been retarded by the twin obstacles of unrealistic standards and organizational training policies, the answer is apparent: Formulate realistic standards and promote unrestricted competition. This has been done, and the resultant forward leap in pistolcraft is the consequence.

Realistic Standards

What do we mean by realistic standards? In view of the tactical mission of the handgun, as used by soldier, policeman, or private citizen, we may start with the idea that a good pistol shot is one who can strike a precise, conclusive blow as quickly as possible

from an unready condition. If we study police surveys we must conclude that the realistic problem must feature a man-sized target at short range, a very limited time interval and probably very dim light. If we study the terminal ballistics of pistols we must further conclude that only heavy-duty cartridges, *fully loaded,* qualify for consideration. If we reflect that the prime virtue of the duty pistol is its instant availability in an unanticipated emergency, we must realize that unless a given pistol problem is commenced with the weapon holstered and safe, it is of limited value.

Hence the rules for new-style practical competition specify targets representing a human adversary or the vital zone thereof without meaningless small graduations in value. (If the ultimate in precision is asked, such target is simply moved out to 100 or 150 yards, emphasizing the fact that this is a rare pistol requirement.) The standard combat target is now a buff silhouette, 18″ x 30″, with a 10″ "K" ring centered. This latter represents the approximate stopping zone of a 38 Special on a full-grown man. Calibers are generally limited to 38 Special "and up," with full service ammunition or equivalent, though in view of the sorry terminal performance of this round, some clubs

specify 357 or big-bore only. Course variety is stressed, since no single course of fire can be varied enough in itself to constitute a definitive measure of skill. All strings of fire must start with the weapon holstered and safe, with the shooter's hands well clear of his equipment. (Whether you call this "quick-draw" or not is up to you. I dislike the term because of its connotations of triviality.) All course problems must represent a tactical

Left—One leg of the obstacle course. ● Right—A modern competition assembly, courtesy of Colt, Andy Anderson, and Smith & Wesson (sights).

Ray Chapman firing stage 1 of the improved Police Pistol Course: From left—Draw; fire 6 shots, reload; fire 6 more without using the master hand, which is presumed disabled. Doctrine holds that the only reason for shooting with one hand is the loss of the other. Time: 12 seconds inclusive. Note empty magazine falling in air (No. 3) as replacement is inserted. Chapman has all shots within K5-5X vital area.

reasonable situation which might actually arise, and which might be solved by the skillful use of a handgun. These, we feel, are realistic standards.

What do we mean by "unrestricted" competition? We mean that, subject to the foregoing "power floor," a competitor should be handed a reasonable problem and permitted to solve it in his own way. His weapon type must not be specified, as long as it is safe and practical. His style of shooting must be left up to him, as long as he hits in the time allowed. He may not be told how to load his weapon, or what position to use, or what procedure to follow in the handling of his piece (except as regards safety technique). Unlike a student undergoing a training procedure, he must be free to use his best judgement and succeed or fail by his own route.

The merits of this are obvious. As long as a man is *required* to use a certain procedure, we will never know if another might not be better. Conventional pistol training and competition has in the past flatly required the competitor to conform to a set of detailed rules which limited his hitting ability for no evident reason. Practical competition gives the contestant a very free hand and encourages innovation. If there is a better way, we want to know what it is, and practical competition has in this manner discovered a whole drawer-full of better ways.

Take the matter of stance and position. The ISU says "Position: Standing, gun held in one hand only, the other hand and arm being used in no way to support the gun." Why? Well, because the pistol was originally conceived as a firearm to be used by a horseman who needed one hand free to control his horse. Also because pistol contests are sporting events with only an indirect concern with the practical problems of combat. Also because "It's just our policy." Actually, of course, there is exactly as much reason to shoot a pistol with one hand as there is to swim with one arm. It's a matter of understanding just what you are trying to accomplish.

But the ISU is not the only wrench in the gears of progress. Current U.S. police trainers permit the use of both hands, but on the close-range stages of the PPC (practical pistol course) they require the pistol to be held at diaphragm level or below, which gives rise to the curious two-hand-belt-high position now seen on magazine covers. I am not without experience in this field, yet I have thought and thought without being able to postulate any conceivable circumstance in which this position could make any sense. If you have time to use two hands (and you do in nearly every case) you have time to come to eye level. If you haven't time to come to eye level you haven't time to use two hands. If the rules encourage a useless technique, the rules are wrong.

In any case, unrestricted competition developed the two-hand-grip, in its most sophisticated form known as the "Weaver Stance." As used by the masters, it is not a noticeable aid to accuracy, but it is absolutely essential to proper swing and burst control, two subjects that would never come up in old-fashioned pistol shooting. A real expert at the ISU game can shoot from offhand just about as well as the pistol will—he's close to a machine rest with that one unsupported arm—but only if he is granted an unrealistic gift of time. Such a performer need only try the International Rapid course—with a fully charged big-bore pistol—to see my point.

Combat Practice

I have claimed a good deal as the product of this new departure in pistol practice, which may be called "practical" or "combat" shooting. Perhaps I should illustrate. To use a widely known example, the new clubs now shoot the P.P.C. of the police circles

Combat pistol competition produces personalized weapons. The 45 Auto is the most favored piece.

in just half the standard time allowance. and clean it. Of course, we shoot it "free style." The Advanced Military course, on which 455 x 500 was originally considered "expert" performance, is now regularly fired without loss of a point. In the 1967 championship match, Ray Chapman completed it with the loss of just two K's in 50 shots. In 1966 the same man (who is probably the greatest pistol shot now in competition) fired a perfect score on the Mexican Defense Course, including the California modification, for the first time in competition, though this had been done before in practice. The Running Man match has by now become a centering contest—a mere "possible" won't get you standing room. And the "Balloon Bust" now calls for *consistent hits* (say 4 out of 5) on a 12″ target at 7 yards at under six-tenths of a second—including time to react to the firing signal! (There will be those — there always are — who will claim this is no special trick. Every August in California there's $500 that says it is.)

In essence, the polished combat shot is not necessarily more accurate than the traditionalist—from offhand he may even be a bit less so—but he strikes a much heavier blow and he strikes it much, much quicker. Hence the motto *Diligentia, Vis, Celeritas* (accuracy, power, speed), which is represented by the DVC monogram on most club insignia. (The combat shot does not shoot from offhand in any event since it is an unrealistic position.)

The value of practical pistol competition would be negligible if only a few super champions had been able to profit by it. After all, a man who starts with talent and develops it for a lifetime can eventually stand on the tip of his index finger. Its real contribution lies in its discovery of systems and techniques that can make the average man about 5 times as efficient as he might otherwise be. Partly because the discovered techniques are inherently superior, and partly because combat shooting is more "fun," newcomers to the game develop with astonishing speed. As an example, one-third of the

entrants in the 1967 Military contest at Oceanside, Calif., kept all their shots in the black on the NRA target at 50 yards—with heavy caliber pistols. Some of these shooters were old hands, of course, but many were not. After over 10 years of observing and competing in practical competition in California, I can sincerely state that the system we have developed makes more men better shots quicker than any other now in use. One season's shooting, necessarily spread out enough so that it could be duplicated by a short program of intensive training, can turn a reasonably well-coordinated novice into a very sharp pistolero, and give him the confidence in his sidearm that is so often lacking in our soldiers and policemen.

Now if all this is true, and I believe I can prove that it is, it seems only reasonable to ask why it has not been accepted and acted upon by all users of handguns—military, police, or civilian. There are several answers. Probably the most significant is that the degree of experiment and innovation essential to the new method makes it necessarily a civilian development, and there is a strong popular belief that the combative use of firearms is not an acceptable study for civilians. The services might possibly evolve a realistic set of marksmanship standards in time, though this does not seem likely, but they could hardly abandon the organizational concept of training. Civilian marksmanship is organized in this country by the National Rifle Association (may its shadow never grow less!), but the NRA wages a continuous defensive war against the anti-gun element and simply cannot sanction a type of civilian marksmanship that is frankly weaponcraft as much as it is competive sport. The police, in the main, are made uneasy by the thought of non-uniformed citizens radically surpassing them in practical handgunning, though many prominent combat shots are police officers; and the military are only vaguely interested in pistols, which obviously do not win wars.

Consequently practical pistol competition is still an orphan, despite the many gifts it offers to established marksmanship. Not only is it not accepted; it is often actually resented. Last year a noted ace who holds the rating of "combat master" was assigned to Viet Nam as a civilian police instructor. His skill was naturally quite evident and he was asked to demonstrate it at the annual pistol championships. His performance was as spectacular as one might expect, and the Vietnamese were delighted. However, his superior, who was of the traditionalist persuasion, did not wish to put this skill to use. He did not even congratulate his new assistant on his work. He growled "So that's your game!," turned his back, and walked away. Reminds one of the initial welcome the rear-engined Grand Prix cars got at Indianapolis.

Obstructionists are prone to condemn practical shooting as "dangerous," but this condemnation is speculative and not borne out by observation. Accidents can happen, but they are not inherent in the game. Organized combat shooting had one minor injury in 1955, none since.

As of this writing, active practical pistol competition programs are in force in Southern California and in the Philippines. The Southwest Pistol League (it was the Southwest *Combat* Pistol League until the incorporation authorities blanched at the fearful word) runs things in the U.S., and the Western Visayas Combat League on Negros Island, the Philippines. The Northeast Combat Pistol League is well started in New England and there is some response from Australia. Individual enthusiasts are scattered throughout the U.S., and there are some in Mexico, but it will probably be at least another 10 years before a really well-knit, nation-wide organization can be expected. Meanwhile the pioneers continue to study the problem, to improve procedures, to recruit newcomers, and to polish their own skills. We hope that we won't have to wait so long to be asked for our help that we will be too old to grant it. ●

For Long Distance Gunning
CALL XXM

An introduction to Winchester—Western's premium shotshells, their high density loads now called Double X Magnums.

by WALLACE LABISKY

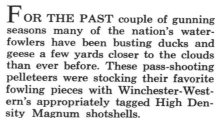

FOR THE PAST couple of gunning seasons many of the nation's waterfowlers have been busting ducks and geese a few yards closer to the clouds than ever before. These pass-shooting pelleteers were stocking their favorite fowling pieces with Winchester-Western's appropriately tagged High Density Magnum shotshells.

These initial loads were in 2¾" magnum persuasion, 12 gauge only, with 1½-oz. shot charges in the two most popular shot sizes for distant work—2s and 4s.

At that time the story was that 3" 12s carrying the super-potent 1⅞-oz. shot charge would follow shortly, and 20-bore magnum shooters were hopefully gazing into their crystal spheres for a glimpse of a 3" offering in that bore size. But to date we have not seen any of the extra-long HDM loads, nor has there been any word from W-W as to what is holding up the show. There obviously is a snag of some kind, one we hope will soon be cleared away.

Just how superior are the new HDM shells? Well, if my pattern board work is any criterion, you will probably swear that dyspeptic Old Betsy has undergone a miraculous cure. If your full-choke tube is now throwing a 70% pattern at 40 yards with the regular Mark 5 loads, you can look for 80% patterns with the

HDM fodder. In other words, roughly a 10% increase is in store, right across the board.

The extra performance built into the HDM shotshells is based on the very same approach that W-W adopted some years back when they upgraded their buckshot loads. A finely granulated polyethylene is employed to fill the pellet interstices, and in addition a conventional plastic sleeve surrounds the shot charge.

Several test loads in both shot sizes were broken down for a close look at the loading details. The use of the poly filler material represents the one and only difference to be found between the HDM offering and the regular Mark 5 loads. All other components are identical, including the hull, this being the exceptionally strong compression-formed plastic job with integral basewad. Crimp is the usual 6-segment fold closure with heat-sealed center "plug."

The height and style of the brass head on the short magnum 2s also parallels that found on the regular Mark 5s, but the short magnum 4s wear brass without the familiar W-W cannelures and with a different headstamp—this reading "W-W" above and "12 GAUGE" below. It is assumed that the latter style will eventually become standard on all HDM shells.

The shot charges run highly uniform in both weight and pellet count. The shot itself is brightly polished and of excellent quality in terms of roundness. Powder charges, too, proved admirably uniform; this came as no surprise because the free-flowing properties of Ball propellants are especially conducive to minimal variations in charge weight.

Being something of a handloading nut, I was anxious to learn the amount of granulated polyethylene that W-W uses with the 1½-oz. shot charge. Give or take a few tenths of a grain, this levels out roughly at 19.0 grains for both shot sizes.

What specific role does the plastic sawdust play? Its purpose is solely that of alleviating pellet damage that occurs when the expanding powder gases impart that initial push to the shot charge.

Even with the "slow" propellants that are used for heavy shot loads, this jolt is of such magnitude that many pellets become misshapen as they are jammed against one another. Those near the base of the shot column fare much worse than those near the top. Once the shot charge clears the muzzle, the damaged pellets quickly begin to stray from the shot cloud. Obviously, the greater the number of damaged pellets, the larger the loss in pattern density.

A simple plastic sleeve encircling the shot charge is of value in eliminating pattern-wrecking pellet dam-

The Double X Magnum Mark V protects shot pellets against in-bore damage with both a polyethylene collar and a special non-abrasive filler that surrounds and cushions the shot.

age, but it helps only the comparatively few pellets that are in bore contact. As a means of preventing pellet jamming the sleeve is largely ineffectual. It is in this latter realm that the plastic sawdust pays generously for its keep, proving a buffering action that goes a long way in retaining pellet roundness.

As we have seen, the shot pellet that escapes deformation is the one that contributes to pattern density out at game-killing distances. In addition to a flight path that is more true, the undamaged pellet also has a lower rate of velocity loss. Thus a two-fold fringe benefit accrues—a shorter flight time and a bit more striking energy at the target.

Another improvement in external ballistics shown by the HDM loading, and which apparently stems from the use of plastic sawdust, is a smaller variation in load-to-load pattern density. For example, in one series of 5-shot 40-yard tests, using an improved modified barrel (.026″ choke constriction), the HDM short magnum with 2s registered a variation of just seven pellets (5%) between high and low patterns (based on the traditional 30″ circle). In contrast, the regular Mark 5 short magnum (same shot size) fired for control purposes gave an extreme spread of 33 pellets (24.6%).

Using the same barrel with 4s, the HDM loading gave an outstandingly low spread of five pellets (2.4%), as compared to 13 pellets (6.2%) for the regular Mark 5 fodder.

The loading which gives a rock-bottom extreme spread has much more value than simply looking good in a pattern summary table. Its advantage in actual gunning practice is that it is a consistent performer in terms of maximum effective range. Flipping the coin over, the loading which delivers erratic percentages lacks reliability at any distance beyond the effectiveness of its weakest pattern.

But that's not all. There is still another side to the HDM story—a

factor sometimes overlooked when assessing the capability of a barrel/load combination for extreme-range gunning. It is simply this: the high-percentage pattern is far from being the whole ball of wax. Pellet distribution is also a factor of paramount importance.

The ultimate in a long-range pattern can be defined as one which combines an extremely high percentage, or efficiency, along with a strong concentration of pellet hits in the *central* area. For a given percentage, such a pattern will chalk up kills at an appreciably greater range than will the pattern which features *balanced* pellet distribution.

Thanks to the buffering action of the granulated polyethylene, these HDM loads do, indeed, toss out patterns with strongly dense centers. As such, the HDM loading measures up to its intended purpose, but in meeting those requirements it imposes a handicap for gunning at moderate ranges.

Consider, for example, my tests with the short magnum 4s. At 40 yards the improved modified barrel was averaging better than 80%, with roughly 55% or two-thirds of the total count printing in a 20″ circle. That left the edges of the 30″ circle with thin, ragged coverage. Needless to say, a perfect hold at that range would just about reduce a duck or a goose to pulp, while a sloppy hold could easily result in either a cripple or a clean miss.

For any gunning under 50 yards the HDM fodder is too efficient; I believe, that the standard Mark 5 loading, delivering more balanced pellet distribution, shapes up as a more suitable choice. But for the pass-shooting *artiste* who considers a 45- or 50-yard chance as so much stale bread, who gets his jollies from watching that webfoot fall and fall and fall, the HDM loading is made to order. In this realm of special use, it seems destined to gain overwhelming approval. ●

Case Capacity Measurement

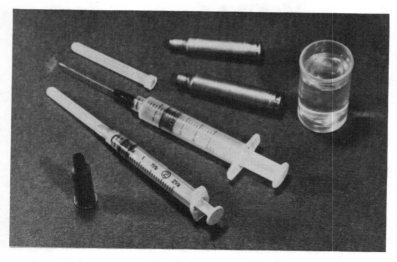

Fig. 1. Disposable plastic hypodermic syringes facilitate cartridge capacity measurement.

A new and simple technique that results in top accuracy for both gross volume and bullet-depth volume.

by HAROLD O. DAVIDSON

MEASURING cartridge case capacities is one of those simple but tedious tasks. The standard method involves weighing the empty case on a powder scale—easy enough. Then the empty case is filled with water, usually with an eye-dropper, put back on the scale carefully, and weighed again. The difference between the two weights, obviously, is the *gross* capacity of the case (without allowance for the space taken up by the seated bullet) expressed in grains of water. The result may be converted into volumetric measure (253 grains = 1 cubic inch; or, 15.4 grains = 1 cubic centimeter). However, in designing his sliderule "Computer for Handloaders" Powley thoughtfully calibrated it directly in grains of water to avoid the need for this conversion.

The trouble with this procedure is that it takes considerable fussing around to get 5% accuracy, and a great deal of care to do substantially better than that. One reason is that the law about water "seeking its own level" doesn't apply over small surfaces. Capillary forces cause the water to reach the mouth of the case at the outside edges before the case is full, giving a concave shape to the surface. Surface tension then allows the case to be overfilled without spilling. These two effects can produce a variation of several grains in apparent capacity. The fact that the drops from an average eye-dropper run about a full grain in weight doesn't help matters either for the handloader seeking maximum precision. These difficulties are easily avoided by using the right tools for the job; which in this case are a couple of disposable plastic hypodermic syringes obtainable from the family physician. The most useful sizes are the 2½ and 5cc graduated syringes shown in Fig. 1, although the 1cc syringe may also be useful. (One cubic centimeter equals .061 cubic inch and one cc of water weighs approximately 15.4 grains.)

The syringe permits rapid filling of the case, yet with such close control that consistently exact measurements are easily made. The majority of handloaders and cartridge collectors, however, have no interest or need for tenth-of-a-grain accuracy in measuring case capacity. For most purposes 5% accuracy is entirely adequate, and this can be achieved without using the scales at all. If the syringe is filled initially to exactly its graduated capacity, the volume of water expelled to fill the cartridge case can be read off directly from the syringe. The con-version scale with this article makes it easy to convert the results into grains of water (for use with the Powley computer) or cubic inches.

Gross Versus Net Capacity

The methods of capacity measurement we've just discussed are all concerned with gross capacity because this seems to be the easiest measurement to make, accurately. To determine net capacity—that is, the volume actually available for powder and its initial combustion—it's necessary to subtract the space taken up by the part of the bullet that's seated into the case. Obviously, the deeper the bullet's seated, the less the net capacity of the case will be. Since *net* capacity is the figure that must be used with the Powley computer (and with

Table 1

Factors for Reduction in Case Volume per Hundredth-inch of Seating Depth

Caliber Nominal	Actual inches	Cubic in. (in.³)	Cubic Centimeters (CC)	Grains water, (gr. H₂O)
22, 5.56mm	.224	.00039	.0065	.10
243,6mm	.243	.00046	.0076	.12
25	.257	.00052	.0085	.13
264, 6.5mm	.264	.00055	.0090	.14
270	.277	.00060	.0099	.15
280, 7mm	.284	.00063	.0100	.16
7.35mm	.300	.00071	.012	.18
30, 7.62mm	.308	.00074	.012	.19
303, 7.7mm	.312	.00076	.013	.19
32	.321	.00081	.013	.20
8mm	.323	.00082	.013	.21
338	.338	.00090	.015	.23
348	.348	.00095	.016	.24
35	.358	.0010	.016	.25
375	.375	.0011	.018	.28
44	.429	.0014	.024	.37
458	.458	.0016	.027	.42

See text for instructions in using this table.

other techniques involving loading density) it might seem that we've taken a backhanded approach to the problem.

The direct approach to net capacity measurement may appeal to some reloaders, so we'll take a moment to explain it before describing how adjustments for seating depth are made in using the indirect method that we prefer. To measure net capacity directly one first determines the combined weight of an empty case and a bullet of the type to be used in a particular load. Then the case is filled approximately full of water, and the *same* bullet used in the first step is pressed into the case to the depth at which it will normally be seated. This should be done very slowly so that the excess water is forced out around the bullet without developing so much hydraulic pressure as to expel the primer or deform the case (it's easiest to do this using un-resized fired cases) The whole works—case, water, and seated bullet—is now weighed. Finally, by subtracting from this total the previously determined weight of bullet and case one finds the net case capacity in grains of water. The direct

243 Winchester brass is 54.6 grains of water. A glance at Table I tells us that each hundredth of an inch of seating depth of a 6mm bullet displaces a .12-grain of water. Thus, for a seating depth of .25-inch (25 hundredths) the adjustment factor will be: 25 (hundredths) x .12 (grains of water per hundredth) = 3.0 grains. Hence, the net case capacity is 54.6 − 3.0 = 51.6 grains of water. Increasing the seating depth to .30-inch would give us an adjustment of 30 x .12 = 3.6 grains, and a net capacity of 54.6 − 3.6 = 51 grains. Note that a change in seating depth did not require a repetition of the water filling and weighing process, as would have been required using the direct method.

In 243 the factor for cubic inches is .00046; for cubic centimeters, .0076.

From the example just given we see that the indirect method of determining net capacity is really quite simple. To summarize: we take the desired seating depth of the bullet in hundredths of an inch, and multiply this figure by a factor selected from Table 1. This result is subtracted from the gross capacity that we've previously

this result by 100 to get the final answer in grains of water; or, multiply it by .39 for cubic inches; or by 6.44 for cubic centimeters. Summarized as mathematical formulas we have:

Correction factor = $100\ L\ (D_1{}^2 - D_2{}^2)$
for grains of water
Correction factor = $.39\ L\ (D_1{}^2 - D_2{}^2)$
for cubic inches
Correction factor = $6.44\ L\ (D_1{}^2 - D_2{}^2)$
for cubic centimeters.

Now let's run through a quick example to see how this works. Assume we've got a 6mm (D_1 = .243) bullet with a boat-tail section .20-inch long (L) tapering to .205-inch diameter (D_2) at the base. We proceed with the calculations as follows:

Step 1: Squaring D_1 = .243x.243 = .058049
Step 2: Squaring D_2 = .205x.205 = .042025
Step 3: Subtracting $D_2{}^2$ from $D_1{}^2$ = .016024
Step 4: Multiplying by L   x .20
                          .0032048
Step 5: Multiply by 100 to get
        grains of water   x 100
                          .32 grains

Going back now to our previous ex-

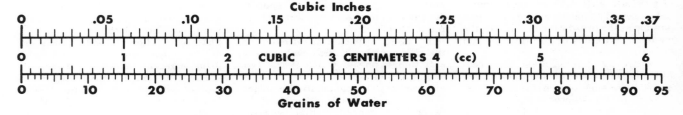

Cubic Inches

0   .05   .10   .15   .20   .25   .30   .35   .37

0   1   2   CUBIC   3   CENTIMETERS   4   (cc)   5   6

0   10   20   30   40   50   60   70   80   90   95

Grains of Water

Cartridge Capacity Conversion Scale

method is a perfectly good one. However, each new bullet and each change in seating depth means a repetition of the entire procedure. Let's see how the indirect method cuts down on the work. We'll look first at square-base bullets.

No matter what the nose shape or weight of our bullet might be, the part seated within the case is always the same shape—a simple cylinder. As we learned in high school math, the volume of a cylinder is the area of its base (d²/4), where d is the diameter, times the height (which in this case is the seating depth). Since the area is the same for all bullets of a given caliber, it's an easy matter to work up one reference table (Table I), which gives the true diameter for all popular calibers. To make matters still easier our table will include the proper conversion factors so that we need only measure the seating depth in hundredths of an inch and multiply this result by the appropriate number from our table to find the correct adjustment factor in terms of cubic inches—or cubic centimeters—or grains of water. Let's run through an example.

A typical gross case capacity for

determined, and which will always be the same no matter what choice of bullet or seating depth we make. This is the procedure for flat base bullets. It may also be used for boat-tail bullets, even though such bullets take up slightly less volume for a given seating depth than regular flat base bullets. Because of this there'll be a small error. However, it'll be consistent from round to round. Furthermore, the error will be on the "safe" side since actual net capacity will be somewhat larger than we calculate it to be.

Correction for Boat-tails

If we want to find out how much the error will be and, perhaps, make an additional adjustment to correct for it, the following procedure may be used. First, take the main bullet diameter in inches, and call this value D_1. Then measure the base diameter and call this D_2. Finally, measure the length of the boat-tail section from the point where the taper begins to the base, and call this value L (also in inches). Now, square D_1 (multiply by itself) and subtract from this value the square of D_2, and multiply the resulting difference by L. Multiply

ample of a 243 Winchester with bullet seating depth of .30-inch, we see that use of our assumed boat-tail bullet would give us about 51.3 (51 + .32) grains of water net capacity instead of the 51 grains that we'd get with a flat-base bullet. As previously noted, this is hardly enough difference to bother with.

Summing Up

We've described two methods of determining gross capacity of cartridge cases. The weight of water method will generally be the most accurate. However, the direct volumetric method using calibrated plastic hypodermic syringes is easier, and accurate enough for some purposes. To find net capacity, the volume taken up by the part of the bullet seated within the case must be subtracted from gross capacity. This adjustment is easily found by multiplying an appropriate factor from Table I by the bullet seating depth. This method works for all flat-base bullets, and gives an approximation for boat-tail bullets that's safe and adequate for almost any purpose. However, a correction factor formula for boat-tail bullets is also provided. ●

the Air Rifle...

With every passing month, more and more air arms make the scene—long guns and handguns, rifled and smooth bore, pneumatic, gas and spring operated. Here's a comprehensive and trustworthy guide out of the maze, from low-cost plinker to top-dollar precision target rifles.

A FINE AIR RIFLE offers manifold uses. The pleasure derived from any arm depends greatly on the amount and kinds of shooting one can do with it.

In my air gun business I'm occasionally surprised at the limited air arms knowledge shown by some customers, people otherwise familiar with firearms. I'm asked to help in selection, but there's a broad area to be covered when you consider caliber choice, models and the three distinctly different methods of pellet propulsion among today's air arms.

Those smitten by the pneumo-bug come from all walks of life, and their reasons for wanting an air rifle are varied: (a) Safer, economical gun training, target practice and plinking. (b) Easier availability of shooting area, be it home, garage, back yard or field. (c) Vermin and pest killing and small-specimen collecting. One man has an impossible cat problem; another has woodpeckers working his house trim. Still another buys the most massive match model he can get. Not to shoot, mind you, but to hang on the wall because "It looks so impressive."

For their first air gun many affluent buyers are drawn to the glamorous match models, only to find later that they're low-powered specialty tools, limited to their intended purpose—precision target shooting at the official ISU 10-meter range. I always try to suggest the lighter-weight, lower-cost, higher-powered sporting variety for the tyro because my experience, logic and sales indicate that for the great majority of new, as well as for veteran

enthusiasts, the better grade sporting air rifles come closest to filling the all-round spot.

To avoid disenchantment later on, the shopper should first evaluate several things, one of which is the type of propulsion he thinks best suited to his needs: CO_2, pneumatic or spring. There is a trade-off of features between them. Since the three types *are* in successful use that's proof enough that no one system is the complete ideal, which each manufacturer or the sometimes over-zealous salesman would like you to believe.

If serious target work or competition is the goal, then a match grade should be selected. This would most likely be a spring type, but it doesn't have to be the so-called "recoilless" versions. These latter have opposing pistons or other methods to counteract the slight spring surge felt when firing, a recent refinement. Those who are experts can fire comparably tight groups without this feature. Try to test both types before deciding if it is worth the extra cost. The mere psychological aspect of sophisticated equipment helps the performance of some shooters.

Ammunition

While it is best to be guided by the manufacturer's recommendations on the type of pellets to use, many tests

S&W Air Rifle

Smith & Wesson's new Model 77 single-shot air rifle combines lever-action loading with pump-up compression via a lever that hinges below the barrels. Some 10 strokes of the lever give maximum power, we understand—which seems like a lot. Made in 22 caliber only, at least so far, there's an automatic safety, and sights are fully adjustable. The 22" barrel is button-rifled, the twist one turn in 16 inches, right hand, and there are 10 grooves. The hardwood stock and fore-end are walnut finished, over-all length is 40 inches and weight goes 6½ pounds ● This is a man-sized air rifle, which we looked over briefly at the NSGA meeting in early 1970. The receiver alone is over 10 inches long, and its depth is over 2½ inches. Prices have not been announced, but will likely be around $40-$50.

Which One?

by LADD FANTA

Opposite page—A Sleeper—the Diana 27 (alias Hy-Score 807, alias Winchester 427). Acclaimed by many experts at home and abroad as the best buy in the Diana line, it has some other nice features besides good power, double-pull match trigger, fine accuracy and low price ● Regardless of the air rifle selected, its ultimate performance depends on the pellets used in it. These two bulk-pack tins show great extremes in quality. Tins with a high percentage of battered and misshapen pellets are a waste of money. Such pellets can be damaging to a spring gun if used regularly.

show that some other brand of pellet may give as good or better accuracy.

The importance of good quality pellets can't be over-emphasized. Regard-less of model or caliber, an air rifle can shoot only as well as the pellets used in it. Many air guns have a surprising affinity for a particular type of pellet. Experiment with different kinds to find optimum performance with *your* rifle, and then use that type for all of your shooting. Frequently, new shooters often make numerous sight changes before realizing that their promiscuous switching of pellet varieties is the cause. In some cases, a change of pellet style can spread group point of impact over 1" at 20 feet, to say nothing of group dispersion itself!

Air gun lead pellets are very vulnerable to damage. It is false economy to use any pellets if the box or tin you bought contains many irregular and misshapen rounds. Continued use of such battered pellets not only gives poor accuracy and lowered power in any gun, but in the spring type it does not provide the necessary braking action for the piston. They may be as damaging to the gun as if you were firing with an empty chamber.

European dimensional designations for 177, 20, 22 and 25 caliber pellets are 4.5mm, 5mm, 5.5mm and 6⅓mm, respectively. British equivalents are #1 bore (177), #2 bore (22) and #3 bore (25).

The large variety of Diabolo pellets available alters shooting characteristics of any gun. For example, the flat-headed match pellets have exceptional short range accuracy, punch paper holes in wad-cutter fashion. The round nose types produce slightly longer range and deeper penetration. Most Diabolo pellets weigh about 8.0 grains in 177, 14.0 in 22. However, weights vary between brands from 7.3 to 9.0 grains in 177 and 12.0 to 15.0 in 22, significantly changing muzzle velocity (MV) and impact point. In England many air gun buffs cast their own pellets, some of the interesting hunting shapes resembling a miniature spitzer type bullet.

Caliber Choice

The virtues of the 177 versus the 22 are oftentimes the subject heatedly debated among air gun advocates; somewhat akin to the small-bore, high-velocity fans versus the large-bore, lower velocity devotees. Size notwithstanding, if an old Webley Mk. II or

S&W Air Pistol

Smith & Wesson has a new gas-operated pellet pistol, the Model 78. As the photograph shows, there is a close resemblance to S&W's Model 41 target autoloader in 22 rimfire —and why not? The M78 CO_2 pistol is made in 22 LR only, its 8¼-inch barrel cut with 10 grooves, right-hand twist or one turn in 16 inches. The Patridge-type rear sight is fully adjustable, the sight radius is 10 inches, and the double-sear trigger is also adjustable. The safety is of cross-bolt type. The S&W 12.5-gram power cartridge lodges in the handle, and there's an option at will of low- or high power. Grips are of thumb-rest target type, in real walnut. We handled this attractive and well-balanced pistol for a few moments, but there's been no chance to test one on the range. Price, while not yet set, should be in the $40-$50 range.

Left—Crosman's Model 160 single shot air rifle is CO_2 operated (2 Powerlets), comes in 22 caliber only, sells for about $42 ● The Benjamin Model 362, a single shot gas-operated (CO_2) air rifle made in 22 caliber. See text for details.

other vintage 25-cal. air rifle in good condition should chance your way, there's no need to turn it down. Bimoco and HN in Germany and Champion in England still make these king size pellets. Champion pellets are currently U.S. marketed in 177, 20, 22 and 25 caliber, all of round-nosed pattern.

The 20-cal. (5mm) Sheridan pellets are truly unique. Their 16-gr. bullet-nosed construction, coupled with the maximum charge pump-up capability of the Sheridan rifle, produces the highest energy of any modern air arm.

Here is the formula for calculating muzzle energy:

$$\frac{MV^2 \times W}{450,000} = ME$$

Where:
MV = Muzzle velocity
W = Weight of pellet in grains
ME = Muzzle energy

In some brands of air guns the 177 version may compute to a greater ME than the 22, a difference that's often questioned.

The final selection must, of course, rest with the user, but it is a conceded fact that the 177, with flatter initial trajectory, is more accurate for target work at short ranges. Also, the bulk-pack 177 Diabolo pellets are cheaper than the 22s, and have a higher muzzle velocity. Various 177 match pellets are available in individually-partitioned boxes of 100; 22s are not. However, quite accurate shooting can be done with a good 22 and other bores when such excellent pellets as the Sheridan, RWS or HN are used; these may equal and even surpass 177 performance at extended ranges.

Despite the apparent advantages of the 177, the 22 has followers aplenty who are quick to point out that 22 pellets are easier to handle; they're not really *that* much more in cost, they're less fragile and, even with lower initial velocity (from an equivalent model of gun), when fired at an elevation of about 30° the 22 carries farther than the 177 because of the former's greater remaining velocity.

In short, the heavier 22 pellet does have better plinking effectiveness, dramatically demonstrable when it comes to tin-can rolling and the like.

Pneumatic, CO_2 or Spring?

Powerful spring-air arms have a definite lunge and recoil as the piston is driven forward to compress the air, the recoil starting while the pellet is traveling down the barrel. This does not occur in pneumatic and gas guns. Pneumatic arms, on the other hand, have problems deriving from the number and type of pump strokes and the valving. These conditions, conversely, do not occur in spring-air arms. Gas arms, as a further illustration, have problems deriving from valving, power source (thermal and CO_2 gas cartridge) variations, and from decreasing pressures as the power supply diminishes.

With some inherent attributes in each power system, the relative advantages and disadvantages are best presented when compared to one or both of the others. Actually, no matter how serious the shortcoming appears to be, with a little positive thinking one can almost always find a compensating good point. In light of this I'm going to divulge some of the less popular characteristics, with special emphasis on the spring guns, since these are currently enjoying the greatest upsurge in model variety and popularity.

The Pneumatic

The ever-popular pneumatic air rifles have, with their flexibility of power, the widest range of usefulness. This feature can be somewhat self-defeating if pumping is not performed uniformly, since shot-to-shot trajectory changes occur from variation in power whether intentional or inadvertent. Pumping must be consistent; not hard and fast one time, slow the next. It takes effort and practice to overcome this normal tendency. Those who persevere and truly become proficient then have a most versatile air arm. The market is limited to Benjamin,

Crosman and Sheridan.

The fine old series 300 Benjamin pneumatics have been replaced by the series 340. Although heralded as "new," there is only minor face-lifting, with the older not-so-safe safety redesigned. Not to be outdone, the Crosman 140 now has become the 1400, but here again, only minor changes. The Crosman self-cocking and air-lock prevention feature is made possible by using the blow-off system of air release when fired, but all at the cost of a progressively harder trigger pull with each successive pump stroke.

The Benjamin and Crosman pneumatics, both rather small in size, are best fitted for the youth.

The "in" crowd likes to refer to the Sheridan as the aristocrat of pneumatic air rifles. Of the three, it is the best proportioned for serious adult use and delivers top power. Let's take a closer look at air gun power in general and the Sheridan in particular.

In Great Britain, under the British Firearms Act of 1968, no one under 17 may buy an air gun or pellets, while those under 14 may legally use them only under the supervision of someone over 21. It is also illegal for anyone under 17 to have an uncovered air gun in a public place. So one might ask: Just how dangerous or even lethal are air guns? It is historical fact that pneumatic air rifles have been made which were powerful enough to kill man. The Austrian Girandoni pneumatic rifles of 51 caliber used against Napoleon's forces had full charge ME of 400 foot pounds! Some of the pneumatic air canes once popular on the Continent and in England were also quite potent; the round balls used in them had power on the order of 1.5 inches of wood penetration at 50 feet.

Something to think about in a more modern vein is an interesting note regarding tiny missiles and small muzzle energies, figures which can be compared to today's typical air gun powers: A recent military report mentions that the new Device 3F67A, a

Sheridan's 5mm under lever rifle—one of the finest pneumatic-type air rifles made. Great power, high accuracy, excellent construction and modest price make this rifle a top favorite. Peep sights, scope and mounts are available, with the basic rifle offered in two finishes—Blue and Silver ● The Sheridan air rifle, the world's most powerful commercially made air arm, uses its own unique 20-cal., 16-gr. bullet-shaped ammunition (left). Champion 20-cal. Diabolo pellets, of only 12.5 grains, give good accuracy and higher velocity with fewer pump strokes ● Sheridan offers two bullet traps. The Model 22, suitable for air rifle pellets and 22 rimfire ammo, is $12.50, with paper targets $1 per C. The other trap (not illus.) takes standard 10-bull 10½x12" targets, and is suitable for regular 38 Special handgun loads. It may be placed on its broad flat base or wall-mounted. $30.

5.56mm training cartridge for the M-16 rifle, fires a 5-gr. bullet at a MV of 1040 feet per second (fps). The 12 ft. lbs. of ME makes the bullet dangerous, and possibly lethal, at extremely close ranges. It is intended to be fired at targets only and all safety precautions must be exercised. Many of our present-day air rifles approach, and even exceed, this ME level. *All air guns should always be handled with the same gun safety rules observed with firearms.*

With chronographed muzzle velocities in the vicinity of 700 fps, the heavily-pumped Sheridan may develop around 20 ft. lbs. of energy. Add to this the fact that, unlike the conventional Diabolo air gun pellet, the solid-nosed, bullet-shaped Sheridan round has far greater penetration, thus allowing some rather unusual, but un-sportsmanlike, animal kills. Keep in mind that whenever any spectacular results such as these are quoted it is never mentioned how much additional game was shot at, wounded, and suffered a long agonizing death.

No manufacturer or thinking person condones the use of air rifles for large game, of course, but it is worth mentioning that the Sheridan has reserve power for the rabbits, squirrels and pests it was intended for, even at 60 yards or more.

Since trajectory changes occur from varying the M/V by the pumping charge, the purist might then ask what about accuracy, since it seems reasonable the rate of rifling twist would be optimized at some power level by the manufacturer. The following is a condensed table showing results from a Sheridan air rifle with receiver peep-sight.

Averages of 5-shot groups, in inches

Pumps	15 ft.	30 ft.	50 ft.
3	.24	.57	.78
4	.22	.55	.62
5	.32	.66	1.00
6	.71	.62	1.28
7	.90	.75	1.37

Obviously the 4-pump velocity produced the most accurate results. Most of us puff a little to get up steam for repeated 5- to 8-pump pneumatic shooting, and scores do suffer from accelerated heart beat. It has been demonstrated that the physical effort of pumping up for 10 or more target shots with a compressed-air arm in a limited period of time results in poorer scores than those made by the same shooter using a CO₂ arm, where the physical effort is avoided. To a lesser degree, this applies also to comparisons with the single cocking stroke of spring-air arms. We shouldn't

despair, though, since a popular pneumatic maker's ads once pointed out how beneficial the pumping exercise is for developing the shoulders!

By repeated pumping, the pneumatic can be charged with enough air to give higher velocities than either the spring or CO₂ types and with no recoil it is easy to shoot accurately (on a slow rate of fire basis). On the other hand, the spring gun needs only one spring-cocking movement as opposed to the multi-stroke pumping of the pneumatic; it has uniform power, faster delivery of shots and simplicity of action. This last point always brings up the delicate subject of the valves used in pneumatic (and CO₂) arms. Their integrity is always pointed to as some sort of Achilles' heel, deservedly or not.

The valves in a pneumatic rifle are the heart of the arm and, if not abused, can last almost indefinitely. Solvents and cleaning fluids may be harmful, and so are extreme pressures from exceeding pumping recommendations. People fail to realize this and there are always those who try to convert their pneumatic into a big game rifle via the strong arm method by over-pumping. Over-charging may spring both barrel and pump tube, may loosen the barrel, buckle the pump lever or linkage; crack the pump handle, may pressure-cut or heat-scorch valve seats and cause air locks. Today, manufacturers use the best possible synthetic material within cost limits for the inlet and outlet valves but are faced with design compromise. A hard valve seat material will withstand high pressures but may seep at low pressures. A too-soft valve seat material readily seals low pressures but is unable to take high pressures without grooving. This problem was solved years ago by using precise ball valves in the Sheridan Super Grade pneumatics, but had to be abandoned because of high manufacturing costs. However, the current Sheridans perform as well as their costly predecessors. They are built to stand all but completely unrealistic pressures, which are ballistically and, from the standpoint of physical effort, quite senseless.

Overly maintenance-conscious pneumatic owners sometimes create their own troubles with too much oiling of the pump, which will temporarily affect both velocity and accuracy. Scrubbing the barrel from the muzzle end is poor policy at any time with any form of arm, but especially so with the Benjamin and Sheridan, which have rifled brass/bronze barrels. Lead/bronze has a better coefficient of friction than lead and steel; normally it is not necessary to clean or oil inside them since they will not lead or rust.

There's a man in the front row who has had his eyebrows raised ever since the mention of brass/bronze material for rifled barrels used by Benjamin and Sheridan. The answer is NO, they will not wear out. These barrels will normally outlast the rest of the gun. The only way to hasten their end is by carelessness or stuffing the wrong kind of fodder through them—like darts, for instance

CO₂ Arms

Perhaps the most important thing going for CO_2 arms is their ease of shooting once the CO_2 supply is installed. Such rifles fire pellets propelled by a jet of carbon dioxide gas released when the trigger pull allows the impact hammer to open a gas outlet valve briefly.

The CO_2 arms have the closest resemblance to regular firearms handling procedures, thus making them best for training and the instruction of beginners. Since no barrel or pump manipulation is needed for firing preparation, the gun is most easily kept pointed "downstream" at the target area; a fast highly appreciated by instructors with novice youngster groups!

Until pressure drops off seriously, the CO_2 arms give reasonably consistent velocity, especially indoors or under normal room temperatures, and

Top—Hammerli's CO_2 Master Target pistol comes in 177 caliber only, has fully adjustable trigger, click sights, and an automatic gas-release system. Their "Single" 177 pistol, also CO_2 type, lacks the gas-release feature but is otherwise similar in performance and high accuracy ● The FWB Model 65 air pistol has the same fixed-barrel, side-lever system found in the FWS air rifles; the lever is on the left side, however.

the rate of fire is higher than a pneumatic's. All this is offset by higher shooting costs (for the CO_2) and lower power versus hard-pumped pneumatics and the stronger spring guns. The CO_2 gas gun is affected by temperature. They shoot with higher velocity when it's hot and considerably slower (than normal) in the cold. When a CO_2 gun is used continuously, the temperature of the gas chamber (reservoir) drops, reducing internal pressure or shooting power because this depends on the volume of gas pressure that escapes when the gun is fired. Allowing sufficient time between shots is the only way to get the most

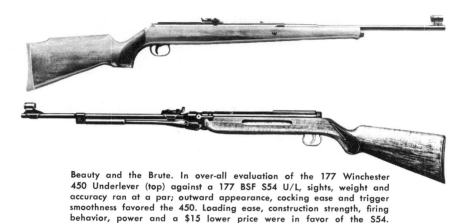

Beauty and the Brute. In over-all evaluation of the 177 Winchester 450 Underlever (top) against a 177 BSF S54 U/L, sights, weight and accuracy ran at a par; outward appearance, cocking ease and trigger smoothness favored the 450. Loading ease, construction strength, firing behavior, power and a $15 lower price were in favor of the S54.

uniform velocity results.

New owners of CO_2 arms sometimes get surprised when the "O" ring on the reservoir or fore-end plug is swollen as removed. This is caused by temporary absorption of CO_2 but waiting a spell between cartridge changes will allow the "O" ring to return to its original size. Oil or grease coatings on "O" rings catch grit and dirt particles, shortening their useful life. A fine material to use on "O" rings is MOS_2 powder, which leaves the surface dry and super-slick for easy conformability.

For those who like the CO_2, the Benjamin 362 and Crosman 160 are good little guns, but come only in 22 caliber. The more advanced target shot will insist on 177, and for him the match grade Hammerli 472 is available, along with the less frilly 471 Junior at less cost.

A minor advantage of pneumatic and CO_2 types is that they're odorless and smokeless on firing. The standard spring guns do produce a detectable smell, even a haze, after continual firing indoors.

Proper pellet seating is important for best accuracy. The single shot pneumatic and CO_2 guns usually have a projection on the loading bolt which chambers the pellet in the same position each time. The barrel-cocking spring gun depends upon the owner's good sense and choice of pellets for exact thumb pressure fit, drop-in-loose fit or snug fit. The use of a loading awl or thimble to push the pellet clear into the chamber can be a big help, otherwise the protruding pellet tail-section gets mashed.

Spring Guns

We'll discuss the more popular and handier sporting rifles first, although the basics are applicable to match arms as well.

First, it should be made clear that in all quality spring-compression air guns only the compressed air generated at the moment of firing is used as a propellant. No mechanical part of the arm (besides the bore) is ever in contact with the missile. The pellet

is *not launched* by a spring-driven plunger.

By far, the largest percentage of all spring-air pellet rifles made today are of the barrel cocking type. You snap the barrel down and it pivots on its hinge, exposing the breech for loading, the mainspring being cocked at the same time. Now insert the pellet into the chamber, snap the barrel shut (a spring-loaded detent provides automatic latching) and the rifle is ready to fire. These operations take only seconds, allowing a very fast rate of fire if desired. A variation has an "underlever" for cocking, is nearly as fast to operate, but has a small loading-port handle to negotiate for each shot; a small crossbolt is turned 90° from firing position to loading position and vice versa. This piece of precise machine work is the chief reason why the underlevers are more costly than similar barrel-cockers. The U/L design allows a fixed barrel-receiver relationship, obviating the breech-sealing problems that can occur with hinged-barrel designs. Anyone who wishes to, or must, use a peep sight or scope, should give preference to the U/L system, for the fixed-barrel design means more freedom from zero changes in sight settings. I don't recommend peep or scope use on barrel-cockers. Keep the air gun simple; it's intended for short range shooting anyway. The barrel-mounted factory sights are there for a good reason, they've evolved from years of experience by their makers, and in whose countries air rifles are serious business.

Those dead set on scope mounting the spring rifle should get a copy of *ARM Vol. 20*, an Air Rifle Headquarters publication. They also offer a whole series of helpful booklets on various imported spring-air arms. Even if your gun is not covered, the general information is applicable.

Is the spring gun the robust, trouble-free shooting iron as frequently envisioned because it has "fewer delicate parts?" Yes, the barrel-cocking spring gun can be a rugged brute, a wonderfully efficient

Right and left side views of the new Feinwerkbau M300. The rifle at top shows the Match stock (buttplate dropped) with pistol grip cap. The other FWB M300 shown has the Tyrolian stock, but also offers the same refinements and adjustability as the Match rifle. The M300, while basically the same rifle as the older M150, has been improved in its trigger system, stock design, lever and leverage, etc. The FWB M300 air rifle in a fine cutaway view. For a large full-color sectional view like this, with all major components keyed and described, write to Air Rifle Headquarters for the "FWB Company News/Winter 1968-69" booklet.

work horse in consistent power and accuracy—but it can have problems, too. For example, the little breech seal, so necessary but failure-prone if abused, neglected or overlooked, can cause low power, ultimate failure of other components and poor accuracy. Also, what the valves are to a pneumatic or CO_2 gun, the spring is to the spring-air rifle. Few industries require the diversified engineering knowledge that is required in the processing of springs. Many people consider a spring a simple component, but it is, in fact, often a very complicated part to design and make. Webley and Scott go so far as to factory-seal their replacement springs to ensure the genuine article for their products. Spring problems in any spring-air rifle arise from: (a) Dry firing without proper pellet in bore, (b) Leaving the gun cocked over a long period of time and (c) Cocking with unnecessary force, hard against the stop, or (d) The promotion of "diesel" firing.

Jerk, Jump, Kick

The slight spring reaction noted when firing a standard spring gun varies among different makes, sometimes among identical rifles. It is called by many descriptive names— recoil, recoil effect, jerk, jump, kick, spring-surge, firing harshness or vibration. Oftentimes, although unrecognized as such, it is a combination of normal firing pulse and vibration. While most annoying to some, and requiring some getting used to, others take it cheerfully, claiming that it lets you know "something happened." Perhaps the best word describing the

end result is "behavior." A well-behaved spring rifle is one you don't have to think about before, during or after firing. You simply aim and fire with just the slightest mental and physical effort. In general, the heavy match-target rifles of 9 to 12 pounds and low power are the best behaved. But if the ratio of spring-driving power and gun weight reverses, as in the sporting rifles, a combined recoil effect can make the gun very unpleasant to shoot if certain conditions exist. The powerful mainsprings can reach a state of resonance upon firing, producing vibrations that have a loosening effect on sights, scopes and bedding screws. In extreme cases—such as with the big Weihrauch HW35— this intensified vibration can actually sting the trigger finger.

With the exception of the "recoilless" match weapons, all spring-air guns have *some* jump, but a normal amount goes unnoticed after familiarization. Some manufacturers claim a "delayed" or "damped" recoil, accomplished by careful design in the relationship between piston speed, barrel length (resistance to pellet) and vent-hole size. The timing is such as to leave a slight cushion of compressed air as the pellet exits the barrel. This critical balance can be upset by a leaky breech seal, loose fitting or grossly underweight pellets and improper lubrication. The "feel" of a properly functioning, well-behaved spring-air rifle is a pleasant sensation; the firing is crisp, smooth, with no after-firing vibration.

While new, the original grease on the mainspring keeps vibration down

to a negligible level, but some manufacturers avoid substantial spring grease-coating because ordinary lubricant, especially when thinned out, eventually causes the very undesirable "dieseling." Besides, conventional greases and oils are not beneficial for the leather piston seals.

Many of the British air guns and the Winchester-Dianas come through practically dry. If their owners do nothing about the mainspring, they'll never enjoy the full potential of an otherwise well-made gun.

Firing any high-power spring-air rifle with a dry mainspring produces some after-firing vibration accompanied in many cases by an audible twang or tinny sound. These make even the better grade gun feel and sound as if solid construction is lacking, to say the least, and hardly instill confidence in the shooter—a vital factor.

Lubrication

I've tried various means of damping mainspring vibrations. One was coating of the spring, an expensive and involved way, while the other was application of a stiff, non-melting silicone compound, which is easier and works well. Results with the latter have been above my hopeful expectations, and sample testing by selected customers to check my findings has brought exuberant requests for more.

To treat the spring, it must be removed from the gun and all old lubricant wiped off. If it's dry, as many will be, an initial light dusting and rubbing with MOS_2 powder over the entire inside area is good insurance

The Slavia Models 620, Czech-made. This is a modest-cost, barrel-cocking, spring air rifle in 177—plain but sturdy, with rifling to highest standards. The man-sized 620 goes 6 lbs., is 43" long, offers a hard-hitting muzzle velocity of 650 fps with a single cocking stroke. The 624 (not illus.), 4 lbs. and 38½" long, gives 460 fps MV, sells for a bit less. Ask Fanta for details of these and any other air arms—complete literature, 25¢.

Czech-made barrel-cocking air rifle in 177 caliber, is of all-steel construction and the Poldi barrel has 10 grooves. About $32 from Continental Arms Corp.

against future fretting or galling. About ½-ounce of this tenacious material rubbed over the spring coils produces a very significant difference in smooth firing of the weapon. After-firing oscillations of the spring cease immediately, and if any of the stuff migrates to the piston seal, fine; it is an ideal lubricant/preservative for leather or synthetics, and the high viscosity resists dieseling.

I've been asked why I always specify an MOS_2 powder (Molykote Z, to be exact) or Molykote G, a paste-like grease containing over 60% Z powder, but don't advocate a dispersion, such as Dri-Slide, which some people consider a veritable cure-all.

The simple facts are that such dispersants contain MOS_2 particles averaging 1 micron in size, thus do not meet any military specifications. On the other hand Z powder particles averaging 12 microns, meet Mil-M-7866A specs for size and purity. For maximum effectiveness I've always found that Z powder or its compounds works best, and substantiation lies in Dow Corning's bulletin 06-027, which says of Molykote G paste: "Its chief component is Molykote Z powder, chosen not only for *preferred particle* size but also for its high quality." (Emphasis mine.)

Hand cast hollow-base lead bullets—177, 20, 22 or 25—for air rifles offer higher penetration. The well-made brass moulds have wood handles, can also be ordered in any shape, caliber or weight for other rifles or pistols. Pellet rifle moulds are $3-$5.50, plus $3.30 postage from L. E. McQuire, 76 Bela Grove, Blackpool, Lancaster, England.

Many imported spring guns are stocked in beech, or beech is optional. Beech makes a fine stock, so there is no need for concern if walnut is not available. Beech is a strong, dense and durable hardwood. Because it normally lacks the attractive figure frequently found in walnut, it is erroneously considered second-rate gunstock material. In fact, from a utilitarian standpoint, it surpasses walnut; few people know that beech is 16% more dense, 12.8% harder, 41% more shock resistant and has 14.7% greater shear strength.

There are so many sporting spring-air rifles to select from that the newcomer is hard put to make a choice between $13.95 close-out specials to $95.00 super-sporters. Price can be an indicator of quality, but only a rough one. Many suffer from *magnumitis* in going from firearms to air arms, with demands on power alone. This is a common mistake, and experience quickly teaches that other considerations are far more important. Likewise, it is pointless to worry about pin-point accuracy, attainable only in a machine rest, from a sporting air rifle.

When offhand ability makes hitting beer cans or the like easy at 30 yards, try 40 yards. With factory open sights, such targets become more challenging at 50-60 yards, bringing greater satisfaction than the same accomplishment with a 22 rimfire. There's really no excuse for limited proficiency with an air rifle because it is such an economical, year-round useful instrument.

Size, weight and other general data on the air rifles currently available are covered in the GUN DIGEST air gun section. Space here doesn't allow comprehensive comment on all suitable models, but we'll cover a representative sampling.

BSA—Birmingham Small Arms

The BSA underlever, recently re-designed, is not currently available in the U.S. However, the barrel-cocking BSA Meteor is, and deserves special attention.

If simplicity is the keynote of good design, then the Meteor should be an award winner in several areas. They reach the buyer in perfect shape by virtue of moulded-foam box. The new owner may be surprised to find that barrel and receiver are not blued, but carry an attractive black enamel finish. This is quickly forgotten as investigation reveals other interesting innovations: one screw only is required to hold the trigger guard and rear of action securely; self-centering piston seal; the crisp trigger is adjustable to a hair trigger if so desired; optional-height front post-sight inserts are available, and it's the only barrel-cocking air rifle made with a perfectly square standing breech; this assures shot-to-shot alignment by a fixed un-

derbolt stop, not by typical slanted face contact between barrel breech and standing breech. This permits the easiest flush-pellet loading and a soft, synthetic breech seal that is unique in being pressure responsive. Add all this to easy cocking, excellent power, quality rifling; broad, generously proportioned forearm, easy take-down (with English instructions) and it becomes evident why it is a good buy at $39.95. True, the new owner can expect to do some accurizing of his own by lubricating, adjusting sights, trigger, etc.

Bayerische Sportwaffen-Fabrik

The BSF firm has a full line of barrel-cocking rifles, ranging from best made miniatures to the most powerful S60, which has a certified muzzle velocity of 729 fps in 177, and 590 in the 22. The BSF S54 is their sturdy under-lever design with three stock options—Standard, Bayern and Match.

BSF makes guns in the best old world traditions, solid and strong, with no use of cost-cutting plastics or synthetics. The hinged-barrel designs all have double-detent breech closure and split cocking rods for easy cocking. A concurrent line, under the "Bavaria" name, starts with the tiny Bavaria 30 and ends with the rugged Bavaria 55, a short-barrelled version of the S60.

Stocks are of beech or walnut; an "N" after the model number stands for Nussbaum, meaning walnut.

For the magnum-power boys the BSF S60 and B55 are the most sought after for field use and hunting. The S54 U/L has S60-B55 power components, including the sturdy trigger assembly, while the U/L rod is rattle-free when in place by virtue of its self-centering, spring-loaded sleeve; this requires pulling back for both release-to-cock and return.

The S54 U/L rifles are more muzzle heavy than the barrel-cockers, but this gives a greater steadiness for aim control when shooting off-hand, in effect the same as the addition of a barrel sleeve weight to match-target rifles.

Slavia

From the great arms center in Brno, Czechoslovakia come the latest Slavia models 620 (177); 624 (177) and the 622 in 22. It is interesting to conjecture what—if given a rightful free reign after WW II—this beleaguered country might have produced in air arms today. In the years before WW II Brno produced some of the finest air rifles, in the form of trainers, ever made.

For serious adult use only the 620 should be considered, and it represents a good value at a rock-bottom price. The gun is simplicity itself functionally, and it's without any such embellishments as an eye-catching

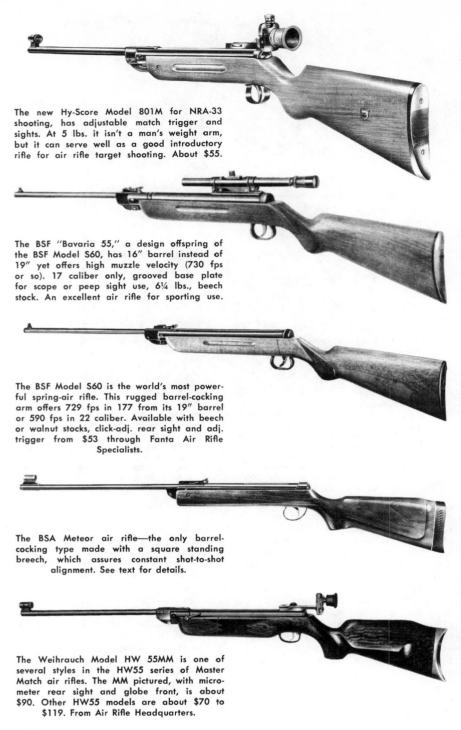

The new Hy-Score Model 801M for NRA-33 shooting, has adjustable match trigger and sights. At 5 lbs. it isn't a man's weight arm, but it can serve well as a good introductory rifle for air rifle target shooting. About $55.

The BSF "Bavaria 55," a design offspring of the BSF Model S60, has 16" barrel instead of 19" yet offers high muzzle velocity (730 fps or so). 17 caliber only, grooved base plate for scope or peep sight use, 6¼ lbs., beech stock. An excellent air rifle for sporting use.

The BSF Model S60 is the world's most powerful spring-air rifle. This rugged barrel-cocking arm offers 729 fps in 177 from its 19" barrel or 590 fps in 22 caliber. Available with beech or walnut stocks, click-adj. rear sight and adj. trigger from $53 through Fanta Air Rifle Specialists.

The BSA Meteor air rifle—the only barrel-cocking type made with a square standing breech, which assures constant shot-to-shot alignment. See text for details.

The Weihrauch Model HW 55MM is one of several styles in the HW55 series of Master Match air rifles. The MM pictured, with micrometer rear sight and globe front, is about $90. Other HW55 models are about $70 to $119. From Air Rifle Headquarters.

finish, swivels, etc. The good accuracy of these rifles is in no small measure attributable to the high quality rifling, perfectly finished right down to the neat muzzle crown, comparing favorably with much higher priced guns.

The simple non-adjustable triggers have been improved in later production. Because a rather novel method of barrel lock-up is used I've been keeping an eye on several local customer's guns for any indication of wear across the standing breech-face vent-hole section, since the spring-loaded detent wipes across this spot

on action closure. After months of use no signs of wear are evident.

The 620s are well-behaved, firing crisply and with a solidity of action-to-stock second to none. This is mostly due to the two forearm screws threading directly into carefully drilled holes in the receiver itself; not into those extended "ears" that are commonly welded or screwed to the action. Also, the rear action hold-down screw comes in from a rearward angle, pulling the action down snug and tight as no ordinary straight up method of screw attachment could do.

Webley & Scott

A top grade firearms maker is expected to have something better than average if he also makes air arms. However, the tiny W & S Ranger and Jaguar models can be discounted, and the W & S Falcon, a well-made barrel cocker of good power and balance has the unfortunate disadvantage of a non-adjustable trigger.

The W & S Mark III under-lever, however, is a superbly made air rifle that simply exudes quality in every respect. Pictures of it fail to reveal the beauty of finish and detail which gladden the connoisseur. The rich, dark walnut stocks are expertly proportioned, and the mirror-finished metal is unequalled at any price. Ever see a *tapered* barrel on an air rifle? To achieve its fine balance, the Mk. III has it; the only one in the business. The big wide trigger is single-stage adjustable, with a setting lock, and the loading-port lever detail is beyond belief—nothing can be that smooth! The rifling is top-notch and if ever needed, this gun comes apart easily, thanks to the English-language instruction booklet included.

The Mk. III has power, elegance and is extremely stable once accurized to the owner's wishes.

Hermann Weihrauch

Firearms production skills are reflected in the HW air arm line—their good triggers seem to be a company hallmark. For example, HW makes the inexpensive Arminius revolvers, which have surprisingly nice triggers considering the price range.

HW air rifles are all barrel-cocking, though some models have special barrel-locking contrivances in the form of manual barrel-release locks instead of, or in conjunction with, the usual spring-powered, cam-faced detent bolts.

The over-sized HW35E, the longest air gun made at 47" over-all, uses a spring-loaded, thumb-wrecking knurled button for barrel releasing prior to each cocking and loading. As · the salesman once said: "—if you ever lose your canoe paddle—."

The HW55MM Match series (not SF, MF) use an external locking lever, operating a half-round cam. Unfortunately the cams are not progressive (slightly eliptical) to take up for wear or possible less-than-perfect fit in production. The HW55MM and 55MF Match stocks are first class, and oftentimes shooters desiring more power will use the stronger HW50 series mainspring in their 55MM or 55MF to make up a hybrid match-sporter.

Diana

Diana air arms, Dianawerk Mayer und Grammelspacher, are marketed in the U.S. under Hy-Score and Winchester labels, each handling at least 10 different models. For serious sporting use the following three rifles are best. Equivalent gun cross-reference is as follows:

Diana	Hy-Score	Winchester
Model 27	Model 807	Model 427
177 & 22	22 only	22 only
Model 35	Model 809	Model 435
177 & 22	22 only	177 only
Model 50	NA*	Model 450
177 & 22		177 only

*NA—Not Available

The Winchester 450 (Diana 50) U/L has a semi-Mannlicher length forearm, effectively hiding the cocking underlever. While handsome in appearance and securely held, stock removal or tightening requires a special spanner which is not supplied. The MV rating, 693 fps in 177, seems questionable. In comparing new, out-of-the-box guns, the BSF S54 U/L's with certified MV of 669 fps in 177, repeatedly showed greater penetration in Ballistic Putty. The W-W435, also rated at 693 fps in 177, likewise fell behind in penetration power. All Winchester literature giving the 427 (22) MV at 660 fps is incorrect; this is the 177 MV figure, not that of the 22. Hy-Score (M807) gives correct MV at 540 fps in 22. Advertised MV of the smaller W-W425 (22) is also incorrect.

New owners of Winchester air rifles should be alert to some ludicrous discrepancies in their Operation and Care booklets supplied with each gun. Under Care and Cleaning one is told to oil the gun chamber after each using, but a few sentences further the statement is made that the compression tube (chamber) and piston are made of a special material that requires no attention and must not be oiled! Again, the directions advise firing the gun several times after oiling, *but no mention is made to load a pellet in the gun each time.* Serious damage could well develop if that suggestion is followed. Also, directions on spreading the oil in chamber are incomplete as stated.

The Diana 27 (W-W 427, Hy-Score 807) is a good buy since it does have some important refinements from the more expensive models. The double-pull trigger is excellent, and would do

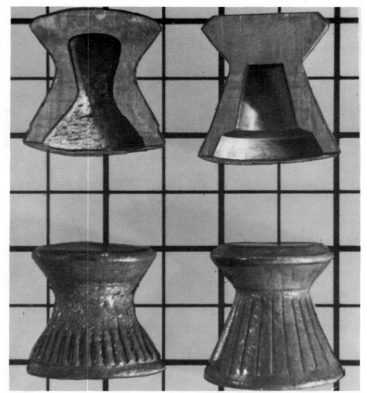

RWS, famous match-winning 177 pellet makers, now offer a new 22-cal. pellet (right, above and below) with improved target and sport shooting performance ● More head weight for better aerodynamic stability, more accuracy ● Thinner tail section for positive expansion, power sealing and easier flush-pellet insertion into tight chambers ● Longer over-all, bearing surfaces farther apart for optimum bore guidance ● Sharp bearing edges reduce friction-drag for higher velocity ● Tail-section grooving for long-flight control is now recessed, allows more metal in the important nose area without changing 14-gr. weight ● Available in tins of 200 and 500 from Fanta Air Rifle Specialties.

justice on a match rifle. It uses annular ball bearings to grasp the piston shaft in cocked position instead of the usual large claw. The mechanism is quite ingenious. Unless the owner is mechanically inclined, spring and trigger-section disassembly should not be attempted. The rear sights, comfortably large and fully adjustable, are partly made of plastic—true of the 35 and 50 also. The trigger on the W-W 427 is plastic; metal on 435 and 450. Rifling is excellent on all models, as well as over-all finish, and the guns are protected by individual carton packaging.

No mechanical device is 100% failure-proof, and no missile-projecting device is any more reliable than the sum of its own elements together with the pellets used, the power supply and the general characteristics inherent in all these when combined. Nevertheless, buying that first serious air rifle can be the beginning of a long and joyous friendship because a sporting air rifle, by one definition that satisfactorily fits it, is a gun that is fun to shoot. When your spirits, the weather, the place and your gun are all in tune, the relationship can indeed be euphoric! ●

The Walther Model LGV precision air rifle, a spring-air barrel-cocking type, has the new Olympia stock and barrel-locking device. Walther LG-55 air rifles are quite similar, but have light or heavy barrels, standard or Tyrolean stocks. Intearms is the importer.

The Herter SL-18 AUTOMATIC SHOTGUN

A fully detailed Testfire Report on a new Japanese-made autoloader. The author found this long-action shotgun performed well, calls it a "best buy."

by LARRY S. STERETT

The SL18 is loaded the same way as the Browning Automatic-5. The magazine holds 4 shells, plus one in the chamber; a plug provided reduces capacity to two rounds.

INSIDE THE shimmering gold-colored box, nestled in white foam, lay a beautiful 12 gauge Browning Automatic-5 shotgun. Did I say Browning? Sorry, a second glance revealed some slight differences. It wasn't a Browning after all, but a new 12 gauge Herter SL18 Automatic shotgun, apparently almost identical to the Browning.

Herter's used over two pages in their 1967 (No. 77) catalog to introduce the new SL18, with delivery to start by September 1967. As often occurs, production problems prevented delivery until late July of 1968. The wait may have been long, but when the product exceeds the expectation it's worth it.

My SL18 barrel is 30″ long, including the chromed barrel extension. The finish is the best I've seen on any new gun in a good many years, being extremely well-polished with a high-luster bluing. The barrel is topped with a .300″ wide ventilated rib having a .155″ stainless steel front bead, and a .070″ brass center post 16½″ from the muzzle; the rib has a wavy pattern on top to break up light reflections, except for the last 4¾″, which are reduced in height and smooth. (The wavy pattern is continued along the top-center of the receiver to provide a continuous sighting plane.) The rib on the Browning is reduced in height for only 3½″, and has a criss-cross pattern its entire length.

Unlike the integral barrel lug of the Browning, the SL18 lug is brazed, with two small openings that make it appear the same type lug could be used on a gas-operated shotgun; may-

be there is another new shotgun in the wind.

The left side of the SL18 barrel is stamped as follows: MADE IN JAPAN BY THE PINE CO. FIREARM DIV., 12 GAUGE (18.5) 30 INCH 2¾ CHAMBER FULL CHOKE, while the right side has: MODEL SL-18—PROOF TESTED FOR MAGNUMS, HERTER'S FIREARMS DIV., WASECA, MINNESOTA. Just ahead of the receiver, on the right side, the barrel is stamped with an H, superimposed with a P, apparently for Herter Proof. It is unusual to see a barrel stamped 12 gauge and 18.5 (its metric bore diameter), but it is a good idea.

The only other difference between the SL18 barrel and that of the Browning is in the rib; the Browning is more openly ventilated. SL18 barrels, all with vent ribs, fit the Browning shotguns perfectly—I tried it—and extra barrels are available in 30″, 28″, and 26″.

The SL18 magazine cap is larger—1.42″ wide and .90″ deep—versus 1.34″ and .77″—than that of the Browning, and the ridged surface is longer and deeper to provide a better gripping area.

From a distance of several feet the most noticeable difference between the two guns is in the SL18 fore-end. Browning's front handle is positioned by the fitting of a tongue into a groove in the front of the receiver, around the magazine tube. The SL18 has the groove plus two additional recesses to receive positioning studs, plus being reinforced at the rear with a ¼-inch band of blued steel with two studs to fit the receiver recesses. The Browning fore-end is reinforced only with a thin scant 1¼″ wide fi-

brous strip about ⅝″ forward of the receiver; this strip retards splitting, but doesn't prevent it.

The barrel lug of the Browning butts against the wood of the fore-end; the SL18 has a ⁹⁄₁₆″ black nylon buffer for this purpose, which should help absorb the action of the barrel returning to battery. Inletted into the front of the fore-end is a ³⁄₁₆″ black nylon cap containing the magazine cap lock plunger assembly; this cap is more decorative than functional, but it may help dampen fore-end vibrations.

The SL18 action is almost identical to that of the Browning, except for a few minor details. The "speed loading" feature advertised in the 1967 Herter catalog does not appear on the actual shotgun, no doubt because it is an exclusive Browning design.

The receiver screws of the two shotguns are in identical positions, but the SL18 screws also have lock screws. Screw slots on the SL18 are large enough to accept regular screwdriver blades, while those on the Browning have long been known for being narrow.

Engraving on the SL18 receiver is good and the edges sharp—it *is* engraving, at least on the sides of the receiver, not rolled on. The edging design is very similar to that of the Browning, but the rest is not. Instead of small leaves, curls and scrolls, the Herter receiver is covered with larger leaves in a vine-like arrangement in basically the same areas. The Browning receiver has the word BROWNING on the left side above a small oval sketch of John M. The SL18 has HERTER'S in the same position, but the sketch is not only larger and facing forward, but is of an oriental-appearing gentleman with a beard. No engraving appears on the upper or lower tang, trigger guard, or on the rear of the SL18 receiver.

The SL18 has a Browning-type magazine cut-off; shells feed automatically from the magazine if the latch is forward during the operating cycle, but are retained in the magazine if the latch is to the rear. This also allows a shell to be ejected from the chamber without disturbing the shells in the magazine.

A large cross bolt safety is located just behind the trigger for easy manipulation. The head is large and deeply checkered, more so than on the Browning, but the receiver is not recessed for the top edge. When in the "off" position a bright red ring is visible on the left side of the safety. (A left-hand safety is available at no extra cost.)

SL18 tangs are shorter than Browning's; 3" to 3½" for the upper tang, 2½" to 3⅛" for the lower. These dimensions permit a full pistol grip on the SL18, one with a more pronounced curve than that of the Browning.

The buttstock on the SL18 is similar to the Browning's with a broad full comb, deeply fluted, and a full pistol grip with slightly convex base. The fore-end and butt are of French walnut, the test gun showing some beautiful dark figuring in the toe and grip areas. The fore-end is checkered 20 lines to the inch, the grip 18 lines. The checkering is good, with no noticeable runouts, and the borders are no more wavy than those found on Brownings. The checkering, fore and aft, is similar to that on the Browning, too. The wood, well-sealed, has a durable and glossy plastic coating, the

wood looking like a piece of fine furniture. The buttplate is black plastic, almost completely covered with checkering.

The metal finish is excellent; better than on some shotguns costing several hundred dollars. The barrel extension, follower and bolt assembly are chromed, the trigger heavily gold-plated.

Shooting the Herter SL18

First test for the SL18 was the patterning board to determine if the full choke barrel had a preference for a particular shot size. It did. The Herter automatic is no different from many shotguns in that it handles the larger stock sizes best. At 40 yards Winchester Super-Speed Mark 5 HD Magnum loads averaged 84.2% of the 1½ ounces of 2s in a 30" circle. Super-X Magnum Mark 5 No. 5s averaged 75.6%.

Smaller shot sizes produced pattern averages ranging from 51.9% for paper-cased 1-oz. Sportloads in 6s to 70.7% for new plastic Alcan Trapmax loads holding 1⅛/7½s. Other 7½ and 8 loads averaged in the 60% to 70% bracket, except for some new Wanda all-plastic shells; these averaged 57.6% with 7½s.

Remington SP 00BK loads were also patterned. All of the 9 pellets were in the 30" circle for all five shots, giving an average of 100%, with 5 to 7 pellets always within a 20" circle. (With the smaller shot sizes the over-all pattern spread was approximately 48", and very close to the aiming point.)

Following the patterning I took the SL18 to the trap range for a session with Blue Rocks and some orange-colored Herter targets. Of particular interest was whether the length of pull—14⅛" compared to the Brown-

ing's 14⁷⁄₁₆"—and the full pistol grip would affect the mounting and swing of the SL18. I needn't have worried. Using Alcan Trapmax loads and some new all-plastic Herter Blue Powermag (2¾/1⅛/8s) loads almost every bird disappeared in a puff of black dust, and thanks to the 8¹⁄₁₆ lbs. of heft the SL18 seemed to have almost no recoil.

Another feature I like on the SL18 is the trigger. The tip is shaped with less curve than the Browning, and the pull has a very even four pounds.

If you like the long-recoil system of operation, try the SL18. I rate it as a "best buy." Try as I would I couldn't find anything wrong with the one I checked out, though I do have a suggestion for all manufacturers or importers of such shotguns.

Long-recoil operated shotguns use a friction ring to retard rearward barrel movement with heavy loads. If light target loads are used the friction ring must be repositioned or the fired cases won't eject—fine for handloaders, since the empties can be extracted manually. This ring changing is not difficult, but if done infrequently it's easy to forget what goes where. The Remington Model 11 used to have a simple set of illustrated instructions glued to the inside of the fore-end to indicate proper location of the friction ring for the load being used. I think this is still a good idea for all long-recoil shotguns; with the fore-end removed you could glance at the illustrations to see what to do next.

The SL18 is not in the current Herter catalog, but you can obtain it over the counter or order through your dealer from Herter's, Inc. R.R. 1, Waseca, Minn. 56093. The current price (mid-'69) is $138.95, plus postage for 12 pounds, for the Trap Model. The shorter barrel hunting models are slightly less. ●

The Herter SL18 automatic shotgun.

THERE WERE SOME people who predicted dire effects upon handgun development as a result of the enactment of GCA 68. Well, that took place over a year and a half ago, and it has, if anything, stimulated development of new models. Probably more new handgun models have been introduced during the past twelve months than any recent similar period. In several instances, specific new models can be tied directly to portions of the law.

For example, take the new Walther PPKS distributed by Interarms. Previously, both the PPK and PP models could be freely imported and were quite popular. Came GCA 68 and the PPK was prohibited; its weight and dimensions prevented it from accumulating enough "points" to qualify for importation. Walther, with Interarms' assistance, crash-developed a slightly larger and heavier version of the PPK which qualified (barely) for importation. It is designated PPKS and is already becoming quite popular. This model would not have come into being without the new law.

In another area, GCA flatly prohibited importation of small pocket-size auto pistols of traditional form. Prior importation of such guns at low prices had killed domestic development and production in this field. Certainly the prohibition of such imports played a part in Smith & Wesson's decision to introduce its Model 61 "Enforcer," a 22 LR, pocket-size, self-loader. As a further result, Colt's will begin producing here the 25 ACP "Junior" auto it has previously imported from Spain. Prohibition of imports has also spurred development of new designs by other companies.

The way ATFD regulations assign point values for importation qualification has had other effects upon imports. A simple, basic autoloader cannot hope to qualify unless it has at least a fair percentage of these features: chamber indicator; target sights; target trigger; magazine safety; firing pin lock; double-action lockwork, etc. Consequently, in order to hang in with the U.S. market, foreign makers are upgrading their designs. Both Astra and Beretta offer new modern double-action 32 autos, prompted at least in part by the importation requirements. Star produced on short notice its shortened, lightweight version of the Model B when the new law cut off importation of its pocket models.

Since GCA 68 eliminated importation of many cheap (often junk) handguns, several factories have been set up to turn out virtually the same guns here at home. It appears that domestic production—which at present is entirely within the law—may very soon exceed previous imports of such guns. Therefore, the import-restriction limitation of the law is totally useless.

This pocket automatic in 25 ACP is made of stainless steel by American Firearms Co.

HANDGUNS 1970
U.S. and Foreign

by GEORGE C. NONTE, Jr.

The newer are fewer, some old have been tolled, but too many junker-klunkers mar the scene. There's good news and bad news.

Junk Handguns

We'd like to elaborate on this particular class of handguns. They introduce two problems. First, in the absence of any industry or governmental standards of quality and serviceability, tens of thousands of these "under $20" guns are actually hazardous to both shooter and bystander. Some produce no more than 30-40% reliability; that is, they actually *fire* only 3 to 4 out of each 10 cartridges. Others are deplorably inaccurate by current standards. Second, because of their price level, they appeal primarily to the less-lawful citizen and are often used criminally.

If the Law permits you to buy a handgun at all, it permits you to buy these junkers; but you do yourself no favor when you do so. You may even wind up short a finger or an eye as a result. If you start handgunning with such a marginal piece of ordnance, you'll only handicap and discourage yourself.

But, as long as people will buy these junkers, some of which cost only $2.50-$3.00 to produce, manufacturers will turn them out by the carload. We don't need them. Wait until you can afford a *good* handgun, and the junkers will soon disappear.

In one respect, the law is producing salutary effects; forcing overseas makers to up-grade guns, and encouraging new domestic models.

To our way of thinking, the domestic (as well as foreign) handgun producers could do with a bit of prodding. Demand has been so good for so long for their products that they've become careless. Generally speaking, quality has deteriorated across the board. I point no specific finger—*all* of our major domestic producers could do better.

Quality Control?

Examples of this deterioration aren't hard to find. In the past year I've examined several 38 Special and 357 Magnum revolvers that malfunctioned right out of the box or within a short period of time. One police officer shelled out over $150 for a premium service gun; by the time it had fired 300 rounds in practice it was so badly out of time it produced 50% misfires. Another similarly priced gun was bought new by a local cop who returned to the dealer with blood in his eye only a few hours later. Before ever being fired, the action locked up tight in double-action. A few queries to other dealers uncovered an identical occurrence with the same make and model. Then there is the new handgun that was delivered to me; extraction was difficult and the front sight flew off after firing less than 75 rounds. Also, a dealer in Michigan reported to me just last week that he had two famous-make revolvers in his shop with cylinder defects apparently originating at the factory.

As I've said, this condition seems to exist across the board. It's bad enough at best, but when new guns delivered to police officers don't function reliably, the situation gets damned hairy. All I can say is that final inspection and testing needs attention. Personally, I'd rather wait a while for a new gun and be certain it would perform properly than get a rush job I'd have to send back for repair. Speeding production to catch up with demand is only good business, but to use that as an excuse for delivering defective firearms to men whose life depends upon them isn't quite my idea of how to stay popular. It may be that more competition in the heavy DA revolver field will help clear up this condition. We hope so.

Some of the new models rumored or even confirmed a year ago still aren't available. For example, the new Ruger Double Action tested (in prototype form) in GD 24 is still conspicuous by its absence. Just when we'll see *production* specimens of this model remains clouded in Southport (Conn.) smog. We don't mind a little lead time, but it does stir up the natives to brag about new items a couple years before they can actually be purchased. On the opposite side of the fence we have the new M61 Smith & Wesson 22 whose existence was virtually denied until thousands of guns were in the warehouse ready for shipment to the trade.

New Items

We can't possibly cover here all of the more common variations and changes occurring since last year. We have, however, sorted out all those de-

Astra Constable is now available from Garcia/Firearms Int. in 32 ACP; 22LR and 380 ACP calibers will be offered later.

velopments of apparent significance, particularly truly *new* models. Each is covered as well as time, space, and availability of samples has allowed. Here is the list, alphabetical, of course.

American Firearms Models

American Firearms Mfg. Co., Inc., is a new entrant to the handgun industry, operating out of San Antonio. Its major effort is in a line of pocket-size autoloading pistols in 22, 25, 32 and 380 calibers. A single design, used for all four calibers, combines the same slide and frame, with only those minor variations necessitated by the different cartridges. In this manner maximum parts interchangeability is achieved.

Only the 25 ACP model is now offered—4.4″ long by 3.5″ high, weight 14 ounces in all-steel. A planned light-alloy version will weigh 7.5 ounces. The design is quite simple, combining major features of the Walther Model 9 and the 1925 Lilliput. Frame and barrel are precision-cast (investment) in a single piece to finish dimensions. The barrel is then drilled and rifled and minor machining and drilling are accomplished. A conventional slide is used with recoil spring under the barrel. A manual safety is at left rear of the frame; magazine catch at butt. A finger-rest spur is provided on the magazine and the very rudimentary sights are cast integrally on barrel and slide.

Uniquely, all major parts are investment cast of #302 stainless steel, then polished bright. The polishing characteristics of this material prevent economical achievement of a really *good* smooth finish, but the no-rust properties outweigh this disadvantage.

Thus far we've examined only prototype 25 caliber guns. They were lacking in fit and finish quality but seemed durable enough. Price of the 25 is $58.50, and 32 and 380 planned

at $67.50 and $74.50, respectively. The 22 will be $69.95. Alloy frame models will be substantially cheaper. Blue finish (actually black chrome over the bright stainless) will be offered later at $15 additional.

American Firearms has ambitious plans, including a 22 Short copy of the Lilliput, double-action pocket pistols, and large-caliber, military-type handguns. We look forward to seeing production specimens of all of them.

Astra Constable

Ever since sales of the 300/3000 series of pocket autoloaders collapsed, Astra (Unceta y Cia) has worked at developing a modern double-action pocket pistol. The result is now with us in the Constable, being imported by Firearms International. At 6½″ long and 25 ounces it makes a nice compact package. Available currently only in 32 ACP caliber, the Constable greatly resembles the Walther PPK in appearance, but is much different internally. It uses a Walther-type manual safety on the slide, but lacks the hammer block of the PP/PPK series. The safety, when engaged, drops the hammer, but prevents the hammer from striking the firing pin.

Slide stop and ejector are combined and have an external thumb button for manual operation. Magazine catch is rearward of the trigger in Colt/Browning fashion—far better than a butt-located type.

Dismounting is done by pressing down a sliding block ahead of the trigger, then drawing the slide fully rearward and lifting it free of the frame tracks, freeing it to be eased forward off the barrel. The barrel is pinned to the frame and is surrounded by the recoil spring. Grips are wrap-around brown plastic grooved horizontally. Finish is blue, but with Spanish liking for ornamentation, I'd expect plated and engraved models to be offered soon.

The sample we examined showed good fit and finish, but with lots of as-cast and unfinished surfaces inside on non-critical areas. This doesn't interfere in the least with reliability and proper functioning. The Constable will be offered also in 22 LR and 380 ACP eventually and will give the Walther series a good bit of competition at its lower price. Exact retail price is vague at the moment. At this time, this is the only new Astra pistol available in this country—quite a change from years gone by when 8 or more models could be had.

Beretta M90

J. Galef & Sons just announced a new Beretta Model 90 32 ACP auto-loader. This is an intriguing pocket-size gun, made as compact as possible while still qualifying for importation. This makes it 6¾" long and weight about 20 ounces.

The M90 possesses the following features: double-action lockwork; re-bounding hammer with safety block; chambered-cartridge indicator; quick-detachable, stationary stainless steel barrel; quick and simple takedown.

Externally the M90 resembles the Walther PP/PPK series, but is vastly different inside, with fewer parts. A simple dismounting lever in the frame above and ahead of the trigger is pressed forward and up to allow the retracted slide to be drawn up and rearward off the frame, then eased forward off the barrel. The barrel may then be removed (no reason to) by turning off its lock nut and drawing it rearward out of its seat in the frame. This opens up the possibility of changing calibers rather simply—perhaps to the more potent 380 ACP cartridge if Beretta could be per-suaded to make barrels.

The manual safety, at the left rear of the frame, also functions as a slide latch. The red colored extractor also functions as a chambered cartridge in-dicator. When a round is in the cham-ber the extractor protrudes to be seen and felt. The magazine catch is con-veniently located on the left of the frame behind the trigger in Colt/Browning fashion. Standard finish is blue; grips are of checked black Ten-ite wrapping around the frame rear. Counting everything—all pins and screws, all magazine parts—the Be-retta M90 contains only 43 parts.

As we go to press, no sample gun has been tested—but it looks good as a working gun. Announced retail price is $110, more or less in line with com-petitive Walther, Mauser, and Astra guns.

Charter Arms
Pocket Target

Having achieved good acceptance of its Undercover 38 Special revolver, Charter Arms introduced a 22 RF

Beretta M-90 has a stainless steel barrel and takes down quickly. Imported by Galef, it is available in 32 ACP only.

version of it called the "Pocket Tar-get." It carries a 3" barrel, ramp front sight, and an adjustable target-type rear sight let into the top strap. Aside from these changes, it is identical to the Undercover. Construction is all steel, with smooth walnut grips and blue finish. Weight is 18½ ounces; length 7⅛" height 4³⁄₁₆".

The Pocket Target is an excellent gun for casual outdoor use or for training in "snub-nose" handling. It's a real handy tackle-box or bedroll gun for taking afield.

Our first sample gun gave extraction difficulties and had the front sight poorly installed. It was returned and a replacement was supplied. It seems the first few guns were produced by a chamber-reaming method that wasn't entirely satisfactory. This was changed and subsequent guns show easy ex-traction. Accuracy of both sample guns was satisfactory, and no malfunc-tions occurred with the second gun. Price is $82.00. A plated presentation model is available in a lined, brass-furnitured mahogany case.

Charter also offers its Undercover 38 Special now with 3" barrel; weight 17 ounces.

Colt's Mark III Series

The long-standing Official Police design, the basis for all Colt double-action revolvers for more than half a century, has finally been relegated to obsolescence. A completely new action design has replaced it in the Trooper and Official Police, and two new mod-els with the new action have been added to the line; Metropolitan and Lawman. All guns with the new action bear the model suffix "Mk III," thus the "Trooper Mk III," etc. Small frame guns continue to be built on the previous design.

The Trooper Mk III is the top of

This cutaway view of Colt's Mk IV series automatics shows the new barrel and bushing design.

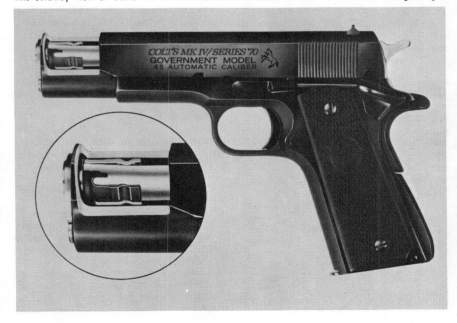

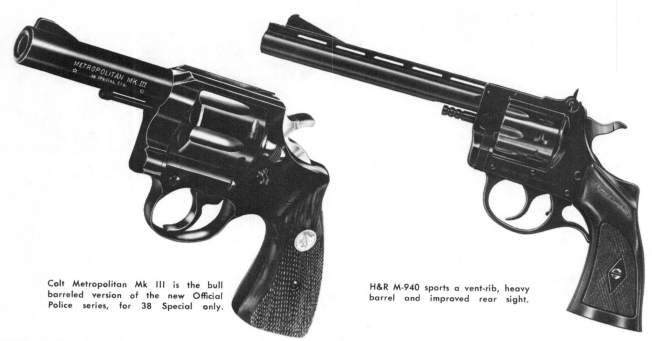

Colt Metropolitan Mk III is the bull barreled version of the new Official Police series, for 38 Special only.

H&R M-940 sports a vent-rib, heavy barrel and improved rear sight.

the line with a fully shrouded ejector rod, integral barrel rib, target sights, and target hammer and trigger in 357 Magnum caliber. The Official Police Mk III is a plain-barrel, fixed-sight service version of the same gun in 38 Special caliber. The Lawman Mk III and Metropolitan Mk III are heavy "bull" barreled (4″ only) versions of the OP in 357 Magnum and 38 Special respectively.

We've examined and shot all of these new guns. Performance has been faultless, but all of them seem—to me —unnecessarily massive and heavy. Frame corners and other areas are

bluff and squarish with little aesthetic appeal. Though all four guns handle well, they *look* clumsy and awkward alongside, say, a S & W Combat Magnum. I'm thoroughly convinced that aesthetics *is* a significant factor in handgun purchases, even among police officers.

Major advances for the Mk III are shortened hammer and trigger travel and smoother double-action pull. The lockwork dispenses entirely with Colt's traditional two-arm, combination mainspring and rebound lever. Coil springs are used throughout except for the hand spring. The safety lever

(hammer block) is a completely new design on the left side and the new cylinder bolt looks suspiciously as if it had been made in Springfield rather than Hartford. This is a completely new action, not just a rehash of the old design. Maximum use is made throughout of investment castings— in fact all major parts except barrel and cylinder are cast.

Price on the Trooper Mk III is $135.50; the other three guns going for $115.

Colt's big autoloading pistols—the 45 Government and Gold Cup models —have also been improved. A new

---

New Tayra Holster

Tayra Corp. sent in a quite new and different "Concealed Weapon" holster, this first version sized to take S&W K-frames, M19s, M&Ps and the like. Made of ethylene vinyl acetate, this interesting holster was designed by F. R. Marburger of Canton, Ohio's detective bureau. Fully washable, it's guaranteed flexible in sub-zero cold, and the back (see illus.) is fully adjustable for a snug fit on belts up to 2 inches wide.

Our sample worked very well—a 4-inch barreled Colt was a smooth fit in the moulded interior, and simply shoving the base of the thumb against the safety strap freed the gun for instant release.

The holster rides upright, thus may be used as a cross-draw carrier as well, and its unusual design lets a better-performing 4″ barreled gun be carried about as easily as a 2″ handgun.

This is a well-thought out design, and we hope that potential customers won't be put off by the unorthodox appearance and materials. Write for prices.

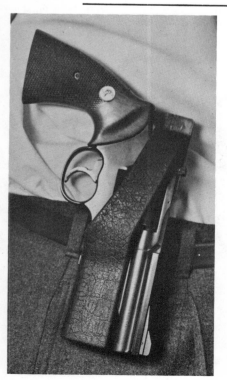

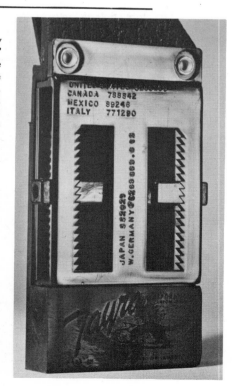

split, collet-type barrel bushing mates with a matching taper on the barrel muzzle, causing the barrel to be gripped tightly and uniformly by the three "finger" portions of the bushing as the slide moves into battery. We've not seen a sample yet, but we hear that the new barrel and bushing produce a great improvement in accuracy.

The new models are designated the "Mk IV/Series 70," that prefix added to their old designations. We expect this Mk IV system will be applied to 38 Super and 38 Special autos in the near future, but Colt says it cannot be made available in Commander pistols; not enough room for the long bushing.

Since GCA 68 prevents importation of the Junior 25 Auto, we are told this little gun will now be manufactured by Colt's.

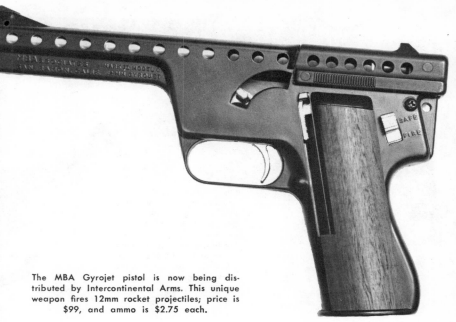

The MBA Gyrojet pistol is now being distributed by Intercontinental Arms. This unique weapon fires 12mm rocket projectiles; price is $99, and ammo is $2.75 each.

H&R M940

H&R has revised its "Sidekick," a solid-frame, side-swing 22 RF revolver, calling it the Model 940. This is the previous key-locked design fitted with a new, round, ventilated-rib, heavy barrel and an improved target-type rear sight.

Also interesting is the fact that H&R continues to import the 4-caliber HK-4 double-action autoloader. This unique outfit qualified for importation under the ATFD "factoring criteria" so will continue to be available.

Newly made copy of the Remington 1875 revolver from Replica Arms in 38 Special or as the original in 45 Long Colt calibers.

Replica Arms Remington

Replica Arms is usually associated only with muzzleloaders, particularly Colt percussion revolver copies, but it now offers a cartridge handgun copy. Oddly enough, this gun fits right in with the front-loaders. It is a modern replica of the Remington M1875 single-action revolver in 45 Colt caliber. This model was a contemporary of the SAA Colt and only some 25,000 were made by Remington.

The Replica Arms Remington contains modern materials and manufacturing methods. The sample we've examined looks good. As of this writing, the retail price hasn't been firmed up.

Dan Wesson's M-12 double action revolver offers interchangeable barrels of 2½", 4" or 6" lengths.

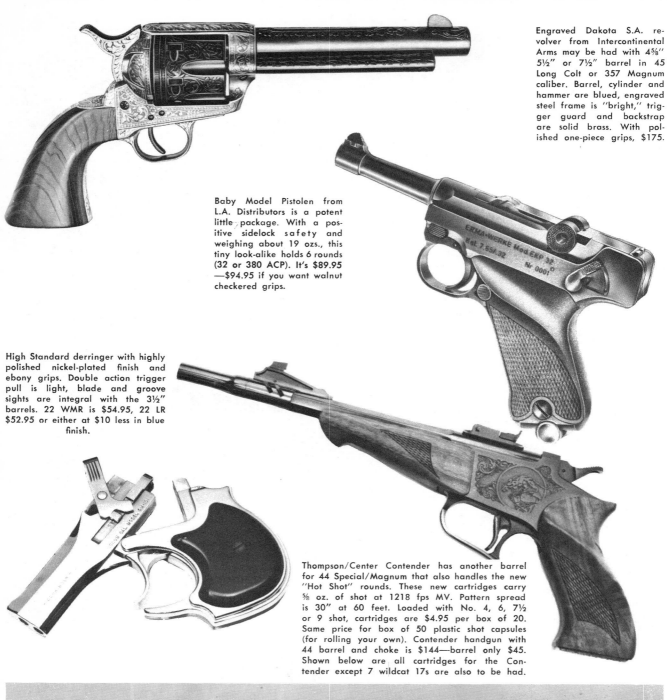

Engraved Dakota S.A. revolver from Intercontinental Arms may be had with 4⅝" 5½" or 7½" barrel in 45 Long Colt or 357 Magnum caliber. Barrel, cylinder and hammer are blued, engraved steel frame is "bright," trigger guard and backstrap are solid brass. With polished one-piece grips, $175.

Baby Model Pistolen from L.A. Distributors is a potent little package. With a positive sidelock safety and weighing about 19 ozs., this tiny look-alike holds 6 rounds (32 or 380 ACP). It's $89.95 —$94.95 if you want walnut checkered grips.

High Standard derringer with highly polished nickel-plated finish and ebony grips. Double action trigger pull is light, blade and groove sights are integral with the 3½" barrels. 22 WMR is $54.95, 22 LR $52.95 or either at $10 less in blue finish.

Thompson/Center Contender has another barrel for 44 Special/Magnum that also handles the new "Hot Shot" rounds. These new cartridges carry ⅝ oz. of shot at 1218 fps MV. Pattern spread is 30" at 60 feet. Loaded with No. 4, 6, 7½ or 9 shot, cartridges are $4.95 per box of 20. Same price for box of 50 plastic shot capsules (for rolling your own). Contender handgun with 44 barrel and choke is $144—barrel only $45. Shown below are all cartridges for the Contender except 7 wildcat 17s are also to be had.

22 LR	22 Hor.	222 Rem.	380 Sup.	9mm	45 Colt
22 WMR	22 K-Hor.	256 Win.	38 Spl.	357/44	44 Mag.
5mm Rem.	22 Jet	30 Carb.	357 Mag.	45 ACP	44 Shot

Browning ISU International Target Medalist is a special version made especially to comply with ISU shooting requirements. Barrel length is 5.9"; over-all length is 10¹⁵⁄₁₆"; weight empty, 42 ozs. Sight radius is 8.6" and thumbrest grip is 1.8", maximum width allowed. All other specs and features are identical with standard Medalist. Price $132.50.

The Targetmaster 38 Special revolver, made in Germany, is imported by L.A. Distributors. Target style accessories are standard equipment—checkered walnut grips, wide hammer spur, trigger and adj. sights. $49.95 with ribbed barrel in 2", 4" or 6" length.

If you like big old Colts, here's Potomac Arms copy of the 4-lb. Colt Dragoon with a 44 caliber 7½" barrel, plus a roll-engraved cylinder scene of a soldier and Indian fight. Finished in satin blue with a color-case hardened frame, brass back strap and trigger guard with genuine walnut grips. Price, $100.

Combat shooters should welcome the 9mm SIG P-210 pistol imported by Benet Arms. Our test sample shows every sign of excellent quality. The fitting is very snug, trigger pull is light and crisp, and the balance is such that it will produce little fatigue during long sessions of dry-firing. A 22 Long Rifle conversion unit (with fixed sights) is also made for inexpensive target practice or plinking. The finish is a deep, almost matte black, and the fully adjustable sights show little tendency to shine. About $230 with walnut grips, plus an extra $100 for the 22 LR conversion unit.

Ruger Security Six

The Ruger double-action police revolver described here in detail one year ago is still not available. Numerous minor changes and improvement have been made on the basic prototype, but they aren't discernible to casual observation. Recent discussion with the Rugermen indicates production guns will be delivered before the end of this year. We can't be more specific as this is written.

This new revolver, now known as the Ruger "Security-Six," will be offered initially only in 357 Magnum and 38 Special calibers; barrel lengths of 2¾", 4" and 6"; price will be $87.50 with fixed sights, $97.50 with adjustable rear. Intentions are to offer a 22 rimfire version later on, we hear.

Smith & Wesson M61

For some time we'd been hearing grapevine stories about a pocket-size Smith & Wesson automatic. As is typical of that firm, queries on the subject were answered with a smiling "What new automatic?" In short, more strengthening than allaying our curiosity.

However, all things come to him who waits, and early this year the first lot of the new S&W M61 "Escort" 22 LR self-loaders was delivered to the trade and simultaneously to writers who hadn't already wormed their way into the Springfield plant to see the little gun perform.

The M61 is pocket-size: 4.82" long by 3.63". high, 0.95" thick (over the grips) and with a 2.18" barrel. Weight, with standard light-alloy frame, is 13½ ounces on my postal scale.

Externally it doesn't at first seem to offer anything out of the ordinary. Then, a cocking indicator may be seen poking slightly through the upper rear corner of the left grip. When cocked, it rises about ³⁄₃₂" above the grip; it's flush when uncocked. Note: it does *not* indicate whether a cartridge is in the chamber.

Closer examination discloses that the barrel is housed in the frame, *beneath* the recoil spring in the slide. This immediately brings to mind the old Bayard M1908-through-1923 pocket pistol series. Further examination "shows" the M61 mechanical layout to be much the same as the Bayard: separate spring housing over the magazine well; barrel in frame; recoil spring over barrel and locked in place by the front sight; underslung breechblock extending below slide proper; ejection port in frame rather than slide, etc. With improvements, of course.

Operation is simple: engage thumb safety by pressing upward; place 5 cartridges in the magazine; seat magazine in butt; draw slide fully back and let it run forward to chamber the first round. The magazine may then be removed and an additional cartridge

Smith & Wesson's new M-61 5-shot 22LR pocket automatic is slim, lightweight, has good sights.

inserted to replace the one chambered. It's ready to fire when you lower the safety.

To clear the gun, engage safety, remove magazine, and draw the slide back to extract the cartridge from the chamber. There is no magazine disconnector, chamber indicator, or slide lock.

Disassembly couldn't be simpler. Remove magazine and make certain pistol is unloaded; depress button in slide over the muzzle (recoil spring guide end); lift out front sight; ease spring and guide out; draw slide fully rearward and lift vertically off the receiver.

The alloy frame is anodized a smooth grayish-black. Top and rear of the steel slide are matted to reduce glare; sides are bright blue.

Sights are the best I've seen on a gun this small. Though fixed, the rear sight has a square notch a full ¹⁄₁₀" wide and nearly as deep. The sloping front blade is .075" wide and neatly squared. Both are high enough to be seen and used in a hurry in poor light. There is some lateral play in the front sight since it is held in place by the recoil spring guide. However, at table-top range this presents no great disadvantage. This gun certainly is not intended for 50-yard target work.

Functionally this little gun does very well. Light pocket guns are notorious for jamming because of light recoiling parts, short travel, and other factors. Thus far the sample M61 has shucked its way through 300 rounds of assorted makes of high velocity 22 Long Rifles without a single failure. Many a pocket gun of similar size hasn't done as well for us. Incidentally, Remington Golden Bullet HV ammunition produces 1145 fps in this sample gun.

From an accuracy standpoint, it will keep all its shots on a dinner plate at 25 feet when the sights are used. Careful two-handed rest shooting (try that sometime with a gun whose butt allows a full grip with *only* one finger) produces 2½" groups at that same range. The rather heavy trigger pull (7½ lbs.) isn't conducive to tiny groups.

In one-hand point shooting, conscious effort is required to avoid shooting low. One instinctively tips the muzzle down, trying to get the front strap deeper into the hand. With a little practice, though, correction for this tendency comes easy and I find no difficulty in getting consistent rapid-fire hits on a life-size head and shoulders silhouette at 15 feet.

The M61 is simple, light and, at $47.50, economical. It's more reliable than most other autos of its size, and its accuracy is entirely adequate. Loaded with 22 LR HV Hollow Points, it's a far more potent defensive gun than any 25 or 32 Auto. As such it seems ideal for the officer or legal gun-toting citizen who must have maximum concealability; or for the officer who feels the need of a second "emergency" gun in addition to his standard service arm. It's no substitute for a good 38 Special or 9mm, but within its obvious limitations, it will do the job well.

Dan Wesson Arms

The unique Wesson M-12 double-action revolver with interchangeable barrels, introduced last year is finally expected to be available late this summer. Some minor design changes have been made, but the general appearance remains the same. Its most distinguishing feature is the interchangeable barrel system, these made in 2½", 4" and 6" lengths. Price is still pegged at $110 for the target-sighted model in blue finish. No other prices are available yet.

Walther PPKS

As mentioned earlier in this section, the ATFD "factoring criteria" prohibited importation of the very popular Walther PPK double-action, autoloading pistol. The slightly larger and heavier PP model qualified for importation. This resulted in a crash program to develop a PPK variation that *could* qualify for importation.

The result is the PPKS with its heavier and longer butt frame and larger capacity magazine. In essence, the changes amount to a PP frame fitted with PPK slide and barrel. The increase in dimensions and weight qualify the new model for importation. It isn't as light and compact as the PPK, but it makes a very fine undercover gun all the same. It is offered in 22 LR, 32 ACP, and 380 ACP; $112, $106 and $106, respectively, including a spare magazine. As far as I'm concerned, they could forget the 32—the other calibers are better for any reasonable handgun use.

Walther has also added the GSP, an improved version of the OSP rapid-fire, target pistol chambered for the 22 LR cartridge. Though built on the same basic action as the OSP, the GSP incorporates internal changes and a slab-sided barrel without weights. Price is $220.

Though not really new, a 22 LR conversion unit is now offered for the P.38. Additionally, the P.38 is now offered in 7.65mm Parabellum (30 Luger) and 22 LR caliber.

As for other new items, several domestic plants are turning out the low-cost guns we mentioned earlier. In most instances they represent *minimum* firearms and some are not even, in our considered opinion, safe. Such items don't merit coverage here. That doesn't mean all guns not listed here are unsafe—far from it. In spite of high-flying advertising claims, you usually get what you pay for. If you see a new gun priced lower than similar types by our top makers, you can bet it's less gun. Guide yourself accordingly.

Foreign revolver makers, Weihrauch, J. P. Sauer, Astra, Taurus, Rossi, Gabilondo (Llama) and others have all introduced "new" models. Almost without exception they are simply previous designs up-graded to qualify for importation. Two-inch, fixed-sight guns can't be imported, so three-inch target-sighted models have been introduced, being then qualified for importation. We don't consider them really *new* models for the purposes of this report. ●

This Walther GSP target pistol replaces the older OSP. Note slab-sided barrel and lack of weights. 22LR only, from Interarms.

Interarms also imports the Mauser-made Parabellum, made in 9mm and 30 Luger calibers, price about $200.

The new Walther PPKS is heavier, longer and has larger magazine capacity than the older PPK. Available in 22 LR, 32 or 380 ACP.

CHECK CHART OF U.S. RIMFIRE HANDGUNS

Make	Model	Sights	Price	Barrel	Notes
AUTOLOADERS					
Browning	Nomad	adj.	71.50	4½-6¾	22 LR, also 2 target models
Browning	Challenger	adj.	86.50 up	4½-6¾	ext. trigger adj. screw
Browning	Medalist	adj.	138.50 up	6¾	target; dry-fire device
Browning	Internat.	adj.	134.50	6½	22 LR, Target
Colt	Huntsman	fix.	71.50	4½-6	10-shot
Colt	Targetsman	adj.	82.50	6	10-shot
Colt	W'man Sport	adj.	100.00	4½-6	10-shot
Colt	MT Woodsman	adj.	115.50	4½-6	10-shot
H. S.	Duramatic	fix.	64.95	4½-6½	quick takedown
H. S.	Sport-King	fix.	75.00	4½-6¾	22 LR or 22 S (Flite King)
H. S.	Sup. Tour.	adj.	95.00	5½, 6¾	also with bull barrel
H. S.	Sup. Citation	adj.	115.00	5½-6¾-7¼	Cit. Military, $110.00
H. S.	Olympic (ISU)	adj.	130.00	5½, 6¾	22 S only (Oly. Mil. 22 LR)
H. S.	Sup. Trophy	adj.	130.00	5½-7¼	Trophy Mil. $125.00
Ruger	Standard	fix.	47.50	4⅝-6½	first Ruger model
Ruger	Mark I Target	adj.	67.50 up	6⅞	9-shot, comp. extra
S & W	46 Target	adj.	112.50	5, 7	22 LR, Heavy bbl. $118.00
S & W	41 Match	adj.	131.50	5, 7⅜	22 LR or 22 S (5½ HB)
S & W	Escort	fix.	47.50	2³⁄₁₆	22 LR, 5 shot
Sterling	Target 300	adj.	105.00	4½-6-8	22 LR
Sterling	Husky	fix.	57.50	4½	10-shot
Sterling	Trapper	fix.	63.50	6	interchangeable safety
Stoeger	Luger	fix.	69.95	4½, 5½	22 LR
REVOLVERS					
Charter	Pocket Target	adj.	82.00	3	Swing-out cyl.
Colt	Frontier Scout	fix.	71.50 up	4¾	22 RF, also 22 RFM
Colt	Buntine Scout	fix.	82.50 up	9½	22 RF, also 22 RFM
Colt	OM Match	adj.	143.00	6	also in 22 RFM
Colt	Cobra	fix.	101.00	3	38 Spl. also
Colt	Diamondback	adj.	135.00	2½-4	also in 38 Spl.
F. I.	Regent	fix.	34.95	3-4-6	8-shot-Swingout cyl.
H & R	622	fix.	37.95	2½-4-6	solid frame
H & R	900	fix.	43.95	2½-4-6	snap-out cyl.
H & R	949	adj.	44.95	5½	9-shot
H & R	929 Side Kick	semi	49.95	2½-4-6	swingout cyl.
H & R	Ultra S'Kick	adj.	62.95	6	vent. rib bbl., safety lock
H & R	999 S'man	adj.	69.95	6	9-shot, top-break
H. S.	Durango	fix.	58.95	4	frontier style
H. S.	Double-9	semi	65.00	5½-9½	frontier style
I. J.	55A, Cadet	fix.	41.50 up	2½-4½-6	solid frame, both models
I. J.	57A	adj.	44.75 up	4½-6	now with loading gates
I. J.	Sidewinder	fix.	44.75 up	6	frontier style
I. J.	Trailsman 66	adj.	53.75 up	6	rebounding hammer
I. J.	Viking 67	adj.	53.75 up	2¾-4½-6	snub model—67S
Ruger	Bearcat	fix.	44.00	4	engr. cyl. walnut-grips
Ruger	Single Six	fix.	64.25	5½	22 RF, 22 RFM, walnut grips
Ruger	S.S. Conv.	fix.	69.50	5½-6½-9½	2 cyls. (9½" bbl. $78.00)
Ruger	S.S.S. Conv.	semi	78.00	5½-6½	2 cyls. New frame profile
S & W	Combat M'piece	adj.	97.50	4	also in 38 Spl.
S & W	22/32 Kit	adj.	98.50 up	2-4	also 3½" Airw'ght & 22 RFM
S & W	22/32 Target	adj.	106.00	6	small frame
S & W	K22 Magnum	adj.	107.50	4, 6, 8⅜	22 RF Magnum
S & W	K22	adj.	107.50	6, 8⅜	also in 32 and 38
MISCELLANEOUS					
Challanger	Derr.	fix.	19.95 up	2½	22
H. S.	Derringer	fix.	42.95 up	3½	O-U, 22 LR or 22 RFM
Merrill	S. S.	adj.	129.50	10½	Int. bbl. $35.00, 22 RF, 22 Hornet, 22 Jet, 357, 38, 256, 44, 45, others
Contender	Single Shot	adj.	135.00	10"-8¾"	convert to 22 WMR, 22 Rem. Jet, 22 Hornet, 22 K-Hornet, 256 Win., 357 Mag., 38 Spl., ($144), 9mm Luger, 30 Carb., 222 Rem., 44 Magnum & shot extra barrels ($36 ea.)

CHECK CHART OF U.S. CENTERFIRE AUTO PISTOLS

Make	Type	Calibers	Sights	Barrel	Price	Notes
AUTOPISTOLS						
American	Pocket	25	fix.	2⅛	58.50	Stainless Steel
Browning	Mil.	9mm	fix.	4⅝	112.50	13-shot clip
Colt	Mil.	45, 38, 9mm	fix.	4¼	125.00	Commander
Colt	Mil.	45, 38	fix.	5	125.00	MK IV series in 45
Colt N.M.	Tar.	45, 38 Spl.	adj.	5	190.00	MK IV series in 45 Gold Cup 45, 38
S&W	Tar. 52-1	38 Spl. WC	adj.	5	197.00	new trigger, sear, etc.
S&W	Mil.	9mm	adj.	4	110.00	double action
Universal	Mil.	30	adj.	10¼	129.95 up	Shortened M1 Carbine

CHECK CHART OF U.S. CENTERFIRE REVOLVERS

Make	Type	Model	Calibers	Sights	Barrel	Price	Notes
REVOLVERS							
Char. Arms	Belly	U'cover	38 Spl.	fix.	2-3	75.23	nickel $85.23 round or square butt.
Colt	Belly	Det. Spl.	38 Spl., 32 NP	fix.	2-3	96.50 up	nickel, $111.00
Colt	Belly	Cobra	38 Spl., 32 NP	fix.	2-3-4	101.00	nickel, $116.15
Colt	Belly	Agent	38 Spl.	fix.	2	101.00	with hammer shroud $107.00
Colt	Med.	Diamondback	38 Spl.	adj.	2½-4	135.00	also in 22 LR
Colt	Med.	Pol. Pos. Spl.	38 Spl., 32 NP	fix.	4-5	96.50	nickel, $111.00
Colt	Med.	Off. Pol. MKIII	38 Spl.	fix.	4-5-6	115.00	
Colt	Med.	Lawman	357 Magnum	fix.	4	115.00	
Colt	Med.	Metropolitan	38 Spl.	fix.	4	115.00	
Colt	Med.	Trooper MKIII	38 Spl., 357 M	adj.	4-6	135.50 up	target, $142.00
Colt	Tar.	U.M. Match	38 Spl.	adj.	6	143.00	
Colt	Lge.	Python	357 Magnum	adj.	2½-4-6	190.00	nickel, $218.50
Colt	Lge.	S.A. Army	357, 45C	fix.	4¼-5½-7½	190.00	also 44 Spl.
Colt	Lge.	Buntline	45 Colt	fix.	12	215.00	
Colt	Lge.	New F'tier	357, 44 Spl., 45C	adj.	5½-7½	225.00	flat-top, Royal Blue
F. I.	Belly	Regent	32	fix.	2½, 4	39.95	
H&R	Small	G'man 732	32 S&W Long	fix.	2½-4	47.95	chrome, $59.95
H&R	Belly	925	38 S&W	semi	2½, 4	59.95	
I.J.	Belly	55S-A	32 & 38 S&W	fix.	2½	41.50	
I.J.	Belly	67S Snub	32 & 38 S&W	adj.	2¾	57.50	
Ruger	Lge.	Blackhawk	357, 41 Mag., 30 US	adj.	4⅝-6½	98.50	41 cal. new
Ruger	Lge.	Blackhawk	357/9mm Convrt.	adj.	4⅝-6½	110.00	2 cyls.
Ruger	Lge.	Super B'hawk	44 Magnum	adj.	7½	125.00	
Ruger	Med.	Sec.-Six	357 Magnum	fix.	2¾, 4, 6	87.50	adj. sights, $97.50
S&W	Belly	Terrier	38 S&W	fix.	2	84.00	nickel, $92.00
S&W	Belly	Chiefs Spl.	38 Spl.	fix.	2-3	84.00	airweight, $86.50 up
S&W	Belly	M60 Chiefs Spl.	38 Spl.	fix.	2	110.00	stainless steel
S&W	Belly	B'guard	38 Spl.	fix.	2	86.50	airweight, $94.50
S&W	Belly	C'tennial	38 Spl.	fix.	2	90.50	airweight, $96.50 up
S&W	Small	Reg. Police	32 & 38 S&W	fix.	2-3-4	84.00	nickel, $92.00
S&W	Small	Hand Ejec.	32 Long	fix.	2-3-4	84.00	nickel, $92.00
S&W	Med.	Mil. & Pol.	38 Spl.	fix.	2-4-5-6	84.00 up	2", 4" airweight, $86.50 up
S&W	Med.	H. B. M&P	38 Spl.	fix.	4	84.00	heavy barrel
S&W	Med.	Mil. & Pol.	41 Magnum	fix.	4	105.50 up	
S&W	Med.	Combat Mas.	38 Spl.	adj.	2, 4	97.50	
S&W	Med.	Combat Mag.	357 Magnum	adj.	4, 6	135.00	target stocks
S&W	Med.	CF Magnum	22 Magnum	adj.	4, 6, 8⅜	144.50	inserts for 22RF
S&W	Tar.	K-32	32 S&W Long	adj.	6	107.50	
S&W	Tar.	K-38	38 Spl.	adj.	6-8⅜	107.50	S.A. type, $119.50
S&W	Lge.	H'way Patrol	357 Magnum	adj.	4-6	107.50	
S&W	Lge.	357 Magnum	357 Magnum	adj.	3½, 5, 6, 8⅜	156.50	
S&W	Lge.	41, 44 Mag.	41, 44 Mag.	adj.	4-6-8⅜	181.00	target grade
S&W	Lge.	1955 Target	45 Auto	adj.	6½	138.50	
Wesson	Med.	M12	357 Magnum	adj.	2½, 4, 6	110.00	

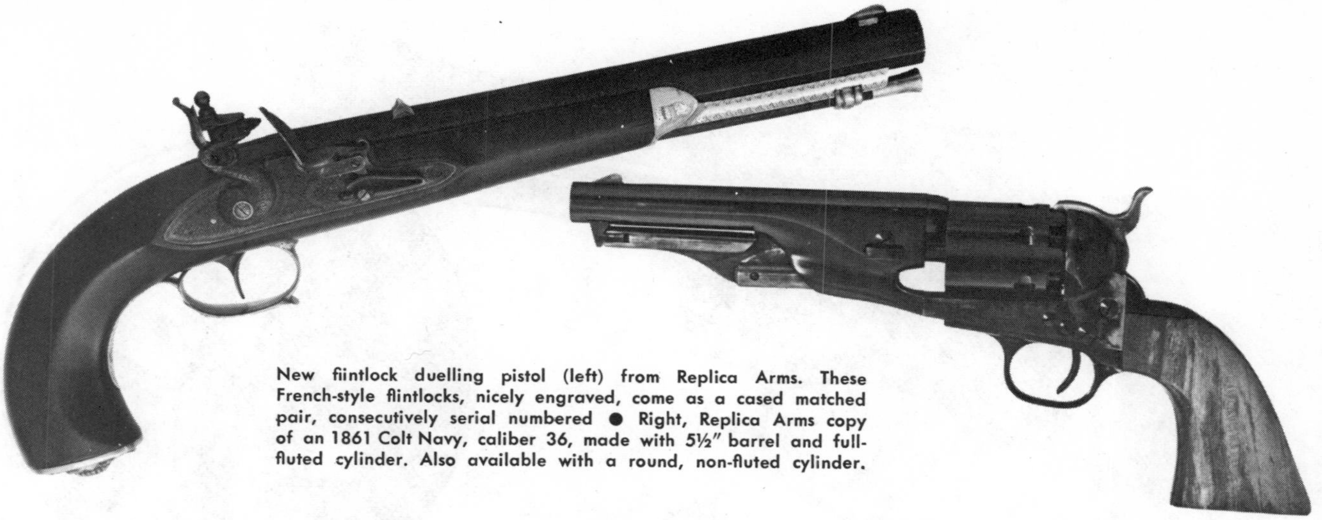

New flintlock duelling pistol (left) from Replica Arms. These French-style flintlocks, nicely engraved, come as a cased matched pair, consecutively serial numbered ● Right, Replica Arms copy of an 1861 Colt Navy, caliber 36, made with 5½" barrel and full-fluted cylinder. Also available with a round, non-fluted cylinder.

CHECK CHART OF FOREIGN CENTERFIRE AUTO PISTOLS

Make	Type*	Calibers	Sights	Barrel	Price	Notes
Astra	P	32	fix.	3½		Constable DA
Beretta	U	32,380	adj.	6	69.95	Puma
Beretta	M	9mmP	fix.	4½	117.50	Brigadier
Beretta	P	32	fix.	3½	110.00	M90 DA
Erma	U	32,380	fix.	3¼	89.95	Luger style
Erma	M	9mmP	fix.	4⅜	129.95	DA
HK-4	P	22, 25, 32, 380	fix.	3½	125.00	Inter. cals., DA
Hawes	U	32	fix.	6	64.95	
Llama	M	38, 45	fix.	5	92.50	Colt Copy
MAB	M	9mmP	fix.	5	109.00	15 shot
Mauser	P	32, 380	fix.	3⅜	110.00	HSc DA
SIG	M	22, 7.65, & 9mmP	fix.	4¾	197.00 up	Convert.
Star	M	9mmP, 38, 45	fix.	5	89.95	Mod. Colt Copy
Walther	P	22, 32, 380	fix.	3⅞	106.00	PP DA
Walther	M	7.65, 9mmP	fix.	$4\frac{15}{16}$	106.00 up	DA
Walther	P	22, 32, 380	fix.	$3\frac{5}{16}$	106.00	PPK/S DA

*P = Pocket, U = Utility, M = Military.

CHECK CHART OF FOREIGN RIMFIRE AUTO PISTOLS

Make	Type*	Calibers	Sights	Barrel	Price	Notes
Beretta	U —	22	adj.	6	69.95	Jaguar
Beretta	T	22	adj.	6	87.00	Sable
Erma	U	22	fix.	3⅜	79.95	Luger style
Gaucho	U	22	fix.	5, 6½	59.95	
Hammerli	T	22	adj.	6, $7\frac{1}{16}$	215.00 up	M206, 7, 8, 9, 10
Star	U	22	fix.	5	59.95 up	Mod. FR
Unique	U	22	adj.	6	65.85	Corsair
Walther	P	22	fix.	$3\frac{5}{16}$, 3⅞, 6	112.00 up	DA
Walther	T	22	adj.	5¾	198.00 up	OSP, GSP
Walther	U	22	fix.	$4\frac{15}{16}$	132.00	P38 DA

*P = Pocket, U = Utility, T = Target.

HGR-28

CHECK CHART OF FOREIGN CENTERFIRE REVOLVERS

Make	Type	Model	Calibers	Sights	Barrel	Price	Cap.
Arminius	M	HW38	32, 38 Spl.	adj.	4, 6	47.95 up	6
Astra	B	Cadix	32, 38 Spl.	adj.	3, 4, 6	64.50	5
Dakota	SA	———	357, 41, 44, 45	fix.	4⅝, 5½, 7½	89.75 up	6
Deputy	SA	———	357 Mag.	fix.	4¾	79.95	6
Hawes	SA	———	357, 44, 45	fix.	5½	89.95 up	6
Herters	SA	Powermag	357, 401, 44	adj.	6½	59.95	6
I.N.A.	B	———	32, 38 Spl.	fix.	3, 4½	52.95 up	5
Llama	M	Martial	38 Spl.	adj.	4, 6	74.50	6
Rossi	B	———	32, 38 Spl.	adj.	3, 4, 6	60.50	5
Sauer	T	Medallion	38 Spl.	adj.	4, 6	119.95 up	6
Solingen	B	———	38 Spl.	fix.	2	59.95	6
Stallion	SA	———	357, 45	fix.	5½, 6½	87.00	6
Taurus	B	———	38 Spl.	fix.	4	60.50	6

M = Medium (size), B = Belly, SA = Single Action, T = Target

HGR-29

CHECK CHART OF FOREIGN RIMFIRE REVOLVERS

Make	Type	Model	Cal.	Sights	Barrel	Price	Cap.
Arminius	U	———	22	fix.	3, 4, 6, 9½	37.95 up	6
Astra	B	———	22	fix.	3, 4, 6	64.50	9
Dakota	SA	———	22	fix.	4⅝, 5½, 7½	89.75 up	6
Deputy	SA	———	22	fix.	4¾	39.95 up	6
Herters	SA	Western	22	adj.	5	27.45	6
Llama	U	Martial	22	adj.	6	74.50 up	6
Sauer	T	Medallion	22	adj.	4, 6	119.95	6
Stallion	SA	———	22	adj.	5½, 6½	87.00	6

U = Utility, B = Belly, SA = Single Action, T = Target.

Ruger Security-Six

Here's the Ruger Security-Six double-action revolver in its production form—a handsome and sturdy holster handgun. Compact and relatively light (33½ oz. in the 4" barrel size), it is at the same time amply strong and massive enough for heavy-duty police and military use, for law enforcement personnel generally.

This genuinely solid-frame revolver—there are no sideplates or sideplate screws to loosen—the new Ruger S.S. is made of steel throughout, except for the checkered walnut grip panels.

The basic components—frame, cylinder, crane, and barrel are made of heat-treated chrome-moly steel, while the coil springs, used throughout are wound from the best steel music wire.

The new Ruger double action can be field stripped in a minute—literally—and reassembled in about as short a time, with only a coin for a tool.

A positive internal safety system interposes a block of steel between the spring-loaded firing pin head and the face of the hammer *only* when the hammer is drawn fully rearward. This safety system was designed to prevent accidental discharge if the gun should be dropped or if the hammer is struck.

Made in 357 Magnum (handles 38 Special as well) or in 38 Special, the Ruger S.S. is offered with a 2¾", 4" or 6" barrel, and with fixed or adjustable sights at $89 and $97.50 respectively.

Pictured here are the 2¾-inch barreled Ruger Security-Six with fixed sights and the same model with 4-inch barrel and adjustable sights. The closeup within the circle shows details of the checkered hammer spur for positive thumb cocking, the adjustable rear sight with its heavy guard walls, and the serrated thumb latch for releasing the swing-out cylinder. The wide trigger is also grooved.

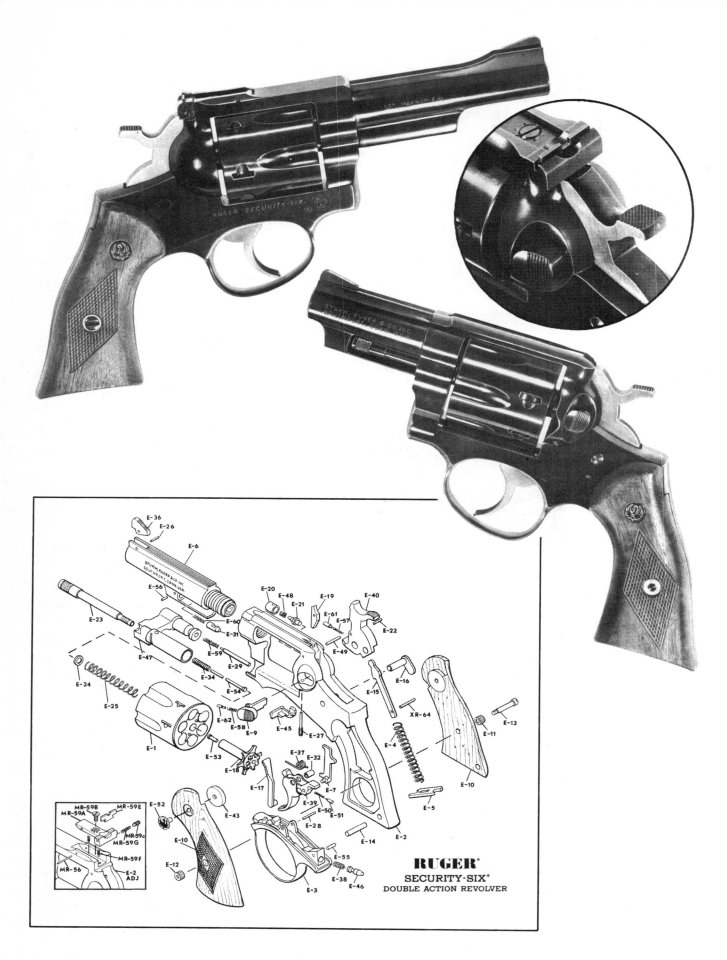

RUGER®
SECURITY-SIX®
DOUBLE ACTION REVOLVER

letters to...

These are some of the letters received
by Jim Hack, distinguished gun editor of *Shooting & Blasting*.
Mr. Hack has been writing about guns, shooting, and hunting
for many years. His shooting feats are legendary, and he is
the recipient of many honors, including the Krautbauer Trophy.
His latest book is *Freeloading Through Life*.

Dear Mr. Hack: I have always wanted to own some fine rifles but unfortunately I have never had the money to buy same. I am sure you have many fine rifles you never use and have no real use for. Therefore I am sure you will be glad to present me with same because I have real need for them. I have just graduated from the Word of God Bible College and am going to Tanzania to bring the Word of God to the natives. While I am engaged in doing the Lord's work I also plan to do some hunting. Therefore I am sure you will be glad to assist me in doing the Lord's work by sending me the following rifles: One 458 Winchester (pre-1964) stocked by Al Biesen with Leupold 3x scope on Griffin & Howe mount, open rear sight. Also send 200 rounds ammunition.

One 375 Magnum (preferably on a square-bridge Magnum Mauser action but if you send pre-1964 Model 70 there will be no hard feelings) with stock by Griffin & Howe or Goens. Redfield 2¾x scope please! 300 rounds of ammunition.

30-06 with 4x scope. I prefer one made by Bob Owens or Alvin Linden before 1940 but good post-war rifle would do. 500 rounds of ammunition.

Joe Jelks
R.D. #1
Broken Knee, Ark.

P.S.—Please send by Express Prepaid.
P.P.S.—The Lord will bless you!

Dear Friend—In the attic of an old house I have found a gun. It is 65 inches long and weighs about 10 or 11 pounds. It has a trigger. The man who owns the house and who said I could have it says he thinks his grandfather or somebody carried it in the Revolutionary War, or maybe it was the Civil War. Please tell me when it was made, who made it and how much I can get for it if I sell it.

John Roe
Titus City, Pa.

Dear Jim: I am 16 years old and I am interested in guns. I have a 22 and a single-shot 410. Last fall I killed two pheasants and 5 cottontails. I have been thinking about My Work in Life. I think I would like to be a Gun Editor. I read where you do a lot of Hunting. Do you pay your way or does *Shooting & Blasting* pay your way? Or do these "Outfitters" and Areoplane Companies give you free trips? How much do you make? How many hours a day do you work? What courses should I take in College so I could be a Gun Editor? How long are your vacations? How did you get your Job? You do not look very smart in your pictures but maybe you are.

Cletus Todd, Age 16
Mary Lou, Idaho

My dear Mr. Hack: I have just finished watching a program on TV in my snug little apartment here in "Sunny Southern California." It showed the *cutest* movie actor you ever saw hunting Lions in Africa. I was simply thrilled to death! It also showed this movie actor and his "white hunter" in their camp. It was simply *darling* and looked *very* comfortable. The "white hunter" was simply a Dream Boat and he had the most darling English accent I ever heard!

After seeing all this I am simply *dying* to go on safari. I am an airline stewardess and we get a perfectly *marvelous* discount to fly on any airline anywhere.

I have seen your pictures in *Shooting & Blasting*. You look awfully old but sort of *nice* and, well, *kind*. I know you go on safaris. I would simply *love* to go along. You must get very lonely with no one to talk to except the white hunter and the gun bearers and things. I would love to go with you. I could take down your notes or type your manuscripts, or *something*.

I have seen your picture so I think it is only fair that I enclose mine. I am 5 feet 3, and 36-22-34.

Annabelle Evans
722 Rodeo Drive
Beverly Hills, Calif

Dear Hack: I am loading my 30-06 with the 135-gr. Winnebago bullet and 56 grains of No. 4320. Please tell me what kind of groups I can shoot with that load. Please give me the pressure and the muzzle velocity. I will sight in at 200 yards. Please give me the drop at 300, 400, 500, 600, 700, 800, 900, and 1,000 yards.

Reply by return mail.

Albin Stumpkin
21-21st St.
Willebago, Pa.

Dear Jim: I read everything you write. I don't always agree with you but some of the time you are on the ball. Some fellows I work with at the factory and I want to hunt in Canada. We will go on our two week vacation. We will drive. Can you recommend an outfitter? We want reasonable prices and because we are all experienced in hunting deer here in Pa. and sometimes over the line in W. Va. we could work our way. We don't want anything fancy. We just want record sheep, caribou, moose, goats, and grizzly, good food, and good equipment.

Steve Nemick
Wilkes Barre, Pa.

Dear Mr. Hack: I was told by the husband of one of my friends (a Mr. Rollo Ashton, who reads *Shooting & Blasting*) that you have a free information service. I have to give a paper at the March meeting of the Daughters of the American Revolution. Please furnish me the history of the Finnegan family in Jones County, New Hampshire.

(Mrs.) Ellen Ring
Goober, Ia.

Dear Mr. Hack: I am taking advantage, as a subscriber to *Shooting & Blasting*, of your Free Information Service. Please answer the following questions at your earliest convenience:

1—What is the diameter of the following bullets, 280 Ross, 416 Rigby, 404 Jeffery, 8x46R, 470, 505 Gibbs, 450-400 Jeffery, 500-465 H&H.

2—Describe in detail the alloy used in the Winchester Model 21 frame and describe the heat treatment.

3—I have a Model 93 Marlin 30/30-cal., Serial number 61145. Please tell me what year, month, and day it was shipped from the factory, to what retailer, and what jobber. Give list price and wholesale price, also original owner if possible and oblige.

**Marvin T. Smith
Yankton, S.D.**

Dear Sir: I have a gun. It was in the closet behind some old boots where my late father died. In the same room, I mean. It has a number on it. It says 83561. Please tell me all about it. Where was it made? How much did it cost? I hear antique guns are very valuable. Is this an antique gun?

*Hyman K. Perkins
Rough & Ready, Ariz.
Gen. Del.*

Dear Mr. Hack: Pleeze tell me all about guns and shouting.

**Bobby Jimson-Weed, Age 9.
6863 Holly St.
Baltomore, Md.**

Dear Mr. Hack: My father and I are interested in hunting in the West. Please tell me the game to be found in the various Western states, the best areas to hunt each, the methods of

hunting, the license fees and hunting regulations of each state and oblige.

William B. Prawn Jr.
40 High Street
Stackbridge, N. J.

Dear Mr. Hack: I recently purchased at a "country" auction a very fine "shotgun." It is very valuable, people tell me. It has two barrels and on them it says "Royal Damascus." It has hammers but one is missing. It is also marked "Empire Special." I have been told it is worth $1000 but if you want it you can have it for $500.

**Julius Williams
Jonesboro, Ala.**

Dear Jim:

Could you please answer the following questions for me. I have checked out one of your books entitled *Jim Hack's Hunting Tales* and have read all three hunting articles about hunting in Sonora: "Santiago and the Cazedora," "Meat for Tamales," and "Plenty of Deer." I know it has been 20 or 30 years since you hunted there but could you please try to answer the following: 1. Where did you hunt in the preceding chapters? 2. Do you think these are still good hunting? 3. Where do you think would be a good place to hunt big Desert Bighorn Sheep, Whitetail and Mule Deer? 4. What problems would there be in obtaining licenses for all three species? 5. How much are licenses and guides? 6. If my Dad and I work up a trip to Sonora could you go and when? Please answer this one. 7. Do you think there is much game in Sonora?

Please answer the following

(1) Which is the best or which do you like the best, a 20 or 25x spotting scope? Why? Which make do you like the best? Why? How much will a good spotting scope cost?

(2) What make and what model knife do you like and use for skinning and gutting game? How do you sharpen your knives?

(3) Could you give me the trajectory of the 270 with 130-gr. bullet out to 600 yards using the Winchester-Western factory ammunition?

(4) What is the drop at 600 and 550 yards with the 130-gr. 270 with your handloaded ammunition sighted in 3" high at 100 yards and on the nose at 275 yards and 38" low at 500 yards?

(5) When you have downed a sheep trophy and are carrying out the head as pictured in *Jim Hack's Hunting Tales* do you carry out the head and the whole skin or just the head and the skin from the shoulders forward or back of the front legs forward? How do you leave the carcass before you return and get it? Do you use a sheet of plastic or a tarp to skin out the animal on to keep the meat from getting dirty? When you cannot skin an animal at once and lay him over a log or large stone so the air can circulate do you put the body cavity where

it's facing up, down, or toward the side?

(6) When one has a 4-minute dot in a 2½x scope and is shooting at game at 300 to 400 yards away doesn't the reticle on deer and sheep, etc., cover up the entire lung, heart, shoulder area so the error of aim is very great? Why do you use a 4-minute dot in a 2½x scope and a 2-minute dot in a 4x scope? What make scopes do you like the best and what happened to the 2½x Lyman Alaskan scope? Which is the best on a 270 for all-round hunting purposes, a 2½x or 4x scope? What reticle and power scopes do you like the best for big game hunting, target shooting, and varmint hunting? Which is the best for hunting purposes, an internally or externally adjustable scope? What make mounts and rings do you like the best? Do you use "Lock-Tite" or any other formula? Why?

(7) What action do you like the best? Why?

(8) On your 270s what are the grip caps and buttplates made out of? Why don't you use recoil pads on 270s and 30-06s, etc.? Which are the best for heavy- and medium-recoil rifles, solid or perforated pads? Why?

(9) On your classic 270s how are the cheekpieces shaped? Which do you like the best? Why?

(10) Could you please give me your phone number in case I want to call you. Here is my phone number, Area Code 721, 68-29264, in case you want to call me.

(11) Could you please give me all your loads and muzzle velocities for the 270. One is 60 grains of 4831. Please give me all your loads and muzzle velocities for the 25-06. Please give lengths of barrels.

(12) What make bullets are best for Whitetail and Mule Deer and sheep? Which kind do you use? Is the Hornady a good bullet? Is it too heavily constructed for light game like Whitetail Deer? Which is best, spitzer or spire point bullets? Why? Which are the best, regular or boat-tail bullets? Why?

Lum Jones
Applet, Tex.

P.S. If you want to you can put your answers on the backs of these pages. Please try to answer all my questions. I have checked out and read *Jim Hack's Hunting Tales* and also *Blasting Through Life*. I have enjoyed them *very much*. Say hello to your wife for me. When and where do you plan your next big game hunt? (I hope it is down to Sonora.)

Dear Hack:

Please tell me where I can get parts for a World War II Germany pistol, where I can get it fixed, and how much it will cost.
Paul Krammer
Glasgow, Pa.

Dear Friend:

Probably 5 or 6 years ago I got in the mail a small newspaper or something, maybe 20-30 pages, and it had a lot of ads about guns, parts, etc. There was one I was interested in, but I didn't buy it at the time. It was a 22 rifle barrel guaranteed accurate, just a "blank." I have always wished

I had bought it. I am sure you have seen the "paper." Please look it up, find out if there are any of those barrels left, how much they cost, etc. Have them send me one C.O.D.

Thank you very much!

A. E. Jones
Suggin, S. D.

Dear Mr. Hack,

I am 29 years old, I am a good shot and very strong. I have hunted deer in Pa., Va., and W. Va. I have decided to take a year off my job and take an extended Big Game Hunt for the following species of game: Jaguar, Ocelot, Jaguarundi, Margay, Bobcat, Cougar, Javelina, Pronghorn, Mule Deer, Stone Sheep, Dall Sheep, Mountain Goat, Caribou, Elk, Moose, Grizzly Bear, Brown Bear.

Please list the best locality for each specie and list the seasons, license fees, etc. Also give me 5 outfitters for each specie.

I want to get all this game before I marry and settle down. I would also like to write stories about these hunts. It would be good if I had a companion. I am sure you could find one who would go with me and pay most of the expenses in return for being mentioned in my stories. Please reply at earliest convenience.

Frank Crumb
Pittsburgh, Pa.

Dear Sir:

I would like for you to make me up a list of recommended loads using the following powders: Hodgdon's, Norma's, Herters, Duponts, Hercules, Etc, Etc, with bullets as follows; 85 grs., 87 grs., 93 grs., 100 grs., 120 grs., 125 grs., 129 grs., 130 grs., 139 grs., 140 grs., 150 grs., 156 grs., 160 grs., 165 grs., and 200 grs., for the 6.5mm Ackley Mag. and for the 6.5x55mm Improved Version 77 grs., to 165 grs. This barrel is 31¼" long, what would be the best range to sight this rifle in at? And on the Magnum with a 29¼" inch long barrel what would be the best range to sight this rifle in at? I have a complete set of reloading dies by RCBS, and case forming dies by the same. The only thing I need is plenty of case's in 6.5x55m-m Norma, and Magnum Brass New or Once-Fired. Also recommended Cast Bullets with gas checks loads, for both rifles. I see the 6.5x61m-m Belted Magnum, by Bob Steindler in August, 1969 *Shooting Times*, is very close to the 6.55m-m Ackley Magnum, the case length of 61m-m translates into 2.44" and the fire-formed case has a 28 degree shoulder. I was thinking of using this loading data as a guide. If you ever want to Test this rifle while here in New York, just drop me a letter saying so and I would have it ready for you to pick it up, and then you will be able to give me your own opinion, as to what loads work best in my rifle. I am enclosing a stamped self-address envelope for your reply. Thanking you ever so much, in your efforts to guide and help me, if there is a cost for the information I seek, I would gladly pay for it.

Wm. P. Schlock
Salmoc, N.Y.

Guns and Game Shooting—

a comparison of American and British practices.

Nilo Farms photo

Despite the author's claim to neutrality, we think
you'll detect a bit of bias for the sportsman's way of going
in the United Kingdom. He could be right, too, but . . .

by DEREK PARTRIDGE

WHY IS IT that most hunting pictures I see in American shooting magazines show a pheasant lumbering up into the air from under the hunter's feet or a mallard careening away from a blind—and both about to be shot at point-blank range? Conversely, why is it that I often hear hunters discussing other hunters who've blasted off at birds so far away they'd need an ICBM to reach them?

Editors I have discussed this with reckon that a small number of these pictures are faked-up for visual impact, but they agree, sadly, that generally they're a fair reflection of how many American hunters shoot. At such ranges, the shot pattern has no time to spread out. A bird hit at this range will be no good for eating. Is this what the American hunter really wants? Let's look at the other side of the coin.

Some American hunters are only after their bag limit, and they're not too fussy how they fill it. Quantity has become the motivating force behind their sport, so-called, as they massacre pathetically easy targets. Is there any easier shot than a cumbersome pheasant trying desperately to

get airborne after being flushed at one's feet? At other times these sportsmen fire hopefully into the skies at wild-fowl that are so far away they look like sparrows. They mistakenly believe that magnum guns and super magnum loads extend the maximum effective 50-yard killing range of the shotgun into hundreds of feet.

I believe there are few hunters in Britain who shoot at birds even at 40 yards. I say this because there is a 120-foot duck tower at the West London Shooting Grounds which throws a target 40 yards high. I've heard many of the country's finest and most experienced game shots swear that these targets are unkillable because they are hopelessly out of range. 40 yards straight up is really quite a distance

Bill Dittman lowers the boom on a Nilo Farms pheasant. This is a crossing shot of about 40 yards, and the bird has a tailwind. Bill cut tailfeathers with his first shot, nailed the bird with his second. He is hunting in a field of native cover—mostly daisy fleabane and foxtail. To his left is a dense hedge of multiflora rose; behind that are cultivated fields of corn and milo sorghum—tailor-made pheasant cover.

when you look at it, yet well within the capabilities of the shotgun.

I know kills are also made at up to 60 yards, but that calls for skill (or luck) to do so consistently, and it is all too likely to result in wounded birds. The control of large areas of British wildfowling by the Wildfowlers' Association of Great Britain is effectively eliminating this type of hunter.

Surveys by wildfowl bureaus in the States have shown large numbers of geese and duck carrying pellets in their feet and undersides. These pellets could never have had the slightest chance of being immediately lethal. The slowly dying birds found are devastating testimony to this form of bad sportsmanship. It is a disgrace, and only brings justifiable, but understandably indiscriminate, public outcry against true sportsmen.

I've used the word "sportsman" several times and with deliberate stress. How does one define the term in relation to hunting? I'm fairly impartial, I think (my father was English and my mother American), but I think Britain provides the answer. I believe, most people accept Britain as the traditional home of the shooting sports and of real sportsman. The English have a reputation for "playing the game" (often to their own detriment!) in most aspects of their dealings with man and beast. Whether that is still true today may be argued, but I'm going back into the not-too-distant past for the origins of the true sporting code. They might also be described as the unwritten, but rigidly respected rules of the game between hunter and hunted.

Rules of the Game

Most young English sportsmen are put through a strict apprenticeship by parents, gamekeepers or pest control officers. Their early shooting is mostly for wood-pigeon, a bird about the size of a bandtailed pigeon, with the flight characteristics of the mourning dove. Wood-pigeons are a serious threat to English agriculture as they eat anything a farmer plants. Flocks, in the thousands, can totally destroy fields in a few days.

Officially classified as pests, wood-pigeon are hunted throughout the country *all year round*. This develops an extremely hardy, fast-moving bird into an unbelievably wary quarry. It can spot you, with your gun, hundreds of yards away. It can also perform the most baffling acrobatics between the moment it sees your gun barrel moving and your firing. This means the young British shooting man is brought up with very difficult, but very rewarding, shooting.

I remember that the most satisfying, but not my largest bag, in terms of good shooting, was in the failing light of a winter's evening in the Lincolnshire fens. In the last 45 minutes before it became too dark to see, I shot 59 wood-pigeons and a pheasant with 83 shells—there are no bag limits in Britain! When I returned next morning to collect them, every one had been devoured by the huge rats that infested that copse!

The average English hunter has a strange quirk that's hard to explain; he has a tremendous degree of respect, almost affection, for his quarry—an unusual attitude towards the creatures he kills.

Most game shot in Britain is driven rather than walked-up, but partridge and grouse are also walked-up, with dogs. As the birds explode from the ground, ahead of the dogs, immediately flying fast and low, they're considered sporting targets. To further insure "sporting" shooting, the dogs flush them a considerable distance from the gunners. Pheasants are scarcely ever walked-up, except by the rough shooter walking the hedgerows, with his dog, for anything that gets up. The pheasant's lumbering ascent and large bulk class it as an unsporting target for walking-up.

With driven game, the idea is to flush birds far enough from the guns so that they're moving at top speed

Ernie Simmons swings on a big Nilo Farms pheasant—not the easiest shot for a right-handed gunner. In hunting this rather dense cover of foxtail edges and heavy milo, Ernie chose an improved cylinder barrel and a Super Trap load of 7½s. An excellent combination for most large upland birds, in the new sleeved shotshells it is effective at longer ranges than most birdhunters think.

Nilo Farms photo

and well up in the air by the time they reach the shooters. This way, they offer a variety of difficult crossing and passing shots. This is further enhanced by the vagaries of the British climate—a normal cocktail of pelting rain well-mixed by high winds! I have often watched skilled game shooters deliberately picking the most difficult shots in preference to the easy ones. Frequently, they lower their guns when a bird appears which they consider too easy and no challenge to their ability.

These people were the backbone of the British sporting scene—true sportsmen and gentlemen. Today taxes, estate and death duties have curtailed the activities of many and closed their estates. Their places are often taken by townsfolk with money. These people are frequently ignorant of the ways and traditions of the country, and have more money than manners. They make many a gamekeeper curse under his breath and wish for the good old days!

The British shoot other game and wildfowl similar to ours in the U.S., but with slightly differing guns and loads. They like the 12 gauge with standard or light loads rather than 12s with heavy loads or smaller gauge guns with heavier loads. There are practical reasons. English game guns are—or were—hand-made to weigh between 6¼ and 6¾ pounds. This eliminates the problem of carrying excessive weight around, but limits one to comparatively light loads to avoid intolerable recoil.

Until the recent introduction of lightweight models, American mass-produced field models weighed roughly between 7¼ and 8¼ pounds, and only the 20 gauge was comparable in weight to the English 12s. Occasionally a 16 gauge is seen at a British shoot—often owned by a man who'd lived in the Middle or Far East. There he had wanted an even lighter gun and a reduction in the weight of the shells he carried on long treks in the heat and humidity. 20s, 28s and 410s are almost exclusively used by women and youngsters, who often graduate, gauge by gauge, until they reach the 12.

This difference in gun weight is also one of the reasons for the different styles of American and British shooting. The British almost invariably use the gun technique known as "swinging-through," their light guns being best suited to this method. The target is passed at overtaking speed and the gun fired at the moment of passing—the overtaking speed itself providing the necessary lead.

In the U.S., the more popular method appears to be pointing-out a sustained lead—a more suitable system for guns of greater over-all weight and often muzzle-heavy. One of the great weaknesses of the sustained lead method is that I defy anyone to accurately measure any distance in mid-air

from 20 to 50 yards away. It is only the individual's idea of what the space between his muzzle and the target appears to be *to him*. Each individual's assessment is going to be different. It is therefore absolutely impossible to try and teach someone to shoot by this method.

Using the swing-through method, the tracking swing starts as the gun is being mounted and the trigger pulled virtually as soon as the gun touches the shoulder. This is possible because British emphasis on the importance of proper gun fit gives us the certain knowledge that when we mount the gun and look at a target, the gun is "looking at"—and therefore shooting at—the same spot.

Americans, in common with many non-British Europeans, tend to use unnecessarily heavy loads. Europeans seem to have a fondness for recoil; when they pull the trigger, they want to know it! Americans seem to think they obtain greater ranges with heavier loads. This is not entirely true. The effective range of a shell—the range at which one can reasonably expect a clean kill from a correctly pointed gun—is dependent on the striking energy of the size of pellet used.

Naturally, large pellets will carry farther and faster than smaller ones (via their increased ability to overcome air resistance—and also maintain their striking energy for a greater distance. But you can't load so many large pellets into a shell, so you leso pattern performance. Therefore, while individual pellets will travel a longer

distance and still be capable of killing, it is a gamble that there will be a sufficient number of these larger pellets striking the bird to insure a clean kill.

To kill, you either need a certain number of pellets each with a certain striking energy (depending on the size of the bird) hitting almost anywhere, or one pellet hitting a vital spot. At extended ranges, there is little chance of the requisite number of pellets being close enough together, and the possibility of hitting a vital spot with one pellet is far outweighed by the likelihood of hitting a non-vital spot, this causing a painful, lingering death. The "sportsman" who causes this doesn't even have the satisfaction of bringing home his bag.

The British standard 12-ga. load is $1\frac{1}{16}$ ounces, but running a very close second to it is a straight 1-oz. load. A considerable number of shooters will use as little as $\frac{7}{8}$-oz., which approximately matches their standard 20-ga. load. A small number will go up to $1\frac{1}{8}$ ounces, but this load is generally preferred by the wood-pigeon shooter rather than the game shooter. The standard duck and goose load is $1\frac{3}{16}$ ounces, although $1\frac{1}{4}$ ounces is also popular. The maximum magnum load is $1\frac{3}{8}$ ounces, while the American magnum load is a full $\frac{1}{4}$-oz. more to make $1\frac{7}{8}$ ounces. Standard British game loads for 16, 20, 28 and 410 gauges are respectively: $\frac{15}{16}$-oz.; $1\frac{3}{16}$-oz.; $\frac{9}{16}$-oz. and $\frac{7}{16}$-oz.

Recommended shot sizes for comparable game are: (shot sizes have been converted from English to American): Pheasant—6 or $7\frac{1}{2}$; partridge

Photo by John Marchington

Photo by John A. Pearce

Above—A very high cock with the second barrel of a magnificent right and left ● Coastal ducks give only a fleeting chance, call for constant alertness by the wildfowler and his dog.

—7½; grouse—6 or 7½; geese—2 or 4; duck—5 or 6 and rabbits—6. The most popular size for all-round game shooting is English No. 6, which comes between the American 6 and 7½, but, strangely enough, does not exist in the U.S.

The most popular barrel length is undoubtedly 28″. Some game shooters are disciples of the late Bob Churchill's 25″ barrel theory, while the wildfowler generally favors 30″. The big majority of game guns are side-by-sides, with only an occasional over-under. One barrel is generally bored improved-cylinder, with improved-modified or full in the second barrel. Also very popular as a first barrel is quarter-choke, which comes between improved-cylinder and modified. Naturally, people have different borings for guns or extra sets of barrels for different types of shooting, with the wildfowler using tighter choking. The chokes mentioned are generally those selected for an all-purpose gun as being the best compromise for all forms of shooting.

Automatics are absolutely taboo at any British game shoot. Some shooters will *say* they object on the grounds of safety. This is a reasonable objection as they like to see a gun broken open to clearly indicate it is safe. But if they were really honest, the majority have nothing more than hide-bound, traditional objections to this "nasty, unsightly, unwieldy, new-fangled, misbegotten . . . " Blood pressures rise and port-infused faces take on a ruddier hue!

I feel this is narrow-minded, since it is not the gun, but how it is handled by its owner that really matters. They also complain about the number of shells that can be loaded into an automatic. Below is a letter I once wrote to the English *Shooting Times* in reply to an item about automatics by a very distinguished writer whose work I greatly respect, normally. His remarks also express the strange attitude the British have towards their quarry—which I mentioned earlier.

The writer, Gough Thomas, had said: "I feel that a game little sporting bird that has successfully run the gauntlet of one shot should not be subjected to a second—not, at least, unless badly needed for the pot—still less to more." I replied: "By what moral right does he presume to allow that it is acceptable to shoot at a bird once and not twice—or more times? Either it is all right to shoot at and kill a bird for sport, or it is not—genuinely for the pot alone being a different matter. Each person must satisfy his own conscience on this issue. The 'game little sporting bird' does not willingly offer its life in the interests of sport—the decision is the sportsman's—the bird has no choice. 'To kill or not to kill, that is the question, not whether 'tis nobler to permit survival after one, two or more attempts.'" (With apologies to Shakespeare!)

I'll end this with a photo caption in the English *Shooting Times*. The picture shows a pheasant which has obviously just been flushed at the shooter's feet—the caption read, "One to leave alone . . . " ●

Photo by John A. Pearce

Photo by John A. Pearce

Above — One to leave alone ● Pigeon shooting over laid corn can give excellent opportunities for getting a dog in trim before the shooting season commences.

The 38 Special

the reports of its death have been greatly exaggerated!

by JAMES R. OLT

ASIDE FROM being the most widely used police and self-defense cartridge in the United States, the 38 Special is also the most maligned and criticized centerfire pistol cartridge in current use. Thousands of policemen and security guards have and will stake their lives without question on the power and accuracy of the 38 Special. Yet many writers and experts on handgun combat state flatly that the 38 Special is not a reliable manstopper.

The 38 Special is certainly no powerhouse when its factory load ballistics are compared to the 41 and 44 Magnums. The fact is, it looks downright puny alongside these hand cannons. However, the 38 comes closer

than you might think to the 357 Magnum — especially in short-barreled revolvers—when handloaded to maximum. But the real niche for the 38 Special, aside from target work, is when a rather powerful cartridge is needed in a small handgun—which takes in a lot of territory these days.

There has been a never-ending chain of development toward more powerful handgun cartridges for the last hundred years or so, culminating in the 357, 41 and 44 Magnums, and that's also how the 38 came about. The cartridge was developed when the 38 Long Colt was found to be woefully inadequate during the Philippine Insurrection. The original revolver chambered for the 38 Special

was the Smith & Wesson Military & Police Model of 1902. The original loading comprised a 158-gr. bullet in front of 21 grains of black powder. Since then, the 38 Special has been chambered in more handguns than Senator Dodd can shake a fist at; from tiny 2-shot derringers to the big, velvet-smooth target revolvers like the Smith & Wesson K-38 and the Colt Officers Model Match Target.

Like the 30-06 Springfield rifle cartridge, the 38 Special is factory loaded in a broad range of bullet weights and styles, and to several velocity levels. There are mildly loaded wadcutter target rounds and high speed, armor-piercing loads designed for blasting away at fleeing automobiles.

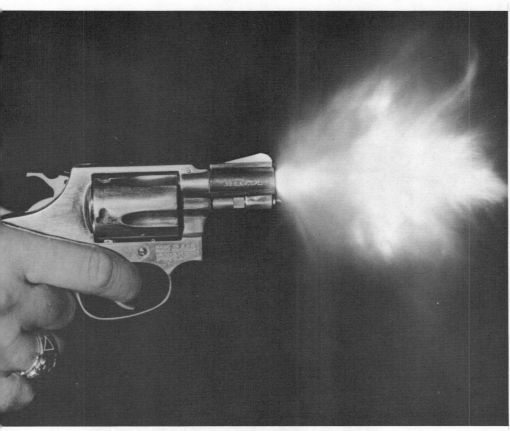

A Smith & Wesson stainless steel Chief's Special being fired at night with the standard Winchester-Western factory load.

fined holes in paper that the wadcutters and semi-wadcutters do. For most purposes, the round nose revolver bullet offends the olfactory organs, but, unfortunately, it is usually what you get when you buy a box of factory loaded 38s.

Also, the muzzle velocity is held way down in the standard 38 Special factory load—and with good reason! There are thousands of ancient (and some not so ancient) 38 revolvers floating around that can only be described as clunkers. Many of them are cheaply constructed foreign jobs that simply won't take the strain of extended shooting with fullhouse loads. So the cartridge is deliberately loaded to low pressure levels to make it safe even in poor revolvers. (Another fine revolver cartridge that suffers the same fate is the venerable 44 Special as far as factory loads are concerned. The handloaded 44 is another story, too.)

In an effort to overcome the built-in limitations of the 158-gr. round nose factory load, many 38 shooters who rely on store bought ammunition turn to the 200-gr. so-called "police load." Here again, a round nose bullet is used and the velocity is low — published figures show 730 fps in a 6-inch barrel. I've used this heavy version of the 38 Special in large and small frame revolvers from time to time and found it to be a big disappointment. It fails to penetrate the side of oil drums from as close as 15 feet. It drops like a rock at medium to long ranges, though ad-

Sad to say, though, probably the most potent version of the 38 Special—a 160-gr. semi-wadcutter bullet loaded to about 1100 fps muzzle velocity in a 6-inch barrel—is *not* available in a factory load.

There are some 15 different factory loaded versions of the 38 Special available today (not counting blanks), using bullets ranging from 110- to 200 grains. The 38 Special Match loads with 148-gr. wadcutter bullets loaded to about 770 fps mv are excellent for both serious target work and casual plinking. They are hard to improve on by handloading except for finding a particular bullet your revolver happens to shoot a little better than the others. Velocity is not the big thing in target shooting.

38 Special Loads

The most commonly seen version of the various 38 Special factory loads, in both yellow and green boxes, is the standard (and much cussed) 158-gr. round nose bullet loaded to the common 158-gr. load. A round nose bullet is simply no good for bringing out the potential of a good pistol cartridge. The round nose bullet doesn't give the slamming, brick-bat impact of the semi-wadcutter style. It leaves smaller entrance and exit wounds in game, holes that tend to close up after the bullet passes through instead of bleeding exten-

sively. The round nose bullet isn't very good for serious target shooting because it doesn't cut the sharply de-

The S&W 38 Chief's Special alongside the S&W 357 Combat Magnum.

Above left—Cartridges compared (from left): 357 Magnum, 38 Spec. 158-gr., 38 Spec. 160-gr. semi-wadcutter handload, 38 Spec. 200-gr. and 45 Auto. ● Right—Closeup comparison of the 38 Special 160-gr. semi-wadcutter handload and standard 158-gr. factory round-nose load. ● Below—Small frame 38 revolvers are ideal hideout arms. Holster shown is the Brauer semi-shoulder model, a spring type that is also usable as a cross-draw rig, as shown.

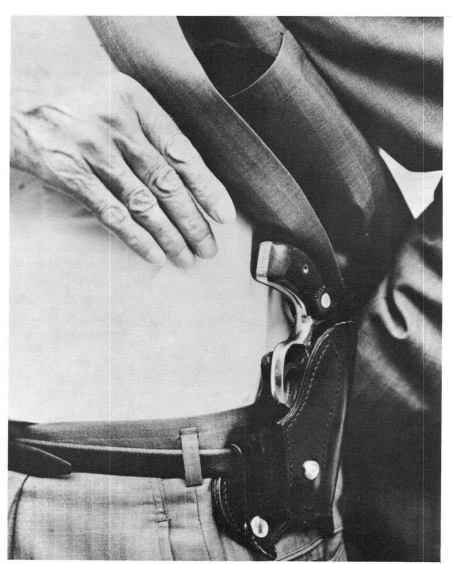

mittedly long range shooting is something the 200-gr. load was never intended for. It doesn't make any more sense, of course, to shoot over-hefty bullets in the limited-powder-capacity 38 Special case than it does to load 220-gr. missiles in 30-30 brass. There should be something of a sensible balance between bullet weight and case capacity.

However, a new and brighter spot in the commercial loading picture is the 38 Special ammunition produced by Super-Vel Co. of Shelbyville, Indiana. Their 38 Special loading consists of a 110-gr. jacketed softpoint bullet at 1370 fps muzzle velocity, which turns up the considerably more impressive muzzle energy figure of 458 ft/lbs. This is a wicked load for varmints, and also for self-defense. The Super-Vel torpedoes are finding more and more acceptance with law enforcement agencies, too.

Now, just after I'd completed this essay, a 1970 Norma catalog reveals four new cartridges in 38 Special. The hottest one is their 110-gr. semi-jacketed HP going 1542 fps at the muzzle for 580 ft./lbs. of energy. Next, their 158-gr. semi-jacketed HP at 900 fps, ME being 285; then the same load but with a full-jacket semi-wadcutter bullet. Last, the new Norma 158-gr. RN lead bullet, which leaves the muzzle at 870 fps, ME 266 ft./lbs. All of these MV figures were got in a 6" barrel, and if the really tight groups shown came from that barrel, it's a good one indeed. One picture shows 10 shots at 50 meters (55 yards) going into a hole that measures a mere .370" on centers!

Remington also announced (late in 1969) two new 38 Special cartridges. A 125-gr. semi-jacketed HP lopes along at a fast 1370 fps. On target at 50 yards, it prints only 0.7" high at mid-range, only 3.0" low at 100 yards! Remington's other new 38 Special load uses the traditional 158-gr. bullet, but here in a semi-jacketed HP. MV is 1150 fps, well over anything they've done in this weight previously and in this caliber.

I wish I'd had a chance to shoot some of these—especially that Norma hotshot—but I haven't seen the ammo yet, at least not on my friendly dealer's shelves. Still, it hardly sounds like the old warhorse is all that spavined and swaybacked yet, does it?

Why the 38 Special

So far, all this sounds rather negative. Why should you want a 38 Special? The answer of many 38 owners is that it's a superbly accurate, mild-recoiling cartridge; quite versatile when handloaded, and with a great many fine revolvers and some automatics chambered for it. Various fine bullets are available for the 38 Special, and it gives excellent accuracy and results with several different powders. It is an easy—and economical—case to load for. For these reasons it is far and away the most popular centerfire target cartridge in the country.

While the ballistics of the 158-gr. RN factory load are rather unspectacular, the cartridge would be improved if it were loaded with the same 158-gr. semi-wadcutter Remington and Winchester use in the 357 Magnum. Nevertheless, to get all the potential out of the 38, a fullhouse handload is necessary. The finest all-round load for the 38 Special, I'm convinced, is a 158- to 162-gr. semi-wadcutter bullet like the Lyman 357446, the Markell SW160, or the Speer and Hornady 160-gr. jacketed softpoint jobs. Load these bullets in front of 11.0 grains of Hercules 2400, and your previously anemic 38 Special suddenly becomes a different proposition. Muzzle velocity is right at 1100 fps in a 6-inch barrel. In heavy frame revolvers like the Smith & Wesson K-38 or the Colt Officers Model this load can be increased by one grain, but this does warm things up a bit! Either load, of course, should be cautiously approached from below.

I don't care for hunting big game with a handgun—any handgun, for

Colt's new Official Police Mk III, a 38 Special double action revolver, comes with 4-, 5- or 6-inch barrel, may be had with smooth or serrated trigger, service or target hammer.

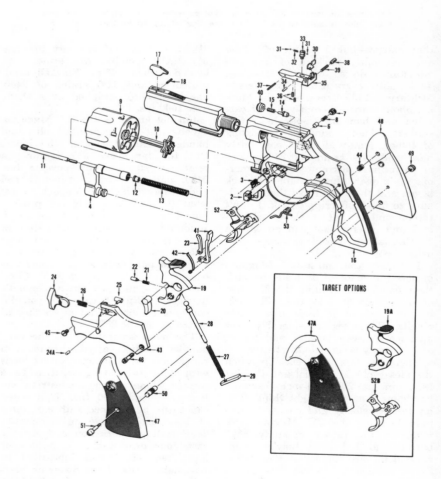

Isometric (exploded) view of the Colt Trooper Mk III, the new internal mechanism system is used in several other Colt double action revolvers.

Colt's new Lawman, a 357 Magnum that carries a 4-inch heavy barrel and fixed sights, is made on the Mk III frame, first introduced for the Trooper 357.

that matter—but a couple of Idaho and Wyoming packers of my acquaintance do so with 38 Specials. They both carry Smith & Wesson Military & Police revolvers, the blueing about worn off from years of carrying and handling. Both lads, fine stalkers, shoot handloads consisting of 160-gr. semi-wadcutters cast fairly hard and 11.0 grains of 2400. Both of them have accounted for numerous mule deer, plus a couple of black bears, and they often use their handguns to finish off crippled elk. I don't recommend it, but it shows what a cool and careful shot can do with a 38 Special at sensible ranges — and using a potent load.

I suspect that most 357 Magnum owners put a lot of 38 loads through their handguns. Loading the 357 case down to mild 38 velocities will work, but 38 loads in 38 brass give better results. There is considerably less airspace between powder and bullet, and accuracy is consistently better.

There is less difference between the mossy old 38 Special and the 357 Magnum in 2- to 4-inch barreled handguns than you might think. The impressive velocity and energy figures published for the 357 Magnum are taken in the rather unhandy 8⅜" barrel, and I believe they're exaggerated upward somewhat. The latest *Speer Reloading Manual* lists an interesting chart showing the effect of barrel length on the velocity of handgun cartridges. The widely-used 357 Magnum handload consisting of 14.0 grains of 2400 with a 160-gr. bullet was shot in the 8⅜" barrel for a chronographed 1301 fps, but in the

3½" barrel its MV was only 1084 fps. My S&W Combat Masterpiece 38, loaded with a 160-gr. Markell semi-wadcutter and 11.0 grains of 2400, has been chronographed at a shade over 1000 fps.

I'm not knocking the 357 Magnum. I believe it is the greatest all-round handgun cartridge ever developed. But the large-case 357 requires a relatively slow-burning powder like 2400, and at least a 4-inch barrel (preferably 6-inch or longer) to get what the case is capable of producing. I can't see the 357 in 2-inch snubnose revolvers at all; matter of fact, the very thought of a snubnose 357 makes my ears ring. However, if I had to part with all my handguns except one, I'd keep my S&W Combat 357 Magnum without a moment's hesitation. Still, I can tell you I'd continue to shoot a lot of 38 Special cartridges in the 357!

The most accurate of all the various 38 loadings at short-to-medium ranges are the mid-range target loads with 148- to 150-gr. wadcutters pushed along at the pedestrian velocity of about 800 fps. This speed can easily be attained with 3.0 grains of Hercules Bullseye or Winchester 240P Ball powder. You can cheaply cast your own wadcutter bullets or buy them sized and lubricated at reasonable prices from Speer or Markell, or from hundreds of individuals around the country who do custom bullet casting to pick up an extra buck. The wadcutter is seated flush with the case mouth, leaving a minimum airspace between the base of the bullet and the powder charge —

something that is conducive to good accuracy. The wadcutter, squared off at both ends, bears evenly on the rifling throughout its barrel travel.

This mild 38 Special load has much to recommend it for both serious target shooting and casual plinking. It is superbly accurate in a decent revolver. It is a joy to shoot; recoil is very mild. Revolvers fed this mild diet last forever, and brass also lasts for many, many loadings. Surprisingly enough, it gives pretty fair killing power for pest shooting.

I got wise to the poor killing power of the standard 158-gr. round nose factory load after plunking a number of Kansas jackrabbits with them. Most of 'em ran off like they weren't even hit. I switched over to some wadcutter target loads I found in a sporting goods store, and immediately saw a big difference. The flat-faced wadcutter, at ranges up to about 30 yards, does a pretty fair job with square body hits even on the big blacktail jacks. From the energy figures published for this load, it doesn't look adequate for anything much larger than a healthy starling. Bullet form and design means a lot in how a handgun bullet will kill, though, and again the flat nose proves its worth.

A wicked 38 wadcutter load for both varmint shooting and self-defense with one of the short-barreled revolvers is the Speer 148-gr. hollow-base wadcutter seated *upside down*. Loaded fairly mildly for small-frame revolvers with 3.5 grains of Bullseye, it's a potent combination for self defense. Loaded in front of 6.0 grains of Hercules Unique for the larger frame S&W Military & Police or the Colt Detective Special, it makes even stouter medicine.

There is a big assortment of 38 Special handguns available these days. The Smith & Wesson K-38 and the Colt Officers Model Match Target offer the epitome of balance and precision for target shooting. While the 38 Special, a rimmed cartridge, has traditionally been made for revolvers, Colt has been chambering their National Match Gold Cup auto for it for some time, as does Smith & Wesson with their Model 52 Master Auto. However, note that both of these automatics are target pistols, and will function only with mid-range wadcutter loads with the bullets seated flush with the case mouth.

There are a pair of superb premium-grade holster revolvers chambered for the 38 Special — the Colt Diamondback and the Smith & Wesson Combat Masterpiece. Both carry excellent adjustable sights. The Diamondback is available with a 2½- or 4-inch barrel; the Combat Masterpiece can be had with either a 2- or a 4-inch tube. Both revolvers have smooth actions and trigger pulls, and

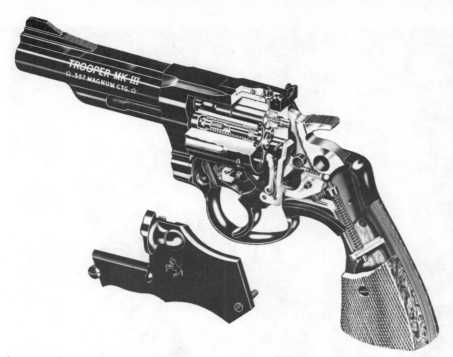

Colt's Trooper Mk III, a cutaway view that reveals the new internal mechanism that is common to several other new Colt revolvers. The Trooper is offered in 38 Special and 357 Magnum, each with 4- or 6-inch barrels; target or service grips, hammer and trigger.

shoot beautifully with a minimum of tuning. They are the choice of a great many policemen serious about what weapon they depend on.

A great many shooters who can't quite afford the sizable layout of cash it takes to buy a double action 357 Magnum revolver find some sort of happiness with the old reliable Smith & Wesson Military & Police, or the Colt counterpart, the Official Police. While the 38 Special is not the 357 Magnum, these last are no-nonsense, workhorse revolvers with a 4- or 6-inch barrel. Feed it that 160-gr. SWC/11.0 grs. 2400 load I've mentioned, and it's still in the ballpark. They can often be found, too, in good condition at reasonable prices.

The New 38s

Latest among quality handguns chambered for the 357/38 Special are Colt's Trooper Mk III, a superb revolver with a new interior design, target sights, the works. Just recently Colt has announced three other revolvers with the same advanced mechanism—one is a 1970 version of an old and tried standby, the new title being the Official Police Mk III, a bit lighter gun than the Trooper. The OP Mk III will be offered with 4", 5" and 6" barrels; fixed sights for police work are standard. Service and target grips will be available, and there's also a choice of triggers and hammers — smooth or serrated for the former, narrow service style or broad and serrated for the latter.

The new 38 Special Colt is called the Metropolitan Mk III. This revolver comes with a 4" heavy barrel, weighs 36 ounces, and features op-

tional equipment like the Colt Official Police Mk III—hammer, trigger, grips, etc.

There's another new 357 Magnum, too, the Lawman Mk III, also with the 4" heavy barrel. Options available are identical to those offered on the other Mk III revolvers just described, but note that none of the three new guns have the reinforced barrels of the Trooper Mk III, and that both the Metropolitan and the Lawman are made only with fixed sights.

Two other new ones I'll mention only briefly because they were covered extensively in the 24th ed. of the GUN DIGEST.

The new Ruger, a 357/38 Special, and the first double action revolver for the Southport company, has an entirely new action design, a frame that has no removable — and hence damageable — sideplates, and an interior assembly that can be dismounted in a few minutes and just as readily re-assembled. These latest Ruger revolvers should be available, in fixed-sight form—by the time you read this — and attractively priced, too.

Dan Wesson's first revolver — entirely U.S.-made, of course — is also a 357 Magnum. It has quite unusual interior mechanism, but the unique feature of this handgun is the ready interchangeability of a short barrel with a long one, or vice versa. A barrel shroud, as it's called, is the key to this new system.

As noted earlier, there is a spot the 38 Special fills better than any other pistol cartridge, as far as I'm

concerned. It's when something powerful is needed in a small handgun, one that can be comfortably carried in a pocket or stowed easily in a purse or briefcase.

The Colt Detective Special, and the lightweight Cobra and Agent, are fine and reliable snubnose guns, as is the Smith & Wesson M&P in either standard or airweight, but for a compact and solid little 38 revolver, the Smith & Wesson 5-shot Chief's Special is in a class by itself. Amazingly accurate, it's a favorite of detectives and off-duty policemen. The steel Chief's Special weighs 19 ounces with a 2-inch barrel, the Airweight versions only 14 ounces. It is that 5-shot cylinder that gives the Chief's Special the edge in compactness compared to the fatter 6-shot 38 snubnose revolvers.

There are more variations of the Chief's Special: the Model 60 is made in stainless steel, but unfortunately they're in very short supply, probably because of the activities in southeast Asia. The S&W Bodyguard is on the same frame (in alloy) as the Chief's Special, but is furnished with an integral hammer-shroud to keep the gun from snagging on clothing when it is drawn rapidly. While the Colt revolvers mentioned can also be obtained with hammer shrouds, they aren't quite as compact as the Chief's Special and Bodyguard.

The 38 Special has been *the* most popular centerfire revolver cartridge for a long time, and it will continue to be bought in great numbers and widely used. Despite all the talk amout its inadequacy for police work, it will still be the No. 1 police cartridge for the forseeable future. Law enforcement agencies have their problems these days; charges of excess force and brutality being dropped at random make many departments hesitant to go to a more powerful pistol. I've talked with a number of police weapons instructors who told me the 38 Special is about all the cartridge many officers can shoot accurately anyway. I wouldn't go so far as to say this, but there is the problem of ammunition interchangeability among individual officers, and this is another reason why the 38 stays up there.

Should you buy a large-frame 38 Special for all-round use, possibly big game hunting? My answer is no. The 357 Magnum in a 6-inch barreled revolver is considerably more suitable. But if you're interested in target shooting, handgun hunting for smaller game or varmints, plinking with a gun larger than a 22, or for possible self-defense and home protection, then the 38 Special has much to offer. Handloaded to its full potential, it is a fine cartridge. In spite of its critics, it's a long way from being dead! ●

Revival of the Sharps

BOB HAGEL

A famous and favorite rifle during the last days
of the buffalo, the Sharps Borchardt won further acclaim
in many thousand-yard matches at Creedmoor.
Here's a Testfire Report on the new Sharps 78—and
its performance afield on elk and deer.

NEARLY A CENTURY ago, 92 years to be exact, the Sharps Rifle Company of Bridgeport, Conn., announced a new falling block, single shot, hammerless action rifle. This rifle, made under the Borchardt patent, was known as the Sharps Borchardt Model 1878.

In many ways this action was years ahead of its time, and compared to the side-hammer single shot actions, it was as slick as a gal in a Bikini alongside a great aunt Emma in hoop skirts. The Sharps Borchardt was made in many styles from military carbine and rifle to sporters and long-range target rifles. It enjoyed a good deal of popularity, and was chambered for some of the most powerful big-bore cartridges of the day, but the demise of the great buffalo herds, and the success of the repeater was already writing the final chapter to the popularity of the big-bore single shot rifle.

It seems, however, that the pages of time have a habit of unfolding to reveal again an almost forgotten page. Popular demand caused Colt to revive the old single action Peacemaker; muzzleloaders again appeared on the scene furnished by many makers; Ruger came along with his Farquharson-oriented No. 1 single shot. Now, nearly 100 years after its inception, the Sharps Borchardt has been revived.

Early in 1969, the Sharps Arms Company of Salt Lake City, Utah, announced that they were in the process of reviving the old Sharps Borchardt rifle in the form of the Sharps Model 78. Art Swanson, who heads the new company, is ably assisted on the technical end by one of the best known gunsmiths and firearms writers in the country, P. O. Ackley. Mike Keesee, former editor of *Guns & Ammo* magazine, is marketing director.

Early in June of 1969, I examined and shot some of the first handmade prototypes, when Mike Keesee was flying around to show them to various editors and gunwriters. Unfortunately, Mike's time and mine was limited that day and, while I looked over several of the new rifles, I had time to test shoot only one. This rifle was chambered for the 257 Ackley Improved cartridge, in which we fired factory 257 Roberts ammo. Considering the chambering and the ammunition being used, along with the light barrel, I was quite impressed with groups that averaged around 1½ MOA. The rifles also impressed me enough to

Two photographs mentioned by the author (p. 174, col. 3 and p. 176, col. 2), are not shown for lack of space.

want to have one around long enough to wring it out and test it with good handloads. Mike promised to see that I got one for hunting season. True to his word, he did even better than that, and late in September, he flew in with a pair of the new rifles, one chambered for the 30-40 Krag cartridge, the other for the 375 H&H. These guns were, of course, both prototypes, the 30-40 bearing serial number 0001 and the 375 number 0005.

As far as the frame of the action is concerned, it is so similar to the original Borchardt that to one who is not thoroughly familiar with the latter there appears to be no difference between the two. As shown by the photo of one of the older Sharps Borchardt actions bearing serial No. 6097, which apparently came from the Mid-Range model, and the new M78, there is little difference in size. It is on the inside, however, that the big difference shows up. In addition, three different lever types will be offered for the new rifles.

Action Data

Coil springs are used throughout

the action and the parts of the one I took down were very smooth and perfectly fitted. One outstanding feature that makes the M78 action open and close like a fine double shotgun, is that the toggle link, referred to by the company as a "planetary cam system," rotates in a double row of Timken needle bearings. There is also a built-in adjustment system that, according to the manufacturer, makes it possible to adjust for wear if any takes place.

The firing pin is set up so that it is fully retracted into the breechblock on the first movement of the lever, and before there is any downward movement of the block. The firing-pin hole in the face of the block is also quite small so that no trouble is encountered with modern high-pressure cartridges. Both of these features are decided improvements over the Sharps Borchardt.

The extractor is designed so that it can be adapted to all types of cartridge heads used today; rimmed, rimless, semi-rimmed and belted. I believe it could also be used with rebated rims as on the 284 Winchester. About the only trouble I found with either rifle, however, was with the 375 which refused to extract cases that were at all tight. This seemed to arise from the fact that for some reason the extractor was a little loose and did not have much spring tension, allowing it to slip out of the extractor groove in the case. As far as camming power is concerned, there seemed to be plenty of that, and the company has indicated that the extractors will be beefed up on production guns. The extractor on the 30-40 worked perfectly. The extractor does not normally throw the case clear of the action, but brings it back to where you can pick it out with your fingers. However, if the lever is slammed ahead smartly, the case will usually clear the action.

The safety is unique in that it can be made either manual or automatic by a simple quarter-turn of a screw that is exposed when the action is open. I do not feel that an automatic safety is desirable on any rifle when hunting, and I set both of these rifles for manual operation, while hunting with them. The auto safety is handy in target and test shooting, or in training the beginner. If you don't like automatic safeties you don't have to use it, if you do, it is there.

I am not especially fond of the location of the safety release lever, which is placed at the rear of the cocking piece shroud. This is a good location

except for one thing, it is on the left side, which is convenient for the south-side shooter, but the percentage of left-handers is pretty small. For shooting with iron sights, it would not bother the right-hander much, but when a scope is mounted on the rifle—they do not come with iron sights—the safety is hard to reach under the eyepiece with the right thumb; especially with gloves on. It seems that if only one safety design is to be used, it should be set up for right-handed shooters.

The Canjar single-set trigger is one of the finest found on any rifle either custom or commercial. Normally it will be used as a conventional trigger and is adjustable from 2 to 5 pounds, and in the rifles I shot, has a clean break. When pushed forward, a little lever protrudes from the center of the trigger shoe which acts as the release. This "set" hookup can be adjusted from a high of 4 ounces down to as little as ¼-ounce. The trigger was used in the set position for nearly

all of my bench accuracy testing. One word of warning about the pull adjustment for conventional trigger use; like many adjustable triggers, if you try to adjust this one for too light a pull, you may find that if the safety is put on before the gun is fired, the firing pin will be released when it is taken off safe. Check this out if you adjust the pull.

As I've said, the M78 is furnished in three lever styles, a full loop, half loop, or a finger piece that extends below the pistol grip and terminates in a flat-sided ball. I am not certain which of these will be standard, but two will be optional extras.

Barrels come in various lengths starting at 26″ and running through 36″ length. They also come in several weights, from the light or #1, to the "bull" or #6. The #2 barrel is standard for the smaller calibers and the #3 is standard for larger calibers like the 375 and up. Some barrel weights and lengths will be available in certain calibers only.

These are the three Sharps Arms Company models in prototype form. The loop-lever version (left) and the hook-lever style at right were used by Bob Hagel in his testing and hunting. The rifle at left has the No. 1 barrel, 26″ long, caliber 30-40 Krag. The author's other Sharps is a 375 H&H Magnum, the barrel a No. 3 of 30″ length.

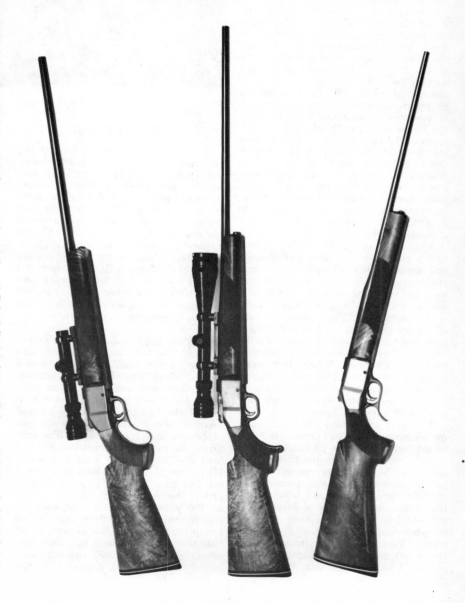

The 375 H&H Sharps and the bull that finally decided to die with his front end up on the beaver dam, the end you take the insides out of is down in a couple of feet of iced mud-pie.

These barrels are unusual in at least one respect; they carry their full diameter forward of the receiver for several inches before starting to taper toward the muzzle. This feature offers a straight surface, parallel to the bore, on which to mount a scope. The barrels are tapped for scope mounts. Neither base is on the receiver, which has certain advantages. It also has the advantage of adding a lot of weight that I feel could be better used to beef up the barrel along its entire length. I see no good reason why this could not be accomplished by the use of a quarter-rib, either integral or otherwise. That way the #2 barrel would have only about the weight of the #1 barrel with its very small muzzle diameter of minus .500-inch as it is now made. This, however, is only one man's opinion.

The fore-end is unusual in the way it is fastened to the receiver. It should be noted that it is not attached to the barrel. A through-bolt runs through the fore-end and is attached solidly to the receiver. The fore-end is held to this by a screw that threads into the end of the bolt. While it is claimed that with this arrangement any amount of pressure desired can be applied to the barrel near the tip of the fore-end, I seriously doubt that stable tension can be held. It seems to me that if the barrel does not shoot its best by floating it, then there isn't much you can do about it. The fore-end is quite large and is suited to varmint shooting more than big game hunting. It is a bit too square to suit me for a hunting rifle.

Stocks on all of the rifles I saw had a classic design with well-shaped full pistol grips without caps, and rubber butt pads. The stocks fit the average rifleman very well and absorbed recoil as well as any classic stock I ever used. They were all made of a very good grade of showy American walnut and well finished. Pistol grip and fore-end were both checkered by hand in various designs that were fairly well done. The stock is, of course, held to the action by a through-bolt. All the metal work is well finished and superbly blued.

Just how production rifles will stack up along side the prototypes is hard to say, but where the prototypes were strictly machined, the production actions will be made for the most part by the investment casting process, including the extractor and lever. Both the actions and barrels of production rifles will be made from 4140 chrome-molybdenum steel which is extremely strong. From my tests in handloading the 30-40 and 375 cartridges for this action, I can assure you that these actions are strong enough for any modern cartridge.

The 375 Sharps

While I have never been a strong advocate of single shot rifles for hunting big game, not seeing much reason to go into reverse when forward gears are available, I thought it might be interesting to go back into the past for one hunting season. I had a moose permit to fill, and the 375 Sharps seemed a logical choice for that chore. However, I had cut my hunting teeth on a 30-40 Krag rifle for which I'd loaded a big bucket full of brass, and I'd always wondered what the old cartridge was capable of in a strong action of modern steels with modern powders.

Needing the 375 first for the moose hunt, I started loading ammo and testing to see what it would do and what it liked. I talked Dave Andrews, the fellow who ramrods the ballistic setup for Speer, into staking me to a few of the 285-gr. 375 bullets he had hoarded away when they went out of production. I also talked him into giving me loading information. His pet load was 70 grains of 4064 in the 375 H&H case. No better load was found for the new Sharps. I never fired a group that was much larger than 1″ at 100 yards with that load, and, as the photo shows, I fired one 3-shot group that went into one not-so-ragged hole that measured only ³⁄₃₂″ center-to-center! While this load was not maximum in this rifle, it clocked 2745 fps with only 10 fps variation between high and low velocities from the 30″ #3 barrel.

This load was good enough and, time being short, I took off for the moose country to make like a buffalo hunter of yesteryear without testing other loads. As things turned out, I was glad I didn't have any more push behind that bullet because it was inclined to come apart at the seams.

One thing had been obvious from the start; with the heavy barrel on the 375, recoil would be very light for this cartridge. Of course, the well-shaped stock had a lot to do with this, but the rifle, complete with the 1x-4x Redfield scope in bridge-type Jr. mounts, weighed just a couple of ounces short of 11 pounds. This weight made itself felt after a few hours of pushing my way through the willow bottoms and windfelled timber on the ridges of the moose country. Even with the 30″ barrel the Sharps was only about the same over-all length as a conventional long-action bolt rifle with a 24″ tube, which made it quite agreeable to worry through the thick stuff.

For several days I pussyfooted around through the willow patches, glassing the meadows at daylight and just before dark. I saw plenty of moose, but nothing that seemed worthy of the big Sharps. Then one evening I spotted a big bull and his girl friend out in the middle of a beaver pond. I was on the point of a ridge above the bull. but he didn't know or care

taken the top off the heart, blowing up somewhere in the middle; only the jacket reached the hide on the far side. This, I have found, is typical moose behavior—they're not so very hard to kill, but it takes quite a while for them to get the word.

Back at the loading bench, I worked up loads using 82 grains of 4350 behind the 285-gr. Speer bullet; that gave 2822 fps, and a 79-gr. load of 4350 behind the 300-gr. Silvertip clocked 2731. Neither of these loads, however, gave nearly the accuracy of the 70/4064 load. I do know, however, that some 270-gr. factory ammo produced groups below 1 MOA in this rifle when it was tested by others.

The 30-40 Sharps

I hadn't loaded a 30-40 or hunted with it for over 20 years, so I bought a box of 180-gr. pointed Remington Core-Lokt ammo for a starter and set to work, to see what the old case would produce in the new action.

Starting with 180-gr. Hornady bullets and H-4895 powder, I worked up to a charge of 47 grains before the red light started flashing. Even that load was far from dangerous in the strong Sharps M78 action, but it did show .001″ head expansion at the forward end of the web where the case body started to expand to fill the chamber. There was no rim expansion, and three of these loads were fired in the same case before the primer pocket became too loose for further use. I backed off to 45 grains, however, and chronographed the load. From the 26″ barrel the 180-gr. bullet steamed along at 2757 fps! This load was almost mild in the rifle, and bullets had to be seated quite deeply because of the very short throat. This velocity intrigued me enough to work up loads with bullets from 110 to 220 grains. The chart shows the results, taken on a chronograph of known accuracy. There are no flies on the 30-40 cartridge when used in a strong action. It will surpass the 308 Winchester and push the 30-06. The rimmed case is also ideal for the single shot action.

About the time I started testing the 30-40 Sharps, Dave Andrews sent me a few of the first experimental 180-gr. 30 caliber magnum bullets. Loading these ahead of 45 grains of 4895, I started hunting with the handy, light Sharps 30-40. This rifle is about the same length over-all as a short-action bolt gun with a 22″ barrel, weighs about 8 pounds with scope, and is a joy to pack in rough hunting country. I shot a small muley buck and a big cow elk, both at about 150 yards, with this rifle and the 180-gr. Speer magnum bullet. One shot did the job very well in both cases, and the bullet exited on both animals with excellent results. The bullet from the elk, dug

—maybe because he was too busy whispering whatever it is that a bull moose whispers into a cow moose's ear.

I slipped down to 175 yards, sat behind a downed log and waited for the bull to get out of the pond onto solid ground, but afraid that if he did he'd evaporate into the 15-foot willows. Finally he splashed over to the edge of the dam, popping through an inch of ice as he went, and stood with his front feet out of the drink. This was the time. The crosshair settled where his heart should be, and I heard the plop of the big bullet. The bull was dead, but he apparently wasn't aware of it. He backed out into the middle of a quarter-acre of mud pie and stood there while I prayed a little

and held my fire. The he came back and put his front feet out on the dam again. Next, seeming to lose momentum, he backed out toward the middle. Three times he backed into the middle of that beaver pond, and three times he tried to climb out on the dam. Then he finally went down with his big front end on the dam, but with the end you take the insides out of laying in a couple of feet of the coldest chocolate pudding south of the Tanana. Did you ever try draining a quarter-acre of beaver pond with a hand axe? Well, that's easier than trying to unfasten 300 pounds of moose guts under two feet of iced soup!

The 285-gr. bullet had punched a fist-sized hole through the lungs and

M78 Sharps 30-40 Loads

26″ barrel. R-P cases, weight 170.7 grains. Federal 210 primers. Oehler No. 10 chronograph, Temp. 60 degrees F. All instrumental velocities converted to muzzle velocities.

Bullet/grs.	Powder/grs.	MV/fps
220 Hornady RN	4350/46	2385
200 Speer Ptd.	4350/49	2532
200 Speer Ptd.	4320/44	2538
180 Hornady Ptd.	H-4895/45	2757
165 Speer Ptd.	H-4895/47	2875
150 Speer Ptd.	H-4895/50	3054
130 Speer HP	4064/50	3120
110 Speer PSP	4064/52	3321
Rem. factory 180 gr.		2425

UNDER NO CIRCUMSTANCES SHOULD ANY OF THESE LOADS BE USED IN KRAG, WINCHESTER MODEL 95 OR OTHER RIFLES ORIGINALLY CHAMBERED FOR THE 30-40 KRAG CARTRIDGE!

out of the dirt on the hillside, still weighed 106 grains. It looks like a winner.

During the hunt these two rifles were subjected to all kinds of weather: rain, snow and below-zero temperatures. They were not babied in any way, and they functioned perfectly at all times.

While it is doubtful that the greatest use of these rifles will be in hunting big game, they do have certain advantages. The most outstanding is the longer barrel length possible with the same over-all length as rifles with other action styles. Also, with proper long throating, many cartridges like the 7mm Remington Magnum and 300 Winchester Magnum can be loaded to the full potential of the case without taking up powder space with the butt-end of the bullet. I am not sure, however, that the very light #1 barrel as used on the 30-40 will give the accuracy desired by some riflemen. While the 375 was highly accurate, I was never able to obtain very tight groups with the 30-40 no matter what load I used in it. Even very mild loads did not help. The smallest groups fired in 3-shot strings were around 1½ inches, with average groups running 2 to 3

inches. This may have been caused partly by the lack of tension exerted by the fore-end on the barrel to damp vibration.

I sincerely hope that the production rifles will have some arrangement for a sling. I don't like a sling fastened to the barrel ahead of the fore-end; it is too far forward for a shooting sling and is also inclined to lower bullet impact if used as such. I'd prefer to see it on the fore-end, and with the new fore-end design promised that location will be feasible.

At this time, it is the intention of the Sharps Arms Company to chamber the M78 for a variety of cartridges ranging from 17- through 50-caliber, and you'll find a list of these with this article. These calibers should be enough to suit most anyone's taste or needs, but company plans are to chamber the M78 for any standard caliber and some wildcats as an optional extra.

If you like a single shot rifle, for whatever purpose, and one that smells strongly of the dust, sage and horse sweat of the Old West, the new Sharps 78 will give you fits of nostalgia, with one eventually winding up in your gun rack. ●

Colt Buys Sharps

Early in May we learned that Colt had bought up the Sharps Arms Company, but we have had no word on what Colt may be planning for the company or its "Sharps 78" rifles. Whether the alteration in style and design outlined below will take place remains to be seen.

(We've been told that some changes in style and configuration will be made in the Sharps 78. The fore-end will no longer be attached *via a bolt running from the tip back, thus a more slender, more graceful fore-end wood treatment will be carried out. At the same time, the buttstock will show a more graceful profile — the stock that has been seen was, admittedly, a bit on the heavy-looking, bulky side. Whether the safety location will be altered to be more suitable for right-handed shooters—as Bob Hagel suggests validly—remains to be seen. J.T.A.)*

Above—Hagel used the 30-40 Krag and the 375 H&H Magnum in hunting with the new Sharps rifles. Three shots were all it took to kill a mule deer, an elk and a moose. ● Left—The 30-40 Sharps 78 was used for hunting elk and mule deer. This small buck is the result of one of those hunts. This short, light-barreled arm is an ideal mountain rifle for those who like single shooters. ● Below—Bullet at left is experimental 180-gr. Speer Magnum taken from hillside after passing through a cow elk broadside. Fired from 30-40 at 2757 fps MV. Other bullet is 285-gr. 375 bullet taken from moose shot through heart, muzzle velocity 2745 fps. It gave poor penetration for a bullet of that weight.

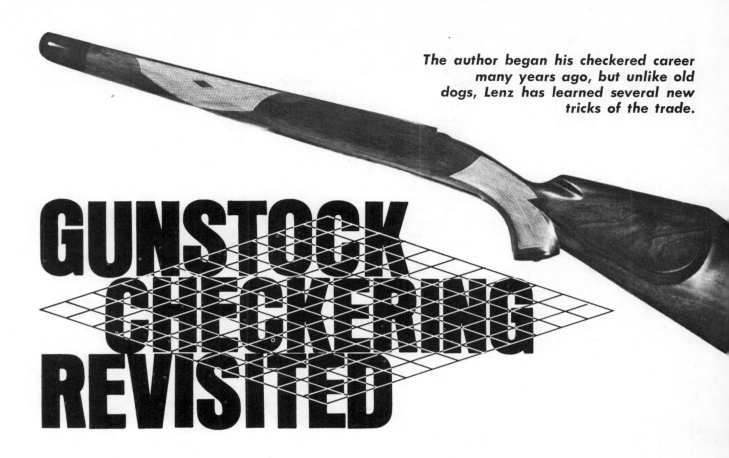

The author began his checkered career many years ago, but unlike old dogs, Lenz has learned several new tricks of the trade.

GUNSTOCK CHECKERING REVISITED

by ELLIS CHRISTIAN LENZ

To ENGAGE IN general gunsmithing it is necessary to be the master of numerous skills, the jockey of suitable machines, and the tenant of a permanent working space. In contrast with these extensive requirements, the gunsmith's tributary craft of checkering may be executed with a few hand tools and in small working quarters. With these modest requirements in mind, we shall examine the craft of gunstock checkering, and possibly gain respect for just one portion of the capable gunsmith's work.

Well-executed checkered areas on the grip and fore-end of a shoulder gun have long marked it as the better piece. Checkering, ideally, provides non-skid holds for the hands, and may also be decorative. Checkering's gun-holding advantage is proportionate to the need for speed and sureness in operating the gun. Thus checkering is most useful if other means of supporting the piece, as with a taut sling or solid rest, are absent. Firm handholds are essential for the fast-swinging shotgunner, and the field rifleman likes the reassuring feel of checkering against his palms. The handgun, least supportable of all small arms, almost invariably has grips checkered or otherwise roughened to insure a secure hold.

Hand-checkering is now seldom seen on American factory-made long guns of otherwise good quality—Ruger is an exception, the Models 77 and Single shot both being hand cut. In bygone days women did much of the shops' checkering. Now, what passes for factory checkering are designs stamped into the gunstock wood. This "instant checkering" benefits the manufacturer more than the customer and, decoratively, has little distinction.

Hand checkering continues to appear on certain domestic guns of better and custom grade, and on good grades of imported, factory-made guns. Also, many checkering jobs are done by specialists who advertise for the work, and by capable hobbyists. As to the latter, who should learn to checker? The deciding factor is an aptitude for manual crafts, especially woodworking.

Some gunsmiths try to avoid the woodworking branches of their craft. They seem to distrust procedures that are not found in a machinist's handbook. It's not that metalworking is the easy life, but precise results are more assured than in woodworking. The natural woodworker enjoys the challenges of his medium; he's somewhat of an artist, and might consider metalworking too restrictive. So it is that few gunsmiths are equally happy, and proficient, in shaping both metal and wood. Checkering is easily one of the less profitable jobs in general gunsmithing, and is sometimes avoided for that reason. Our bustling economy seems bent on closing the price gap between checkering's diamonds and those of the jeweler.

The situation today settles down to having a checkering specialist do one's work or attempting the job at home. The latter course would appeal to the somewhat talented soul who values do-ability above financial reward. He can also avoid contumely—a suitably old-fashioned word—of the time-is-money crowd by assuming the title of Gentleman Checkerer.

My own interest in checkering began in the 1920s. There followed some years of casual but firsthand instruction from master stockmakers, such as the late Harvey Rodgers and Robert Owen. During that period I cut a few stocks and did a considerable amount of checkering. Checkering then interested me to the extent of preparing working instructions for publication in *The American Rifleman* in 1933. I later expanded the checkering and tool material for inclusion in my book *Muzzle Flashes,* first published in 1946.*

---

*Standard Publishing Co., Huntington, W.Va.

Fig. 9 shown above—The left side of the Krag rifle described in the text covers the metal sideplate, helps to strengthen the stock.

GUNSTOCK CHECKERING REVISITED

In 1968 my practical interest in checkering was revived. A Bishop-stocked Krag sporter and a factory-stocked Savage 222 invited my efforts. I did not view the task with confidence, for I had not used my Whiteman checkering tools in 30 years. However, during that time hobbyists and new-generation gunsmiths had told me that the old *Rifleman* instructions had helped them to become checkerers. After such nice recommendations, I reread my advice to the tyro and felt encouraged to proceed!

In checkering the 222 stock I regained some facility in using the old tools. In their day they were of accepted professional design, but apparently they'd become passé during the years, if I were to believe maker's claims for tools of somewhat different design. I would try the "store bought" tools on the Krag stock. My reason for doing this was two-fold: a desire to compare operation of the newer tools with the old ones, and also to dispel any learner's thought that the old "professional" tools lent some otherwise unattainable ease to the effort. In actual practice I found ease of use an important advantage of the newer tools. The old tools may now attain some dignity as collector items.

I consider a stocking cradle essential to this work. One is easily constructed. As shown in Fig. 1, it allows the stock to be turned and rotated as the work proceeds. Cradle designs vary, even to the extent of cradling the assembled gun. But one checkerer, a lady and most expected to favor a cradle, simply rests the gun stock in her lap. I suppose it is no more diffi-

cult to do lap checkering than diapering a squirming infant.

In checkering a 2-piece stock, the buttstock is supported by means of a ⅜" steel rod held in a bench vise. The rod, inserted friction tight in the butt, permits rotation of the work, and vise adjustment allows other positions. The forearm is checkered in the cradle while secured to a suitable wooden rod.

The manual procedures of checkering are readily learned. The student's first concerns are choice of suitable designs and their subsequent transfer to the stock areas. First comes the development of a fore-end design. In some instances commercial transfer designs might prove useful, also templates. I prefer tailoring the design to the individual stock. Any design of adequate size must adapt itself to all combinations of fore-end curve and taper. The method which we shall use is too time consuming for the pro, but shortcuts are the dividends of experience and he is entitled to collect.

Location of the fore-end checkering is best determined by grasping the stock as in the offhand shooting stance and noting the extended hand's location. Then, with grease pencil, mark the front and rear limits of the proposed design area, preferably on the fore-end's left side. Over these marks we wrap a piece of tracing tissue, around the fore-end, and secure the underside with tabs of adhesive tape. Then, with the tissue held snugly to the wood, we locate with pencil marks points A and B, Fig. 2. AB shall be the top border line, ⁵⁄₁₆" from the fore-end's top edge. Locate points C and D in similar fashion. Remove the tissue from the stock; on it are just four penciled dots.

A few simple drafting tools will now prove useful. The tissue is placed on a several-inches-larger piece of bond paper and the points ABCD are transferred to it by means of pin pricks. Discard the tissue. Rule pencil lines between pinpricks AB and CD. With dividers we halve the area laterally and establish points EF. Using this centerline as the base for right angles,

lines AC and BD are ruled in. We now have an accurately drawn keystone-shaped area that compensates for fore-end curve and taper.

Next, we halve the keystone with line OO, and pencil in the pilot diamond, G. It shall be of 3-to-1 proportion, three times as long as it is wide. Such a proportion is considered a better design—and quite rightly—than a more square one. Most importantly, projections of the pilot's sides now dictate the pitch of all straight lines in the pattern, excepting the top border line.

Planning the Layout

Development of the actual design determines its appearance on a visible side of the fore-end. Its width is the established line AB. The rest of the design "hangs" on this line. In this instance the design's depth and balance are promoted by the mild downward curves Aa and Bb. Instead of these curves, angular scallops fulfill the same purpose, as shown on the

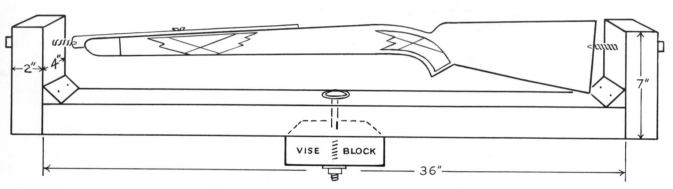

Fig. 1 A homemade checkering cradle which allows all working adjustments. Rotation of the stock in the cradle is had by means of 4" blunted lag screws snugly self-threaded in the cradle's end members.

stock in Fig. 1, but the many angles involved create needless tooling work for the beginner. The use of scallops is traditional, but also vanishing from modern fore-end design.

With the aid of a draftsman's triangle sliding along a straightedge, we project sides of the pilot diamond to establish the design's lower boundaries ah and bh. Care is taken to keep the junction point, h, well away from the centerline, EF. We now have a design area that is well proportioned and apparently suitable for its location on the stock.

The master lines are now ruled in, 1-2 and 3-4. They'll control all subsequent cutting of the diagonal lines that form the checkering's diamond shapes. The master lines are placed well within the pattern area for reasons to be understood as we commence actual work with the tools.

With the left-side panel penciled in, it is not difficult to complete the matching side. Lower points of the opposed patterns, h and g, are ¾" apart. Between those points I have made provision for an ivory inlay, a

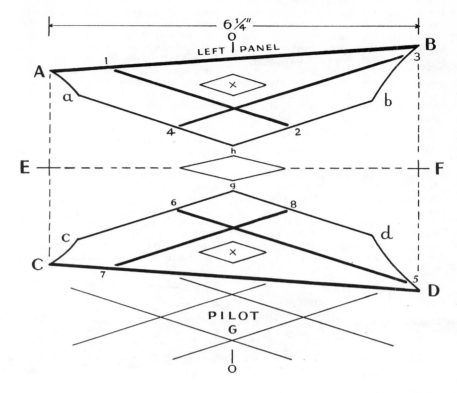

Fig. 2　The complete fore-end pattern.

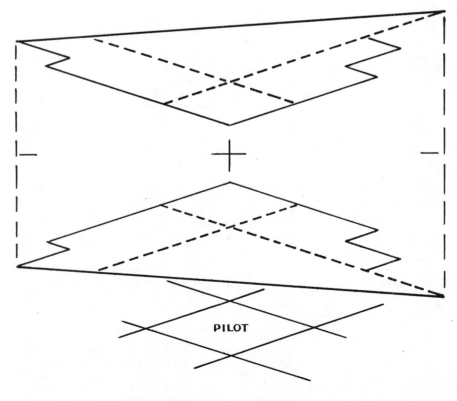

Fig. 2a　An alternate fore-end pattern.

matter of personal taste. Also, not to be included in these basic instructions is my provision for the larger diamonds, x and x, to appear in the finished work. Such special touches, and inlaying, are to be undertaken only after one has had some practical experience in the craft. Tasteful inclusion of decorative spots invest the work with a bit more character than otherwise.

With both panels completed, the paper is trimmed, leaving only the keystone shape with a $\frac{1}{16}''$ margin. (The pilot is put aside for use in planning the pistol grip's pattern.) The keystone is now carefully positioned on the fore-end and tacked with tape to prevent shifting. We pierce the pattern and the wood underneath with a sharp stylus at every juncture of the pencil lines. These small punctures in the wood will vanish in the checkering cuts. The pattern is stripped from the fore-end.

Points A and B are now visible on the stock and ready to receive common pins. But first we check to see that this top border line remains parallel with the top of the fore-end. Any slight deviation is now correctable. The pins in place, they act as stakes to steady a straightedge as the first line, AB, is scribed into the wood. Resetting the pins, lines are scribed to similarly connect every puncture mark. Border lines ah and bh swing over the fore-end's curve and are scribed with the aid of a small flexible rule. The curves Aa and Bb and their counterparts are most accurately scribed by means of a draftsman's plastic curve, which will also be useful in defining outlines of the pistol grip pattern. Next, the master lines are scribed into the panels. Preliminary work on the fore-end is now completed. All essential work lines of the pattern are visible on the wood and tooling can follow.

Choice of Tools

As to tools, I chose the Dem-Bart make, Fig. 3. Even before testing them I felt certain that they, or most any tools of later design, would prove easier to use than my old ones. Trial cuts proved them a delight to use. The interchangeable cutting heads are small gems of milled precision. The basic handle, and the steel shank to which the cutter is pinned, are properly shaped and proportioned. This tool says "go."

From the large variety of Dem-Bart cutters listed, I needed but a few for this project—the No. 1 fine V-cutter; No. 3 spacer to space 16 lines-per-inch, and Special S-1, an additional tool fitted with a shorter cutter for deepening border curves and cleaning up tight corners in the work.

Although checkering lines may be spaced as close as 32 per inch, I chose 16 lines, the coarsest. This spacing usually proves most practical to cut on wood of indifferent quality. It is

GUNSTOCK CHECKERING REVISITED

also most durable on much-used guns. It is wise to learn control of the tools, and working methods, on wood of less immediate importance than that of the fore-end waiting to be checkered. Fig. 4 shall be the practice pattern. It is penciled and then scribed on a flat piece of wood, preferably walnut. Assuming the right hand holds the V-cutter, deepen the scribed line **AD**, starting at **D**. The cutter handle is held lightly, the index finger steadying the metal shank. It

the first row of diamond shapes appears. Continue spacing to **DC**. The pattern area is now well defined, and actual tool spacing has caused final cuts to fall on, or very near, the scribed lines **BC** and **DC**. Had these border lines been previously cut, instead of scribed, it would have been a distinct gamble that actual spacing might coincide with those cuts. The Gentleman Checkerer is not to be caught with his borders down! It's bad form.

Shaping the Diamonds

With the V-cutter we start to shape the diamonds. The work sequence follows that of the spacer. The first pass does not greatly deepen the lines. The third over-all pass usually fixes the depth and surface texture of the finished job. My preference is to allow small plateaus on the individual diamonds in the English fashion. They are not harsh to the touch and are

square diamonds. Also, the mid-pattern master lines permit the borders to be finally located through normal spacing, as was noted in tooling the practice pattern.) At this time lines **Aa** and **Bb** are cut with the short cutter, S-1. Some workers prefer to use a bent needle file in cutting border curves. This design has no added border, sometimes a device to hide tooling runovers. Here the final spacing line is deepened to become a neat border.

In cutting the opposite panel one should approach its lower point with caution. Cumulative error in spacing of either panel can throw its point a bit to one side or the other. Such misalignment is corrected by eliminating or adding a final spacing line, whichever will shift the point of the panel to bring it directly opposite the finished one. This chance for correction is another reason for not cutting the borders before actual spacing

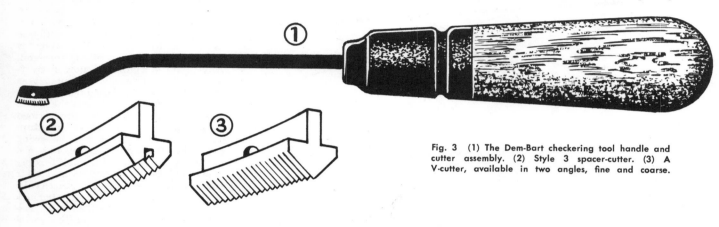

Fig. 3 (1) The Dem-Bart checkering tool handle and cutter assembly. (2) Style 3 spacer-cutter. (3) A V-cutter, available in two angles, fine and coarse.

is quite important that the wrist and arm move nearly as possible in line with the cut being made. Any application of force at even a slight angle invites the cutter to wander from its guide line. This precaution and a light approach allows the cutter to find and follow its prescribed path. The actual cutting is done with a nudging motion of the tool, forward and back, but progressively forward. Wood dust is blown away and progress noted. The line completed, another pass of the cutter provides a more distinct furrow, but not deep.

We are ready to use the spacer, with **AD** as the master line. This spacer, as shown in Fig. 3, has its guiding edge on the left side, requiring the cutter to progress from **D** to **A**. The spacer's *smooth* edge follows its guide line as the *serrated* edge begins to cut line (1). An additional pass with increased pressure on the cutter will firmly establish line (1) as the next guide line. Thus we progress across the area to **BC,** the farther scribed boundary. Turning the work, line **AB** is defined with the V-cutter. Then, spacing from **A** to **B** forms line (2) and

structurally stronger when not pointed. However, any shaping of the diamonds is largely regulated by the lines-per-inch spacing and subsequent use of a fine or coarse V-cutter. The latter, of wider angle, points the diamonds quickly. These factors are for the judgment of the craftsman.

Checkering over curved surfaces is not difficult to do, but before tooling the fore-end it would benefit to lay out a design on a discarded military stock. A diamond-shaped area involving the sides and bottom of the fore-end would do. This preliminary tooling is a good investment in working ability, and any booboos can be filed under highly classified information.

The Krag fore-end is waiting to be tooled; we'll start on the lefthand panel, Fig. 5. The top border line is deepened with the V-cutter; next, the master lines. (Here is why the master lines have been placed well within the working area: In spacing we thus work away from each side of a master line, reducing the effect of any small errors in tooling. The sum of such errors can produce noticeably

finally establishes them. This area is shown in Fig. 6.

Completion of the fore-end checkering has yielded increased familiarity with wood textures, which are seldom uniform throughout a gunstock. We've found cross-grain tooling most easily done, with precision; whereas in cutting with the grain, or nearly so, one must proceed carefully to keep the grain from influencing the progress of the V-cutter. An initial, persistent runout tendency may be reduced by temporarily reversing the working direction. The denser grain structures of selected woods cut and finish most smoothly and best receive finer-line checkering.

The design and checkering of the pistol grip presents few problems at this stage of our progress. Starting with the right side, Fig. 7, an appropriate pattern is sketched with grease pencil. The design should harmonize in some respect with the fore-end pattern. A forward curve does that. It is not advisable (for the novice, at least) to include much space on the grip's under side, for tooling in that area becomes unnecessarily awkward

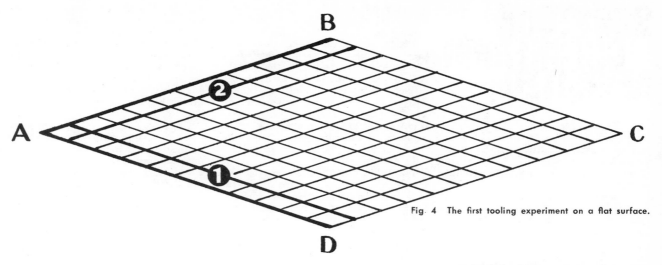

B

A

C

D

Fig. 4 The first tooling experiment on a flat surface.

as the center line is approached. Leave at least 1″ of free space between the opposed patterns.

The grip's pattern curves are now trued with the draftsman's curve and scriber. The flexible rule is used in scribing the bottom border. This border and the curves can now be deepened with the V-cutter as their exact location is not regulated by the spacer. The fore-end's paper pilot diamond is now used in establishing this pattern's master lines. The diamond is taped into the grip pattern, pointing forward and slightly upward. Lines can now be extended from the pilot onto the wood. Removing the paper, these lines are completed with scriber and rule. As master lines they also determine the pitch of the scallop included at the rear of this pattern.

The design on the left side of the grip, Fig. 8, is not a precise copy of the right side, provision being made to accept the beginning of the cheekpiece. This is typical of the minor irregularities attending the work. Here I have avoided a close approximation of the pattern's normal lines; the angle is unusual, to avoid the appearance of compromise. This departure from the lines of the pattern produces some incomplete diamonds along the border, also unavoidable wherever the pattern is bounded by a curved border.

Final Touches

To finish newly cut checkering one

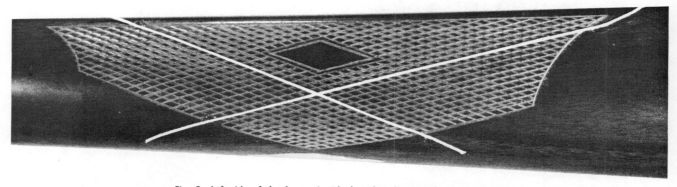

Fig. 5 Left side of the fore-end with threads indicating the master lines used in cutting the checkering. Threads are for illustrative purposes only.

Fig. 6 Detail of the bottom of the fore-end.

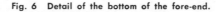

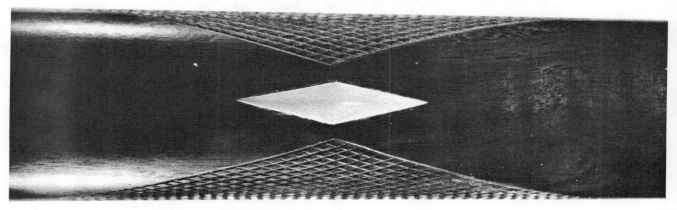

GUNSTOCK CHECKERING REVISITED

may brush into it satin varnish, much thinned with turpentine. This mixture effectively seals the raw cuts without clogging the work, nor does it affect the stock's existing finish. In fact it is not desirable to checker a stock before an over-all finish has been applied. To finish after checkering would result in dulling the checkered area and clogging it with finishing compound.

Fig. 9 shows the Krag stock with its checkering completed, lacking only the preservative finish in the panels. As viewed in its entirety, the work reflects simplicity and usefulness with only touches of embellishment. The more eye-arresting designs and fine feats of execution we leave to the masters. Unfortunately some who would aspire to the master rating are only expert tool pushers. A "de luxe" job is full of meaningless curves and unrelated areas. I'm sure it is far easier to ignore a few "dutchmen" (tool runouts) in a consistently designed panel than to be saddled with a poor design filled with perfect dia-monds. It is good to realize that relevant and attractive checkering areas are not difficult to plan, and they also invite few tooling problems.

It doesn't take long for the hobby-checkerer to attract the favorable attention of fellow gun owners; and what can be more soothing than earning a bit of income while enjoying oneself?

Up to a few years ago checkering was a simon-pure handicraft, its tool as muted in operation as grandpa's folding razor. But no longer. These days the production-minded pro deftly guides an electric checkering tool. He is the driver of a souped-up cutter. More power to him, and may his brakes hold at every border! ●

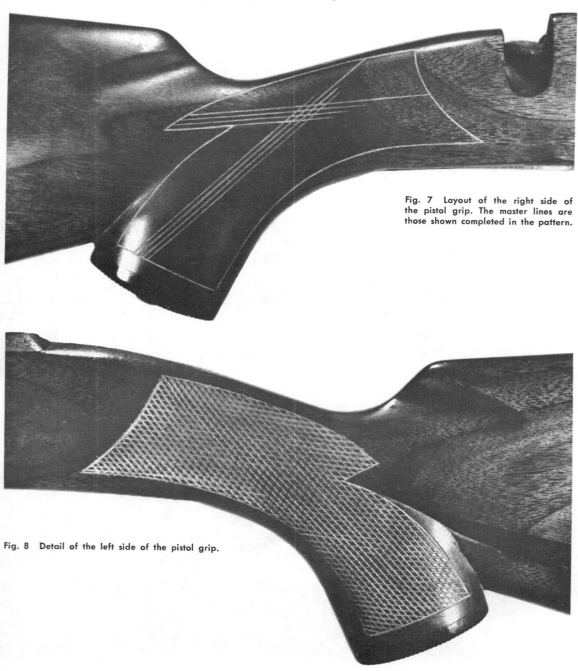

Fig. 7 Layout of the right side of the pistol grip. The master lines are those shown completed in the pattern.

Fig. 8 Detail of the left side of the pistol grip.

What Interchangeable 9mms?

by George C. Nonte, Jr.

Can you use — efficiently and safely — one or more of the several 9mm cartridges in Star and Astra auto pistols? Here are the results of a careful and extended survey — which could have been direr!

A FELLOW DROPPED by my office not long ago—a local occasional shooter—to ask if I could spare him some cheap 9mm Luger (Parabellum) ammunition to use in a couple of pistols he had. Just happening to have a fresh case of Canadian military ammunition at hand, I was glad to help him out in view of the fact that the local shops had none.

His guns were a Star Model A and Astra Model 400, both in excellent condition. Both were marked "9mm/38," indicating they were chambered for the 9mm Bergmann-Bayard cartridge.

When it was tactfully pointed out to this lad that the cartridges he had asked for were not correct for his guns, answered that with "These guns were especially made so they would handle all sorts of different 9mm ammunition so a soldier could use whatever was handy;" and on to tell me that it was foolish to pay 10¢ or 12¢ per round for the proper ammunition when 9mm Luger cartridges cost only about a third of that. He went on to say that several magazine articles and advertisements for surplus pistols had clearly stated that the Luger cartridge

and a number of others were perfectly safe to use in his guns.

That fellow had a point. He was only repeating what he had been told and what he had read in supposedly authoritive publications. From time to time since World War II there have been various lots of obsolete military pistols offered for sale without necessarily being accompanied by an adequate supply of ammunition. Many of these guns were chambered for cartridges either no longer in production or not readily available in this country.

About the same time a few individuals discovered that under *certain conditions,* Spanish guns chambered for the 9mm Bergmann-Bayard cartridge (also known as the 9mm Largo or the 9mm/38) would fire other 9mm cartridges. That this was a sometime thing, and that it also might produce undesirable results was not included in the comments these gentry made. These discoveries were somehow distorted into the statement "Guns chambered for the 9mm Bergmann-Bayard cartridge are *designed* to use most other 9mm cartridges, such as 9mm Luger, 9mm Steyr, 9mm Brown-

ing short, 9mm Browning long, etc.

Shortly thereafter ad writers picked up the statement and used it to enhance the saleability of their merchandise. It just so happened the practice worked often enough that no great amount of furor arose from the users.

Nevertheless, I have proved to my own satisfaction and that of numerous associates that the practice of promiscuously interchanging various 9mm pistol cartridges in guns chambered for the 9mm Bergmann-Bayard cartridge isn't always a good idea. It produces at best indifferent reliability and, at worst, definite damage to the gun and potential damage to the shooter.

9mm History

Let us disprove the statement that the 9mm Bergmann-Bayard cartridge and chamber were deliberately designed to accept other cartridges. The 9mm Bergmann-Bayard originated about 1898 by Theodore Bergmann, being developed concurrently with the Bergmann No. 6 Military pistol. We assume then, that the cartridge existed for some time prior to 1903, and that

Llama Extra, cal. 9mm Largo (Bergman-Bayard)

Star Model B, cal. 9mm/38 (9mm Bergman-Bayard)

Astra Model 400, cal. 9mm (Bergman-Bayard)

by then both performance and dimensions had been standardized for some time. In 1903, *none* of the allegedly interchangeable 9mm cartridges had been introduced, with the exception of the Colt 38 ACP. It had been around since the late 1890's. It becomes apparent that the 9mm Bergmann-Bayard chamber could not possibly have been designed to accept cartridges not even in existence. In chronological order, those allegedly interchangeable 9mm cartridges were developed as follows.

1) 38 ACP: Formally introduced to the public in 1900, it is known to have been produced in modest quantity between 1897 and 1899. While it is likely that the developers of the 9mm Bergmann-Bayard were aware of the existence of the 38 ACP, there is no reason to believe they copied it. On the contrary, since both cartridges were intended primarily for military use, it is more likely that the European designers would have avoided interchangeability. In those days most nations set great store by having their *own* cartridges, and were not concerned with interchangeability.

2) 9mm Luger (Parabellum): In 1904 the Imperial German Navy adopted the Luger Pistol in 9mm caliber, indicating that the cartridge had been standardized dimensionally at least some months prior to that time.

The 9mm Luger case is of the same type as the Bergmann-Bayard—a rimless, tapered design, However, the Luger case is some .160″ to .170″ shorter. Inasmuch as both cases are specifically designed to headspace on the case mouth against a shoulder in the chamber, it is clearly evident there was never any intention of interchangeability between the two.

3) 9mm Browning long: In 1908 the Fabrique Nationale of Belgium offered a new Browning military automatic pistol, the M-1908—chambered for the 9mm Browning long cartridge of somewhat less power and velocity than the 9mm Parabellum.

This cartridge had been developed in 1907 specifically for the new Browning pistol. It is slightly semi-rimmed case fully 0.10″ shorter than the 9mm Bergmann-Bayard.

4) 9mm Browning short (380 ACP): In 1908 Colt announced the 380 CAPH, (Colt Automatic Pistol Hammerless). It is a true rimless case,

without body taper, and measures only .670″—.683″ in length—a great deal shorter than the 9mm Bergmann-Bayard. It was of relatively low velocity and power, intended purely for pocket-size, unlocked-breech pistols. This cartridge was designated the 9mm Browning short.

5) 9mm Steyr Auto Pistol: Chronologically the last of the lot, this cartridge was adopted by the Austrian government in 1912—indicating it had been under development and finalized in dimensions and performance as early as 1911—long after the advent of the Bergmann-Bayard. It is a rimless case of the same nominal length as the Bergmann-Bayard, without body taper. It headspaces on the mouth of the case, and of all of the 9mm cartridges under discussion, it is the most nearly like the 9mm Bergmann-Bayard. While the two cartridges are not

Left to right: Factory cartridges; 9mm Steyr; 9mm Bergman-Bayard; 9mm Browning long; 9mm Parabellum; 380 ACP; 38 Super.

Left, 9mm Parabellum fired in Llama 9mm/38. Note obliteration of head marking and pierced primer.

Three cases on right fired in assorted 9mm/38 guns; from left: 9mm Steyr, 38 Super, 9mm Bergman-Bayard.

precisely the same dimensionally, manufacturing tolerances cause a certain amount of overlap. Within that overlap it is impossible to differentiate between the *cases* dimensionally. The bullets do differ, the Steyr weighing 114 to 118 grains, the Bergmann-Bayard 125 to 136 grains, and they're of different nose shape.

It can be seen from the above that if any true interchangeability exists, it is between the 9mm Bergmann-Bayard and the 9mm Steyr. Since the latter followed the former by some six or more years, any copying or deliberate interchangeability took place at Austrian hands, not the designers of the Bergmann-Bayard.

The foregoing facts should debunk the popular tale that assorted Spanish pistols in 9mm Bergmann-Bayard caliber were *intended* to accept other cartridges. Another factor also tends to specifically contradict the statement that 9mm Luger cartridges may be substituted: This is that the Spanish Astra, Llama and Star pistols, about which the statement is made, are or have been manufactured in both 9mm Bergmann-Bayard *and* 9mm Luger calibers.

Now Spanish manufacturers are just as sharp as any to be found— it is unlikely they would have spent money to produce guns in 9mm Luger caliber if those in 9mm Bergmann-

Bayard were *intended* to function properly with the former. What do you think?

9mm Testfire

Let us take a look at what happened when we attempted to use the aforementioned cartridges in the 9mm Bergmann-Bayard pistols. Several guns were used: Two Astra M-400s; one Star Model A; one Llama Extra; and one M-12 Austrian service pistol chambered for the 9mm Steyr cartridge. All guns ranged from good to near-new condition.

38 ACP and 38 Super Automatic: Functioned perfectly, both when single-loaded and when fed from the magazine. They failed to chamber in the 9mm Steyr, inasmuch as the breech block face counterbore was just a wee bit too small to accept the semi-rim of the 38 cases. On the other hand, all of the 9mm Bergmann-Bayard guns provided adequate clearance for the 38 rim. Even when the 38 cases are heavily crimped upon the bullet, eliminating positive contact between the case mouth and the chamber shoulder, the rim is supported sufficiently well by the mouth of the chamber to insure proper functioning and headspacing. There are those, I suppose, who will say that this was intended by the designers of the guns, but I doubt it.

9mm Luger (Parabellum): This is the substitute most often recommended, though it proved to be by far the worst of the lot. Several makes of 9mm Luger cartridges were found to drop freely into the 9mm Bergmann-Bayard chambers until brought to rest on the chamber shoulder. This placed the head of the Luger cartridge approximately ⅛" away from the face of the breechblock, which should normally support it at the instant of ignition.

When 9mm Luger cartridges were dropped manually into the chamber, the slide allowed to slam forward, and the trigger then pulled, the results were most interesting, if not to say pyrotechnic. Some would fire, others would not. The firing pins of most of the test guns protruded through the breechblock face sufficiently to strike the Luger primers lightly. This resulted in an occasional misfire. When the cartridge did fire, the results were at best a badly-flattened primer, and at worst a completely blown primer which allowed gas to escape into the action. Recoil was excessive, cases were mangled in varying degrees, and primer pockets more often than not badly distorted.

Why? Simple—the wholly unsupported primer began to move rearward out of the case the instant it was ignited by the firing pin, to be followed

Left to right: 9mm Parabellum; normal 9mm Parabellum case fired in correct chamber; two 9mm Parabellum cases fired in Llama 9mm/38 chamber. Note how extractor wiped rims forward as case was blown rearward upon firing.

Left to right: Normal fired 9mm Parabellum case; 9mm Parabellum case fired in Astra 9mm/38; case head remains picked out of Astra action from previous round.

by the case as chamber pressure built up. The case with partially protruding primer was then driven rapidly rearward (no doubt faster than the bullet was driven forward, due to the difference in weight and inertia) and slammed violently into the face of the breech, moving back over the primer. If the primer had moved only slightly out of the case at the time of impact, the only result was a badly flattened primer. If, on the other hand, the primer was clear or almost clear of the case, gas under high pressure began to escape. Impact of case against breechblock sealed off this gas and, in so doing, produced further mutilation of both primer and case.

When 9mm Luger cartridges were fed from the magazine, more often than not the rim slipped under the extractor hook. The cartridge would then fire normally, because the extractor held it in reasonably close contact with the breechblock. Functioning of the pistol was normal. Both cases and primers appeared normal and suffered no damage. However, approximately 15 to 20% of the time, a cartridge would be driven into the chamber without being caught by the extractor hook. Those cases were mangled as mentioned previously. Some guns functioned perfectly through several magazines of 9mm Luger ammunition before driving a

cartridge into the chamber to misfire or come apart at the seams. Others produced as many as two or three such malfunctions from a single magazine. Apparently, minor differences from gun to gun make the difference between almost-reliable and terrible functioning with the 9mm Luger cartridge.

When the 9mm Luger cartridge was tried in the Steyr M-12 pistol essentially the same results were produced. 9mm Browning long: Only a limited amount of this caliber, imported by Blackhawk Small Arms Ammunition, was available, so testing was not as extensive as with the other calibers. This cartridge's .400"—.405" diameter semi-rim prevented it from dropping too deeply into the chamber, even though the case is 0.10" shorter than the 9mm Bergmann-Bayard cartridge. Consequently, it functioned well when single loaded, headspacing on the rim. When fed from the magazine, the 9mm Long functioned properly in the Astra and Star pistols. However, it apparently did not produce sufficient recoil energy to drive the slide of the Llama Extra consistently far enough to the rear to pick up fresh cartridges from the magazine. Several failures to feed for this reason were encountered. In the 9mm Steyr M-12 pistol, the rim of the 9mm Browning long pre-

vented complete chambering, as with the 38 ACP.

9mm Browning short (380 ACP): Here we have a straight, rimless case ³⁄₁₆-inch shorter than the 9mm Bergmann-Bayard. It drives a lighter bullet at less velocity, producing less recoil energy. When fed directly into the 9mm Bergmann-Bayard chamber and allowed to go fully forward, the primer was not ignited. Firing pin protrusion simply wasn't great enough to ignite the primer. When fed from the magazine, only a modest percentage were caught by the extractor. Those that were caught would fire normally, but failed to drive the slide back sufficiently for normal functioning. From a functional view, this cartridge is by far the poorest of the lot in the 9mm Bergmann-Bayard.

9mm Steyr Auto Pistol: As mentioned earlier, this cartridge is so like the 9mm Bergmann-Bayard in dimensions that it is sometimes impossible to differentiate between the two. Consequently, we expected no difficulty with any of the guns—certainly not with the M-12 Pistol which was chambered for it. The results were as expected. All test guns functioned perfectly with it.

Conclusions

So, it can be seen that the most commonly recommended substitution of the 9mm Luger cartridge in 9mm Bergmann-Bayard pistols is at best potentially dangerous. Of the other sometimes-recommended substitutions, the 9mm Browning long and the 9mm Steyr are safe, but the availability and quality of them tend to make the substitution generally impractical. However, if you are able to pick up a reasonably good supply of either cartridge at low enough price, then there is no particular reason for not using them, other than that the cases will be Berdan-primed—difficult or impractical to reloaad. The 9mm Browning short is out because of its failure to operate semi-automatically the actions of the various pistols.

This, then, leaves us with two choices—first the original and proper 9mm Bergmann-Bayard. It is available only as military surplus. Berdan and corrosive primed, and not particularly well distributed. Last and best of the lot, the 38 ACP or Colt 38 Super Automatic cartridge. It not only functions perfectly in the 9mm Bergmann-Bayard guns, but is available almost anywhere you care to look. In addition, its case takes standard Boxer-type primers which facilitates reloading.

These features all combine to make the 38 the best choice for both the reloader and the factory-ammunition shooter who wants to take advantage of the relatively low priced surplus arms chambered for the 9mm Bergmann-Bayard cartridge.

There are other ways to get good, reliable Boxer-primed cases to fit the various 9mm Bergmann-Bayard guns. George Spence, Steele, Missouri shortens 38 Special cases, turns off the rim, and cuts a proper extraction

Left, 9mm Bergman-Bayard cartridge seated properly (headspacing on case mouth in Astra M400 barrel.) Right, 9mm Parabellum, having shorter case, seats too deep in Astra M400 chambered for 9mm Bergman-Bayard unless held back by extractor.

groove in his lathe. The resulting case is just a wee bit undersize at the base, but loaded to normal velocity and pressure holds up quite well. Another solution is to cull out all of your 222, 222 Magnum, and 223 Remington cases which have neck splits or other front-end defects. Trim them to 9mm Bergmann-Bayard length, chamfer, and expand the mouth to accept .355″ diameter bullets. The result is also a bit undersized at the base, but is of sturdier construction than the 38

Special, and therefore can be loaded hot without any trouble. The above methods may also be used to produce reloadable cases in most of the other 9mm calibers mentioned.

No doubt about it, those Spanish 9mm Bergmann-Bayard pistols at prices ranging from $20 to $40 are excellent bargains. Just because you got the gun cheap, though, don't be so penurious as to attempt dangerous cartridge substitutions simply because they are cheap. ●

Caliber	9mm Bergmann Bayard	38 ACP	9mm Parabellum	9mm Browning long	380 ACP	9mm Steyr
Country	Germany	USA	Germany	Belgium	USA	Austria
Developed	1903	1897-99	1904	1907	1908	1911
Introduced	1903	1900	1904	1908	1908	1912
Bullet, grs.	130	130	125	108	95	118
MV	1116	1270	1275	1029	962	1112
ME	359	465	450	254	195	323
Rim dia.	.392	.405	.393	.404	.374	.381
Head dia.	.390	.382	.392	.384	.373	.380
Neck dia.	.375	.382	.380	.376	.373	.380
Case length	.900	.900	.760	.800	.686	.900
Bullet dia.	.355	.358	.355	.355	.356	.355
Cart. length	1.300	1.280	1.160	1.100	.980	1.300
Case type	Rimless, straight taper	Semi-rim, straight	Rimless, straight taper	Semi-rim, straight taper	Rimless, straight	Rimless, straight
Principal Weapons	Star, Astra, Llama, Bayard	Colt	Colt, Radom, Beretta, Luger, P-38, Browning	Browning	Beretta, Colt, Walther, Browning	M-12

THE AMERICAN AND HIS GUNS . . . .

and why he wants to keep them

by PEYTON AUTRY

Despite the many new and highly restrictive gun laws plaguing the law-abiding citizen-sportsman— *laws which have not averted the rising crime rate—* we are now faced with the open threat of full registration and confiscation. Everyone of us must combat these incredibly naive and ill-considered attacks to the utmost.

IN 1968, TWO PROMINENT Americans, Dr. Martin Luther King and Senator Robert F. Kennedy, were killed by assassins' bullets.

These appalling acts, added to the increase in the American crime rate in the last decade, have brought cries to regulate, or even abolish, individual ownership of firearms in the United States. It seems that many Americans, acting from a deep-rooted sense of guilt in these tragedies, seek to do some form of penance. As a result, some insist that gun ownership by individuals should be discouraged or even outlawed.

Those opposing strong gun-control legislation do not argue about the increasing number of crimes. They, too, were shocked by the 1963 assassination of President Kennedy and other tragedies that followed. Unquestionably, crimes of the most atrocious types are on the increase.

It does not appear, however, that all the facts about firearms and their legitimate use are known to most advocates of stronger gun-control legislation.

John F. Kennedy's assassination focused on firearms the attention of many ordinary citizens who know little about guns. In fact, many otherwise-educated legislators, newsmen, public officials and non-gun-owning citizens appeared totally unaware that it was perfectly legal for a law-abiding citizen to own and use a firearm. Since 1963, many of these persons have rendered opinions which vary all the way from recognition of the broad scope of the subject to the narrower view that ownership of a gun by anyone other than the police or military is unnecessary and should be abolished immediately.

"Why *not* abolish private ownership of guns?" ask the uninitiated. "They are dangerous weapons. They *cause* crime. Except for the criminal, who wants or needs them?"

In a few years, it may not be remembered that Lee Harvey Oswald was a political radical who renounced the United States and had lived in Russia. It certainly will be recalled, however, that Oswald killed Kennedy with a "mail-order" rifle. That rifle continues to receive more of the apparent blame for the assassination than Oswald himself.

Why should firearms control be controversial in the face of facts such as the slaying of President Kennedy, bank holdups, hoodlums using guns with reckless abandon, and snipers shooting helpless citizens to death? The uninitiated may ask: "Since it seems obvious that gun laws are needed to curb these crimes, why do millions of law-abiding, honest and upright citizens oppose such laws?"

As usual, there are two sides to the question. Those millions of Americans who own and use guns morally and legally offer convincing and logical arguments that no restrictions should be placed on the rightful and lawful use of firearms—firearms of any kind. They point with every justification to the vast difference between their sane and peaceful use of guns and the *misuse* of firearms by criminals.

Of these millions of privately-owned firearms in America, the overwhelming majority are in the hands of law-abiding citizens. The percentage of guns in criminal hands is exceedingly small—and it is an incontrovertible fact that most guns used in committing crimes are *stolen* guns.

The Second Amendment to the Constitution of the United States is not familiar to many of those who do not own guns or who have no interest in hunting or shooting as a sport. Article II of the Bill of Rights reads as follows: *Right to Keep and Bear Arms. A well regulated militia being necessary to the security of a free state, the right of the people to keep and bear arms shall not be infringed.* The only amendment that was put ahead of this is the First, which guarantees freedom of religion, speech, the press, and the right of petition for redress of grievances. All other personal liberties follow the "right to keep and bear arms." Anti-gun proponents claim that "militia" refers to the National Guard rather than to individuals or their rights. Yet all of the dictionaries of the English language appear to define *militia* as both *organized* and *unorganized*. The latter consists of all *able-bodied males.* It is regulated by selective service and the manpower needs of the armed forces. The majority of State Constitutions authorize individuals to have firearms for defense of home, person or property.

There are more than 40 million gun owners in the United States. About 20 million of them are hunters, about one million of whom are women. They are already regulated by approximately 20,000 federal, state and local firearms laws, most passed long before 1963. Thus, sportsmen and other gun owners are now decidedly skeptical about one or two more federal gun laws being able to control or reduce crime. After all, the 20,000 laws now on the books are either not doing the job, or they are not being enforced.

Hunters are highly important to the American economy. They spend more than $1.5 billion a year on hunting—most of it for travel, food, clothing and related equipment.. *Shooting enthusiasts pour more money into the American economy than any four spectator sports combined!*

Guns are owned for other legal purposes. For instance, there are over one million active arms collectors in America.

Adults using guns are joined by more than 350,000 boys and girls who participate in the annual National Rifle Association junior marksman-ship programs. Youngsters are naturally curious about guns, and this valuable program teaches them respect for firearms in an atmosphere of good judgment, intelligent and safe gun use and sportsmanship. A number of states require completion of such a program before those under a certain age can obtain a hunting license. The NRA program is available in nearly every community in the country.*

Gun users may be the only people who have ever asked to have their taxes raised. To support wildlife research and conservation, hunters and the shooting industry asked for and got an 11 per cent excise tax levied on the sale of sporting arms and ammunition. Over 300 million dollars already has been collected and used, some of it to buy land for wildlife ranges. The hunters' tax money supports many non-hunted species and the sportsmen are glad of it.

The U.S. Fish and Wildlife Service is in the middle of a 7-year program to acquire 115 million acres of wetlands, all to be paid for by the hunters' purchase of duck stamps (each at $3.00 a year). The duck stamps are required for hunting all migratory water wildfowl, such as ducks and geese. The land being acquired is open to the public for year-round outdoor recreation, whereas hunters, as such, use this land only two or three months a year.

Judge William G. Long, of Seattle's Juvenile Court, is convinced that outdoor sports can help prevent juvenile delinquency. Judge Long, who heard 45,000 cases over 20 years, says that not one of the boys or girls who came before him had a wholesome outdoor hobby.

FBI Director J. Edgar Hoover, writing in *Uniform Chime Reports,* (July 28, 1966, Page VIII), says:

"Crime is a social problem and the concern of the entire community. The law-enforcement effort is limited to the factors within its control. Some of the conditions which will affect the amount and type of crime that occurs from place to place are:

1. Density and size of the population of the community and the metropolitan area of which it is a part.

2. Composition of the population with reference to age, sex and race.

3. Economic status and mores of the population.

4. Relative stability of population, including commuters, seasonal and other transient types, climate including seasonal weather conditions.

5. Effective strength of the police force.

6. Policies of the prosecuting officials and the courts.

7. Attitude of the public toward law-enforcement problems.

8. Administration and investigative efficiency of the law-enforcement agency."

On a per capita basis, fewer people are killed by guns now than a decade or two ago. From 1930 to 1965, homicides by firearms decreased 50 per cent on a per capita basis. Accidental deaths due to sporting firearms have fallen one-third in the last 30 years despite population growth and a doubling in the number of licensed hunters.

Shooting attracts many participants outside the United States, with 78 countries being represented in the International Shooting Union. Worldwide, only track and field sports attract more participants than does competitive shooting.

Perhaps the best known national or international shooting organization is the National Rifle Association of America, the oldest of many such national organizations in the United States. The NRA, which strongly opposes laws restricting ownership and the lawful use of guns by individuals,

In 1963 Johnny L. Davis, Jr. of Columbia, S.C., won the world's sub-junior Skeet championship at Rochester, N.Y., with a score of 96x100 with his 12-gauge gun. The annual event is for boys and girls under the age of 13.

has for years fought actively and just as hard *for* legislation to stop the *misuse* of guns, contrary to the considerable criticism it has received in the press, television and radio. The NRA has, for many years, supported firearms legislation aimed at differentiating between the law-abiding gun owner and the armed criminal.

Organized in 1871, the NRA has grown to over 1,000,000 members, all of whom are required to be American citizens. The association over the years counts among its members and officers many distinguished Americans from all walks of life. These include lawyers, judges, high-ranking military officers, civil servants and even several Presidents of the United States.

The NRA, a non-profit organization, is open to any American citizen who can present specific character references from other members or members of the U.S. Armed Forces. Its objectives are to promote social welfare, public safety and national defense; to train and educate citizens in the safe, efficient handling of *small arms,* and generally to encourage the lawful ownership of firearms. These objectives help NRA members to become more proficient in the use of small arms. This has been done for years through the sponsoring of competitive matches among civilian and military shooters alike.

The NRA is also the parent organization of shooting clubs and police and military marksmanship units. It initiated civilian marksmanship training in 1871, and young shooters' training in 1907. It was active in establishing the National Board for Promotion of Rifle Practice in 1903. Since 1903 it has been active in the operation of the national rifle and pistol matches. The NRA cooperates with the Director of Civilian Marksmanship (DCM) in determining eligibility of government shooting equipment sales to clubs and individuals for the promotion of civilian marksmanship.

The NRA's aim, to train civilians in the use of arms, has for many years been recognized and encouraged by the U.S. government. War experience has shown that the young recruit with previous civilian training in firearms stands a much better chance of survival.

Switzerland and certain other countries *require* all males to train in the use of small arms. In Switzerland, each male must accept a rifle and ammunition, given to him free of charge, to keep in his home.

What about firearms mishaps? Well, here are the National Safety Council figures for 1968 on the principal accidental causes of death:

Motor vehicles, 55,200; falls, 19,900; burns, 7500; drowning, 7400; poisons, 4000; firearms, 2600; machinery, 2100.

In 1968, there were 101 million motor vehicles and 105 million drivers in the United States. By comparison, there were about 40 million gun owners.

The number of firearms in private hands is estimated at a quarter-billion to a billion. Conservatively, the best guess is probably a half-billion.

What do these figures boil down to? About 1900 automobile drivers per death, against one death per 15,000 gun owners. In other terms, about 1800 vehicles per death versus about 200,000 guns per death. Past statistics have shown that about the same number of persons choke to death on food as those who die accidentally from guns.

Other organizations have joined the National Rifle Association in steadfastly opposing misguided firearms legislation. Among them are the National Society of the Daughters of the American Revolution (DAR), the National Police Officers Association and the National Shooting Sports Foundation.

The latter two organizations joined in a resolution which reads in part: *Restrictive anti-gun laws do not succeed in disarming the criminal, but do disarm the law-abiding citizen, thus denying the law-abiding citizen effective self defense, as well as jeopardizing his opportunities for training in the use of firearms, and discouraging his hunting and gun sports afield.*

Many other shooting and conservation organizations are opposed to strong unrealistic and needlessly restrictive anti-gun legislation, such as the National Skeet Shooting Association, the Amateur Trap Shooting Association, the National Muzzle Loading Rifle Association, the National Wildlife Institute and many others.

Many of those who clamor for more federal laws on guns do not realize that there already are two very wide-ranging U.S. statutes controlling firearms.

*Further information is available from: National Rifle Association, 1600 Rhode Island Ave., N.W., Washington, D.C. 20036.

The National Firearms Act of 1934, modified in 1954 and 1968, levies a $200 tax on the making or transfer of any fully-automatic weapon; shotguns with under 18-inch barrels; rifles with under 16-inch barrels; mufflers, silencers and certain other apparatus.

The Federal Firearms Act of 1938 (modified in 1968 as the 1968 Gun Control Act) controls the movement in interstate and foreign commerce of all types of firearms. Among other things it specifies federal licenses for all manufacturers, dealers, importers and collectors of firearms. It prohibits interstate shipment of firearms between unlicensed individuals (except for certain antique arms), and also requires the license holder to maintain records of all firearms and most ammunition sales. Where collectors are licensed, their transactions are severely restricted on guns made after 1898. Most sportsmen and collectors strongly feel the 1968 law was ill-advised and passed in panic. As a result, several bills have been introduced in Congress seeking repeal of the 1968 law.

Both the 1934 and 1938 laws now provide a fine of $5000 and $10,000 or imprisonment for 5 and 10 years respectively, or both, for conviction under either statute.

Note, please, that the 1934-1938 Federal Firearms Acts specifically prohibited the sale to and the ownership by a convicted felon or one under indictment, drug addicts, those with a

Mrs. John B. (Kathleen Fitchett) Dinning of Ruxton, Maryland, holds the women's 12-gauge record for the NSSA world championships with a score of 249x250 posted in 1962.

history of mental aberation and those under age.

What did the federal authorities do from 1934-1938 on to enforce these firm and desirable provisions? Virtually nothing. The very *first* prosecution under the old acts took place in 1968!

Millions of Americans agree with Lowell E. Krieg, formerly with the Olin Mathieson Chemical Corp., who pointed out in 1963 that:

(a) No responsible person—in or out of the firearms industry, sportsman or not—

wants guns to be freely used by criminals or other maladjusted members of society.

(b) But no responsible person should decide to attempt to limit the free use of sporting firearms by other responsible members of that same society.

(c) A gun never killed anyone, robbed a bank, threatened or molested a defenseless person. It is inanimate and harmless until a human being provides the energy to give it action.

(d) It is ridiculous to assume that a criminal intent on armed robbery will register his gun before he commits the crime.

(e) The criminal himself provides the key to the prevention of crime. Society misleads itself when it tries to punish a knife, rope, gun or the frequently mentioned "blunt object."

(f) The only way to really restrict the use of firearms by criminals is to make the penalty for use of guns or any deadly weapon in the commission of a crime so severe that criminals will be afraid to use them. The deterrent penalty must far outweigh any possible criminal gain. This would penalize the criminal and not the honest citizen.

It has only been in the last several decades that firearms have not been owned by almost every American family. Most of those who do not own guns today are members of a non-outdoor, metropolitan segment of society.

Privately owned firearms, used in the settling of this country, helped win the very freedom of America. As mentioned before, it is estimated that some 40 million Americans own firearms. This is about half the adult population.

What are these guns used for?

Some guns are used for protection of the home, others are used for hunting. Great numbers are used for target shooting by the millions of people who belong to thousands of Skeet, trap and rifle clubs. Millions of sportsmen think of firearms in the same way that others think of fishing rods and golf clubs. There are tens of thousands of guns filling private and public arms collections, many of them of high artistic merit.

The variety of arms is infinite. The subject of firearms is truly monumental. An expert on firearms history is automatically an expert on history itself. The hoodlum with a cheap stolen pistol, or the sniper with a rifle, is a microscopically tiny and foreign part of this subject; so small and different as to be attended only by criminologists.

Unlike automobiles and household

An air-rifle competition among youngsters.

Skeet shooters are always glad to help youngsters. R. Bogie of Loon Lake, N.Y., gives pointers to 14-year old Jimmy Downing, Jr. of So. Hadley Falls, Mass., during Skeet shooting competition at Lordship, Conn.

appliances, guns seldom wear out. As a result, there may be as many as a billion guns in the United States today. Many are cherished family heirlooms which symbolize the role of pioneer forebears. The members of hundreds of clubs throughout the nation actually fire these old weapons, many in fine condition, some of which hark back 200 years or more.

The National Muzzle Loading Rifle Association was formed in 1930 for the express purpose of collecting, shooting and preserving the tradition of that long, muzzle-loading art form which originated in early America—The Kentucky-Pennsylvania rifle. Today, the NMLRA has grown to over 10,000 members, with a national shooting site at Friendship, Indiana, where an annual National Shoot is held.

Other guns have been handed from father to son and are reminders of days, when as a youth, one was taught sportsmanship in a duck blind, over the family setter, or perhaps on a mountainside in the early dawn looking for the movement of deer or elk. Any man who has gazed into the depths of a painting by Winslow Homer or A.B. Frost will understand this same feeling. In this atmosphere, millions of American boys learned genuine respect for the safety and welfare of others.

Not only are some antique weapons unique, but collections are often extremely valuable. The worth of some old American guns would make the prices on paintings in some galleries appear to be bargain-basement priced. Some of these old American firearms command up to $10,000 each.

Antiques are not the only guns of high value. Some modern sporting arms bring prices running to several thousand dollars, may require several years to complete, because of the artistically engraved metal and carved wood.

Gun ownership in America is a subject of monumental scope. It is legal by constitutional right; it is non-criminal in nature with respect to the overwhelming majority of firearm users; and it is made up for the most part of solid patriotic citizens.

The subject is so big that further legislation should only be drawn up by experts. This is why some presumably capable Congressmen and Senators have offered anti-firearm legislation faulty in the extreme, acts that if passed would leave law-abiding, decent citizens unprotected in their homes, unable to hunt our fields and forests, and would affect the economy in a severely serious way. Happily—at least for the time being—such inept, ill-conceived bills have not passed. These naive—to be charitable—lawmakers have also overlooked the fact that nearly 100 per cent of gun owners are law-abiding citizens, and that this group makes up nearly half of the adult population. ●

DOUBLE GUNS

by MERRILL K. LINDSAY

Photos by BRUCE PENDLETON

Double barreled guns and rifles have come a long way since 1500—about when the first twin-tubes were made. Here's a thorough review of the many systems developed over four centuries, with a bow to the resurgent interest in doubles today.

WITH TODAY'S multi-barreled aircraft cannon firing at unbelievable cyclic rates of more than 10,000 shots a minute, who cares about earlier weapons that shot from a mere one or two barrels. That is, unless you are interested in history, and want to know how the modern weapons came into being. It was a bigger step forward in the history of firearms from the one-barreled gun to two-barreled guns than the later advance from two to 12 or 20. If the first hand-held weapon was built and shot some time around 1300, and we think that it was, it took more than 200 years for gunmakers to progress from single barrel guns to any sort of practical working double guns.

During the same 200 years, all kinds of experiments were made. Bunches of iron barrels were tied together in an effort to create a multi-firing weapon. In another direction of design, more than one charge was placed in the same barrel. The majority of these weapons discharged all of their loads at once with a hell of a roar. The effect was not always what the designer of the gun was hoping for. Sometimes a multiple burst was the intention, but more often it was an accident, resulting from one charge igniting another. Sometimes the effort to produce multi-firing weapons resulted in guns that

were just too cumbersome to be practical. The frightened citizens of Verona, Italy, fearing the possible attack of a combination of neighboring princes, built a marvellous monster. Did it have pipes! It looked like the guts of the world's biggest steam boiler. It had rows on rows of barrels stacked 20 deep. The idea of the inventive genius was that one man on each level of the staging that supported the barrels would light a train of powder on his particular floor. The powder train would then burn merrily along and ignite the charge in each successive barrel on that level. Of course, there was no provision for moving this piece of artillery nor for aiming it at anything. It was an early example of the man building a boat in his garage that wouldn't come out through the doors. In this case the Veronese never did get anybody to pose long enough in front of all those barrels to prove anything.

When loose powder or matches were used for ignition of guns, it was work enough to fire one single barrel with any degree of success. De Gheyn, in his book, *The Exercise of Armes for Calivres, Muskettes . . .* (matchlocks) illustrates the 37 steps required to fire a matchlock and reload it. This was in 1607, when the matchlock was still the chief weapon used by the infantry of European armies. More than 60 years

before De Gheyn, nevertheless, the first successful double guns had been built, using the new system of firing, the wheel-lock.

Wheel-locks

The wheel-lock made the double gun a practical possibility, because its system of cigarette lighter ignition eliminated the need of an open fire or a burning match, which could and often did lead to a double barreled explosion. Instead, the wheel-lock mechanism, with its covered pans—left and right, or over and under—made doubles shooting almost as safe as single shots.

The earliest double barrel firearms that I have seen have all been pistols. This might have to do with the additional weight of a two-barrel gun, and two pistol barrels should weigh less than two rifle barrels. I don't think that this is necessarily the answer, however. As we have seen, the infantry were still equipped with the cumbersome matchlocks, while that elite branch, the cavalry, got the newer model guns, the wheel-locks. The cavalry, of course, needed wheel-locks, as it was a near-impossibility keeping a match lit on horseback. Naturally, short barrels were preferred, as they were less cumbersome on horseback, so the early wheel-lock weapons were apt to be pistols or short carbines.

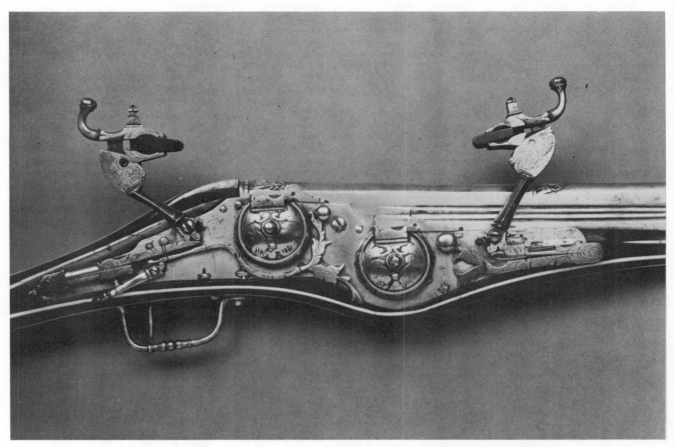

Peter Peck over-and-under double wheel-lock pistol, made circa 1553. Joe Kindig, Jr., collection.

A double barrel wheel-lock horse pistol, then, would have been a good thing to invent as it would save the horseman having to dismount, or at least take both hands off the reins of his beast in order to reload. As necessity is well known to be the mother of invention, the double barrel dagger handled pistol in the Porte de Hal Museum in Brussels, Belgium should, by rights, be signed *M. Neccessite*. Alas, there is not only no name, there's not even a proofmark, a date, or a clue to the country or place where it was made. It is a very early piece, as one can see by the shape of the grips or handle. True pistol grips had not even been invented, and single barrel guns with grips like this, which can be dated to the early 1500s, are in some of the collections of the north Italian museums. Incidentally, the ball on the end of the grip not only kept the hand from sliding off, but it opened up to make two hinged halves of a box holding spare pyrites and balls.

Another help in dating this early double gun is a two-barreled pistol in the Metropolitan Museum of Art. The Met piece has all kinds of clues indicating not only where it came from, but who made it and when. The barrel is signed with the initials *P. P.* and we know that one Peter Peck, a matchlock and wheel-lock maker, lived in Munich

throughout a very long lifetime. He was born in 1503 and died in 1596. Between 1519 and 1555 the Emperor Charles V reigned over most of Europe. The double barreled pistol in the Metropolitan has the crest and motto of Charles engraved on the wheel-lock cover. Peter Peck could not have been old enough or skilled and famous enough to have been given a commission to build this gun until some time in the 1530s or '40s, so it is possible to date not only this gun but the one in Brussels. The invention of the double barreled pistol can, therefore, be pretty well tied down to an exact time in history, though there are no patent dates.

Early double barreled guns had two locks and, quite naturally also, two triggers. The skill of the Nuremberg gunsmiths was such that it was no time at all before double guns were built to fire both barrels from a single trigger, one lock and one barrel at a time. The very earliest of these double barreled pistols, with their large frizzen springs cupped around the wheel, were of the two-trigger variety. If they were over-and-under designed guns, each trigger had its own trigger guard, and the two barrels were inlaid into the opposite sides of a tapered stock. The gun was fired, then turned over on the other side to fire the second barrel.

Such an over and under wheel-lock can be seen in the collection of the Musee de L'Armee in Paris. Unfortunately, somewhere during its long life, and in its travels from Germany to France, it has lost one of its barrels. The French museum people — being broke, as usual — replaced the missing barrel with a neatly whittled piece of broomstick. There is enough left of the gun to make it one of the early important pieces.

Other early double pistols had one shooting position for both barrels. One barrel was laid on top of the other, and two locks, one ahead of the other, were situated on the right side of the gun. As each lock served its own barrel, and one lock was ahead of the other, the barrels were, of necessity, of different length. This is true of both the Porte de Hal pistol and the Peter Peck pistol in the Metropolitan Museum.

All of these early guns and the ones that immediately succeeded them had barrels which were bedded independently. Usually the barrels were inletted into a wooden stock. An exception to this can be seen in a few surviving Nuremberg metal pistols, where even at an early date, the barrels were brazed to an iron rib which separated them. Either system seems to have satisfied the 16th century shooter as long as the gun functioned as it was supposed to, and two shots could be fired in succession. No thought was wasted on accuracy, or on having the two barrels shoot in the same direction. This is easy to understand as the (usually) smoothbored barrels were intended for shooting at point blank range. Therefore the fact that one barrel shot above or below another, or a few feet to the left or the right of the other barrel was purely academic. The trick in those days was to gallop up to your enemy, avoid his swinging saber, point the pistol at his cuirass-covered chest and yell "you're dead" as you pulled the trigger.

Cavalry Use

This tactic, employed by masses of

The system didn't work too well, however, when the enemy was quicker than the heavily armed Germans on their heavy horses. In a recorded encounter with lightly armed Polish or Cossack horsemen, the reiters took a beating. The Poles simply melted away instead of facing the organized pistol attack of the Germans. Instead, they swept around the flank of the German circle on their speedy light ponies and used their sabers with great effectiveness against the temporarily unarmd part of the circle which was trying to reload.

This example and others led the commanders of troops of cavalry to abandon the use of the pistol. Human nature being what it is, the individual

At first, after guns were invented, it was considered unsporting to use them for sport. Beside that, the early guns wouldn't shoot fast enough and were too cumbersome to hit any kind of moving game. It wasn't until the beginning of the 16th century that we find any evidence of guns being used instead of the traditional hunting swords, boar spears, and hunting crossbows. The first picture of a man hunting with a gun was made in 1504. It is in the "Hunting Book" of the Emperor Maximilian. The illustration shows Maximilian holding on a chamois which is perched above him on a little promontory jutting out over a lake. His was not the only gun being used for this purpose. He complains in his

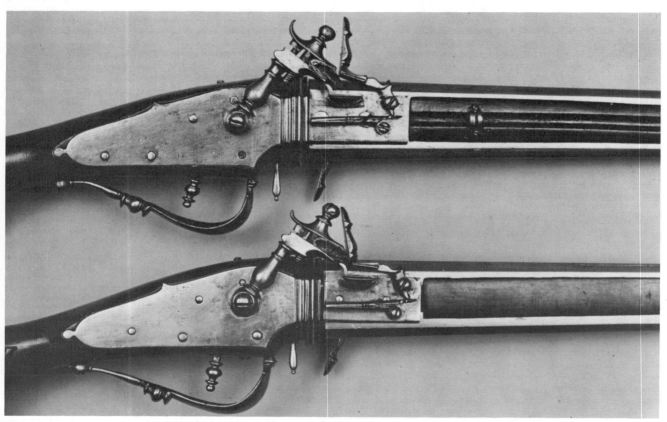

Wender-type pistols, marked *Lazarino Cominazzi*, with straight stocks, made before 1637. Length overall 22¼", 14" barrels, 52 caliber. Nos. 3777-3778, Museo Storico Nazionale d'Artiglieria, Turin.

trained cavalry, was very effective. It worked especially well when horses were in on the act. A maneuver which was drilled into both men and horses was called the caracole. It was practiced by the *reiters* of the German states with great effectiveness. A troop of cavalry rode in a circle with the horses doing a side step so that they were facing the enemy at all times. The riders in the front of the circle fired their guns at point blank range. As the circle rotated, they reloaded in a hurry so that they would be ready the next time that their turn came up. The effect on stationary ground troops was devastating as they were subjected to a continuous barrage of pistol fire.

cavalryman was apt to fire his pistol at a safe distance from a saber cut, and too far away to score a hit. Not being accustomed to using a sword or a lance, he felt at a disadvantage and took for the hills. This made for lost wars, so the commanders of cavalry regiments in the 17th century often forbade the use or even the carrying of pistols in a charge. Whatever effect this may have had, there were still a great number of single and double barrel pistols being made, and some of these pistols found their way home with the soldiers after their particular war had ended. In this way, what were essentially military or guard weapons wound up being used for hunting.

memoirs that the peasants were making "develish use of fire-guns" and killing off the rare ibex. Maximilian considered that ibex hunting was his royal prerogative, and he laid down harsh laws to prevent the ibex being shot at.

Maximilian was only one of many 16th century European hunters to use a gun. Guns are mentioned in the hunting regulations of Francis I (1515-1547) and even Cellini, who had no hunting preserves of his own, built his own light hunting rifle and used it to shoot rabbits which he found in the grass-covered ruins of Roman temples.

Once hunting with guns had become a popular pastime, the double gun real-

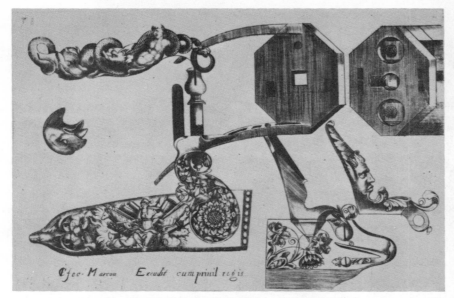

From Francois Marcou's *Plusieurs Pieces d'Arquebuzerie.*

Wender Doubles

No one knows who invented the Wender. Among the very early examples are a pair of straight stocked pistols with 14-inch barrels in the Artillery Museum in Turin. These pistols, almost long enough to be classed as carbines—22¼"—could have been used for hunting or military purposes. The stocks are plain, unlike most hunting weapons. They were made in Brescia, in northern Italy, by Lazarino Cominazzo before 1637, and so are the first known Wenders to survive.

Not long after these pistols were made, a pattern book design for decorating Wender long guns turned up in the Paris pattern book of Francois Marcou. Marcou's book of designs was first printed in 1657, so the Wender gun must have been around in France before that. There are examples of Danish, German and Swedish Wenders dating from around the 1650s and continuing right on into the 19th century. The Wender could very properly be considered the most popular hunting weapon of Germany and Austria.

The Wender was not the only double gun to make the scene during this long period. There were also fixed barrel over-and-under guns built with two locks, one mounted on either side of the gun. One lock fired the top barrel and the other communicated the flash by means of a short tube to the under barrel. This type was not as popular as the Wender either because they were more awkward, having the cocks sticking out on both sides, or because of the additional cost of the extra lock. The cost of the lock was a very impor-

ly came into its own. In its earliest form, the double gun was an over-and-under. A European type which was most popular, from its introduction in 1650, was the Wender. This gun was used all over Europe for more than a century, and was brought to America by the German settlers who came to Pennsylvania. Fine "Kentucky" Wenders were subsequently built in Lancaster and York. The Wender is an over-and-under double gun with barrels which rotate. After the top barrel is fired, the bottom barrel is swung up into firing position and held there by a spring-loaded pin. The pin release lever is usually handily located ahead of the trigger guard so that it can be worked with the trigger or index finger. Most of these guns (if flintlock) have a single lock and cock, but on each barrel there is a separate pan and pan cover. This assembly comes up into the correct operating position when the barrel to which it is attached is brought into firing position. The barrels of the Wender are inletted into a full length wooden forestock, and the ramrod is located on one side between the barrels.

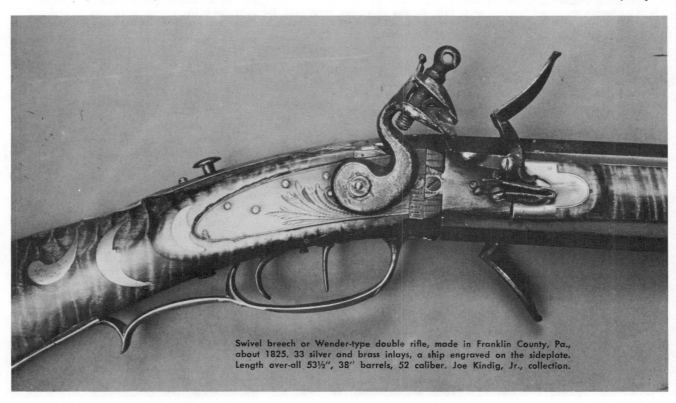

Swivel breech or Wender-type double rifle, made in Franklin County, Pa., about 1825. 33 silver and brass inlays, a ship engraved on the sideplate. Length over-all 53½", 38" barrels, 52 caliber. Joe Kindig, Jr., collection.

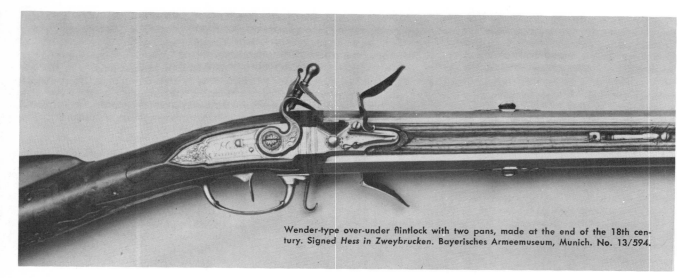

Wender-type over-under flintlock with two pans, made at the end of the 18th century. Signed *Hess in Zweybrucken*. Bayerisches Armeemuseum, Munich. No. 13/594.

tant element in the total price of a gun.

Up to this point, shotguns and guns used for hunting in general had tremendously long barrels. Such length was necessary in order to give the uncertain, slow-burning powders a chance to develop their maximum pressures. Later, when gunpowder was corned and the size of the corned pellets could be controlled, it became possible to speed up the rate of burning and, correspondingly, shorten the length of the barrels. Shorter, lighter barrels made the side-by-side double a likely possibility.

The lightest, strongest barrels in all of Europe, which had been thus made consistently for hundreds of years, starting in the 1550s, were the barrels of the Comminazzo family—the same family of gunmakers who built the earliest surviving Wender. It is not surprising, then, to find that the earliest side-by-side double was also built by one of them, Lazari Cominaz some time around 1600. This is a wheel-lock with interchangeable barrels now in the Bavarian Army Museum in Munich. This and later side-by-side doubles of the 17th century were made the same way that the Wenders had been. That is, the barrels were separated by wood, not soldered. Wood had many advantages. It was easier to work than metal, and the alignment of the barrels could be improved with a piece of sandpaper wrapped over a dowel. Even of more importance was the fact that the wood absorbed the vibration of both barrels when one was being shot. Solving this problem was to be a bugaboo to double gunmakers for hundreds of years.

It wasn't until the 1730s that the modern double barrel shotgun, with two barrels soldered together, was first made in St. Etienne in France. Its maker, Jean Le Clerc, used solder; soldered ribs were commonly used in Paris during the next 30 years. Now

Napoleon's Boutet flintlock with extra percussion barrels and locks made for Prince Osten-Sachen, military governor of Paris in 1814. The barrels are signed *Manufacture de Versailles* and were made about 1815. The percussion barrels are signed *Leopold Bernardo, Canonnier de Paris*. The percussion locks are signed *Zaoue*. No. 42.50.7, Metropolitan Museum of Art, New York, the Dick Fund, 1942.

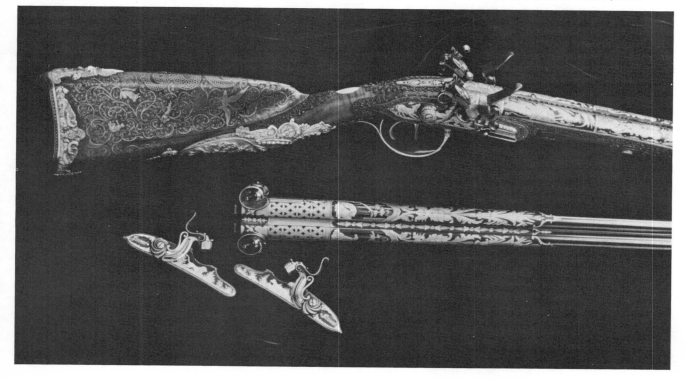

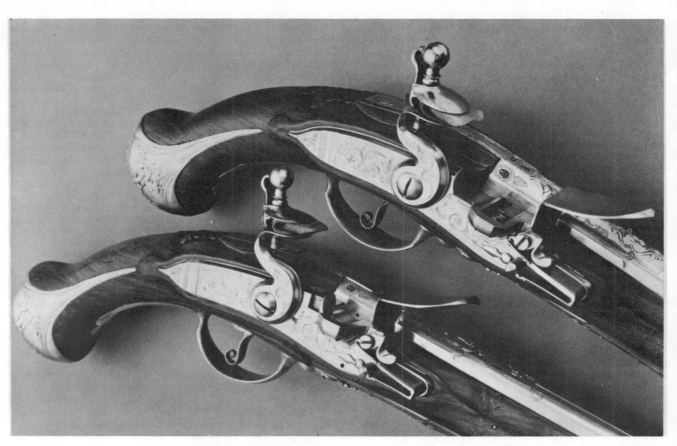

Pair of over-and-under flintlock holster pistols from the collection of the Grand
Duke of Saxe-Weimar. Tower of London collection. Nos. 12/1556 and 1557.

English 16-gauge breech-loading shotgun with barrels
that move forward, made about 1820. Length over-all
38", 21½" barrels. No. M/61, Armeria Reale, Turin.

the gunsmiths really had an alignment problem, and it's one that has hung around ever since.

More and more was demanded by hunters and bird shooters of their double guns. As game became scarce from over-hunting, and what game was left was understandably shy of the hunter and his gun, the range from which the hunter had to shoot increased. Also wing shooting became a sport, where formerly it had been impossible to hit a bird on the wing. These conditions created a demand for accuracy at reasonable distances.

Barrel Alignment

The first and most obvious way to make the two barrels of a shotgun or rifle shoot together at approximately the same point was to line up the bores of the two barrels. If there had been no other problems, this would have meant that two solid bullets fired from the two barrels would have followed a parallel course, the track being as wide as the center of the two bores. Unfortunately, that didn't work because of recoil and lateral movement, left and right, of side-by-side barrels at the moment of discharge. The next trick was to try to make the two barrels shoot to the same exact point at a given distance, usually 40 yards with a shotgun, and 100 yards or less with a double rifle. In order to accomplish this feat, the two barrels ordinarily

have to have their bore axes converge (or even cross each other) to correct for the change in impact caused by recoil. Altering the bullet weight, and the increase or decrease of the powder charge will affect the point of impact. For this reason, double rifles are regulated for a given bullet weight and powder charge. So far, so good, but now a problem arose which no one had contemplated before the first gunsmith soldered together his first set of barrels.

When you fire a single barrel gun, the barrel vibrates from the shock of the explosion. If the barrel is bedded in the wood of a forestock, the vibration may be damped somewhat, but when you fire one barrel of a double gun, the barrel is not free to vibrate independently because of the inert mass of steel attached to one side, namely, the other barrel and the rib. The lopsidedness of the structure sets up unpredictable vibration which can radically affect accuracy as well as point of impact.

The cure for this lopsidedness was not an easy one. It took years of painful trial-and-error experimentation, to get a practical solution. Even today there is no easy shortcut to building a fine double gun. Here, taken from *One Hundred Great Guns,* are the painstaking steps which have to be followed in the manufacture of a double gun.

"Between the barrels is a fitted and

tapered iron rib, to which both barrels have been brazed. (In order to do this) the two barrels are set up in rough position, held apart by clamped-on iron wedges, and shot to see what happens. Each barrel is shot independently of each other; they are then pushed together or pulled apart at the muzzle by driving in or pulling out a muzzle wedge until the two barrels shoot approximately to the same point at a given distance. When the barrels are being aligned, barrels, solder, wedges and all are tightly wrapped with iron wire. Then red hot iron rods are placed in the barrels until the barrels themselves are hot enough to melt the hard solder —thus acting as their own soldering iron. This process is repeated over and over — soldering and unsoldering — until the alignment is perfect. Top and bottom ribs are then soldered in place, sights attached, and the barrel struck and polished — the alignment of barrels is a subtle and difficult job."

All of this requires the most skilled kind of hand work, and there are few skilled craftsmen anywhere who can or will build double guns today. A handful of gunmakers are building good double guns in Austria, Belgium, England and Italy. The best English guns, traditionally the finest, take three to four years to build on custom order. In the United States, no double rifles are being built, and the finest double barreled shot-gun, the Win-

Damascus double barrel percussion shotgun with sliding safety **cover** to protect the eye from exploding caps. Musée d'Armes, Liège.

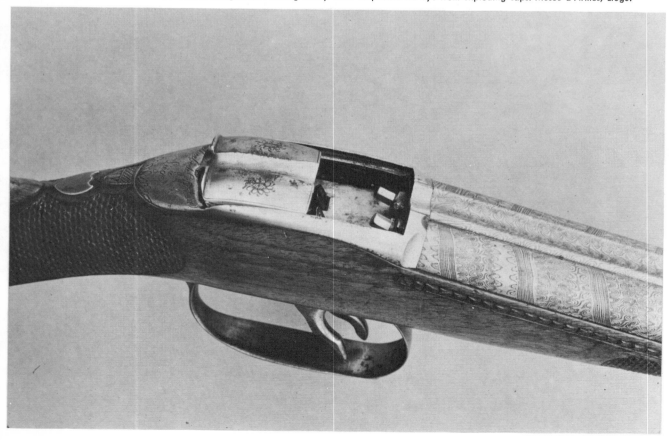

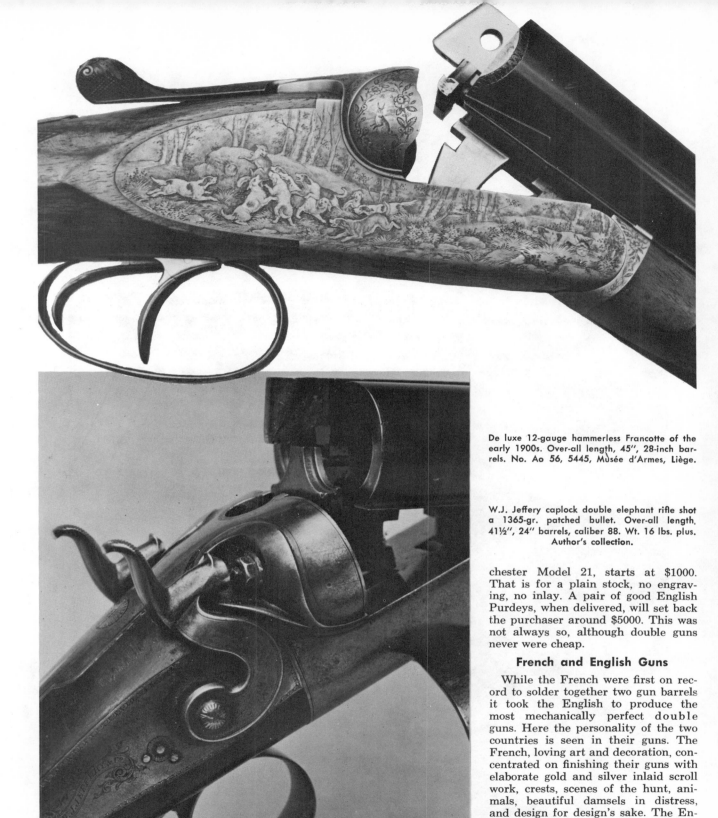

De luxe 12-gauge hammerless Francotte of the early 1900s. Over-all length, 45″, 28-inch barrels. No. Ao 56, 5445, Musée d'Armes, Liège.

W.J. Jeffery caplock double elephant rifle shot a 1365-gr. patched bullet. Over-all length, 41½″, 24″ barrels, caliber 88. Wt. 16 lbs. plus. Author's collection.

chester Model 21, starts at $1000. That is for a plain stock, no engraving, no inlay. A pair of good English Purdeys, when delivered, will set back the purchaser around $5000. This was not always so, although double guns never were cheap.

French and English Guns

While the French were first on record to solder together two gun barrels it took the English to produce the most mechanically perfect double guns. Here the personality of the two countries is seen in their guns. The French, loving art and decoration, concentrated on finishing their guns with elaborate gold and silver inlaid scroll work, crests, scenes of the hunt, animals, beautiful damsels in distress, and design for design's sake. The English guns are plainer. The ambition of the English gunsmith was to make a gun which functioned perfectly in all kinds of weather and was as perfect on the inside as on the outside. The English gun trade had plenty of home encouragement. Never has a nation produced so many avid sportsmen.

The English hunter not only raised game scientifically at home in order

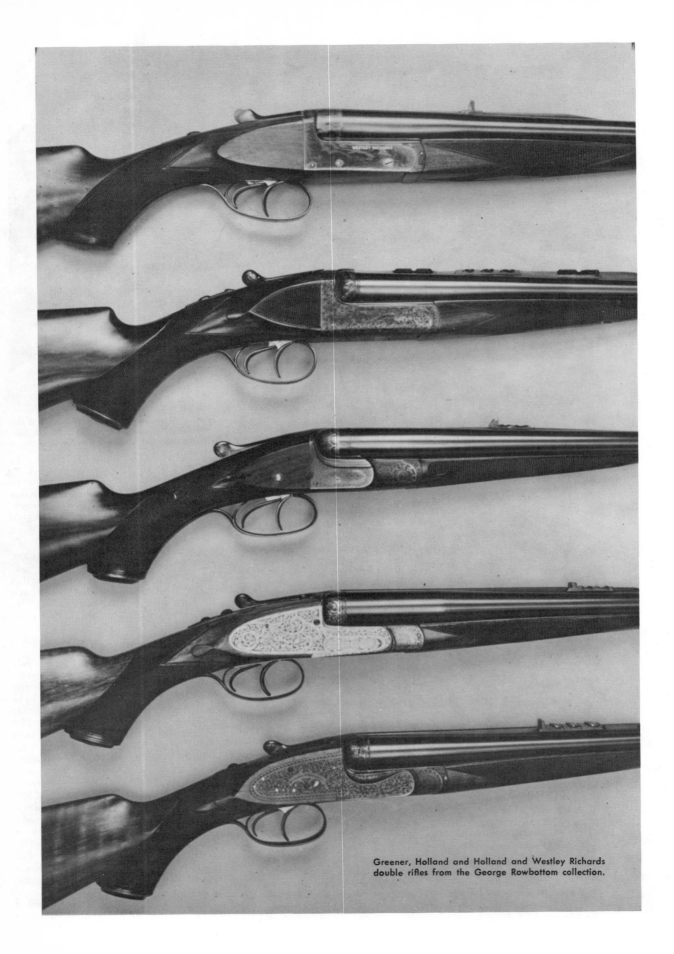

Greener, Holland and Holland and Westley Richards double rifles from the George Rowbottom collection.

to provide for the enormous shoots which are still part of the British sporting scene, but they took their double guns and rifles into every corner of the world. The British made the finest double rifles in black powder 500, 577 and 600 calibers for hunting tiger in India. They built monster 8, 4, and 2 bore double rifles to shoot elephant and rhino in Africa. English bird guns in all bores, were the treasured possessions of Hungarian noblemen and Turkish pashas. Even in America, the double rifle went west with English sportsmen who were hunting in the plains states and the Rockies before 1850.

bolt action and automatic rifles. In any event, hunters who have had an opportunity to shoot a double gun seldom revert to other types of actions. The model '94 Winchester lever action is reputed to have killed more deer in the United States and Canada than any other gun. Similarly, the double rifle has accounted for more big game in Asia and Africa than all the bolt actions, lever actions, trombone actions and automatics.

The Scene Today

With today's game shortages and resultant bag limitations, there is little need for an automatic away from the Skeet field. A double gun will kill all

sporting guns in Liege. The firm of Francotte is still going strong after more than 100 years, and the Browning over-and-under is very popular today. In Austria fine double guns and rifles are being made in Ferlach, these not as expensive as English guns.

In the United States, in addition to the Model 21 Winchester, there are a number of good, serviceable double guns being made for a price. They lack the finish and smoothness of the better guns, but then you are not paying so much. The United States used to produce a number of fine double guns. There were none better than the Parker shotgun made in Meriden, Conn.,

Westley Richards double rifle, caliber 375 Magnum, with hand-detachable locks. George Rowbottom collection.

The great value of a double gun as a hunting weapon is described by professional white hunter John Taylor, in his book *African Rifles and Cartridges,* published in a U.S. edition in 1948. He says that if you are sure of a kill on your first shot, it makes no difference whether you shoot a single shot rifle, an automatic, a bolt action, or a double, but if you need more than one shot, which is often the case with thick skinned African game, the working of a bolt and the resultant clicks will give away the location of the hunter to the wounded animal. This, he points out, has often proved unhealthy for the hunter. Taylor also likes double rifles because they are positive. The extreme heat that is absorbed by a gun exposed to the hot midday African sun, can cause expansion and jamming of both

the game you will normally have a chance to shoot at, and the knowledge that you have only two shots may make you hold a little more carefully. The pleasure of owning and shooting a good double cannot be exaggerated. If you are a millionaire or a dedicated shooter you won't be happy until you own a pair of the finest English guns, but fortunately you can own a double without all that dough or dedication.

In the last few years, some very good doubles have been made in Japan by the same kind of skilled mechanics who build the Nikon camera. In Brescia and Turin, where guns have been made for 500 years, good, reasonably priced 12, 20, 28 and 410 gauge double shotguns are being manufactured to American specifications for the U.S. market. Belgium has always made

the Dan Lefevers, the original Foxes, or the fine hand-finished L. C. Smith.

Don't take my word for it, and don't rush out and buy a double gun that doesn't fit you, but if you have a friend about your own size who shoots a double, ask him to let you try it out. If you see a good second-hand double barreled gun that fits you, grab it if the price is right. After all, you own a gun because you are a hunter, not a machine adjuster; as you may have noticed, those who are the deadliest shots are the ones who make it simple for themselvs. All their attention is focused on the game they're after, not the adjustments on the gun they are going to shoot. A good double, difficult as it may be to build, is a simple, honest weapon that delivers two shots as fast as you can pull the trigger. ●

The KNIFE

Man's oldest tool, ever the same and ever-changing. Modern steels, new handle materials make today's knives, handmade or factory, better than ever before —and different!

by KEN WARNER

SOME FIVE editions ago, when the GUN DIGEST first covered handmade knives, it was easy to be an expert; easy to know all the knifemakers; easy to know all about knives. Things have changed. A list appended to this treatment contains 42 names—42 knifemakers who sell at least part of their work. Something over 15 of those names are serious—they make knives for a full-time living.

There'll be a handmade knife for anybody and everybody in the 1970s, individual creations that will be sold in the tens of thousands.

What brought this on? Well, it's more than simple affluence. The knifemaker's craft is one of the oldest trades and there appears to be a growing appreciation of craftsmanship; the use of a really good knife is a constant delight; more people than ever (numbers, not percentages) are getting outdoors, where a knife is useful—the list of factors is lengthy. The genus *collector* is heavily involved— aside from those who collect one each of all the types a given knifesmith produces, others ardently search out new smiths to add to their collection of one each by every knifemaker.

There is a strong military relationship, too. Carrying a good knife to South-East Asia may not bring a young man back for certain, but it's a very sensible piece of insurance, and a useful confidence-builder. The soldiers across the Pacific have enough on their minds. They don't want to worry about a knife breaking when that blade is being used to make them comfortable or to provide shelter or, *in extremis* and quite rarely, as a weapon.

Five editions back we said a custom knife, a good hand-made knife, was "pretty good for stout and awful good for sharp." We said it was made of steel with a carbon content of .9% to 1.4% or thereabouts; that some smiths forged and some smiths simply ground the steel away. We said the knife was made in the fire—heat treatment and the resulting temper were the big factors. We said these smiths worked hard with the best materials they could find, taking few shortcuts.

That's all still true. About the only material change is that stainless steel makes more sense now than it did then. There is evidence—discussed below—that the *absolute top edge-holding ability* still goes to non-stainless steels, but 440C and some other 400-series steels that are stainless have proven over the past 5 years to be very, very good indeed.

Sixteen Top Makers

Don't get the idea that nothing has changed, however. In design, in shape, in aptitude, in variety, in weight, in style—it's a whole new ball game. New names on the list—some of them —are way, way up there in quality; others are asking first-class prices for honest but second-echelon work. In knife-making, as in tool design and rifle-making, the eye of the artist shows. Some fellows are just not as artistic as other fellows.

Nevertheless, readers of this article are entitled to opinions. The following opinions are this writer's:

W.F. "Bo" Randall is, thus far, the unquestioned dean of 20th century knifesmiths. His work is original with him; the quality is there; the looks are unmistakably Randall. He is the most-imitated, which means that his designs outsell everybody, taking into account all brands.

D.E. Henry is the best workman in the bunch. The craft evident is unmatched, even in the eyes of other knifemakers. He confines himself almost exclusively to replicas of 19th century knives, which in some ways takes him out of the running, but the lines, the work are plain to see, regardless of the style.

Draper knives are the best-finished available. It is doubtless possible to bring steel and nickel-silver and Micarta and stag and suchlike to a brighter, smoother and cleaner finish, but it would be very difficult indeed.

Moran knives are, with little argument, the highest-finished, most-solid hard-use knives in the traditional mode. Second only to Draper (whose knives are "modern," whatever that

means) in finish, Moran knives reveal the hand of the maker in detail, in workmanship and construction, as a master. Moran is one of the few who do it all—every licking bit of work—without power tools, save for grinders and sanders, perhaps a drill press.

R.W. Loveless, who began making knives 16 years ago for sale at Abercrombie & Fitch (marked "Delaware Maid" for you collectors) and unabashedly admits they were Randall types, is going to reshape fine knife design just as Randall did, but differently. He is the top designer, an artist with the grinding wheel and a fine craftsman. He has something else going for him, too, which will be discussed below.

There are 11 more full-time, superior knifemakers. Perhaps a word about all 16 of them is in order.

Ralph Bone: Sound solid knives, quite derivative of Randall shapes and sizes. Excellent workmanship, very professional and up to standards. From about $30. Makes a stout folding knife, push daggers and boot knives.

Cooper: Wide variety of shapes and sizes, some derivative, but more original. No variety in handle treatment—Micarta all the way. Well thought of. Made by John N. Cooper; marketed by George J. Cooper. From about $30.

Dowell: Trademarked TMD, these are sportsmen's "using" knives. There are 8 models, not derivative. Uses some ⅛" stock, which is often an advantage. Has one useful $20 knife; the rest start at about $35. Good simple designs.

Draper: Catalogs hard to come by. Highly finished; wide range of handle material, blade shapes.. Heavy duty knives. Prices in the middle ranges.

Fischer: A Texas maker and his original designs with a traditional flavor show it. YO Ranch guides use many Fischer knives and they are good. Has 9 main designs at prices from $40 and $50.

Henry: Makes reproduction Bowies and several original full-use designs, all with the highest quality workmanship. Lowest priced knife is $125; makes Bowies at a base price of $25 per inch of blade, takes 8 to 10 months to deliver.

Hibben: Heavyweight knives of mostly derivative design. Very tough stuff and nicely finished. Actually, there have been two Hibben knife grades, Standard and Signature, the difference being the degree of finish. Prices from about $50.

Kneubuhler: Pronounced "kuh-ny-bew-ler" and the maker of W-K knives, Kneubuhler has his own special niche. He makes largely Mountain Man gear

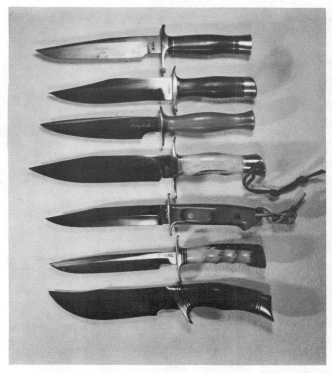

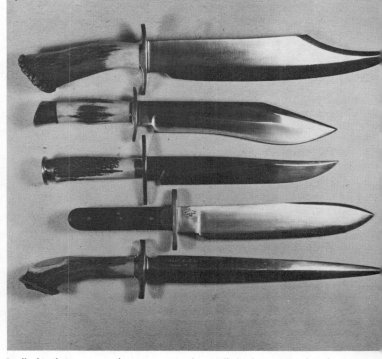

These fighting knives—excepting the Sparks heavy-duty hunting knife at the bottom—present the approximate range of 20th century design in this class. From top, they are made by: Stone, Hibben, Lile, Draper, Loveless, Randall, Sparks. Prices from $45 to $150. Most are bevel-ground on both edges; the Loveless is double hollow-ground. Blades are 6½-7½". Note (except Sparks) the double guards, and that the heavy-bladed specimens carry heavy butt caps to bring the balance back into the hand.

Really big knives, as in this group, are almost all display pieces, though the center three are within the range of practicality with 10" blades. From the top: Lile Bowie; Hibben special-order Bowie with Kukri features; Kneubuhler *Colter's Hell* Mountain Man knife; oversize special-order Moran Rio Grande camp knife; Lile Arkansas toothpick. The Hibben was an attempt by its buyer to meet jungle conditions, was later abandoned; the *Colter's Hell* is quite light and handy, despite its size; the Moran was built for a Viet Nam trip that didn't happen, was meant to be unbreakable and probably is; the two Lile knives are replicas of fighting knives from 19th century America.

and fixings, uses the same guard-and-pommel design—his own—throughout, makes authentic stuff of high finish and quality at quite low prices—$35 for a 5" skinner to $50 for a 9½" 19th century fighting knife plus specials at up to $125 in the Bowie types. The W-K sheaths are notably sturdy—each has a fitted cloth and rigid fiberglass liner. Also makes such muzzleloader's fixings as hunting bags and the like.

Lile: Jimmy Lile just turned full-time professional, after building 1000 knives or so. He has conventional and derivative designs; also produces some of his own styles, original to him. He forges or grinds, customer choice. Produces nicely balanced large Bowies and "toothpicks." Prices from $40 to $125. He's making 100 engraved Bowies commemorating Arkansas River navigation, cased at $500.

Loveless: Most Loveless knives come ready to use at 62C Rockwell—they are very hard. Completely original designer and master grinder. Quality features like taper tang, nickel-silver handle wrap, decorative glue lines at joints, full-tang slab handles, choice of

handle style. Excellent heavyweight sheaths. Prices from about $80.

Moran: Eye-tempered in the charcoal, severely tested, then polished to a mirror finish—that's a Moran knife. Moran forges. Produces *Cinquecento* daggers, and the like as combat-quality replicas; other work is traditional but distinctly Moran in design. Handsome knives; very superior sheaths; top drawer workmanship. Prices from $55.

Morseth: The original Morseth's grandson now runs the shop and makes the knives. Morseth blades are ground from bars laminated in Norway—1/16" of very hard steel between two 1/16" layers of soft steel—and they work well. New blade designs are coming along; the same old good workmanship at relatively low prices, the same great fiber-lined sheath.

Randall: The shop is getting bigger and sometimes one slips by, but in the main the sound structure and good workmanship is there, along with the excellent and handsome design. Prices are medium low—the 13 sporting knives and the famous #1 and #2 fighting knives are all between $35

and $45—and they are Randalls.

Ruana: This is an old name, highly respected by every knifemaker. Ruana casts handles in place, doesn't finish surfaces cleanly, but makes his own designs and his knives stand up. They are remarkable bargains in handmade knives—some under $10.

Seguine: This Alaskan knifemaker shows high competence, though you will likely wait up to 3-4 years to get one. We've had more than several complaints about slow, slow delivery. Prices medium.

Stone: Started with derivative designs—tough and heavy knives of thick stock are still his best sellers, but he's now putting out some originals of interesting and useful shape. Prices in the high middle range.

Workmanship

Leaving aside for the moment a number of part-time knifemakers, a couple of whom turn out small amounts of work in the same class as the big 16, what is it about those men that makes them good? Well, you already know they make hard tough blades that get sharp and stay

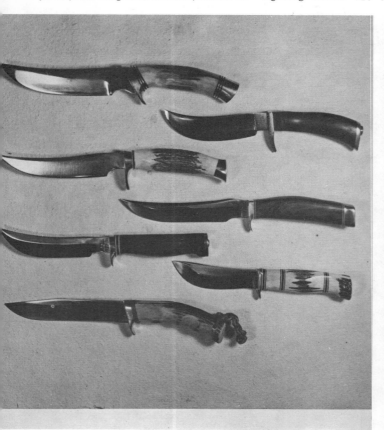

Above—These heavy game knives are favorites among fine knife buyers. Mostly, they have blades from ¼" stock. Made by, from the top: Sparks, Moran, Lile, Hueske, Heath, Morseth, Loveless. Properly, the Morseth is a skinner and the Loveless, with its straight blade, is a heavy-duty camp/utility knife. Prices from $30 to $90, single-edged blades up to 6½" ● In the Randall smithy, they still use hammers. In the foreground, Randall's newest series of military knives.

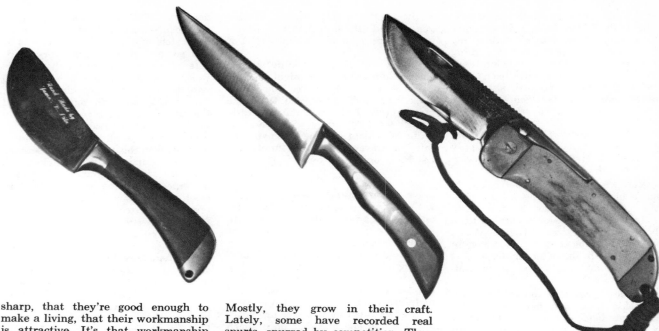

sharp, that they're good enough to make a living, that their workmanship is attractive. It's that workmanship that makes the difference.

If any of them by happenstance turned out a knife where the blade edge, point, the guard and the butt of the knife weren't all lined up, and you sent the knife back, you'd get about the most apologetic letter you ever saw. The solder joint—where used—at the blade and guard isn't sloppy. The handles *fit*—any edge is clean, adjoining materials butt smoothly. The grinds are clean and bobbles don't show. The knife is symmetrical.

That isn't true of some of the newcomers. Make no mistake—it isn't easy to keep an edge straight and in line, particularly on a big knife. It isn't easy to run a clean grind-and-polish line. It isn't easy to throw away $5 worth of ivory when the drill slips.

It takes a good man about 300 knives to get a good start on these skills, and 1000 knives is likely more like it.

Below that level there are hobbyists and part-timers and some superb craftsmen who make a dozen knives or so a year. That accounts for the other 25-odd names on the list below.

Some of them are doing right well. Heath of Wisconsin is very good with a grinding wheel and his blades, though the designs are familiar, are prettily made. Hueske, a Texan, has found out what balance is and shapes up a knife nicely. Sparks' knives are very well-finished and well-made, and he'll be right up there soon. H.G. Bourne of Ohio—the writer has seen only pictures—appears to make excellent knives. Another Texan named Martin does right well, B.R. Hughes says, and the prices quoted seem low enough. Sewell makes knives strictly to order to customer designs—and so it goes.

Another thing apparent to the student is that knifemakers change.

Mostly, they grow in their craft. Lately, some have recorded real spurts, spurred by competition. They get technical advice, change methods and materials; they see other designs and change their own; they reach enough success to want more. The best thing of all happens when a knifemaker decides he's good enough to do his own thing exclusively. Some hard-nosed and tough individuals start out that way, of course. The result is always a superior knife, and generally a superior design.

Knife Design

There's this thing about knives. They all have handles, edges, points, usually guards or at least something

Special designs spark a lot of interest, revealing a lot about their makers—who sell conventional knives for a living. At right is an early Seguine answer to the pocketknife problem, a heavy knife, good enough to dress and skin big game, made first-class. Seguine may have stopped making these, but other makers seem to be starting to offer folding knife designs. The two wood-handled knives at the left are Lile's skinner and caper.

R. W. Loveless at the finishing bench. The knife he holds is his Big Bear model, with an extra guard. He no longer makes this model, but another knifemaker is reported ready to try it.

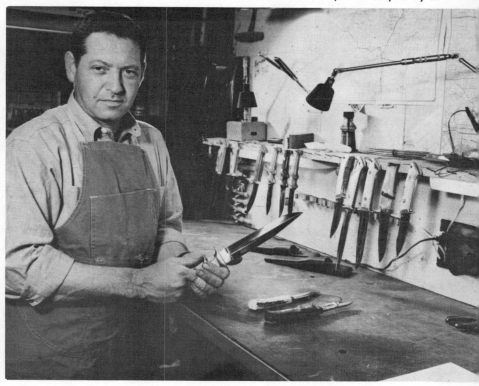

at the joint between blade and handle. The knife is the basic tool, and has been since Man started killing big things to eat. So just about everything has been tried. For long generations, most practical knives have been 2" to 10" in the blade, and their shape has fallen somewhere between the broad, curved, sweeping, nearly pointless blade of the skinning knife and the thin long pointed blade of the fillet knife used on fish. A butcher-supply catalog will give you a review of useful knife shapes.

Yet knifemakers keep trying to come up with something a little classier, a little stouter at the same weight, a little easier to use, a little better suited to some particular chore, and very often they try to come up with a length, shape and material that creates something close to an all-round knife.

It doesn't exist, of course. You cannot skin mice and fight bears with the same blade. In jungles, you carry a machete or bolo; in the North Country, you carry an axe; maybe you carry butchering tools in a pack. For such people an all-round knife is possible because they're not asking it to do machete or axe or heavy butchering work. The fighting man out there? He figures his knife as a weapon. He needs about 6" in the blade, a point in line with the center of the handle, and he wants a double guard—and those primary requirements take a lot of handiness out of a knife.

Finally, my all-round knife is your case of the uglies. We might be able to wear the same gloves, shoot the same rifle and dance with the same girl, you and I. There is damned little chance we'll be happy with the same knife. We might even agree on special-purpose knives, but we absolutely will not agree on the all-rounder.

Knife Steel

Knives are steel—useful knives—with a hardness range upwards of 52C on the Rockwell scale. That 52C to 55C range is a pretty soft steel, but usually tough; at 56C to 58C and even 60C, we are getting into the real edge-holding range whilst maintaining some ruggedness; 60C and even higher is possible given very highly advanced metallurgy and heat treatment on very pure steel. Such hard knives are bears to hone and sharpen, but once sharp they stay that way. If the steel is right, they are as tough or tougher than softer blades.

Recently, quite a few knifemakers exhibited at a Las Vegas gun show. One of them had Rockwell test gear along. One maker's blades tested at 64C, yet those are not brittle knives.

That's Bob Loveless. He loses as many as 20% of his blades in heat treatment—some batches—because he is stretching the design as far as it will go, and then pushing very intricate procedures on top of that. He is working with a single batch of 660 pounds of a very pure kind of steel. The tensile strength figures and all the other measurements are pretty technical, but in essence he and his professional metallurgists are able to push steel to this performance because they are starting with a single batch that has so few impurities it cannot be ordered on the market—that is, steel makers simply won't take the order. All except one, which took Loveless 5 years to find.

Why are impurities important? Well, it seems when you get out on the knifemakers' limb, pushing a knife all the way, blade fractures start at microscopic non-metallic inclusions—chunks, so to speak, of stuff that isn't steel—that act as stress risers. Eliminate most of these, and you get a blade that doesn't start to fracture easily, so you can make it hard, and if you have a very hard and very tough blade, you can make it thinner or you can hollow-grind it deeply. The idea is that there are advantages.

It also costs a lot of money to do it this way. The metallurgists are doing it for the education involved, but everything else runs into dough.

One of the most fascinating knives made today is this Loveless boot knife—a miniature fighting knife, with 5" blade, double-hollow-grind, and of immaculate workmanship. It's $150 or so, but nearly everyone with $150 who has seen one buys it.

Loveless designs for the hunter are, from the top: straight hunter, hollow-ground; gut-hook skinner; semi-skinner; straight hunter with lifted point. These four are full-tanged, with slab handles. The top knife has Loveless' conventional handle and guard shape; the other three show his improved handle, which he makes in micarta, wood or stag. The bottom knife, a narrow-tang model with the handle milled away, shows his first-class handling of the strength problem.

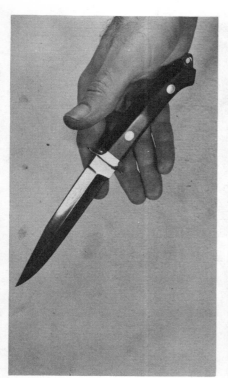

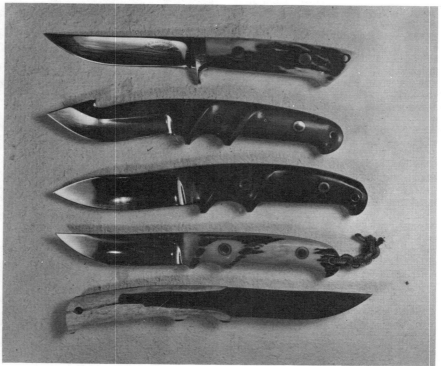

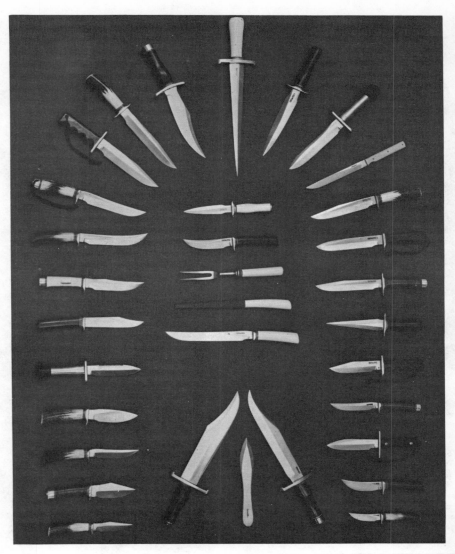

are called survival knives—have chopping back edges and the like—and, in truth, serve often as knives for combat soldiers.

Medium Game Knives These are deer knives. When they are longer than 5" they are lightly constructed. In the main, these are straighter than the big game knives, but still have some belly in the edge for skinning, and generally a dropped or clipped point to get the point out of the way when gutting. A knife of this type is a useful knife all day, so it has to be handy. The design variations are myriad, and again the shape depends on the designer's leanings—toward meat-cutting and skinning or toward general work. The balance generally comes back into the hand. Single edge and a single guard, if any.

Skinning Knives Whether pure skinner, meaning with rounded point, or nearly so—enough point to start cuts—this is a broad-bladed type with a very rounded curve to the edge. When thin-bladed, it is useful in preparing food in camp, but its *metier* is the separation of hide from flesh. In size, useful

This photo shows one of everything Randall, the dean of knifesmiths, makes. The range is from 12" Bowies and toothpicks down to 3" small-game knives, with heavy emphasis on attack, survival and fighting knives.

A handmade H.H. Frank folding knife, with ivory handle and full blade engraving. These knives, in small quantities and at relatively high prices, are available through R.W. Loveless.

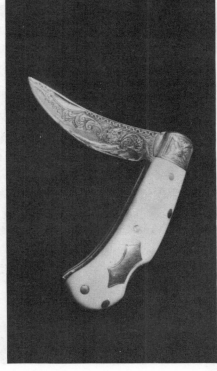

Of course, for 90% of uses, it isn't necessary. Steel companies haven't been standing still on the kinds of steel they *will* deliver. The past 5 years have seen lots of improvements, particularly in 400-series stainless steels, and 56C and 58C hardnesses are damned tough. Given a $\frac{3}{16}$" or $\frac{1}{4}$" bar to start with, there is hardly any way a single man can hit or pry hard enough to bust an honest workman's blade.

The blade is still made in the fire, though some blades and some fires have improved. The forging *vs.* grinding controversy continues, but it's still true that the key to the quality of a knife, given the basic materials, is in the hands of its maker. Good men don't make bad knives.

The Kinds of Knives

Fighting Knives The purest type is the double-edged dagger, and the knife as a weapon almost always has at least 1½ edges—that is, the back is sharpened for 3-4". The typical American

fighting knife makes some concessions toward field utility, has a 6" to 8" clipped blade (the clip portion being sharp) and double guards. The fighting style taught to most American fighting men suits this knife. Individual makers lean toward the dagger when they make their knife narrow and straight, and toward the utility side when the blade is broader and there is some rounded curve in the forward edge. There are many variations, of course, but the key points are the presentation of the point at the mid-line of the handle and blade, the sharpened back edge, the double guards. The balance is back in the hand, for maneuverability.

Heavy Game Knives These are big fellows. They are stylish large butcher knives, in truth, with the balance forward. Edges are quite curved, and blade lengths are 6" and up. Some knives in this category are quite massive, in order to do some chopping, and often broad-bladed, to get the weight. Some designs in this category

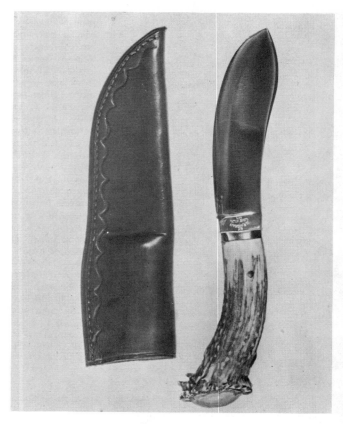

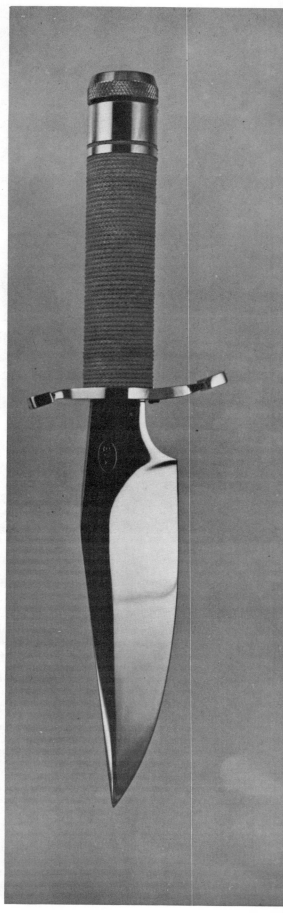

Above—George W. Sears, writing as "Nessmuk," inspired many an out-doors-oriented boy. Townsend Whelen was one. Sears had a knife that looked like this and Moran copied it for a customer, calling it, naturally, the Nessmuk model. ● Right—H.G. Bourne makes this knife as a survival type. It has a hollow handle, wrapped with nylon cord, various blade and guard features designed to make it function as an all-round military/backwoods type. ● Harry (left) and Steve Morseth in their shop. They turn out very good values in hand-built knives of laminated steel.

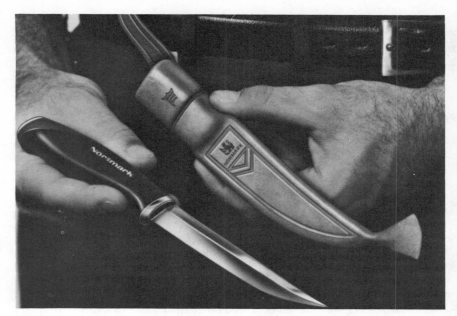

skinners range from 3″ to 8″ in the blade, the difference being, of course, the size of the hide you're taking.

Small Game Knives These are little knives, thin-bladed and not wide, offering a good sharp point, and meant for dressing small things, from quail to rabbits to turkeys, and useful for a careful job of caping the big game trophy, too. They should go 2″ to 3½″ in the blade, but the light construction is the real key, and important in use.

Fish Knives There are two—a good chopping knife, strong enough to handle big fish, and a long thin flexible blade for filleting. These are best in stainless. Straight edges and fine points are useful—fish are not very complicated. A serrated back edge will help scale most fish.

Variations This section could be longer than all the others, given free rein. It's worth looking at some, however: *Boot knife* small, light fighting knife. *Chute knife* jumper's tool, double-

Above—Among commercial knives the latest Normarks are excellent values at their attractively low prices—$9.95 for the Presentation Hunter pictured, complete with lined top-grain leather-sheath. Their Presentation Fillet Knife, with slenderer 6″ blade, is also $9.95. ● W.F. Moran, Jr., stands at his anvil, the glowing coal-fired forge behind him—the ancient armorer at his craft.

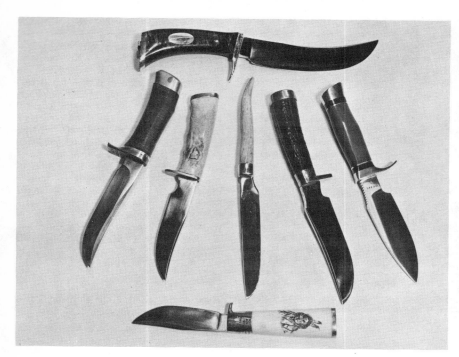

Knives—A Custom Group

At top, a special Moran blade, 6½″ long, the handle of burly wood, the guard and pommel of fluted brass. From left—A 5¼″ forged blade by Baker (not now producing), the handle of leather washers, guard and pommel of brass and aluminum. Next, a semi-skinner by Merle Seguine, the handle of fossilized ivory, mounted in brass. Third, a Walt Kneubuhler blade for cutting patches in muzzle-loading shooting, the handle of horn. Next, another WK-blade of 5½ inches with a dark bone handle. Fourth—a 5″ blade by Stone (Model MK), the handle of phenolic resin, the furniture brass. Below—A Ladow (Doc) Johnston special skinner with 4″ blade. The ivory handle is scrimshawed by Milt Barringer after a drawing by John Barsotti.

Knives—A Mixed Lot

Above and clockwise, from noon—German-made pocket hunting type, with sawblade and hook blade. Sheffield-made semi-skinner from A&F that works well. Kabar Sea Scouts' model, used long ago in the Navy and in several hunts. The sheath holds a marlinspike as well. An old Dall de Weese pattern sold by Marble, a gift from Ned Roberts. Buck's M103 skinner, a good blade. Another German type, similar to the other but with fixed main blade. This last, in its slim sheath, is carried in the stocking of the *lederhosened* hunter. Center, a matched pair of special skinning and caping blades by Stone, both solid stainless steel.

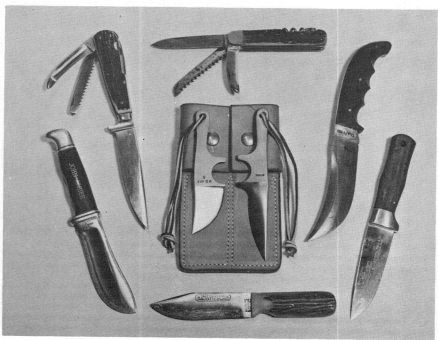

edged to get shroud lines in a hurry, plus survival design. *Gut-hook knife* the back edge has a sharpened hook ground in it, used to zip open the gut cavity. *Bowie knife* technically, the big broad fighting and survival knife with a clipped point of the 1840s to 1870; currently, most biggish clipped-point knives with double guards and wide blades. *Push dagger* knife with T-handle, meant to fit across palm as blade protrudes from fist, and useful as concealment knife. *Toothpick* often called "Arkansas toothpick," a very long double-edged dagger. *Ooloo* spelled different ways, it means the nearly semi-circular pointless Eskimo skinning and chore blade. *Patch knife* generally a small blade, flat on one side, the other beveled to an edge, used for cutting the patch at the rifle muzzle by black powder shooters. *Caper* short light thin knife, often with blunted point, designed for careful cutting on a trophy head.

All this can be taken seriously, or a fellow can pick a good compromise and go all the way with it. The combination of features makes the difference. For example, a small-game size, but with a curved and narrow blade of 4″ or so can do nearly anything that doesn't take a lot of punch, given some time spent learning to handle it. That describes the "personal knife" of one H.H. Buck, an important knife-maker whose sons have gone commercial. Unfortunately, they have straightened out the curve in the Buck personal knife.

Knife Care

Knives don't need much, except common sense. Don't let them rust, or get too dull, and just use them as knives. Don't leave them in the sheath in storage.

When it comes to sharpening, there are several considerations, and the first of these is your location; that is, are you touching up an edge in the field, or working on the bench? The bench is the place for a serious edge. The stone—regardless of type, and we'll get to that later—should be fixed in place, either by nailing down its box, surrounding it with quarter-round, or whatever. You should have plenty of lubricant on hand, whether it be water, saliva, light oil or honing oil. And you should have your mind on what you are doing, because you'll find these instructions a little different.

They come, incidentally, from A.G. Russell, who purveys Arkansas Oilstones from P.O. Box 474, Fayetteville, Ark. 72701, and believes his grade of *novaculite* called Washita/ Soft Arkansas is the best possible single stone for working knife edges. This writer feels there are none better, at any rate. Russell's one single added instruction is probably as important as his stone.

Deer-sized knives show most design-variety. From top, left column: Morseth, Seguine, TMD, Loveless, Olsen. Right: Ruana, Draper, Randall, Heath, Lile. About $10 to $60. All offer a straight shape for chores, enough edge sweep for skinning, enough point for gutting. Blades are 4" to 5½", weight about 7-9 ounces.

A. G. RUSSELL'S LIST OF KNIFEMAKERS

Some known; some unknown; some great; some so-so. Most have catalogs. Some charge for them, as indicated.

Arnold Knives, Box 1427, Grand Prairie, Tex. 75050
Lee Biggs, 3816 Via La Silva, Palo Verde, Ca. 92266
Ralph Bone Knife Co., 806 Ave. J, Lubbock, Tex. 79401
D. L. Brown, 1803 Birdie Dr., Toledo, O. 43615
L.E. "Red" Brown, 301 E. Neece St., Long Beach, Ca. 90804
H.G. Bourne, 1252 Hope Ave., Columbus, O. 43212
Pete Callan, 17 Sherline Ave., New Orleans, La. 70124
J.N. Cooper, 2200-D Burbank Blvd., Burbank, Ca. 91502 (25¢)
Phillip Day, Rt. 1, Box 465T, Bay Minetter, Ala. 36507
Dan Dennehy (Dan D), Box 4479, Yuma, Ariz. 85364
Charles E. Dickey, 803 N. E. A St., Bentonville, Ark. 72712
T.M. Dowell, 139 St. Helen's Pl., Bend, Ore. 97701 (25¢)
Draper Knives, Box 94, Ephraim, Utah 84627
John Ek, 3214 NW 54th St., Miami, Fla. 32142
Clyde Fischer, Rt. 1, Box 170-M, Victoria, Tex. 77901
H.H. Frank, c/o Loveless, Box 837, Lawndale, Ca. 90260
James Furlow, 4838 Santa Fe Trail SW, Atlanta, Ga. 30331
L.A. Hale, 4857 Shallen Ave., Riverside, Ca. 92503
Pete Heath, 119 Grant St., Winnecone, Wis. 54986
D.E. Henry, Star Route, Mountain Ranch, Ca. 95246
Geo. H. Herron, 920 Murrah Ave., Aiken, S.C. 29801
Gil Hibben, Box 7, Manti, Utah 84642
Chubby Hueske, 4808 Tamarisk Dr., Bellaire, Tex. 77401
LaDow Johnston, 2322 W. Country Club Parkway, Toledo, O. 43614
Jon Kirk, 800 N. Olive St., Fayetteville, Ark. 72701
Walter Kneubuhler, Box 327, Pioneer, O. 43554 (50¢)
James B. Lile, Route 1, Box 56, Russellville, Ark. 72801 ($1)
R.W. Loveless, Box 837, Lawndale, Ca. 90260 ($1)
Bob Ludwig, 1028 Pecos Ave., Port Arthur, Tex. 77640
Joe S. Martin, Box 6652, Lubbock, Tex. 79413
John T. Mims, 1509 W. 7th St., Hattiesburg, Miss. 39401
Mitchell Knives, 511 Ave. B, So. Houston, Tex. 77587
W.F. Moran, Route 5, Frederick, Md. 21701 (50¢)
Steve Morseth, Box 406, Redmond, Wash. 98052
Randall Knives, Box 1988, Orlando, Fla. 32802 (25¢)
R.H. Ruana, Box 574, Bonner, Mont. 59823 (50¢)
Jack D. Schmier, 16787 Mulberry Cr., Fountain Valley, Ca. 92708
Merle Seguine, Box 989, Juneau, Alaska 99801
Blackie Sewell, 894 Kings Ct., Atlanta, Ga. 30306
W.J. Sonneville, 1050 W. Chalet Dr., Mobile, Ala. 36608
Bernard Sparks, Dingle, Id. 83233
Stone, D. W. Knives, 703 Floyd Rd., Richardson, Tex. 75080
Thunderbird Custom Knives, 912 So. 2nd St., Blackwell, Okla. 74631
Don Zaccagaino, 2256 Bacon Pt. Rd., Pahokee, Fla. 33476

COMMERCIAL KNIFE SPECIALISTS

Buck Knives, 6588 Federal Blvd., San Diego, Ca. 92114
Gerber Knives, 14200 S.W. 72nd St., Portland, Ore. 99223
Olsen Knives, 7 Joy St., Howard City, Mich. 49329

In the main, you've heard it all: Lift the back of the knife so the blade makes a 20° angle with the stone, sweep the knife from back to point on each side while maintaining this angle, and keep it up until you have an edge that won't reflect light anywhere and will shave hair. You may have to hone (a piece of gray cardboard, suitably backed, is just abrasive enough to make a good hone) by drawing the edge backwards across the honing surface if your knife produces a "wire edge." The new and important thing is this: Bear down as hard as you can and never let up —on a good knife, those delicate little strokes don't do a damned thing but make you feel good. Bear down and get that edge clean and quick. That's why you pay attention—if you do it right, you're putting a lot of force into it. An 8″ stone is OK for this stuff, but a 12″ stone is better. In the field, you hold the knife if it's largish, and move the stone; don't bear down now —you're just touching things up.

Carborundum stones, GE's Carboloy stones, aluminum oxide — they all work. Some of them sludge up ahead of the edge, given these hard strokes, and that limits the fine work, but they'll still produce an edge quickly. You might experiment to see if you want the long dimension of the stone toward you and work from side to side, or work from the end of the stone, pushing and pulling the blade.

Factory Knives

Not everyone has $30 and up to spend on a hand-built knife; not everyone wants to wait while one is built; some might not even believe (and I think they're wrong) the good hand-built knife is better. If you're in this category, try a Buck, a Gerber or an Olsen knife. They're good stuff, even if they are standardized. Olsen's are, as a matter of fact, as much hand-made as many small shop knives. You'll find their addresses with the rest.

You might want to build your own. Indian Ridge Traders, Box 50, Ferndale, Mich. 48220, imports Sheffield blades in a variety of shapes and sizes. They are pretty good stuff, though not, in this writer's view, as hard as a better knife should be. The blades are cheap enough to try without busting the pocketbook and good enough not to be a waste of time.

If you want to try them as knives without building your own handle, you can buy finished knives from Indian Ridge in some styles, and at least two sources handle finished knives made from IRT blades—Thunderbird Custom Knives, 912 S. 2nd St., Blackwell, Okla. 74631 or LaDow Johnston, 2322 W. Country Club Pkwy., Toledo, O. 43614.

The big commercial factories are getting into the quality knife business.

Loveless knives—superb in form and quality, durability and made to be used.

Make no mistake—they have always built good knives that gave good value. Now that the general price level is up, they can put more time and effort into a knife, and they're now demonstrating they can build good ones. Case, Western, KaBar, Schrade-Walden—all four have special knives.

Future Trends

Knives are going to get tougher, no doubt of that. This writer thinks they are going to get lighter, too. As users get more sophisticated, they're going to start thinking of ¼-inch-thick knives as sort of sharpened pry bars and start getting back to the real cutting instruments. One smith said to me "I got no business shooting at anything I can't get the hide off of with an eight-inch blade."

Pocket knives are coming along. A fellow in Ohio is going to market his fine hand-made folding knives — engraved all over—through R.W. Loveless at prices above $100. W.F. Moran just made his first folding knife. Merle Seguine used to make a heavy folding knife. There are more and better folding commercial knives around already, heavy-duty type, that is.

Bone, I've just learned, offers a heavy folder at about $65.

Some importers, seeing the light, are importing only very good knives, a trend that will probably step up. Some foreign cutlers can make very good knives, once they are convinced there is a market for them at high prices.

Five years from now, however, it's going to be a design story. We'll be seeing lots of different things. A case in point is the little back-packer set shown here by Stone—two little slips of steel, one for skinning, one for sticking and both for cutting, that do the whole job without handguard, handle material or anything. It's going to be very interesting, this knife story, a few years hence. ●

Handloading

A detailed report on new tools, components and accessories.

by the Technical Editors

Lyman Universal Case Trimmer

Part 1—Equipment

New Avtron Chronographs

Avtron has a new digital counter chronograph, the Model K233.

The Model K233 features bright, in-line, 4-digit readout, easily visible in the brightest sunshine. It is completely portable, built into a rugged steel case.

A 1,000,000 cycle crystal-controlled time base gives high resolution, and special circuitry allows screen spacings of 5, 10, and 20 feet to eliminate errors associated with small screen spacing. The new K233 may be used with expendable screens or Avtron's new solid state photoelectric screens, Model K100 or K101, which we've described earlier. A provision for checking screen continuity is included.

The K233 can be ordered with an AC power supply or battery power, but not both. We haven't had one for test yet, but I'm sure the same dependability and accuracy for which Avtron chronographs are noted will be maintained.

The Model K233 sells for $389, the K233C at $585.

Bair Machine Co. has dropped one shotshell press and offers another improved tool in its stead, and at the *same price*. An unusual occurrence these days.

Newest Bair shotshell loader is the Honey, reported capable of 225 rounds per hour by an experienced operator. This $59.50 tool is an up-graded, more compact version of last year's Panda and uses the same dies. It has a vertical sliding die head riding on a square steel column attached to a heavy round base. It features positive rod ejection of cases from the resizing die; a drawer in the base to catch fired primers; and a nylon bushing in the sizing die. This bushing greatly reduces friction and sizing effort, and also removes one more area susceptible to rust. Powder and shot flow may be cut off by rotating the transparent hoppers. In addition, the hoppers are slightly tapered, permitting stacking to increase capacity. Gauge conversion kit costs $26.50, but does not include powder and shot bushings.

Honey Bair is also available with an automatic primer feed actuated by movement of the charge bar. Primers are carried to the primer seater by a tubular magazine. The press won't jam—inverted primers won't seat, of course—and shotshell production is faster and less troublesome. Price with auto-primer feed is $79.50 complete for one gauge, including a primer tube filler.

Bahler Die Shop continues to produce a line of rifle and handgun bullet swaging dies for the RCBS Rockchucker press. In handgun calibers they will make either ½- or ¾-jacketed bullets and are priced at $60 for soft point or $65 for hollow point form.

Rifle dies will sell for $150-$200. These are shipped complete with ram, 3 die bodies and extruder—exact price depends on make of press to be used.

Fred Wood also tells us he's about to produce 20- and 14-cal. jackets. Write for prices and availability.

Brown Precision Co., makers of the Little Wiggler case spinner, have made some improvements in the design of their tool. There are now two springs, one to each case-holding lever, that permit all cases to be measured. A longer bar permits the dial indicator to be located farther down the case—away from the mouth—when desired. One other option, and one to be recommended, is the stainless steel mandrel used to hold either bullet point or case mouth. This is a mere $1.50 extra, but will extend the usefulness of the tool and eliminate the cleaning/polishing chore if you have rust problems in your area. The price of the Little Wiggler is still $34.95—extras are $1.50 for the 375 and larger stainless steel mandrel and $1.50 for the double spring modification.

C&H (Owen, Wis. 54460) have a small number of the 203 Swag-O-Matic tools on hand, these being designed to make ½- and ¾-jacket bullets. These later jackets should be available about when you read this, and presumably they'll result in bullets with the jacket top running over the ogive. Write for their new catalog-price sheet, which shows some discount prices on discontinued items as well.

The reorganization of the C-H Tool & Die Co. has posed many problems for its new owners. If final production of the redesigned tools has all the qualities outlined in some correspondence with the officers of C-H we can expect some very high quality items with a lot of thought behind them.

First off, the new hexagonal-form dies will feature a carbide expander ball—making inside neck lubrication unnecessary. The die for making these expanders cost the company $750 each, therefore the popular 30 caliber dies will be the first ones out of the plant, with other calibers to follow—probably in order of popularity. No prices have been announced as yet.

A couple of red plastic items that are well thought out are: a plastic powder dripper with a large, square-flanged base and a base insert that can be filled with sand, shot, etc., $2.45. The big-capacity 5-sided powder funnel fits all cases from 22 to 45 cal., 75¢.

Camdex, Inc., introduced a new high-production automatic reloading machine at the NRA show this spring. Made for 38 Special only at this time, it has a loading capacity of over 2000 rounds per hour. This AC-powered machine costs $3500, has a capacity of 135 primers and 400 bullets. Powder is metered to within 1/10-gr. and primer seating depth and crimp are fully adjustable. This tool will shut itself off when primer magazine is down to 5 primers, or if powder charge deviates more than 1/10-gr. It will feed cases automatically (on full-auto) or can be "jogged" to check functioning. This is one of the best we've seen, and undoubtedly a few custom reloaders and clubs could use its capability.

A separate automatic primer feeder is available to fill the primer tubes, cost $425. At 135 per tube, it would take a good man to keep up with the hungry needs of this press. For more information, write Camdex for their informative, descriptive brochure.

Chronograph Specialists

Chronograph Specialists have introduced a new low-cost chronograph of digital type. The crystal controlled oscillator in this circuitry operates at

500,000 cycles, and recommended screen separation is a mere 2 feet. The new unit, called the CS-200, is constructed throughout with silicon transistors and integrated circuits, and there is a check switch to test and verify continuity and screen connections—screens are not supplied, but any of the popular types such as those made by Avtron may be used.

The CS-200 is quite light, some 2 pounds only, and its long-life small battery is self-contained within the unit. With screen cables, velocity charts and full instructions, the CS-200 is available in kit form at $49.50 or at $80 fully assembled and ready to go. This latter figure includes both a 12-volt adaptor for use via a car cigarette lighter, and a 115-volt AC adaptor.

Lester Coats, 416 Simpson St., North Bend, Ore. 97459, recently sent us a well-machined lead wire core cutter for producing precision cores prior to bullet swaging. It has 6 holes, bored to standard wire sizes, and an adjustable stop that can be moved under any one of them. In use the Coats core cutter is screwed to the bench, the wire inserted into the appropriate hole and the lever is turned to move the two discs against each other in a shearing action. Cores drop from below the cutter and may be caught in a box. Made to handle all calibers from 22 thru 45, it costs $15.

Ellwood Epps, who operates one of the top sporting goods/gunshops in Canada, at Clinton, Ontario, is a sort of ingenious guy. He recently sent along a quite different case-reduction outfit (see photo) that will size down about any metallic case you might name—as the two cases pictured will testify.

Some 13 short-cylinder sleeves — each of different inside diameter-plus-taper—came with the die body shown; the latter will hold any 3 of these sleeves, selected according to the case being squeezed down.

It took a bit of trial-and-error, of course, to insure I didn't push the shoulder down too far, but once that was set (using a Wilson combination case gauge to check cone-to-head dimension), one trip through the Epps 3-die setup did the trick. I lost only one case out of 40, and for this trial run I used a batch of WW II brass.

As far as I know, Epps doesn't of-

Ellwood Epps, Clinton, Ontario, Canada uses this die set in his shop to size cases and the two multi-shouldered rounds at left show what can be done. See text for details.

fer this sleeve/die outfit for sale, but we thought you'd like to know about this phase of the art.   J.T.A.

Herter's Inc. sent us quite a few new products from Herter for testing and evaluation recently. Most were early production or pilot products and were received without instruction manuals or directions—we had very little difficulty putting these tools through their paces, even so.

The Model 6 shotshell press charge bar was difficult to move when throwing a shot charge—we received a pair of neoprene washers a few days later, along with a 6-pt. crimper, which cured that problem. The M-6 is a progressive tool that does a nice job of crimping (2-stage). All loaded rounds gave little evidence of swelling a few days after loading. We did find, however, that when crimping new plastic cases a couple of lever strokes in the final crimper finished the case with a nicely rounded crimp.

The new shotshell crimp cutter received gave difficulty because we had one less hand than was needed! Holding the tool in a vise let shells, paper and plastic, be cut quickly to proper length for roll-crimping. After our tests were completed a pamphlet was received and—you guessed it—it read: "The crimp cutter, held in a vise..."

Hulme long-time supplier of automatic case feeders for the Phelps and Star reloading machines has up-dated his tools—they're both self-lubricating and are now supplied with three 48″ long clear plastic case feeder magazines. The Mark-III handles 5 calibers, Mk-IIIA 8 calibers. Ten calibers can be loaded (not-simultaneously) if both base plates are purchased.

Lachmiller Eng. Co. introduced many new items—one is a cast iron lead pot, capacity 10 lbs.; with both a lip and an "ear" opposite to facilitate pouring the melt into ingot moulds. $2.50 only. An extra large capacity, square shaped dipper for use with multiple cavity moulds is $2.

The casting equipment above supplements a new series of moulds just added to the LEC tool catalog.

Double- or triple-cavity blocks are now available and can be had in rifle calibers from 243 through 30 and most pistol and some round ball calibers. The blocks are well vented between their mating surfaces and have an "X" vent across the top. The sprue cutter locks into place when mould is closed—an Allen head screw and domed, circular washer holds this unit snug and flat to the mould surface.

Lee Engineering is producing a number of new, small, pocketable tools for the reloader. The newest is a case spinner for use with your ¼″ electric drill and a shell holder head (for Lee Case Trimmer, extra). If you have one of their case trimmers, this 58¢ gadget will turn it into a power trimmer, chamfering tool or polishing machine. As usual, the design is extremely simple—it has a ¼″ shaft on one end and is threaded for the shell holder head ($1.70) at the other.

Cleaning primer pockets is easy with Lee's newest tools. These come in two sizes and are priced at 49¢ each. They fit the primer pockets well and clean them neatly. Be careful with these, we lost a couple in a jacket pocket, they're that small.

A decapper and base are also made for removing crimped-in primers from GI brass. Lee must feel very confident about this product since they guarantee it unbreakable and offer free replacement. $2.45.

New Lyman Universal Case Trimmer

Lyman's new case trimmer has a universal chuck that accepts all sizes of metallic cartridge cases. The easy-to-use Universal Trimmer is designed for maximum precision, for each case is locked in positive position to insure case-to-case accuracy. Variations in rim thickness don't affect accuracy, either. There are both fine and coarse length adjustments. The cutter shaft rotates in a self-lubricating bronze bearing.

The new Universal Trimmer sells for $22, one cutter head and one pilot of your choice included. Extra pilots are 90¢ each, and calibers from 17 to 45 are available.

A drill press model is also offered, using the same Universal chuck and the same pilots. For those with quantities of cases to trim, this is an excellent item. $14, including one pilot and one cutter head.

Herter's Shotshell Crimp Cutter

Lee case trimmer

Ohaus Dial-O-Grain scale

Mayville Engineering Co. (MEC) has made several changes in their popular MEC 600 Jr. shotshell loader. The ejection stroke at the resizing station has been lengthened to handle either high brass or low brass cases. It will carry, as standard equipment, the "Pro-Check" device available for all 600 Juniors; a small arm attached to the charge bar to hold the wad guide in its lower position after dropping the powder charge, thus eliminating the need for pushing the guide down by hand and saving a useful amount of time each cycle.

The Versamec features a longer-stroke new Platform Cam for ejecting field shells at the ejector station—no adjustments are required, no matter the case length. Another new aspect is the Pro-Check, a device that programs the measure assembly to position the charge bar in correct sequences automatically. There's a new paper-case crimp starter, too. Changing from plastic-case 6- or 8-point star crimps to paper-case cone closures takes only seconds! All of this makes the new Versamec a top tool for the hunter as well as the Skeet and trap shooter.

Ohaus Dial-O-Grain scale is the latest offering to handloaders who are after real precision. This is an extremely sensitive laboratory type scale with magnetic damping and a capacity of 3100 grains. The most unusual feature of the M-304 is an adjustable vernier dial calibrated by tenths of a grain up to 100 grains, after which counter poise weights are used.

Pacific Gun Sight Company's new plant is now in operation, turning out thousands of Pacific items. If you've been waiting for something from Pacific, that wait should be over.

A new pistol powder measure, which replaces the one dropped from the line a few years ago, incorporates a square bar that can be pushed from

left to right as is done on most shotshell presses. This new design eliminates the binding problem encountered with the old model. The charge bar uses interchangeable bushings and 22 sizes are made. A chart on page 13 of their catalog lists charge weights for each of eight powders in most cases. Price of the new pistol measure is $14 (less bushing) and bushings are $1.50 each.

Ponsness-Warren has no new tools to offer this year—their excellent tools leave little to be desired from a design aspect. However, they do have a few new accessories to make their tools more convenient.

The Du-O-Matic press has been adapted in 410 tooling so that it is now capable of handling the latest Federal plastic cases and one-piece wads in that gauge. Dies for the Du-O-Matic will have a new sizing ring inside in all gauges so that all cases—high or low brass, or steel head—can be resized full-length.

Until recently, the Size-O-Matic and Du-O-Matic would not easily handle high brass or steel shells. These heads were so hard to resize that once loaded (P-W presses hold the cases in the size dies until ejection after final crimping) the completed rounds were almost impossible to eject from the press. A spacer-ring is now used inside all dies that allows any shell to be loaded.

An 8-point crimp starter is now available that is ball bearing lined. P-W has changed the angle of the wire pick-up finger as well, making the crimp starter more sensitive and alignment quicker and more precise than before.

RCBS has dropped the massive A-3 press from the line. Seems like the Rockchucker can do most everything that the A-3 did and at a lesser price to you. We're sorry to see that big tool go, but if you've used the Rockchucker, you'll know there is nothing lacking but size and weight.

The needs of the 17-cal. wildcatters haven't been overlooked by the Huntington firm. New for this year is a chamfering/deburring tool which will handle the 17s and the larger calibers,

too. A case-neck brush, a funnel and a drop tube have been added, so there are few tools for this sub-caliber sport not supplied by RCBS.

Redding-Hunter tools have been with us for a number of years, and have undergone little change. The R-H firm has, however, decided that there are a few things still to be done, and here is the first.

A redesigned Model 25 Turret Press is offered by Redding-Hunter. This unit has been popular because of its 4- or 6-hole turret, permitting two 3-die setups at once, for example.

Heavy-duty construction is used throughout the Model 25 tool; the frame, press and turret are of high quality cast iron, and precision machining assures smooth operation and continuous, trouble-free service. The 13¼" handle is blued steel. Weight of the redesigned M25 is about 23 lbs. The tool carries a life-time warranty against defects in materials and workmanship.

SAECO Reloading Inc. is the new name for the old firm still headed by Bob Modisette. SAECO is justly famous for producing top quality loading tools, bullet moulds, electric lead pots, a superb bullet lubricator/sizer and dies.

New calibers have been added to expand their line of bullet moulds. These are all round ball: 31, 36 (three cavity) 44, 45 (two cavity) and 58 caliber (single cavity). Later this year moulds for 32 S&W, 9mm and 375 H&H will be available.

Sil's K-Spinner MK-11 is the updated version of a long-time favorite case polishing tool. The older model used a chuck-type holder that gripped the case head, the new one uses a caliber-size mandrel which not only speeds case changing, but can be used for a number of different case configurations of the same caliber—30-06, 30-30, 300 H&H, etc. The price is less —a surprise these days—only $1.75 per caliber.

Speer's new *Manual for Reloading Ammunition #8* should be available at gun and book shops as you read this. The new *hard-bound* book contains 3200 new-tested loads within its 448 pages!

New calibers include 240 Weatherby, 6mm/287, 25/284, 6mm Rem., 444 Marlin and seven pistol calibers.

The handgun section has 1400 additional new loads. As an example, the 38 Special—a popular caliber—shows 2 loads for each of 27 powders using Speer's 158-gr. lead semi-wadcutter bullet.

Shotgunners will find 40 pages added to their section, these containing the latest dope compiled from data supplied by powder manufacturers.

Our congratulations to Ray Speer, Dave Andrews and the Speer staff for

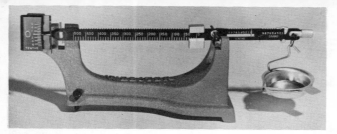

having done a fine job on this book—as were past editions. One last thought—Ray will appreciate it—the hardbound book sells for $3.95.

Webster Scale Mfg. Co. is an old and well-respected name in the handloading field. They've made good scales for as long as I can remember, which is perhaps testimony of their good design. All of them used hydraulic damping—until now.

The latest MB-5, magnetically damped, has a maximum capacity of 510 grains and is pleasant to use. The beam, of aluminum alloy, has deep notches for the poises and has large easy-to-read numerals. We've had an MB-5 here for testing and it performed well, showing little or no variation when weighing the same "standard" test weight. The MB-5 is a good value at $17.50.

L. E. Wilson has a fine 17 cal. burring tool priced at $3.25—that's only 25¢ more than the one we've used for years. This new one has a special, small guide pin and the cutter is milled a bit differently on both ends to accommodate the 17s.

Another item of note seen in one of the recent bulletins is a wall thickness micrometer, somewhat similar to those available about 5 years ago. Using a ball anvil, the latest mike measures wall thickness of cases or jackets of .190" to 1", inside diameter, and to ½" in depth. The new mike sells for $30 (add 60¢ for insurance).

H. A. Zimmerman makes a small, hand-held case trimmer that performs well and is preset for one caliber. Other calibers can be trimmed, but a new pilot-cutter ($2) and base-cap (75¢ $1) may be needed for the change. A new series has just been announced, these being for the 17s. Name your cartridge when ordering, and for $4 plus 15¢ shipping you'll get a trimmer that puts cases back to correct size every time.

Part 2—Components

Ballistics Research Labs Sabot Slugs

At long last, to coin a phrase, there's something new in shotgun slugs—or at least new in this application.

The use of "sabots" or sleeves to encase the basic projectile is not all that novel, but the Kelly-McAlvain design is a real breakthrough, I think, as far as shotguns go. The K-A projectile is a lead bullet in 50 caliber that weighs 437 grains (1 oz.), thus it's longer than a 12-bore "rifled slug," and it maintains velocity and energy better. The makers claim 100% less air resistance for the semi-hourglass shaped bullet versus ordinary 12 bore slugs, and a 100% increase in range, penetration, killing power and accuracy.

A 2-piece plastic sleeve surrounds the bullet, making for a near-perfect fit down the bore and holding the slug central to the barrel axis. The smooth plastic increases muzzle velocity, too.

Two versions are offered. The MK8 type uses a hardened alloy for police use in penetrating car bodies, engine blocks and the like. The MK9 sabot-slugs, intended for game shooting, use a Shock Point bullet of softer alloy.

A 12 bore Winchester M1200 brush gun was hurriedly borrowed and 10 K-A loads were put into the paper at 50 meters. All 10 printed single holes from the straight cylinder-bored gun, and in good groups—two 5-shot strings. I'd have preferred a scope, but the open iron sights had to serve, with the result that one group ran 3.65 inches, the other 5.15, though 4 of the latter about into 3.25 inches.

Under the conditions, I think those are quite good figures, but I understand that Elmer Keith—with a

scoped shotgun—has been doing considerably better, getting tight groups at 100 and more yards.

Write to BRI (116 N. Main, Sebastopol, Ca. 95472) for prices and availability.

DuPont's current issue of their *Handloader's Guide to Powders for 1970-71* is very much worth having. There's a tremendous amount of valuable data in the new booklet, especially for shotshell stuffers, 4 pages cover centerfire metallics, but all popular calibers are shown, and one page gives handgun loads. Write for your copy.

Federal Pushin'-Cushion wad

Federal Cartridge Corp., having introduced the 2½" plastic 410 shotshell and one-piece wad last year, were not satisfied to rest on their laurels. Here's more that's new from Federal.

Federal now has plastic tubes in all gauges: 12, 16, 20, 28 and 410. However, paper tubes are still offered in some of the company's light 12, 16 and 20 gauge loads and in 12 and 20 gauge target loads.

The "Pushin'-Cushion," a one-piece 20 gauge plastic wad column, will be offered to handloaders in April, 1970.

Federal for 1970 rounded out its centerfire cartridge line with 6 more basic numbers. Notable among these is their 357 Magnum with 158-gr. jacketed soft point bullet at about 1550 fps, albeit from an 8⅜" barrel! The others are: a 30 carbine 110-gr. SP load, a 25 Auto 50-gr., a 32 Auto 71-gr., a 9mm Luger 123-gr. and the 380 Auto with a 95-gr.

Green Bay Bullets now offers a molybdenum disulfide (MoS_2) cast bullet lubricant in sticks, solid or hollow, at 70¢ each. "Moly" works itself into the pores of the metal reducing friction and bore leading. Its stiff consistency works cleanly through the lubricator/sizer without smearing, yet adheres firmly in the grease grooves, nor will it melt or run into the powder of a loaded round under normal conditions.

Hercules, Inc. has a new, 1970-dated *Smokeless Powder Guide,* a 24-page (with covers) 8½x11 manual for handloaders that is yours for the asking. The new manual has just double the number of pages of last year's effort, most of the new space given over to shotshell loads—there are lots of them.

Consult our Directory pages for the location of firms or individuals mentioned.

Hodgdon Powder Co. The new Hodgdon Loading Data Manual #21 is now available. Devoted totally to new loading information, the columnized matching information charts covering rifle, pistol, shotgun, and lead bullet loads is a new idea. There's also complete information on all Weatherby calibers, expanded data on shotshell loading and good dope on the popular new 17 calibers. The book is a darn good one —it's clearly written, and it's only $2. See your dealer or order direct.

Hornady Mfg. Co. Late in 1969 Joyce Hornady announced a new bullet for the 375 H&H, a 270-gr. Spire Point that makes it the heaviest pointed bullet available for that caliber.

The new 375/270-gr. Spire Point will give, of course, a considerably flatter trajectory than did the old soft point of the same weight, so it should make a far better bullet for those longer-range elk shots.

The 270-gr. Round Nose has been dropped, as has been Hornady's Short Jacket 300-gr. 45 bullet. His 100-gr. 30-cal. SJ bullet is continued.

Two new handgun bullets are offered this year, both 45s: there's a 258-gr. HP for 45 Long Colt chambers, and a 185-gr. HP for the Colt 45 auto, with both having "long" jackets that positively won't permit leading of the bore. These two bring the Hornady handgun bullet line to 8 now, including a 9mm/115-gr. HP, a 38/125-gr. HP, two other 158-gr.. 38s, and a 44/240-gr. HP. All of these have over-the-ogive jacketing—non-leading.

Three other bullets are about to be released or soon will be: a 210-gr. ¾-jacketed 41 Magnum; a 125-gr. for the 8x57, and a 120-gr. Spire Point in 257 caliber, prices not so far set for any of these.

S. E. Laszlo is the main importer of Eley/Hy-Score products into the U.S. Components include plastic shotshell monowads (12 ga.) and 209 shotshell primers; unprimed brass (Boxer) for 308 Win., 30-06, 270 Win., 303 British, 243 Win. and 30-30 calibers. Fixed ammo in the calibers above, 12 gauge shotshells and the complete Eley 22 rimfire line, including the 1968 Mexico Olympic-winning match ammo, Tenex, and a true CB cap will also be part of Laszlo catalog. Savage, too, will be distributing the 22 RF Tenex match ammo from Eley.

JASCO has supplied self-adhesive labels and plastic cartridge boxes for some time. A new addition is the Shell Caddy. Made of rigid, light weight plastic, the Shell Caddy holds 50 shotshells of any gauge including the 410. Two of these, worked left and right of the press, keep the bench orderly, speed up loading and reduces the spilling of powder and shot. A real convenience at $2.10 each.

Hornady"s 270-gr. for 375 H&H

Norma-Precision powders have been seen on many more dealers' shelves of late. Evidently their distribution system is improved or you, the reloader, have been demanding more from your dealer or both!

Norma for 1970 has three new publications that we consider well worth writing for. The first is their *Ballistics Tables,* a booklet, covering all cartridges loaded and offered by Norma. All data therein is presented in 6 languages! The load- and full ballistic data—using Norma bullets, powders and primers, of course—is published in English-American style and in the metric system as well. 32 rifle cartridges are covered, from the 22 Hornet to the 375 Magnum, and 14 handgun cartridges—25 ACP to 45 ACP. Pressure figures, please note, are given for every load.

The second publication is the *Norma Loading Data* booklet, again using Norma powders and bullets generally, though no primers are indicated. Rifle, handgun and shotshell loads are covered in detail, pressures included. In this publication, 41 rifle calibers are shown, including a number of U.S. rounds that Norma does not offer—the 225 Winchester, 30-40 Krag, 300 and 338 Winchester Magnum, etc. Numerous handgun and shotshell loads are listed, too many to enumerate here.

Write for these items—you'll find them valuable indeed—and ask also for the new *Norma Ammunition and Components* catalog for 1970 and the price list that goes with it.

Nosler 6mm Zipedo

Nosler Bullet Company makes great hunting bullets, to say the least. They have little new to offer, but we can report some results on tough game the average reader is not likely to encounter. But first a news note.

Late in 1969 a new Solid Base (formerly Zipedo) bullet was announced —an 85-gr. 243 (6mm) spitzer S.P. that should make a fine long-range varmint load.

I used Nosler's exclusively in Zambia in 1969 for all of the soft-skinned game, and for follow-up shots on buffalo. For the 7mm Remington Magnum I loaded 160-gr. Nosler ahead of 69.6 grains of Norma 205, while in the 338 Winchester Magnum I used 76.0 grains of Norma 205 with the 250-gr. Nosler, and 79.9 grains of N205 for the 210-gr. Nosler.

I never had a failure to put down any game hit with any of these loads —not that I didn't miss entirely a couple of times! As I've noted elsewhere I shot Hornady 250-gr. solids at Cape buffalo, where I wanted to break those great shoulders, but for anything else you simply can't go wrong with Nosler soft points—a truly superb and reliable bullet.

Omark CCI has, free for the asking, a 16-page booklet containing information on primers—history, application and function. Profusely illustrated with action photos, drawings, graphs and a table for primer selection, this booklet should help you to better understand this component. Write CCI if you want a copy and if you're a 22 rimfire shooter they have another booklet on that subject, too.

New Case-Cleaner Lube

Reloader's No. 7 Case Cleaner & Lubricant is a new, non-toxic, non-acidic liquid that cleans cases very well indeed—I'll get to the lubricant part later on. The directions call for mixing the 8-oz. bottle of clear reddish liquid with an equal amount of water, then dropping average-dirty cases into this mixture for an hour, but cases may be left in over night without harm, as a matter of fact, if the brass is extremely dirty. I dumped 20 unprimed old 220 Swift cases into the solution for one hour, and when these moderately-dirty cases were removed they were all bright and clean. Even the primer pockets were 95% cleaned; a bit of cloth at the end of a matchstick removed any traces of fouling or dirt remaining in the pockets. I had kept one case aside as a control of sort, so I had a comparison.

The makers say that after removing the cases from the solution, they can be resized in the wet state, using no other lubricant except in the case of sizing dies that are getting their first workout. I tried this, using a dozen 30-06 cases, and the results were really surprising—these cases went into and out of the dies a bit easier than with the usual case lubricants.

Reloaders No. 7 seems to offer a quick and safe way of cleaning cases, and one we can highly recommend. Write to Sports Distributors Co., Rte. 1, Box 19, Rapid City, S.D. 577761 for a bottle—the price is $1.50.

Remington Arms Co. has released two new 38 Special cartridges of high potency—and intended for use only in modern revolvers designed for hot loads. The 125-gr. semi-jacketed (¾ jacket) HP load has a MV of 1570 fps, no less, while the new 158-gr. bullet of the same design leaves the muzzle (of a 6″ barrel) at 1150. The new non-leading 38 bullets are available to handloaders now—or soon will be.

Sharps Arms Co. has been bought by Colt, and from what we've been able to gather, the company will continue to operate as it did but its distribution will be aided by the experience of the Colt firm.

The Sharps bullet line continues to expand, and who knows how many may be made to match some of those scarce collectors' items now dormant.

Sierra Bullets

Sierra has just announced 4 new 38-caliber handgun bullets—2 jacketed soft points and 2 ditto hollow points. The latter are made to a new design, as the sketch illustrates—note the unusual form of the cavity, and also that the jacketing runs over the ogive, eliminating any bore leading.

The SP bullets come in 125- and 158-gr. weights, the HP form going 110 and 125 grains.

These new bullets show high accuracy, we were told, and better than a 70-80% weight retention when fired in water- and oil-based clay, with expansion up significantly, too.

These new Sierras are priced at $4.35-$4.50 per 100, and in the near future Sierra will introduce 4 similar-construction bullets in 9mm and 44 caliber.

Sierra also has a new hunting bullet, a boat-tail hollow point in 30 caliber said to give a quick expansion/deep penetration balance that makes it an excellent choice on medium- to big game animals. No opportunity to try these yet. They're $5.85 per C.

Speer, Inc. Five new Speer bullets were introduced in January, 1970—described further on—these following closely three handgun bullets made in 1968-1969.

The 70-gr. bullet in .224″ is meant for use in any of the 22 centerfires that will allow a velocity at the muzzle of over 3000 fps in a 14″ twist barrel. Load data for this new semi-spitzer heavyweight 22 bullet shown here were developed in a 22-250 Remington M700 with 24″ barrel, 1-14″ twist.

Speer's new 158-gr. R.N. bullet is

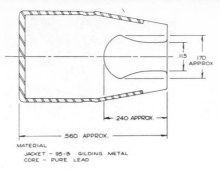

MATERIAL
JACKET – 95-B GILDING METAL
CORE – PURE LEAD

Cross section of Sierra's unique new hollow-cavity design for its 4 new 38-cal. bullets.

designed for general 38 Special use, while the two long-jacketed 357 bullets are high velocity types for 357 Magnum and 38 Special. Happily, leading won't be a problem with either of these.

The new 200-gr. bullet for the 45 ACP or 45 Auto Rim use carries a soft-lead core, thus should be an excellent choice for handgun hunting as well as for defense purposes. Good velocity should result, too.

Some of the 70-gr. 224 bullets should reach us soon, and if time allows, we'll add some 100-yd. accuracy test results to these notes.

Super Vel Cartridge Corp. has just finished compiling all the load dope and pressure figures for handgun cartridges using Super Vel bullets. This new manual should be available as you read this, though Lee Jurras hasn't told us the price.

Williams Custom Guns

Bill Williams has become a 17-caliber specialist. Perhaps his best-known products are 17-cal. bullets in 18, 20, 22.5 and 25-gr. weights, particularly his Epoxy-Bonded bullets (same weight range) for deep penetration on game and larger varmints. These E-B bullets have shown much less tendency to break up early, compared with normal 17-cal. bullets, over a lengthy and diverse test project.

These E-B bullets can't be called cheap, going at $10 per 100 (Williams regular line are $6 per C), but they're worth the extra dough if it's penetration and killing power on bigger animals that you're looking for.

Williams also supplies a full line of cleaning gear for the 17s, loaded ammo in 17 Mach IV, 17 Javelin, 17-222 and 17-223 at about $5 for 20, and also cleaned and formed cases in these calibers at some $15 per 100.

I imagine Bill is ready—I know he's able—to create custom rifles in any of the popular 17s, but you'll have to write to him about that.

However, he's also converting 221, 222, 222 Magnum and 223 rifles to 17s at a $60 basic price ($10 to $20 extra for premium-grade barrels, etc.) for a new barrel which he'll chamber, fit and blue, matching the contour of your original barrel. He fully guarantees these jobs—money back, no questions raised. Better write first, though,

because these costs may have gone up a little, times being what they are.

We received a sample lot of bullets from Williams, late in 1969 in both types, but we could only shoot them at paper targets—no game or varmints being available this past rough winter. Accuracy—in a light-barreled H&R 17-222 Magnum prototype—was excellent for that rifle. Normally the H&R shoots into ⅞″-1″ with best loads—21-22 grains of 3031 and good bullets of 22-25 grains—and the Williams E-B bullets did that well and better. Out of five 5-shot targets, two were .75″, the others going .81″, .89″ and .91″, using 21.6/3031 and Remington 7½ primers. I was wishing I'd still had the A&M 17-Javelina on hand, a heavy-barreled rifle for a 17, in which to give these Williams bullets a whirl. That A&M was a ½″ group rifle usually!

Too Late To Classify

Brownell's Inc. supplies a great variety of tools to the gunsmiths of the U.S., many of whom keep abreast of trade developments by Bob's frequent newsletters. In a recent issue, Bob mentioned a *plastic* vernier caliper, and from his glowing discription we had to see and use one. His ad was unbelievable—"Again right on the 1/-1000th and mostly within 1/10,000 . . . comparing with my $50 mike."

Most things made of plastic are serviceable for a while, but not generally that accurate. We asked Bob to send one, and within a few days it arrived. This caliper sells for $3.14—three dollars and fourteen cents, so there is no mistake. Yes, there is a difference in weight but not in quality. It is easy to read (both English and metric systems simultaneously) and is consistent, too, if the operator is. The caliper is made in the same dies used to produce an identical tool (but of steel) selling for $70. Brownell's guarantees them 100%.

Hensley & Gibbs have discontinued their dealer distribution system, will now sell their moulds direct to the customer — which permits them to maintain the high level of quality and still maintain the same prices. To find out what is available—or what you'd like to have — send them a long, stamped envelope and you'll get all the dope on the H&G line.

McKillen & Heyer have made their maximum case length gauge for quite a few years, but it wasn't until now that we've had the chance to see and use one. This multiple-length gauge, hard chrome plated, is recommended for measuring fired and sized cases. Calibers are marked in raised letters that won't wear off and are easy to read. Most popular calibers are shown, price $5.25. This gauge sure makes setting a trimmer to size a lot quicker than measuring each cut with a micrometer or caliper.

The Gun Digest Presents

Guns of the World in Color

A pleasing parade of fine firearms—specially photographed in brilliant color—for the sportsman, the gun enthusiast, the collector.

The sketches below identify and describe the arms pictured on pages 225 to 256 in sequence.

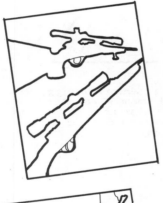

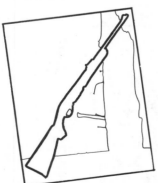

Harrington and Richardson (page 1)

H&R's New Model 370 (top) Ultra "Medalist" rifle features a Mauser Supreme action, fully adjustable trigger, and sliding safety with a 24" barrel. The 330 Standard rifle (bottom) has a fully adjustable rear sight, gold bead front sight and a 22" tapered barrel.

Bausch and Lomb (page 2)

Bausch and Lomb's extensive line of optics for the shooter is complete and justifiably well regarded. To illustrate the wide range of shooter's accessories we show their Balvar 8B variable-power rifle scope, a Zoom 60 spotting scope, a pair of Decot shooting glasses and—to guard against hearing losses—a pair of Quiet Ears.

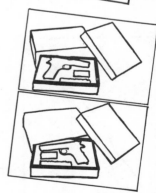

Remington Arms Company (page 3)

Remington's 742 Autoloader is representative of the company's line of quality firearms. The rifle pictured is in 243 Winchester caliber with a 22" barrel. Other calibers available are 6mm and 280 Remington, 308 Winchester and 30-06. A 742 carbine, 308 and 30-06 only, is also offered.

R.C.B.S. (page 4)

RCBS loading tools and related accessories are "precisioneered" to produce the highest quality ammunition, to facilitate handloading. From left—the big-capacity Uniflow powder measure, the heavy-duty Rock Chucker press, the new RCBS powder scale and the Dirak, a useful device for storing dies.

Colt Industries (page 5)

Colt marks the end of WW II with two cased and engraved 25 Anniversary commemoratives, both 45 ACP nickeled autos, one for the European-African-Mid-East theater, the other for the Pacific-Asiatic theater. The appropriate cases carry seven inert cartridges and a special 640-page issue of the American Heritage **Picture History of WW II.**

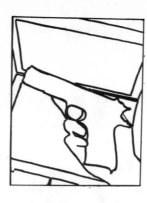

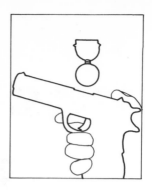

Colt Industries (page 6)

Colt's European-African-Middle Eastern theater 25th Anniversary commemorative is furnished in a rich walnut case that includes a color photograph of the surrender ceremony at Rheims, May 7, 1945. The gun is engraved with palm leaves and the historic actions occurring in this theater of operation.

Colt Industries (page 7)

The Pacific-Asiatic theater commemorative comes in an Obeche-wood case with a scene depicting the Japanese surrender aboard the **USS Missouri** at Tokyo Bay, September 2, 1945. Grips of this gun are of exotic Brazilian rosewood.

Colt Industries (page 8)

Another of the Colt Commemoratives is the Meuse-Argonne 45 Automatic which honors the World War I victory. The gun is engraved with a World War I battle scene and has a medallion inset in the grip.

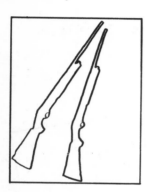

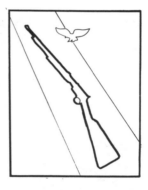

Garcia Sporting Arms (page 9)

These two Beretta AL-2 autoloading shotguns demonstrate that autoloaders can be both functional and beautiful. Pictured are a trap model, with Monte Carlo stock, in 12 gauge (left) and a light and graceful upland-game field gun in 20 gauge.

Garcia Sporting Arms (page 10)

The BL-5—a de luxe boxlock over-under shotgun—illustrates Beretta's Aristocrat grade hand-engraving and their superb handling of excellent European walnut in buttstock and fore-end. The gun pictured is a 20 gauge with an extra set of hand-fitted barrels.

Garcia Sporting Arms (page 11)

The made-in-Brazil Rossi "Gallery Model" slide action 22 rimfire rifle is a re-creeation of one of the most famous, most dependable 22 rifles ever made—the long-gone Winchester Model 1892.

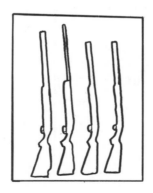

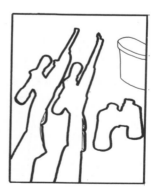

Garcia Sporting Arms (page 12)

The Sako Forester carbine is an example of the strong, rugged and precision rifles the Finns are noted for. Pictured is a Mannlicher (full length) stocked light sporting arm in 243 caliber, complete with peep sight and sling.

Charles Daly (page 13)

Four quality shotguns that display the Daly mark of excellence. From left—the Model 572 Diamond grade stocked in finest French walnut with fully engraved receiver; the Model 300 Superior grade single-barrel trapgun; the LTD Field grade 100, a new lightweight Daly, and the Superior Model 200 Skeet gun.

Williams Gun Sight (page 14)

Williams' new booklet describes in detail how to sporterize every popular firearm. Pictured here, and currently being featured, are a Williams Guide Line equipped Remington Model 742 and a Winchester Model 94.

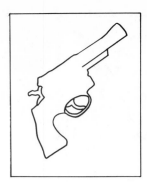

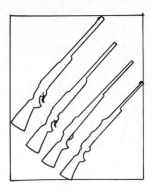

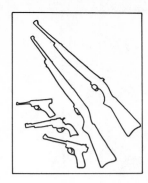

Sturm, Ruger & Co (page 15)
Ruger's new Security-Six double-action solid-frame revolver is constructed on a truly unique design. There are no side-plates. A compact holster revolver, the new Ruger is yet sturdy and massive enough for police and military use.

Sturm, Ruger & Co. (page 16)
Pictured are two Ruger Number 1 Single Shot rifles, the Tropical Model in 458 caliber and the Medium Sporter in 300 Magnum, plus two Model 77 bolt action rifles—the 77 RS and the heavy-barreleed 77 VR, both in 22-250 caliber.

Sturm, Ruger & Co. (page 17)
Ruger's full line of fine firearms includes those shown here—the Model 10/22 Carbine, the Model 44RS Carbine, the Single Six revolver, the Standard autoloading 22 pistol and the Mark I Target auto pistol, also in 22 rimfire.

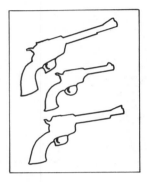

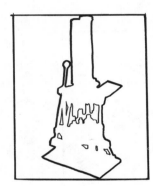

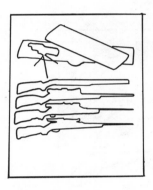

Sturm, Ruger & Co. (page 18)
Ruger's fame can well rest on the quality and popularity of their famed single action revolvers. Pictured are the Blackhawk, the Super Blackhawk and the Bearcat. A 45 Colt-45 ACP version will be available soon.

Ponsness-Warren (page 19)
The superb P-W high-quality, high-precision 8-station shotshell press pictured is a semi-automatic progressive loading tool that handles paper and plastic shells, a tool that assures the operator of reloads second to none.

Weatherby, Inc. (page 20)
Top to bottom, the new Regency 12-gauge shotgun, the Mk V rifle in 300 Weatherby Magnum caliber with Weatherby Imperial scope, the new Vanguard rifle in 30-06 with 3-9x Premier scope, and the Mark XXII DeLuxe 22 rimfire rifle with Mark XXII 4x.

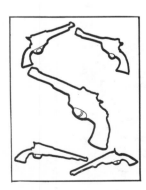

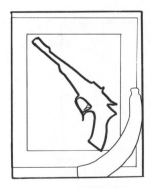

Hawes Firearms Co. (page 21)
Pictured are the Montana Marshal single action (top left), the Chief Marshal single action (top right), the J.P. Sauer double action target revolver (center), the 1858 New Army Remington percussion revolver (lower left) and the Navy 1851 percussion revolver (lower right).

Lee Custom Engineering (page 22)
The Lee Loader makes it possible to reload rifle, handgun and shotgun ammunition with a minimum investment and with a maximum of simplicity. The tool is available for most popular calibers—pictured is the 30-06 model.

Thompson/Center Arms (page 23)
The Contender, a single shot, break-open target pistol offers the unique feature of interchangeable barrels for a wide selection of calibers—both rimfire and centerfire. Pictured here in 357 Magnum, the gun is available with 10" or 8¾" tapered octagon barrels.

W. R. Weaver Co. (page 24)

Weaver's Classic 600 6-power scope —one of a new scope line introduced this year—incorporates all the accuracy, dependability and quality features of the famed K models plus elegant styling, sparkling satin-black finish and aluminum alloy construction.

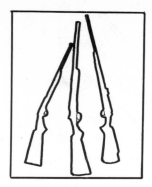

Browning Arms Co. (page 25)

Browning displays (from left) the Grade III 22 Automatic rifle, a Diana grade superposed shotgun and the Olympian grade bolt action rifle—firearms that show the highest quality and the finest hand-fitting by expert craftsmen.

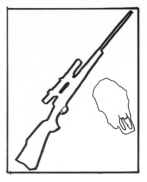

Winslow Company (page 26)

Winslow's lighter-weight Bushmaster Regimental custom rifle, specially designed for bush country, displays a special modified beavertail fore-end for quick and sure grasping, and a gracefully slender pistol grip.

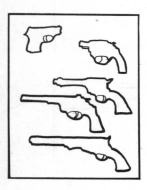

Firearms Import and Export (p. 27)

Importers of such guns as (from top) the 25-cal. Titan auto pistol, the Western Duo Combo revolver in 22 LR and 22 WMR, the Titanic 32-cal. revolver, the Arminius double action 22 revolver and the Navy percussion revolver, a replica of the 1861 Colt.

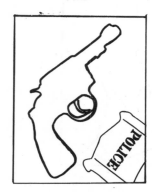

Colt Industries (page 28)

Colt's Mk III Lawman—a power-packing protector with pin-point accuracy for police use—is one of several new handguns on the new Mk III frame. This Lawman has a 4" barrel, is chambered for the 357 Magnum load.

Colt Industries (page 29)

Colt's Woodsman-Huntsman, an auto pistol in 22 LR, is specially designed to fit easily into pocket, pack or tackle box, is the ideal beginner's handgun. It offers quick-aligning fixed sights, a 10-shot magazine capacity and wide trigger.

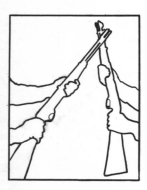

Colt Industries (page 30)

The Colteer autoloader 22 (left), lightweight and easy handling, fires up to 15 rounds as fast as the trigger is squeezed. The Stagecoach 22, stocked in American black walnut, Western straight-grip style, has a 13-shot tubular magazine, fore-end barrel band, engraved receiver.

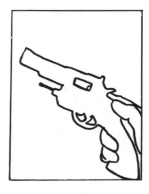

Colt Industries (page 31)

For a smooth double action, Colt's 357 Trooper Mk III was specially designed to eliminate drag and uneven pull. All working parts are designed for longer wear and durability plus a fail-safe firing pin and cylinder-hammer safety interlock.

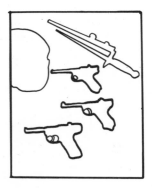

L A Distributors (page 32)

A trio of the German-made Erma pistols. From the top—the 32 caliber autoloading Baby Model Pistolen, the 8 shot 22-caliber automatic Pistolen and the KGP 70—a 9mm Parabellum caliber copy of the famed German P-08 pistols.

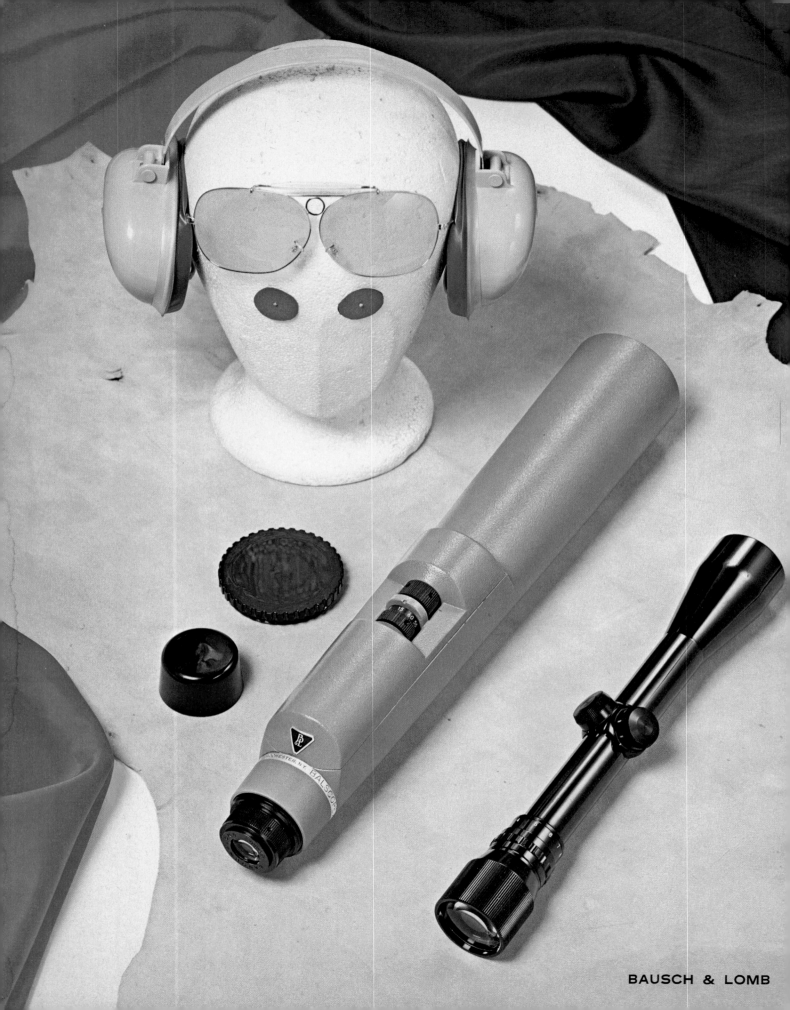

BAUSCH & LOMB

REMINGTON

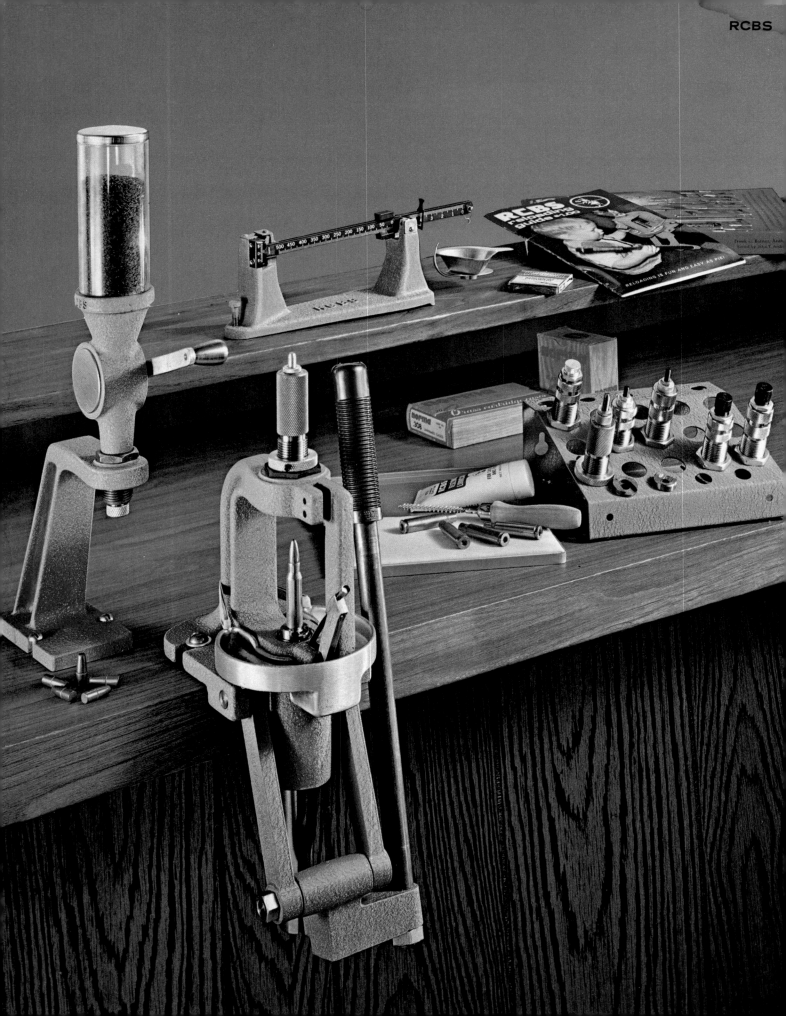

COLT

COLT

GARCIA·BERETTA

GARCIA

GARCIA

RUGER

RUGER

RUGER

PONSNESS-WARREN

LA DISTRIBUTORS·ERMA

Shooters who don't wear ear protectors are inviting dire trouble.
Not only may hearing suffer, says Matt Helm's creator, but worse problems
may develop. Here's a tale of deer hunting with a difference.

THE QUIET GUN

by DONALD HAMILTON

AT DAWN OF opening day we spotted four deer on an open hillside far up the valley, but we had to wait almost half an hour to make sure there were some bucks in the bunch. When there was light enough at last to see antlers on two of the shadowy forms, we tucked away our binoculars and planned our strategy.

Well, to be honest, the battle plan was laid out chiefly by my friend and companion, Ozzie Washburn, bear hunter and hound-dog man, acting general of our two-man army. A city dweller myself—I write books for a living—I was the soldier in the ranks.

"You swing over that way," Ozzie whispered, pointing east across the valley. "Stick to the trees, be real quiet, and keep going until you hit a fence. Follow it up through the woods over there. Hunker down in the cover at the edge of the meadow. . . "

I ventured a mild protest. "I doubt if I can hit anything from there, Ozzie. That's a long shot across the valley for a lousy little 30-30 with iron sights."

"I know," he said patiently. "So you just hunker down in the bushes like I say, and I'll sneak up the ridge

above them on this side and try to send them over there past you. I think there's a pretty good rack on one of them. You take him. After you've got him down, I'll try for the smaller buck with my 270, if I can get a clear shot from up there. All I want is some venison for the freezer, anyway." He added, as I started to turn away. "But take it easy now and don't forget your earmuffs. Remember your doctor's orders."

We were hunting on Ozzie's ranch in northern New Mexico, and I was working under some medical handicaps. For the past few years I'd been bucking a persistent jinx where hunting was concerned. Every summer, it seemed, just about the time I started thinking about sighting in the guns and oiling up the boots for the coming fall, I'd wind up with a health problem of one kind or another.

This year had been no exception; an ear operation had left me fairly

---

Above—A full moon rising over the mountains the evening before the hunt seemed like a bad omen but it didn't affect the feeding habits of the deer adversely.

shaky and prevented me from indulging in any pre-season practice with my hunting firearms. I'd done what I could with a Sheridan air rifle, but loud bangs were strictly out of bounds for a while. Now that I had more or less recovered, I'd managed to talk the doctors into letting me do a bit of hunting, but only on condition that I get myself the quietest gun possible and use full ear protection at all times, hence the little 30-30 and the earmuffs, so-called, actually a pair of headphone-type hearing protectors.

Having squeezed that much of a concession out of the medical dictators, I'd got Ozzie on the phone and asked if he could provide me with an easy deer, since I still wasn't in shape for any rugged wilderness missions. He'd thought he could oblige—and there was my deer, now, up the long valley, with the season less than an hour old. At least he was mine if I could get him.

It was a clear, still, late-October morning. The air was crisp and there was heavy frost on the grass. I eased through the woods, found a barbed-wire fence, and started making my way along it as instructed, but paused to free the ear protectors hooked into the pocket of my jacket. I put them on, just in case I should jump a buck in the timber ahead and have to shoot fast.

I worked the lever to chamber a cartridge, and lowered the hammer cautiously to half-cock, hoping that this was the safe and proper way to carry the unfamiliar firearm in the presence of game. I looked down at it ruefully, wishing for my faithful old 308 bolt action M70 with its fine clear scope, hanging on the wall back home. I'd never used a lever gun before, nor had I ever hunted with iron sights.

I've called it a little gun, but it wasn't really so small in spite of its underpowered cartridge. In many ways, it was a crazy firearm to lug into these rugged foothills on a serious hunt; its nickelplated receiver and fore-end cap shone like mirrors in the gray dawn light. It also had a long and heavy octagon barrel.

Sacrilege!

Collectors of Winchester 94 commemoratives will wince when I confess that I'd taken a perfectly good specimen dedicated to the memory of President Theodore Roosevelt and fixed it up with a carrying sling and a Williams Foolproof peep sight. I'd even—horrors!—fired it several times to sight it in, probably ruining it forever as a collectors' item.

But I was not a collector. I was just a hunter with ear trouble looking for a gentle, soft-spoken firearm with which to clobber a deer. Now that I had it, the question was whether or not I could actually hit anything with it, and if I did, whether or not it would kill what I hit. I slipped forward cautiously. My first concern was to get close enough to give the unfamiliar gun, the unfamiliar sights, and me, a fair chance. As I picked my way gingerly along the fence line, keeping low, moving very slowly and placing each foot with extreme care, it occurred to me that, for having hunted as many years as I had—never mind the exact number—I'd actually made very few real stalks of this kind.

Most of my former hunts, whether on foot, on horseback, or in a 4-wheel-drive vehicle, had resulted, sooner or later, in kind of blundering onto an animal standing in plain sight within range of my scope-sighted rifle. Or I'd been waiting on a stand and let the animal blunder into me. Almost all I'd ever had to do was find myself a steady rest, if the range required it, and shoot.

This was different. I discovered that just knowing that the deer were up there across the valley, and that I had to get into position opposite them without being seen, heard, or smelled, made me breathe more heavily than the exertion justified—even though I kept telling myself firmly that there was really nothing to get excited

about. Just the same, my hands were sweating.

I paused to catch my breath and check the wind. There still wasn't much of it, just a slight movement of air down the valley from the deer to me. Perfect. The bushes ahead were too thick to get through silently. I saw an opening to the left and moved that way carefully, bending low to avoid scraping against an overhanging pine branch. Starting to straighten up, I found myself looking right into the eyes of a big mule deer doe.

I suppose that's a slight exaggeration. Actually, she was well out in the open meadow ahead, some 200 yards away, but she certainly seemed to be

With earmuffs on and quiet, long-barreled rifle in hand, the author begins his stalk.

looking straight at me, and there wasn't a speck of cover between us. To the left of her, partially screened from me by more brush and trees, were the other three deer, browsing peacefully, but the big doe was watching, ready to give the warning if I moved a muscle . . . .

Deers and Ears

Well, that's a pickle any dumb deer hunter can get himself into and, with luck, out of. Some of my recent ear problems can also be acquired by any careless shooter, or even a careful shooter who believes everything he reads and hears about ear protection. Since these problems are more serious —there are lots of deer but you've only got two ears—I feel that while we're waiting for that suspicious doe to relax her vigilance, I ought to pass on what I've learned the hard way about ears and shooting, hoping to prevent others from making the mis-

takes I did.

To start with, my case is not quite typical. Some of my troubles are due to an inner-ear condition which, the doctors assure me, has nothing whatever to do with shooting. However, there are other problems definitely and admittedly noise-connected, and I've had a few of those, too.

Here's where the uninformed layman firing his souped-up magnum makes his first mistake. He thinks that when he neglects to protect his ears he is gambling only with his hearing, but he is wrong.

Certainly exposure to loud gunfire can result in some degree of deafness, large or small, and often does, but it's not only the sounds you can't hear that can become troublesome, but the sounds you can hear that aren't there. *Tinnitus,* or ringing of the ears, is no fun. Most shooters have experienced temporary cases of it after sessions at the trap club or rifle range, but it can become permanent, it can do so without warning, and once it does there's no real cure.

Furthermore, in addition to the hearing mechanism, the human ear also contains the body's balance center. This can also be affected by extremely loud, explosive sounds. Dizziness and vertigo are uncomfortable at best. They can be disabling.

So you're actually risking a certain amount of lifetime discomfort and inconvenience, if not worse, when you step up to the firing line and pull the trigger. The extent of the risk depends on the gun you use, the precautions you take, and just how sensitive your ears happen to be. There are

Instant replay shows the author sighting his quiet, long-barreled 30-30 Commemorative at the same stump from which the actual shot was made.

people whose hearing seems capable of tolerating almost indefinite exposure to the thunderous crash of a 458; others react badly to the comparatively insignificant pop of a 22.

The best way to determine your own sensitivity is to have your ears checked by a competent specialist. He can determine to what extent, if any, the shooting you've already done has affected your hearing. Knowing this, you can judge how careful you need to be in the future. It has been suggested that everyone who shoots a great deal should have his hearing checked at least every couple of years, and there's a lot to be said for the idea.

The problem is finding a specialist qualified to do the checking. In a big city you'll probably have no trouble, but in a small town you may be dealing with an ear-nose-throat man who is great on tonsils and sinuses but doesn't really have too much experience with noise-induced hearing problems. But any reputable ENT man anywhere should be glad to steer you to the nearest clinic where you can have a hearing test performed, and this is what you must get. Without it, you don't know where you stand.

Audiograms and Tinkling Bells

Let me emphasize: what you want is a thorough hearing test, which is an examination conducted in a sound-proof room or booth containing certain electronic equipment for piping sounds of known volume and frequency into a pair of headphones worn by the patient. From this, the examiner can draw up a response curve—an *audiogram*—showing whether or not the patient's ears have been affected by shooting, or by certain types of disease.

That is a true hearing test. Anything a doctor does in his own office with tuning forks or other gadgets is not a real hearing test. If he insists that it is, and that you don't need any further examination, you should rise gracefully, walk out of his door and find yourself another doctor, one who'll refer you to a place with proper equipment.

Suppose, then, that after being tested you learn that your ears are perfectly normal in all respects, in spite of the fact that you've scorned all types of hearing protection and made a hobby of firing the biggest cannon you could lay your hands on. Well, lucky you. In this case, you can go on shooting as you have been, but please get checked again in a year or two—or when and if it seems to you that people who used to speak quite clearly have suddenly started mumbling.

Most likely your situation will be the opposite. Most likely you will have used some ear protection, perhaps not while hunting, but at least at Skeet, traps, or at the rifle range. Even so—if you've been around for a while and done fair amounts of shooting—you will find that your hearing has suffered somewhat in the high-frequency range. The question is, what can you now do to protect yourself from further hearing losses, or, if your hearing is still perfect, how can you make sure of keeping it that way?

Unfortunately, there's very little you can do, and you can't be absolutely sure if you continue to shoot exactly as before. At present, there is no protection available that will totally defend your ears against the amount of noise produced by the firearms you're most likely to be using.

Here is the second place where the uninformed layman goes wrong. First, as we have said, he thinks he is only risking a slight loss of hearing when he, bare-eared, touches off his bellowing Super Magnum, but there are other things besides deafness that can happen to his ears, and they may. His second error is to believe that when he finally condescends to use a highly touted protective device of some kind he is perfectly safe no matter what he shoots or where. This is not so.

The damage done to my hearing, disease apart, occurred while I was wearing both earplugs and earmuffs simultaneously. Granted that my ears weren't quite healthy to start with, the fact remains that all the protection I could give them wasn't enough. There just isn't that much protection around for the guns I was using.

Unfortunately, this is a field in which accurate information is hard to come by. I've spent considerable time, written a great many letters, read a great many articles, and asked a great many questions, trying to get scientific data on the sound levels reached by a number of our most popular sporting firearms, and the protection afforded by the various devices available on the market, but all I can pass along are some rather shaky figures gleaned here and there along the way. However, they will suffice to show what I'm driving at.

Decibel Levels

The average person speaking in normal tones in a quiet room puts out some 60 decibels of sound. A hard-driving band of the kind popular with the younger generation may turn up 120 decibels or more. (This does not mean that the band is only twice as loud as the person speaking; decibels work on a logarithmic scale and it takes a mere 3 decibels to indicate a doubling of the noise.)

The kids love it, but quite apart from musical tastes, a lot of older people can't stand the sheer volume of sound put out by such a band, for any length of time. (It has been shown that many young people addicted to this music suffer significant hearing losses.) Luckily for us middle-aged shooters, a firearm produces only a brief blast of sound, otherwise most of us would find shooting quite intolerable, since gun noises go much higher.

For example, while a 22 rifle puts out only a little over 100 decibels, a 12 gauge shotgun with ordinary target loads is said to turn up about 140. A 30-06 rifle kicks up a 150-165 decibel fuss (the exact figure seems to depend on the rifle, the load, and who's doing the testing) I'm told, and the big magnums reach 170 decibels and more.

Under certain circumstances the effective noise reaching the ear can be increased, for a given firearm. Indoor ranges and covered firing points, for instance, tend to reflect a gun's report and give it several cracks at you. Such accessories as muzzle brakes and compensators may not add to the total noise output, but they direct more of it back towards the shooter. (My downfall was due largely to a 300 Winchester Magnum with muzzle brake.)

Consider the figures above, and then ponder the fact that 90-100 decibels is generally accepted as the region in which hearing trouble can begin. Obviously, even a nice, quiet 22 rifle isn't totally safe.

Now let's see what's offered us in the way of protection. One manufacturer claims, for his device, up to 40 decibels attenuation (noise reduction) at some, but not all, frequencies. He seems to feel that this is a spectacular achievement, and it may well be, since the most optimistic figure I've come across, for headphones and earplugs worn simultaneously, is only a little higher—45 decibels—and this figure is considered unrealistically high by some specialists.

Even if we accept the higher figure, it follows that a trapshooter using a 12-gauge shotgun and mild target loads will be exposed to repeated

shocks amounting to at least 95 decibels (140 minus 45) even if he wears full protective paraphernalia. According to some medical sources, the amount of sound getting through to him will still be enough to cause damage in the long run.

If he's firing a 30-06, the figures say he hasn't got a chance. At least 105 decibels (150-45) are still getting through, and he's in the danger zone despite the fact that his head is all cluttered up with noise-reducing gear.

So there is what we may call an audibility gap here: the most popular firearms develop more noise than the best protective devices can reduce to a perfectly safe level. Yet people do shoot 12-gauge shotguns and 30-06 rifles for years without noticeable trouble, indicating that the medical profession—perhaps with specially sensitive individuals in mind—may have set the limits a bit conservatively as far as the average person with healthy ears is concerned.

My daughter, for instance, became very interested in trapshooting a few years ago. Since she was studying mu-

sic, I was careful to get her hearing checked and insist that she protect it carefully. Some 20,000 rounds of 12-gauge ammunition later, it was checked again. The doctor found absolutely no sign of deterioration.

Earplugs and Earmuffs

Figures to the contrary notwithstanding, experience indicates, then, that the average person born with fairly durable hearing is moderately safe in shooting guns in this general category if he uses the protection currently available. The suitable devices on the market fall into two classes: earplugs and headphones. The choice is quite simple. Earplugs are generally cheaper, more convenient, and more comfortable to wear. Headphones keep your ears warm and give much better protection.

This is, of course, only one man's opinion. However, I have plugged my ears with everything from free cotton to forty dollars' worth of individually fitted plastic plugs. I've covered them with headphones ranging in price from eight to $100. As far as I'm con-

Hamilton with rifle, earmuffs and 4-point buck.

cerned, there's no comparison. The phone-type gizmos are bulky, uncomfortable damn nuisances that invariably get in the way of your hat, generally display some flashy metal to alert the game, and often interfere with cheeking the gun properly, but if you really need protection, my tender ears say that they do by far the better job of blocking out noise.

This finding contradicts to some extent the opinions of other writers, most of whom advise earplugs of one kind or another. I can't help thinking that, while I'm speaking only of protection, these men are giving considerable weight to the comfort factor in making their recommendations. Most of them are professional outdoors writers, meaning that they are tough-eared characters who've been firing off big guns all their lives without a great deal of discomfort (although most of them admit to some degree of deafness, and some confess to hearing crickets chirping where there aren't any.) They realize the need for protection, all right, but I don't think they quite realize how much protection some of us tender-eared gents—and ladies—require.

If you can get by with earplugs, fine, but just remember that there are better defenses available. I won't venture to plug any specific plugs (pardon me!) since I haven't checked the entire field. I'll merely suggest that the trickier varieties, that are supposed to function—in one way or another—to let ordinary conversation come through, while shutting out damaging gunfire noise, don't seem to give as reliable protection, in my experience, as those that simply block the ear canal, period.

In this connection, I should point out that many plugs aren't allowed to work at maximum efficiency because they aren't seated properly by the user. The National Rifle Association recommends the following procedure: to insert a plug in the left ear, reach around behind the head with the right hand, grasp the ear, and pull it backward, straightening the ear canal so that the plug can be seated deeply with the left hand. Then reverse the procedure for the other ear.

I'd be the last to deny that acoustic earmuffs are lousy things to wear, particularly while hunting. However, shooting with them on beats no shooting at all, and that's the choice my doctors gave me. Perhaps the best compromise, if your ears aren't all that delicate, is to use the plugs for hunting and the muffs for target shooting (although you might consider bringing both to the duck blind if you and your companions plan to do much blasting with compensator-rigged magnums.)

As for specific headphone recommendations, all the ones I've tested worked O.K. except the backband models, which on me tend to sag

down and interfere with the gunstock. Two hints: pick a hunting cap whose lower edge doesn't lift the earpieces and let the sound come through; and use shooting glasses with thin wire temples, not heavy bone or plastic jobs that'll be ground into your skull by the pressure of the muffs, and interfere with the fit.

Among the devices practical for general shooting use, headphone-type protectors are the best insurance currently available for continued healthy hearing. However, you should keep in mind that this insurance is just barely good enough. In fact, according to the official figures it's not quite good enough, even with guns of no more power and noise than the standard 12-gauge and 30-06. If you switch to more powerful and louder firearms you are definitely in danger *no matter what you put on your ears*. The catch is that even if the eardrum is completely protected, sounds above a certain level will be conducted by the bones of the skull, and the hearing nerves will still take a beating.

Danger Ahead!

You have been warned. There is nothing you can wear that will render shotguns and rifles of magnum dimensions safe for your ears. The chances are good that every time you pull the trigger of one of these howitzers, smoothbore or rifled, you are injuring your hearing to some extent. However, I won't venture to advise you to quit using the big guns, because I know that if you're an addict you'll ignore such advice. If the big thing in your life is bowling over moose with a 375 or knocking geese out of the stratosphere with a 10-gauge, you may figure that it's worth the microscopic (you hope) damage you're incurring with each shot. After all, nobody lives forever, and if your ears last as long as you do, they've lasted long enough.

I will say, however—speaking from personal experience—that the man is a fool who goes out and needlessly exposes himself to noises at this level by firing such cannon when it doesn't mean meat in the freezer or antlers on the wall. Once I wrote a piece advising magnum advocates to do their plinking and practicing with lighter artillery lest they kick themselves into a raging flinch. I wasn't aware then of the hearing angle—at the time I'd had no trouble along those lines—but if I'd taken my own advice, my ears would be in much better shape than they are today.

So much for the fortunate characters who are having no trouble, who suffer no reactions from a day at the rifle range or trap club, whose audiograms show no significant drop in hearing. That leaves those more sensitive shooters whose ears are beginning to rebel against the constant battering in spite of careful protection and the use of only moderately noisy firearms.

Dr. Howard House (Chairman of the Conservation of Hearing Committee of the American Academy of Ophthalmology and Otolaryngology), who was kind enough to check the medical facts in this article, suggests that I should emphasize here that if you experience any ringing of the ears after shooting, or any loss of hearing acuity however temporory, it's a sign that your ears are sensitive to the amount of noise they've been receiving, and damage is being done. If you're already using all the protection you can get, you have no choice but to lower the sound level somehow.

The simple and obvious answer is to put silencers on the guns, but the practice is frowned upon by the federal government. The alternative is to see what can be done to reduce the noise output of your shooting irons by legal means.

That brings up the question: just what makes one gun noisier than another? It may come as a shock to you —it did to me—but the answer is that nobody seems to know, except in the most vague and general way.

Questions Without Answers

If you ask a simple question (I did) like what is the exact decibel difference between the sound output of a

Bausch & Lomb Quiet-Ear

standard 30-30 carbine with a 20-inch barrel and a 26-inch barreled rifle in the same caliber, you get a blank and wondering stare. Apparently nobody's ever bothered to find out. Ask just how much a muzzle brake or compensator adds to the effective noise of a given firearm and you find that most ear specialists never even heard of such gadgets. Yet these are important questions for the patient with ear trouble looking for a gun he can use with reasonable safety.

But the work has apparently not been done, or if it has been done it's hidden where some of the best specialists in the field can't find it. So all I can do is indicate the factors probably involved, in the hope that somebody'll do the necessary research and come up with some useful tables and equations that will let a shooter figure out, before he buys a gun, exactly how hard it's going to batter his hearing.

Obviously, the primary factor determining the loudness of a firearm is the size of the powder charge it fires. Anyone who has ever taken his trap gun into a duck blind knows that, in the very same gun, the heavy waterfowling loads using 3¾ drams of powder bang a great deal more loudly than 2¾-dram light trap loads. The magnum loads bang more loudly still.

But the powder charge is not the only element involved in noise making. That mild and relatively quiet shotgun charge of 2¾ dram-equivalents, roughly 75 grains, is just about the amount of powder fired in the heavy 300 Winchester Magnum rifle that I had to get rid of because it was so ferociously noisy. (Yes, yes, Virginia, I know we're talking about different kinds of powder that may not weigh up quite the same, but let's not start splitting hairs so early in the game.)

In this connection, the significant difference between a shotgun and a rifle would seem to be that a modern rifle operates with a chamber pressure in the 50,000 psi area, while a shotgun doesn't develop much more than 12,000 psi. We can deduce, then, that pressure is another factor influencing the noise output: the greater the pressure, the louder the noise.

But is it the *chamber* pressure that determines the noise developed by a given charge of powder? If so, why should my son's M70 in 243 caliber, with a 22-inch barrel, be considerably easier on the ears than my Fajenstocked Sako carbine in the same caliber, with an 18-inch barrel?

Presumably the main reason the longer barrel makes less noise is that it allows room for more expansion of the powder gases—and therefore a greater drop in pressure—before these gases are blasted into the atmosphere. Apparently it's the pressure at the muzzle, not in the chamber, that really counts. The fact that the longer barrel carries the sound a little farther from the shooter's ear is also a consideration.

Essentially, then, we can say that, for any firearm, the smaller the powder charge, the lower the operating pressure, and the longer the barrel, the more comfortable it will be to shoot as far as noise is concerned. This is still very general and fairly obvious, but in the absence of quantitative research I'm afraid it's the best we can do. The question then is, as hunters—target shooters have somewhat different problems—how light can we go?

What Price Magnums?

Well, it doesn't really take a 10-gauge magnum load of two ounces of lead and 5 dram-equivalents of powder to kill a goose except at extreme ranges, distances most shooters can't cope with anyway. I've killed several geese—admittedly in Mexico, where they don't fly quite so high—with a light, mild-mannered 20-gauge Browning O/U with 28″ barrels, firing an ounce of #4 shot driven by 2¾ drams of powder. I've killed quite a few limits of ducks with the same weight of #6 shot, but using only 2½ drams of powder—a very peaceful load—and they weren't all decoying right into my lap, either.

I've even killed ducks with a 410 Browning o/u, again with 28″ barrels—very easy on the ears—but I don't recommend this unless they are coming in very well, or unless you've got a retriever handy who just loves to chase cripples. However, the same 410, with the smallest standard shotgun load made, a mere half-ounce of shot, has accounted for plenty of doves and quail. It is quiet enough for anybody's ears, and with tight, full-choke barrels it throws an adequate pattern just as far as an open-bored gun in a much heavier gauge. You merely have to point it straighter, that's all!

So much for shotguns. As for rifles, it doesn't really take 4- or 5,000 magnum foot-pounds of energy to massacre a moose. I've brought down a couple of specimens of the smaller European variety quite dead with my old 308—dead enough that I wouldn't hesitate to use the same gun on one of the Alaskan giants offering a good shot at reasonable range.

There are spots where only a magnum will suffice, of course—extremely long shots, or point-blank confrontations with dangerous, wounded game —but you can stay out of those spots

Lee Sonic Ear Valve by Sigma

David Clark Co. earmuffs

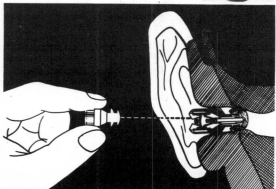

American Optical Hear-Guard

if you really try. Or, if you don't want to stay out of them, you can at least reduce the wear and tear on your hearing apparatus by reserving the outsize cannon for just that kind of hunting, and using a lighter rifle for less demanding situations.

What lighter rifle? Well, for my own use, given plenty of time, I'd probably order a singleshot rifle I've seen advertised with a 30″ barrel. That long a tube should take the curse off my favorite 308 Winchester cartridge, a load that's always been lucky for me.* However, since time was short, I picked a quicker and less expensive solution for this hunting season, as already described: the ancient, relatively low-pressure 30-30 throwing a blunt 170-gr. slug through the 26″ barrel of an M/94 commemorative. It turned out to be ideal from a noise standpoint. As for whether or not it would kill deer . . .

* * * * *

The big doe was still staring my way. I felt my knees begin to tremble from the strain of holding the awkward position in which she had caught me. Obviously something had gone badly wrong. The deer were supposed to be way over on the far hillside, not down here standing guard over the approach I had to use. (Later, I learned from Ozzie that a pickup truck full of hunters had come clattering along the ranch road just over

_____
*Since writing this I've put in my order for a Sharps 78.

the ridge, spooking the whole bunch my way prematurely.)

At last the doe dropped her head and began to browse. I lowered myself with infinite caution and squirmed across the open lane between the trees. Reaching the shelter of some heavy brush, I saw another deer out there, even closer, and it seemed to me that I could detect antlers but I wasn't quite sure. I carefully worked my binoculars out of the front of my jacket and tried to hold them steady, at which point I realized that I either had buck fever or St. Vitus dance.

The image wouldn't stay still in the glasses, even though they weren't very powerful. I did manage to determine that I was looking at a buck with antlers big enough to be legal. However, I didn't think it was the bigger buck of the pair we'd seen. I knew Ozzie would be ashamed of me if I settled for the little one, but then, Ozzie tends to have a touch of the Boone-and-Crockett syndrome, particularly where his guests are concerned. He feels obliged to send us all home with great big horns. I guess he's caught the complaint from some of the tape-measure-happy characters he's guided.

These compulsive trophy-seekers make it very tough on us simple folk who just plain like to hunt and shoot, love to eat venison, but don't really give a damn what the beast wears on its head as long as it's legal. Maybe when I've shot so many big-game animals that it all begins to seem tame

Willson Sound Silencer

and uninteresting, I'll start playing this game of whose-antlers-are-bigger-than-whose. In the meantime, I find it exciting enough to sneak up on just any legal deer . . . the big buck was over to the left somewhere behind a lot of brush, while the smaller one was now looking straight at me, and I wasn't even in position for a shot at him.

The Bead Looked Bright

I needed to wiggle out about four feet farther. I'd be lucky to make even that distance right under his eyes, since he was less than 150 yards away. If I tried for any more, I could lose the whole jackpot.

Again there was an interminable wait until the head came down. I squirmed forward until I could rest an elbow on a low stump. As I worked myself very slowly into a position from which I could line up the sights, I was wondering just how a real deer was going to look over iron sights after all my years with a scope.

To my surprise, when I got the sight picture at last, it looked very good. The bright front bead, centered in the rear aperture, was clear and sharp against the gray-brown deer-shape out there, and there was no shake at all. Maybe those oldtimers had something with their long, muzzle-heavy guns, I reflected. Despite my nervousness and breathlessness, the old style rifle lay in there like a rock, and the lack of scope magnification added to the confidence-inspiring feeling of total steadiness. Gaining assurance, I remembered to ease back the unfamiliar hammer. The slight click brought the deer's head up once more. Then I was putting pressure on the trigger and waiting for the piece to fire . . .

With the shot, my target went down as if clubbed. Working the lever, I jumped up and hurried forward—and was almost run over by the larger buck and a doe. As they veered away sharply and disappeared into the woods, I heard Ozzie's 270 crash across the valley, but it was a long shot at a running target and the 8-pointer didn't flinch. Well, we'd have to get Ozzie his deer later. (We did.)

Meanwhile, after a couple of years of big-game-hunting inactivity, I had a nice 4-pointer down in the frosty grass, on opening day, with the sun just appearing over the mountains to the east. I advanced cautiously, watching for movement, with the long Roosevelt rifle cocked and ready in my hands. I'd once had an apparently dead antelope jump up and run away, and I wasn't going to be caught like that again, not today.

I was aware of Ozzie coming down the hill to scold me for taking second best, but it didn't bother me a bit. I'd had my stalk and I had my deer. At that moment, the size of the trophy made no difference whatever. ●

Precision Rifle Ammunition and its creation

Handloading for the highest degree of accuracy demands refinements in techniques that many reloaders are unaware of. A master riflesmith and veteran competition shooter, the author explains in exact detail how to put together match quality cartridges.

by ROY DUNLAP

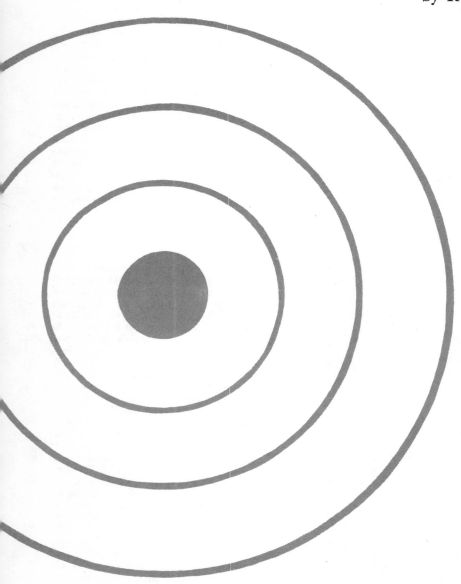

HANDLOADING or reloading of rifle, handgun and shotgun ammunition falls into three separate, almost completely different fields, alike only in the basic principles calling for a casing, primer, propellant and projectile. This article covers only the procedures involved in loading for the modern centerfire rifle calibers in general use today.

While every person who reads this book probably knows something about reloading, not one out of a hundred experienced loaders really understands what he is doing. There are a dozen or more loading manuals or booklets available, giving basic principles of safe loading techniques, recommended loads, etc., data which will permit anyone with an IQ higher than his hat size to load respectable ammunition. However, in what will be told here, such loads are where we'll start—the aim will be to produce not just safe and reliable cartridges, but to turn out precision stuff, capable of using to the utmost the accuracy of the rifle. In other words, ammunition so good it proves the adequacy or inadequacy of the rifle it tests. Any competitive bench-rest shooter, target rifleman, or riflemaker knows a few loads in a few calibers that, precision loaded, can tell in 20 rounds whether a new barrel is good, needs a recheck with different bullets, or should be scrapped immediately. They rely almost entirely on the ammunition for a decision.

Within the past 10 years a new class of rifle and handgun shooters has developed in this country—in the main, young men (to me anybody under 40 is a boy!—who have an intense interest in firearms for sport shooting; tar-

J&G Rifle Ranch offers several cartridge case tumblers. Pictured is the Model AR-6 (left)—their most popular size—which handles 70-80 rifle cases or 150-250 handgun cases and Model B with more than twice the AR-6's capacity. Other tumblers are available from J&G, larger and smaller, and all do an excellent job. As J&G points out, tumbling cleans case necks on the inside, radically reduces expander-ball friction, lessens case-neck stretching.

gets, varmints, modified and competition bench-rest shooting, and from muzzle-loading black powder arms to the high intensity rifle. These young men have created a vast, expanding market to serve them—constant change (and some improvements) in arms, scopes and loading equipment. It would be a safe guess that today we have at least 5 times the number of products in each of these departments as we had just 15 years ago. Some 25 years ago we had but one "gun" magazine—American Rifleman, journal of the National Rifle Association, plus GUN DIGEST and three or four outdoor magazines with small firearms sections. Today there are a dozen or so publications devoted solely to publicizing, advertising and reviewing every product and development in the world of firearms. Many of their writers have limited or narrow experience, often familiar only with their specialty calibers or the uses of these calibers. Within their corridors they are experts, their data reliable, but they're often tempted to transfer their information out of its slot, ending up with articles only half-correct, thus misleading the uninformed reader.

The new class of riflemen have, as a rule, started as individuals, not as members of a rifle club with experienced men to advise and recommend —not that all experienced men give sound advice, but it helps to have a few opinions before spending a lot of money on anything! These new shooters frequently derive their information from the magazines and the loading booklets. In too many cases they suffer much disappointment and needless expense before learning enough to really enjoy their sport.

I hope to provide a short-cut or two . . .

There are some 15 centerfire rifle calibers (barrel diameters) in the U.S., ranging from 17 to 45 (not counting a few oddball wildcat bores), and uncountable case variations among them. All have an accuracy potential —some greater than others, of course —and the object is to load ammo that makes the smallest group the individual rifle is capable of firing. Here we enter the fascinating field of experimentation—will a different make of bullet group better? A different weight, or shape, or diameter; more or less powder, a different primer? The combinations are almost endless. Any rifle can be worn out checking less than half of the possibilities! This can be, and often is, the most fun in handloading, but I personally hate to burn out a good barrel shooting experimentally. It really isn't necessary either, because you can eliminate about 80% of the unsatisfactory results ahead of time by precision loading.

Getting Started

Precision loading simply means you take precise care in every phase of every operation in loading, and in the selection and preparation of bullets, cases and primers. Cartridge cases are the most overlooked factor—even experienced men often mix up once-fired and 3-times-fired cases, different lots or even brands, dirty cases, and so on. Cleaning is necessary and quite easy. It is the first operation of all. A fired case should have its neck cleaned out by a brass brush—a regular barrel brush turning in a drill press—or mo-

tor chuck if you have one, otherwise just clamp the brush shank in a vise and run the case over the brush a few times. Always use a size larger brush —a 25 caliber for 6mms, a 30 for 270, etc. The case is then ready for measuring neck thickness, for you can't expect a great deal from a case that has a neck several thousandths of an inch thicker on one side than the other. There are a couple of reasonably inexpensive tools made for the purpose, but a case-neck or tubing micrometer—while more costly—is far more exact and about as fast. I check necks in three places, rotating about a third of a turn over the mike's ball-anvil for each check. You don't want more than .001″ variation in thickness anywhere around the neck, or in total thickness between cases; that is, you don't want necks .011″ plus or minus .0005″ mixed with cases running .013″, plus or minus the same half. Not in the same batch or lot you are loading.

L. S. Starrett has a good one, the No. 220, with pin anvil that accepts cases from 17 caliber on up, priced about $30 or so. With this Starrett tool, other rod anvils of different sizes may be substituted.

Case necks should be miked where neck will hold bullet tightest—in neck sizing, $\frac{1}{16}$″ from mouth. Neck thickness sometimes varies, tapering from thin at mouth to thick at shoulder junction. Repeated firing in some calibers (like 30/338) causes brass to flow into the neck and thicken at junction of the neck and shoulder. If the die has a straight neck section you can see how full sizing can give you an inside-neck situation like a reversed funnel! This is why fired cases usually shoot

This small and precisely made case-neck turning/reducing tool is made by Bob Simonson. Available with interchangeable arbors and case holders, its carbide cutter is fully adjustable for depth and arbor-position depth. A fine tool.

better with short neck-sizing only, while on first firing the same case might do well with a full neck size.

Uniformity is the key word in ammunition, and in all components and measurements.

Two "lots" of brass can shoot equally well if shot separately, but with mixed cases the group may suffer. When all necks in a given batch of cases are of uniform thickness, you've made a big step toward tight groups. For ultimate uniformity outside or inside neck-reamers are used to remove brass from the thick side of the neck and so make it uniform. This involves special tools, often special dies and expanders and, as you are reducing all case necks to the level of the thinner portions, you may even require a special tight-necked chamber in the rifle. The average man seeking accuracy is better off *selecting* cases for uniformity.

Primer Pockets The next step is de-priming or de-capping, cleaning the primer pocket and sizing the flash-hole. Rotary brushes are best, but you can do a satisfactory job just scraping with a small screwdriver bit. Next, primer pocket flash-holes must have no "flash" (raised metal burrs) around the hole, inside the case or in the pocket, and hole diameters must be uniform. Flash-hole diameters may vary a few thousandths of an inch between different lots or brands of cases, but you can usually find a number-size drill bit that fits the average hole and enlarges the small—just clamp the bit in a vise with a half-inch of the point exposed and run cases down on it. You also can use a larger bit, 1/8″ to 3/16″ in diameter, with a sharp point, to remove "flash" and slightly chamfer the flash-hole, both inside the case and in the pocket. If the flash-hole is a wee bit off center, don't worry about it—this has been checked out many times and doesn't seem to affect accuracy. Away off, it can.

Weighing Cases Since the cases are now the same size outside, a heavy one obviously has more brass in it and so must be smaller inside. Weighing them and segregating them into classes having one or two grains' weight difference is a very important factor in achieving accuracy with high-pressure or full bore loads. Case size or caliber means quite a bit in the weight check as the percentage of tolerance—the degree that won't hurt accuracy—will vary with the mass involved. A one-grain variation in 300 Winchester Magnum cases can't mean much, but one grain in a 17 or a 22 Hornet case counts for perhaps four times as much. In proportion this would mean a 4- or 5-grain difference in the magnum case. Common sense will give you an idea of proportionate weight tolerance for your specific cartridge.

(I have long felt that most successful wildcat cartridges owe much of their reputation to the fact that their rifle owners really had to work on the cases—neck 'em down, expand, trim, fire-form, etc. In so-doing they've ended up with pretty uniform matched cases, whereas men dealing with standard factory calibers often pay little or no attention to the same details they would check carefully in the wildcat.)

By now you are beginning to understand that just because you have 40 cases you can't load 40 rounds of super-good ammunition. It'll be more like 20 and, in some calibers, like 10! No, you don't throw away the rejects. In any caliber they are good for practice, for preliminary test groups in which you ignore the flyers—shots away from the main group; for pressure checks, general field shooting and plinking. Pressure checks are an important matter—you'll have noted that all loading manuals tell you to "drop maximum loads two grains and work up" or words to that effect. So, you load two or three cartridges of each load or loads, starting with two grains low, then two or three of each with a half-grain more, and so on until flattened primers or hard extraction, or both, indicate you're up to maximum. Then you should drop the powder charge a little and start loading your good selected or matched cases.

With new, unfired cases, you also check neck thickness, weight and primer pockets. If the cases are already primed, decap them when you neck size, using slow, steady pressure on the tool handle. Those primed cases may be new or they may have been stored for months or years, or their primers may have deteriorated slightly from damp storage, etc.

Components There are places to save money in shooting, but don't try to do so on components. For the utmost accuracy you need good building blocks —good cases, good bullets, good powders, reliable primers. If you want to play with pick-up cases, bullet "seconds," powders and primers of unknown shelf-life and storage conditions, you can have fun, but don't expect too much and don't be misled by an occasional good group. You need several good groups with a particular load before you can depend on it.

Loading Tools Let's talk about loading tools for awhile. As intimated earlier, the present-day loader has a wide choice in equipment. There are hand tools, not much different from those of almost 100 years ago; C-presses, of which I believe the old Pacific Company made the first, over 40 years ago; the H-type press; the columnar-toggle type such as the Hollywood, about 25 years old, and the O-type, exemplified by the RCBS tools, notably. Tools can be had in varying price ranges and quality or material and workmanship.

Consult our Directory pages for the location of firms or individuals mentioned.

All will do sizing and decapping well, many are strong enough to take bullet-swaging dies and so be used to make jacketed bullets—which phase of this field won't be covered in this article. Most tool presses have immensely strong frames and toggle systems— linked with the same semi-hard steel pin the lighter tools had a generation ago. But pins are easy to replace. Strength of the press is not very important unless you're considering bulletmaking. Any of the tools should handle full-length sizing of the largest rifle cases without trouble—though some will work easier than others—if your cases are clean, lubricated but not over-lubricated, and the dies smooth. For preparing very accurate ammunition we'll seldom full-length size anyway—we'll just size the neck back 1/16″ or thereabouts, enough to hold the bullet in place in handling, and in the magazine against recoil if cartridges are to be used in repeating fire, as in western varmint hunting. So, the tool needs only be made well enough to keep dies in line with shell-holders, which usually have enough tolerance to allow a case to center itself in the die, and to last a lifetime without breaking anything more than a pin or two. You don't need any turret heads, automatic primer feeds or multiple this-or-that features. These are for people who want to load lots of ammo fast. Right now we are concerned with super-quality, not speed, and only you, not production equipment, can do the job. Primarily, you want a tool that is convenient to handle—easy to put cases into the shell holder, change dies, adjust, etc.

Powder Scales I have gone through a great many scales, now have several, and I generally use one that is about the cheapest on the market—it does the work without being pampered! Some of the newer scales may be faster for powder weighing, I don't know, but any scale made for reloading is accurate enough for the best loading if it's used properly; many, however, must be handled and watched very carefully. Many scales have faults you should know about; side-canting or lateral movement of the arm in its bearings; that is, the arm moves out of its exact vertical-travel plane, the pointer swinging behind or in front of its graduated plate. This fault gives non-uniform weights while *registering* a uniform weight. The common second problem is when a different charge weight results if powder is added to bring the pan *up to balance* than when the pan has an overcharge and powder is removed to bring the pan *down to balance*. These faults are easily noted and corrected by making sure the beam pointer is always centered in its correct vertical plane or swing. Also, develop a technique of always weighing charges the same way. The commonest system—and a good one—is to adjust the powder measure to throw a slightly light charge for the scale pan, then use a "trickler" to add individual granules of powder to bring the pan up to balance.

The only way to check scale performance is to re-weigh several charges. Weigh out 10 charges, dump them in cases, then go back and dump each one back on the pan and see if they all check out the same as they did the first time. Shocking how often they won't—if you haven't been careful. Graduated scales often do not check out exactly with weights, varying up to several tenths of a grain sometimes. This is not especially important since uniformity between your own charges is what's desired. For example, your 41.5-gr. load might actually be 41.4, and your friend's 41.5-gr. load be 41.7. Scales are adjustable for zero, so you can use a known scale weight or a bullet checked out on several other scales, or a laboratory balance, to adjust your own.

Many modern scales have dampers of various types, designed to slow the swinging of the beam and speed up operations. I don't think much of them in general because they can give pretty wide load variations unless used very carefully. Oil in the oil-paddle type slows the beam too quickly, frequently affecting sensitivity; better to use plain water in the jar or tank. Mechanical dampers that I have tried are totally worthless. The magnetic-field type can be pretty good. Sensitivity of these remains high because with the beam in balance, the magnetic field is cut off, so to speak. If someone will invent an electro-magnetic type working off a flashlight battery, operated by a button, maybe we'll have something!

I just hold the pointer centered with the fingers when putting the loaded pan on the scale, or when adding powder prior to trickling on the final few granules.

Powder Measures While not essential tools for rifle loading—you *must* have a scale to set the measure, so the scale can be used for measuring all charges—the measure can be used to speed up weighing with all powders. With small-grain powders a measure can give very uniform charges. The successful use of a measure depends primarily on the operator, and secondarily on the powder in use. The loader must train himself to an absolutely unvarying routine in using the knocker (if any) to settle the powder, in throwing the handle or lever with the same force and speed every time, and in keeping a reasonably uniform level of powder in the measure. Small-grain or ball powders pack well in the charging recess of the measure and so contribute to uniformity of weight. Large-grain rifle powders don't do so well. The powder measure is absolutely required for pistol and shotgun loading but for top-drawer rifle fodder

At top, RCBS primer pocket cleaner handles large and small holes. Next, the RCBS case-neck brush followed by the S.S.&D. primer pocket cleaner, a new and well-designed tool. Next, Lee Engineering's pair of pocket scrubbers, then the twin Herter tools for cleaning pockets. Last, Herter's GLH pedestal/crank cleans all pockets with stiff wire brushes.

it is just an accessory to the scale. If you have a measure, keep it clean. Never leave powder in it for more than a day or two. Even though nearly all have chromed steel or non-ferrous metal working parts that come in contact with the powder, you must keep on the lookout for rust and corrosion. You must not oil them so keep them clean and dry.

Getting the powder into the case isn't always easy. Buy, make or have made individual funnels for each caliber you load for—don't try to use one small size for everything. Powder should flow freely into a case. Today we load many cartridge cases to capacity *and beyond*—using charges greater than the case will hold with normal loading! This is done by use of a "drop-tube funnel," a funnel extended to 8″ or more by fitting a brass, aluminum, or even glass tube down which the powder is poured more or less slowly. The added distance the powder falls help it pack in the case and so take up less space. You will find such loads listed as "compressed," meaning that the bullet when seated compresses the powder. Some such loads will fill the case to overflowing unless a drop-tube is used, in which case the charge settles to the bottom of the neck and so permits the bullet to enter.

Loading Dies Sizing and seating dies are made by many people, several of whom should return to making pipe fittings. This is one area in which things are not as good as they were in the good old days, say 15 or 20 years ago. Anyone with a turret lathe and a few reamers can make dies very cheaply. Unfortunately, it is a hard and rather expensive job to make them really good—constant care of the reamers, careful hardening and polishing, maintaining very close tolerances on diameters and angles, plus careful inspection and gauging. I've seen more bad dies in the past three years than in the preceding 30. All you can do is clean and inspect the interior to see if it is really polished, without toolmarks, and then try out for a check of dimensions—and fire back at the maker if they don't work right on clean, once-fired brass. Now, don't expect them to reduce brass to unfired-case dimensions at the base—they're all designed to reduce diameters to just under the chamber specifications, which are greater than those for new cases. "Minimum" dies are available, to reduce even more, but these special, down-to-new case type you don't want, they are hard to use, require much pressure in the tool and cannot be used at all if cases are not perfectly clean and smooth, because you end up squeezing down the case in the *solid-base area*, and solid brass just doesn't compress easily. (Normal brass alloys will extrude cold at from 70,000 to 80,000 pounds per square inch (psi), and, believe it or not, there are loading tools which approach these figures.)

A neck die, of course, should only size the neck of the case, so the body portion is unimportant. The lock rings should lock the die in the tool freely, the rings bottoming all around, and they should never show any indication of pulling the die out of line. Because dies are usually used in many different makes of tools it is necessary that threading be on the loose side. This isn't necessarily bad. European target sight makers construct their rear sight discs on the same system—the thread is sloppy, but a big, square shoulder pulls the disc into perfect alignment when tightened. The rings on the disc should do the same thing when the die thread is a loose fit in the press head.

Die Troubles Whenever you have to full-length size doubtful cases—those that may be hard to get in and out of the chamber—always remove the ex-

standard-head cases (30-06 size at base) a 5/16" drill and 3/8" coarse tap work best. No, you won't hurt the die.

When a case separates in a die, leaving only the thin-walled front section inside, the problem isn't so tough nowadays—it just takes a little time. Turn the stripped die up, expander assembly removed, put a little wad of cloth or paper down into the shoulder of the case, mix up a little epoxy bedding material, plastic steel, etc., and pour it down into the case. Let it harden, then beat the works out from the top with the little rod and your ever-present hammer. Naturally, you don't get any of the epoxy inside the die, only inside the case that's inside the die!

Keep your dies clean, wiping 'em out every 10 cases anyway, and lubricate your cases. Anything from liquid soap to engine oil will do, but it is far better to use lanolin or the synthetic lanolins sold for case lubricants. For

you feel your way as you start cases into sizing dies, holding the case with one hand and moving the tool handle with the other. The expanders must be kept smooth, of course; the best way is with a small motorized buffing wheel, which gives 'em a mirror finish. Then, when you finish a loading session, oil them.

Uniformity of cases extends to sizing also—the expanding plug will tell you the story. If three cases come out over the plug with uniform pull, but the fourth comes out easier or harder, set it aside. For best accuracy all cases must register the same resistance or pull effort to the expander. A tighter neck holds the bullet tighter, so the powder builds up a little higher pressure forcing it out of the case, a loose neck gives the opposite; result—high and low shots in the group. The strength with which the case holds the bullet is known as bullet pull, simply the amount of force needed to pull the bullet from the case. It can vary from one to 100 pounds, literally. Only arsenals and ammunition-factory laboratories have the equipment to actually measure bullet pull. The handloader can only strive to keep it uniform by the feel of the loading-tool lever in his hand as he pulls case-necks over the expander, and he can pretty well equalize varying pull by eliminating most of the bullet-pull through neck-sizing just enough to hold the bullet. Also, as bullets are seated it is pretty easy to feel any that seat with more or less pressure than the rest.

Primer- and bullet-seating are the most neglected parts of loading, as far as advances in tool design goes. Cases are still held by the rims for priming, bullets just forced into cases.

Primers Primers are necessarily taken for granted by literally all loaders. Except for good storage (kept in their boxes or in large-mouthed jars or other air-tight and moisture-tight containers), and not keeping them more than a year or so, there just isn't much we can do about them. If you have machine-shop facilities it is easy to make test equipment in which a weight dropped for specific distances will fire all primers and from a lesser won't, but this is not really needed. Primers today are very, very uniform. All are of the lead styphnate, noncorrosive type, originally based on a German formula of the 1920s. There are small variations in sizes—one brand may fit a particular batch of cases better than another. The "Magnum" type primers are made to give a hot, longer-burning flash than standard, for the purpose of igniting large-grain slower-burning powders in large cases. They are usually not suited to small and medium-capacity rifle cases and often give poorer groups.

(About here I'd like to recommend a book all handloaders should be compelled to read in about their second or third year of loading—*Principles and*

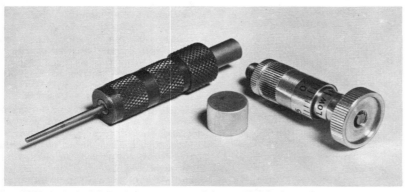

Herter's flash-hole diameter gauge (left) quickly checks uniformity, gives decimal diameter as well. Zenith Primer Mike tests depth of seated primer to .001", guards against too-high primers. Furnished with zeroing block.

panding plug assembly, leaving the top of the die open. Should you tear the head or rim off the case, a short rod through the top and a belt with a hammer gets the ruined case out. If the expanding unit is in the die and you tear the rim out with the shell-holder, you've got problems. Like needing a drill and a bit larger than the expanding plug, a tap-wrench and a tap that'll thread into the hole the bit will cut, and the aforementioned short steel rod and hammer. You take the die with stuck case out of the tool and put it in a vise; unscrew the expander-decapping assembly and pull it up to the top of the case so you can run the drill in through the primer pocket. Next you pull the expander setup very tightly against the neck of the stuck case inside the die, and unscrew the expander; now the expander and decapping pin can be dropped out through the drilled hole and the threaded rod removed through the top of the die. You now thread the tap into the hole in the primer pocket until it is tight and solid, drop the short rod into the die against the end of the tap and hammer away. For

neck sizing you can get good results with no lubricants at all in the larger cases, or you can do this: oil a cleaning patch well, lay it flat in a can-lid on the bench, press the mouth of each case on it, then into a lid or paper with Scientific Lubricant's Motor-Mica on it, thus leaving a tiny ring of lubricant inside and outside the case mouth, enough for short neck-sizing without leaving any excess lube inside the case or on the outside of the neck. This plan will not build up excess lubricant inside the die, to eventually put dimples in the case shoulder, as in full-length sizing, so you don't have to take the die out frequently and clean it during loading. Expanding plugs or balls—the part that expands neck for holding the bullet after the sizing die reduces the neck diameter—come with various tapers, usually insufficient in that every now and then the plug doesn't enter the case but hits on the mouth and makes dents. This occurs because the shellholder doesn't hold the case truly vertically but allows it to tilt out of line. You lose the case, too, because you can't ever straighten it out perfectly. So,

Practice of Loading Ammunition, by Earl Naramore.* This is a 452-page book with few "recommended" loads in it. The section on primers alone is worth the price. Read this book and you will begin to really understand ammunition and everything about it!)

The American Boxer-type primer with the anvil in the primer cup (invented by a European) has one large central flash-hole which makes reloading quite easy compared to the European Berdan-type primer (invented by an American!). The latter has the anvil as an integral part of the case base, this being a raised lump in the center of the primer pocket, with two little flashholes (sometimes 3), one on each side of the anvil. The Berdan primer cap has no anvil: it is just a cup with the priming compound in it, like a percussion cap. Seating Berdan primers requires care and a priming tool with a stop on it so that you can't go too far—there isn't anything to stop you. Decapping Berdan cases is quite a chore since you don't have a large central flash-hole to push a strong decapping pin through. The common tool, a hand type, hooks over the case rim and then forces a sharp point at an angle through the fired primer, near the edge, and then you lever it out. Cases can be damaged. The best way is messy—hydraulic pressure. First you size the cases or full-size the necks, without a decapping pin in the assembly, of course, and drop them in a pan of water. You must have a base to hold the cases—just something the case will go down into, or a shell-holder, with a clearance hole for the old primers to fall into or through. The remaining tool is a steel rod, just small enough to enter the sized case necks, one end cut off and then threaded to fit back on exactly like the joint in a take-down cleaning rod. In that joint you fit a tiny disc of leather to make a washer, sanding it to size for a tight force-fit in the case neck. With this setup and a hammer you're in business to decap Berdans. Put the water-filled case in the holder, the washer-end of rod in the neck and tap the other end with the hammer. The primer is forced out, and so is the water! Once you have the gadgets, decapping is fast and easy but, as I said before, messy. Since the cases are already wet, it's a good time to clean them.

Fresh Berdan primers are seated with a controlled-depth primer punch as found on H-frame and Hollywood presses, or by separate priming tools such as the Lachmiller, which I use for Berdans.

Centerfire Boxer-type primers are used in U.S., Canadian and foreign-made cases designed for the U.S. market. This primer is just pushed into the pocket until it hits bottom—*firmly.* If a primer is not seated full depth so

---

*Harrisburg, Penna. 1954.

The RCBS Rockchucker O-form press which has superseded Fred Huntington's great A-2 press, offers same high leverage and superb construction of its predecessor. Shown here with primer arm and primer catcher.

Pacific's Multi-Power press, of modified C-form, offers enhanced leverage, is seen here with auto primer feed and spent-cap catcher.

that the anvil legs rest on the bottom of the pocket, your ammunition isn't going to be so good. In this situation the firing pin has first to drive the entire primer down to bottom, then continue to force cap and compound against the top of the anvil to ignite it. You'll get spotty ignition, elevation errors and poor groups. You can seat primers with great pressure but it must be done slowly, and it should take some side pressure just to get them into the pocket. If they go in very easily, it usually means the pockets have been stretched a little from previous high-pressure loads. I have shot loads with these "loose" primers but, while I felt accuracy was not impaired, such ammunition is not to be depended upon. Such a loose primer could fall out of a loaded cartridge under recoil in a magazine.

Many C-type tools seat primers at a slight angle; the necessary pressure required for seating will show this as a flattening at the front edge of the primer cup. Fussy loaders with these tools have long seated primers with good moderate pressure, then turned the case half-way around and again pressed the seating punch against the primer to sort of equalize things.

Several years ago I got disgusted and made myself a straight-line primer seater. The case is held head up and upright by an inside-the-case rod —not by the rim—and I drive primers straight into pockets against solid support. It's a sort of Rube Goldberg miniature arbor-press arrangement, but it works. I've been doing long-range target shooting for 30 years— and not too badly—but after I started using this primer seating tool I could notice an improvement at 1000 yards. The tool is pictured so I won't go into a detailed description. However, I mentioned earlier that primer seating often takes effort; when I started out to make the tool I tried to use a chamber (as in a sizing die) to hold the case instead of a rod. Ha! Sufficient pressure to seat primers crumpled or set back the shoulders of the cartridge cases. While this gave me added respect for the strength of case rims, it didn't solve anything, so I ended up with the swinging rod to hold the case, as described above. The rod, by the way, is a push fit for a neck-sized 30-caliber case. Set-screws at the case-head area adjust to center magnum or standard-base cases so that the case is held in line with the primer punch. For other calibers, rods would have to be made to fit. The tool shown would cost too much to make to be a marketable accessory, but I believe that with a little experimentation a similar tool, using a cam arrangement, could be worked out to let the tool be made in semi-production at a fair price. Anyone interested? Take off with my blessing.

There are several straight-line or nearly so primer seaters available—

Lachmiller's, Bonanza, Gun Clinic, Lee, et al. In all of these a conventional shell holder is used, thus a case can tip out of true axis if the case is a bit loose in the holder. The only tool that does seat a primer into a tightly held case is one made by John Nuler, and it isn't exactly cheap or readily available. Nuler makes them more or less on order at $25 each for one caliber (extra calibers $5), and certainly the Nuler tool is a bit slow. It does do a fine job, though, and it's fully adjustable, of course.

Primer seating for precision ammunition must always be a separate operation because you must clean the primer pockets before seating a new primer. Primer fouling acts as a cushion for the anvil, hence prevents perfect ignition.

Bullet Seating I ain't licked this yet! The best method is through the use of such hand-operated straight-line seaters as the B&M or Wilson, next

press is just too great, defeats the idea of feeling the bullet into the case. However, a sensitive arbor press could do a good job, and there are at least two available. Both are used by a number of bench-rest shooters, and with full satisfaction. One is made by Gene's Gun Shop, the other by Pat McMillan (see our Directory pages), and prices run about $25 - $30.

I predict the next advance in loading equipment will be a bullet seater with a pressure scale incorporated. Perhaps it will be a straight-line die as mentioned above, with a hand lever and torque bar or spring-scale system that will register how many pounds each bullet takes to seat. I'm sure the design wouldn't be too hard or expensive to work up. A dial or a free-sliding scale plate that would register the pressure and hold the reading as the bullet reached seating depth, to be reset to zero, manually or automatically as the tool handle passes some

meaning all but the boat-tail match types, maximum accuracy comes below the maximum velocity obtainable. In the smaller bores—under 30 caliber —only a few will give top accuracy with maximum loads and a particular bullet, usually the heavier ones. Bench-rest and target riflemen have almost no interest in velocity as such for their loads. The latter almost universally work with maximum ones but use bullets giving accuracy at highest velocities. They couldn't care less what the muzzle figures are—all they want is uniform accuracy.

Flat-based bullets are greatly in the majority, but today boat-tail types are available in calibers under 270. The boat-tail aspect has little streamlining value, which doesn't take any effect until velocity has dropped below 1400 fps, but it serves to sort of balance the bullet, giving it length without a long bore-bearing surface to raise pressures. Long bearing areas in high velocity

Lyman-Ohaus D5 scale has 505-gr. capacity, is magnetically damped.

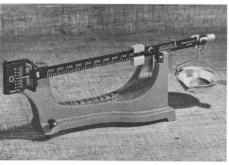

High virtue of this MB-5 Webster scale is separation of increments into tenths, grains and 10-gr. units, making for deep and wide poise notches, hence they're not easily dislodged. Capacity 509-plus grains, magnetically damped.

The new RCBS scale has a capacity of 505 grains, is made with the care and precision always expected in Fred Huntington's products.

the Vickerman or Bonanza type of straight-line seating die for use in the loading press, last the conventional seating die for press use. All have drawbacks—the hand seaters work well only with boat-tail bullets or with cases expanded almost to bullet diameter, and when the case is not full of powder. True, a small arbor press solves these problems. Several modern cases, notably the 7.62mm NATO (better known as the 308 Winchester), shoot best with compressed loads—but you aren't about to compress powder in seating a bullet with a *hand* seater! Don't try it, either, unless you like painfully bruised hands. Using a mallet or a hammer on a hand seater is ridiculous, for the whole idea is to feel the bullets seat uniformly; if one goes in hard, you set that cartridge aside; if too easy, you set it aside too. Luckily for 308 shooters, most dies in this caliber are made for the commercial case, which is a little smaller in diameter than the military National Match 7.62mm brass used by a great many loaders in this country. These tighter seating dies do a respectable job of straight-line seating in a good loading press. They fit the case snugly enough to steer it straight onto the bullet. However, Vickerman or Bonanza dies are a good investment in this caliber.

Why not use an ordinary arbor press? Well, the leverage in the usual

point during its release or cartridge-withdrawal cycle, would be needed. The same setup could be rigged for a separate bullet-seating tool made like a hand-seater but with the seating punch moved by some kind of torque-wrench application, I've passed this idea on to others for years, but nobody wanted to work on it. Let me know what you ingenious people out there come up with—better yet, send me one. In 308.

Bullets The subject of bullets is just too much to cover, since we are talking in general, not covering a single caliber in which detailed comment on types and weights can be made. For generalities—we have lots of bullets available in most calibers, by makers large and small. Each reader is familiar with the weights available for his calibers, and most of the time he'll be using bullets too light, and pushing them too fast. Because the average rifle handloader is fascinated by muzzle velocity figures, he wants speed; with hunting-type bullets,

Consult our Directory pages for the location of firms or individuals mentioned.

rifles creates more metal fouling, also. The jacket material, of course, has a great deal to do with this fouling—softer jackets, coppery-looking because they have a higher copper content, give more fouling at higher velocities than the harder gilding-metal types. In a rough or dirty barrel any bullet can foul, but the softer the jacket the more fouling. You must keep your barrel clean for accuracy. If it is smooth and doesn't easily metal-foul, just run a patch with solvent through it every 20 rounds. Use a brass brush only if it is needed, as at the end of a day of shooting.

The hardest part of precision loading is getting the *right* bullets for *your* barrel. They should never be smaller than the groove diameter of the barrel they are to go through and, if possible, up to .0003" larger. Your groove diameter isn't easy to even find out—you have to force a soft lead slug through your barrel, then carefully mike it. (If the slug doesn't go through with even pressure, but resists every now and then, showing tight and loose spots, the barrel isn't so good, and if loose at the muzzle, you need a new barrel right now!) Then mike bullets in the store to see what they measure. The figures on the box mean nothing really—it's the ten-thousandths that mean accuracy! Undersize bullets— those which won't fill up the grooves

—often shoot very well for a few rounds, 100 to 400. Then the accuracy drops off and the throat of the barrel shows much erosion where hot gas has escaped around the bullet as it started up the rifling. Nearly all custom barrel-makers now have air-gages, instruments that can measure barrel diameter at any point inside. If your barrelmaker owns an air-gage, find out the figures for your barrel; you'll then know what bullets to try first. Also, if the barrel is a bit tighter at the muzzle than at the breech, you have received a bonus—it will shoot better and longer. Go by the breech figures in matching bullets.

Barrel Life No one can figure this out exactly. We know that some steels last longer than others, that some powders are hotter than others and give more throat erosion, that rapid-fire wears a barrel much more than slow fire, that frequent cleaning prolongs barrel life, but there are some things we still don't understand. Take two identical barrels—same maker, same steel, same measurements, same exact dimensions, used with the same ammunitions—one can give twice the accuracy life of another! Stainless steel barrels are good in slow-fire uses, but life can be cut in half if much rapid-fire shooting is done.

Please understand we're talking about the *accuracy* life of barrels. A rifle will continue to shoot as long as the hole goes all the way through the

Belding & Mull, RCBS and Redding-Hunter powder measures, in that order from top to bottom.

barrel. What we're concerned with is the point at which groups begin to open up, when accuracy starts to go downhill. In sporters you can often change to a different bullet and regain accuracy for a few hundred more rounds. The 30 caliber target shooter can't—he has to use specific bullets, and when the barrel no longer handles them it means a new barrel. The average rifleman rarely knows the accuracy life of his barrel; usually he

over-estimates it. With most modern high-velocity calibers, it is under 2000 rounds; with magnum cases it's under 1000. At muzzle velocities under 3000, barrel life increases greatly.

In some calibers it is hard to match bullets and barrels. The 6.5mm is the kid with too many relatives. It is like the 22 centerfires in the U.S.—22 Hornet, .2235"; 22 Swift, 22-250, 222, et al, 2240"; the 22 Savage, .227". In Europe there are 5 sets of 6.5mm land-and-groove measurements. The largest is the 6.5x54mm Mannlicher/Schoenauer—and this is the set used by most U.S. barrelmakers for their 6.5mm tubes. Mannlicher bullets are long, heavy and on the small side to keep pressures down, so American-made 6.5mm bullets are often under-size for American-made 6.5mm barrels. The 264 Winchester Magnum is a 6.5mm, of course, the factory using a sort of two-diameter bullet to get velocity without too much pressure. You can have a wild time trying to handload for this cartridge with some of the bullets on the market!

Some 6.5mm bullets run .2630", others go .2640" but most U.S. barrels in 6.5mm show a groove dimension of .2640". I'm having A&M make an air-gauged 6.5mm barrel for me, groove to be .2637" to .2640", not larger, for use with the new Sierra 140-gr. HP match bullets and—hopefully—with the Lapua 144-gr. bullet, though the latter is not yet available.

Any 6.5mm is difficult to obtain high velocity with—you get pressure signs before velocity rises. However, with 139- or 140-gr. long-point bullets you can get flatter trajectories at lower velocities in 6.5mms than with any other caliber.

Some time ago, switching from a 270 to a 6.5x55mm, I had a hell of a time for awhile. I automatically equated flat trajectory with high velocity, but when sighted-in at 200 yards, I found I'd better hold the same elevation a lot farther out. But if a deer was walking slowly at some 300 yards, I'd have to lead him about three lengths!

Situations like this call for experimentation—5-shot groups are enough to tell whether loads are worthless or worth further development. Here is where you can use the cases and cartridges rejected because of weight, sizing differences, etc. They'll give good groups, they just won't give the best.

You select bullets as best you can. Look them over for seams in the jackets, dents or nicks in bases. Put these duds aside for the miscellaneous shooting. Weigh the bullets. Not because you want to shoot only those of exactly the same weight—a very little plus-or-minus variation won't really hurt accuracy, though we always feel better if they are very close. No, we weigh them because any that turn up a half-grain or so light might be that way because of an air bubble

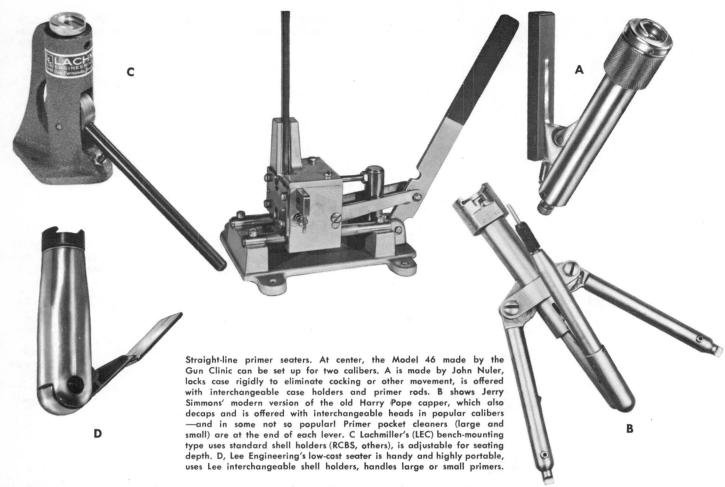

Straight-line primer seaters. At center, the Model 46 made by the Gun Clinic can be set up for two calibers. A is made by John Nuler, locks case rigidly to eliminate cocking or other movement, is offered with interchangeable case holders and primer rods. B shows Jerry Simmons' modern version of the old Harry Pope capper, which also decaps and is offered with interchangeable heads in popular calibers—and in some not so popular! Primer pocket cleaners (large and small) are at the end of each lever. C Lachmiller's (LEC) bench-mounting type uses standard shell holders (RCBS, others), is adjustable for seating depth. D, Lee Engineering's low-cost seater is handy and highly portable, uses Lee interchangeable shell holders, handles large or small primers.

inside the bullet, between core and jacket. That will make the bullet unbalanced as it spins through the air, causing it to take itself outside your group. For the same reason, clean out the tips of hollow-point bullets, for they may have sawdust, particles of corncobs or other polishing agents in the hollows. For short-range shooting this doesn't seem to matter, but at long range, as the rotational speed diminishes, you do get an effect—ring-like groups often result, the bullets apparently going into a spiral flight as they slow down. A few years ago I tried to check this, asking Joyce Hornady for some 168-gr. boat-tailed HP bullets, both polished and unpolished—that is, some which had never been in the tumbler with polishing agents. Shooting both types at 200 yards showed no real difference in groups—on a given day either bullet might give the smaller group. However, at 300 yards, the unpolished bullets won out, by just a little, almost every time.

Rate of Twist Rifling twist, of course, has some bearing on the bullets to be used for highest accuracy. However, velocity is also a factor since the whole idea of rifling is to give the bullet sufficient spin to stabilize it, but not to over-stabilize—in which case the groups are smaller at longer range

than at short! There is usually quite a bit of latitude—in 30 caliber a 308 with 10″ twist equates with a 30-06 with a 12″ twist or a 300 Winchester Magnum with 1-14″, yet all three work very well with any of the three twists. With the slower-velocity 308 stability at longer rangers suffers only with bullets heavier than 168 grains to the 14″ twist.

In smaller calibers there is a wide range of bullet weights and lengths, but the "standard" twist for the caliber seems best-suited to bullets in the middle range; accuracy falls off (usually) with the lightest and heaviest bullets. A good example of twist/accuracy relationship was the 244 Remington, designed for light, short varmint bullets. It wouldn't handle the heavier ones—you couldn't load 244 cases heavy enough to get stability and accuracy without running into excessive pressures. The caliber and the rifle flopped. Remington then gave barrels a faster twist, renamed the 244 the 6mm Remington, and the caliber is back in favor. It works. Choose bullets in the medium and heavy weights

For a complete survey of loading tools and accessories, see our just-released HANDLOADER'S DIGEST V. Specifications and prices are shown as well.

for accuracy.

Absolutely every rifle cartridge for which loading dies are available is capable of high accuracy, minute of angle (MOA) or less within its distance range, *if its rifle and barrel are good enough, and the bullet is right*. Some cartridges are easier to load for accuracy, certainly, examples being the 22-250 and the 270 Winchester—almost anything you can concoct in these calibers will shoot well, again assuming a proven barrel, etc. Others are more difficult; you really have to experiment to get the best groups. The 30-06, perhaps the caliber most reloaded of all, is not one of the easy ones.

Powders Powders and their burning rates have much effect on accuracy. Years ago, working with a big chronograph setup, one of the tests I made was to load cartridges in a given caliber—using the same bullets, cases and primers throughout—to uniform velocities with different powders. The results were wild—like one powder giving a group 4 times the size of another! On the face of things, bullets leaving a barrel at uniform velocity should automatically shoot the same, but they don't. The rate of bullet acceleration in the barrel, and the pressure curve while the bullet is still in the barrel, have much to do with accuracy, and I don't mean just barrel vibration.

Work with powders suited to your caliber and bore: one will usually prove definitely better than all others. Case capacity has a bearing on the type of propellant best suited. As a rule of thumb, use the fastest-burning powder your cartridge can handle without running into excessive pressures. There is a pronounced tendency toward using the big-grain or other forms of slow-burning powders in all calibers. In my own experience these belong in nothing smaller than a 270 Winchester with 150-gr. or heavier bullets, or in 30 calibers with 180-gr. or heavier bullets. Such powders as 4350 or 4831 are only for high-capacity loading—full-case or compressed-load charges. Under no circumstances should you use reduced loads of either. Such loads can be very dangerous—the powder is not only slow-burning, but slow to ignite, really requiring magnum primers for best performance. With such powders, if any appreciable air-space remains in the cartridge, the powder may not burn progressively; instead, the entire charge may ignite all at once (or detonate, as in an explosion), wrecking the rifle and maybe the rifleman. This has happened several times. A full case of "slow" powder may give only mild pressure, but 10 grains less may blow up! 4350 and 4831 belong in large cases, as full loads behind heavy bullets.

The most flexible powder for a generation has been DuPont 4064. A medium-fast burning type, it is usable in more case sizes, in more calibers, and with more bullet weights than any other. 4320, while smaller-grained, is inhibited to burn a little slower; it is also flexible, usable in cases from the 22-250 to the 30-06. Like some other powders, of course, it "peaks out" at a certain point in each caliber, that is, it reaches a stage where more powder creates more pressure but no more velocity. In large cases you can't reach this point in safety, but in medium-capacity brass you can. In a 308 with 180-gr. bullets, for instance, you're wasting time and powder if you use more than 41 or 42 grains of 4320. Nothing is gained.

DuPont's 4895, a powder developed for military use in the 30-06 with 150-gr. bullets, has proved to be very, very good in smaller cases and will often give the maximum accuracy possible in medium-capacity cartridges. A little faster-burning than 4064, it has, to quite a degree, replaced 3031 in this medium-capacity-case field. Which is a good thing, as 3031 is pretty fast and has a deceptively-fast pressure curve —from safe to excessive may mean only one-grain change in the charge. In such larger cases as the 270 or the 30-06 you can get into trouble real sudden with 3031. In the medium and small-medium cases it is capable of superb accuracy.

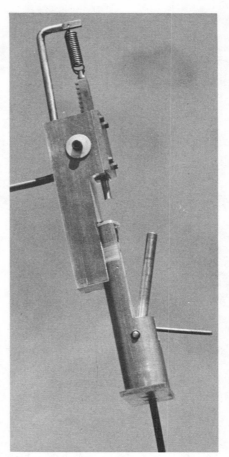

The author's straight-line priming tool. Essentially an arbor press, it looks way out, maybe, but it works.

The smaller-grain, fast-burning powders are, of course, for the small cases. They're seldom used otherwise, except when used for very light or half-loads in large cases. In this instance, the loader may put two charges in one case, this being very easy to do! Fired, such a cartridge disassembles the rifle all by itself at worst; at best the case lets go and gas escapes through the action. This can be even worse for the rifleman if the rifle is not built to deflect gas coming back around and through the bolt; it can, and has, reached the eye in some such accidents. Normally, when a cartridge blows up a bolt action rifle, gas blows the extractor off, opens the magazine, splits the stock and may or may not blow the top of the receiver ring out. The bolt usually stays put. The shooter is seldom injured beyond a stock-splinter, perhaps, in his hand or arm—if he was wearing glasses. Without glasses, he can get gas-burned slightly on the cheek if the rifle was scope-sighted, or perhaps eye-burned if his eye was low, as in using metallic sights. When a defective barrel splits, the fore-end also opens up, and the hand holding it may be cut badly by escaping gas if the split happens to be in line with the fingers, etc. Shooting glasses or sunglasses with hard-

ened lenses should always be worn while doing any shooting. They not only protect, but you can see better and they keep the wind out of the eyes so you can sight better.

When a closed-breech autoloader, pump or lever type fails for any reason, not much happens beyond a bulged receiver and a financial setback. Just a few weeks ago I saw a current model 30-06 pump which had fired before completely closing and locking. It was bulged, jammed, etc., but the boy who had fired it had not even noticed anything especially wrong when it went off!

Talking about guns blowing up in an article on handloading may be getting out of line, but the two matters can be allied, to be delicate about it, and I'd like to point out a few facts. Handloaders, by the very fact that they are interested enough in ammunition to start loading, are usually 99% safety-minded, but even the most experienced men may accidentally load the wrong powder someday—*the principal cause of loading accidents.* The safety rules for handloading are mostly plain common sense—you don't mix powders, you carefully label any that are put into unmarked containers, you store powder and primers in dry, reasonably cool places where the kids can't get at them to use in rocket experiments, you don't smoke while loading or allow yourself to be distracted while loading. Don't load while you're watching the football game on TV and/or while trying to keep the kids out of trouble. Don't ever use an unknown or new powder without some starting data to go on.

I have wandered all around in this article on purpose! I don't want this to be just a step-by-step set of direction for putting together cartridges. I want this to be read three or four times so the general data will sink in. Precision loading for maximum accuracy is nothing new—perhaps the most efficient level was reached between 1890 and 1915, when the Schuetzen game was at its height, using ultra-accurate black powder rifles by Zischang, Pope, Schoyen and others. Lead bullets were very carefully cast and swaged for utmost uniformity, and were usually seated via a false muzzle, pushed down to the throat of the barrel. Thus the bullet was in the rifling, already engraved and fitting, no variation in bullet pull because there wasn't any, and the barrel was clean for every shot. The case was cleaned, primed and loaded with powder, then chambered, the same case often being used for all the shooting, just cleaned and reprimed, no sizing needed. I can remember the heavy brass Ideal "everlasting" cases, made just for this purpose. You just can't get more uniformity in ammunition than those old boys did—today's competitive bench-rest shooters, with the finest modern equipment in rifles,

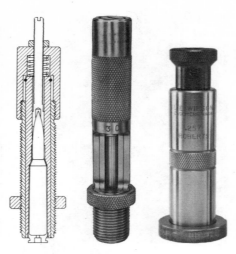

Straight-line bullet seaters. Belding & Mull, Bonanza (usable in ⅞-14 threaded presses), Vickerman and Wilson.

telescopic sights and bullets, took about 50 years to beat the old records, shot by Schuetzen riflemen.

A pretty sneaky way to get to lead-bullet loading, wasn't it?

Seriously, the use of cast bullets in high-power rifles can be very interesting, and even useful and rewarding if you live in wild turkey country. Back in the 1930s, when almost every American rifleman owned a 30-06 Springfield—along with his other arms —nearly all of them did some lead-bullet shooting. The post-war advent of a wide choice of jacketed bullets, and money in the pocket to buy them, just about killed the activity, but it seems to be coming back a little. There are several reasons and advantages besides economy—it appeals to the real do-it-yourselfer, and believe me, you do it yourself. You wouldn't trust your twin brother to do anything right about your own lead bullets! The rifle barrel will last forever as lead bullets and their charges not only don't hurt it, they polish it smoother. Cost is negligible once you have the mould, pot and sizing equipment. Very, very good short-range accuracy can be achieved, but only with effort. The challenge is tremendous—almost everything depends on the bullet and you have to make the bullet. The velocity range is really quite wide. Years ago for winter-time gallery shooting at 50 feet indoors men used to load the 30-06 with three grains of Bullseye pistol powder behind round 30-caliber buckshot, and they didn't do badly. They'd load hard linotype-metal bullets up to 2500 fps for 200- and 300-yard summer shooting. In New York City there is or was an old annual 100-yard indoor tournament for 22 rimfires, but they didn't always say so. An unreconstructed character showed up once with a 30-40 Krag and ammunition loaded with an old Pope-designed lead bullet. He won the shoot —which was immediately limited to rimfires thereafter. Fun can be had with lead bullets.

Admittedly, ranges are short. While lead bullets will travel far, the accuracy range must be considered 300 yards at the most, at least in small modern calibers. Tom Eason, my successor and former apprentice, recently did quite a bit of lead-bullet loading in the 308 Winchester. He did this with very accurate heavy-barreled match rifles, finding out quite a few things new to me and, I hope to you. He discovered his best accuracy came with bullets cast in single-cavity moulds, using pure high-speed Babbitt bearing-metal, which has a high tin content. Pointed or spitzer type bullets would not shoot as well as the round-nosed Loverin gas-check types in the lightweight bullet loads used. Bullets come from the mould about .313", the gas-checks put on by hand, then the bullets run through a .313" size-lube die to seat the gas-checks squarely and to lube the bullets. Finally the bullets are sized to .3080" (contrary to old lead-bullet sizing custom) in a Lyman 310 or SAECO bullet-sizing die, for straightness and final diameter. Cases are trimmed only enough to obtain a square mouth, then chamfered and bell-mouthed on a Lyman M-type die so they won't shave the edges of the bullet in the seating operation. The bullets are seated, then crimped separately. They seem to shoot a little better than if left uncrimped. (With very light loads this might not always be true in all calibers). It was found that the Loverin 150-gr. bullet (Ideal 311456), weighing around 153 grains in Babbitt with gas-check and lubrication, gives very good results with 37 grains of 4064, using a little cotton wad over the powder. This has to be getting around 2300 fps, well out of the pop-gun class and right up there with the full factory 30-30 cartridge. Accuracy—one inch at 100 yards, 2½" at 200.

At 100-yard range the 120-gr. Ly-

Consult our Directory pages for the location of firms or individuals mentioned.

man 311465 bullet does very well with 20½/4198, same loading procedures, and it's fun to play with. Good accuracy, no recoil, etc. It was discovered that primers can be a big factor. With the above loads, for instance, Alcan primers gave markedly better groups. Yet with jacketed bullets, or other lead bullet loads or calibers, no brand shows any unusual difference over another.

Lead bullets barrels develop personalities of their own, too. The loads mentioned above, in the rifle used, showed individual traits: they wouldn't group most times from a clean barrel, sometimes needed 10-12 shots fired before the groups tightened up and stayed tight. Changing to another load, even using the same bullets, sometimes required the same number of fouling shots! With some barrels a completely clean barrel groups best —that is, wiped out with patch and solvent before each shot. You never know until you try. Tom says he has never licked the close flyers—a one-inch group usually consisted of 8 or 9 shots in one ragged hole, with one or two separate bullet holes bringing the spread up to a one-inch total. Some lead-bullet men are now using Dacron fibers rather than cotton for over-powder fillers, on the theory that Dacron will be completely consumed when the cartridge fires, or more so than cotton.

In the small calibers cast bullets are even trickier, and velocities must be held down more to prevent barrel leading. Not much has been written about 22 centerfire lead-bullet shooting for years, but I think a lot of riflemen in squirrel country are missing some-

This small arbor press, made by Gene's Gun Shop, handles neck sizing, straight-line bullet seaters, can be rigged for priming, too.

thing. Think how nice that 222 or 223 would be so loaded. There can be beneficial side effects, too. Years ago, when the 220 Swift was the popular varmint caliber, people used to foul barrels, have all sorts of accuracy-loading troubles. I'd give them a handful of sized and lubricated 22 cast bullets, tell them to pick out any light load in any book they had and go shoot them into a bank somewhere. Four times out of 5 those few lead bullets lapped the barrel enough to make it shoot better with the jacketed bullets. Or it did when the guy remembered to clean out all the metal-fouling before he shot the cast ones!

In the calibers above 30, the lead bullet really comes into its own. Pressures are low in big cases even with jacketed bullets and full loads, so you can get gas-check cast-bullet loads with high accuracy and velocity that compare favorably with the "real thing." They're effective in the field, too, for all but the heaviest and most dangerous big game. Don't sneer—remember that lead killed a helluva lot more game in this country than jacketed bullets ever have. I shot a buffalo once with a 30 Newton using a 180-gr. soft point, but the real buffalo hunters a century ago dropped millions with big lead slugs!

The heavy-caliber rifles seldom see real use in the field—how often does one hunt anything needing a caliber from 338 to 458? With full factory (expensive, that is) cartridges that kick you sick if you fire more than a few from any position but standing, these rifles just don't get much use. Loaded with cast bullets, that super rifle can be used a lot, give a lot of fun and make the owner a skilled and confident rifleman. When he runs into that grizzly on the big hunt he won't be concerned about finding the bear in the sights and hitting it; he'll be perturbed if the bullet hits more than an inch or two from where he aimed!

In loading for the large calibers we do run into a few problems not encountered with the smaller, whether with lead or jacketed bullets. Most, incidentally, are quite accurate with almost all the bullets available for them. In powders, you go back to the medium-capacity-case types. In the 300 H&H you use 4350 or 4831, but in a 375 H&H these sort of go "poo." You can damn near throw a bullet faster unless heavily-compressed charges are used. Faster-burning powders are required to get pressures up. The 35 Whelen cartridge was a pre-World War II favorite and did pretty well. After the war, with 4895 powder, the cartridge came into its own and gave very good results indeed. The 35 Whelen is simply the 30-06 case with neck expanded up for 35-caliber bullets, works perfectly in any action that will handle the 30-06, and shoots well with light or heavy loads.

35 Whelen owners liked to shoot the

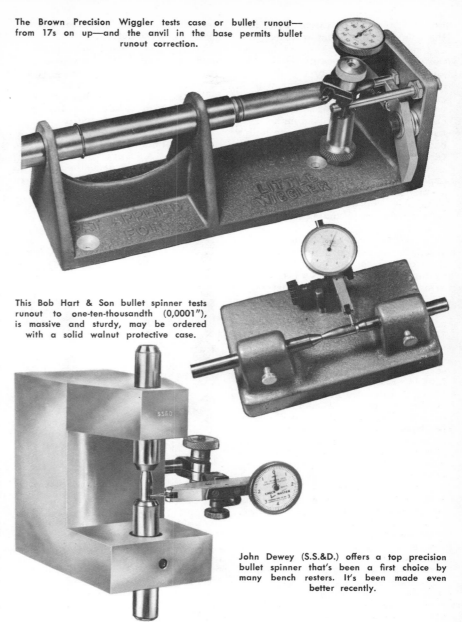

The Brown Precision Wiggler tests case or bullet runout—from 17s on up—and the anvil in the base permits bullet runout correction.

This Bob Hart & Son bullet spinner tests runout to one-ten-thousandth (0.0001"), is massive and sturdy, may be ordered with a solid walnut protective case.

John Dewey (S.S.&D.) offers a top precision bullet spinner that's been a first choice by many bench resters. It's been made even better recently.

accurate light cast-bullet loads for fun and shot lots of them; the cartridges developed so little pressure that they didn't even expand to fill the chambers fully. Firing-pins drove cases forward in firing, and after a few shots the rifleman had short cases and long headspace! This happens with light loads in all calibers, so be guided accordingly. Headspace gauges for cases (not chambers) don't cost so much. The short cases will continue to fire light loads as long as the firing pin reaches the primer, but if you suddenly load a full load in one you can have lots of trouble—separated case heads, at worst a blown rifle. To salvage too-short cases dent the shoulder and load bullets far enough out to hold the case against the bolt face. You can now fire it and form the case to full headspace.

Because breech pressure is comparatively low, the big calibers are easy on brass. Cases last a long time and lead bullets shoot very well—anyone who owns one of the "cannons" is missing a big bet if he doesn't load lead bullets for it.

Because every individual part of shooting is interdependent on all other aspects, let's talk a little about the rifles made to use our precision-loaded ammunition, about bench shooting for testing both, and about scope sights.

Seating Depth Some of you have probably wondered why I forgot to say anything about seating depth when we were on bullet seating. Well, the individual rifle regulates this for single-loading cartridges, as does the magazine box for magazine-loading ammo. Lead bullets seem to shoot best if forced into the rifling, jacketed bullets perform best when they are as close as possible to the throat, or the beginning of the rifling, without touching. Depending on the original throating, the amount of throat wear and the shape of the bullet involved, you can see that there just can't be any positive, universal seating depth for any caliber! However, it's easy to determine the correct seating with a given bullet—just barely neck-size a case, 1/32″ or less, seat a bullet way out, then chamber this dummy cartridge. The throat will push the bullet back in the case to maximum over-all cartridge length: use this to set your seating die, increasing your seating depth about 1/16″ or less. This applies to single loading, of course. For magazine use, you just seat to an over-all length that'll work freely through the box.

In certain rifle/ammunition relationships headspace and chamber dimensions are factors in accuracy. For example, the 7.62mm NATO on 308 Winchester rounds are nominally the same, using the same headspace gauges theoretically. However, there's a difference, specifically with the 7.62 U.S. National Match ammunition. A rifle closely and correctly chambered for the 308 commercial cartridge will not accept National Match brass, which is up to .005″ larger in diameter at the base, ahead of the extraction cut, and the N.M. cartridge requires about .004″ more headspace, mainly because of a greater neck-shoulder radius. As the military cases are very popular for handloading, and most current factory rifles are now chambered to accept them, we have a situation in which the commercial cases are a little small, are of thinner brass, weigh much less and therefore contain more powder. The 308—being a caliber in which the more powder you get into the case the better it shoots with most bullets—has us going in circles. Under this chamber/cartridge setup new commercial cases cannot always give the best accuracy because some of the firing pin's energy is lost in forcing the cartridge to a full forward seat in the chamber, before firing; and this itself is variable depending on how the extractor grips the rim of each case. Best accuracy will be obtained from cases fired in the rifle and then neck-sized for precision loading. This is also true in most other calibers to a lesser degree.

With belted magnum cases there's a different problem. When first loading new magnum brass, seat the bullets so they do *not* hold the case back against bolt face; in this instance you want the firing pin to drive the case forward so the belt gets to its forward position or seat in the chamber, as the cartridge fires. If a long-seated bullet holds the case back against the bolt the belt may not be fully seated, and cases may come out with a tiny step ahead of the belt, having expanded into the belt-cut in chamber. They can be hard to chamber fully, for even full-length sizing won't reduce this

step. If you order a barrel custom-made for a belted case, instruct the gunsmith to chamber it with minimum headspace, using new cases instead of gauges to check it. So made, you'll have little trouble with cases in loading, although you may have to reject a case once in awhile, one that won't go in the rifle to start with!

While I'm no exponent of ultra-tight, minimum chambers, I do like them close. A sloppy, oversize chamber can be an enduring headache to a handloader. Cases fired in it will

Forster Bros. combination gauge (left) checks cone-to-head dimensions of bottle-neck cases, guards against over-sizing. Their chamfering tool is at right.

separate at the base if subsequently full-length sized to "normal" more than a couple of times. Cartridges may lie on the bottom of such chambers, or be held out of line by extractor or ejector pressure, hence expand unevenly; these fired cases won't again enter the chamber except in the same position they were fired in. You could mark case bases so that they are always inserted with the same side "up," permitting the accuracy wanted. These loads won't check out so well when rolled on a glass plate or otherwise checked for concentricity, perhaps, but they'll shoot if lined up properly in the chamber.

Sometimes a rifle with a good chamber won't accept its own fired cases freely, the reason usually being that the bolt face does not lie exactly 90° to the case base when the bolt is locked and the cartridge fired. The base expands to fit the slanted bolt face. Check by placing fired cases base down on a smooth surface, close together, then rotate them. If their angle changes as the cases turn, you've got it. You'll have to mark such cases so they go back in the same position every time, as just mentioned. Try several such cases in the rifle, turning each a little until you find the position in which the bolt closes best,

then check the firing-pin indent in fired primers. It will usually be a bit off-center, and it will be the same on all fired cases; now mark them for top or indexing position.

Ignition Good ignition is vital. A sluggish firing pin just won't make it. Put in a new mainspring every couple of years just for insurance. The firing pin should hit the primers dead center for best and most uniform ignition, for the primer anvil is centered in the primer. A wee bit out of center is common and won't hurt, but away off is bad. In bolt actions, there isn't anything less straight than a forged bolt, and in each receiver they can lock up a little differently. If you have an old type Model 70, a Springfield or a Mauser in which the firing pin hits far off-center, about the only thing you can do is to locate some extra bolts. Then try those (with correct headspace) by firing primed-only cases. Often a bolt out of line in one rifle will be perfect in another.

Falling-block single shot rifles usually hit the primer a little high or low —this can be controlled by the linkage between lock and lever sometimes, but it may depend on barrel fitting.

Rifles The rifle must be bedded correctly, have a good barrel (repeat, have a good barrel), trigger pull and a scope without parallax. Failure in any of these defeats your good ammunition. The ammunition will tell you about the bedding and barrel, your finger the pull, and a fast check with the rifle at rest will tell you if the scope has parallax—if you move your eye and the cross-hairs move, without having moved the rifle you have it. Target scopes and most fixed-power hunting scopes of 8x and more can be focussed for exact ranges, eliminating all parallax. Hunting scopes of 6x and lower power, usually parallax corrected for 150 yards and beyond, may have some error at shorter ranges. With parallax present you only sight at the same spot when your face is in exactly the same position on the stock; if you have a minute of parallax you have a minute of error to start with, meaning the group you shoot can be a minute larger than the rifle and ammunition are really capable of shooting.

Bench Rests The bench rest is the mainstay for testing, but even in using one it isn't easy to hold for the same exact point of impact for every shot, despite the sandbags under the fore-end and buttstock. Still, you can at least see the errors and allow for them. Machine rests san be made, but they're quite a project. They are generally set up to test pressure barrels rather than complete rifles unless these have special fittings on the butt, etc. Some competitive riflemen have made them to handle target rifles, primarily for 600-yard testing of both rifles and loads. They get groups at that distance of 4″ and less with 308s, which would indicate everything is working—the best target so far is 2⅛" for 10 shots at 600 yards!

To sum up: for precision loading you must select cases by weight and measurement. With some calibers cases lengthen more than others, may require trimming every second firing or so. Cases must be clean. Over-all cleaning with case-cleaning compounds, automotive carbon cleaners such as "Gunk," etc., is easy. The cases should be fitted to your rifle, that is, fired in the chamber to start with, though in larger cases you can often get full accuracy with new un-

spring will be maximum or more in hot weather. A maximum summer load can be mild when the snow covers the ground, too.

Don't discount yourself if you can't shoot well yet on target range or hunting field. Always load the very best you can. The dub shooter needs better accuracy than the expert—a top-notch prone shooter who can hold dead center can take a rifle that shoots a 12" group at 200 yards and shoot a 12" group; the tyro who can only hold in a 12" circle can shoot in 12" if he's shooting a rifle-load combo good for a one-hole group, but if he's

with any bolt action, and minute-of-angle groups from M1 Garand rifles and M-14s.

You need a smooth and clean chamber in your non-bolt action and the cases kept clean to get reliable functioning, more so than with the bolt. You have to find out how much sizing of cases is the minimum, to obtain useful case life. Loads must usually be below velocity of the bolt action in the same calibers—the rifles just work better with less pressure. The nature of construction of some rifles cannot be expected to give MOA accuracy but good loading can bring

Bob and Wally Hart's new rifle rest is the best of its kind we've seen. Heavier at 11 lbs., and with longer legs, it offers great stability on the bench. A double-rise, lockable elevation system lets it be used at any range, and there's an extra-fine adjustability of the rear leg, the other two legs being fully adjustable as well. Varmint class and BR bars are available, about $40 with either. Sandbags and postage extra.

Center—Gene Beecher's fine rifle rest for bench shooters was one of the first such offered, is still in great demand. Right—The Wichita Precision rifle rest is a favorite among many shooters. It's offered by Basil Tuller, maker also of top-grain leather sand bags.

fired cases on the first loading. Primers must be fresh, seated cleanly and firmly. Powder charges must be exact, bullets inspected, weighed, and seated as straight as possible. Don't keep ammunition too long—three years maximum, unless loaded in new cases. In the varmint calibers graphite wads are sometimes used (Ipco, usually); these can prolong barrel life, aid accuracy, prevent fouling, etc., but they soon deteriorate in hot weather, ruining accuracy. Store ammunition, bullets and cases in air-tight containers such as surplus military ammo cans with clamp lids. Brass and copper alloys corrode easily, and you can find industrial contaminents in the air almost anyplace in the U.S. today! Try to keep components and ammunition stored where they won't suffer prolonged exposure to temperatures over 100 degrees F. or below freezing.

When on the range, don't let your ammunition sit in the sun on hot days. A 15° temperature rise means about a one-minute change in elevation, just like adding a couple of grains of powder. This means, of course, that a good load worked up to just under maximum in winter or

using that 12" grouper, he may well get a 36" group since every shot can be 12" from his hold! You dig? It always irritates the hell out of me to hear someone say he doesn't need a better rifle or ammunition because he can't shoot any better anyway. He can, but he doesn't know it and won't learn. Good equipment helps every rifleman at any level.

In loading ammunition for lever, pump, autoloading or single-shot falling-block action rifles you must learn your own rifle. Chambers are often given more taper or made larger in diameter on the theory that loose chambers make for easier extraction; these actions don't have the initial extraction power of the bolt action. The old belief that these rifles weren't inherently accurate, and that cases had to be full-length sized every time, aren't easy to disprove, but I've seen it done—groups from a 99 Savage 250-3000 that would be hard to beat

For a complete survey of loading tools and accessories, see our just-released HANDLOADER'S DIGEST V. Specifications, prices are shown, too.

groups from 5" at 100 yards down to 1½"—a worthwhile improvement in the meat rifle! Falling block single shots are limited only by their over-all strength rating and what they'll do in extraction; in my judgment they can be loaded for as if they were bolt actions. In some tubular-magazine rifles bullets with sharp, hard points, such as some of the hollow-points now made or bronze-points, can be dangerous; the point can act as a firing-pin against the cartridge ahead of it in the magazine, and if the rifle has sharp recoil, you can guess what might happen. Also, handloads with short neck-sizing cannot be used in any magazine if recoil is hard enough to move the bullets in the neck.

Our grandfathers loaded lots of ammunition for their hunting rifles long before bolt actions appeared in the hands of anyone but military shooters—they had poor powders, corrosive primers and jacketed bullets that metal-fouled barrels badly.

You can load better ammunition for any rifle—the more accurate your loads, the more careful you'll be shooting them. You'll become a better rifleman in all respects. ●

A History of

This is the 4th installment of the new and fully up-to-date series "History of Proof Marks" initiated in our 22nd edition. The author, Mr. Lee Kennett, is highly qualified to have undertaken the definitive research required, and we feel certain his comprehensive and detailed work will prove reliable, interesting, instructive and valuable.

While Mr. Kennett used the framework of the late Baron Engelhardt's "The Story of European Proof Marks" as a structural guide, he personally visited and talked with Proof House officials in many countries in his research. He will continue to do so until all nations in the survey have been covered. When that time arrives, we will publish the complete book.

With this issue we present "Proof Marks in Spain." The completed and published book will carry a full account of the origins and historical back ground of proof marks.

SPAIN
Origins to 1915

By THE 16th century Spain had taken her place among the arms-producing nations of Europe, Spanish guns being highly regarded and widely exported. Individual makers generally did their own proving, but according to one authority 16th century barrelmakers of Eibar and other centers often had their products tested at the Royal Arsenal at Placencia. Proof remained, however, an individual matter until 1847, when the government authorized the gunmakers of Eibar, the most important arms center, to establish a local proof house. The house was publicly authorized but privately run; it administered voluntary proof only.[1] This arrangement remained in effect until the beginning of the 20th century.

Proof practices and marks remain something of an enigma; many valuable records were destroyed during the Spanish Civil War of 1936-1939, and what is known is rather fragmentary. In the case of shotguns, there were both provisional and definitive proofs designated by marks 1 and 2 respectively. Subsequently, proof was somewhat amplified. All smoothbores underwent provisional proof in the rough (mark no. 1). Finished barrels were tested again and given mark no. 3. This constituted

a definitive proof for muzzleloaders, but was only a second provisional proof for breechloaders. After breeching the latter underwent definitive proof, depending upon their breeching system. Those having the locking lever under the trigger guard received mark no. 4. Shotguns having the locking lever incorporated in the fore-end received mark no. 5. These were proofs at moderate pressures, suitable for arms of these systems, often having only one locking lug. Shotguns with two or more locking lugs underwent one of the above proofs and then a heavier definitive proof generating 10,700 psi (mark no. 6). An optional superior definitive proof was also possible, designated by mark no. 7. There were two optional smokeless powder proofs, one at 12,000 psi (mark no. 8), and a superior smokeless with Schultze powder at 12,800 psi (mark no. 9).

By the beginning of the 20th century the privately operated voluntary proof system was no longer adequate. The nature of gunmaking had changed; what had formerly been a craft had now become an industry of sizable proportions. In 1909 Eibar alone produced a half-million guns. The export market had become an important one, but because of *compulsory* proof in other countries Spanish gun exporters were faced with that obstacle. The private proof house at Eibar would hardly do in this situation. First of all, it received no support from the government, but was obliged

Proof Marks

Gun Proof in Spain

by Lee Kennett

to meet expenses from proof fees. Yet these could not be very high or gun makers would not submit arms to its proof. About the only arms submitted were shotguns, but very often makers preferred to prove and stamp their own guns, sometimes with marks that *resembled* foreign proof marks! (This was the source of many complaints in Liége at the beginning of the century). More serious, the Eibar proof house marks were not registered or protected from counterfeiting, with results that can well be imagined.[2]

There was considerable agitation for compulsory official proof at the beginning of the century, but the proposal encountered much opposition from some gunmakers. At a meeting in Eibar in 1907 these makers argued that they operated on a minimal cost basis, and that proof fees would raise their costs too much. Moreover, they feared the delays involved in submission to proof—the Eibar proof facilities being inadequate to handle a large volume of guns.[3] A compromise was reached in 1910, whereby the government took over the direction of the proof facilities and protected the proof marks, though proof remained voluntary. Three new basic proof marks were introduced, undoubtedly to replace former marks that had been fraudulently applied. These were marks 11, 12 and 13. At the same time, a new stamp was introduced to indicate gauge (mark no. 14).

Beginnings of Compulsory Proof

Continual agitation for compulsory proof culminated in a law of 31 January, 1915, establishing this principle. The 1915 law only laid the basis of compulsory proof; subsequent enactments were to bring it into effect. These were slow in forthcoming, perhaps because of continued resistance among some gunmakers. The provisional proof house regulations were not formulated until 1919; even then, compulsory proof did not begin, for new installations had to be prepared. Originally, proof houses were planned at Eibar and Oviedo. Only the former came into existence then, gun proof finally getting under way at Eibar in January, 1923; to give makers even more time to adjust to the new system, proof did not actually become obligatory until April, 1924. A short time later a second proof house was opened in Barcelona, but proving firearms there ceased in 1935. Since that time the only Spanish proof house has been at Eibar.

The new regulations, issued in final form in 1923, conformed to the Brussels' standards, for Spain signed the Convention in that same year. At the same time Spanish laws were changed so as to protect foreign patents from infringement by local gunmakers (the imitation Colt and Smith and Wesson revolvers occasionally seen resulted from this abuse). The establishment of the new system

Spanish Proof Marks
1847-1970

In this table the mark numbers at left are those assigned by the author, and keyed by him to the text for reference. The 2nd column shows the true form of the proof mark and gives the period of its use. The last column tells the marks' significance.

Voluntary Proof System
1847 - 1923

1		Two variant marks for provisional proof. The oval form is thought to be the older.
2		Definitive proof mark; current in the 1880s.
3		Proof of finished barrels; constituted definitive proof for muzzle-loaders and 2nd provisional proof for breechloaders.
4		Definitive proof of shotguns with locking lever under the trigger guard. May also be found on guns with two or more locking lugs.
5	2ᴬP	Definitive proof of shotguns with locking lever in the fore-end. May also be found on guns with two or more locking lugs.
6		Black powder definitive proof of shotguns with two or more locking lugs at 10,700 psi.
7	3ᴬP	Superior black powder definitive proof.
8		Smokeless definitive proof of shotguns at 12,000 psi.
9		Superior smokeless definitive proof of shotguns at 12,800 psi.
10	**12**	Gauge designation.

New Marks Introduced in 1910

11		Replaced mark no. 1.
12		Replaced mark no. 3.
13		Replaced mark no. 5.
14		Replaced mark no. 10.

Compulsory Proof System, 1923 to Date

15	1923-1931	Eibar house mark.
16	1931-	Replaced mark no. 15.
17	1925?-1931	Barcelona house mark.
18	1931-1935	Replaced mark no. 17.
19	1923-	Single black powder proof of muzzle-loading single barrel smoothbore at 9000 psi **and** provisional proof of unjoined barrels of muzzle-loading doubles at 13,000 psi until 1929. Thereafter single proof for all muzzle-loading smoothbores at 10,300 psi.
20	1923-1929	Definitive black powder proof of double barreled muzzle-loading smoothbores.

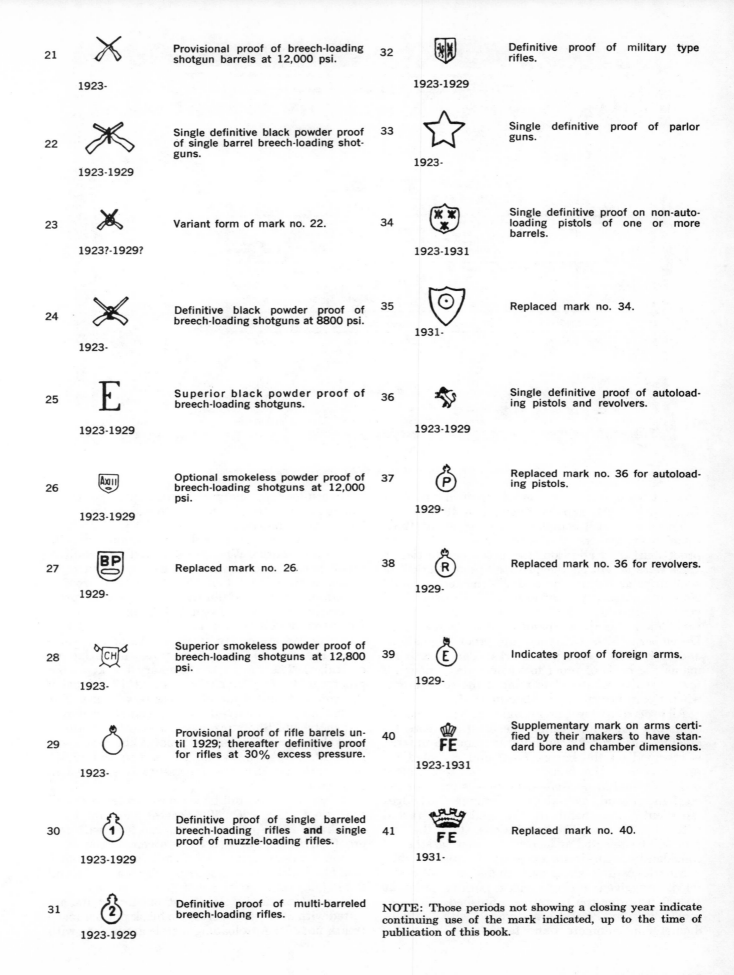

21   1923-   Provisional proof of breech-loading shotgun barrels at 12,000 psi.

22   1923-1929   Single definitive black powder proof of single barrel breech-loading shotguns.

23   1923?-1929?   Variant form of mark no. 22.

24   1923-   Definitive black powder proof of breech-loading shotguns at 8800 psi.

25   1923-1929   Superior black powder proof of breech-loading shotguns.

26   1923-1929   Optional smokeless powder proof of breech-loading shotguns at 12,000 psi.

27   1929-   Replaced mark no. 26.

28   1923-   Superior smokeless powder proof of breech-loading shotguns at 12,800 psi.

29   1923-   Provisional proof of rifle barrels until 1929; thereafter definitive proof for rifles at 30% excess pressure.

30   1923-1929   Definitive proof of single barreled breech-loading rifles **and** single proof of muzzle-loading rifles.

31   1923-1929   Definitive proof of multi-barreled breech-loading rifles.

32   1923-1929   Definitive proof of military type rifles.

33   1923-   Single definitive proof of parlor guns.

34   1923-1931   Single definitive proof on non-autoloading pistols of one or more barrels.

35   1931-   Replaced mark no. 34.

36   1923-1929   Single definitive proof of autoloading pistols and revolvers.

37   1929-   Replaced mark no. 36 for autoloading pistols.

38   1929-   Replaced mark no. 36 for revolvers.

39   1929-   Indicates proof of foreign arms.

40   1923-1931   Supplementary mark on arms certified by their makers to have standard bore and chamber dimensions.

41   1931-   Replaced mark no. 40.

NOTE: Those periods not showing a closing year indicate continuing use of the mark indicated, up to the time of publication of this book.

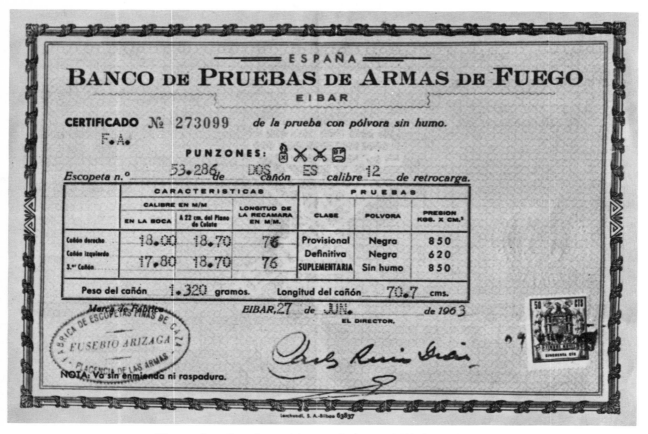

Eibar proof certificate for an Arizaga twelve gauge double barrel shotgun.

brought with it recognition of Spanish proof by Belgium in 1924, and by England in 1927.

There were still complaints abroad about those Spanish gunmakers' marks that resembled foreign proof marks; in addition, the proof authorities in 1924 were accepting the private "proof marks" of such firms as Remington and Winchester as valid.[4] This, of course, was contrary to the Brussels Convention—to which the U.S. had not been a signatory. As a result, a Spanish royal decree of 14 December, 1929, tightened up proof regulations and introduced some new marks. This decree remains the basis of proof in Spain today, though a few marks were altered to remove the royal crown when Spain became a republic in 1931.

All arms must bear, on arrival at the proof house, a factory mark and caliber designation. Bore diameter, measured 22 centimeters from the muzzle, is stamped on the barrel. Each gun accepted for proof receives the house mark (no. 16). Before proof, a visual inspection—viewing—is made of the mechanism and over-all functioning. Cartridges must enter the chambers, fire, and be extracted without difficulty. The regulations state that no arm will be rejected at inspection from "aesthetic" considerations or if its accuracy is questionable.

Muzzle-loading shotguns, single- or multi-barreled, are given a single black powder proof at 10,300 psi after the barrels are finished. They receive mark no. 19 and are stamped with the bore diameter in millimeters and tenths.

Breech-loading shotgun barrels undergo provisional proof in the finished state except for chambering and final polishing at 12,000 psi, receiving mark no. 21 and the bore diameter stamp in millimeters and tenths. When resubmitted for definitive proof, bore diameter must not have been enlarged by more than 0.4mm or the provisional proof is considered invalid. Definitive black powder proof generates 8800 psi, designated by mark no. 24. Definitive bore diameter, chamber length and barrel weight in grams are stamped. Automatic shotguns are proved by firing three magazine-fed cartridges. The first is the ordinary black powder proof charge, or a smokeless one at 12,000 psi if the gun is intended for smokeless powder use. The second and third cartridges are ordinary commercial shotshells. Shotguns may undergo two optional smokeless powder definitive proofs. The first generates 12,000 psi (mark no. 27), the second 12,800 psi (mark no. 28). Proof pressure is stamped in each case.

Rifles, including military types, undergo definitive proof only, with 30% excess pressure loads (mark no. 29). Automatic rifles are fired with two proof cartridges followed by two commercial ones. Saloon (parlor) arms take definitive proof from a case filled with the standard powder loaded behind the regular commercial bullet (mark no. 33).

Non-automatic pistols, of one or more shots, are tested with 30% excess pressure black powder loads (mark no. 35). Autoloading pistols are proved with

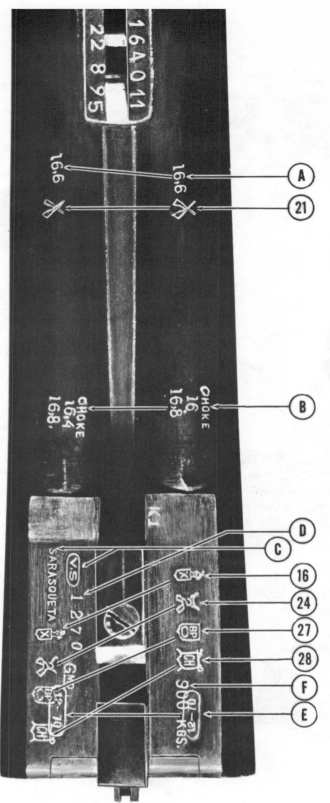

two 30% excess pressure loads followed by two commercial ones (mark no. 37). Revolvers are proved definitively in each chamber (mark no. 38).

Altered or repaired arms are subject to reproof, but no special marks are designated. These arms are to be treated as "new guns." Individuals may submit old arms for proof as well—the ordinary definitive marks being affixed to them if proof was successful. Foreign arms without sanctioned marks undergo definitive proof and bear a special mark (no. 39). Arms certified by their makers as having "standard" chamber and bore dimensions receive mark no. 41.

Shotshell Proof

One of the most interesting aspects of Spanish proof is the voluntary proof of shotshells. Manufacturers may submit these in lots of 1000, along with a sufficient number of rounds to replace those used in testing. Three types of proofs are offered—pressure, velocity, and general serviceability. For the pressure test, the proof authorities pick 20 shells from the lot; 8 are unloaded to verify uniformity in powder and shot charges and wadding. The other 12 are fired in a pressure gun. Shells with 65mm cases and 12 and 16 gauge cases in 70mm, must not generate an average pressure over 8400 psi. For other shells the maximum permissible average pressure is 9100 psi. No single shell may greatly(?) exceed these averages.

For velocity tests, 10 cartridges are fired, velocity being measured at 10 meters. Average velocity must conform to specifications of shot weight for each gauge. A general serviceability test is made with 10 cartridges fired from an ordinary shotgun. To pass this test there must be no misfires, ruptured cases or other defects.

Those batches of cartridges which pass these tests are returned to the manufacturer with a proof house certificate attached to each box of shells indicating the proofs they have passed. Should a lot of shells pass the pressure test but fail the others, they are returned to the manufacturer without a certificate. If a lot fails the pressure test, each of the 1000 cartridges must be unloaded in the presence of a proof official! ●

References

1. Gregorio de Mujica, *Eibar, monografía histórica,* 2nd ed., Zarauz, 1956, pp. 77, 89-90.
2. "Banc d'épreuves des armes à feu d'Eibar," *Armurerie liégeoise,* Liége, February, 1907, p. 947.
3. "L'Epreuve obligatoire des armes à feu en Espagne," *Armurerie liégeoise,* Liége, October 1907, p. 1009.
4. "Dans les bancs d'épreuve étrangers," *Armurerie liégeoise,* Liége, June 1924, p. 55.

Bibliography

In addition to the works cited in the references, an excellent work has recently appeared on Spanish arms: J.D. Lavin, *A History of Spanish Firearms,* New York, 1965; it contains several references to proof in the 16th, 17th and 18th centuries, as well as some makers' marks. For information regarding current proof practices, and a copy of the proof house rules, the author is indebted to Lt. Col. Carlos Ruiz Diaz, Director of the Eibar Proof House.

Proof marks on a Sarasqueta 16-gauge double gun made in 1965. The "12-70" stamp at lower left is wrong, the workman having been misled, probably, by the weight—"1270 Gmos." Such errors are not uncommon. (A) Shows bore diameter at provisional proof. (B) Indicates degree of choke and diameter of cylindrical sections. Choke in left barrel has 0.8mm constriction; right has 0.4mm. (C) Makers' name and mark. (D) Weight of barrels in grams. (E) 12-70, gauge and chamber length in millimeters, but should read "16-70." (F) shows maximum definitive proof pressure in kilograms.

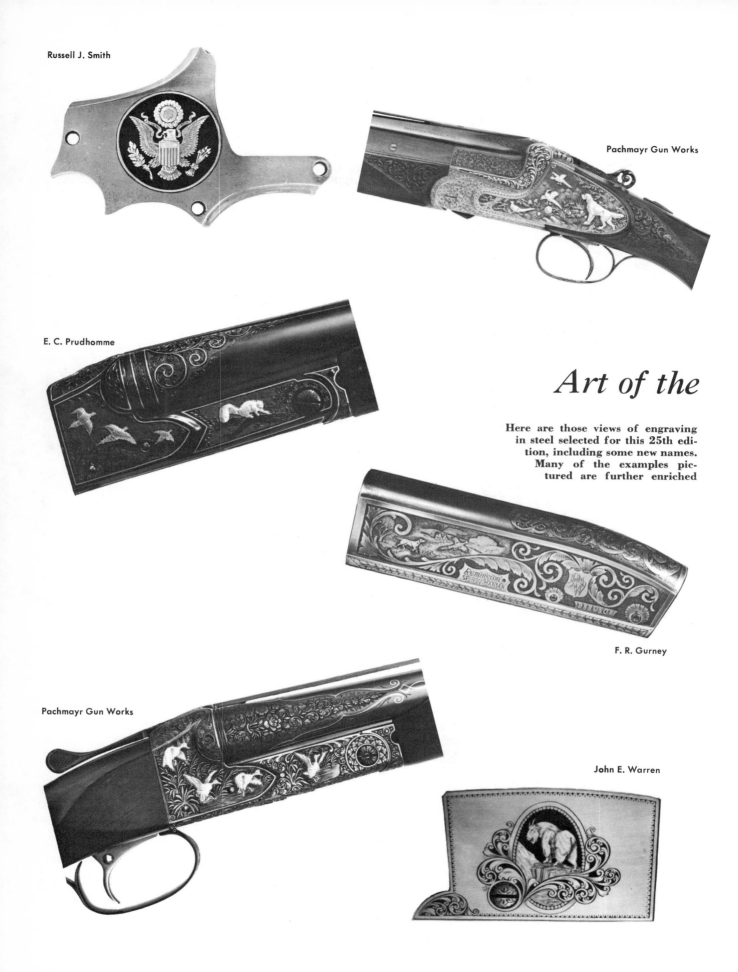

Russell J. Smith

Pachmayr Gun Works

E. C. Prudhomme

Art of the

Here are those views of engraving in steel selected for this 25th edition, including some new names. Many of the examples pictured are further enriched

F. R. Gurney

Pachmayr Gun Works

John E. Warren

Russell J. Smith

Pachmayr Gun Works

Engraver

with inlays of gold and silver, some in relief, some not.

The addresses of the artists displayed here will be found in our Directory of the Arms Trade.

Arnold Griebel

John E. Warren

John E. Warren

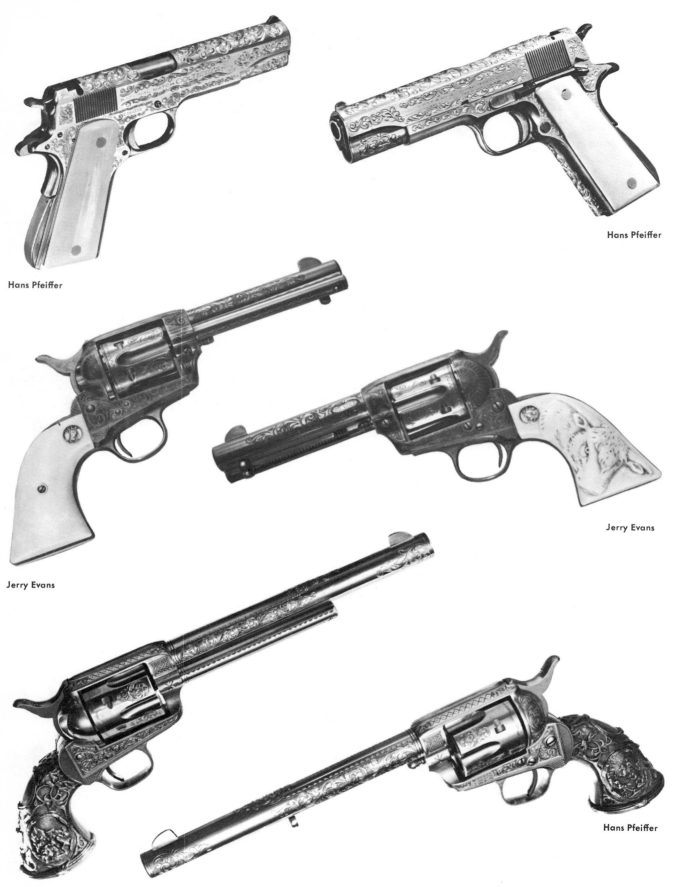

Hans Pfeiffer

Hans Pfeiffer

Jerry Evans

Jerry Evans

Hans Pfeiffer

Hans Pfeiffer

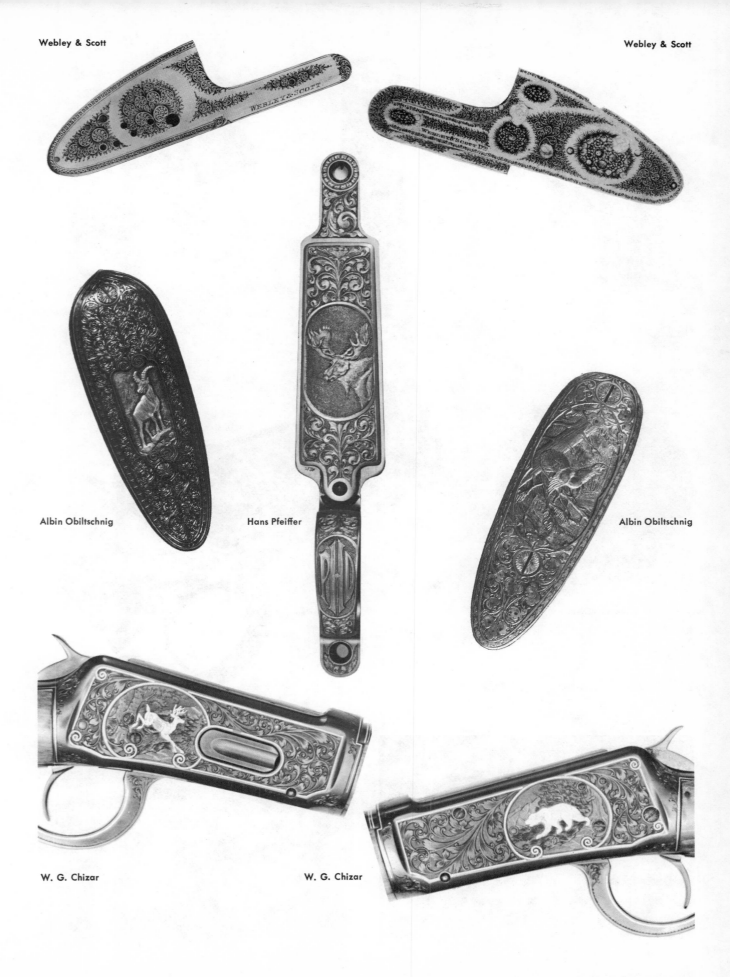

Albin Obiltschnig

Hans Pfeiffer

Albin Obiltschnig

W. G. Chizar

W. G. Chizar

Hans Pfeiffer

Bill Dyer

Hans Pfeiffer

Lynton McKenzie

John E. Warren

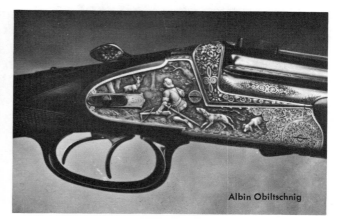

Albin Obiltschnig

Albin Obiltschnig

STANDARD BALLISTICS tables fall considerably short of telling riflemen all they want to know about the performance of their favorite cartridge, and this is especially true where the longer ranges are concerned. The pages of various magazines constantly admonish sportsmen that what a bullet does *out where the game is hit* is what counts. Yet such information in meaningful form is not so easy to find.

Tell the average hunter that his bullet has 1190 foot pounds of striking energy remaining at 300 yards, and what does it mean to him? He has a figure it's true, but will most likely have difficulty assessing its significance.

Perhaps he believes that kinetic energy ($\frac{1}{2}MV^2$) is not the true measure of a bullet's ability to down large game most reliably? If so, he'll be more interested in knowing its momentum $\frac{MV}{(700)}$, at a given range. But where does he find this?

for a different loading or a more powerful rifle.

For large game, where bullet weight and penetration are felt to be more important indexes of killing power than velocity, our column giving pounds-feet of momentum should fill one more informational void. In this regard it is not my intention here to argue the merits of this system of judging power as against the more usual foot-pounds of kinetic energy, but simply to present the figures for those who may want them. A comparison of the results obtained with these alternate methods may even furnish a basis for some animated discussions between readers.

Drop (bullet fall below the line of sight) can be most important if we are to score hits at ranges beyond that for which our rifle is sighted-in. This too has been given, as has the length of barrel on which ballistics of each cartridge are based.

The tables have been divided into

where Table I shows bullet strike at 300 and 500 yards when rifles are sighted for 200 yards, while Table II is based upon a 100-yard sighting common for the shorter woods hunting ranges, hence are projected only to 200 and 300 yards.

All calibers and all ranges could not be covered in our tables. For those who may wish to produce comparable data for some cartridge or load not shown, or for a particular range, this is how the calculated figures were arrived at.

(A) In Tables I and II, where the velocities of factory cartridges were available from published Remington or Winchester ballistics tables, they were used. In those instances where remaining velocity at 500 yards wasn't listed, it was necessary to first determine the ballistic coefficient (C) of the factory bullet, using the formula $C = \dfrac{X}{S(v)-S(V),}$ in which X is the base range of 300 yards expressed

Ye Compleate Exterior Ballistics

or

Retained Efficiency of Rifle Cartridges

by KEN WATERS

where does he find this?

Or maybe our rifleman would like to know how much his bullet has dropped out at 300 and 500 yards from a 200-yard zero? Remington-Peters tables give this data for certain selected loads, but not for all, and the Winchester-Western pamphlet lists only Mid-Range Trajectory heights, which are far less useful.

To provide interested readers with this much-needed information in ready-reference form, the author has constructed a comprehensive set of tables that obviate the necessity of referring to other sources. Where available, commercial data has been used, but in many instances it was found necessary to resort to computations to supply data on what is happening at typical game ranges. Particularly important are the several columns of new data that help answer the questions just posed. In order to give a clearer picture of retained velocity and energy an easily understood medium was needed, and percentages seemed the logical answer.

Knowing that only 50% of a bullet's initial velocity and 25% of its energy remains at, say, 500 yards, could influence a hunter's decision as to whether to attempt such a long shot, or perhaps make him realize the need

three sections: The first one covers factory ammunition capable of long-range performance; the second, those cartridges suitable for the shorter woods ranges; the third, some selected handloads in the more popular calibers. By this means a truer perspective of cartridge suitability can be gained, besides which bullet drop can be based upon the most practical sighting-in range in relation to velocity.

In using these tables, it is especially important that readers note carefully the range specified at the top of each column! The figures given are correct *only* for that range, and the ranges selected as typical for woods cartridges are different from those representative of long range loads. They cannot, therefore, be compared directly, either between our tables, or with those of others.

For example, in Table I (Long Range Loads), the figures for momentum are calculated for 300 yards, while in Table II (Woods Cartridges), momentum is taken at 100 yards. Elmer Keith's book, *Keith's Rifles for Large Game,* lists the momentum of several cartridges at the muzzle. Obviously, all three tables give differing values.

The same is true for bullet drop,

in feet (900), V is the muzzle velocity, "v" is the remaining velocity at range X (300 yards), and S(v) and S(V) are velocity functions from the Ingall's Ballistic Tables, (columns "u" and "Su" in his Table I). *Hatcher's Notebook** contains these tables, along with a clear explanation of their use in connection with this formula. It is highly recommended reading.

(B) Once the ballistic coefficient of a given bullet is known, we are then in a position to solve for remaining velocity at 500 yards by means of the equation $S(v) = S(V) + \dfrac{X}{C}$. Again the Ingall's Tables are used, interpolating where necessary, avoiding any need for higher math. Also, any range desired could be substituted for the 500 yards which we used, but it should be remembered that in these calculations, yards must *always* be changed to feet. Thus, 1500 was used for X, in place of 500 yards.

(C) Arriving at terminal velocities for handloads is far easier if you use Hornady bullets and consult the ballistic tables in the Hornady Handbook. Those tables list the ballistic coefficient (C) for each Hornady bul-

---

*1957 and later editions only. Publ. by Stackpole Co., Harrisburg, Penna.

let, thereby saving Step A, and by knowing the muzzle velocity of your load, it is a simple matter of reading remaining velocity at a number of selected ranges *directly* from the tables. The work of performing Step B is thus avoided also. For most accurate results, muzzle velocity should be determined by the use of a chronograph.

(D) The percentage of retained velocity, at any given range, is obtained by simple long division. Divide the remaining velocity (v), by the muzzle velocity (V), and your answer will be remaining velocity out at the farther distance expressed as a percentage of the original, considered as 100% at muzzle.

(E) Exactly the same procedure is followed to find the percentage of bullet energy remaining at stated ranges. Simple judgment will tell a hunter that although his cartridge may have plenty of energy at 100 and even 200 yards for the game sought, a retained energy figure of 50% at 300 yards means that at that range it only has half as much power as it had at the muzzle, and is therefore marginal. A figure of 25% or 30% at 500 yards generally means that it is inadequate or nearly so for any but the smallest animals.

(F) Regardless of whether you prefer the old and still correct term "Momentum," or the recently applied title "Potence," you'll be multiplying bullet weight (in grains) times velocity (in feet per second) at the desired range, then dividing by 7000 (the number of grains in a pound) in order to arrive at the number of pounds-feet (p/f) momentum developed by a bullet. There's nothing new about this, except that momentum figures given in previous tables have almost always been calculated at the muzzle rather than at typical game ranges. In our tables momentum is shown at 300 yards for long-range cartridges, and at 100 yards for woods calibers. You can do this for any range you wish just by knowing the remaining velocity at that range and using *it* as a multiplier, rather than muzzle velocity.

For example, if you wished to know the momentum (M) of the 100-gr. 6mm Remington factory bullet at 100 yards (not given in our table), you would look up the velocity listed in Remington tables for that range (2920 fps), multiply by bullet weight (100 grains), and divide by 7000.

$$M = \frac{mv}{7000} = \frac{100 \times 2920}{7000}$$
$$= \frac{292000}{7000} = 41.7 \text{ p/f (pounds-feet).}$$

Nothing difficult about that, is there? Still, if you're satisfied with the ranges we've based our calculations on, you won't even need to do that much arithmetic.

Reduced to the simplest possible form of explanation, it may be noted that in the kinetic energy formula, velocity is *squared,* whereas in arriving at momentum figures, velocity is used as a straight multiple. Obviously then, kinetic energy places greater emphasis on velocity, while bullet weight assumes equal importance as a factor of momentum. You take it from there and use either one that suits you. Our tables give *both* for purposes of comparison.

(G) A recommended application of the data in these tables is the comparison of light and heavy bullet loads in the same cartridge. Hunters often debate the relative merits of various bullets within a single caliber for some specific purpose. Say a 6mm Remington owner wonders if the faster 80-gr. load is preferable to the 100-gr. for antelope at long range.

Table A provides the answer. Although the 80-gr. factory load in 6mm starts out 350 fps faster than the 100-gr., the latter has higher retained velocity and energy at 300 yards, while at 500 long steps the 100-gr. bullet is traveling 190 fps faster and possesses over half-again as much striking energy (870 vs. 570). Another way to say it is that the 100-gr. retains 38% of its original energy, as compared to 26% for the 80-gr. Obviously, the 100-gr. load would be the better choice.

The same thing applies to the 300 Winchester Magnum, where the 180-gr. load retains 45% of its energy at 500 yards as against only 31% for the 150-gr. That this trend in favor of heavy bullets can be overdone, however, is illustrated by the figures given for the 338 Winchester Magnum, where the 300-gr. bullet is less efficient at long range than the 250-gr.

An interesting example of how a bullet with better ballistic coefficient, coupled with a suitable handload, can improve a cartridge's long range performance, is to be seen in the data for the 257 Roberts handload (Table III), versus that of the 257 factory load.

(H) Calculation of bullet drop at various ranges is far more complicated —too complicated to detail here. However, I have worked out a simple method which, while not precisely accurate, provides answers sufficiently close to serve the average hunter's purposes.

Let's assume we have a 30-06 rifle sighted in for 200 yards with the 180-gr. Remington Bronze Point factory load, and wish to know how much our bullet will drop below the line of sight at 500 yards:

(1) First we must find the *approximate* time of flight between the 200-yard point (our zero range) and 500 yards:

(2) In the Remington Ballistic Tables, look up the remaining velocities of this load at 200 and 500 yards: (2280 fps @ 200; 1730 fps @ 500).

(3) Add the velocity at 500 yards to that at 200 and divide the total by 2.

This gives *average* velocity of the bullet over the last 300 yards of flight. Example:

$$1730 + 2280 = \frac{4010}{2} = 2005 \text{ fps average.}$$

(4) Since velocity is expressed in feet per second, we'll change this distance of 300 yards to feet, calling it 900.

(5) Now divide 900 feet by the average velocity, 2005 fps:

$$\frac{900}{2005} = .448 \text{ seconds.}$$

Our answer is the approximate decimal part of a second it takes this bullet to travel the distance (time of flight) between the 200- and 500-yard points.

(6) Knowing the time of flight (T), only one step further is required, using our abbreviated method, to determine the amount of bullet drop (D) at 500 yards from the 200-yard zero. During the first second of flight after leaving the muzzle, a bullet falls 16.1 feet, but since modern high velocity bullets take considerably less than a second to cover 500 yards, the fall below the line of sight will be only a fraction of that amount of drop.

To simplify things, we have developed an easily-worked formula in which the time of flight between our 200-yard zero and the target at 500 yards is *squared,* and then multiplied by a "constant" based upon the effect of gravity over the intervening 300 yards. Including a conversion from feet to inches, this constant works out to *260* at 500-yards. Thus, in our example:

$$D = 260 \times T^2$$
$$= 260 \times .448 \times .448$$
$$= 52.18 \text{ inches, or } 52.2''.$$

By our rough formula, then, we have come up with a bullet drop of 52.2″ at 500 yards. Again consulting the Remington tables, we find that the correct amount of drop at that range for the 180-ga. 30-06 Bronze Point is given as 52.7″. I believe that's close enough for all practical purposes. It should be pointed out, however, that our "constant" of 260, is *not* applicable in figuring the amount of drop at ranges other than 500 yards. A different constant is necessary for each range in relation to sighting-in distance, and here are some:

At 500 yards from 200-yard zero = 260.
At 300 yards from 200-yard zero = 456.
At 300 yards from 100-yard zero = 227.
At 200 yards from 100-yard zero = 307.

Neither the caliber of your rifle nor the bullet's weight or shape need be considered in this final computation since they have already been taken into account in the time of flight. Simply substitute the time of flight figures for your cartridge in this formula, and you should be able to calculate the amount of drop below the line of sight at these ranges without any difficulty. ●

TABLE I — Long Range Factory Cartridges

Cartridge	Bullet	Velocity yards Muzzle	300	500	% Retained MV 300	500	Energy Yards Muzzle	300	500	% Retained ME 300	500	p/f Momentum 300	Drop/Ins. 200-yd. Zero 300	500	Barrel lgth./ins.
243 Win.	80 HP	3450	2330	1735	69	50	2115	965	535	46	25	26.6	6.3	40.5	26
243 Win.	100 PSP	3070	2320	1940	76	63	2090	1190	835	57	40	33.1	6.9	42.0	26
6mm Rem.	80 HP	3540	2400	1790	68	50	2220	1018	570	46	26	27.4	6.0	38.3	26
6mm Rem.	100 PSP	3190	2420	1980	76	62	2260	1300	870	58	38	34.6	6.5	38.7	26
250 Savage	100 ST	2820	1870	1390	66	49	1760	775	429	44	24	26.7	10.3	67.6	24
257 Roberts	100 ST	2900	1920	1424	66	49	1870	820	450	44	24	27.4	9.6	63.7	24
6.5mm Rem Mag.	120 PSP	3030	2230	1790	74	59	2450	1330	850	54	34	38.2	7.5	45.4	20
264 Win. Mag.	140 PSP	3200	2480	2100	78	66	3180	1910	1370	60	43	49.6	6.1	36.7	26
270 Win.	130 BP	3140	2400	1980	76	63	2840	1660	1130	58	40	44.5	6.5	39.7	24
270 Win.	150 PP	2900	2160	1746	74	60	2800	1550	1016	55	36	46.3	7.9	49.4	24
280 Rem.	125 PSP	3190	2320	1840	73	58	2820	1490	940	53	33	41.4	6.7	41.5	24
280 Rem.	150 PSP	2900	2250	1870	78	64	2800	1680	1160	60	41	48.2	7.8	45.5	24
284 Win.	125 PP	3200	2310	1819	72	56	2840	1480	918	52	32	41.3	6.8	43.3	24
284 Win.	150 PP	2900	2160	1746	74	60	2800	1550	1016	55	36	46.3	7.9	49.4	24
7mm Rem Mag.	125 PSP	3430	2450	1900	71	55	3260	1660	1010	51	31	43.8	5.7	36.2	26
7mm Rem. Mag.	150 PSP	3260	2450	1990	75	61	3540	1990	1310	56	37	52.5	6.3	37.7	26
7mm Rem. Mag.	175 PSP	3070	2430	2060	79	67	3660	2290	1640	63	49	60.8	6.7	39.0	26
300 Savage	150 PSP	2670	1890	1480	71	55	2370	1190	729	50	31	40.5	10.7	64.7	24
300 Savage	180 PSP	2370	1770	1445	75	61	2240	1250	833	56	37	45.5	13.4	72.5	24
308 Win.	150 PSP	2860	2050	1590	72	56	2730	1400	840	51	31	43.9	8.5	53.7	24
308 Win.	180 PSP	2610	1970	1613	75	62	2720	1540	1039	57	38	50.7	11.2	58.9	24
30-06 Spfld.	150 BP	2970	2240	1820	75	61	2930	1670	1100	57	38	48.0	7.5	45.7	24
30-06 Spfld.	180 BP	2700	2080	1730	77	64	2910	1730	1190	60	41	53.5	8.5	52.7	24
300 H&H Mag.	180 PSP	2920	2220	1830	76	63	3400	1970	1340	58	39	57.1	7.6	45.5	26
300 H&H Mag.	150 PSP	3400	2430	1890	71	56	3850	1970	1190	51	31	52.1	6.1	37.7	26
300 Win. Mag.	180 PSP	3070	2440	2060	79	67	3770	2380	1700	63	45	62.7	6.9	38.9	26
338 Win. Mag.	200 PP	3000	2170	1714	72	57	4000	2090	1304	52	33	62.0	7.8	49.4	25
338 Win. Mag.	250 ST	2700	1940	1531	72	57	4050	2090	1300	52	32	69.3	9.7	61.2	25
338 Win. Mag.	300 PP	2450	1690	1308	69	53	4000	1900	1140	48	29	72.4	12.7	81.3	25
375 H&H Mag.	270 SP	2740	1990	1620	73	59	4500	2370	1570	53	35	76.8	9.8	56.0	25
375 H&H Mag.	300 ST	2550	1830	1449	72	57	4330	2230	1395	52	32	78.4	10.9	69.2	25

KEY: HP = Hollow Point   ST = Silver Tip   PP = Power Point
      PSP = Pointed Soft Point   BP = Bronze Point   SP = Soft Point

TABLE II — Woods Factory Cartridges

Cartridge	Bullet	Velocity yards Muzzle	100	200	% Retained MV 100	200	Energy yards Muzzle	100	200	% Retained ME 100	200	p/f Momentum 100	Drop/Ins. (100-yd. Zero) 200	300	Barrel lgth./ins.
30-30 Win.	150 SP	2410	1960	1620	81	67	1930	1280	875	66	45	42.0	8.3	29.5	26
30-30 Win.	170 SP	2220	1890	1630	85	73	1860	1350	1000	73	54	45.9	8.2	29.6	26
32 Win. Spcl.	170 SP	2280	1920	1630	84	71	1960	1390	1000	71	51	46.6	8.5	29.8	26
303 British	180 SP	2540	2300	2090	91	82	2580	2120	1750	82	68	59.1	5.8	19.0	26
35 Rem.	200 SP	2100	1710	1390	81	66	1950	1300	855	67	44	48.9	10.9	39.4	22
358 Win.	200 ST	2530	2210	1910	87	75	2840	2160	1610	76	57	63.1	6.5	21.9	22
358 Win.	250 ST	2250	2010	1780	89	79	2810	2230	1760	79	63	71.8	7.7	25.5	24
350 Rem. Mag.	200 PSP	2710	2410	2130	89	79	3260	2570	2000	79	61	68.9	5.1	18.0	20
350 Rem. Mag.	250 PSP	2410	2190	1980	91	82	3220	2660	2180	83	68	78.2	6.4	21.5	20
44 Rem. Mag.	240 SP	1750	1360	1110	78	63	1630	985	655	60	40	46.6	17.5	64.5	18½
444 Marlin	240 SP	2400	1845	1410	76	59	3070	1815	1060	59	35	63.3	9.6	36.7	24
458 Win. Mag.	510 SP	2130	1840	1600	86	75	5140	3830	2900	75	56	134.1	9.2	32.1	25

TABLE III — Handloaded Cartridges

Cartridge	*Bullet Grs. powder	Velocity yards Muzzle	300	500	% Retained MV 300	500	Energy yards Muzzle	300	500	% Retained ME 300	500	p/f Momentum 300	Drop/Ins. (200-yd. Zero) 300	500	Barrel lgth./ins.
243 Win.	100 47.0 N205	3120	2366	1936	76	62	2157	1243	832	58	39	33.8	6.8	40.4	26
6mm Rem.	100 48.0 N205	3157	2398	1968	76	62	2208	1276	858	58	39	34.3	6.7	38.9	26
257 Roberts	100 48.0 N205	3092	2310	1870	75	60	2116	1183	776	56	37	33.0	7.1	41.6	24
264 Win. Mag.	140 63.0 #4831	3177	2520	2132	79	67	3132	1974	1413	63	45	50.4	5.9	35.6	26
270 Win.	130 59.0 N205	3156	2425	2010	77	64	2869	1697	1166	59	41	45.0	6.5	37.8	26
270 Win.	150 56.5 N205	2990	2352	1983	79	66	2978	1842	1310	62	44	50.4	6.8	40.3	26
280 Win.	139 58.5 N205	3020	2308	1904	76	63	2815	1642	1119	58	40	45.8	6.7	41.0	26
284 Win.	139 59.0 #4831	3014	2302	1900	76	63	2804	1635	1113	58	40	45.7	6.7	41.1	24
7mm Rem. Mag.	154 68.0 #4831	3160	2494	2108	79	67	3406	2127	1522	62	45	54.9	5.9	35.3	26
308 Win.	165 48.0 H380	2704	2030	1650	75	61	2680	1510	997	56	37	47.9	9.1	55.5	26
308 Win.	180 47.0 H380	2624	2040	1700	78	65	2752	1663	1154	60	42	52.5	9.1	55.6	26
30-06 Spfld.	165 57.0 #4350	2840	2142	1748	75	62	2955	1681	1119	57	38	50.5	7.8	48.8	24
30-06 Spfld.	180 57.0 #4350	2742	2136	1788	78	65	3004	1823	1276	61	42	54.9	8.4	49.6	24
300 H&H Mag.	180 67.0 #4350	2927	2293	1928	78	66	3424	2101	1485	61	43	59.0	7.2	42.8	24
300 Win. Mag.	180 75.0 N205	3071	2416	2036	79	66	3769	2333	1656	62	44	62.1	6.5	38.4	24

*Hornady Spire-Point bullets used in all loads listed above. If different bullets are used, figures will change.

Scopes & Mounts 1970

by BOB BELL

*A full and comprehensive report, both critical and commending,
with a backward glance at the glassware of years gone by.*

DID YOU EVER stop to wonder how many pieces of game have been bagged with scope-sighted rifles in the last 25 years—which is to say, since the first edition of the GUN DIGEST? Obviously, there's no way of knowing for certain, but I've got a hunch that if I had a penny for each one I'd be on the list of immediately retired fellows—those guys who can forget about working and devote all their time to such useful pursuits as hunting, shooting and writing about the same. Unfortunately I see no prospects of collecting that penny-per-piece, so I'm limited to spending scarcely half my time with a gun in my hand, but we can dream, can't we?

Twenty-five years is a good chunk out of anyone's life, and a lot of changes can occur in that period. Consider scopes and mounts, the subjects of this review. In GD-1, only five scope makers were mentioned: Fecker, who made the 1½", 1⅛" and ¾" target scopes and his externally-mounted Small Game scope in three low powers; Litschert, with his Models A and B target scopes and Model C varmint glass, plus attachments for raising low power hunting scopes to 6x or 8x normally, though one booster went to 15x; Mossberg's No. RFI Automatic Range Finder 4x for 22 rimfires and No. 5M4 4x for Hornet class loads; Lyman's Super-Target-spot, Targetspot, Junior Targetspot, M438 4x Field Scope, and the Alaskan All-Weather 2½x; and Weaver, who then produced the 440, 330, 29S (my first scope, obtained in the late '30s and still in my possession), 329, 333, 335 and 1x shotgun scope.

Mounts listed were Weaver's T (bracket) and B (bridge) models, Redfield's Senior and Junior, Stith's Streamline and the similar Install-It-Yourself version, Mossberg's side and top models, and Griffin & Howe's single- and double-lever models, the latter also available with micrometer windage adjustment.

A check of the catalog pages in this 1st edition will give some idea of how interest in optical sighting instruments has grown in the past quarter-century. It also indicates some of the changes by showing which of the 1944 scopes have disappeared; for instance, all of the Weavers listed above, which of course were replaced by the popular K models, which in themselves have been upgraded a number of times since their introduction just after WW II, the Alaskan and small Targetspots, all of the Feckers . . .

GD 1 also ran a 3-page article, "Scope Dope," by Milton M. Izdal, O.D., which gave a good idea of the basic principles of scope design, written in language easily understood by the layman. In following editions, other aspects of this field were covered by Claude Parmalee, Warren Page, Col. Townsend Whelen, Bill Schumaker, and others, including the present writer.

There were a few other scopes around when the first GUN DIGEST came out. One of the best early hunting models was the Noske, now long gone. Others appeared and have disappeared since. Among these were the G-88, a 2½x from Maxwell Smith Co. of Los Angeles; the original 2½x

Texan from Norman-Ford of Tyler, Texas, called by Jack O'Connor "an Alaskan with a southern accent," the Stith Bear Cubs (which evolved through the Kollmorgens into the Redfields); various Leupolds; the Lyman Challenger and Wolverines; the Boone Scope, a small prism design, and others.

Mounts came and went too. The Stith Streamline, which had a strong solid tube enclosing the front end of the scope and binding it to the barrel, was to my eyes the best looking mount ever made, but it has been unavailable for years, reportedly because varying scope dimensions made it impossible to mass produce this item. I have a couple of these on rifles that I wouldn't part with. That tube really protected the objective end of the scope. Then there were the Stith Master, Bengert, Forster, Fischer, Miller Kodiak Dreamount, MyKrom, and Weather-Matic (which swung the scope aside when a lever was worked on top-ejecting models), to name a few. Some of these were real Rube Goldberg creations, both in appearance and action. Nevertheless, most seemed to work and I expect that many hunters still are using them. Possibly some are yet available commercially, though we've seen no recent literature on them.

(For the record, the German-made Zeiss and Hensoldt hunting scopes scope were also available before WW II. The Noske noted by Bob Bell was made in the U.S. by Rudolph Noske—the first really successful big game glass to be native made. In the same period Adolph Niedner had made a few quick-detchable side mounts for scopes; in one version the removable element slid on and off tapered dovetails, running fore-and-aft—a valuable system, because with every shot the scope got tighter.

Niedner had, in fact, made at least one telescope—in target type—for **Dr. F. W. Mann** sometime before the Big War, WW I, that is. Your editor has owned this Niedner-Mann two-diameter tube, 16x scope for many years. It came with one of the last rifles the grand old man made, a fairly heavy muzzleloader for target shooting—false muzzle, a wide array of tools, moulds, etc.—J.T.A.)

There have been notable trends in scopes during the last quarter-century. One is the general increase in size. The early Weaver line was based on ¾″ tubes, while the Alaskan, Texan, G-88, 2½x Stith, Leupold and others went ⅞″, or thereabouts. This larger diameter was close to ideal for a 2½x glass, giving plenty of light and a good size exit pupil, but when Weaver went to a full inch tube with the K2.5 and K4 (the latter having a further enlarged objective section) the style which endures yet today was set. I've often thought that this size, understandable with the K4, was used with the K2.5 just to simplify materials inventory, etc.

For a time some odd-size tubes, particularly the 26mm diameter (1.023″), were used—on the Lyman Challenger, the Stith Bear Cubs and the Kollmorgens, primarily—but this aberration soon vanished in the U.S., though many foreign scopes are made with such minute variations. It complicated the mount inventory and gave little in return.

A straight inch tube gives enough light for most hunting, even on a 4x scope, and for a time Stith offered one of these (apparently Weaver-made) as the design made it easy to use their Streamline mount. But the trend was to ever-larger lenses and eventually an objective of about 32mm, which gives an 8mm exit pupil, became standard for 4x scopes.

Other trends were the regular increases in magnifications offered in response to the demands for "better seeing ability" as shooters grew more scope educated; the importation of European- and Japanese-made scopes at many price levels (and corresponding values); the offering of short, hunting-type varmint scopes of medium power, such as the Edwards V model, Weaver K8 and K10, Unertl Vulture, Bushnell Scopemaster and Lyman Wolverine; and perhaps most important, the development of variable power scopes.

The Variable Appears

Variables had been made for many years in Europe but to most of us

Bob Bell (left) and Don Lewis look at some of Bell's guns. Bell holds his old 348 Win. M71 with 2½x Texan, 6″ Lee Dot, Stith Streamline mount. Lewis holds old standard M52 Win., Unertl 1½″ 18x.

here they were brand new and fascinating when we got our first glimpse around 1950. Hunters spent countless hours in gun shops, squinting through one scope or another and watching the image magically recede or come closer as he twisted the adjustment rings.

Bausch & Lomb's little 2½-4x Balvar was one of the first here, and a fine scope it was, but neither it nor the Weaver KV, a 2¾-5x model that had its power switching mechanism under a cap on the adjustment turret, attracted a large following, if those few seen in the field were any indication. But the B&L Balvar 8 did! A 2½-8x which appeared about 1956, this optically beautiful, medium-size scope seemed to be what American hunters had been waiting for. Not everyone was happy with the adjustable mount (necessitated by the Balvar's lack of internal windage and elevation machinery), but no one faulted the scope's ruggedness or its optics. It was, and is, an outstanding glass.

Many other manufacturers soon produced variables of similar power spread, but most had one annoying factor in common—the apparent increase in reticle size when power was increased. Actually, the reticle subtended the same at all powers as image size went up with magnification, but it didn't seem that way to the shooter. Bausch & Lomb had avoided this in the Balvar by use of a tapered crosshair (actually a deposit of metallic iconel on a plane lens) which was smaller in diameter at the intersection than at any other

point and, because the outer edges of the field disappeared as power was increased, cutting off the thicker portions, it appeared to be the same thickness at all magnifications. Other manufacturers, using regular metallic crosswires, had what appeared to be a coarse reticle at the top setting and one that almost disappeared at bottom setting.

This occurred because the reticle was installed in the focal plane of the objective lens unit, thus was ahead of the power-switching apparatus and varied directly with it. The obvious solution was to move the reticle into the focal plane of the eyepiece, where it would be behind that apparatus and not be magnified along with the target. Redfield did this in 1963 and the effect was to make the reticle appear smaller at top power, as was desired for long range shooting, and coarse at low power, which made it ideal for fast work at close range when the power was cranked down. The best of all possible worlds! as Voltaire might have said had he been with us a scant decade ago.

All of which brings us up to the present, though we fully realize that many excellent scopes—the legendary Zeiss and Hensoldts, for example—have received short shrift here, despite the fact that these German models were the direct antecedents of our scopes of today. But as always space is limited, and over the 800 miles stretching from Chicago I can hear Ye Ol' Ed bellowing, "%!#&*$, Bob, c'mon, get with it, tell 'em what's new!"

So here it is.

⊕ **American Import Co.** A half-dozen L. M. Dickson "Signature" scopes are offered by this San Francisco importer, the latest being the V20/154, a 1½-4x variable with unenlarged objective. Priced at $39.95, it fits the general design of switch-power scopes gaining favor with average range hunters, giving a 50-plus foot field at bottom power and 28 feet at top. All these Dicksons—2½, 4, 6, 2½-7 and 3-9 powers, in addition to the V20/154—are built on 1-inch tubes and all have crosswire reticles, with a post optional in the 2½x and 4x. Eye relief is about 3″ in each. A fair number of these are seen in the Pennsylvania deer woods, and they seem to give good service.

⊕ **Anderson & Co.** makes the useful Storm King and Storm Queen lens covers, the former having watch-crystal type lenses which may be aimed through for fast shots or swung aside on hinges if you have an extra mount. Made in 12 sizes to fit most popular scopes, $3.45. Storm Queens are offered in full caps or end caps, with a connecting rubber band. These can be flipped off, using the band's elasticity to free them, for instant scope use, $2.95.

⊕ **Bausch & Lomb** has no new scopes or mounts this year, but does offer some new reticles for their fine Trophy scopes. According to product supervisor Howard Palmer, 7 reticles are now available—standard crosshair, post, dot and tapered crosshair (these 4 still offered in the older Custom scope line), plus the new Dualine, Taper-Dot and Rangefinder.

The Dualine is similar to a reticle available from numerous others and consists of 4 thin posts which become thinner crosshairs at the intersection. This design is gaining popularity rapidly, as it combines the best features of both post and crosswires. The Rangefinder is essentially B&L's tapered crosshair with an additional set of horizontal crosshairs in the upper part of the field. Knowing the average size of the game being hunted and the distance between these crosswires in minutes-of-angle, it's possible to compute the animal's distance with a good degree of accuracy—always assuming you have a clear view of the animal, a rest which permits precise use of the crosshairs, and so on (problems which accrue to all makes of scopes using any kind of reticle rangefinder).

The Taper-Dot is also a variation on the familiar tapered crosshair. In this reticle, the crosshairs don't meet at the center. Instead, at the point where their intersection normally would be, a small dot is located. This dot measures 1¼ MOA in the Balfor B4x and 1½-½ MOA in the Balvar B8 variable, the only scopes in which this reticle is currently available.

Dualine, Rangefinder and Taper-Dot reticles are each $5 extra, the

The latest Buehler mount is made for the Thompson/Center Contender handgun.

Consult our Directory pages for the location of firms or individuals mentioned.

Dualine being offered in the Balfor B4x and Balvar B8, and the Rangefinder in the Balvar B8 only.

Bausch & Lomb made one of the first variables in this country, a 2½-4x, but that's now gone. However, they still make a fine medium-power variable, the Balvar 5. This 2½-5x scope gets little mention for some reason or another—probably because the 2½-8x is so popular—but it's an excellent choice for big game, giving all the magnification spread needed, while the scope itself is only about the size of a regular 4x. Actually, this is a zoom arrangement, so you can have any power between 2½x and 5x, if needed. The Balvar 5 has no internal adjustments, so it requires a movable mount such as the B&L Custom.

⊕ **Browning Arms.** Two new scopes have been added to the Browning line —a 5x "Wide Angle" having a 30-foot field, a length just under a foot, a weight of less than 10 oz. and a choice of CH, post, 2-minute dot or 4 Plex reticle. This glass has an amazing resemblance to a line of telescopes built in Colorado! Price, $74.95, plus $10 for dot. The second is a 3-9x of high quality, listing at $109.95. For the fella who likes consistency, these make fitting sights on the fine Browning rifles, and you can tie them together with Browning bridge-type mounts. Still offered are the popular 2-7x and, for rimfires, the ¾″-tube 4x, a handsome, sturdily built model.

⊕ **Buehler, Inc.,** has for several decades been making strong bridge mounts for most popular rifles, and some years back, when scoping handguns became

the thing with a lot of shooters, Buehler began accommodating them too. Latest handgun mount is their Code TC, for the T/C Contender single shot, at $11.25. I've never liked the looks of a scope on a revolver, but I don't mind one on the Contender, probably because of this gun's somewhat futuristic appearance regardless of the sighting equipment. There's no doubt that a low-power scope is a big help for the comparatively long range shooting that this gun will handle when chambered for the 357, 22 Jet or other high-speed loads.

Buehler mounts will handle all American scopes, of course, and one length or another permits considerable adjustment in eye relief position; many of the foreign scopes with odd tube diameters also can be fitted with Buehler rings. Currently, they're made in 26mm, 26½mm, 27mm and 28mm diameters, often in several heights. So, if you have an old Zeiss or Hensoldt that you never got aboard a rifle because of its non-American-standard size, give a thought to Buehler.

⊕ **Bushnell Optical Corp.** With three complete lines of big game scopes— the Scopechief IVs, Custom Ms and Banners—plus smaller versions for rimfires and the handgun Phantoms, it's obvious that Bushnell has a glass sight for about everyone. Their Command Post has proven to be a highly useful reticle, one that many hunters have come to prefer for varied-light use. Still, someone out in Pasadena apparently has a thing about seeing where he's shooting under miserable

Bushnell 4x Scope Chief V with battery powered "Lite Site."

Bushnell Scope Chief IV, a 1x shotgun scope.

conditions, for the latest item is a new scope, the 4x Scopechief V, with the new "Lite-Site" reticle. Used normally, it's simply a good scope of standard specs with conventional crosswires. But when you gotta shoot and it's simply too dark to see the reticle, you can switch on a battery-powered light which is seen as a white dot at the crosswire intersection—and instantly your aiming point is visible against the darkest target! Oughta work even against black bears in a coal mine, if they hang out in such places. Seriously, I can think of more than one occasion when it would have been darn handy to have such an arrangement, and I have a hunch many hunters are going to give this Lite-Sited Scopechief a whirl. Various small filters are furnished, too, giving the user a choice of color shades instead of white light. The replaceable battery, incidentally, is a #640, 1.4 volt. Scope price, $69.50.

Also new from Bushnell this year is a 1x shotgun/rifle scope with 92-foot field and 6-inch eye relief. With a constantly-centered, PCH or Command Post reticle and length under 10 inches, it's of handy size, except for a large eyepiece (1.8″ diameter) which might make mounting bothersome on a gun whose bolt comes rearward under the glass during operation. But on the usual pump or auto shotgun, it should be no problem. $59.50.

The Banner line now boasts a 4-12x variable with adjustable objective unit ($64.50) and a straight 10x, which also can be range focused. For rimfire shooters, the Scopechief IV-M and

Custom M scopes are available with a mount to fit grooved-receiver 22s, while handgunners who like the Ruger auto can now fit a Phantom scope in Bushnell's All Purpose Dual mount at $5. This rig has two legs which fit hardened chrome-moly studs on the bottom and grip the Phantom's mount rail on top. As with any scoped handgun, the looks are somewhat Buck Rogerish, but it works.

A new spotting scope is the 20-45x Zoom Spacemaster II, a prismatic design with 60mm objective. A built-in baffle system has made the lens shield formerly used unnecessary. Price, $109, or $95 if wanted as a single 15x power, 20x standard or wide angle, 25x 40x or 60x.

Bushnell has just announced a new version of their good low-cost spotting scope, the Sentry II. This short (12⅝″) and compact prismatic scope has fully coated inner-shielded optics —no sunshade needed—and the objective lens is big at 50mm. A standard thread-mount boss attaches to a tripod, shooter's stand or car-window mount, and a 20x, 32x or 48x eyepiece may be ordered, and extra eyepieces ($19.50 ea.) are quickly interchanged. Cost with one eyepiece, $54.50.

⊕ **Conetrol** has expanded their line of mounts by adding the Gunnur grade, which fits neatly between the Custom—which is tops with this Texas outfit (and with many hunters too!)— and the Huntur line, which might be called their no-frills setup, though it is a solid, dependable mount.

The Gunnur grade, $25.85 complete with split rings, comes in three heights, bridge or two-piece base, for tubes of one inch, 26mm or 26½mm, split or solid rings. Dovetail bases are also available for certain rifles.

Whereas Conetrol's Custom mounts have a mirror finish, contoured edges and Nylok cone screws, and the Huntur line has non-reflecting finish, angular edges and no stud screws, the Gunnur sorta splits the difference with high-gloss finish, non-contoured edges and no stud screws in the rings.

For our new readers the Conetrol mount, a bridge design, is known for its sleek, no-bulge rings and a base which permits windage correction without projecting adjusting screws.

⊕ **Herter's, Inc.,** of Waseca, Minn., supplies an extensive number of outdoor items, including numerous "Hudson Bay Official Rifle Scopes." These are offered in all normal fixed powers from 2¾x to 8x, plus 3-9x and 4-12x variables; a long-eye relief 2x for Winchester lever actions, a 1½x handgun scope, 1x models for rifle and shotgun, plus several lower priced "Perfection" models of conventional design. The 4-12x, the most expensive at $59.95, is

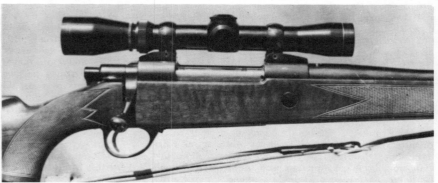

Conetrol "Gunnur" rings and SRS (short ring spacing) base on a Sako L-61R receiver.

fitted with a rangefinder/point of aim reticle—what looks like a fairly complicated collection of various size circles and horizontal lines grouped around the regular crosswire's intersection. Being a feller who prefers simple sighting arrangements, this sort of overawes me, but you might like it fine. A buck will get you the complete Herter catalog, wherein it's all explained at length. Herter's also has mounts of the Weaver type and an adjustable set of their own design.

⊕ **J. B. Holden Co.,** maker of the Ironsighter mount—sort of a set of figure 8 blocks, the top part holding the scope, the bottom hole to permit aiming with iron sights—is going strong after getting started a year or so ago, according to boss Jerry Holden. The Ironsighter is made for many popular rifles, and will soon be available for shotguns, 22s with grooved receivers, and for long eye relief scopes on the M94 Winchester. Basic list is $14.95, with rimfire models at $6.95, the M94 design at $19.95. About one-sixth of the Ironsighter's production goes to my home state of Pennsylvania, Holden says, which maybe gives some idea of our weather in deer season.

Holden Ironsighter scope mounting ring.

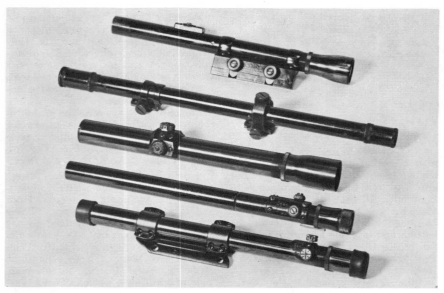

Some Scopes of Yesteryear

FROM TOP—Lyman Alaskan 2½x made *circa* 1938, Serial No. 2760, made without weatherproof caps, and shown in an Echo side mount. Mounted on a very early Model 70 standard sporter in 30-06 caliber (serial No. 3338), the combination shot at worst into 2 MOA with most factory loads, frequently bettered 1 inch with good handloads. Now, some 6,000 rounds later, much of it Frankford Arsenal corrosive-primer loads, the rifle still shoots into 2-3 inches despite frosty groove erosion from breech to muzzle, and lands rounded off for several inches ahead of the lead. A *good* barrel is a "thing of beauty and a joy forever." Second scope from the top is a Winchester of

2¾ power with external mounts, one of several found in England after WW II. While the click adjustments for windage and elevation are crude by today's standards, once on target it stays put and good groups can be had. Third in line is an early 4x K-series Weaver with flat-top tapered post reticle, also made without dust or weather caps. It has given excellent service in the field on several big game rifles.

The last scope but one is an early ¾" tube Weaver, the Model 330, an excellent small glass for its day; but this one has never been mounted—it is normally kept in its original black and silver carton. Last is also an

old Weaver, a 29S, held in a Weaver side mount. Though not as luminous as it might be, it was a popular scope at one time, being suitable even for high power rifles in spite of its rather delicate-appearing adjustment knobs. I used it on a Model 40 Savage bolt action in 300 Savage caliber for two or three seasons.

Pictured elsewhere on this page is the earliest American-made big game scope. Made by Rudolph Noske in California, *circa* 1930, the power is a low 2¼, the reticle a tapered post-with-crosswire, the post at top subtending a full 6 inches. The mount is one of Adolph Niedner's sliding dovetail side-attaching types, fitted to an early Super Grade Model 70 Winchester in 270 caliber. This rare Niedner mount was an excellent design—every shot locked it on more firmly—and of Niedner's typical superb construction and machining.

The long 2-diameter scope—with its handmade cowhide case—shown on this page may well be unique. It was made in 1913 by Adolph Niedner for Dr. Franklin W. Mann, the author of *From Muzzle to Target,* during the period when Niedner worked extensively on various gunsmithing-gunmaking projects for Mann. It is optically and mechanically a fine glass, even by today's standards, though it needs a good cleaning. Of 16 power, it is 22½ inches over-all, weighs 25 ounces with mounts and caps, and has ¼-minute micrometer adjustments for windage and elevation. The all-steel tube is marked, at the rear end, MANN-NIEDNER/1913/MALDEN, MASS./U.S.A. Range focus is obtained by rotating the eyepiece.

This early target scope came to me as one of many accessories with the last muzzle-loading heavy target rifle Adolph Niedner made—a precision instrument of 40 caliber, false-muzzled and in near-mint condition.

A full length view of the Model 70 Super Grade in 270 caliber carrying the Niedner-Noske scope-mount described above is also pictured. The full fancy-figured crotch walnut stock —with the then typical Winchester feather-grain fails to show here because the wood has darkened through heavy over-oiling. The trapped steel buttplate, the scope caps, the Lyman 48 sight and the silver grip cap—also with a small trap—are fully engraved.

J.T.A.

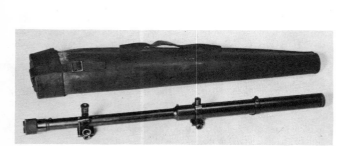

⊕ **Paul Jaeger** can do just about anything in the gunsmithing field that anyone might dream up. Among other things, he makes a Quick Detachable single-lever side mount which permits removal and replacement of a scope with insignificant, if any, change in zero. This is the sort of shenanigan I've never had any desire to try in the field, but a hunting pal does it routinely, claiming he adjusts his sighting equipment to the conditions. It's still a shock to see him unlatch his scope and stick it in the back of his hunting coat along with the Hershey bars, ham 'n cheese sandwiches, etc., and blithely amble down through the dripping woods with his old Remington. But he bags bucks and other assorted stuff, with both glass and iron sights, so the idea must work.

Jaeger makes bases to fit most popular rifles and rings in three heights and two diameters, one-inch and 26mm. The high mount allows use of iron sights. Price, $38.

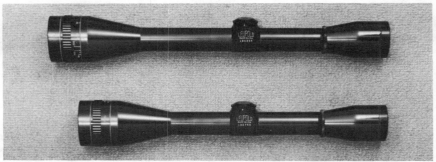

Leupold M8 Gold Ring 12x and 10x scopes.

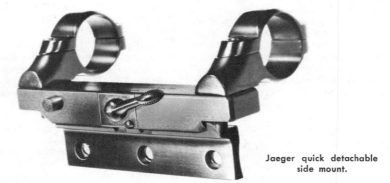

Jaeger quick detachable side mount.

⊕ **T. K. Lee Co.** installs the famous Tackhole Dot in many hunting and target scopes.

Lee Dots will be made in any size desired, but their recommendations (which, after 24 years of dot use we agree with completely) are:

2½x or 3x scope for general big game, 4"; brush shooting 5"-6"; 4x, 2"-3"; 6x for big game, 2"; 8x for varmints, ¾"; 12x, ½"; 1½-4½x, 9"-3"; 2-7x, 4½"-1½"; 3-9x, 3"-1"; 4-12x, 1½"-½". Dot coverage given is at 100 yards, proportionate at other ranges. The most important thing with dots is, don't get them too small. $7.50 to $15 for most American scopes.

⊕ **Leupold & Stevens** some time back sent along a pair of their M8 Golden Ring varmint scopes, one in 10x, the other 12x. Though advertised for quite a while, few have been seen. But they were worth waiting for. It's a pure joy to look through these scopes. Lenses are as clear as spring water in the Oregon high country where Leupolds are so often used, they don't leak—which also can be important in that region—and the adjustments are accurate. Though not particularly small or light (the 12x weighs 14 oz., is about 14½" long), this is not objectionable

on a varmint rifle, in fact may be something of a help as the weight adds to the rifle's inertia. I've had these on a number of rifles, including the 222, 22-250 and 243 (around here, it's rare for a given scope to stay on the same rifle more than a few weeks at a time, which often has me mumbling in my beard as I try to recall which is zeroed in for what when a sudden opportunity for chuck shooting arises), and found them ideal for the shooting suited to such cartridges. They'd also do for pronghorns and deer, in wide open country where most shots are at long range. We have quite a bit of this in northern Pennsylvania, where it's common to shoot at whitetails from one ridge to another across a narrow valley, total distance being maybe a quarter-mile or more. Fields of view are too small for close shooting on moving game, of course.

As expected from Leupold, the tubes are high-gloss black, to match today's rifles, with gold trim and distance markings on the adjustable objective unit.

One possible problem might be pointed out. The 10x and 12x are different lengths, the 12x having more distance between the adjustment housing and the enlarged objective bell. This makes it possible to mount the 12x on the Ruger Single Shot's integral scope rib and still have the scope project rearward far enough that eye relief is no problem. With the 10x, mounting rings have to bracket the adjustment turret, which moves the scope so far forward that many shooters won't be able to get close enough to see a full field. This

problem occurs only with this particular rifle. It would be helpful if the Ruger's scope rib had another set of notches to permit spacing the scope rings at different distances.

The other Leupolds, fixed powers of 2x (with long eye relief for the 94 Winchester), 3x, 4x and 7½x, and variables of 2-7x and 3-9x have been covered in earlier GUN DIGEST issues, so won't be gone into here in detail. All are top quality glasses. The Detacho Mount and Model 3 also are still available and made for many popular American rifles plus various Mausers.

⊕ **Lyman Gun Sight Corp.** As mentioned earlier, the fabled Lyman Alaskan All-Weather scope is gone, along with the Challenger and Wolverines, but except in a nostalgic sense there's no good reason to miss them. The All-American line, which stretches from 2½x to 10x, covers all hunting situations except possibly ultra-long range varmint busting, and for such specialists the Super-Targetspot is available. As a friend remarked, if he had to limit himself to only one make of scope he'd just as soon have Lyman as anything in the world.

In recent years I've been doing a lot of shooting with Lymans. The 3x on a Mannlicher-stocked 284 Mauser has proved fast and dependable on Pennsylvania whitetails in the woods, and the 10x on a heavy 22-250 has watched the final moments of many chucks and crows.

Every Lyman I've seen—and I've used all of the current line—has had sharp clear lenses and unusually accurate adjustments, though in most cases these have unusual values—³⁄₁₀" in the 10x, for instance.

For woods hunters, a simple tapered-post reticle is offered—no crosswire, unless wanted—and this would seem one of the finest choices for fast use in bad light in a low power scope. Few other makers offer this one. You can, of course, have a standard CH or dot if desired. Hunting scopes run from $49.50 to $84.50.

The Super-Targetspot, made in powers from 10x to 30x, has been a longtime favorite with all classes of shooters who demand precision. Its weight, 25 oz., is lighter than might be expected with a target scope. $135.

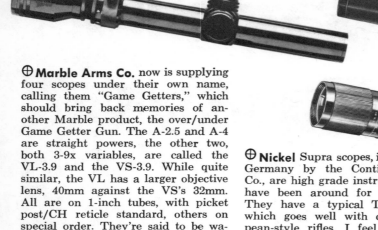

⊕ **Marble Arms Co.** now is supplying four scopes under their own name, calling them "Game Getters," which should bring back memories of another Marble product, the over/under Game Getter Gun. The A-2.5 and A-4 are straight powers, the other two, both 3-9x variables, are called the VL-3.9 and the VS-3.9. While quite similar, the VL has a larger objective lens, 40mm against the VS's 32mm. All are on 1-inch tubes, with picket post/CH reticle standard, others on special order. They're said to be waterproof, but samples have not yet arrived so we can't report on this. Prices, $39.50 to $69.50.

The Game Getter mount raises the scope a bit, allowing the use of iron sights through a tunnel in the base. It's currently available for most modern Remington high-powers, the Ruger 44 Magnum, Savage 110, 99 and 24V, Weatherby, Winchester 70, 88 and 100, Marlin 62 and 336, Mossberg, Browning, H&R and FN Mausers. $14.95.

⊕ **Marlin Firearms Co.** has for some years been marketing their "Plus Power" scopes, often in a package deal with their rifles. Two new ones are out this year, the M850, a 2-5x big game scope, and the M275, a ¾"-tube 4x for rimfires, which sells for $10.

Bill Clede sent along an 850 for testing, and an interesting little scope it is. Just over 10" long, it has an unenlarged objective, ¼-minute internal adjustments, weighs 11 oz., and has a field of 50 feet at bottom power, about 17 at 5x.

An interesting item offered in all Marlin big game scopes is their Tri-Post reticle—three heavy posts, one from each side and the bottom. This is practically identical to a design popular in Germany in years past... and maybe still... though these Marlins are built in Japan. There was a time when most Americans, myself included, scorned such an arrangement. I guess we felt we wanted to aim within a sixteenth-inch of some exact spot on that buck bouncing through the dripping hemlocks, and a coarse reticle like this wouldn't serve. Well, experience has shown that fine crosswires won't either, for the simple reason that they're too often invisible under typical shooting conditions. But this Tri-Post isn't invisible, *nohow*, and for the guy who lugs his Marlin lever action into close range deer or bear cover, this rig will be hard to beat. Scope price, $39.95; Marlin High Power mount, $6.95; less when bought with some Marlin guns.

⊕ **Nickel** Supra scopes, imported from Germany by the Continental Arms Co., are high grade instruments which have been around for a long time. They have a typical Teutonic look, which goes well with certain European-style rifles, I feel. They're offered with both w. and e. adjustments, or just with elevation alone, and in either steel or light metal tubes. Some models have a dovetail mounting rib. Lenses are coated, and a special Diflex coating, claimed to be superior to the standard method, is available. Some of these Supras have very large objective lenses, which gives them good light-gathering characteristics. In combination with one of the coarse reticles (10 different designs are available, to fit many different conditions), they should be very good for use in dim light.

⊕ **Pacific Gunsight Co.** Over the last few years we've had occasion to do quite a bit of shooting with one Pacific scope, a 3-9x, and a fair amount with a 4x and a 6x—all their Supreme models. All have proved satisfactory, though the crosswires seem a bit finer than we like them. This is a subjective thing, though, and depends a lot on the area being hunted. Being based in Nebraska, these Pacifics could well be tailored with that open country in mind. I've often thought that Weaver's crosswires were on the fine side, too, and have a hunch it's because the maker is used to the clear desert light that's normal outside of El Paso. Be that as it may, we've been getting good service from these several Pacific scopes, and their large objectives—40mm—make for big exit pupils, which simplifies fast aiming.

⊕ **Peter's Gun Shop,** formerly P.G.S, Inc., makes rubber shields for scope lenses to keep off rain, snow, debris. There are 4 sizes, one of which will fit practically any hunting scope, and a special split cover adaptable to objective tubes over 1.625". A spiral ring inside helps keep rain off lenses when the gun is carried at normal angles, plus there's a drain slot at the bottom. They ain't handsome, when the weather is miserable they certainly do help. $3.95 per pair.

⊕ **Premier Reticles** has deserted the chilly hills of West Virginia for the warm flatlands of Florida, Bob Thom-

Left, Marlin M850 2-5x big game scope ● Above, Nickel Supra 4-10x Varipower ● Realist fixed power 4x scope.

as tells me. A new reticle factory has been built at Ocala, where the emphasis is on installing dots and other reticles for several scope manufacturers, who then of course supply the complete, ready-to-go units to jobbers, dealers or customers.

⊕ **Realist, Inc.** The Camputer Auto/Range scopes announced by Realist a few years back have somewhat overshadowed their regular line of hunting scopes, so perhaps this is a good time to bring them up. At present Realist has fixed-power models of 2½x, 4x and 6x, as well as a pair of variables, the 3-9x and 1½-4½x. For hunters who prefer more light than a straight-tube variable of low power gives, the 1½-4½x could well be the answer. Its enlarged objective gives a 7mm exit pupil even at 4½x, which is all the human eye can handle, no matter how dark it gets. This adds a bit of weight—it goes 11½ ozs., noticeably more than some other variables of similar magnification—but it's impossible to get something for nothing in optics.

As mentioned last year, the Camputer design is now available in 3-9x and 1½-4½x, as well as straight 4x and 6x. We've described how the Auto/Range works in several earlier GDs, so we won't go into it again; however, we've tried both of the switch-powers, checking them against a target of known size at known distances, and they work. At the same time it should be pointed out that, while it's not difficult to use the A/R or any other rangefinding reticle on a benchrest with sandbags while sighting at a motionless, clearly defined black-and-white target, the same can't be said about using it from an improvised field position against an indistinct or partly hidden, neutral-colored animal. Things are never the same in the bush as in the lab. Still, under proper conditions this rig can take all the guesswork out of the range question, and it can usually keep you from making the gross errors common to eye-only guessing.

⊕**Redfield Gun Sight Co.** The most interesting scope news of the year, in my opinion, comes from Redfield, a company which has the knack of coming up with new ideas—on the production level—quite often. The previously-mentioned non-magnifying reticle and their internally adjusted target scopes are examples. Now there is the "Widefield" concept.

Consult our Directory pages for the location of firms or individuals mentioned.

What Redfield designers have done is enlarge the horizontal dimension of their 2¾x, 4x and 6x scopes by some 25 percent. Note that I said the *horizontal* dimension. The vertical dimension is essentially unchanged. And so the field of view is roughly oval in shape—and if that isn't a bit unusual I don't know what is. It's something of a shock to look into one of these Widefields and for the first time in your life not see a circular field. Takes a few minutes of getting used to, but there's no doubt that the extra width makes it easier to find running game.

Field widths are: 2¾x, 55½ feet; 4x, 37½, 6x, 25. There's no doubt that the added area makes the 4x usable even on the fastest moving short range whitetail, and truth is, many scope fans will doubtless switch to the 6x for routine shooting, as it has enough field for the average woods use where the 4x formerly reigned, while its added power will be ideal for the occasional open country long shot.

I have a 6x with CH Peep reticle (an open dot, in effect, whose inner measurement is about 2¼" at 100 yards), and it's quite a scope. It's currently on a Ruger Single Shot 243, proving itself on Keystone State chucks as a warmup for pronghorns later on. As usual with Redfields, the windage and elevation adjustments (half-minutes in the 6x) are almost exactly as advertised. Dunking in hot water disclosed no leaks in this sample. In general, the Widefield looks pretty much like the standard model, except that the eyepiece is 1.6" wide by 1.4" high, rather than being round.

All the new Redfield Widefield scopes. From top: 2¾, 4 and 6 power. These Widefields offer 25% wider field of view horizontally while vertically they have the same field as other Redfields of like power.

As background, we might say that the Widefield concept has been in the works for quite some time. Ed Hilliard, Redfield executive, told me that the idea had been suggested to Kollmorgen for the Bear Cub, years ago, but they had higher priority things on their mind then. Some additional work was done in the early 1960s, and a few years later a highly sophisticated optical design was worked out. This one, however, wasn't economically feasible, so a complete new optical system was worked out. This is not just a revised eyepiece, Hilliard says, but rather an optical system. Patents have been applied for.

Available reticles include the CH, PCH, dot, 4PCCH and 4-Plex, in addition to the CH Peep.

Another new item is a high-power variable, with magnification range of 6-18x. Priced at $149.95 ($10 more for dot), this one apparently is slanted toward the long range big game hunter who uses the same rifle for varmints and occasional bench shooting. Despite the increase in power it is the same size as the 4-12x but weighs 4 oz. more (18 oz.). Field varies from 16 feet down to 5½. Eye relief is about 3½", which makes it usable on a magnum. The objective bell is adjustable for range, a necessity on scopes above about 8x if parallax is to be eliminated and image degradation minimized.

This much weight is a scope, particulary when mounted fairly high, as the 2" objective bell requires, makes a strong, immovable mount a necessity. The Redfield Jr., of course, has these qualities so long as the screws remain tight. Loc-tite or some similar substance should be used wherever possible, and it might be a shrewd idea to help solidify the contact between scope mount base and receiver bridge by the use of epoxy. The weakest link in the whole scope/mount/gun setup is those miserable little 6-48 screws that most factory-drilled holes require. Some companies are going to larger sizes, at least in some models, and I hope they'll all come to that soon.

A new Redfield accessory for the paper-puncher or sheep-shooter is the "Fifteen-Sixty," a variable power spotting scope with a magnification spread of 15x to 60x. This spotter has a 60mm objective and uses an erector lens system instead of prisms. Eye relief of about ¾" permits use with shooting glasses. Price is $149.50, with a tripod stand at $27.50 and molded plastic carrying case, $29.95.

(Our sample of this new variable spotter proved to be an excellent optical instrument—even at the full 60 power there was fine sharpness and definition as long as little or no mirage is present. Our first trial was on a clear and very cold day in February, so it was amazing to see 22 caliber holes looming up in 50 caliber size seemingly.

In addition to the power ring adjustability, there are two other adjustments—the eyepiece can be set for the operator's vision requirements, while there's another ring, forward of the power ring, that is marked Plus and Minus. This one is essentially used to snap the image into best sharpness, but there's a dividend for target shooters—turn this No. 3 ring left or right, and wind or mirage conditions can be judged. A good glass.
(J.T.A.)

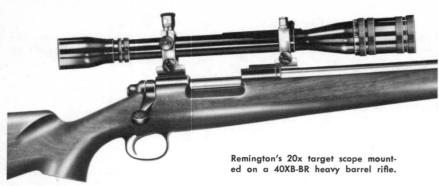

Remington's 20x target scope mounted on a 40XB-BR heavy barrel rifle.

⊕ **Remington Arms** quite likely has the distinction of putting out the most exclusive scope line in the country. It consists of exactly one model. But that one is a honey. A short, lightweight 20x target model designed by accuracy aficionado Mike Walker, it can be mounted on the action alone—even a short action such as the Remington 40XB for the 222—which means that no scope weight bears on the barrel, an important point when single-caliber group sizes are the goal.

This scope was announced in last year's GD, and since that time we have had numerous opportunities to use one on a 40XB-BR 222. The entire outfit is highly impressive. Weighing less than 10½ lbs., it usually groups in a half-inch or so at 100, and has given groups under a quarter-inch when we were holding well. For this shooting we used the 52-gr. Sierra BR bullet, with several powder charges. Since each gun is an individual in its likings, we won't mention the loads, except to say they were standard for the 222.

The short length of this scope makes it easy to focus precisely for range while looking into it (even with my short arms I can reach the movable objective unit), and the fine crosswire permits precise aiming—particularly important when you want to hold off a fraction of an inch for changing conditions rather than take time to make an adjustment.

Mounts, incidentally, are Unertl target models, a design of proved efficiency. However, in a conversation with Walker last summer he expressed some interest in modifying the scope to use internal adjustments. This would necessitate, among other things, a reduction in field of view, but since this is on the large side now

the loss would be no great inconvenience. In return, it would be possible to have solid mounting, which eliminates one area where variation sometimes occurs in the rifle/scope setup.

Quite a few of these Remington scopes are seen at bench shoots and doubtless more will be in the future, as the supply increases. Dick Dietz tells me that at this time—April 1970—they can't keep up with the demand. Price, $159.95.

⊕ **S & K Mfg. Co.,** maker of the Insta-mounts that've made life simpler for the guy who wants to scope a military rifle, now has mounts to fit some 70 commercial and GI rifles. Average price is about $18.50 complete, or $22.50 for the mount and the UN (Under Neath) see-through riser blocks. A recent addition is an Insta-mount for the M1—Garand, if you prefer—which Sid Haight says is possibly the sleeper of the line, for it's selling surprisingly well. Don't know why it shouldn't, myself. I can remember a few times I wished I had a scope on an M1.

S. & K.'s address, incidentally, is PO Box 247, Pittsfield, Pa. 16340—*not* Pittsburgh.

⊕ **Savage Arms.** celebrating its 75th Anniversary this year, has announced a new item in the scope field, the M420, a 1½-4x variable built on a straight one-inch tube. We've had one of these awhile now and find it an impressive little glass. Made in Japan to Savage's specs, it has noticeably bright lenses, as does the older 3-8x which we've used for several years.

Incidentally, brightness of the field is not solely a matter of relative brightness or lens diameter. RB can be calculated by dividing the clear objective lens diameter in millimeters by the true power and squaring the result. However, you can take several scopes having the same RB rating and by direct comparison see that one is brighter than another. The kind of glass used in the lenses, the formulas by which compound lenses are ground in order that one lens can compensate for another's deficiencies, etc., affect image brightness.

Field in the M1420 is listed at 64-25 feet, length is 10¼", weight 10 oz.,

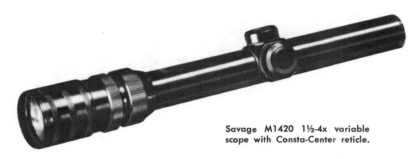

Savage M1420 1½-4x variable scope with Consta-Center reticle.

with Consta-Center reticle. Our sample has medium crosswires, no doubt the first choice for most shooters. Tested for leakage by submerging in hot water, we got one small leak from under an adjustment cap. $47.50.

Besides the two variables mentioned, Savage has a 2½x and a 4x for big game, choice of CH or post, and 4x, 6x and 3-7x models for rimfires, the latter ones equipped with tipoff mounts and priced $9.75-014.95.

The current Savage catalog shows QD mounts for the big game scopes similar in design to Lyman's. But a mount sent with the 1½-4x was somewhat different, having a transverse rod on the ring bases to match a relieved portion in the top of the base, to prevent slippage. Either way works well. It's mentioned only to keep you from being surprised when you open the box. Mounts are Japanese made too.

⊕ **Scope Instrument Corp.** has about a dozen scopes in its lineup now, including several for rimfires. Models not mentioned here previously include a straight 3x with 34-foot field and 10mm exit pupil, and a 1½-5x having a 32mm objective lens. With either CH or post, the 3x sells for $24.95, the variable for $37.95.

S & K Insta-mount for the M-1 Garand.

Tasco #610W, a 2-5x variable big game scope.

⊕ **Stoeger Arms,** besides acting as a supplier for many other makes of scopes, also markets 4 models under their own name. These are fixed powers in 4x, 6x and 8x, and a 3-9x variable. All have inch tubes, ½-minute internal adjustments, and coated lenses. Weights run from 9 to 13 oz., all are about 12″ long, and all have 3″ eye relief.

⊕ **Tasco** has an extensive line of scopes, primarily in the medium-price bracket. Two new ones this year come at each end of the size range. The first is a 2-5x big game model with an advertised field of 58 feet at bottom power. No test sample so far, so we can't comment directly on this scope, or on the big M705, a 6-18x target-type variable with 40mm objective. This scope has external mounts with ¼-minute clicks, is 22½″ long and weighs 36½ oz. $99.95. It's also available as a straight 12x, 16x or 20x at $79.95.

Samples of the new Tasco 6-18x and 20x target scopes—big and impressive looking—came into the editorial offices a while back, but testing one or the other attached to a rifle wasn't possible. Both of these scopes use the type of mount that slides fore-and-aft over a dovetailed steel base—as has been the regular practice with such other target scopes as Lyman and Unertl for many years.

However, somewhere along the line a dimensional error crept into the Tasco mounts, particularly the rear member. It proved impossible to tighten the rear mount enough to remove all shakiness, and the front mount took a lot of effort to get tight.

A further handicap in tightening the mount screws lies in their not having any drive slots in the knurled heads to help leverage. A pliers had to be used, but even so the leverage obtained wasn't enough to fully tighten the back mount.

The dimension of target-scope bases (except for length and hole locations) have been well-standardized for years,

so the problem can only lie in the Tasco mount—or mounts.

A letter has been sent to Tasco, but it's too early—as this is written—for a reply. Perhaps we'll be able to report further later on. J.T.A.

⊕ **Unertl Optical Co.** It's no exaggeration to say there are no better target scopes in the world than Unertls. A visit to any benchrest shoot or an any-sight rifle match—whose contestants are among the world's most finicky citizens—will prove this, just by counting the number of big Unertls in use, compared to the number of entries. So when a new Unertl scope is announced, it's big news.

Unertl's new scope is called the BV-20 (for Benchrest-Varmint, which indicates the groups it's slanted toward) It's a 20x only 17⅞″ long, weighs but 21¼ oz. with caps removed, is supplied with ¼-minute POsa mounts (less bases), Magnum clamp, recoil spring and screw-on dust covers, at $139.95. With standard target mounts (less bases) and plain clamp ring, weight is 19 oz., price $131.95.

Objective lens is 43mm in diameter and the tube length and shape is such that mounts can be installed at full 7.2″ separation for true ¼-inch click adjustments.

The advantages of such a design to benchresters and varminters are obvious, and there's still one big design change to mention. Range focusing is *not* accomplished by screwing the objective in or out, but rather by turning a graduated sleeve just forward of the ocular lens group. To adjust for range and parallax, a lock ring is loosened, a graduated sleeve is rotated to the desired setting and held there while the lock ring is tightened. The scope can be focused down to 50 feet for gallery shooting.

Focusing is *not* accomplished by shifting the erector lens system, as was done with the old Fecker, but the maker does not want to announce the mechanics of the system at this time.

Patents on it have been applied for.

This rearward location of the adjustment unit is very convenient for anyone who has occasion to shoot at various distances and where precise focusing is required, such as in benchrest or target shooting, where eyestrain is noticeable after a few shots if the image is not exact, and it's necessary to aim with the smallest degree of error. This new location permits easy changes while looking at the target through the scope—something that's almost impossible with the objective focusing designs. Varmint shooters rarely have this trouble, as they usually focus at about 200 yards and let it go at that, accepting some image degradation at closer ranges since their targets are comparatively big and only an occasional shot is being taken. Still, for those who want to make adjustments, the system on this new Unertl is bound to be more convenient than on any other current target scope.

Unertl still offers all the other target, varmint and hunting scopes covered in past issues of the GUN DIGEST, of course. Specs and prices are in the catalog section.

As a matter of interest, Unertl literature gives the following information on click values of their external target mounts (¼-MOA at 7.2″ is standard separation) when other separations are used:

Base Separation	Click Value
12.6″	1/7-MOA
10.6″	1/6-MOA
9.0″	1/5-MOA
7.2″	1/4-MOA*
5.4″	1/3-MOA

⊕ **E. D. Vissing Co.** is located in Idaho, reason enough for developing the Supreme lens covers. I've seen the sun there in hunting season, once. These covers slip over the scope's lenses to make dust- and rain-proof shields. To use, a release on each cap is pressed—one to a thumb as the rifle is raised—and the spring-loaded shields swing away. We've used a set on a favorite 2-7x Redfield, and they're highly useful in typical hunting weather. $4.95 per set.

*For the record 7.2 inches between centers does not give true minutes of angle, but rather inches at 100 yards, etc., assuming that target-mount screw adjustments are still being made to .001-inch increments. For true MOA a separation of base centers must be 6.86 inches for like conditions.

Unertl BV 20 is their newest offering for benchrest and varmint shooting.

Weaver Classic 400   Weaver Classic 600

⊕ **W. R. Weaver Co.** has been turning out rifle scopes since 1930, which adds up to about 40 years and only the Good Lord knows how many. I've been using them myself for well over 30 years, a right good stretch. To keep coming back that long does suggest satisfaction, I feel.

This year brings some additions and changes to the Weaver line. Three new big game scopes are offered. Called the Classics, they are the 300, 400 and 600 models, 3x, 4x and 6x respectively, with prices of $49.95, $57.95 and $62.95. They differ from the well-known K series in several ways, the most notable being a glittery bright finish that doubtless will appeal to shooters who like glittery bright guns. I'm not one of those guys, but that matters not. These tubes, incidentally, are an anodized aluminum alloy rather than the traditional steel of the K models, which saves a couple of ounces on weight. Eyepieces are fully adjustable for focusing to the user's vision but designed to prevent accidental removal, which makes weather sealing simpler. Reticles are constantly centered, of course, with a choice of CH, PCH, Dual X or Rangefinder, or center dot at $7.50 extra.

The three Classic models cover all kinds of big game shooting, of course, and the nearer varmints. Still, it wouldn't surprise me to see other powers, particularly a variable or two, being offered in a year or so with this glossy finish.

Our sample Classic is a 4x, and it has all the makings of a fine hunting scope. Haven't had it long enough to say how it takes the gaff, but I've noticed over many years that one of the outstanding characteristics of Weaver scopes is their toughness. I've shot some scopes apart on heavy-

recoiling rifles, but never a Weaver. I'll bet this Classic holds up just as well. If it doesn't, you'll hear about it.

The changes mentioned earlier are in the rimfire models. The C4 and C6 scopes, formerly built on ¾" tubes, have been discontinued. Their replacements are the D4 and D6, made with ⅞" tubes to accommodate larger lenses and transmit more light. This should make them especially popular with young squirrel hunters who do most of their shooting in the dim light of the tall timbers. The D4 and D6 have CH reticles, 1" friction lock adjustments, and come with Tip-Off or N mounts. $10.95 and $12.95.

Rimfire riflemen who want a variable can still get the V22, a 3-6x, with either CH or Dual X. For several years. I've been using one of these on a Sheridan 5mm pellet gun, which makes an ideal outfit for eliminating barn pigeons, starlings, sparrows, and the like when noise—or lack of it—is important. This is an amazingly accurate little rifle, incidentally, well worthy of a scope.

The Classic scopes do not replace any of the 8 K models, but simply supplement them. These Ks range from 1½x to 12x plus, of course, the 4 big game variables described in earlier editions of GD, making a total of 18 models in the Weaver lineup.

(This new small scope has an anodized alloy tube, too, like the new Classics, thus it weighs some 2 ounces less than before. I've used the new V22 on Remington's 5mm rifle with excellent results—several groups that ran just over an inch at 100 yards, despite a fresh breeze running. I found I could hold that Dual-X reticle onto the target very well indeed, its definitive being jet black on the crisply clear target. J.T.A.)

Since writing the above data two other Classic scopes, the 300 and 600, came in. As always with such new items, several tests were run so we'd have some idea what to expect in the field. Basically, what we do is simply compare a scope's advertised specifications with those obtained by direct measurement of the samples. Obviously, anything made by man is subject to some manufacturing tolerances, but it's nice to know that a given item comes close to what you've been led to expect, if only for the confidence this gives the user.

Magnification is easily checked by focusing the fixed scope on a small, conspicuous object and looking into the scope with one eye while looking at the object with the unaided eye at the same time. With a little practice, two images will be seen—one magnified, the other normal. By overlapping these, you can see how many times larger the one image is than the other, and this is the magnification. Fields also can be measured, as can eye relief. Specs on the three Classics checked out as listed, except for a full 4 inches of eye relief on the 6x against the 3¾ inches indicated.

Since weatherproofing is important in a hunting scope, we submerged each in water heated to about 140 degrees. This heats the gas inside the scope tube immediately, causing it to expand and escape through any joint not sealed. A line of bubbles indicates any leak. Not a single bubble escaped from any of these three Classics, which shows an excellent sealing job.

We found a trace of parallax in each scope at 100 yards, perhaps a half-inch. Any scope which cannot be focused precisely for a given range (as target scopes can) will have some parallax at every range except the one used in adjusting the glass at the factory. With these Classics that's probably 150 yards, a common distance for such settings. There's no point in getting worked up about an inch or so at any range. It's been many years since we've seen a fixed-power hunting scope that had enough parallax to be concerned about, though it's still a top topic of conversation among shooters.

These Classics have internal click adjustments protected by black plastic caps. Their value is listed as ½-MOA in the 3x, ¼-MOA in the 4x and 6x. We tested these with a colli-

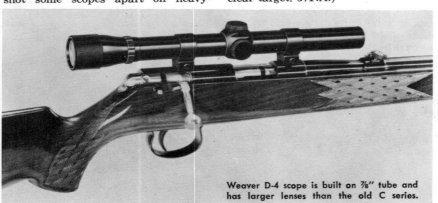

Weaver D-4 scope is built on ⅞" tube and has larger lenses than the old C series.

Williams Guide Line 3-9x variable scope.

mator having a 4 MOA grid; that is, a grid made up of squares, each one 4 MOA on a side. With the scope attached in its regular mounts and the collimator in the muzzle, the reticle was adjusted to coincide with a grid square. Then elevation and windage adjustments were made to see how many clicks were necessary to get the reticle onto the adjacent intersection.

Since the 3x is rated as having half-minute clicks, it should have taken 8 clicks per 4-minute square. Actually, it repeatedly took 12 clicks with the sample at hand. This gives a value of ⅓ MOA, rather than ½. The 4x and 6x did have ¼-minute clicks, as the spec sheet indicates.

During this work, the adjustment values were not tested just at the midpoint, but as far out as the grid would allow.

There are other ways of testing adjustments—with a fixed scope focused on a 100-yard target, say, or by shooting on an accurate rifle—but the former offers no particular advantage over the collimator and the latter introduces whatever variables are inherent in the rifle, ammo and shooter.

Anyway, all indications are that these Classics are fine additions to the Weaver line. We hope we can give you some results based on hunting experience later on.

⊕ **Weatherby, Inc.** has three new scopes this year—so new they aren't available at this writing, but should be by the time this edition is in print, according to Roy Weatherby. Called the Premier line, they are of 2½x, 4x and 3-9x, all built on one-inch tubes, of course, and all having objective lenses of 1.575" clear aperture. An objective this large gives a tremendous exit pupil of 16mm in the 2½x, which makes for ultra-fast aiming. It's 10mm in the 4x, still somewhat larger than average, and varies from 13mm to 4½mm in the variable, thus gives all the light the eye can *use,* even at top power.

(While it is quite true that the average human eye can handle no more light than is transmitted by an exit pupil of 5mm diameter, the exit pupil larger than 5mm or so allows more rapid sighting because the eye has more latitude, more vertical and lateral leeway.)

Available reticles are CH, PCH, Duplex, Lee Dot and Open Dot. Ob-

jective lenses are recessed more than usual, making the tube in effect a sunshade. Focusing for individual eyesight is of the binocular type—just by turning the eyepiece. Reticles are centered and non-magnifying, which means they appear to grow smaller as power is upped in the variable. Adjustments are by ¼-minutes and internal. You will remember that the Olympian line of scopes from Weatherby, announced last year, had no internal adjustments. That line is no

Williams "Guide" reticle.

longer available, apparently because of its lack of w and e within the tube.

Prices on the Premiers are: 2½x, $39.50; 4x, $44.50, and 3-9x, $59.50.

Another new optical item from Weatherby is the Sightmaster, a zoom spotting scope giving powers from 20x to 45x. Only 12¼" long, this spotter weighs 33.7 oz., has a 60mm objective, a field at 100 yards of 10½ to a scant 7 feet, an exit pupil of 3mm at 20x, which gives an unusual amount of light at this power, and 1.3mm at 45x. Scope price, $99.50, tripod, $14.95.

With this power spread, the Sightmaster doubtless will be highly useful on the range. Its size should make it handy in the varmint pastures, too,

but I'd think it'd have special appeal for chuck, sheep, pronghorn and similar hunters if offered in a lower power combination—say 12x to 30x. The times when atmospheric conditions permit the use of 35x or 45x are pretty rare, and there are times when even 20x is too much.

⊕ **Williams Gun Sight Co.,** which for many years has supplied the dependable Quick Convertible scope mount (with Ace-in-the-Hole peep) in either top or side position for the base, and with a number of variations for offsetting, etc., has branched out. They now are offering the Williams Guide-Line scopes, hunting models in straight 4x or variables of 1½-4½x, 2-6x, or 3-9x. Mebbe it was to be expected. After all, the Williamses have mounted many thousands of scopes over a period of some decades, and usually this leads to thoughts of what a glass sight should be—thus the Guide-Line.

All are on one-inch tubes, the small variable having an unenlarged objective, and all have half-minute internal adjustments. Made in Japan, apparently, to Williams' specs, they are said to have a minimum of 70 MOA adjustment, to have point of impact vary by less than one MOA when magnification is switched, and to be waterproof. No sample yet, so we can't report test results.

Four reticles are available, CH, dot, TNT (Thick-N-Thin)—the now common, and useful, combination of crosswires and posts), and the Williams "Guide," a post that tapers to a "neck," then flares out and comes to a point, something like a diamond sitting atop a tapered post. A horizontal crosswire just touches the top of the diamond. I don't know if the form offers any real advantage over a conventional post, but it might appeal to your eyes. Knowing the mount it subtends at various ranges might be useful for their estimation on occasion, as can the dot size (3 MOA at 4x) and the distance between the heavy portions of the TNT reticle, 16 MOA. Scopes, $69 to $108.

Besides the QC mounts mentioned, Williams has a new "Sight-Thru" design; this raises the scope up so you can look through circular openings in the bases to aim with iron sights. $15.

Consult our Directory pages for the location of firms or individuals mentioned.

Weatherby Premier 3-9x variable scope.

DOUBLE ACTION SHOOTING-- THE SECRETS OF SUCCESS

by PAUL B. WESTON

The author shooting precision double action with a 38 Colt Python in preparation for a bullseye pistol shoot. The locked-in double action grip ties in with the grip used in shooting auto pistols and contributes to the total accuracy when shooting the standard three competition guns: 22, 38 and 45.

Relatively few handgunners realize the precision shooting that can be done when firing double action. The author—a long time master of the straight-through technique—raises the curtain.

DOUBLE ACTION revolver shooting has achieved new heights of speed and accuracy. Today, the supremacy of single action shooting exists only in the minds of shooters who have never probed the secrets of double action. The major undisclosed fact about double action is that the basic design of modern revolvers pre-supposes the weapon will be fired as a "self-cocker," and this rejection of thumb cocking permits shooting with a locked-in grip and super-concentration on sighting and aiming. Also unrevealed has been the fact that the heavy and lengthy trigger motion can be *braked* to insure accuracy without any loss of the great rapidity of fire inherent in double action. Lastly, and always treated confidentially by initiates of shooting, is

that certain revolvers are superior for shooting double action, and may be modified to enhance this capability. Knowledge of the intricacies of the pull-and-squeeze trigger motion of double action and the capability of various revolvers challenge handgunners to a testing, a reappraisal, in this controversial area of double action shooting.

The Self-cocking Mechanism: 1877-1968

Police officers and sheriff's deputies along the American frontier were the first individuals to seek out revolvers known as "self-cockers." The single-action revolver was commonly available, yet these early law-enforcement agents paid from 5 to 15 dollars above

the standard prices for double action guns to obtain weapons with a self-cocking mechanism. A sheriff in California's Barbary Coast area in 1875 is quoted by John E. Parsons in his fine book, *Smith and Wesson Revolvers,** as commenting that a revolver with a double action mechanism would be the best weapon that a sheriff or policeman could possibly carry and had long been sought by law enforcement agents. Colt satisfied this demand initially, in 1877; Smith and Wesson marketed their first double action revolver in 1880.

Possibly, the error of gun designers in making these weapons both self-cocking and thumb cocking is the bas-

---

* Wm. Morrow & Co., N.Y.C., 1957.

ic reason for the failure of double actions to become popular among American target and sporting shooters. It is likely the thumb-cocking capability, with its 3- to 5-lb. single action trigger pull, as opposed to the 13- to 15-lb. trigger pressure required for double action, served to tout gun owners into using the single action characteristics of these guns for recreational shooting, but buying them in preference to single action weapons because the self-cocking mechanism could be used in emergencies for rapid fire.

Despite the basic mechanical merit of the double action locking mechanism, the modern concept of shooting double action with a *braked* trigger pressure did not emerge until the fabulous Ed McGivern proved that shooting double action revolvers by the double action method delivered greater accuracy combined with speed than any other method by which revolvers have been fired! On the evening of January 23rd, 1934, on the indoor shooting range at Lewiston, Montana, four reputable citizens and gun enthusiasts subscribed and swore to an affidavit stating they witnessed Ed McGivern fire 5 shots double action from a Smith and Wesson revolver and place all of them within the span of a playing card at 15 feet in *exactly ⅖ths of a second!*

However, McGivern's proof of the efficiency of the double action mechanism in revolvers ran contrary to the opinion of every local handgun marksman across the United States. As late as 1947, in my own book, *Target Shooting Today,** I wrote about attempting to teach double action shooting to U.S. Navy aviation personnel and reported a complete lack of success. It was not until 1950, when Bill Peterson and George Phillips of New York's Roslyn Club began to win Eastern pistol shoots using a two-stage double action trigger pull which braked the heavy double action trigger pressure of their Smith and Wesson target guns, that shooters (including the author) began to believe in the basic merit of double action. A year later, members of the Federal Bureau of Investigation's famed firearms training units began to shoot phenomenal scores double action on the silhouette targets of the FBI's Practical Pistol Course. These agents shot their issue Colt 4-inch revolvers, either using the audible click signal of Colt revolvers or Ed McGivern's straight-through trigger motion to brake the heavy double action trigger pressure to a cushioned stop.

During the intervening years, the author shot double action at all stages of many pistol shoots, winning several time and rapid fire 20-shot matches over the NRA courses of fire at 25 yards by shooting 198x200 with a 38

* Greenberg, N.Y.C., 1950.

Mirror training—Ed McGivern's method of detecting such faults as "milking" and "bumping" the trigger. The mirror reflects any movement at the moment the hammer falls.

John S. Hunt, student-coach at Sacramento State College, demonstrates double action shooting from the combat sitting position. Gun is the author's worked-over long-action Smith and Wesson.

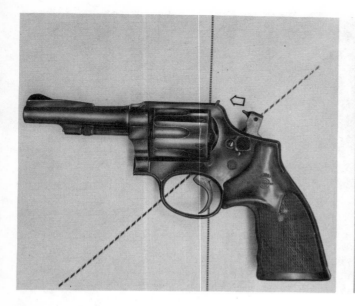

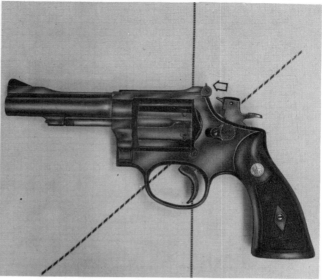

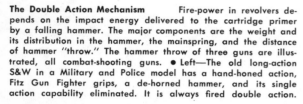

The Double Action Mechanism Fire-power in revolvers depends on the impact energy delivered to the cartridge primer by a falling hammer. The major components are the weight and its distribution in the hammer, the mainspring, and the distance of hammer "throw." The hammer throw of three guns are illustrated, all combat-shooting guns. ● Left—The old long-action S&W in a Military and Police model has a hand-honed action, Fitz Gun Fighter grips, a de-horned hammer, and its single action capability eliminated. It is always fired double action.

● Center—A recent, shorter-action S&W of the same model, not modified in any way except for hand-honing the action. ● Right —The Colt Python has a factory-honed action; the only modification has been a pair of Herret's Shooting Star grips. ● Far right—Tuning the mechanism of the S&W revolver: The hammer on the left is untouched, the other has been de-horned (for holster wear under a coat and quick-draw potential), and its single action capability eliminated (single arrow). The author believes this shortening and squaring of the hammer sear face

caliber long-action Smith and Wesson revolver; John Brownfield became top shooter on the FBI's clandestine pistol team, the Peekskill Gun Club, shooting double action; and George Phillips went on to win the National Pistol Championship, shooting double action in the centerfire matches.

In the words of Ed McGivern: "The double action guns, tested against electrically operated timing machines, seem to be capable of speed combined with accuracy and bullet grouping that cannot be equaled by any single action or other type of revolver."

Improved Accuracy Possible in Double Action

The accuracy potential of any handgun shooter can be improved in double action shooting because a locked-in grip can be used and the rejection of thumb cocking permits full concentration by a shooter on sighting and aiming.

In single action shooting, the grip pressure often changes when shooting timed and rapid fire because of the need of thumb cocking after each shot and the requirement of shooting 5 shots in time limits of 20 or 10 seconds. These changes in grip pressure may result from tension associated with shooting under the pressure of a time limit or in order to hold a gun "creeping" upward after each shot, but each change in pressure is likely to move the sights out of alignment

and to move the bullet's point of impact on target.

The locked-in grip for double action can be firm and constant. Its unchanging characteristic from shot to shot in any type of speed firing assists in maintaining the same point of impact shot after shot, and aids in holding the aligned sights in the same relationship at all times from the first to the last shot. Since the need of cocking the hammer is no longer present, the high thumb position common to single action shooting can be junked and a more natural low-thumb position assumed. It is this low-thumb position that stretches the web between the shooter's thumb and trigger finger, giving the double action grip its feeling of being locked in place.

Double action shooters are only confronted with two operations in firing: trigger pressure and watching the sights. Unlike single action shooters, they do not have to think of reaching up to cock the hammer between shots and replacing the thumb in the same position on the gun and with the same pressure—and avoiding the "thumbing" of a shot which is always possible in single action shooting. Double action is a cock-sure technique, and the shooter has only to think of watching his sights between shots in speed shooting as he moves through the trigger motion which cocks the hammer and fires the gun.

Moreover, the amount of practice

usually required to learn the trigger motion of double action is sufficient to reduce it to a mechanical operation: a response of the muscular system to the visual cues of sighting and aiming. Any in-depth study of Ed McGivern and today's combat police shooters indicates that the combining of speed with accuracy in double action primarily results from an intense visual concentration on sighting and aiming and a below-conscious attention to the operation of the gun. The concentration is on looking, the doing takes care of itself!

Braking Double Action Trigger Motion

The road block to greater use of the double action mechanism in modern revolvers has been the tendency of most uninformed shooters to "milk" the trigger with an upward-downward motion just as the shot is fired, or to "bump" the final motion of the heavy trigger pull against the rear of the trigger guard. "Milking" is a convulsive sudden pressure to overcome the weight of the heavy double action trigger pull and is a fault common with persons attempting double action for the first time. Trigger "bumping" is a potential hazard to attaining accuracy in double action until a shooter learns to cushion the final stage of the trigger motion by easing off on the trigger pressure *just before the hammer falls and the shot is fired.*

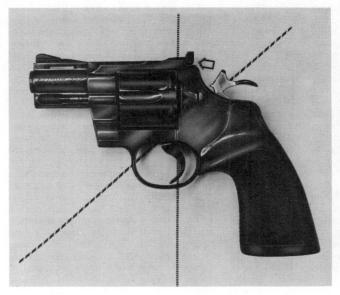

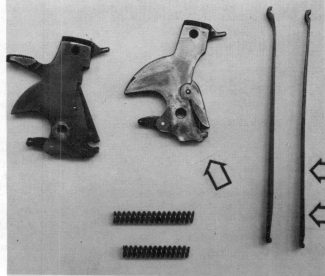

offers a "clean break" when the hammer is released by the trigger. ● The thick base section of the S&W blade mainspring has been ground down (double arrow). Ticklish tinkering—the author ground down 5 of these springs in 1954 and had 4 of them break off in the area of grinding. The fifth spring is still in action in 1968. The objective is to lessen the trigger weight by making the spring more flexible and to add a little "zip" to the hammer throw. The spring at the left is factory-fresh. ● The trigger rebound coil spring at top has not been cut, the other one has had three coils cut off. This also lessens the weight of

the trigger pull, but in the second stage. Most shooter-tinkerers start by nipping off one link at a time; when this spring is too short the trigger does not return to its forward position, so watch it. ● The hammer, trigger rebound spring, and mainspring pictured were last modified in 1954, and the gun has been fired weekly to date: 1968. From 1954 to 1958 the author carried this gun as his service 38 revolver on duty with the New York City Police Dept. ● Shooters who fancy Colt guns, but don't have or can't afford the Python, should consult a good pistolsmith. These experts can work wonders with the flying horse, old or new.

The concept of accurate double action shooting is based on braking the energy of trigger pressure and reducing it to a minor force which will not move the aimed or pointed gun off target as the trigger releases the hammer and the weapon fires.

More precisely, this braking of the double action trigger motion is a pull-and-squeeze upon the trigger. The hammer is brought back rapidly by a strong rearward pull on the trigger through 75%-85% of its rearward travel, and held at this point until the shooter begins the final steadily-increasing trigger squeeze which will fire the shot. In the final phase of this trigger technique there is little perceptible motion in the trigger as it lifts the hammer the short-short distance necessary for it to slip off the sear of the trigger and into the forward motion which will fire the gun.

In 1967, during firing tests at the State College in Sacramento, Calif., the author was able to repeat day after day for the two weeks of the tests a pull-and-squeeze trigger motion that moved through the initial phase rapidly to a point of temporary hesitation that left no more than a 2- to 3-lb. trigger pull during the second stage of squeezing off the shot. While it is true the author used a two-stage trigger motion, with a pressure point to warn of the impending second stage, it is also true that shooters using a straight-through pressure, or the audible "click" of Colt revolvers, have

achieved similar uniformity in this braking of trigger motion in double action.

The Two-stage Trigger Motion

The author watched Bill Peterson cushion the second stage of double action against a rubber eraser inserted into the rear of his trigger guard on many Sundays at the Roslyn Club's pistol range, but developed little interest in double action until another club member—George Phillips—began to shoot "possibles" in timed fire by cushioning the tip of his trigger finger against a "pressure point" at the rear of the trigger guard of his gun.

This use of a pressure point on the gun to warn the shooter when the first pulling motion has been completed, and to permit the momentary rest which dissipates the energy of pulling back on the trigger, can be developed into an amazingly accurate signal-response. It is also an excellent cushion against which to squeeze the remaining trigger pressure to guard against any trigger bump of any kind.

In shooting this two-stage trigger motion, the first joint of the trigger finger should be pushed through the trigger guard to position the trigger against the second joint of this finger. This grip will permit most shooters to touch the rear edge of the trigger guard, where it joins the frame of the revolver, as they move the trigger back through the first *pulling* motion. Shooters with short fingers will find

it necessary to move their grip to the right slightly, and they may require custom grips or some homework with plastic wood to build up a point within reach of the tip of their trigger finger as it completes the first movement of this two-stage pull.

The pressure point should offer a rounded area that will not stop the rearward movement of the trigger finger. Shooters who have learned an unusual discrimination will not need to move their finger any noticeable distance in the second stage, often *squeezing* the trigger by exerting pressure against the pressure point until the slack in the fleshy tip of their finger is taken up and the weapon fires. Others will require a slight sliding of the finger tip to complete the second stage of the double action pull. A light pressure against this point insures a sliding motion without friction.

Two-stage double action shooters start the first portion of this trigger motion as they move from the *raise pistol* command into aiming position for a first shot, and during the recovery of the aim for following shots. It is a firm, fast and smooth motion. The amount of hesitation in this trigger position before the squeezing motion is started, and the final steadily-increasing pressure put on the trigger to fire the gun, depends upon the type of fire. It might be a lengthy pause in slow fire, to give the weapon a chance to settle down into the shooter's aiming area; and it would be aligned

DOUBLE ACTION SHOOTING -- THE SECRETS OF SUCCESS

with the shooter's need for speed in timed and rapid fire, or in combat shooting. However, it is a real squeeze in the final motion of increasing pressure which fires the gun.

Straight-Through Trigger Pressure

Ed McGivern's fabulous rapidity of fire along with his equally remarkable accuracy was achieved by shooting double action with a straight-through trigger pressure. Ed taught himself muscular control and developed the musculature in his arm and hand to sweep back the trigger in a *pulling* motion through three-fourths to seven-eighths of its travel, to discriminate as to the peak point for temporary hesitation, and to move smoothly into the second stage of squeezing the remaining pressure on the trigger. Ed's method does achieve everything inherent in the two-stage trigger motion without the warning signal or assistance of a pressure point. Proof that straight-through trigger pressure can be controlled without ending in a massive trigger bump is readily available in the tight groups shot by McGivern in all of his double action shooting. Anyone who has read his shooting classic, *Fast and Fancy Revolver Shooting,** has noted the manner in which McGivern consistently grouped his shots in test after test.

McGivern's instructions on attaining the necessary skill is simple: practice with the empty gun. His words have been repeated by police instructors and shooting coaches for years. Most of the emphasis on such "dry-shooting" has been on learning to make this movement without bumping the trigger as the hammer is released and the gun is fired. Secondary emphasis has been on keeping the two sights in alignment with each other and within an aiming area while the straight-through pressure is being applied. Lastly, the shooter's concentration was directed toward keeping his sights in alignment as *he released this straight-through pressure.*

I believe the failure of most shooters attempting this straight-through pressure has been due to a misunderstanding of the mechanics of controlling a single finger of one hand. Most of us teaching shooting have been captivated over the years by McGivern's

*King, Richardson Co., Boston, Mass., 1938.

step-by-step instructions. Recently, in gunnery classes at the State College in Sacramento, Calif., I've reversed the emphasis!

I now advise concentration on the release of the trigger. I think it is this motion that builds the muscles and furnishes the cues for the rearward pressure. I have found that shooters who can hold their sights in alignment as the trigger is released have learned how to cushion the final straight-through squeeze. As this "cushioning" is learned, these shooters have no difficulty in holding their sights in alignment all through the trigger movement. The breakthrough appears to be this: learning to promptly release the trigger without disturbing the aiming picture is the best way of learning to stop the rearward pressure smoothly without any bumping motion. It appears to be a conditioning of the muscles to oppose one another for a single coordinated rearward - and - forward movement, rather than to learn two movements. I think this is the lost key to McGivern's amazing trigger control despite the speed of his finger movements.

The 'Click' Signal

The double action mechanism of modern Colt revolvers makes a noise when the trigger is moved through about two-thirds of its rearward motion. The noise emanates from the release of the spring-loaded cylinder bolt by the rebound lever. It is a very distinct click. Strangely, while it is not a loud sound, I have known shooters who could hear it on a noisy indoor range while several other shooters were firing. It is also possible that through practice these shooters learn to pick up a supplementary signal, a slight unevenness in the trigger motion at the moment the meshing of the interior moving parts emit the distinctive click signal.

However, this click signal is nothing more than a warning at the end of the initial *pulling* movement of the trigger motion. It must be integrated with a cushioning of the final *squeezing* segment of the double action trigger motion. Since the pressure point in the two-stage trigger pressure serves as its own warning, this audible signal is more commonly associated with a straight-through trigger pressure. It is a bona fide technique of controlling double action trigger pressure and is very helpful to new shooters firing Colt revolvers. Extensive practice usually develops the ability to control a straight-through pressure and negates the need for this signal.

Revolvers for Double Action

Smith and Wesson revolvers have a functional design more adaptable to modern double action shooting than Colt revolvers, and among Colt revolvers the extra-cost Python series adapts more readily to double action.

The major characteristic of the Smith and Wesson mechanism is that the cylinder is moved through its turning motion and locked in place during the initial *pulling* phase of the trigger motion. In addition, the major tension of the blade mainspring is compressed during the first portion of this trigger pull. Therefore, the final *squeeze* of the trigger motion in a Smith and Wesson mechanism does little more than compress the trigger rebound spring—a slight opposition pressure that aids in cushioning the trigger finger to a faultless stop as the gun fires. In the Colt mechanism, the cylinder must be swung through some of its circular motion and the major tension of the leaf mainspring compressed during the final stage of double action trigger motion. The work of turning the cylinder and cocking the mainspring in the early stages of double action trigger motion is a definite asset.

The moving parts of any double action mechanism should be smoothed and honed to a friction-free surface. Friction between the surfaces of two moving parts add to the drag factor of the double action trigger pull, and a free-falling hammer speeds up lock time and delivers the little bit of extra impact energy that is often the difference between firing a cartridge and having a misfire. While Smith and Wesson has always polished up a greater percentage of their moving parts than the Colt people, the metal parts of Colt revolvers will take a high polish. This honing is within the skill of any shooter, if he can procure the necessary stones for hand polishing—particularly the very fine white oil stones for the final honing. The basic metal surfaces of these gun parts are not removed; it is a case of leveling the surface to a glass-like smoothness.

The hand-honed, highly polished action of the Colt Python is one of the major reasons for its ready adaptability to double action. The mechanism can honestly be termed a friction-free environment. In addition, I've always suspected the mainspring of the Python series has been worked over or is different in its flexibility in comparison with the standard Colt mainsprings. Once, when Fred Roff was president of the Colt firm, I thought I had an admission about the Python mainspring, but he claimed it is no different than any of their mainsprings and that the additional hand-fitting of parts in the Python smoothed out the action.

Shooting any revolver double action creates a basic problem in ignition. The hammer fall is shortened by the fact that the hammer is not thumb-cocked to full cock. Originally, the design of the double action mechanism allowed for a long hammer fall which would make ignition positive, but the popularity of short actions in revolv-

The Two-Stage Trigger Motion

1st position—no pressure on trigger. ● Center: 2nd position—at the point of momentary hesitation. The pulling pressure has been completed and the squeezing pressure has started. Arrows on cylinder indicate complete rotation of S&W cylinder during the first stage of the double action trigger motion. ● Below: 2nd position, continued, showing low thumb position and tip of trigger finger touching the pressure point at the rear of the trigger guard where it joins the revolver's frame. The pressure point is a warning signal; contact with it alerts the shooter that he has completed the

1st stage of this trigger motion and must ease off and *squeeze* the few pounds of pressure necessary to lift the hammer slightly and let it fall and fire the cartridge. ● The revolver illustrated is a long-action S&W, M&P Model 38 Special. It has been hand-honed by the author to reduce friction between the moving parts, a heavy K-38 barrel has been installed, and its single action capability removed. It can only be fired double action. The special order grips by S&W are full-bodied, with a small build-up behind the trigger guard to enlarge the pressure point.

ers led to a restriction on the cocking movement of the hammer and on its falling distance. Of course, the short action for thumb cocking is a wee bit shorter when fired double action. The late Bob Nichols, in writing the *Secrets of Double Action Shooting*** recommended the long-action Smith and Wesson revolver because the impact energy of its long hammer fall guarded against misfires. I can support this position on the basis of almost 20 years of experience. The older long-action Smith and Wesson revolver is the most dependable weapon for double action shooting. Misfires are almost unknown in tests and field shooting of these guns, while the more recent short action revolvers will misfire now and then.

It's not that modern handguns misfire regularly, they don't. When they do, it is usually because of a hard primer in the cartridge or an improperly seated primer cushioning the impact of the firing pin. On the other hand, even hard or improperly seated primers will fire with a very satisfactory bang in the long-action Smith and Wesson revolver.

Tinkering for Double Action

I like to tinker with guns. Shooting double action invites modification of the double action mechanism. Usually, it will start with a shooter unwinding the mainspring strain screw at the bottom of the grip of Smith and Wesson revolvers to test the amount of tension which can be taken from the mainspring before the revolver starts to misfire with some regularity. Of course, low tension on this spring means less weight to the double action trigger motion. In Colts, the tinkering may start with a little bending of the lower section of the leaf mainspring— for the same goal. Then, the home gunsmith may seek improved functioning by such action as taking a couple of links off the trigger rebound lever (in Smith and Wesson guns), or adding metal to the cylinder bolt or the lug of the rebound lever (in Colt guns). I've even ground down the base of Smith and Wesson mainsprings, and Bill Gunn, now President of Smith and Wesson, turned out U-shaped and extra-flexible mainsprings for double action shooters who liked to tinker with their guns.

The objective of home gunsmithing is to lighten the heavy trigger pull of double action, speed up the lock time and in doing so to add some additional impact energy to the fall of the hammer in order to guarantee positive ignition of every shot fired. There's a conflict in this juxtaposition: When the trigger pull is lightened too much, the weapon will lose the necessary impact energy. However, there is little need to have more than enough impact energy when it means wheeling

---

* Coward-McCann, N.Y.C., 1950.

back and squeezing off additional pounds of trigger pressure. Since the impact energy from the hammer's fall is a composite of the shape and weight of the hammer, the tension-energy in the mainspring, and the drag factor of friction between moving parts, it can be readily seen that work in these areas will affect trigger pressure.

However, any modification of a revolver for better performance in double action should always favor high impact energy. A few pounds of trigger pull is almost meaningless in comparison with the threat of a misfire or malfunction. This is particularly important when the revolver is the service weapon of a police officer, a personal defense gun, or depended upon for protection against attack in home or place of business.

The author's confidence in his own "tinkering" is based on two years of gunsmithing in the handgun field — and explains a willingness to carry a worked-over gun on police patrol. Unless a shooter has similar experience or has an unusual mechanical know-how and skill with tools, it is advisable to seek out a local gunsmith with an excellent professional reputation and discuss modifications with him. This is particularly true of Colt revolvers. Of course, a shooter can hone the action and might even lessen the tension of the mainspring by some judicious trial-and-error bending, but other modifications usually require the skilled hands and the special tools of a professional gunsmith.

"Precision" vs. Combat Shooting

Double-actioneers term shooting at bullseye targets, in competition against single action and auto pistol shooters, precision shooting. Combat shooting includes aimed as well as directed fire, with the unaimed fire being delivered from the hip or shoulder level. Many precision shooters confine their double action to the speed shooting stages of firing against time limits, but the author and an increasing number of other shooters now fire their slow-fire stage with this double-action technique. Shooting slow, timed, and rapid fire double action appears to improve an over-the-course average, and compensates for the loss of a point or two in slow fire. Today's requirements for combat gunnery cite only one acceptable method of shooting: double action. Some areas permit single action shooting at the longer ranges during the aimed fire stages, but the trend nationally is to demand double action at every range and in every position of combat gunnery.

While precision shooting offers no support for its one-handed target shooting position, and combat gunnery allows the support of barricades and portions of the shooter's body, there is no problem in changing from the standing target position to the sitting, kneeling, and prone positions of com-

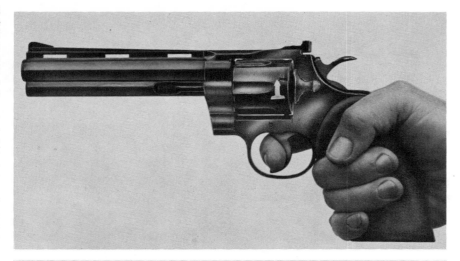

Straight-Through Trigger Motion Above —The start: Note trigger finger position; there is no need to push the finger well into the trigger guard, as in the two-stage motion, for it does not contact any pressure point. ● Below —Halfway: The rapid pulling motion of the first stage has been completed. The shooter now moves into the squeezing motion which will fire the gun. This is the position of the signal click of Colt revolvers—a warning to double action shooters. Note: The arrows indicate the late-moving rotation of cylinders on Colt revolvers. The second stage of double action trigger pulls is heavier on Colt revolvers because the cylinder does not revolve completely during the first stage. ● The gun, a 357 Colt Python, is an extra-cost revolver, but its hand fitted action, hand-honing of the moving parts and "floating" firing pin, more than justify the cost. Grips are standard "target" and ideal for double action as they offer a slight build-up of wood behind the trigger guard which is useful for two-stage double action. The author has fitted a beavertail trigger shoe to afford greater control in this straight-through motion.

bat shooting—or in moving to the more difficult unsupported standing position.

There is a definite transition of double action shooting skill between these two types of shooting. There is also a transfer between the skill attained in one type of trigger motion to the other. Shooters who have learned the two-stage trigger motion using a pressure point can change without any real difficulty to a straight-through trigger motion. In fact, many of America's combat shooters use the two-stage method at the long-range aimed-fire stages of combat firing, and switch to the faster straight-through technique for close-range hip shooting and firing from the point-shoulder position.

This transfer of skill from target shooting to combat gunnery to possible situations in real life requiring defense shooting may be the chief attraction of double action. It may be that double action is a search for the ultimate in handguns and hand gunning. There is a great deal of personal satisfaction in learning new skills, and in probing these disclosures about the area of new horizons for gun enthusiasts willing to invest time and effort intricacies of double action. It is an area of new horizons for gun enthusiasts willing to invest time and money in learning a new total skill in handgun shooting.　　　　　●

Dale W. Goens

Ruger No. 1 Single Shot rifle with very handsomely figured exhibition grade French walnut—and very handsomely handled, too! Note smooth flow of cheekpiece lines, checkering and fore-end treatment.

Custom Sporting Arms

Left and right views of a Model 70 Winchester, in classic style, stocked in a superb piece of Circassian walnut by Duane Wiebe for Wm. G. Chizar of Chizar Engraving.

Custom Guns

Gus F. Butterowe

Right and left views of a 17-222 wildcat, barrel by P. O. Ackley, the maple stock with rosewood tips and inlays. 4x B&L scope in Conetrol mount.

Lou Williamson

Fine classic styling and checkering in dense Texas walnut on a Douglas barreled FN Mauser in 22-250. Leupold 7½x scope in Redfield mount.

R. E. Anderson
30-06 varmint rifle in the modern manner on an FN Mauser, 26" Douglas barrel. Exhibition grade myrtlewood stock cut with skip-line checkering. Leupold 7½x scope in Buehler mount.

Len Brownell
Short action K Mauser in 250-3000 made for Mrs. Brownell. A light rifle in the classic manner, the metal engraved by John Warren. Note fine checkering, graceful cheekpiece, levered floorplate.

Hurst Custom Gunstocks
A Danzig Mauser with a Douglas barrel in 308 NATO caliber. The tiger-tail maple stock, in the classic style, carries 24-line checkering, shows fine control of line and proportion.

Richards Micro-Fit
Dual-grip thumbhole design lets shooter use normal grip or hole optionally. These production stocks are quite inexpensive, good values.

Richards Micro-Fit
Custom-look stocks at low cost. This classic design, well-handled, starts at $16.95 in maple, $19.95 in walnut with spacers, as shown.

A

Shaw's Custom Guns
This Browning O-U was completely re-engraved and gold inlaid by Shaw, stocked in top grade French walnut and checkered 32 lines per inch.

B

Shaw's Custom Guns
Exhibition grade Claro walnut on a Sako in 300 H&H caliber, carved to oak leaves in modern style, and "satin oil" finished—12 coats!

C

Hal Hartley
A muzzleloader in the Hawken style, caliber 54, that Mr. Hartley made for himself. The 33" barrel is ⅞" at the muzzle, was made by Bill Large of Ironton, O.

D

Pachmayr Gun Works
Special stocking of a Browning O-U trap gun shows attractive checkering pattern, a gold inlaid and engraved game scene.

E

Pachmayr Gun Works
Model 42/410 Winchester pump stocked in "marble-cake" French walnut with matching fore-end. 28-line checkering.

F

Russell Zeeryp
Model 12 Winchester trap gun stocked in fancy-figured maple and checkered in an unusual and full pattern.

Crest Carving Co.
FN Mauser-actioned sporter in their Supreme Grade with fancy walnut, the fore-end flared in semi-beavertail style. Caliber, barrel lengths, weights to order.

Clayton N. Nelson
This handsome stock was created for a Champlin barreled action (actions available barreled or not), the wood best fancy French walnut checkered 24 lines to the inch.

Smitty's Gun Shop
A short Mauser action stocked in Zebra wood, chambered for Smith's 450 Magnum. Good lines and good checkering.

Swanson Custom Firearms
Unusual straight-grip stocking in French walnut of a pre-war M70 Winchester, cal. 270. Trim, light and graceful for mountain hunting.

R. J. Maberry
Unusual wood! Buttstock is American walnut grafted to English walnut in the fore-end. The Remington M700 action holds a Douglas barrel in 222; the scope is a Leupold 3x-9x in Buehler mount.

John Bivins, Jr.
Flintlock rifle in Revolutionary war style is iron-mounted, stocked in fine fiddleback maple showing raised carving. Flared and tapered 50-caliber octagon barrel by Bob Paris (Gettysburg, Pa.) and lock by C. E. Siler of Asheville, N.C.

Keith Stegall
M70 Winchester barreled by Ed Shilen in 280 Imp., classic-stocked in Exhibition grade French walnut that's well and extensively hand checkered.

Sportsman's Den
A high-wall Winchester single shot in 22-250, the wood feather-grain walnut with stippled grip and fore-end.

Barber's Southpaw Conversion
Remington 700 in 243 caliber, made into left-hand style with thumbhole stock. Bushnell Scopechief 1.5-4.5x variable in Bushnell mounts, safety in trigger guard.

Snapp's Gun Shop
High-wall Winchester S.S. rifle, Douglas barreled in 225. Super fancy black walnut, nicely handled. Shortened tang, through bolt; shoots ½ MOA with factory ammo.

Mike Conner
7x57 on a Sako action with a part-octagon ribbed barrel, the French walnut stock the essence of simplicity. Note fleur-de-lis, ribboned checkering, cheekpiece treatment, fore-end tip.

John Bivins, Jr.
Federal period flintlock rifle in the Virginia-Carolina style, entirely handmade by Bivins except for the lock and 40-caliber Douglas barrel. Sterling silver inlaying, brass furniture. Note raised carving.

Varmint Rifle Variables

The varmint rifle can be whatever you want it to be — lever, pump, auto or bolt action. It all depends on how and where you're going to use it.

by Jon R. Sundra

In the close quarters of a blind the short-barreled carbine really earns its keep.

THERE HAVE probably been more articles devoted to varmint and predator hunting these past few years than to any other type of hunting. These articles usually consist of the author giving a rundown of the current crop of varmint cartridges followed by his expounding on the merits and demerits of each, starting with the 222 Rem. and working up. But rather than re-hash the same old ballistic data that most of you are pretty familiar with, let's take a close look at varmint rifles *per se;* their size, weight, and function as specialized firearms. Is a varmint rifle the classic heavy-barreled job with the high-power target-type scope, or is the term "varmint rifle" determined strictly by the use to which the gun is put? I'm inclined to favor the latter. Any type of rifle used successfully in potting vermin and pests is a varmint rifle, regardless of what the books say! It's not very convincing to tell the owner of an 18″ barreled carbine that he's made the wrong choice if he's the best chuck hunter in town. Not that a carbine is the most accurate; but then accuracy is not always the primary consideration in determining the type of rifle best suited to a specific varminting job.

Back around the turn of the century the lever action Winchester in 25-20 was a real demon of a varmint rifle. Compared to the other combinations of the day it provided the accuracy and flat trajectory needed to make those "long" shots of 100-125 yards on small game. By today's standards, however, its value is that of a collector's item. The reason for its obsolescence is not that varmints have got any harder to kill; it's simply that, like the passing of the general practitioner, things have become specialized. Just as advances in medicine and surgical techniques have made it improbable for the same doctor to proficiently perform—by present-day standards—a brain operation one day and open-heart surgery the next, so too have advances in rifle and cartridge design make the "one-gun" man relatively ill-equipped. The old saying, "What was good enough for dad is good enough for me" is now meaningless. I'm not shooting a 30-40 Krag, and have no desire to. Sentimentality has its place but the choosing of one's rifle battery should be done from pragmatic considerations. In many instances there are as many varmints and predators around today as in dad's day, but the ratio of hunters per critter has risen tremendously while the total area of hunt-able land has decreased. The competition thus created results in fewer shots at warier animals and at longer ranges. These conditions have stimulated the development of more accurate rifles and flatter-shooting cartridges. As in any area of development, these improvements have led to specialization not only in cartridge design but in the rifle's physical characteristics as well.

Choosing the Rifle

It has never ceased to amaze me how much deliberation a fellow goes through in choosing the "right" caliber for his new varmint rifle and how little thought he gives to the more important considerations such as barrel length and weight, stock design and type of wood. For every shot the hunter is presented with, there is a specific type of rifle better suited to that particular job than others. I'm speaking of the choice between the carbines, the medium-weight sporters, and the heavy-barreled target types. Since we can't carry three rifles of different design on every varmint hunt, we have to do the next best thing; we must determine the most frequently occurring circumstances under which the average shot is taken. Let's take a few hypothetical cases

Representative rifle types, from the top: Heavy-barreled varminter at 13 lbs. 2 oz., 47 inches; medium-weight sporter at 8 lbs. 14 oz., 44 inches; and carbine at 7 lbs. 3 oz., 37½ inches.

and, given a few facts as to the quarry and conditions, i.e., car cruising, walk and stalk, or predator calling, prescribe the rifle best suited to the job.

Let's begin with the eastern groundhog hunter who slowly cruises along the back-country roads, glassing the rolling fields of the fertile farming areas. A typical shot would consist of spotting the critter, perhaps several hundred yards off, getting out of the car and then stalking a short distance to a vantage point within range. Now here's a hunter who could take full advantage of a 26″ or 28″ barrel tapering to .700″ to .900″ at the muzzle. The stock can be of the target type having a wide beavertail fore-end and extra thickness through the mortise area and butt. Unless the gun is to double as a target rifle, we need not concern ourselves about the 13½-lb. limit imposed by the NBRSA for rifles in the "Heavy Varmint Class." However, 15 pounds is about the upper limit one could go and still retain some handling and carrying qualities. Topping this rig would be a target type scope of 8X or more in the form of a Unertl, Lyman, or a Balvar 6-24. With the proper tuning and tailored handloads, this type of outfit should deliver at least ¾ MOA (minute of angle) or better. The long bar-

rel will deliver the highest velocity—hence flatter trajectory—than its shorter-barreled brothers in the same caliber. Since it is seldom carried for any distance or length of time, its heavy weight and somewhat delicate optics need not be considered serious drawbacks. Where long-range accuracy is the primary requisite, the heavy-barreled varminters have no equal.

On the other side of the specialized rifle spectrum we find the carbines with their 18″ and 20″ barrels. Completely equipped with scope and carrying sling these little bantams tip the scales at a mere 6¾ to 7½ lbs. Because of their light weight and short length (37-39 inches) they're a sheer joy to carry. In the unpredictable sport of predator calling, where the action could come from any direction, you've got to be ready for anything—and fast! If you've ever tried swinging at 24″ barreled sporter 180° while kneeling in heavy cover or in a camo-cloth blind you'll know why the carbine is the only choice. Since most shots are taken at relatively short ranges, the need for tack-driving accuracy and high velocity/flat trajectory are only lesser considerations. This is one area where the firepower provided by the semi-autos, pumps

and lever actions has distinct advantages over the bolts. A fast second shot is often needed when Mr. Predator is weaving in and out of the brush, presenting anything but a good target. A motionless fox, coyote, or bobcat standing broadside is a rare bird indeed! The optics should have the high luminosity and large field of view provided by the 2½ or 3X scopes; higher magnification makes it difficult to pick up a moving animal at close range. The reticle should be of the heavy crosshair, duplex or post variety to provide better visibility in the dim light of early morning and late evening when calling is most productive. A good combination reticle is the Command Post—crosshair or flat-top post and crosshair—found in the Bushnell scopes.

With the heavy varminter and carbine we sacrifice versatility for excellence in limited applications. Now, let's take a look at a rifle specifically designed for versatility: the sporter. Any smokepole that is light enough to be carried several hours without undue fatigue, one that handles well and can perform any task with a fair degree of efficiency, is a compromise at best. Nevertheless, a well-tuned sporter performs many varminting chores well.

Author's wife using "buffalo sticks" to give solid support to her 22-250 for a long shot.

Sundra with a day's take of 'chucks. Here's proof that sporters can deliver the goods!

Although author feels that cartridge choice is a secondary consideration, here are some of the better ones, from left: 225 Win., 22-250 Rem., 220 Swift, 243 Win., 6mm Rem., 25-284, 6.5-284 and 6.5-06.

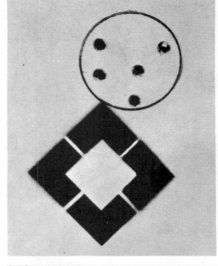

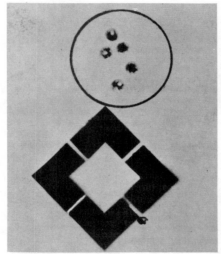

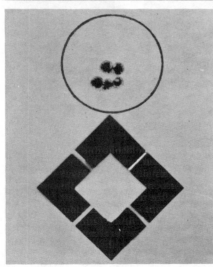

Targets showing average accuracy obtainable from varmint rifle types. Top: M600/6mm Rem. carbine, 4x scope, using 46.5/4350/85 Sierra SP. Middle, custom sporter in 6mm Rem., 9x variable scope, load 50/4831/85 Sierra SP. Third: Heavy-barreled Mauser in 243 Win., 15x scope, load 43.5/4350/90 Speer SP. All groups about 75% full size, all shot at 100 yards.

Ruger No. 1 single-shot rifle, in 222, 22-250, 243 and 6mm is versatile enough to be used in all categories mentioned in the article.

Savage M24-V, an over-under 222 and 20 ga., is a fast-handling gun for short to medium range.

Remington 760 Gamemaster, available as a 223 carbine, is fast for a follow-up shot yet is short in over-all length for quick swinging.

The average sporter has a barrel of 22″ to 24″ tapering to about .610″ to .650″ at the muzzle. Depending on whether the trigger guard/floorplate assembly is steel or alloy, type of wood and density, and scope/mount combo, the gun will weigh anywhere from about 8 to 9½ lbs. complete with sling. Since we are striving for versatility, the choice of scope should be a variable of the 2X-7X or 3X-9X variety. These will provide enough magnification for those long shots at chucks and crows and also enable you to cut back to 2X or 3X for close-range work, as in predator calling in heavy cover and/or dim light.

Although being rather light, the sporter is often capable of astounding accuracy. Two of my favorites are a Douglas-barreled 6mm Remington on a Mauser action and a Douglas-barreled 22/250 based on a Reming-

ton 722 action. Both of these rifles deliver constant MOA groups or better, some of which measure as small as ⅜″. That's excellent accuracy for any kind of rifle! The new Model 788 Remington in the same pair of calibers are giving excellent accuracy, I hear, and total weight is low.

The Debit Side

Now that we've reviewed the advantages of each type of rifle, let's look at the drawbacks. In all fairness, though, the "drawbacks" occur only when we expect a rifle to perform a function at which another type was designed to excel. Therefore, any comparison is invalid, and useful only in demonstrating the fact that you "can't have your cake and eat it too."

The heavy-barreled jobs are the most specialized of the group, hence the least adaptable. Their heavy

Winchester 100 carbine, here in 243 caliber, for those who like the speed of a semi-auto in close-quarters shooting.

Remington 660 carbine is fast-handling and the good ballistic factors of the 243 and 6mm make it a fine medium-range varmint rifle.

Savage's 99, also in 243 Win., makes a good choice for those who prefer a lever action.

Winchester 70 Varmint has a heavy barrel, and can be had in 22-250, 225 or 243. Add a high-power scope for the long shots.

Remington's 700 BDL is built as a heavy barrel varminter in 222, 223, 22-250, 6mm Rem. and 243 caliber for long-range shooting.

weight and long barrels make them a penance to carry for any length of time. Their target-type scopes and mounts are delicate compared to standard hunting scopes, making them suitable only for the car-cruising type of hunting. The carbines, on the other hand, are a pleasure to carry but because of their light weight they're hard to hold steady for really precise long-range shooting. Their short barrels will cut up to 200 fps from the velocity of a 24″ barrel and up to as much as 300-350 fps from a 26″ and 28″ barrel respectively. There would also be an increase in mid-range trajectory height at any given distance. The sporters with their 22″ and 24″ barrels are the type of gun you sling over your shoulder, along with your binoculars, and head for the fields prepared for come-what-may. It may not excel in any particular type of

varmint or predator hunting but it'll do a pretty darn good job at either.

Although I promised not to mention ballistics and trajectories, no discussion would be complete without a review of some of the better cartridges. Of the .22 centerfires, I'll take the 22-250 Rem. with the 225 Win. close behind, both loaded with 60-gr. Hornady bullets. In the 6mms I'd have to take the 6mm Rem. over the 243 Win., these loaded with either of the two 85-gr. Sierras or the 87-gr. Hornady. Of the 25's I'd pick the 25-284 followed by the venerable old 25-06, both with 100-gr. pills. In the 6.5s which is about the practical upper limit for a varmint-predator cartridge) I'd take the 6.5 Rem. due to its commercial status followed by the 6.5-284 loaded with the 100-grainers. I've purposely left out such hotshots as the 6mm-284, the 257 Weatherby and 264 Win-

chester because their case capacity/bore ratio makes them pretty hard on barrels. Between finding a load, potting predators, and paper punching, you're going to use lots of ammo. For this reason I would suggest you leave these, along with similar cartridges, for small and medium big game.

So, it all boils down to the old axiom, "You don't get nothin' for nothin'." To achieve excellence in one area you sacrifice some attribute in another, and the most important question to ask yourself is: "Do I do enough of a specific type of hunting to warrant a specialized rifle?" If the answer is "yes" or if, unlike me, money is no problem, you owe it to yourself to take full advantage of the respective attributes of the heavy-barreled varminter and/or the carbine; if you can't justify it on them, then the sporter is the rifle for you. ●

Testfire Report

A shooting and field evaluation of six sporting arms. There's handload data on a couple of them, too, plus critical notes on performance, construction and appearance.

- Charter Arms Pocket Target
- Colt's Mark III Sixguns
- Browning Lever Action BL-22
- Remington 5mm Rim Fire Magnum
- Browning Single Barrel Trap Gun
- Remington 25-06 in the Model 700 BDL

Charter Arms' latest, the Pocket Target, a 22 rimfire 6-shot revolver with adjustable sights, a new safety system and a lifetime firing pin.

by RUSS CARPENTER

Charter Arms Pocket Target

After years of lying nearly dormant, development of new hand guns is again going strong. To illustrate, Colt has their new Mk III on the market, Ruger's new Security Six is in production and Thompson/Center is offering a whole batch of new chamberings for their Contender pistol. These new developments are news of the current times and show the optimistic thinking of these manufacturers. All this in spite of the dim view given the future of handguns by the ill-advised Eisenhower Crime Commission. But, when a new company enters the handgun manufacturing field under these conditions I call it a real display of optimism. This is just what Doug McClenahan and his crew at Charter Arms Corp. have done. Of course, I view the progressiveness of these people with delight. The fact is that Charter Arms could not have picked a better time to market their snubnosed Undercover pistol, inasmuch as the handgun industry has been bogged down with shortages of good undercover pistols for several years. Needless to say, the Undercover 38 Special has been a success.

Now Charter is entering the sporting handgun field with a pocket pistol chambered for the 22 RF. It's the type of pistol most outdoorsmen know as a kit gun for it fits into a small section of the hunter's pack or the fisherman's kit. Charter Arms calls it the Pocket Target 22 LR and, while I found it quite accurate, the only target shooting it's suited for is the informal kind so many of us enjoy while afield.

The action of the Pocket Target is identical to Charter's 5-shot 38 Special Undercover model, but it has a 3-inch barrel and is a 6-shooter. It weighs a bit under 19 ounces and features adjustable sights.

The frame of the Pocket Target is made in two pieces. The main frame is steel and supports the cylinder and houses the working parts. An aluminum die cast extension holds the grips, retains the mainspring and forms the trigger guard.

The cylinder swings out and may be unlatched by either pushing the serrated cylinder latch button forward or pulling forward on the ejector rod. When the cylinder is closed the rear end of the ejector rod locks into a hole in the frame, while forward of the frame a collar on the front section of the ejector rod locks into a hole counterbored in the forward end of the frame. From the standpoint of safety this seems a satisfactory lock up, but there is quite a lot of play in the forward end of the cylinder and the crane. This play seems to have little or no effect as accuracy has been very good for a snub-nosed pistol. Evidently, it must lock up close to dead center or this would not be so.

The action of the Pocket Target has built-in insurance against accidental firing. The system used to prevent this is the same as Colt is using on their new Mk-III revolvers. It consists of a bar called the hammer block which moves between the face of the hammer and the firing pin as the trigger is pulled to the rear. Unless the trigger is pulled the bar is not in position to complete the linkage between these parts and the hammer can only hit the frame. This is a very sure safety feature that prevents an accidental blow, such as dropping the pistol, to cause the gun to fire.

The front sight is of the accepted square or Patridge type with a ⅛-inch blade. Adjustments are in the rear sight, with a screw on the left side for windage and a spring-loaded rocker adjusted by an opposing screw for elevation. The windage screw has no clicks or graduations, but the elevation screw, while lacking graduations, is click loaded. The adjustments work in a satisfactory manner, but on one pistol I tested it took all of the available left windage to center the point of impact.

The walnut grips are made in two styles—plain or oversized at the buyer's option. The plain grips fit the frame rather poorly—in some places they overhang while in others they're over ¹⁄₃₂-inch from the edge. I switched grips on two different Charter Arms 22s and they fit differently on each. Quality control in manufacturing the grip frame and the grips themselves should be given more tender loving care. The plain grips are quite small, but I like their feel. Those shooters who prefer a more hand-filling grip can spend $6.50 more and get the oversized Bulldog style. The fit of the Bulldog grips is excellent, and they cover the entire frame—not just the sides. They are checkered and undoubtedly give the shooter a firmer grip.

Trigger pull on the Pocket Target I've been carrying on walks afield is 3 pounds when fired single action, and

11 pounds in double action. The single action pull is clean and free from any sign of creep. The double action pull weight increases smoothly as the trigger is pulled, with no final click or build up as the point of firing is reached. While this may sound great to anyone without experience at double action shooting, combat trained shooters of the old school had their pet double action revolvers tuned so build up came exactly at a point that told them—through the trained feel of their educated trigger finger—that the pistol was ready to fire. This is the only way that proper control can be exerted to achieve good hits in double action shooting. However, I wouldn't worry about double action work with the Pocket Target, for nothing the sportsman will shoot at ordinarily requires a speed faster than single action. Single action let offs are the only way to shoot a revolver of this kind if you want to hit your mark.

The steel parts of the gun are blued, the aluminum elements black anodized. The hammer is color case-hardened and the grips are oil finished. Over-all quality of finish is good.

I experienced no malfunctions of any kind in using various brands and types of ammunition. Extraction was generally good, although a cylinder full of certain brands of ammo did show rather hard extracting, but not enough to be really bothersome. These were shotshells; but I've found that the long brass of shot loads stick in most of my revolvers. I test such shotshells, of course, because they'll be used for snake control by fishermen who carry the Pocket Target.

The new Charter Arms 22 revolver is a good choice for the outdoorsman who wants a handy and compact handgun for use afield or around camp.

Colt's Mk III Trooper 357 Magnum, the leader among a group of new-design revolvers. The Mk III Official Police has no barrel rib or ejector-rod housing, comes in 38 Special and has fixed sights only.

Colt's Mark III Sixgun

A completely new revolver from Colt, not just a surface revamp, is truly a rare bird, but the Mk III I've been testing for nearly a year is all new. Not only is the gun new, the plant it's made in is new, manufacturing equipment and methods are new and, not least, many of the parts are made from new materials.

Hints of a new revolver had been coming out of Hartford for over two years. I was hoping to see a considerably simplified revolver mechanism, but the innards of a double action revolver are a complicated affair at best. Still, while the Mk III isn't really all that simple, much has been done in that direction. When you compare a pre-Mk III with the new model the latter's less complex mechanism is easily seen.

It may be that the all-new plant and their new and unusual automatic machinery will interest some readers, but that story will have to wait—we don't have the space here.

The outside appearance of the Mk III shows no hint of radical change, in fact it looks like most other Colt revolvers. It's when you remove the sideplate that you find the major changes. The first thing I noticed was the absence of the old hard-to-time rebound lever and cylinder-locking bolt. These parts as well as most of the other parts in a Colt (and many others) were never readily interchangeable. In truth, they required the service of a better-than-average gunsmith when repair or replacement was needed. The old locking bolt is a delicate bar that has to slide off a lug on the side of the action bar. These parts as well as others in the old system had to be precisely fitted if the gun was to function. The new bolt resembles the one used by S&W. It is a heavy part, spring-loaded and activated by a lever built into the upper forward part of the trigger—no fitting of these parts is required, but they are strong and efficient. The new bolt drops off its lever very fast and quickly wears a line on the cylinder. I don't like this from an appearance standpoint, but it is as it was designed to be.

Sintered Metal

The hammer and trigger, the two most complicated pieces in this new revolver are made of sintered metal, and I assume there may be other small parts so made. Sintering is a process in which an alloy or mixture of powdered metal is formed in a die under pressure, then heated, but not melted, until it becomes a very dense, non-porous finished piece. In the case of these parts it appears that no after machining or fitting was necessary. A good feature for Colt's manufacturing because of the shortage of skilled labor. Assembly of the Mk III offers no real problem. To my way of thinking this feature makes the Mk III truly a simpler revolver; Colt now has a handgun that, at long last, uses interchangeable parts, so now repair on any Colt in the new series becomes a simple matter of changing parts.

The working parts are very hard and can be expected to give exceptional wear. Colt claims to have fired 20,000 live rounds and 250,000 dry firings with one Mk III, and all of this without measurable wear — a truly tough test! I've shot my Mk III for about a year, but I've only fired about 1700 rounds—I don't think I'll live long enough to duplicate Colt's endurance tests.

The usual V-type mainspring, which always drove the hammer and returned the trigger after firing in the old Colt action, has been replaced by two stainless steel coil springs. I have never been a fan of coil springs in revolver actions, although I must admit there is much less breakage with the coil type. It has been my experience that many revolver actions using coil springs don't exhibit a crisp, clean feel on both cocking and firing. The Colt Mk III, however, has a better-than-average feel for a coil spring action. One spring drives the hammer and another returns the trigger, hand and hammer bar after each shot.

Short Action?

Colt claims a short action in the Mk III, but I can't agree. It seems to me to be not much shorter than my old Colt Trooper, and it's noticeably longer than my old 44 Special Model 1950 S&W Target. Most double actions have a shorter fall on the double action pull than with the single action pull—a necessity of design. The Mk III has a reasonable hammer fall when fired double action, but a full half-inch longer fall when shot single action. This is measured from the top of the hammer to the frame and in my opinion is too much.

The double action weight of pull in the Mk III is quite heavy, I thought, but after I compared its pull with that of several other revolvers I was surprised—all the popular double action revolvers on the market take from 9 to 12 pounds to let them off double action. I tested 3 S&Ws and 4 Colts, all new from factory boxes.

Colt's data sheet says the typical Mk III in double action breaks at 10½ pounds, but mine took a full 12. I wasn't happy with this so I decided to try to improve it. I tried various lubrications, but that didn't help. Next I filed and stoned the milling cutter tool marks inside the action until I got them smooth. I also stoned the bearing and friction surfaces of the working parts. There *was* an improvement, but it was slight. The next thing I did is not recommended to anyone without some gunsmithing experience. I shortened the mainspring a bit at a time testing the pull meanwhile, and when I had removed two turns the pull was down to 10 pounds. I was doing so well I tried a bit more, and when I'd removed a total of 3 turns the double action pull was down to 9 pounds;

the hammer felt spongy under my thumb, though, and while all the single action shots went off without failure, the double action letoffs produced two misfires in 15 shots! Needless to say, I replaced the mainspring with a new one, but I removed a turn-and-a-half from it, ending up with Colt's "typical" 10½-pound D.A. pull.

I'm not much of a fan of the double action technique for revolver shooting—getting old, I guess. I feel the way to place a shot where it counts is to cock the revolver and aim. Gone are the days when cheating river boat gamblers were shot across a card table, and any range much farther than that is too far for most shooters to hit anything firing double action. Sure, there are some highly trained pistolmen who can shoot and hit firing double action, even at fair distances, but they're few and far between. Most handgunners—cops and others—will do better if they stick to single action shooting. My Mk III, by the way, has a very nice 3-pound single action pull, though at first I could detect a slight creep. However, that bit of honing I did and the amount of shooting I've done has seen this disappear.

Colt calls the Mk III a strong and safe handgun, and so it seems to me. For instance, you could strike the rear of the hammer or even drop it from a great distance yet it could not fire unless someone or something held the trigger all the way to the rear. When the trigger is in full firing position it has moved a steel bar up *between* the front of the hammer and the firing pin. This completes the linkage, the bar transmitting the hammer energy to the firing pin. Without this bar in position the only thing the hammer can hit is the revolver frame.

The cylinder has ample wall thickness over the chambers to handle heavy loads, but Colt advertising says "Cylinder is not weakened by location of bolt notches." While I have no fear of my Mk III cylinder splitting, even with heavy loads, I must say Colt is not telling it quite like it is. The fact is that the deepest part of each bolt notch is located very near the center of the chamber, which is the thinnest section of the cylinder

wall. For this reason, if the chamber were fired with an over-loaded cartridge this would be the weakest point, and here is where I would expect it to fail. I repeat, though, that I feel it's amply safe and in reality I'm finding fault with advertising rather than engineering.

Field Tests

The real proof of any gun is how well it performs at the job it was designed to do. The Mk III was unquestionably designed for police work, but this doesn't mean it can't do double duty and serve well for the outdoorsman. My personal Mk III is a 4-inch 357 Magnum—though I would prefer a 6-inch version for hunting. I have used it afield and can find no fault with its performance.

For every hot 357 Magnum load I've fired in this Mk III I've shot two or more mid-range 38 Special handloads. Most of this mid-range shooting has been informal plinking with my two sons. To check accuracy and sight setting we use a sand bag rest, and at 25 yards these mild loads usually reward us with half-dollar-size clusters.

For a service or hunting type load I went the modern route pioneered by Lee Jurras with his Super Vel ammo. This is a lighter-than-normal-bullet driven at its highest safe velocity. My favorite load in this 357 is 19 grains of Hercules 2400 under Speer's 125-gr. jacketed bullet. From the sand bag rest groups were a bit larger than the mid-range load, but the explosive power and greater penetration is there for the highway patrolman who needs to stop a getaway car, or for the outdoorsman who wants to hunt with a handgun. The Colt Mk III, I believe, is a fine arm for the policeman or the outdoorsman.

The Mk III action will be applied to other Colts over the next few years (there are several already—the new Official Police is one), so we can expect a full updated line of Colt revolvers. I predict that this new and rugged, simplified handgun is going to be in high demand by shooters looking for high performance in a revolver—our misguided naive Solons permitting.

Browning's BL-22

When you combine the Western lever action carbine look with Browning quality craftsmanship you have the makings of a winner, and the new Browning BL-22 is just that. The fact that Browning's newest plinker is a lever action 22 rimfire makes it truly a natural for this company. I say this because John Browning was the de-

signer of the most popular lever-action rifles our shooting world has ever known. The Winchester Models 92, 94, 86 and 95 lever actions, as well as numerous other guns, were designed by this great man. He was undoubtedly the most productive of all gun designers. John Browning is long gone from the shooting scene, but one

glance at this sleek little carbine and it's easy to see that his influence is still with us.

There is one thing, though, that's different about this lever action—it's the first Browning gun to be stamped *Made In Japan*. I don't make the point to stigmatize this fine little rifle, for such other staid old companies as

Winchester and Ithaca have proved beyond a shadow of a doubt that great guns can be—and are—made by Japanese craftsmen. It's a first from Browning, but others are following—in fact, later in this same Test Fire section I'll be telling you about a second Japanese Browning. It's a new single barrel trap gun.

The first thing to catch my eye about this little carbine is the finish on wood and metal. The wood is walnut, and it's filled to perfection and topped with a high gloss finish. Personally I'm of the classic satin-finish school, but I must admit the stocks on this little carbine are very attractive.

Most gun manufacturers, Browning included, don't seal the end-grain wood of their stocks, under the buttplate. I suggest that a coat of sealer or stock finish is needed in this area, which requirement I discovered the hard way. I got caught out in a quick shower, getting the BL-22 pretty wet, and a bit later on the finish started to lift near the buttplate. Needless to say, I've since slapped a couple of coats of stock finish onto the end grain.

to flick the rifle opened and closed without releasing my grip on the stock. The lever houses the trigger and the gun cannot be fired unless the lever is fully closed; also, were you to hold the trigger back and close the lever the gun still won't fire. You must release the trigger to engage the sear and the gun will now fire the next time you pull the trigger. The trigger is also disengaged when the hammer is at half-cock. While on the subject of built-in safety there is another BL-22 feature I like; even with the hammer all the way forward, striking the hammer or dropping the gun on the hammer will not fire the BL-22! Why? Because the firing pin is *shorter* than the distance between the rear of the receiver and the cartridge head. This is an inertia-type pin, lightly spring-loaded to hold it rearward; when the hammer falls the blow is enough to drive the pin forward, striking the primer. It's quite safe and it's sure. I like the exposed hammer, especially for young shooters, because it's easy to tell at a glance if the gun is in its safest position.

Browning's dope sheet says most

Iron Sights

Like so many other rifles the open sights on the BL-22 leave a bit to be desired. The bead front sight is only blued steel, and I find it impossible to see it unless I'm shooting at a conventional black bull on a white target. For shooting a squirrel in dull woodslight, forget it. I suggest you replace it with either a gold or ivory bead for hunting or plinking. The rear sight is an adjustable folding leaf and unless you plan to install a receiver sight (the receiver is not drilled for one) why have a folding leaf? I found that all scope sights designed for 22 rimfires clear the leaf when it's in the up position. For a shooter who prefers open sights the leaf is apt to be folded about the time he wants to pot a squirrel. I would prefer a conventional solid sight here.

All this about sights will mean very little to you if you do as I did. The receiver is grooved for the tip-off type mount and I installed a Bushnell Custom 3x-7x variable scope on my test BL-22. This is a modestly priced ($15.95), dependable scope with a glossy finish that well-matches the fin-

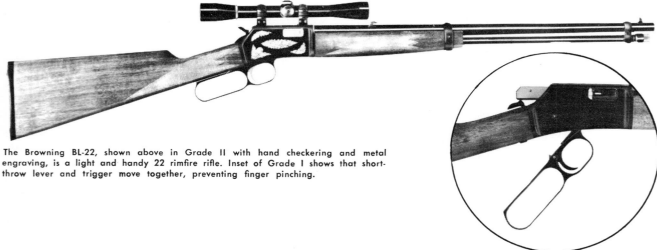

The Browning BL-22, shown above in Grade II with hand checkering and metal engraving, is a light and handy 22 rimfire rifle. Inset of Grade I shows that short-throw lever and trigger move together, preventing finger pinching.

The metal of the BL-22 is blued to the same degree of high gloss as is the wood finish. Most of the metal is machined steel, the magazine bands and the internal fire-control housing the only exceptions, and they are machined from aluminum.

When I disassembled the action I also found all internal parts were also machined from solid steel except for the ejector and one internal lever. While these two items are formed by a punch press, they show evidence of hand finishing—as do all of the internal parts. Such good care in manufacturing undoubtedly accounts in great part for the ease with which this carbine operates.

Short Lever Throw

The lever has a very short throw—Browning's specifications say that it moves 33 degrees. I found it quite easy

BL-22s have a 5-lb. trigger pull, but mine is a slight bit less—4¾. The best thing about the pull is that there's no noticeable creep. Many of you shooters may think 5 pounds is excessive and, were this a target rifle, it would be. But this is a plinker that will see a lot of service from inexperienced shooters, and I find it a perfect trigger for informal shooting. In fact we've had great sport shooting this little rifle at beer cans tossed out 60 or 70 feet in a gravel pit—and in no time at all those cans are chewed to pieces.

Another feature I especially like is the tubular-magazine latch. It's positive in any position—just push it closed and it catches. It also opens from any position. There is no fumbling with a pin in the flimsy slot that's found on many 22s.

ish on the BL-22. It's compact, the adjustments are positive, and the grooved mount is very secure.

The BL-22 takes down by removing the screw in the right hand side of the receiver, lowering the lever and pulling the buttstock, lever, fire control parts and breechblock out to the rear. While this is rather an easy takedown I don't recommend it to any one except a gunsmith, as several parts are loose when the gun is apart. Browning does not give direction for taking down in the BL-22 literature, so let this be a word to the wise—leave the BL-22 together except for a periodic cleaning by your gunsmith.

The BL-22 is sold by authorized Browning dealers, and the cost of $74.50 is truly a modest price for such quality. It's an ideal choice for young-at-heart plinkers between eight and eighty.

Remington's Model 592 is the tubular-magazine 5mm Rim Fire Magnum, shown here being tested at Creedmoor Farm. See "Sporting Arms of the World" in this issue for further shooting data.

Remington 5mm RF Magnum

Late in 1967 Remington invited a group of gun writers to Merrymeeting Bay in the state of Maine to do a bit of waterfowl shooting and take a peek at the new Remington offerings for that year. Among other things, they showed us a new rimfire cartridge called the 5mm Rim Fire Magnum. They even gave each of the writers there a sample cartridge, and that was the last we saw or heard about the new 20-caliber cartridge.

That was the situation until late in 1969 when Remington invited the same group of writers to the YO Ranch in Texas for some whitetail hunting plus another preview of "what's new at Remington." Part of the news was a reintroduction of the 5mm RF Magnum, and the promise that it really was ready this time! I'd about begun to think it would never be marketed, with visions of my one sample cartridge becoming a rare collector's item. But no—the 5mm is here, and I've been testing it for several weeks.

I've learned that the reason for this great delay was a series of problems —unexplainable excess pressure and how to lick it plagued both the cartridge and the rifle. So, back to the drawing board for two years, but now I can tell you that both rifle and cartridge have been perfected, and that it is the hottest rimfire cartridge I've ever fired.

Before I tell you about the cartridge, though, let me describe the rifle Remington developed for this hot little rimfire. Back in 1966 Remington introduced a new line of bolt action rifles chambered for the 22 rimfires, calling them the 580 series. Those new rifles featured a rear lock-up system with 6 locking lugs on the bolt—two rows of 3. It was quite evident that here was an action with many times the strength needed for the regular 22 RF cartridges. At the time I felt sure that Remington had bigger and better things in mind for this strong little action. My prediction has come true, too, for Remington has modified the very same action to accommodate the new 5mm load.

As Remington has used an action and basic rifle you're undoubtedly familiar with, I'm not going to tell you here all the details of the rifle, but there are some points well worth covering.

The Model 591, a clip repeater, is the type I've been testing. (There is also a tubular version, the M592.) The clip holds 4 cartridges and, if you put one in the chamber, you're good for 5 shots. The clip is made of a light, tough plastic material — it loads easy, and it's also easy to insert or detach from the rifle.

The stock on my Model 591, identical in specifications to that on my Model 582, is a well-designed stock— it's slender, but has a full sized feel. The comb is the proper height to put your eye perfectly in line for a scope sight.

The 24-inch barrel carries open sights. The front sight, dovetailed to the barrel, is quite high and has a silver bead. The rear sight, a flat-topped leaf with a U notch, is adjustable for windage and elevation.

The trigger is designed with a falling sear as found on more expensive high powered rifles, but it's not adjustable. I found the trigger pull to be free from creep, but too heavy— it was 5½ pounds. I removed the trigger, stoned the engaging surfaces and removed a couple of coils from the trigger return spring. I ended up with a clean 3-pound pull. I don't recommend this trigger improvement job to any one without gunsmith experience, but your local gunshop can adjust this trigger to perfection for about 5 bucks.

The extraction system developed for the 5mm is truly unique, I think. It's a double stage mechanism that allows the cartridge head to be completely supported when the bolt is closed. The first stage is part of the chamber wall and, as the bolt is pulled to the rear, this section hooks to the bolt and comes back, drawing the cartridge with it. This first stage comes out about ⅜", then separates from the bolt and returns to its original position in the chamber wall. At this point a conventional hook extractor takes over and finishes the job of pulling the cartridge completely from the chamber to a point where it's tossed out the ejection port. The secondary hook doesn't do the entire job because the chamber wall would have to be cut away, at least in the area of the rim, to let the hook catch hold of the cartridge rim. With the high pressure present in the 5mm case any unsupported area might blow out. With the system Remington uses there are no unsupported areas in the chamber walls. In my test shooting extraction and ejection were perfect.

The receiver is grooved for scope mounts, and for range testing I installed the reasonably priced Weaver V22 3x-6x variable scope with Weaver tip-off mounts. The reticle is Weaver's Dual-X, which has heavy outer wires supporting fine cross wires at the center. I strongly recommend this style for varmint hunting.

The 5mm/20 caliber cartridge is really all new, its bullets miking .204" in diameter, and weighing 38 grains. The bottle-neck case gives an impression of high power, and it is, certainly, the fastest and most-energy rimfire on the market today. The 5mm bullet, of hollow point form, is made in the popular "Power-Lokt" construction, which has earned a high reputation for accuracy The listed velocity is 2100 fps at the muzzle, and at 150 yards down range it's still traveling 1400 fps. I checked velocity on my Oehler Model 10 chronograph, recording an average MV of 2033 fps. My reading was taken 5½ feet from the muzzle, so I feel Remington's 2100 MV figure is acceptably correct. From Remington's ballistic charts and my own tests I feel that the 5mm RFM is a good choice for woodchuck-sized varmints out to 150 yards.

For accuracy I test-fired the 5mm from a bench rest at 100 yards. Results were good. The average of ten 5-shot groups was about 1½₂″—the largest was 1⅞″, the smallest ⅝-inch. I feel this is good accuracy for varmint shooting up to that practical range of 150 yards I've suggested.

The Model 591 clip repeater sells for $64.95, the Model 592 tubular repeater for $69.95. The Weaver V22 scope complete with a tip-off mount is only $15.95, and I simply don't know how they do it at that price!

I think the M591-Weaver V22 combination, at a total cost of $80.90, represents a hell of a good buy for a 150-yard varmint rifle, though the ammo at some 7¢ a round may prevent a lot of casual plinking!

Remington 25-06

Our oldest wildcat cartridge has gone legitimate. I really don't know the year the late Adolph O. Niedner first squeezed the neck of a 30-06 cartridge down to 25 caliber, but I do know he was ahead of the times with his 25-06, becausee it was years before fully suitable powders became available. I made up my first 25-06 about 1950, but it was many years earlier when Niedner had started the 25-06 ball rolling. At the time I made my reamer the in thing was to give wildcats a sharp 40-degree shoulder, but I made my reamer with the standard 17.5 degree slope of the 30-06. I never regretted the decision to make it this way, and since then I've probably chambered two dozen barrels to the old standard 25 Niedner. I still shoot the first rifle I made in this caliber and, though it's probably been fired over 1500 rounds, it still puts 5 shots in less than two inches at 200 yards.

Remington's new 25-06 is an exact copy of Niedner's' original version, and they are chambering it in their Model 700 bolt action rifle. The Model 700 is a great rifle, but it's not so new I'm going to bore you with a lot of gab about a rifle you already know.

At present the new 25-06 Remington is loaded with a varmint type 87-gr. Power-Lokt bullet. But Remington promises that by the time you read this a 120-gr. Core-Lokt big game load will be on your dealer's shelf.

A rifle like the 25-06 would be worthless without a good telescope sight. In fact, selection of the scope can make or break the efficiency of any rifle, whatever the cartridge or caliber. For the 25-06 I picked one of the new Redfield Widefield models in 6 power. As the 25-06 is a dual-purpose load, equally suitable for varmints and big game, this scope is a good choice. In other words a 6x

scope is minimal for varmints and more than enough for big game.

The new Widefields are made in three fixed-power models—2¾x, 4x and 6x. The field of view is a full 25% wider than other scopes I compared it against. It's almost like looking out a picture window. The eyepiece of the scope is flatted top and bottom, but according to Ed Hilliard of Redfield, Redfield has not simply ovalized the ocular lens—a new optical principle, up for patent, is involved. By doing this Redfield made it possible, however, to have the advantages offered by a large diameter ocular, and still mount the scope low to the rifle.

The test scope has Redfield's 4-PLEX reticle. This is the type with heavy posts from four directions and fine cross wires at the center. The heavy section tends to attract or direct your eye to the center even in poor light, and the finer center section makes an aiming point that's usable on the smallest of targets.

Throughout my tests of the 25-06 the Redfield Widefield performed to perfection. It's a great choice for a rifle of this type, but I'd advise less power than 6x for the average big game rifle.

The 87-gr. factory cartridge, loaded with that super-accurate Power-Lokt HP bullet, lives up to the reputation earned by this bullet in the 22s and 6mms. Were I to average all my groups the chart would show well over an inch, but I shot many 5-shot targets under an inch, and I have a few 3-shot strings that are just over half an inch.

Remington's spec. sheet says this load gives 3500 fps velocity at the muzzle. They correct or estimate to the muzzle, and they test in a 26-inch barrel. Seven-and-a-half feet from the Model 700 muzzle I recorded 3266 fps using the standard 24-inch barrel. This is a lot less than 3500 fps, but with handloads it's well with-

in safe limits to boost the velocity of an 87-gr. bullet up to 3500 fps. The powder in the few loads I pulled apart appears to be quite like Du Pont's IMR 4350, and the load is 53 grains. I never advise anyone to copy a factory load by looks, but this load is well under accepted and published loads for this cartridge, so should therefore be safe to copy. I loaded 53 grains of 4350 behind a Sierra 87-gr. SP spitzer. Velocity was only 27 fps slower than the Remington Power-Lokt load. As the different make bullet with it's different bearing surface could cause this amount of variation I'm quite sure Remington is using a powder very close to 4350. While looks and the chronograph made this appear to be so, the primers in the Remington load had the appearance of near maximum pressure. Perhaps the primers used by Remington are made of a softer material than the 250 CCI Magnum primers I was using. However, I loaded the 87-gr. Sierra bullet up to 56/4350 and velocity averaged 3428 fps. There were no sign of excess pressure, and accuracy was good.

Over the many years I have shot my old 25-06 I've used 4350 for most of my loads though I have always leaned toward heavier bullets in this caliber. Other powders will undoubtedly load well in the 25-06, but 55 grains of 4350 will push the 100-gr. Speer close to 3300 fps and 52/4350 gives the 120-gr. Speer 3025 fps. Loads that have worked well in my old rifle gave like results in the new Remington.

The 25-06 is a medium/heavy cartridge suitable for bigger varmints or up to such game as whitetail and mule dear. I know it will be used on heavier game, and will probably make some fine kills, but it's still not to be recommended. It's a great cartridge that long ago proved itself, and I expect to see it enjoy a new lease on life as a member of Remington's growing family.

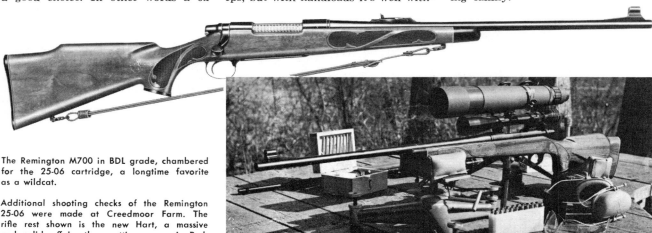

The Remington M700 in BDL grade, chambered for the 25-06 cartridge, a longtime favorite as a wildcat.

Additional shooting checks of the Remington 25-06 were made at Creedmoor Farm. The rifle rest shown is the new Hart, a massive and solid affair; the spotting scope is Redfield's 15-60, a new variable glass that works well indeed.

Browning's New Single Barrel Trap Gun

The competitive trapshooter who wants a single barrel trap gun in the old traditional style can find it in the new Browning Model BT-99. Here's a trap gun of the kind that Parker, Ithaca, LeFever and like companies built—mostly by hand—in the early years of this century.

The BT-99 is an import, though, made under Browning's close supervision in far away Japan, but I'm pleased to be able to say that it displays the fine quality we've come to expect from Browning.

The buttstock is the usual long, high-combed design needed by the trapshooter to positively align his eye over the barrel, to insure the same sight picture shot after shot. My BT-99 has a 14½-inch pull, the drop a bit less than the Browning spec sheet

fore-end checkering wraps around both sides and the bottom. All this checkering is deeply cut, and sharp enough to improve the shooter's grip. The wood has a high gloss finish, plastic probably, times being what they are.

My test gun has a 34-inch barrel, but though most of the experienced trapshooters who tried this gun on clays liked the long tube, I believe the 32-inch version would handle easier for those of slight build. In other words, the 34-inch barrel is a bit muzzle heavy. I like this as it swings and follows through well, but it could be a bit tiring for some shooters.

The barrel is topped with a ventilated rib that is quite high at the breech end and quite low at the muzzle. This causes the gun to shoot high, which is as it should be with a trap

rected mine by lengthening the ejector actuating rod. After this adjustment there were no malfunctions of any kind. The trigger pull is a clean, crisp 3½ pounds. There is no safety, as a trap gun is never closed till the shooter is ready to fire.

Before testing the BT-99 at the traps I tried it out on pattern sheets. The barrel is marked FULL CHOKE, and after I'd fired a few shots I knew the barrel was properly marked. The way that barrel squeezes the pattern down makes this shotgun a handicap shooter's dream. Patterns ran better than 90% using Remington All-American 7½ trap loads at 40 yards. I measured the bore and found .040" constriction, whereas .025" usually gives a full choke pattern in many field guns. The BT-99 can be had, how-

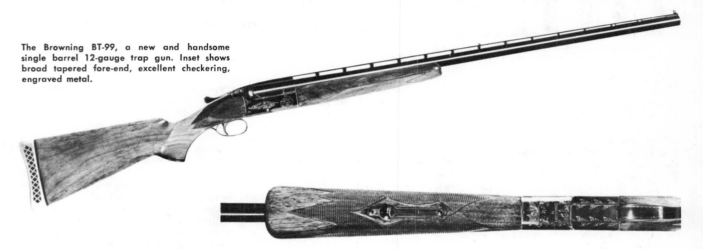

The Browning BT-99, a new and handsome single barrel 12-gauge trap gun. Inset shows broad tapered fore-end, excellent checkering, engraved metal.

calls for—1⅜-inch at the comb and 1½ inches at the heel. Because many trapshooters reshape their stocks—hoping they'll obtain that will o' the wisp—a perfect fit for them, the high comb on the new Browning gives these customizers a little more wood to work with. As for me, I had no problem with the fit of the stock—it suited me fine, and I liked the curved, concave recoil pad that's standard on the BT-99.

The fore-end is a hand filling beavertail type that tapers from a narrow 1½ inches wide at the rear to 2⅜ inches across at the front. This tapered shape is considered by many shooters to give good forward control of the gun. The fore-end fastens to the barrel with a catch that uses a spring-loaded lever — similar to the method used on most high grade doubles and singles. There are three screws on the inside and a through bolt to the forward tip, so this fore-end should never shoot loose.

The pistol grip and fore-end carry an abundance of well-cut, 20 lines to the inch checkering. There are two large side panels that just touch at the top of the pistol grip, while the

gun. Your targets are rising, therefore as you swing up and under them, the high shot charge will hit. The top of the rib is serrated to prevent glare, and there are two white bead sights. The forward one is a medium-sized Bradley type, the rear bead a small round one set flush with the rib, about mid-way up the barrel.

The receiver is attractively scroll engraved, and all the metal is nicely blued—not in a glossy finish, either, but more of a subdued matting.

Inside the action all the working parts are heavy, hardened and well finished. I was especially impressed by the ruggedness of these parts. I don't expect to see many *broken* BT-99s—but here's what occurred in mine. An automatic ejector lifts an unfired shell from the chamber or kicks a fired shell out. The auto ejector malfunctioned regularly on my test gun. When I dry fired the gun it worked fine, but when a shell was actually fired the resistance from the primer held the actuating mechanism back enough to prevent the engagement of the ejector sear. I know of no other BT-99 having this trouble, and I cor-

ever, with a choice of three different chokes — full, improved modified or modified. As I've said, the full choke version is a fine choice for the handicap shooter, but I recommend the improved modified for most trapshooters. If you are a rather casual, once-in-a-while type trapshooter the regular modified choke might be the best choice. With the middle bead lined up at the base of the front bead, and the bird flying just over the front bead, I found that this sight picture centered the pattern right on the clay. This is the picture most trapshooters want.

I'm not a hotshot trap gunner, so I don't shoot many straight 25s, but my average with the BT-99 has been 21 x 25—scores that are over my head normally! Friends who are better at the game do very well indeed with this good looking trap gun.

The BT-99 is made in Grade I only and sells for a modest $295. Yes, that's a "modest" figure for a gun built to fire tens of thousands of shotshells. The BT-99 should last for years of trouble-free service, and I think it's a lot of trap gun for the money.

British Military Cartridges ---

Pistol, Revolver, SMG

by P. LABBETT

A detailed study of England's service cartridges for handguns and submachine guns.

British cartridges, from left: Mk 2, 450 Adams revolver; Mk 3, 476 Enfield revolver; 442 R.I.C. Webley; Mk 1, 455 Blank and Mk 2, 455 Blank.

BRITAIN BEGAN tentatively to arm her Army and Navy with revolvers in 1854. Before that date, early revolver types had been viewed with official distrust: they were prone to misfire or jam, and single shot percussion pistols had continued in service. These were, in terms of reliability and strength, more suitable than the percussion revolvers then commercially available. Pistols were normally carried by officers of both services, and by cavalry troopers. In addition the Royal Navy used large quantities, especially to arm boarding parties.

From 1854 however, the position changed, and from that time more reliable revolvers became available. That year the Select Committee on Small Arms recommended the purchase of Adams revolvers for both the Navy and Army. In the following year large quantities of 45 cal. Adams and 36 cal. Colt revolvers, both percussion guns, were purchased. The latter were mainly for the Royal Navy, but both types were used in the Crimea campaign, against the Russians (1854-1856), and during the Indian Mutiny (1857). The Royal Navy bought no more Colts after about 1860, but maintained existing Colts in service well into the 1870s. The Army began to convert its Adams to centerfire in 1868, and obtained further quantities of Adams revolvers originally made as centerfire weapons.

The Adams revolver, whatever its other virtues, lacked punch, its 450 cartridge being comparatively puny. However, for the next 12 years it remained Britain's standard revolver. Officers of the Army during this period often armed themselves with privately purchased revolvers, or multi-barrel pistols, taking heavier cartridges, up to 577 caliber. The British Army, between 1860 and 1900, waged a whole series of hard-fought campaigns, mostly in Africa or Asia, against savage enemies who took a lot of killing. Few officers fancied their chances in these wars, if caught in hand to hand combat, armed with the 450 Adams. The following list shows the type of campaign referred to.

Pekin	1860
Ashantee	1873-74
Afghanistan	1878-80
Kabul	1879
Kandahar	1880
Egypt	1882
Nile	1884-85
Burma	1885-87
Khartoum	1898

Britain replaced the Adams with the Enfield 476 revolver in 1880. While an advance over the Adams, it was not basically a good design. It was a self-ejecting top hinge model, of rather clumsy appearance. Its cartridge, however, was a good deal more powerful than that of the Adams, and the Enfield went a long way to satisfying the need for a worthwhile revolver. It was, even at the time of its introduction, inferior to the then commercially available Webley revolver.

In 1894 Britain introduced the first of its long line of Webley revolvers for Army service—the Mark I. Up to the replacement of the Webley in the early 1930s, a total of 6 different Marks were adopted. The Webley series, all of 455 caliber, earned their reputation for toughness and reliability. Although replacement of the 455 Webley began when the 380 Enfield was introduced,

Webleys remained in service, especially as a wartime substitute weapon, until 1945. Some are still used in Commonwealth country Armies.

The last of Britain's revolvers was the 380 Enfield revolver No. 2 which, although now partially replaced by the Browning automatic pistol, is still in use today. Although the 380 Enfield was the last of the official line, Britain pressed into service large numbers of Smith and Wesson 380 revolvers during the WW II. Then, as in the first world war, she had to meet requirements for handguns by using a number of substitute weapons — Colts, Smith and Wessons, even old Adams revolvers.

One other revolver should be mentioned, although one not used by the British regular forces. This was the 442 Royal Irish Constabulary Webley. The weapon was officially introduced and recorded by the Army, because the Royal Irish Constabulary was a para-military force, highly trained and well-armed, working in close liaison with the Army. The R.I.C. had internal security duties far different from normal British police duties. Ireland was torn by internal strife, amid which turmoil the normally unarmed British police would have been helpless, thus a para-military organization came into being. The present day Royal Ulster Constabulary, which came into existence on the partition of Ireland in 1922, is the direct descendant of the old R.I.C. It is still the only permanently armed police force in the United Kingdom.

The Royal Irish Constabulary adopted the 442 Webley before the Army adopted the 455 Webley, later

Enfield Mk 2 revolver,
Model 1882, cal. 476.

Power pistol at the end of the 1939-45 war.

The 9mm Browning was first issued to British airborne troops in WW II. After that its use was extended greatly, but at no time has it completely replaced the 380 Enfield revolver. Where handguns are still carried, it is often the Enfield.

Britain's choice of 9mm caliber for auto pistols was natural, for apart from the efficiency of this cartridge, it was already in extensive use in British submachine guns. Britain's first domestic SMG was the 9mm Lanchester, an outright steal of the Bergmann design. Short of submachine guns at the outbreak of the 1939 war, Britain put into service large quantities of 45-cal. U.S. Thompsons. As the war progressed the Thompson was gradually replaced by the 9mm Sten submachine

augmenting them with Enfield and Webley revolvers of Army origin.

From 1900 onwards, Britain carried out fairly extensive trials with various automatic pistols. The Army, while still sold on revolvers, felt that experience in alternatives was lacking, and the trials were mainly held to rectify this lack, and to give the Army an insight into the design, functioning and limitations of auto pistols generally. Between 1900 and 1911 the Small Arms Committee tested the following auto pistols — Borchardt, Bergman, Steyr, Roth, Browning, Colt, Mars, Mauser, Frommer, Glisenti and Webley. Many of these were tried in different models or calibers, and some of the individual trials were of a comprehensive nature. At the end of them, the Army still had a marked preference for the revolver. The Royal Navy had shown interest in the Webley auto pistol, adopting them on a partial basis in 1912, but said at the same time that they intended to keep the Webley revolver as their basic weapon. In 1915 the use of the Webley pistol was extended to the Royal Flying Corps. This 455 cal. Webley auto was the only official auto pistol until the adoption of the 9mm Browning Hi-

Webley Mk 1 revolver, c. 1894, cal. 455.

gun. In all, 6 service Marks of Stens were introduced, eventually replacing the Thompson altogether. In the 1950s the 9mm L2A2 SMG (the Sterling) was introduced, now the sole SMG in British service.

The ammunition for British service pistols and SMGs, past and present, therefore, falls into the following main types:

450 revolver	380 revolver
442 revolver	455 auto
476 revolver	45 ACP
455 revolver	9mm Parabellum

These types, described below, were all manufactured in British government ammunition factories except the 45 ACP. Britain, although producing this caliber commercially, did not manufacture it for military purposes, relying on imported ammunition, of U.S. manufacture. 45 ACP ammunition was, however, made in Australian and Canadian government factories.

450 for Adams revolver. Three Marks of this type were issued, all cartridge cases 17mm long.

450 Mark I. Approved November, 1868. Has brass case with iron base-disc. 13-gr. charge of black powder. 25-gr. lead bullet with two cannelures. Boxer primed.

450 Mark 2. Approved September, 1877. Differs from the Mark I in having a brass base-disc instead of iron. Boxer primed.

4-barreled Lancaster pistol, cal. 476.

British cartridges, from left: Mk 1, Black Powder 455 Ball (Mk 1, Cordite is similar but has cannelured case); Mk 2, 455 Ball Cordite; Mk 3, 455 Ball Cordite; Mk 4, 455 Ball Cordite (Mk 5 is similar in appearance); Mk 6, 455 Ball and Mk 1, 455 Drill D.

450 Mark 3. During WWI the Adams revolver was taken back into service as a reserve weapon. The Mark 3 cartridge was introduced at this time; unlike earlier marks it had a normal, solid-drawn, one-piece brass case, further identified by a heavy cannelure missing from earlier Marks. Berdan primed.

455/476 for Enfield revolver. Three Marks of this ammunition were issued, all with cases 22mm long, all with solid, drawn-brass cases using Boxer primers. 18 grs. black powder.

Mark I. Introduced 1880. Only a small number were ever made, and these were sent to India. Bullet diameter .455″, and somewhat shorter than the Mark 2 bullet.

Mark 2. Introduced 1880. 265-gr. lead bullet with base cavity, diameter .455″. Charge was 18 grains of black powder. Small diameter primer. After June, 1881, the bullets were additionally secured via 3 indentations into the case. Boxer primed.

Mark 3. Introduced end of 1881. 265-gr. lead bullet has three cannelures, diameter .477″. Unlike the Mark 2, it has a clay plug in the base cavity. Charge was 18 grains black powder. Identifiable by top cannelure visible above case mouth. Boxer primed.

442 for R.I.C. Webley. One Mark of ball and one of blank were issued for this series. Brass case was 16.5mm long. The ball and blank both used Boxer primers.

Mark I, Ball. Approved 4 June, 1892. 219-gr. lead bullet with one cannelure. Charge was 10 grains black powder.

Mark I, Blank. Approved 4 June, 1892. Charge was 11 grains of black powder.

455 for Webley revolver (also originally intended for use in existing stocks of Enfield revolvers). The following marks of this type were issued, all with .455″ diameter bullets:

Ball, black powder—1 Mark.
Ball, Cordite—6 Marks.
Blank—2 Marks.
Dummy/drill—2 Marks.
Proof—1 Mark.

The Mark I black powder and Mark I Cordite used cases 21.5mm long, both Boxer primed, while the Mark 2 through Mark 6 Ball used cases 19mm long. The remaining Ball rounds were Berdan primed. Details of various marks are:

Mark I, Ball, Black powder. Approved July, 1891. Solid, drawn-brass case. 265-gr. lead bullet with three cannelures, base cavity. Charge was 18 grains black powder.

Mark I, Ball, Cordite. Approved Sept., 1894. Similar in appearance to Mark I black powder except case has single cannelure. 265-gr. lead bullet has 3 cannelures, base cavity. Charge was 6.5 grains Cordite.

Mark 2 Ball, Cordite. Approved July, 1897, but almost immediately withdrawn in favor of the Mark 3. The Mark 3, because of its bullet design having a dum-dum or expanding effect was withdrawn from service, and in 1900 manufacture of the Mark 2 was recommended. The Mark 2 continued as the basic 455 cartridge until replaced by the Mark 6. The Mark 2, first of the short (19mm) cased 455 rounds, carried a 265-gr. lead bullet having 3 cannelures and a base cavity.

Webley Mk 4 revolver, c. 1899, cal. 455.

Webley 455 auto pistol, Mk 1 Naval, adopted 1913.

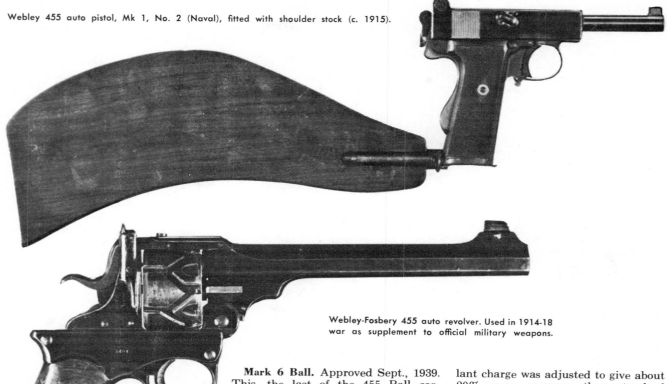

Webley 455 auto pistol, Mk 1, No. 2 (Naval), fitted with shoulder stock (c. 1915).

Webley-Fosbery 455 auto revolver. Used in 1914-18 war as supplement to official military weapons.

The charge varied between about 5 and 6 grains of chopped Cordite.

Mark 3 Ball, Cordite. Approved February, 1898, issued in place of Mark 2 but withdrawn in 1900 due to bullet shape. The Mark 3 used the same case as the Mark 2, but the lead bullet, in addition to its base cavity, had a deep nose cavity, which gave it an "explosive" effect. Bullet weight, 220 grains; charge 6 grains Cordite.

Mark 4 Ball, Cordite. Approved May, 1912. Designed to give better man-stopping capability than the Mark 2, the lead bullet was flat nosed, without cavity, although there was the usual base cavity. The bullet had 3 cannelures and weighed 220 grains. The charge was about 5.5 grains of Cordite. Because of its blunt nose it also came under the "dum-dum" classification, thus was not kept in service.

Mark 5 Ball. Approved May, 1912. Quite similar to the Mark 4, but the bullet had an antimony content. Used as a march cartridge.

Mark 6 Ball. Approved Sept., 1939. This, the last of the 455 Ball cartridges, was introduced to overcome the objections raised to the maintenance of a lead bullet for service. It replaced the Mark 2, its jacketed bullet being of similar shape to the Mark 2, and weighing the same. The bullet had one cannelure, and the cartridge was loaded with Cordite (5.5 to 7.5 grains) or nitrocellulose powder (5.5 grains). Although replaced in official British use now, certain Commonwealth armies still use this cartridge, and some post-war, British-made contract ammunition for these armies has used a small size primer.

Mark I, Proof Q. This cartridge, identified by its copper-washed case, and incorporating in the headstamp either "PROOF" or (later) "Q", was approved in April, 1914. It used a normal Mark 2 type bullet, and its propel-

lant charge was adjusted to give about 20% more pressure than standard Ball.

Mark I, Blank. Approved May, 1897. Used a crimped brass case, measuring 18.5mm long, with 10-gr. powder charge, black.

Mark 2, Blank. Approved, March 1899, and later designated "Blank L. Mark 2.T." The crimped brass case was 18mm long, the charge 8 grains powder. The case had a larger flash hole than the Mark 1. Black powder.

Mark I, Drill D. First approved as a "Dummy" cartridge in June, 1920, the designation was later changed to "Drill," and so approved in March 1922. Consists of a normal service case, but the primer pocket holds a red fiber pad, and three red flutes are impressed into the sides of the 19mm long case. Mark 2 type lead bullet was used and, while most of this mark had

British cartridges, from left: Mk 1, 380 Ball; Mk 2, 380 Ball; Mk 1.T, 380 Blank L; Mk 1, 380 Drill D and Mk 2, 380 Drill D.

a white metal case, some specimens are found with brass cases.

Though not bearing an official designation, there was a 455 Instructional or Drill cartridge issued in 1893, consisting of the Mark I Black Powder Ball case and bullet, but without charge or cap composition. First filled with coal dust, this practice was abandoned, and from 1899 two holes were bored through the walls of the case for

jacketed bullet. Powder charges were similar to the Mark 1. Date of introduction of the Cordite version was October 1937; of the N.C., March, 1941.

Mark I, Proof Q. Similar to the Mark I Ball, and with the same bullet, the case was copper washed and included the letter "Q" in the headstamp. The charge was 5 grains of Cordite.

British cartridges, from left: Mk 1, Ball 455 Webley auto; Mk 1.z, 9mm Ball (Mk 2.z is similar in appearance); Mk 1, 9mm Inspectors' Dummy U; Mk 1, 9mm Drill D; Mk 2, 9mm Drill D and Mk 1.z, 9mm Blank (Canadian).

Automatic Arms Ammunition

455 for Webley semi-automatic pistol. Only one type of cartridge was officially issued for use with this pistol, as below.

Mark I, Ball. Approved April, 1912. The brass case, Berdan primed, was 23.5mm long. The case was, of course, rimless, and took a charge of 7 grains of pistol Cordite. The bullet, round nosed and jacketed, with one cannelure, weighed 224 grains.

Although not officially listed, a 455 Auto proof cartridge was produced commercially, but bore no military headstamp. Instead, it had a purple stripe across the base, over the commercial headstamp. Otherwise it was similar to the Ball cartridge.

9mm for Browning Autoloading pistol, and for SMG. The following Marks of this ammunition were issued.

Ball—2 Marks.
Tracer—1 Mark.
Proof—1 Mark.
Inspector's Dummy—1 Mark.
Drill—2 Marks.

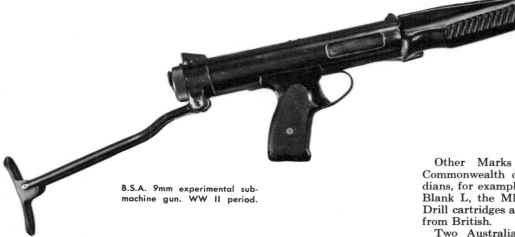

B.S.A. 9mm experimental submachine gun. WW II period.

Other Marks were produced in Commonwealth countries. The Canadians, for example, produced the 9mm Blank L, the Mk I.z, and Australian Drill cartridges are distinctly different from British.

Two Australian Drill types were made: one had a brass case, pierced with two pair of holes; the service bullet positioned by a redwood "distance" piece; the case was without flash-hole or anvil. The other Drill cartridge had a tinned case, the service bullet blackened, no flash-hole or anvil.

Both of these Drill cartridges had the letter D in their headstamp.

Little is known about the 9mm Blank cartridges, except that the slightly bottlenecked case was 29.5mm long and crimped. The charge was a nitrocellulose powder, weight unknown.

Service ammunition had brass cases, rimless, 19mm long. Some experimental production of light alloy cases took place in the 1950s. Details of 9mm ammunition follows:

Mark I.z., Ball. Introduced in 1941. Had a 115-gr. jacketed bullet, with a propellant charge of about 5 grains nitrocellulose.

identification.

380 for Enfield revolver. The 380 cartridge case was 19.5mm long, and was based on the standard Smith and Wesson 38 S&W cartridge. The following Marks of 380 ammunition were issued.

Ball—2 Marks   Blank—1 Mark
Proof—2 Marks   Drill—2 Marks

Mark I, Ball. Both Cordite and nitrocellulose loadings were manufactured, and the date of introduction was November, 1930. The bullet was lead, round nosed, with two cannelures weighing 198 grains. The charge was 3.7 grains of Cordite or 2.5 grains of N.C.

Mark 2, Ball. Mainly because of the objections to lead bullets, the Mark 2 was introduced, having a 197-gr.

Mark 2, Proof Q. Like Mark I, Proof Q, but the charge was 5 grains of Cordite or 4 grains of N.C.

Mark I.T., Blank L. Approved August, 1934. Consisted of a crimped brass case 18.5mm long. The charge was 5.5 grains of black powder.

Mark I, Drill D. White metal case with three red-painted flutes, loaded with lead bullet similar to Mk I Ball. Primer pocket filled with red fiber pad.

Mark 2, Drill D. Like Mark I, Drill D, but with jacketed bullet similar to Mark 2 Ball. Primer pocket painted red.

Beginning with the 455 Webley revolver ammunition all British service revolver ammunition is fully headstamped, including the Mark numeral. Most earlier revolver ammunition was not headstamped.

Sterling 9mm Model P.G.4 submachine gun (Lanchester) c. 1940.

Austen 9mm Mk 1 submachine gun, folding butt extended. (Australia, WW II)

Sten 9mm Mk 4 submachine gun, with silencer and folding buttstock extended (c. 1944).

Mark 2.z., Ball. Introduced in 1944. Like Mk I.z. Ball but carries 6 grains N.C.

Mark I.z., Tracer G. Introduced for limited issue in the war. Details not published, but it is based on a normal case with standard ball type headstamp, hence identification not apparent except by reference to the box label.

Mark I, Proof Q. This proof cartridge was produced with both Cordite and nitrocellulose loadings. Identification was by the copper-washed case, the yellow painted primer annulus, and the inclusion of the letter "Q" in the headstamp.

Non-standard Proof. Early in the war, prior to the introduction of the Mark I Q, the United States supplied 9mm proof ammunition to Britain. These cartridges had tinned cases and bore the headstamp "W.R.A. 9mm."

Mark I, Drill D. Introduced in 1944, this was the service brass case, without primer, and with the standard bullet. An internal wood dowel prevented the bullet from receding into the empty case, which had 4 holes bored through it for identification. Brass cases are occasionally found blackened.

Mark 2, Drill D. This cartridge, produced in the 1950s, consisted of a white metal case with three red-painted flutes, an empty primer pocket and the standard service bullet. The cap chamber is painted red.

Mark I, Inspectors Dummy U. Introduced in the 1950s and is used by armorers for weapon testing. Two basic variants exist. The first is entirely of steel, bullet and case being in one piece. The center of the cartridge is bored out, from the base, the whole having a dull finish. The other has a brass head screwed into a steel body, the latter and the bullet being in one piece. The center of this round is also bored out from the base. It may be found finished in the original brass and steel, or tinned over-all. Both variants are fully headstamped.

Since the war a number of 9mm special cartridges have been developed. Included are a number of different cartridges for silenced weapons, and like the original German 9mm *Nahpatrone* (close shooting), heavy bullets have been the means of achieving silenced effect. Both 150- and 170-gr. bullets have been produced. Apart from use in cloak-and-dagger operations, there would seem to be a potential use for cartridges such as these in the Viet Nam operations, where clearing of Viet Cong tunnels could be facilitated by silenced weapons. To clear

them with normal weapons causes deafness, and explosives or fire can damage any documents or equipment therein.

All British automatic pistol ammunition is fully headstamped, the headstamp including the Mark numeral.

The standard British system of headstamp code letters, which became operative from about WW I days, applies to revolver and auto pistol ammunition, per the following code letters:

C Cordite loading (This code "C" was discarded after about 1908)
D Drill (These cartridges are used in troop training for magazine filling, loading, etc.)
G Tracer
L Blank
Q Proof
U Inspector's Dummy. Weapons testing
Z Nitrocellulose loading
T Black powder loading for blank ammunition (not for Ball ammunition)

The 9mm cartridge is now a standard NATO caliber, subject to a common specification and proof, and British 9mm Ball ammunition now bears the NATO mark—a cross within a circle on the headstamp.   •

The Shooter's Showcase

Canjar Triggers

These top-quality triggers—offered in Set, DeLuxe and Improved types —are too well known to need elaboration here, but we can report that Canjar has a new, fully informative full-color brochure describing his triggers and various other shooters' products he's marketing—barrel stabilizers, slings, fore-end stops, palm rests, adjustable buttplates, and so on—and it's yours for the cost of a letter.

● *Keeping clean* in the wilderness can be a problem. Trak is a new super soap in a super-mini package yet does about everything.

Trak soap can be used to wash the body, your clothes and just about anything else. It works well as a shave cream, leaving the face feeling squeaky clean. Just a small button of Trak is needed for most chores, and it won't cause high suds contamination since it is bio-degradable. $3 from Freeman Industries, Tuckahoe, N. Y. 10707.

● *Winnebago,* one of the largest recreational vehicle makers in this country, recently sent a directive to their dealers urging them to avoid the use of billboards. The company considers such advertising another kind of pollution that clutters the landscape, reducing the quality of outdoor America. We are in full agreement, and it may be that a respect for our environment can stimulate good business.

● *A versatile tool* that will appeal to many gun tinkerers is called Clamdown. This combination machinists clamp/horizontal vise has a cast aluminum base 4x5" and a jaw opening of 2¼" max. Three movable pegs permit the Clamdown to be used as a jig with quick, positive alignment and clamping facilities. It's $9.98 from Ditto, 527 N. Alexandria Ave., Los Angeles, Calif. 90004.

"CLAMDOWN"

● *Container Development Corp.* has expanded their line of Handibins, now offers a series of Plastiboxes and divider bins. They're made of polypropylene, impervious to most everything, and can be had in green, yellow or blue. The PB-2 Plastibox shown is 6x3½x2½ inches, costs about $1. They're handy to have around the shop for sorting brass, storing bullets or shotgun wads. They also have racks that can be mounted to the wall or used for stacking. Write them for their catalog—it shows a wide selection of types and sizes to choose from.

● *Jim Baiar,* Rt. 1B, Box 352, Columbia Falls, Mont. 59912, offers Hex Socket guard screws for all popular bolt actions—Mauser, M70 Winchester, Remington (40X and 700), Springfield, et al. Baiar will also custom-make these sets to match your guard screws, in case he can't supply you from stock, at his regular prices.

Two-screw sets sell for $3.95, 3-screw packages are $4.95. Our sample set shows excellent finish and blueing, and a hex-socket wrench is supplied with each set. Made of a tough alloy steel, the Hex Socket guard screws can be easily tightened too much, so go carefully. I like these hex guard screws—it's hard to avoid butchering conventional slotted screws if the action-barrel has to be removed from the stock frequently.

● *Lathe owners* can turn tapers readily with the E-Z Taper, an attachment made by E-Z Tool Co., 918 Douglas, Des Moines, Iowa 50313. This $39.95 accessory has over 6" of travel, sealed-bearing live center, requires no tailstock set-over or "steps" when making longer cuts. This unit clamps on the tailstock quill (1.5" dia. or less) and due to the sliding feature, multiple tapers may be cut on the same piece of stock with little effort. Duplicating tapers is simple since the original piece is used for set-up. Here's a real time and money saver for the lathe operator/owner. Give exact diameter of tailstock quill (to second decimal) when ordering.

Focusing a Scope

Telescopic sights are used by most big game rifle shooters and by virtually all varminters. Scopes give the hunter a clearer picture of his target, making for better accuracy, quicker identification and increased safety. Scopes brighten the sight picture, allowing the hunter to see clearly during those final, crucial moments of dusk when wildlife is on the move.

Yes, the odds favor the hunter who uses a scope, but how many scope users know how to focus the instrument properly? When a shooter acquires his first scope and takes a peek through it, he often finds it out of focus for his eyes. If he doesn't know any better, he keeps staring at his sight picture while turning the eyepiece for a sharper image. What he doesn't know is that his eyes tend to adapt themselves to the out-of-focus picture during the process. He settles for an image that looks clear to him at the time, but he'll find the scope out of focus the next time he uses it.

Here's how to avoid this. First, turn the eyepiece to the left until both the object being sighted and the reticle appear blurred. (Don't unscrew it all the way or you'll let out the nitrogen that prevents fogging.) Now move the eyepiece clockwise, but look away frequently to prevent your eyes from adjusting to a picture still out of focus. Continue to turn the eyepiece to the right each time you re-sight until you get the sharpest image on both the center reticle and the object being sighted. Your scope is now in focus for you.

● *Sunglass Facts For The Sportsman* is the name of a new booklet offered free by Bausch and Lomb, Rochester, N. Y. 14602. It contains a lot of information on selection of lens color, density and quality as well as suggestions on appropriate types to be used for a variety of outdoor sports.

● *Jet-Aer Corp.,* well known for their G-96 gun cleaning and finishing materials, have some new items.

Their waterproofing Leather & Boot aerosol spray was applied to a pair of boots worn around Chicago last winter, but not a bit of salt or water penetrated. 7 ozs., $1.49.

Their Fabric Waterproofing, applied to a pair of Clark's desert boots made them easy to keep clean—just a wipe with a damp cloth and a brushing kept 'em like new. 7 ozs., $1.25.

● *J&G Rifle Ranch* sent us a couple of their Thumlers Tumblers and we've been using them for cleaning many of the cartridges, cases and bullets shown in this book and for shooting ammo, too. The AR-6 is relatively small—about 200 pistol cases per load—sells for $29.95 and gives a lot of service while occupying little bench space. Model B at $41.95 polishes about 10 boxes of rifle cases at one loading. Using ground walnut hulls as a polishing agent, cases came out sparkling clean in about an hour. Other models are available from $21.95 to $64.95—write J&G for further information at Turner, Montana 59542.

● *Safe-T-Planer,* made by Gilmore Pattern Wks., 1164-R North Utica, Tulsa, Okla. 74110, attaches to radial arm saw ($15.95) drill press or multi-purpose tool ($12.75) to make an endless variety of panel edges or mouldings.. It's also useful as a shaper and can be used to make rabbets, bevels, fancy rosettes, etc. A truly versatile attachment at an economical price. Name your tool when ordering for a perfect fit.

● *Looking for a place* to hunt? Sportsmen will want to order a free copy of the new *North American Shooting Preserve Directory* from: National Shooting Sports Foundation, 1075 Post Rd., Riverside, Conn. 06878.

The directory lists preserves in 42 states and Canada which are open to the public on a fee basis. Most of them have seasons of 5 to 6 months. In addition to offering upland hunting and clay-target shooting, many preserves feature father-son programs— a good way to bridge the generation gap.

Butts Bullet Trap

Made to absorb without trouble all rimfire loads and centerfire handgun loads, including 38 Special (no HV centerfires, please), this 19-lb. steel receptacle features a replaceable deflector plate, an easily-removed front for cleaning, and it can be hung up or set on a flat surface for support. 14¼" tall by 12" wide, it lists for $26.95 from Recreation Products Research, 158 Franklin Av., Ridgewood, N.J. 07450.

RPR also offers a plastic-coated metal bipod rest for rifles, a spring-loaded clamp-on-the barrel type that stands 10½" high, weighs only a pound, sells for $4.95. A small caution: if you want to use a rest—any rest—that attaches to the barrel, be sure to do your sighting-in with the rest in position. Otherwise you'll find your point of impact higher, usually, when you fit the rest to the barrel.

● *Hobby-Carve* is a three-dimensional pantograph of sorts that makes duplicates of relief carvings in wood, plastic or other soft materials. It uses a router (supplied at $40 additional if you don't have one) and comes with cutters, tracers, work shield and in knock-down form for easier, less expensive shipping at $79. We cut a few small plaques and found less effort needed to set up the Hobbi-Carve than required to duplicate using only a router. The tool will also work in depth (up and down) almost an impossibility with a router and less difficult than making a copy with a flex-shaft tool. Finished work is a very close duplicate of the original. St. Paul Machinery Mfg. Co., 21 - 4th St. SW, Osseo, Minn. 55369, has these in stock and will answer any questions we haven't answered.

Lock's Philadelphia Gun Exchange

A varmint hunter's adjustable (8" to 12") bipod is offered, the rifle rest fleece covered, and on elastic band furnished for attaching the bipod to the rifle. Weighing only 9 oz., this handy rifle rest is finished in black and polished aluminum, and there's a "D" ring for attaching it to the shooter's belt. $9.95.

● *Making gadgets* for your own use can be fun, but many times there is need for a gear, spring or odd sized mirror or lens that makes completing the project an impossibility. If you've had such problems, try Edmund Scientific Co., 555 Edscorp Bldg., Barrington, N. J. 08007 next time. They have a free catalog that is jammed full of goodies.

There's a product we picked out of the book that should interest shooters/handloaders—a 4" dial caliper (No. 60,452) with a stainless steel body and hardened measuring surfaces at $19.25 postpaid, including a leather case.

● *Eating well* on a trip afield is a big part of having a good time. A new line of freeze-dried foods is offered by Sportsmen's Choice, Micro Dr., Woburn, Mass. 01801. Carrying the Tony Bolton brand name, these main dishes for 4 include such delectable repasts as: beef and gravy with rice ($2.25), beef stew ($2.65), chicken dinner with rice ($2.65) and a number of others. Quite a few 2-serving dishes may be had at from 30¢ to 77¢ and all come packed in sealed, lightweight moisture - proof packages that need no refrigeration. At these prices, don't forget to take more than the usual amount; outdoor appetites are generally bigger.

● *Cut circles* just about as easy as drawing them with "Accu-Orb" from Technological Devices, Box 3491, Stamford, Conn. 06950. A complete kit, including the plastic/steel circle-cutting tool, an 8½x11" cutting board and 10 extra blades, costs $7.95. With it you can make circles, rings or holes in most materials up to ¹⁄₁₆" thick (a little more if the stock is soft) from ⅛" to 24" diameter. This is the best hole maker we've seen, and the tool gets a lot of use here at the office.

● *Colt Firearms* is just out in its 6th edition. Written by one of our most respected authors, James E. Serven (see his "Guns of the Western History Makers" elsewhere in this edition), it now runs to 416 pages with 100 of them fully revised. You can easily tell the new book—it has a plastic cover rather than a dust jacket. Priced at $19.95 it is still a good buy.

● *Hugger Hook* has a new type of peg-board (large-hole type) hanger that is bent at a right-angle horizontally. Insert this in a handgun barrel and support the rest of the weight near the trigger guard with one of the regular type Hugger Hooks—your pistol or revolver now looks good on the wall and has less chance of falling than with other systems.

● *Time Target Patches* are 1"x1" self-sticking square pasters, black or white, come in a handy dispenser box holding 500 patches at 98¢. We've found them easy to use, and easy to apply—not having to lick 'em is a convenience.

● *Knife collectors* will be happy to know that American Reprints, Box 6023, St. Louis, Mo. 63139 has just published in facsimile the 1936 Remington knife catalog. Filled with line drawings, it looks much like the original. Priced at $2.50 this 36 page, 6½x 10" soft cover book is to be had direct from the publisher.

A couple of other reprints are the 1872 J.H. Johnston, Great Western Gun Works catalog—46 pages, 6½x 9¾" soft cover at $2 and the 1884 Hibbard, Spencer & Bartlett catalog —96 pages, 8½x11" soft cover at $5. Both of these carry muzzleloaders and breechloaders, ammunition, components and shooting accessories for the shooter.

● *Modern chemicals* continue to appear on the market all promising to cure the woes of the world. Dri-Slide is termed a "penetrating-inhibiting dry-film reaction lubricant" which means that this dual-function product reduces friction and imparts an effective corrosion inhibitor at the same time, protecting tools and guns, etc. Now available in 8 oz. aerosol cans at your dealers or direct.

● *Karl A. Neise,* Moderntools Corp. is selling a new Triple-05 series of dial calipers. A micro-screw adjustment lets you open or close the jaw spacing by as little as ½-thousandth of an inch (the indicator proper has red dots between the .001" line divisions). If you have reasonably good eyesight, discrimination can be made between a line and a dot for close estimates to .00025". They're not cheap—4" at $25 to 10" at $59.60—but a dial caliper has many uses around the shop, therefore it pays to buy a good one.

Aldrin-Dieldrin Banned

The U.S. Department of Agriculture on March 9, 1970 canceled federal registrations for all uses of aldrin and dieldrin insecticides in water areas in an effort to further reduce pollution of the nation's water resources and potential contamination of fish and other aquatic life.

The cancellation action is similar to that taken in November, 1969, by the USDA to limit the amount of DDT in the environment. Aldrin and dieldrin, both persistent pesticides, are from the same chemical family as DDT. Dieldrin is the most widely found pesticide in the environment, after DDT, and is a breakdown product of aldrin.

Seymour Shell Catcher

This new device, designed to grab fired shotshells as they're ejected from automatic shotguns, will be welcomed by shooters who reload. It fits Remington Models 1100, 11-48, and 58, in 12, 16, or 20 gauge (not intended for use on doubles).

To use, remove the bolt handle by pulling straight out and insert the Shell Catcher in its place. Load the gun by dropping the shotshell into the receiver, brass end first, and close the action. When the gun is fired, the empty shell will be caught between the twin prongs.

Simple to install or remove, this U.S. patented gadget *does* work, and well. $5.95 from Old Mill Trap & Skeet, 300 Mill Ridge Rd., Secaucus, N.J. 07094.

Eyeglass Accidents

Nothing spoils a day in the field like an essential pair of eyeglasses falling off and breaking. Here's a simple way to prevent the accident. Drill a small hole near the extreme end of each temple piece with a No. 60 wire gauge drill, then thread a length of 20-30 lb. Nylon monofilament (fishing line) through the holes, from the inside, tying a figure-8 knot on the outside of each temple, first having shortened the line to a length that just barely permits the glasses to be slipped over the head. This way they can't slip very far out of normal wearing position, while at the same time the wearer is spared the bulk and annoying pressure of elastic retainers.

● *The Classic Decoy Series,* a portfolio of 24 watercolors by Milton C. Weiler, has just been printed by Winchester Press. This limited edition of 1,000 copies, each numbered and signed by the artist, depicts the work of master craftsmen decoy carvers. This magnificent work carries a text describing each decoy and its maker written by the inimitable Ed Zern. Reproduced on fine paper, loosely bound and ribboned, the portfolio sells for $100 from Winchester Press, 460 Park Ave., N. Y., N. Y. 10022.

● *Rust and corrosion,* the sportsman's gremlins, have been with us for years. Liquid Wrench is a compound of solvents that will, in many cases, make equipment serviceable again by removing gum, rust, corrosion, scale and varnish. It leaves a protective film behind to prevent further problems. Available in 3- and 8-oz. spout cans or in 6-oz. spray can.

A companion product is L-S-C, a moisture-displacing micro-oil that lubricates and protects metal, helps start wet engines, and will protect most corrosion-prone metals during storage. Available in 4- and 12-oz. spray cans and in one-gallon cans for shop use.

● *Al Popper* (614 Turnpike St., Stoughton, Mass. 02072) offers a big variety of tie tacks, tie bars, cuff links, etc., with gun motifs of all kinds —pistol, revolver, rifles and shotguns. Nicely done in gold or silver colors, these are $1.50 each plus postage. Popper also makes, on order, name badges that are durable and good looking, with or without guns attached. Dealer discounts are available also, and a price list may be had free.

● *Warm feet* in the woods can make a trip much more enjoyable and less fatiguing. A new product offered by Forest City Products is Woodsman insulating insoles. These are made of a cushioning, insulating foam covered with a thick layer of 100% virgin wool plaid. With every pair— they look big enough for the abominable snowman—a trimming chart is included to cut these down to your exact boot size. FCP has other products too—first aid kits for house, boat or auto, safety treads for bathtub or boat deck and self-adhesive flannel.

● *Work and enjoy* the outdoors without getting chills up the back and across the shoulders with the series 80-30 electric tunic vest from Visa-Therm, Box 486, Bridgeport, Conn. 06601. Selling for $19.95 and made of Nylon for men and women, this vest provides up to 4 hours of continuous warmth on 2 "D" cells. Windproof, waterproof and completely washable, this insulated jacket retains 80% of the body heat, providing a comfortable 60° inside temperature when it is below zero. Electrically-heated socks, mittens and suits are also made.

● *Remington's Wild Game Cookbook* ($2.95), now in its second printing, is the 4th book in their Sportsmen's Library. Written by Bill Johnson, the revised and expanded edition carries some far-out dishes: barbecued beaver, potted pigeon, roast raccoon, braised bear, moose meatloaf, etc. Order by mail from Remington, Box 731, Bridgeport, Conn. 06601.

● *Improvement of camping* facilities is the aim of Family Camping Federation. They're encouraging everyone to make the litterbug aware of himself by using the Morse code symbol "L"—to be played upon your auto or boat horn when one is spotted. Horn language for this is "Beep, Beeeeeep, Beep, Beep." So you don't become a litterbug, too, they offer imprinted plastic litterbags at 3 for 25¢ or $25 per thousand, from FCF, Bradford Woods, Martinsville, Ind. 46151.

● *Chainsaw, lawnmower* and other two-cycle engine users will welcome Sta-Bil—it permits gas/oil mixtures to remain in the tank, carburetor, etc., without gumming.

To use, one ounce of Sta-Bil is added to a gallon of fuel and the engine run 3 to 5 minutes. That amount will stabilize the fuel for a year, and give instant starts in most cases—a good idea also if you have any 4-cycle stand-by equipment with automatic starting. 8 ozs. for $2.95 or $6.95 per quart from Knox Laboratories, 2335 S. Michigan, Chicago, Ill. 60616.

● *Lightning Loaders* may be just what you need for additional firepower from your tubular-magazine 22 rimfire rifle. Preload the Lightning Loader at home (5 metal tubes, each holding 15 Long Rifle, 18 Longs or 22 Shorts), then dump a full load into your rifle smoothly and quickly. The five brass-alloy tubes, supplied with a leather holster, are $8.95; an economy model, with plastic tubes, is $5.95 from Hunter Mfg. Co., Box 2882, Van Nuys, Ca. 91404.

● *Calling game* or varmints is a lot of fun—getting wildlife close-up so the kids can see them in a natural habitat or for shooting with rifle or camera. An electronic caller we highly recommend is made by Johnny Stewart Game Calls, Box 1909, Waco, Texas 76703. These rugged, lightweight, high-fidelity record players are powerful and dependable. It can double as public address system or two-speed record player for parties, etc. Battery operated, it will work anywhere.

On a recent trip to Texas, Johnny Stewart demonstrated what can be done with a quality caller and why the design must be good to fool game. On the first call we lured 7 coyotes within 25 yards of the horn-type speaker—all at the same time, and we have pictures to prove it. Good enough?

Later this year a cassette tape player will be released, but picking out a particular track on a record, or repeating, may be just a little more flexible.

● *Working Together for a Livable Land* is the title of the latest in the series of cartoon-type booklets put out by the Soil Conservation Society of America. These sell for 25¢ a copy, less in quantities. Emphasis is on cleaning up our polluted environment and what can be done to make the earth habitable for the years to come. Back cover is blank for imprinting, should some dealers so choose. SCSA has other booklets and imprinting services at 7515 NE Ankeny Rd., Ankeny, Iowa.

The Facts About Hunting

Hunting often is referred to by the modern day outdoor planner as a declining sport, an activity diminishing in importance. Here are a few facts that refute that premise.

Distribution of Federal funds collected through excise taxes on hunting and fishing equipment totaled $24,000,000 during the first 6 months of 1969, an increase of $1,900,000 over 1968.

The greatest part of the increase was due to a jump in sales of sporting firearms and ammunition.

Through this same tax, sportsmen have paid nearly $400,000,000 in the past 30 years on guns and ammo alone, equal to $22 per minute. For waterfowl shooting specifically, sportsmen have paid more than $100,000,-000 in duck stamp fees since passage of the law in 1934. In pursuing their sport, hunters spend nearly $300,000,-000 yearly in automobile travel expenses alone.

That's a lot of money being spent for a sport supposedly declining in popularity. You might mention these facts the next time someone tries to sell you such nonsense.

● *If it moves,* it probably needs lubrication. Trouble is, many of these jobs would require less attention and attract less dirt if the lubricant was dry rather than oily. Dry-Lube is a fine, dry, silvery powder that makes moving parts more efficient by reducing friction. It won't stain fingers or fabrics and can be used most anywhere. A poly-bottle costs 40¢, but we liked the slim pencil type (at 59¢) that slips into a pocket and is handier in the field. Works well on guns, zippers and camera gear. Made by Reardon Products, 323 N. Main St., Roanoke, Ill. 61561.

Storing Powder Samples

Plastic vials available from any pharmacy solve the problem of storing powder samples. Photo shows sample charge of 26.2 grains of flake powder removed from the 7.92 x 39 Russian cartridge, as used in the Ak-47 assault rifle. Round label is self-sticking type; comes in packets or sheets available from most office supply stores.

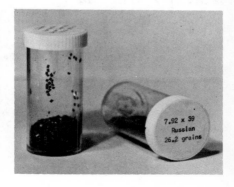

AMERICAN BULLETED CARTRIDGES

by KENNETH L. WATERS

> A check list of current metallic cartridges, domestic and imported, plus a guide to performance and selection.

LATEST DEVELOPMENTS IN METALLIC CARTRIDGES

The year behind us has been one of extensive readjustments involving both sellers and buyers of firearms and ammunition, as a result of the GCA of 1968. With tighter restrictions on imports, especially the shut-down on military surplus, two distinct trends appear to be emerging in the field of metallic cartridges:

(1) A resurgence of interest in our own American-made ammunition involving not only new factory rounds, but also witnessing several long-needed improvements in standard loadings.

(2) An increased emphasis on the reloadability of cases for foreign metric calibers. As stocks of surplus military ammo dry up or increase in price, this trend is certain to accelerate.

Improved bullets, new powders and higher costs—even the legal controls themselves—seem to have worked to promote the growth of handloading with most interesting results. We have found, for instance, that our older pistol cartridges can readily be made far more effective through the use of better bullets at higher velocities, and this discovery has sparked a demand sufficient to induce the manufacturers of commercial ammo to bring forth improved versions of factory cartridges in standard calibers.

A curious occurrence worthy of note has been the increased longevity given the old 30-30 cartridge by the issuance of commemorative rifles in that caliber.

In 1970 however, the spotlight was on Remington. As producers of the only two new standard metallic cartridges to appear in that year, they would have had an automatic claim to that position, but with one of this new pair holding the distinction of being the world's highest velocity rimfire cartridge, they were doubly sure. They thus bear looking-into first.

RIFLE CARTRIDGES

Remington 5mm Rim Fire Magnum

Remington says this round "looks like a centerfire cartridge," and indeed it does, resembling a smaller scale version of the fine old K-Hornet. The fact that it is instead a rimfire will be good news to the farm boy too busy to reload, yet desirous of having a true varmint rifle less costly to shoot as well as own, than are the various centerfires.

Factory literature compares the new 5mm round with a 22 Long Rifle High Speed cartridge thus:

Cartridge	Bullet/grs.	MV/fps	ME/fp	Trajectory/yds. 50	100	150	Wind Deflec./ ins. 100 yds.
5mm R.F. Mag.	38 PLHP	2100	372	+ .9	0	− 4.3	5.5
22 Long Rifle	40, lead	1285	147	+2.9	0	−10.8	9.0

The above figures assume an iron sight height 0.7″ above the bore axis, rifles sighted in at 100 yards, and a wind of 15 mph perpendicular to the line of fire. 24″ test barrel in 5mm.

The ballistic differences between these two cartridges are obvious, the 5mm at 150 yards still being slightly superior to the 22 Long Rifle at its muzzle. Nor does this comparison take into account the better mushrooming qualities of the 5mm's Power-Lokt jacketed hollow-point bullet.

As a varmint cartridge designed for maximum destructiveness, the 5mm Remington is simply beyond comparison with the old Long Rifle, and a closer relationship will be found between it and the 22 Winchester Magnum Rimfire:

Cartridge	Bullet/grs.	MV/fps	V/100 yds.	ME/fp	E/100 yds.
5mm Remington	38	2100	1605	372	217
22 WMR	40	2000	1390	355	170

Based on field experience with the 22 WMR on varmints, it seems reasonable that the 5mm Remington should be effective to 150 yards on the smaller species, and to a full 100 yards on the larger.

It should be noted that bullet diameter of the 5mm is only .2045″ in contrast to the usual .224″ of centerfire 22 calibers, so shooters will have to buy or make their own cleaning rod since many 22-cal. rods won't go into this 5mm. However, 17-cal. rods could serve, too. 5mm bullets, being jacketed rather than lubricated, bores should be cleaned after each shooting session precisely the same as with centerfire rifles.

Remington's latest, the 591 rifle in 5mm RFM caliber

Remington's 5mm RFM, hotter than any other rimfire.

25-06 Remington

The gap in the caliber sequence at 25 that had existed since chambering for the 250-3000 Savage and 257 Roberts had ceased, has become more rather than less noticeable with the passage of time. Over the past couple of years it has been obvious that something would have to be done to fill that gap, and the first major loading company to move in this area would almost surely reap the rewards of shooter enthusiasm.

From the writer's perch, the two most likely possibilities appeared to be factory adoption of either of two popular and practical wildcats—the 257 Improved or the 25-06. Remington's decision to go with the 25-06 is not surprising when it is considered that ballistics from this larger case would, with modern slow-burning powders, be superior to those possible from a blown-out 257 Roberts case with equal pressures, added to which the use of the '06 hull as a base would almost certainly endear the new cartridge to a considerable segment of shooters. Remington explains it by saying simply: "Growing familiarity with its (the 25-06) performance potential among shooters has led to increasing demand for it as a commercial load in recent years."

Wisely, I think, in spite of a variety of case shoulder angles in the various wildcat versions, Remington chose to standardize the original 25-06, which is nothing more than the 30-06 case necked down to 25-caliber, retaining the same shoulder angle of 17½ degrees.

The move that will likely surprise many is their choice of bullet weight for the initial issue, but appearing as it did in the spring, the 87-gr. hollow-point Power-Lokt bullet, designed to combine high accuracy and flat trajectory for long range varmint operations, makes good sense. Remington has already announced that a second loading with 120-gr. Core-Lokt PSP bullet will be available in time for the 1970 big game season. Most odd is the absence of any mention of a 100-gr. load. Even without such a medium-weight, however, the 25-06 promises just the sort of versatility and flat shooting that riflemen have hankered for.

Factory ballistics for the 87-gr. 25-06 Remington load follow:

25-06 Remington with 87-gr. JHP Bullet

	Muzzle	100	200	300	400	500
Velocity (fps)	3500	3070	2680	2310	1990	1690
Energy (fp)	2370	1820	1390	1030	765	550
Trajectory (in.) Sighted-in @ 200 yds.	—	+1.4	0	−6.3	−19.2	−40.9

The above figures are based upon firing from a 26″ barrel with a rifling twist of 1-in-10″, and assume the use of iron sights with line of sight 0.9″ above the bore axis.

Comparison with other popular cartridges shows this new round to be equally as flat in its trajectory as the 6.5 Remington Magnum with 100-gr. bullets, and slightly flatter than the 270/130 grain. Out to 300 yards, it even equals the big 7mm Magnum 150-gr. Remaining energy at 300 yards is very nearly as great as that of a 100-gr. 250 Savage at 200 yards.

With only 3 weeks in which to test the 25-06 Model 700 rifle for accuracy before writing our report, and no opportunity to try it on game, I can only say that it has displayed remarkable grouping ability with factory ammunition, and bullet expansion that is close to being explosive. Look for much activity with this cartridge in the years ahead, including a ready acceptance by the handloading fraternity.

Remington's 25-06, made legitimate after all these years as a wildcat.

6.5mm Remington Magnum 100-grain Core-Lokt

Remington also announced in 1970 a new 100-grain Core-Lokt PSP loading for their 6.5 Magnum, extending the versatility of that cartridge into the varmint field. Note, however, that the type of bullet used is one customarily employed in game shooting. This is confirmed by Remington's statement that the new loading makes the 6.5 Magnum ". . . a most effective selection for hard-to-reach game such as antelope, mountain goats and sheep."

6.5mm Remington Magnum with 100-gr. PSP Bullet

	Muzzle	100	200	300	400	500
Velocity (fps)	3450	3070	2690	2320	1990	1700
Energy (fp)	2640	2090	1610	1190	880	640
Trajectory (in.) Sighted-in @ 200 yds.	—	+1.4	0	−6.3	−19.1	−41.0

The above figures are based upon firing from a 26″ barrel with a rifling twist of 1-in-9″, and assume the use of iron sights with line of sight 0.9″ above the bore axis.

Federal Cartridge

Our old friends at Federal have also been busy this past year, rounding out their line of centerfire cartridges with the addition of 6 additional basic calibers, all but one in the handgun line:

    25 ACP with 50-gr. bullet
    32 ACP with 71-gr. bullet
    380 Auto with 95-gr. bullet
    9mm Luger with 123-gr. bullet
    357 Magnum with 158-gr. JSP bullet
    30 Carbine with 110-gr. S.P. bullet

The entire Federal list now includes 16 rifle and 7 pistol calibers, with more additions to come.

Their 357 Magnum loading with 158-gr. JSP bullet, rated at 1550 fps and 845 fp from an 8⅜″ barrel, is especially noteworthy, these bullets rising only ½″ above the line of sight midway to 50 yards.

Remington's new and fast 38 Special load, using 125-gr. HP bullets.

HANDGUN CARTRIDGES

38 Special

Remington has also been active in improved loads for handguns, and their new 38 Special rounds are sure to excite renewed interest and restore confidence in the effectiveness of that most popular revolver cartridge. There are two new loads, one with 158-gr., the other with 125-gr. bullets. They show two notable advances. First, their bullets are semi-jacketed hollow-points designed to withstand higher velocities without leading bores, and give increased expansion upon impact. These better bullets are really the key to the whole thing, but the substantially-boosted velocities of 1150 fps for the 158-gr. and 1370 fps for the 125-gr. (from 6″ barrels) provide the remaining good news.

Muzzle energies are 465- and 520 f.p. respectively, with both still delivering 400 fp at 50 yards. This is far and away superior to the 9mm Luger, and even compares quite favorably to the 357 Magnum and the lead bullet police loading of the 41 Magnum when those rounds are used in 6″ or shorter barrels.

A certain U.S. Congressman to the contrary, straight thinking folks will not compare dangerous criminals to soldiers fighting for their country—even enemy soldiers—and this writer can't think of a good reason why our hard-pressed police officers shouldn't take full advantage of this Remington development to give them greater life assurance as well as increased power to apprehend the criminal. From here it looks like the 38 Special is just now coming into its own.

Norma 38 Special High Speed

Not to be outdone in the race to modernize the 38 Special round, Norma has produced a new loading with 110-gr. JHP bullet which they list as developing 1542 fps from a 6″ barrel while holding pressures to 18,600 psi! Quite a neat trick, and it is a most efficient looking cartridge to boot. The hollow point is amply large in a lead nose with flat point that can't possibly contact the bore, a copper jacket extending well over the ogive. Too, the nickeled case has no cannelure, which should prevent stretching and please reloaders.

Energy of the new round amounts to 580 fp at muzzle, making this a very potent little package indeed. It should be especially well received by field shooters, where its flatter trajectory and increased expanding characteristics will prove particularly effective.

Speer-DWM

Because of the vagaries of imports these days, Speer has been struggling valiantly to clear their DWM line of foreign loaded ammunition through customs, or so I hear. I asked for an up-dated listing of what is currently available, both in standard U.S. calibers and the much needed metrics. Dave Andrews of Speer has supplied me with a series of lists, including components and prices.

Unfortunately there isn't room here to reprint those pages, but it is a good, comprehensive collection of calibers. There are, for instance, in the metrics, such cartridges as the 6.5x57, the 7x64 and 7x65R, the 8x56 Mannlicher, 8x57 JS and JRS (.318″), 8x60S, 8x64 and 8x65R, 9.3x62, 9.3x72R, 9.3x74R and 10.75x68, among others. Several, but by no means all of these cartridges, are pocketed for American primers. In some instances, there still may be a wait involved. Best bet would be to write Speer for these lists and inquiring as to availability.

In American rifle calibers, a round dozen are listed in 22 different loadings from 222 Remington to 300 Winchester Magnum, and it's more than usually accurate factory ammo, judging from our bench-rest trials.

If you're one who likes to tote a 6-gun afield, Speer has come out with 4 modern fast-stepping loads packed in compartmented re-usable plastic boxes. Two are in 38 Special with 125-gr. JSP and 140-gr. JHP, while the other pair are in 357 Magnum using the same bullets. These bullets have a blunt round-nose with soft lead core for optimum expansion, and because of their smoothly rounded contour, without shoulder, are more easily loaded into the cylinder in a hurry.

Super Vel 357 Magnum and 9mm Parabellum loads.

Super-Vel Additions

Since I last reported on Super Vel's high performance handgun cartridges (1969 GUN DIGEST), the line has been greatly expanded. For the auto pistol shooter there is now a high speed 380 ACP loading with 80-gr. JHP bullet at 1026 fps; to the earlier 90-gr. JHP 9mm Luger loading has been added a 112-gr. JSP; there are two loadings for the 38 Super Automatic, one with 107-gr. JHP and the other a 112-gr. JSP; and finally a dandy 190-gr. JHP load for the 45 ACP.

For the 6-gunner there are now a pair of 41 Magnum rounds with 170-gr. jacketed bullets in a choice of hollow or soft points; a medium-weight 357 Magnum loading with 137-gr. JSP; 38 Specials in either 158-gr. semi-wadcutter "Kopperkote" or 147-gr. hollow-base full-wadcutter "Match"; and, to be available late in 1970, a 125-gr. half-jacketed hollow-point for the 38 S&W.

The jacketed hollow- and soft point loadings in particular have exerted an effect on handgun ballistics that is literally tremendous. No longer is it necessary to hold down velocities in order to prevent leading, or to rely solely on mass and momentum for stopping power.

This year also, Super Vel has made these highly effective bullets available to reloaders as separate components. Under GCA-1968 regulations, you'll have to order them through your dealer, but this isn't difficult, and while you're at it, the SV people also offer both large and small pistol primers under their own brand name, plus empty un-primed cases in eight calibers. Too, there is now an interesting and helpful sheet of loading data for Super Vel bullets to be had, complete with pressures, so if you're curious you can now find out how they manage to get their high velocities.

Part I. RIFLE CARTRIDGES
The Centerfires

22 HORNET One of the most useful smallbore cartridges, and the first standard 22 specifically for varmint hunting. Since its appearance in 1930 it has earned a reputation for fine accuracy, flat trajectory, and quick bullet expansion. Effective to 175 yards on foxes, woodchucks, and jack rabbits, excellent for wild turkeys, it should definitely not be used on deer.

218 BEE Introduced in 1938 for the lever action Model 65 Winchester, its use was extended to bolt actions where its greater powder capacity, higher velocity and flatter trajectory from a stronger case made it a better choice than the Hornet. Effective on the same game species as the Hornet. Not available in any rifle today.

219 ZIPPER Introduced by Winchester in 1937, this rimmed cartridge acquired a poor reputation for accuracy in the Model 64 lever action, but in custom bolt action and single shot rifles, it groups excellently. Bullets are same diameter as Hornets and Bees regardless of name. Powerful enough for coyotes but still not adequate for deer. Discontinued 1964.

22 REMINGTON JET See Part II — Handgun Cartridges.

220 SWIFT Highest velocity standard rifle cartridge ever commercially produced in the U.S., its 48-grain bullet leaving the muzzle at 4110 fps is virtually a bomb, unfit for use on big game animals. As a long range varmint cartridge it is one of the finest, needing only a longer, heavier bullet less sensitive to wind. With full power loads cases stretch and bore wear is accelerated — which would occur with any cartridge of similar intensity. Popularity of the Swift has accordingly declined to the point where Winchester has discontinued chambering rifles for it, although factory cartridges are still produced.

222 REMINGTON One of our newer and most accurate cartridges, the 222 has climbed rapidly to fame as a bench-rest target and varmint load. Its bullets are better shaped than its predecessors, extending the range to about 225 yards, and it is chambered only in strong bolt action rifles. Production of this cartridge has resulted in decreased sales of Hornet, Bee, and Zipper ammo.

222 REMINGTON MAGNUM Big Brother to the standard 222 Rem., this newer and slightly longer cartridge has nicely combined power and wind-bucking ability with the fine accuracy of its forerunner to give varmint hunters one of the best balanced, most practical 'chuck cartridges ever developed. 55-gr. bullets of factory loads have a resistance to wind deflection superior to the 50-gr. standard 222 bullet, and handloaded 60-gr. bullets are still better in this respect. Also these heavier Magnum bullets arrive at a 200-yard target with some 25% more energy than the 50-gr. standard 222's.

222 SUPER RIMMED Developed in Australia, this rimmed version of our 222 Remington emigrated first to Canada and thence to the U.S. An ideal choice for chambering in single shot rifles, case dimensions (except for the rim), ballistics and loading data all duplicate those of the standard 222. Velocities may be somewhat higher however, in the longer barrels common to single shot rifles.

223 REMINGTON Adopted by the U.S. military forces as the 5.56mm with full metal jacketed 55-gr. bullets, its civilian name is 223 Remington, under which headstamp a soft point bullet is loaded. Identical ballistically to the 222 Magnum, the 223's case dimensions differ enough so that they should never be fired in a 222 Magnum chamber; they'll go in, but hazardous excess headspace will be present with a probability of case separations. Rifles for the 223 have a twist rate of 1-in-12" rather than the 1-in-14" of most 22 centerfires, this to insure bullet stability all the way out to 600-yards. Case capacity is about a grain less than the 222 Magnum and its neck is about 1/16" shorter, making the 222 Magnum a better choice for handloaders. Future government surplus ammunition will probably be available for the 223, however.

225 WINCHESTER Intended as a successor to the 220 Swift (in Winchester rifles), this new high performance cartridge has done more than that; it has also superseded the discontinued 219 Zipper in its role as the most powerful rimmed 22 centerfire. Although officially classified as "semi-rimless," the 225 does have a rim, easily sufficient to permit its use in single shot rifles while still fitting the bolt heads and extractors (of 270, 30-06 dimensions) of modern standard rimless cartridge repeaters. Closely similar in design to the 219 Improved Zipper (but differing in certain vital dimensions), the 225 Winchester is loaded to higher pressures than the old standard 219 Zipper, developing 540 fps greater muzzle velocity for a trajectory that is almost twice as flat. Factory cartridges in this new caliber are loaded with outstanding uniformity and provide excellent accuracy.

22/250 REMINGTON A long time favorite wildcat with both varminters and benchrest shooters, the 22/250 was standardized by Remington in 1965 and shows signs of rapidly growing popularity. Generally considered to be better designed than the Swift, it will give nearly as high velocities with bullets of the same weight. Because it is slower, case and barrel life are longer. Case capacity to bore ratio in the 22/250 is most favorable, and its short over-all loaded cartridge length of 2.35" makes it readily adaptable to short-action box magazine repeaters. Either new 22/250 Remington or Norma cases, or reformed 250 Savage brass may be used for reloading.

243 WINCHESTER One of the new 6mm or 24 caliber compromises between 22 and 25 calibers, having in large measure the best features of both. A 100-gr. bullet with high sectional density at 3,070 fs for deer and antelope, and an 80-gr. at 3,500 for long range varmints, provide accuracy equal to the Swift and far better wind-bucking and killing power. Excellent for the one-gun hunter of game not larger than deer.

244 REMINGTON Another new 6mm, but because of Remington's 1-in-12-inch rifling twist, bullet weights are restricted to 75 and 90 grains. Thus the 244 is not considered quite the equal of the 243 on big deer, despite the greater powder capacity of the 244. On targets or varmints however, it is doubtful if the shooter — or the chuck — would notice any difference, assuming rifles of equal accuracy. In custom barreled rifles with 10" twist, 100- or 105-gr. bullets can be handloaded to give 243 power.

6mm REMINGTON Identical in case dimensions to the older 244 Remington, this newer cartridge is loaded with the 100-gr. bullet demanded by deer hunters. Remington lists MV as 3190 fps, and barrels have a rifling twist of 1-in-9" to stabilize the longer bullet. Despite the fact that 75- and 90-gr. 244 cartridges can also be used in 6mm rifles, shooters wanted a varmint round bearing the 6mm headstamp. Hence, in 1965 Remington announced an additional load using their new 80-gr. Power-Lokt bullet, which has proven exceptionally accurate and flat shooting. The 6mm is therefore an even better dual purpose cartridge than the 243.

25-20 WCF Prior to the coming of the Hornet and Bee, this was the top combination small game and varmint cartridge, dating back to 1893. Today, a choice of 3 loads is available, (requiring different sight settings), including the older 86-gr. lead or soft point bullets at 1,460 fs, and a later 60-gr. H.P. at 2,250 fs. The slower, heavier bullets are good for game from squirrels to turkey, while the 60-gr. is strictly a varmint cartridge. Neither should ever be used on deer.

25-35 WINCHESTER Another cartridge from the 1890's, this one can be used for deer. Currently obtainable only as a 117-gr. soft point at 2,300 fs, the 25-35's chief claim to fame lies in its reputation as one of the most accurate cartridges ever developed for lever action rifles, and one of the lightest recoiling.

250 SAVAGE Popularly known as the "250-3000" because of its velocity with an 87-gr. bullet, this fine cartridge appeared in 1915 as one of our earliest really high speed loads. 100-gr. bullets are loaded to 2,820 fs. Quick killing power, flat trajectory, and light recoil have kept this cartridge popular for over 40 years. Use 100-gr. bullets for deer and 87's for varmints. In wind-swept areas, the 100 grain is preferred, even for varmints.

256 WINCHESTER MAGNUM See Part II—Handgun Cartridges.

257 ROBERTS Named for its famed originator, Ned Roberts, this was to be an extra-long-range varmint cartridge, but with its adoption by Remington for factory production, loaded with both 100- and 117-gr. bullets, it was recognized as an excellent medium game cartridge as well. The 87-gr. at 3,200 fs is for varmints. It is thus a speeded-up 250 for bolt actions, with greater powder capacity and a 10-inch twist, permitting the heavier 117-gr. factory and 125-gr. custom bullets which make this the finest all-around cartridge where game no larger than deer will be hunted. Biggest fault of the 257 is its deep-seated bullets, loaded thus for short actions. Seated out for custom long-throated chambers, accuracy improves noticeably.

6.5 REMINGTON MAGNUM Second of the short-case belted magnums. This cartridge is available only with the 120-gr. Pointed Soft Point Core-Lokt bullet so far. MV lists as 3030 foot seconds for the 20" barreled Remington 660 carbine. With a powder capacity very close to that of the 270, ballistics are also similar in barrels of the same length. In game killing power, it stands midway between the 6mm Remington and the larger 7mm Remington Magnum.

264 WINCHESTER MAGNUM This is the third in a series of short belted cartridges designed to deliver magnum velocities and power from standard length bolt actions. The 264 Magnum is a cartridge with a specific purpose—the delivery of a controlled-expanding bullet with flat trajectory and high residual energy at ultra long ranges. This it does exceptionally well. At 500 yards the 140-gr. bullet has 1370 fp of energy, 37% more than the 270 WCF 130-gr. and 23% more than a 30-06 180-gr. Velocity at that far-out point is still 2100 fps—close to 30-30 muzzle speed, and bullet drop is about 6" less than the 270. The 100-gr. 264 varmint load is even flatter-shooting, dropping some 9" less than the 140-gr. The 140-gr. loading should be adequate for medium soft-skinned game up to and including elk and moose.

270 WINCHESTER Superior to the 257 and 6mms for western use and for game larger than deer, the 270 has earned a good reputation among open country hunters. Its flat trajectory and high velocity with 130-gr. bullet at 3140 fps makes hitting easier over long, difficult-to-estimate ranges. Thus, as a mule deer, sheep and goat cartridge it is all anyone could ask for. For larger and heavier game of the caribou, elk and moose species, Winchester loads a 150-gr. Power-Point bullet to an increased muzzle velocity of 2900 fps, while Remington offers a 150-gr. round nose Core-Lokt at 2800 for woods hunting. The 100-gr. load is excellent for varmints, and is a good choice on antelope, too.

7mm REMINGTON MAGNUM Rifle cartridge of 1962, this short-case belted magnum mates the striking power of a 180-gr. 30-06 with the velocity and flat trajectory of a 130-gr. 270. The 175-gr. load has 21½% greater muzzle energy than the 180-gr. 30-06, and the 150-gr. is traveling 12% faster than the 130-gr. 270 bullet out at 300 yards. Various "wildcat" 7mm Magnum cartridges have evidenced their game killing ability in all corners of the globe, and now we have a factory standard cartridge capable of doing the same.

In 1965, Remington added a 175-gr. factory loading having a pointed Core-Lokt bullet designed to retain high velocity over longer ranges. Starting out at the muzzle with the same 3070 fps as the round-nose bullet, remaining velocity of the new spitzer slug is 340 fs higher at 300 yards and 460 fs faster at 500 yards, even equaling the 150-gr. bullet by the time 300 yards is reached.

In 1967, Remington added still another loading, this time a 125-gr. PSP at 3430 MV, thus making available a lightweight, high speed bullet with correspondingly flat trajectory for use on the smaller species of big game under long range conditions. This load should **not** be used in taking really large game, especially at short to medium ranges where velocity is still high.

280 REMINGTON Competitor of the 270 Winchester for open country hunting, and challenger of the 30-06 for "all-around cartridge" title in U.S. hunting fields, the 280 combines the best features of the 270 and the 7mm Mauser, providing slightly better ballistics **with factory loads** than either of those two. Four bullets—100-, 125-, 150- and 165-gr.—make the 280 "right" for a large variety of game; it combines flat shooting, a choice of either quick expansion or deep penetration, and easy recoil. This is one cartridge that is suited for practically any kind of hunting country or terrain, open or wooded, long or short range. For larger game such as moose, its 165-gr. bullet makes it preferable to the 270 unless the latter cartridge is handloaded to equal bullet weight. This is a "true" 7mm, bullets measuring .2835", and any 7mm bullet with a diameter of .283" to .284" may be used.

284 WINCHESTER Unusual for American cartridges, this short-cased round has a body diameter larger than its rim, giving it a powder capacity only about 1 grain less than the 280 Remington, even though ½-inch shorter, while retaining a "standard" size rim (common to such calibers as the 270, 280, 308 and 30-06), in order to permit use of the 284 cartridge with existing bolt face dimensions. Designed to give short action rifles (specifically the Winchester M88 lever action and M100 autoloader) ballistics equaling the longer 270 Winchester and 280 Remington cartridges, there is no reason why bolt action rifles shouldn't be chambered for it.

7mm MAUSER Originating as the Spanish military cartridge of 1893, the 7x57mm became popular the world over and today's factory loadings are better than ever. It will handle any game that the 270 will, but if used for antelope or other plains game at long range, either Federal's or Dominion's 139-gr. at 2900 fps, or Norma's 150-gr. load at 2756 fps should be specified. For varmints, Norma offers a 110-gr. bullet loading at 3068 fps MV. These modern high velocity versions have given the 7x57 new appeal. However, the standard U.S. cartridge with 175-gr. round-nose bullet of high sectional density is still the best choice for big game, especially when hunting in brush or woods.

30 CARBINE Commercial jacketed SP cartridges are loaded by both W-W and R-P for the 30 M-1 carbine. Remington's 110-gr. is a round nose SP whereas Winchester's is a hollow point SP. MV is 1980 fps, for only 955 fp energy. At 100 yards only 575 fp energy remains, so this cartridge should not be used on deer or any other big game species. As a small game load it is of course adequate, but may ricochet badly if fired at varmints in open fields.

30-30 WCF & 32 WINCHESTER SPECIAL Old favorites of the deer hunter and rancher, these cartridges continue to be popular more because of the light, handy carbines which use them than because of any attribute of the cartridges themselves. For the indifferent marksman they are wonders, having neither great bullet weight nor high velocity. These are deer cartridges and should not be "stretched." They're neither flat shooting nor accurate enough for varmints, nor do they have the power to be good moose killers.

30 & 32 REMINGTON Rimless versions of the 30-30 and 32 Special for the Remington line of autoloaders and slide action rifles (Models 8, 81, 14 and 141), bullet weights and velocities are the same (except no 150-gr. bullets), and there is no difference in killing power. Depends solely on which rifle action the shooter chooses as to which cartridge he uses.

300 SAVAGE Developed by Savage to approximate early 30-06 ballistics in their Model 99 lever action, this cartridge had a phenomenal acceptance for a time. It has an extremely short case neck, making it difficult to reload, but with 150- and 180-gr. factory loads it is a quick killer on deer. The lighter bullet should be chosen where flat trajectory and rapid expansion counts, but for wooded country, or for bear, moose and caribou, use the 180-gr. bullet.

30-40 KRAG Generally called the "Krag", this old military cartridge looks good in "civies." Rifles are no longer made for it, but the Krag bolt actions and Winchester Model 95 lever actions just don't seem to wear out. 180- and 220-gr. bullet loadings are available, with the former as best choice for deer, or mountain hunting requiring the flattest possible trajectory, while the latter is a long brush-cutter slow to open up and offering deeper penetration on heavy game than the faster 30-06, assuming like bullets.

308 WINCHESTER Commercial version of the 7.62mm NATO cartridge, the 308 is a big stick in a small bundle. A stubby cartridge, resembling the 300 Savage with a longer neck but still half-an-inch shorter than the 30-06, this hot little number comes within 100 fs of equaling 30-06 velocities. When first brought out, only 150- and 180-gr. bullets were available in factory loads, but now there is a 110-gr. varmint load and a dandy 200-gr. for the heavier stuff. As the new service cartridge, it will prove increasingly popular for target work as well as hunting.

30-06 SPRINGFIELD American military cartridge since 1906, this has been the standard by which all other big game cartridges were compared. Many have called it our most versatile all-round cartridge, for there are many bullets available, from the 110-gr. for varmints, through the flat-shooting 150-gr. to the 180-gr. "all-purpose," and finally up to a 220-gr. for big game and timber hunting. Except for Alaskan brown bear, buffalo, and rear-angling shots on elk, it is probably adequate for any North American game.

300 H&H MAGNUM Introduced in 1925 as the "Super-Thirty," this was the first factory cartridge giving a velocity in excess of 3000 fps with a 150-gr. bullet. Re-named "300 H&H Magnum" by Americans, it soon demonstrated its superiority as a big game cartridge and, starting in 1935, as a long range target load in the Wimbledon Cup Match at Camp Perry. By virtue of its larger belted case and heavier powder charge, the 300 H&H moves 180-gr. bullets 220 fps faster than the 30-06 with an additional quarter-ton of energy. This gives the shooter who is able to handle the increased recoil flatter trajectory with less wind deflection and more remaining knock-down power. Match Target loads are also offered.

300 WINCHESTER MAGNUM Recognizing the average American hunter's predilection for 30-cal. rifles as the favorite all-round bore size, Winchester in 1963 introduced this modern 300 Magnum, thereby spelling the doom of the fine old 300 H&H after 38 years. MV of the new round runs 150 to 200 fps higher than the 300 H&H with equal bullet weights, delivering almost 24% greater remaining energy at 400 yards (180-gr. bullet), and 13% flatter trajectory at the same range. Ballistics also exceed by a considerable margin those of smaller bore magnums. The 300 Winchester Magnum with proper bullet weights is adequate for all our big game from deer and antelope to elk, caribou, moose and even the great bears, plus African game of similar weight.

303 BRITISH British service cartridge for over half a century, the 303 has long been popular in Canada, and now with thousands of surplus military rifles in the hands of U.S. shooters its use on this side of the border has increased enormously. Consequently, a wide variety of factory loads have been made available including the old standard 215-gr. round-nose from Remington, Norma and Dominion at 2180-2200 fps; a 180-gr. from Remington, Winchester, Federal, Dominion and Norma averaging 2540 fps (Dominion, 2610); 150-gr. Dominion and Norma at 2720 fps. and even a 130-gr. Norma load traveling 2790 fps. The 303 has thus become a quite effective multi-purpose cartridge for North American game.

303 SAVAGE Another light deer cartridge of the 30-30 class, but in this one some velocity was traded for more bullet weight, 180- and 190-gr. bullets being given 100 to 200 fs less speed. 30-30 killing power, with penetration slightly increased at the expense of a more arched trajectory.

32-20 WCF An almost obsolete little shell which simply refuses to die, it should have been named the 30-20, for it uses a 30-cal. bullet. Too light and under-powered for deer. OK on turkeys, and up to 100 yards it will do a good job on 'chucks. Use the 80-gr. high-speed H.P. for varmints and the 100-gr. "standard" for edible game.

32-40 WINCHESTER Another old timer for which rifles are no longer made, this one began life as a single shot target cartridge, but was soon adapted to repeating hunting rifles. Its 165-gr. bullet lacks the velocity and punch of a 30-30, especially since the high velocity loading was discontinued, but it is still sometimes seen in the deer woods.

8mm MAUSER Underloaded by American ammunition makers because of the wide variations in quality and bore diameter of foreign rifles chambering it, this cartridge has ballistics about like the 30-40 Krag and is a good deer slayer. As loaded by Norma and imported into this country it is quite different, acquiring 30-06 powers. Caution here is to make sure of your rifle. Strength and accuracy vary widely with the individual rifle. Given a good one, this can be a fine big game cartridge using the stepped-up loadings. Do NOT mix with 30-06 rounds!

8mm LEBEL French Army cartridge for many years and until now loaded (only) by Remington, the Lebel has surprisingly good ballistics but is only used in sporterized military rifles or carbines and hence has never found wide favor in this country. Its fat rimmed case is not well adapted to modern bolt actions, but it is a powerful deer load. Discontinued 1964.

338 WINCHESTER MAGNUM Long awaited by many big game hunters, the 338 has shown itself to be a leading contender for the all-round rifle crown, killing large game such as brown bear and bison with the aplomb of a 375 H&H, or whitetail deer with less meat destruction than a quick-expanding 270 bullet. This is a modern, high-efficiency cartridge with flat trajectory slightly bettering the 30-06-180 gr. and 270-150 gr. loads, while delivering about 25% more striking energy at 200 and 300 yards than the 30-06. The great sectional density of the heavier bullets insures penetration and resistance to deflection by wind or brush, especially when the 275-grain Speer bullets are handloaded. Recoil is greater than with lesser cartridges, but not excessive for the shooter used to firing heavy 30-06 loads in light sporting rifles. The 338 will become increasingly popular with hunters who mix elk and moose with their regular deer menu.

348 WINCHESTER Lever action cartridge for really big game as well as deer, this is one of our most powerful rimmed cases. It appeared in 1936 for the Winchester Model 71 and was chambered in that one rifle only. Some versatility is provided by a triple range of bullet weights—150, 200, and 250 grains—but the heavier pair are best bets and all that are really needed. While more powerful than necessary for deer, it will do a sure job without wasting any more meat than an explosive 270 or 30. The 250-gr. bullet has ample stopping power for our largest American game. With its flat-nose bullets it is a deadly cartridge whose principal limitations are a rather heavy recoil and medium range.

35 REMINGTON With 200-gr. bullet, the 35 has been found to have considerably more anchoring power than the smaller 30's and 32's. Then too, it's good for getting through brush without deflection, and leaves a better blood trail. To 200 yards there's little difference in trajectory from the 30-30 and it has the advantage of being effective on larger game such as moose at moderate ranges, without excessive recoil. Highly recommended for Eastern deer and black bear, this praise does **not** include the pointed 150-gr. load. Stick to the 200-gr. for best results.

351 WINCHESTER SELF-LOADER Chambered only in the now-obsolete Winchester '07 autoloading rifle, the 351 hangs on because of its widespread use by police departments. For close wood ranges it can be used for deer and will kill with a proper hit.

358 WINCHESTER New and rimless brother of the 348, this one develops almost the same ballistics at the muzzle but its more pointed bullets retain that punch further out. The 358 is simply the 308 Winchester, neck-expanded to take 35-cal. bullets. The 358 is a splendid cartridge for moose and elk, and even the large bears can be tackled with it using the 250-gr. Trajectory is the same as that of the 30-40 Krag with 220-gr. bullet.

350 REMINGTON MAGNUM First commercial cartridge to deserve the term Short Magnum, and one of the most practical big game rounds to appear in recent years, the 350 Magnum is especially notable for the restraint built into its design. Either standard length or short actions will accommodate its squat hull and deep-seated bullets, and its power is an almost perfect compromise, for American big game, between too much and not enough. This stems directly from its powder capacity, about 7% more than that of a 30-06 when both cases are filled to the base of their necks. 200-gr. bullets have a MV of 2710 fps, while 250-grainers reach 2410 fps, both from only a 20" carbine barrel. The old 35 Remington is thus hopelessly outclassed and the 35 Whelen challenged by a cartridge that is still within the recoil limitations of once-a-year hunters. Deer hunters and those who are recoil-shy should use the 200-gr. load, which delivers noticeably less kick.

375 H&H MAGNUM World-wide big game cartridge and champion of the "mediums," the 375 H&H dates back to 1912 but can still boast no peer as an all-round load for big and dangerous game. It will dispatch the largest American game as well as most African species. If necessary, it will kill an elephant, and yet its big 270-gr. slug will travel over long ranges as flat as a 180-gr. 30-06 to kill mountain game without excessive meat destruction. There is also a 300-gr. bullet turning up over 2 tons of muzzle energy. Cartridges may be purchased in almost all of the big game regions of the world. Its one disadvantage is its quite heavy recoil.

38-40 WINCHESTER This "38" actually measures 40 caliber and should have been named "40-40." Many deer are still killed yearly by its 180-gr. bullet, loafing along at 1,330 fs, mostly because it punches a big enough hole to let out a lot of blood. It's obsolete and there are a lot of better cartridges, but for short ranges (under 100 yards), it will still do the trick.

38-55 WINCHESTER Like the 32-40, this cartridge started out as a target load for single shot rifles, in which it quickly established a reputation for fine accuracy. Its use spread to repeating hunting rifles where the 255-gr. bullet proved to be a more sure stopper than the 30-30. It tends to ignore brush, but its low velocity means a rainbow-trajectory and so it lost the popularity race. No rifles are made for it.

44-40 WINCHESTER Big brother of the 38-40, this is the same type of short, low-velocity cartridge, varying only by being slightly larger in bullet diameter and weight (200 grains). Under 100 yards it will kill as well as a 30-30.

44 REMINGTON MAGNUM See Part II—Handgun Cartridges.

444 MARLIN In essence a "super" 44 Magnum since it uses the same 240-gr. .429" jacketed SP bullet but in a long, straight 2.22" case, 444 Marlin provides 30% higher MV with 88% greater ME! At the muzzle its energy is greater even than that of the 30-06, at least on paper, but the blunt, relatively short bullet sheds velocity so fast that at only 100 yards it is down to the power level of the 7mm Mauser and 300 Savage. However, the 444 will be hitting as hard at 200 yards as the 35 Remington at 150, making it a fine deer and black bear cartridge to this range, while at 100 yards or less it is capable of handling just about any North American big game. Its biggest need is for a heavier constructed bullet that will not break up on the tough muscles and bone structure of such game or any intervening brush. Such bullets are already available to handloaders.

45-70 Still potent after 85 years, some of which was on the battlefield, but even more in the hunting fields, this old timer asks only to be used within ranges where its trajectory isn't too steep. Other than that, its user can count on a kill (if he does his part) whether the game be a small deer or a big moose. Excessive drop makes hitting tough beyond 150 yards, despite its ability to kill well beyond that distance.

458 WINCHESTER Most powerful commercial American cartridge, the 458 has already won its spurs in Africa; the special Model 70 rifle chambered for it is known as the "African" Model. It is well named, for the massive 500-gr. full-steel-jacketed and 510-gr. softpoints are an "over-dose" for practically all other game with the exceptions of Indian tiger, Asian gaur, and Alaskan brown bear. Heavy bullet weight and high speed for its caliber combine to make this more than just a good killing cartridge—it is a "stopping cartridge," designed to break down the most ponderous and dangerous beasts, and this it will do. For an American going to Africa for elephant, buffalo and rhino it is top choice. The soft point should be used on even the largest soft-skinned game, for the solid bullet is a specialized number for elephants. Has greatest recoil of all American cartridges.

THE WEATHERBY CARTRIDGES

Weatherby Magnum cartridges have been factory produced for many years now, and are sold at sporting goods stores all over America and in many foreign countries. The brass cases are produced in Sweden, but all other components are American-made and assembled. They therefore qualify as American ammunition and merit inclusion in this analysis of cartridges on the U.S. market.

224 WEATHERBY VARMINTMASTER Smallest of the Weatherby's, the 224 also has the smallest capacity of any belted case. Despite its modest size, however, velocities over 3700 fps with 50-gr. bullets and 3600 fps with 55-gr. have been chronographed, making it a close competitor of the 22-250. It is thus an efficient case which, in combination with the added safety features of good base thickness and positive headspacing provided by the belt, rates as an impressive performer. For those varminters who feel a need for more velocity than the 222 or 222 Magnum, but are willing to settle for less than the 220 Swift, the 224 Weatherby is an outstanding choice.

240 WEATHERBY MAGNUM Highest velocity of all factory-loaded 24 calibers, with the single exception of Holland & Holland's 244 Magnum, this medium capacity Weatherby features an entirely new belted case of reduced dimensions, capable of driving 70-gr. 6mm bullets to 3850 fps, 90-gr. to 3500, and 100-gr. to 3395 fps. It is thus some 200-300 fs faster than the 6mm Remington, and 300-400 fs ahead of the 243 Winchester. With loads giving sufficiently fine accuracy, this should prove to be an outstanding cartridge for open country deer and antelope shooting in combination with summer use as a long range varmint round.

257 WEATHERBY MAGNUM For varmint shooting at extremely long range or for the lighter species of big game in open country, where a premium is placed on flat trajectory and rapid bullet expansion, this cartridge is outstanding. Offering the flattest trajectory of any known 25-caliber cartridge, it utilizes the maximum loads of present-day powders that can be efficiently burned in this caliber to provide the highest striking energy for its bore size. In these combined respects, it is exceeded only by the 264 Winchester Magnum in cartridges under 270 caliber, and even there the difference is negligible.

270 WEATHERBY MAGNUM Next step up in the Weatherby line, the 270 WM is also a better choice for those who place more emphasis on big game hunting, but would still like to use the same rifle for off-season varminting. Bullets of 100, 130 and 150 grains are available with energies and trajectories close to Winchester's 264 Magnum with, however, a somewhat better bullet selection for greater flexibility. While 270 WM muzzle velocities are around 300 fps faster than the standard 270, at 300 yards the speed differential is little more than 100 fs with the lighter bullets but some 270 fs ahead in 150-gr. loadings.

7mm WEATHERBY MAGNUM This cartridge so closely parallels the 270 WM in almost all respects that little more need be said about it, except to note that there's a .007" bigger bore and heavier bullet selection (to 175 grains) in the 7mm. In any event, there is little to choose between the 7mm WM and the newer 7mm Remington Magnum.

300 WEATHERBY MAGNUM Weatherby says this is his most popular and versatile caliber, and it's not hard to see why. With equal bullet weights, the 300 Weatherby develops from 285 to 355 fps more muzzle velocity than the 300 H&H Magnum for a noticeable increase in power. This cartridge is also liked for the nice balance it strikes between the large and small bores. For example, the 180-gr. 300 WM load offers some 500 fs velocity advantage over the 270-gr. 375 H&H Magnum with a consequent flattening of trajectory by 27%, and yet when loaded with a 150-gr. spitzer bullet it is both faster and flatter shooting than either the 270 or 7mm Weatherby Magnums. Despite some rather extreme claims for it the 300 Weatherby Magnum is doubtless one of the finest all-round big game cartridges.

340 WEATHERBY MAGNUM This is Weatherby's newest big game cartridge, produced to satisfy those hunters who want still more bullet weight than the 300's 220 grains, but at the same time wish to retain the 300's velocity and trajectory characteristics. This it does, giving a 250-gr. bullet only 55 fs less muzzle velocity than the 220-gr. 300 WM. Recoil is up, however, and the man who selects the 340 in preference to a 300 should be reasonably sure he needs its extra punch. For the great Alaskan bear it would appear to be a better choice, but for an all-round rifle involving mostly smaller game, the 300 would get the nod. The 340 WM uses the same bullets as the 338 Winchester Magnum, but boosts bullet speeds by 150 to 210 fps. An excellent moose, elk and bear cartridge.

378 WEATHERBY MAGNUM With this truly "magnum-size" cartridge we enter the field of specialized big game calibers. The latest Weatherby catalog states that it was "designed for the purpose of killing thick-skinned animals where extremely deep penetration is needed." With bullet weights of 270- and 300-gr. at velocities of 2900 to 3180 fps, it should be obvious that while striking power is unquestionably great, so is its recoil; entirely too much, in fact, for the average hunter not used to handling such heavy comeback. Experienced African and Arctic hunters, however, accustomed to the slam of the 375 H&H and larger rifles, report the 378 WM to be a most effective cartridge for the big stuff. With the adoption of the 378, Weatherby has discontinued production of the 375 WM, although ammunition for the older caliber is still being made. Despite its designation, the 378 uses the same bullets as the 375 Weatherby and the 375 H&H Magnum.

460 WEATHERBY MAGNUM Comments made on the 378 WM apply with even greater force to this largest and most powerful of all American cartridges. Using the same oversize belted case as the 378 Weatherby, its energy of 8000 fp with 500-gr. bullet is so great that it would normally be selected for only the very largest and dangerous game including elephant, rhino and buffalo. Some authorities feel that the 378 Weatherby would be adequate for such animals were it not for African game laws requiring rifles of 40 caliber or over for those species. Here again the name may be misleading, since the 460 WM uses the same size bullets as the 458 Winchester, only at a phenomenal increase of 570 fps muzzle velocity and nearly 3000 foot pounds of ME.

AMERICANIZED IMPORTED CARTRIDGES

We include here summaries on some of the popular and significant cartridges produced in Europe for the U.S. market. Some were actually designed in this country, others of overseas origin were specifically intended for export to the States; since most of them are encountered with increasing frequency, it is reasonable to think of them as "American" by use if not by manufacture. Only those loaded with American-type "Boxer" primers are included.

6.5x54 MS An old but still liked cartridge for the Mannlicher-Schoenauer carbines, Norma offers five different versions with bullet weights of 77, 139 and 156 grains at muzzle speeds of 3117, 2580 and 2461 fps. A modest capacity round, the 6.5 MS built its reputation as a game cartridge **not** on velocity, but rather on the deep penetration of its long pencil-like round nose bullets. In its heaviest bullet weight, it has been well-liked in Maine as an effective black bear load.

6.5x55 SWEDISH Long the military cartridge of Sweden and Norway, the 6.5x55 has become quite common in the U.S., partly because of thousands of imported surplus military rifles and the fine Schultz & Larsen target rifles. With its light recoil, resistance to wind deflection and excellent accuracy, it has justified its Scandinavian reputation and is seen increasingly on our target ranges. Norma offers 6 different loadings with bullet weights of 77, 93, 139 and 156 grains at velocities somewhat above those of the smaller Mannlicher cartridge. The 139-gr. load is probably the most popular here.

7x61 S&H A modern high velocity big game round with Norma short belted case, the brain-child of Americans Phil Sharpe and Dick Hart, this shell is only 4mm longer than the old 7x57 Mauser case but velocity with 160-gr. boat-tails is 3100 fps at muzzle of a 26" barrel, according to the Norma table.

In 1968, Norma improved the 7x61 case by changing its interior dimensions to provide thinner but stronger case walls. Known as the Super 7x61, exterior dimensions remain exactly the same as formerly, hence the new version will fit all rifles chambered for the older 7x61 S&H, but due to a slightly increased powder capacity, velocity is rated 50 fs higher; (3150 with 160-gr. bullet from 26" barrels).

30 U.S. CARBINE To satisfy the demand for 30 Carbine ammo, Norma produces one with full metal jacket, the other in soft point, both 110 grain. This last, the one hunter-owners most sought, is at best little more than a small game cartridge, since velocity and energy are down to 1595 fs and 622 fp respectively at only 100 yards. Fast repeat shots should not be counted on to make up for inadequate power; this cartridge should not be selected for deer or other big game hunting.

308 NORMA MAGNUM A short magnum tailored to American big game fields. Its 180-gr. bullet steps out at a velocity 400 fs faster than the 180-gr. 30-06, is 180 fs ahead of the great 300 H&H, equals the new 300 Winchester Magnum and even approaches the much larger 300 Weatherby. Advantage of the Norma cartridge (true also of the 300 Win. Mag.) is that it has the same over-all length as a 30-06, will fit in '06 magazines and only requires re-chambering the barrel and opening up the bolt face, plus an extractor alteration, to convert an '06 to 308 Magnum. Pressures run pretty high in this case, so only rifles with strong actions should be converted to the new cartridge. Only factory load is with 180-gr.

"Dual-Core" bullets, but the cases may be reloaded with American primers and any 30-cal. bullets from 110- to 220-gr. weight. It is thus a versatile as well as powerful high performance cartridge.

NORMA 7.62mm RUSSIAN Imported by Norma-Precision for American owners of Winchester Model 1895 and surplus military rifles in this caliber, the 7.62mm is furnished with the Tri-Clad soft point 180-gr. bullet developing 2625 fps muzzle velocity and more than 2750 fp energy. This is a rimmed bottle-necked case, ballistically almost identical to our 308, thus only slightly inferior to the 30-06. Formerly loaded in this country with either 145-gr. or 150-gr. bullets at 2820 fs, those ballistics may be reproduced in these new cases by handloaders desiring a lighter, faster bullet loading.

303 BRITISH HV Another modernized old cartridge is Norma's high velocity loadings of the 303 British. As loaded by Remington with a 215-gr. bullet and by Winchester with a 180-gr., pressure limitations of the Lee-Enfield action have held velocities to a sedate 2180-2540 fps, and owners of surplus 303's have wondered how they could obtain higher speeds. The safest way is to decrease bullet weight, and this is just what Norma has done. Two Norma factory loads include a 150-gr. bullet at 2720 fps and a 130-gr. at 2789, either of which will shoot flatter and open quicker on impact than the heavier bullets. If you use a 303 for open country hunting of deer or antelope, give these new loads a try.

7.65 ARGENTINE Originally known as the 7.65mm Belgian Mauser, this cartridge was once loaded in the U.S. and chambered in such popular rifles as the Remington 30-S and Winchester 54 and 70, but was discontinued about the time of WW 2 for lack of demand. Importation of surplus Argentine military Mausers has reversed the picture and there is once again a need for this surprisingly efficient round. Norma offers a single 150-gr. soft point with 2920 fs muzzle velocity and 2105 fs at **300** yards for a midrange trajectory height of only 5.8". Regardless of the fact that this cartridge was designed over 70 years ago, in its modern version it is still an excellent deer cartridge. Bullet (not cartridge) size is the same as a 303 British—.311"-.312".

8x57-JR and 8x57-JRS Rimmed versions of the famous 8x57 Mauser case, the 8x57-JR is loaded by Norma with a 196-gr. .318" bullet, while the 8x57-JRS has the same weight but in .323" diameter. Post-war rifles generally have the larger bore size, while pre-war rifles usually have (but not necessarily) the .318" bore. In any event, the proof markings on the barrel should be carefully examined and only those cartridges with the proper size bullets used. Both of the 8x57 rimmed rounds are good deer and black bear cartridges.

358 NORMA MAGNUM First of the new line of Norma Magnums, this 35-caliber number was offered to the market in 1959 and since then has steadily gained favor among big game hunters here and abroad. In the Scandinavian countries, the 358 Norma has become a favorite of moose hunters, a use for which it is well-fitted almost anywhere. A 250-gr. bullet at 2790 fps from a 23" barrel gives 4322 fp energy—some 1500 more than a 220-gr. 30-06—and energy close to the 4500 fp of a 375 Magnum. With a 200-gr. bullet, 3100 fps can be reached with permissible pressures, so that the 358 Norma may be thought of as a direct competitor of the 338 Winchester, both ballistically and as concerns adaptability to game species. It should fill the bill as a powerful "medium" bore for African hunting, and of course is a natural for Canadian and Alaskan large game.

RIMFIRE CARTRIDGES

5mm REMINGTON RIMFIRE MAGNUM Although announced in the fall of 1967, this 20-cal. bottle-necked rimfire cartridge had still not been offered for sale by spring of 1969. Various troubles are said to have been experienced with early production runs. If eventually able to meet predicted ballistics, calling for a 38-gr. jacketed soft point at 2100 fps MV, performance at 50 yards will about equal that of the 22 WMR at its muzzle, and still deliver as much punch at 150 yards as does the 22 Long Rifle High Speed at the muzzle. Object of this round is to provide lower cost small-game stopping effectiveness with fine accuracy to 150 yards from light, relatively inexpensive rifles.

22 SHORT The economical shooting gallery cartridge. Accurate to 50 yards, this old load is still a popular number. Three loadings—Standard, High Speed and Gallery—give it a usefulness second only to the indispensable 22 Long Rifle. It is **not** a game cartridge, however, and its use on live targets should be restricted to rats, snakes, starlings and the like, since even in the high speed load its light bullet gives but half the energy of the Long Rifle.

22 LONG Only the High Speed loading of this little "betwixt and between" cartridge survives. Having neither the accuracy of the Short nor the power of the Long Rifle it is not recommended except for those few old repeating rifles chambered especially for it.

22 LONG RIFLE Finest and most versatile rimfire cartridge ever developed, it is today better than ever. Four loadings fit it for just about everything except big game hunting. This is everybody's cartridge, with the gilt-edged accuracy of the special Match loads for serious competition, the Standard rounds for economical practice, the High Speeds for small game hunting (with hollow-point bullets), and the Shot cartridges for pest destruction. The High Speed with plain bullet is not recommended for **any** of these uses. For hunting, better use the hollow-point for humane kills, and even try for a head shot. Pass up shots beyond 75 yards and be content with squirrels, rabbits and birds.

22 WINCHESTER AUTOMATIC Useful only to owners of the old Winchester Model 1903 autoloader, it is less powerful than the Long Rifle.

22 WRF (or REMINGTON SPECIAL) More powerful than any Long Rifle load and a far better hunting cartridge, it deserves to be more popular. Its flat-nose bullet, of slightly greater diameter and 5 grains more weight than a Long Rifle, is faster, and turns up a third more energy. For squirrel hunters it is hard to beat, and rifles for it should again be made.

22 WINCHESTER MAGNUM RIMFIRE This newest and most potent rimfire cartridge offers the highest velocity, flattest trajectory and greatest striking power of any rimfire cartridge currently available. Its ballistics in a 6½" barrel exceed even those of any other rimfire when used in a rifle. This new cartridge is a top-flight choice for the 100-125 yard varmint shooter who doesn't handload; similarly, for the farmer's gun kept against raiding hawks, foxes, etc., **and** for the handgunner who prefers to use his "short gun" for hunting.

Part II. HANDGUN CARTRIDGES
(Rimfire & Centerfire)

22 SHORT RF This little cartridge is currently experiencing a revival of popularity because of its adaptability to rapid-fire International-type shooting in the autoloading pistols made especially for it.

22 LONG RF See Rifle Cartridge Section.

22 LONG RIFLE RF Just as with rifles, this cartridge has done more than any other to popularize shooting and training with the handgun. In either revolver or "automatic" it is highly accurate and makes a fine companion for hunter and trapper. Ammo is easily carried, yet will kill small game better than some larger centerfires. Use high speeds for hunting and standards for target work.

22 REMINGTON JET First of the CF handgun cartridges to appear, this little bottleneck was introduced in March of 1961 when Smith & Wesson announced their Magnum M53 revolver. Besides the 22 Jet this gun handles (via cylinder inserts) 22 Shorts, Longs and Long Rifles. The factory-announced muzzle velocity of 2460 fps (obtained in closed-breech test barrels) has not been achieved in revolvers with their open gap between cylinder and barrel. However, the 1870 fps reached with 6" barrels (2100 with 8⅜") makes this a respectable handgun varmint cartridge in any man's language.

221 REMINGTON FIREBALL The second 22-cal. CF cartridge to be introduced by Remington, it established a precedent in 1963 by being chambered in the first American commercial bolt action pistol. 2650 fps has been reached with a 50-gr. bullet from its 10½" barrel, equal to a factory 22 Hornet with 45-gr. bullet fired in a full-length rifle barrel.

256 WINCHESTER MAGNUM Winchester's entry in the high speed, flat trajectory handgun cartridge field had trouble getting off the ground after it was announced in April, 1961, but it has finally developed as *both* a handgun and rifle cartridge. Early published factory velocities were *lower* than those actually attained, first tables saying 2000 fps for the 60-gr. SP bullet, whereas independent chronographs registered 2350 fps from the 8½" barrel of a Ruger Hawkeye.

25 AUTO Smallest of production centerfires, this is strictly for use in defensive weapons—tiny automatics lacking both power and accuracy, firing 50-gr. metal case bullets with less energy than even the standard velocity 22 LR.

30 CARBINE In producing his Blackhawk revolver chambered for the 30 Carbine cartridge, Bill Ruger has made this round properly classifiable as a handgun load. For the considerable number of today's pistol shooters seeking a high speed, flat-shooting revolver cartridge without the heavy recoil of a 44 or 41 Magnum, but with more bullet weight and diameter than a 22 caliber, the 30 Carbine may provide the answer. Factory and GI loads produce velocities varying from 1400 to 1530 fps from our 7½" barrel test revolver, giving them some 40% more muzzle energy than the 22 Jet. As a revolver load it will be liked particularly by owners of carbines in the same caliber as a companion piece.

30 LUGER A bottle-necked cartridge for automatic pistols firing a 93-gr. metal case bullet at 1,220 fs. Flat shooting with high paper energy, expansion is lacking due to bullet construction, severely limiting its game-killing or man-stopping capabilities. However, it far out-classes the 32 ACP.

30 MAUSER Early high velocity champion, this is still one of the world's hottest cartridges, boasting 1,410 fs with 85-gr. metal case bullet. Like the 30 Luger, it makes long range hitting easier but the bullet falls short of adequate killing power, and it must be used in the awkward Mauser pistol.

32 AUTO Next step up in the caliber scale for automatics, this is a very popular cartridge here and abroad for pocket pistols. Many are used by foreign police where it is known as the 7.65mm, but again a small (71-gr.) round nose metal case bullet gives energy only in the high speed 22 Long Rifle class and no bullet expansion. Not recommended for hunting or defense use.

32 S&W & 32 S&W LONG These are the most popular of the 32's for revolvers, the shorter load used in innumerable old "bureaudrawer specials," the accurate Long in target and light police revolvers. The Long should always be chosen if the gun will handle it. A good small game cartridge but lacks power for police work.

32 COLT SHORT & LONG A pair of "obsolete" cartridges used in old-model Colt pocket revolvers, they are less accurate and less powerful than the 32 S&W Long, and will not chamber in modern 32-caliber revolvers.

32-20 WINCHESTER Best of all the 32's for revolvers, using 100-gr. bullets in both lead and soft point types with flat nose, this is the smallest caliber practical for serious police and defensive use. Trajectory is also flatter due to higher velocity, making this a good hunting cartridge for varmints and small game. Do NOT use the "High Velocity" rifle loads in revolvers.

38 AUTO and 38 SUPER AUTOMATIC The 38 Automatic cartridge is intended to be used in the original Colt 38 Automatic pistols, Models of 1900 and 1902. When the Colt Super 38 appeared about 1925, a new, more powerful loading was offered under the name of Super 38 for this stronger pistol. These Super 38 Automatic cartridges should not be fired in the early model Colt pistols in view of their system of slide attachment and the higher pressures of the Super cartridge. Even the regular 38 Automatic is closely comparable to the 9mm Luger in power, and the 38 Super will give the 357 Magnum a run for its money in barrels of equal length. If loaded with soft point bullets, both of these 38 Auto cartridges would make good game killing loads. Either cartridge will function properly in the Super automatic pistol.

380 AUTO Designed to give more power in a straight blow-back automatic pistol than is provided by the 32 ACP cartridge, and yet keep down chamber pressure and recoil to stay within the limitations of small pocket pistols, it is the smallest auto pistol cartridge which can be recommended for defense.

9MM LUGER This is a more practical load for automatic pistols, using a heavier (124-gr.) bullet at good velocity (1,120 fs), and with considerable accuracy. It is the closest thing to a world or international military pistol cartridge and its popularity here is on the increase with the new S&W automatic and the Colt Commander chambered for it.

38 S&W A favorite cartridge for pocket revolvers, with 146-gr. bullet, and adopted by the British military during World War II, when it was known as the 38-200 (as it was loaded with a 200-gr. bullet). Nothing smaller is recommended for defensive use.

38 COLT SHORT & LONG The 38 Short was used in early Colt house defense guns and the Long was the cartridge which failed to stop fanatical Moros during the Philippine Insurrection. Either may be used in a 38 Special revolver, but both are out-classed by that cartridge for any purpose, hence seldom used.

38 SPECIAL Known as the "S&W" when loaded with round nose bullets, and as the "Colt Special" with flat-points, this is undoubtedly the most popular revolver cartridge in existence. Highly accurate for match shooting, adequately powerful for police and defensive work, yet light enough in recoil to permit its use in small, featherweight belly guns.

357 MAGNUM A high velocity revolver cartridge ideally suited to the needs of police officers and field shooters, its 158-gr. bullet travels at a far higher velocity and delivers an even greater increase in striking energy than the same weight bullet from a 38 Special of equal barrel length. With metal piercing bullet it will penetrate an automobile body, and with the flat-point lead bullet it will kill game of considerable size. An even better choice of bullet for field use is the soft point Remington or Norma half-jacket which will not lead up barrels as do the ordinary lead bullets at high velocity. One of our three best long range revolver cartridges, a gun in this caliber has the added advantage of chambering all 38 Special cartridges for target work.

38-40 WINCHESTER See Part I—CF Rifle Cartridges.

41 LONG COLT Chambered only in old model Colt revolvers, this slow moving, heavy bullet (195 grains) load is suited only for short range shooting where the blunt shape of its lead bullet makes it a good stopper.

41 MAGNUM Produced by Remington for Smith & Wesson revolvers in response to demands for a more potent police cartridge, this new 41 Magnum fills the gap between the 357 and 44 Magnums. Two loads are offered, one a 210-gr. SP at 1500 fps, the other a 210-gr. lead bullet at 1050 fps, both MV figures from 8¾" bbls. In the more common 6" bbl., velocities run 1342 and 986. A potent and accurate cartridge in SP version, trajectory is practically as flat as the 44 Magnum is; it penetrates even deeper, though bullet energy is less. Recoil, only 75% of a 44 Magnum's, makes it a much more pleasant load to shoot. It may well find more use in the game fields than on the policeman's beat. Recoil and gun weight are both heavy for police use, and so far the lead bullet loads have shown only mediocre accuracy. Bullet diameter is .410" and will not interchange with the old 41 Long Colt.

44-40 WINCHESTER See Part I—CF Rifle Cartridges.

44 S&W SPECIAL Developed as a target cartridge from the earlier 44 S&W Russian, the 44 Special has never been loaded by the factories to its velocity potential. The 246-gr. lead bullets travel slowly (755 fs), which is of no matter on target ranges where their high accuracy is paramount. Only when properly handloaded is its true power capacity realized.

44 REMINGTON MAGNUM 44 Special and 44 Russian cartridges may be used in 44 Magnum revolvers when light loads are desired, but for a serious matter afield or on the highway, the new Magnum load is in a class by itself. A flat point, copper-base bullet of 240 grains at 1,570 fps gives the unprecedented muzzle energy of 1,310 fp or nearly *twice* that of the 357 Magnum. Power, recoil and cost are all high, making this a cartridge for specialized use by veteran handgunners. A 44 Magnum is now available specifically designed for use in rifles and carbines. Remington uses a jacketed soft point bullet with a muzzle velocity of 1750 fps claimed; Winchester's ammo has a hollow, soft point that leaves the muzzle at 1750 fps.

45 COLT Most famous of all American revolver cartridges and still one of the best, whether the target be criminal or beast. For close range work we would prefer its big 250-gr. bullet to the 357 Magnum. Now that new guns are again being made for the old 45, its historical background as well as its effective power should ensure a continued popularity and long life.

45 AUTO (or ACP) Official U.S. Army sidearm cartridge for over a half-century and spanning three wars, this largest American cartridge for automatic pistols has thoroughly proven itself both in combat and on the target range. Difficult load to control, but inherently accurate, it has now been given assists in the form of a new light wadcutter target loading, and in late 1957 a new target model pistol of the Colt Model of 1911. There is even a metal-penetrating load for highway patrolmen. This is a good choice for the bigbore shooter, but needs a soft point bullet for field work on game.

45 AUTO RIM Companion of the 45 ACP, this thick-rimmed cartridge was developed for use without half-moon clips in revolvers chambered for the automatic cartridge. For either game shooting or police work it is a better choice than the ACP because of its 230-gr. lead bullet.

CENTERFIRE RIFLE CARTRIDGES — BALLISTICS AND PRICES

Winchester-Western, Remington-Peters, Federal and Speer-DWM

Most of these centerfire loads are available from Winchester-Western and Remington-Peters. Loads available from only one source are marked by a letter, thus: Winchester (a); Western (b); Remington (c); Peters (d); Speer-DWM (f). Those fewer cartridges also available from Federal are marked (e). Contrary to previous practice, W-W and R-P prices are not necessarily uniform, hence prices are approximate. Federal prices are generally slightly lower.

Cartridge	Bullet Wt. Grs.	Bullet Type	Velocity (fps) Muzzle	Velocity (fps) 100 yds.	Velocity (fps) 200 yds.	Velocity (fps) 300 yds.	Energy (ft. lbs.) Muzzle	Energy (ft. lbs.) 100 yds.	Energy (ft. lbs.) 200 yds.	Energy (ft. lbs.) 300 yds.	Mid-Range Trajectory 100 yds.	Mid-Range Trajectory 200 yds.	Mid-Range Trajectory 300 yds.	Price for 20*
218 Bee*	46	HP	2860	2160	1610	1200	835	475	265	145	0.7	3.8	11.5	$9.60
22 Hornet*	45	SP	2690	2030	1510	1150	720	410	230	130	0.8	4.3	13.0	9.00
22 Hornet* (c, d)	45	HP	2690	2030	1510	1150	720	410	230	130	0.8	4.3	13.0	9.00
22 Hornet*	46	HP	2690	2030	1510	1150	740	420	235	135	0.8	4.3	13.0	9.00
222 Remington (e)	50	PSP, MC, PL†	3200	2660	2170	1750	1140	785	520	340	0.5	2.5	7.0	3.75
222 Remington Magnum (c, d)	55	SP, PL†	3300	2800	2340	1930	1330	955	670	455	0.5	2.3	6.1	4.10
223 Remington (c, d, e)	55	SP, PL†	3300	2800	2340	1930	1330	955	670	455	0.5	2.1	5.4	4.10
22-250 Remington (a, c, d)	55	PSP, PL†	3760	3230	2745	2305	1730	1275	920	650	0.4	1.7	4.5	4.10
225 Winchester (a, b)	55	PSP	3650	3140	2680	2270	1630	1200	875	630	0.4	1.8	4.8	4.10
243 Winchester (e)	80	PSP, PL†	3500	3080	2720	2410	2180	1690	1320	1030	0.4	1.8	4.7	5.20
243 Winchester (e)	100	PP, CL, PSP	3070	2790	2540	2320	2090	1730	1430	1190	0.5	2.2	5.5	5:20
6mm Remington (c, d)	80	PSP, HP, PL†	3450	3130	2750	2400	2220	1740	1340	1018	0.4	1.8	4.7	5.20
6mm Remington (c, d)	100	PCL	3190	2920	2660	2420	2260	1890	1570	1300	0.5	2.1	5.1	5.60
244 Remington (c, d)	90	PSP	3200	2850	2530	2230	2050	1630	1280	995	0.5	2.1	5.5	5.20
25-06 Remington (c, d)	87	HP	3500	3070	2680	2310	2370	1820	1390	1030	Not Available			5.65
25-06 Remington (c, d)	120	PSP	Not Available				Not Available				Not Available			5.65
25-20 Winchester*	86	L, Lu	1460	1180	1030	940	405	265	200	170	2.6	12.5	32.0	7.35
25-20 Winchester*	86	SP	1460	1180	1030	940	405	265	200	170	2.6	12.5	32.0	8.20
25-35 Winchester	117	SP, CL	2300	1910	1600	1340	1370	945	665	465	1.0	4.6	12.5	5.10
250 Savage	87	PSP, SP	3030	2660	2330	2060	1770	1370	1050	820	0.6	2.5	6.4	4.90
250 Savage	100	ST, CL, PSP	2820	2460	2140	1870	1760	1340	1020	775	0.6	2.9	7.4	4.90
256 Winchester Magnum* (b)	60	OPE	2800	2070	1570	1220	1040	570	330	200	0.8	4.0	12.0	9.00
257 Roberts (a, b)	87	PSP	3200	2840	2500	2190	1980	1560	1210	925	0.5	2.2	5.7	5.35
257 Roberts	100	ST, CL	2900	2540	2210	1920	1870	1430	1080	820	0.6	2.7	7.0	5.35
257 Roberts	117	PP, CL	2650	2280	1950	1690	1820	1350	985	740	0.7	3.4	8.8	5.35
6.5 Remington Magnum (c)	100	PSPCL	3450	3070	2690	2320	2640	2090	1610	1190	Not Available			7.05
6.5mm Remington Magnum (c)	120	PSPCL	3030	2750	2480	2230	2450	2010	1640	1330	0.5	2.3	5.7	7.05
264 Winchester Magnum	100	PSP, CL	3700	3260	2880	2550	3040	2360	1840	1440	0.4	1.6	4.2	7.05
264 Winchester Magnum	140	PP, CL	3200	2940	2700	2480	3180	2690	2270	1910	0.5	2.0	4.9	7.05
270 Winchester	100	PSP	3480	3070	2690	2340	2690	2090	1600	1215	0.4	1.8	4.8	5.65
270 Winchester (e)	130	PP, PSP	3140	2880	2630	2400	2850	2390	2000	1660	0.5	2.1	5.3	5.65
270 Winchester	130	ST, CL, BP, PP	3140	2850	2580	2320	2840	2340	1920	1550	0.5	2.1	5.3	5.65
270 Winchester (c, d)	150	CL	2800	2440	2140	1870	2610	1980	1520	1160	0.6	2.9	7.6	5.65
270 Winchester (a, b, e)	150	PP	2900	2620	2380	2160	2800	2290	1890	1550	0.6	2.5	6.3	5.65
280 Remington (c, d)	125	PCL	3190	2880	2590	2320	2820	2300	1860	1490	0.5	2.1	5.3	5.65
280 Remington (c, d)	150	PCL	2900	2670	2450	2220	2800	2370	2000	1640	0.6	2.5	6.1	5.65
280 Remington (c, d)	165	CL	2820	2510	2220	1970	2910	2310	1810	1420	0.6	2.8	7.2	5.65
284 Winchester (a, b)	125	PP	3200	2880	2590	2310	2840	2300	1860	1480	0.5	2.1	5.3	5.65
284 Winchester (a, b)	150	PP	2900	2630	2380	2160	2800	2300	1890	1550	0.6	2.5	6.3	5.65
7mm Mauser (e)	175	SP	2490	2170	1900	1680	2410	1830	1400	1100	0.8	3.7	9.5	5.65
7mm Remington Magnum	125	CL	3430	3080	2750	2450	3260	2630	2100	1660	0.6	1.8	4.7	7.05
7mm Remington Magnum (e)	150	PP, CL	3260	2970	2700	2450	3540	2940	2430	1990	0.4	2.0	4.9	7.05
7mm Remington Magnum (e)	175	PP	3070	2720	2400	2120	3660	2870	2240	1750	0.5	2.4	6.1	7.05
7mm Remington Magnum (c, d)	175	PCL	3070	2860	2660	2460	3660	3170	2740	2350	0.5	2.1	5.2	7.05
30 Carbine* (e)	110	HSP, SP	1980	1540	1230	1040	950	575	370	260	1.4	7.5	21.7	8.95
30-30 Winchester (c, d)	150	CL	2410	1960	1620	1360	1930	1280	875	616	0.9	4.5	12.5	4.45
30-30 Winchester (e)	150	HP	2410	2020	1700	1430	1930	1360	960	680	0.9	4.2	11.0	4.45
30-30 Winchester (a, b)	150	PP, ST, OPE	2410	2020	1700	1430	1930	1360	960	680	0.9	4.2	11.0	4.45
30-30 Winchester (e)	170	PP, HP, CL, ST, MC	2220	1890	1630	1410	1860	1350	1000	750	1.2	4.6	12.5	4.45
30 Remington	170	ST, CL	2120	1820	1560	1350	1700	1250	920	690	1.1	5.3	14.0	5.20
30-06 Springfield	110	PSP	3370	2830	2350	1920	2770	1960	1350	900	0.5	2.2	6.0	5.65
30-06 Springfield	125	PSP	3200	2810	2480	2200	2840	2190	1710	1340	0.5	2.2	5.6	5.65
30-06 Springfield (c, d)	150	BP	2970	2710	2470	2240	2930	2440	2030	1670	0.5	2.4	6.0	5.65
30-06 Springfield (e)	150	PP	2970	2620	2300	2010	2930	2280	1760	1340	0.6	2.5	6.5	5.65
30-06 Springfield	150	ST, PCL, PSP	2970	2670	2400	2130	2930	2370	1920	1510	0.6	2.4	6.1	5.65
30-06 Springfield	180	PP, CL, PSP	2700	2330	2010	1740	2910	2170	1610	1210	0.7	3.1	8.3	5.65
30-06 Springfield (e)	180	ST, BP, PCL	2700	2470	2250	2040	2910	2440	2020	1660	0.7	2.9	7.0	5.65
30-06 Springfield	180	MCBT, MAT	2700	2520	2350	2190	2910	2540	2200	1900	0.6	2.8	6.7	8.40
30-06 Springfield	220	PP, CL	2410	2120	1870	1670	2830	2190	1710	1360	0.8	3.9	9.8	5.65
30-06 Springfield (a, b)	220	ST	2410	2180	1980	1790	2830	2320	1910	1560	0.8	3.7	9.2	5.65
30-40 Krag	180	PP, CL	2470	2120	1830	1590	2440	1790	1340	1010	0.8	3.8	9.9	5.75
30-40 Krag	180	ST, PCL	2470	2250	2040	1850	2440	2020	1660	1370	0.8	3.5	8.5	5.75
30-40 Krag	220	ST	2200	1990	1800	1630	2360	1930	1580	1300	1.0	4.4	11.0	5.75
300 Winchester Magnum	150	PP, PCL	3400	3050	2730	2430	3850	3100	2480	1970	0.4	1.9	4.8	8.35
300 Winchester Magnum	180	PP, PCL	3070	2850	2640	2440	3770	3250	2790	2380	0.5	2.1	5.3	8.35
300 Winchester Mag (a, b)	220	ST	2720	2490	2270	2060	3620	3030	2520	2070	0.6	2.9	6.9	8.35
300 H&H Magnum (a, b)	150	ST	3190	2870	2580	2300	3390	2740	2220	1760	0.5	2.1	5.2	8.35
300 H&H Magnum	180	ST, PCL	2920	2670	2440	2220	3400	2850	2380	1970	0.6	2.4	5.8	8.35
300 H&H Magnum	220	ST, CL	2620	2370	2150	1940	3350	2740	2260	1840	0.7	3.1	7.7	8.35
300 Savage (e)	150	PP	2670	2350	2060	1800	2370	1840	1410	1080	0.7	3.2	8.0	5.55
300 Savage	150	ST, PCL	2670	2390	2130	1890	2370	1900	1510	1190	0.7	3.0	7.6	5.55
300 Savage (c, d)	150	CL	2670	2270	1930	1660	2370	1710	1240	916	0.7	3.3	9.3	5.55
300 Savage (e)	180	PP, CL	2370	2040	1760	1520	2240	1660	1240	920	0.9	4.1	10.5	5.55
300 Savage	180	ST, PCL	2370	2160	1960	1770	2240	1860	1530	1250	0.9	3.7	9.2	5.55
303 Savage (c, d)	180	CL	2140	1810	1550	1340	1830	1310	960	715	1.1	5.4	14.0	5.70
303 Savage (a, b)	190	ST	1980	1680	1440	1250	1650	1190	875	660	1.3	6.2	15.5	5.70
303 British (e)	180	PP, CL	2540	2300	2090	1900	2580	2120	1750	1440	0.7	3.3	8.2	5.70
303 British (c, d)	215	SP	2180	1900	1660	1460	2270	1720	1310	1020	1.1	4.9	12.5	5.70
308 Winchester	110	PSP	3340	2810	2340	1920	2730	1930	1340	900	0.5	2.2	6.0	5.65
308 Winchester (a, b)	125	PSP	3100	2740	2430	2160	2670	2080	1640	1300	0.5	2.3	5.9	5.65
308 Winchester (e)	150	PP	2860	2520	2210	1930	2730	2120	1630	1240	0.6	2.7	7.0	5.65
308 Winchester	150	ST, PCL	2860	2570	2300	2050	2730	2200	1760	1400	0.6	2.6	6.5	5.65
308 Winchester (e)	180	PP, CL	2610	2250	1940	1680	2720	2020	1500	1130	0.7	3.4	8.9	5.65
308 Winchester	180	ST, PCL	2610	2390	2170	1970	2720	2280	1870	1540	0.8	3.1	7.4	5.65
308 Winchester (a, b)	200	ST	2450	2210	1980	1770	2670	2170	1750	1400	0.8	3.6	9.0	5.65
32 Winchester Special (c, d, e)	170	HP, CL	2280	1920	1630	1410	1960	1390	1000	750	1.0	4.8	12.5	4.60
32 Winchester Special (a, b)	170	PP, ST	2280	1870	1560	1330	1960	1320	920	665	1.0	4.8	13.0	4.60
32 Remington (c, d)	170	CL	2120	1800	1540	1340	1700	1220	895	680	1.0	4.9	13.0	5.40
32 Remington (a, b)	170	ST	2120	1760	1460	1220	1700	1170	805	560	1.1	5.3	14.5	5.40
32-20 Winchester HV* (1)	80	OPE, HP	2100	1430	1090	950	780	365	210	160	1.5	8.5	24.5	8.00
32-20 Winchester*	100	SP, L, Lu	1290	1060	940	840	370	250	195	155	3.3	15.5	38.0	6.40
8mm Mauser (e)	170	PP, CL	2570	2140	1790	1520	2490	1730	1210	870	0.8	3.9	10.5	5.65
338 Winchester Magnum (a, b)	200	PP	3000	2690	2410	2170	4000	3210	2580	2090	0.5	2.4	6.0	7.65
338 Winchester Magnum (a, b)	250	ST	2700	2430	2180	1940	4050	3280	2640	2090	0.7	3.0	7.4	7.65
338 Winchester Magnum (a, b)	300	PP	2450	2160	1910	1690	4000	3110	2430	1900	0.8	3.7	9.5	7.65

CENTERFIRE RIFLE CARTRIDGES—BALLISTICS AND PRICES (continued)

Cartridge	Bullet Wt. Grs.	Bullet Type	Velocity (fps) Muzzle	100 yds.	200 yds.	300 yds.	Energy (ft. lbs.) Muzzle	100 yds.	200 yds.	300 yds.	Mid-Range Trajectory 100 yds.	200 yds.	300 yds.	Price for 20*
348 Winchester (a)	200	ST	2530	2220	1940	1680	2840	2190	765	509	0.4	1.7	4.7	$7.95
348 Winchester (c, d)	200	CL	2530	2140	1820	1570	2840	2030	1470	1090	0.8	3.8	10.0	7.95
35 Remington (c, d)	150	CL	2400	1960	1580	1280	1920	1280	835	545	0.9	4.6	13.0	5.15
35 Remington (e)	200	PP, ST, CL	2100	1710	1390	1160	1950	1300	860	605	1.2	6.0	16.5	5.15
350 Remington Magnum (c, d)	200	PCL	2710	2410	2130	1870	3260	2570	2000	1550	Not Available			7.05
350 Remington Magnum (c, d)	250	PCL	2410	2190	1980	1790	3220	2660	2180	1780	Not Available			7.05
351 Winchester Self-Loading*	180	SP, MC	1850	1560	1310	1140	1370	975	685	520	1.5	7.8	21.5	11.25
358 Winchester (a, b)	200	ST	2530	2210	1910	1640	2840	2160	1610	1190	0.8	3.6	9.4	6.90
358 Winchester (a, b)	250	ST	2250	2010	1780	1570	2810	2230	1760	1370	1.0	4.4	11.0	6.90
375 H&H Magnum	270	PP, SP	2740	2460	2210	1990	4500	3620	2920	2370	0.7	2.9	7.1	9.05
375 H&H Magnum	300	ST	2550	2280	2040	1830	4330	3460	2770	2230	0.7	3.3	8.3	9.05
375 H&H Magnum	300	MC	2550	2180	1860	1590	4330	3160	2300	1680	0.7	3.6	9.3	9.05
38-40 Winchester*	180	SP	1330	1070	960	850	705	455	370	290	3.2	15.0	36.5	9.50
44 Magnum* (c, d)	240	SP	1750	1360	1110	980	1630	985	655	510	1.6	8.4	—	9.75
44 Magnum (b)	240	HSP	1750	1350	1090	950	1630	970	635	480	1.8	9.4	26.0	4.00
444 Marlin (c)	240	SP	2400	1845	1410	1125	3070	1815	1060	675	Not Available			5.60
44-40 Winchester*	200	SP	1310	1050	940	830	760	490	390	305	3.3	15.0	36.5	11.45
45-70 Government	405	SP	1320	1160	1050	990	1570	1210	990	880	2.9	13.0	32.5	7.05
458 Winchester Magnum	500	MC	2130	1910	1700	1520	5040	4050	3210	2570	1.1	4.8	12.0	16.85
458 Winchester Magnum	510	SP	2130	1840	1600	1400	5140	3830	2900	2220	1.1	5.1	13.5	11.10

* Price for 50   HP—Hollow Point   SP—Soft Point   PSP—Pointed Soft Point   PP—Power Point   L—Lead   Lu—Lubaloy   ST—Silvertip
HSP—Hollow Soft Point   MC—Metal Case   BT—Boat Tail   MAT—Match   BP—Bronze Point   CL—Core Lokt   PCL—Pointed Core Lokt
OPE—Open Point Expanding   †PL—Power-Lokt (slightly higher price)   (1) Not safe in handguns or Win. M73.

WEATHERBY MAGNUM CARTRIDGES—BALLISTICS AND PRICES

Cartridge	Bullet Wt. Grs.	Bullet Type	Velocity (fps) Muzzle	100 yds.	200 yds.	300 yds.	Energy (ft. lbs.) Muzzle	100 yds.	200 yds.	300 yds.	Mid-Range Trajectory 100 yds.	200 yds.	300 yds.	Price for 20
224 Weatherby Varmintmaster	50	PE	3750	3160	2625	2140	1562	1109	1670	1250	0.7	3.6	9.0	$4.95
224 Weatherby Varmintmaster	55	PE	3650	3150	2685	2270	1627	1212	881	629	0.4	1.7	4.5	4.95
240 Weatherby	70	PE	3850	3395	2975	2585	2304	1788	1376	1038	0.3	1.5	3.9	6.60
240 Weatherby	90	PE	3500	3135	2795	2475	2444	1960	1559	1222	0.4	1.8	4.5	6.60
240 Weatherby	100	PE	3395	3115	2850	2595	2554	2150	1804	1495	0.4	1.8	4.4	6.60
257 Weatherby	87	PE	3825	3290	2835	2450	2828	2087	1553	1160	0.3	1.6	4.4	6.60
257 Weatherby	100	PE	3555	3150	2815	2500	2802	2199	1760	1338	0.4	1.7	4.4	6.60
257 Weatherby	117	SPE	3300	2900	2550	2250	2824	2184	1689	1315	0.4	2.4	6.8	6.60
270 Weatherby	100	PE	3760	3625	2825	2435	3140	2363	1773	1317	0.4	1.6	4.3	6.60
270 Weatherby	130	PE	3375	3050	2750	2480	3283	2685	2183	1776	0.4	1.8	4.5	6.60
270 Weatherby	150	PE	3245	2955	2675	2430	3501	2909	2385	1967	0.5	2.0	5.0	6.60
7mm Weatherby	139	PE	3300	2995	2715	2465	3355	2770	2275	1877	0.5	1.9	4.9	6.60
7mm Weatherby	154	PE	3160	2885	2640	2415	3406	2874	2384	1994	0.5	2.0	5.0	6.60
300 Weatherby	150	PE	3545	3195	2890	2615	4179	3393	2783	2279	0.4	1.5	3.9	7.70
300 Weatherby	180	PE	3245	2960	2705	2475	4201	3501	2925	2448	0.4	1.9	5.2	7.70
300 Weatherby	220	SPE	2905	2610	2385	2150	4123	3329	2757	2257	0.6	2.5	6.7	7.70
340 Weatherby	200	PE	3210	2905	2615	2345	4566	3748	3038	2442	0.5	2.1	5.3	7.70
340 Weatherby	210	Nosler	3165	2910	2665	2435	4660	3948	3312	2766	0.5	2.1	5.0	9.70
340 Weatherby	250	SPE	2850	2580	2325	2090	4510	3695	3000	2425	0.6	2.7	6.7	7.70
378 Weatherby	270	SPE	3180	2850	2600	2315	6051	4871	4053	3210	0.5	2.0	5.2	15.00
378 Weatherby	300	SPE	2925	2610	2380	2125	5700	4539	3774	3009	0.6	2.5	6.2	15.00
460 Weatherby	500	RN	2700	2330	2005	1730	8095	6025	4465	3320	0.7	3.3	10.0	17.50

Trajectory is given from scope height. Velocities chronographed using 26″ bbls. Available with Nosler bullets; add $2.00 per box.
SPE—Semi-Pointed Expanding   RN—Round Nose   PE—Pointed Expanding

RIMFIRE CARTRIDGES—BALLISTICS AND PRICES

Remington-Peters, Winchester-Western, Federal & Cascade Cartridge, Inc.

All loads available from all manufacturers except as indicated: R-P (a); W-W (b); Fed. (c); CCI (d). All prices are approximate.

CARTRIDGE	WT. GRS.	BULLET TYPE	VELOCITY FT. PER SEC. MUZZLE	100 YDS.	ENERGY FT. LBS. MUZZLE	100 YDS.	MID-RANGE TRAJECTORY 100 YDS.	HANDGUN BARREL LENGTH	BALLISTICS M.V. F.P.S.	M.E. F.P.	PRICE FOR 50
22 Short (a, b, c)	29	C, L*	1045	810	70	42	5.6	6″	865	48	$ .85
22 Short Hi-Vel.	29	C, L	1125	920	81	54	4.3	6″	1035	69	.85
22 Short HP Hi-Vel. (a, b, c)	27	C, L	1155	920	80	51	4.2	—	—	—	.95
22 Short (a, b)	29	D	1045	—	70	—	—	—	—	(per 500)	8.50
22 Short (a, b)	15	D	1710	—	97	—	—	—	—	(per 500)	7.62
22 Long Hi-Vel.	29	C, L	1240	965	99	60	3.8	6″	1095	77	.90
22 Long Rifle (a, b, c)†-1	40	L*	1145	975	116	84	4.0	6″	950	80	1.50
22 Long Rifle (b)†-3	40	L*	1120	950	111	80	4.2	—	—	—	1.50
22 Long Rifle (b)†-3	40	L*	—	—	—	—	—	6¾″	1060	100	1.50
22 Long Rifle (d)†-4	40	C	1165	980	121	84	4.0	—	—	—	.95
22 Long Rifle Hi-Vel.	40	C, L	1335	1045	158	97	3.3	6″	1125	112	1.00
22 Long Rifle HP (Hi-Vel. (b, d)	37	C, L	1365	1040	149	86	3.4	—	—	—	1.10
22 Long Rifle HP Hi-Vel. (a, c)	36	C, L	1365	1040	149	86	3.4	—	—	—	1.10
22 Long Rifle (b, c)	No.	12 Shot	—	—	—	—	—	—	—	—	1.85
22 WRF [Rem. Spl.] (a, b)	45	C, L	1450	1110	210	123	2.7	—	—	—	2.50
22 WRF Mag. (b)	40	JHP	2000	1390	355	170	1.6	6½″	1550	213	3.21
22 WRF Mag. (b)	40	MC	2000	1390	355	170	1.6	6½″	1550	213	3.21
22 Win. Auto Inside lub. (a, b)	45	C, L	1055	930	111	86	4.6	—	—	—	2.50
5mm Rem. RFM (a)	38	PLHP	2100	1605	372	217	Not Available				3.49

†—Target loads of these ballistics available in: (1) Rem. Match; (2) W-W LV EZXS, Super Match Mark III; (3) Super Match Mark IV and
EZXS Pistol Match; (4) CCI Mini-Group.   C—Copper plated   L—Lead (Wax Coated)   L*—Lead, lubricated   D—Disintegrating
MC—Metal Case   HP—Hollow Point   JHP—Jacketed Hollow Point   PLHP—Power-Lokt Hollow Point

NORMA C.F. RIFLE CARTRIDGES—BALLISTICS AND PRICES

Norma ammunition loaded to standard velocity and pressure is now available with Nosler bullets in the following loads: 270 Win., 130-, 150-gr.; Super 7x61 (S&H), 160-gr.; 308 Win., 180-gr.; 30-06, 150-, 180-gr.; 375 H&H, 300-gr., all at slightly higher prices. All ballistic figures are computed from a line of sight one inch above center of bore at muzzle.

Cartridge	Bullet Wt. Grs.	Type	Velocity, feet per sec.				Energy, foot pounds				Max. height of trajectory, inches			Price for 20
			V Muzzle	V 100 yds.	V 200 yds.	V 300 yds.	E Muzzle	E 100 yds.	E 200 yds.	E 300 yds.	Tr. 100 yds.	Tr. 200 yds.	Tr. 300 yds.	
22 Hornet*	45	SPS	2690	2030	1510	1150	720	410	230	130	Not Available			$7.45
220 Swift	50	PSP	4111	3611	3133	2681	1877	1448	1090	799	.2	.9	3.0	4.35
222 Remington	50	PSP	3200	2660	2170	1750	1137	786	523	340	.0	2.0	6.2	3.50
223	55	SPP	3300	2900	2520	2160	1330	1027	776	570	.4	2.4	6.8	3.80
22-250	50	SPS	3800	3300	2810	2350	1600	1209	885	613	Not Available			3.80
	55	SPS	3650	3200	2780	2400	1637	1251	944	704	Not Available			3.80
243 Winchester	75	HP	3500	3070	2660	2290	2041	1570	1179	873	.0	1.4	4.1	4.80
	100	PSP	3070	2790	2540	2320	2093	1729	1433	1195	.1	1.8	5.0	4.80
6mm Remington	100	SPS	3190	2920	2660	2420	2260	1890	1570	1300	.4	2.1	5.3	4.80
250 Savage	87	PSP	3032	2685	2357	2054	1776	1393	1074	815	.0	1.9	5.8	4.50
	100	PSP	2822	2514	2223	1956	1769	1404	1098	850	.1	2.2	6.6	4.50
257 Roberts	100	PSP	2900	2588	2291	2020	1868	1488	1166	906	.1	2.1	6.2	4.95
	120	PSP	2645	2405	2177	1964	1865	1542	1263	1028	.2	2.5	7.0	4.95
6.5 Carcano	156	SPRN	2000	1810	1640	1485	1386	1135	932	764	Not Available			5.80
6.5 Japanese	139	PSPBT	2428	2280	2130	1990	1820	1605	1401	1223	.3	2.8	7.7	5.80
	156	SPRN	2067	1871	1692	1529	1481	1213	992	810	.6	4.4	11.9	5.80
6.5 x 54 MS	139	PSPBT	2580	2420	2270	2120	2056	1808	1591	1388	.2	2.4	6.5	5.80
	156	SPRN	2461	2240	2033	1840	2098	1738	1432	1173	.3	3.0	8.2	5.80
6.5 x 55	139	PSPBT	2789	2630	2470	2320	2402	2136	1883	1662	.1	2.0	5.6	5.80
	156	SPRN	2493	2271	2062	1867	2153	1787	1473	1208	.3	2.9	7.9	5.80
270 Winchester	110	PSP	3248	2966	2694	2435	2578	2150	1773	1448	.0	1.4	4.3	5.30
	130	PSPBT	3140	2884	2639	2404	2847	2401	2011	1669	.0	1.6	4.7	5.30
	150	PSPBT	2802	2616	2436	2262	2616	2280	1977	1705	.1	2.0	5.7	5.30
7 x 57	110	PSP	3068	2792	2528	2277	2300	1904	1561	1267	.0	1.6	5.0	5.30
	150	PSPBT	2756	2539	2331	2133	2530	2148	1810	1516	.1	2.2	6.2	5.30
	175	SPRN	2490	2170	1900	1680	2410	1830	1403	1097	.4	3.3	9.0	5.30
7mm Remington Magnum	150	SPSBT	3260	2970	2700	2450	3540	2945	2435	1990	.4	2.0	4.9	6.55
	175	SPRN	3070	2720	2400	2120	3660	2870	2240	1590	.5	2.4	6.1	6.55
7 x 61 S & H (26 in.)	160	PSPBT	3100	2927	2757	2595	3415	3045	2701	2393	.0	1.5	4.3	6.85
30 U.S. Carbine	110	SPRN	1970	1595	1300	1090	948	622	413	290	.8	6.4	19.0	3.35
30-30 Winchester	150	SPFP	2410	2075	1790	1550	1934	1433	1066	799	.9	4.2	11	4.15
	170	SPFP	2220	1890	1630	1410	1861	1349	1003	750	.7	4.1	11.9	4.15
308 Winchester	130	PSPBT	2900	2590	2300	2030	2428	1937	1527	1190	.1	2.1	6.2	5.30
	150	PSPBT	2860	2570	2300	2050	2725	2200	1762	1400	.1	2.0	5.9	5.30
	180	PSPBT	2610	2400	2210	2020	2725	2303	1952	1631	.2	2.5	6.6	5.30
	180	SPDC	2610	2400	2210	2020	2725	2303	1952	1631	.7	3.4	8.9	5.80
7.62 Russian	180	PSPBT	2624	2415	2222	2030	2749	2326	1970	1644	.2	2.5	6.6	5.80
308 Norma Magnum	180	DC	3100	2881	2668	2464	3842	3318	2846	2427	.0	1.6	4.6	7.45
30-06	130	PSPBT	3281	2951	2636	2338	3108	2514	2006	1578	.1	1.5	4.6	5.30
	150	PS	2972	2680	2402	2141	2943	2393	1922	1527	.0	1.9	5.7	5.30
	180	PSPBT, SPDC	2700	2494	2296	2109	2914	2487	2107	1778	.1	2.3	6.4	5.30
	220	SPRN,	2411	2197	1996	1809	2840	2358	1947	1599	.3	3.1	8.5	5.30
300 H & H	180	PSPBT	2920	2706	2500	2297	3409	2927	2499	2109	.0	1.9	5.3	6.70
	220	SPRN	2625	2400	2170	1986	3367	2814	2301	1927	.2	2.5	7.0	6.70
7.65 Argentine	150	PSP	2920	2630	2355	2105	2841	2304	1848	1476	.1	2.0	5.8	5.80
303 British	130	PSP	2789	2483	2195	1929	2246	1780	1391	1075	.1	2.3	6.7	5.30
	150	PSP	2720	2440	2170	1930	2465	1983	1569	1241	.1	2.2	6.5	5.30
	180	PSPBT	2540	2340	2147	1965	2579	2189	1843	1544	.2	2.7	7.3	5.30
7.7 Japanese	130	PSP	2950	2635	2340	2065	2513	2004	1581	1231	.1	2.0	5.9	5.80
	180	PSPBT	2493	2292	2101	1922	2484	2100	1765	1477	.3	2.8	7.7	5.80
8 x 57 JR	196	SPRN	2362	2045	1761	1513	2428	1820	1530	996	.4	3.7	10.6	5.80
8 x 57 JS	123	PSP	2887	2515	2170	1857	2277	1728	1286	942	.1	2.3	6.8	5.30
	159	SPRN	2723	2362	2030	1734	2618	1970	1455	1062	.2	2.6	7.9	5.30
	196	SPRN	2526	2195	1894	1627	2778	2097	1562	1152	.3	3.1	9.1	5.30
358 Winchester	200	SPS	2530	2210	1910	1640	2843	2170	1621	1195	.4	3.1	8.8	6.40
	250	SPS	2250	2010	1780	1570	2811	2243	1759	1369	.6	3.9	10.4	6.40
358 Norma Magnum	250	SPS	2790	2493	2231	2001	4322	3451	2764	2223	.2	2.4	6.6	7.30
375 H & H Magnum	300	SPS	2550	2280	2040	1830	4333	3464	2773	2231	.3	2.8	7.6	8.40
44 Magnum	240	SPFP	1750				1640				Not Available			3.95

P—Pointed SP—Soft Point HP—Hollow Point FP—Flat Point RN—Round Nose BT—Boat Tail MC—Metal Case
DC—Dual Core SPS—Soft Point Semi-Pointed NA—Not announced *Price for 50

CENTERFIRE HANDGUN CARTRIDGES—BALLISTICS AND PRICES

Winchester-Western, Remington-Peters, Norma and Federal

Most loads are available from W-W and R-P. All available Norma loads are listed. Federal cartridges are marked with an asterisk. Other loads supplied by only one source are indicated by a letter, thus: Norma (a); R-P (b); W-W (c). Prices are approximate.

Cartridge	Bullet Grs.	Bullet Style	Muzzle Velocity	Muzzle Energy	Barrel Inches	Price Per 50
22 Jet (b)	40	SP	2100	390	8⅜	$9.00
221 Fireball (b)	50	SP	2650	780	10½	4.20
25 (6.35mm) Auto*	50	MC	810	73	2	5.10
256 Winchester Magnum (c)	60	HP	2350	735	8½	9.00
30 (7.65mm) Luger Auto	93	MC	1220	307	4½	8.05
30 (7.63mm) Mauser Auto	85	MC	1410	375	5½	8.05
32 S&W Blank (c)	No bullet	—	—	—		3.85
32 S&W Blank, BP (c)	No bullet	—	—	—		3.85
32 Short Colt	80	Lead	745	100	4	4.40
32 Long Colt, IL (c)	82	Lub.	755	104	4	4.60
32 Colt New Police	100	Lead	680	100	4	5.40
32 (7.65mm) Auto*	71	MC	960	145	4	5.80
32 (7.65mm) Auto Pistol (a)	77	MC	900	162	4	5.35
32 S&W	88	Lead	680	90	3	4.40
32 S&W Long	98	Lead	705	115	4	4.65
7.5 Nagant (a)	104	Lead	722	120	4½	7.35
32-20 Winchester	100	Lead	1030	271	6	6.40
32-20 Winchester*	100	SP	1030	271	6	8.00
357 Magnum (b)*	158	SP	1550	845	8⅜	7.65
357 Magnum	158	MP	1410	695	8⅜	7.40
357 Magnum	158	Lead	1410	696	8⅜	6.45
357 Magnum (a)	158	JSP	1450	735	8⅜	6.90
9mm Luger (a)	116	MC	1165	349	4	6.70
9mm Luger Auto*	124	MC	1120	345	4	7.20
38 S&W Blank (c)	No bullet	—	—	—		4.00
38 Smith & Wesson	146	Lead	685	150	4	5.45
38 S&W (a)	146	Lead	730	172	4	5.05
380 MK II (a)	180	MC	620	153	5	5.45
38 Special Blank (c)	No bullet	—	—	—		5.45
38 Special, IL (c)	150	Lub.	1060	375	6	5.70
38 Special, IL (c)	150	Lub.	1060	375	6	7.10
38 Special	158	Lead	855	256	6	5.50
38 Special	200	Lead	730	236	6	5.75
38 Special	158	MP	855	256	6	6.85
38 Special (b)	125	SJHP	Not available			6.85
38 Special (b)	158	SJHP	Not available			6.85
38 Special WC (b)	148	Lead	770	195	6	5.70
38 Special Match, IL (c)*	148	Lead	770	195	6	5.70
38 Special Match, IL (b, c)*	158	Lead	855	256	6	5.60
38 Special Hi-Speed	158	Lead	1090	425	6	6.10
38 Special (a)	158	RN	900	320	6	5.15
38 Colt New Police	150	Lead	680	154	4	5.05
38 Short Colt	125	Lead	730	150	6	4.95
38 Short Colt, Greased (c)	130	Lub.	730	155	6	4.95
38 Long Colt	150	Lead	730	175	6	5.50
38 Super Auto (b)	130	MC	1280	475	5	6.15
38 Auto, for Colt 38 Super (c)	130	MC	1280	475	5	6.15
38 Auto	130	MC	1040	312	4½	6.15
380 Auto*	95	MC	955	192	3¾	5.95
38-40 Winchester	180	SP	975	380	5	9.50
41 Long Colt, IL (c)	200	Lub.	730	230	6	6.15
41 Remington Magnum (b)	210	Lead	1050	515	8¾	8.50
41 Remington Magnum (b)	210	SP	1500	1050	8¾	9.70
44 S&W Special	246	Lead	755	311	6½	7.45
44 Remington Magnum	240	SP	1470	1150	6½	10.00
44 Remington Magnum	240	Lead	1470	1150	6½	9.75
44-40 Winchester	200	SP	975	420	7½	11.45
45 Colt	250	Lead	860	410	5½	7.50
45 Colt, IL (c)	255	Lub., L	860	410	5½	7.50
45 Auto*	230	MC	850	369	5	7.80
45 ACP (a)	230	JHP	850	370	5	8.00
45 Auto WC*	185	MC	775	245	5	8.20
45 Auto MC (a, b)	230	MC	850	369	5	8.25
45 Auto Match (c)	185	MC	775	247	5	8.00
45 Auto Match, IL (c)	210	Lead	710	235	5	8.00
45 Auto Rim (b)	230	Lead	810·	335	5½	7.95

IL—Inside Lub.   JSP—Jacketed Soft Point   WC—Wad Cutter
RN—Round Nose   HP—Hollow Point   Lub—Lubricated
MC—Metal Case   SP—Soft Point   MP—Metal Point
LGC—Lead, Gas Check   JHP—Jacketed Hollow Point

SUPER VEL HANDGUN CARTRIDGES—BALLISTICS AND PRICES

The cartridges listed below are perhaps the most powerful and destructive of these calibers commercially manufactured. Bullets listed can be had as components — other weights (not loaded by Super Vel) are also available.

Cartridge	Bullet Gr.	Bullet Style	Muzzle Velocity	Muzzle Energy	Barrel Inches	Price Per 50
380 ACP	80	JHP	1026	188	5	$6.45
9mm Luger	90	JHP	1422	402	5	7.45
9mm Luger	110	SP	1325	428	5	7.50
38 Special	110	JHP/SP	1370	458	6	6.45
38 Special	147	HBWC	775	196	6	5.35
38 Special Int.	158	Lead	1110	439	6	5.85
357 Magnum	110	JHP/SP	1690	697	6	7.45
44 Magnum	180	JHP/SP	2005	1607	6	†4.10
45 Auto	190	JHP	1060	743	5	8.45

JHP—Jacketed Hollow Point   SP—Jacketed Soft Point
HBWC—Hollow Base Wad Cutter   †Price per 20

SHOTSHELL LOADS AND PRICES

Winchester-Western, Remington-Peters, Federal & Eley

In certain loadings one manufacturer may offer fewer or more shot sizes than another, but in general all makers offer equivalent loadings. Sources are indicated by letters, thus: W-W (a); R-P (b); Fed. (c); Eley (d). Prices are approximate.

GAUGE	Length Shell Ins.	Powder Equiv. Drams	Shot Ozs.	Shot Size	PRICE FOR 25
MAGNUM LOADS					
10 (a¹, b)	3½	5	2	2, 4	$8.80
12 (a, b, c)	3	4½	1⅞	BB, 2, 4	5.80
12 (a¹, b)	3	4¼	1⅝	2, 4, 6	5.35
12 (a¹, b, c, d)	2¾	4	1½	2, 4, 5, 6	4.90
16 (a, b, c, d)	2¾	3½	1¼	2, 4, 6	4.25
20 (a, b, c)	3	3¼	1¼	2, 4, 6, 7½	4.40
20 (a¹)	3	Max	1³⁄₁₆	4	3.95
20 (a¹, b, c, d)	2¾	3	1⅛	2, 4, 6, 7½	3.90
28 (a, c)	2¾	Max	1	6, 7½, 8, 9	3.90
LONG RANGE LOADS					
10 (a, b)	2⅞	4¾	1⅝	4	5.20
12 (a¹, b, c, d)	2¾	3¾	1¼	BB, 2, 4, 5, 6, 7½, 9	4.25
16 (a, b, c, d)	2¾	3¼	1⅛	4, 5, 6, 7½, 9	3.90
16 (a¹, b, c)	2¾	3	1⅛	4, 5, 6, 7½, 9	3.90
20 (a¹, b, c, d)	2¾	2¾	1	4, 5, 6, 7½, 9	3.70
28 (a, c)	2¾	2¼	¾	4, 6, 7½, 9	3.70
FIELD LOADS					
12 (a, b, c)	2¾	3¼	1¼	7½, 8, 9	3.80
12 (a, b, c)	2¾	3¼	1⅛	4, 5, 6, 7½, 8, 9	3.60
12 (a, b, c)	2¾	3	1⅛	4, 5, 6, 8, 9	3.55
12 (a, b, c)	2¾	3	1	4, 5, 6, 8	3.40
16 (a, b, c)	2¾	2¾	1⅛	4, 5, 6, 7½, 8, 9	3.40
16 (a, b, c)	2¾	2½	1	4, 5, 6, 8, 9	3.25
20 (a, b, c, d)	2¾	2½	1	4, 5, 6, 7½, 8, 9	3.30
20 (a, b, c)	2¾	2¼	⅞	4, 5, 6, 8, 9	3.00
SCATTER LOADS					
12 (a, b, c)	2¾	3	1⅛	8	3.75
16 (a, b, c)	2¾	2½	1	8	3.40
20 (a, b, c)	2¾	2¼	⅞	8	3.25
TARGET LOADS					
12 (a, b, c)	2¾	3	1⅛	7½, 8, 9	3.55
12 (a, b, c)	2¾	2¾	1⅛	7½, 8, 9	3.55
16 (a, b, c)	2¾	2½	1	8, 9	3.25
20 (a, b, c)	2¾	2¼	⅞	8, 9	3.00
28 (a, c)	2¾	2¼	¾	9	3.70
410 (a, b, c, d)	3	Max	¾	4, 5, 6, 7½, 9	3.40
410 (a, b, c, d)	2½	Max	½	4, 5, 6, 7½, 9	3.40
SKEET & TRAP					
12 (a, b, c, d)	2¾	3	1⅛	7½, 8, 9	3.55
12 (a, b, c)	2¾	2¾	1⅛	7½, 8, 9	3.55
16 (a, b, c, d)	2¾	2½	1	8, 9	3.25
20 (a, b, c)	2¾	2¼	⅞	8, 9	3.00
BUCKSHOT					
12 (a, b, c)	3 Mag.	4½	—	00 Buck—15 pellets	6.65
12 (a, b, c)	3 Mag.	4½	—	4 Buck—41 pellets	6.65
12 (b)	2¾ Mag.	4	—	1 Buck—20 pellets	5.80
12 (a, b, c)	2¾ Mag.	4	—	00 Buck—12 pellets	5.80
12 (a, b, c)	2¾	3¾	—	00 Buck— 9 pellets	5.15
12 (a, b, c)	2¾	3¾	—	0 Buck—12 pellets	5.15
12 (a, b, c)	2¾	3¾	—	1 Buck—16 pellets	5.15
12 (a, b, c)	2¾	3¾	—	4 Buck—27 pellets	5.15
16 (a, b, c)	2¾	3	—	1 Buck—12 pellets	5.15
20 (a, b, c)	2¾	2¾	—	3 Buck—20 pellets	5.15
RIFLED SLUGS					
12 (a, b, c, d)	2¾	3¾	1	Slug	6.35
16 (a, b, c)	2¾	3	⅞	Slug	6.00
20 (a, b, c)	2¾	2¾	⅝	Slug	5.80
410 (a, b, c)	2½	Max	1/5	Slug	5.45

W-W 410, 28- and 10-ga. Magnum shells available in paper cases only, as are their scatter and target loads; their skeet and trap loads come in both plastic and paper.

RP shells are all of plastic with Power Piston wads except: 12 ga. scatter loads have Post Wad: all 10 ga., 410-3" and rifled slug loads have standard wad columns.

Federal magnum, long range and field loads are available in both plastic and paper. Buckshot, slug and all 410 loads are made in plastic only.

Eley shotshells are of plastic-coated paper.

1—These loads available from W-W with Lubaloy shot at higher price.

CIL Ballistics

BALLISTICS

KKSP—'Kling-Kor' Soft Point
PSP—Pointed Soft Point
SP—Soft Point
CPE—Copper Point Expanding

MC—Metal Cased (Hard Point)
PNEU—Pneumatic
HP—Hollow Point
ST—'Sabretip'

DESCRIPTION	Bullet Wt. Grains	Type	Velocity in Feet per Second Muzzle	100 Yds.	200 Yds.	300 Yds.	400 Yds.	500 Yds.	Energy in Foot Pounds Muzzle	100 Yds.	200 Yds.	300 Yds.	400 Yds.	500 Yds.
22 HORNET	45	PSP	2690	2030	1510	1150	—	—	720	410	230	130	—	—
22 SAVAGE	70	PSP	2800	2440	2110	1840	—	—	1220	925	690	525	—	—
222 REMINGTON	50	PSP	3200	2600	2170	1750	—	—	1140	785	520	340	—	—
243 WINCHESTER	75	PSP	3500	3070	2660	2290	1960	1670	2040	1570	1180	875	640	465
243 WINCHESTER	100	PSP	3070	2790	2540	2320	2120	1940	2090	1730	1430	1190	995	835
244 REMINGTON	75	PSP	3500	3070	2660	2290	1960	1670	2040	1570	1180	875	640	465
6.5 x 53 MM MAN.-SCH.	160	SP	2160	1950	1750	1570	—	—	1660	1350	1090	875	—	—
6.5 x 55 MM	160	SP	2420	2190	1960	1760	1580	1420	2080	1700	1360	1110	885	715
25-20 WINCHESTER	86	SP	1460	1180	1030	940	—	—	405	265	200	170	—	—
25-35 WINCHESTER	117	SP	2300	1910	1600	1340	—	—	1370	945	665	465	—	—
250 SAVAGE	100	PSP	2820	2460	2140	1870	—	—	1760	1340	1020	775	—	—
257 ROBERTS	117	PSP	2650	2280	1950	1690	—	—	1820	1350	985	740	—	—
270 WINCHESTER	100	PSP	3480	3070	2690	2340	2010	1700	2690	2090	1600	1215	890	640
270 WINCHESTER	130	PSP	3140	2850	2580	2320	2090	1860	2840	2340	1920	1550	1260	1000
270 WINCHESTER	160	KKSP	2800	2530	2280	2050	1840	—	2790	2270	1850	1490	1200	—
7 x 57 MM MAUSER	139	PSP	2800	2500	2240	1990	1770	1580	2420	1930	1550	1220	965	770
7 x 57 MM MAUSER	160	KKSP	2650	2330	2040	1780	1550	1350	2500	1930	1480	1130	855	645
7 MM REMINGTON MAGNUM	175	SP	3070	2720	2400	2120	1870	1640	3660	2870	2240	1750	1360	1040
30-30 WINCHESTER	150	PNEU	2410	2020	1700	1430	—	—	1930	1360	960	680	—	—
30-30 WINCHESTER	170	KKSP	2220	1890	1630	1410	—	—	1860	1350	1000	750	—	—
30-30 WINCHESTER	170	ST	2220	1890	1630	1410	—	—	1860	1350	1000	750	—	—
30-30 WINCHESTER	170	MC	2220	1890	1630	1410	—	—	1860	1350	1000	750	—	—
30-30 WINCHESTER	150	ST	2410	2020	1700	1430	—	—	1930	1360	960	680	—	—
30 REMINGTON	170	KKSP	2120	1820	1560	1350	—	—	1700	1250	920	690	—	—
30-40 KRAG	180	KKSP	2470	2120	1830	1590	1400	—	2440	1790	1340	1010	785	—
30-06 SPRINGFIELD	130	HP	3150	2730	2470	2170	1920	1690	2870	2160	1770	1360	1060	820
30-06 SPRINGFIELD	150	PSP	2970	2670	2400	2130	1890	1670	2930	2370	1920	1510	1190	930
30-06 SPRINGFIELD	150	ST	2970	2670	2400	2130	1890	1670	2930	2370	1920	1510	1190	930
30-06 SPRINGFIELD	180	KKSP	2700	2330	2010	1740	1520	—	2910	2170	1610	1210	920	—
30-06 SPRINGFIELD	180	CPE	2700	2480	2280	2080	1900	1730	2910	2460	2080	1730	1440	1190
30-06 SPRINGFIELD	180	ST	2700	2470	2250	2040	1850	1670	2910	2440	2020	1660	1370	1110
30-06 SPRINGFIELD	220	KKSP	2410	2120	1870	1670	1480	—	2830	2190	1710	1360	1070	—
300 WINCHESTER-MAGNUM	180	ST	3070	2850	2640	2440	2250	2060	3770	3250	2790	2380	2020	1700
300 HOLLAND & HOLLAND MAGNUM	180	PSP	2920	2670	2440	2220	2020	1830	3400	2850	2380	1970	1630	1340
300 SAVAGE	150	PSP	2670	2390	2130	1890	1660	—	2370	1900	1510	1190	915	—
300 SAVAGE	150	ST	2670	2390	2130	1890	1660	—	2370	1900	1510	1190	915	—
300 SAVAGE	180	KKSP	2370	2040	1760	1520	1340	—	2240	1660	1240	920	715	—
300 SAVAGE	180	ST	2370	2160	1960	1770	1600	—	2240	1860	1530	1250	1020	—
303 SAVAGE	190	KKSP	1980	1680	1440	1250	—	—	1650	1190	875	660	—	—
303 BRITISH	150	PSP	2720	2420	2150	1900	1670	1470	2460	1950	1540	1200	930	720
303 BRITISH	150	ST	2720	2420	2150	1900	1670	1470	2460	1950	1540	1200	930	720
303 BRITISH	180	KKSP	2540	2180	1860	1590	1360	—	2580	1900	1380	1010	740	—
303 BRITISH	180	CPE	2540	2330	2130	1940	1760	1600	2580	2170	1810	1500	1240	1020
303 BRITISH	180	ST	2540	2300	2090	1900	1730	1580	2580	2120	1750	1440	1200	1000
303 BRITISH	215	KKSP	2180	1900	1660	1460	1250	—	2270	1720	1310	1020	750	—
308 WINCHESTER	130	HP	2930	2590	2290	2010	1770	1560	2480	1940	1520	1170	905	700
308 WINCHESTER	150	PSP	2860	2570	2300	2050	1810	1590	2730	2200	1760	1400	1090	840
308 WINCHESTER	150	ST	2860	2570	2300	2050	1810	1590	2730	2200	1760	1400	1090	840
308 WINCHESTER	180	KKSP	2610	2240	1920	1640	1400	—	2720	2010	1470	1070	785	—
308 WINCHESTER	180	ST	2610	2390	2170	1970	1780	1600	2720	2280	1870	1540	1260	1010
308 WINCHESTER	200	KKSP	2450	2210	1980	1770	1580	1410	2670	2170	1750	1400	1110	875
8 MM MAUSER	170	PSP	2570	2300	2040	1810	1600	—	2490	2000	1570	1240	965	—
32-20 WINCHESTER	115	SP	1480	1220	1050	940	—	—	560	380	280	225	—	—
32 WINCHESTER SPECIAL	170	KKSP	2280	1920	1630	1410	—	—	1960	1390	1000	750	—	—
32 WINCHESTER SPECIAL	170	ST	2280	1920	1630	1410	—	—	1960	1390	1000	750	—	—
32 REMINGTON	170	KKSP	2120	1800	1540	1340	—	—	1700	1220	895	680	—	—
32-40 WINCHESTER	170	KKSP	1540	1340	1170	1050	—	—	895	680	515	415	—	—
35 REMINGTON	200	SP	2100	1710	1390	1160	—	—	1950	1300	865	605	—	—
351 WINCHESTER SELF-LOADING	180	SP	1850	1560	1310	1140	—	—	1370	975	685	520	—	—
358 (8.8 MM) WINCHESTER	200	KKSP	2530	2210	1910	1640	1400	—	2840	2160	1610	1190	870	—
38-40 WINCHESTER	180	SP	1330	1070	960	850	—	—	705	455	370	290	—	—
38-55 WINCHESTER	255	SP	1600	1410	1240	1110	—	—	1450	1130	880	700	—	—
43 (11 MM) MAUSER	385	LEAD	1360	1150	1030	940	—	—	1580	1130	910	750	—	—
44-40 WINCHESTER	200	SP	1310	1050	940	830	—	—	760	490	390	305	—	—
44 REMINGTON MAGNUM	240	SP	1850	1450	1150	980	—	—	1820	1120	710	510	—	—

Short Range Sighting-in—It is preferable to sight-in a rifle at the "recommended sighting" range. However, it is sometimes necessary to sight-in a rifle at a distance shorter than the "recommended sighting" range because you don't have the necessary yardage available. To do this, find from the range table at what distance the bullet will first cross the line of sight. Put up a target at this distance and from a firm rest fire

and Range Table

RANGE TABLE—Values shown in this table are based on a sight height 1½" above line of bore. RECOMMENDED SIGHTING: ⊕ indicates the most favourable sighting range in order to minimize the sighting problem at shorter and longer ranges. + Indicates inches high; — Indicates inches low.

RANGE

First Crosses Line of Sight App. Yds.	50 Yds.	75 Yds.	100 Yds.	125 Yds.	150 Yds.	200 Yds.	250 Yds.	300 Yds.	400 Yds.	500 Yds.	Wt. Grains	Type	DESCRIPTION
29.0	—	+1.5	—	—	⊕	—4.0	—	—	—	—	45	PSP	22 HORNET
25.0	—	—	+2.0	—	—	⊕	—4.5	—	—	—	70	PSP	22 SAVAGE
30.0	—	—	+2.0	—	—	⊕	—3.5	—	—	—	50	PSP	222 REMINGTON
30.0	—	—	—	+2.5	—	—	⊕	—3.0	—15.5	—36.5	75	PSP	243 WINCHESTER
27.5	—	—	—	+3.0	—	—	⊕	—3.5	—16.5	—35.5	100	PSP	243 WINCHESTER
30.0	—	—	—	+2.5	—	—	⊕	—3.0	—15.5	—36.5	75	PSP	244 REMINGTON
25.5	—	+1.5	—	—	⊕	—4.0	—	—	—	—	160	SP	6.5 x 53 MM MAN.-SCH.
21.0	—	—	+3.5	—	—	⊕	—5.0	—13.0	—39.0	—	160	SP	6.5 x 55 MM
16.0	+2.0	—	⊕	—4.0	—	—	—	—	—	—	86	SP	25-20 WINCHESTER
23.0	—	+1.5	—	—	⊕	—4.5	—	—	—	—	117	SP	25-35 WINCHESTER
27.5	—	—	+2.0	—	—	⊕	—3.5	—	—	—	100	PSP	250 SAVAGE
24.0	—	—	+2.5	—	—	⊕	—4.5	—	—	—	117	PSP	257 ROBERTS
31.5	—	—	—	+2.5	—	—	⊕	—3.5	—14.5	—33.5	100	PSP	270 WINCHESTER
27.5	—	—	—	+3.0	—	—	⊕	—4.0	—16.0	—35.5	130	PSP	270 WINCHESTER
28.5	—	—	+2.0	—	—	⊕	—4.0	—25.0	—	—	160	KKSP	270 WINCHESTER
27.0	—	—	—	+4.0	—	—	⊕	—4.5	—18.5	—41.0	139	PSP	7 x 57 MM MAUSER
29.0	—	—	—	+2.5	—	⊕	—4.0	—28.5	—	—	160	KKSP	7 x 57 MM MAUSER
25.0	—	—	—	+3.5	—	⊕	—	—4.0	—18.0	—43.0	175	SP	7 MM REMINGTON MAGNUM
27.0	—	+1.5	—	—	⊕	—4.0	—	—	—	—	150	PNEU	30-30 WINCHESTER
23.0	—	+1.5	—	—	⊕	—4.5	—	—	—	—	170	KKSP	30-30 WINCHESTER
23.0	—	+1.5	—	—	⊕	—4.5	—	—	—	—	170	ST	30-30 WINCHESTER
23.0	—	+1.5	—	—	⊕	—4.5	—	—	—	—	170	MC	30-30 WINCHESTER
27.0	—	+1.5	—	—	⊕	—4.0	—	—	—	—	150	ST	30 REMINGTON
20.0	—	+2.0	—	—	⊕	—5.0	—	—	—	—	170	KKSP	30-30 KRAG
21.0	—	—	+3.0	—	—	⊕	—5.5	—	—41.0	—	180	HP	30-06 SPRINGFIELD
27.0	—	—	—	+3.0	—	⊕	—	—4.0	—19.5	—47.0	130	HP	30-06 SPRINGFIELD
25.0	—	—	—	+3.5	—	⊕	—	—4.0	—17.5	—41.0	150	PSP	30-06 SPRINGFIELD
25.0	—	—	—	+3.5	—	⊕	—	—4.0	—17.5	—41.0	150	ST	30-06 SPRINGFIELD
24.0	—	—	+2.5	—	—	⊕	—4.0	—32.5	—	—	180	KKSP	30-06 SPRINGFIELD
21.0	—	—	—	+4.0	—	⊕	—4.5	—20.5	—46.0	—	180	CPE	30-06 SPRINGFIELD
20.0	—	—	—	+4.0	—	⊕	—4.5	—21.0	—48.5	—	180	ST	30-06 SPRINGFIELD
21.0	—	—	+3.0	—	—	⊕	—5.5	—41.0	—	—	220	KKSP	30-06 SPRINGFIELD
27.5	—	—	—	+3.0	—	⊕	—	—3.5	—14.5	—32.5	180	ST	300 WINCHESTER-MAGNUM
25.0	—	—	—	+3.5	—	⊕	—	—4.0	—17.5	—39.0	180	PSP	300 HOLLAND & HOLLAND MAGNUM
26.0	—	—	+2.5	—	—	⊕	—3.5	—29.0	—	—	150	PSP	300 SAVAGE
26.0	—	—	+2.5	—	—	⊕	—3.5	—29.0	—	—	150	ST	300 SAVAGE
20.0	—	—	+3.5	—	—	⊕	—5.5	—43.0	—	—	180	KKSP	300 SAVAGE
21.5	—	—	+3.0	—	—	⊕	—5.5	—35.0	—	—	180	ST	300 SAVAGE
17.5	—	—	+3.0	—	—	⊕	—5.5	—	—	—	190	KKSP	303 SAVAGE
22.0	—	—	—	+4.5	—	—	⊕	—5.0	—23.0	—53.5	150	PSP	303 BRITISH
22.0	—	—	—	+4.5	—	—	⊕	—5.0	—23.0	—53.5	150	ST	303 BRITISH
23.0	—	—	+3.0	—	—	⊕	—5.0	—41.0	—	—	180	KKSP	303 BRITISH
19.0	—	—	—	+4.5	—	—	⊕	—5.0	—23.0	—52.5	180	CPE	303 BRITISH
17.5	—	—	—	+5.0	—	—	⊕	—5.5	—26.5	—71.0	180	ST	303 BRITISH
16.0	—	—	+4.5	—	—	⊕	—7.0	—54.0	—	—	215	KKSP	303 BRITISH
23.5	—	—	—	+3.5	—	—	⊕	—4.5	—23.5	—59.0	130	HP	308 WINCHESTER
25.0	—	—	—	+3.5	—	—	⊕	—4.5	—20.0	—47.5	150	PSP	308 WINCHESTER
25.0	—	—	—	+3.5	—	—	⊕	—4.5	—20.0	—47.5	150	ST	308 WINCHESTER
23.0	—	—	+3.0	—	—	⊕	—5.5	—38.0	—	—	180	KKSP	308 WINCHESTER
22.0	—	—	—	+4.5	—	—	⊕	—5.0	—21.5	—51.5	180	ST	308 WINCHESTER
22.0	—	—	+3.0	—	—	⊕	—5.0	—12.0	—35.0	—48.5	200	KKSP	308 WINCHESTER
22.5	—	—	+3.5	—	—	⊕	—5.5	—33.5	—	—	170	PSP	8 MM MAUSER
16.5	+2.0	—	⊕	—3.5	—	—	—	—	—	—	115	SP	32-20 WINCHESTER
23.0	—	+2.0	—	—	⊕	—4.5	—	—	—	—	170	KKSP	32 WINCHESTER SPECIAL
23.0	—	+2.0	—	—	⊕	—4.5	—	—	—	—	170	ST	32 WINCHESTER SPECIAL
20.0	—	+2.0	—	—	⊕	—5.0	—	—	—	—	170	KKSP	32 REMINGTON
21.0	+1.0	—	⊕	—2.5	—	—	—	—	—	—	170	KKSP	32-40 WINCHESTER
19.5	—	+2.5	—	—	⊕	—6.0	—	—	—	—	200	SP	35 REMINGTON
16.0	—	+3.0	—	—	⊕	—7.5	—	—	—	—	180	SP	351 WINCHESTER SELF-LOADING
20.5	—	—	+3.0	—	—	⊕	—5.0	—38.5	—	—	200	KKSP	358 (8.8 MM) WINCHESTER
14.5	+2.5	—	⊕	—4.0	—	—	—	—	—	—	180	SP	38-40 WINCHESTER
13.5	—	+4.0	—	—	⊕	—8.5	—	—	—	—	255	SP	38-55 WINCHESTER
16.0	—	—	⊕	—3.5	—	—	—	—	—	—	385	LEAD	43 (11 MM) MAUSER
12.5	+3.0	—	⊕	—4.5	—	—	—	—	—	—	200	SP	44-40 WINCHESTER
13.0	—	+4.5	—	—	⊕	—8.0	—	—	—	—	240	SP	44 REMINGTON MAGNUM

a three-shot group. The centre point of the group is the "centre of impact"—the average spot where the bullets strike. Adjust sights to bring the centre of impact to the centre of the target then fire another group. If the centre of impact is on target the rifle will be sighted in at the range recommended in the range table. It is, however, desirable to fire a target at that range as soon as possible as a double check.

SPEER-DWM C.F. RIFLE CARTRIDGES—BALLISTICS AND PRICES

These DWM metric calibers are imported by Speer, Inc. The Starkmantel (strong-jacket, soft-point) bullets have apparently been discontinued. Metric cases and bullets for calibers listed may be special-ordered from Speer. U.S. calibers offered by Speer-DWM will be found elsewhere in this section.

Caliber	Bullet Wt. Grs.	Bullet Type	Velocity Muzzle	100 yds.	200 yds.	300 yds.	Energy Muzzle	100 yds.	200 yds.	300 yds.	Mid-Range Trajectory 100 yds.	200 yds.	300 yds.	Price for 10
5.6 x 35R Vierling*	46	SP	2030	1500	1140		418	224	130		1.2	7.5		$6.65
5.6 x 50R (Rimmed) Mag.*	50	PSP					Not Available							6.65†
5.6 x 52R (Savage H.P.)	71	PSP	2850	2460	2320	2200	1280	947	846	766	.3	2.3	6.5	4.70
5.6 x 61 SE	77	PSP	3700	3360	3060	2790	2350	1920	1605	1345	.1	1.1	3.4	11.85
5.6 x 61R	77	PSP	3480	3140	2840	2560	2070	1690	1370	1120	.1	1.3	4.0	11.85
6.5 x 54 MS	159	SP	2170	1925	1705	1485	1660	1300	1025	810	.5	4.1	11.5	4.05
6.5 x 57 Mauser	93	PSP	3350	2930	2570	2260	2300	1760	1350	1040	.1	1.7	4.8	4.35
6.5 x 57 R	93	PSP	3350	2930	2570	2260	2300	1760	1350	1040	.1	1.7	4.8	4.70
7 x 57 Mauser	103	PSP	3330	2865	2450	2060	2550	1890	1380	977	.1	1.7	5.2	4.05
	162	TIG	2785	2480	2250	2060	2780	2200	1820	1520	.3	2.4	6.7	4.70
7 x 57 R	103	PSP	3260	2810	2390	2000	2430	1820	1320	920	.1	1.8	5.3	4.25
	139	SP	2550	2240	1960	1720	2000	1540	1190	910	.3	2.9	8.6	4.25
	162	TIG	2710	2420	2210	2020	2640	2120	1750	1460	.3	2.4	6.9	5.25
7 x 64	103	PSP	3572	3110	2685	2283	2930	2230	1670	1190	.1	1.4	4.4	4.35
	139	SP	3000	2570	2260	1980	2780	2040	1570	1200	.2	2.2	6.4	4.35
	162	TIG	2960	2603	2375	2200	3150	2440	2030	1740	.2	2.0	6.0	6.10
	177	TIG	2880	2665	2490	2325	3270	2820	2440	2130	.2	2.0	5.6	6.80
7 x 65 R	103	PSP	3480	3010	2590	2200	2770	2100	1540	1120	.1	1.5	4.7	4.90†
	139	SP	3000	2570	2260	1980	2780	2040	1570	1200	.2	2.2	6.4	4.90†
	162	TIG	2887	2540	2320	2140	3000	2320	1930	1650	.2	2.2	6.3	6.95†
	177	TIG	2820	2600	2420	2255	3120	2660	2300	2000	.2	2.1	5.9	7.60†
7mm SE	169	ToSto	3300	3045	2825	2620	4090	3480	3010	2600	.1	1.4	3.9	11.85
7 x 75 R SE	169	ToSto	3070	2840	2630	2430	3550	3050	2620	2240	.1	1.6	4.5	11.85
30-06	180	TUG	2854	2562	2306	2077	3261	2632	2133	1726	.2	2.2	6.3	5.20†
8 x 57 JS	123	SP	2968	2339	1805	1318	2415	1497	897	477	.2	2.7	8.8	3.85
	198	TIG	2732	2415	2181	1985	3276	2560	2083	1736	.3	2.5	7.1	4.55
8 x 57 JR	196	SP	2391	1991	1742	1565	2488	1736	1316	1056	.5	3.9	11.2	3.70
8 x 57 JRS	123	SP	2970	2340	1805	1318	2415	1497	897	477	.2	2.7	8.8	4.05
	196	SP	2480	2140	1870	1640	2680	2000	1510	1165	.4	3.3	9.4	4.05
	198	TIG	2600	2320	2105	1930	2970	2350	1950	1620	.3	2.7	7.6	4.90
8 x 60 S	196	SP	2585	2162	1890	1690	2905	2030	1560	1245	.4	3.2	9.2	4.55
	198	TIG	2780	2450	2205	2010	3390	2625	2130	1770	.3	2.4	6.9	5.75
9.3 x 62	293	TUG	2515	2310	2150	2020	4110	3480	3010	2634	.3	2.8	7.5	5.90†
9.3 x 64	293	TUG	2640	2450	2290	2145	4550	3900	3410	3000	.3	2.4	6.6	8.75†
9.3 x 72 R	193	FP	1925	1600	1400	1245	1590	1090	835	666	.5	5.7	16.6	6.05†
9.3 x 74 R	293	TUG	2360	2160	1998	1870	3580	3000	2560	2250	.3	3.1	8.7	8.00

*Price for 20   †Boxer Primed   FP—Flat Point   SP—Soft Point   PSP—Pointed Soft Point   TIG—Brenneke Torpedo Ideal
TUG—Brenneke Torpedo Universal   ToSto—vom Hofe Torpedo Stopring

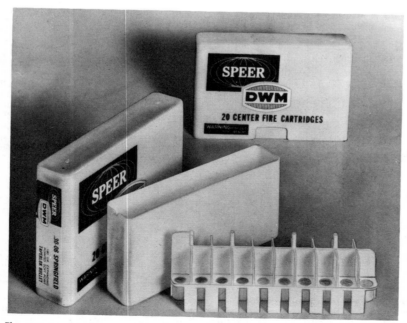

The new reusable 4-way cartridge box in which all Speer-DWM ammo will be packed.

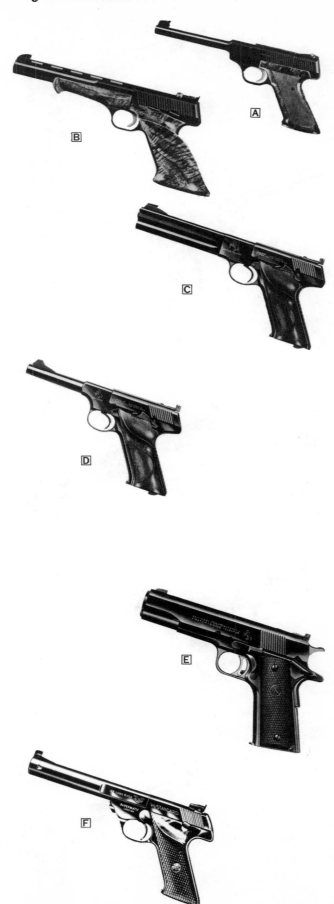

A BROWNING 22 AUTO CHALLENGER PISTOL
Caliber: 22 LR, 10-shot magazine.
Barrel: 4½ inches or 6¾ inches.
Length: 8⅞" over-all (4½" bbl.). **Weight:** 35 oz. (4½" bbl.).
Stocks: Select walnut, hand checkered, wrap-around.
Features: Steel frame, manual stop-open latch (automatic after last shot); gold plated grooved trigger; trigger pull adjustment screw on rear face of frame.
Sights: ⅛" non-glare blade front; frame-mtd. rear, screw adj. for w. & e.
Price: Blued, either bbl. $86.50   Engraved and gold inlaid. . **$254.50**

B BROWNING 22 AUTO MEDALIST PISTOL
Caliber: 22 LR, 10-shot magazine.
Barrel: 6¾", med.-heavy vent. rib.
Length: 11⅛" over-all. **Weight:** 46 oz. less weights.
Stocks: Full wrap-around thumbrest of select checkered walnut; matching fore-end. Left hand grips available.
Features: Dry-fire mechanism permits practice without mechanical harm. Fore-end holds variable weights. Trigger adj. for weight of pull and backlash.
Sights: ⅛" undercut removable blade front; rear frame-mtd., has micrometer clicks adj. for w. and e. Sight radius, 9½".
Price: Blued . . . . . . **$138.50**   Engraved and gold inlaid **$334.50**

BROWNING 22 AUTO INTERNATIONAL MEDALIST PISTOL
Caliber: 22LR, 10-shot magazine.
Barrel: 5.9", med.-heavy vent. rib.
Length: 10¹⁵⁄₁₆" over-all. **Weight:** 42 oz.
Stocks: Select walnut, full wraparound with thumb rest, 1.8" max. width.
Features: The International Medalist pistol meets all International Shooting Union regulations. The regular Medalist qualifies under N.R.A. pistol regulations.
Sights: Identical to those of standard Medalist, sight radius is 8.6".
Price: Blued **$132.50**

C COLT WOODSMAN MATCH TARGET AUTO PISTOL
Caliber: 22 LR, 10-shot magazine.
Barrel: 4½ inches, 6 inches.
Length: 9 inches (4½" bbl.). **Weight:** 40 oz. (6" bbl.), 36 oz. (4½" bbl.).
Stocks: Walnut with thumbrest; checkered.
Features: Wide trigger, automatic slide stop.
Sights: Ramp front with removable undercut blade; ⅛" standard, ¹⁄₁₀" on special order; Colt-Elliason adjustable rear.
Price: Colt Blue only **$115.50**

D COLT WOODSMAN SPORT and TARGET MODEL
Caliber: 22 LR, 10-shot magazine.
Barrel: 4½ inches, 6 inches.
Length: 9 inches (4½" bbl.). **Weight:** 30 oz. (4½" bbl.), 32 oz. (6" bbl.).
Stocks: Walnut with thumbrest; checkered.
Features: Wide trigger, automatic slide stop.
Sights: Ramp front with removable blade, adjustable rear.
Price: Colt Blue only **$100.00**

COLT TARGETSMAN
Same as Woodsman S&T model except: 6" bbl. only; fixed blade front sight, economy adj. rear; without auto. slide stop. **$82.50**

E COLT NAT'L MATCH 38 SPECIAL GOLD CUP AUTO
Caliber: 45 ACP or Wad Cutter; 38 Spec. W.C. 5-shot magazine.
Barrel: 5", with new design bushing.
Length: 8½ inches. **Weight:** 37 oz.
Stocks: Checkered walnut, gilt medallion.
Features: Arched or flat housing; wide, grooved trigger with adj. stop; ribbed-top slide, hand fitted, with improved ejection port.
Sights: Patridge front, Colt-Elliason rear adj. for w. and e.
Price: Colt Royal Blue **$190.00**

COLT NAT'L MATCH Mk IV SERIES 70 45 GOLD CUP AUTO
Identical to 38 Gold Cup except fitted with a split-finger, collet-type barrel bushing and reverse-taper barrel to match for improved accuracy.
Price: **$190.00**

F HI-STANDARD SUPERMATIC STANDARD CITATION
Caliber: 22 LR, 10-shot magazine.
Barrel: 5½" bull weight.
Length: 10 inches (5½" bbl.). **Weight:** 42 oz. (5½" bbl.).
Stocks: Checkered walnut with or w/o thumbrest, right or left.
Features: Adjustable trigger pull; anti-backlash trigger adjustment; double acting safety; rebounding firing pin. Back & front straps stippled.
Sights: Undercut ramp front; click adjustable square notch rear.
Price: 5½" bull barrel **$110.00**

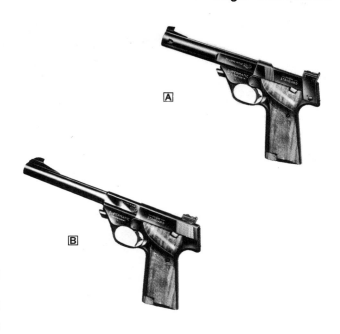

A HI-STANDARD S'MATIC CITATION MILITARY AUTO
Caliber: 22 LR, 10-shot magazine.
Barrel: 5½" bull, 7¼" fluted.
Length: 9¾ inches (5½" bbl.). **Weight:** 44½ oz.
Stocks: Checkered walnut with or w/o thumbrest, right or left.
Features: Same as regular Citation plus military style grip, stippled front- and backstraps, positive magazine latch.
Sights: Undercut ramp front; frame mounted rear, click adj.
Price: Either bbl. length.................................**$115.00**

B HI-STANDARD S'MATIC TOURNAMENT MILITARY AUTO
Caliber: 22 LR, 10-shot.
Barrel: 5½" bull, 6¾" tapered.
Length: 9¾" (5½" bbl.). **Weight:** 45 oz.
Stocks: Checkered walnut, thumbrest for either hand.
Features: Military type grip; 5½" bbl. notched for stabilizer; non-adj. trigger; positive magazine safety; otherwise like regular Citations.
Sights: Ramp-mounted undercut front blade, adj. rear on slide.
Prict: Either bbl. length...................................**$95.00**

C HI-STANDARD (*ISU) OLYMPIC AUTO PISTOL
Caliber: 22 Short, 10-shot magazine.
Barrel: 6¾" round tapered, with stabilizer.
Length: 11¼". **Weight:** 40 oz.
Stocks: Checkered walnut w or w/o thumbrest, right or left.
Features: Integral stabilizer with two removable weights. Trigger adj. for pull and anti-backlash; Citation grade finish.
Sights: Undercut ramp front; click adj., square notch rear.
Price: Blued **$130.00**
*Complies with all International Shooting Union regulations.

D HI-STANDARD (*ISU) OLYMPIC MILITARY AUTO
Caliber: 22 Short, 10-shot magazine.
Barrel: 6¾" round tapered, with stabilizer.
Length: 11 inches. **Weight:** 40½ oz.
Stocks: Checkered walnut w or w/o thumbrest, right or left.
Features: Integral stabilizer with two removable weights; adj. trigger with anti-backlash screw. Grip as on military 45.
Sights: Undercut ramp front; frame mounted rear, click adj.
Price: Blued **$135.00**

E HI-STANDARD SUPERMATIC TROPHY MILITARY AUTO
Caliber: 22 LR, 10-shot magazine.
Barrel: 5½" heavy, 7¼" fluted.
Length: 9¾ inches (5½" bbl.). **Weight:** 44½ oz.
Stocks: Checkered walnut with or w/o thumb rest, right or left.
Features: Grip duplicates feel of military 45; positive action mag. latch; front- and backstraps stippled. Adj. trigger, anti-backlash screw.
Sights: Undercut ramp front; frame mounted rear, click adj.
Price: Either bbl. length **$130.00**
Accessories for Hi-Standard Supermatics
Stabilizers (furnished on Olympics) **$5.50**
2 oz. wgt., **$2.00**. 3 oz. wgt., **$2.50**. Extra magazines **$4.75** to **$6.50**

F RUGER Mark I TARGET MODEL AUTO PISTOL
Caliber: 22 LR only, 9-shot magazine.
Barrel: 6⅞" or 5½" bull barrel (6-groove, 14" twist).
Length: 10⅞ inches (6⅞" bbl.). **Weight:** 42 oz. with 6⅞" bbl.
Stocks: Checkered hard rubber.
Features: Rear sight mounted on receiver, does not move with slide; wide, grooved trigger. Muzzle brake (fits Mark I Target only) $6.00 extra.
Sights: ⅛" blade front, micro click rear, adjustable for w. and e. Sight radius 9⅜" (with 6⅞" bbl.).
Price: Blued, either barrel length..........................**$67.50**
Price: Checkered walnut panels with left thumbrest..........**$71.50**

A SMITH & WESSON 22 AUTO PISTOL Model 41
Caliber: 22 LR or 22 S, 10-shot clip.
Barrel: 5" or 7⅜", sight radius 9⁵⁄₁₆" (7⅜" bbl.).
Length: 12", incl. detachable muzzle brake, (7⅜" bbl. only).
Weight: 43½ oz. (7⅜" bbl.).
Stocks: Checkered walnut with thumbrest, usable with either hand.
Features: ⅜" wide, grooved trigger with adj. stop; wgts. available to make pistol up to 59 oz.
Sights: Front, ⅛" Patridge undercut; micro click rear adj. for w. and e.
Price: S&W Bright Blue, satin matted bbl., either caliber......$131.50

B SMITH & WESSON 22 MATCH HEAVY BARREL Model 41
Caliber: 22 LR, 10-shot clip.
Barrel: 5½" heavy, without muzzle brake. Sight radius, 8".
Length: 9". **Weight:** 44½ oz.
Stocks: Checkered walnut with modified thumbrest, usable with either hand.
Features: ⅜" wide, grooved trigger; adj. trigger stop.
Sights: ⅛" Patridge on ramp base. S&W micro click rear, adj. for w. and e.
Price: S&W Bright Blue, satin matted top area.............$131.50

S & W 22 AUTO HEAVY BARREL EFS Model 41
Same as Model 41 Heavy Barrel but with extendible ⅛" front sight. Without muzzle brake or weights. Blued..................$144.50

C SMITH & WESSON 22 AUTO PISTOL Model 46
Caliber: 22 LR only, 10-shot clip.
Barrel: 5", 7", or 5½" heavy.
Length: 10⁹⁄₁₆" (7" bbl.). **Weight:** 42 oz. (7" bbl.).
Stocks: Checkered nylon with modified thumbrest, usable with either hand.
Features: ⅜" wide, grooved trigger; adj. trigger stop.
Sights: Front, ⅛" Patridge undercut on 7"; ⅛" ramp on 5". Micro click rear adj. for w. and e.
Price: S&W Satin Blue....$112.50   5½"Heavy Barrel....$118.00

SMITH & WESSON CONVERSION KIT
Converts Models 41 and 46 from 22 Short to 22 LR and vice versa. Consists of barrel, slide, magazine, slide stop and recoil spring.
Price, parts only $61.70
Price, factory installed and tested 70.60
Price, 5½ heavy bbl. only with sights for M41 or M46.......53.30

D SMITH & WESSON 38 MASTER Model 52 AUTO
Caliber: 38 Special (for Mid-range W.C. with flush-seated bullet only). 5-shot magazine.
Barrel: 5".
Length: 8⅝". **Weight:** 41 oz. with empty magazine.
Features: Top sighting surfaces matte finished. Locked breech, moving barrel system; checked for 10-ring groups at 50 yards. Coin-adj. sight screws. Dry firing permissible if manual safety on.
Stocks: Checkered walnut.
Sights: ⅛" Patridge front, S&W micro click rear adj. for w. and e.
Price: S&W Bright Blue....................................$197.00

E STERLING TARGET "CUP" SERIES AUTO PISTOL
Caliber: 22LR, 10-shot magazine.
Barrel: 4½", 6", and 8".
Length: 9" (4½" bbl.). **Weight:** 36 oz. (4½" bbl.).
Stocks: Checkered plastic.
Features: Adjustable trigger and balance weights; sear lock safety.
Sights: ⅛" blade front; Click adj. square notch rear.
Price: Blued (M283) $105.00
Price: Blued with 6" tapered barrel (M284) 105.00

. . . Target Revolvers

F COLT DIAMONDBACK REVOLVER
Caliber: 22 S, L or LR, or 38 Special, 6 shot.
Barrel: 2½" or 4", with ventilated rib.
Length: 8⅜" (4" bbl.). **Weight:** 26 oz. (2½" bbl.), 29 oz. (4" bbl.).
Stocks: Checkered walnut, target type, square butt.
Features: Ventilated rib; grooved, crisp trigger; swing-out cylinder; wide hammer spur.
Sights: Ramp front, adj. notch rear.
Price: Colt Blue $135.00

G COLT OFFICERS MODEL MATCH REVOLVER
Caliber: 22 LR or 38 Special, 6 shot.
Barrel: 6 inches.
Length: 11¼". **Weight:** 43 oz. (22 cal.), 39 oz. (38 cal.).
Stocks: Checkered walnut, square butt.
Features: Grooved trigger, wide hammer spur, hand fitted swing-out cyl. action.
Sights: Undercut ⅛" removable blade front, adjustable rear.
Price: Blued $143.00

H COLT NEW POLICE PYTHON REVOLVER
Caliber: 357 Magnum (handles all 38 Spec.), 6 shot.
Barrel: 2½", 4" or 6", with ventilated rib.
Length: 9¼" (4" bbl.). **Weight:** 41 oz. (4" bbl.).
Stocks: Checkered walnut, target type, square butt.
Features: Ventilated rib; grooved, crisp trigger; swing-out cylinder; wide hammer spur.
Sights: ⅛" ramp front, adj. notch rear.
Price: Colt Royal Blue......$190.00   Nickeled.........$218.50

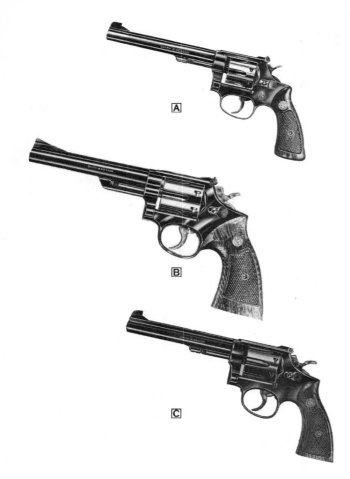

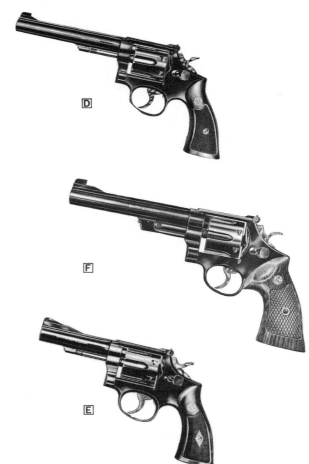

A SMITH & WESSON 1953 Model 35, 22/32 TARGET
Caliber: 22 S, L or LR, 6 shot.
Barrel: 6 inches.
Length: 10½ inches. Weight: 25 oz.
Stocks: Checkered walnut, Magna.
Sights: Front, 1/10" Patridge, micro click rear, adjustable for w. and e.
Price: Blued...$106.00

B SMITH & WESSON 22 CENTER FIRE MAGNUM Model 53
Caliber: Rem. 22 Jet and 22 S, L, LR with inserts. 6 shot.
Barrel: 4", 6" or 8⅜".
Length: 11½" (6" bbl.). Weight: 40 oz.
Stocks: Checkered walnut, target.
Features: Grooved tangs and trigger, swing-out cylinder revolver.
Sights: ⅛" Baughman Quick Draw front, micro click rear, adjustable for w. and e.
Price: Blued $144.50
Price: Extra cylinder for 22 RF. (fitted)..................$35.30

C SMITH & WESSON MASTERPIECE TARGET MODELS

Model: K-22 (M17).	K-22 (M48).
Caliber: 22 LR, 6 shot.	22 RF Magnum, 6 shot.
Barrel: 6", 8⅜".	4", 6" or 8⅜".
Length: 11⅛" (6" bbl.).	11⅛" (6" bbl.).
Weight: 38½ oz. (6" bbl.).	39 oz. (6" bbl.).
Model: K-32 (M16).	K-38 (M14).
Caliber: 32 S&W Long, 6 shot.	38 S&W Special, 6 shot.
Barrel: 6 inches.	6", 8⅜".
Length: 11⅛ inches.	11⅛ inches.
Weight: 38½ oz. (loaded).	38½ oz. (6", loaded).

Features: All Masterpiece models have: checkered walnut, Magna stocks; grooved tang and trigger; ⅛" Patridge front sight, micro. adj. rear sights. Swing out cylinder revolver.
Price: Blued, all calibers............................$107.50

D SMITH & WESSON K-38 MASTERPIECE Single Action
   Same as the M14 K-38 Masterpiece except single action only, and is supplied with target type hammer and trigger. Price: blued..$119.50

E SMITH & WESSON COMBAT MASTERPIECE REVOLVER
Caliber: 38 Special (M15) or 22 LR (M18), 6 shot.
Barrel: 4" (2" available in 38 Spec.).
Length: 9⅛" (4" bbl.). Weight: Loaded, 22, 36½ oz., 38 (2" bbl.) 30 oz.
Stocks: Checkered walnut, Magna. Grooved tangs and trigger.
Sights: Front, ⅛" Baughman Quick Draw on ramp, micro click rear, adjustable for w. and e.
Price: Blued...$97.50

F SMITH & WESSON 1955 Model 25, 45 TARGET
Caliber: 45 ACP and 45 AR, 6 shot.
Barrel: 6½" (heavy target type).
Length: 11⅞ inches. Weight: 45 oz.
Stocks: Checkered walnut target. Tangs and target trigger grooved, checkered target hammer.
Features: Tangs and trigger grooved; target trigger and hammer standard. Swing-out cylinder revolver.
Sights: ⅛" Patridge front, micro click rear, adjustable for w. and e.
Price: Blued $138.50

SMITH & WESSON ACCESSORIES
   Target hammers with low, broad, deeply-checkered spur, and wide-swaged, grooved target trigger. For all frame sizes, $4.65 (target triggers not available for small frames). Target stocks: for large-frame guns, $9.95 to $11.45; for med.-frame guns, $7.85-$9.95; for small-frame guns, $6.60. These prices applicable only when specified on original order.
   As separately-ordered parts: target hammers and triggers, $7.65; stocks, $10.35-$11.65.

A AMERICAN FIREARMS STAINLESS PISTOL
 Made entirely of stainless steel, finished bright. Calibers 22 LR, 25, 32 and 380 ACP using same frame and slide. 4.4" long, 3.52" high, .90" wide, 14 oz. (25 cal.) in steel. 7½ oz. with alloy frame. 7-shot magazine (25 cal.).

Price: 25 Cal., bright...**$58.50**	Blued **$44.50**
Price: 32 Cal.,.......... 67.50	380 Cal. 74.50
Price: 22 LR Cal. 69.95

B BROWNING HI-POWER 9mm AUTOMATIC PISTOL
Caliber: 9mm Parabellum (Luger), 13-shot magazine.
Barrel: 4²¹/₃₂ inches.
Length: 7¾ inches over-all. **Weight:** 32 oz.
Stocks: Walnut, hand checkered.
Features: External hammer with half-cock safety, thumb and magazine safeties. A blow on the hammer cannot discharge a cartridge; cannot be fired with magazine removed.
Sights: Fixed front; rear adj. for w.
Price: Blued $112.50

C BROWNING RENAISSANCE HI-POWER 9mm AUTOMATIC
 Same as Browning Hi-Power 9mm Auto except: fully engraved, chrome plated, polyester pearl grips $284.50

D BROWNING 22 AUTO NOMAD PISTOL
Caliber: 22 LR, 10-shot magazine.
Barrel: 4½ inches or 6¾ inches.
Length: 8⅞" over-all (4½" bbl.). **Weight:** 34 oz. (4½ bbl.).
Stocks: Novadur plastic, checkered, wrap-around.
Features: Steel frame; thumb safety; bbls. interchangeable via lock screw on front of frame.
Sights: ⅛" non-glare blade front; frame-mtd. rear, screw adj. for w. & e.
Price: Blued, either bbl. $71.50

E COLT GOVT. SUPER 38 AUTO PISTOL
Caliber: 38 Super Auto, 9 shot.
Barrel: 5 inches.
Length: 8½ inches. **Weight:** 39 oz.
Stocks: Checkered Coltwood. Grooved trigger.
Features: Grip and thumb safeties; grooved trigger and hammer; arched mainspring housing.
Sights: Fixed, glare-proofed ramp front, square notch rear.
Price: Blued ....$125.00   Nickeled $143.75

F COLT Mk IV/SERIES 70 45 GOV'T MODEL AUTO PISTOL
Identical to 38 Super and previous 45 Government Model except for addition of a split-finger, collet-type barrel bushing and reverse-taper barrel to match for improved accuracy.
Price: Blued............$125.00   Nickeled $143.75

COLT CONVERSION UNIT
 Permits the 45 and 38 Super Automatic pistols to use the economical 22 LR cartridge. No tools needed. Adjustable rear sight; 10-shot magazine. Designed to give recoil effect of the larger calibers. Not adaptable to Commander models. Blue finish $70.00

G COLT COMMANDER AUTO PISTOL
Caliber: 45 ACP, 7 shot; 38 Super Auto, 9 shot; 9mm Luger, 9 shot.
Barrel: 4¼ inches.
Length: 8 inches. **Weight:** 26½ oz.
Stocks: Checkered Coltwood.
Features: Grooved trigger and hammer spur; arched housing; grip and thumb safeties.
Sights: Fixed, glare-proofed ramp front, square notch rear.
Price: Blued $125.00

A COLT HUNTSMAN AUTO PISTOL
Caliber: 22 LR, 10-shot magazine.
Barrel: 4½ inches, 6 inches.
Length: 9" (4½" bbl.). **Weight:** 30 oz. (4½" bbl.), 31½ oz. (6" bbl.).
Stocks: Checkered walnut. Wide trigger.
Sights: Fixed ramp front, square notch rear, non-adjustable.
Price: Colt Blue $71.50

B CHALLANGER PONY DERRINGER
Caliber: 22 Short, single-shot.
Barrel: 2½", side swing, blued.
Length: 4¹⁵⁄₁₆" overall. **Weight:** 7¾ oz.
Stocks: Brown plastic, smooth.
Features: Fixed open sights, stud trigger, auto. ejection, single action, storage case.
Price: Gold frame (M2204)................................$19.95
Price: Nickel frame, white plastic grips (M2205) 21.95
Price: 14K Gold frame, white plastic grips (M2206) 29.95

C HI-STANDARD MODEL D-100 and DM-101 DERRINGER
Caliber: 22 S, L or LR; 22 Rimfire Magnum. 2 shot.
Barrel: 3½", over and under, rifled.
Length: 5 inches. **Weight.** 11 oz.
Stocks: Smooth ivory plastic.
Features: Hammerless, integral safety hammerblock, all steel unit is encased in a black, anodized alloy housing. Recessed chamber. Dual extraction. Top break, double action.
Sights: Fixed, open.
Price: Blue .... $42.95   Nickel $52.50
Price: 22 WMR, Blue.... 44.95   Nickel 54.95

D HI-STANDARD DURA-MATIC AUTO PISTOL
Caliber: 22 LR, 10-shot magazine.
Barrel: 4½ or 6½ inches.
Length: 9 inches (4½" bbl.). **Weight:** 32 oz. (4½" bbl.).
Stocks: Checkered plastic grips. Grooved trigger.
Features: Non slip trigger, interchangeable bbls., moulded target grips.
Sights: Fixed, ramp front, square notch rear.
Price: Blued $64.95

E HI-STANDARD SPORT KING ALL-STEEL AUTO PISTOL
Caliber: 22 LR, 10-shot magazine.
Barrel: 4½ or 6¾ inches.
Length: 11¼" (6¾" bbl.). **Weight:** 42 oz. (6¾" bbl.).
Stocks: Checkered laminated plastic.
Features: Wide, scored trigger; new hammer-sear design; new "jam-free" ejection. Slide lock, push-button take down.
Sights: Fixed, ramp front, square notch rear.
Price: Blued, either bbl. $75.00

F RUGER STANDARD MODEL AUTO PISTOL
Caliber: 22 LR, 9-shot magazine.
Barrel: 4¾ or 6 inches.
Length: 8¾" (4¾" bbl.). **Weight:** 36 oz. (4¾" bbl.).
Stocks: Checkered hard rubber.
Sights: Fixed, wide blade front, square notch rear.
Price: Blued $47.50
Price: With checkered walnut grips 53.50

G SMITH & WESSON 9mm MODEL 39 AUTO PISTOL
Caliber: 9mm Luger, 8-shot clip.
Barrel: 4 inches.
Length: 7⁷⁄₁₆". **Weight:** 26½ oz., without magazine.
Stocks: Checkered walnut.
Features: Magazine disconnector, positive firing pin lock and hammer-release safety; alloy frame with lanyard loop; locked-breech, short-recoil double action; slide locks open on last shot.
Sights: ⅛" serrated ramp front, adjustable rear.
Price: Blued ....$110.00   Nickeled $118.00

J SMITH & WESSON M61 PISTOL
Caliber: 22 LR, 5-shot.
Barrel: 2⅛"
Length: 4¹³⁄₁₆". **Weight:** 14 oz.
Stocks: Checkered with cocking indicator pin protruding through left grip.
Features: Elementary blow-back pocket pistol with alloy frame.
Sights: Fixed square notch.
Price: Blued $47.50

H STERLING "CUP" SERIES AUTO PISTOL
Caliber: 22LR, 10-shot magazine.
Barrel: 4½" (Heavy) or 6" (tapered).
Length: 9" (4½" bbl.). **Weight:** 36 oz. (4½" bbl.).
Stocks: Checkered plastic.
Sights: Fixed ramp (6" bbl.) or blade (4½" bbl.) front. Square notch rear.
Features: Interchangeable safety (4½" bbl.).
Price: Blued (M286) 6" $63.50
Price: Blued (M285) 4½" 57.50

K STOEGER LUGER 22 AUTO PISTOL
Caliber: 22 LR, 12-shot (11 in magazine, 1 in chamber).
Barrel: 4½" or 5½".
Weight: 30 oz.
Stocks: Checkered, identical to P-08.
Features: Action remains open after last shot and as magazine is removed. Grip and balance identical to P-08.
Price: 4½" Barrel $69.95
Price: 5½" Barrel 72.95

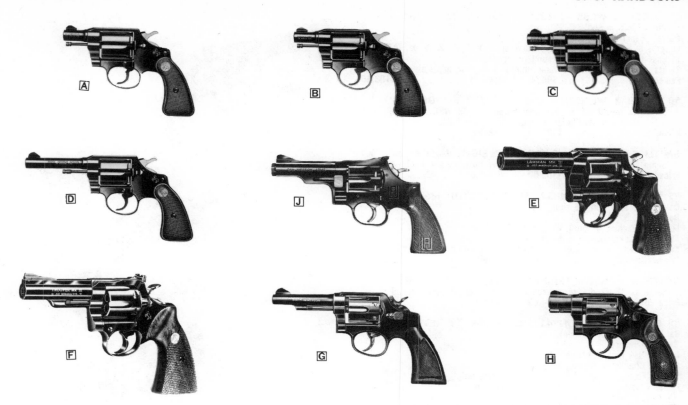

A COLT DETECTIVE SPECIAL
Caliber: 32 New Police or 38 Special, 6 shot.
Barrel: 2″, 3″ (32 NP available in 2″ only).
Length: 6¾″ (2″ bbl.). **Weight:** 21 oz. (2″ bbl.).
Stocks: Checkered walnut, round butt. Grooved trigger.
Sights: Fixed, glare-proofed ramp front, square notch rear.
Price: Blued.............$96.50   Nickeled $111.00
Price: Blued, 38 Spec., 2″, with hammer shroud installed...... 102.50

B COLT COBRA REVOLVER
Caliber: 32 New Police or 38 Special, 6 shot.
Barrel: 2″, 3″ (22 LR available in 3″ only. 4″ available in 38 Spec. only).
Length: 6¾″ (2″ bbl.). **Weight:** 15 oz. (2″ bbl.), 17 oz. (4″ bbl.).
Stocks: Checkered walnut, round butt. Grooved trigger.
Sights: Fixed, glare-proofed ramp front, square notch rear.
Price: Blued.............$101.00   Nickeled $116.15
Price: Blued, 38 Spec. With hammer shroud installed....... 107.00

C COLT AGENT REVOLVER
Caliber: 38 Special, 6 shot.
Barrel: 2″ (Twist, 1-16) .
Length: 6¾″. **Weight:** 14 oz.
Stocks: Checkered walnut, round butt. Grooved trigger.
Sights: Fixed, glare-proofed ramp front, square notch rear.
Price: Blued....$101.00   With a hammer shroud installed..$107.00
COLT HAMMER SHROUD
     Facilitates quick draw from holster or pocket. Hammer spur projects just enough to allow for cocking for single action firing. Fits only Colt Detective Special, Cobra and Agent revolvers. Factory installed on new guns, $5, or as a kit for installation. Blued only..............$6.00
     Factory installed on your gun (listed above). Blued only...... 7.50

D COLT POLICE POSITIVE REVOLVER
Caliber: 32 New Police or 38 Special, 6 shot.
Barrel: 4″, 5″. (32 NP available in 4″ only).
Length: 8¾″ (4″ bbl.). **Weight:** 23 oz. (38 cal.).
Stocks: Checkered walnut, round butt. Grooved trigger.
Sights: Fixed, glare-proofed ramp front, square notch rear.
Price. Blued........$96.50   Nickeled, 4″ bbl. only......$107.50

COLT OFFICIAL POLICE Mk III REVOLVER
Caliber: 38 Special, 6 shot.
Barrel: 4″, 5″ and 6″.
Length: 9¼″ (4″ bbl.).
Weight: 36 oz. (38 cal., 6″ bbl.).
Stocks: Checkered walnut, square butt.
Sights: Fixed, glare-proofed ramp front, square notch rear.
Price: Blued $115.00

E COLT LAWMAN Mk III REVOLVER
     Same as Official Police Mk III but with 4″ heavy barrel. Weight 36 oz. 38 Special only. Also as Metropolitan Mk III in 357 Magnum caliber.
Price: $115.00

F COLT TROOPER MK III REVOLVER
Caliber: 38 Special or 357 Magnum, 6-shot.
Barrel: 4″, 6″ (357 only).
Length: 9¼″ (4″ bbl.). **Weight:** 40 oz. (4″ bbl.), 39 oz. (6″ bbl.).
Stock: Checkered walnut, square butt. Grooved trigger.
Sights: Fixed ramp front with ⅛″ blade, adj. notch rear.
Price: Blued $135.50. With wide spur hammer and target stocks **$142.00**

G SMITH & WESSON M&P Model 10 REVOLVER
Caliber: 38 Special, 6 shot.
Barrel: 2″, 4″, 5″ or 6″.
Length: 9″ (4″ bbl.). **Weight:** 30½ oz. (4″ bbl.).
Stocks: Checkered walnut, Magna. Round or square butt.
Sights: Fixed, ⅛″ ramp front, square notch rear.
Price: Blued.............$84.00   Nickeled $92.00

SMITH & WESSON 38 M&P Heavy Barrel Model 10
     Same as regular M&P except: 4″ ribbed bbl. with ⅛″ ramp front sight, square rear, square butt, wgt. 34 oz.
Price: Blued.............$84.00   Nickeled $92.00

H SMITH & WESSON 38 M&P AIRWEIGHT Model 12
Caliber: 38 Special, 6 shot.
Barrel: 2 or 4 inches.
Length: 6⅞″ inches. **Weight:** 18 oz. (2″ bbl.)
Stocks: Checkered walnut, Magna. Round or square butt.
Sights: Fixed, ⅛″ serrated ramp front, square notch rear.
Price: Blued.............$86.50   Nickeled $94.50

J DAN WESSON MODEL 12 REVOLVER
Caliber: 357 Magnum, 6-shot.
Barrel: 2½″, 4″, 5″ or 6″ interchangeable.
Length: 9″ (4″ bbl.). **Weight:** 30 oz. (4″ bbl.).
Stock: Three sets of stocks supplied in varying size, angle and style.
Sights: Two adj. rear sights (target or combat) supplied. ⅛″ front sight adj. for E.
Features: Wide spur (⅜″) hammer; barrel shroud offered in aluminum or steel for weight and balance preference. Tools supplied for barrel and grip changing.
Price: Blue (approx.) $110.00

A SMITH & WESSON 1953 Model 34, 22/32 KIT GUN
Caliber: 22 LR, 6 shot.
Barrel: 2 inches, 4 inches.
Length: 8 inches (4" bbl. and round butt). **Weight:** 22½ oz. (4" bbl.).
Stocks: Checkered walnut, round or square butt.
Sights: Front, ¹⁄₁₀" serrated ramp, micro. click rear, adjustable for w.&e.
Price: Blued.............$98.50   Nickeled $106.50

B SMITH & WESSON Model 51 22/32 KIT GUN
Same as Model 34 except chambered for 22 WRF Magnum; 3½" barrel; weight, 24 oz. Choice of round or square butt.
Price: Blued............$105.50   Nickeled $113.50

SMITH & WESSON KIT GUN AIRWEIGHT (Model 43, not illus.)
Same as M34 except 3½" barrel, square butt; weight 14¼ oz. 22LR.
Price: Blued............$105.50   Nickeled $113.50

C SMITH & WESSON 32 HAND EJECTOR Model 30
Caliber: 32 S&W Long, 6 shot.
Barrel: 2", 3", 4".
Length: 8 inches (4" bbl.). **Weight:** 18 oz. (4" bbl.).
Stocks: Checkered walnut, Magna.
Sights: Fixed, ¹⁄₁₀" serrated ramp front, square notch rear.
Price: Blued.............$84.00   Nickeled $92.00

SMITH & WESSON TERRIER Model 32 REVOLVER
Same as 32 Hand Ejector except: 38 S&W cal.; 2" bbl. only; 5 shots.
Price: Blued.............$84.00   Nickeled $92.00

D SMITH & WESSON 41 M&P Model 58 REVOLVER
Caliber: 41 Magnum, 6 shot.
Barrel: 4 inches.
Length: 9¼ inches. **Weight:** 41 oz.
Stocks: Checkered walnut, Magna.
Sights: Fixed, ⅛" serrated ramp front, square notch rear.
Price: Blued............$105.50   Nickeled $113.00

E SMITH & WESSON 41 MAGNUM Model 57 REVOLVER
Caliber: 41 Magnum, 6 shot.
Barrel: 4", 6" or 8⅜".
Length: 11⅜ inches (6" bbl.). **Weight:** 48 oz. (6" bbl.).
Stocks: Oversize target type checkered Goncala Alves wood and target hammer. Tang and target trigger grooved.
Sights: ⅛" red ramp front, micro. click rear, adj. for w. and e.
Price: S&W Bright Blue or Nickel $181.00

F SMITH & WESSON 44 MAGNUM Model 29 REVOLVER
Caliber: 44 Magnum, 44 Special or 44 Russian, 6 shot.
Barrel: 4", 6½", 8⅜".
Length: 11⅞" (6½" bbl.). **Weight:** 47 oz. (6½" bbl.), 43 oz. (4" bbl.).
Stocks: Oversize target type, checkered Goncala Alves. Tangs and target trigger grooved, checkered target hammer.
Sights: ⅛" red ramp-front, micro. click rear, adjustable for w. and e.
Price: S&W Bright Blue or Nickel $181.00

G RUGER SECURITY SIX REVOLVER
Caliber: 357 Magnum and 38 Special, 6 shot.
Barrel: 2¾", 4" and 6".
Weight: 33½ oz. (4" bbl.)
Stocks: Checkered walnut, semi-target style.
Features: Solid frame with barrel, sighting rib and ejector rod housing combined in one integral unit. Can be "taken-down" using only a coin.
Sights: Fixed, or w. and e. adjustable rear.
Price: With fixed sights $89.00
Price: With adjustable rear sight 97.50

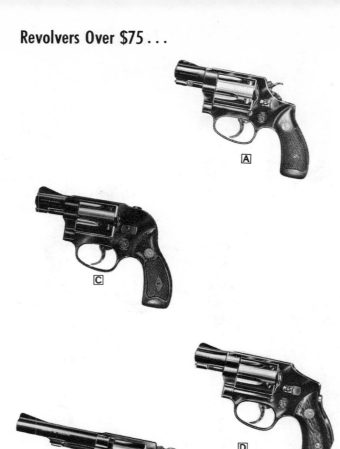

A SMITH & WESSON 38 CHIEFS SPECIAL & AIRWEIGHT
Caliber: 38 Special, 5 shot.
Barrel: 2 inches, 3 inches.
Length: 6½ inches (2" bbl. and round butt). **Weight:** 19 oz. (2" bbl.; 14 oz. AIRWEIGHT).
Stocks: Checkered walnut, Magna. Round or square butt.
Sights: Fixed, 1/10" serrated ramp front, square notch rear.
Price: Blued std. M-36. .**$84.00**   Standard weight **$92.00**
Price: Blued AIR'W M-37   86.50   AIRWEIGHT 94.50

B SMITH & WESSON CHIEFS SPECIAL STAINLESS Model 60
Same as Model 36 except: 2" bbl. and round butt only.
Stainless steel...**$110.00**

C SMITH & WESSON BODYGUARD Model 38 REVOLVER
Caliber: 38 Special; 5 shot, double action revolver.
Barrel: 2 inches.
Length 6⅜ inches. **Weight:** 14½ oz.
Features: Alloy frame; integral hammer shroud.
Stocks: Checkered walnut, Magna.
Sights: Fixed, 1/10" serrated ramp front, square notch rear.
Price: Blued............**$86.50**   Nickeled **$94.50**

SMITH & WESSON BODYGUARD Model 49 REVOLVER
Same as Model 38 except steel construction. Weight 20½ oz.
Price: Blued............**$86.00**   Nickeled **$94.00**

**D SMITH & WESSON CENTENNIAL Model 40
& AIRWEIGHT Model 42 REVOLVERS**
Caliber: 38 Special, 5 shot.
Barrel: 2 inches.
Length: 6½". **Weight:** 19 oz. (Standard weight), 13 oz. (AIRWEIGHT).
Stocks: Smooth walnut, Magna.
Sights: Fixed 1/10" serrated ramp front, square notch rear.
Price: Blued, standard wgt. **$90.50** Nickeled, standard wgt. **$ 98.50**
Price: Blued AIRWEIGHT.... 96.50 Nickeled, AIRWEIGHT ...104.50

E SMITH & WESSON 32 & 38 REGULATION POLICE
Caliber: 32 S&W Long (M31), 6 shot. 38 S&W (M33), 5 shot.
Barrel: 2", 3", 4". (4" only in 38 S&W).
Length: 8½ inches (4" bbl.).
Weight: 18¾ oz. (4" bbl., in 32 cal.), 18 oz. (38 cal.).
Stocks: Checkered walnut, Magna.
Sights: Fixed, 1/10" serrated ramp front, square notch rear.
Price: Blued..... ....**$84.00**   Nickeled **$92.00**

F SMITH & WESSON HIGHWAY PATROLMAN Model 28
Caliber: 357 Magnum and 38 Special, 6 shot.
Barrel: 4 inches, 6 inches.
Length: 11¼ inches (6" bbl.). **Weight:** 44 oz. (6" bbl.).
Stocks: Checkered walnut, Magna. Grooved tangs and trigger.
Sights: Front, ⅛" Baughman Quick Draw, on plain ramp. micro click rear, adjustable for w. and e.
Price: S&W Satin Blue, sandblasted frame edging and barrel top **$107.50**
Price: With target stocks **$115.00**

G SMITH & WESSON 357 MAGNUM Model 27 REVOLVER
Caliber: 357 Magnum and 38 Special, 6 shot.
Barrel: 3½", 5", 6", 8⅜".
Length: 11⅜" (6" bbl.). **Weight:** 44 oz. (6" bbl.).
Stocks: Checkered walnut, Magna. Grooved tangs and trigger.
Sights: Any S&W target front, micro click rear, adjustable for w. and e.
Price: S&W Bright Blue or Nickel..................**$156.50**

H SMITH & WESSON 357 COMBAT MAGNUM Model 19
Caliber: 357 Magnum and 38 Special, 6 shot.
Barrel: 2½", 4", 6".
Length: 9½ inches (4" bbl.). **Weight:** 35 oz.
Stocks: Checkered Goncala Alves, target. Grooved tangs and trigger.
Sights: Front, ¼" Baughman Quick Draw on 2½" or 4" bbl., ⅜" Patridge on 6 bbl., micro click rear adjustable for w. and e.
Price: S&W Bright Blue or Nickel..................**$135.00**

A CHARTER ARMS "UNDERCOVER 2" REVOLVER
Caliber: 38 Special, 5 shot.
Barrel: 2" or 3.
Length: 6¼" (round butt). **Weight:** 16 oz.
Features: Wide trigger and hammer spur.
Stocks: Smooth walnut, round or square butt available.
Sights: Fixed; matted ramp front, ⅛" wide blade.
Price: Polished Blue......**$80.00** Nickel **$85.23**
Price: With checkered, finger-rest bulldog grips (blue)........ **86.50**

L CHARTER ARMS POCKET TARGET
Same as Undercover but in 22 LR caliber, and has 3" bbl. Fitted with adjustable rear sight, ramp front. Weight 18½ oz.
Price: Blued **$87.50**
Price: With checkered, finger-rest bulldog grips **94.00**

B FIREARMS INTERNATIONAL REGENT
Caliber: 22 LR, 8-shot or 32 S&W Long, 6-shot.
Barrel: 37", 4" or 6" round (2½" or 4" in 32 S&W Long).
Weight: 28 oz. (4" bbl.).
Features: Swing-out cylinder, recessed for cartridge rims.
Stocks: Checkered composition.
Sights: Fixed; ramp front.
Price: Blued, 22 LR **$34.95**
Price: Blued, 32 S&W Long **39.95**

C H&R Model 940 Ultra "Side-Kick" REVOLVER
Caliber: 22 S, L or LR, 9 shot.
Barrel: 6", target weight with ventilated rib.
Weight: 33 oz.
Features: Swing-out, safety rim cylinder; safety lock and key.
Stocks: Checkered walnut with thumbrest.
Sights: Ramp front; rear adjustable for w. and e.
Price: H&R Crown-Luster Blue **$62.95**

D HARRINGTON & RICHARDSON Model 732 Guardsman
Caliber: 32 S&W or 32 S&W Long, 6 shot.
Barrel: 2½" or 4", round barrel.
Weight: 23½ oz. (2½" bbl.), 26 oz. (4" bbl.).
Features: Swing-out cylinder with auto. extractor return. Pat. safety rim cylinder. Grooved trigger.
Stocks: Checkered, black Cycolac.
Sights: Blade front; adjustable rear on 4" model.
Price: Blued..**$49.95** Chromed (Model 733) 2½" bbl. only **$54.95**

E HARRINGTON & RICHARDSON Model 900 REVOLVER
Caliber: 22 S, L or LR, 9 shot.
Barrel: 2½", 4" or 6" round bbl.
Weight: 20 oz. (2½" bbl.), 26 oz. (6" bbl.).
Features: Snap-out cylinder; simultaneous push-pin extraction; coil springs; safety rim cylinder; Round-grip frame with 2½" bbl.
Stocks: Checkered, black Cycolac.
Sights: Fixed, blade front, square notch rear.
Price: Blued **$43.95**

F HARRINGTON & RICHARDSON Model 622 REVOLVER
Caliber: 22 S, Lor LR, 6 shot.
Barrel: 2½", 4" or 6" round bbl.
Weight: 22 oz. (2½" bbl.).
Features: Solid steel, square-built frame; snap-out cylinder; simultaneous push-pin ejection; non-glare finish on frame; coil springs.
Stocks: Checkered black Cycolac.
Sights: Fixed, blade front, square notch rear.
Price: Blued, 2½", 4" or 6" bbl. **$37.95**

G HARRINGTON & RICHARDSON Model 926 REVOLVER
Caliber: 22 S, L, or LR, 9 shot.
Barrel: 4". **Weight:** 31 oz.
Features: Top-break, double or single action.
Stocks: Checkered walnut.
Sights: Fixed front, read adj. for w.
Price: Blued **$64.95**

H HARRINGTON & RICHARDSON SPORTSMAN Model 999 REVOLVER
Caliber: 22 S, L or LR, 9 shot.
Barrel: 6", top-break (16" twist), integral vent.-rib.
Length: 10½". **Weight:** 30 oz.
Features: Wide hammer spur; rest for second finger.
Stocks: Checkered walnut, semi-thumbrest.
Sights: Front adjustable for elevation, rear for windage.
Price: Blued **$69.95**

J HARRINGTON & RICHARDSON Model 925 "Defender"
Caliber: 38 S&W, 5 shot.
Barrel: 2½" or 4".
Weight: 22 oz. (2½" bbl.), 31 oz. (4" bbl.). **Length:** 9" (4" bbl.)
Features: Top-break double action, push pin extractor.
Stocks: Smooth walnut, birshead style (2½" bbl.) or square butt (4" bbl.).
Sights: Rear with windage adj., front adj. for elevation, 4" bbls. only.
Price: H&R Crown Luster Blue **$59.95**

K HARRINGTON & RICHARDSON Model 929 "Side-Kick"
Caliber: 22 S, L or LR, 9 shot.
Barrel: 2½", 4" or 6".
Weight: 26 oz. (4" bbl.).
Features: Swing-out cylinder with auto. extractor return. Pat. safety rim cylinder. Grooved trigger. Round-grip frame.
Stocks: Checkered, black Cycolac.
Sights: Blade front; adjustable rear on 4" and 6" models.
Price: Blued, 2½", 4" or 6" bbl. **$49.95**
Price: Chromed (Model 930), 4" bbl. **54.95**

A HARRINGTON & RICHARDSON Model 949 FORTY-NINER
Caliber: 22 S, L or LR, 9 shot.
Barrel: 5½" round with ejector rod.
Weight: 31 oz.
Features: Contoured loading gate; wide hammer spur; single and double action. Western type ejector-housing.
Stocks: One-piece smooth walnut frontier style.
Sights: Round blade front, adj. rear.
Price: H&R Crown-Luster Blue $44.95

C HI-STANDARD DOUBLE-NINE REVOLVER
Caliber: 22 S or LR, 9 shot.
Barrel: 5½", dummy ejector housing fitted.
Length: 11 inches. **Weight:** 27¼ oz.
Stocks: Stag ivory finish plastic. (Ebony with nickel only.)
Features: Western styling; rebounding hammer with auto. safety block; spring-loaded ejection, gold anodized trigger guard and back strap.
Sights: Blade front; movable notch rear.
Price: Blued............$65.00   Nickeled $70.00

B HIGH STANDARD DURANGO
A variation of the High Standard Double-Nine with a brass-finished trigger guard and backstrap. 4½" bbl., 10" over-all; 26¼ oz. 22 LR; blued.
Price: $58.95

HIGH STANDARD HOMBRE
Same as the Durango but 4" bbl., no ejector, 24¾ oz.
Price: Blued............$49.95   Nickeled $54.95

D HI-STANDARD LONGHORN REVOLVER
Same as Double-Nine except: 9½" bbl. only; smooth walnut grips; wgt. 35 oz.; over-all 15". Blued $75.00

E IVER JOHNSON MODEL 50A SIDEWINDER REVOLVER
Caliber: 22 S, L, LR, 8 shot.
Barrel: 6 inches.
Length: 11¼". **Weight:** 31 oz.
Features: Wide spur hammer, half-cock safety, scored trigger, Flash Control cylinder, recessed shell head, push rod ejector.
Stocks: Plastic Stag Horn.
Sights: Fixed, blade front.
Price: Blued..$44.75

F IVER JOHNSON TARGET MODEL 57A REVOLVER
Caliber: 22 S or LR, 8 shot, double action.
Barrel: 4½", 6".
Length: 10¾" (6" bbl.). **Weight:** 30½ oz. (6" bbl.).
Features: Flash Control cylinder, adj. mainspring.
Stocks: Checkered thumbrest, Tenite: (walnut, **$5.80,** checkered walnut, **$9.20** extra).
Sights: Adjustable Patridge type.
Price: Blued, in flocked case...........................$39.95

IVER JOHNSON TARGET MODEL 55A REVOLVER
Same as Model 57A except without adjustable sights. Price, blued, in flocked case. $36.75

IVER JOHNSON CADET Model 55SA
Same as Model 55 except with 2½" barrel only, rounded tenite grips; weight 24 oz. Price, blued, in flocked case............$41.50
Also available in 32 or 38 S&W caliber, 5 shot...........   41.50

G IVER JOHNSON MODEL 67 VIKING REVOLVER
Caliber: 22 S or LR, 8 shot.
Barrel: 4½" or 6", chrome-lined heavy.
Length: 9½" (4½" bbl.). **Weight:** 34 oz. (6" bbl.).
Features: Cyl. front recessed for Flash Control, chambers also recessed for cartridge rims. Matted top, wide trigger. "Hammer-the-Hammer" action.
Stocks: Checkered, thumbrest plastic.
Sights: Adjustable Patridge type.
Price: Blued $49.95

IVER JOHNSON VIKING 67S SNUB REVOLVER
Same as M67 Viking except has 2¾" barrel, smooth rounded stocks, 7" over all, weighs 25 oz. (target stocks available)..........$53.75
Also available in 32 and 38 S&W caliber, 5 shot..........   57.50

IVER JOHNSON TRAILSMAN 66 REVOLVER
Same as M67 Viking but with rebounding hammer. 6" bbl. only.
Price: $47.50

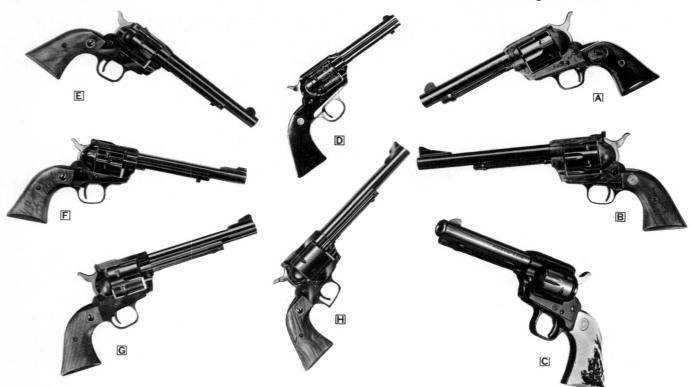

A COLT SINGLE ACTION ARMY REVOLVER
Caliber: 357 Magnum or 45 Colt, 6 shot.
Barrel: 4¾", 5½" or 7½". (357 Mag. 5½" only).
Length: 11½" (5½" bbl.). **Weight:** 40 oz. (5½" bbl.).
Stocks: Checkered hard rubber. (Walnut stocks $5.00 extra).
Sights: Fixed. Grooved top strap, blade front.
Price: Blued and case hardened in color.................**$190.00**
Price: Nickel with walnut stocks..........................225.00
Price: Buntline Spec., cal. 45 only. 12 bbl., st'd. stocks..... 215.00

B COLT SINGLE ACTION ARMY—NEW FRONTIER
Same specifications as standard Single Action Army except: flat-top
frame; high polished finish, blue and case colored; ramp front sight
and target rear adj. for windage and elevation; smooth walnut stocks
with silver medallion **$225.00**

COLT SINGLE ACTION FRONTIER SCOUT REVOLVER
Caliber: 22 S, L, LR, 6 shot.
Barrel: 4¾" or 9½" (Buntline), steel.
Length: 9⁵/₁₆" (4¾" bbl.); 14¾" (9½" bbl.).
Weight: 24 oz. (4¾" bbl.); 28½ oz. (9½" bbl.).
Stocks: Black checkered composition.
Sights: Blade front, fixed notch rear.
Features: Alloy frame; blued finish. Walnut stocks $5.00 extra.
Price: 4¾" bbl. ......**$71.50** Blued, 9½" Buntline......**$82.50**

C COLT FRONTIER SCOUT '62 REVOLVER
Same as "K" Scout except "Midnight Blue" only, "Staglite" stocks,
wgt. 30 oz., Price, 4¾" bbl. ....**$82.50** 9½" Buntline....**$93.50**

COLT FRONTIER SCOUT NICKEL REVOLVER
Same as Standard Frontier Scout except: heavier frame, walnut
stocks. Weight 30 oz. Price, 4¾" bbl. **$93.50**
Price: 9½" Buntline 105.50

COLT FRONTIER SCOUTS with Dual Cylinders
Same as regular Frontier Scouts except: furnished with two inter-
changeable cylinders; one chambered for 22 LR; the other for 22 RF
Magnum.
Frontier Scout **$83.50** Nickel Scout **$105.50** "62" Scout **$94.50**
Frontier Buntline **94.50** Nickel Buntline **116.50** "62" Buntline **105.50**

D RUGER BEARCAT REVOLVER
Caliber: 22 S or LR, 6 shot.
Barrel: 4" round, fixed blade front sight.
Length: 8⅞ inches. **Weight:** 17 oz.
Stocks: Genuine walnut with medallion.
Sights: Fixed; Patridge front, square notch rear.
Features: Alloy solid frame, patented Ruger coil-spring action; non-
fluted, engraved cylinder.
Price: Blued **$44.00**

E RUGER SINGLE SIX REVOLVER
Caliber: 22 S, L or LR; also available in 22 RF Magnum; 6 shots.
Barrel: 5½" (6 groove, 14" twist).
Length: 10⅞". **Weight:** 36 oz.
Stocks: Smooth walnut.
Sights: Fixed; blade front, square notch rear.
Features: Independent firing pin in frame; coil springs throughout;
recessed chambers.
Price: Blued **$64.25**

RUGER SINGLE SIX CONVERTIBLE REVOLVER
Same as regular Single Six except furnished with two interchangeable
cylinders: one chambered for 22 S, L or LR; the other for 22 RF Magnum. Choice of 5½", 6½" or 9½" barrel.
Price: with 5½" or 6½" barrel....**$69.50** 9½" barrel....**$78.00**

F RUGER SUPER SINGLE SIX CONVERTIBLE REVOLVER
Same as the Single Six except: frame with integral ribs, which protect the adj. rear sight, similar to the Blackhawk; blade front sight on
ramp base. 5½" or 6½" bbl.
With extra 22 Magnum cylinder in cloth pouch..............**$78.00**

RUGER 30 CARBINE BLACKHAWK REVOLVER
Same as the 357 Magnum except 7½" bbl. only (6 groove, 20"
twist), weight 44 oz., 13⅛" over-all. Blued only.............**$98.50**

RUGER 357 MAGNUM—9MM/38 SPECIAL
CONVERTIBLE BLACKHAWK
Same as the 357 Magnum except furnished with interchangeable
cylinders for 9mm Parabellum and 38 Special cartridges.....**$110.00**
9mm cylinder, fitted to your 357 Blackhawk............. 16.00

G RUGER 357 or 41 MAGNUM BLACKHAWK REVOLVER
Caliber: 41 or 357 Magnum, 6 shot.
Barrel: 4⅝" or 6½" (6-groove, 16" twist).
Length: 12⅛" (6½" bbl.). **Weight:** 39 oz.
Stocks: Smooth genuine walnut.
Sights: Ramp front ⅛", micro click rear adj. for w. and e.
Features: Coil springs throughout, flat-top frame, long sight radius,
floating alloy firing pin in frame. Solid frame.
Price: Blued **$98.50**

H RUGER SUPER BLACKHAWK 44 MAGNUM REVOLVER
Caliber: 44 Magnum, 6 shot. Also fires 44 Spec.
Barrel: 7½" inches (6-groove, 20" twist).
Length: 13⅜ inches. **Weight:** 48 oz.
Stocks: Smooth genuine walnut.
Features: Large grip solid frame of steel; square-back guard; flat top-
strap; non-fluted cylinder; wide, serrated trigger; wide-spur hammer.
Price: **$125.00**

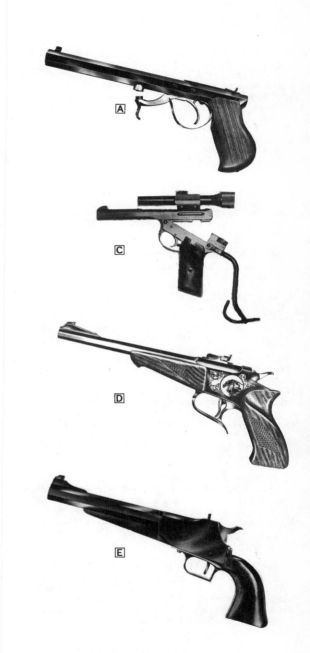

A CHALLENGER HOPKINS & ALLEN M-L BOOT PISTOL
Caliber: 36 or 45, single shot percussion.
Barrel: 6 inch octagonal, regular or gain twist.
Length: 13 inches. **Weight:** 34 oz.
Stocks: Smooth walnut, birdshead style.
Features: Underhammer lockwork; match trigger.
Sights: Fixed blade front, adj. rear.
Price: **$39.95**

C MERRILL SPORTSMAN'S SINGLE SHOT
Caliber: 22S, L, LR, 22WMR, 22WRF, 22 Rem. Jet, 22 Hornet, 117 K Hornet, 357, 38 Spl., 256 Win. Mag., 45 Colt/410 (3″).
Barrel: 9″, hinged type break-open. Semi-octagon.
Length: 10½″. **Weight:** 54 oz.
Stocks: Smooth walnut with thumb & heel rest.
Sights: Front 125″ blade, square notch rear adj. for w. & e.
Features: .355″ rib on top, grooved for scope mounts, auto. safety, cocking indicator, hammerless.
Price: **$129.50**
Price: Extra bbls. . . . . . **$35.00**   Wrist rest attachment **7.95**

B REMINGTON MODEL XP-100 Bolt Action Pistol
Caliber: 221 Fireball, single shot.
Barrel: 10½ inches, ventilated rib.
Length: 16¾ inches. **Weight:** 60 oz.
Stocks: Brown nylon one-piece, checkered grip with white spacers.
Features: Fits left or right hand, is shaped to fit fingers and heel of hand. Grooved trigger. Rotating thumb safety, cavity in fore-end permits insertion of up to five 38 cal., 130-gr. metal jacketed bullets to adjust weight and balance. Included is a black vinyl, zippered case.
Sights: Fixed front, rear adj. for w. and e. Tapped for scope mount.
Price: Including case **$99.95**

D THOMPSON-CENTER ARMS CONTENDER
Caliber: 22 S, L, LR, 22 WMR, 22 Rem. Jet, 22 Hornet, 22 K Hornet, 256 Win., 9mm Parabellum, 38 Super, 357/44 B & D, 38 Spl., 357 Mag., also 222 Rem., 30 M1, 45 ACP, 44 Mag.
Barrel: 8¾″, 10″, tapered octagon. Single shot.
Length: 13¼″ (10″ bbl.). **Weight:** 43 oz. (10″ bbl.).
Stocks: Select checkered walnut grip and fore-end, with thumb rest. Right or left hand.
Sights: Under cut blade ramp front, rear adj. for w. & e.
Features: Break open action with auto-safety. Single action only. Interchangeable bbls., both caliber (rim & center fire), and length. Grooved for scope. Engraved frame.
Price: Blued **$135.00**
Price: Extra bbls. . . . . **$36.00**   Fitted Walnut case. **29.50**
Price: Bushnell Phantom scope base. **5.00**

E TINGLE BLACK POWDER M1960 PISTOL
Caliber: 40, single shot, percussion.
Barrel: 8″, 9″, 10″ or 12″ octagon.
Length: 11¾ inches. **Weight:** 33 oz. (8″ bbl.).
Stocks: Walnut, one piece .
Features: 6-groove bbl., easily removable for cleaning; 1-in-30 twist.
Sights: Fixed blade front, w. adj. rear.
Price: **$64.95**
Price: With detachable shoulder stock, **$19.50** extra.

F UNIVERSAL ENFORCER AUTO CARBINE
Caliber: 30 M1 Carbine, 30-shot magazine.
Barrel: 10¼″ with 12-groove rifling.
Length: 17¾″. **Weight:** 4½ lbs.
Stocks: American walnut with handguard.
Features: Uses surplus 5- or 15-shot magazine. 4½-6 lb. trigger pull.
Sights: Gold bead ramp front. Peep rear adj. for w. and e. 14″ sight radius.
Price: Blue finish **$129.95**
Price: Nickel plated finish **149.95**
Price: Gold plated finish **175.00**

Rifles in this section include autoloaders, pump, lever, and bolt action designs, wherein the bulk of the design/manufacturing process is of United States origin. To the great variety of designs is added an even greater variety of cartridges for which these rifles are chambered. If the user is a handloader, the combinations become limitless. Proper selection of a cartridge/rifle combination can hardly be covered in a paragraph (books sometimes fail to cover the subject), but selection of the appropriate cartridge is a good first step. The type of action, and the choice of manufacturer can then be left to taste and pocketbook.

A

A MARLIN PRESENTATION 336 LEVER ACTION RIFLE
Centennial matched pair consists of custom engraved Marlin Model 336 in 30-30 and a Model 39 22 carbine. Centerfire carbine has tapered octagon barrel, straight-grip, selected fancy American walnut with fluted comb. Receiver is hand engraved with inlaid Centennial medallion, curved butt plate and fore-end cap are cartridge brass, 24 K gold-plated trigger, square lever. Other specs identical to those of M336. The Centennial M39 has the same 100th anniversary finishing details as the centerfire gun. Matched pair comes in presentation case, carries identical serial numbers on the top tang. Offered only during 1970. Matched Pair. **$750.00**

B MARLIN 336C LEVER ACTION CARBINE
6-shot, full length magazine. Solid top receiver sand blasted for non-glare; slide ejection. 20" Micro-Groove bbl. Bead front sight; open rear. Offset hammer spur furnished at no charge. Gold plated trigger. Walnut p.g. stock and fore-end. Wgt. 7 lbs. 38½" over-all. Cal. 30-30. 35 Rem. **$105.00**

MARLIN 336T L.A. CARBINE
Same as 336C except: straight stock; cal. 30-30 only. Brass saddle ring. Wgt. about 7 lbs. **$105.00**

C GARCIA SAKO FINNWOLF RIFLE
Hammerless lever action rifle with a gear-operated short-throw lever. Solid frame with side ejection; detachable 4-shot box magazine; cross-bolt safety behind trigger. One-piece walnut stock (13¾"x1½"x2⅝") with Monte Carlo cheekpiece, fluted comb, checkered p.g. cap. 23½" bbl. has bead front sight on hooded ramp; no rear sight. Drilled and tapped for scope mounting. Wgt. about 7 lb., 42¼" over-all. Cals. 243 and 308.
Standard Sporter **$245.00**
Also offered as left hand model, same price.
Deluxe Sporter also available in left hand version...........**$305.00**

D GLENFIELD 30 LEVER ACTION CARBINE
Same as Marlin 336 Carbine except: 4-shot, ⅔ magazine. 20" bbl., walnut finish stock with semi-beavertail fore-end. 38½" over-all, wgt. 7 lbs. Cal. 30-30 only **$99.95**

E MARLIN 444 MAGNUM RIFLE
Same as 336 Carbine except: 4-shot, ⅔ magazine. Tapped for scope and receiver sights. 24" bbl. of special steel. Lyman folding leaf rear sight adj. for w. & e.; hooded ramp blade front. Walnut straight grip Monte Carlo stock with fluted comb, Marlin recoil pad; detachable sling swivels and carrying strap. Wgt. 7½ lbs., 42¼" over-all. Cal. 444 Magnum **$135.00**

F MARLIN 1894 LEVER ACTION CARBINE
10-shot, full length magazine. Solid top receiver; side ejection. 20" Micro-Groove barrel. Bead front sight; open rear. Offset hammer spur furnished at no charge. Gold plated trigger. Walnut straight grip stock and fore-end. Wgt. approx. 6 lbs. 37½" over-all. Caliber .44 Magnum. A re-creation of the Marlin M1894 discontinued in 1917. Available September '69. ....**$105.00**

G SAVAGE 99E LEVER ACTION RIFLE
5-shot rotary mag. 20" bbl. Cocking indicator on tang, safety on right side of receiver. Walnut-finished checkered stock (13½"x1½"x 2½"). Ramp front sight with step adj. sporting rear. Tapped for scope mounts. Wgt. 7 lbs., 39¾" over-all. Calibers: 300 Savage, 243 and 308 Winchester **$129.75**

SAVAGE 99F LIGHTWEIGHT CARBINE
Same as 99E except: 22" lightweight bbl. Damascened bolt, gold plated trigger. Improved sear mechanism, tang safety locks trigger and lever. Mag. indicator on left side. Select walnut stock with checkered p.g. and fore-end, steel buttplate. Gold bead ramp front, folding semi-buckhorn rear. Wgt. 6½ lbs., 41¾" over-all. Cals. 300 Sav., 243, 284, and 308 Win. **$156.50**

Ⓐ SAVAGE 99C LEVER ACTION CLIP RIFLE
Similar to M99F except: Detachable staggered clip magazine with push-button ejection (4-shot capacity; 3 in 284). Wgt. about 6¾ lbs., 41¾" over-all with 22" bbl. Cals. 243, 284, 308 . . . . **$156.00**

Ⓑ SAVAGE 99DL CARBINE
Same as 99F except: High comb Monte Carlo stock; anodized aluminum buttplate; slim fore-end; sling swivels. Wgt. 6¾ lbs., 41¾" over-all. Cals: 300 Sav., 243, 284 and 308 Win. **$160.00**

SAVAGE 99-PE PRESENTATION GRADE RIFLE
Full hand-engraved, including tang and lever; game scenes on action. Choice American walnut Monte Carlo stock, hand checkered. Weight, 6¾ lbs., 22" bbl. Tapped fortopmount. 243, 284, 308 Win. . . . **$360.00**

Ⓒ SAVAGE 99-DE CITATION GRADE RIFLE
Slightly less luxurious than Presentation Grade, same cals. . . **$285.00**

Ⓓ SAVAGE 1895 LEVER ACTION RIFLE
An authentic re-creation of the original lever action model made by Arthur W. Savage. Offered in serialized limited edition to mark 75th anniversary of company during 1970. Both sides of receiver carry commemorative engraving, special brass medallion is inlaid in stock, brass butt plate is crescent shaped as in original. Brass blade front sight. Octagon barrel 24", 44" over-all. Choice walnut stock custom finished, schnabel fore-end, wt. 8 lb. Cal.: 308 Win. only **$195.00**

Ⓔ SEARS 54 LEVER ACTION CARBINE
Solid frame, 6-shot tubular mag. 20" bbl. Half-cock hammer safety. Walnut finished hardwood straight grip stock with nickelplated checkered steel buttplate. Bead front sight on ramp; open notch rear windage adj. Tapped for receiver sights and Sears 3x scope. Wgt. 6½ lbs., 37¾" over-all. Cal. 30-30 only **$94.95**

Ⓕ WESTERN FIELD 740 LEVER ACTION CARBINE
6-shot full length mag., 20" bbl., solid top receiver, side ejection. Walnut stock and fore-end, fluted comb; recoil pad, 1" leather sling strap with swivels. Hammer spur for cocking with scope mounted. Open rear, beaded front sight. Wgt. 7½ lbs., 38½" over-all. Cal. 30-30 only. **$91.95**

Ⓖ WINCHESTER 88 LEVER ACTION RIFLE
Hammerless, rotating 3-lug front-locking bolt. Side ejection, cross-bolt safety. Solid frame with one-piece p.g. stock (13¾"x1½"x2⅝"), basket-weave checkered. Short stroke, fast operating lever. 22" round bbl. Bead front sight on ramp, with cover; folding leaf rear. Tapped for scope mounts; 4-shot detachable magazine, (3-shot in 284). Weight 7¼ lbs., 42½" over-all. Calibers: 243 Win., 284 Win., (10" twist), 308 Win., (12" twist) **$152.95**
Extra 4-shot magazine 5.50

Ⓗ WINCHESTER 88 CARBINE
Similar to 88 rifle. Same stock dimensions. No checkering, bbl. band on fore-end. 39½" over-all, bbl. 19". 7 lbs. **$143.95**

Ⓙ WINCHESTER 94 LEVER ACTION CARBINE
Solid frame, 6-shot tubular magazine. 20" bbl. Walnut-finished straight grip stock and fore-end (13"x1¾"x2½"). Bead front sight on ramp with removable cover; open rear. Tapped for receiver sights. Weight 6½ lbs., 37¾" over-all. Cals. 30-30, (12" twist), 32 Special (16" twist). **$99.95**

WINCHESTER 94 44 MAGNUM CARBINE
Similar to 94 lever action, except 10-shot magazine, wgt. 6⅛ lbs. and 38" twist. **$109.95**

WINCHESTER 94 ANTIQUE CARBINE
Same as M94 except: color case-hardened and scrolled receiver, brass-plated loading gate and saddle ring. 30-30 only **$109.95**

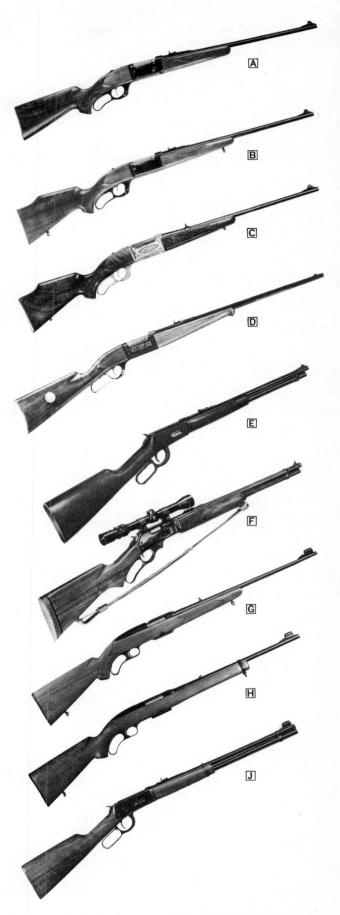

A WINCHESTER MODEL 94 CLASSIC RIFLE
Solid frame, 26" octagon bbl., 8-shot tubular mag. Gold-plated loading gate, scroll-engraved receiver, metal fore-end tip, sling ring straight grip, high gloss semi-fancy walnut stock. 43¾ over-all, wgt. 8 lbs. In 30-30 only (12" twist) $134.95

WINCHESTER MODEL 94 CLASSIC CARBINE
Similar to 94 Classic Rifle, except: 6-shot capacity, 20" octagon bbl., 37¾" over-all, 7 lbs. 30-30 only.........................$134.95

WINCHESTER 94 CLASSIC MATCHED SET
One rifle and one carbine with consecutive serial numbers..$294.90

B WINCHESTER GOLDEN SPIKE COMMEMORATIVE 94
Similar to M94 Classic carbine, except receiver and tang commemorative engraved, receiver, upper and lower tang and twin barrel bands gold plated. A special Centennial medallion struck by the U. S. Mint is imbedded in the stock $119.95

C WINCHESTER THEODORE ROOSEVELT COMMEMORATIVES
Similar to M94 Classics, except receiver and tang commemorative engraved, crescent buttplate, half pistol grip and contoured lever, receiver, fore-end cap, and upper tang are plated in white gold. Commemorative medal imbedded in stock. Rifle has two-thirds (6-shot) magazine and weighs 7½ lbs. Price rifle or carbine........$134.95
Matched set with consecutive numbers..................$294.90

D WINCHESTER COWBOY COMMEMORATIVE CARBINE
Similar to M94 Classic carbine, except for bright nickel plating on receiver, upper and lower tang, lever and barrel bands. Curved stainless steel butt plate with tang extending onto top of classic square comb carbine stock. Cowboy commemorative medallion inset in stock, saddle ring on left side of receiver, 30-30 only. Carbine......$125.00
Matched set with consecutive numbers..................$275.00

E WINCHESTER LONE STAR COMMEMORATIVE
Similar to M94 Classic, this special issue was designed to commemorate achievement of statehood of Texas 125 years ago. All fittings are brass, unique half-round, half-octagon barrel, contoured lever. Special medallion is inset in stock. 30-30 only.
Rifle $140.00
Carbine $140.00
Matched set, rifle and carbine......................$305.00

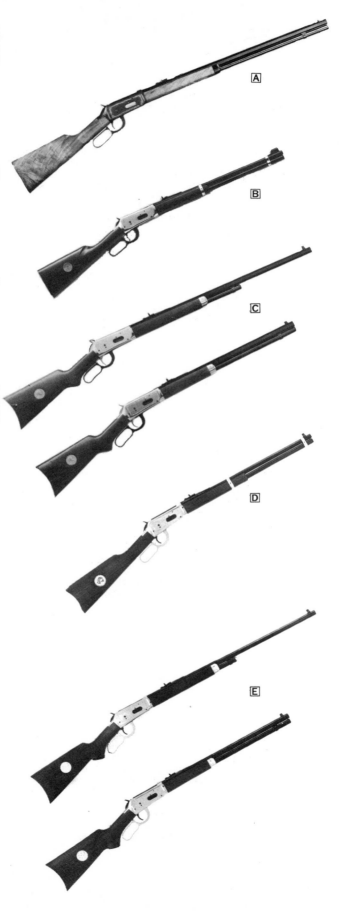

A ARMALITE AR-180 SPORTER CARBINE

Semi-automatic, gas operated carbine, cal. .223. Barrel, bolt, recoil buffer unit and stock assembled as straight-line unit, minimizes barrel jump on recoil. Over-all 38″, bbl. 18¼″, weight 6½ lbs. Flip-up "L" type sight adj. for w.&e., post front adj. for e. Safety lever on both sides of receiver. Nylon folding stock, phenolic fiber-glass heat dissipating fore-end. Flash-hider compensator. Price includes two 5-rd. magazines **$237.00**
3 power (2.75x20mm) telescope available with mounts **68.75**

B BROWNING HIGH-POWER AUTO RIFLE

Gas-operated semi-automatic rifle. Bolt locks via 7-lug, rotary-head bolt. Detachable 5-shot trap-door mag., 22″ bbl. with adjustable folding-leaf rear sight and hooded ramp front. French walnut p.g. stock (13⅝″x2″x1⅝″) and fore-end, with hand checkering. Wgt. 7⅜ lbs., 43½″ over-all. Cals. 270, 308, 243 Win., and 30-06. Grade I .. **$187.50**
Grade II. Same as Grade I except hand-rubbed, selected French walnut stock, and receiver hand engraved **$204.50**

BROWNING MAGNUM AUTO RIFLE

Same as the standard caliber model, except weighs 8½ lbs., 45¼″ over-all, 24″ bbl., 3rd mag., Cals. 7mm Mag., 300 Win. Mag. and 338 mag.   Grade I .....**$189.50**   Grade II **$204.50**

C EAGLE "APACHE" CARBINE

Recoil operated semi-automatic rifle, handles the 45 ACP cartridge from a 30-shot detachable magazine. Only 4 moving parts. Over-all length 36½″, bbl. length 16½″, weight 9 lbs. Protected post front sight, aperture rear. Black finish. **$129.95**

D HARRINGTON & RICHARDSON 360 ULTRA AUTOMATIC

Gas-operated, semi-auto rifle. Side ejection, recessed bolt face, manual bolt stop. Sliding trigger guard safety. 3-round detachable box mag., 22″ bbl. Open adj. rear sight, gold bead ramp front. Receiver tapped for scope. One-piece American walnut Monte Carlo stock, rollover cheekpiece; checkered pistol grip and fore-end. 43½″ over-all, wgt. 7½ lbs. Cals. 243, 308. ....**$189.00**
Also available with full roll-over cheekpiece as Model 361 .. **199.95**

E J & R 68 SEMIAUTOMATIC CARBINE

Recoil operated carbine fires from a closed bolt. Cal. 9mm parabellum, 30-shot staggered box magazine. 28½″ over-all, 16¼″ bbl., wgt. 7 lbs. unloaded. Sights: protected blade front; fixed peep rear. High impact plastic stock and fore-end.
Aircraft aluminum receiver. **$149.95**

F PLAINFIELD MACHINE CO. CARBINE

Newly manufactured gas-operated cal. 30 M1 Carbine which duplicates size and appearance of popular GI model, including click adj. rear sight. Glossy finish stock. 18″ bbl. Wgt. 5½ lb. 35½″ over-all. mag., 22″ Douglas bbl. Open adj. rear sight, gold bead ramp front. Metal or wood handguard **$105.00**
Paratrooper. With telescoping wire stock, front vertical hand grip. **$125.00**
Plainfielder. With Monte Carlo checkered sporting stock (also available with no checkering, at $6.00 less) **$125.00**

REMINGTON 742 WOODMASTER AUTO RIFLE

Gas-operated "Power-Matic" action reduces recoil. Rotary multiple lug breechbolt locks into 22″ bbl., fully encloses cartridge. Hammerless, solid frame, side ejection. Gold bead front sight on ramp; step rear sight with windage adj. Walnut p.g. stock (13⅜″x1⅝″x2¼₁₆″) and fore-end, deluxe checkered 4-shot detachable magazine, Wgt. 7½ lbs. 42″ over-all. Cals: 243 Win., 6mm Rem., 280 Rem., 308 Win. and 30-06.
....**$164.95**
  Extra 4-shot magazine **5.25**
  Sling strap and swivels (installed) **9.10**
  Peerless (D) and Premier (F) grades .... **$595.00** and **1295.00**
  Premier with gold inlays **1950.00**

G REMINGTON 742 BDL WOODSMASTER

Same as 742 except: "stepped" receiver, Monte Carlo stock with cheekpiece (right or left), whiteline spacers, basket-weave checkering on p.g. and fore-end, black fore-end tip, RKW finish. (13⁵⁄₁₆″x1⅝″x 1¹³⁄₁₆″x2½″). Cals. 30-06, 308 ....**$184.95**

REMINGTON 742 CARBINE

Same as M742 except: 18½″ bbl., 38½″ over-all, wgt. 6¾ lbs. Cals: 30-06, 308 Win. **$164.95**

A RUGER 44 AUTOLOADING CARBINE
Gas-operated, cal. 44 Magnum. 18½" bbl. 4-shot tubular magazine and one-piece walnut p.g. stock (13⅜"x1⅝"x2½"). Sourdough front, folding leaf rear sights. Crossbolt safety. Magazine release button. Receiver tapped for scope mounts. Weight 5¾ lbs., 37" over-all **$115.00**
Model 44-RS Deluxe, with built-in receiver sight, carbine stock and swivels **$125.00**

B RUGER 44 SPORTER CARBINE
Same as Ruger autoloader except: sporter stock with Monte Carlo comb, flat buttplate; full pistol grip with cap; longer streamlined fore-end, relieved for fingertips; sling swivels. Cal. 44 Magnum....**$120.00**

C UNIVERSAL 1000 AUTOLOADING CARBINE
Gas operated, hammerless. 5-shot magazine. 18" bbl., 12-groove rifling. Walnut stock inletted for "issue" sling and oiler; handguard; forward one-piece swivel and bayonet stud; front blade sight with protective wings, adj. rear aperture. Crosslock safety. Wgt. 5½ lbs., 35½" over-all. Cal. 30 M1..............................**$116.95**
Universal also offers other versions of their basic M1000 Carbine, including two models handling the 256 cartridge, at prices ranging from ....**$129.95 to $175.00**

D UNIVERSAL 1020 TEFLON CARBINE
Same as the 1000 Carbine but has soft, dull Teflon finish said to be self-lubricating, water and scuff resistant. Available in black, tan, blue, green and olive colored finishes, with a high finish American walnut Monte Carlo Stock...................**$149.95**

E WINCHESTER 100 AUTOLOADING RIFLE
Gas-operated with cam action rotating bolt. Hammerless, solid frame; side ejection and crossbolt safety. Tapped for scope mounts. One piece walnut p.g. stock (13¾"x1½"x2⅝"), semi-beavertail fore-end, basket-weave checkered; 22" bbl. Bead front and folding leaf rear sights. 4-shot detachable magazine (3-shot in 284). Wgt. 7¼ lbs., 42½" over-all Cals. 243, 284 (10" twist), and 308 (12" twist).........**$164.95**
Extra magazine 5.50

WINCHESTER 100 AUTOLOADING CARBINE
Similar to 100 Autoloading rifle, with same stock dimensions. No checkering. Bbl. band on fore-end. 39½" over-all. Bbl. 19". Wgt. 7 lbs. Cals. 243, 284 (10" twist), and 308 (12" twist)..............**$156.95**
Extra magazine 5.50

F REMINGTON 760 GAMEMASTER SLIDE ACTION
Hammerless, solid frame, side ejection rifle. Rotary multiple-lug breechbolt locks into 22" bbl., fully encloses cartridge. Trigger must be released and action fully closed for each shot. Checkered walnut RKW finish p.g. stock (13⅜"x1⅝"x2¹⁄₁₆") and for-end; black fore-end tip, non-slip buttplate, all with white spacers. Cross-bolt safety. Gold bead front sight on matted ramp, open sporting rear. Tapped for scope mounts. 4-shot detachable magazine. Wgt. 7½ lbs. 42" over-all. Cals.: 6mm Rem., 243, 270, 308 Win., 30-06.....................**$139.95**
Sling strap and swivels (installed)..................... 9.10
Extra 4-shot clip................................... 4.50

G REMINGTON 760 BDL GAMEMASTER
Same as 760 except: "stepped receiver," Monte Carlo stock with cheekpiece (right or left), whiteline spacer, basket-weave checkering on p.g. and fore-end, black fore-end tip, RKW finish. (13⁵⁄₁₆"x1⅝"x 1¹³⁄₁₆"x2½"). Cals. 270, 30-06, 308.......................**$159.95**

REMINGTON 760 GAMEMASTER CARBINE
Same as M760 except has 18½" barrel. Wgt. 6¾ lbs., 38½" over-all. Cals: 308 Win., and 30-06...........................**$139.95**
Also in Peerless (D) and Premier (F) grades.....**$595.00 and 1295.00**
(F), with gold inlay............................... 2000.00

H SAVAGE MODEL 170 SLIDE ACTION
Hammerless, solid frame, side ejection rifle. Short 3¾" pump stroke, 22" bbl., checkered p.g., finger rail in slide handle. Top-tang safety locks trigger and sear. Walnut stock (14"x1½"x2½"), hard rubber butt plate, gold bead ramp sight, folding leaf rear sight, drilled and tapped for scope mounting, holds 3 rounds in magazine, one in chamber, 30-30 only. 41½" over-all, 6¾ lb. **$99.75**

SAVAGE SCOPEGUN MODEL 170
Standard Model 170 equipped by factory with mounts and 1½X4X Variable scope. **$137.50**

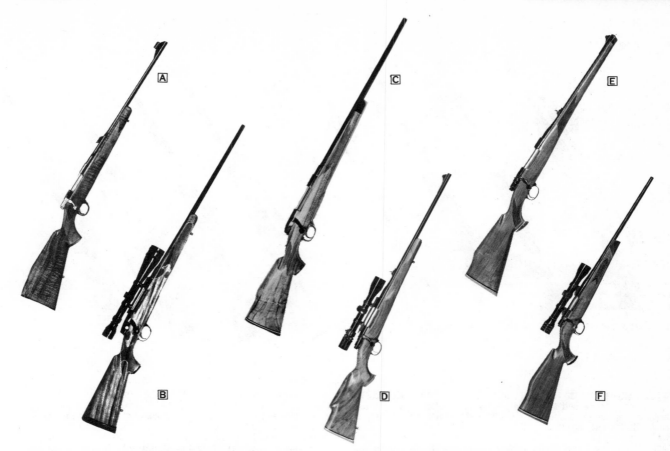

A BROWNING HIGH POWER RIFLE Safari Grade

Short and medium Sako or standard Mauser action with hinged floorplate, hand engraved. 3-position sliding safety. Grooved factory adjusted trigger; engraved trigger guard. Checkered walnut p.g. stock, Monte Carlo comb and cheekpiece, 13⅝"x1⅝"x1⅝"x2⅜". Swivel eyelets fitted. 22" lightweight or 24" heavyweight bbls. specifically contoured for each caliber. Hooded ramp front sight, removable adj. folding leaf rear sight. Cals. 222, 222 Mag., 22-250 or 243 (heavy bbl.) without sights; 243, 270, 284, 30-06 or 308 sights optional. Wgt. 6⅛ to 6¾ lbs. (light bbl.), 43" over-all................**$231.50** to **$239.50**
Heavy bbl. available in 222, 222 Mag., 22-250 or 243. Wgt. 7½ to 7¾ lbs. 45" over-all.................**$231.50** to **$239.50**
Also available in 7mm Rem., 300 Win., 300 H&H, 308 Norma, 338 Win., 375 H&H and 458 Win. Magnum calibers. 24" bbl., wgt. 8¼ lbs., 45" over-all including recoil pad.............**$249.50** to **$256.50**

BROWNING HIGH POWER RIFLE Medallion Grade

Same cals. as Safari. Figured walnut stock with skip-line checkering, rosewood grip cap and fore-end tip. Hand engraved receiver and bbl., high-polish blue. Polished bolt, bolt sleeve, bolt handle. Gold plated trigger. All except 458 are without sights.

All Short and medium action models	**$374.50**
30-06 and 270 calibers	**387.50**
Magnum calibers	**394.50**
458 Magnum	**399.50**

BROWNING HIGH POWER RIFLE Olympian Grade

Same as Medallion except with finest figured walnut stock; 32-line checkering with hand carved scroll borders; gold initial medallion inset into grip cap. Receiver, floorplate and trigger guard satin-chrome finished. Engraved with animal scenes.

All short and medium action models	**$624.50**
30-06 and 270 calibers	**647.50**
Magnum calibers	**654.50**
458 Magnum	**659.50**

B CHAMPLIN PREMIER RIFLE

Six locking lugs hold the jewelled bolt at both ends of the tri-rail action. Has checkered bolt knob, 24" octagon bbl., Redfield scope mts., Camjar adj. trigger. Hand inletted oil finished select Claro walnut stock (13½"x1"x⅝"x½") of Monte Carlo design has ebony fore-end tip, black Pachmayr recoil pad, steel p.g. cap, det. sling swivels. Cals. 270, 30-06, 7mm Rem. and 300 Win. Mag. Choice of RH or LH action.................**$636.56**

C CHAMPLIN CUSTOM CROWN RIFLE

Similar to the Premier except: stock built to order, 22 line checkering, optional checkered steel p.g. cap, round or dragoon style trigger guard. Choice of high-gloss or non-glare blueing, barrel length and recoil pad style. Customers name engraved on bbl..........**$850.00**
Other modifications and changes are offered such as tapered octagon barrel with integral quarter-rib, ramp and sling swivels, one or three-leaf sights and many more.

D HARRINGTON & RICHARDSON 300 BOLT ACTION

Mauser Supreme bolt action with hinged floorplate, adj. trigger, sliding safety. 22" bbl., adjustable rear sight, gold bead ramp front; receiver tapped for scope. American walnut stock, hand checkered p.g. and fore-end, Monte Carlo comb, roll-over cheekpiece. Sling swivels. Wgt. 7¾ lbs., 42½" over-all. Cal. 22-250, 243, 270, 308, 30-06 (5-shot), 7mm Rem. Mag., 300 Win. Mag. (3-shot).............**$225.00**
With Ultragon barrel, $12 extra, 22-250 and 30 cals.
Model 330, same as M300 except: stock w/o fore-end or p.g. caps; spacers; no checkering on fore-end. Monte-Carlo stock. No swivels. Not available in 22-250..................**$139.95**

E HARRINGTON & RICHARDSON 301 ULTRA CARBINE

Similar to M300, except: Mannlicher style stock (no roll-over cheekpiece) metal fore-end tip. 18" bbl., 39" over-all, wgt. 7¼ lbs. **$239.00**

F HARRINGTON & RICHARDSON 317 ULTRA WILDCAT

Sako bolt action, adj. trigger, sliding thumb safety, receiver dovetailed for scope. 20" barrel. Hand polished, hand checkered walnut p.g. stock, capped fore-end and p.g. Monte Carlo comb. Wgt. 5¼ lbs., 38½" over-all. Cals. 223 Rem. and 17/223 Mag. (handloads), 6 shot.
.................**$249.00**

HARRINGTON & RICHARDSON 317 PRESENTATION GRADE

Similar to above, except special selected walnut stock, basketweave checkering on p.g. and fore-end.................**$450.00**

A HARRINGTON & RICHARDSON 370 ULTRA MEDALIST

Mauser Supreme bolt action, 24″ heavy varmint-target bbl. Receiver and bbl. tapped for scope and metallic sights. Fully adj. trigger, receiver drilled and tapped for sight or scope. Oil finished, hand rubbed walnut p.g. stock, roll-over comb, semi-beavertail fore-end, recoil pad and adj. swivels. Target scope ribbed base optional at extra cost. Wgt. 9½ lbs., 44¾″ over-all. Cals. 22-250, 6mm Rem., and 243, 5 shots. $245.00

B ITHACA LSA-55 BOLT ACTION RIFLE

Available in cals. 243, 308, 22-250 & 6mm. 23″ bbl., 42½″ over-all, wgt. approx. 6½ lbs. Hand checkered selected walnut Monte Carlo stock (13⅝″ pull) with palm swell; sling swivels. Removable rear sight adj. for w. & e. Ramp front sight. Adjustable single-stage trigger. Receiver has integral scope mounting bases and detachable box magazine. $169.95

ITHACA LSA-55 DELUXE BOLT ACTION

Same as the std. except rollover cheekpiece, fore-end tip and pistol grip cap of rosewood with white spacers.... ....$214.95

C MOSSBERG 800 BOLT ACTION RIFLE

4-shot mag. with hinged floorplate. Recessed bolt face; 6 locking lugs. Top thumb safety. 22″ AC-KRO-GRUV bbl. Gold bead ramp front, adj. folding leaf rear sight. Monte Carlo cheekpiece walnut stock, checkered and carved, with whiteline spacers, sling swivels. Wgt. 6½ lbs., 42″ over-all. Cals. 22-250, 243, 308...................$109.95

MOSSBERG 800SM SCOPED RIFLE

Same as M800 except has Mossberg M84 4x scope. Wgt. 7½ lbs. $128.00

MOSSBERG 800D DELUXE RIFLE

Super grade M800 with special finish and Monte Carlo rollover-comb stock. Wgt. 6¾ lbs...$170.00

MOSSBERG 800V TARGET-VARMINT RIFLE

Model 800 with heavy 24″ barrel, target scope bases, no iron sights. Cals. 243 and 22-250 only. 44″ over-all, wgt. about 9½ lbs..$124.95

MOSSBERG 800M MANNLICHER RIFLE

Same as M800 except has one piece Mannlicher style stock, flat bolt handle, 20″ bbl., 40″ over-all and weighs 6½ lbs.....$139.00

RANGER ARMS TEXAS MAVERICK RIFLE

All grades in cals. 22-250, 243, 6mm Rem., & 308. Choice of 22″ or 24″ bbl. and right or left hand stock and action. English or Claro walnut Monte Carlo stock (13⅝″ pull) with cheekpiece, skip-line checkering, recoil pad, sling swivel studs, rosewood p.g. cap with maple spacer, polyvinyl epoxy finish. Wgt. 7¾ lbs.

Stateman's Grade has minimum coverage checkering, standard grade and finish barrel $325.00

Senator's Grade has medium coverage checkering, premium grade standard finish barrel $375.00

Governor's Grade has full coverage checkering, premium grade deluxe polish barrel, hand honed and lapped action with jeweled bolt body and knurled bolt knob $425.00

RANGER ARMS TEXAS MAGNUM RIFLE

Same as the Maverick except in 270, 30-06, 7mm, 300 and 358 Norma Magnum calibers. Optional 24″ or 25½″ bbls. Wgt. 8¼ lbs. Stateman's **$300.00**.   Senator's **$350.00** and Governor's **$425.00**

F RANGER ARMS BENCH REST RIFLE

Single shot in choice of left or right hand models. Cals. 222 or 22-250. Thumb hole stock of laminated walnut strips with wide beavertail fore-end. 24″ stainless steel bbl. Wgt. 11¾ lbs. 13½″ pull. $500.00

Barreled action (std. or Mag.), in the white, from **$139.50** to **$249.50**. Action from **$97.50** to **$149.50**.

G REMINGTON 660 BOLT ACTION CARBINE

Monte Carlo stock, checkered p.g. and fore-end (14″x1⅞″x2″). Brass-bead ramp-blade front sight, "U" notch adj. rear. Forward angled bolt, 2-position safety. Capacity 5 rds. in 6mm Rem., 243, 308; 222 Rem. Barrel 20″, over-all 38¾″. Wgt. 6½ lbs. $124.95

Sling and swivels (installed)........................... 9.10

H REMINGTON 660 MAGNUM CARBINE

Same as 660 Carbine except has laminated beech and walnut stock with recoil pad and quick-detachable swivels; strap supplied. 4-shot capacity in cals. 6.5mm and 350 Rem. Mag. $154.95

J REMINGTON 700 ADL BOLT ACTION RIFLE

Walnut, RKW finished p.g. stock, impressed checkering, with Monte Carlo comb and cheekpiece (13⅜″x1¹¹⁄₁₆″x2⁵⁄₁₆″); blind magazine. Adj. trigger. Gold bead front sight on ramp, removable step-adj. rear sight with windage screw. Bolt handle checkered top and bottom. Cals. 222, (24″ bbl.), 43½″ over-all). 6-shot; 22-250 (24″ bbl., 43½″ over-all), 6mm Rem., 243, 25-06 and 308 Win. (22 bbl., 41½″ over-all), 270 Win., 30-06, (22″ bbl., 42½″ over-all), 5-shot. 7 lbs........$139.95

264 or 7mm Mag., 4-shot 24″ stainless steel bbl., 44½″ over-all, recoil pad, 7½ lbs. $154.95

REMINGTON 700 BDL BOLT ACTION RIFLE
Same as 700-ADL except: fleur-de-lis checkering; black fore-end tip; white line buttplate and fore-end tip spacers; quick release hinged floorplate; matted-top receiver; 1″ sling and quick detachable swivels. Hooded ramp front sight **$159.95**
6.5 Rem. Mag., 350 Rem. Mag., 264, 300 Win. or 7mm Rem. Mag., 4-shot, 264, 300 & 7mm has stainless steel bbl., 44½″ over-all, recoil pad, 7½ lbs. **$174.95**
375 H&H or 458 Win. Mag., 4-shot, 26″ bbl., 46½″ over-all, recoil pad, 9 lbs. . . . . **$ 334.95**
Peerless Grade . . . . **$595.00**   Premier Grade **1295.00**

A REMINGTON 700 BDL VARMINT
Same as 700 BDL, except: 24″ heavy bbl., 43½″ over-all, wgt. 9 lbs. Cals. 222, 223, 22-250, 6mm Rem., 243 . . . . **$174.95**

B REMINGTON 700C CUSTOM RIFLE
Same as the 700BDL except choice of 20″, 22″ or 24″ bbl. with or without sights. Jewelled bolt, with or without hinged floor plate. Select American walnut stock is hand checkered. Has rosewood fore-end & grip cap. Hand lapped barrel. 16 weeks for delivery after placing order **$345.00**
Optional extras: recoil pad **$12.00**, oil finish **$13.75** and left hand cheekpiece **$25.00**.

C REMINGTON 788 BOLT ACTION RIFLE
4-shot detachable mag. in cals. 22-250, 6mm Rem., 243, 30-30, 308 and 44 Mag. 5-shot in 222. Walnut finished Monte Carlo hardwood stock (13⅝″x2⅝″x1⅞″) with p.g. Bbl. 22″ except 222 (24″). Sights; front blade on ramp, open rear, screw adj. for w. & e. Rear-sight mounting holes correct for target scope block. Receiver tapped for scope and receiver sights. Weighs 7 lbs. (44 Mag.); 7¼ lbs. (6mm, 243, 30-30, 308); 7½ lbs. (222, 22-250) **$89.95**

REMINGTON 788 LEFT HAND BOLT ACTION
Same as 788 except cals. 6mm & 308 only and left hand stock and action. **$94.95**
Sling strap and swivels, installed **$5.40**. Extra Mag . . . . . . **$ 4.50**

D RUGER 77 BOLT ACTION RIFLE
Cals. 22-250, 6mm Rem., 243 & 308. Short stroke bolt on one-piece construction with two locking lugs. Adj. trigger, hinged 5-shot magazine. 22″ bbl., 1″ tip-off type rings supplied as standard. Checkered American walnut stock (13¾″x2⅛″x1⅝″) with p.g. cap; sling swivel studs and recoil pad. 42″ over-all; Wgt. 6½ lbs **$160.00**
With iron sights **175.00**

RUGER 77 MAGNUM RIFLE
Cals. 284 Win. (5-shot), 6.5mm or 350 Rem. Mag. (3-shot). Otherwise same as standard cal. 77. . . . . **$160.00**

RUGER MODEL 77 LONG ACTION
Action length of the standard Model 77 has been increased so that the longer cartridge chamberings are now also available in this rifle. Cals. 270 and 30-06 with 22″ barrel, 25-06 and 7mm Rem. Mag. with 24″ barrels. Prices and specs same as for short action. Delivery to start July 1970.

SAVAGE 110 E BOLT ACTION RIFLE
Cals. 30-06, 243, 308 (4-shot) & 7mm Rem. Mag. (3-shot). 20″ (7mm, 24″) bbl., walnut finished hardwood stock (13½″x1⅝″x1½″x 2½″) with checkered p.g. and fore-end with Monte Carlo comb. Hard rubber butt plate (7mm, recoil pad). Gold bead front sight on removable ramp; step elevator rear, tapped for peep or scope sights. Wgt. 6¾ lbs. (7mm, 7¾ lbs.); 40½″ over-all (20″ bbl.) **$117.50**
7mm Mag. **132.50**
Model 110-EL same except left hand action **125.50**
7mm Mag. **138.50**

E SAVAGE 100D BOLT ACTION RIFLE
Same as the 110E except: 22″ bbl. (24″, 22-250, 6 Mag. cals.); walnut stock; aluminum butt plate (magnum, recoil pad); folding semi-buckhorn rear sight (22-250 no sights); 22-250 weighs 8 lbs.; Cals. 30-06, 22-250, 243, 270 & 308 . . . . **$141.50**
7mm Rem., 264, 300 & 338 Win. Mag. **147.50**
Model 110DL same except left hand action **156.50**
Magnum calibers **160.50**

F SAVAGE 110C BOLT ACTION RIFLE
Same as the 110D except: Detachable 4-shot box magazine. Not available in 22-250 . . . . **$146.50**
Model 110CL same except left hand action **152.50**

G SAVAGE 110 PREMIER GRADE RIFLE
Same as the Model 110D except: selected French walnut stock with roll-over cheekpiece, skip-line hand checkered p.g. and fore-end. Rosewood fore-end tip and butt cap with white spacers. Sling swivel studs. Folding leaf rear sight. Right or left hand action. Wgt. 7 lbs., 7¾ in 7mm. Cal. 243 and 30-06 . . . . **$199.50**
Same in 7mm Rem. Mag. with 24″ stainless steel bbl. **212.50**

H SAVAGE 110-PE PRESENTATION GRADE RIFLE
Similar to M110 Premier Grade except: choice French walnut stock; receiver, trigger guard and floor plate fully engraved, right or left hand action. 243-30-06 . . . . **$345.00**, 7mm Rem. Mag. **$355.00**

SAVAGE 110 Barreled Actions. Same as used in 110MC & 110 Magnum. No stock or sights. Right-hand action, 22-250, 243, 270, 308, 30-36 . . . . . **$94.00**; 7mm Rem., 264, 300, 338 Win. **$104.00**
With left-hand action, standard calibers . . **$98.00**, magnums . . **108.00**
Actions only. Write to Savage for price.

J SAVAGE 340 CLIP REPEATER
Bolt action, 4-shot clip rifle. 225 Win. 222 Rem. (24″ bbl.) or 3-shot 30-30 (22″ bbl.). Walnut p.g. stock with fluted comb, white spacers, checkering on p.g. and fore-end. 13½″x1½″x2½″. Ramp front sight with gold bead; folding stepped rear. Thumb safety. Wgt. about 6½ lbs., 42″ over-all (24″ bbl.) **$84.75**

A SEARS 53 BOLT ACTION RIFLE

Hinged floorplate. Walnut finished Monte Carlo stock with checkered p.g. and fore-end. Tapped for receiver sights and scope mounts. Bolt face encloses cartridge head; bolt handle flat on underside. Serrated trigger. 3-position thumb safety on bolt head. White metal bead front sight on ramp. Semi-buckhorn folding rear adj. for elevation. Wgt. about 6¾ lbs. Cals. 243 and 30-06 (5-shot, 22″ bbl., 42⅜″ over-all)................$129.99

B SEARS 53 TED WILLIAMS RIFLE

Same as Sears 53 except: 30-06 only; 22″ bbl., 10″ twist, 42⅜″ over-all, wgt. 6¾ lbs. Wide trigger. American walnut stock, Monte Carlo comb, checkered p.g. and fore-end (13⅝″x1⅜″x1¾″x 2⅜″). Recoil pad, black fore-end tip, 1″ detachable swivels and sling, medallion on p.g., engine turned bolt, scrolled floor plate.....$165.00

C SMITH & WESSON BOLT ACTION RIFLES

All have Mauser 3-lug actions, hinged magazine floor-plates, jewelled bolts, single-stage trigger. Silver bead ramp front & open sporting rear sights, sling swivels. Available in cals. 270, 30-06, 308 & 243 with 23¾″ 4-groove bbls. (243 has 6). 5-shot mag.

Model C has walnut stock with high-gloss plastic finish, checkered p.g. and fore-end (illustrated)...........................$192.50

Model B has Monte Carlo stock.........................202.50

Model A has cheekpiece, rosewood p.g. cap and fore-end tip with white spacers 215.50

Model D has full length (Mannlicher type) stock..........221.00

Model E has full length Monte Carlo stock...............225.00

All models are available with oil finished, instead of plastic, stocks in cal. 30-06. Deduct $17.00 from prices.

D WEATHERBY MARK V BOLT ACTION RIFLE

Designed especially for the Weatherby Magnum cartridge line, the Mark V action features: nine locking lugs; low-lift (54°) bolt handle; counter-bored bolt face and bbl. breech fully enclose the cartridge; three gas ports; streamlined, shrouded bolt sleeve; cocking indicator; adj. trigger; hinged floorplate and thumb safety. Barrels have cold-swaged rifling and are profiled in proportion to caliber. Deluxe checkered walnut Monte Carlo stock with high luster finish, recoil pad. 13½″ pull. Sights are optional extras. Cals: 224, 22-250 (4-shot, 6½ lbs., 43¼″ over-all, 24″ bbl., 14″ twist).....................$299.50

With 26″ semi-target bbl. 309.50

Cals., 257, 270, 300, (12″ twist), 240, 7mm 30-06 (10″ twist) 3-shot, 7¼ lbs., 44½″ over-all 24″ bbl. $329.50

Cal. 340 (3-shot 8½ lbs., 46½″ over-all, 26″ bbl., 10″ twist) 339.50

Cal. 378 (13½″ pull, 2-shot, 8½ lbs., 46½″ over-all, 26″ bbl., 12″ twist) $425.00

Cal. 460 (California Mesquite stock, 13⅞″ pull, 2-shot, 10½ lbs., 46½″ over-all. 26″ bbl., 16″ twist, muzzle brake)...........$495.00

Calibers 240, 257, 270, 7mm and 300 WM, or 30-06 may be ordered with 26″ bbls. for $10.00 extra. 378s with muzzle brake, $37.50 extra.

WEATHERBY MARK V RIFLE Left Hand

Available in all Weatherby calibers except 224 and 22-250. Complete left handed action; stock with cheekpiece on right side. Prices are $10 higher than right hand models except the 460 WM is unchanged.

E WEATHERBY VANGUARD BOLT ACTION RIFLE

Strongly modified Mauser action with 2 bolt lugs, hinged floor plate, drilled and tapped for scope mounting. Fully adjustable trigger, 24″ hammer forged barrel. American walnut stock with p.g. cap and contrasting wood fore-end, 13½″ pull, side safety. Stock is hand checkered and inletted. 44½″ over-all. Cals. 243 and 308 (5 round magazine), 264, 7mm Rem. Mag., 300 Win. Mag. (3 round mag.)..........$199.50

WESTERN FIELD 770 BOLT ACTION RIFLE

Mauser-type action with recessed bolt head and locking lugs; side safety locks trigger; non-slip bolt handle; 4-shot magazine capacity. Hand finished French walnut stock; p.g. and fore-end are hand checkered. Hooded front ramp, adjustable open rear sights. Sling swivels included. Cals. 270, 30-30. 42″ over-all. $135.00

F WESTERN FIELD 780 BOLT ACTION RIFLE

Mauser-type action. Monte Carlo stock with cheekpiece, checkered p.g. and fore-end, whiteline spacers, 1″ sling swivels. Gold bead front ramp, adj. folding leaf rear sight. 22″ bbl., 42″ over-all. Cals. 243, 308 ....$96.95

WESTERN FIELD M-780

Super grade with roll-over cheek piece stock of American walnut with rosewood p.g. cap and fore-end tip, white line spacers, cushion rubber buttplate. Cal. 308 or 243 Win. $165.00

G WINCHESTER 70 STANDARD RIFLE

Bolt action; wide adj. trigger; 3-position safety on fully enclosed bolt head. Red cocking indicator. Recessed bolt face. Engine-turned bolt. Floating swaged bbl. with hooded bead front sight, adj. open rear. Action tapped and sights removable for scope mounting. Walnut stock with Monte Carlo comb and cheekpiece (13½″x1¾″x1½″x2⅛″), checkered p.g. and fore-end, sling swivels. Cals. 222, 22-250, 225, 243, 270, 30-06 ,308, 6-shot (222, 4-shot), wgt. 7½ lbs., 42½″ over-all, 22″ bbl., 10″ twist (225, 222 and 22-250 have 14″ twist, 308 has 12″).
....$169.95

A WINCHESTER 70 AFRICAN
Same as M70 Standard except: 458 Win. Mag. only. 4-shot; open rear sight. 22" non-floating heavy bbl. 14" twist. Stock measures 13½"x1⅜"x1¾"x2⅜", has black plastic fore-end tip and grip cap; wgt. 8½ lbs., recoil pad and special rear sight.............. **$349.95**

B WINCHESTER 70 DELUXE RIFLE
Same as M70 Standard except: presentation-checkered semi-fancy walnut stock, ebony p.g. cap and fore-end tip with white spacers, knurled bolt knob, non-slip rubber buttplate. 225, 243, 270, 30-06, 300 Win. Mag. (recoil pad)............................... **$339.95**

C WINCHESTER 70 MANNLICHER
Same as M70 Standard except: 19" barrel bedded full-length in Mannlicher-style stock of American walnut with Monte Carlo profile and raised cheek-piece. Length 39½" over-all, weight about 7 lbs. Available in 243, 270, 308 Win. or 30-06.................... **$239.95**

D WINCHESTER 70 MAGNUM RIFLE
Same as M70 Standard except with recoil pad and in these magnum cals.: 7mm Rem., 264, 300, 338 Win., 375 H&H, 3-round mag. capacity. Wgt. 7¼ lbs. (8½ lbs. in 375), 24" bbl., 44½" over-all. R.H. twist: 9" in 264, 9½" in 7mm, 10" in 300, 338, 12" in 375............ **$184.95**

E WINCHESTER 70 VARMINT RIFLE
Same as M70 Standard except: 222 Rem., 22-250, 225 and 243 only, target scope blocks, no sights, 24" heavy bbl., 14" twist in 22-250, and 225, 10" twist in 243. 44½" over-all, 9¾ lbs. Stock measures 13½"x⅞"x1⁵⁄₁₆"x⅜" from bore line...................... **$184.95**

Standard, Magnum and Varmint 70s feature: New anti-cramp bolt; stainless steel follower; black chromed steel guard and floorplate. Newly designed stocks have wider cheekpieces, slimmer fore-ends, new grip caps.
DeLuxe, Target and African 70s have some of these new features.

WINCHESTER 70 TARGET RIFLE
Heavy 24" barrel, contoured aluminum handstop that fits left and right hand shooter, high comb target stock. Tapped for micrometer sights, clip slot in receiver, cals. 308 and 30-06........... **$229.95**

Winchester 70 Barreled Actions. No stock, sights or scope blocks; receivers tapped and plugged. **Standard:** 222 Rem., 22-250, 225, 243, 270, 308, 30-06....**$124.95; Magnum;** 264, 7mm Rem., 300 Vin., 338......**$139.95; Varmint:** 22-250, 225, 243.....**$139.95; Target:** 308, 30-06...**$171.95**

F WINCHESTER 670 BOLT ACTION RIFLE
Similar to Winchester 70. Sliding, 2-position safety; recessed bolt face; red cocking indicator; wide, serrated trigger; ramp front sight and adj. open rear (both easily detachable for scope-only use). Monte Carlo stock (13½"x1¾"x1½"x2⅛"), checkered p.g. and fore-end. 22" floating bbl. 10" twist. Wgt. 7 lbs., 42½" over-all. Cals. 243, 270, 30-06 ....**$124.95**

G WINCHESTER 770 BOLT ACTION RIFLE
Available in cals. 222, 22-250, 243, 270, 30-06 & 308 (4-shot). 42½" over-all, 22" bbls. Walnut stock (13½"x 1¾" x 2⅛" x 1½") with Monte Carlo, undercut cheekpiece, fluted comb, checkered p.g., with caps and fore-end, sling swivels. Ramp-and-hood front and sporting rear sights are detachable. Wgt. 7½ lbs. 10" (243, 270, 30-06), 12" (308) and 14" (222, 22-250), twist............. **$139.95**

WINCHESTER 770 MAGNUM BOLT ACTION
In cals. 264, 7mm Rem. and 300 Win. (3-shot) Magnum. Same as the 770 except: rubber recoil pad, 24" bbl., 44½" over-all; wgt 7¼ lbs. 9" (264), 9½" (7mm) & 10" (300) twist................ **$154.95**

H WINSLOW BOLT ACTION RIFLES
FN Supreme actions, Douglas barrels, custom treatment of metal and wood in 3 stock types and in 7 grades. Made in all popular cartridges.
Regal Grade Plainsmaster, with more extensive checkering, roll-over comb, ivory and ebony inlays........................... **$390.00**
Regent, Regimental, Crown, Emperor and Imperial Grades in ascending order of carving, engraving and inlaying, to........... **$3,500.00**
Regal grade Varmint with Bushmaster stock in custom calibers 17/222, 17/222 Mag. and 17/223. Priced from............ **$430.00**
Extra, for magnum calibers **10.00**

[A] HARRINGTON & RICHARDSON 158 TOPPER RIFLE
Single shot, takedown, side lever break-open rifle. Auto. ejector. Walnut finished stock and fore-end; recoil pad. 22" bbl. Lyman folding adj. rear and ramp front sights. Wgt. 5¼ lbs., 37½" over-all. Cal. 30-30 ....$42.95
Extra interchangeable 20 ga., 26" Mod. choke shotgun bbl... 15.00

[B] CHALLENGER HOPKINS & ALLEN HERITAGE
Single shot, underhammer percussion muzzle loader. Straight grip walnut stock and fore-end. Curved buttplate, inset cap box and extended trigger guard of brass. 32" octagonal bbl., uniform or gain twist rifling. Blade front sight and both open and peep rear sights. Barrel and action blued. 8½ lbs. Cals. 36 or 45....................$99.95
Offhand Deluxe. Plain version of the Heritage........... 87.95

[C] CHALLENGER HOPKINS & ALLEN BUGGY CARBINE
Single shot, underhammer percussion muzzle loader. Straight grip walnut stock and fore-end, flat buttplate, 20" octagonal bbl. All metal parts blued. Blade front sight, open adj. rear. Wgt. 5½ lbs. Cals. 36 or 45..$84.95

CHALLENGER HOPKINS & ALLEN DEER STALKER
.58 Cal. muzzle loading underhammer percussion rifle. 32" octagonal bbl., 1 turn in 72", .575 bore uses .580 gr. slug. Wgt. approx. 9½ lbs. $139.95

CHALLENGER HOPKINS & ALLEN 45 TARGET
Single shot, underhammer percussion muzzle loader. Heavy 32" octagonal bbl., straight grip walnut stock. Blade front, open rear sight. Cal. 45 only...................................$84.95

[D] CHALLENGER HOPKINS & ALLEN MINUTEMAN
Muzzle-loading, Kentucky-style flintlock rifle. 39" octagonal bbl. brass-mounted stock of maple, walnut or cherry. 55" over-all. Cals. 36 or 45. ....$179.50
Same, except percussion ignition....................... 179.50

CHALLENGER HOPKINS & ALLEN OVER & UNDER RIFLE
Fire the first barrel and rotate the breech and the second barrel comes up ready to fire. Each barrel has its own set of sights targeted to the same point of impact. 45 cal. with walnut stock and crescent butt-plate. 28" blued octagonal barrels. 43" over-all. Wgt. 8½ lbs. $139.95

[E] RUGER NUMBER ONE SINGLE SHOT
Dropping block underlever action with internal hammer, selectable full ejector or extractor, tang safety. Trigger adj. for weight, travel, and overtravel. Two piece checkered walnut p.g. stock for scope use, with recoil pad. Choice of semi-beavertail or sporting fore-end. Sling swivels (on barrel band with sporting fore-end). Bbl. 26" (24" 375HH, 45-70 & 458). Barrel scope mount (1" rings) furnished, open sights an optional extra. Cals. 222, 22-250, 243, 6mm Rem., 270, 30-06, 7mm Rem. Mag. (7x57, 280, 264, 6.5 Rem. Mag., .300 Win Mag., 375H&H, 45-70 & 458 Mag. available on non-cancellable special order). 42" over-all (26" bbl.). Wgt. 7¾ to 8¼ lbs........$265.00
For gold bead front and folding leaf rear add $15.00.
For sporting fore-end add................................$ 20.00
Rifle in 375H&H, 458 Mag. & 47-50 with sights and sporting fore-end .,..$265.00

[F] SHARPS 78 SINGLE SHOT
Falling block underlever action with internal hammer; extract adaptable to any type cartridge rim (i.e. rimmed, semi-rimmed, rimless or belted). Breech block safety is selective from manual to automatic. Classic style lever interchanges with optional extra loop or continental (English) lever. Trigger is a combination single stage (adj. for pull, sear engagement and over-travel and set trigger. Single stage adjusts from a pull of 2 to 5 lbs., set adjusts from 4 oz. to ¼ oz. Choice of barrel lengths (26" to 36"), weights and contours. Tapped for scope mounts. Sights are an optional extra. Forearm available in two lengths and styles. Walnut stock with rubber butt plate is standard with optional extra choices of woods, cheekpieces, butt-plates and checkering. Cals. available from 17 through 50 with several new "Sharps" calibers plus old Sharps cals. in modern loads. Weighs from 6¾ lbs. to 16 lbs. (Std. unit with 30" No. 2 bbl. weighs about 7¾ to 8¼ lbs.).
Deluxe Grade I Std. or Lightweight.....................$295.00
Premier Grade II Std. or Lightweight................... 399.50
Custom grades from $495.00 to $5,000.00.

SHARPS GOLDEN SPIKE CENTENNIAL MODEL 78
A commemorative model (Series A) available in 50-70 cal. with 30" bbl. only. Features hand checkered fancy walnut stocks, engraved receiver and cartridge well traps, inlaid pistol grip caps. Priced Grade III, $495.00; Grade VI, $1,250.00 and Grade VIII, $2,500.00.

[G] TINGLE M-1962 MUZZLE LOADING TARGET RIFLE
A half-stock percussion target rifle of 36 or 44 cal., 52" twist. 32" octagon hook-breech bbl. is easily removed. Blade front and V notch adj. rear sight. One-piece walnut stock, concave cheekpiece, brass fittings. Double set triggers. Coil spring lock. Right or left hand models. Wgt. 10 lbs. 48" over-all..............................$129.95

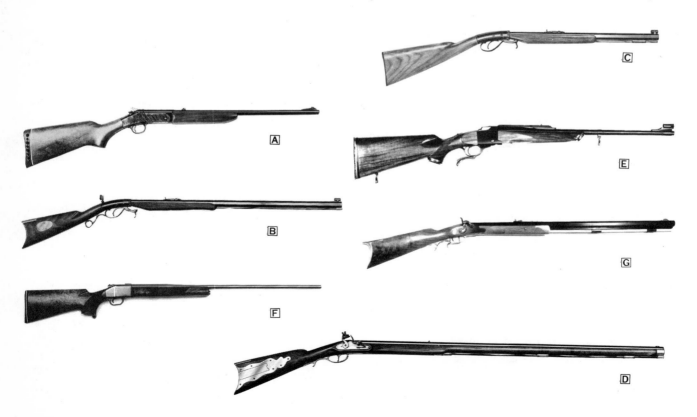

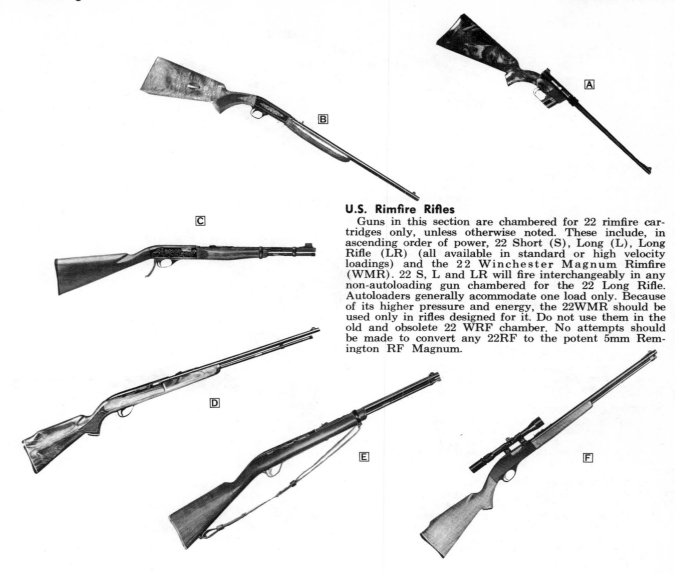

U.S. Rimfire Rifles

Guns in this section are chambered for 22 rimfire cartridges only, unless otherwise noted. These include, in ascending order of power, 22 Short (S), Long (L), Long Rifle (LR) (all available in standard or high velocity loadings) and the 22 Winchester Magnum Rimfire (WMR). 22 S, L and LR will fire interchangeably in any non-autoloading gun chambered for the 22 Long Rifle. Autoloaders generally acommodate one load only. Because of its higher pressure and energy, the 22WMR should be used only in rifles designed for it. Do not use them in the old and obsolete 22 WRF chamber. No attempts should be made to convert any 22RF to the potent 5mm Remington RF Magnum.

A ARMALITE AR-7 EXPLORER CARBINE

8-shot autoloading cal. 22 LR rifle. Wgt. 2¾ lbs., and floats. 16" alloy bbl. (steel lining), alloy receiver; moulded fiberglass stock houses barrel and action when disassembled. 16½" over-all when stowed. Peep rear and blade front sight. Over-all length, 34½" $49.95
   With walnut Monte Carlo cheekpiece stock. 64.50

B BROWNING AUTOLOADING RIFLE

Lightweight auto with tubular magazine in buttstock holding 11 LR cartridges, 19¼" barrel easily removed with fore-end. Checkered French walnut p.g. stock (13¾"x1³/₁₆"x2⅝") and semi-beavertail fore-end. Folding leaf rear sight; gold bead front sight. Engraved receiver grooved for scope mount. Wgt. 4¾ lbs., 37" over-all.
   Grade I . . . . $97.50   Grade II . . . . $145.00   Grade III $260.00
   Grade I available for 22 S cartridges, 22¼" barrel, mag. holds 16 rounds. Grooved receiver or left hand safety optional without cost.
Price $97.50

COLT COLTEER CARBINE

Autoloading rifle with 15-shot tubular magazine. Straight grip black walnut stock (13¾"x1⅝"x2¼") beavertail fore-end. 19½" bbl. with hooded gold bead front sight with notch rear adj. for w. and e. Receiver grooved for Tip-Off mount. Cross-bolt safety. Wgt. 4¾ lbs., 37" over-all. 22 LR only. $65.00

C COLT STAGECOACH CARBINE

Similar to Colteer except: 16½" bbl., 33¾" over-all. Scroll engraved receiver, with saddle ring. 22 LR only $75.00

D HI-STANDARD SPORT-KING DELUXE RIFLE

22 LR, L or S tubular autoloader. Mag. holds 15 LR, 17 L or 22 S. 22¼" round tapered barrel. Checkered p.g. stock with Monte Carlo comb, semi-beavertail fore-end. Open sights, slide safety. Wgt. 5½ lbs., over-all 42¾" $54.95

E HI-STANDARD SPORT-KING CARBINE

Same action as Sport-King Deluxe. 18¼" bbl. has bead post front and open rear sight. Western-style straight grip stock with sling swivels and brass buttplate. Tubular mag. holds 17 S, 14 L or 12 LR. Golden trigger guard, trigger and safety. Receiver grooved for scope mounts. Wgt. 5½ lbs., 38½" over-all. $54.95

F MARLIN 49 AUTOLOADING RIFLE

Based on the Marlin 99 action this rifle has a rustproof solid-top receiver, grooved for scope mounting, with a manual hold-open device (similar to the GI carbine) for cleaning and inspection. Bolt is engine-turned; trigger is gold plated. Tubular magazine holds 19 22 LR cartridges. Front ramp, step-adjustable open rear sights. Walnut stock with white-line spacers at grip cap and buttplate. 40½" over-all; weight, about 5½ lbs. 22 LR only. $59.95
   With Marlin 300 4x scope as illustrated. $65.00

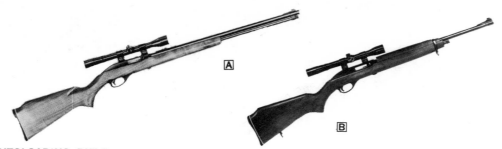

A MARLIN 99C AUTOLOADING RIFLE
19-shot auto rifle with tubular mag. 22" bbl. with open rear and hooded ramp front sights. Walnut Monte Carlo p.g. stock. Crossbolt safety. Tapped for receiver sights, grooved for Tip-Off mounts. 40½" over-all, wgt. 5½ lbs. Cal. 22 LR only....................$49.95
   With Marlin 300 4x scope as illustrated..................57.75

B MARLIN 99 M1 CARBINE
Same as the Marlin 99 rifle except: Walnut handguard with band; removable rear sight, ramp front cover; swivels. 18" barrel, 37" over-all, wgt. 4¾ lbs. 9-shot tubular magazine..................$49.95
   With Marlin 300 4x scope as illustrated..................57.75

MARLIN 989 M2 CARBINE
Clip magazine version of the Marlin 99 M1 Carbine. Cal. 22 LR. Two 7-shot clips....................$49.95
   With Marlin 300 4x scope............................57.75

C GLENFIELD 60 AUTOLOADER
19-shot tubular mag., 22-cal. auto rifle. 22" bbl., chrome-plated trigger. Receiver grooved for Tip-Off mounts. Monte Carlo stock of American hardwood. 22 LR only..........................$43.95

D MOSSBERG MODEL 350K RIFLE
Autoloading rifle with 7-shot, 3-way clip that handles 22 S, L or LR. Walnut p.g. stock with cheekpiece and Monte Carlo comb. 23½" "AC-KRO-GRUV" barrel. Sling swivels. Open rear sight, bead front. Tapped for peep sight, grooved for scope mount. Wgt. about 6 lbs., 43½" over-all. $48.95

E MOSSBERG MODEL 351K RIFLE
Autoloading rifle with one-piece walnut stock, Monte Carlo comb. Tubular magazine in buttstock holds 15 LR cartridges. Open rear and bead front sights. Receiver grooved for scope mount. 24" "AC-KRO-GRUV" barrel. Wgt. 6 lbs., 43" over-all. Cal. 22 LR only. Price $49.95

MOSSBERG MODEL 351C CARBINE
Same as Mossberg 351K except: 18½" bbl., bbl. band, sling swivels; wgt. 5½ lbs., 38½" over-all. $51.95

F MOSSBERG MODEL 352K CARBINE
Autoloading rifle with 18½" "AC-KRO-GRUV" barrel. 7-shot, 3-way clip handles 22 S, L or LR. Walnut pistol grip stock with Monte Carlo comb. Hinged moulded fore-end forming a 5" hand grip. Open rear and bead front sights. Sling on left side of stock. Grooved for scope mount. Wgt. 5 lbs., 38" over-all....................................$49.95

G MOSSBERG MODEL 430 RIFLE
Autoloading rifle with two piece walnut stock. Gold plated trigger and damascened bolt, top tang safety. Hand checkered, butt plate and p.g. cap with white liners. Open rear U-notch sight, gold bead front sight. Tubular magazine holds 18 22 LR cartridges. 24" bbl., grooved for scope mount. Wgt. 6¼ lb., 43½" over-all........$59.95

H MOSSBERG MODEL 432 WESTERN STYLE CARBINE
Identical to Model 430, but barrel is 4" shorter, grip is straight. Sling swivels, but no checkering. Magazine holds 15 22 LR cartridges. Wgt. 6 lb., 39½" over-all................................$54.95

A NOBLE 285 AUTO RIFLE
22-cal. autoloading rifle with round 22" bbl. Tubular mag. holds 15 LR. Walnut finish p.g. stock. Ramp front and adj. open rear sights. Top thumb safety. Receiver grooved for Tip-Off mount. Wgt. 5½ lbs. 40" over-all. **$39.95**

B REMINGTON 552A AUTO RIFLE
An autoloading rifle designed to "match" the Model 742 big game rifle in style and handling. Uses all 22 rimfires without adjustment; capacity 15 LR, 17 L or 20 S in tubular magazine. 23" barrel, full size walnut stock, Crossbolt safety with positive disconnection of hammer and trigger; spent case deflector fitted. Bead front and step-adjustable rear sights, receiver grooved for Tip-Off mount. Wgt. about 5¾ lbs., 42" over-all. **$64.95**
Model 552GS. Same as above except 22 Short only. **76.95**

REMINGTON 552 BDL AUTO RIFLE
Same as Model 552A except: p.g. cap, checkered grip and fore-end, ramp front and fully adjustable rear sights. RKW finish. **$74.95**

REMINGTON 552C CARBINE
Same as Model 552A except: 21" barrel, wgt. 5¼ lbs., 40" over-all. **$64.95**
Sling and swivels (installed). **7.50**

C REMINGTON NYLON 66 AUTO RIFLE
An ultra-lightweight autoloading rifle with moulded, checkered Mohawk Brown Nylon stock and diamond-inlaid fore-end. Tubular mag. in stock holds 14 LR. 19⅝" barrel. Open rear and blade front sights. Grooved for Tip-Off mount. Thumb safety on top of grip. Wgt. 4 lbs., 38½" over-all **$54.95**
With Apache Black stock, chromed bbl. and action. **59.95**
Model 66GS. Same as M66 except 22 Short only. **64.95**
Sling strap & swivels, installed. **5.40**

D REMINGTON MODEL 550 AUTOLOADER
Auto rifle, tubular mag. holds 22 S, 17 L, 15 LR interchangeably. Walnut p.g. stock. 24" round tapered barrel. Thumb safety. Receiver grooved for scope mounts. Wgt. 6¼ lbs. Open rear and bead front sights. Over-all 43½". Cal. 22 S, L, or LR. **$59.95**

E REMINGTON NYLON 77 RIFLE
Similar to Nylon 66, but with removable clip magazine that holds 5 22LR cartridges **$49.95**
Extra 5-shot clip. . . . .**$2.75**   Extra 10-shot clip. **3.50**

RUGER 10/22 AUTO CARBINE
22 LR carbine with a 10-shot rotary, detachable magazine that fits flush with the stock. Bolt hold-open latch. Crossbolt safety. American walnut stock. Receiver tapped for scope mounts. Ivory bead front sights, folding-leaf rear. 37" over-all, 18½" bbl., wgt. 5 lbs. **$54.50**

F RUGER 10/22 AUTO SPORTER
Same as 10/22 Carbine except: Sporter style Monte Carlo stock with straight buttplate, p.g. cap, fluted fore-end and sling swivels **$64.50**

G SAVAGE 60 AUTOLOADING RIFLE
20" bbl., top tang safety. Tubular magazine takes 15 22 LR ctgs. Checkered walnut Monte Carlo stock with semi-beavertail fore-end. Blade front sight with bead, open rear with step elevator. Receiver grooved for scope. 40½" over-all; wgt. about 6 lbs. **$59.50**

H SAVAGE 90 AUTOLOADING CARBINE
Tubular magazine takes 10 22 LR ctgs. 16½" bbl., Walnut Monte Carlo stock with sling swivels. Receiver grooved for scope. 37½" over-all; wgt. about 5¼ lbs. **$57.50**

A SEARS MODEL 3T AUTO RIFLE
Autoloading rifle with tubular magazine holding 21 S, 17 L or 15 LR. Shoots all three interchangeably. 20½" round bbl. 16" twist Crossbolt safety; burnished bolt handle, trigger and mag. cap. Walnut finished p.g. stock. Ramp front and step adjustable rear sights. Receiver grooved for scope mount. Wgt. 5 lbs., 39" over-all............**$46.99**

B SEARS TED WILLIAMS 3T AUTO
Same as 3T except: Magazine cap, bolt handle and trigger are nickel plated; fluted walnut stock, checkered p.g. and fore-end, p.g. cap; white line buttplate spacer......................**$75.00**

D STEVENS 88 AUTOLOADING RIFLE
Tubular magazine takes 15 22LR ctgs. 22" bbl., 40½" over-all; wgt. about 6 lbs. Top tang safety. Walnut finished hardwood stock with checkering. Receiver grooved for scope..............**$49.75**

E WEATHERBY MARK XXII RIFLE
A semi-automatic 22-cal. rifle with 24" contoured barrel. 3-leaf folding rear, ramp front sights. Walnut p.g. stock with Monte Carlo comb and cheekpiece, high polish finish. Rosewood p.g. cap and fore-end tip with white line spacers. Single pin release for quick takedown. Shotgun type safety on rear tang. Action can be converted to single shot by thumb-operated lever. Grooved for Tip-Off mount. 42½" over-all, wgt. 6 lbs. **$119.50**

F WESTERN FIELD MODEL 836 RIFLE
Autoloading rifle with tubular mag. holding 22 S, 17 L or 15 LR. Shoots all three interchangeably. 20" round bbl. Grooved for Tip-Off mount. One-piece walnut finished p.g. stock. Bead front and step adjustable rear sights. Flash shield over action port protects shooter. Thumb safety. 40" over-all.....................................**$45.95**

WESTERN FIELD MODEL 850 RIFLE
Autoloading rifle with 3-way clip hold 7 22 S, L or LR cartridges. 18½" bbl. Thumb operated safety. Bead front, step adjustable rear sights. Streamline walnut finished p.g. stock. 39" over-all....**$38.99**

G WESTERN FIELD MODEL 846 RIFLE
Autoloading rifle with tubular mag. holding 15 LR cartridges. 18½" round bbl. Crossbolt safety. Walnut finish p.g. stock and fore end. Plastic buttplate. Bead front and step adjustable rear sights. Wgt. 5¼ lbs. Caliber: 22 LR only. 38½" over-all. **$46.95**

H WINCHESTER 290 AUTO RIFLE
Autoloading rifle with tubular mag. holding 21 S, 17 L and 15 LR. 20½" bbl. (16" twist). With square post on ramp front and square notch adj. rear. Walnut finished p.g. stock and fore-end (13⅝"x1¾"x 2¾"). Receiver grooved for Tip-Off scope mounts. Cross lock safety in front of trigger guard. Engine turned bolt. 39" over-all, wgt. 5 lbs. Cal. 22 ....**$59.95**

WINCHESTER 290 DELUXE
Same as M290 except: Selected walnut stock with Monte Carlo comb (drop 2¼"), cheekpiece, white spacer, basket-weave checkering, swivels. Gold-plated trigger and safety. **$79.95**

WINCHESTER 190 AUTO RIFLE
Same as M290 except: No checkering, pistol grip cap or buttplate spacer **$49.95**
M190 auto carbine. Same as M190 Rifle, except with barrel band, swivels **$52.95**

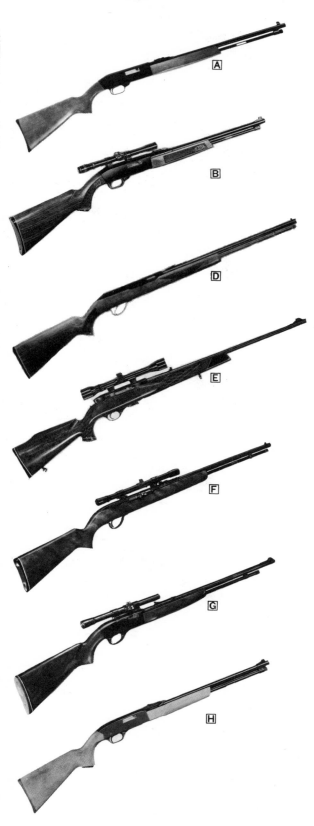

Bolt Action . . .

BROWNING T-BOLT T-1 REPEATING RIFLE
Straight pull, hinged bolt action rifle. 5-shot clip with single shot adapter. Thumb safety locks trigger and bolt. 22" bbl. Blade ramp front and fully adj. peep rear. Receiver grooved for Tip-Off mount. One-piece walnut p.g. stock (13½" x 1⁵⁄₁₆" x 3"). Wgt. 5½ lbs. 39¼" over-all. Available with either right-hand or left-hand bolt. Cal. 22 LR (S and L also, with single-shot adapter)......................**$62.50**

A BROWNING T-BOLT T-2 REPEATING RIFLE
Same as T-1 except: 24" bbl.; stock of figured walnut with checkered p.g. and fore-end; wgt. 6 lbs.; 41¼" over-all................**$84.50**

B HARRINGTON & RICHARDSON 865 PLAINSMAN RIFLE
5-shot clip mag. with exclusive ejector. Thumb safety 22" bbl. Monte Carlo stock in walnut finish. Open rear and blade front sight. Grooved for scope or rear peep sight. Bolt action. 39" over-all, wgt. 5 lbs. Cal. 22 S, L or LR.................................**$39.95**

C MARLIN 81-C RIFLE
Bolt action rifle. Tubular mag. holds 26 S or 18 LR. Thumb safety. 22" Micro-Groove bbl. Bead front sight. Walnut p.g. stock with Monte Carlo comb. Grooved for Tip-Off mount. Gold plated trigger. 40½" over-all, wgt. 6 lbs. Cal. 22 S, L or LR..................**$46.95**
  Marlin 300 4x20 scope..............................**13.95**

D MARLIN 80-C BOLT ACTION RIFLE
Bolt action rifle. Clip mag. version of the 81-C. 8-shots. Wgt. 5½ lbs. Cal. 22 S, L or LR..............................**$44.95**
  Marlin 300 4x20 scope..............................**13.95**

GLENFIELD 20 BOLT ACTION REPEATER
Similar to Marlin 80-C, except: Walnut finish stock, without Monte Carlo, conventional rifling..............................**$37.95**

E MARLIN 980 BOLT ACTION RIFLE
22 RF Magnum bolt action rifle. 8-shot clip mag. Thumb safety. 24" Micro-Groove alloy steel bbl. Open rear sight, ramp front sight with hood. Walnut p.g. stock, Monte Carlo comb. Swivels and leather carrying strap. Grooved for Tip-Off mount. Gold plated trigger. 43" over-all, wgt. 6 lbs.......................**$49.95**
  With Marlin 500 3x-7x Variable scope as illustrated........**61.00**

F MOSSBERG MODEL 342K CARBINE
Bolt action carbine with 3-way adjustable 7-shot clip. 18" "AC-KRO-GRUV" barrel, thumb safety. Walnut-finished p.g. stock, Monte Carlo comb. Hinged moulded fore-end forming a 5" hand grip. Adj. open rear and bead front sights. Sling on left side of stock. Grooved for scope mount. Wgt. 5 lbs. Over-all 38". Caliber S, L or LR......**$39.95**

MOSSBERG 340K RIFLE
Same as 342K Carbine except: 24" "AC-KRO-GRUV" bbl. Does not have hinged fore-end. Sling swivels. Tapped for peep sight. Wgt. 6½ lbs., 43½" over-all.................................**$39.95**

MOSSBERG 340B RIFLE
Same as Model 340K except has hooded ramp front sight with bead and aperture, and Mossberg S330 peep with ¼-minute clicks for w. and e. **$48.95**

MOSSBERG 340M SPORTER
Same as 342K, but with one-piece Mannlicher stock with Monte Carlo cheekpiece, p.g., butt plate with white spacer. Sling swivels and leather sling. Wgt. 5¼ lb., 38½" over-all..................**$54.95**

G MOSSBERG 346K RIFLE
Hammerless bolt action rifle with 24" "AC-KRO-GRUV" bbl. Tubular mag. holds 25 S or 18 LR. Thumb safety. Walnut finished p.g. stock with cheekpiece and Monte Carlo comb. Adjustable open rear sight, sporting Front. Grooved and tapped for scope or peep. Detachable sling swivels. Grooved for scope mount. 43½" over-all, wgt. 6½ lbs. **$44.95**

H MOSSBERG MODEL 640K CHUCKSTER
Hammerless bolt action rifle. Cal. 22 Magnum rimfire. 24" "AC-KRO-GRUV" barrel. Thumb safety and grooved trigger. Open rear and post front sight. Walnut p.g. stock with cheekpiece and Monte Carlo comb. Sling swivels. 5-shot clip. Wgt. 6 lbs., 44¾" over-all........**$49.95**

J MOSSBERG 640M MAGNUM
Hammerless bolt action rifle especially designed for the 22 WRF Magnum round. 5-shot detachable clip, double extractors, thumb operated safety, American walnut Mannlicher stock, hand checkered p.g. and fore-end. Sling swivels with leather sling. Adj. rear sight, bead front sight, receiver grooved for tip-off scope mounts. Front sight slot will accept Mossberg S320 hooded ramp sight, receiver drilled and tapped for Mossberg S330 receiver peep sight. Wgt. 6 lb., 40¾" over-all, bbl. 20" **$64.95**

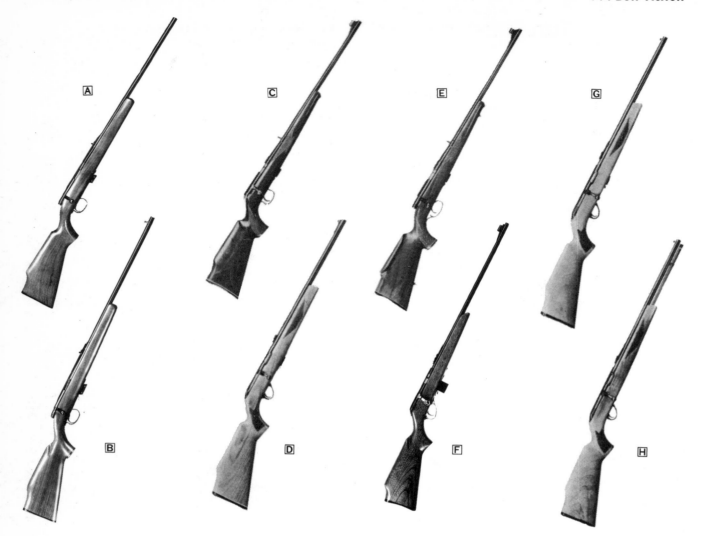

A REMINGTON 581 RIFLE

Bolt action, 5-shot box mag., with 24" bbl. Thumb safety, 6 locking lugs at rear of bolt. Receiver grooved for scope mounts. Bead front, screw adj. open rear sights. Full size Monte Carlo stock. 42⅜" over-all, wgt. 5¼ lbs. 22 S, L, LR............................**$49.95**
Sling swivels & strap, installed............................ **5.40**
Available in left hand model............................**54.95**

REMINGTON 582 RIFLE

Same as M581, except: tubular mag. under bbl. holds 20 S, 15 L, 14 LR. Wgt. 5½ lbs. **$54.95**

B REMINGTON 591 RIFLE

Bolt action rifle especially designed for the powerful 5mm Remington Rimfire Magnum round. Bolt completely encases cartridge case head, two stage extraction, six heavy rotary locking lugs, plus extra fast lock time, make this the strongest rimfire action currently produced. Side safety, receiver grooved for scope mounts. Plastic grip cap carries maker's name and caliber. Dovetail bead sight in front and adjustable rear sight can be removed. 4-shot clip, wgt. 5½ lb. 42⅜" over-all **$64.95**

REMINGTON 592 RIFLE

Identical to the Model 591, except for tubular magazine that holds 10 5mm Remington Rimfire Magnum rounds...................**$69.95**
Extra clip for M591....**$3.50**   Sling and swivels installed... **5.40**

C SAVAGE 164 BOLT ACTION RIFLE

4-shot clip mag. with a 24" bbl. Single stage adjustable trigger. Hand checkered walnut stock with cheekpiece and schnabel fore-end. Receiver grooved for scope. 42" over-all; wgt. 6 lbs. Chambered for 22 LR only...**$89.95**
Also in cal. 22 RF Magnum (4-shot mag.) as the 164M..... **95.00**

D SAVAGE 65 RIFLE

Bolt action rifle, cal. 22 S, L or LR; 5-shot clip, 20" lightweight bbl. Thumb safety locks trigger. Recessed bolt face, double extractors. Monte Carlo walnut stock. Ramp front sight, open rear sight with elevator; grooved for scope mount. Wgt. 5 lbs. 39" over-all.....**$46.50**
Available chambered for 22 WMR as 65M................. **49.50**

E SAVAGE ANSCHUTZ 54 SPORTER

Bolt action 5-shot repeater based on the Match 54 action. Detachable magazine. Trigger adjustable for weight of pull and travel. Wing safety locks firing pin and bolt. 22½" barrel. Front sight hooded bead on ramp, rear adj. folding leaf, receiver grooved and tapped for scope. Checkered French walnut p. g. stock, with roll-over comb, schnabel fore-end, sling swivels. 22 LR only. Wgt. 6¾ lbs.....**$150.00**

F SEARS MODEL 2 RIFLE

Bolt action rifle with 6-shot clip, independent thumb safety. 20¾" bbl., gold bead front sight, open rear sight. Monte Carlo fluted comb p.g. stock, walnut finished. Sling swivels. Receiver grooved for scope mount. Wgt. 5 lbs., 40" over-all. Cal. 22 S, L or LR............**$36.99**
Available chambered for 22 WRM as Model 2M............. **40.79**
With tubular mag. holding 19 S, 15 L, or 13 LR as Model 27.. **39.99**

G STEVENS 34 RIFLE

Bolt action 22 rifle, 5-shot clip, floating bbl., thumb safety. Recessed bolt face. Fluted comb stock with full pistol grip; corrugated buttplate. Open rear, post front sights. 4¾ lbs., 20" bbl. 39" over-all. **$39.75**
Available chambered for 22 WMR as 34M................. **44.50**

H STEVENS 46 RIFLE

Tubular magazine bolt action 22 rifle; capacity, 22 S, 17 L, 15 LR. Otherwise same as M34...................................**$44.50**

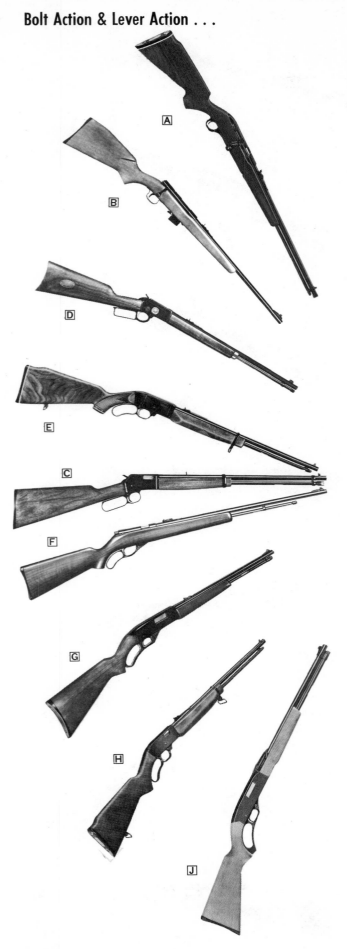

A WESTERN FIELD MODEL 842 RIFLE
Bolt action repeating rifle with tubular mag. holding 25 S or 18 LR. Thumb safety. 24" round bbl. Walnut p.g. stock with Monte Carlo comb; buttplate with white line spacer. Bead front and step adjustable open rear sights. Grooved for Tip-Off mount. Weight 6¼ lbs., 43½" over-all. Caliber: 22 S, L, LR...................................$39.99

WESTERN FIELD MODEL 830 BOLT ACTION RIFLE
Same as Model 842 except 7-shot clip mag. Wgt. 6 lbs. $33.99

WESTERN FIELD MODEL 822 BOLT ACTION RIFLE
Same as Model 830 except chambered for the 22 RF Magnum cartridge. 5-shot clip mag. Sling swivels furnished. 44¾" over-all..$42.99

B WINCHESTER 131 BOLT ACTION REPEATER
Seven-shot mag., walnut finish Monte Carlo stock (13½"x1½"x2½"). Red cocking and safety indicators. Bead-post front sight on ramp, adj. rear. Wgt. 5 lbs. 40" over-all, 20¾" barrel. 22 S, L, and LR.
....$39.95

WINCHESTER 141 BOLT ACTION REPEATER
Similar to 131, except tubular magazine in stock, holds 19 shorts, 15 longs, 13 long rifles...................................$44.95

C BROWNING BL-22 LEVER ACTION RIFLE
Tubular magazine holds 22S, 17L or 15LR. Visible Hammer. 20" bbl. Short throw lever travels through an arc of only 33 degrees and carries trigger with it. Disconnect system prevents firing until lever and breech are fully closed. Walnut straight stock and fore-end. Adj. folding leaf rear and raised bead front sights. Receiver grooved for rifle scope. 36¾" over-all, wgt. 5 lbs. Grade I..........$74.50
Same, except Grade II with gold plated trigger, hand engraved receiver with scroll design...................................$92.50

ITHACA 49R SADDLEGUN REPEATER
Lever action carbine with 20" bbl., tubular mag. Cal. 22LR only. Checkered walnut stock, open sights (rear adj. for w. & e.). Rebounding hammer safety, mag. cap. 15 LR. Wgt. 5½ lbs., over-all 37½" $59.95

D MARLIN 39 CENTURY LTD. CARBINE
This commemorative version of the Model 39 is offered only during 1970 to mark company's 100th anniversary. Western-style lever action carbine with squared-off lever, tubular magazine holds 21 Shorts, 16 Longs, 15 Long Rifle cartridges. 20" tapered octagon Micro-Groove barrel with adjustable semi-buckhorn rear and brass bead front sight. Selected American walnut stock and fore-end, butt plate, fore-end cap and engraved name plate in stock are cartridge brass. Centennial medallion is inlaid in receiver. Drilled and tapped for receiver sights and scope mounts, scope adapter base and offset hammer spur included. 24K gold-plated trigger. Wgt. 6 lb., 36" over-all......$125.00

E MOSSBERG 402 PALOMINO CARBINE
Hammerless lever action carbine with tubular magazine (20 S, 15 L, 13 LR). Walnut Monte Carlo stock, beavertail fore-end. Receiver has removable sideplate; non-glare top finish, grooved for scope mounts. Open rear and bead front sights. 20" round bbl. Grooved trigger. Wgt. 4¾ lbs., 36½" over-all. Cal. 22 S, L or LR.................$63.95

F NOBLE 275 LEVER ACTION RIFLE
Hammerless, tubular magazine repeater rifle (21 S, 15 LR) with one-piece walnut stock (13½"x1¾"x2¾"), serrated hard rubber buttplate. Short-throw lever, visible straight-line loading. Thumb safety. Patridge type ramp front sight. Open notch rear adj. for elevation. Receiver grooved for Tip-Off scope mount. 24" bbl., 42" over-all, wgt. about 5½ lbs. Cal. 22...................................$49.95

G SEARS MODEL 5 LEVER ACTION RIFLE
Hammerless repeating lever action rifle with tubular magazine holding 21 S and 15 LR ctgs., interchangeably. Receiver grooved for Tip-Off mounts. Cross-bolt safety in front of trigger guard. Walnut finished hardwood p.g. stock. Nickel trigger. Tapered post front sight on ramp; notch rear adj.: for elevation. 20½" bbl., 16" twist, 39" over-all, wgt. about 5 lbs. Cal. 22...................................$55.99

H WESTERN FIELD MODEL 865 CARBINE
A short-throw, lever action carbine with tubular magazine holding 20 S, 15 L or 13 LR. 20" round tapered barrel. Walnut finished p.g. stock with Monte Carlo comb; beavertail fore-end; sling swivels and barrel band. Bead front and step adjustable open rear sights. Wgt. 4¾ lbs., 36½" over-all...................................$53.95

J WINCHESTER 250 RIFLE
Lever action rifle with tubular magazine (21 S, 17 L or 15 LR). 20½" bbl., 1 in 16" twist; square post front sight on ramp and square notch adj. rear. Walnut finished p.g. stock and fore-end (13⅝"x1¾"x2¾"). Receiver grooved for Tip-Off scope mounts. Cross lock safety in front of trigger guard. Trigger disconnects when lever is moved. Engine turned bolt. Cal. 22, 39" over-all, wgt. 5 lbs. $61.95
Same, except M255, cal. 22 WRM, 11-shot...............71.95

WINCHESTER 250 DELUXE
Same as M250 except: Selected walnut stock with Monte Carlo comb (drop 2¼"), cheekpiece, white spacer, basket-weave checkering, swivels; gold-plated trigger and safety $81.95
Same, except M255 DL, cal. 22 WRM, 11 shot............89.95

WINCHESTER 150 LEVER ACTION CARBINE
Same as M250 except straight stock (no p.g.), no checkering or spacers. With barrel band and swivels......................$55.95

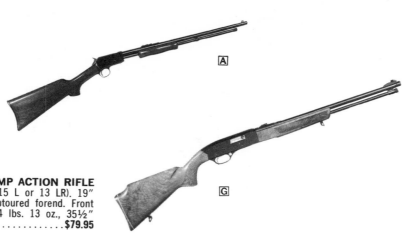

A HARRINGTON & RICHARDSON 749 PUMP ACTION RIFLE

Tubular magazine 22 cal. slide action (18 S, 15 L or 13 LR). 19" bbl. Walnut finished carbine style stock with contoured forend. Front dovetail blade and read adjustable sights. Wgt. 4 lbs. 13 oz., 35½" over-all. **$79.95**

B HI-STANDARD SPORT-KING RIFLE

Tubular magazine 22 cal. slide action rifle with side-loading port, holds 24 S, 19 L or 17 LR. Checkered Monte Carlo stock, semi-beavertail grooved fore-end. Steel-to-steel breech lock-up. Receiver grooved for Tip-Off mount, 24" barrel. 5½ lbs., 41¾" over-all. **$64.95**

C NOBLE 235 PUMP RIFLE

Slide action rifle with tubular magazine (21 S or 15 LR). Hammerless. Thumb safety. 24" bbl. Walnut p.g. stock (13½"x1¾"x2¾") and grooved slide handle. Open rear sight adj. for elevation, bead front sight on ramp. Receiver grooved for Tip-Off mount. Wgt. 5½ lbs., 42" over-all. Cal. 22 S or LR. **$45.95**

D REMINGTON 572 FIELDMASTER PUMP RIFLE

Solid frame, slide action rifle. Tubular magazine holds 20 S or 14 LR, removes to convert to single shot. Streamlined hammerless action. 24" bbl. Cross-bolt safety. Genuine walnut p.g. stock, grooved slide handle. Open rear and bead front sights. Grooved for Tip-Off mount. Wgt. 5½ lbs. 42" over-all. Cal. 22 S, L or LR. **$64.95**
Model 572 BDL Same as the 572 except: p.g. cap, RKW finish, checkered grip and fore-end, ramp front and fully adjustable rear sights. **$74.95**
Model 572 SB Similar to the 572, but has smoothbore bbl. choked for 22 LR shot cartridges. **$74.95**
Sling and swivels, installed. **7.50**

F WINCHESTER 270 PUMP ACTION

Slide action hammerless rifle with tubular magazine; holds 21 S, 17 L and 15 LR. Grooved for Tip-Off mount. Square post front sight on ramp; square notch rear adj. for w. and e. Cross lock safety on trigger guard. Engine turned bolt. 20½" bbl., 1 in 16" twist. Walnut finished hardwood stock (13⅝"x1¾"x2¾") with checkered fore-end. 39" over-all, wgt. 5 lbs. Cal. 22 S, L or LR. **$64.95**
Same, except M275, cal. 22 WRM, 11 shot. **71.95**

G WINCHESTER 270 DELUXE

Same as M270 except: Selected walnut stock with Monte Carlo comb (drop 2¼"), cheekpiece, white spacer, basket-weave checkering, swivels; gold-plated trigger and safety. **$84.95**
Same, except M275 DL, cal. 22 WRM, 11 shot. **89.95**

H BRONCO 22 RIFLE

Ultra lightweight single shot 22 featuring a swing-out chamber, skeletonized 1-pc. receiver and p.g. stock, push-button safety. Wgt. 3½ lbs. **$15.95**

J HARRINGTON & RICHARDSON 750 PIONEER

Single shot rifle. Self cocking bolt with cocking indicator. "Fluid-Feed" loading platform. Thumb safety 22" bbl. Open rear and blade front sights. Grooved for scope or rear peep sight. Monte Carlo stock in walnut finish. Wgt. 5 lbs., 39" over-all. Cal. 22 S, L or LR. . . .**$28.95**

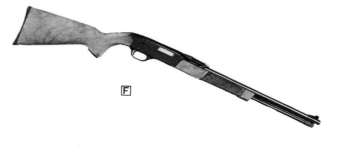

A HARRINGTON & RICHARDSON 755 SAHARA
Single shot rifle with automatic extraction, ejection and cocking. 18″ bbl. with protected front and adj. rear sight. Thumb safety. Mannlicher style, walnut finish p.g. stock with Monte Carlo comb. Wgt. 4 lbs., 36″ over-all. Cal. 22 S, L or LR...............$28.95

B HARRINGTON & RICHARDSON 760 RIFLE
Same as Sahara except: Blade dovetail front sight; Monte Carlo half-length stock; wgt. 4 lbs...............$23.95

C ITHACA 49 SADDLEGUN
Single shot, lever action (Martini type) for 22 S, L, LR. Rebounding hammer safety, 18″ button rifled bbl. Walnut stock and fore-end. Wgt. about 5½ lbs., over-all 34½″...............$29.95
Ithaca 49 Saddleguns are also available in a shortened stock, boy's model at $26.95, chambered for the 22 RF Magnum at $34.95; with a finely figured walnut stock; sling and swivels at $39.95; with extra fancy figured walnut stock with gold-shield inlay; owner's name engraved at no extra charge; receiver is hand engraved by Ithaca's master engraver; gold-plated hammer and trigger, for $150.00; or the same in 22 RF Magnum, $150.00

D MARLIN 101 SINGLE SHOT RIFLE
Single shot bolt action rifle. 22″ Micro-Groove bbl. Walnut finished p.g. stock with Monte Carlo comb. Adjustable rear and bead front sights. Grooved for Tip-Off mount. Cocking piece must be pulled before rifle can be fired. White line spacers. 40″ over-all, wgt. 4½ lbs. Cal. 22 S, L or LR...............$29.95
Marlin 275 4x20 scope...............10.00

E GLENFIELD MODEL 10 RIFLE
Similar to the Marlin 101 except standard walnut finish pistol grip stock...............$26.95

F MOSSBERG M320B RIFLE
Hammerless, single shot, bolt action rifle with 24″ AC-KRO-GRUV bbl. Auto. thumb safety. Walnut finished stock with Monte Carlo comb. Hooded ramp front with bead and aperture, and peep rear with ¼-minute clicks for w. and e...............$39.95

G NOBLE MODEL 222 SINGLE SHOT RIFLE
Single shot bolt action rifle, designed for young shooters. Barrel and receiver made from one piece of steel. Must be manually cocked after bolt is closed. 22″ round bbl.; peep rear sight, interchangeable with V-notch, adj. for w. & e. Walnut finished stock. 13¾″ x 1½″ x 2⅝″). Weight about 5 lbs., 38″ over-all. Cal. 22 S, L or LR...............$22.50

H REMINGTON 580 SINGLE SHOT RIFLE
Single shot bolt action 22-cal. rifle. American walnut stock, 24″ bbl. with bead front sight, adj. open rear. 6 rear-located locking lugs. Automatic thumb safety. Double extractors. Receiver grooved for Tip-Off mount. Wgt. 5 lbs., 42⅜″ over-all...............$39.95

REMINGTON 580 SB
Same as 580 except smoothbore bbl...............$44.95

J REMINGTON MODEL 514 SINGLE SHOT RIFLE
Single shot bolt action, handles 22 Shorts, Longs, and Long Rifle cartridges. 24″ bbl., rear sight adjustable for elevation, front sight for windage. Rotary safety on rear of bolt. Walnut finished hunting-type stock with corrugated butt plate. Wgt. 4½ lb., 41″ over-all. $26.95
Model 514BR, same rifle as Model 514, but stock is 1″ shorter for young shooter...............$26.95
Sling swivels installed, leather sling...............5.40

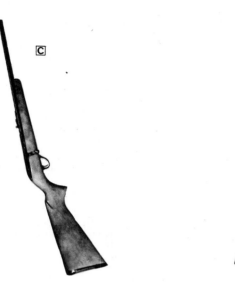

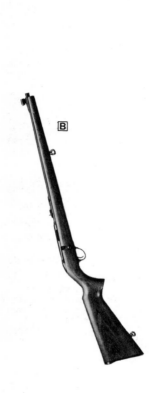

A CHALLENGER 2268 FRONTIERSMAN RIFLE
Single shot lever action (Martini type) for 22S, L or LR. Positive lock hammer safety, 18" bbl., walnut finish stock and fore-end. Wgt. approx. 5½ lbs., 34" over-all. Blade front & adj. notch rear sights. Blued finish **$29.95**
Also available in 22RF Magnum (M2269) **$34.95**; with gold plated hammer & trigger in 22S, L or LR (M2271) **$34.95**; or in 22RF Magnum (M2272) **$39.95.**

B SAVAGE 63K BOLT ACTION CARBINE
Bolt action single shot rifle with a 18" tapered bbl. Cocks on opening. Automatic safety. Bolt lugs lock in bbl. extension. One-piece, full length, walnut finish stock with sling swivels and corrugated butt-plate (14" pull). Hooded ramp front and open rear sight with adj. for elevation. Grooved for Tip-Off mount. Wgt. 4 lbs., 36" over-all. Cal. 22 S, L or LR...**$32.50**
Also available chambered for the 22 RF Magnum as the 63M. **35.50**

C SEARS MODEL 1 SINGLE SHOT RIFLE
Bolt action self-cocking rifle, with cocking indicator automatic thumb safety, bead front sight, adj. rear. Walnut finished birch p.g. stock. 20¾" bbl., 40" over-all, wgt. 5 lbs. Receiver grooved for scope mount. Cal. 22...**$23.99**

D STEVENS 73 RIFLE
Single shot bolt action 22 rifle. Safety goes on automatically when bolt is opened. 20" bbl., 14" buttstock; wgt. 4¾ lbs., 38½" over-all. Walnut-finished p.g. stock. Cal. 22 S, L or LR............**$25.50**
Available as Youth's Model, **73Y**, with 12½" stock........ **25.50**

E WESTERN FIELD MODEL 815 RIFLE
Hammerless bolt action single shot rifle. 24" round bbl. with 8-groove rifling. Automatic safety; straight line loading platform. Walnut finished p.g. stock with Monte Carlo comb; 13" pull. Bead front and step adj. rear sight; receiver-grooved for scope mount. Weight 5¾ lbs., 43½" over-all..**$22.94**

F WINCHESTER 121 BOLT ACTION RIFLE
Single shot. Safety engages automatically when bolt is lifted. Red cocking indicator. Receiver grooved for scope mounts. Semi-Monte Carlo, walnut-finished stock 13½"x1½"x2½". Bead front, adj. rear sights. Wgt. 5 lbs., 40" long, 20¾" barrel. 22 S, L, LR........**$25.95**

WINCHESTER 121 BOLT ACTION YOUTH RIFLE
Similar to 121 Standard, but with stock 12¼"x1½"x2¼", 38¾" over-all. Wgt. 5 lbs. 22 S, L. LR...........................**$25.95**

WINCHESTER 121 BOLT ACTION DELUXE RIFLE
Similar to 121 Standard except: fluted comb, ramp front sight, sling swivels, deluxe trigger mechanism. 22 S, L, LR..............**$29.95**

A ANSCHUTZ 1411 MATCH 54 RIFLE

Bolt action single shot target rifle. Bbl. 27½"x¹⁵⁄₁₆" dia. Polished action has double locking lugs. Wing type safety locks both bolt and firing pin. Short firing pin travel. Adj. trigger. French walnut prone-style American stock with Monte Carlo comb, cast-off cheekpiece. Checkered p.g., adj. rubber buttplate. Beavertail fore-end has swivel rail and adj. swivel. Receiver grooved for micro. sights. Bases for globe front sight and target scopes. Wgt. 11 lbs. 46" over-all. Cal. 22 LR. No sights **$172.50**
   Left hand stocked model without sights...............**185.00**

B ANSCHUTZ 1413 SUPER MATCH 54 RIFLE

Same as the 1411 Match except: International type stock with thumb-hole. Adj. palm shelf on p.g. Aluminum Schutzen hook buttplate with horizontal, vertical and lateral adjustments. New yoke-type adj. palm rest. Wgt. 15½ lbs., 50" over-all. Without sights.......**$340.00**
   Left hand stocked model without sights.................**$355.00**

D ANSCHUTZ 1407 MATCH 54 TARGET RIFLE

Very similar to M1411, except: Built to meet International Shooting Union standard rifle requirements. Wgt. 10 lbs. with sights; 26" hand-lapped bbl., ⅞" diam., adj. 500 gram (1.1 lb.) trigger, with replacement spring to convert to 3 lb. pull. Rubber buttplate, adj. vertically. Receiver grooved for Anschutz micrometer sight (adaptable to Redfield International and Olympic). Checkered fore-end and pistol grip. Without sights. Cal. 22 LR only......................**$172.50**
   Left hand stocked model, without sights.................**185.00**

E SAVAGE ANSCHUTZ 64 MATCH RIFLE

Bolt action single shot target rifle. Bbl. 26"x¹¹⁄₁₆" dia. Bases for front sight and target scopes. Action grooved for micro. sights. Slide safety, adj. trigger. Monte Carlo stock with cheekpiece and deeply fluted, high comb. Contoured checkered p.g., adj. rubber buttplate. Beavertail fore-end has swivel rail and adj. swivel. Wgt. 7¾ lbs., 44" over-all. Cal. 22 LR rimfire. Without sights...................**$79.95**
   Left hand stocked model without sights...................**89.95**
F M64-S, with Redfield Olympic sight **$105.00**; left hand model **$115.00** 7 lb. M64 may be ordered, at the same price, to conform with Canadian match regulations or for those who desire a lighter rifle.

SAVAGE ANSCHUTZ MARK 10 TARGET RIFLE

Similar to M 64 except: bbl. 26"x¹³⁄₁₆" dia. Walnut-finished stock with cheekpiece, thumb groove, adj. fore-end hand stop and swivel. Fixed buttplate, no blocks for target scope. Wgt. 8½ lbs. Right hand only. Price **$75.00**

ANSCHUTZ Optional Sight Equipment

International micro. sight (¼-minute click) adj. for w. and e.; slide-on bases fit receiver grooves, adj. for eye relief; interchangeable 1.1mm and 1.2mm peep sight discs. Price $41.80. Rubber eyeshade, slips onto peep sight disc, price $1.80. Globe protects front sight and controls light (sight inserts not included), $9.00. Front sight post-type inserts, set of 5, $1.65; aperture-type, set of 10, $3.30. Complete front and rear sight set includes all items above plus mounting tool..**$49.75**

G MOSSBERG 144-LS TARGET RIFLE

Bolt action, 7-shot clip. Thumb safety. 26" heavy bbl. Walnut p.g. target type stock with cheekpiece and high comb. Adj. trigger. Mossberg S-331 ¼-minute rear and Lyman 17A front sights. Grooved for Tip-Off mounts. Sling swivels, adj. hand stop. Wgt. 8 lbs., 43" over-all. Cal. 22 LR **$64.95**

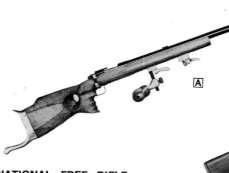

[A] REMINGTON INTERNATIONAL FREE RIFLE

Single shot; 27¼" heavy bbl., 40-XB action. Semi-finished walnut laminated stock enables shooter to finish to individual needs. Adj. hook buttplate and palm rest. Front sling swivel. 2 oz. adj. trigger. Wgt. about 15 lbs. Chambered for 222 Rem., 222 Rem. Mag., 22-250, 223 Rem., 6mm Rem., 6mm Int., 6mmx47, 6.5mm Rem. Mag., 7mm Rem. Mag., 7.62 Nato, 30-06, 30-338, 300 Win. Mag., 22 LR. Other cals, to special order..**$365.00**
    With left hand stock **390.00**

REMINGTON 40-XB RANGEMASTER TARGET Rimfire

Bolt action single shot. Loading platform gives straight-line feed. Trigger click adj. for weight of pull. 28" standard or heavy bbl. Walnut p.g. stock with high comb and beavertail fore-end. Adj. swivel base and removable fore-end stop. Redfield Olympic receiver and front sights. Scope blocks. Cal. 22 LR only. Wgt. without sights: Standard, 10 lbs.; Heavy, 12 lbs. 50½" over-all. Either model, no sights.......**$184.95**
    With Redfield sights **219.95**

[B] REMINGTON 40-XB RANGEMASTER TARGET Centerfire

Same as 40-XB Rimfire except: 27¼" bbl., chambered for 222, 222 Mag., 223, 22-250 (14" twist); 6x47mm, 6mm International (12" twist); 6mm Rem. (10" or 12" twist); 6.5mm Rem. Mag., 7mm Rem. Mag. (9" twist); 7.62 Nato 30-06, 30-338, 300 Win. Mag. (10" twist). 2-ounce trigger, $40 extra. Wgt. 11¼ lbs. Heavy, 9¾ lbs. Standard. Single shot. **$235.00**
    Factory accuracy requirements (MOA): 222, 222 Mag., 223—.45; 22-250, 6x47mm—.55; 6mm Int., 6mm Rem.—.60; 6.5x55mm—.70; 7mm Mag., 7.62—.75; 30-06, 30-338—1.00. 300 Win. Mag.—not available.
    Repeating model (5-shot, clip slots) in 222, 222 Rem. Mag., 223, 6x47mm, 6mm Int., 6mm Rem., 22-250, 7.62................**$255.00**
    Extra for stainless steel bbls.......................... **20.00**

[C] REMINGTON 540X MATCH TARGET RIFLE

Bolt action, single shot; 22LR; 26" bbl.; wgt. 8 lbs., 2 oz. Thumb safety; tapped for iron sights, scope mounts, rear sight bracket. Stock has 12¾" to 15½" pull, 4-way adj. butt-plate & thumb cuts. ....**$ 99.95**
    With Redfield No. 63 front & 75 rear sights.............. **119.95**
    For sling strap with front swivel block assembly installed add   **6.95**

[D] WINCHESTER 52D BOLT ACTION TARGET RIFLE

Cal. 22 LR, single shot. No sights, tapped for front sight base and receiver sight; scope blocks fitted. Walnut target stock with full length accessory channel and adj. bedding device (13⅝"x¼"x¾" with std. wgt. bbl., from line of bore). Non-slip rubber butt pad. Choice of 28" std. wgt. (9¾ lbs.) or heavy bbl. (11 lbs.) 46" over-all.......**$167.95**

WINCHESTER 52D BARRELED ACTIONS

No stock or sights. Receiver and bbl. tapped for blocks. Standard or heavy bbl. **$130.50**

[E] WINCHESTER MODEL 70 TARGET RIFLE

Marksman walnut stock with high comb, beavertail fore-end; (13¼"x ½"x⅞" from line of bore), adj. front swivel base, aluminum hand stop. No sights; scope bases mounted on bbl. Tapped for front sight base and receiver sight. Serrated rubber butt pad. Clip slot in receiver. Cal. 308, 30-06, 5-shot, 10¼ lbs., 24" free-floating heavy bbl., (10" twist), 44½" over-all.................................**$229.95**

[F] WINCHESTER 52 INTERNATIONAL MATCH RIFLE

Single shot in 22LR. 44½" over-all; 28" heavy bbl., wgt. 13½ lbs. 1 in 16" twist. Features adj. hand stop and trigger. Receiver tapped for sights and scope bases, scope blocks are included, sling attachment. Laminated thumb-hole stock with butt plate assembly complete with hook and rubber butt-plate. Adj. for cant, horizontal and vertical movement. Has full length accessory track. Aluminum trigger guard with trigger adj. holes. Palm rest assembly, fore-end stop assembly with felt base, detachable swivel and clamping bar.
....**$350.00**
    With Kenyon Trigger, installed........................ **385.00**

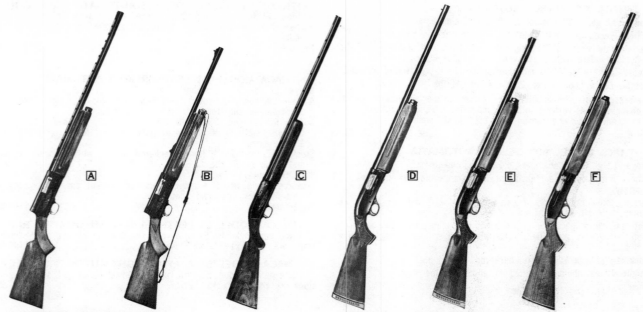

A BROWNING AUTO-5 Standard
Gauge: 12 only (5-shot; 3-shot plug furnished). 2¾″ chambers.
Action: Recoil operated autoloader; takedown; extra bbls. interchange without factory fitting; mag. cut-off; cross-bolt safety (left-hand available).
Barrel: 26″ (Cyl., Imp. Cyl.); 28″ (Mod., Full); 30″, 32″. (Full). Matted top, medium bead sight.
Stock: 14¼″x1⅝″x2½″. French walnut, hand checkered half-pistol grip and fore-end.
Weight: 7¾ to 8¼ lbs., depending on barrel.
Features: Receiver hand engraved with scroll designs and border; double extractors; bbl. and guide ring forged together.
Price: . . . . $194.50   With vent. rib $209.50

Browning Auto-5 Light 12, 20 and Sweet 16
Same as Std. Auto-5 except: 26″ bbls. (Skeet boring in 12 & 20 ga., Cyl., Imp. Cyl., Mod. in 16 and 20 ga.); 28″ bbls. (Skeet in 12 ga., Full in 16 ga., Mod., Full); 30″ (Full in 12 ga.). Gold plated trigger. Wgt. 12 ga. 7¼ lbs., 16 ga. 6¾ lbs., 20 ga. 6⅜ lbs. $204.50
Price: With vent. rib. Wgt. 12 ga. 7½ lbs., 16 ga. 6⅞ lbs., 20 ga. 6½ lbs. $219.50

Browning Auto-5 Magnum 12
Same as Std. Auto-5 except: chambered for 3″ magnum shells (also handles 2¾″ magnum and 2¾″ HV loads). 28″ Mod., Full; 30″ and 32″ (Full) bbls. 14″x1⅝″x2½″ stock. Recoil pad. Wgt. 8¾ lbs.
Price: . . . . $207.50   With vent. rib. Wgt. 9 lbs. . . .$222.50

Browning Auto-5 Magnum 20
Same as Magnum 12 except barrels 28″ Full or Mod., or 26″ Full, Mod. or Imp. Cyl. 7 lbs. $207.50
With ventilated rib, 7½ lbs. 222.50

B Browning Auto-5 Buck Special
Same as Std. A-5 except: 24″ bbl. choked for slugs, gold bead front sight on contoured ramp, rear sight adj. for w.&e. Wgt. (12 ga.) 7⅝ lbs.
Price: $207.50
Browning Auto-5 Light 12, 16, 20 or 12 Buck Special
Same as Std. Buck Special except: with gold trigger and of less weight. Wgt. 12 ga. 7 lbs.; 16 ga., 6⅜ lbs.; 20 ga., 6 lbs. 2 oz.; 3″ Magnum 12, 8¼ lbs.
Price: $217.50
All Buck Specials are available with carrying sling, detachable swivels and swivel attachments for $6.00 extra.

Browning Auto-5 Standard Trap
Same as the Auto-5 Standard except: Stock (14⅜″x1⅜″x1¾″), 30″ vent. rib bbl. (Full). Wgt. 8¼ lbs. $209.50

Browning Auto-5 Light Trap
Same as Standard Trap except: Wgt. 7¾ lbs. $219.50

Browning Auto-5 Light Skeet
Same as Light Standard except: 12 and 20 ga. only, 26″ or 28″ bbl. (Skeet). Wgt. 6¼-7¼ lbs. $204.50
With vent. rib. Wgt. 6⅜-7½ lbs. 219.50

C BROWNING DOUBLE AUTOMATIC
Gauge: 12 only (2-shot).
Action: Short recoil autoloader; takedown. Trigger guard safety.
Barrel: Twelvette: 26″ (Mod., Imp. Cyl., Cyl., or Skeet); 28″ (Mod., Skeet and Full); 30″ (Full). Twentyweight: 26½″ (all chokes).
Stock: Hunting and Skeet, 14¼″x1⅝″x2½″. Trap, 14⅜″x1⅜″x1¾″. French walnut, hand checkered, full p.g.
Weight: Twelvette, 6⅞ lbs.; Twentyweight, 6 lbs.
Features: Soft recoil; visible side loading; shoots all 2¾″ loads without adjustment; hand engraved receiver, black and gold finish; crisp, gold plated trigger. Safety in rear of trigger guard, convenient to either hand. Low, ¼″ wide vent. rib optional.
Price: Twelvette, matted bbl. . . . .$239.50   Vent. rib bbl. $254.50
Price: Twentyweight, matted bbl. . 254.50   Vent. rib bbl. 269.50
Price: Extra Twentyweight bbls., matted rib. 88.50
         Vent. rib 103.50
Price: Extra Twelvette bbls., matted rib. 78.50
         Vent. rib 93.50
Price: Trap, standard vent. rib. .$209.50   Lightweight vent. rib. 219.50
         Offered in 12 ga. only.
Price: Skeet models, in 12 and 20 ga.
         Lightweight plain matted barrel. . .$204.50, vent. rib. . 219.50

D HI-STANDARD SUPERMATIC DELUXE AUTOS
Gauge: 12 or 20 (5-shot; 3-shot plug furnished).
Action: Gas operated autoloader (12 ga. 2¾″, 20 ga. 3″ chambers).
Barrel: 12 gauge, 30″ (Full), 26″ (Imp. Cyl.), 12 and 20 gauge, 28″ (Mod. or Full). Plain barrel.
Stock: 14″x1½″x2½″. Walnut, checkered p.g. and semi-beavertail fore-end. Recoil pad. 20 ga. guns have longer fore-end with sloped front.
Weight: 7½ lbs. (12 ga.). 47¾″ over-all (12, 28″).
Features: 12 ga. uses all 2¾″ shells, 20 ga. all 2¾″ or 3″ shells, including rifled slugs, without adjustment.
Price: Field. . . .$149.95   Special, with adj. choke (27″ bbl.). .$157.95
Price: Deluxe Rib, checkered stock, vent. rib, w/o adj. choke. . 174.95
Price: Checkered stock, vent.-rib, adj. choke. 182.95
Price: Duck, 3″ Magnum, 12 ga., 30″ Full, recoil pad,
         with vent. rib. bbl. 184.95

E Hi-Standard Supermatic Deer Gun
Same as Supermatic Auto except: 12-ga. only, 22″ plain bbl., Cyl. bore, with rifle sights. Checkered walnut stock and fore-end, recoil pad. Receiver tapped for aperture sight. 41¾″ over-all, 7¾ lbs. $184.95

F Hi-Standard Supermatic Skeet
Same as Supermatic DeLuxe except: 26″ Skeet choke bbl.; all external parts high polished; internal parts super finished; better grade American walnut stock (no recoil pad) and fore-end with cabinet finish. Weight about 7½ lbs. $179.95

Hi-Standard Supermatic Trap
Same features as Supermatic Skeet except: 30″ full choke barrel; stock (14⅜″x1½″x1⅞″); recoil pad. Wgt. 8 lbs. 12 ga. only. .$184.95

Hi-Standard Supermatic Executive Trap
Same gun as Supermatic Trap, but with Fajen Monte Carlo stock, selected wood $274.95

ITHACA MODEL 300 AUTOMATIC

Gauge: 12 ga. 2¾″ chambers, 20 ga. 3″ chambers.
Action: Recoil-operated, takedown, interchangeable barrels.
Barrel: Roto-Forged 30″ 12 ga. only (Full), 28″ (Full or Mod.), 26″ (Imp. Cyl.). Standard without rib, vent. rib, $15.00 extra.
Stock: 14″x1½″x2½″. Hand checkered walnut, p.g., fluted fore-end.
Weight: 12 ga. about 7 lbs., 20 ga. about 6½ lbs.
Features: Positive cross-bolt safety, automatic magazine cutoff permits changing loads without unloading magazine. 20 ga. guns are designed to permit quick changeover from 2¾″ to 3″ shells.
Price: $149.95

ITHACA MODEL 900 DELUXE AUTOMATIC

Gauge: 12 ga. 2¾″ chambers, 20 ga. 3″ chambers.
Action: Recoil-operated, takedown; interchangeable barrels, cross-bolt safety.
Barrel: Roto-Forged; 30″ 12 ga. only (Full), 28″ (Full or Mod.), 26″ (Imp. Cyl.) all with vent. rib.
Features: White spacers in grip cap and butt plate; attractive engraving on receiver is gold-filled, gold-plated trigger and nameplate inlaid in stock.
Stock: 14″x1½″x2½″, hand checkered walnut, p.g.
Weight: 12 ga. about 7 lbs., 20 ga. about 6½ lbs.
Price: $179.95

ITHACA MODEL 900 DELUXE AUTOMATIC SLUG GUN

Identical to the Model 900 Deluxe, except with 24″ barrel that carries rifle sights for slug shooting. 12 ga. 2¾″ chamber, 20 ga. 3″ chamber.
Price: $169.95

ITHACA MODEL 51 FEATHERLIGHT AUTOMATIC

Gauge: 12 ga. 2¾″ chamber.
Action: Gas-operated, rotary bolt has three locking lugs. Takedown. Self-compensating for high or low base loads.
Barrel: Roto-Forged, 30″ (Full), 28″ (Full, Mod., or Skeet), 26″ (Imp. Cyl. or Skeet). Extra barrels available. Raybar front sight. Vent. rib $30.00 extra.
Stock: 14″x1⅝″x2½″. Hand checkered walnut, white spacers on p.g. and under recoil pad.
Weight: About 7½ lbs.
Features: Hand fitted, engraved receiver, 3 shot capacity, safety is reversible for left hand shooter.
Price: Standard $164.95

ITHACA MODEL 51 FEATHERLIGHT AUTOMATIC TRAP

Same gun as Model 51 with vent. rib, trap recoil pad, stock dimensions are 14¼″x1½″x1⅞″. **Price:** $199.95

ITHACA MODEL 51 FEATHERLIGHT AUTOMATIC SKEET

Same gun as Model 51 with vent. rib, skeet recoil pad, stock dimensions are 14″x1⅝″x2½″. **Price:** $197.95

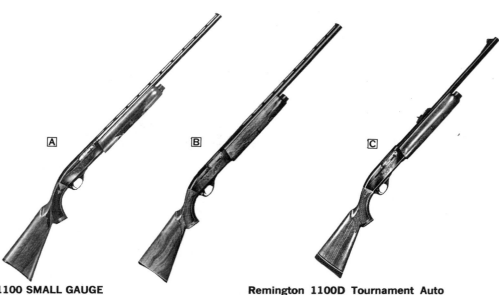

Ⓐ REMINGTON 1100 SMALL GAUGE

Same as 1100 except: 28 ga. 2¾″ (5-shot) or 410, 3″ (except Skeet, 2½″ 4-shot). 45½″ over-all. Available in 25″ bbl. (Full, Mod., or Imp. Cyl.) only.
Price: Plain bbl........$179.95   With vent. rib........$204.95

REMINGTON 1100 20 GA. LIGHTWEIGHT

Basically the same design as Model 1100, but with special weight-saving features that retail strength and dependability of the standard Model 1100.
Barrel: 28″ (Full, Mod.), 26″ (Imp. Cyl.).
Weight: 6½ lbs.
Price: ....$179.95   With vent. rib...........$204.95

Ⓑ REMINGTON MODEL 1100 AUTO

Gauge: 12, 16, 20 (5-shot); 3-shot plug furnished.
Action: Gas-operated autoloader.
Barrel: 26″ (Imp. Cyl.), 26″ Mod. in 12 and 20 ga. only), 28″ Mod., Full), 30′ Full in 12 ga. only.
Stock: 14″x1½″x2½″ American walnut, checkered p.g. and fore-end.
Weight: 12 ga. 7½ lbs., 16 ga. 7⅜ lbs., 20 ga. 7¼ lbs.; 48″ over-all (28″ bbl.).
Features: Quickly interchangeable barrels within gauge. Matted receiver top with scroll work on both sides of receiver. Crossbolt safety.
Price: ....$169.95   With vent. rib...........$194.95

Remington 1100 Magnum

Same as 1100 except: chambered for 3″ magnum loads. Available in 12 ga. (30 Full) or 20 ga. (28 Full). 14″x1½″x2½″ stock with recoil pad. Wgt. 7¾ lbs...$184.95
With vent. rib 209.95

Remington 1100D Tournament Auto

Same as 1100 Standard except: vent. rib, better wood, more extensive engraving $595.00

Remington 1100F Premier Auto

Same as 1100D except: select wood, better engraving.....$1295.00
With gold inlay 2000.00

Remington 1100 SA Skeet

Same as the 1100 except: 26″ bbl., special skeet boring, vent. rib, ivory bead front and metal bead middle sights. 14″x1½″x2½″ stock. 20 and 12 ga. only. Wgt. 7½ lbs.
Price: ......$199.95   1100 SB (better grade walnut)......$224.95
For Cutts Comp add.................................... 25.00

Ⓒ REMINGTON 1100 Deer Gun

Same as 1100 except: 12 ga. only, 22″ bbl. (Imp. Cyl.), rifle sights adjustable for w. and e.; recoil pad with white spacer. Weight 7¼ lbs...$189.95

Remington 1100 TB Trap

Same as the 1100 except: better grade wood, recoil pad. 14⅜″x 1⅜″x1¾″ stock. Wgt. 8¼ lbs. 12 ga. only. 28″ (Mod., Full) or 30″ (Mod., Full) vent. rib bbl. Ivory bead front and white metal middle sight.
Price: ....$234.95   With Monte Carlo stock........$244.95

Remington 1100 Extra bbls.: Plain $45.45. Vent. rib $68.15. Vent. rib Skeet $72.40. Vent. rib Trap $72.40. Deer bbl. $54.50. Skeet, with cutts comp. $94.47. Available in the same gauges and chokes as shown on guns.

Autoloading . . .

A SEARS TED WILLIAMS 300 AUTO
Gauge: 12 and 20 (3-shot) 2¾" chamber.
Action: Gas operated autoloader with self-compensating system for light or heavy loads.
Barrel: 27", 12 and 20 ga. (with adjustable choke), 28", 12 ga. only (Mod or Full), ventilated rib.
Stock: American walnut, checkered p.g. and fore-end, recoil pad.
Weight: 7 lbs. (7¼ in 12 ga. w/adj. choke); 48⅝" over-all length (47⅝" w/adj. choke).
Features: Push button action release.
Price: 12 ga. (Mod or Full). .$165.00   With adjustable choke. .$175.00

UNIVERSAL AUTO WING SHOTGUN
Gauge: 12 only (5-shot; 3-shot plug furnished). 2¾" chamber.
Action: Recoil operated autoloader; takedown; extra bbls. interchange without factory fitting; cross-bolt safety.
Barrels: 26", 28" or 30" (Imp. Cyl., Mod., & Full). Vent. rib, Ivory bead front & middle sights.
Stock: 14¼"x1⅝"x2½". Walnut checkered, full p.g. and grooved fore-end.
Weight: About 7 lbs.
Price: $159.95

B UNIVERSAL DUCK WING SHOTGUN
   Same features as Auto Wing except: exposed metal parts are coated with Teflon - S camouflage olive green to avoid reflection; retard rust or corrosion and resist scratches. 28" or 30". Full choke only. $164.95

C WESTERN FIELD MODEL 600 AUTOMATIC
Gauge: 12 only.
Action: Gas operated, take-down.
Barrel: 30" (Full), 28" (Mod.) or 26" (Imp. Cyl., vent. rib model only).
Stock: Walnut, checkered fore-end and p.g. with cap.
Weight: Not available.
Features: Cross-bolt safety at rear of trigger guard; engraving on receiver; recoil pad installed.
Price: ....$144.95   With vent. rib $164.95

D WINCHESTER 1400 AUTOMATIC MARK II
Gauge: 12, 16 and 20 (3-shot).
Action: Gas operated autoloader. Front-locking 4-lug rotating bolt locks in bbl. Alloy receiver. Push button action release.
Barrel: 26" (Imp. Cyl.), 28" (Mod., Full), 30" (Full, 12 ga. only). Metal bead front sight.
Stock: 14"x1⅜"x2⅜". American walnut, new-design checkered p.g. and fore-end; fluted comb, p.g. cap, recoil pad.
Weight: With 26" bbl., 20 ga. 6½ lbs., 16, 12 ga. 6¾ lbs.; 46⅝" over-all.
Features: Self-compensating valve adjusts for std. or magnum loads. Bbls. interchangeable without fitting. Crossbolt safety in front of trigger guard.
Price: ....$159.95   With vent. rib............$184.95
Winchester 1400 Auto Deer Gun
   Same as M1400 except: 12 ga. only, 42⅝" over-all with 22" bbl. specially bored for rifled slugs. Ramp front sight, adj. open rear. Stock: 14"x1½"x2⅜". Wgt. 6½ lbs............................$174.95

E WINCHESTER 1400 AUTO TRAP
   Same as M1400 except: 12 ga. only, 51" over-all with 30" full choke bbl. Stock: 14⅜"x1⅜"x1⅞". Wgt., 8¼ lbs. Metal, middle, red front sights. $214.95.   With Monte Carlo stock 14⅜"x1½"x2⅛"x 1½"). Extended rib $224.95
   With field grade M.C. walnut stock, specially tuned trigger, rib extension $199.95
Winchester 1400 Auto Skeet
   Same as M1400 except: 12 and 20 ga. only, 26" bbl., Skeet choke, wgt. 7½ lbs. Stock: 14" x 1½" x 2½". Metal, middle, red front sights. 46⅝" over-all..$214.95
   Field grade walnut stock and forearm....................189.95
   Winchester 1400 Extra Barrels: Field, 12, 16, 20 ga. **$37.95**; with vent. rib **$68.95**; Deer Gun **$48.95**; Trap, Skeet................**$79.95**
Winchester Recoil Reduction Stocks
   Spring-loaded, compressible plastic stock (12-ga. only) for M12, 1200, 1400. Drop at comb increased ⅛" on Field models with vent. rib, and on Skeet model. Trap model unchanged. Weight increases ¾ lb. on Field models only.
   Ordered with Skeet or trap models, additional............$ 5.00
   Ordered with Field models, additional....................10.00
   Not available for Deer Gun, Trap w/o Monte Carlo, or Pigeon Grade.
   Winchester 1400 field model available in a left-hand version in 12 ga. 28" Mod. only **$167.95**. With vent. rib **$194.95**. Skeet **$219.95** and Trap **$229.95**.
   Winchester 1400 with interchangeable choke tubes which are screwed into the barrel and tightened with supplied wrench. Available in 12, 16 and 20 ga. (28") Full, Mod., and Imp. Cyl. tube.
Price: Field **$169.95**, Vent. **$194.95**. Also, L. H. in 12 ga. only plain **$177.95**. L. H. Vent. **$204.95**. Extra tubes in Full, Mod. or Imp. Cyl. **$4.95**. Wrench **$1.50**.

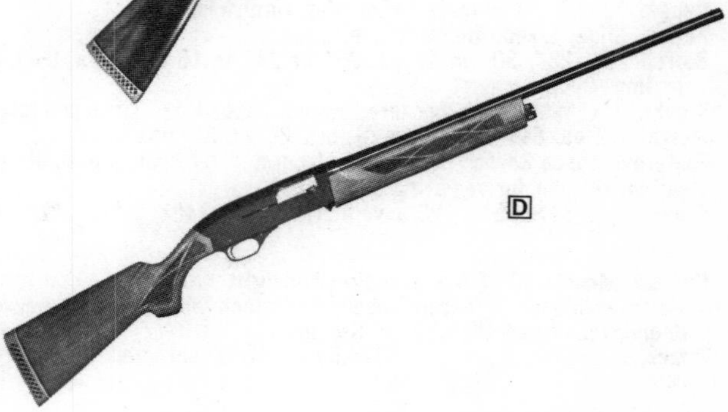

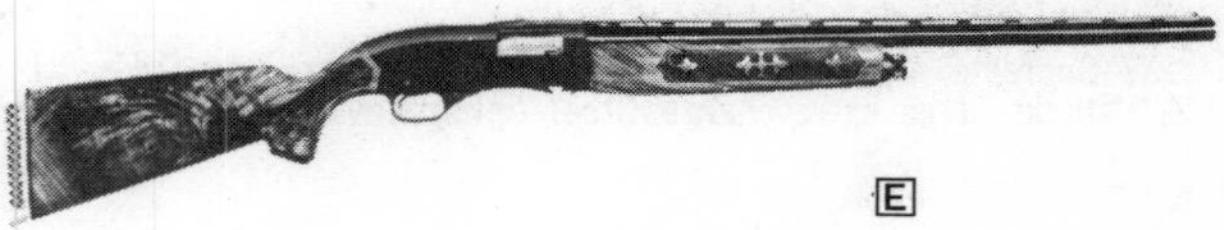

Ⓐ HARRINGTON & RICHARDSON 440 PUMP
Gauge: 12, 20 (2¾" and 3" chamber), 16 (2¾"). 4 shots.
Action: Hammerless, side ejecting, slide action.
Barrel: 24", 12 and 20 ga. (Imp. Cyl.); 26", 12 and 20 ga. (Imp. Cyl. and Mod.); 28", 12 ga. (Full and Mod.), 16 ga. (Mod. only), 20 ga. (Full and Mod.); 30", 12 ga. (Full only).
Stock: Walnut p.g. stock and fore-end recoil pad.
Weight: 6¼ lbs. 47" over-all.
Price: **$104.95**

HARRINGTON & RICHARDSON 442 PUMP
Same as the 440 except: Full length vent. rib, checkered p.g. and fore-end **$139.95**

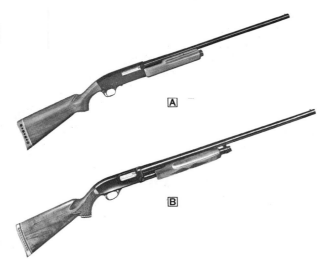

Ⓑ HI-STANDARD FLITE-KING DELUXE PUMP GUNS
Gauge: 12, 20, 28 and 410 (6 shots; 3-shot plug furnished).
Action: "Free-falling" slide action.
Barrel: 12 ga., 30" (Full); 12, 20 ga., 28" (Mod. or Full), 26" (Imp. Cyl.); 410, 26" (Full).
Stock: 14"x1½"x2½". Walnut, checkered p.g. and fore-end. Recoil pad except: 410 & Skeet guns.
Weight: 12 ga. 7¼ lbs., 20, 410 ga. 6 lbs.
Features: Side ejection.
Price: Field ....**$ 99.95**
Price: 12 ga., with adj. choke, 27" bbl................. 109.95
Price: De Luxe Rib, with vent. rib, w/o adj. choke.......... 122.95
Price: 12 and 20 ga., as above with adj. choke............. 129.95
Price: Brush, 12 ga. only with 20" cyl. bbl., grooved fore-end, adj. rifle sights. Stock: (14¼"x1½"x1⅞") 39¾" over-all.....**$112.95**
Price: Brush Deluxe, 12 ga. only with 20" cyl. bbl., checkered p.g. and f.e., sling swivels with sling, adj. peep sight.........**$132.95**

Hi-Standard Flite-King Skeet
Same as Flite-King DeLuxe except: No recoil pad; 26" Skeet choke bbl.; all external parts high polished; internal parts super finished; better grade American walnut stock (14"x1½"x2½") and fore-end with cabinet finish. Wgt. 12 ga. 7½ lbs., 20, 6¼ lbs., 410 ga. 6 lbs. **$132.95**

Hi-Standard Flite-King Trap
Same features as Flite-King Skeet except: 30" full choke; (14⅜"x 1½"x1⅞") has recoil pad. About 7¾ lbs. 12 ga. only.......**$144.95**
Executive with Fajen M.C. stock........................ 229.95

Ⓒ ITHACA MODEL 37 FEATHERLIGHT
Gauge: 12, 16, 20 (5-shot; 3-shot plug furnished).
Action: Slide; takedown; bottom ejection.
Barrel: 26", 28", 30" in 12 ga. 26" or 28" in 16 or 20 ga. (Full, Mod. or Imp. Cyl.).
Stock: 14"x1⅝"x2⅝". Checkered walnut capped p.g. stock and fore-end.
Weight: 12 ga. 6½ lbs., 16 ga. 6 lbs., 20 ga. 5¾ lbs.
Features: Ithaca Raybar front sight; decorated receiver; crossbolt safety; action release for removing shells.
Price: .....**$119.95**   With vent. rib stock (14"x1½"x2½").**$144.95**

Ithaca Model 37 De Luxe Featherlight
Same as Model 37 except: checkered stock with p.g. cap; beavertail fore-end; recoil pad. Wgt. 12 ga. 6¾ lbs.
Price:....................**$124.95**....With vent. rib **$149.95**

Ithaca Model 37 Supreme
Same as Model 37 except: hand checkered beavertail fore-end and p.g. stock, Ithaca recoil pad and vent. rib **$199.95**
37 Supreme also with Skeet (14x1½"x2½") or Trap (14½"x1½"x 1⅞") stocks at no extra charge. Other options available at extra charge.

Ⓓ Ithaca Model 37 Deerslayer
Same as Model 37 except: 26" or 20" bbl. designed for rifled slugs; sporting rear sight, Raybar front sight; rear sight ramp grooved for Redfield long eye relief scope mount. 12, 16 or 20 gauge. With checkered stock, beavertail fore-end and recoil pad.
Price:...**$139.95**
Price: As above with special select walnut stock........... 159.95

Ⓔ MOSSBERG MODEL 500 PUMP GUN
Gauge: 12, 16, 20; 3" (6-shot; 3-shot plug furnished).
Action: Slide, takedown; safety on top of receiver.
Barrel: 26" (Imp. Cyl.), 28" (Full or Mod.), 30" (Full), 12 ga. only. Also 12 ga. 18½" cylinder, for police only).
Stock: 14"x1½"x2½". Walnut p.g., extension fore-end. Recoil pad. 13 oz. steel plug furnished for use with Magnum barrel.
Weight: 12 ga. 6¾ lbs., 45¼" over-all (26" bbl.).
Features: Easy interchangeability of barrels; side ejection; disconnecting trigger makes doubles impossible; straight-line feed.
Price: Standard barrel **$91.25**
Price: C-lect Choke, 3" Mag., 24" Slugster bbls.............. 96.95
Price: Extra barrel, 2¾" chamber.......................... 21.60
Price: Extra Magnum, C-Lect Choke or Slug. bbl.............. 28.10

Mossberg Model 500 Super Grade

Similar to the Model 500 except: vent. rib bbls. in 12 ga. (2¾") or 20 ga. (3"); 26" (Skeet), 28" (Mod., Full), and 30" Full (12 ga. only) 2¾" or 3" mag. Checkered p.g. and fore-end stock with fluted comb and recoil pad (14"x1½"x2½").
Price: 12 or 20 ga. $111.50
Price: 12 ga. 3" Magnum or C-Lect Choke 12 and 20 ga..... 118.45

Mossberg Model 500E

Similar to Model 500 except: 410 bore only, 26" bbl. (Full, Mod. or Imp. Cyl.); holds six 2¾" or five 3" shells. Walnut stock with checkered p.g. and fore-end, fluted comb and recoil pad (14"x1¼"x2½"). Weight about 5¾ lbs., length over-all 46".
Price: Standard barrels ....$ 91.25
Price: C-Lect Choke barrel 96.95
Price: Super Grade, 26" Full, Mod., or Skeet bbl., vent. rib... 111.50
Price: Super Grade, C-Lect Choke and vent. rib............. 118.45

A Mossberg Model 500 APR Pigeon Grade

Similar to Model 500, but with vent. rib, rubber recoil pad, hand checkering, scroll engraving on action.
Price: $139.00
Price: 500 APKR with C-Lect-Choke $145.00
Price: 500 APTR trap gun 30" full choke barrel, M.C. stock, 14½"x 1½"x2", additional barrels available. **Price:** $145.00

B NOBLE 66 PUMP GUNS
Gauge: 12 ga. (3" chamber), 16 ga. (2¾" chamber). 6-shot, 3-shot plug furnished.
Action: Slide, solid frame, side ejection, tang safety.
Barrel: 28" (Mod. or Full)
Stock: Walnut p.g. (13¾" x 1¾" x 2¾"), with impressed checkering.
Weight: About 7½ lbs. 48" over-all.
Features: Key Lock, protects against unauthorized use. Damascened bolt.
Price: M66XLP ....$ 86.92
With Vary-Check Choke, checkered grip recoil pad, as M66 CLP 93.79
With vent. rib, checkered grip recoil pad, as M66 RLP.... 109.06
Same as M66 RLP, with Vary-Check Choke, as M66 RCLP... 115.94

C NOBLE 166L DEERGUN

Same as Model P66XLP except: 24" rifled slug bbl. guaranteed to shoot 3" groups at 100 feet. Hard rubber buttplate. Sling swivels and detachable carrying strap. Lyman adj. peep rear sight and post ramp front. Wgt. 7⅜ lbs., 44" over-all.......................$101.40

D & E NOBLE 602 AND 70 SERIES PUMP GUNS
Gauge: 20 (as 602 Series), 410 (as 70 Series), 3" chambers, 5-shot; 3-shot plug furnished.
Action: Slide, solid frame; tang safety; side ejection.
Barrels: 20 ga., 28", 410 26" (Mod. or Full).
Stock: Walnut, p. g. (13¾" x 1½" x 2⅝"), impressed checkering on fore-end.
Weight: About 6½ lbs. (20 ga.), 6 lbs. (410 ga.) 48" over-all (20 ga.).
Features: Key Lock protects against unauthorized use. Damascened bolt.
Price: M602XLP $86.92
With Vary Choke, recoil pad, checkered grip, as M602 CLP, ...$93.79
With vent. rib, recoil pad, checkered grip, as M602 RLP, ...$¹09.06
Same as RLP Models with Vary Choke, as RCLP.........$115.94
Same as RCLP Models, with alloy bbls. wgt. about 4½ lbs., as M662, 20 ga. only.........$113.75   Vent. rib........$135.75
410 ga. 70X1 $84.68, 70CL $90.57, 70RL $106.85, and 70RCL $113.06.

F REMINGTON 870 WINGMASTER PUMP GUN
Gauge: 12, 16, 20 (5-shot; 3-shot wood plug. 12 oz. Vari-Weight steel plug furnished in 12 ga.).
Action: Takedown, slide action.
Barrel: 12, 16, 20 ga., 36" (Imp. Cyl.); 28" (Mod. or Full); 23 and 20 ga., 26"(Mod.), 12 ga., 30" (Full).
Stock: 14"x1⅝"x2½". Checkered walnut, p.g.; fluted extension fore-end; fitted rubber recoil pad.
Weight: 7 lbs., 12 ga. (7¾ lbs. with Vari-Weight plug); 6¾ lbs., 16 ga.; 6½ lbs., 20 ga. 48½" over-all (28" bbl.).
Features: Double action bars, crossbolt safety. Receiver machined from solid steel. Hand fitted action.
Price: Plain bbl...........$119.95   Vent. rib.........$144.95
Price: Riot gun, 18" or 20" Riot bore..................... 109.95
Price: Riot gun, 20" Imp. Cyl., rifle sights................. 119.95

G Remington 870 Magnum

Same as M870 except: 3" chamber, full choke. Plain bbl.; 12 ga., 30" or 20 ga., 28". Vent. rib bbl.; 12 ga., 30", 20 ga., 28" or 30.". Recoil pad. Wgt., 12 ga. 8 lbs., 20 ga. 7½ lbs.
Price: Plain bbl........$139.95   Vent. rib bbl........$164.95

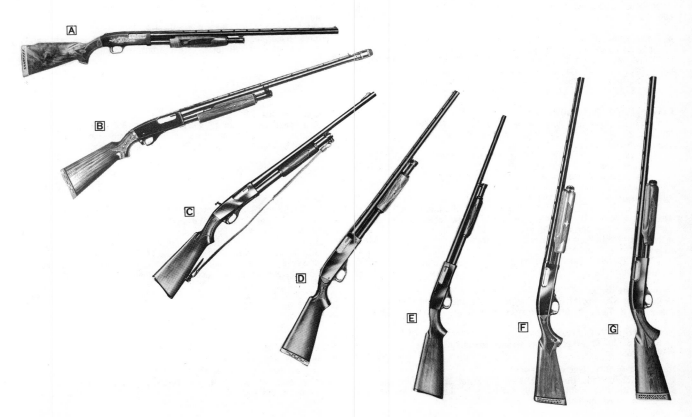

A Remington Model 870 Brushmaster Deluxe
Carbine version of the M870 with 20″ bbl. (Imp. Cyl.) for rifled slugs. 40½″ over-all, wgt. 6½ lbs. Recoil pad. Adj. rear, ramp front sights $139.95

Remington Model 870 Standard Deer Gun
Same as Brushmaster except: lacquer finish, no checkering or grip cap; short fore-end $119.95

B Remington 870 SA Skeet
Same as the M870 except: 26″ bbl. Skeet bored. Vent. rib with ivory front and white metal middle beads. 14″x1⅝″x2½″ stock with rubber recoil pad. 12 or 20 ga. only...............................$149.95
870 SC (better grade and finish of walnut. Hand checkering). 224.95
Add $25.00 for Cutts comp.

Remington 870 Small Gauges
Exact copies of the large ga. Model 870, except that guns are offered in 28 and 410 ga. 25″ barrel (Full, Mod., Imp. Cyl.).
Plain barrel ....$ 29.95
Vent. rib.......$154.95   Vent. rib, skeet choke........ 159.95
Match Weight Skeet Cap for small ga. M870.............. 9.95
D and F grade prices same as large ga. M870 prices.

C Remington 870 TB Trap
Same as the M870 except: 12 ga. only, 28″ (Mod. Full) or 30″ (Mod., Full) vent. rib. bbl., ivory front and white metal middle beads. Special sear, hammer and trigger assy. 14⅜″x1½″x1⅞″ stock with recoil pad. Hand fitted action and parts. Wgt. 8 lbs...........$184.95
With Monte Carlo stock............................. 194.95
870 TC (better Hand checkering)..................... 259.95
With Monte Carlo stock............................. 269.95

Remington 870D Tournament
Same as 870 except: better walnut, hand checkering. Engraved receiver & bbl. Vent.-rib. Stock dimensions to order...........$595.00

Remington 870F Premier
Same as M8700, except select walnut, better engraving....$1295.00
With gold inlays 2000.00

Remington 870 Extra Barrels
Plain $35.70. Vent. rib $58.75. Vent. rib Skeet $61.55. Vent. rib Trap $61.55. With rifle sights $46.10. Available in the same gauges and chokes as shown on guns.

D SAVAGE MODEL 30 PUMP GUN
Gauge: 12, 20 and 410, 5-shot (410, 4-shot) 3-shot plug furnished. All gauges chambered for 3″ Magnum shells.
Action: Slide, hammerless, take-down; side ejection; cross-bolt safety.
Barrel: Vent. rib. 12, 20 ga., 26″ (Imp. Cyl.); 28″ (Mod. or Full); 12 ga., 30″ (Full); 410, 26″ (Mod. or Full).
Stock: 14″x1½″x2½″. Walnut, checkered p.g., grooved extension fore-end, recoil pad.
Weight: 7 lbs. (410, 6¼ lbs.). Over-all 49½″ (30″ bbl.).
Features: Decorated lightweight receiver; gold plated trigger and safety; damascened bolt. Stainless steel front and middle bead sights.
Price: $111.75

Savage Model 30-T
Same specifications as 12 ga., M30 except: 30″ Full choke bbl. with 3″ chamber; Monte Carlo stock with trap dimensions (14⅝″x1½″x 1½″x2¼″). Recoil pad. Over-all 50″. 8 lbs................$118.75

E SEARS MODEL 200 PUMP GUN
Gauge: 12, 16 and 20 (3″ chamber) (5-shot; 2-shot plug installed).
Action: Slide, front-locking rotating bolt.
Barrel: 28″ Full or Mod., 26″ Imp. Cyl. 12 ga only.
Stock: Walnut finished buttstock and fore-end; recoil pad.
Weight: About 6½ lbs.; 48⅝″ over-all (28″ bbl.).
Features: Alloy receiver, non-glare serrated top; cross-bolt safety. Interchangeable bbls., no special tools required, $24 extra.
Price: $89.99
Price: 20 gauge with 27″ barrel and variable choke........... 99.99
Price: 12 ga. with 30″ barrel (Full)........................ 91.99

Sears Ted Williams 200 Pump
Same as Standard 200 except: 12 and 20 ga. only; vent. rib; 3-shot capacity; engine-turned bolt, checkered p.g. and fore-end; p.g. cap, whiteline spacers and name plate. Wgt. 12 ga. 6⅞ lbs., 20 ga. 6⅝ lbs. $135.00. With var. choke. $135.00.

B STEVENS MODEL 77 PUMP SHOTGUN

Gauge: 12, 16, 20, 410, 5-shot (410, 4-shot); 3-shot plug furnished. All but 16 ga. chambered for 3" Mag.
Action: Slide, solid frame; side ejection; crossbolt safety.
Barrel: Plain. 12, 16, 20 ga. 26" (Imp. Cyl.); 28" (Mod. or Full); 12 ga. 30" (Full); 410, 26" (Mod. or Full).
Stock: 14"x1½"x2½". Full p.g., grooved extension fore-end.
Weight: 6¾ lbs. (410, 6¼ lbs.)
Features: Alloy steel receiver. Over-all 49½" (30" bbl.).
Price: $90.50

Stevens Model 77-AC

Same as Model 77 except: with Savage Adjustable Choke and recoil
Price: $97.50

C WESTERN FIELD 550 PUMP SHOTGUN

Gauge: 12, 20 and 410.
Action: Slide action, takedown: top tang safety.
Barrel: 12 ga., 30" (Full), 28" (Mod.). 20 ga., 28" (Ful or Mod.). 410, 26" (Full).
Stock: Walnut finished p.g. stock, plastic buttplate, serrated fore-end.
Weight: Not available.
Features: Straight-line feed, interchangeable bbls., trigger disconnector prevents doubling.
Price: ....$72.95   410 (with rubber buttplate)....$81.95
As above, but with variable choke in 12 or 20 ga. only...... 86.95
Slug gun with 24 bbl. without choke..................... 87.95
Magnum 12 ga., 30" bbl. (Ful choke).................... 87.95
Trap gun, 30" (Full) bbl., vent. rib and trap stock, 12 ga. only 121.95
Vent rib models available, fixed or variable choke as above.. 99.75
to 102.95

D WINCHESTER 12 SUPER PIGEON PUMP GUN

Gauge: 12 only, 6-shot (2-shot plug installed).
Action: Slide, one-piece receiver, takedown, side ejection.
Barrel: 26", 28", 30", floating vent. rib, any standard choke.
Stock: Full fancy American walnut, dim. to order within mfg. limits, hand-finished, "A" checkering or carving (see Win. catalog), Monte Carlo, cheekpiece or offset avail. at extra charge.
Features: Receiver engraved, "1A," "1B," or "1C" type (see Win. catalog). Working parts hand fitted.
Weight: 7¾ lbs.
Price: $875.00

E WINCHESTER 1200 FIELD PUMP GUN

Gauge: 12, 16 and 20 (5-shot; 3-shot plug installed).
Action: Slide; front locking 4-lug rotating bolt locks into bbl. Alloy receiver, cross-bolt safety in front of trigger guard. Take-down.
Barrel: 26" (Imp. Cyl.), 28" (Mod., Full) and 30" Full (12 ga. only). Metal bead front sight.
Stock: 14"x1⅜"x2⅜". American walnut with new-design checkered p.g. and fore-end; fluted comb, recoil pad. Steel p.g. cap.
Weight: 12 ga. 6½ lbs. with 26" bbl. 46⅝" over-all.
Price:.................$114.95   With vent. rib........$139.95

Winchester 1200 Skeet

Same as M1200 except: 12 and 20 ga., 26" vent. rib bbl., b. t. fore-end, metal, middle red front sights.......................$194.95

Winchester 1200 Trap

Same as M1200 except: 12-ga. only, 30" Full choke vent. rib bbl., 50⅝" over-all. 14⅜"x1⅜"x1⅞" stock with recoil pad, b. t. fore-end. Metal, middle, red front sights...........................$194.95
With Monte Carlo stock, 13⅜"x1½"x2⅛"x1½".......... 204.95
Field grade walnut stock, Monte Carlo.................... 159.95

Winchester 1200 Field 3" Magnum

Same as 1200 except: 12 and 20 ga. only, 2¾" or 3" shells, 28" and 30" full choke bbls., 7⅝ lbs. with 28" bbl., 48⅝" over-all.
Price:.................$134.95   With vent. rib........$159.95

Winchester 1200 Deer Gun

Same as M1200 except: 12 ga. only, 22" bbl. bored for rifled slugs; rifle-type sights, rear adj. for e. only.....................$129.95

Winchester 1200 Extra Barrels: Field and Riot w/o sights, 12, 16, 20 ga. **$35.95.** Field with vent. rib, 12, 16, 20 ga. **$66.95.** Riot with sights and Deer Gun, 12 ga. **$46.95.** Trap, 12 ga., Full choke 30" only, Skeet, 12, 20 ga. 26" only..........................**$77.95**
Winchester 1200 with interchangeable choke tubes which are screwed into the barrel and tightened with supplied wrench. Available in 12, 16 and 20 ga. (28") Mod. tube. Price: Field **$124.95** Vent. rib **$149.95.** Extra tubes in Full, Mod. or Imp. Cyl. **$4.95.** Wrench **$1.75.**

Winchester Recoil Reduction Stocks

Spring-loaded, compressible plastic stock (12-ga. only) for M12, 1200, 1400. Drop at comb increased ⅛" on Field models with vent.-rib, and on Skeet model. Trap model unchanged. Weight increases ¾ lb. on Field models only.
Ordered with trap models, additional.....................$50.00

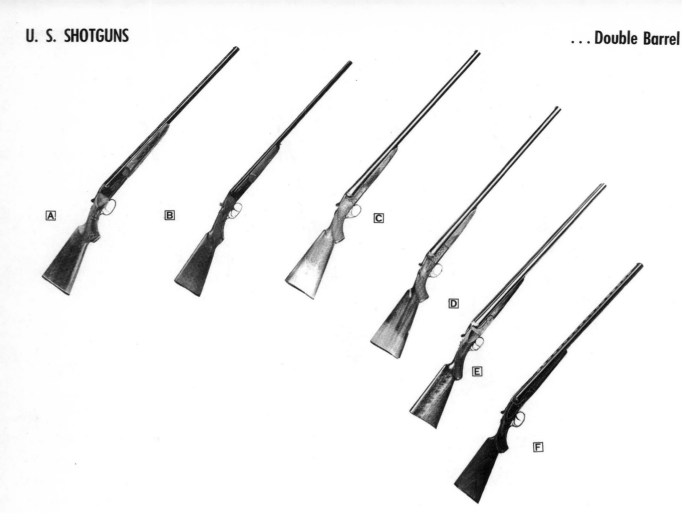

A FOX MODEL B-SE Double

Gauge: 12, 16, 20, 410 (20, 2¾" and 3"; 410, 2½" and 3" shells).
Action: Hammerless, takedown; non-selective single trigger; auto. safety. Automatic ejectors.
Barrel: 12, 16, 20 ga. 26" (Imp. Cyl., Mod.); 12, 16, 20 ga. 28" (Mod., Full); 12 ga. 30" (Mod., Full); 410, 26" (Full, Full). Vent. rib on all.
Stock: 14"x1½"x2½". Walnut, checkered p.g. and beavertail fore-end.
Weight: 12 ga. 7 lbs., 16 ga. 6¾ lbs., 20 ga. 6½ lbs., 410 ga. 6¼ lbs.
Features: Decorated, satin black finish frame; white bead front and middle sights.
Price: $164.50
Also available with double triggers, case hardened frame, without white line spacers and auto. ejectors as Model B............$137.50

B HARRINGTON & RICHARDSON MODEL 404 DOUBLE

Gauge: 12, 20 and 410 (2¾" and 3" shells).
Action: Top lever break-open action, top tang safety, double triggers.
Barrel: 12 ga. 28" (Mod. and Full), 20 ga. 26" (Imp. Cyl. and Mod.), 410 ga. 26" (Full and Full)
Stock: Walnut finished hardwood, hand checkered p.g. and fore-end.
Weight: 12 ga. 7¼ lbs., 20 ga. 6½ lbs., 410 ga. 5½ lbs.
Price: $99.95

C ITHACA SKB 100 GRADE FIELD DOUBLE

Gauge: 12 and 20.
Action: Top lever, hammerless, boxlock, automatic safety, single selective trigger, non-automatic extractor.
Barrel: 12 ga. 26" (Imp. Cyl., Mod.). 28" (Imp. Cyl., Mod. or Mod., Full), 30" Mod., Full), 2¾" chambers. 20 ga. 28" (Mod., Full). 25" (Imp. Cyl., Mod.), 3" chambers
Stock: 14"x1½"x2⅝". Walnut, checkered p.g. and fore-end, p.g. cap, fluted comb.
Weight: 7 lbs. (12 ga.); 6 lbs. (20 ga.).
Features: Automatic safety. Chrome lined action and barrels.
Price: $179.95

D ITHACA SKB 200E DELUXE FIELD GRADE DOUBLE

Same as 100 Grade Field except: automatic selective ejectors, bead middle sight and scroll engraving on receiver, beavertail fore-end. White line spacers. Not avail. in 28" 12 ga. (Imp. Cyl., Mod.). Gold plated trigger and nameplate $225.00

Ithaca SKB 200E Skeet Grade

Same as 200E Deluxe Field Grade except: recoil pad, non-auto. safety. Bbls. 26" 12 ga. or 25" 20 ga. (Skeet, Skeet). Wgt. 7⅜ lbs.
Price: $230.00

E NOBLE MODEL 420 Double

Gauge: 12, 16, 20, 28, 410 (2¾" chambers).
Action: Hammerless, top lever opening, double triggers, auto. safety. Etched hunting scene on frame.
Barrel: 12, 16, 20 ga. 28" (Mod., Full); 12, 16, 20, 28 ga. 26" (Imp. Cyl., Mod.), 410 (Mod., Full). Matted rib.
Stock: 14"x1⅝"x2⅝". Walnut, checkered p.g. and fore-end.
Weight: About 6-6⅞ lbs. 44¾" over-all (28" bbls.).
Features: Double lug locks and cross-bolt lock to bbl. extension.
Price: $109.95

NOBLE MODEL 450E DOUBLE

Gauge: 12, 16, 20 (2¾" chamber).
Action: Demi-block with triple lock, with automatic selective ejectors, double triggers.
Barrels: 28" (Mod. & Full)
Stock: Hand checkered Circassion Walnut with p.g. beavertal fore-end.
Weight: About 6⅞ lbs., 44¾" over-all.
Features: Recoil pad, hand engraved action, gold inlay on top lever. Front and middle bead sight.
Price: $139.17

F MARLIN L. C. SMITH FIELD DOUBLE

Gauge: 12.
Action: Sidelock, double trigger.
Barrel: 28" (Mod. & Full).
Stock: Select walnut with capped p.g. checkered, (14"x1½"x2½").
Weight: 6¾ lbs.
Features: Vent. rib, standard extractors, top auto. tang safety.
Price: $300.00

Double Barrel . . .

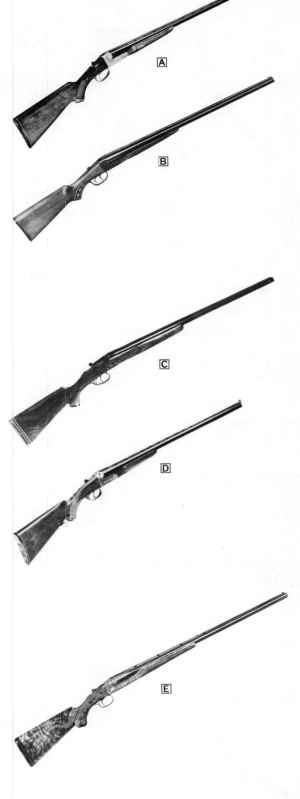

A SEARS DOUBLE BARREL GUN
Gauge: 12, 20, 410. (20 and 410, 3" chambers).
Action: Hammerless, takedown. Double trigger, auto. safety.
Barrel: 12 ga. 30" (Full, Mod.); 20 ga., 28", (Full, Mod.); 12, 20 ga., 26" (Mod., Imp. Cyl.); 410 ga. 26" only (Full and Full).
Stock: 14"x1⅝"x2⅝", walnut finished, p.g.
Weight: 7½ lbs. (12 ga.), 6½ lbs. (20 ga.), 6 lbs. (410).
Features: Black epoxied frame; bbl. and bbl. lug forged in one piece.
Price: $109.99

B STEVENS MODEL 311 DOUBLE
Gauge: 12, 16, 20, 410 (20 and 410, 3" chambers).
Action: Top lever, hammerless; double triggers safety.
Barrel: 12, 16, 20 ga. 26" (Imp. Cyl., Mod.); 12, 16, 20 ga. 28" (Mod., Full); 12 ga. 30" (Mod., Full); 410 ga. 26" (Full, Full).
Stock: 14"x1½"x2½". Walnut finish, p.g., fluted comb.
Weight: 7-6¼ lbs. Over-all 45¾" (30" bbl.).
Features: Box type frame, case-hardened finish.
Price: $109.50

C UNIVERSAL DOUBLE WING DOUBLE
Gauge: 12 and 20, 3" chambers.
Action: Top break, boxlock.
Barrel: 26" (Imp. Cyl., Mod.); 28" or 30" (Mod., Full).
Stock: Walnut p.g. and fore-end, checkered.
Weight: About 7 lbs.
Features: Double triggers; Recoil pad. Beavertail style fore-end.
Price: $129.95
Price: 10 ga. 3½" chamber 32" Full and Full (M2030)...... 149.95

WESTERN FIELD DOUBLE Standard
Gauge: 12, 16, 20, 410 (20 and 410, 3" chambers).
Action: Hammerless, boxlock frame.
Barrel: Matted rib, white metal bead front sight. 12 ga. 30" (Mod., Full), 16 ga., 20 ga., 28" (Mod., Full), 410 ga. 26" (Mod., Full).
Stock: Walnut-finished birch, full p.g., fluted comb.
Weight: 12, 16 ga. 7 lbs.; 20, 410 ga. 6½ lbs.
Features: Coil springs, auto safety, black epoxy finish action.
Price: $86.99

D WESTERN FIELD DOUBLE DELUXE
Same as Standard except: 12 and 20 ga. only; non-selective single trigger; satin chrome finished receiver; 28" bbls. (Mod., Full) with vent. rib. 20 ga. has 3" chambers. Select walnut p.g. stock, checkered, white-line spacers, recoil pad $139.95

WINCHESTER 21 Custom Double Gun
12, 16 or 20 ga. Almost any choke or bbl. length combination. Matted rib, 2¾" chambers, rounded frame, stock of AA-grade full fancy American walnut to customer's dimensions; straight or p.g., cheekpiece, Monte Carlo and/or offset; field. Skeet or trap fore-end.
Full fancy checkering, engine-turned receiver parts, gold plated trigger and gold oval name plate (optional) with three initials $1,200.00

WINCHESTER 21 Pigeon grade
Same as Custom grade except: 3" chambers, available in 12 and 20 ga.; matted or vent. rib, leather covered pad (optional); style "A" stock carving and style "6" engraving (see Win. catalog); gold inlaid p.g. cap, gold nameplate or 3 gold initials in guard........$2,750.00

E WINCHESTER 21 GRAND AMERICAN
Same as Custom and Pigeon grades except: style "B" stock carving, with style "6" engraving, all figures gold inlaid; extra pair of bbls. with beavertail fore-end, engraved and carved to match rest of gun; full leather trunk case for all, with canvas cover..........$3,750.00

A BROWNING SUPERPOSED Standard

Gauge: 12 & 28, 2¾" chamber; 20 & 410, 3" chamber. Any combination of Full, Imp. Mod., Mod., Imp. Cyl., Skeet, and Cyl. chokes.
Action: Takedown; single selective gold plated trigger; automatic ejectors, manual safety combined in thumb piece with bbl. selector mechanism. Actions in proportion to gauge.
Barrels: 12, 20, 28 and 410 ga., 26½" or 28", vent. rib. Solid raised rib available on special order. Steel bead front sight.
Stock: 12 ga. 14¼"x1⅝"x2½"; 20, 28 and 410 14¼"x1½"x2⅜". French walnut, hand rubbed finish, 20-line hand checkering on semi-p.g. and fore-end. Deluxe models have fancier, finer checkering.
Weight: With 28" bbls. 12 ga. 7¾ lbs.; 20 ga. 6¾ lbs.; 28 ga. 6⅜ lbs.; 410 ga. 6½ lbs.
Features: Grade 1, blued steel with hand engraved scroll and rosette designs. Pigeon and Diana grades, steel in silver gray tone with hand engraved game scenes showing greater artistic design with each successive grade. Midas grade has specially blued steel with deeply hand carved background and hand engraved 18K gold-inlaid game birds.
Price: Grade 1, 12 or 20 ga..... **$440.00**   28 or 410 ga..... **$475.00**
Price: (28 & 410 ga. only) Pigeon Grade **$675.00**, Diana **$895.00**, Midas **$1,255.00**.

Browning Superposed Magnum 12

Same as Browning Standard 12 ga. Superposed except 3" chambers; 30" (Full and Full or Full and Mod.) barrels. Stock, 14¼"x1⅝"x2½" with factory fitted recoil pad. Weight 8 lbs. Grade 1, **$445.00**, Pigeon **$675.00**, Diana **$895.00**, Midas **$1,255.00**.

B BROWNING SUPERPOSED LIGHTNING

Same as Standard except: 7-7¼ lbs. in 12 ga. 6-6¼ lbs. in 20 ga. Grade 1 **$455.00**, Pigeon **$675.00**, Diana **$895.00**, Midas **$1,255.00**.

Browning Superposed Lightning Trap 12

Same as Browning Lightning Superposed except: semi-beavertail fore-end and ivory sights; stock, 14⅜"x1⅜"x1¾". 7¾ lbs. 30" (Full & Full, Full & Imp. Mod. or Full and Mod.). Grade 1 **$465.00**, Pigeon **$685.00**, Diana **$905.00**, Midas **$1,270.00**.

Browning Superposed "New Model" Skeet

Same as the Superposed Lightning except: full pistol grip stock; recoil pad; beavertail fore end and front and center ivory sights.
Price: GD-1, 12 or 20 ga. only..........................**$450.00**

C SUPERPOSED BROADWAY TRAP 12

Same as Browning Lightning Superposed except: ⅝" wide vent. rib; stock, 14⅜"x1⅜"x1¾". 30" or 32" (Imp. Mod., Full; Mod., Full; Full, Full). 8 lbs. with 32" bbls. Grade 1 **$485.00**, Pigeon **$705.00**, Diana **$925.00**, Midas **$1,290.00**.

Browning Superposed Standard Skeet

Same as Superposed Standard except: 26½" or 28" bbls. (Skeet, Skeet). Wgt. 6½-7¾ lbs. 12 and 20 ga. Grade 1 **$450.00**; (28 and 410 ga). **$485.00**, Pigeon **$705.00**, Diana **$925.00**, Midas **$1,290.00**

Browning Superposed Lightning Skeet

Same as Standard Skeet except: 12 and 20 ga. only. Wgt. 6-7¼ lbs. Grade 1 **$465.00**, Pigeon **$685.00**, Diana **$905.00**, Midas **$1,270.00**

D BROWNING SUPERPOSED SUPER-LIGHT

Gauge: 12, 2¾" chamber.
Action: Boxlock, top lever, single selective trigger. Bbl. selector combined with manual tang safety.
Barrels: 26½" (Mod. & Full, or Imp. Cyl. & Mod.)
Stock: Straight grip (14¼" x 1⅝" x 2½") hand checkered (fore-end and grip) French walnut.
Weight: 6⅜ lbs., average.
Features: Slender, tapered solid rib. Hand rubbed finish, engraved receiver.
Price: **$485.00**

Browning Superposed Combinations

Standard and Lightning models are available with these factory fitted extra barrels: 12 and 20 ga., same gauge bbls.; 12 ga., 20 ga. bbls.; 20 ga., extra sets 28 and/or 410 gauge; 28 ga., extra 410 bbls. Extra barrels may be had in Lightning weights with Standard models and vice versa. Prices range from **$750.00** (12, 20 ga., one set extra bbls. same gauge) for the Grade 1 Standard to about **$2,160.00** for the Midas grade in various combinations, all as cased sets.

E ITHACA MX-8 TRAP GUN

Gauge: 12 only, 2¾" chambers.
Action: Boxlock type, single non-selective trigger; interchangeable trigger-hammer group offers choice of firing order.
Barrel: 30" or 32", especially bored for international clay target shooting. High concave vent rib has 5" ramp.
Stock: Custom, finely checkered (oiled or lacquer finish) European walnut, interchangeable with other models, 9 available including Monte Carlo.
Weight: About 8 lbs.
Features: Ventilated middle rib has additional vent ports for maximum heat dissipation, better balance and smoother swing.
Price **$1,500.00**
    Extra trigger-hammer group **75.00**
    Extra stock **85.00**

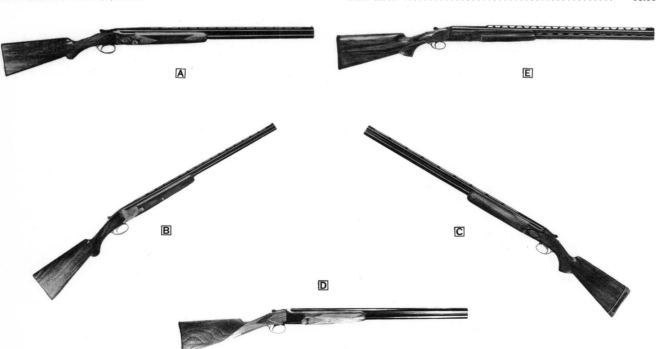

ITHACA COMPETITION I TRAP O/U

Gauge: 12 only, 2¾″ chambers.
Action: Boxlock type, interchangeable hammer-trigger group. Single non-selective trigger, specify choice of firing order.
Barrel: 29¼″, upper Full; lower, Imp.-Mod., vent rib has concave surface with deep cuts.
Stock: Interchangeable, 6 standard (1³⁄₁₆″ to 1½″ at comb x1⅜″ to 1⅞″ at heel) and 3 Monte Carlo (1⅜″ to 1⁹⁄₁₆″x1⅜″ to 1⁹⁄₁₆″) of walnut; all have 14½″ pull. Fore-end has slight taper and finger groove for firm grip.
Weight: About 7¾ lbs.
Features: Extra trigger-hammer groups are available to change firing sequence and/or trigger pull. Custom stocks also available.
Price: **$825.00**
   Extra trigger-hammer group 75.00
   Extra stock 85.00

ITHACA COMPETITION I SKEET O/U

Gauge: 12 only, 2¾″ chambers.
Action: Boxlock type, interchangeable hammer-trigger group. Single non-selective trigger.
Barrel: 2/¾″ (Skeet & Skeet). Vent rib has concave surface with deep cuts.
Stock: 14½x1½″″x2⅜″, interchangeable walnut, custom stocks available.
Weight: About 7¾ lbs.
Features: Extra trigger-hammer groups to change firing order and/or weight of pull. Leather faced recoil pad has bevelled heel that will not catch. Extra stocks interchange for different style and dimension.
Price: **$900.00**
   Extra trigger-hammer group 75.00
   Extra stock 85.00

A ITHACA SKB 500 FIELD GRADE O-U

Gauge: 12, 20.
Action: Top lever, hammerless, boxlock; gold-plated single selective trigger; automatic ejectors, non-auto safety.
Barrel: 26″ vent. rib (Imp. Cyl., Mod.); 28″ (Imp. cyl., Mod. or Mod. Full); 30″ (Mod., Full); 12 ga., 2¾″ chambers. 26″ (Imp. Cyl., Mod.); 28″ (Mod., Full); 20 ga., 3″ chambers.
Stock: 14″x1*″x2⅝″. Walnut, checkered p.g. and fore-end, p.g. cap, fluted comb.
Weight: 7½ lbs. (12); 6½ lbs. (20).
Features: Border scroll engraved receiver. Chrome lined bbls. and action. Regular front sight.
Price: **$249.95**

B ITHACA SKB 600 TRAP GRADE O-U

   Same as 500 Field Grade except 30″ bbl. (Imp. Mod., Full, or Full, Full), fine scroll engraved receiver; bead middle sight; Monte Carlo stock (14½″x1½″x1½″x2″), p.g. white line spacer and recoil pad. Wgt. 7¾ lbs. **$295.00**
   Field Grade 600, no recoil pad or Monte Carlo............. 289.95
   Field Grade 12 ga., 3″ Magnum........................ 289.95
   Trap Grade 700, select walnut oil finished stock and band engraved receiver **$395.00**

Ithaca SKB 600 Skeet Grade O-U

   Same as 600 Trap except: 26″ or 28″ bbls. (Skeet, Skeet), stock (14″x1½″x2⅝″), standard buttplate and whiteline spacer. Wgt. 7½ lbs. **$289.95**
   Skeet Grade 700, select walnut oil finished stock and band engraved receiver **$395.00**

C SAVAGE MODEL 24-S O-U

Gauge: Top bbl. 22 S, L, LR; bottom bbl. 410 or 20 ga., 3″ chambers.
Action: Side lever opening; hammer has spur for bbl. selection. Separate extractors.
Barrel: 24″; top rifled; Full choke shotgun bbl. below.
Stock: 14″x1½″x2½″. Walnut finish, p.g., corrugated buttplate.
Weight: 6¾ lbs. Over-all 40″.
Features: Open rifle sights, rear adj. receiver grooved for scope mount.
Price: **$61.75**
   With top bbl. for 22 RF Magnum........................ 61.75

D Savage Model 24-DL

   Same specifications as Model 24-S except: two-way top lever opening, select walnut stock with Monte Carlo comb and beavertail fore-end, white line spacers, checkered; satin black, decorated receiver, trigger guard and lever **$76.50**
   With top bbl., for 22 RF Magnum...................... 76.50

E Savage Model 24-V

   Same as Model 24-DL except: 222 Rem. and 20 ga. only; satin-black frame and trigger; barrel band; folding leaf rear sight; rec. tapped for scope (scope base $2 extra) .... **$ 98.50**
   With 4x scope as Model 24 V/S........................ 128.95

SAVAGE MODEL 330 O/U

Gauge: 12, 2¾″ chambers, 20 ga. 3″ chambers.
Action: Top lever, break open. Selective single trigger, auto safety locks trigger, coil springs.
Barrel: 26″ (Mod. & Imp. Cyl.), 28″ or 30″ (Mod. & Full).
Stock: 14″x1½″x2½″). Walnut, checkered p.g. and fore-end, hard rubber plate.
Weight: About 7 lbs., 46½″ (30″ bbl.) over-all.
Features: Monoblock locking rails are engaged by locking shield that snaps forward as gun is closed. This shield overlaps the breech for added strength.
Price: **$199.50**

F SAVAGE MODEL 440 O/U

Gauge: 12, 2¾″ chambers, 20 ga. 3″ chambers.
Action: Top lever, break open. Non selective single trigger, auto. safety, all coil springs.
Barrel: 26″ (Skeet & Skeet or Mod. & Imp. Cyl.), 28″ (Mod. & Full), 30″ (Mod. & Full), all with vent rib and hard-chrome lined.
Stock: 14″x1½″x2½″. French walnut, hand checkered p.g. and fore-end, hand rubbed finish, hard rubber buttplate.
Weight: 6½ lbs., length 42½″-46″ over-all.
Features: Hand engraved steel receiver. Simple extractors. Fast hammer fall.
Price: **$237.50**
   Trap Grade 440-T, with manual safety, extra wide trap style vent. rib, extractors, semi-beavertail fore-end, Monte Carlo stock and recoil pad **$285.00**
   Deluxe Grade 444, with ejectors, single selective trigger and semi-beavertail fore-end **$289.50**

G CHAMPLIN OVER & UNDER SHOTGUN

Gauge: 12 only, 2¾″ Chambers.
Action: Fully engraved, choice of frosted or color case hardened, specifications not yet available.
Barrel: Any length or choke desired. Vent rib.
Stock: Custom made to customers specifications with choice of straight or p.g.
Weight: Average 7 to 8 lbs.
Price: **$642.50**
   Deluxe Grade, with finer engraving and walnut.......... 847.50
   Custom Grade, with engraving by one of America's foremost engravers **$1,100.00** and up.

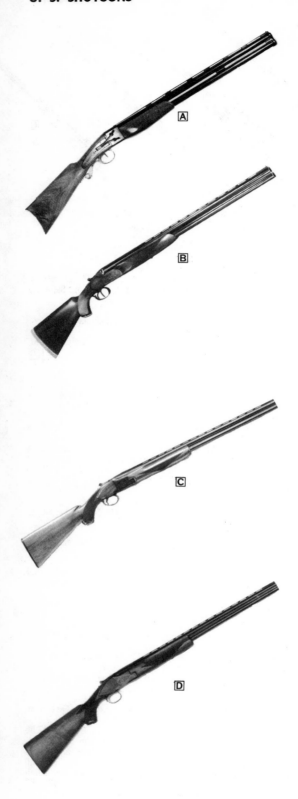

A TINGLE MUZZLE LOADING O-U M1965 SHOTGUN
Gauge: 10 or 12.
Barrels: 30″ over and under, open bores; easily removed for cleaning.
Stock: Walnut (beavertail fore-end).
Features: Barrels, lock and trigger plate blued; buttplate and trigger guard brass. Mule-ear side hammers. Double triggers.
Weight: 8½ lbs., 46″ over-all.
Price: With ventilated rib..............................$169.95

B UNIVERSAL OVER WING O/U SHOTGUN
Gauge: 12, 20. 3″ chamber.
Action: Top lever, hammerless, box lock, double triggers.
Barrel: 26″ vent. rib (Imp. Cyl., & Mod.); 28″ or 30″ (Mod. & Full). Front & Middle sights.
Stock: 14″x1½″x2⅝″. Walnut, checkered p.g. and fore-end. Recoil Pad.
Weight: 7½ lbs. (12); 6½ lbs. (20).
Price: $199.95
With single-trigger, engraved receiver and fancier stock... 249.95

C WINCHESTER 101 OVER-UNDER Field Gun
Gauge: 12 and 28, 2¾″; 20 and 410, 3″.
Action: Top lever, break open. Manual safety combined with bbl. selector at top of receiver tang.
Barrel: Vent. rib 26″ 12, 26½″, 20 and 410 (Imp. Cyl., Mod.), 28″ Mod & Full), 30″ 12 only (Mod. & Full). Metal bead front sight. Chrome plated chambers and bores.
Stock: 14″x1½″x2½″. Checkered walnut p.g. and fore-end; fluted comb.
Weight: 12 ga: 7¾ lbs.; Others 6¼ lbs.; 44¾″ over-all (28″ bbls.).
Features: Single selective trigger, auto ejectors. Hand engraved receiver.
Price: 12 or 20 ga.....................................$350.00
Price: 28 or 410 ga....................................370.00

Winchester 101 Trap Gun
Same as the 101 Field gun except: Metal front and middle bead sights. 30″ (Full & Full) bbl. only. 14⅜″x1⅜″x1⅞″ stock with 1¼″ pitch down and recoil pad. 12 ga. only....................$360.00
With Monte Carlo stock (14⅜″x1⅜″x1⅜x1⅞″), 30″ or 32″, Full and Full or Imp. Mod. and Full..............................$370.00

Winchester 101 Single Barrel Trap Gun
Same as M101 Trap except: Single bbl. 34″ (Full), 32″ (Full) or 32″ (Imp.-Mod.) Vent.-rib. 12 ga. only. Monte Carlo stock.........$350.00

Winchester 101 Combination Trap Set
Same as M101 Trap except: Single bbl. 32″ or 34″ (Full) and extra over-under bbls. 30″ or 32″ (Imp.-Mod. & Full). Includes fitted trunk case $560.00
3-bbl. set: 32″ single bbl. (Full), 32″ single bbl. (Imp.-Mod.), and 32″ over-under bbls. (Imp.-Mod. & Full)....................$735.00

D Winchester 101 Skeet
Same as M101 except: 12 ga., 26″ bbls., 20, 26½″, 12, 20, 28 & 410, 28″. Bored Skeet and Skeet only.....................$350.00

Winchester M101 Combination Skeet Set
Same as M101 20 ga. Skeet except: Includes Skeet bbls. in 410 & 28 ga. Vent. ribs match 20 ga. frame. With fitted trunk case..$750.00

Winchester 101 Magnum Field Gun
Same as 101 Field Gun except: chambers 3″ Magnum shells; 12 & 20 ga. 30″ (Full & Full) bbls. only; hand-engraved receiver, select French walnut stock with fluted comb, hand-checkered pistol grip and beavertail fore-end with recoil pad........................$350.00

A H & R TOPPER MODELS 158 and 198
Gauge: 12, 20 and 410. (2¾″ or 3″ chamber), 16 (2¾″ only).
Action: Takedown. Side lever opening. External hammer, auto ejection. Case hardened frame.
Barrel: 12 ga., 28″, 30″, 32″, 36″; 20 and 410 ga., 28″. (Full choke). 12, 16, 20 ga. available 28″ (Mod.).
Stock: Walnut finished hardwood; p.g., recoil pad. (14″x1¾″x2½″).
Weight: 5 to 6½ lbs., according to gauge and bbl. length.
Features: Self-adj. bbl. lock; coil springs throughout; automatic rebound hammer.
Price: M158 ....$36.95
   Model 198. Chrome frame, ebony stock. 20 ga. and 410, 28″ bbl.
....$42.95

H & R TOPPER JR. MODEL 490
Like M158 except ideally proportioned stock for the smaller shooter. Can be cheaply changed to full size. 20 ga. (Mod.) or 410 (Full) 26″ bbl. $37.95

B H & R TOPPER BUCK MODEL 162
   Same as M158 except 12 ga. 24″ cyl. bored bbl., adj. Lyman peep rear sight, blade front $42.95
Weight: 5½ lbs.; over-all 40″.
Features: Cross bolt safety; push-button action release.

C ITHACA 66 SUPERSINGLE
Gauge: 12, 20, 410 (3″ chamber).
Action: Non-takedown; under lever opening.
Barrel: 12, 20 ga. 28″ (Mod., Full); 12 ga., 30″ (Full); 410, 26″ (Full).
Stock: Straight grip walnut-finish stock and fore-end.
Weight: About 7 lbs.
Features: Rebounding hammer independent of the lever.
Price: $34.95
   With vent. rib, 20 ga. only............................. 49.95

Ithaca 66 Supersingle Youth
   Same as the 66 Standard except: 20 (26″ Bbl., Mod.) and 410 ga. (26″ Bbl., Full) shorter stock with recoil pad.....................$36.95
   With vent. rib, 20 ga. only............................. 51.95

D ITHACA MODEL 66 RS SUPERSINGLE Buckbuster
   Same as the Model 66 Standard except: 12 and 20 ga. only, 22″ bbl. with rifle sights, designed to shoot slugs...............$42.95

E ITHACA 4E GRADE SINGLE BARREL TRAP GUN
Gauge: 12 only.
Action: Top lever break open hammerless, dual locking lugs.
Barrel: 30″ or 32″, rampless rib.
Stock: (14½″x1½″x1⅞″). Select walnut, checkered p.g. and beavertail fore-end, p.g. cap, recoil pad. Monte Carlo comb, cheekpiece. Cast-on, cast-off or extreme deviation from standard stock dimensions $100 extra. Reasonable deviation allowed without extra charge.
Features: Frame, top lever and trigger guard engraved. Gold name plate in stock.
Price: Custom made: Write factory for price.

Ithaca 5E Grade Single Barrel Trap
   Same as 4E except: Vent. rib bbl., better wood, more extensive engraving, and gold inlaid figures. Custom made: Write factory for price.

Ithaca $4500 Grade Ejector
   Same as 5E except: Special wood, better engraving, figures inlaid in green and yellow gold and platinum, gold plated trigger.

F SAVAGE MODEL 220L SINGLE
Gauge: 12, 16, 20, 410 (12, 20 and 410, 3″ chambers).
Action: Side lever break open; automatic top tang safety; hammerless; auto. ejector.
Barrel: 12 ga. 30″; 16, 20 ga. 28″; 410 ga. 26″. Full choke only.
Stock: 14″x1½″x2½″. Walnut, p.g. full fore-end.
Weight: About 6 lbs. Over-all 46″ (30″ bbl.).
Features: Unbreakable coil springs; satin black finish.
Price: $47.50

G GARCIA BRONCO 410 SHOTGUN
   Lightweight single shot (3″ chamber), featuring swing-out chamber, skeletonized 1-pc. receiver and p.g. stock, push-button safety. 4½ lbs.
Price: $24.50

A SEARS SINGLE BARREL GUN
Gauge: 12, 20, 410 (All 3" ga.)
Action: Side button release. External hammer, auto. ejector, coil springs.
Barrel: 12 ga., 30"; 20 ga., 28"; 410, 26". Full choke only.
Stock: 14"x1½"x2½". Walnut finish hardwood, p.g.
Weight: About 7 lbs.
Features: Wide cocking lever; decorated frame.
Price: $39.99
 Youth's Model. 12½" stock with recoil pad; 20 ga. 26" bb., Mod. choke, or 410 ga., 26" bbl., Full choke. Wgt. about 6½ lbs.
Price: $39.99

B STEVENS MODEL 940 Single Barrel Gun
Gauge: 12, 16, 20, 410 (12, 20 and 410, 3" chambers).
Action: Side lever break open; hammer; auto. ejector.
Barrel: 12 ga. 28", 30", 32", 36"; 16, 20 ga. 28"; 410 ga. 26". Full choke only.
Stock: 14"x1½"x2½". Walnut finish, p.g.
Weight: About 6 lbs. Over-all 42" (26" bbl.).
Features: Satin black, decorated frame, low rebounding hammer.
Price: 26" to 32" bbls. ....$37.50 36" bbl.........$38.75

Stevens M940 Youth's Gun
 Same as Model 940 except: 26" bbl., 20 ga. Mod. or 410 Full, 12½" stock with recoil pad. Wgt. about 5½ lbs...................$38.75

C Stevens M94-C
 Similar to M940 except: top lever opening, case hardened finish, checkered p.g.........$39.75 12 ga. 36" bbl.........$41.00

D STEVENS MODEL 94-Y
 Identical to Stevens M94-C, except for shorter stock with rubber recoil pad. 20 ga. 26" bbl. Mod., 410 26" bbl. Full.
Price: $41.00

E UNIVERSAL SINGLE WING SHOTGUN
Gauge: 12 only, 3" chamber.
Action: Top break, takedown, external hammer.
Barrel: 28", full or mod. choke.
Stock: Walnut, p.g.
Weight: About 7 lbs.
Features: Beavertail fore-end. Automatic ejection.
Price: $41.50

F WESTERN FIELD 100 Single Barrel Gun
Gauge: 12, 16, 20, 410 (410, 3" chamber).
Action: Hammerless; thumb slide break open.
Barrel: 12 ga., 30"; 16, 20 ga., 28"; 410 ga., 26". All Full choke.
Stock: Walnut finished, p.g., recoil pad. 13¾"x1½"x2¼".
Weight: 6¼ to 7 lbs.
Features: Automatic safety, auto ejector.
Price: $36.99
 Also available as Youth's Model. 12½" stock, 20 or 410 gauge. Wgt. 6 lbs., 41" over-all...................................$37.99

G WINCHESTER MODEL 370 Single Barrel
Gauge: 12, 20, 410 (3" chamber); 16, 20 and 28 (2¾").
Action: Top break, takedown, external hammer.
Barrel: 12 ga., 30", 32", 36"; 16 ga., 30", 32"; 20 and 28 ga., 28"; 410 ga., 26". Full choke only.
Stock: Hardwood p.g. (14"x1⅜"x2⅜"), full fore-end.
Weight: 5½ to 6¼ lbs. Over-all 48¼" (32" bbl.).
Features: Auto. ejection, rebounding hammer. Top snap opens left or right.
Price: ....$39.95 **Price:** 12 ga. 36" bbl. $40.50
 Also available as Youth's Model. 12½" stock, 20 or 410 ga. Wgt. 5½ (410) or 6 lbs., 26" bbl., 40¾" overall.................$40.50

A MARLIN GOOSE GUN BOLT ACTION
Gauge: 12 only, 3-shot (3″ chamber).
Action: Takedown bolt action, thumb safety, detachable clip.
Barrel: 36″, Full choke.
Stock: Walnut, p.g., recoil pad, leather strap & swivels.
Weight: 7¼ lbs., 57″ over-all.
Features: Double extractors, tapped for receiver sights. Swivels and leather carrying strap. Gold-plated trigger.
Price: $59.95

Glenfield Model 50 Bolt Action
Same as the Marlin Goose Gun except: 12 and 20 ga., 3″. No sling or swivels. Recoil pad on 12 ga. Bbls. 12 ga. 28″, 20 ga. 26″ (Full). Wgt. 6¾ lbs., 49″ over-all (28″ bbl.)......................$49.95

B MOSSBERG MODEL 183K BOLT ACTION
Gauge: 410, 3-shot (3″ chamber).
Action: Bolt; top-loading mag.; thumb safety.
Barrel: 25″ with C-Lect-Choke.
Stock: Walnut finish, p.g., Monte Carlo comb.
Weight: 5½ lbs. 44½″ over-all.
Features: Moulded trigger guard with finger grooves.
Price: $46.45
Also available in 410 ga. with 24″ bbl., detachable Full and Mod. choke tubes, as M183D $44.45

C MOSSBERG MODEL 395K BOLT ACTION
Gauge: 12, 3-shot (3″ chamber).
Action: Bolt; takedown; detachable clip.
Barrel: 28″ with C-Lect-Choke.
Stock: Walnut finish, p.g. Monte Carlo comb; recoil pad.
Weight: 6¾ lbs. 47½″ over-all.
Features: Streamlined action; top safety; grooved rear sight.
Price: $56.95
Also available in 20 ga. 3″ chamber 28″ bbl. 6¼ lbs. as M385K, $52.45, and in 16 ga. 28″ bbl., 6¾ lbs., as M390K...........$55.95

MOSSBERG MODEL 395S BOLT ACTION
Same as Model 395K except 24″ barrels with adjustable folding leaf. rear sight and ramp front, for use with slugs. Sling supplied...$58.95

D SEARS BOLT ACTION 410
Gauge: 410, single shot, 3″ chamber.
Action: Top loading, self-cocking bolt.
Barrel: 24″, Full choke.
Stock: Walnut finished hardwood, p.g., corrugated buttplate.
Weight: 4¾ lbs. 43″ over-all.
Features: Automatic thumb safety.
Price: $34.99
Same, except a repeater with 2-shot detachable clip. Wgt. 5½ lbs. $41.99

E SEARS MODEL 140 BOLT ACTION
Gauge: 12, 20; 3-shot.
Action: Self-cocking bolt.
Barrel: 25″, with adj. choke.
Stock: Walnut finished, p.g., corrugated buttplate.
Weight: 7½ lbs. (12 ga.); 7 lbs. (20 ga.); 46″ over-all.
Features: Double extractors; thumb safety; 2 shot detachable clip.
Price: 12 ga. ....$49.99   20 ga..............$49.99
Price: with adj. choke 54.99

F STEVENS MODEL 51 SINGLE SHOT BOLT ACTION
Gauge: 410, 3″ chamber.
Action: Top loading, streamlined bolt action.
Barrel: 24″ Full choke.
Stock: Walnut finish, checkered fore-end and p.g.
Weight: About 4¾ lbs. Over-all 43½″.
Features: Band extractor, automatic thumb safety.
Price: $37.50

G STEVENS 58 BOLT ACTION SHOTGUN
Gauge: 12, 16, 20 2¾″ chambers. 20 ga. also in 3″. (2-shot detachable clip).
Action: Self-cocking bolt; double extractors; thumb safety.
Barrel: 25″, Full choke.
Stock: Walnut finish, checkered fore-end and p.g., recoil pad.
Weight: 7-7½ lbs. Over-all 46″ (43½″ in 410)
Features: Crisp trigger pull.
Price: $53.50
Also available in 410 ga., 3″ chamber, 3-shot detachable clip, 5½ lbs. $44.75

Stevens 59 Bolt Action
Same as Model 58 410 ga. except: tubular mag. holding five 3″ or six 2½″ shells; 3-shot plug furnished; no recoil pad. Wgt. 6 lbs. 24″ bbl., 44½″ over-all..$54.50

H WESTERN FIELD 172 BOLT ACTION SHOTGUN
Gauge: 12 (3″ chamber).
Action: Self-cocking bolt. Thumb safety, double locking lugs, detachable clip.
Barrel: 28″ adj. choke, shoots rifled slugs.
Stock: Walnut, Monte Carlo design, p.g., recoil pad.
Features: Quick removable bolt with double extractors, grooved rear sight.
Price: $42.95
M175 Same as above except 20 ga., **$39.95**   Without recoil pad and adj. choke $34.95

A BERETTA JAGUAR AUTO PISTOL

6″ bbl. with an over-all length of 8¾″. Wgt. approx. 19 oz. 10-shot magazine with finger spur. 22 LR only. Two piece wrap-around plastic grips are checkered. Adj. rear sight, external hammer, thumb lever safety. Slide stays open on the last shot. Blued. From Galef.
....**$69.95**

B BERETTA PUMA AUTO PISTOL

External-hammer auto pistol. 32 Auto. 10-shot magazine with finger spur. 6″ bbl., weighs approx. 19 oz., 9½″ over-all. Adj. rear sight, thumb lever safety, wrap-around plastic checkered grips. Blued. From Galef. **$69.95**

C BERETTA SABLE AUTO PISTOL

Cal. 22 LR, 10-shot magazine with finger spur. 6″ bbl., 8¾″ over-all, wgt. approx. 26 oz. Adj. rear sight, 3 blade front sight. Crossbolt safety, external hammer. Wrap-around checkered plastic grips. Blued. From Galef. **$87.00**

F ERMA KGP 9mm AUTO PISTOL

9MM version of the P-08. 8-shot magazine. Checkered walnut grips. Toggle-bolt stays open on last shot. Fixed barrel with double action feature and falling block thumb safety lever. Open notch rear and blade front sight. Weighs 38½ oz., 4⅜″ bbl., 8½″ over-all. Blued. L. A. Distributors, importer......................**$129.95**

G BERETTA M90 PISTOL

A new double action pocket pistol. 3½″ bbl., 6¾″ over-all length, 8 round magazine; 19 oz., blue finish; checked black plastic wrap-around grips; fixed sights; sighting rib on slide. Rod extractor functions as chamber indicator. Slide stays open on last shot. In 32 ACP only. From Galef...**$110.00**

D BERETTA BRIGADIER AUTO PISTOL

Military and police auto pistol in 9mm Luger (Parabellum) caliber. Single action, external hammer, side safety. 4½″ barrel, 31 oz., 8″ over-all. Fixed sights. Black plastic wrap-around grips. 8-shot capacity. Slide stays open on last shot. From Galef. Blued..........**$117.50**

E ERMA KGP BABY

Made in 32 and 380 auto., 6-shot magazine and 2¾″ barrel, this toggle-bolt pistol is reminiscent of the Luger design. Blue-black finish; checkered walnut grips; sidelock safety. Length 5¼″ over-all, weight about 19 oz. L. A. Distributors, importer...................**$89.95**

Autoloading Pistols . . .

A ERMA FB1 PISTOL
Lightweight (14 oz.) 25-caliber pistol has 6-shot magazine. 5⅜"
over-all with 2½" barrel, all steel frame with walnut grips and thumb
safety. Blued finish. LA Distributors, importer.................$39.95

B ERMA 22 PISTOLEN
22 version of the famous Model P-08. 8-shot magazine takes 22 LR.
Checkered walnut grips. Familiar toggle-bolt stays open on last shot.
Open notch rear and blade front sight. 9" over-all, wgt. 36 oz. with a
4⅝" bbl. Blued. L. A. Distributors, importer.................$79.95
    ERMA 22 "NAVY" PISTOLEN
Similar to Erma 22 Luger, except with 12" barrel, walnut fore-end,
adj. rear sight. 16½" over-all, 48 oz. LA Distributors, importer..$99.95

HAWES WASP MARK I PISTOL
A basic hammerless blowback smallbore pocket pistol. 6-shot magazine, 4½" over-all, weight 12 oz., smooth white plastic grips.
25 ACP, blue:........$29.95   Chrome..............$30.95
22 LR, blue...........30.95   Chrome..............31.95

HAWES WASP MARK V PISTOL
Long-barreled version of a typical blowback pocket pistol. Fixed
sights, blue finish, checked plastic grips; exposed hammer, 6" barrel,
10-shot in 22 LR, 8 in 32 ACP. 22 LR, blue.................$59.95
Chrome.................$62.95   32 ACP, blue.......64.95

HAWES OLYMPIC PISTOL
Built on a typical rimfire rifle bolt action. One piece wood stock;
open sights; 11⅛" bbl. 22 LR only......................$49.95

D LLAMA MODEL IXA AUTO PISTOL
45 ACP cal. Blued finish, ribbed slide, broad hammer spur and
adj. square notch rear and blade front target sights. 7-shot magazine.
Wgt. 2 lbs. 6 oz., 5⅜" high, 8½" over-all, 5" bbl. Thumb and grip
safeties. Stoeger, importer............................$92.50

LLAMA MODEL VIII AUTO PISTOL
Same as above except: Super cal., 9-shot, 2 lbs. 6½ oz.....$92.50

F MAB AUTOLOADING PISTOL
Uses a rotary unlocking system, exposed hammer. 8 or 15 shot
magazine, thumb safety, fixed sights. Blued finish. Cal. 9mm, wgt.
38 oz. Mars Equipment, importers.....................$109.00

G MAUSER HSc AUTO PISTOL
This commercial model is made in West Germany by the original
Mauser organization. In cals. 32 (8-shot) and 380 (7-shot) Auto. Pistol
is 6⅜" over-all, with a 3⅜" bbl. and weighs 23 oz. Features exposed
hammer spur, double action with thumb safety lever and magazine
disconnect safety. Also, walnut checkered grips, blued finish and
fixed sights. Interarms, importer.....................$110.00

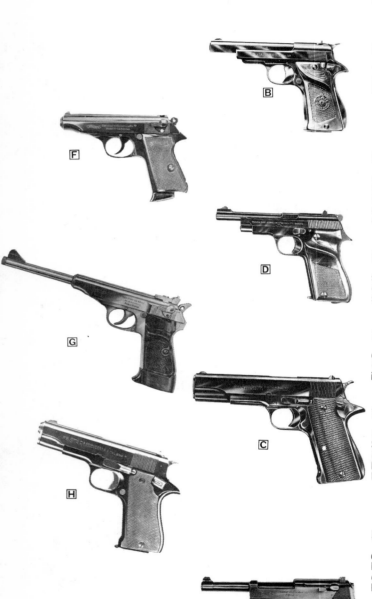

A SIG 210 AUTOMATICS

Available in 22 LR, 7.65 Luger or 9mm Luger, 8-shot 4¾" bbl., 8½" over-all, wgt. approx. 34 oz. Double pull trigger. Fixed notch rear, blade front sights. Grooved wooden grips. Thumb safety. Polished blue finish. Imported by Grieder, Benet Arms Co., & Casanova Guns......**$220.00**

With checkered hard rubber grips and matte finish....... 197.00

Conversion unit, available with all components necessary to convert to cal. 22.................................**$100.00**

SIG 210 TARGET AUTOMATICS

Same as the M210 except: 7.65mm and 9mm only. 6" bbl., adj. target trigger, micro. rear sight adj. for w. and e.; adj. front sight. Hard rubber grips and matte finish. Wgt. 38⅓ oz., 9⅔" over-all..**$249.00**

Same, but with 4¾" bbl............................ 225.00

B STAR MODEL FR AUTO PISTOL

All feature quick takedown, thumbrest grips, checkered backstrap, thumb- and half-cock safeties. 22 LR, 10-shot magazine; extra mag. furnished at prices shown. Garcia, importer. Standard, 5" bbl. 26 oz. Fixed sights.

Blued....**$59.95**　　Chromed....**$69.95**　　Chromed, engr. ..**$94.95**

Star Sport, same as the "FR" except: 6" bbl., 28 oz., adj. sights.

Blued............**$59.95**　　　　　Chromed............**$69.95**

C STAR MODEL A, B & P AUTOS

Based on the U. S. Pistol, M1911A1 short recoil system with half-cock and thumb safeties, exposed hammers, these pistols feature 9-shot (.38 Super Model A & 9MM Para. Model B) and 7-shot (45ACP Model P) magazines. Weigh approx. 2 lbs. 6 oz., have 5" bbl., and are 8½" over-all. They have checkered walnut grips, fixed sights and are blued. Garcia, importer.........................**$89.95**

H STAR STARLIGHT PISTOL

A recoil-operated, Browning-type design with light alloy frame. A shortened, lightened version of the Star Model B, 9mm Parabellum cal. only. 4¼" bbl., 25 oz. blue finish, checked wood grips, fixed sights. Garcia, importer **$89.95**

D UNIQUE CORSAIR AUTO PISTOL

Has thumb and magazine safeties as wel as a half-cock position on the exposed hammer. Thumbrest checkering plastic grips, adj. sights. 6" bbl., 9⅛" over-all, wgt. 26 oz., blued, 10-shot. Cal. 22 LR. Garcia, importer. **$65.95**

E WALTHER P-38 AUTOMATIC PISTOL

This commercial model is made in W. Germany of lightweight alloys, in polished blue finish. Weight 27½ oz., 8⁷⁄₁₆", over-all; 4¹⁵⁄₁₆" barrel. Safety locks firing pin, blocks action and drops the hammer; signal pin indicating when chamber is loaded; single or double action, external hammer. 8-shot magazine (2 furnished), checkered plastic grips and lanyard swivel are standard. Interarms, importer...........**$140.00**

Same but with matte finish 106.00

Same but in 22 LR cal. with matte finish 132.00

F WALTHER MODEL PP PISTOL

A line of pocket auto pistols that feature an exposed hammer, double or single action. Indicator pin shows if chamber is loaded. Bbl. length, 3⅞"; wgt., 23 ozs., over-all, 6⁵⁄₁₆", Mag. capacity, 8 shots except 380 cal. holds 7. Cals. 32 or 380. Blued. Interarms....**$106.00**

In 22 LR caliber 112.00

G WALTHER SPORT MODEL PISTOL

Basically the Walther PP in 22 LR, this pistol offers a longer barrel (6"), click rear sight, thumb rest grips, extension mag. Interarms, importer. **$120.00**

WALTHER PPKS

A shortened version of the PP, replacing the PPK which did not qualify for importation. It is the PP fitted with PPK slide and barrel. White-insert combat sights. In 22 LR, 10 shots; 32, 8; 380, 7. 3⁵⁄₁₆" bbl, 6³⁄₁₆" over-all, 4⁵⁄₁₆" high. 32 and 380..**$106.00**　　22..**$112.00**

A HAMMERLI INTERNATIONAL AUTO PISTOLS 206-207
Adj. precision trigger set for 2 lbs. 7¹¹/₁₆" bbl., high speed action, micro. rear sight adj. for w. and e. ⅛" front sight. Muzzle brake and bbl. wgt. standard. Thumbrest, checkered grips. 22 S or LR....**$215.00**
Model 207, same as 206 except: adj. French walnut grips made to ISU rules **$245.00**

B HAMMERLI INTERNATIONAL AUTO PISTOLS 208-209-210
M208 is like the M206 but has 6" bbl., is without muzzle brake, and has a 3-lb. trigger pull. Designed for Ladies Matches, it weighs only 35 oz. Price....................................... **N.A.**
M209 is like the M206 but offers several advanced features: 6 gas ports over chamber permit adj. of leakage for balancing to various cartridge brands or types; new combination muzzle brake and new light bolt for less jar. Cal. 22 Short only.
M209, standard walnut grips.......................... **N.A.**
M210, adj. walnut grips............................... **N.A.**
Regular grips with thumbrest and checkering **$15.00**. Adj. grips with checkering **$40.00**. Magazine for cal. 22 S or LR **$9.00**. Additional wgt. **$6.00**. Muzzle brake **$4.00**. Grieder, importer.

C HAMMERLI MATCH PISTOLS 104-105
Single shot pistol has 5-lever set-trigger, adj. to fractions of an ounce. Round 11⅛" bbl. Micro. rear sight with click adj. for w. and e. ⅛" front sight. Selected French walnut grips with adj. shelf, trigger-finger ramp and custom finish. Martini action. Cal. 22 LR. Imported by Grieder **$255.00**
Model 105, same as 104 except: octagonal bbl. and deep blue finish **$320.00**

D WALTHER OSP RAPID FIRE MATCH PISTOL
A newly designed pistol, complying with International Rules. 22 Short only; 5-shot magazine. Simple barrel take-down; bolt held open after last shot. Weight, about 41 oz., 11⅞" over-all. 5¾" bbl. Supplied with spare magazine, barrel weight, cleaning rod, brush and wrench. Interarms, importer **$198.00**
Walther GSP variant of OSP with slabside heavy barrel, no weights.
.... **$220.00**

E ARMINIUS REVOLVERS
Solid-frame, double-action, swing-out cylinder revolvers with lockwork assembled to grip frame. Ventilated rib, 3", 4", 6" and 9½" bbls. Floating firing pin, checked one-piece plastic grip. LA Distributors, importer.

Standard model, 22 RF, blue....**$37.95**		22 WMR, blue....**$41.95**
Chromed....**$41.95**	Combination, 22 and 22 WMR, blue....**$50.95**	
With target sights, blue......**$55.95**	Chromed 55.95	
Target model, 22 RF, blue.... **41.95**	Chromed 44.95	
Target model, 32 CF, blue..... **44.95**	Chromed 47.95	
Target model, 38 Spl., blue.... **49.95**	Chromed 54.95	

F ASTRA CADIX REVOLVERS
Double action revolvers with adj. rear sight; shrouded ejector rod; one piece checkered stocks and swing out cylinder. Cals. 22 LR (9 shots) or 38 Spec. (5 shots) with 4" or 6" bbl. Wgt. 25 to 27 oz., blued, Garcia, importer................................ **$64.50**

G DAKOTA REVOLVERS
Single action revolvers with case hardened receivers; brass trigger guard and backstrap; fixed sights; floating firing pin and one-piece smooth walnut grips. 4⅝", 5½, or 7½" barrels ($2.25 extra for 7½") in 22 rimfire, 22 WMR, 357 Magnum or 45 Colt caliber. Intercontinental Arms. **$89.75**
With extra 22 WMR cylinder............................. **97.20**
Also as Super Dakota in 41 and 44 Magnum calibers, 5½" and 7½" bbls. with flat-top frame, adj. sights front and rear, long magnum grip, square-back guard................................. **$99.75**

H Dakota Engraved Models Identical to $89.75 models above, and in same calibers, but heavily engraved in scroll and floral pattern on frame, cylinder and hammer. Guard and straps polished bright brass, frame finished bright, rest blue. One-piece smooth walnut grips.
4⅝" and 5½" bbls........**$165.00**   7½".......**$175.00**

[A] DEPUTY 22 SINGLE ACTION REVOLVER

6-shot, loading and ejection through loading gate. 4¾" bbl. Fixed front sight, notch rear. Black satin finish, checkered walnut grips. 22 S, L, LR. LA Distributors, importer..................**$39.95**
Also, as the Adjusto with adj. target sights................**47.95**
Available as Deputy Combo with interchangeable cylinder for 22WMR **$49.95**
Also, as the Adjusto with adj. target sights................**59.95**
The Deputy is also available as a 6-shot single action revolver in 357 Magnum. Satin black finish, except for color case-hardened frame; walnut grips..**$79.95**

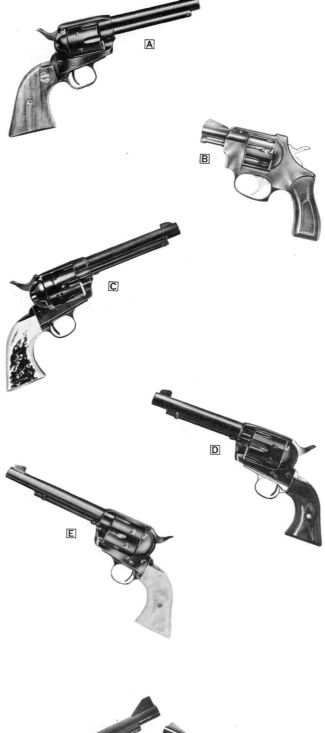

[B] GUARDIAN REVOLVER

Solid-frame, double-action, swing-out cylinder revolver. 5-shot, blue finish, fixed sights, checked plastic grip, 2¼" bbl. Firearms Import & Export, importer.
Black chrome ....**$39.95**   Bright chrome **$44.95**

[C] HAWES WESTERN MARSHAL REVOLVERS

Single action, frontier style 6-shot revolvers made in 45 Long Colt, 357 or 44 Mag. Moulded stag grips, floating firing pin, 5½" barrel, fixed sights. All working parts of steel, blue finish over-all. Weight, 40 oz. **$89.95**
As above, but with an extra cylinder compatible with the barrel, 357 Mag./9mm, 44 Mag/44-40, 45 Colt/45ACP...............**$99.95**
As above but in 22 S, L or LR cal....**$54.95**   22 WMR.... **57.95**
With both 22 cal. cylinders..........................**64.95**

[D] HAWES MONTANA MARSHAL REVOLVERS

Same as Western Marshal except: solid brass backstrap and trigger guard, hand-rubbed rosewood grips.......................**$99.95**
As above, but in 22 cal. rimfire.......................**64.95**

[E] HAWES TEXAS MARSHAL

Same as Western Marshal except: revolver is fully chromed with black or white Pearlite grips.......................**$104.95**
As above, but in 22 cal. rimfire.......................**69.95**

[F] HAWES CHIEF MARSHALL REVOLVER

Single action, frontier style, 6-shot revolver in 357, 44 Magnum or 45 Colt caliber. Ramp front sight, click adjustable target rear sight let into raised boss on top strap. Blue finish; smooth rosewood grips; 6" bbl., 48 oz. 11¾" over-all **$109.95**

HAWES VIRGINIA CITY MARSHALL REVOLVER

Same as Western Marshall except frame and barrel are blue, cylinder, guard and backstrap in bright nickel plate; pearlite grips......**$99.95**

[G] HERTER'S GUIDE REVOLVERS

Solid-frame double-action, swing-out cylinder revolver with lockwork assembled to removable trigger guard/grip frame. Click-adjustable rear sight, ventilated rib, one-piece checked plastic grip.
22 LR, 8-shot, 4" or 6" bbl., blue....**$39.95**   Chromed....**$44.95**
38 Spl., 6-shot, 4" or 6" bbl., chromed..................**49.95**

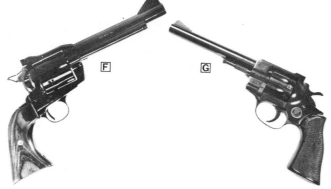

LLAMA MARTIAL 38 REVOLVER
Similar to the Martial 22 above except 38 Spl. cal., 4" (29 oz.) or 6" bbl. $74.50
Llama Martials also available in chrome or blue engraved..$112.50
In chrome plate 89.95

ROSSI REVOLVERS
32 S&W Long and 38 spl. (6-shot) revolvers with swing-out cylinders, simultaneous ejection. 3" or 4" bbls. Wgt.: 32, 19 oz. 7" over-all. In presentation case. Garcia, importer.
   32 S & W, 4" bbl. blue or nickel plated finish...........$65.00
   38 Spl., 4" bbl., blue or nickel plated finish........... 65.00

F J. P. SAUER MEDALION REVOLVER
6-shot swing-out cylinder double action revolver. With adj. rear sight, checkered walnut grips, wide trigger and hammer spur. Cal. 38 S&W Spl. with 3", 4" or 6" bbl.; or 22 LR with 4" or 6" bbl. 11⅛" over-all, wgt. about 39 oz. (6"). Blued. Hawes Firearms Co., importer.
....$119.95

G J. P. SAUER TROPHY REVOLVER
Same as above except with walnut thumbrest target grips and vent. rib, 6" bbl. only. $129.95

SOLINGEN LIBERTY CHIEF REVOLVER
6-shot revolvers with swing-out cylinder, simultaneous ejection. Fixed sights, adj. trigger, checkered, rounded walnut grips. Cal. 38 Spl., 16½" over-all (2" bbl.) Solingen Cutlery, importers.
   Blued $59.95

STALLION SINGLE ACTION REVOLVER
6-shot, loading and ejection through loading gate. Cals. 22 LR or 22 WMR, 5½" or 6½" bbl., 11⅝" over-all (6½"), wgt. 2 lbs. 6 oz. Rear sight adj. for w.&e., ramp front. Smooth walnut grips with interior fastening. Blued. Galef, importer...................$87.00
   Also in 357 Mag. or 45 Colt.......................... 89.95

J TAURUS REVOLVER
Swing-out cylinder, checkered grips, fixed sights. Cal. 38 Spl., 4" round bbl., 6-shot. Wgt. 32 oz. Blued or nickel. Garcia, importer. $60.50

A HERTER'S POWERMAG REVOLVER
Single action, frontier-style 6-shot revolver made in Herter's own 401 Powermag caliber. Cartridges and ctg. components available from them. 6½" bbl. 12½" over-all. Extra-long grips, adj. rear and ramp front sights. $59.95

HERTER'S CUSTOM GRADE SUPER REVOLVER
Same as the Powermag except in 357 Mag. or 44 Mag. cal.
....$59.95

B HERTER'S WESTERN SINGLE ACTION
22 rimfire, 6-shot single action revolver with 5" bbl., plastic staghorn grip, blade front sight, rear adj. for w & e. Blued......$27.45

C I.N.A. TIGER REVOLVERS
5 shot, walnut grips, swing-out cylinder. 3" or 4½" barrel. Weight 13½ oz. (3" bbl.) 38 Spl. Firearms I & E. Corp., importer.
   Blued.............$52.95   Nickeled.............$55.95
   Same, only 32 S&W Long, 6 shot cylinder.
   Blued $50.95

D LLAMA MARTIAL 22 REVOLVER
A match revolver in 22 LR cal. with 6" vent. rib bbl. Micro rear sight adj. for w. and e. Wide, grooved trigger and hammer. Recessed cyl. Target style, checkered walnut grips. Wgt. 26 oz. Stoeger, agents.
....$74.50

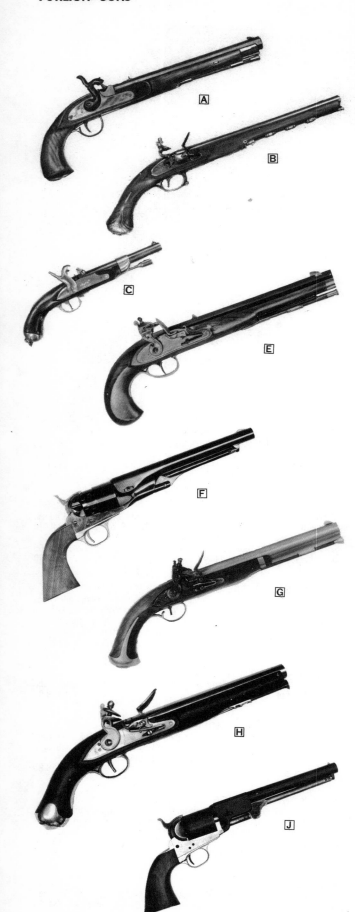

Ⓐ DIXIE KENTUCKY PERCUSSION PISTOL
Muzzle-loading caplock single shot with 9″ octagonal rifled barrel, cal. 40. Maple stock, brass furniture, open sights. Black powder only **$62.50**
Same as above except flintlock...........................**69.50**
Dixie shows numerous other flintlock and percussion revolvers and pistols in their catalog 118 cost $1.00 post paid.

Ⓑ DIXIE FLORENTINE HOLSTER PISTOL
A flintlock with a 13″ smoothbore barrel, 21″ over-all. Walnut full stock. All furniture is ornamented in high relief and silver plated; barrel polished bright. **$145.00**

Ⓒ DIXIE M1822 FRENCH PISTOL
Replica of the French Model 1822 flintlock converted to percussion. Smoothbore, 71 caliber. Ramrod cupped to form powder measure. Brass furniture, walnut stock. **$69.95**

Ⓓ HAWES FAVORITE PISTOL
Replica of the famous Stevens Favorite tip-up target pistol, with chrome frame and blued 8″ barrel, moulded checkered white plastic grips. Fires 22 S, L or LR single-shot. Weight, 20 oz.; length 12″ over-all **$35.95**

Ⓔ KENTUCKIAN FLINTLOCK or PERCUSSION PISTOL
A single shot pistol designed for black powder only. 9½″ octagon barrel, caliber 44, rifled. Brass front and steel rear sights are dovetailed into barrel. Case hardened, engraved lockplate. Trigger guard, barrel cap, ramrod tip and thimbles solid brass. Polished one-piece full-length stock of select walnut. Weight about 40 oz.; 15½″ over-all. Imported by Intercontinental Arms. Either form..............**$59.95**

Ⓕ MARS EQUIPMENT 44 ARMY
Exact replica of Colt's 1860 Army revolver. Caliber 44, using .451″ round ball, black powder and caps. 8″ round barrel, walnut stocks, blue finish with case hardened frame. Weight, 44 oz...........**$89.95**
Similar in 36 cal. Navy, brass mounted...................**49.95**

Ⓖ MARS EQUIPMENT FLINTLOCK PISTOLS
Replica of the Harpers Ferry, model 1805. 16″ over-all, 10″ bbl., 54 cal. rifled bore. Varnished wood, brass mountings. Casehardened lockplate marked with eagle, "U.S." and "Harpers Ferry 1807"....**$99.95**
Also, Virginia model similar to the M-1805 but with swivel ramrod and shorter grip. Marked "Virginia" and "Richmond 1812"....**$99.95**

Ⓗ MARS EQUIPMENT BRITISH FLINTLOCK PISTOL
A replica of the British cavalry weapon of the Geoge III period. 69 caliber, smoothbore, for BLACK POWDER ONLY. Full length walnut finished stock, steel barrel (9″) and lock, brass fittings. Lock is marked "TOWER" and GR under a crown. Weight about 3½ lbs., 15¼″ over-all **$39.95**

Ⓙ NAVY ARMS 1861 COLT REVOLVER
A replica of the Colt 1861 Navy, 36 caliber percussion revolver. 7½″ blued steel barrel; case hardened frame; brass back strap and trigger guard; one-piece walnut grips. Wgt. 41 oz., 13″ over-all. **$90.00**
In presentation walnut case with powder flask, bullet mould and capper at **$125**. Engraving extra; **$60**, **$80**, **$120**, depending on style.

A NAVY ARMS 1860 ARMY REVOLVER
A percussion Army revolver, a copy of the 1860 Colt, with a pol-walnut grips. Cal. 36 or 44...........................$45.00

B NAVY ARMS TARGET REVOLVER
Identical to Navy 1860 Army Revolver but with full-length barrel rib extending back to form a top strap. Fitted with click-adjustable target type rear sight, hand-tuned action. In 36 or 44 percussion caliber.
....$125.00

NAVY ARMS WELLS FARGO REVOLVER
A replica of the 1848 cal. 31 Colt, without rammer. Case hardened frame and hammer; 3" or 5" bbl., polished brass guard and straps.
....$75.00

C NAVY ARMS DRAGOON REVOLVERS
Accurate copies of Colt 44 1st, 2nd and 3rd Model Dragoon revolvers. 7½" bbls., wt. 4 lbs. 2 oz., length 14"...................$100.00

D NAVY ARMS BABY DRAGOON
Replica of the 31 cal. Colt 1848 with 3" or 6" barrel......$75.00

NAVY ARMS SHOULDER STOCK of highly polished walnut, fits all Navy Arms percussion revolvers...........................$30.00

NAVY ARMS "YANK" AND "SHERIFF'S" REVOLVERS
Replicas of the Colt 1851 Navy revolver. Caliber 36, percussion. 7½" octagon barrel (Yank only); case hardened frame and loading lever; silver plated backstrap and trigger guard..............$90.00
Also available as Sheriff's model, with barrel length to customer order, with or without loading lever. Special order only........$90.00
Engraved Yanks, $60, $80, $120 extra, depending on style.

E NAVY ARMS ROLLING BLOCK PISTOL
Exact copy of Remington Number 3 rolling block pistol. Cal. 357 Magnum, with blued steel barrel, case-hardened frame, and walnut stock. Cased with accessories $125.00

NAVY ARMS KENTUCKY PISTOL
Flintlock, with rifled steel barrel, blued. Case hardened, engraved lockplates. Cal. 44, 15½" over-all. Navy Arms, importer....,$80.00
Engraved with carved stock $25.00 extra.

F NAVY ARMS 1858 NEW MODEL ARMY REVOLVER
A replica of the Remington 44 caliber Civil War percussion revolver. 8" octagon barrel; brass trigger guard; two-piece walnut grips. Weight 46 oz., 13¾" over-all. Blued.............................$90.00
Also available in 36 caliber with 7⅜" barrel.............. 90.00
Engraving extra; $70, $90, $130, depending on style.
Navy also supplies a full line of M.L. accessories, cappers, pouches, holsters, flasks and moulds. Brochure on request.

G POTOMAC ARMS WALKER REVOLVER
A replica of the 1847 Colt Walker, the first of the typical Colts. 9" bbl., 15¾" long; 4 lbs. 8 oz., case-hardened frame, hammer and rammer. Brass square-back guard, one-piece walnut grip, engraved cylinder. 44 caliber. $110.00

H POTOMAC ARMS WELLS FARGO REVOLVER
Copy of the rammerless 1848 Colt 31 cal. revolver supplied to Wells Fargo. 3" or 6" bbl., case-hardened frame and hammer. Etched cylinder, square-back brass guard and straps, one-piece grip. $75.00

J POTOMAC ARMS DRAGOON REVOLVER
Replica of the Colt 1st Model 4 Dragoon of 1848. 7½" bbl., 14" long, 4 lbs. 2 oz. Engraved cylinder, case-hardened frame, hammer and rammer; polished brass guard and straps; one-piece smooth walnut grip. $110.00

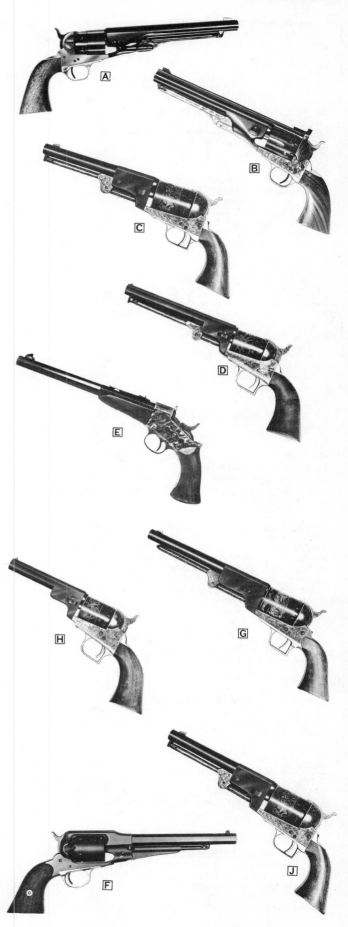

A RENEGADE PERCUSSION MODEL
Double barreled pistol, rifled, in 36 or 44 caliber, for black powder only. 8¼" blued barrels; case hardened frame. Sideplates, hammers, brass trigger guard and brass buttcap engraved. Proofed with 30% overload, certificate furnished. Weight 32 oz. Intercontinental Arms.
....**$39.95**

B REPLICA ARMS 44 DRAGOON
6-shot 44-cal. replica of the 2nd Dragoon Model percussion muzzle-loading revolver. 7½" bbl., blued and case-hardened. Square-back brass trigger guard. For black powder use........................**$104.50**
Flask **19.95**

C REPLICA ARMS 1861 NAVY-1860 ARMY
36-cal., 6-shot black powder percussion Navy revolver, duplicating the Colt 1861 Navy. Frame, lever and hammer are case-hardened, rest of metal is blued. Iron or brass back strap is cut for stock....**$89.95**
Same, but 44-cal. Army **89.95**
Shoulder stock, either................................ **35.00**

D REPLICA ARMS WALKER REVOLVER
A replica of the big Walker Colt, this caplock gun weighs about 4½ lbs., measures 15¾" over-all. 6-shot. Case-hardened frame, hammer and lever; brass trigger guard. Cylinder has rolled engraving scene. 44 caliber, for black powder only. 9" octagon-round bbl. Left hand twist. From Replica Arms...........................**$115.00**
Walker powder flask...................................... **19.95**
Walker mould, single cavity.............................. **11.50**
Walker tool **3.00**
Cased, with all accessories............................. **188.50**

E REPLICA ARMS TEXAS PATERSON of 1836
Cal. 36 round ball only 6", 7½", 9" or 12" bbls. 11 groove, slow right hand twist. 17" over-all with 12" bbl. Folding trigger; smooth walnut grips. Case-hardened frame and hammer. Notch in hammer is rear sight, brass blade post front. 5-shot, blued, engraved cyl., for black powder only. From Replica Arms **$104.50**. With 12" bbl., **$109.50**
Paterson powder flask...**$20.00** Mould 12.50
Capper .... 12.00 Rod 1.50

F REPLICA ARMS BABY DRAGOON of 1848
Cal. 31, 5-shot. 4", 5", 6" octagon bbl. revolver, 10⅜" (6" bbl.) over-all, wgt. 25 oz. Case-hardened frame. Square brass trigger guard and back strap. One-piece smooth walnut grips. Notched hammer rear and post front sights. Polished blue finish, etched cyl. For black powder only. From Replica Arms...................................**$76.25**
Brass bullet mould, double cavity........................ **11.50**
Powder flask, small....................................... **9.50**

G REPLICA ARMS WELLS FARGO REVOLVER
Like the Baby Dragoon except: made with 3", 4", 5" or 6" bbl. without loading lever....................................**$73.00**

REPLICA ARMS REMINGTON 45
A modern copy of the Remington 1875 single-action revolver. In 45 Colt and 38 Spl. calibers only, blued, 6 shot. Modern automatic safety bar. **$149.95**

REPLICA ARMS SINGLE SHOT PISTOL
Modern solid-frame, single-shot 44 cal. percussion pistol in frontier revolver style. 9" blued bbl., smooth one-piece wood grip, case-hardened frame and hammer. Available with interchangeable 28-gauge bbl. ....**$69.50.** With extra 28-gauge bbl. **$89.50**

H NAVY ARMS DERRINGER
A shooting replica of the sharps 4-barrel pistol. Polished brass frame; 2⅝" blued steel bbls. Black plastic carved grips. Spur trigger. Barrels move forward for loading, firing pin rotates to each bbl. position. 22 Short only. Weight 10 oz., 5" over-all...............**$40.00**
Also available in presentation walnut case at **$45.00.**

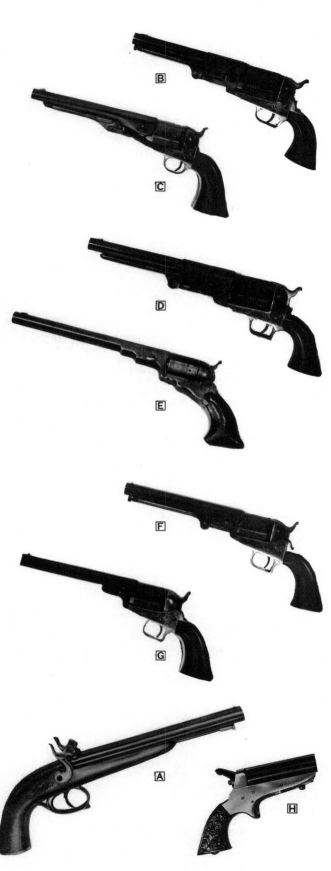

A CENTURY SQUIBMAN AUTOLOADING RIFLE
A semiautomatic rifle with 15 round clip. Contoured 19½″ barrel with muzzle brake. Cocking indicator, grooved receiver for scope mounting, bead front sight, blade rear sight adj. for elevation. Shell deflector can be removed, hold-open bolt provision. 22LR only. Wgt. 5¾ lbs., 40½″ over-all. Century Arms, Inc., importer.
Price: $39.50

B ERMA M22 CARBINE
A close copy of the U.S. M1 in 22 LR. 10-shot mag., 17¾″ barrel, 35⁵⁄₁₆″ over-all, original type sights. Receiver grooved for scope. 15-shot mag. also available at extra cost. 5¾ lbs. LA Distributors, importers $69.95

C FRANCHI CENTENNIAL AUTOLOADING RIFLE
A semi-automatic rifle with tubular magazine in the buttstock holds 11 22 L R cartridges (16 Shorts in Gallery model) Push-button cross-bolt safety, receiver grooved for scope mounting. Quick takedown feature. 21″ barrel with gold bead ramp front and step adjustable open rear sights. Stock is walnut with checkered p.g. and finger-grooved semi-beavertail fore-end. Weight 5 lbs., 2 oz., 39″ over-all. Stoeger, importer ....$ 86.95
Deluxe model with fully engraved receiver 124.95

D GEVARM E1 AUTOLOADING RIFLE
Carbine style take down rifle. Detachable 8 shot clip, cal. 22 LR. 19½″ bbl. (6 grooves, 17½″ twist). Reversible spring guide. Striker bar on breechblock, fires from open bolt, automatic ejection. Receiver grooved for Tip-Off mounts. Blade front sight, open adj. rear. Bolt handle safety. French walnut two-piece p.g. stock and fore-end, p.g. cap. 36⅞″ over-all. Under 21″ taken down. Gevelot, Canada, importers, U.S. dists., Blumenfeld Co...................$73.70

E GEVARM A3 AUTOLOADING SPORTER
Same as E1 except 19½″ bbl., tunnel front sight with 5 interchangeable inserts, tangent sliding leaf rear. French walnut one-piece p.g. stock, schnabel-type fore-end tip....................$92.40

HERTER'S G-90 22 AUTO RIFLE
Tubular magazine holds 12 22 LR; side safety, bolt holds open on last shot, 20″ bbl. Walnut p.g. stock and fore-end. Receiver grooved for tipoff scope mounts.. Blade front sight, adj. rear. 40½″ over-all, 5¾ lbs. Herter, importers...........................$39.55
With 4x scope and mount............................. 50.55

F NAVY ARMS 66 RIFLE
Lever action 22 rimfire rifle built to resemble the Winchester 66. Full length tubular magazine, 14 LR capacity, brass frame and buttplate. 18″ blued bbl. Blade front sight, open leaf rear. Straight-grip walnut-finish stock, not checkered. 39½″ over-all, wgt. 7 lbs. Navy Arms, importer $120.00

G SARMCO MODEL TZ-17 RIFLE
5-shot bolt action hunting carbine in 22 LR. Walnut half-p.g. stock, adj. trigger pull, blade front sight, open tangent adj. rear. Wgt. 5.9 lbs. Sarmco, importer $70.00

TRADEWINDS MODEL 311A RIFLE
Bolt action 22 LR repeater with detachable 5-shot clip magazine; sliding safety on receiver locks trigger and bolt handle. Open 3-leaf rear sight, hooded ramp front; receiver grooved for scope mounting. Monte Carlo walnut stock with checkered p.g. and fore-end; sling swivels. Wgt. 6 lbs., 41¼″ over-all. Tradewinds, importer.....$84.50
5-shot clip...........$4.75   10-shot clip...........5.75

H TRADEWINDS AUTOLOADING RIFLE
Detachable 5-shot mag., 23¾″ bbl. cal. 22 LR. Bead front sight, 3-leaf folding rear. Receiver grooved for scope mounts. Walnut p.g. stock with cheekpiece, schnabel fore-end. 41½″ over-all, 5¾ lbs. Tradewinds, importer $89.50

J WALTHER KKJ—22 RF & HORNET SPORTER
Bolt action sporting rifle, cal. 22 LR, 22 WMR or 22 Hornet. 22″ barrel; 5-shot detachable clip magazine; open rear sight adjustable for w. and e. and bead front sight. Checkered Monte Carlo walnut p.g. stock (13⅞″x1⅜″x1¾″x2½″). Cross-bolt safety, receiver grooved for tip-off mounts. 41⅛″ over-all, wgt. 6 lbs. Double set triggers $10 extra. Interarms, importers................................$144.00
22 Hornet or 22 RF Magnum calibers.................. 144.00

A ALASKAN BOLT ACTION RIFLES

Made in Belgium, these rifles are available in three styles. Magnum rifles are chambered for 338, 300 Win. 7mm Rem. and 300 Weatherby. All have Monte Carlo stock of French walnut, p.g. and fore-end checkered and capped with rosewood; sling swivels and recoil pad attached. 24" barrel on rifles, 20" barrel on Magnum Carbine which has full length Mannlicher stock. No sights. Standard rifle can be had in 30-06, 243 or 7x57 but does not have recoil pad. Skinner's Sportsmans Supply, importer ....$200.00 to $225.00

B BSA MONARCH DELUXE RIFLES

Available in 222, 243, 270, 308, 30-06 and 7mm Mag. BSA rifles feature a fully adjustable trigger, a bolt head that encloses the cartridge and is in turn enclosed by the barrel extension, a gas-proof cocking piece, hinged floorplate, silent safety with cocking indicator, integral scope dovetails, and a checkered, walnut stock with cheekpiece and recoil pad. Weight about 6¼ lbs. From Galef. $149.95

BSA MONARCH DELUXE VARMINT RIFLE

Same as Monarch DeLuxe except has heavy barrel, and made in 222 Rem. or 243 Win. only. About 8½ lbs. From Galef..........$169.95

C CETME-SPORT AUTO RIFLE

5-shot autoloader with unusual roller and cam breech-locking mechanism. Available with wood or steel (with bipod) fore-end. Flip-up aperture rear sight, protected blade front. Muzzle brake, carrying sling, spare mag., cleaning kit furnished. Cal. 308, 17¾" 4-groove bbl. (9.4" twist), 40" over-all, 10½ lbs. Cannot be converted to full auto. fire. Mars Equipment, importers.............................$229.95
    Scope mounts with 1" or 26mm rings................... 12.00
    20-shot magazine 9.00

CONTINENTAL ARMS RIFLE

Bolt action rifle with hinged floorplate has Siemens Martin barrel; integral half rib with express rear, hinged hooded front ramp sights; swivel holder. Stock is of French walnut, checkered fore-end and p.g. with trap in grip cap; horn or ebony tip. Available in 338, 458 Win. Mag.; 244, 375 H&H, 8x68S, 416 Rigby, 505 Gibbs or custom chambered in other calibers. Continental Arms, importer...../......$450.00

D CONTINENTAL ARMS DOUBLE RIFLE

Boxlock action, engraved with single selective trigger and auto. ejectors. Blade front and express rear sights. Straight two-piece stock with checkered p.g. and fore-end. Chambered for 270 Win., 30-40, 8x57JRS, 303, 30-06, 375 H&H, 450 500, 450 Nitro Express, 465 or 470 Rigby. Continental Arms, importer. Write for prices.

E HENRI DUMOULIN CUSTOM RIFLES

F.N. Mauser Supreme action, 24" button rifled barrel, jeweled bolt, sliding side safety. Tapped for standard scope mounts. Select French walnut with beavertail fore-end, scottish hand checkering, rosewood p.g. cap and fore-end cap, Pachmayr recoil pad, Q.D. swivels. Calibers: Group A: 22-250, 243, 6mm, 25-06, 270, 280, 308 Win., 30-06, 358 Win.; Group B: 264, 7mm Rem., 300 Win., 308 Norma, 7x61 S&H, 338, 350 Rem.; Group C: 240, 257, 7mm, 300 and 378 Weatherby's Magnums, 300 H&H, 375 H&H; Group D: 404 Jeffrey, 416 Rigby, 425 Westley Richards, 458 Win., 505 Gibbs, 460 Weatherby.
Price: Rifle, in all four caliber groups, from **$239.50**, extra charge for group B, C, and D chamberings.
Price: Varmint rifle, same as above, but with medium heavy varmint barrel, action tapped for scope, group A calibers **$249.50**, group B calibers **$15.00** extra, group C calibers, **$29.00** extra.
Price: Carbine with 20" bbl. Mannlicher stock, from **$253** up, in group A, B and C.
    Premium wood, especially selected, from **$72.00** up, special checkering from **$36.00**. Custom engraving, silver and gold inlays, engraved name plate, etc., write for quotations to JBL Arms Co., Box 323, Dover, Pa.

F FERLACH DOUBLE RIFLE

Anson & Deeley engraved. silvered action, treble lock with Greener cross bolt. 22", 24" or 26" bbls., all popular calibers from 7x57mm to 300 Win. Mag. Two triggers each settable. Auto. safety and ejectors. Circassian walnut checkered p.g. stock and fore-end, with cheekpiece. horn p.g. cap and buttplate; ramp front sight and express rear. Wgt. 7½-8 lbs. Flaig's, importer. $1,000.00

FERLACH SPORTER RIFLE

98 Mauser action with all milled steel parts, Sako trigger side safety. Bolt knurled and forged for low scope mounting. Boehler steel barrel 24" long, button rifled, 6 grooves. Sights: 100 and 200 yard rear, hooded ramp front with gold bead. Tapped and drilled for scope mounting. Hand checkered Circassian walnut stock with Monte Carlo cheekpiece, rubber recoil pad, rosewood fore-end tip and p.g. cap, sling swivels. Calibers: 243, 7X57, 270, 308 Win., 30-06.....**$139.00**
In 25-06.......**$149.00** (For test fired case in this caliber, add $10.)

G FERLACH DOUBLE O-U RIFLE

Like the Ferlach side-by-side double rifle except: double Greener 4-lock action, calibers 270 to 458 Win., matted-rib bbls. Left- or right-hand cheekpiece stock. 8½-9½ lbs. Flaig's, importer. ..**$1,100.00**
Other rifles and drillings available. Write for catalog.

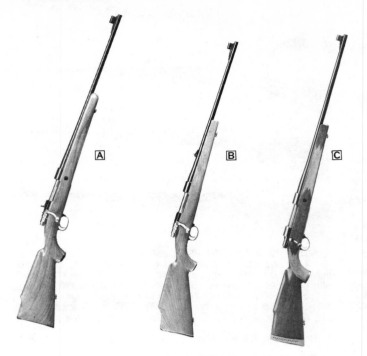

Ⓐ GARCIA F.N. SUPREME RIFLES

Available in all popular calibers, incl. Magnums. 24″ barrel (22″ in 308), Checkered Monte Carlo p.g. stock of French walnut. Streamlined bolt sleeve; 5-shot magazine (3-Mag., 4-243, 308); sliding side safety, hinged floorplate; adjustable trigger. Hooded ramp front and Tri-Range rear sight; tapped for scope. Weight about 7¾ lbs., 44½″ over-all. Garcia Sporting Arms Corp., importer. Standard calibers: **$328.00;** Magnum (264, 300 Win. Mag., 7mm Mag.) **$360.00;** Barreled action, standard: **$175.00,** Magnum calibers: **$195.00.**

Action only from $96.50 to $108.00; Benchrest actions from $98.70 to $110.00; Magnum action from $100.00 to $106.00.

Ⓑ GARCIA MUSKETEER RIFLE

FN Mauser Supreme bolt actions, checkered walnut, Monte Carlo stock with p.g., sling swivels. 24″ barrel with Williams Guide open rear sight, hooded ramp front sight, adj. trigger, sliding thumb safety; hinged floorplate. Wgt. about 7 lbs., 44½″ over-all. Garcia Sporting Arms Corp., importer. Calibers: 243 264, 270, 30-06, 308 Win., 308 Norma Mag., 7mm Rem. Mag., 300 Win. Mag.
Price: **$159.00**

Ⓒ GARCIA SAKO FINNBEAR RIFLE

3-lug, long L-61 action, bolt handle safety lug, cold-swaged barrel, recessed bolt face. Checkered walnut stock with Monte Carlo comb, recoil pad and sling swivels. Calibers: 264, 270, 30-06, 300 Win. Mag., 338, 7mm. Mag., 375 H&H. Garcia Sporting Arms Corp., importer.
Price: Sporter rifle **$237.00**
Price: Mannlicher stocked carbine, 20″ bbl., 39″ over-all. 267.00
Price: Deluxe sporter 325.00

Ⓓ GARCIA SAKO VIXEN RIFLES

Using the L-461, shortest of Sako actions, otherwise like Garcia Sako Forrester. Four styles: standard sporter 23½″ bbl., carbine with Mannlicher stock 20″ bbl., Heavy Barrel 23½″ bbl., and Deluxe sporter with French walnut stock, skipline checkering, engraved trigger guard and floor plate, contrasting wood p.g. and fore-end cap. Calibers: 222, 222 Mag., 223. Garcia Sporting Arms Corp., importer.
Price: Standard sporter **$199.00**
Price: Carbine 230.00
Price: Heavy Barrel 222.00
Price: Deluxe sporter 280.00
Light barreled action. . .**$128.00**   Heavy barreled action. . . . 132.00
Sako L-461 action, short and benchrest. 85.00
Sako L-579 action, medium and benchrest. 88.00
Sako L-61 action, long action for std. and mag. cartridges. . . . 97.00
Sako scopt mount, 1″ ring, low or medium. 18.95
Sako scope mount, 26mm ring, low or medium. 18.95
Sako scope mount, high, either 1″ ring or 26mm ring. 20.95
Sako adj. trigger #2 **$9.95;** #4 safety and trigger combo. 15.95
Sako Dual Range Peep Sight 9.50

GARCIA SAKO FORESTER RIFLES

Sako L-579 medium length action and cold formed 23″ barrel. Action has integral tapered dovetail scope blocks, adjustable trigger, Monte Carlo walnut stock, checkered at p.g. and fore-end. 42″ over-all, wgt. 6½ lbs. Calibers: 243, 308 Win., 22-250. Garcia Sporting Arms Corp., importer.
Price: Sporter rifle **$215.00**
Price: Mannlicher stocked carbine, 20″ bbl., 39″ over-all. 243.00
Price: Heavy barrel rifle 240.00
Price: Deluxe sporter 299.00
Barreled action, lightweight, **$135.00,** heavy barrel. 145.00

Ⓔ GARCIA SAKO FINNWOLF RIFLE

Hammerless lever action rifle with gear-operated, short lever throw. Solid frame with side ejection, detachable 4 shot box magazine, cross-bolt safety behind trigger. One piece walnut stock with Monte Carlo cheekpiece, fluted comb, checkered p.g. and fore-end. Also offered with left side ejection port at no extra cost. Wgt. about 7 lbs.; 42½″ over-all. Hooded ramp sight, no rear sight, mount blocks for tip-off scope mount, 243 and 308 Win. Garcia Sporting Arms Corp., importer.
Price: Standard sporter **$245.00**
Price: Deluxe Sporter 305.00

Ⓕ HERTER'S MARK U9 RIFLES

Bolt action sporters with BSA-type (British) action. Hooded, gas-diverting cocking piece, recessed bolt face encloses cartridge head, side safety, integral dovetail scope mount bases, fully adjustable trigger, hinged floorplate. Monte Carlo p.g. stock. Q.D. swivels, ramp front sight, adj. rear. 23½″ bbl., about 6¼ lbs., all popular calibers, including Magnus. Custom Supreme Grade. . . . **$107.75** With Douglas bbl. **$114.95**
Same, except without sights. 103.35
Same, except Presentation grade. Has selected wood stock, checkered and flared p.g. and fore-end, both capped with black plastic and white spacers. . . . . **$122.75.** With Douglas bbl. **$138.15**
Same, except without sights. .**$118.35.** With Douglas bbl. . . 131.55
Bbld. actions, polished & blued **$71.45.** With Douglas bbl. . . 87.95
Action only, in the white specify length or cartridge. 57.75
Varmint Model, with heavier stock, beavertail fore-end. 109.45
Same without sights 104.45

HERTER MARK J9 RIFLES

Similar to U9 Models except: Based on improved Mauser type action (with adj. trigger), low-scope safety, integral scope mounting blocks on receiver. Cals. 22-250, 243, 6mm, 264, 270, 7mm Rem. Mag., 308, 30-06, 300 Win. Mag. Custom Hunter Grade. **$87.95**
Without sights 83.50
Same, with Mannlicher stock. .**$96.75.** With varmint stock. . 96.75
Same, Presentation Grade, checkered choice walnut stock, roll-over comb, black fore-end tip and p.g. cap with white-line spacers. . 96.75
Without sights. 91.25
Bbld. actions, blued 62.65
Actions, in the white (short). .**$47.25.** Long. 50.04

A HUSQVARNA LIGHTWEIGHT RIFLES Series 4100

Mauser-type rifle in 243, 6.5x55, 270, 308, 30-06 with 20½" bbl. 41½" over-all. Adj. open rear, hooded ramp front sights; receiver tapped for peep and scope sights. Oiled French walnut stock with cheekpiece, checkered grip and fore-end. Hinged floorplate. Sling swivels. Wgt. about 6½ lbs. Tradewinds. $175.00

Series 4000, same as S-4100, but has high, Monte Carlo stock with cheekpiece. $182.50

Series 3000 Crown Grade, same as S-4000 but 23¾" bbl., 44¾" over-all; stock has ebonite p.g. cap and fore-end with white spacers; jeweled bolt. Wgt. about 7¼ lbs. Same cals. plus 7mm Magnum. Monte Carlo stock. $198.50

Series 456-458, same as S-4000 except with full length stock, and not available in 6.5x55. Straight-comb stock. $198.50
With Monte Carlo. 210.00

Presentation Rifle, same as Crown Grade except specially selected Monte Carlo stock; adjustable trigger; engraved action, guard and bbl. breech. Wgt. 7½ lbs. Cals. 7mm Magnum, 30-06, 270 and 243, 44" over-all $410.00

HUSQVARNA 6000 IMPERIAL RIFLES

Same as S-3000 Crown Grade rifles except: Select European walnut Monte Carlo stock with cheekpiece, high gloss finish, 3-leaf folding rear sight and adjustable trigger. 243, 270, 308, 30-06 and 7mm Rem. Mag. Tradewinds, importer. $257.50

HUSQVARNA 7000 IMPERIAL RIFLES

Same as S-4000 lightweight rifles except: Select European walnut Monte Carlo stock with cheekpiece, high gloss finish. Fully adjustable trigger, 3-leaf folding rear sight. 243, 270, 308 and 30-06 calibers. Tradewinds, importer. $227.50

HUSQVARNA ACTIONS & BBLD. ACTIONS

Same actions used in HVA rifles (5-shot std., 3-shot Mag.)..$ 82.50
Barreled actions (same calibers as in Crown Grade).......... 119.95

B INTERNATIONAL BOLT ACTION RIFLE

British made Mauser-type action with jeweled bolt and hinged floorplate. Magazine holds 5 rounds, 3 in mag. cals. 24" barrel chambered for 243, 270, 308 Win., 30-06, 22-250 or 7mm Rem. Mag. Equipped with Williams ramp front and open mid sights. Monte Carlo stock of French walnut; checkered, capped p.g. and rosewood fore-end tip; sling swivels and Pachmayr recoil pad attached. Weight, 7½ lbs., 44" over-all. International Distributors, importer $169.50

C MANNLICHER SCHOENAUER RIFLES AND CARBINES

Made in carbine style with 20" bbl. (18¼" in 6.5mm), wgt. about 7½ lbs. In rifle style with sporter stock and 22" bbl., wgt. 7½-8 lbs. Carbine comes in 243, 6.5mm, 7mm, 270, 30-06, 308 and 358 Win. cals.; rifle in 243, 270 and 30-06 only. Hooded ramp front sight and folding leaf rear. Dummy sideplate aids fitting scope mount; tapped for Steyr mount. 5-shot rotary magazine. Spooned bolt handle. Walnut stock with medium high Monte Carlo comb, checkered p.g. (with cap and white spacer) and fore-end; rifle has black fore-end tip with white spacer; sling swivels. Adjustable single- or double-set trigger. From Stoeger. $348.95

Magnum model rifles available in 257 Weatherby, 264 Win., 338 Win. and 458 Win. with single trigger.....................$379.95

Alpine Carbine available with high grade, hand carved wood, hand engraving, in 243 and 30-06. ....$554.95

D PARKER-HALE MAUSER RIFLE

Imported by JANA International, the 1200 Super series bolt action rifle has adj. trigger; hinged floorplate; hooded ramp front and folding middle sight; receiver tapped for scope mounts; sling swivels with sling and recoil pad. Monte Carlo stock with checkered p.g. and fore-end. Contrasting color fore-end tip and p.g. cap, both with white line spacers. 22" bbl. 43" over-all, wgt. 7½ lbs. Cal. 243, 270, 30-06, 308 Win. (5 shot) $154.95

7mm Rem. Mag. 300 Win. Mag. or 308 Norma Mag. 164.95

PRESENTATION RIFLE, same as the 1200 Super except with French walnut stock, fully scroll engraved action, trigger guard and magazine floor plate. Also, no sights. Std. Cals. $209.95. Mag. Cals....$219.95

VARMINT RIFLE, same as the 1200 Super except with a glass bedded free floating 24", 4 lb. target bbl., target scope base blocks. Wgt. 9½ lbs. In cals. 22/250, 6mm Rem & 243.............$174.95

E SCHULTZ & LARSEN 68DL RIFLE

A 4-lug bolt action rifle with tubular receiver, 24" bbl., adj. trigger; thumb safety; hinged floorplate. Walnut Monte Carlo stock (13½" pull) with checkered p.g. and fore-end; white line recoil pad and grip cap; 1" swivels. 44½" over-all, 7½ lbs. Without sights. Cal. 264 Win., 7x61 S&H, 7mm Rem., 308 Norma 300 Win., 338 Win. Magnum, 22-260, 242 Win., 6mm Rem., 6.5x55, 270 Win., 308 Win. Fessler, importer. $485.00

Same except 458 Win. Mag. 588.00

F SHIKAR BOLT ACTION RIFLE

A sporter weight rifle with select walnut p.g. stock, basket-weave checkered on p.g. and fore-end. Contrasting wood fore-end tip, recoil pad, both with white-line spacers. Without sights. Cals. 243, 270, 7mm Rem. Mag., 30-06, 308 and 300 Win. Mag. LA Distributors, importer. $249.50

STEYR-MANNLICHER MODEL SL RIFLE

Receiver is machined from solid steel and has a detachable 5-shot rotary-drum magazine. Bolt has six locking lugs, cocking indicator and recessed face. Open rear, hooded ramp front sights. Safety locks bolt and sear. Choice of single- or double-set trigger. Monte Carlo stock, checkered p.g. and fore-end, epoxy finished. Available in 222 Rem., 222 Rem. Mag., or 223. Weight 6¼ lbs. Stoeger, importer....$199.95

Carbine with full-length Mannlicher stock............... 210.95
Target rifle with 28" heavy bbl., without sights......... 210.95

STEYR-MANNLICHER MODEL L RIFLE

Similar to Model SL, but with long action for caliber 22-250 Rem., 225 or 243 Win. $199.95

Chambered for 308 Win. 219.95
Target rifle with 26" heavy bbl., without sights......... 210.95
Carbine with full-length Mannlicher stock............... 210.95
Carbine chambered for 308 Win. 229.95

STEYR-MANNLICHER MODEL M RIFLE

Similar to Model L, but cals. 7x57, 270 or 30-06..........$249.95
Carbine with full-length Mannlicher stock............... 259.95

STEYR-MANNLICHER MODEL S RIFLE

Similar to Model M, but in cals. 7MM Rem. Mag., 257 Wby., 264 Win. Mag., 300 HH Mag., 338 Win. Mag., 375 HH Mag., & 458 Win. Mag. $275.95

G TRADEWINDS "HUSKY" LIGHTWEIGHT RIFLE

HVA action. 21½" Swedish steel barrel with hammer-forged bore. Bead front and fixed rear sights. Italian walnut stock, hand checkered, with Monte Carlo comb; cal. 22-250, 243, 270, 7mm Mag., 30-06. About 6½ lbs., 43" over-all.................................$157.75

TRADEWINDS 600 VARMINT RIFLE

Short HVA action has 23¾" medium-wgt. barrel in cals. 222 Rem., 222 Rem. Mag., 22-250, 223, 243 and 308 Win. No sights, tapped for standard scope mounts. 4 shot (3 in 22-250, 243 or 308) detachable box magazine, adjustable double set trigger. Monte Carlo European walnut stock with cheekpiece, checkered p.g. and fore-end. About 6¾ lbs. Tradewinds, importer. Test target accompanies rifle. $169.50

Same as above except with adj. single trigger, steel trigger guard, front sight and folding rear sight.........................$172.50

TRADEWINDS ACTIONS & BBLD. ACTIONS

Same actions used in 600 rifles (4-shot std., 3-shot Mag.)..$ 89.95
Barreled actions (same calibers as 600 rifles).............. 129.95

A BSA MARTINI-INTERNATIONAL MK III 22 RIFLE

Made by Birmingham Small Arms Co., the MK III features the Martini action; new free floating barrel press-fitted into action and locked in place by two cross bolts. Available in left or right hand cheekpiece models, the loading port and sight base are also reversed for southpaw shooters. 29" barrel, 12 to 14½ lbs. Trigger adjustable from ½ to 3½ lb. pull. Dovetail base on action for tube sight mounting, regular bases on bbl. for scope mounts. Al Freeland, importer.

Without sights, light or heavy model....................$210.00
Available with Parker-Hale, Freeland or Redfield International sights at extra cost.

B PARKER-HALE 1200 TX TARGET RIFLE

Cal. 7.62mm NATO (308 Win.), 5-shot magazine. 26" free floating (1" dia.) glass bedded bbl. Mauser '98 action (commercial) with adj. single stage trigger and triple (trigger, bolt & sear) locking sliding thumb safety. Oil finished walnut target stock (13⅜"x1¹¹⁄₁₆"x1¹⁵⁄₁₆") has high comb beavertail fore-end, full p.g. recoil pad and adj. hand stop. 46¾" over-all, wgt. 10½ lbs. Jana International, importer.
Price: $219.95

C HAMMERLI-TANNER MATCH RIFLE

Designed for 300 meter competition, this heavy (16¼ lbs.) single shot "free" rifle is available in most popular centerfire calibers. Barrel length 29½". Micrometer click rear sight has variable aperature and is adjustable for w. and e.; globe front sight has 4 inserts. Walnut thumbhole stock has adjustable palm rest and sling swivel; buttplate adjusts to any position. Available only on special order with 6- to 10-month delivery. H. Grieder, importer............................$590.00

D SCHULTZ & LARSEN 61 MATCH RIFLE

22 LR single shot bolt action rifle meeting International Match requirements. Has a 28" free-floating bbl., globe front sight with removable inserts. Micro. peep rear sight with removable iris discs, adj. for w. and e. 32" sight radius. 2 adj. buttplates furnished for offhand and prone positions. Adj. palm rest. Walnut thumbhole stock with cheekpiece and adj. handrest. Full length rail undner stock to adj. forward sling swivel, hand stop and palm rest. Choice of trigger systems: adj. "hair"; adj. double pull or slack trigger (4-14 oz.); or adj. double pull (3-4 lbs.). 49" over-all; wgt. approx. 16½ lbs. Fessler, importer.**$565.00**

SCHULTZ & LARSEN 62 MATCH RIFLE

Same as the S&L 61 except: for centerfire calibers. 4-lug bolt action, 27½" bbl., 33½" sight radius; 50" over-all; wgt. approx. 17 lbs. Cal. 6.5x55 Swedish, 7.62 Nato, or any other standard caliber. Fessler, importer. $585.00

E WALTHER KKS-D STANDARD 22 MATCH RIFLE

A bolt action single shot rifle with double locking lugs; wing safety on bolt; light trigger pull; 25.6" bbl. and 44" over-all. Walnut stock with checkered p.g. and fixed sling attachment on fore-end. Globe front sight, aperture rear sight adj. for w. and e. Wgt. 8½ lbs.; cal. 22 LR. Interarms, importer $114.50

As the KKM Matchmaster; like the KKS-D except: adj. trigger pull. Checkered fore-end also; rubber butt with dove-tail bar; slide bar on fore-end with adj. sling attachment, two extra front sight inserts. Wgt. 10 lbs. $119.50

As the KKM-11; same features as the KKM except: with adj. alloy hook buttplate plus regular buttplate and adj. palm rest. Wgt. 12 lbs., 44½" over-all $139.50

As the KKM International; same as the KKM-11 except: 28" heavy tapered bbl. (heavier bbbl. without taper available). Heavy walnut stock with thumbhole and adj. hand shelf. 8 sight inserts incl. Wgt. 15½ lbs. (with straight bbl. 17 lbs.), 46" over-all...................$198.50

F CARL GUSTAF MODEL 63

Swedish Mauser action match rifle. 29.1" barrel is free-floating, has outside diameter of 0.748". Front sight and match sling supplied, three sight inserts are furnished; CG rear sight $30.00, but any other match sight can be installed. Trigger and trigger guard are knurled for maximum control. Stock is designed for match shooting. cheekpiece appears on both sides of stock. Rubber recoil pad and adjustable butt plate are optional. Calibers: 6.5x55 and 7.62 Nato. Sight radius 32.7", 49" over-all, wgt. 9.9 lbs. Action cocks on closing. Century Arms, Inc., importer.

Price: M63 without rear sight $130.00
Price: Carl Gustaf rear sight 30.00
Price: Model 63E for Parker-Hale sight 140.00
Price: Parker-Hale 5C sight 40.00

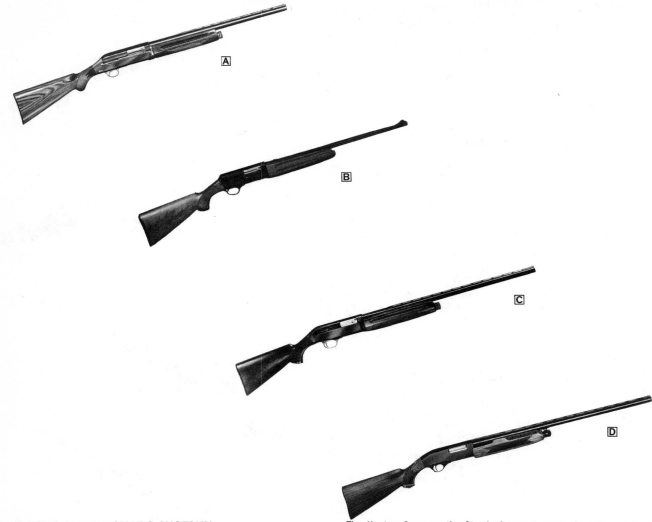

BERETTA AL-2 AUTOMATIC SHOTGUN

Gas-operated in 12 or 20 ga., 2¾" chambers. 28" Full or Mod., 26" Imp. Cyl. chokes, ventilated-rib interchangeable barrels. Hand-checkered p.g. walnut stock (14⅛"x1½"x2½") and fore-end. 3-shot mag. can be emptied without working shells through action. Engraved receiver. Crossbolt safety. Wgt. 7¼ lbs. Garcia, importer....**$217.00**

Also with middle bead as the AL-2 Skeet (12 ga. 26", Skeet) and AL-2 Trap (14⅜"x1⅜"x1¾") 12 ga. 30" Full............... **227.00**

Extra barrels **84.00**

A BREDA AUTOMATIC SHOTGUNS

Italian made in 12 or 20 ga., 2¾" or 3" chambers. Magazine holds four 2¾" or three 3" shells; extension tube (extra) for 7 shots. Nickel-chrome steel barrel with vent. rib or plain has muzzles threaded for "Quick Choke" tubes; 24½" length. Barrel bore, breech and bolt assembly are hard chromed. Auto. magazine cut-off; push-button holds carrier latch in loading position; depressing cartridge retaining lever unloads magazine. Adjustable stock of Italian walnut has checkered p.g. and beavertail fore-end, 14"x2½"x1⅝". Continental Arms, importer......................................**$169.50 to $194.50**

B FRANCHI AUTOMATIC SHOTGUNS

Made in 12 and 20, 2¾" chamber. These Stoeger imports have alloy receivers, chrome-lined bbls., auto. cut-off, 4-shot cap., walnut checkered pistol grip and fore-end. Adj. friction piece sets recoil for standard or hi-vel. loads. 24" or 26" (Imp. Cyt.), 28" (Full or Mod.) or 30" Full (12 only). Wgt. 12, 6¼ lbs., 20, 5 lbs. Plain bbl. **$176.95** ● Vent. rib bbl. **$207.95** ● 3" Magnum models in 12 (32") or 20 (28") Full, with steel receivers and recoil pads. Wgt. 12, 8¼ lbs. 20, 6 lbs. Plain bbl. 12, **$185.95** ● 20, **$175.95** ● Vent. rib bbl. 12, **$212.95** ● 20 **$202.95**

The Hunter. Same as the Standard except: vent. rib only; engraved receiver, high finish select walnut stock, chromed trigger.....**$239.95**

Slug Gun, 12 or 20, 22" Cyl. bbl. with blade front and rear sight adj. for w. and e.; sling swivels. 12 ga., choice of steel or alloy receiver. 20 ga., alloy only **$219.95**

Dynamic 12. Same as the Standard except: 12 only, steel receiver, chromed breech bolt and lifter, **$189.95** ● With vent. rib **$221.95** ● Skeet Gun, **$219.95** ● Slug Gun........................**$219.95**

Wildfowler. Same as Standard Mag. except: ventilated rib bbl. 20 has alloy receiver. 12, **$279.95** ● 20...................**$275.95**

Eldorado. Same as the Standard except: vent. rib only. Receiver scroll engraved; gold plated trigger, chromed breech bolt. Also made with 3" (magnum) chambers in 12 (32") or 20 (28") Full choke bbls. **$345.95**

Other highly decorated Franchis, Crown **$846.95**, Diamond **$1,129.95** and Imperial **$1,359.95**.

Extra bbls. Plain **$52.95**. (Mag. **$60.00**), Vent. rib. (V.R. Mag. **$82.95**). Slug or Skeet **$74.95**.

C TRADEWINDS H-150 & H-170 AUTO SHOTGUNS

Light alloy receiver, 5-shot tubular magazine. 12 gauge only, 2¾"; 26" (Imp. Cyl.), 28" (Mod. or Full), 30" (Full). Select Italian walnut stock, p.g. and fore-end hand checkered. Wgt. 6¾ lbs. Ramp-mounted bead front sight....**$159.95** H-170, Same except vent. rib....**$179.95**

Deluxe 200 series, same as 170 except engraved receiver **$227.50** ● Trap model (14⅜"x1⅜"x1⅞"), 30" bbl....................**$227.50**

D BERETTA SL-2 SLIDE ACTION SHOTGUN

Slide action 12 ga., 2¾" chambers. 28" Full or Mod., 26" Imp. Cyl., ventilated rib interchangeable barrels. Hand-checkered walnut p.g. stock (14⅛"x1½"x2³⁄₁₆") and fore-end. 3-shot magazine can be emptied without working shells through action. Crossbolt safety. Wgt. 7¼ lbs. Garcia, importer **$185.00**

Extra barrels **72.00**

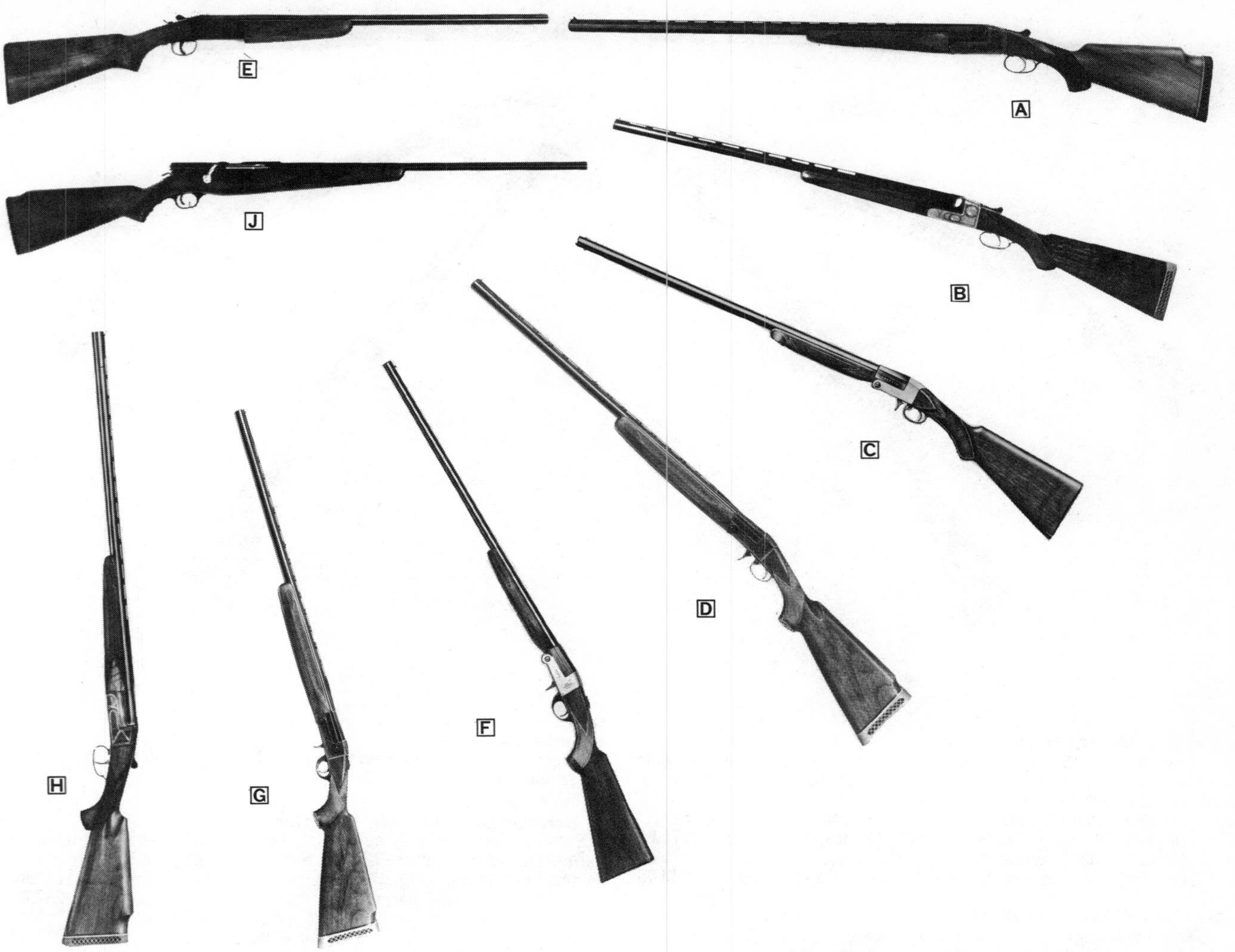

A A & F SINGLE BARREL TRAP GUN
Made in Italy, this 12 ga. gun has a vent. rib barrrel, checkered walnut p.g. stock with Monte Carlo comb, and recoil pad. Abercrombie and Fitch, importer **$395.00**

B ATLAS SINGLE BARREL TRAP GUN
30" or 32" vent. rib barrel of Boehler steel; chromed bore; 12 gauge only. Checkered walnut Monte Carlo stock (14½"x1⅜"x1⅞"x2¼") and beavertail fore-end; recoil pad; engraved action and auto. ejector, weighs about 8 lbs. **$365.00**
With custom engraving, gold trigger and gold lettering **425.00**

C BERETTA FS-1 FOLDING SHOTGUN
This hammerless single is made in 12 (30"), 20 (28"), 28 or .410 ga. (26") full choke bbl.; stock has checkered walnut grip and fore-end, the latter permanently attached. Barrel is made in Beretta mono-bloc construction. Cocks on opening; crossbolt safety in trigger guard. Wgt. from 4½ lbs. (410) to 5½ lbs. (12 ga.). Garcia, importer. **$69.95**

D BERETTA TR-1 MONTE CARLO TRAP SHOTGUN
12 ga. only, 2¾" chambers, 32" single barrel trap-choked, with vent. rib. Crossbolt safety, auto. ejector. Engraved receiver. Checkered Monte Carlo p.g. stock of European walnut (14⅜"x1⅜"x1¾") with beavertail fore-end and trap-style recoil pad. Bbl. release in front of guard. Front and middle bead sights. Garcia, importer. Wgt. about 8¼ lbs. **$160.00**
Also, with extended vent. rib as the TR-2 . . . . **185.00**

F COMPANION FOLDING SHOTGUN
Monobloc receiver is machined from solid stock and satin chrome-plated. Available in 12, 20 and 410 ga. (3" chambers) and 16 or 28 ga. (2¾") with 28" (Full) barrel (30" Full also in 12 ga., 26" Full only in 410). European walnut stock (14"x1½"x2⅝") has checkered fore-end and capped p.g., plastic buttplate. Weight 4½ to 5½ lbs. Galef, importer **$49.95**
With vent. rib **54.95**

CHARLES DALY SUPERIOR GRADE TRAP GUN
12 ga. (2¾"), 32" (Full) Vent rib (4/10") bbl., double beads. Scroll engraved receiver is nickel finished. Manual safety, auto ejector, recoil pad. Checkered Monte Carlo p.g. stock and beavertail forearm with Greener type lock. Daly, importer **$340.00**

J DICKSON BOLT ACTION SHOTGUN
.410 (3") Spanish made weighs 5½ lbs. 3-shot capacity. 25" full choke bbl. Checkered p.g. and fore-end. Sliding thumb safety. American Import, importer **$34.95**

E DICKSON SINGLE BARREL SHOTGUN
Exposed hammer gun with auto ejector, brass bead sight, oil finished stock. M612 12 ga. 28" Full 2¾"; M620 20 ga. 26" Full 3"; M6410 410 ga. 26" Full 3". American Import, importer. . . . **$30.75**

KRIEGHOFF SINGLE BARREL TRAP
12 ga. (2¾") 32" or 34" (Full) vent. rib bbls. Internal parts are hardened heat treated steel. Mechanical trigger, short hammer fall. Monte Carlo stock with checkered p.g. and groover beavertail fore-end. Thumb safety. Wgt. about 8½ lbs. Europa, importer. (Standard) **$750.00**
Also, San Remo grade, **$1,150.00**; Monte Carlo grade, **$2,750.00**; Crown grade, **$2,850.00** and Super Crown grade, **$3,150.00.**
Extra bbls. **$295.00**

G MONTE CARLO TRAP GUN
Made in Italy, this single barrel 12 ga. trap gun has a 32" vent. rib barrel; engraved, blued receiver with automatic extractor and gold-plated trigger. Monte Carlo stock has recoil pad and hand-checkered p.g. and fore-end. Weight 8¼ lbs. Galef, importer **$149.95**

GARCIA-ROSSI SINGLE BARREL SHOTGUN
Available in all gauges with 29" full-choked barrel and 2¾" chamber, except 3" 410. Tip-up action has exposed hammer; stock has checkered p.g. Made in Brazil. Garcia Arms Corp., importer **$29.95**

H STOEGER 27 TRAP GUN
Boxlock action, single bbl., double under-locking lugs, Greener type crossbolt, ejector, has no safety. 12 ga., 30" (Imp. Mod.) or 32" (Full) chrome lined bbl. (Full), with vent. rib. Checkered Monte Carlo p.g. stock (14½"x1⅜"x2⅛"), with beavertail fore-end. 49" over-all. wgt. 8¼ lbs. Stoeger Arms Corp., importer **$498.95**

A A & F PERAZZI O-U
Made in Italy, this 12 ga. features interchangeable stocks for Trap or Field, and interchangeable double or single trigger assemblies. All models have vent. ribs, hand-checkered p.g. walnut stocks with beavertail fore-ends, bright-finished actions. Abercrombie & Fitch, importer.
Trap, with 29" bbl., parallel rib, wgt. 7½ lbs............$875.00
Pigeon, 28" bbl., tapered rib, wgt. 7¼ lbs.............. 875.00
Skeet, 26" bbl., tapered rib, wgt. about 7 lbs. 950.00

B ATLAS GRAND PRIX OVER-UNDER
Merkel-type sidelock action, fully engraved, 12 or 20 gauge, 26" or 28" vent. rib barrels in choice of chokes. Auto. ejectors, SST, straight or p.g. stock to order; about 7¼ lbs. Atlas, importer.
From ....$700.00 up

C ATLAS MODEL 750 OVER-UNDER
Merkel-type action, highly engraved; 12, 16 or 20 gauge, vent. rib barrels 26" or 28" in standard chokes; non-ejector, non-selective single trigger. Straight or p.g. stock, hand checkered (14½"x1½"x2½"), 6¼-7 lbs. Atlas, importer..........................$245.00
Same as M750 but 3" Magnum in 12 or 20 ga. 245.00
Same as M750 but 30" bbls., and auto ejectors......... 265.00

D ATLAS MODEL 87 OVER-UNDER
Similar to M750 but p.g. stock only (14"x1½"x2½"), silvered or case-hardened action. Atlas, importer $230.00
Same, but in 3" Magnum (as M95).,.................... 235.00
Same, but boxlock action, 26" bbls. only, double triggers, and 3" in 28 or 410 ga. only (as M65)..........................$195.00
Same, but with non-selective ST (as M65-ST)............. 225.00

ATLAS 150 SERIES OVER-UNDER SHOTGUN
12 and 20 ga. Bbls. 26" (IC & M or Skeet), 28" (M & F), 30" (F & extra F). Vent. rib. Boxlock action with crossbolt. Chromed bores, silver-plated or case-hardened engraved receiver. Single non-selective triggers. Straight or p.g. stock, checkered. Wgt. 6½-7¼ lbs. Atlas Arms, importer......$275.00   With ejectors..........$325.00
With better engraving, as the M160....................... 295.00
M160 with auto-ejectors, as the M180 (12 ga. only)........ 345.00

F BERETTA BL-1 OVER-UNDER SHOTGUN
Low-profile Monoblock boxlock action, 12 ga., with 30" or 28" M&F or 26" IC&M chrome-moly steel barrels. Double triggers, front trigger hinged, w/o ejectors. Walnut p.g. stock (14¼"x1⅝"x2½", 2" pitch down) and fore-end hand checkered. Auto safety, 2¾" chambers. Ramp front sight, 4 fluorescent inserts. Wgt. 7 lbs. Garcia, importer. $199.00
Extra bbls. 125.00

Beretta BL-2 O-U
Selective single trigger version of BL-1. Trigger selector located on upper tang, integral with safety $239.00
Extra bbls. 125.00

Beretta BL-3 DeLuxe O-U Shotgun
Same as Beretta BL-2, but with gold-plated SST, and ventilated-rib barrel. Engraved receiver. 12 ga., with 30" or 28" M&F or 26" IC&M chrome-lined barrels. Wgt. 7⅛ lbs. $282.00
3" Mag., 30" M&F barrels, 7⅜ lbs....................... 282.00
20 ga., (3") or 28 ga. (2¾"), 28" M&F or 26" IC&M barrels, stock 14¼"x1½"x2⅜", 2¼" pitch down, 6 lbs.................$282.00
Trap 14⅜"x1⅜"x1¾", 1½" pitch down, with p.g. cap and contoured recoil pad. Wgt. (12) 7¼ lbs.....................$314.00
Skeet, 12 (2¾"), 28 (2¾") or 20 (3") ga., 26" S1 & 2 barrels. Stock (12 ga.) 14¼"x1⅝"x2½" (20 ga.) 14¼"x1½"x2⅜"; both with 2" pitch down. Wgt. (12) 7 lbs.; (20) 6 lbs. $314.00
Extra bbls. Field $146.00   Trap or Skeet............. 155.00

Beretta BL-4 DeLuxe O-U Shotgun
Similar to BL-3, with addition of selective auto. ejectors, extensive receiver engraving, deluxe hand checkering......$349.00 to $374.00
Extra bbls. Field $173.00   Trap or Skeet............. 182.00

Beretta BL-5 Premium O-U Shotgun
Same as BL-4, except fully engraved receiver, specially selected walnut stock and fore-end, capped p.g. ....$475.00 to $495.00
Extra bbls. Field $190.00   Trap or Skeet............. 199.00

G BERETTA S02 PRESENTATION OVER-UNDER SHOTGUN
Sidelock action, special chrome-nickel receiver, Boehler anti-rust barrels. All interior parts chromed. Receiver, tangs, screws, lever, guard, fore-end release, safety and standing breech scroll engraved, with a silver pigeon inlaid in the top lever. Trigger, safety and top lever checkered. 12 ga., ventilated rib barrels only, Skeet and trap models available. 26" Imp. Cyl. & Mod. or 28" Mod. & Full standard. Other borings to order without extra cost. Straight or p.g. stocks, perfectly matched from one-piece selected European walnut (14½"x1⅜"x 2³⁄₁₆"). Double triggers standard. Wgt. from about 7¼ lbs. Garcia, importer. $950.00
Same, Model S03, profusely scroll and relief engraved, fancy selected walnut $1,100.00
Same, Model S04, sidelocks are hand detachable, more elaborate engraving, full grain walnut stock and fore-end............$1,325.00
Same, Model S05, gold Crown Grade symbol inlaid into top lever. Built to customer's complete specifications if desired, the whole virtually hand-made $1,750.00
All SO series Presentation Models may be had with stocks to customer's specifications (at small or no extra charge) or with selective or non-selective single trigger at little or no extra cost.

A BRETTON OVER-UNDER SHOTGUN

Made in France, this 12 ga. shotgun weighs only 4½ lbs. Receiver is of heat-treated Dural; steel barrels may be unscrewed and replaced with 16 ga. or slug barrels. Continental Arms, importer **$285.00**
Deluxe engraved model........................... 365.00

B BRNO OVER-UNDER SHOTGUNS

Made in Czechoslovakia, available in 12 or 16 ga. only. Simple design has 25 fewer parts; all parts interchange without hand fitting. Double-single trigger (rear trigger acts as selector). Skeet (illustrated), trap or field grades available. Continental Arms, importer.... **$210.00**

C CONTINENTAL ARMS OVER-UNDER SHOTGUNS

The Nikko (illustrated) is a Japanese made gun available in either 12 or 20 gauge. Boxlock action is hand engraved; jeweled frame, automatic ejectors and lugs. Barrels of hard-chromed vanadium steel with vent. rib. Oil finished, checkered p.g. stock and fore-end which is completely detachable **$285.00**

Other high-grade shotguns are available from Continental. These are made in Belgium and have engraved boxlock actions; 4-way locking system; single selective trigger; selective ejectors and vent. rib. Available in all gauges for 12 through 28.
Royal Crown grade .... **$ 975.00**
Imperial Crown grade 1250.00

D CHARLES DALY OVER-UNDER SHOTGUNS

12 ga., 2¾" (3" mag. in 30" F&F), 20 (3"), 28 ga. (2¾") or 410 (3") chambers. Boxlock action, scroll engraved; firing pins quickly removable. Auto safety (manual on Skeet & Trap models), combined with bbl. selector; auto. selective ejectors. Single selective inertia type gold-plated trigger. Checkered walnut semi-pistol grip stock and fore end (14"x1½"x2½"). Recoil pad on magnums. Vent. rib bbls. with steel bead. 20 ga. in 26" (IC&M); 28" (M&F). 12 ga. in 26" (Skt., & Skt., IC&M, plus M&F in 28" only), 30" (M&F or F&F). Wt. 12 ga. 7⅜ lbs.) 20 ga. 6¾ lbs.; in 28" bbls. (12 or 20 ga.)................**$350.00**
28 or 410 gauge..................................... 369.00
12 ga., 3" mag., F&F, 30" bbls., 8 lbs. 355.00
Superior Grade. Same as Field Grade except: figured walnut, full p.g. stock with p.g. and grooved fore-end; special checkering..... **$370.00**
28 or 410 gauge..................................... 398.00
Superior Skeet. Same as Superior Grade except: 12 or 20 gauge; 26" & 28" bbls., manual safety. Skeet and Skeet bored.......... **$370.00**
28 or 410 gauge..................................... 398.00
12 or 20 ga. with Selexor* 415.00
Superior Trap. Same as the Superior Skeet except: 12 ga. 30", M&F, IM&F or F&F. Manual safety. Standard trap stock (14⅜"x1⅜"x1¾") or Monte Carlo (14⅜"x1½"x1½"x2½") with recoil pad....... **$370.00**
With Monte Carlo stock 379.00
With Selexor* (M. C. only)......................... 415.00
With ½" wide (Flat-Top) vent. rib. With or w/out M. C. stock 410.00
Venture Grade. Similar to Field Grade except: 12 or 20 ga. (2¾" chambers) only, 28" (Mod. & Full) or 26" (Mod. & Imp. Cyl.) barrels with vent rib, single non-selective trigger and non-auto. safety. Weight, about 7 lbs..**$275.00**

CHARLES DALY DIAMOND GRADE OVER-UNDER
Same as Daly Superior Grades except finest French walnut, more extensive checkering and a fully engraved receiver, guard, etc.**$650.00**
* Selexor: Allows either automatic selective ejection or extraction. A button on each side of the receiver provides control. RH button for lower bbl. or LH button for the upper.

ALLEN O-U SHOTGUNS
These Italian O-U guns are offered in a variety of grades in field and trap style. All carry vent. rib. Models are available with single non-selective, single selective, and double triggers, extractors and ejectors, extra wide trap ribs, standard and selected wood. C&M Sporting Arms Co., importer. **Price: M68 $198.95** to Model Mexico 68 at **$385.00**.

E DICKSON GRAY EAGLE O-U

Zoli boxlock action, auto. safety, double triggers, 3" chambers. In 12, 20 ga., 26" bbl. (Imp. Cyl. & Mod.), 28" (Mod. & Full). Wgt. about 7 lbs. (12 ga.), 6 lbs., 20 ga.\ Vent. rib. Hand checkered walnut p.g. stock and beavertail fore-end (14"x1½"x2½"). American Import Co.
....**$217.50**

F FERLACH O-U TURKEY GUN

Boxlock action, Greener cross bolting, top snap, double triggers, Boehler steel bbls., 22" or 24". Top bbl., 12, 16 or 20 gauge; lower, 22 Hornet, 222 Rem., 243 257, 6.5x55, 270, 7x57, 30-06. Engraved action, Circassian stock, hand checkered at p.g. and fore-end. About 6½ lbs. Flaig's importer. **$525.00**
Write for catalog of drillings and combination guns.

G FOREVER YOURS O-U SHOTGUNS

Ferlach-made, Anson & Deeley 4-lock type action, double Greener cross-bolt, Boehler proof steel barrels, ventilated rib, auto ejectors, double triggers, engraved action, checkered Circassian walnut pistol grip stock & split fore-end. Available with or without cheekpiece. Horn p.g. cap and buttplate. Weight 7-7½ lbs. Available in standard gauges, chokes and barrel lengths. Imported by Flaig's, **$675.00**. With single set trigger. **$750.00**

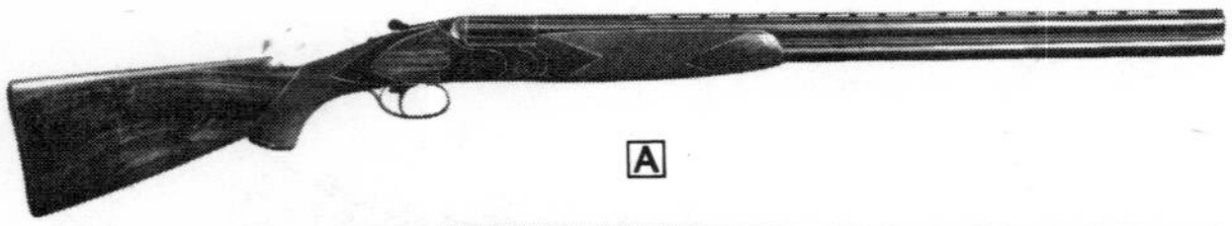

A

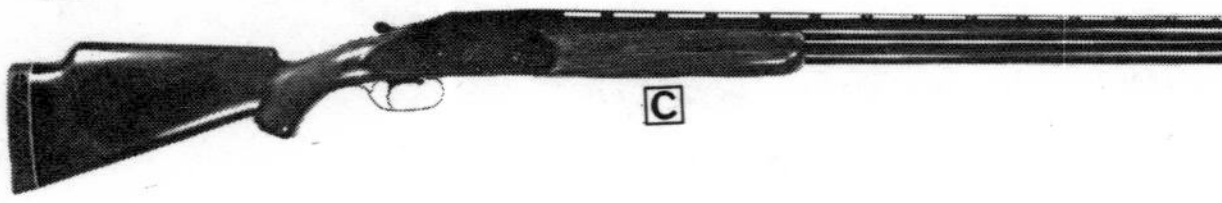

C

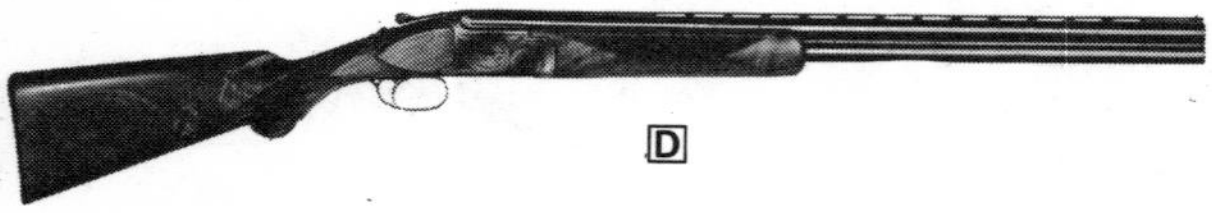

D

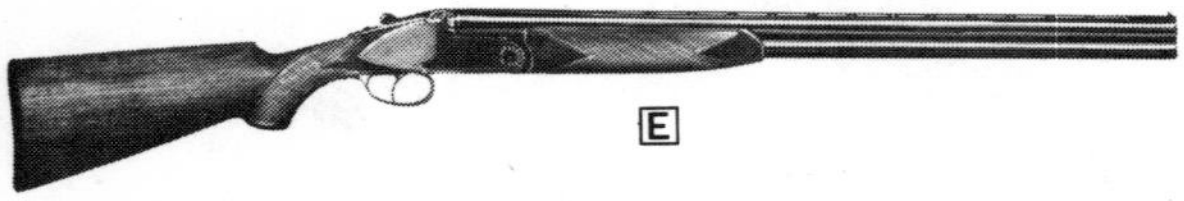

E

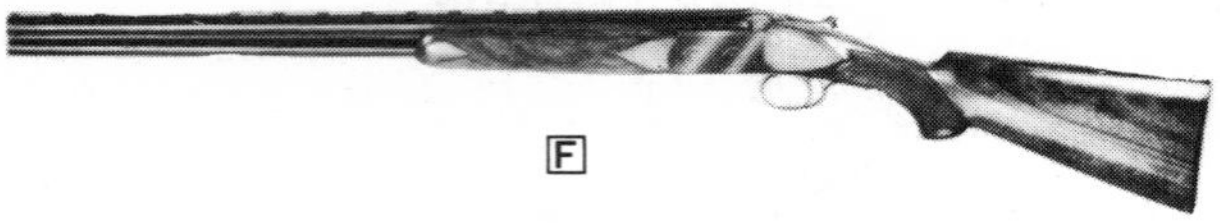

F

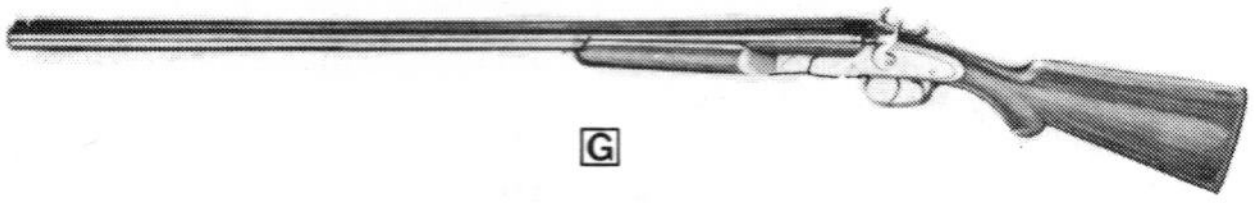

G

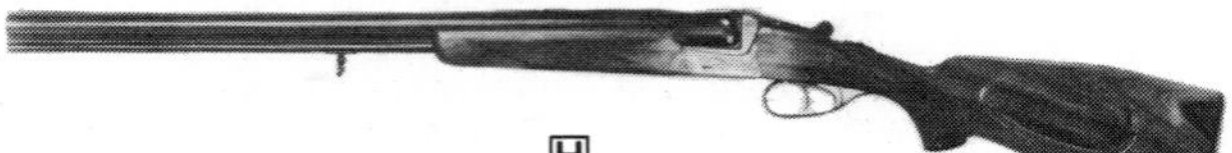

H

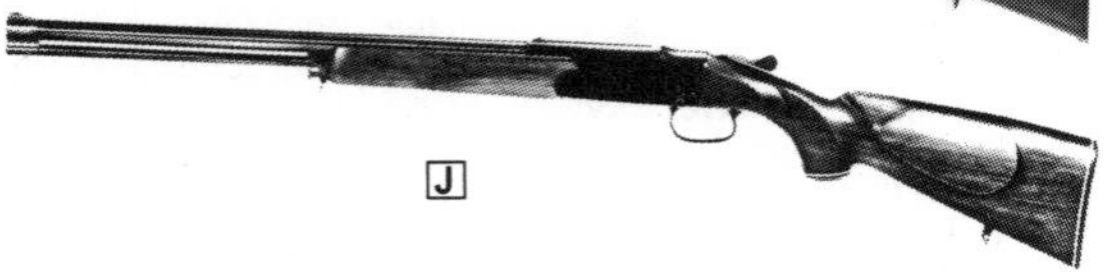

J

A FRANCHI FALCONET OVER & UNDER
Italian-made, this shotgun features easy-cocking action, short, fast hammer fall. Walnut stock, checkered pistol grip and fore-end; 14¼"x 1⅜"x2¼", pitch down 2¾"; stocks or order within limits (¼" in comb hgt., ½" in pull). Skeet stock, 14¼"x1⅝"x2½". Trap, 14⅜"x 1½"x1⅞". 12 Gauge only with vent. rib, single selective trigger and automatic ejectors. Field model has automatic safety. Field—26" (Imp. Cyl. & Mod.), 28" (Mod. & Full), or 30" (Mod. & Full). Skeet—26" (Skeet #1 & #2); Trap—30" (Mod. & Full) bbls. Chromed bores, engraved receiver. Stoeger.
Falconet Ebony (12 & 20) **$295.95**, Buckskin (12 & 20) **$305.95**, Silver (12 only) **$325.95.** Standard Skeet (12 only) **$395.95** or Std. Skeet with 12 and 20 ga. bbls. **$595.95.** Standard Trap **$395.95** or Super Trap **$495.95.** Imperial Grade **$1,099.95** or Monte Carlo Grade **$1,499.95.**

C KRIEGHOFF MODEL 32 OVER-UNDER
The Europa Corp. imports this near-duplicate of the old Remington 32. A three-way safety (manual, auto or inoperative) and Boehler special steel bbls. are standard on all M32's. Made in 12 and 20 only, with selective single trigger, ejectors and ventilated rib, the M32 is available as a Skeet or field gun with 28" bbl. or as a trap gun (30" bbls.) at **$595.00.** • Other bbl. lengths and chokes to order, as is a Monte Carlo stock. The San Remo grade, with fancier walnut and relief engraving, is **$995.00.** • The Monte Carlo carries extra fancy wood, elaborate engraving and silver inlays, Monte Carlo stock at **$2,650.00.** • The Crown Grade is like the Monte Carlo but has gold inlays, at **$2,750.00.** • The Super Crown, like the Crown, has both gold and silver inlaid figurines, at **$2,950.00.** Extra bbls. with standard borings .... **$275.00** to **$295.00**

D LAMES OVER-UNDER SHOTGUN
Boxlock action is hand engraved, all parts are blued except single selective trigger which is gold plated. European walnut stock has hand-checkered p.g. and fore-end. Available in 12 ga. only, with 26" (Imp. Cyl. & Mod.), 28" (Imp. Cyl. & Mod. or Mod. & Full), 30" and 32" (Mod./Imp. and Full or Full and Full). LA Distributors, importer **$329.95**

LAURONA OVER-UNDER SHOTGUN
Boxlock 12 ga. shotgun has vent. rib barrels choked Mod. and Full. Stock has checkered p.g. and fore-end. Twin-single triggers. Receiver is lightly engraved. Mars Equipment, importers.............. **$199.00**

E RICHLAND ARMS 844 OVER-UNDER SHOTGUN
Boxlock action of nickel-chrome steel, blued, non-selective single trigger and simple extractors. Stock (14"x1⅝"x2¼") of European walnut with checkered p.g. and fore-end. Barrels of English Vickers steel, 12 ga. only, 30" (Full & Full) 7 lbs., 3 oz., 28" (Mod. & Full) 7 lbs., or 26" (Imp. Cyl. & Mod.) 6¾ lbs......................... **$189.50**

F RICHLAND 828 OVER-UNDER
Casehardened receiver. Rosette engraving. Walnut stock (1½"x 2¼"x14¼") has skip-line hand checkering with matching quick-detachable fore-end. Ventilated rib. Non-selective single trigger. Plain extractors, non-automatic safety. Sliding bolt cross lock. In 28 ga. (2¾" chamber) with 28" (F&M) or 26" (IC&M) barrels. Weighs 5¼ lbs. (26"). **$268.00**

G GARCIA-ROSSI OVERLAND EXPOSED HAMMER DOUBLE
12 ga. (3") with 28" & 20" (F&M, IC&M)) bbls; 20 ga. (3") with 26" and 20" (F&M) bbls. and 410 (3") 26" (F&F) bbls. Double triggers and hammers. Semi pistol grip stock and beavertail fore-end. Thumb lever release, bead front sight. Garcia Sporting Arms Corp., importer. . **$79.95**

SAUER 66 OVER-UNDER
Based on the Purdey-System with Holland and Holland type removable sidelocks. Has a single selective trigger, selective automatic ejectors and the field model features an automatic slide safety. Krupp-Special steel barrels with ventilated rib, ivory front and middle bead, a selected fancy walnut stock (14¼"x1½"x2¼") with p.g., ventilated recoil pad and fine line hand checkering. Available in three grades of engraving. 12 ga. only (other gauges to be announced later). Barrel length and choke: 26" (IC&M) 28" (F&M) 30" (F&M). Wgt. 7¼ lbs. Weatherby, importer. Grade I **$495.00,** Grade II **$595.00** & Grade III **$695.00.**
Trap model available with special trap stock and ventilated rib. 30" and 32" (F&F, F&M). Grade I **$550.00,** Grade II **$650.00** and Grade III, **$750.00.**
Skeet with 26" (S&S) barrels. Grade I **$550.00,** Grade II **$650.00** & Grade III **$750.00.**

H SAUER BBF OVER-UNDER RIFLE-SHOTGUN
Stock (14½"x1⅝"x2¾") made of selected walnut, with p.g., cheekpiece and hand checkering, and is built in the classic tradition. The trigger guard is steel. 16 ga. (2¾"). Rifle barrel: 222, 243, 30-30, 30-36 and 7x65R. Barrel length: 25"; Krupp-Special gun barrel steel; Shotgun barrel full choke; rifle barrel hammer-forged; matted rib; bead front sight; folding leaf rear sight. Blitz action with Kersten lock; centrally guided firing pins; front trigger for rifle barrel designed as adjustable single-set trigger; sear safety manually operated by slide on upper tang. Wgt. 61 lbs. Weatherby, importer.
Standard Model (with arabesque engravings on action and fine hand checkering) **$550.00**
De Luxe Model (with Scotch checkering on selected walnut stock, white line spacers at p.g. and butt plate, and hunting scene engravings on action). **$645.00**

VOERE O-U RIFLE-SHOTGUN
Available in 20 ga., 3" chamber, over 222, 222 Mag. or 223 rifle caliber. 23⅝" barrels with simple extractor and folding rear and blade front sights. Single trigger. Locking lever is pushed left for cocking, right to open the breech. Walnut cheekpiece stock; checkered p.g. and fore-end; white spacers at grip cap and buttplate. Sling swivels attached. Weight, 6½ lbs.; length, 40" over-all. L. A. Distributors, importer **$219.95**

J ZOLI SILVER SNIPE OVER-UNDER
Purdey type boxlock action with crossbolt, 12 or 20 ga. (3" chambers); satin chrome-plated receiver, single selective trigger, simple extractors and auto. safety. Chrome-lined barrels with vent rib; 30" (12 ga. only, Mod. & Full), 28" (Mod. & Full), or 26" (Imp. Cyl. & Mod.). Walnut stock (12 ga., 14⅜"x1⅜"x2¹⁄₁₆"; 20 ga., 14⁵⁄₁₆"x1⅝"x 2⁹⁄₁₆") with checkered p.g. and fore-end, plastic buttplate. Weight about 6½ lbs. Galef, importer.......................... **$229.95**
Trap, Skeet models have non-auto. safety, wide non-glare vent. rib and suitable stock dimensions, 2¾" chambers.............. **$259.95**

ZOLI GOLDEN SNIPE OVER-UNDER
Same as Silver Snipe except selective auto. ejectors...... **$274.95**
Trap, Skeet models **304.95**

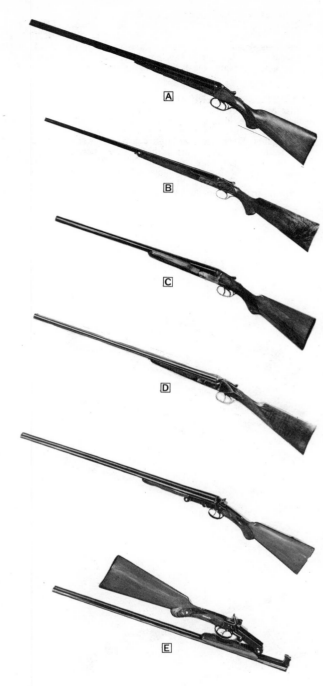

A&F KNOCKABOUT DOUBLES

Made in Italy to A&F's specifications, the Mark I Knockabout is a side-by-side, in 12 (26" or 28" bbls.), 20, 28 or 410 (26"). All gauges have double triggers, plain extractors, color case-hardened action and checkered walnut p.g. stock and fore-end. About 6½ lbs. (12 ga.); 5½ lbs. (20 ga.); 5¼ lbs. (28, 410). 12 or 20 ga., **$150.** 28 and 410 **$25.00** higher. The Mark II is similar to the Mark I, but has vent. rib, ejectors and a beavertail fore-end. 12 and 20 gauge, **$259.50.** The Mark III is a 12, 20 or 28 ga. over-under with single trigger, vent. rib, engraved action with antique silver finish. 26" and 28" barrels only, with choice of choke. Weight, 6¾ lbs. (12 ga.); 5½ lbs. (20 ga.).

12, 20 ga. **$289.50**, 28, 410 ga. **$297.50**

A A&F ZANOTTI SHOTGUN

A custom made side-by-side double in 12 ga. (26" Mod. & Imp. Cyl. or 28" Mod. & Full); 20 and 28 ga. (26" Mod. & Imp. Cyl). 12 ga. has semi-p.g. walnut stock and beavertail fore-end; 20 and 28 ga. have straight grip and slim fore-end. All have single non-selective triggers, ejectors, gold stock inlay for initials, etc. Abercrombie & Fitch, importer.

12 or 20 gauge ...... **$675.00**   28 gauge **$750.00**

B A&F FINEST QUALITY SHOTGUNS

Abercrombie & Fitch import the famous Purdey, Holland & Holland, Boss and Westley Richards shotguns. All are custom-made and hand-finished and, while A&F carries a few models in stock, guns ordered with custom specifications usually require 1 to 2 years for delivery. All have full side locks, single or double triggers and ejectors. Westley Richards side-by-side doubles start at **$900.**, the others at **$2800.**; over-under models start at **$3400.**

C ATLAS 200 SERIES DOUBLE GUNS

12, 16, 20, 28 and 410 ga., 26". (Imp. Cyl. and Mod.), or 26" and 28" (Mod. and Full), bbls. Engraved Anson & Deeley-type action. Vickers steel bbls. with chromed bores. Walnut stock with checkered semi-p.g. and beavertail fore-end. Wgt. approx. 6-7 lbs. Double trigger. .**$180.00** M204 with single trigger **$210.00**. M206 with single trigger, auto ejectors **$230.00**. Note: 410, 28 ga. in M200 only.

M208 Magnum same as M200 except 12 or 20 ga., 3" chambers, **$185.00**; with single non-seleceive trigger **$195.00**

ATLAS 145 DOUBLE SHOTGUN

Similar to M200 except: Vent. rib, choice of p.g. or straight stock, full hand engraving, entire gun of nickel-chrome steel. 12 & 20 ga. only. Atlas Arms, importer **$290.00**

With two sets of bbls., 26" (Skeet 1 & 2); 28" (M & F).... **395.00**

ATLAS 500 MAGNUM DOUBLE SHOTGUN

Similar to M200 Magnum except; 10 ga., 3½ chambers, 32" bbls. (F & F); 12, 20 ga., 3" chambers, 28" (M & F). Vent. rib, double triggers, recoil pad. Action especially built for magnum loads. Atlas Arms, importer **$210.00**

ATLAS 300 DOUBLE SHOTGUN

12 and 20 ga., 26" bbls. ((IC & M); 28" (M & F). Holland & Holland type sidelock action with Purdey-type lock. Hand engraved, auto ejectors. Superior walnut stock, checkered on p.g. and fore-end. Non-selective single trigger. Wgt. 7¼ lbs. (12 ga.). 6¼ lbs. (20 ga.). Atlas Arms, importer **$440.00**

Model 310, with single selective trigger **485.00**

BERETTA GR-2 DOUBLE

Greener type boxlock action, engraved receiver, coil mainsprings. Folding front trigger, auto. safety. Walnut hand-checkered stock (14"x 1½"x2½", 2¼" pitch down) and semi-beavertail fore-end. 12 ga., 2¾" chambers, 30" or 28" (M&F), 26" (IC&M) barrels. 20 ga., 2¾" chambers, 28" (M&F) or 26" (IC&M) barrels. 7⅛ lbs **$277.00**

Extra bbls. **140.00**

BERETTA GR-3 DOUBLE

Same as GR-2 except single selective trigger **$294.00**

12 ga. (3" chambers), 30" M&F barrels, stock 14"x1½"x2½", (2½" pitch down), recoil pad, 8 lbs **$294.00**

Extra bbls. **147.00**

BERETTA GR-4 DOUBLE

Same as GR-3 except fully hand-engraved receiver, selective auto. ejectors, full p.g. stock with grip cap. 12 ga. 2¾" **$371.00**

Extra bbls. **198.00**

D BERNARDELLI GAMECOCK DOUBLES

Boxlock action, double underlugs, case-hardened with light engraving; plain extractors, double triggers, auto. safety. Checkered straight grip walnut stock and fore-end (14"x1½"x2¼"). 12 or 20 ga. with 25" bbls., 2¾" chambers (IC, M), 28" (M, F), wgt. 6-6½" lbs. Stoeger, importer **$230.00**

Deluxe Gamecock, like above except: sideplate action, engraved, chrome-lined bbls., selected fancy wood **$330.00**

Premier Gamecock, similar to Deluxe, except auto-ejectors, non-selective single trigger, Greener-type cross bolt, 3" chambers. .**$440.00**

BERNARDELLI ITALIA HAMMER DOUBLES

Made from modern steel, but with old-style external hammers. 12 ga. only 30" chrome-lined bbls. (M, F), 2¾" chambers. Action has Greener-type crossbolt, double triggers, engraved sideplates, double underlugs, half-cock safety. Checkered fancy walnut stock and fore-end. Stoeger, importer **$220.00**

Brescia model, similar to Italia except: 12 ga., 28" or 30" bbls., 20 ga., 26" bbls. (IC, M) **$160.00**

E CENTURY FOLDING SHOTGUN

Hammer gun with side lever that opens gun, depressing button on forward part of left frame allows complete folding of this Spanish double. Chambered for the 410 3" Magnum, 27¾" barrels are choked Full and Full. Wgt. 4¾ lbs. Century Arms, Inc., importer.......**$54.50**

A CONTINENTAL ARMS DOUBLE GUNS

The Centaure is a hand made Belgian shotgun with triple locking lugs and side clips. French walnut stock, hand-checkered p.g. and fore-end. 12 ga., 30″ barrels only **$137.50**

Supra De Luxe Model 5 is a better quality gun made in Belgium. Boxlock action with Greener cross-bolt and engraved game scene. Available in all gauges and barrel lengths from 26″ to 32″; Skeet, trap and field models **$395.00**

Model 62 is like the Model 5 but also in 12 ga. Magnum; vent. rib; Anson Deeley boxlock action, engraved; selective auto. ejectors; horn grip cap and buttplate. **$495.00**

Model 40 is like the Model 5 but chambered for 10 ga. Magnum; double underlugs; 32″ barrel full-choke; double triggers; weight about 10 lbs. **$495.00**

The best quality sidelock gun (illustrated) is hand made in Belgium and has engraved locks, double triggers and a straight buttstock with hand checkering at the wrist and fore-end. Available singly or in matched pairs, each **$2500.00**

B CHARLES DALY EMPIRE GRADE DOUBLE

12 ga., 2¾″ (3″ in 30″ F&F), 16 ga. 2¾ or 20 ga. (3) chambers, 26″ (IC&M), 28″ (M&F) and 30″ (F&F) bbls. with tapered, raised vent rib. Boxlock action, double locking lugs and triggers; auto safety. Blued receiver is engraved. Walnut, checkered pistol grip stock and beavertail fore-end; recoil pad on magnum model. Wgt., 12 ga. 7¼ lbs., 16 ga. 6½ lbs., 20 ga., 6¼ lbs. in 28″ bbls. **$236.00**

DARNE DOUBLE BARREL SHOTGUN

The unique action whose protruding double "ears," pulled rearward, slide the entire breechblock back exposing the chambers for loading. All models have raised ribs, French walnut checkered pistol grip and fore-end stocks, (14¼″x1⅝″x2½″) double triggers and selective ejectors. Stoeger, importer. Bird Hunter in 12 or 20 ga., 25½″ bbls. (Imp. Cyl. & Mod.). Wgt. approx 6¼ lbs. (12)—5¾ lbs. (20)........ **$235.00**
● Pheasant Hunter De Luxe. Same as the Hunter except: 12 ga. 28″ (Mod. & Full) fancy wood and engraving, **$315.00** ● Quail Hunter Supreme. Same as the Deluxe but in 20 or 28 ga. only, 25½″ (Imp. Cyl. & Mod.) bbls. Elaborate hand engraved action, hard-chromed bores, carrying strap and swivels.................................. **$410.00**

C DAVIDSON 63B DOUBLE SHOTGUN

12, 16, 20, 28, 410 ga. Anson & Deeley crossbolt action (28 & 410 w/o crossbolt). Automatic tang safety. Manual extractors. Brushed nickel finish, engraved. 28 ga., 25″ bbls. (IC & M); 410, 25″ (F & F); 12, 16, 20 gauges; 26″, 28″, 30″ bbls., all popular chokes. Front and middle bead sights. Spanish walnut p.g. stock hand checkered, with grip cap, white-line spacers. Davidson, importers. ...... **$ 99.50**
Magnum, 12 and 20 ga., 3″ chambers, 26″, 28″, 30″ bbls... 119.50
Magnum, 10 ga., 3½″ chambers, 32″ bbls. (F & F)........ 149.50
Model 63BDL. A deluxe version of the Model 63B with select walnut stock, 18 line checkering and more receiver engraving. 20 ga. (Mod. & Full or Imp. Cyl. & Mod.) 2¾″ chambers, weight 6 lbs. 7 oz. or 410 (Full & Full) 3″ chambers, 5 lbs. 11 oz. **$109.50**
12 ga. with single trigger........................... 124.50

DAVIDSON 69SL SIDELOCK DOUBLE

12 ga. (2¾″) with 30″, 28″ (M&F) or 26″ (IC&M) bbls. Also 20 ga. (2¾″) with 28″ (M&F) or 26″ (IC&M) bbls. Checkered walnut p.g. stock and forearm with white-line spacers. Nickel finish, engraved detachable sideplates with cocking indicators. Automatic safety, manual extractors, gold plated trigger, two brass sighting beads. Wgt. 7 lbs. (12 ga.) Davidson, importer............................ **$129.50**

D DICKSON COMPACT DOUBLE

Anson & Deeley type action, case-hardened receiver, auto-safety, single trigger. Hand-checkered walnut p.g. stock (14″x1⁹⁄₁₆″x2½″). 12 ga., 28″ (M&F, IC&M), 3″ chambers. Wgt. about 6 lbs. 12 oz. Standard Extractors, vent. rib, rubber recoil pad. American Import Co., importer.
.... **$146.50**

DICKSON FALCON MAGNUM DOUBLE

Scroll-engraved Anson & Deeley type action, Holland type extractors, raised matted rib. auto. safety, double triggers. Checkered p.g. stock and beavertail fore-end. Recoil pad. 32″ bbls., Full and Full, 3½″ chambers, 10-gauge Magnum. American Import Co....... **$150.00**

DICKSON FALCON DOUBLE SHOTGUN

Same as Magnum 10 except: 12 or 20 ga. in 28″ M&F, or 26″ IC, 3″ chambers. Black plastic butt plate and p.g. cap with white spacers. American Import Co. **$121.00**

DIXIE BREECH-LOADING HAMMER DOUBLES

Of modern Belgian, Italian or Spanish manufacture, proofed for heaviest smokeless powder loads, these double guns are available in 12, 16, 20 and 410 ga., regular or Magnum with 28″ to 32″ barrels. Case-hardened frames with modest engraving. Straight, semi-pistol or full pistol-grip halfstocks, some with checkered grip and fore-end, some smooth. Dixie Gun Works, importers....... **$100.00** to **$140.00**

E FERLACH COMPANION DOUBLE GUN

12, 16, 28 (2¾″ chambers), 20, 410 (3″ chambers). Choice of bbl. lengths and chokes. Anson & Deeley action, two triggers, auto. ejectors, semi-beavertail fore-end. Circassian walnut stock of standard dimensions, checkered p.g. cap, cheekpiece optional. Choice of recoil pad or horn buttplate. 6½-7 lbs. Flaig's, importer. **$500.00**

F KRIEGHOFF AMERICAN DRILLING

Blitz action, engraved receiver. Shotgun locks are auto-cocking with indicators. Rifle lock cocks by moving tang-mounted slide forward. Split extractors lift rifle case higher than shotshells. Wide black nylon trigger guard. Stock has checkered p.g. and beavertail fore-end, Pachmayr recoil pad. Gun comes with 22 WMR insert barrel fitted inside right shotgun tube. Available in double 12 ga. over 30-06 or 7mm Mag. 25″ barrels, 41″ over-all; weight, 7 lbs. Harry Owens, importer **$1,500.00**
Extra insert barrel for 22 LR.......................... 24.00

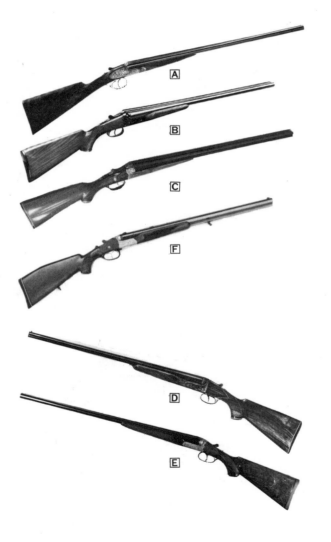

A MERCURY MAGNUM DOUBLES

10 (3½"), 12 or 20 ga. (3") magnums. 12 and 20 ga. have 28" (F&M) brazed rib bbls., 10 ga. in 32" F&F. Triple-lock Anson & Deeley type action with double triggers, front hinged; auto safety, extractors; safety gas ports; engraved frame. Walnut, checkered pistol grip stock and beavertail fore-end; (14"x1⅝"x2¼") with recoil pad. Wgt. 12 ga., 7¼ lbs., 20 ga., 6½ lbs. 45" over-all. Tradewinds, importer......$134.50
10 ga., 10⅛ lbs., 49" over-all.........................159.95

B P.O.S. 10 GAUGE MAGNUM DOUBLE

Made in Spain, this shotgun uses Anson & Deeley top lever type action, Purdey type locks. Case hardened action, checkered Spanish walnut p.g. stock, with recoil pad, beavertail fore-end. 32" (Full) bbls., 3½" chambers. Wgt. 11 lbs. Sloans Sporting Goods Co., importer. $150.00

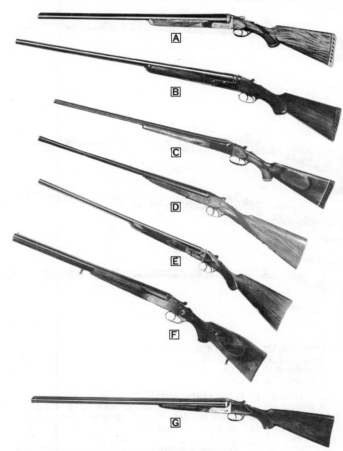

PREMIER DOUBLE BARREL SHOTGUNS

The Continental model is an exposed hammer side-lock gun with two triggers available in 12, 16, 20 or 410. All have 26" barrels choked Mod. & Full except 410, 26". French walnut stock (14"x1⅝"x 2½") checkered at p.g. and fore-end. Length 44½" over-all;; weight about 7 lbs. Ed Paul's Sporting Goods, importer $131.25
Ambassador model is similar to above except: hammerless side-lock action with auto. safety on tang. $144.30
Brush King has a boxlock action and is fitted with 22" barrels choked Mod. and Imp. Cyl. available in 12 or 20 ga. only. Length 39" over-all; weight about 6 lbs. $113.95
Other models and grades are available. Write importer for catalog.

C RICHLAND ARMS SHOTGUNS

Imports from Spain and Italy. The 200 is a demibloc side-by-side double with auto. safety, two triggers, long beavertail fore-end, walnut p.g. stock with cheekpiece and recoil pad. 12, 16, 20, 28 or 410 ga. 410 and 20 ga. with 3" chambers, others 2¾". 30", 28", 26" or 22" (20-ga. only) bbls., all standard chokes..................$129.50
202 is the 200 with extra set of 12 or 20 ga. bbls........179.50
711 is a 10-ga., 3½" chambered long range double with 32" F&F bbls. $149.50
Same, 3" chambers 12 ga., 30" F&F bbls...............139.50
707 is a lightweight (6½ lbs.) 20 ga. Magnum double with improved forcing cones, chokes and borings for 80%-85% patterns with 4's. 26" (IC&M), 28" (M&F) or 30" (F&F) bbls. Checkered walnut p.g. stock, beavertail fore-end, recoil pad.........................$179.50
707-2, with two sets of barrels. 30" (M&F) & 26" (IC&M).. 249.50

D SANDERSON SHOTGUNS

Illustrated is the Classic Bird Gun, M200 S-I, a lightweight double in 28 (4½ lbs.) to 12 gauge (6 lbs.); standard 2¾" or 2" chambers, with barrels from 25" up. The walnut stock has a straight grip and classic fore-end. Auto ejectors, hinged front trigger and engraved action. $425.00 up. 2" and 2½" shells are available from Sanderson. Belgian-made Neumann shotguns imported by Sanderson include the 10 gauge Magnum double from $385; 12, 20 and 410 3" doubles from $249.50 and 20 gauge bird guns.

E WEBLEY & SCOTT 700, 701, 702 DOUBLE GUNS

12 or 20 ga. Anson & Deeley action, boxlock. hammerless, top lever, no extension, solid tumbler, auto. safety. 26" bbls. (Mod. & Imp. Cyl.), 28" (F. or M. & F., M., I.P.), 30" (Full & Ful, Mod. or Imp. Cyl.). Straight or semi-pistol grip stock, hand checkered (14⅝"x1½"x2¼"). Custom fitting, recoil pad, single non-selective trigger, optional at extra cost. About 6¾ lbs. (12-28") to 5¾ lbs. in 20x28". Service Armament Co., importers.

Model 700, light scroll engraving, selected French walnut..$375.00
Model 702, more scroll engraving, better French walnut.... 550.00
Model 701, profusely scroll engraved, fancy French walnut.. 750.00
Write for information on other W&S guns; from.......... 30.00

SAUER ROYAL SIDE BY SIDE

Anson & Deeley action with Greener cross bolt; double underlocking lugs; single selective trigger; automatic slide safety; side firing pin indicators. Krupp-Special steel barrel with ivory bead, matted rib. Fine arabesque engraving on grey case hardened action. Selected walnut stock (14¼"x1½"x2¼") with fine line hand checkering. White spacers at p.g. cap and ventilated recoil pad. The beavertail fore-end is furnished with a patented spring snap. 12 ga. (2¾") with 28" & 30" (F&M) bbls. 20 ga. (3") with 28" (F&M) & 26" (IC&M) bbls. Wgt. 12 ga., approx. 6½ lbs.; 20 ga. approx. 6 lbs. Weatherby, importer.
....$345.00

F SAUER DRILLING 3000-E RIFLE-DOUBLE SHOTGUN

Finest walnut is used for the modified Monte Carlo stock (14½"x 1⅝"x2¾") with p.g., cheek-piece, sling swivels, metal trigger guard and fore-end with checkering. Features a patent spring snap. 12 ga. bbls. chambered for 2¾" shells. Calibers of rifle barrels: available in 222, 243, 30-30, 30-06 and 7x65R. 25" bbl. Krupp-Special gun barrel steel; matted rib; bead front sight; automatically operated folding leaf rear sight; right barrel modified, left barrel full choke; rifle barrel hammer-forged. Blitz action with Greener cross bolt; double underlocking lugs; separate rifle cartridge extractor; front trigger acts as set trigger, adjustable fo pull; vertical firing pin indicators; Greener side safety mechanism locks all 3 bbls.; sear slide safety on upper tang locks right shotgun barrel when firing rifle barrel. Wgt. 6½ to 7¼ lbs., depending on rifle caliber. Weatherby, importer.
3000-E Standard Model (with arabesque engravings on action and fine line hand checkering)..................................$625.00
3000-E De Luxe Model (with Scotch checkering on selected walnut stock, white spacers at p.g. and butt plate and hunting scene engravings on action).......................................$715.00

SAUER ARTEMIS SIDE BY SIDE

12 ga. (2¾") with 30" & 38" (F&M) bbls. 20 ga. (3") with 28" (F&M) & 26" (IC&M) bbls. With Holland and Holland type removable side-locks with double sear safeties and automatic selective ejectors. Stock (14¼"x1½"x2¼") and beavertail fore-end, with fine line hand checkering, are made of highly figured walnut. Krupp-Special steel barrels with ivory bead front sight, Greener cross bolt, double under locking lugs, automatic slide safety and single selective trigger. Weight about 6½ lbs. Weatherby, importer. Grade I (with fine line engraving)...$1,295.00
Grade II (with full English arabesque engraving),....... 1,495.00

G ZOLI SILVER HAWK DOUBLE

Modified Anson & Deeley boxlock action with Purdey triple locks, 12 or 20 ga. (3" chambers); satin chrome-plated receiver with light engraving; double triggers, plain extractors, auto. safety, pins indicate loaded chambers. Chrome-lined barrels, 26" (Imp. Cyl. & Mod.), 28" (Mod. & Full); in 12 ga. only, 30" (Mod. & Full) and 32" (Full & Full). European walnut stock (14⅜"x1⅜"x2⁵⁄₁₆"), hand-checkered fore-end and p.g. with cap, plastic buttplate. Weight about 6¼ lbs. Galef, importer $179.95

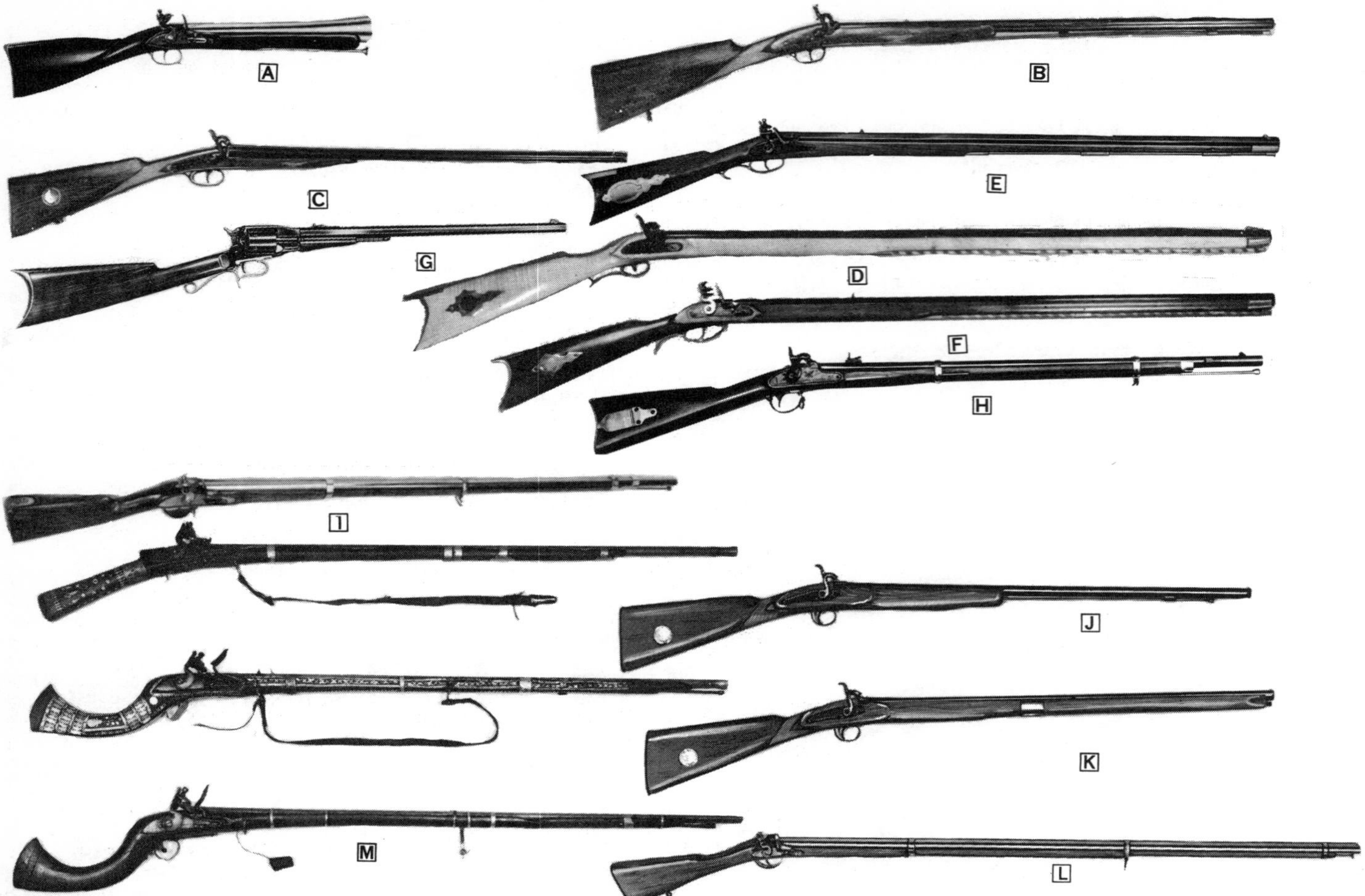

CENTURY MUZZLE LOADERS
[I] Belgian made Charleville 1763 Flintlock Musket. Round barrel, 45″ long smooth bore, 69 caliber. Stock walnut finished wood, brass barrel bands and trigger guard. Overall length 60″. Weight 8½ lbs. Proof tested for black powder by Belgian Official Proof House. Century Arms Importers **$99.50** [J] Percussion action ⅔ stock, 28″ blued barrel. Checkered pistol grip. Weight 3½ lbs. Ramrod, patch box. **$19.50.** Flintlock action. **$29.50.** [K] Percussion action, full length stock. 28″ blued barrel. Checkered pistol grip. Weight: 4 lbs. Ramrod, patch box **$24.50.** Flintlock action **$34.50.** [L] Also, Military flintlock model, 50″ barrel 12 ga. Ramrod **$54.50.** [M] Antique rifles—Genuine antiques, made over a century ago, no two alike. **$99.00.**

[A] COACH GUARD BLUNDERBUSS
A close copy of the flintlock muzzleloaders used against highwaymen. Metal parts blued, wooden stock has polished, ebonized finish. Proof tested. Mars Equipment, importers **$99.95**

[B] DIXIE HALFSTOCK RIFLE
Percussion lock 40-cal. rifle, 32″ round bbl., 6 grooves. Checkered stock and fore-end, open sights, wood ramrod in two thimbles. Steel furniture. Wgt. about 7½ lbs. **$72.50**

[C] DIXIE PERCUSSION SHOTGUNS
Newly made in Belgium from old parts. Most have cap boxes. Barrels average 32″. 6 lbs., single shot, 410 to 32 ga. **$24.95**
Similar, except double barrel, about 20 ga., 8 lbs. **79.95**

[D] DIXIE SQUIRREL RIFLE
Percussion cap 40-cal. rifle with 40″ bbl., 48″ twist, six lands. Full length hard maple stock, stained and varnished, with patchbox. Brass furniture. Kentucky rifle sights, two, "candy-striped" cleaning rods furnished. Wgt., about 10 lbs. For black powder only. Dixie Gun Works, importer. **$139.50**
Flintlock version **149.50**
Double set triggers (installed by purchaser) **8.50**

[E] KENTUCKIAN FLINTLOCK RIFLE
Built in the image of the early Pennsylvania "Kentuckies." Fullstock, 33½″ octagonal barrel, 44 caliber. Weight about 6¼ lbs., over-all 48″. Engraved lockplate and brass patchbox, solid brass furniture, open sights, hardwood ramrod. Intercontinental Arms, importer **$125.00**
Also available in percussion **125.00**

KENTUCKIAN FLINTLOCK CARBINE
Same as Kentuckian rifle, but with 25½″ barrel, 40″ over-all. Intercontinental Arms, importer. **$125.00**
Also available in percussion **125.00**

[F] KENTUCKIAN FLINTLOCK RIFLE
A modern cal. .40 version of the Pennsylvania-Kentucky. Blued 40″ octagon barrel, 13/16″ across the flats, 6 lands. Case-hardened, engraved lockplate, European walnut full-length stock with patchbox, brass furniture. Black powder only. 55″ over-all, wgt. about 10 lbs. Dixie Gunworks, importers. Percussion model **$125.00**
Flintlock model **125.00**

[G] NAVY ARMS CARBINE
6-shot revolving carbine based on the Remington 44 Army revolver. 16″ or 18″ bbl., buckhorn rear sight, adjustable silver blade front. Straight grip wooden stock, curved metal buttplate, scrolled trigger guard. Navy Arms, importers **$125.00**

STOEGER FLINTLOCK ARMS
M4910 is a red-painted full-stocked 12 ga. single shot, 51″ bbl., fittings are brass. 9¼ lb. **$69.95**
M6475 is ⅞ stocked in walnut, with 14 ga., 36″ barrel. **59.95**
M5033 is a half-stock double in 14 gauge, bbls. 31″, straight-grip walnut stock. 7 lbs. **$106.95**
M4957B is a checkered half-stock single bbl., 33″ long in 14 gauge, iron fittings, 6 lbs. **$62.95**
M6494 is 34″ bbld. 4 gauge of 9¾ lbs., with hook buttplate and ⅞-stock with metal bands. **$71.95**
M6475W is a plain ⅞-walnut stock in 14 gauge, with 36″ single bbl. Iron fittings, 7½ lbs. **$59.95**

[H] ZOUAVE RIFLE
A percussion muzzle-loading rifle, cal. 58, that duplicates the Civil War Remington Model 1863. Walnut ⅞-length stock with steel ramrod, sling swivels and brass patchbox in stock. Case-hardened lock, blued 33″ barrel and brass furniture. Bead front and open rear sights. Wgt. 9½ lbs., 52″ over-all. Navy Arms, importer **$100.00**
Zouave Carbine, 22″ bbl. **100.00**
A rifle made to similar specifications is offered by Mars Equipment. **$99.95**

Guns in this section are compression powered by: A) disposable CO₂ cartridge; B) by hand pumping of air; C) by cocking a spring which compresses air. This air is released when the trigger is pulled. Calibers are 177 (BB or pellet) and 22 pellet, except for Sheridan rifles, these using a special form of 20-cal. bullet. Pellet guns are usually rifled, those for BBs only are not; 177-cal. rifles can shoot BBs also, of course.

BENJAMIN 262 SUPER CO² ROCKET (not illus.)
Caliber: 22, single shot.
Barrel: 5¾", rifled bronze liner.
Length: 9¼". **Weight:** 3 lbs.
Power: Standard CO² cylinder, 2-stage power.
Features: Plastic stocks. Adj. rear sight. Fingertip safety. Target outfit includes pellets, Bell target and paper targets, one CO² cartridge; $4.00 extra.
Price: $27.00

A BENJAMIN 422 SEMI-AUTOMATIC PISTOL
Caliber: 22, 10-shot.
Barrel: 5⁹⁄₁₆", rifled bronze liner.
Length: 9". **Weight:** 2 lbs.
Power: Standard CO² cylinder. Muzzle velocity about 400 fps.
Features: Trigger and hammer safeties, checkered plastic thumbrest grips, adj. rear sight, blade front.
Price: Blued $27.50

B BENJAMIN SUPER S. S. TARGET PISTOL SERIES 130
Caliber: BB, 22 and 177; single shot.
Barrel: 8 inches; BB smoothbore; 22 and 177, rifled.
Length: 11". **Weight:** 2 lbs.
Power: Hand pumped.
Features: Bolt action; fingertip safety; adj. power.
Price: M130, BB..**$32.00**   M132, 22..**$32.00**   M137, 177..**$32.00**

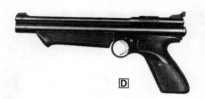

C BSF MATCH EXPORT PISTOL
Caliber: 177 single shot
Barrel: 7" rifled
Length: 15¾ inches. **Weight:** 2 lbs. 10 oz.
Power: Spring (barrel cocking).
Features: One piece walnut grip with thumb-rest. Adjustable trigger. Bead front, rear adjustable for w. and e. Air Rifle Hdqtrs, importer.
Price: $34.50

D CROSMAN MODEL "1300" MEDALIST II
Caliber: 22, single shot.
Barrel: 8", button rifled.
Length: 11¾". **Weight:** 32 oz.
Power: Hand pumped.
Features: Moulded plastic grip, hand size pump forearm. Cross bolt safety, self-cocking.
Price: $29.95

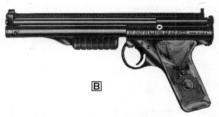

E CROSMAN 600 SEMI-AUTOMATIC PISTOL
Caliber: 22, 10-shot.
Barrel: 5¼ inches, button rifled.
Length: 9½ inches. **Weight:** 40 oz.
Power: Crosman Powerlet CO² cylinder.
Features: Thumbrest plastic grips; adj. rear sight; thumb safety; ammo-count magazine.
Price: $32.50

F CROSMAN PEACEMAKER "44"
Caliber: 22, 6 shot.
Barrel: 4¾", button rifled.
Length: 10⅜". **Weight:** 34 oz.
Power: Crosman CO² Powerlet
Features: Revolving cylinder, walnut finished grips. Simulated gold hammer and trigger, positive valve design. Single-action.
Price: $24.95

G CROSMAN FRONTIER "36"
Caliber: BB, 18-shot.
Barrel: 4¾", smoothbore.
Length: 10⅜". **Weight:** 34 oz.
Power: Crosman CO₂ Powerlet
Features: Single-action, steel barrel, revolving cylinder. Walnut finish grips.
Price: $24.95

A CROSMAN MARK I TARGET PISTOL
Caliber: 22, single shot.
Barrel: 7¼ inches, button rifled.
Length: 10⅝ inches. **Weight:** 43 oz.
Power: Crosman Powerlet CO_2 cylinder.
Features: New system provides same shot-to-shot velocity, adj. from 300- to 400 fps. Checkered thumbrest grips, right or left. Patridge front sight, rear adj. for w. & e. Adj. trigger.
Price: 22 or 177 ....$27.95

CROSMAN MARK II TARGET PISTOL
Same as Mark I except 177 cal. $27.95

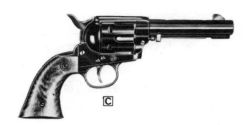

C DAISY 179 SIX GUN
Caliber: BB, 12-shot.
Barrel: Steel lined, smoothbore.
Length: 11½ inches. **Weight:** NA.
Power: Spring.
Features: Forced feed from under-barrel magazine. Single action, molded wood grained grips.
Price: $8.95

B CROSMAN 38 TARGET REVOLVER M9
Caliber: 22, 6-shot.
Barrel: 6 inches, rifled.
Length: 11 inches. **Weight:** 38 oz.
Power: CO_2 Powerlet cylinder.
Features: Double action, revolving cylinder. Adj. rear sight.
Price: $34.95

CROSMAN 38 COMBAT REVOLVER
Same as 38 Target except 3½" bbl., 38 oz...............$34.95

D DAISY 177 BB PISTOL
Caliber: BB, 150-shot.
Barrel: Formed steel, smoothbore.
Length: 10⅜ inches. **Weight:** NA.
Power: Spring.
Features: Gravity feed, adjustable rear sight, molded plastic thumbrest grips.
Price: $8.95

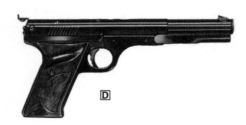

E DAISY CO_2 200 AUTOLOADING PISTOL
Caliber: BB, 175-shot semi-auto.
Barrel: 7½ inches, steel-lined, smoothbore.
Length: 11⁵⁄₃₂", sight radius 9". **Weight:** 24 oz.
Power: Daisy CO_2 cylinders, 8½ grams (100 shots) or 12 grams (160 shots).
Features: 175-shot magazine; constant full power; valve system eliminates gas leakage; checkered thumbrest stocks; undercut ramp front sight and adjustable rear.
Price: $23.95

DIANA 5 TARGET PISTOL
Same as the Hy-Score 815 except: Air Rifle HQ degreases, inspects, test fires, adjusts, sights-in and repackages.................$34.50
Without accurizing 29.95

DIANA 6 TARGET PISTOL
Same as the Hy-Score 816 but with accurizing done as described above $57.50
Without accurizing 49.95

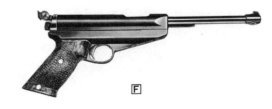

F FEINWERKBAU 65 TARGET PISTOL
Caliber: 177, single shot.
Barrel: 7½", rifled, fixed to receiver.
Length: About 15". **Weight:** 42 oz.
Power: Spring, cocked by left-side lever.
Features: Recoiless operation, may be set to give recoil; Micro. rear sight, 14" radius. Adj. trigger; normal 17.6 oz. pull can be raised to 48 oz. for training. Checkered, thumbrest target grips. Air Rifle Hdqtrs. or Daisy, importer.
Price: $144.50

A HAMMERLI MASTER CO² TARGET PISTOL
Caliber: 177, single shot.
Barrel: 6.7", rifled, 12 grooves, R.H.
Length: 16". **Weight:** 38 oz.
Power: 8g. or 12g. CO² cyl., 40-60 plus shots.
Features: Easy manual loading; residual gas vented automatically; 4-way adj. trigger; ramp front sight, ⅞" blade (other widths avail.), micro-click rear; sight radius adj. 11½" to 13⅜". Bbl.- and grip weights available, $4 and $3.50.
Price: $54.00

B HAMMERLI SINGLE TARGET PISTOL Model 452
Caliber: 177, single shot.
Barrel: 5.2 inches, rifled.
Length: 12 inches. **Weight:** 34 oz., including CO² cylinder.
Power: Standard CO² cylinder.
Features: Auto spring loader; adj. trigger; valve permits emptying CO² cylinder. Micrometer adj. rear sight. ⅛" blade front sight on ramp. H. Grieder, importer. Price incl. 10 CO² cylinders, 100 pellets.
Price: $41.00

C HEALTHWAYS ML 175 CO² AUTOMATIC PISTOL
Caliber: BB, 100-shot repeater.
Barrel: 5¾", smooth.
Length: 9½". **Weight:** 28 oz.
Power: Standard CO² cylinder.
Features: 3 position power switch. Automatic ammunition feed. Positive safety.
Price: $21.00

HEALTHWAYS MA22 CO² AUTOMATIC PISTOL
Same as Healthways ML175 except rifled 22 cal. bbl., rear sight adj. for w. and e., cap. 50 lead balls. $24.00

D HY-SCORE 816 M TARGET PISTOL
Caliber: 177, single shot.
Barrel: 7" precision rifled.
Length: 16 inches. **Weight:** 50 oz.
Power: Spring, bbl. cocking.
Features: Recoil-less firing, adj. trigger. Hooded front sight with 3 apertures, click adj. rear with 4 apertures. Plastic thumbrest target grips.
Price: In plastic case $49.95

HY-SCORE 814 JUNIOR PISTOL
Caliber: 177 darts, BBs, single shot.
Barrel: Smoothbore.
Length: About 10 inches. **Weight:** N.A.
Power: Spring, compressed by screwing in breech plug.
Features: Checkered wooden grips.
Price: Blued $5.95

HY-SCORE 815 TARGET PISTOL
Same as Hy-Score M816 except: without recoil-less system; is slightly shorter and lighter; has fixed aperture front sight. In plastic case. Also in 22 cal. $29.95

A HY-SCORE 802 AUTOLOADING PISTOL
Caliber: 22, 6-shot repeater.
Barrel: 10¼ inches, rifled.
Length: 10¼ inches. **Weight:** 30½ oz.
Power: Spring.
Features: Thumbrest target grips. Recoil comparable to standard target pistols. 3-pound trigger pull. Shutter type loading.
Price: Blued **$29.95.** M800, same except single shot..........**$24.95**

LUFT PISTOLE 210 TARGET
Caliber: 177, single shot.
Barrel: 4¾" rifled.
Length: 8". **Weight:** 45 oz.
Power: Spring.
Features: Same size, weight & shape as a standard auto. pistol. Simulated slide lifts, cocking the gun, as the breech is loaded. Navy Arms, importer.
Price: **$17.50**

B MARKSMAN REPEATER PISTOL
Caliber: 177, 20-shot repeater.
Barrel: 2½ inches, smoothbore.
Length: 8¼ inches. **Weight:** 24 oz.
Power: Spring.
Features: Thumb safety. Uses BB's, darts or pellets. Repeats with BB's only.
Price: Black finish **$9.95**

E WALTHER MODEL LP2
Caliber: 177, single shot.
Barrel: 9.4", rifled.
Length: 12.8"   **Weight:** 20 oz.
Power: Spring-air.
Features: Recoil-less operation, cocking in grip frame. Micro-click rear sight, adj. for w. & e. 4-way adj. trigger. Plastic thumbrest grips; wood grip at extra cost. Interarms, importer.
Price: **$72.00**

F WALTHER MODEL 53 PISTOL
Caliber: 177, single shot.
Barrel: 9⅜", rifled.
Length: 12¼". **Weight:** 42 oz.
Power: Spring.
Features: Micrometer rear sight. Interchangeable rear sight blades. Adj. trigger. Target grips. Bbl. weight available at extra cost. Interarms, Alexandria, Va.
Price: **$38.00**

G WEBLEY AIR PISTOLS

Model:	Junior	Premier
Caliber:	177	177 or 22
Barrel:	6⅛"	6½"
Weight:	24 oz.	33 oz.
Power:	Spring, barrel cocking	Same
Sights:	Adj. for elev.	Adj. for w.&e.
Trigger:	Fixed	Adj.
Price:	$19.95	$27.50

Features: Come with cardboard storage case, pellets, spare washer. Service Armament, importer.

H WINCHESTER 363 TARGET PISTOL
Caliber: 177, Single shot.
Barrel: 7" rifled.
Length: 16". **Weight:** 3 lbs.
Power: Spring, barrel cocking.
Features: Recoil-less firing, adj. double pull type trigger, hooded front sight with 3 apertures, click adj. rear sight. Plastic thumbrest target grips. M.V. 378 fps.
Price: **$52.95**

J WINCHESTER 353 TARGET PISTOL
Caliber: 177 or 22, single shot.
Barrel: 7" rifled.
Length: 16". **Weight:** 2 lbs. 11 oz.
Power: Spring, barrel cocking.
Features: Plastic thumbrest target grips. Adj. double pull trigger, Micro rear sight, detachable bead front with hood. M.V. 378 fps.
Price: **$32.95**

[A] ANSCHUTZ 250 TARGET RIFLE
Caliber: 177, single shot.
Barrel: 18½", rifled, one piece with receiver.
Length: 45". **Weight:** 11 lbs. with sights.
Power: Spring, side-lever cocking, 11 lb. pull.
Features: Recoilless operation. Two-stage adj. trigger. Checkered walnut p.g. stock with Monte Carlo comb & cheekpiece; adj. buttplate; accessory rail. Air Rifle Hdqtrs., importer.
Price: Without sights **$152.00**
　　　　Add **$22.75** for utility aperture sights or **$44.75** for premium aperture sights.

BAVARIA/WISCHO 55N SPORTING RIFLE
Caliber: 177 or 22, single shot.
Barrel: 16½", rifled.
Length: 40½". **Weight:** 6.4 lbs.
Power: Spring (barrel cocking).
Features: High velocity (728 fps in 177, 590 fps in 22) and accuracy combined with rapid loading, can be reloaded in 5 seconds. Stock is of walnut with checkered p.g. and buttplate. Open rear, bead front sights; receiver grooved for scope mounting. Trigger is adjustable. Air Rifle Hdqtrs, importer.
Price: **$56.50**

[B] BSA METEOR SUPER
Caliber: 177 or 22, single-shot.
Barrel: 18½", rifled.
Length: 42". **Weight:** 6 lbs.
Power: Spring, bbl. cocking.
Features: Beechwood Monte Carlo stock, recoil pad. Adjustable single-stage trigger. Bead front, adjustable rear sight. Positive relocation of barrel for same zero shot to shot. Galef, importer.
Price: **$39.95**

[C] BENJAMIN 3030 CO² REPEATER
Caliber: BB only.
Barrel: 25½", smoothbore, takedown.
Length: 36". **Weight:** 2 lbs. 13 oz.
Power: Standard CO² cylinder.
Features: Bolt action. 30-shot repeater with permanent-magnet, shot-holder ammo feed.
Price: **$25.50**

[D] BENJAMIN SERIES 3100 SUPER 100 SHOT RIFLES
Caliber: BB, 100-shot; 22, 85-shot repeater.
Barrel: 23", rifled or smoothbore.
Length: 35". **Weight:** 6 lbs.
Power: Hand pumped.
Features: Bolt action. 100-shot, piggy back full view magazine. Bar V adj. rear sight. Walnut-finished p.g. stock.
Price: M3100, BB . . . . **$38.50**　M3120, 22 rifled **$38.50**
　　　Also available with custom stock at $3 extra.

[E] BENJAMIN SERIES 362 SUPER CO² SINGLE SHOT
Caliber: 22 only.
Barrel: 23", rifled.
Length: 35". **Weight:** 6 lbs.
Power: Standard CO² cylinder. 2 power settings.
Features: Bolt action. Bronze-lined steel bbl. Adj. rear sight. Walnut-finished stock. Two-stage power.
Price: **$31.50**
　　　Also available with custom stock at $3 extra.

[F] BENJAMIN SERIES 340 RIFLE
Caliber: 22 and 177 pellets or BB; single shot.
Barrel: 23", rifled.
Length: 35". **Weight:** 6 lbs.
Power: Hand pumped.
Features: Bolt action, walnut stock and pump handle. Adj. V sight.
Price: M340, BB . . **$35.95**　　M342, 22 . . **$35.95**　　M347, 177 . . **$35.95**
　　　Available with custom stock at $3 extra.

[G] CROSMAN M-1 CARBINE
Caliber: BB, 22-shot.
Barrel: Smoothbore, steel.
Length: 35⅝". **Weight:** 4½ lbs.
Power: Spring.
Features: Patterned after U.S. M1 carbine, uses slide action cocking, military type adj. sights. Hardwood stock.
Price: **$19.95**

A CROSMAN 99 REPEATER RIFLE
Caliber: 22, 14-shot.
Barrel: 19½ inches, button rifled steel.
Length: 40 inches. **Weight:** 5 lbs. 10 oz.
Power: Crosman Powerlet CO_2 cylinder.
Features: Lever action pellet rifle with swing-arm loading principle; has size and balance of firearm counterparts. Two-stage power selector. Adj. rear sight.
Price: $37.50

B CROSMAN 1400 RIFLE
Caliber: 22, single shot.
Barrel: 19½ inches, rifled steel.
Length: 35 inches. **Weight:** About 6 lbs.
Power: Hand pumped.
Features: Bolt action. Air-Trol valve prevents air lock from over-pumping. Adj. trigger, left or right hand safety. Scope and mount optional.
Price: $36.95

C CROSMAN 160 RIFLE
Caliber: 22, single shot.
Barrel: 21 inches, button rifled steel.
Length: 40 inches. **Weight:** 5⅜ lbs.
Power: 2 Crosman Powerlet CO_2 cylinders.
Features: Bolt action. Monte Carlo stock, hard rubber butt plate. Adj. receiver sight. Turning cross-lock safety. Scope and mount optional.
Price: $41.50

D CROSMAN POWERMATIC "500"
Caliber: BB, 50 shot semiautomatic.
Barrel: 18", smoothbore steel.
Length: 37¾". **Weight:** 4½ lbs.
Power: Crosman CO_2 Powerlet.
Features: Positive safety, over 100 shots from one Powerlet. Walnut finished stock, grooved receiver for optional scope or peep sight. Rear sight is adjustable for windage and elevation.
Price: $22.95

E CROSMAN MODEL 3500 SLIDEMASTER
Caliber: BB, 22 shot slide action.
Barrel: 18", smoothbore steel.
Length: 36". **Weight:** 4 lbs.
Power: High compression spring.
Features: Fast and easy cocking, hooded post front sight and fully adjustable rear sight. Scope and mount optional. High comb Monte Carlo stock.
Price: $16.95

F CROSMAN PELLMASTER 700
Caliber: 22
Barrel: 18 inches, rifled steel.
Length: 36¾ inches. **Weight:** 4 lbs.
Power: Crosman Powerlet CO_2 cylinder.
Features: One stroke cocking and safety knob, hooded post front and adjustable rear sight, high Monte Carlo comb walnut finished hardwood stock. Uniform velocity from shot to shot, designed for NRA 10 meter competition.
Price: $27.95

CROSMAN PELLMASTER 707
Same as Pellmaster 700 except 177 cal. and BB.......... $27.95

G CROSMAN MODEL 760 POWERMASTER
Caliber: BB, 180 shot.
Barrel: 19½", smoothbore steel.
Length: 35½". **Weight:** 4½ lbs.
Power: High compression spring.
Features: Short stroke, power determined by number of strokes. Walnut finished checkered stock and forearm. Post front sight and adjustable rear sight. Cross-bolt safety. Scope and mount optional.
Price: $24.95

H CROSMAN TRAPMASTER SHOTGUN
Gauge: .380 inch, chambers Crosman CO_2 shotshells.
Action: One-stroke, side cocking single shot.
Barrel: 28" true cylinder bore, full length rib.
Stock: 14¼"x1"x2", contoured hardwood, walnut finished.
Weight: 6¼ lbs. 46" over-all.
Power: Crosman Giant CO_2 Powerlet.
Features: Pattern is about 14" dia. at 40 feet (effective range). Plastic shotshells contain about 55 No. 8 pellets. Looks and feels like other shotguns.
Price: $49.95

CROSMAN CO_2 SKEET SET
Includes Trapmaster shotgun, box of 25 reusable plastic break-away targets, 100 shotshells, 10 giant Powerlets and Skeet trap with remote foot release $89.95

A DAISY 21 DOUBLE BARREL RIFLE
Caliber: BB, 48-shot.
Barrel: 23½ inches, smoothbore.
Length: 37¾ inches. **Weight:** 4½ lbs.
Power: Spring, barrel cocking.
Features: Two barrels and triggers; automatic safety; beaded front ramp
and open rear sights.
Price: **$23.95**

B DAISY 25 PUMP GUN
Caliber: BB, 50-shot.
Barrel: 18 inches, smoothbore.
Length: 37 inches. **Weight:** NA.
Power: Pump cocking spring.
Features: Ramp front and adj. rear sights. BBs are spring-force fed.
Price: **$16.95**

C DAISY 1894 SPITTIN' IMAGE CARBINE
Caliber: BB, 40-shot.
Barrel: 17½ inches, smoothbore.
Length: 35 inches.
Power: Spring.
Features: Cocks halfway on forward stroke of lever, halfway on return.
Price: **$19.49**
Price: With 4X Scope, as M3894 . . . . 26.95
Price: With fluted receiver, cocking lever, saddle ring, loading port,
fore-arm cap and contoured butt plate, as 3030 . . . .**$21.49**

D DAISY 99 TARGET SPECIAL RIFLE
Caliber: BB, 50-shot.
Barrel: 18 inches, smoothbore.
Length: 36 inches.
Power: Spring.
Features: Wood stock, beavertail fore-end; sling; hooded front sight
with four insert apertures, adj. aperture rear.
Price: **$19.95**

E DAISY RIFLES

Model:	96	95	111	102	1776
Caliber:	BB	BB	BB	BB	BB
Barrel:	18″	18″	18″	13½″	13½″
Length:	36″	35⅛″	35″	30½″	30½″
Power:	Spring	Spring	Spring	Spring	Spring
Capacity:	700	700	700	500	500
Price:	$16.95	$12.95	$11.95	$8.95	$9.95

Price: Model 96 with 4X scope, as M496 . . . .**$24.45**
Features: 96 has M.C. stock and oversize fore-end; 95 stock is wood,
fore-end plastic; 111 and 1776 have plastic stocks; 102 has wood
stock; 1776 has sighting tube w/aperture and is gold finished.

F DAISY HIGH POWER RIFLES

Model:	160	220	230	250
Caliber:	177 & BB	177	22	22
Barrel:	12″	14½″	15¾″	15¾″
Rifled:	No	Yes	Yes	Yes
Length:	33″	36″	38″	38″
Weight:	3 lbs.	3¾ lbs.	5 lbs.	5½ lbs.
Power:	Spring	Spring	Spring	Spring
Price:	$16.45	$22.95	$27.95	$32.95

Features: All are barrel cocking with beechwood stocks. 160 and 220
have bead front and adj. rear sights. 230 and 250 have blade front
and adj. rear target sights.

G DAISY CO² 300 REPEATER
Caliber: BB, 5-shot semi-auto.
Barrel: 22 inches, smoothbore.
Length: 37⅞ inches. **Weight:** 2 lbs. 14 oz.
Power: Daisy 8.5 or 12 gram CO² cylinder.
Features: Free-style stock, cross-bolt safety, 200 shot magazine capac-
ity, blade front daj: open rear sights, receiver grooved for scope.
Price: **$31.49**
Price: With 4X scope, as CO² 3300 . . . . 38.95

H DAISY 572 SPITTIN' IMAGE SLIDE ACTION RIFLE
Caliber: BB, 45-shot.
Barrel: 22½ inches, smoothbore.
Length: 42¼ inches.
Power: Spring.
Features: Pump-cocking, cross-bolt safety, takedown bbl., adj. rear
sight, under bbl. magazine, wood-grained stock and fore-end.
Price: **$21.95**
Price: With 4X scope, as 2572 . . . . 29.45

J DAISY 2299 QUICK SKILL RIFLE KIT
Caliber: BB, 50-shot
Barrel: 24 inches, smoothbore.
Length: 37⅝ inches (adult stock). **Weight:** 3¼ lbs.
Power: Spring.
Features: Kit includes rifle, shooting glasses, ammo, official targets and
instruction manual. No sights, meant for instinct shooting instruction.
Price: **$25.95**

A DAISY VL SHOOTING SYSTEM
Caliber: 22VL caseless ctg., single shot.
Barrel: Solid steel, 6 lands and grooves 1 in 16" twist.
Length: 38 inches. **Weight:** 51 lbs.
Power: Fires 29 gr. bullet at 1,150 fps.
Features: Cartridge has no case or primer. Action has no firing pin or ejector. Cocking by recessed lever. Ignition is by air released under high pressure causing friction to ignite material at base of bullet. Also has auto. safety, plastic wood finished stock with checkered p.g. and fore-end. Rear sight adj. for w. & e.; blade front.
Price: Model 0002 ....$39.95
PRESENTATION VL
Same as above but with walnut stock, storage gun case with foam cushion lining, brass wall hangers and 300 rounds of ammunition. Model 0003. ....$125.00

DIANA 60 TARGET RIFLE
Caliber: 177, single shot.
Barrel: 18", rifled.
Length: 43½". **Weight:** 9½ lbs. with sights and detachable bbl. sleeve.
Power: Spring (barrel cocking).
Features: Recoil-less type action, no jar. Micro. aperture rear sight, globe front with 4 inserts. Two-stage, adj. trigger, pull less than 1 lb. Checkered walnut p.g. stock with Monte Carlo comb & cheekpiece, rubber buttplate. Air Rifle Hdqtrs., importer.
Price: $118.50
Add $19.00 for Tyrolean Stock.

DIANA 65 TARGET RIFLE
Same as the M60 except weighs 11 lbs., has adj. stock length; M.V. 50 fps., double trigger, (Available about July 1969).
Price: $169.75

C FEINWERKBAU 300 MATCH RIFLE
Caliber: 177, single shot.
Barrel: 19½" rifled steel, one piece with receiver.
Length: 42". **Weight:** 9¾ lbs.
Power: Hand cocked by side lever. Less than 10 lbs. pull required.
Features: Barrel and receiver recoil together, independent of stock, to eliminate felt recoil, are locked up when gun is cocked. Micro. rear peep sight, globe front with inserts. Trigger fully adj. Muzzle velocity 575 fps. Checkered walnut stock with Monte Carlo cheekpiece, palmswell p.g. Daisy or Air Rifle Hdqtrs., importers.
Price: 150S (9 lb. Std.) **$169.75**; 150SL (L.H.) **$188.75**; 150ST (Tyrol. stock), 150STL (L.H. Tyrol. stock) **$199.50**

FEINWERKBAU 200 RIFLE
Same as F'bau 300 except: has slight recoil effect; 20" bbl., 640 fps. M.V. Available from A.R.H. or Daisy.
Price: $144.50

E HAMMERLI CO² MATCH RIFLE Model 472
Caliber: 177, single shot.
Barrel: 23¼", rifled steel.
Length: 41½". **Weight:** 9 lbs. 11 oz.
Power: Standard CO² cylinder or CO² Powerlets.
Features: Walnut p.g. stock with Monte Carlo comb and cheekpiece; adj. trigger; curved rubber buttplate. Micrometer rear sight, globe front sight. H. Grieder, importer.
Price: $124.00

M471 Junior Same except has bbl. post front sight and bbl. mounted rear sight, no pad, weight 6 lbs. $74.00

F HEALTHWAYS PLAINSMAN MC22 AUTO RIFLE
Caliber: 22, 75-shot.
Barrel: 20½ inches, rifled for round lead balls.
Length: 41 inches. **Weight:** 4½ lbs.
Power: CO² (8- or 12-gram cylinder).
Features: Up to 50 shots automatically with 12-g. cylinder; no cocking, pumping, etc. Full size p.g. wood stock.
Price: $35.00

G Plainsman MX175. Same as MC22 except 175" smoothbore for BBs; weighs 8 oz. less. $30.00

HY-SCORE 809M TARGET RIFLE
Caliber: 22, single shot.
Barrel: 19 inch rifled.
Length: 44 inches. **Weight:** 7 pounds.
Power: Spring, bbl. cocking.
Features: Adj. target receiver sight, aperture front with 4 inserts, in addition to open adj. middle sight also with 4 apertures.
Price: $64.95

A HY-SCORE RIFLES

Model:	808	806	813	801	807
Caliber:	177	177	22	22	22
Barrel:	12″	14½″	14¼″	15¾″	17⅜″
Rifled:	No	Yes	Yes	Yes	Yes
Length:	33″	36½″	36½″	38½″	41¾″
Weight:	3 lbs.	3¾ lbs.	4 lbs.	5 lbs.	5 lbs. 14 oz.
Power:	Spring	Spring	Spring	Spring	Spring
Price:	$14.95	$19.95	$25.95	$29.95	$39.95

Features: All are barrel cocking. All have adj. sights and regular triggers except 807, which has an adj. trigger. Staeble 2.2X scope and mt. available for all but 808, **$14.95.**
M813 and scope available at a combination price of **$33.40**
M801 available as 801M with click adj. receiver sight......**$49.95**

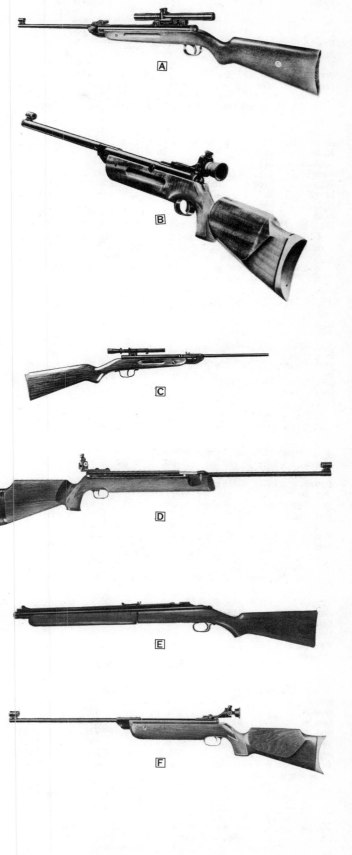

B HY-SCORE 810M OLYMPIC INTERNATIONAL RIFLE
Caliber: 177, single shot.
Barrel: 19¼″ 12-groove rifled.
Length: 44″. **Weight:** 9½ lbs.
Power: Spring (barrel cocking).
Features: Full cheekpiece, Monte Carlo stock, hand checkered; grooved fore-end, curved rubber buttplate. Adj. target receiver sight (includes 4 apertures), hooded front sight (includes 4 inserts).
Price: **$99.95**

M810SM SUPER MATCH
As above but with weight increased to 14 lbs., bbl. locking device, adj. stock, replaceable mainspring, MV 650 fps, accuracy tested: ¼″ spread at 33′ **$169.95**

C PIC MINUTEMAN M77 RIFLE
Caliber: 177; 22, single shot.
Barrel: 14″, 6- and 10-groove rifled.
Length: 36″. **Weight:** 3¼ lbs.
Power: Spring (barrel cocking).
Features: Adj. sights, grooved for scope, light wood p.g. stock., finger-grooved fore-end.
Price: 177...............**$13.50**   **Price:** 22...............**$14.00**
With 4x tip-off mount scope **$5.50** extra.

D SAVAGE-ANSCHUTZ 250 TARGET RIFLE
Caliber: 177, single shot.
Barrel: 18½″, rifled steel fixed to receiver, movable compression cylinder.
Length: 45″ **Weight:** 11 lbs. with sights.
Power: Hand cocked by side lever, about 11 lbs. cocking effort.
Features: Recoiless shooting via oil damper and compensating piston. Two-stage trigger adj. for finger length. French walnut, Monte Carlo stock and beavertail fore-end; checkered p.g. with Wundhammer swell. Accepts Anschutz target sights.
Price: Without sights **$152.00**

E SHERIDAN BLUE AND SILVER STREAK RIFLES
Caliber: 5mm (20 cal.), single shot.
Barrel: 18½″, rifled.
Length: 37″. **Weight:** 5 lbs.
Power: Hand pumped (swinging fore-end).
Features: Rustproof barrel and piston tube. Takedown. Thumb safety. Mannlicher type walnut stock.
Price: Blue Streak ....**$38.75**   Silver Streak **$39.75**
Sheridan accessories: Intermount, a base for ⅜″ Tip-Off scope mounts, **$6.75**; Sheridan-Williams 5DSH receiver sight, **$7.00**; Model 22 Targetrap, **$12.50**; Model 38 Targetrap **$30.00**; Sheridan 5mm pellets, **$2.50** for 500.

F WALTHER LG 55-M RIFLE
Caliber: 177, single shot.
Barrel: 16″, rifled.
Length: 41⅜″. **Weight:** 9 lbs. (9.7 lbs. with bbl. sleeve).
Power: Spring (barrel cocking).
Features: Micro. click adj. receiver sight, globe target front, 3 inserts. Walnut cheekpiece Monte Carlo, checkered p.g. stock. Tyrolean stock $10 extra. Interarms, importers.
Price: **$96.00**
Double set triggers available with any LG 55-M for $12 extra.

WALTHER LG 53-ZD RIFLE
Caliber: 177, single shot.
Barrel: 16″, rifled.
Length: 41⅜″. **Weight:** 6 lbs.
Power: Spring (barrel cocking).
Features: Micro. click adj. receiver sight; globe front with 3 inserts. Adj. trigger. Checkered p.g. stock. Interarms and other importers.
Price: **$68.00**

A WEBLEY AIR RIFLES

Model:	Jaguar	Falcon	Mark III
Caliber:	177	177, 22	177, 22
Barrel:	NA.	17¼"	18½"
Length:	37"	41½"	43½"
Weight:	4 lbs.	6 lbs.	6 lbs.
Power:	spring	spring	spring
Sights:	open, adj.	open, adj.	globe front
Price:	$27.50	$39.95	$75.00

Features: Wooden p.g. stocks. Receivers grooved for scope mounts. Jaguar comes with target holder, target cards, 500 pellets, 12 darts, oil. Mk III is lever-cocking, others bbl.-cocking. Service Armament, importer.

B WEIHRAUCH 30 & 50 SERIES RIFLES

Model:	30 M-II	30S	50 M-II	50S	50 E
Caliber:	177	177	177	177	177
Barrel:	16⅞"	16⅞"	18½"	18½"	18½"
Trigger:	fixed	fixed	fixed	adj.	adj.
Length:	40"	40"	43½"	43½"	43½"
Wgt., lbs.:	5½	5½	7	7	7¼
Price:	$36.50	$44.50	$44.50	$49.95	$56.50

Features: All are rifled and spring-operated by single stroke cocking. Post and ramp front sights (except 50S and 50E have globe fronts with 4 inserts). Open click rear sights, adj. for w. & e., except 30 Mk-11 has lock-screw windage. Walnut finished stocks. 50E has cheek-piece, checkering, ¾" sling swivels. MV of all 660-67 fps. Air Rifle Hdqtrs., importer.

C WEIHRAUCH 35 TARGET RIFLES

Model:	35	35L	35E
Caliber:	177	177	177
Barrel:	19½"	19½"	22"
Wgt. lbs.:	7½	7½	8
Rear sight:	open	open	open
Front Sight:	All with globe and 4 interchangeable inserts.		
Power:	All with spring (barrel cocking).		
Price:	$67.50	$74.50	$89.95

Features: Trigger fully adj. and removable. Open rear sight click adj. for w. and e. P.g. high comb stock with beavertail fore-end, walnut finish, except 35E have checkered walnut with standard cheekpiece. 35L has Tyrolean cheekpiece stock. Air Rifle Hdqtrs., importer.

F WEIHRAUCH 55 TARGET RIFLES

Model:	55SF	55SM	55MM	55MM	55MM-L	55T
Caliber:	177	177	177	177	177	177
Barrel:	18½"	18½"	18½"	18½"	18½"	18½"
Wgt. lbs.:	7¼	8½	8½	7½	8½	8½
Rear Sight:	open	aperture	aperture	open	aperture	aperture
Front Sight:	All with globe and 4 interchangeable inserts.					
Power:	All with spring (bbl. cocking) .600 fps.					
Price:	$64.50	$78.50	$94.50	$84.50	$109.50	$109.50

Features: Trigger fully adj. and removable. Micrometer rear sight adj. for w. and e., on all but 55SF and 55MM. P.g. high comb stock with beavertail fore-end, walnut finish stock on 55SF, SM. Walnut stock on 55MM, Tyrolean stock on 55T. Air Rifle Hdqtrs., importer.

G WINCHESTER AIR RIFLES

Model	416	422	423	425
Calibers:	177	177	177	22
Length:	33"	36"	36"	38"
Wgt. lbs.:	2¾	3¾	4	5
Velocity, fps:	363	480	480	543
Price:	$16.95	$23.95	$28.95	$33.95

H WINCHESTER HIGH POWER AIR RIFLES

Model	427	435	450	333
Caliber:	22	177	177	177
Length:	42"	44"	44½"	43¼"
Wgt. lbs.:	6	6½	7¾	9½
Velocity, fps:	660	693	693	576
Price:	$40.95	$55.95	$85.95	$169.95

Features: All are rifled, except 416 (smoothbore), and spring operated by single stroke cocking. Triggers: 416, 422 & 423—double pull type triggers. 425, 427 & 435—adjustable double pull type triggers. 333—two stage trigger adj. for wgt., pre-travel & sear-off. Front sights: 416 & 422—bead post front sights; 423—blade front sight with ramp. 425 & 427—hooded front sights; 450 & 333—interchangeable front sight assemblies. Rear Sights: 416, 422 & 423—adj. screw, 425, 427, 435 & 450—Adj. micro. 333—Adj. diopter. Also, 425, 427, 435 & 450 have dovetail bases for scope mounting. 435, 450 & 333 have rubber butt pads, cheekpieces & checkered p.g. areas. 333 has an auto. safety, when bbl. is open and red indicator when bbl. is closed.

Chokes & Brakes

Cutts Compensator

The Cutts Compensator is one of the oldest variable choke devices available. Manufactured by Lyman Gunsight Corporation, it is available with either a steel or aluminum body. A series of vents allows gas to escape upward and downward, reducing recoil without directing muzzle blast toward nearby shooters.

For the 12-ga. Comp body, six fixed-choke tubes are available: the Spreader — popular with Skeet shooters; Improved Cylinder; Modified; Full; Superfull, and Magnum Full. Full, Modified and Spreader tubes are available for 16, 20, 28, and .410, and an Adjustable Tube, giving Full through Improved Cylinder chokes, is offered in 12, 16, 20 and 28 gauges.

Barrel adaptors in various internal diameters are available at $1.00 to permit exact fitting of Cutts Expansion Chambers.

The Comp body with wrench and adaptor sells for $13.00; Comp Tubes are $3.25 each, steel or aluminum, and the Adjustable Tube is $9.75. Factory installation is $7.00, plus transportation.

Dahl Muzzle Blast Controller

Only 1½″ long by ¾″ in diameter, this device is claimed to reduce recoil up to 40%. An outer sleeve, threaded onto the gun muzzle, is threaded on the inside to accept a machined plug which is bored through for bullet passage. Gas behind the bullet is bled off through slots in the plug. swirled through a number of tiny passages while contained by the sleeve, and then vented upward, this final action somewhat offsetting muzzle jump. Standard model, $12; Deluxe $14. 2″ long Streamlined, no flaps. Custom, $15. Installation, $5.

The 1½″ collet length is fully backed-up to prevent blown patterns arising from the springiness and vibration found in unsupported collet sleeves. A U.S. patent (No. 2,977,702) was obtained on this feature some time ago.

Emsco Choke

E. M. Schacht of Waseca, Minn., offers the Emsco, a small diameter choke which features a precision curve rather than a taper behind the 1½″ choking area. 9 settings are available in this 5 oz. attachment. Its removable recoil sleeve can be furnished in dural if desired. Choice of three sight heights. For 12, 16 or 20 gauge. Price installed, $21.95. Not installed, $16.50.

Herter's Rifle Recoil Eliminator

The Recoil Eliminator is a metal tube—1¹⁵⁄₁₆″ long and ⅞″ diam. in the standard model, same length and 1⅛″ diam. in target type — which is screwed to the muzzle. Angled ports direct escaping gas upward and rearward, reducing recoil and muzzle jump. The target model has a shield to prevent muzzle blast from annoying nearby shooters. Weights are 2 oz. and 3 oz. respectively. Made for calibers 25 to 32. Price of standard, $2.50; $5.50 installed. Target, $3.50 and $6.50.

Vari-Choke

Herter's, Inc., supplies the Vari-Choke, which features a ball-bearing micro-click adjustment of the pattern sleeve, rather than the spring system used by others. This model has 8 choke settings, from Full to Improved Cylinder. With Recoil Eliminator, price is $15.95 installed; without Eliminator, $12.25.

Jet-Away

Jet-Away Choke

Arms Ingenuity Corp., makers of the Jet-Away, say that this device controls patterns through partial venting of the powder gases which normally enlarge patterns. The Jet-Away has a series of three slots in the top of the tube and a sliding control sleeve. When the sleeve is in its rearward position, all slots are uncovered, the maximum of gas is vented and patterns are densest. To obtain more open patterns, the sleeve is moved to cover one or more slots. In 12 or 20 gauge only, the Jet-Away is made of aluminum, weighs 3 ozs. $24.95 installed.

Lyman CHOKE

The LymanCHOKE is similar to the Cutts Comp in that it comes with fixed-choke tubes or an adjustable tube, with or without recoil chamber. The adjustable tube version sells for $21.95 with recoil chamber, $19.50 without, in 12. 16 or 20 gauge.

Lyman also offers a Single-Choke Adaptor at $12.25 installed. This permits use of any of the Cutts Comp tubes or an adjustable choke tube, with or without recoil chamber. If recoil chamber is desired, add $2.45.

Pendleton Dekicker

This Dekicker is unusual in that it is not a separate tube added onto a rifle muzzle but is machined into the barrel itself. Obviously, it cannot be installed by the customer. It must be sent to J. F. Mutter's Pendleton Gunshop, where a section of the bore a short distance behind the muzzle is relieved into an expansion chamber. Exit holes drilled at precise locations vent gas to lower apparent kick. Because metal is removed instead of being added, there is a small decrease in gun weight.

Installation, including barrel polishing, is $35 in calibers from the 220 Swift to 358 Magnum; $40 for 375 to 458; $40 for 460 Weatherby and large single barrel express calibers.

Poly-Choke

Poly-Choke Co., Inc., now is offering the Deluxe Signature Poly-Choke. It provides 9 choke settings (marked in 24 karat gold) to cover the complete pattern range as well as handle rifled slugs. It comes in two versions, the standard at $24.95, and the ventilated model at $27.95 installed. Fits 12, 16, 20 or 28 gauge. The Poly-Choke has been on the market for more than 30 years and is still gaining popularity.

Rex Sha-Cul Rifle Muzzle Brake

C. R. Pedersen & Son engineered the Rex Sha-Cul muzzle control tube to cut down recoil and blast. The manufacturers state that the device helps eliminate bullet wobble, thus aiding accuracy. 3″ long and 1³⁄₁₆″ in diam., the Sha-Cul can accommodate all calibers from 22 to 458. It requires ½″ of barrel thread to install. Sold on an "unconditional money-back guarantee," the price is $17.50, plus $3.50 installation.

INTERNATIONAL GUNS INC.
Handles the complete line of Parker-Hale (British) metallic sights. Write for catalog.

LYMAN No. 48
¼-min. clicks for w. & e. Any disc. Target or Stayset (hunting) knobs. Quick release slide, adjustable zero scales. Made for almost all modern big-game rifles. Price: **$17.50**   With long slide......**$19.50**

LYMAN No. 57
¼-min. clicks. Target or Stayset knobs. Quick release slide, adjustable zero scales. Made for almost all modern rifles. Price......**$9.50**

LYMAN No. 60
¼-min. clicks for w. and e. Extension arm permits choice of 3 positions of eye relief. Designed for use on medium-weight, small bore target rifles. Price...........................**$9.75**

LYMAN No. 66
Fits close to the rear of flat-sided receivers, furnished with target or Stayset knobs. Quick release slide, ¼-min. adj. For most lever or slide action or flat-sided automatic rifles. Price...............**$9.50**

LYMAN No. 524 HI-LO EXTENSION RECEIVER-SIGHT
Apertures above and below for metallic and scope lines of sight. ¼-min. adj. For Win. 52 Sporter, 52 Standard (old and new), 52 Heavy Barrel (target and marksman stocks); Rem. 40X. Price.........**$19.50**

REDFIELD TROPHY
Aluminum construction. Staff detaches for scope use. Point-blank screw returns sight to same zero position. Features hunter-type knobs with coin slots, ¼-min. clicks. For most popular rifles. Price....**$10.95**

REDFIELD MICRO-STEEL
Made entirely of machined tool steel. ¼-min. micrometer click adj. with Hunter knobs. Quick detachable staff. Made for many centerfire rifles **$14.95**

REDFIELD No. 75
For Junior Target rifles. ¼-min. clicks for w. and e. Quick detachable extension, adj. to two positions. Available in two heights, scope or standard. For 75HW—Win. 75: 75HG and SG—Sav. 19; 75HV and SV—Stev. 416, Sears Ranger; 75HM and SM—Mossberg, master actions; 75HB and SB—Ballard; 75HR and SR—Win. SS, High Wall action only; Walnut Hill and 417; 75RT—Rem. 513T; 75RS—Rem. 513S; 75RX—Rem. 521. Price **$16.95**

REDFIELD INTERNATIONAL MATCH
Spring loaded windage and elevation adjustments eliminate lost motion or backlash. Large adjusting screws. ¼-min. click values. Base and ⅞" disc. Fits same base as Olympic. Price.................**$32.95**
With base and "Sure-X" disc (see Sight Attachments). Price..**$44.85**

REDFIELD INTERNATIONAL MARK 8
⅛-min. click adj. for windage and elevation distinguishes the Mark 8 which has all of the refinements of Redfield's International Match. Equipped with standard base and ⅞" disc. Price............**$39.95**
With base and Sure-X disc (see Sight Attachments). Price..**$51.85**

REDFIELD OLYMPIC
Elevation, windage, and extension adjustments. New elevation compensation. ¼-min. click. Base and ⅞" disc. Made for practically all target rifles. Price...............................**$24.95**
Extra bases. Price.............................. 3.95
With base and Sure-X disc (see Sight Attachments). Price....**$36.85**

TRADEWIND SNAP-SHOOTER
Micrometer click elevation adjustment, sliding windage adjustment with locking screws. Designed to fit rear scope mount holes in Husqvarna HVA and FN Mauser actions. Price......................**$9.50**

WILLIAMS "FOOLPROOF"
Internal click adjustments. Positive locks. For virtually all rifles, plus Win., Rem. and Ithaca shotguns. Price.................**$12.00**
Add .50 for Twilight aperture. Extra shotgun aperture...... 2.00

B-SQUARE SPRINGFIELD
For 03A3. Windage and elevation by means of allen screws. Locks on dovetail. Wrench furnished. Price.........................**$5.00**

B-SQUARE SMLE (LEE-ENFIELD)
For No. 4 and Jungle carbine. No drilling or tapping required. ³⁄₃₂" disc furnished. Price.............................**$3.95**

BURTON ROUGH SERVICE
Adj. for w. & e. Mounts with two 6-40 screws. For most rifles..**$8.75**

BUEHLER
"Little Blue Peep" auxiliary sight used with Buehler and Redfield scope mounts. Price **$3.35**
Mark IV front sight for above............................ .95

FREELAND TUBE SIGHT
Uses Unertl 1" micrometer mounts. Complete with bases for 22-cal. target rifles, inc. 52 Win., 37, 40X Rem. and BSA Martini. Price..**$42.50**

KUHARSKY AUXILIARY
Fits onto B&L or Kuharsky mounts to give emergency sighting. Includes peep rear and post front sights; extension rail slides forward for increased sight radius. Price.............................**$9.95**

LYMAN No. 40
Mounts on left side of receiver. By releasing locking lever, slide can be adjusted for elevation. Slot in aperture permits horizontal alignment. Target disc. for Sav. 40, 45, 340, 342, Stevens 58, 322, 325, Marlin 55, Moss. 185K and H&R 349. Price....................**$6.50**

LYMAN No. 53
Shotgun receiver sight, mounts compactly near rear of receiver. For most Win., Rem., Sav., Marlin, Mossberg, J. C. Higgins and Ithaca shotguns. Price **$4.40**

LYMAN No. 55
Located at rear of receiver; compact, easily adjusted. For almost all low-priced bolt action rifles. Price........................**$4.40**

REDFIELD RECORD
Aluminum construction with detachable staff for scope use. Adj. by means of locking screws. Point-blank screw returns sight to zero position. For most rifles. Price.............................**$7.95**

REDFIELD RE-22
1965 model for all dovetail-grooved 22 rifles (takes place of SS sights). Adj. for w. and e. **$7.95**

REDFIELD RE-SG
Shotgun receiver sight; mounts compactly at rear of receiver. Fits most shotguns by use of slotted base installed on receiver wall. Price **$9.95**

REDFIELD RE-24
For Savage M24's over-under rifle-shotgun.................**$9.95**

REDFIELD X-TUBE
For use with Redfield Olympic or International Match rear sights. Front telescope-type mount attaches to scope block. Price....**$24.95**

WILLIAMS 5-D SIGHT
Low cost sight for shotguns, 22's and the more popular big game rifles. Adjustment for w. and e. Fits most guns without drilling or tapping. Also for Br. SMLE. Price...........................**$7.00**

WILLIAMS ACE-IN-THE-HOLE PEEP
Auxiliary sight that slips into the Williams QC scope mount. Adj. for w. and e. Price.............................**$2.50**

WILLIAMS GUIDE
Receiver sight for .30 M1 Car., M1903A3 Springfield, Savage 24's, Savage-Anschutz rifles and Wby. XXII. Utilizes military dovetail; no drilling. Double-dovetail W. adj., sliding dovetail adj. for E. Price.**$7.00**

Sporting Leaf and Tang Sights

HOPKINS & ALLEN NUMRICH MUSKET SIGHT
Three-way rear leaf sight designed for 58 cal. muzzle loading military rifles. Fixed V-notch for 50-yard range, flip-up aperture for 100 yards and V-notch for 200 yards. Particularly suited to Springfield and Zouave rifles. Price..................................$4.95

LYMAN No. 16
Middle sight for barrel dovetail slot mounting. Folds flat when scope or peep sight is used. Sight notch plate adjustable for e. White triangle for quick aiming. 3 heights; A—.400" to .500", B—.345" to .445", C—.500" to .600". $2.95

MARBLE FALSE BASE
New screw-on base for most rifles replaces factory base. ⅜" dovetail slot permits installation of any Marble rear sight. Can be had in sweat-on models also. Price $2.00

MARBLE FOLDING LEAF
Flat-top or semi-buckhorn style. Folds down when scope or peep sights are used. Reversible plate gives choice of "U" or "V" notch. Adjustable for elevation. Price....................$4.50 — $5.96
Also available with both w. and e. adjustment.............$4.90

MARBLE SPORTING REAR
With white enamel diamond, gives choice of two "U" and two "V" notches of different sizes. Adjustment in height by means of double step elevator and sliding notch piece. For all rifles; screw or dovetail installation. Price ....$4.30—$5.50

MARBLE SPORTING REAR
Single step elevator. "U" notch with white triangle aiming aid. Lower priced version of double step model. Price....................$2.30

O.S.E. WINDAGE OPEN REAR
Screw set windage adjustment of .025" per graduation. Dovetail installation, choice of short or long base and flat top or semi-buckhorn. Full w. & e. adjustment with use of O.S.E. Adjustable height front sight. Original Sight Exchange. Price, open rear only.................$3.95

REDFIELD SEMI-BUCKHORN FOLDING LEAF
Semi-buckhorn sight for dovetail slot mounting. Sturdy spring holds sight in upright position. No. 47L .375"-.475"; No. 47H .375"-.562" high. Price $4.45

REDFIELD FLAT TOP FOLDING LEAF
Same as above except flat top style. No. 46L .375"-.475"; No. 46H .375"-.562" high. Price $4.45

REDFIELD SEMI-BUCKHORN SPORTING REAR
Reversible sighting plate gives choice of "U" notch or "V" notch. Five-step elevator. Fits standard dovetail slot. No. 49L for most rifles, No. 49S for 22's and carbines. Semi-buckhorn. Price...........$4.45

REDFIELD FLAT TOP SPORTING REAR
Same as above except flat top style. No. 48L for most rifles, No. 48S for 22's and carbines. Price..................................$4.45

WILLIAMS GUIDE
Open rear sight with w. and e. adjustment. Bases to fit most military and commercial barrels. Choice of square "U" or "V" notch blade, ³⁄₁₆", ¼", ⁵⁄₁₆", or ⅜" high...$5.00
Extra blades, each...1.25

Globe Target Front Sights

FREELAND SUPERIOR
Furnished with six 1" plastic apertures. Available in 4½"-62½" lengths. Made for any target rifle. Price with base.............$16.00
Price with 6 metal insert apertures........................19.00

FREELAND JR
Same as above except standard dovetail mounting, various heights.
Price with base and 6 plastic apertures....................$14.00
Price with 6 metal insert apertures.........................17.00

FREELAND TWIN SET
Two Freeland Superior or Junior Globe Front Sights, long or short, allow switching from 50 yd. to 100 yd. ranges and back again without changing rear sight adjustment. Sight adjustment compensation is built into the set; just interchange and you're "on" at either range. Set includes base and 6 plastic apertures. Twin set (long or short).$28.00
Price with 6 metal apertures............................32.00
Price, Junior Twin Set (long or short) plastic apertures......26.00
Price, Junior Twin Set (long or short) metal apertures.......30.00

FREELAND MILITARY
Short model for use with high-powered rifles where sight must not extend beyond muzzle. Screw-on base; six plastic apertures. Price $15.00
Price with 6 metal apertures..............................18.00

LYMAN No. 17A
7 interchangeable inserts which include 4 apertures, one transparent amber and two posts .050" and .100" in width. Price..........$3.75

LYMAN No. 17A XNB
For Springfield 03 and 03A3. Replaces issue front sight and barrel band. With seven inserts. Price.............................$6.00

LYMAN 77
Similar to M17A, except mounts to a separate base, is quickly detachable. Base $1.50.   Sight.............................$5.00

REDFIELD Nos. 63 and 64
For rifles specially stocked for scopes where metallic sights must be same height as scopes. Instantly detachable to permit use of scope. Two styles and heights of bases. Interchangeable inserts. No. 64 is ¼" higher. With base, Price.....................................$7.95

REDFIELD No. 65
1" long, ⅝" diameter. Standard dovetail base with 7 aperture or post inserts which are not reversible. For any rifle having standard barrel slot. ¹³⁄₃₂" height from bottom of base to center of aperture. No. 65NB same as above with narrow base for Win. 54 N.R.A., 70, and Savage 40, 45, and 99 with ramp front sight base. Price..........$5.95

REDFIELD No. 66
Replaces entire removable front sight stud, locked in place by screw in front of barrel band. ¾" from bottom of base to center of aperture. For Spgfld. 1903. Price.......................................$5.95

REDFIELD No. 68
For Win. 52, heavy barrel, Sav. 19 and 33, and other rifles requiring high front sight. ¹⁷⁄₃₂" from bottom of base to center of aperture. Standard dovetail size only. Price.................................$5.95

REDFIELD OLYMPIC
Detachable. 10 inserts—5 steel, sizes .090", .110", .120", .140", .150"; one post insert, size .100"; four celluloid, sizes .090", .110", .120", .140". Celluloid inserts in clear, green, or amber, with or without cross hairs. For practically all rifles and with any type rear sight. Fits all standard Redfield, Lyman, or Fecker scope blocks. With base, Price. $15.90

REDFIELD INTERNATIONAL SMALLBORE FRONT (Illustrated)
Similar to Olympic. Drop-in insertion of eared inserts. Outer sleeve prevents light leakage. Two-step base allows quick forward-backward change between 100 and 50 yards.........................$18.90
with standard base and inserts........................17.90

REDFIELD INTERNATIONAL MILITARY BIG BORE
Same as International Match except tube only 2¼" long. For 30 cal. use. $17.90

REDFIELD 285 S RAMP
No. 285 ramp designed for 22's fits without drilling by use of dovetail filler block. Redfield Sourdough, gold tip and ivory bead front sights fit dovetail slot on ramp. Short, streamlined design. Price without front sight.......................................$3.25

WOMACK DUAL RANGE
Instant change from 50 to 100 yards by rotating front knurled sleeve ½ turn. Choice of 6" or 10" length. Price, including 6 apertures, base and screws...$21.00

Ramp Sights　　Front Sights

Williams Streamlined Ramp

Lyman ramp and front sight

JAEGER
Band type with detachable hood, gold or ivory bead. When ordering, give height and muzzle diameter. Price........................$7.95

LYMAN SLIP-ON RAMP AND FRONT SIGHT
No soldering or brazing necessary, has tapered hole. Inside dia. .550″ to .640″. Removable hood. Price for ramp, sight and hood..$8.20

LYMAN SCREW-ON RAMP AND SIGHT
Used with 8-40 screws but may also be brazed on. Heights from .110″ to .350″. Price with sight...........................$4.95

MARBLE COUNTOUR RAMP
For late model Rem. 725, 740, 760, 742. ⁹/₁₆″ between mounting screws. Price $4.50

MARBLE RAMPS
Available in either screw-on or sweat-on style. 5 heights; ³/₁₆″, ⁵/₁₆″, ³/₈″, ⁷/₁₆″, ⁹/₁₆″. Standard ³/₈″ dovetail slot. Price............$4.25
Hoods for above ramps.................................1.00

PEDERSON "REX"
Offered as the "Rex" ramp, this is a hoodless type without barrel band. Heights available are ¼″ to ⁹/₁₆″. Blued or in the white, and without sights. Price $2.50

REDFIELD SWEAT-ON RAMPS
Standard ³/₈″ dovetail with screw for holding position while sweating. ⁵/₁₆″, ³/₈″, or ⁹/₁₆″ high, 3⅜″ over all. Price, without hood..$4.95

REDFIELD SCREW-ON RAMPS
Same as sweat-on except has two screws for mounting. Price, without hood $4.95
Hoods for above ramps.................................1.00

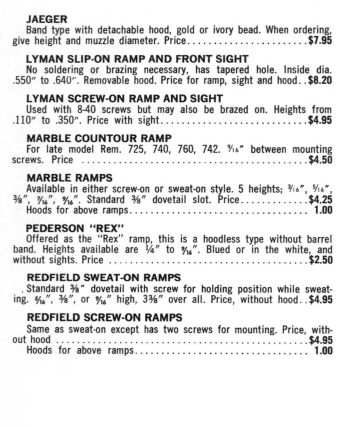

WILLIAMS SHORTY RAMP
Companion to "Streamlined" ramp, about ½″ shorter. Screw-on type, it is furnished in ⅛″, ³/₁₆″, ⁹/₃₂″, and ³/₈″ heights without hood only. Price $3.50

WILLIAMS STREAMLINED RAMP
Hooded style in screw-on or sweat-on models. Furnished in ⁹/₁₆″, ⁷/₁₆″, ³/₈″, ⁵/₁₆″, ³/₁₆″ heights. Price with hood.................$5.50
Price without hood.................................4.50

WILLIAMS SHOTGUN RAMP
Designed to elevate the front bead for slug shooting or for guns that shoot high. Diameters to fit most 12, 16, 20 ga. guns. Fastens by screw-clamp, no drilling required. Price, with Williams gold bead.$3.50
Price, without bead 2.75

LYMAN BLADE & DOVETAIL SIGHTS
Made with gold, silver or red beads ¹/₁₆″ to ³/₃₂″ wide and in varying heights for most military and commercial rifles..from $1.70 to $2.00

LYMAN No. 22
Ivory bead front sight for Savage 24 series. O-U. Price......$2.50

MARBLE STANDARD
Ivory, red, or gold bead. For all American made rifles. ¹/₁₆″ wide bead with semi-flat face which does not reflect light. Specify type of rifle when ordering..$1.90

MARBLE-SHEARD "GOLD"
Show up well even in darkest timber. Shows same color on different colored objects; sturdily built. Medium bead. Various models for different makes of rifles so specify type of rifle when ordering. Also made for 30 or 9 mm Lugers, Colt's Single Action Army, Bisley Model, with plain sight or any other Colt's or S & W revolver with stationary front sight. Price..$3.20

MARBLE COUNTOURED
Same contour and shape as Marble-Sheard but uses standard ¹/₁₆″ or ³/₃₂″ bead, ivory, red or gold. Specify rifle type................$2.20

O.S.E. ADJUSTABLE HEIGHT FRONT
Screw adjustment gives .025″ change in height for each turn. 5 models give adjustments from .260″ to .880″. Fits ³/₈″ dovetail barrel or ramp slots. White or gold bead. Original Sight Exchange. Price.$2.95

REDFIELD SOURDOUGH PATRIDGE
Gold face set at 45° angle; blackened, it serves as a target sight. Blade or dovetail styles; width .070″. Square block of phosphor bronze inlaid to provide visibility in poor light. Price.................$3.45

REDFIELD-CARBINE BLADE TYPE
Sourdough patridge, ivory bead or gold tip, ¹/₁₆″ only. For Win., Sav., Krag, Spgfld., Rem. Price................................$3.45

REDFIELD IVORY BEAD OR GOLD TIP
¹/₁₆″. For practically all rifles, carbines, pistols and revolvers. Price $2.45

REDFIELD FULL BLOCK
For Springfield 03 (not 03A3) in Sourdough, ¹/₁₆″ gold or ivory bead. $4.45. Mauser Dovetail—For narrow Mauser and other European dovetail slots. Sourdough, gold or ivory bead. $2.45—$3.45. De Luxe Ramp Blades—Sourdough, ¹/₁₆″ gold or ivory bead. Price............$2.00

TRADEWIND SNAP-SHOOTER
Silver inlay post. Fits ³/₈″ dovetail; height, ³³/₆₄ from bottom of dovetail. Price $1.50

WILLIAMS BRILLIANT BEAD
Large bright bead. In .250″ and .340″ base widths; 7 heights from .260″ to .538″. Price....................................$3.25

WILLIAMS IVORY & GOLD BEAD
Has flat sides. Made for Williams .250″ ramps. Also available in .340″ width, ¹/₁₆″ and ³/₃₂″ bead sizes. 10-heights.............$2.25

WILLIAMS GUIDE BEAD SIGHT
Fits all shotguns. ⅛″ ivory, red or gold bead. Screws into existing sight hole. Various thread sizes and shank lengths...........$1.75

Handgun Sights

Left—FDL revolver sight.
Above—Micro handgun sight.

BO-MAR DE LUXE
Gives ⅜" w. and e. adjustment at 50 yards on Colt Gov't 45, sight radius under 7". For Colt, Hi-Standard, Ruger and S&W autos. Uses existing dovetail slot. Has shield-type rear blade. $16.00

BO-MAR LOCK-UP RAMP
For Colt 38, 45 autos. Has locking barrel feature which positions and centers the barrel in relation to the slide to assure free functioning and barrel lock-up. To be installed by competent pistolsmith only. $22.50

BO-MAR HIGH STANDARD RIB
Full length, 8¾" sigh radius, for all bull barrels and military. Slide alteration required. $30.00

BO-MAR LOW PROFILE RIB
Streamlined rib with front and rear sights; 7⅛" sight radius. Brings sight line closer to the bore than standard or extended sight and ramp. Weighs 4 oz. Made for Colt Gov't 45, Super 38, and Gold Cup 45 and 38. ....$28.00
Extended sight and ramp, 8⅛" radius, 5¾ oz. 34.00
Rib & tuner—inserted in Low Profile Rib—accuracy tuner. Adjustable for barrel positioning. 39.95

BO-MAR FRONT SIGHTS
⅛" tapered post, made for Colt, Hi-Standard, Ruger and S&W autos. ....$3.00—$4.00

F.D.L. WONDERSIGHT
Micrometer rear sight for Colt and S&W revolvers. 1-min. clicks for windage. Sideplate screw controls elevation....................$4.95

HEG TRIANGLE REAR
Standard has small blade, w. & e. adj. gives ½" at 50 yds. for Colt, High-Standard and Luger target guns. $10.00

HEG TRIANGLE REAR DELUXE
As above but extends sight radius slightly and has over-size blade for least distraction....................................$12.00

HEG PISTOL RIB
Made for 45-cal. autos. Must be installed by gunsmith. Adds 3¾ oz. to slide. Made in two models. With std. 7¹/₁₆" radius and the extended 8¹¹/₁₆" radius $25.00

MICRO
Click adjustable w. and e. rear with plain or undercut front sight in ¹/₁₀", ⅛", or ⁵/₃₂" widths. Standard model available for 45, Super 38 or Commander autos. Low model for above pistols plus Colt Service Ace. Also for Ruger with 4¾" or 6" barrel. Price for sets.........$15.50
Price with ramp front sight. 18.50

MICRO
Non-adjustable sight set for 45 auto....................$7.50

Shotgun Sights

FOR DOUBLE BARREL SHOTGUNS (PRESS FIT)
Marble 214—Ivory front bead, ¹¹/₆₄"....$1.00; 215—same with .080" rear bead and reamers....$2.95. Marble 220—Bi-color (gold and ivory) front bead, ¹¹/₆₄" and .080 rear bead, with reamers....$3.95; Marble 221—front bead only....$1.90. Marble 223—Ivory rear .080....$1.00. Marble 224—Front sight reamer for 214-221 beads....$0.75; Marble 226—Rear sight reamer for 223.........................$0.75

FOR SINGLE OR DB SHOTGUNS (SCREW-ON FIT)
Marble 217—Ivory front bead ¹¹/₆₄"..$1.20; with tap and wrench..$2.50
Marble 218—Bi-color front, ¹¹/₆₄".... 1.60; with tap and wrench...3.05
Marble 223T—Ivory rear .080.......1.60; with tap and wrench..3.05
Marble Bradley type sights 223BT—⅛", ⁵/₆₄" and ¹¹/₆₄" long. Gold, Ivory or Red bead $1.60

MARK FRONT SIGHT
Screw-on type, with bead to fit plain bbls., and ribs ¼", ⁵/₁₆", ⅜" and ½" wide. Precision Gun Sight Company...................$3.50

POLY-SIGHT
Luminous bead ramp front and aperture rear, connected and supported by a 12" bridge, for use on shotguns with slugs or buckshot. Adj. for windage, elevation. Not for break-open guns. Price, including installation at Poly-Choke Co., and postage $36.70

SLUG SITE
A combination V-notch rear and bead front sight made of adhesive-backed formed metal approx. 7" over-all. May be mounted, removed and re-mounted as necessary, using new adhesive from the pack supplied. $5.00

Sight Attachments

BARRETT IRIS SIGHTING DISC
For all American extension receiver sights. Standard model includes rubber eye guard......................................$13.50
With rotating colored filters........................... 16.75

FREELAND LENS ADAPTER
Fits 1⅛" O.D. prescription ground lens to all standard tube and receiver sights for shooting without glasses. Price without lens..$10.50
Price lens ground to prescription. 11.50

MERIT ADAPTER FOR GLOBE FRONT SIGHTS
An Iris Shutter Disc with a special adapter for mounting in Lyman or Redfield globe front sights. Price...........................$9.00

MERIT IRIS SHUTTER DISC
Eleven clicks give 12 different apertures. No. 3 and Master, primarily target types, .022" to .125"; No. 4, ½" dia. hunting type, .025" to .155". Available for all popular sights. The Master Disc, with flexible rubber light shield, is particularly adapted to extension, scope height, and tang sights. All Merit Deluxe models have internal click spring; are hand fitted to minimum tolerance. Price..............$8.00—$11.00
Master..............$10.00   Master Deluxe.......... 13.00

MERIT LENS DISC
Similar to Merit Iris Shutter (Model 3 or Master) but incorporates provision for mounting prescription lens integrally. Lens may be obtained locally, or prescription sent to Merit. Sight disc is ⁷/₁₆" wide (Mod. 3), or ¾" wide (Master). Lens, ground to prescription, $7.60. Standard tints, $9.10. Model 3 Deluxe.....................$13.00
Master Deluxe......................................$16.00

REDFIELD VARD (Variable Diopter)
For shooters with visual problems. By adjusting the focus ring to focus the lens system at a point between the front sight aperture and the bull and controlling the size of the iris diaphragm, a crisp sharp high-contrast sight picture can be achieved. Provision is made for a prescription lens holder for shooters whose requirements exceed the focus capability of the VARD. Comes with smoke-gray filter. Front thread is ⁹/₃₂—32NS and will fit International and Olympic sights now being produced. Older O/I sights with ⁷/₃₂ thread will be converted at the plant for $3.45 on request. Maximum magnification is 1.3X. Use of the VARD adds approximately 1.5" to the sight. Extension attaching bases listed allow the sight to move forward 1.5" to accommodate for this extra length. Prices: VARD-IRIS Combination with filter $39.95
Iris Diaphragm only with filter........................ 19.95
Prescription lens holder 1.95
Set of 3 filters—Yellow, Sage Green and Gray........... 3.95

REDFIELD SURE-X SIGHTING DISC
Eight hole selective aperture. Fits any Redfield target sight. Each click changes aperture .004". Price......................$7.95

REDFELD SIGHTING DISCS
Fit all Redfield receiver sights. .046" to .093" aperture. ⅜", ½" and ⅞" O.D. Price, each.................................$ .95

WILLIAMS APERTURES
Standard thread, fits most sights. Regular series ⅜" to ⅝" O.D., .050" to .125" hole. "Twilight" series has white reflector ring. .093" to .125" inner hole. Price, regular series..$.75. Twilight series..$1.25
New wide open ⁵/₁₆" aperture for shotguns fits 5-D and Foolproof sights. Price $2.00

MERIT OPTICAL ATTACHMENT
For revolver and pistol shooters. Instantly attached by rubber suction cup to regular or shooting glasses. Any aperture .020" to .156". Price, $8.00. Deluxe (swings aside).........................$10.00

HUNTING, TARGET♦ AND VARMINT♦ SCOPES

Maker and Model	Magn.	Field at 100 Yds. (feet)	Relative Brightness	Eye Relief (in.)	Length (in.)	Tube Diam. (in.)	W&E Adjustments	Weight (ozs.)	Other Data	Price
American Import Co.										
Dickson 250	2½	43	64	3½	—	1	Int.	—	CH standard, Post available in 2½x and 4x. Aluminum tubes, centered reticles, nitrogen filled. 1" adj.	$24.95
Dickson 400	4	30	67	3½	—	1	Int.	—		27.95
Dickson 600	6	19	30	3	—	1	Int.	—		34.95
Dickson V20/154	1½-4	53-28	177-25	4-3	—	1	Int.	—		
Dickson V33/257	2½-7	43-16	174-22	3	—	1	Int.	—		45.95
Dickson V40/39	3-9	30-12	196-21	3	—	1	Int.			51.00
Bausch & Lomb										
Custom Baltur A	2½	43	64	3¼	12¼	1	Ext.	9½	Custom models must be used with B&L or other adj. mount. Trophy models have internal ½ MOA adj. Custom variables have tapered CH. Straight powers have CH, Post $5, dot $10. Balfor B has CH; post, tapered CH, dualine, taper-dot $5, dot $10. Balvar 8B has CH; post, tapered CH, RF, dualine, taper-dot $5, dot $10.	49.95
Custom Balfor A	4	30	56	3¼	12¼	1	Ext.	9		59.95
Custom Balvar 5	2½-5	40-20	164-41	3½	12¾	1	Ext.	9½		79.95
Custom Balvar 8A	2½-8	40-12½	256-25	3½	12¾	1	Ext.	10½		99.95
Trophy Baltur B	2½	42	164	3	12⅛	1	Int.	11		49.95
Trophy Balfor B	4	30	64	3	11⅞	1	Int.	11		59.95
Trophy Balsix B	6	20	36	3	11⅞	1	Int.	10¾		69.95
Trophy Balvar 8B	2½-8	40-12½	207-20	3½	11⅞	1	Int.	12½		99.95
Browning										
22 Scope	4	24	56	2½-4	9⅜	.75	Int.	6¼	22 Scope w/mount $41.45-$42.45. CH, Post or 4-Plex optional in big game models; dot $10 extra.	31.95
Wide Angle	5	30	58	3	11½	1	Int.	9¾		74.95
	3-9	35-12	159-19	3½	12¾	1	Int.	12½		109.95
Browning	2-7	44-16	241-20	3-4½	11¼	1	Int.	11½		99.95
Bushnell										
Scopechief IV	2¾	43	58	4	10	1	Int.	8½	Scopechief models have Command Post reticle with Magnetic Control Ring. Constantly centered reticles in Scopechiefs, Customs and Banners. Integral mounts $15 extra on Scopechiefs. Phantoms intended for handgun use.	54.50
Scopechief IV	4	32	64	3¾	11¾	1	Int.	10½		64.50
Scopechief IV	6	20	40	4	12½	1	Int.	11½		79.50
Scopechief IV	1½-4½	78-26	216-23	4¼-3¼	9¼	1	Int.	7¾		79.50
Scopechief IV	2½-8	44-15	160-16	4-3¼	11	1	Int.	11		89.50
Scopechief IV	3-9	39-13	160-18	3¾-3¼	11½	1	Int.	12¼		94.50
Scopechief 22	3-8	30-12	55-6	2½	11	⅞	Int.	7½	Mount rail. Similar 4x at $14.95.	19.95
Scopechief V	4	30	96	3½	12¼	1	Int.	10¾	Battery powered Lite-Site reticle.	69.50
Custom M	2½	49	64	4¼	10½	1	Int.	7¾		37.50
Custom M	4	27	64	3¾	11½	1	Int.	9¾		44.50
Custom M	6	19	40	3¼	13	1	Int.	10¾		47.50
Custom M	3-9	35-12½	159-18	3¾-3	12¼	1	Int.	12½	Mount rail. Similar 4x at $10.95.	64.50
Custom 22	3-7	29-13	28-5	2	10	⅞	Int.	6½		15.95
Banner	2½	45	64	4¼	10½	1	Int.	8		29.50
Banner	4	30	64	4	11¾	1	Int.	10		36.50
Banner	6	19½	29	3¾	13¼	1	Int.	10½		39.50
Banner	10	12	26	3½	14¼	1	Int.	14½	Obj. focuses for range.	56.50
Banner	1½-4	63-28	169-25	4¼-3¼	10	1	Int.	10¼		46.50
Banner	3-9	39-13	115-13	3¾-3	11¼	1	Int.	12		49.50
Banner	4-12	29-10	181-18	3¼	13¼	1	Int.	15½	Obj. focuses for range.	64.50
Phantom	1 1/3	24	441	6-17	7⅝	⅞	Int.	5		24.50
Phantom	2½	10	100	7-16	9¼	⅞	Int.	5½		34.50
Shotgun	1	92	337	6	9⅞	1	Int.	11½		64.50
Collins										
Bulittco	2½	40	164	3	11¼	1	Int.	9½	One-piece duralumin tube with oilproof rubber packings at lens/ metal joints. Nitrogen filled.	34.95
Bulittco	4	30	64	3	11¼	1	Int.	9½		36.95
Bulittco	6	20	28	3	11¼	1	Int.	9½		38.95
Colt										
Coltmaster Jr.	4	30			12½	.75	Int.	7	Coltmaster Jr. scopes have tip-off mounts.	10.75
Coltmaster Jr.	6	20			14½	.75	Int.	8		13.75
Davis Optical										
Spot Shot 1½"	10, 12, 15, 20, 25, 30	10-4		2	25	.75	Ext.		Focus by moving non-rotating obj. lens unit. Ext. mounts included. Recoil spring $3.50 extra.	89.50
Spot Shot 1¼"	10, 12, 15, 20	10-6		2	25	.75	Ext.			69.50
Habicht										
4 S-D	4	30	64	3¼	11	1.18	Int.	13	From Del-Sports. With e. only, $62.75. With light alloy tube. (27mm), mounting rail, $69.75; same, e. only, $65.75.	63.90
Herter's										
Perfect	1	100	256	3-5	9¾	1	Int.	10¼	A variety of reticles including dots and rangefinders available in different scopes at small price increase. Hudson Bay rimfire scopes: 4x, $17.95; 6x, 3-9x, $30.95.	33.95
Mark II	2¾	44	58	3½	10¼	1	Int.	8½		31.95
Mark IV	4	30	64	3½	11½	1	Int.	9½		31.95
Mark VI	6	20	38	3½	12¾	1	Int.	10½		31.95
Mark VIII	8	15½	22	3½	12½	1	Int.	14½		38.49
Mark IA	3-9	14-41	157-18	3½	12½	1	Int.	14½		49.95
Mark XXI	4-12	11½-34	100-14	3½	13¼	1	Int.	12½		53.95
Hy-Score										
No. 467	4	26	14	1¾	12	.75	Int.	7¼	Alloy tubes. Weather and fog-proof. 400 series scopes are made in Japan.	8.95
No. 469	6	19	6	1¾	12	.75	Int.	7½		11.95
Model 461-466	2½	35	64	3	9⅞	1	Int.	8		19.95
Model 462-468	4	28	64	3	11⅝	1	Int.	10		19.95
Model 463	6	22	28.1	3	11¾	1	Int.	10		20.95
Vari-Power 464	3-9	36-16	126-12	3¼	12½	1	Int.	14		29.95
Vari-Power 471	3-9	35-14	193-18	3¼	12½	1	Int.	14		36.95
Jason										
860	4	27¼	64	3½	12	1	Int.	9	Constantly centered reticles, ball-bearing click stops, nitrogen filled tubes, coated lenses.	19.95
864	6	17½	28	3¼	12	1	Int.	9		21.95
861	3-9	31½-12	112-12	3	13¼	1	Int.	13¾		29.95
865	3-9	31½-12	177-19	3	13½	1	Int.	15¼		34.95

Hunting, Target and Varmint Scopes—Continued

Maker and Model	Magn.	Field at 100 Yds. (feet)	Relative Bright-ness	Eye Relief (in.)	Length (in.)	Tube Diam. (in.)	W&E Adjust-ments	Weight (ozs.)	Other Data	Price
Leupold										
M8	2	25	100	8-18	8.45	1	Int.	7.25	Constantly centered reticles; in addition to the crosshair reticle the post, tapered (CPC), post and duplex, and duplex reticles are optional at no extra cost. Dot reticle $10.00 extra. 2x suitable for handguns and Win. 94. A new M8/6x, recently announced, sells for $74.50.	46.50
M8	3	43	45	3.85	10.13	1	Int.	8.25		59.50
M8	4	30	50	3.85	11.50	1	Int.	9.00		64.50
M8	7½	14	32	3.60	12.60	1	Int.	12.75		79.50
M8	10	10	16	3½	13	1	Int.	13¾		94.50
M8	12	9	11	3½	14½	1	Int.	14		99.50
Vari-X II	2-7	42-18	144-17	3.7-4.12	11.00	1	Int.	10.75		87.50
Vari-X II	3-9	30.5-13	208-23	3.5-4.12	12.60	1	Int.	13.75		97.50
Lyman										
All-American	2½	43		3¼	10½	1	Int.	8¾	2, 3, or 4 minute dot reticle $10 extra. Choice of standard CH, tapered post, or tapered post and CH reticles. All-weather reticle caps. All Lyman scopes have new Perma-Center reticle which remains in optical center regardless of changes in W. & E.	49.50
All-American	3	35		3¼	11	1	Int.	9		49.50
All-American	4	30		3¼	12	1	Int.	10		59.50
All-American	6	20		3¼	13⅞	1	Int.	12¼		67.50
◆All-American	8	14		3¼	14⅜	1	Int.	13		84.50
◆All-American	10	12		3¼	15½	1	Int.	13½		84.50
◆Super Targetspot	10, 12, 15, 20, 25, 30	12, 9.3, 8.9, 5.6, 4.3, 4	86%	2-1⅞	24-24⅜	.75	Ext.	24¼-25	Non-rotating objective lens focusing. ¼ MOA click adjustments. Sunshade, $2 extra. Steel case, $9 extra. 5 different dot reticles, $10.00 extra.	135.00
Marble										
A-2.5	2¾	43	164	3½	11¾	1	Int.	10¾	Duralumin tubes, nitrogen filled. Post, CH, dot or 3-post reticle. Variables have ½ MOA adj.	39.50
A-4.0	4	30	64	3½	11¾	1	Int.	10¾		39.50
VL-3.9	3-9	38½-12½	177-19	3¼	13½	1	Int.	15½		68.50
VS-3.9	3-9	37-10½	114-12	3¼	13½	1	Int.	13½		69.50
Marlin										
300	4	23	25	1½	11¾	⅞	Int.	9	Coated lenses, non-magnifying reticles. Tri-Post reticle. A 4x Glenfield M200, suitable for 22 rifles, and with ½-minute adj., is $8.00.	13.95
500	3-7	24-10	49-16	1¾	12	⅞	Int.	9½		16.95
600	3	29	144	3½	12½	1	Int.	10		32.95
700	5	20	64	3½	12½	1	Int.	11		34.95
800	1½-5	55-19	256 49	3½	11⅜	1	Int.	13½		42.95
850	2-5	50-17½	100-16	3	10¼	1	Int.	11		39.95
900	3-9	35-12	169-19	3¼	12¾	1	Int.	14		44.95
Glenfield 400	4	28	64	3½	12	1	Int.	9		20.00
Nickel										
Supra	2½	42	72	3½	11½	1.18	Int.	7½	¼ MOA click adjustments. Steel or alloy tubes. Weatherproof reticle caps. Crosshair, post and c.h. or post and crossbar reticles are standard. New "Diflex" coated lenses. Continental Arms Co.	75.00
Supralyt	4	33	30	3½	11½	1.18	Int.	8		75.00
Supra	4	32	81	3½	11¼	1.18	Int.	9		85.00
Supra	6	21	36	3½	12½	1.18	Int.	9		85.00
◆Supra Varminter	6	24	56	3¼-5	12¼	1.18	Int.	11½		89.50
Supra Vari-Power	1-4	66.5-27.3	153-28	3½	10½	1.18	Int.	13.1		115.00
Supra Vari-Power	1½-6	60-21.6	176-36	3½	12	1.18	Int.	14.8		150.00
Supra Vari-Power	2½-6	38-21	125-36	3½	11¾	1.18	Int.	11		125.00
Supra Vari-Power	2½-9	42-15.6		3½	14½	1.18	Int.	17.3		160.00
Supra Vari-Power	4-10	30-12	100-18.5	3½	12½	1.18	Int.	12½		135.00
Pacific										
2.5x Supreme	2½	36		3½	11¾	1	Int.	10	All Pacific scopes have constantly centered reticles, coated lenses and ¼ MOA adj. Nitrogen filled. Choice of crosshair or post and crosshair.	27.95
4X Supreme	4	31		3½	12½	1	Int.	12		36.95
6x Supreme	6	20		3½	11½	1	Int.	11		33 95
3-9x Supreme	3-9	34-14		3½	12½	1	Int.	13		52.95
Precise Imports										
NR-15	4	23	14	2	11	.75	Int.	6¾	Price with mount. All scopes have constantly centered reticle.	7.95
20257	3-7	23-13	43-8	3	11½	.75	Int.	7½		13.95
20265	2½	32	164	3¾	12	1	Int.	9.6		24.95
20244	4	29	64	3½	12	1	Int.	9		24.95
20249	3-9	36-13	177-19	3	13⅓	1	Int.	15		39.95
20260	10	12.2	16	3	12½	1	Int.	10½		29.95
Realist										
Apache	4	30	6	2	12½	.75	Int.	7	Scope price includes mount. Constantly centered reticles in Riflescopes. CH or P&CH standard. Dot $10 extra. Sunshades available $6.95 — $8.95. Nitrogen processed. Aluminum construction.	9.95
Apache	6	20	4	2	13¾	.75	Int.	8		12.50
Riflescope	2½	44	66	3-5	10½	1	Int.	8		51.50
Riflescope	4	31	73	3-5	12⅜	1	Int.	9		61.50
Riflescope	6	20	38	3-5	14	1	Int.	10		71.50
Brushscope	1½-4½	65-26	225-49	3-5	11	1	Int.	11½		79.50
Riflescope	3-9	34-12	144-16	3-5	13¼	1	Int.	11		99.50
Camputer	6	20	38	3-5	14⅝	1	Int.	18	Supplied with special mounts and range cams for most popular rifles and calibers.	119.50
Auto/Range	4	31	73	3-5	11	1	Int.	17		119.50
	1½-4½	65-26	225-49	3-5	12¼	1	Int.	17		129.50
	3-9	34-12	144-16	3-5	12¾	1	Int.	17		129.50

Left—Realist 4x Auto-Range scope.
Right—Redfield 6x Widefield scope.

Maker and Model	Magn.	Field at 100 Yds. (feet)	Relative Brightness	Eye Relief (in.)	Length (in.)	Tube Diam. (in.)	W&E Adjustments	Weight (ozs.)	Other Data	Price
Redfield										
Sportster 4X	3.9	24.5	27	3-3¾	9½	.75	Int.	6¼	Constantly centered reticles; scratchproof Tuf-Coat finish; W. & E. dials adjustable to zero; weatherproof sealed. Reticle same size at all powers. Add $10 for Accu-Range, $10 for dot (not avail. in Sportster). 12X has separate parallax adj. knob, ¼" clicks.	31.95
Widefield 2¾	2¾	55½	49	3	10½	1	Int.	8		59.95
Widefield 4	4	37½	46	3	11½	1	Int.	10		69.95
Widefield 6	6	25	44	3	13½	1	Int.	11½		84.95
Magnum 12X	12	10	13.7	3-3¾	14⅞	1	Int.	13.5		119.95
Magnum Variable	1-4	85-30	289-31	3½	9¾	1	Int.	10¼		89.95
Magnum Variable	2.3-7	44-16	182-20	3-3¾	11¾	1	Int.	11½		99.95
Magnum Variable	3.3-9.1	37.5 12.5	159-19	3-3¾	12¾	1	Int.	12½		109.95
Magnum Variable	4-12	28-9	100-12	3-3¾	13⅞	1	Int.	14		129 95
3200 Target	12, 16, 20, 24,	6½, 5¼, 4, 3¾	9, 6, 3¼, 2¼	2½	23¼	1	Int.	21	Mounts solidly. Fine CH, Med. CH, ¼" dot.	169.95
Sanders										
Bisley 2½x20	2½	42	64	3	10¾	1	Int.	8¼	Alum. alloy tubes, ¼" adj., coated lenses. Two other scopes are also offered: a 3-9x at $52.50, and a 6x45 at $42. Rubber lens covers (clear plastic) are $2.50; with amber-colored lenses, $3.50. Choice of reticles in CH, PCH, 3-post.	34.00
Bisley 4x33	4	28	64	3	12	1	Int.	9		38.00
Bisley 6x33	6	19	28	3	12½	1	Int.	9½		40.00
Bisley 8x33	8	18	16	3¼	12½	1	Int.	9½		42.00
Bisley 10x33	10	12½	10	2½	12½	1	Int.	10¼		44.00
Bisley 8x45	8	18	30	3¼	12½	1	Int.	11¼		44.00
Bisley 5-13x40	5-13	29-10	64-9	3	14	1	Int.	14		56 50
Savage										
2520	2½	43		3	10¾	1	Int.	8.5	Coated lenses, duralumin tubes. Reticles permanently centered.	31.50
0433	4	30		3	12	1	Int.	10		37.50
1420	1½-4	64-25	—	3	10¼	1	Int.	10		47.50
3833	3-8	35-13		3	11½	1	Int.	12		59 50
2037	3-7	25-14		2	11¼	.875	Int.	8	For 22 rifles; price includes mounts.	14.95
0420	4	25½		2	11½	.75	Int.	8.5		9.75
0620	6	17½		2	11½	.75	Int.	8.5		12.50
Scope Instruments										
2650	2½	32	164	3½	11½	1	Int.	10	Constantly centered reticles—CH or post. Nitrogen filled. Yellow haze filter.	24.95
2652	4	29	64	3¼	11½	1	Int.	9½		24.95
2654	6	21	28	3	11½	1	Int.	9½		24.95
2658	3-9	29-13	113-12	3	13¼	1	Int.	14¼		37.95
2656	3-9	29-12	177-19	3½	13¼	1	Int.	16		39.95
Sears										
No. 53801	4	30		2	11½	.75	Int.	6	First three scopes for 22's only, complete with rings for grooved receivers. Crosshair or post and crosshair reticle. Big game scopes come with mount rings. Bases available to fit almost all H.P. rifles. Fixed crosshair reticle remains in center regardless of adjustment. No. 53824 for Sears M54.	12.75
No. 53802	4	28		2	11½	.75	Int.	8		8.75
No. 53803	3-6	30-16					Int.	6½		13.50
No. 53824	3	37		3-6	10⅜	1	Int.	8½		34.50
No. 53821	4	30		3¼	11¼	1	Int.	12		39.50
No. 53901	1				8	1	Int.	8½		39.50
Southern Precision										
562	2½	40	144	3½	12	1	Int.	9¼	Centered reticles, CH or post. All elements sealed.	21.95
564	4	30	64	3½	12	1	Int.	9¼		23.95
566	6	21	28	3¼	12	1	Int.	9¼		23.95
Stoeger										
4x	4	30	64	3	12	1	Int.	9	CH only. ½" clicks. Obj. tube diam. 1½" in fixed powers, 1⅞" in variable.	24.95
6x	6	20	28	3	12¾	1	Int.	9		29.95
8x	8	16	25	3	12	1	Int.	13		35 95
3x-9x	3-9	38-11	170-20	3	11½	1	Int.	12¾		46.95
Swift										
Grizzly	2½	32	159	3	11.7	1	Int.	8.5	Dot, tapered post & CH or Rangefinder reticles available on all but Zoom & Game, $2.50 extra. Rangefinder optional on Zoom & Game. All have self-centering reticles.	24.00
Stag	4	28½	64	3	11 7	1	Int.	8.5		24.50
Gamescope	4	30	64	3	11.7	1	Int.	9		36.00
Bighorn	6	18½	28	3	11.7	1	Int.	8.5		27.50
Yukon	2½-8	32½-13	164-16	3	13¼	1	Int.	11.3		38.00
Zoomscope	2½-8	41-15½	256-25	3½	12½	1	Int.	16.1		67.50
Tasco										
Zoom Target	3-7	28-12	130-24	2¼	12	⅞	Int.	9½	Lens covers furnished. Constantly centered reticles. Write the importer, Tasco, for data on complete line.	19.95
Pistol Scope	1½	23	216	19	8⅝	⅞	Int.	7½		19.95
Sniper	2-5	36-18	150-24	3¼	11¼	1	Int.	10		39.95
Super Marksman	3-9	35-14	266-29	3.2	12⅜	1	Int.	12½		49.95
Tops										
4X	4	28½	64	3	11½	1	Int.	9½	Hard-coated lenses, nitrogen filled, shock-proof tested. Write Ed Paul, importer, for data on complete line.	23.95
8X	8	14½	16	3	13	1	Int.	10		29.95
3X-9X	3-9	33-15	175-19	3	12¾	1	Int.	14		39.95

Unertl BV-20 target scope.

Hunting, Target and Varmint Scopes—Continued

Maker and Model	Magn.	Field at 100 Yds. (feet)	Relative Bright-ness	Eye Relief (in.)	Length (in.)	Tube Diam. (in.)	W&E Adjust-ments	Weight (ozs.)	Other Data	Price
Tradewinds										
TW-4	4	31	81	3¼	10.8	1	Int.	11	Lightweight dural tubes. Dot reticles same price, leather scope caps included. Tradewinds, Inc., importer.	54.50
TW-VARI	2.5-8	35.4-14.8	100-20.25	3¼	12¼	1	Int.	12.7		69.50
TW-Zoom	1.5-4	62-28	144-20	3¼	9.7	1	Int.	11.6	Diamond Dot reticle.	57.50
United										
Golden Hawk	4	30	64		11⅞	—	Int.	9½	Anodized tubes, nitrogen filled. Write United for data on complete line.	44.50
Golden Grizzly	6	18½	44		11⅞	1	Int.	11		55.00
Golden Falcon	4-9	29½-14	100-20		13½	1	Int.	12¼		89.50
Golden Plainsman	3-12	33-12½	169-11		13½	1	Int.	12¾		110.00
Unertl										
Falcon	2¾	40	75.5	4	11	1	Int.(1')	10	Black dural tube in hunting models. (2 oz. more with steel tube.)	50.00
Hawk	4	34	64	4	11¾	1	Int.(1')	10.5		54.00
Condor	6	17	40	3-4	13½	1	Int.(1')	12		68.00
◆1" Target	6,8,10	16-10	17.6-6.25	2	21½	.75	Ext.	21	Dural ¼ MOA click mounts. Hard coated lenses. Non-rotating objective lens focusing.	67.00
◆1¼" Target	8,10,12,14	12-6	15.2-5	2	25	.75	Ext.	25		90.00
◆1½" Target	8,10,12,14 16,18,20,24	11.5-3.2		2¼	25½	.75	Ext.	31		105.00
◆2" Target	8,10,12,14 16,18,24 30,36		22.6-2.5	2¼	26¼	1	Ext.	44		145.00
◆Varmint, 1¼"	6,8,10,12	14.1-7	28-7.1	2½	19½	.875	Ext.	26	¼ MOA dehorned mounts. With target mounts.	92.00 95.00
◆Ultra Varmint, 2"	8,10, 12,15	12.6-7	39.7-11	2½	24	1	Ext.	34	With dehorned mount. With calibrated head.	115.00 132.00
◆Small Game	4,6	25-17	19.4-8.4	2¼	18	.75	Ext.	16	Same as 1" Target but without objective lens focusing.	49.00
◆Vulture	8 10	11.2 10.9	29 18½	3-4	15⅝ 16⅛	1	E or I	15½	Price with internal adj. Price with ¼ MOA click mounts.	82.00 98.00
◆Programer 200	8,10,12,14 16,18,20,24 30,36	11.3-4	39-1.9		26½	1	Ext.	45	With new Posa mounts.	192.00
◆BV-20	20	8	4.4	—	17⅞	1	Ext.	21¼	Range focus unit near rear of tube. Price is with Posa mounts, Magnum clamp. With standard mounts and clamp ring, $131.95.	139.95
Universal										
Deluxe UC	2½	32	172	3½	12	1	Int.	9¼	Aluminum alloy tubes, centered reticles, coated lenses. Similar Standard series available at lower cost.	24.95
Deluxe UE	4	29	64	3½	12	1	Int.	9		24.95
Deluxe UG	6	17½	28	3¼	12	1	Int.	9		26.95
Deluxe UL	3-9	34-12	177-18	3	12¾	1	Int.	15¼		42.95
Weatherby										
Mark XXII	4	25	50	2½-3½	11¾	⅞	Int.	9¼	Focuses in top turret. ¼ MOA adj. for e., 1 MOA for w. in all models. Reticles: CH, post and CH, Lee Dot or Open Dot ($12.50 extra).	29.50
Imperial	2¾	47½	90	3¼-5	10½	1	Int.	9¼		69.50
Imperial 4x	4	33	81	3¼-4½	11⅛	1	Int.	10¼		79.50
Imperial 6x	6	21½	62	3¼-4½	12½	1	Int.	12⅜		89.50
Imperial Variable	2-7	48-17¾	324-27	4.3-3.1	11 3/16	1	Int.	12		99.50
Imperial Variable	2¾-10	37-14.6	296-22	4½-3½	12½	1	Int.	14⅛		109.50
Premier 2½	2½	44	256	3½	13¼	1	Int.	12.9	Premiers have binocular type focusing, centered non-magnifying reticles, ¼ MOA adj.	39.50
Premier 4	4	31	100	3½	13¼	1	Int.	12.9		44.50
Premier 3-9	3-9	38½-12½	177-19	3½	13¼	1	Int.	14.4		59.50
Weaver										
Classic 300	3	37	—	4	10⅜	1	Int.	7	Classics have glossy anodized alloy tubes, non-removable eyepieces, choice of all five reticles, dot $7.50 extra.	49.95
Classic 400	4	31	—	4	11¾	1	Int.	8		57.95
Classic 600	6	20	—	3¾	13⅝	1	Int.	9		62.95
K1.5	1½	56		3-5	9¾	1	Int.	7		29.95
K2.5	2½	43		3-6	10⅜	1	Int.	8½		39.95
K3	3	37		3-6	10⅜	1	Int.	8½		39.95
K4	4	31		3-5½	11¼	1	Int.	9½		46.95
K6	6	20		3-5	13⅝	1	Int.	11	Crosswires, post, rangefinder or Dual X reticle optional on all K and V scopes (except no RF in K1½, post in K8, 10, 12, or RF in V22). Dot $7.50 extra in K and V models only. Objective lens on K8, K10, K12, V9 and V12 focuses for range.	52.50
K8	8	15		3-5	15⅜	1	Int.	12¼		59.95
K10	10	12		3-5	15½	1	Int.	12½		64.95
K12	12	10		3-5	15¾	1	Int.	12½		72.95
V4.5	1½-4½	54-21		3-5	10	1	Int.	8½		57.95
V7	2½-7	40-15		3-5	11⅝	1	Int.	10½		64.95
V9	3-9	33-12		3-5	13	1	Int.	13		72.95
V12	4-12	24-9		4	13		Int.	13		84.95
V22	3-6	30-16		2	12½	.875	Int.	4½		15.95
D4	4	28	—	2	11⅝	.875	Int.	4	D model prices include N or Tip-Off mount.	10.95
D6	6	18	—	2	12	.875	Int.	4		12.95
Williams										
Guide Line	4	29½	64	3¾	11¾	1	Int.	9½	Coated lenses, nitrogen filled tubes, ½ MOA adj. CH, dot, TNT or Guide reticle. Dot covers 3 MOA at 4x in all models.	69.00
Guide Line	1½-4½	78-26	196-22	4⅓-3¼	9½	1	Int.	7¾		99.00
Guide Line	3-9	39-13	161-18	3¾-3¼	12	1	Int.	14½		108.00
Zeiss										
Diatal D	4	31.5	64	3⅛	10½	1.18	Int.	11	Alloy tubes. Leather caps furnished. Turret dials not calibrated. Carl Zeiss, Inc., importer.	135.00
Diatal D	6	21	49	3⅛	12½	1.18	Int.	13½		147.00
Diavari D	1½-6	60-21	161-36	3⅛	12¼	1.18	Int.	16¼		199.00

◆Signifies target and/or varmint scope.

Hunting scopes in general are furnished with a choice of reticle—crosshairs, post with crosshairs, tapered or blunt post, or dot crosshairs, etc. The great majority of target and varmint scopes have medium or fine crosshairs but post or dot reticles may be ordered.

W—Windage E—Elevation MOA—Minute of angle or 1" (approx.) at 100 yards, etc.

TELESCOPE MOUNTS

Maker, Model, Type	W and E Adjust.	Scopes	Suitable for	Price
Bausch & Lomb			Most popular rifles.	38.90-52.90
Custom One Piece (T)	Yes	B&L, other 1" scopes.		
Custom Two Piece (T)	Yes			26.90
Trophy (T)	No	1". With int. adj.		21.90-37.90
Browning				
One Piece (T)	W only	1" split rings	Browning FN rifles.	24.25
One Piece (T)	No	¾" split rings	Browning 22 semi-auto	4.50
One Piece Barrel Mount Base	No	Groove mount	22 rifles with grooved receiver.	6.00
Two Piece	No~	¾" ring mount.	For Browning T-bolt 22	9.50
B-Square Co.				
Mono-Mount	No	Leupold M8-2x (mounts ahead of action)	M94 Win.	11.50
			M1 Carbine.	9.50
Buehler				
One Piece (T)	W only	¾" or 1" solid rings; ⅞", 1" or 26mm split rings. 4" or 5" spacing.	All popular models.	Solid rings—21.75 Split rings—26.75
One Piece "Micro-Dial" Universal	Yes	Same. 4" ring spacing only.	Most popular models.	Solid—28.25 Split—33.25
Two Piece (T)	W only	Same. Rings for 26.5—27mm adjust to size by shims.	Rem. 700, 721, 722, 725; Win. 70, 52; FN; Solid—21.75 Rem. 37; Mathieu; Schultz & Larsen; Husq. Split—26.75	
One Piece Pistol Base	W only	Uses any Buehler rings.	S&W K, Colt and Ruger.	Base only—11.25
One Piece (T)	W only	Same.	Rem. 600 rifle and XP100 pistol.	Base only—11.25
Bushnell				
Universal (T)	W only	1" split rings	All rifles with top of action tapped for 6/48 screws. Two steel 6/48 studs are screwed into receiver holes, eliminating conventional base. Rings drop over studs, are held by opposing screws which give rough windage adj. Economy mount set,	14.95 9.95
Dual Purpose	No	Phantom	V-block bottoms lock to chrom-moly studs seated in two 6-48 holes.	5.00
Rigid	No	Phantom	Heavy loads in Colt, S&W, Ruger revolvers, Rem. XP100, Ruger Hawkeye.	5.00
94 Win.	No	Phantom	M94 Win., end of bbl. clamp or center dovetail.	5.00
Collins				
Bulittco (T)	E only	1" split rings	Rimfire rifles with grooved receivers.	4.98
Conetrol				
One Piece (T)	W only	1" solid or split rings.	Sako dovetail bases (14.95); Solid rings—19.40-21.40	
Two Piece (T)	W only	Same.	for S&K bases on M1 Carb., Split rings—22.90-24.90 SMLE 4 & 5, $9.90. Huntur line, $10.90-$14.90. Gunnur line, $14.90-$20.90.	
Griffin & Howe				
Standard Double Lever (S)	No	All standard models.	All popular models. (Garand $37.50; Win. 94 $30.00).	30.00
E. C. Herkner Echo (S)	No	All standard models.	All popular models. Solid or split rings.	14.50—19.75
Holden				
Ironsighter (T)	No	1" split rings	Many popular rifles. Rings have oval holes to permit use of iron sights. For 22 rimfire grooved receivers, ¾, ⅞ or 1 inch tubes, $6.95. For long eye relief scopes on M94, $19.95.	14.95

International Guns Inc. handles the complete line of Parker-Hale (British) Roll-Over and other scope mounts.

Maker, Model, Type	W and E Adjust.	Scopes	Suitable for	Price
Jaeger				
QD, with windage (S)	W only	1", 26mm; 3 heights.	All popular models.	38.00
QD Railscope Mount	W only		For scopes with dovetail rib	38.00
Jaguar				
QD Dovetail (T)	No	1", 26mm and 26½mm rings.	For BSA Monarch rifle (Galef, importer).	16.95
Kesselring				
Standard QD (T)	W only	¾", ⅞", 1", 26mm—30mm split or solid rings.	All popular rifles, one or two piece bases.	12.50-20.00
See-Em-Under (T)	W only	Same.	Rem. 760, 740, 788, Win. 100, 88, Marlin 336	16.50
QD Dovetail (T)	W only	1", 26mm.	Steyr 22, Sako, B.S.A., Brno, Krico	16.50
Kwik-Site (T)	No	1" split rings	Fits Weaver type bases. Mounts scope high to permit iron sight use.	11.95

Kwik-Site see-thru rings.

TELESCOPE MOUNTS—Continued

Maker, Model, Type	W and E Adjust.	Scopes	Suitable for	Price
Leupold				
Detacho (T)	No	1" only.	All popular rifles. Instantly detachable, leaving W. & E. adjustable peep sight available.	13.50
			Bases for Rem. 600 series	9.95
M3 (T)	Yes	1" only.	Bases for Win. M94 and Rem. XP100.	5.00— 7.50
			Rem. 700, 740, Win. 70, 88, 100, Wby. Mark V, FN, others. Bases reversible to give wide latitude in mounting.	24.50
Lyman All-American				
Tru-lock (T)	No	¾", ⅞", 1", 26mm, split rings.	All popular post-war rifles, plus Savage 99, 98 Mauser. One or two piece bases.	9.50
Marble				
Game Getter (T)	No	1" only.	Many popular rifles. Has see-through base to permit use of iron sights.	14.95
Marlin				
One Piece QD (T)	No	1" split rings	Most popular models. Glenfield model. 5.00.	6.95
Mashburn Arms				
Positive Zero (T)	With or w/o W	All standard models.	All popular models, solid or two-piece base, solid or split rings.	17.50—32.50
Numrich				
Side mount	No	1" split rings	M1 carbine.	6.95
Pachmayr				
Lo-Swing (S)	Yes	¾", ⅞", 1", 26mm solid or split loops.	All popular rifles. Scope swings aside for instant use of iron sights.	20.00
Lo-Swing (T)	Yes	¾", ⅞", 1", 26mm split rings.	Adjustable base. Win. 70, 88; Rem. 721, 722, 725, 740, 760; Mar. 336; Sav. 99.	25.00
Precise Imports				
M-21 (rings only)	No	1" tube; not over 32mm obj.	Fit Weaver bases.	3.95
M-22 (rings only)	No	1" tube; 40mm obj. scopes		3.95
Realist				
V lock QD (T)	No	1" split rings.	Most popular rifles.	13.00
Redfield				
JR-SR (T)	W only	¾", 1", 26mm.	Low, med. & high, split rings. Reversible extension front rings for 1". 2-piece bases for Mannlicher Schoenauer and Sako. JR-SR comes with integral folding peep sight.	19.90—40.90
Swing-Over (T) base only	No	1". (Not for variables.)	Standard height split rings. Also for shotguns.	14.95
Ring (T)	No	¾" and 1"	Split rings for grooved 22's.	5.95— 9.95
S&K				
Insta-Mount (T) base only	No	Takes Conetrol, Weaver, Herter or United rings.	M1903, A3, M1 Carbine, Lee Enfield #3, #4, #5, P14, M1917, M98 Mauser, FN Auto, AR-15. For M1 Garand, steel rings.	6.00-27.00 / 41.50
Conventional rings and bases	No	1" split rings	Most popular rifles. For "see through underneath" risers, add $4.	19.00
Sako				
QD Dovetail (T)	W only	1" or 26mm split rings.	Sako, or any rifle using Sako action. 3 heights and extension rings available. Firearms International, importer.	18.95—20.65
Savage				
Detachable (T)	No	1" split rings.	Most modern rifles. One or two piece bases. 9.75-10.25	
No. 40 (S)	No	1"	For Savage 340	3.00
Tasco				
700(T) and 800(S) series	No	1" split rings, regular or high.	Many popular rifles. Swing mount, 9.95.	4.50—10.45
M722	No	Split rings.	For 22s with grooved receivers.	3.00
Tradewinds				
Two Piece (T)	W only	26mm or 1" split rings.	Husqvarna, HVA rifles, actions. Scope removable w/o changing sighting. Tradewinds, imp.	14.95—18.95
Unertl				
Posa (T)	Yes	¾", ⅞", 1" scopes	Unertl target or varmint scopes.	25.00—26.00
¼ Click (T)	Yes	¾", 1" target scopes	Any with regular dovetail scope bases.	23.00—24.00
Dehorned Varmint (T)	Yes	¾", ⅞", 1" scopes	Same, less base.	20.00—23.00
Weaver				
Detachable Mount (T & S)	No	¾", ⅞", 1", 26mm.	Nearly all modern rifles. Extension rings, 1" $11.00	10.50
Type N (S)	No	¾" scopes only.	Same. High or low style mounts.	2.00
Pivot Mount (T)	No	¾", 1", 26mm.	Most modern big bore rifles.	13.00
Tip-Off (T)	No	⅞".	22's with grooved receivers.	2.00, 3.00
Tip-Off (T)	No	1", two-piece	Same. Adapter for Lee Enfield—$1.75	8.00
Williams				
Offset (S)	No	¾", ⅞", 1", 26mm solid, split or extension rings.	Most rifles (with over-bore rings, $17.50). Br. S.M.L.E. (round rec.) $2.50 extra.	15.00
QC (T w/peep)	No	Same.	Same. Add $4.50 for micro. windage ring.	20.00
QC (T w/o peep)	No	Same.	Most 22 rifles, plus Mar. 36, 39, 93, 336, Sav. 23D, Win. 05, 07, 10.	17.50
QC-TM-B22	No	Same.	For Browning 22 autoloader and Rem. 241.	17.50

(S)—Side Mount   (T)—Top Mount.   22mm = ⅞"   25.4mm = 1"   26mm = 1.18"   26.5mm = 1.045"

Conetrol "Custum" bridge base and low rings.

SPOTTING SCOPES

BAUSCH & LOMB BALSCOPE Sr.—60mm objective. 20X. Field at 100 yds. 11.1 ft. Relative brightness, 9. Wgt., 48 oz. Length closed, 16⁷⁄₁₆". Rapid prismatic focusing **$129.95**
   Also 15X, 30X, and 60X eyepieces, each................. **29.95**
   Triple eyepiece turret (without eyepiece)............. **19.95**
   Combination auto window/camera tripod adaptor......... **24.95**
   Carrying case **24.95**
   Tele-Master camera adapter **34.95**
BAUSCH & LOMB BALSCOPE ZOOM—15X to 60X variable power. 60mm objective. Field at 1000 yards. 150 ft. (15X) to 37½ feet (60X). Relative brightness 16 (15X) to 1 (60X). Wgt., 48 oz., 16¹¹⁄₁₆" overall. Integral tripod lug. Straight eyepiece **$159.95**
   With 45° eyepiece **169.95**
BAUSCH & LOMB BALSCOPE 20—40mm objective. 20X. Field at 100 yds., 7.5 ft. 15³⁄₈" over-all, Wgt., 22 oz. **$29.95**
BAUSCH & LOMB BALSCOPE 10—30mm objective. 10X. Field at 100 yds., 7.5 ft. 10¼" over-all, weight, 9 oz. **$9.95**

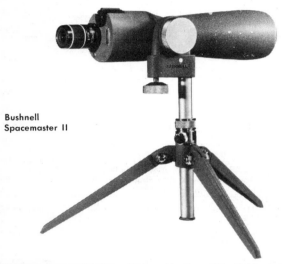

Bushnell
Spacemaster II

BUSHNELL SPACEMASTER—60mm objective, 25X. Field at 100 yds., 10.5 ft. Relative brightness, 5.76. wgt., 39 oz. Length closed, 15¼". Prism focusing, sliding sunshade **$95.00**
   15X, 20X, 25X, 40X and 60X eyepieces, each............. **22.50**
   20X wide angle eyepiece **27.50**
BUSHNELL SPACEMASTER 45°—Same as above except: Wgt., 43 oz., length closed 16¼". Eyepiece at 45° **$99.50**
BUSHNELL SPACEMASTER II—20X-45X zoom. 60mm objective. Field at 100 yards 12-7.2 ft. Relative brightness 9-1.7. Wgt. 36 oz., length 11⅝". **$109.00**
BUSHNELL SENTRY II—20X. 50mm objective. Field at 100 yards 12 ft. Relative brightness 6.25 .... **$54.50**
   Also 32X and 48X eyepieces, each **19.50**
BUSHNELL ZOOM SPOTTER—40mm objective. 9X-30X var. power... **$29.50**
HY-SCORE MODEL 460—60mm objective. 15X, 20X, 25X, 40X and 60X eyepieces included. Field at 100 yds. 15.8 to 3.2 ft. Length closed 11". Wgt., 35 oz. With tripod and case **$182.00**
PACIFIC ZOOM—60mm objective, 15X to 50X variable. Field at 100 yds., 7½-3½ ft. Aluminum body. With adj. tripod **$94.50**
PACIFIC 15x60—60mm objective, 5 eyepieces (15X, 20X, 30X, 40X, 50X), adj. tripod. 100-yd. field, 12-3¼ ft. **$89.50**
PRECISE IMPORTS, T-15—60mm objective, 15X to 30X zoom scope. About 15" long, weighs approximately 6 lbs. with adj. tripod. **$49.95**
PRECISE IMPORTS, T-19—60mm objective, interchangeable eyepieces of 15X, 20X, 30X, 40X, 60X. Sliding sunshade. Weighs about 6 lbs. with adj. tripod. **$69.95**
REDFIELD FIFTEEN-SIXTY—15X-60X zoom. 60mm objective. Field at 100 yards 15.6-3.7 ft. Relative brightness 16-1. Wgt. 48 oz., length 16¾" **$149.50**
   Tripod stand **27.50**
   Carrying case **29.95**
SATURN RANGER—60mm objective. 20X. Field at 100 yds., 10.4 ft. Relative brightness, 9. Eye relief, ⁹⁄₁₆". Wgt., 33 oz. Length closed, 15⁵⁄₁₆". Spiral adjustment of eyepiece. Chilford Arms.......... **$54.50**
SATURN SCOUT—44mm objective. 20X. Field at 100 yds., 6.7 ft. Relative brightness, 4.84. Eye relief, ½". Wgt., 23 oz. Length closed, 13". Draw tube plus spiral focusing. Chilford Arms................ **$29.50**
SOUTHERN PRECISION MODEL 549—60mm objective and 5 eyepieces from 15X to 60X; extensible sunshade and folding tripod. Closed, 14¾", Wgt., 4¼ lbs. **$79.50**

SOUTHERN PRECISION MODEL 550 — 60mm objective and 4 turret-mounted eyepieces from 20X to 60X; ext. sunshade and folding tripod. Closed, 16¼", wgt., 5½ lbs. with tripod (included) **$75.00**
SOUTHERN PRECISION ZOOM MODEL 547—60mm objective, 25X to 50X; ext. sunshade folding tripod. Closed, 18", wgt. 4½ lbs. with tripod (included) **$69.50**
SOUTHERN PRECISION MODEL 546—50mm objective, 25X. Folding tripod, leather case included. Closed, 13", wgt. 3 lbs. **$27.00**
SWIFT TELEMASTER M841—60mm objective. 15X to 60X variable power. Field at 1000 yards 160 feet (15X) to 40 feet (60X). Wgt. 3.4 lbs. 17.6" over-all **$135.00**
   Tripod for above................................. **30.50**
   Photo adapter **10.95**
   Case for above **23.00**
SWIFT MODEL 821—60mm objective. 15X, 20X, 30X, 40X and 60X eyepieces included. Field at 100 yds., 158 to 32 ft. 18" tripod with friction clutch adj. handle. Length 13½" (without sunshade). 6 lbs. ... **$96.00**
SWIFT MODEL 822—40mm objective. 20X eyepiece, tripod adapter, sunshade and dust cap. Length closed 10". Wgt. 27 oz. **$46.50**
TASCO 8TOZ—60mm objective. 20X to 60X variable power. Field at 1000 yards 158 feet (16X) to 40 feet (50X). Wgt. 4½ lbs. 18" over-all **$79.95**
UNERTL RIGHT ANGLE—63.5mm objective. 24X. Field at 100 yds., 7 ft. Relative brightness, 6.96. Eye relief, ½". Wgt., 41 oz. Length closed, 19". Push-pull and screw-focus eyepiece. 16X and 32X eyepieces $18 each. **$110.00**
UNERTL STRAIGHT PRISMATIC — Same as Unertl Right Angle except: straight eyepiece and wgt. of 40 oz. **$92.00**
UNERTL 20X STRAIGHT PRISMATIC — 54mm objective. 20X. Field at 100 yds., 8.5 ft. Relative brightness, 6.1. Eye relief, ½". Wgt., 36 oz. Length closed, 13½". Complete with lens covers **$74.00**
UNERTL TEAM SCOPE—100mm objective. 15X, 24X, 32X eyepieces. Field at 100 yds. 13 to 7.5 ft. Relative brightness, 39.06 to 9.79. Eye relief, 2" to 1½". Weight, 13 lbs. 29⅞" overall. Metal tripod, yoke and wood carrying case furnished (total weight, 80 lbs.) **$450.00**
WEATHERBY—60mm objective, 20X-45X zoom **$99.50**
   With fixed power eyepiece **85.00**
   Tripod for above **14.95**

SCOPE ATTACHMENTS

DAVIS TARGETEER—Objective lens/tube units that attach to front of low power scopes, increase magnification to 8X. 1¼" lens, **$25**, 1½" lens **$29.50**
HERMANN DUST CAPS—Connected leather straps, hand made, natural color. For all popular scopes. **$4.00**
LEE TACKHOLE DOTS—Various size dots for all scopes.
Price .... **$7.50—$15.00**
LYMAN HAZE FILTER—For morning and late afternoon hunting. Filters out blue and violet rays allowing only the best part of the spectrum to transmit through your telescope lenses. For all reflescopes... **$2.75**
PGS SCOPE SHIELDS—Flexible rubber, usable at front and rear, protect scopes from snow or rain. Made for all scopes. **$3.95**
PREMIER RETICLES—Various size dots for all scopes, also special reticles to order. Price—**$7.00** to **$18.50**. **PREMIER WEATHER CAPS**—transparent, high light transmission. For all popular scopes. Price **$3.50**. Special sizes **$5.00**
RING MOUNTS—Custom made for German-type claw bases. Don's Gun Shop.
STORM KING LENS CAPS—A hinged glass-and-rubber protector set (2), made in various sizes for all scopes. May be unhinged or sighted through. Anderson Gun Shop. Per pair................... **$3.45**
VISS'S SUPREME LENS COVERS — Hinged protectors for most scope models, front and rear lenses shielded. E. D. Vissing Co. Per pair, postpaid. **$4.95**

SPOTTING SCOPE STANDS

DAVIDSON MARK 245 — Bipod adjustable for elevation, 9½"-14½". Side mount with two straps. Black crinkle finish. Length folded 16½". Price **$23.95**
FREELAND ALL ANGLE—Tripod adjustable for elevation. Left or right side mount with worm drive clamp. Folding legs. Clamps available for any scope tube size. Black, gray, or green crinkle finish. Price. .. **$20.75**
   Also 12" 18", 24" extensions available. **$3.00-5.00**
FREELAND OLYMPIC—Bipod adjustable for elevation. All angle mount with padded worm drive clamp. Folding legs. Clamps available for any scope tube size. Black, grey, or green crinkle finish. Price. ... **$23.75**
   Also 12", 18", 24" extensions available. **$3.00-5.00**
   Zoom head for tripod or bipod. **$10.00**
FREELAND REGAL BIPOD—Choice of saddle or zoom head. All adjustment knobs are oversize for easy adjusting. Large "ball" carrying knob. Gray or green finish. **$26.75**
   Above with stability weight. **33.25**
   Extensions 12"-24" **$3.00-5.00**
O. S. E.—Tripod adjustable for elevation. Top mount with worm drive rubber-covered clamp. Folding legs. Clamps available for any scope tube size. Black or green crinkle finish. Price **$13.95**

ARMS ASSOCIATIONS IN AMERICA AND ABROAD

Alabama Gun Collectors Assn.
Mrs. T.M. Stewart, 601 Eastwood Pl.,
Birmingham, Ala. 35216

Alamo Arms Collectors
Bill Brookshire, 410 Rector,
San Antonio, Tex. 78216

Amateur Trap Shooting Assn.
P.O. Box. 246, Vandalia, O. 45377

American Military Inst.
Box 568, Washington, D.C. 20044

American Ordnance Assn.
R. E. Lewis, 616 Transportation Bldg.,
Washington, D.C. 20006

American Reloaders Assn.
Dean Grennell, Box 4007, Covina, Calif. 91722

American Single Shot Rifle Assn.
Dr. John P. May, 13 E. Prospect Ave.,
Mt. Prospect, Ill. 60056

American Society of Arms Collectors, Inc.
Rob. F. Rubendunst, 6550 Baywood Ln.,
Cincinnati, O. 45224

Antique Arms Coll. Assn. of Conn.
A. Darling, 35 Stanley St.,
New Haven, Conn. 06511

Arapahoe Gun Collectors
Bill Rutherford, 2968 S. Broadway,
Englewood, Colo. 80110

Arizona Gun Collectors
Mike Welker, 1940 E. Clarendon,
Phoenix, Ariz. 85016

Arkansas Gun & Cartridge Coll. Club
M. Cutrell, 2006 E. 7th, Pine Bluff, Ark. 71601

Ark-La-Tex Gun Collectors Assn.
Ray Franks, 1521 Earl St., Shreveport, La. 71108

Armor & Arms Club
J. K. Watson, 51 W. 51st St.,
New York, N.Y. 10019

Arms Collectors of the Southwest
Robert Kuban, Box 543, Yuma, Ariz.

Arms and Armour Society of London
F. Wilkinson, 40 Great James St.,
Holborn, London, W.C.I.

Barberton Gun Collectors Assn.
R. N. Watters, 1108 Bevan St., Barberton, O.

Bay Cities Arms Coll. Assn.
P. Oldham, 8714 Hollywood Blvd.,
Los Angeles, Ca. 90069

Bay Colony Weapons Collectors
Carl Majesky, 42 Cabot Rd., Danvers, Mass.

Bayou Gun Club
John West, 825 Ida, New Orleans, La.

Belton Gun Club
J. K. Phillips, P.O. Box 235, Belton, S.C. 29627

Boone & Crockett Club
400 Forbes Ave., Pittsburgh, Pa.

Calif. Hunters & Gun Owners Assoc.
V. H. Wacker, 2309 Cipriani Blvd., Belmont, Cal.

Calif. Muzzle Loader Assn.
A. Moore, 3960 Palos Verdes Dr. N.,
Palos Verdes Estates, Ca. 90274

Canadian Historical Arms Soc.
John R. Hunter, P.O. Box 901,
Edmonton, Alb., Canada

Carolina Gun Collectors Assn.
N. C. Bill Harvey, P.O. Box 464,
Wilson, N.C. 27893

Cedar Valley Gun Coll.
R. L. Harris, 1602 Wenig Rd., N.E.,
Cedar Rapids, Iowa 52402

Central Illinois Gun Collectors Assn., Inc.
Paul Peterson, 1251 South East,
Jacksonville, Ill. 62650

Central Indiana Gun Coll. Assn.
Paul E. Daugherty, 421 E. Washington St.,
Hartford City, Ind. 47348

Central Ohio Gun and Indian Relic Coll. Assn.
Coyt Stookey, 134 E. Ohio Ave.,
Washington C.H., O. 43160

Central Penn Antique Arms Assn.
Geo. Smithgall, 549 W. Lemon St.,
Lancaster, Pa. 17603

Central States Gun Collectors Assn.
Chas. J. Versluis, 701 Broadway,
Waterloo, Ia. 50703

Chippewa Valley Weapons Collectors
J. M. Sullivan, 504 Ferry St.,
Eau Claire, Wis. 54701

Chisholm Trail Antique Gun Coll. Assn.
Carney Pace, 2632 So. Ellis, Wichita, Kans. 67216

Colorado Gun Collectors
Larry Jones, 1348 So. Yates, Denver, Colo. 80219

Connecticut Gun Guild
R. Harris, P.O. Box 67,
Cornwall Bridge, Conn. 06754

Cowtown Gun Traders & Collectors
W. Morgan, 1401 Jacksboro Hwy., Ft. Worth, Tex.

Crawfordsville Gun Club, Inc.
Rob. J. K. Edmonds, R.R. 2,
Crawfordsville, Ind. 47933

Cumberland Valley Arms Collectors Assn.
N. Naylor, Rte. #2, Hagerstown, Md. 21740

Dallas Gun Collectors Assn.
D. Jackson, 8603 Angora, Dallas, Tex. 75218

Delaware Antique Arms Collectors
C. Landis, 2408 Duncan Rd.,
Wilmington, Del. 19808

Dixie Arms Collectors
Ruth Greecy, 1509 W. 7th,
Hattiesburg, Miss. 39401

Dixie Gun Collectors Assn.
Albert E. Lewis, Box 6027, Daytona Beach, Fla.

Eastern Iowa Gun and Cartridge Collectors Assn.
F. Fitzpatrick, 305 N. Eliza St.,
Maquoketa, Ia. 52060

Edwardsville, Ill. Gun Collectors
A. W. Stephensmeier, 317 N. Grand Bl.,
St. Louis, Mo. 63103

Egyptian Gun Collectors Assn. Inc.
George W. Harlow, 312 Main St.,
Mt. Vernon, Ill. 62864

Experimental Ballistics Associates
Ed Yard, 110 Kensington, Trenton, N. J. 08608

Florida Gun Collectors Assn.
Bob Marvin, P.O. Box 12206, Plantation, Fla.

Forks of the Delaware Weapons Assn.
John F. Scheid, 348 Bushkill St.,
Easton, Pa. 18042

Fort Dearborn Frontiersmen
Art Pardi, 434 W. Hickory, Lombard, Ill. 60148

Fort Lee Arms Collectors
W. E. Sammis, R.D. 776 Brookridge Dr.,
Valley Cottage, N. Y. 10989

Ft. Smith Dealers & Coll. Assn.
Tony Smith, 2317 No. 53, Ft. Smith, Ark. 72901

Fox Valley Arms Fellowship, Inc.
Graham Burnside, 203 Oregon Ave.,
Dundee, Ill. 60118

Four State Collectors Assn.
M. G. Wilkinson, 915 E. 10th,
Pittsburgh, Kan. 66762

Georgia Arms Collectors
James F. Watterson, 2915 Paces Lake
Ct., N.W., Atlanta, Ga. 30339

Great Lakes Weapons Coll. Assn., Inc.
E. Warnke, 7207 So. 36th St.,
Franklin, Wis. 53132

Greater Calif. Arms & Collectors Assn.
Donald L. Bullock, 8291 Carburton St.,
Long Beach, Cal. 90808

Historical Firearms Soc. of South Africa
"Minden" 11 Buchan Rd., Newlands,
Cape Town, South Africa

Houston Gun Collectors Assn.
C. McKim, 5454 Stillbrooke, Houston, Tex. 77035

Hudson-Mohawk Arms Collectors Assn., Inc.
Bennie S. Pisarz, R.D. 2, Ilion, N.Y. 13357

Illinois Gun Collectors
P. E. Pitts, P.O. Box 1524, Chicago, Ill. 60690

Illinois State Rifle Assn.
2800 N. Milwaukee Ave., Chicago, Ill. 60618

Indian Territory Gun Collectors Assn.
Joe Wanenmacher, Jr., P.O. Box 4491,
Tulsa, Okla. 74104

International Benchrest Shooters
Emory L. Tooly, 8 Cline St.,
Dolgeville, N.Y. 13329

International Cartridge Coll. Assn., Inc.
A. D. Amesbury, 4065 Montecito Ave.,
Tucson, Ariz. 85711

Iroquois Arms Collectors Assn.
Dennis Freeman, 14144 McNeeley Rd.,
Akron, N. Y. 14001

Jefferson State Arms Collectors
Art Chipman, 2251 Ross Lane,
Medford, Ore. 97501

Jersey Shore Antique Arms Collectors
Bob Holloway, 1755 McGalliard Ave.,
Trenton, N. J. 08610

John Hunt Morgan Gun Coll. Assn.
James Hyde, 243 Eastridge Dr., Paris, Ky. 40361

Kentuckiana Arms Coll. Assn.
John F. Harder, Box 1776, Louisville, Ky. 40201

Kansas Cartridge Coll. Assn.
Bob Linder, Box 84, Plainville, Kans. 67663

Kentucky Gun Collectors Assn.,
Ben Johnson, Box 64. Owensboro, Ky. 42301

Lakeshore Gun Collectors
R. N. Watters, 1108 Bevan St.,
Barberton, Ohio 44203

Lancaster Muzzle Loading Rifle Assn.
James H. Frederick, Jr., R.D. 1, Box 447,
Columbia, Pa. 17512

Les Arquebusiers de France,
Mme. Marckmann, 70 rue des Chantiers,
78-Versailles, France

Little Fort Gun Collectors Assn.
Ernie Robinson, P.O. Box 194, Gurney, Ill. 60031

Long Island Antique Gun Coll. Assn.
Frank Davison, 8 Johnson Pl.,
Baldwin, N.Y. 11510

Los Angeles Gun & Ctg. Collectors Assn.
F. H. Ruffra, 1254 9th St., Santa Monica, Calif.

Lower Canada Arms Collectors Assn.
Secretary, P.O. Box 1162, St. B, Montreal 101,
Quebec, Can.

Maple Tree Gun Coll. Assn.
E. P. Hector, Meriden Rd., Lebanon, N.H. 03766

Maryland Arms Coll. Assn., Inc.
H. R. Moale, 2602 Hillcrest Ave.,
Baltimore, Md. 21234

Massachusetts Arms Collectors
John J. Callan, Jr., 15 Montague St.,
Worcester, Mass. 01603

Maumee Valley Gun Collectors Assn.
J. Jennings, 3450 Gallatin Rd., Toledo, O. 43606

Memphis Antique Weapons Assn.
F. Dauser, 3429 Jenkins, Memphis, Tenn. 38118

Memphis Gun Collectors Assn.
T. C. Lee, Jr., 166 Picardy Pl.,
Memphis, Tenn. 38111

Meramec Valley Gun Collectors
L. W. Olson, Star Route, St. Clair, Mo.

Michigan Antique Arms Coll., Inc.
W. H. Heid, 8914 Borgman Ave.,
Huntington Woods, Mich. 48070

Michigan Rifle & Pistol Assn.
John W. Novitch, 124 Moss Ave.,
Highland Park, Mich. 48023

Mid-State Arms Coll. & Shooters Club
B. Pisarz, R.D. 2, Ilion, N.Y. 13357

Midwest Gun Collectors Assn.
Jim VanEvery, 10924 Fisher Rd.,
Ft. Wayne, Ind. 46808

Mineral Belt Gun Coll. Assn.
G. W. Gunter, 1110 E. Cleveland Ave.,
Monett, Mo. 65708

Minnesota Weapons Coll. Assn., Inc.
W. Nemitz, P.O. Box 5098,
Minneapolis, Minn. 55406

Mississippi Gun Collectors Assn.
Mrs. J. E. Swinney, Box 1332,
Hattiesburg, Miss. 39401

Mississippi Valley Gun & Cartridge Coll. Assn.
Mel Sims, Box 426, New Windsor, Ill. 61465

Missouri Valley Arms Collectors
Edw. E. Vaughn, 9216 W. 95 St.,
Overland Pk., Kans. 66212

Montana Arms Collectors Assn.
Chris Sorensen, 175 6th Ave., W.N.
Kalispell, Mont. 59901

Muzzle Loaders' Assn. of Great Britain
D. R. Hawkes, 12 Monument Green,
Weybridge, Surrey, Eng.

National Bench Rest Shooters Assn., Inc.
Bernice McMullen, 607 W. Line St.,
Minerva, O. 44657

National Muzzle Loading Rifle Assn.
Box 67, Friendship, Ind. 47021

National Police Officers Assn. of America
Natl. Police Academy Bldg., 1890 So. Trail,
Venice, Fla. 33595

National Reloading Mfrs. Assn., Inc.
Robert Matt, 433 Silas Deane Highway,
Wethersfield, Conn. 06109

National Rifle Assn.
1600 Rhode Island Ave., Washington, D.C. 20036

National Rifle Assn. (British)
Bisley Camp, Brookwood, Surrey, England

National Shooting Sports Fdtn., Inc.
Charles Dickey, 1075 Post Rd.,
Riverside, Conn. 06878

National Skeet Shooters Assn.
George W. White, 212 Linwood Bldg.,
2608 Inwood Rd., Dallas, Tex. 75235

Nebraska Gun & Cartridge Collectors
E. M. Zalud, 710 West 6th St.,
North Platte, Neb. 69101

New Hampshire Arms Collectors Inc.
James Tillinghast, Box 5, Marlow, N. H. 03456

New Jersey Arms Collectors Club, Inc.
D. Blake, 82 Southgate Rd.,
Murray Hill, N.J. 07974

New Mexico Gun Collectors Assn.
Leroy Walton, P.O. Box 175, Tijeras, N.M. 80759

New York State Arms Collectors Assn., Inc.
Marvin Salls, R. D. 1, Ilion, N. Y. 13357

New Zealand Deerstalkers Assn.
I. D. Wright, P.O. Box 263,
Wellington, New Zealand

Niagara Arms Collectors
Box 468, Beamsville, Ont., Canada

North Alabama Gun Coll. Assn.
Maj. Richard Keogh, P.O. Box 564,
Huntsville, Ala. 35804

Northeastern Ohio Gun Coll. Assn.
John T. Kanne, 1715 Walnut Blvd., Ashtabula, O.

Northern California Historical Arms Coll. Assn.
John L. Moss, 156 Mirada Dr.,
Daly City, Ca. 94015

Northern Indiana Gun Collectors Assn.
Joe Katona, 16150 Ireland Rd.,
Mishawaka, Ind. 46544

Northern Tier Antique Gun Collectors
Cliff Breidinger, Trout Run, Pa.

North-South Skirmish Assn.
F. Schoch, 1247 Croyden Rd.,
Lyndhurst, Ohio 44124

Ohio Gun Collectors Assn., Inc.
Mrs. C. D. Rickey, 130 S. Main St.,
Prospect, O. 43342

Old Fort Gun Collectors Assn.
Jim Hemminger, Box 156, Van Buren, Ark.

Ontario Arms Collectors Assn.
P. Peddle, 174 Ellerslie Ave.,
Willowdale, Ont., Canada

Oregon Arms Coll. Assn. Inc.
Dan Scherlie, 204 N.E. 47th, Portland, Ore. 97213

Oshawa Antique Arms Guild
Frank Folkmann, 296 Grenfell St., Apt. 38,
Oshawa, Ont., Canada

Paso Del Norte Gun Collectors Assn.
Ken Hockett, 1216 Mescalero,
El Paso, Tex. 79925

Patch & Ball Gun Collectors
J. Falerias, 1417 Raspberry Ln., Flint, Mich. 48507

HUNTERS ASK TO BE TAXED

THE AMERICAN hunter is about one in ten in terms of the U.S. population, but when it comes to paying taxes and supporting his recreation, he is one in a million.

The behavior of the hunter has been questioned by many different people for many different reasons, but without doubt one of the hunter's strangest habits is his willingness to pay taxes. What many people do not know, including some hunters, is that hunters pay a 11% excise tax on their sporting longarms and ammunition— an 11% tax that the hunter asked for.

Through staunch hunter support, the Pittman-Robertson Aid in Wildlife Restoration Act was passed in 1937, placing this 11% tax on sporting rifles, shotguns and ammunition. But it was in 1965 that the hunter really threw the public a curve. In 1965, when excise taxes were being lifted from a number of consumer items, a new generation of hunters joined the shooting industry in insisting that the tax be kept, according to Ray Speer, vice president of the National Shooting Sports Foundation.

Revenue from this tax — over $30 million a year—is prorated back to the states through a formula based on land area and the number of licensed hunters in the state. Since the program's birth, these funds have provided more than $400 million to state fish and game departments. Prior to the Pittman-Robertson program, state fish and game departments had to operate primarily on license revenue alone. They now receive 75% reim-

bursement from the P-R program for approved wildlife projects.

Nearly half of the excise tax revenue is used to improve game range by planting feed and cover, restocking game, constructing marshes and ponds for waterfowl and providing watering places for wildlife in arid areas.

The other two major uses of these funds are research and fact-finding that contribute to improved wildlife

management, disease control and the purchase of wildlife lands. Almost every state in the union has used P-R funds to obtain refuges, wintering ranges, wetlands and public hunting grounds, adding up to more total acreage than the entire state of Delaware. The funds actually benefit more nongame birds and animals than game species.

State land acquisition from this self-imposed hunter tax has provided the non-hunting public, as well as the hunter, with state-owned recreation grounds that will benefit the needs of our future generations.

Further benefit could be drawn if Congress were to pass a bill recently introduced by Congressmen John D. Dingell and George A. Goodling. This bill (H.R. 16005) would divert the proceeds from a present 10% tax on handguns from general revenue to the Federal Aid in Wildlife Restoration program. The bill would also extend the 10% handgun tax to archery equipment.

Congressman Goodling, in introducing the bill, explained that it was proposed to give archers an opportunity to contribute to the future well-being of their own sport. The bill has already received pledges of support from much of the archery industry and archers themselves.

Free copies of H. R. 16005, which has been referred to the House Committee on Merchant Marine and Fisheries, is available from the National Shooting Sports Foundation, 1075 Post Road, Riverside, Conn. 06878.

Pelican Arms Collectors
B. Thompson, 9142 Cefalu Dr., Baton Rouge, La. 70811
Penn-Mar-Va Antique Arms Soc.
T. Wibberley, 54 E. Lincoln Ave., Hagerstown, Md. 21740
Pennsylvania Antique Gun Collectors Assn.
Ray Petry, 801 N. Jackson, Media, Pa. 19063
Pennsylvania Gun Collectors Assn.
Arch Waugh, RD 2, Washington, Pa. 15301
Pikes Peak Gun Collectors Guild
Charles Cell, 406 E. Uintah St., Colorado Springs, Colo. 80903
Pine Ridge Gun Coll.
Loren Pickering, 509 Elm St., Crawford, Neb. 69339
Pioneer Gun Collectors Assn.
J. O. Wingate, 4611 Cherokee, Amarillo, Tex. 79109
Potomac Arms Collectors Assn.
Bill Summerfelt, P.O. Box 93, Riverdale, Md. 20840
Presque Isle Gun Collectors Assn.
James Welch, 156 E. 37th St., Erie, Pa. 16506
Quad City Arms Coll. Assn.
A. Squire, 1845 W. 3rd St., Davenport, Ia. 52802
Redlands Arms Collectors
Harold W. Cleveland, 140 The Terrace, Redlands, Calif.
Royal Oak Gun Collectors
Margaret Parker, 13143 Borgmann, Huntington Woods, Mich. 48070
Sabine Gun Collectors Club
Mrs. J. Nugent, Rt. 1, Box 176-B, Orange, Tex. 77630
San Bernardino Valley Gun Collectors
F. Schaperkotter, 2697 Acacia Ave., San Bernardino, Cal. 92405
San Fernando Valley Arms Coll.
L. Campbell, 232 S. 6th, Valinda, Cal. 91744
San Gabriel Valley Arms Collectors
J. Mandeville, 16831 Holton, Valinda, Cal. 91744
Santa Barbara Antique Arms Coll. Assn., Inc.
Tom McKissock, 205 San Napoli Dr., Goleta, Cal. 93017

Santa Fe Gun Collec. Assn.
Ernie Lang, 1085 Nuggett, Los Alamos, N.M. 87544
Sauk Trail Gun Collectors
L. D. Carlock, Rte. 1, Box 169 Prophetstown, Ill. 61277
Shasta Arms Collectors Assn.
L. C. Lacey, Box 715, Project City, Cal. 96079
Shenandoah Valley Gun Coll. Assn.
Daniel E. Blye, P.O. Box 926, Winchester, Va. 22601
Shooting Sports Assn., Inc.
Dan Fales, 1075 Post Rd., Riverside, Conn. 06878
Smoky Mountain Gun Collectors Assn.
W. Brundage, 111 Dixie Ln., Oak Ridge Tenn. 37830
Solomon Valley Gun Collectors
Frank Wheeler, Box 230, Osborne, Kan. 67473
Somerset Rifle & Pistol Club
J. Richard Ross, 2 Stein Bldg., Somerset, Pa. 15501
South Carolina Arms Coll. Assn.
J. W. McNelley, 3215 Lincoln St., Columbia, S.C. 29201
Southern California Arms Collectors Assn.
Frank E. Barnyak, 4204 Elmer Ave., No. Hollywood, Cal. 91602
Southern Indiana Gun Collectors Assn., Inc.
Harold M. McClary, 509 N. 3rd St., Boonville, Ind. 47601
Sporting Arms and Ammunition Manufacturers' Inst.
420 Lexington Ave., N. Y., N. Y. 10017
Stark Gun Collectors, Inc.
Russell E. McNary, 147 Miles Ave., Canton, O. 44708
Stratford Gun Collectors Assn., Inc.
F. Santora, 351 Grovers Ave., Bridgeport, Conn. 06605
Tampa Bay Gun Collectors Assn.
Col. Emmet M. Jeffreys, 401 49th St., N., St. Petersburg, Fla. 33710
Tennessee Gun Collectors Assn., Inc.
M. H. Parks, 3556 Pleasant Valley Rd., Nashville, Tenn. 37204
Texas Gun Collectors Assn.
Mrs. Audra Bradshaw, 4600 Pine, Waco, Tex. 76710

Tippecanoe Gun and Cartridge Collectors Club
Leonard Ledman, RR 12, Box 212, Lafayette, Ind.
Tri-State Gun Collectors
Laurence Stombaugh, 2223 Makin Dr., Lima, O. 45804
Two Lick Valley Gun Collectors
Zenas Hoover, 222 Phila. St., Indiana, Pa. 15701
U. S. International Trap and Skeet Assn.
Box 1437, Huntington Beach, Ca. 92647
U. S. Revolver Assn.
Stanley A. Sprague, 59 Alvin St., Springfield, Mass. 01104
Utah Gun Collectors Assn.
S. Gerald Keogh, 875 20th St., Ogden, Utah 84401
Vermont Gun Coll. Assn.
C. E. Reynolds, 25 Simpson Ct., So. Burlington, Vt. 05403
Virginia Arms Collectors & Assn.
W. H. Bacon, 4601 Sylvan Rd., Richmond, Va. 23225
Wabash Valley Gun Collectors Assn., Inc.
Mrs. Betty Baer, 1002 Lincoln Pk. Ave., Danville, Ill. 61832
Waco Gun Collectors
C. V. Pruitt, 4021 N. 26th, Waco, Tex.
Washington Arms Collectors, Inc.
L. A. Funk, 9404 Woodland Rd., Puyallup, Wash. 98371
Westchester Arms Collectors Club, Inc.
F. E. Falkenbury, Jr., 75 Hillcrest Rd., Hartsdale, N. Y. 10530
Western Illinois Gun Collectors Assn.
Verne Geer, 421 Pearl, Macomb, Ill.
Willamette Valley Arms Coll. Assn.
M. Brooks, 2110 W. 20th, Eugene, Ore. 97405
Wisconsin Gun Collectors Assn., Inc.
Mrs. Harold Molzahn, 427 S. 23 St., La Crosse, Wis.
Wyoming Gun Collectors
Bob Funk, 224N. 2W., Riverton, Wyo. 82501
Ye Conn. Gun Guild
Rob. L. Harris, U.S. Rte. 7-Kent Rd., Cornwall Bridge, Conn. 06754

Shooting Publications

Write directly to the sources noted for titles listed and ask for their latest catalog. Do not order from the GUN DIGEST.

A Joint Resolution—A 4-page statement by the National Police Officers Assn. and the National Shooting Sports Foundation, outlining the role of firearms in U.S. history and voicing their stand against ill-planned restrictive gun laws. Free.[1]

Basic Pistol Marksmanship—Textbook for basic pistol courses. 25¢[2]

Basic Rifle Marksmanship—Textbook for basic rifle courses. 25¢ ea.[2]

The Elk—125-page report on the hunting and management of this game animal, more properly called *wapiti*. Extensive biblio. $1.00.[4]

Free Films—Brochure listing outdoor movies available to sportsmen's clubs. Free.[1]

The Gun Law Problem—Information about firearms legislation. Free.[2]

How to be a Crack Shot—A 14-page booklet detailing everything necessary to becoming an outstanding shot. Free.[3]

Fundamentals of Claybird Shooting—A 39-page booklet explaining the basics of Skeet and trap in non-technical terms. Many diagrams. 25¢ ea.[4]

Hunter Safety Instructor's Guide—How to conduct an NRA Hunter Safety Course. 25¢ ea.[2]

Hunting and Shooting Sportsmanship—A 4-page brochure defining the "true sportsman" and giving information on the outdoor field. Free.[1]

Junior Rifle Handbook—Information about the NRA junior program with short instruction course. (25 copies issued to each new affiliated junior club without charge.) 25¢ ea.[2]

NRA Hunter Safety Handbook—Textbook for students. 10¢ ea.[2]

National Shooting Preserve Directory—Up-to-date listing of small game preserves in the U.S. and Canada. Free.[1]

Ranger Targets— To be used in qualifying for the NRA Ranger emblem; supplied free in reasonably large quantities.[1]

Shooting's Fun for Everyone—The why, when, where, and how of riflery for boys and girls. 20 pp. 5¢ ea.[1]

Trap or Skeet Fundamentals—Handbooks explaining fundamentals of these two sports, complete with explicit diagrams to start beginners off right. Free.[3]

25 Foot Shooting Program—Complete information on a short range shooting program with CO_2 and pneumatic rifles and pistols. 35¢[2]

What Every Parent Should Know When a Boy or Girl Wants a Gun—Straightforward answers to the 15 questions most frequently asked by parents. 8 pp. 5¢ ea.[1]

The Cottontail Rabbit—56-page rundown on America's most popular hunting target. Where to find him, how to hunt him, how to help him. Bibliography included. $1.00 ea.[4]

For the Young Hunter—A 32-page booklet giving fundamental information on the sport. Single copies free, 15¢ each in bulk.[4]

Gray and Fox Squirrels—112-page paperbound illustrated book giving full rundown on the squirrel families named. Extensive bibliography. $1.00 ea.[4]

How to Have More Pheasant Hunting—A 16-page booklet on low cost hunting, including data on in-season stocking and how to start a small preserve. 25¢.[1]

The Mallard—80-page semi-technical report on this popular duck. Life cycle, laws and management, hunting—even politics as they affect this bird—are covered. Bibliography. $1.00 ea.[4]

NRA Booklets—Ranging from 12 to 36 pages, these are articles on specific arms or arms types. Titles available are: Sighting In; The 45 Automatic; The M1 Rifle; Telescopic Sights; Metallic Sights; Duck Hunting; U.S. Cal. 30 Carbine; Remodeling the 03A3; Remodeling the 303 Lee-Enfield; Remodeling the U.S. 1917 Rifle; M1903 Springfield Rifle; Military Rifles and Civil War Small Arms, 50¢ ea. Gun Cabinets, Racks, Cases & Pistol Boxes, 75¢. Deer Hunting, $1.00.[2]

Under the heading of "Range Plans" are 15 booklets priced from 10¢ to $1.00. All are described in an order form pamphlet available from the NRA.

NRA Digest of the Federal Gun Control Act of 1968—A 12-page booklet clearly explaining the new law and its provisions. Free to NRA members.[2]

NRA Federal Firearms Laws—A 28-page booklet digesting the several U.S. gun laws affecting the citizen today. Free to NRA members.[2]

NRA Firearms & Ammunition Fact Book—352-page book of questions and answers, ballistic charts and tables, descriptions of firearms and ammunition. NRA, Washington, D.C., 1964. $2.00 ea. ($1.75 to NRA members).

NRA Firearms Assembly Handbook, Volumes I and II—Articles describing the assembly and disassembly of various arms. Vol. I, 160 pp., covers 77 guns, Vol. II, 176 pp., 87 guns. Illustrated with exploded-view and supplementary drawings. NRA, Washington, D.C., 1960 and 1964. $3.50 ea. (2.50 to NRA members).

NRA Firearms Handling Handbook—21 major articles on the proper useage of most types of small arms available to civilians. Illus. NRA, Washington, D.C., 1962, 80 pp. $2.75 ($1.75 to NRA members).

NRA Gun Collectors Handbook—20 feature articles on all phases of gun collecting, plus a listing of all important museums. NRA, Washington, D.C., 1959. 48 pp., illus. $2.50 ($1.50 to NRA members).

NRA Handloader's Guide—Enlarged & Revised. A successor to the *NRA Illustrated Reloading Handbook*, this excellent new work covers all aspects of metallic-case and shotshell reloading. Washington, D. C., 1969, fully illus. $5.00 (NRA members, $4.00).

NRA Hunters Handbook—51 major pieces, 18 shorter ones. NRA, Washington, D.C., 1960. 72 pp., illus. $3.00 ($2.00 to NRA members).

NRA Illustrated International Shooting Handbook—18 major articles detailing shooting under ISU rules, training methods, etc. NRA, Washington, D.C., 1964. $2.50 ea. ($1.50 to NRA members).

NRA Illustrated Shotgun Handbook—50 articles covering every phase of smoothbore shooting, including exploded views of many shotguns. NRA, Washington, D.C. 1964. 128 pp. $3.00 ea. ($2.00 to NRA members).

NRA Questions and Answers Handbook—150 queries and replies on guns and shooting. NRA, Washington, D.C., 1959. 46 pp. with index, illus. $2.50 ($1.50 to NRA members).

NRA Shooters Guide—40 articles of high interest to shooters of all kinds. Over 340 illus. NRA, Washington, D.C., 1959. 72 pp., $3.00 ($2.00 to NRA members).

NRA Shooting Handbook—83 major articles plus 35 shorts on every phase of shooting. NRA, Washington, D.C., 1961. 224 pp., illus. $4.50 ($3.50 to NRA members).

Principles of Game Management—A 25-page booklet surveying in popular manner such subjects as hunting regulations, predator control, game refuges and habitat restoration. Single copies free, 15¢ each in bulk.[4]

The Ring-Necked Pheasant—Popular distillation of much of the technical literature on the "ringneck." 104-page paperbound book, appropriately illustrated. Bibliography included. $1.00 ea.[4]

Ruffed Grouse, by John Madson—108-page booklet on the life history, management and hunting of *Bonasa umbellus* in its numerous variations. Extensive biblio. $1.00.[4]

Start A Gun Club—All of the basic information needed to establish a club with clay bird shooting facilities. 24 pp. 50¢[1]

Where To Shoot Muzzle Loaders In The U.S.A.—Publ. for black powder burners, and lists more than 100 muzzle loading clubs. 10¢.[1]

The White-Tailed Deer—History, management, hunting—a complete survey in this 108-page paperbound book. Full bibliography. $1.00 ea.[4]

You and Your Lawmaker—A 22-page citizenship manual for sportsmen, showing how they can support or combat legislation affecting shooting and outdoor sports. 10¢ ea.[1]

[2]National Rifle Association of America, 1600 Rhode Island Ave., Washington, D. C. 20036

[3]Remington Arms Company, Dept. C—Bridgeport, Conn. 06602

[4]Olin Mathieson Conservation Dept., East Alton, Ill. 62024

[1]National Shooting Sports Foundation, Inc. 1075 Post Road, Riverside, Conn. 06878

Publishers: Please send review copies to John T. Amber, P.O. Box 0, Chicago, Ill. 60690

PERIODICAL PUBLICATIONS

Alaska Sportsman
Alaska Northwest Pub. Co., Box 4-EEE, Anchorage, Alaska 99503. $6.00 yr. Hunting and fishing articles.

American Field†
222 W. Adams St., Chicago, Ill. 60606. $9.00 yr. Field dogs and trials, occasional gun and hunting articles.

The American Rifleman (M)
National Rifle Assn., 1600 Rhode Island Ave., N.W., Wash., D.C. 20036. $6.00 yr. Firearms articles of all kinds.

The American Sportsman Quarterly (Q)
239 Great Neck Rd., Great Neck, N.Y. 11021. $18.00 yr.

The American West*
American West Publ. Co., 577 College Ave., Palo Alto, Ca. 94306. $9.00 yr.

Argosy
Popular Publ., Inc., 205 E. 42nd St., New York, N.Y. 10017. $6.00 yr.

Army (M)
Assn of the U.S. Army, 1529 18th Ave. N.W., Wash., D.C. 20036. $6.00 yr. Occasional articles on small arms.

Deutsches Waffen Journal
Journal-Verlag Schwend GmbH, Postfach 340, Schwabisch Hall, Germany. $8.00 yr. Antique and modern arms, their history, technical aspects, etc. German text.

Ducks Unlimited, Inc. (M)
P.O. Box 66300, Chicago, Ill. 60666.

The Field†
The Harmsworth Press Ltd., 8 Stratton St., London W.I., England. $27.00 yr. Hunting and shooting articles.

Field & Stream
Holt, Rinehart and Winston, Inc., 383 Madison Ave., New York, N.Y. 10017. $5.00 yr. Warren Page on firearms plus hunting and fishing articles.

Fishing and Hunting Guide
Fishing and Hunting Guide Ltd., P.O. Box 48, Dolton, Ill. 60419. $3.00 yr.

Fur-Fish-Game
A. R. Harding Pub. Co., 2878 E. Main St., Columbus, Ohio 43209. $3.50 yr. "Gun Rack" column by M. H. Decker.

Gunfacts Magazine
Hazard Publications, Inc., Box 9335, Arlington, Va. 22209. $6.00 yr. (8 issues, mo./bi-mo.)

The Gun Report
World Wide Gun Report, Inc., Box 111, Aledo, Ill. 61231. $6.00 yr. For the gun collector.

Gun Week†
Sidney Printing & Publishing Co., P.O. Box 150, Sidney, Ohio 45365. $4.00 yr. U.S. and possessions; $4.50 yr. Canada; $6.00 yr. foreign. Tabloid paper on guns, hunting, shooting.

Guns & Ammo
Petersen Pub. Co., 8490 Sunset Blvd., Los Angeles, Calif. 90069. $5.00 yr. Guns, shooting, and technical articles.

Guns
Guns Magazine, 8150 N. Cenral Park Ave., Skokie, Ill. 60076. $7.50 yr. Articles for gun collectors, hunters and shooters.

Guns Review
Ravenhill Pub. Co. Ltd., Standard House, Bonhill St., London E.C. 2, England. $6.50 yr. For collectors and shooters.

Gun World
Gallant Publishing Co., 116 E. Badillo, Covina, Calif. 91722. $5.00 yr. For the hunting, reloading and shooting enthusiast.

The Handgunner (M)
U.S. Revolver Assn., 59 Alvin St., Springfield, Mass. 01104. $3.50 yr. General handgun and competition articles.

The Handloader Magazine*
Dave Wolfe Pub. Co., Box 3482, Rte. 4, Peoria, Ill. 61614. $5.00 yr.

Hobbies
Lightner Pub. Co., 1006 S. Michigan Ave., Chicago. Ill. 60605. $5.00 yr.; Canada $6.00; foreign $6.50. Collectors departments.

International Shooting Sport*
Union Internationale de Tir, 62 Wiesbaden-Klarenthal, Klarenthalerstr., Germany. $3.60 yr., p.p. For the International target shooter.

The Journal of the Arms & Armour Society (M)
F. Wilkinson (Secy.), 40 Great James St., Holborn, London WC1, England. $4.00 yr. Articles for the collector.

Law and Order
Law and Order Magazine, 72 W. 45th St., New York, N.Y. 10036. $4.00 yr. Articles on weapons for law enforcement.

The Luger Journal
Robt. B. Marvin, Publ., P.O. Box 12206, Plantation, Fla. 33314. $6.00 yr.

Muzzle Blasts (M)
National Muzzle Loading Rifle Assn.; P.O. Box 67, Friendship, Ind. 47021. $6.00 yr. For the black powder shooter.

National Rifle Assn. Journal (British)
Natl. Rifle Assn. (BR.), Bisley Camp, Brookwood, Surrey, England.

National Sportsman's Digest
National Sportsman's Club, Box 2003, Dallas, Tex. 75221. $8.00 yr. Subs. includes membership in the Club, etc.

National Wildlife*
Natl. Wildlife Fed. Inc., 381 W. Center St., Marion, O. 43302. $5.00 yr. w/Assoc. membership.

New Zealand Wildlife (Q)
New Zealand Deerstalkers Assoc. Inc., P.O. Box 263, Wellington, N.Z. $2.00 U.S. and Canada, elsewhere on application. Hunting and shooting articles.

Ordnance* (M)
American Ordnance Assn., Transportation Bldg., Wash., D.C. 20006. $8.00 yr. $7.00 to members. Occasional articles on small arms and related subjects.

Outdoor Life
Popular Science Pub. Co., 355 Lexington Ave., New York, N.Y. 10017. $5.00 yr. Arms column by Jack O'Connor.

Outdoor World*
Preston Publications, Inc., 1645 Tullie Circle, N.E., Atlanta, Ga. 30329. $6.00 yr. Conservation and wildlife articles.

Police*
Charles C Thomas, publisher, 301-327 E. Lawrence Ave., Springfield, Ill. 62703. $9.50 yr. Articles on identification, etc.

Police Times (M)
7777 N.E. 3rd Court, Miami, Fla. 33138.

Popular Mechanics
Hearst Corp., 575 Lexington Ave., New York, N.Y. 10022. $4.00 yr., $4.50 Canada, $6.00 foreign. Hunting and shooting articles.

Precision Shooting
Precision Shooting, Inc., 8 Cline St., Dolgeville, N.Y. 13329. $5.00 yr. Journal of the International Benchrest Shooters.

The Rifle Magazine*
Dave Wolfe Publishing Co., Rt. 4, Box 3482, Peoria, Ill. 61614. $5.00 yr. Journal of the NBRSA.

The Rifleman (Q)
National Smallbore Rifle Assoc., 113 Southwark St., London, S. E. 1, Englnd. $7.00 (5 yrs.). Data on British Matches and International Matches, and technical shooting articles.

Rod and Gun in Canada
Rod and Gun Pub. Corp., 1475 Metcalfe St., Montreal 2, P.Q. Canada. $3.00 yr., $5.00 2 yrs., out of Canada, postage $1.00 p. yr. extra. Regular gun and shooting articles.

Saga
Gambi Public., 333 Johnson Ave., Brooklyn, N.Y. 11026. $5.00 yr. U.S., $5.50 Canada.

The Shooting Industry
Publisher's Dev. Corp., 8150 N. Central Pk., Skokie, Ill. 60076. $7.00 yr.

The Shooting Times (England)†
Cordwallis Estate, Clivemont Rd., Maidenhead, Berksh., England. $20 yr. Game shooting and firearms articles.

Shooting Times
Peoria Journal-Star, Inc., News Plaza, Peoria, Ill., 61601. $5.85 yr. Gun ads plus articles on every gun activity.

The Shotgun News‡
Snell Publishing Co., Columbus, Nebr. 68601. $3.00 yr. Sample copy 50¢. Gun ads of all kinds.

The Skeet Shooting Review
National Skeet Shooting Assn., 212 Linwood Bldg., 2608 Inwood Rd., Dallas, Tex. 75235. $6.00 yr. Scores, averages, skeet articles.

Sporting Goods Business
7 E. 43rd, New York, N.Y. 10017. Trade journal.

The Sporting Goods Dealer
2018 W. Washington Ave., St. Louis, Mo. 63166. $4.00 yr. The sporting goods trade journal.

Sports Afield
The Hearst Corp., 57th St. at 8th Ave., New York, N.Y. 10019. $4.00 yr. Pete Brown on firearms plus hunting and fishing articles.

Sports Age Magazine
P.O. Box 67, Minneapolis, Minn. Trade journal.

Sports Illustrated†
Time, Inc., 540 N. Michigan Ave., Chicago, Ill. 60611. $9.00 yr. Articles on the current sporting scene.

Trap & Field
Review Pub. Co., 1100 Waterway Blvd., Indianapolis, Ind. 46202. $7.00 yr. Scores, averages, trapshooting articles.

True
Fawcett Publ., Inc., Fawcett Bldg., Greenwich, Conn. 06830. $5.00 yr. U.S. Poss., and Canada; $7.00 yr. all other countries.

Valor
Natl. Police Offic. Assoc., Natl Police Academy Bldg., 1890 South Trail, Venice, Fla. 33595. $5.00 yr.

Wildlife Review (Q)
Fish & Wildlife Branch. Dep't of Rec. and Conservation Parliament Bldgs., Victoria, B.C. $1.00 2 yrs.

---

* Published bi-monthly M Membership requirements; write for details.
† Published weekly Q Published Quarterly.
‡ Published twice per month

The Arms Library for

COLLECTOR · HUNTER · SHOOTER · OUTDOORSMAN

A selection of books—old, new and forthcoming—for everyone in the arms field, with a brief description by . . . RAY RILING

ballistics and handloading

Ballistics in the Seventeenth Century, by A.R. Hall. 1st J.&J. Harper ed. 1969 [from the Cambridge University Press ed. of 1952]. 186 pp., illus., with tables and diagrams. $13.50.
A profound work for advanced scholars, this is a study in the relations of science and war, with reference principally to England.
The Bullet's Flight, from Powder to Target, by F. W. Mann. Ray Riling Arms Books Co., Phila., Pa. 1965. A reprint of the very scarce original work of 1909. Introduction by Homer S. Powley, 384 pp. illus. $9.95.
One of the best known and scholarly-developed works on basic ballistics.
Cartridges of the World, by Frank C. Barnes, John T. Amber ed., Gun Digest Co., Chicago, Ill., 1969. 8½"x11", 378 pp. Profusely illus. Paperbound. $6.95.
The second edition of a comprehensive reference for hunters, collectors, handloaders and ballisticians. Covering over 1000 cartridges, loads, components, etc., from all over the world.
Centerfire American Rifle Cartridges, 1892-1963, by Ray Bearse, A. S. Barnes & Co., S. Brunswick, N.J., 1966. 198 pp., illus. $15.00.
Identification manual covering caliber, introduction date, origin, case type, etc. Self-indexed and cross-referenced. Headstamps and line drawings are included.
Centerfire Pistol and Revolver Cartridges, by H.P. White, B. D. Munhall and Ray Bearse. A. S. Barnes, N.Y., 1967. 85 pp. plus 170 pp., illus. $10.00
A new and revised edition covering the original Volume I, Centerfire Metric Pistol and Revolver Cartridges and Volume II, Centerfire American and British Pistol and Revolver Cartridges, by White and Munhall, formerly known as Cartridge Identification.
Complete Guide to Handloading, by Phil Sharpe. Funk & Wagnalls, N. Y., 1953 (3rd ed., 2nd rev.). 734 pp., profusely illustrated, numerous line and halftone charts, tables, lists, etc., $10.00.
The bible of handloaders ever since its first appearance in 1937, but badly dated now.
Handbook for Shooters and Reloaders, by P. O. Ackley. Priv. publ., Salt Lake City, 1962-1965. Illus. Vol. I, 567 pp., $8.00; Vol. II, 495 pp., $8.00. The two volumes, special at $15.00.
Storehouse of technical information on ammunition and its use by a noted authority, with supplemental articles by other experts. Ballistic charts plus loading data for hundreds of cartridges, standard and wildcat.
Handloader's Digest, ed. by John T. Amber. Gun Digest Publ., Northfield, Ill., 1970. 320 pp., very well illus., stiff paper covers. $4.95.
This 5th edition contains the latest data on ballistics, maximum loads, new tools, equipment, reduced loads, etc., plus a fully illus. catalog section, current prices and specifications.
Home Guide to Cartridge Conversions, by Geo. C. Nonte, Jr., Stackpole Books, Harrisburg, Pa., 1967. 404 pp., illus. $8.95.
A new, revised and enlarged ed. of instructions, charts and tables for making ammunition no longer available, or which has become too expensive on the commercial market.
Hornady Handbook of Cartridge Reloading. Hornady Mfg. Co., Grand Island, Nebr., 1967. 360 pp., illus. $3.50.
Handloader's reference, with much detail on projectiles, ballistics, etc., on many popular U.S. and imported firearms. An excellent new work with particularly needed ballistic detail.
The Identification of Firearms and Forensic Ballistics, by G. Burrard. A. S. Barnes, New York, 1962. 217 pp., illus. $3.95.
A standard, reliable, authoritative English work in the criminal-legal field of ballistics.
Interior Ballistics, How a Gun Converts Chemical Energy to Projectile Motion, by E. D. Lowry. Doubleday and Co., N.Y., 1968. 168 pp., including index and bibliography., illus. with 4 halftones and 17 line drawings. $4.50.
An introduction to the history of small arms and weapons relative to the science of internal ballistics, especially for the layman and student.
Lyman Handbook No. 44. Lyman Gunsight Corp., Middlefield, Conn., 1967. $3.50
Latest edition of a favorite reference for ammunition handloaders, whether novice or veteran.
Methods in Exterior Ballistics, by F. R. Moulton. Dover Publ., N.Y.C., 1962. 257 pp., paper covers, $1.75.
A standard work on the mathematics of advanced theoretical and experimental exterior ballistics.
The NRA Handloader's Guide. Ashley Halsey, Jr., ed. Nat'l Rifle Assn., Washington, D.C., 1969. 312 pp., illus., paperbound. $5.00.
Revised edition of a reloading handbook, based on material published in *The American Rifleman.*
Pocket Manual for Shooters and Reloaders, by P. O. Ackley. Publ. by author, Salt Lake City, Utah, 1964. 176 pp., illus., spiral bound. $3.25.
Good coverage on standard and wildcat cartridges and related firearms in popular calibers.

Principles and Practice of Loading Ammunition, by Lt. Col. Earl Naramore. Stackpole Books, Harrisburg, Pa., 1954. 915 text pages, 240 illustrations. $14.95.
Actually two volumes in one. The first part (565 pp.) deals with ballistics and the principles of cartridge making—and the chemistry, metallurgy, and physics involved. The second part (350 pp.) is a thorough discussion of the mechanics of loading cartridges. 1967 printing.
Professional Loading of Rifle and Shotgun Cartridges . . . , by G. L. Herter's. Herter's, Waseca, Minn., 1970. 430 pp., illus. Paper covers. $4.50.
Loading and reloading data for everyone.
Note: A new third printing, more extensive, of this book is available hard-bound. 830 pp. $7.50.
Shooter's Bible Black Powder Guide, by George Nonte. Shooter's Bible, Inc., S. Hackensack, N.J., 1969. 214 pp., well illus. $3.95.
Information on black powder weapons, ammunition, shooting, etc.
Shooter's Bible Reloader's Guide, 2nd ed., by R. A. Steindler. Shooter's Bible, Inc., S. Hackensack, N.J., 1968. 220 pp., fully illus. $3.95.
Comprehensive coverage of technology and methods of handloading all types of small arms ammunition. This is a useful work.
Shotshell Handbook, by Lyman Handbook Staff. Lyman Gunsight Corp., Middlefield, Conn., 1969. 160 pp., illus., stiff paper spiral-binding. $3.00.
The first book devoted exclusively to shotshell reloading. Considers: gauge, shell length, brand, case, loads, buckshot, etc., plus excellent reference section. Some color illus.
Small Arms Ammunition Identification Guide. Panther Publ., Boulder, Colo., 1968. 151 pp., illus., paperbound. $3.00.
Facsimile of a U.S. Army text on cartridge identification, which includes data on foreign ammunition used in Vietnam and elsewhere.
Small Arms Design and Ballistics, by Col. T. Whelen. 1945. Stackpole Books, Harrisburg, Pa. Vol. I, 352 pp., Vol. II, 314 pp., both illus. Each, $6.00.
Authoritative technical data on firearms. Vol. I covers design, function, and operation. Vol. II deals with interior and exterior ballistics.
Speer Manual for Reloading Ammunition No. 8. Speer, Inc., Lewiston, Idaho, 1970. 382 pp., illus. $2.95.
A popular manual on handloading, with authoritative articles on loading, ballistics, and related subjects. Decorated paper wrappers.
Why Not Load Your Own? by Col. T. Whelen. A. S. Barnes, New York, 1957, 4th ed., rev. 237 pp., illus. $5.95.
A basic reference on handloading, describing each step, materials and equipment. Loads for popular cartridges are given.
The Winchester-Western Ammunition Handbook. Thomas Nelson & Sons, N.Y.C., 1964. 185 pp., illus. $1.95.
Called the world's handiest handbook on ammunition for all types of shotguns, rifles and handguns. Full of facts, photographs, ballistics and statistics.

COLLECTORS

Accoutrement Plates, North and South, 1861-1865, by Wm. G. Gavin. Geo. Shumway, York, Pa., 1963. 236 pp., 220 illus. $12.00.
The 1st detailed study of Civil War belt buckles and cartridge box insignia. Dimensions, materials, details of manufacture, relative and dollar values given.
The Age of Firearms, by Robert Held. Gun Digest Publ., Northfield, Ill., 1970. New, fully rev. and corrected ed., paper covers. 192 pp., fully illus. $4.95.
A popular review of firearms since 1475 with accent on their effects on social conditions, and the craft of making functional/artistic arms.
Air Guns, by Eldon G. Wolff. Milwaukee Public Museum, Milwaukee, Wis., 1958. 198 pp., illus. Paper, $6.00.
A scholarly and comprehensive treatise, excellent for student and collectors' use, of air gun history. Every form of arm is described, and a list of 350 makers is included.
The American Bayonet, 1776-1964, by A. N. Hardin, Jr. Geo. Shumway, York, Pa., 1964. 252 pp., profusely illus. $20.00.
First comprehensive book on U. S. bayonets of all services, a standard reference for collectors. All bayonets made for long arms are described in full detail, with outstanding photographs, and historical development of principal types. Full references and bibliography.
American, British & Continental Pepperbox Firearms, by Jack Dunlap. H. J. Dunlap, Los Altos, Calif., 1964. 279 pp., 665 illus. $15.00.
Comprehensive history of production pepperpots from early 18th cent. through the cartridge pepperbox. Variations are covered, with much data of value to the collector.
American Engraved Powder Horns, by Stephen V. Grancsay. Originally published by The Metropolitan Museum of Art, at N.Y.C., 1945. The 1st reprint publ. by Ray Riling Arms Books Co., Phila., Pa. 1965. 96 pp. plus 47 full-page plates. $13.50.
A study based on the J. H. Grenville Gilbert collection of historic, rare and beautiful powder horns. A scholarly work by an eminent authority. Long out of print and offered now in a limited edition of 1000 copies.

American Knives, the First History and Collectors' Guide, by Harold L. Peterson. Scribner's, N.Y.C., 1958. 178 pp., well illus. $5.95.
A timely book to whet the appetite of the ever-growing group of knife collectors.

American Polearms, 1526-1865, by R. H. Brown. N. Flayderman Co., New Milford, Conn., 1967. 198 pp., 150 plates. $14.50.
Concise history of pikes, spears, and similar weapons used in American military forces through the Civil War.

American Socket Bayonets, 1717-1873, by D. B. Webster, Jr. Museum Rest. Service, Ottawa, Can. 1964. 48 pp., 60 illus. paperbound. $1.50.
Concise account of major types, with nomenclature, characteristics, and dimensions. Line drawings.

Ancient Armour and Weapons in Europe, by John Hewitt. Akademische Druck- u. Verlagsanstalt, Graz, Austria, 1967. 3 vols., 1151 total pp., illus. $50.00.
Reprint of a renowned British work first published 1855-1860; covers armor, weapons, military history and tactics through the 17th century.

The Ancient Art of Warfare, by Robert Laffont. New York Grafic Society, Greenwich, Conn., 1968. (2 vols.). 1086 pp., illus. Boxed. $60.00.
A summary on warfare since 1300 B.C., covering the principal campaigns known to history, with much on weapons, equipment, and military customs of all types. Many illustrations in full color.

Antique Firearms, by Frederick Wilkinson. Guinness Signatures, London. 1st ed., 1969. 256 pp., well illus. $15.00.
Sixteen monographs on important aspects of firearms development from the 14th century to the era of the modern repeating rifle. Shows museum-quality arms, many in full color.

Antique Pistols, by S. G. Alexander, illus. by Ronald Paton. Arco Publ. Co., New York, 1963. 56 pp., 12 color plates. $15.00.
The large 8-color plates show 14 examples of the pistol-maker's art in England and U.S.A., 1690-1900. Commentary on each by a knowledgeable English collector.

Antique Weapons, A-Z, by Douglas J. Fryer. G. Bell & Sons, London, 1969. 114 pp. illus. $7.50.
A concise survey of collectors' arms, including firearms, edged weapons, polearms, etc., of European and Oriental design, classified by types.

Armes a Feu Francaises Modeles Reglementaires, by J. Boudriot. Paris, 1961-1968. 4 series of booklets: 1st and 2nd series, 5 booklets; 3rd and 4th, 6 booklets. Each series, $6.75, $9.75, $10.75, $11.75, resp.
Detailed survey of all models of French military small arms, 1717-1861, with text in French and fine scale drawings. Each series covers a different period of development; the last covers percussion arms.

Armes Blanches Militaires Francaises, by Christian Aries. P. Petitot, Paris, 1968. Unpaginated, paperbound, 11 volumes. $9.50 per vol., $95.00 complete.
Pictorial survey of French military swords, in French text and line drawings in exact detail. The classifications in the various volumes are the author's own and do not follow any specific sequence. The work must be used as a complete set for maximum benefit.

Le Armi da Fuoco Portatili Italiane, dalle Origini al Risorgimento, by Gen. Agostino Gaibi. Bramante Editrice, Milan, Italy, 1962. 527 pp., 320 illus. (69 in color), in slip case. $65.00
A magnificently produced volume covering Italian hand firearms from their beginning into the 18th cent. Italian text. Superb illus. of historic weapons, engraving, marks, related equipment. A companion book to *Armi e Armature Italiane.*

Armi E Armature Europee, by B. Thomas-O. Gamber-H. Schedelmann, Bramante Editrice, Milano, Italy, 1965. 246 pp., magnificently illus., mainly in full color. $40.00. Ed. ltd. to 1600 copies.
Italian text version of *Arms and Armor of Europe* by the same authors in German text. Text and commentary cover 50 pp., and there are 196 pp. of illus.

Armi e Armature Italiane, Fino al XVIII Secolo, by Aldo Mario Aroldi. Bramante Editrice, Milan, Italy, 1961. 544 pp., profusely illus. (much in color). In slip case, $65.00.
A luxurious work on the golden age of Italian arms makers through the 18th cent., emphasizing body and horse armor, edged weapons, crossbows, early firearms. Italian text. Beautiful and scholarly work for the advanced collector.

Armi E Armature Orientali, by Gianni Vianello, Bramante Editrice, Milano, Italy, 1966. 423 pp. Magnificently illustrated, mainly in full-color tip-ins. $56.00 with slip case. Ed. ltd. to 1600 copies.
A new addition to a notable series of fine books in the arms and armor field. The introduction is 68 pp., 105 pp. of commentary on the 250 pp. of illus.

Arming the Troops, by Paul C. Boehret. Publ. by the author at Chalfont, Pa., 1967. 39 pp., illus. $7.50. The same in paper wrappers $5.00.
A catalog of arms makers of the early years of U.S. history, from 1775 to 1815.

The Armourer and his Craft, by Charles ffoulkes. Frederick Ungar Publ. Co., N.Y., 1967. 199 pp., illus. $9.95.
Standard British reference on body armor, 11th-16th cent.; covering notable makers, construction, decoration, and use. 1st ed. 1912, now reprinted.

Armourers Marks, by D. S. H. Gyngell. Thorsons, Ltd., England, 1959. 131 pp., illus. $7.95.
Some of the marks of armourers, swordsmiths and gunsmiths of almost every foreign country.

Arms Archives, by H.B. Lockhoven. International Small Arms Publishers, Cologne, W. Germany, 1969. Unpaginated. Illus. English and German text, loose-leaf format. Available in 3 series: "A" Handguns, "B" Automatic Weapons, "C" Longarms. Each series in 3 installments at $7.50 per installment. Binders for each series, $4.50 each.
A major breakthrough in weapons literature. Scaled photographs of arms and their cartridges, fully desc. A 4th series "D" on Antique Firearms due sometime in 1970, same prices.

Arms and Armor, by Vesey Norman. Putnam's, N.Y.C., 1964. 128 pp., 129 illus. $3.98.
Authoritative, compact coverage of European armor and weapons prior to the age of firearms. Excellent illus., many in color.

Arms & Armor from the Atelier of Ernst Schmidt, Munich, by E. Andrew Mowbray, compiler. Mowbray Co., Providence, R.I., 1967. 168 pp., well illus. $11.95.
Principally a compilation of plates from the extremely rare Schmidt catalog displaying the famous replicas of medieval armor and weapons made in his shop from about 1870 to 1930. Limited edition.

Arms and Armor in Colonial America, 1526-1783, by H. L. Peterson. Crown, New York, reprint ed., 1964. 350 pp., illus. $3.95.
Well-organized account of arms and equipment used in America's colonization and exploration, through the Revolutionary period.

Arms and Armour, by Frederick Wilkinson, A.&C. Black Ltd., London. Reprint of 1969, 63 pp., well illus. $2.95.
A concise work for young readers describing edged weapons, polearms, armor, etc., mainly of European origin.

Arms and Armour, 9th to 17th Century, by Paul Martin. C.E. Tuttle Co., Rutland, Vt., 1968. 298 pp., well illus. $15.00.
Beautiful illustrations and authoritative text on armor and accessories from the time of Charlemagne to the firearms era.

Arms and Armour of the Western World, by B. Thomas, O. Gamber & H. Schedelmann. McGraw Hill, N.Y.C., 1964. 252 pp., illus. (much in color), $27.50.
Museum quality weapons and armor shown and described in a magnificent book, which gives the association of specimen arms with the men and events of history. Superb photographs in color. Pub. 1963 in German as "Die Schönsten Waffen . . ." price $25.00.

Arms Collection of Colonel Colt, by R. L. Wilson. Herb Glass, Bullville, N.Y., 1964. 132 pp., 73 illus. Lim. deluxe ed., $16.50; trade ed., $6.50.
Samuel Colt's personal collection is well-described and photographed, plus new technical data on Colt's arms and life. 51 Colt guns and other revolving U.S. and European arms are included.

Arms Making in the Connecticut Valley, by F.J. Deyrup. George Shumway Publ., York, Pa., 1970. Reprint of the noted work originally publ. in 1948 by Smith College. 290 pp., line maps, $10.00.
A scholarly regional study of the economic development of the small arms industry 1798-1870. With statistical appendices, notes, bibliography.

The Art of the Gunmaker, by J. F. Hayward; Vol. I, 1500-1660; Vol. II, 1660-1830. St. Martin's Press, New York, 1962-64. Vol. I: 303 pp. plus 64 pp. of illus., $15.00; Vol. II: 352 pp., 220 illus., $18.50.
Comprehensive survey of firearms development and ornamentation by leading makers in Europe and the U.S. Prepared by a museum expert with excellent illus., this book offers valuable new information.

Artillery and Ammunition of the Civil War, by Warren Ripley. Van Nostrand Reinhold Co., New York, N.Y., 1st ed., 1970. 384 pp., well illus. with 662 black and white photos and line drawings. $22.50.
A fine survey covering both Union and Confederate cannon and projectiles, as well as those imported.

Arts of the Japanese Sword, by B. W. Robinson. Chas. E. Tuttle Co., Rutland, Vt., 1961. 110 pp. of descriptive text with illus., plus 100 full page plates, some in full color. $10.00.
An authoritative work, divided into 2 parts—the first on blades, tracing their history to the present day; the second on mounts and fittings. It includes forging processes; accounts of the important schools of swordsmiths; techniques employed, plus a useful appendix on care and cleaning.

Ballard Rifles in the H. J. Nunnemacher Coll., by Eldon G. Wolff. Milwaukee Public Museum, Milwaukee, Wisc., 2nd ed. 1961. Paper, 77 p. plus 4 pp. of charts and 27 plates. $2.50.
A thoroughly authoritative work on all phases of the famous rifles, their parts, patent and manufacturing history.

The Bannerman Catalogue 1903, Francis Bannerman Sons, New York, N.Y. Reprint released in 1960. 116 pp., well illus., $3.50.
A reprint in facsimile of this dealer's catalog of military goods of all descriptions, including weapons and equipment.

The Bannerman Catalog 1965, Francis Bannerman Sons, Blue Point, N.Y. The 100th anniversary ed., 1966. 264 pp., well illus. $5.00.
Latest dealer catalog of nostalgic interest on military and collector's items of all sorts.

Basic Documents on U.S. Martial Arms, commentary by Col. B. R. Lewis, reissue by Ray Riling, Phila., Pa., 1956 and 1960.
Rifle Musket Model 1855. The first issue rifle of musket caliber, a muzzle loader equipped with the Maynard primer, 32 pp. $2.00.
Rifle Musket Model 1863. The typical Union muzzle-loader of the Civil War, 26 pp. $1.25.
Breech-Loading Rifle Musket Model 1866. The first of our 50 caliber breechloading rifles, 12 pp. $1.25.
Remington Navy Rifle Model 1870. A commercial type breech-loader made at Springfield, 16 pp. $1.25.
Lee Straight Pull Navy Rifle Model 1895. A magazine cartridge arm of 6mm caliber. 23 pp. $2.75.
Breech-Loading Rifle Musket Model 1868. The first 50-70 designed as such. 20 pp. $1.50.
Peabody Breech-Loading Arms (five models)—27 pp. $2.25.
Ward-Burton Rifle Musket 1871—16 pp. $2.00.
Springfield Rifle, Carbine & Army Revolvers (cal. 45) Model 1873 including Colt and Smith & Wesson hand arms. 52 pp. $2.25.
U.S. Magazine Rifle and Carbine (cal. 30) Model 1892 (the Krag Rifle) 36 pp. $2.50.

Bayonets, an Illustrated History and Reference Guide, by F. J. Stephens. Arms and Armour Press, London, 1968. 76 pp., stiff paper wrappers, 134 photographs. $3.75.
A general historical survey of all categories of the weapon, from the U.S. and many other countries.

Bellifortis [The War Hero], by Conrad Kyeser. Verlag des Vereins Deutscher Ingenieure, Dusseldorf, W. Germany. 1967. Two large facsimile volumes, 391 pp., combining Latin and German text. Superbly illus.
For the advanced collector, this is a reproduction of the oldest [A.D. 1405] German manuscript on weapons and warfare. Limited to 1,000 copies, bound in white half-vellum and boxed. $120.00.

Bilderatlas zum Grundriss der Waffenlehre, by K.T. vonSauer. Pawlas, Nurnberg, Germany, 1968. Paper folder containing 28 pp. text and 26 plates. $7.50.
Facsimile of an 1869 set of plates depicting military rifles of Germany, with explanatory pamphlet in German text.

Blunderbusses, by D.R. Baxter. Stackpole Books, Harrisburg, Pa., 1970. 80 pp., 60 illus. $4.95.
Traces blunderbuss development from the 16th century, covering basic designs, firing systems, the double blunderbuss and revolving pepperbox design.

The Book of the Continental Soldier, by Harold L. Peterson. Stackpole Books, Harrisburg, Pa., 1968. 287 pp., of large format profusely illus. with halftone, line, and including art work by H. Charles McBarron, Jr., Clyde A. Risley and Peter Copeland. $12.95.
A thorough and commendable work in every pertinent aspect. Covers in satisfying detail every facet of the soldier's existence.

Book of the 22, by Richard Arnold. Barnes & Co., N.Y.C., 1962. 188 pp., illus., $2.95.
Authoritative data for the 22 rifleman and pistoleer, detailing arms of this caliber in use throughout the world, history of the weapons and cartridges.

Bowie Knives, by R. Abels. Pub. by the author, N.Y.C., 1960. 48 pp. profusely illus. Paper covers. $2.00.
A booklet showing knives, tomahawks, related trade cards and advertisements.

Brass Spikes & Horsehair Plumes: A Study of U.S. Army Dress Helmets, 1872-1903, by Gordon Chappell, Arizona Pioneers Hist. Soc., Tucson, Ariz. 1966. 50 pp., illus. Paper covers. $2.00.
Historical monograph on military headgear of the period.

The Breech-Loader in the Service, 1816-1917, by Claud E. Fuller, N. Flayderman, New Milford, Conn., 1965. 381 pp., illus. $14.50.
Revised ed. of a 1933 historical reference on U.S. standard and experimental military shoulder arms. Much patent data, drawings, and photographs of the arms.
A voluminous work that covers handloading—and other things—in great detail. Replete with data for all cartridge forms.

British and American Infantry Weapons of World War II, by A.J. Barker. 1st ed., 1969. Arco Publishing Co., New York, N.Y. 76 pp., illus., $3.50,
A British officer's survey that includes numerous specialized weapons, all are illustrated and described.

British Military Bayonets from 1700 to 1945, by R.J.W. Latham. Arco Publ. Co., N.Y.C., 1969. 94 pp., illus. $8.50.
History and identification catalog of British bayonets, with fine illustrations, marks, dimensions, and equipment of various British army units.

British Military Firearms 1650-1850, by H. L. Blackmore. Arco Publ. Co. Inc., New York, 1962. 296 pp. and 83 plates of photographs, line drawings, appendices and index. $10.00.
This excellent work admirably and authoritatively covers the subject in every detail. Highly recommended.

British Military Swords, From 1800 to the Present Day, by J. W. Latham, Crown Publishers, N.Y., 1967, 91 pp., illus. $3.95.
Survey of British swords used by various branches of the Army, with data on their manufacture, specifications, and procurement.

British Pistols and Guns, 1640-1940, by Ian Glendenning. Arco Publ. Co., N.Y., 1967. 194 pp., photos and drawings. $7.50.
Historical review of British firearms, with much data and illustration of furniture and decoration of fine weapons.

British Smooth-Bore Artillery, by Maj.-Gen. B.P. Hughes. Stackpole Books, Harrisburg, Pa., 1969. 144 pp., illus. $14.95.
On the muzzle-loading artillery of the 18th and 19th centuries, covering dimensions, ammunition, and application.

The British Soldier's Firearm, 1850-1864, by C. H. Roads. Herbert Jenkins, London, 1964. 332 pp., illus. $12.50.
Detailed account of development of British military arms at the acme of the muzzle-loading period. All models in use are covered, as well as ammunition.

The Canadian Gunsmiths 1608-1900, by S. James Gooding. Museum Restoration Service, Canada, 1962. 322 pp., illus. $17.50.
Comprehensive survey of the gunmakers of Canada and the products of their skill, from early settlement to the age of the breech-loader.

Cartridge Headstamp Guide, by H. P. White and B. D. Munhall. H. P. White Laboratory, Bel Air, Md., 1963. 263 pp., illus. $10.00.
An important reference on headstamping of small arms ammo, by manufacturers in many countries. Clear illus. of 1936 headstamps of every type.

Cartridges, by H. C. Logan, Standard Public., Inc., Huntington, W. Va., 1948. 204 pp., illus. $2.98, Deluxe First ed. $10.00.
"Pictorial digest of small arms ammunition," with excellent line illus. and competent text for collectors of obsolete ammunition. In very limited supply, being the scarce out-of-print and best original edition.

Cartridges for Collectors, by Fred A. Datig. Borden Publishing Co., Alhambra, Calif., Vol. I (Centerfire), 1958; Vol. II (Rimfire and Misc. Types, 1963; Vol. III (Additional Rimfire, Centerfire, and Plastic), 1967. Each of the three volumes 176 pp., well illus. and each priced at $7.50.
Vol. III supplements the first two books and presents 300 additional specimens. All illus. are shown in full-scale line drawings.

Cavalry Equipment 1874. A reprint of *U.S. Ordnance Memoranda No. 18* by Francis Bannerman Sons, Blue Point, N.Y., 1969. 119 pp., 12 plates. $6.50.
An officers' report on details of equipment issued to U.S. cavalry units.

Civil War Carbines, by A. F. Lustyik. World Wide Gun Report, Inc., Aledo, Ill., 1962. 63 pp., illus. paper covers. $2.00.
Accurate, interesting summary of most carbines of the Civil War period, in booklet form, with numerous good illus.

Civil War Collector's Encyclopedia, by Francis A. Lord. Stackpole Books, Harrisburg, Pa., 1963. 384 pp., 350 illus. $17.95.
A reference work on Civil War relics, for museums, students, writers, and collectors of Union and Confederate items. Identifies arms, uniforms, accoutrements, ordnance material, currency, postage, etc. Many patent drawings. Lists of manufacturers and vendors, North and South, are given.

Civil War Guns, by Wm. B. Edwards. Stackpole Books, Harrisburg, Pa., 1962. 464 pp., over 400 illus. $15.00.
Comprehensive survey of Civil War arms, identification data, procurement procedures, and historical data. Important information on replicas, imitations, and fakes.

Classic Bowie Knives, by Robert Abels. R. Abels, Inc., N.Y., 1967. 97 pp., illus. with numerous fine examples of the subject. $7.50.
A nostalgic story of the famous blades, with trade adverts on them, and photos of users.

Collecting Duelling Pistols, by W. Keith Neal. Arms and Armour Press, London, 1968 reprint of the 1966 original. 15 pp., 23 plates, paper covers. $2.50.
A monograph on museum-quality duelling pistols. Fine photographic plates.

The Collecting of Guns, ed. by Jas. E. Serven. Stackpole Books, Harrisburg, Pa., 1964. 272 pp., illus. $24.50.
A new and massive compendium of gun lore for serious collectors by recognized experts. Separate chapters cover major categories and aspects of collecting. Over 600 firearms illus. Handsomely designed, deluxe binding in slip case. Reprint of 1966, $5.95.

Collector's Guide to American Cartridge Handguns, by DeWitt E. Sell. Stackpole Books, Harrisburg, Pa., 1963. 234 pp., illus. $3.98.
Catalogs the important U.S. makers in its field, with histories of the firms and their production models. Photos, descriptions and features of many older and current handguns are included.

Collectors' Guns, by Don Myrus. Arco Publ. Co., Inc., New York, 1962. 128 pp., illus. $3.50.
The fascinating story of firearms—from the early hand cannon to the Peacemaker—with over 200 rare photographs and illus.

Colt Firearms from 1836, by James E. Serven. Foundation Press, La Habra, Cal., 1969. 6th printing, 398 pp., very well illus. $19.95.
A dependable survey of the Colt company and its products. In addition to historical data, each Colt model is illus. and described, with production figures.

Colt Gun Book, by Lucian Cary. Arco Publ. Co. Inc., New York, 1961. 142 pp., profusely illus. $3.50.
A Colt picture book, showing the guns and the men who used them, with much data on the noted outlaws and touching on the inventor.

Colt's Variations of the Old Model Pocket Pistol, 1848 to 1872, by P. L. Shumaker. Borden Publishing Co., Alhambra, Calif., 1966. A reprint of the 1957 edition. 150 pp., illus. $6.00.
A useful tool for the Colt specialist and a welcome return of a popular source of information that had been long out-of-print.

The Complete Book of Gun Collecting, by Charles E. Chapel. Coward-McCann, Inc., N.Y.C., 1960. 222 pp., illus. $4.95.
Answers hundreds of questions for the beginner, and is a reference for the advanced collector and student of firearms. It covers hand cannon of the 14th century to arms of the present day.

Confederate Arms, by Wm. A. Albaugh III, and E. N. Simmons. Stackpole Books, Harrisburg, Pa., 1957. 278 pp., illus. $12.50.
Contains much heretofore unpublished information on the arms and associated material of the Confederacy.

Confederate Handguns, by Wm. A. Albaugh III. Hugh Benet Jr., and Edw. N. Simmons. Geo. Shumway, York, Pa., 1963. 272 pp., 125 illus. $16.00.
Every known true Confederate pistol and revolver is described and illus., with the story of its maker and procurement by the C.S.A. Much new information. Includes listing of C. W. makers and dealers, information on replicas and fakes. Indispensable to the collector and student of these arms and their period.

The Crossbow, by Sir Ralph Payne-Gallwey, Bramhall House, New York, 1968. A reprint in facsimile. 328 pp., well illus. including appendices and a treatise on Oriental bows. $4.95.
The standard, respected work on medieval and later military and sporting crossbows—their construction, history and management.

Cut and Thrust Weapons, by E. Wagner. Spring Books, London, 1967. 491 pp., line drawings. $17.50.
English translation of a survey of European edged weapons, their traditions, manufacture, and use.

Deanes' Manual of the History and Science of Fire-arms, by J. Deane. Standard Publications, Huntington, W. Va. 1946 facsimile reprint of the rare English original of 1858. 291 pp., three folding plates. $6.00.
A history of firearms, plus design and manufacture of military and sporting arms.

Digest of Patents Relating to Breech-Loading and Magazine Small Arms (1836-1873), by V. D. Stockbridge, Washington, 1874. Reprinted 1963 by E. N. Flayderman, Greenwich, Conn. 180 pp., 880 illus. $12.50.
An exhaustive compendium of patent documents on firearms, indexed and classified by breech mechanism types. Valuable reference for students and collectors.

Duelling Pistols, by J. A. Atkinson. Stackpole Books, Harrisburg, Pa. 144 pp., illus. (incl. color plates), $12.95.
Account of duelling practice in Great Britain, with data on various types of pistols, their makers, and their users. Memorable duels are recalled, and a bibliography is included.

Early American Gunsmiths 1650-1850, by H. J. Kauffman. Bramhall House, N.Y., 1968. 2nd reprint. 94 pp., illus. $1.98.
A record of the men and the arms they made.

Early Indian Trade Guns—1625 to 1775, by T.M. Hamilton. Museum of the Great Plains, Lawton, Okla. 1969. 34 pp., well illus., paper covers. $2.50.
Detailed descriptions of subject arms, compiled from early records and from the study of remnants found in Indian country.

Early Percussion Firearms, by Lewis Winant. Wm. Morrow & Co., Inc., N.Y.C., 1959. 292 pp., illus. $2.98.
A history of early percussion firearms ignition—from Forsyth to Winchester 44-40, from flintlocks of the 18th century to centerfires. Over 230 illus. of firearms, parts, patents, and cartridges—from some of the finest collections here and abroad.

Edged Weapons, by Fred. Wilkinson. Guinness Signatures, London, 1970. 256 pp., plus 14-page index. Excellently illus., many in full color. $12.95.
Scholarly treatment of all kinds of blades—from flint to steel, rapiers, smallswords, knives, daggers, hunting weapons, polearms, etc., plus construction and decoration.

The Encyclopedia of Military History, by R. Ernest and Trevor N. Dupuy. Harper & Row, New York, N.Y., 1970. 1st ed., 1406 pp., well illus., in line and halftone. $20.00.
This massive single volume covers the subject from 3500 B.C. to the present time. A complete reference guide to the world's military history; narration of war and combat, tactics, strategy and weaponry. Over 250 maps, illus. of weapons, fortifications, etc.

English, Irish and Sottish Firearms, by A. Merwyn Carey. Arco Publishing Co., Inc., N.Y., 1967. A reprint. 121 pp., illus. in line and halftone. $6.50.
Out-of-print since 1954, this work covers the subject from the middle of the 16th century to the end of the 19th.

English Pistols & Revolvers, by J. N. George. Arco Publ. Co., Inc., N.Y.C., 1962. 256 pp., 28 plates. $6.00.
The 2nd reprinting of a notable work first publ. in 1938. Treats of the historical development and design of English hand firearms from the 17th cent. to the present. A much better book than the former reprint, particularly as to clarity of the tipped-in plates.

English Sporting Guns and Accessories, by Macdonald Hastings. Ward Lock & Co., London. 1st ed., 1969. 96 pp., well illus. $4.00.
A delightful monograph on shotguns and accessory equipment for hunting from 1800 to the advent of the breechloader, including historic arms and ammunition.

European & American Arms, by Claude Blair. Batsford. London, and Crown Publ., N.Y.C., 1962, 192 pp., 9" x 12". Profusely and magnificently illus. $6.95.
A complete visual encyclopedia on all sorts of arms of Europe and America with over 600 photographs of pieces from nearly all the major collections of Western Europe, America, and Russia, from about 1100 to 1850. A splendid text describes histroical and technical developments.

European Armour in the Tower of London, by A.R. Dufty. H.M. Stationery Office, London, England, 1968. 17 pp. text, 164 plates. $12.60.
Pictorial record of almost 400 pieces of armor, helmets, and accouterments in the famous Tower of London collection.

European Arms & Armour, by Chas. H. Ashdown. Brussel & Brussel, N.Y., 1967. A reprint. 384 pp., illus. with 42 plates and 450 drawings. $5.95.
Historical survey of body armor up to the era of gunpowder, with some coverage on weapons and early firearms.

European Arms and Armour, Wallace Collection, by Sir James Mann. The Wallace Collection, London, 1962. 2 vols. 714 pp., 208 plates. $15.00.
A new edition of the catalog of an important British collection, containing historical notes and fine illus. Vol. I, on armor; Vol. II on arms of all types and accessory equipment.

European Hand Firearms of the 16th, 17th, and 18th Centuries, by H.J. Jackson and C.E. Whitlaw. Bramhall House, New York, N.Y. A reprint of the noted original. 108 pp., fine photographic plates. $5.95.
A work for scholars and collectors, including a list of arms makers. Not without error.

The Evolution of the Colt, by R. L. Wilson, R. Q. Sutherland, Kansas City, Mo., 1967. 54 pp., illus. $3.00.
Pictures the fine Colt arms of the publisher from percussion to cartridge. Includes a Colt bibliography.

Famous Guns from the Smithsonian Collection, by H. W. Bowman. Arco Publ. Co., Inc., New York, 1967. 112 pp., illus. $3.50.
The finest of the "Famous Guns" series.

Famous Guns from the Winchester Collection, by H. W. Bowman. Arco Publ. Co., N.Y.C., 1958 and later. 144 pp., illus. $3.50.
The gems of the hand and shoulder arms in the great collection at New Haven, Conn.

Feuerwaffen von 1300 bis 1967, by Hans-Bert Lockhoven. International Small Arms Publ., Cologne, W. Germany, 1969. 96 pp., illus. $6.95.
Review of the principal developments in military smallarms from early times. German text.

'51 Colt Navies, by N. L. Swayze. Gun Hill Publ. Co., Yazoo City, Miss., 1967. 243 pp., well illus. $15.00.
The first major effort devoting its entire space to the 1851 Colt Navy revolver. There are 198 photos of models, sub-models, variations, parts, markings, documentary material, etc. Fully indexed.

Firearms Curiosa, by Lewis Winant. Ray Riling, Philadelphia, Pa. 2nd and deluxe reissue 1961, 281 pp., well illus. $8.50.
Two reissues publ. by Bonanza Books, N.Y., 1965. Same size as above, $2.98. A smaller size, 1968. $1.98.
An important work for those with an interest in odd, distinctive and unusual forms and firing

The Firearms Dictionary, by R.A. Steindler. Stackpole Books, Harrisburg, Pa., 1970. 256 pp., nearly 200 illus. $7.95.
A super single-source reference to more than 1800 English and Foreign gun-related words, phrases and nomenclature, etc. Highly useful to all armsmen—collectors, shooters, hunters, etc.

Firearms in England in the Fourteenth Century, by T.F. Tout. Geo. Shumway, York, Pa., 1958. 58 pp., illus., paper covers. $4.00.
Reprint of a 1911 monograph on the history and manufacture of early British firearms, by a distinguished historian.

The Flintlock, Its Origin and Development, by Torsten Lenk; J. T. Hayward, Editor. Holland Press, London, 1964. 192 pp., 134 illus. $6.95.
First English-text version of the 1939 Swedish work termed "the most important book on the subject." Original illus. are reproduced, and a new index and bibliography complete this valuable book.

Flintlock Pistols, by F. Wilkinson. Stackpole Books, Harrisburg, Pa., 1968. 75 pp., illus. $4.95.
Illustrated reference guide by a British authority, covering 17th-19th century flintlock pistols.

Forsyth & Co.—Patent Gunmakers, by W. Keith Neal and D.H.L. Back. G. Bell & Sons, London. 1st ed., 1969. 280 pp., well illus. $12.95.
An excellent study of the invention and development of the percussion system by the Rev. Alexander Forsyth in the early 19th century. All Forsyth types are covered, plus a diary of events from 1768 to 1852.

The French Army in America, by E. P. Hamilton. Museum Restoration Service, Ottawa, 1967. 108 pp., illus. $3.00.
Concise historical coverage, illus. with contemporary documents and manual-of-arms plates. Text in English and French. Paper wrappers.

French Military Weapons, 1717-1938, by James E. Hicks. N. Flayderman & Co., New Milford, Conn. 1964. 281 pp., profusely illus. $9.50.
A valuable reference work, first publ. 1938 as *Notes on French Ordnance,* this rev. ed. covers hand, shoulder, and edged weapons, ammunition and artillery, with history of various systems.

The Fuller Collection of American Firearms, by H. L. Peterson. Eastern National Park & Monument Assn., 1967. 63 pp., illus. $2.50.
Illustrated catalog of principal military shoulder arms in the collection. Decorated paper wrappers.

Gamle Danske Militaervaben, by Th. Moller. Host & Sons, Denmark. 1st reprinting, 1968. 64 pp., well illus. in line. Heavy paper covers. $4.00.
Old Danish military weapons, with Danish and English text, covering weapons from 1791 to 1832, plus accoutrements.

The Gatling Gun, by Paul Wahl & D. R. Toppel. Arco Publ., N.Y.C., 1965. 168 pp., illus. $5.95.
History of the famed rapid-fire weapon used by many of the world's armies and navies from 1861.

German Mauser Rifle—Model of 1898, by J.E. Coombes and J.L. Aney. A reprint in paper covers by Francis Bannerman Sons, New York, N.Y., of their 1921 publication. 20 pp., well illus. $1.50.
Data on the subject weapon and its W. W. I development. Bayonets and ammunition are also described and illus.

German Pistols and Holsters 1934 to 1945, by R.D. Whittington III. Brownlee Books, College Station, Tex., 1969. 1st ed., limited to 2000 numbered copies. 223 pp., well illus., in halftone. $15.00.
A manual for collectors on subject items issued to the military, police and NSDAP. Covers all models of various designs, including those of foreign manufacture.

German Submachine Guns and Assault Rifles. WE, Inc., Old Greenwich, Conn., 1967. 161 pp. $5.95.
Aberdeen Proving Ground reports on over 50 models of World War II German rapid-fire weapons are reprinted.

Die Geschichtliche Entwicklung Der Handfeuerwaffen, by M. Thierbach, Akademische Druck, Graz, Austria, 1965. Vol. I, 590 pp., German text; Vol. II, 36 plates. $37.00.
The famous German work on history and development of firearms, accessories and ammunition, first published in 1886 in Dresden.

A Glossary of the Construction, Decoration and Use of Arms and Armor in all Countries and in all Times, by Geo. C. Stone, Jack Brussel, New York, 2nd reprint, 1966. 694 pp., illus. $9.95.
The outstanding work on its subject, authoritative and accurate in detail. The major portion is on oriental arms.

The Gun and its Development, by W. W. Greener. Bonanza Books, N.Y., 1967. A reprint. 804 pp., profusely illus. $5.95.
A facsimile of the famous 9th edition of 1910. Covers history and development of arms in general, with emphasis on shotguns.

The Gun Collector's Handbook of Values, by C.E. Chapel. Coward-McCann, N.Y.C., 1968. 398 pp., illus. $10.00.
The 8th rev. ed. of the best-known values reference for collectors, with prices for 1969-1970.

Gunmakers of Indiana, by A.W. Lindert. Publ. by the author, Homewood, Ill., 1968, 3rd ed. 284 pp., illus. Large format. $15.00.
An extensive and historical treatment, illus. with old photographs and drawings.

Guns of the Old West, by C. E. Chapel. Coward-McCann Inc., N.Y.C., 1961. 306 pp., illus. $6.95.
A definitive book on American arms that opened the frontier and won the West. Shows arms, rare pictures, advertisements, and pertinent associated material.

Guns Through the Ages, by Geoffrey Boothroyd. Sterling Publ. Co., N.Y.C., 1962. 192 pp., illus. $1.69.
A detailed illustrated history of small arms from the invention of gunpowder to today. Covers ignition methods, proof marks, fakes, ammo, etc. Bibliography.

Haandskydevaabens Bedommelse, by Johan F. Stockel. Udgivet Af Tojuhusmuseet, Copenhagen, Denmark. 2nd.limited reprint, 1966. Vol. I, 397 pp., plus 6 plates, Vol. II, 1080 pp. illus. Both $30.00.
Printed in Danish but considered by scholars to be the finest and most complete source for the "marks" and "touches" of gunmakers. Both are well illus.

Handbuch Der Waffenkunde, by Wendelin Boeheim. Akademische D. u. V., Graz, Austria, 1966. 694 pp., illus. $14.00.
One of the famous works of 1890—long out-of-print. Now in a new printing. German text. Historical weapons and armor from the Middle Ages through the 18th century.

Die Handfeuerwaffen, by Rudolf Schmidt. Vienna, Austria, 1968. Vol. I, text 225 pp., Vol. II, 76 plates. $20.00.
Reprint of an important 1875 German reference work on military small arms, much prized by knowledgeable collectors. The fine color plates in Vol. II show detailed and exploded views of many longarms and handguns.

Henry Deringer's Pocket Pistol, by John E. Parsons. Morrow, N.Y.C., 1952. Over 70 illustrations. $7.50.
An excellent and complete account of this famous maker, coupled with an extensive story on Deringer's imitators, the later cartridge derringers, etc.

Hints to Riflemen, by H. W. S. Cleveland. Distributor, Robert Halter, New Hope, Pa., 286 pp., illustrated. $6.50.
A reprint of the original 1864 edition, to which *Practical Directions for the Use of the Rifle* has been added.

A History of the Colt Revolver, by C. T. Haven and F. A. Belden. Bonanza Books, N.Y., 1967. A reprint. 711 pages large format, profusely illus. in line and halftone. $8.95.
A great and massive work, including details on other Colt arms from 1836 to 1940. A must for every Colt collector.

A History of Firearms, by W. Y. Carman. Routledge & Kegan Paul Ltd., London, England, 1955. 207 pp., illus. $4.50.
A concise coverage, from earliest times to 1914, with emphasis on artillery.

A History of Firearms, by H. L. Peterson. Chas. Scribner's Sons, N.Y.C., 1961. 57 pp., profusely illus. $3.50.
From the origin of firearms through each ignition form and improvement to the M-14. Drawings by Daniel D. Feaser.

History of Modern U.S. Military Small Arms Ammunition, by F. W. Hackley, W. H. Woodin and E. L. Scranton. Macmillan, N.Y.C., 1967. 315 pp., 8½"x11", over 500 exact-scale drawings and 100 photos. $25.00.
A superb work based on years of research by the capable authors. Covers cartridges for handguns, rifles and machine guns; miscellaneous, experimental and unidentified rounds, etc.

A History of Shooting, by Jaroslav Lugs. Spring Books, Feltham, England. 1st printing, 1968. 227 pp., well illus. with contemporary drawings and photographs. $4.98.
Historical survey dealing mainly with marksmanship, duelling and exhibition shooting in Europe and America.

A History of Spanish Firearms, by James D. Lavin. Arco Co., New York, 1965. 304 pp., illus. $9.95.
This history, beginning with the recorded appearance of gunpowder in Spain, traces the development of hand firearms through their golden age — the eighteenth century — to the death in 1825 of Isidro Soler. Copious reproductions of short and long arms, list of gun makers and their "marks" a glossary, bibliography and index are included.

A History of Weaponry, by Courtlandt Canby, Hawthorne Books, Inc., New York, 1963. 112 pp., illus. $2.98.
From the caveman's club to the M-14 rifle, from Greek fire to the ICBM.

The History of Winchester Firearms 1866-1966, ed. by T. E. Hall and P. Kuhlhoff, Winchester-Western Press, New Haven, Conn., 1966. 159 pp., illus. $10.00.
Called the collector's item of the century, this 3d ed. of Geo. R. Watrous' work rises to new glory in its scope and illustrations. Beautifully produced, with a slip case showing old hunting scenes by A. B. Frost and Frederic Remington. Limited ed.

Identifying Old U.S. Muskets, Rifles & Carbines, by Col. A. Gluckman. Stackpole Books, Harrisburg, Pa., 1965. 487 pp., illus. $10.00.
Collector's guide to U.S. long arms, first publ. 1959. Numerous models of each type are described and shown, with histories of their makers.

An Introduction to British Artillery in North America, by S. J. Gooding. Museum Rest. Serv., Ottawa, 1965. 54 pp., illus., Paperbound. $1.50.
Concise account of such equipment used in America 1750-1850.

Japanese Armour, by L. J. Anderson. Stackpole Books, Harrisburg, Pa., 1968. 84 pp., illus. $4.95.
British reference on museum quality armor made by the Myochin and Saotome families between the 15th and 20th centuries.

Japanese Polearms, by R. M. Knutsen. Holland Press, London, 1963. 271 pp., well-illus. Line drawings and photos. $18.00.
Each category of Japanese spear is described and illus. in this hist. treatment, including schools of spear and sword fencing. Lists leading makers and glossary.

Japanese Sword Blades, by Alfred Dobree. George Shumway, York, Pa., 1967. 39 pp., illus., in paper wrappers. $4.50.
A two-part monograph, reprinted from a notable work.

The Kentucky Rifle, by J. G. W. Dillin. Geo. Shumway, York, Pa., 1967. 5th ed. 202 pp., illus. $20.00.
A respected work on the long rifles developed in colonial days and carried by pioneers and soldiers. Much information of value to collectors and historians. Limited ed.

Longrifles of North Carolina, by John Bivins, Jr. Geo. Shumway, York, Pa., 1968. 200 pp., profusely illus. $24.00.
Historical survey of North Carolina gunmakers and their production during the 18th and 19th centuries. Over 400 gunsmiths are included. Fine photographs.

Longrifles of Note, by Geo. Shumway, Geo. Shumway, York, Pa., 1967. 90 pp., illus. Paper covers. $3.95.
A review of 35 fine American long rifles, with detailed illustrations showing their art work, plus descriptive material.

The Luger Pistol, by Fred A. Datig. Privately published, Los Angeles, Calif., 1962. 328 pp. well-illus. $8.50.
Larger, revised ed. of the story behind the most famous pistol of all time.

Manhattan Firearms, by Waldo E. Nutter, Stackpole Books, Harrisburg, Pa., 1958. 250 pp., illus., in halftone. $10.00.
Complete history of the Manhattan Firearms Mfg. Co., and its products. Excellent specialized reference.

The Mantons: Gunmakers, by W. Keith Neal and D. H. L. Back, Walker & Co., New York, 1966. 300 pp., illus. $10.95.
Well-documented account of the life and work of John and Joseph Manton, and others of the British gunmakers. A long list, with serial numbers, etc., of Manton guns, is included.

The Manufacture of Armour and Helmets in 16th Century Japan, by Sakakibara Kozan. Holland Press, London, 1963. 156 pp., 32 pp. of illus. $20.00.
Important reference on styles and steps of making Japanese armor, first publ. Tokyo, 1800. Eng. trans., revised by H. R. Robinson of Tower of London Armouries.

Metal Uniform Insignia of the US Army in the Southwest, 1846-1902, by S. B. Brinckerhoff, Arizona Pioneers Hist. Soc., Tucson, Ariz., 1965. 28 pp., illus. Paper covers. $1.00.
Monograph on buttons, badges, buckles, and other uniform insignia.

Metallic Cartridges, T. J. Treadwell, compiler. The Armoury, N.Y.C., 1959. Unpaginated. 68 plates. Paper, $2.95. Cloth, $5.95.
A reduced-size reproduction of U.S. Ordnance Memoranda No. 14, originally publ. in 1873, on regulation and experimental cartridges manufactured and tested at Frankford Arsenal, Philadelphia, Pa.

Militaria, by Frederick Wilkinson. Hawthorn Books, New York, N.Y., 1969. 1st U.S. ed. 256 pp., well illus. in halftone. $5.95.
Introduction to military items of interest to collectors, including prints, medals, uniforms, military miniatures, weapons, badges etc.

Military Arms of Canada, by Upper Canada Hist. Arms Soc. Museum Restoration Serv., West Hill, Ont., 1963. 43 pp., illus. $1.50.
Booklet cont. 6 authoritative articles on the principal models of Canadian mil. small arms. Gives characteristics of each, makers, quantities produced.

Military Edged Weapons of the World, 1880-1965, by H. A. Maeurer. Mauerer, College Pt., N.Y., 1967. 151 pp., illus. $4.50.
Various swords, blades, etc., in a private collection are dimensioned, described, and photographed. A guide for collectors. Paper wrappers.

Military Headgear in the Southwest, 1846-1890, by S. B. Brinckerhoff, Arizona Pioneers Hist. Soc., Tucson, Ariz., 1963. 16 pp., illus. Paper covers. $1.00.
Historical monograph, reprinted from the journal *Arizoniana*. With bibliography.

Military Sharps Rifles and Carbines, by R. E. Hopkins. Hopkins, Campbell, Calif., 1967. 141 pp., illus. $11.50.
A guide to the principal types, with photographs, patent data, technical details, etc.

Miniature Arms, by Merrill Lindsay. Winchester Press, New York, N.Y., 1970. 111 pp., illus. $8.95.
A concise study of small-scale replicas of firearms and other weapons of collector interest. Fine color photographs.

Montgomery Ward & Co. 1894-95, reproduction of a 600-page catalog, ed. by Jos. J. Schroeder, Jr. Gun Digest Co., Northfield, Ill., 1970. Profusely illus. $4.95.
A nostalgic look at the past, and for the gun enthusiast a look at models and prices prevailing in the late 19th century.

More Single-Shot Rifles, by James J. Grant. Wm. Morrow & Co., Inc., N.Y.C., 1959. 332 pp., illus. $7.50.
In this new work, a companion book to the author's *Single-Shot Rifles,* will be found new facts on U.S. and other single shot arms. 19 pages from a German catalog are featured, plus patent drawings of Borchardt, Farquharson, Henry and others.

Louis Napoleon on Artillery: The Development of Artillery from the 14th to the 17th Century, by W. Y. Carman, Arms and Armour Press, Middlesex, England, 1967. 24 pp., illus. Paper covers. $2.75.
A reprinting of rare original material—10 finely engraved plates, with 70 drawings, on the development of artillery, plus brief text.

The New Highland Military Discipline, by Geo. Grant. Museum Restoration Service, Ottawa, 1967. 32 pp., illus. $1.50.
Reprint of a Scottish drill manual, regimental history, with illus. contemporary and modern. Paper wrappers.

The 9-pdr. Muzzle Loading Rifle, by J. D. Chown. Museum Restoration Service, Ottawa, 1967. 32 pp., Illus. $1.50.
Reprint of an early Canadian artillery manual, with historical notes. Paper wrappers.

Notes on Canadian Shotshells, by N. Krevosheia and A. M. Provick, compilers. N. Krevosheia, Edmonton, Canada, 1967. Paper wrappers, 32 pp., illus. $2.00.
An illustrated handbook for collectors with line drawings and photos of domestic, contract, export and miscellaneous shells and their boxes, etc.

One Hundred Great Guns, by Merrill Lindsay. Walker & Co., N.Y., 1967. 379 pp., fine color illus. $9.95.
Deluxe illus. history of firearms, covering all principal types of small arms and their makers. Bibliography.
A super-deluxe edition is available at $75.00.

Oriental Armour, by W.R. Robinson. Reprint by Outlet Book Co., New York, N.Y., 1970. 256 pp., well illus. $4.95.
Traces the subject material from earliest times until it was finally discarded.

The Original Mauser Magazine Sporting Rifles. Shooter's Bible, S. Hackensack, N.J. 56 pp., illus., paperbound. $1.00.
Facsimile reprint of a Mauser firearms brochure, with English text.

An Outline of the History and Development of Hand Firearms, from the Earliest Period to About the End of the Fifteenth Century, by R.C. Clephan [Original ed., 1906]. A reprint in 1946 by Standard Publications, Inc., Huntington, W.Va. 60 pp., illus. $4.00.
A worthy facsimile of a very scarce, concise and scholarly work.

The Peacemaker and Its Rivals, by John E. Parsons. Morrow, N.Y.C., 1950. 140 pp., illustrated. Appendix, bibilography, and index. $7.50.
Detailed history and development of the Single Action Army Colt, with an over-all study of the six-shooter's significance in American history.

The Pennsylvania-Kentucky Rifle, by Henry J. Kauffman. Bonanza Books, N.Y., 1968. A reprint. 374 pp., illus. $3.95.
A classic work first publ. in 1960 on early long rifles. Makers, descriptions, and manufacturing methods are covered.

Photographic Supplement of Confederate Swords, by Wm. A. Albaugh III. Wm. A Bond, Vernon, Tex., 1963. 205 pp., 300 photos. $6.95.
Over 200 specimens of C. W. edged weapons are shown, with data on their owners and makers. Useful for collectors and students.

The Powder Flask Book, by Ray Riling. Bonanza Books, N. Y. 1968. A reprint. 520 pp., large format, profusely illus. First re-issue of the 1953 original ed. $9.95. A limited number of the originals are available for inscription and autograph at $50.00.
Covers the literature on flasks, their makers, and users—hunters, shooters and the military—as well as showing the arms, cased or not, short and long. A relative price listing for collector advantage is included.

Price List of the U.S. Cartridge Company's Ammunition. A 1969 reprint of the 1891 original, publ. by J.C. Tillinghast, Marlow, N.H. 29 pp., illus., paper covers. $2.50.
Displays many of the now hard-to-find cartridges.

Quellen zur Geschichte der Feuerwaffen, by A. Essenwein [ed./compiler] Akademische Druck, Graz, Austria, 1969. One volume of text [German] plus another of fascinating plates. 178 pp., text and 197 plates. $50.00.
A fine facsimile of a rare and most interesting German source book on the "History of Firearms," taken from original drawings of 1390-1700. A treasury for the serious scholar and/or artillery buff.

The Rampant Colt, by R.L. Wilson. Thomas Haas, Spencer, Ind., 1969. 107 pp., well illus. $10.00.
Study of Samuel Colt's coat-of-arms and the rampant colt figure used on Colt firearms and in advertising.

Rapiers, by Eric Valentine. Stackpole Books, Harrisburg, Pa., 1968. 76 pp., 58 photos., 3 drawings. $4.95.
A desirable monograph, first on its subject, to be publ. in English. Covers methods of authentication, renovation, cleaning and preservation.

Red Coat and Brown Bess, by Anthony D. Darling. Museum Restoration Service, Ottawa, Ontario, Can., 1970. Paper covers, 63 pp., very well illus., in line and halftone. $3.00.
An unusually excellent treatise on the British Army in 1774-1775. Includes detailed text and illus. of various models of the "Brown Bess," plus "Records of the Battles, Sieges and Skirmishes of the American Revolution."

Remington Catalog [price List] of 1885, a reprint in facsimile, by The Wyoming Armory, Inc., Cheyenne, Wyo., 1969. 48 pp., well illus., paper covers. $2.50.
All rifles, handguns, cane gun, sights, cartridges, shotguns, accessories etc. A priced catalog.

Remington Handguns, by C. L. and C. R. Karr. Crown, N.Y.C., 3rd ed., 1956, 60 plates, 166 pp. $2.49.
An enlargement of their fine first edition, the Karrs have added 12 new illustrations and considerable text material. Valuable and informative. The standard reference on Remington pistols.

The Remington Historical Treasury of American Guns, by Harold L. Peterson. Thomas Nelson & Sons, N.Y.C., 1966. 199 pp., illus. $1.95.
A historical saga woven into first-rate Americana through the facts and details of the Remington firm and their products.

The Revolver, Its Description, Management, and Use, by P. E. Dove. Arms and Armour Press, London, 1968. 57 pp., 6 engravings, stiff paper wrappers. $3.75.
A facsimile reprint of a rare classic, dealing principally with the Adams revolver compared to the qualities of the Colt.

Revolving Arms, by A. W. F. Taylerson, Walker and Co., New York, 1967. 123 pp., illus. $8.50.
A detailed history of mechanically-rotated cylinder firearms in Europe and the U.S. Primarily on handguns, but other types of revolving guns are included.

Rifled Infantry Arms, by J. Schon; trans. by Capt. J. Gorgas, USA. Dresden, 1855; facsimile reprint by W. E. Meuse, Schuylersville, N.Y., 1965. 54 pp., illus. $2.50.
Reprint of classic essay on European military small arms of the mid-19th century. Paper covers.

The Rifled Musket, by Claud E. Fuller. Stackpole Books, Harrisburg, Pa., 1958. 302 pp., illus. $4.95.
The authoritative work of the late Claud E. Fuller and basically an account of the muskets whose model dates fell within the Civil War years—1861, 1863 and 1864. Part Two treats of the contract muskets. Some reproduced material, notably Bartlett & Gallatin's "Digest of Cartridges," is almost wholly illegibile, as is much of an 1860 Ordnance Dept. report.

G. Roth Aktiengesellschaft. Horn Co., Burlington, Vt., 1968. 28 pp., illus., paperbound. $2.50.
Reprint of a German cartridge catalog of 1913, with drawings and dimensions.

Royal Sporting Guns at Windsor, by H.L. Blackmore. H.M. Stationery Office, London, England, 1968. 60 pp. text, 52 plates. $9.54.
Catalog of the most decorative and interesting guns in the Royal Armoury collection at Windsor Castle.

Russian Pistols in the 17th Century, by L. Tarassuk. Geo. Shumway, York, Pa., 1968. 35 pp. plus plates. $4.00.
Monograph on museum quality Russian handguns of the 17th century. Fine, detailed photographs.

Samuel Colt Presents. R. L. Wilson, compiler. Wadsworth Atheneum, Hartford, Conn., 1961. 293 pp., profusely illus. $15.00.
Showing and describing a profusion of rare and super-rare museum-quality Colt arms exhibited at the Atheneum, it is one of the most important and desirable books on rare Colt arms.

Samuel Colt's New Model Pocket Pistols, by S. G. Keogh. Priv. publ., 1964. 31 pp., 20 illus., paperbound. $3.00.
"The story of the 1855 Root model revolver," with detailed classification data and descriptions. Well-illus.

The Samurai Swords, by J. M. Yumoto. Tuttle Co., Rutland, Vt., 1958. 191 pp., illus. $4.50.
Detailed information on evaluation of specimens, including origin and development of the Japanese blade.

Savage Automatic Pistols, by James R. Carr. Publ. by the author, St. Charles, Ill., 1967. A reprint. 129 pp., illus. with numerous photos. $6.50.

Collector's guide to Savage pistols, models 1907-1922, with features, production data, and pictures of each. A reprint of the circa 1912 Savage promotional and instructive booklet titled *It Banishes Fear* is recommended to accompany the above. Paper wrappers, 32 pp. $1.50.

Schuyler, Hartley & Graham Catalog. Publ. by Norm Flayderman, Greenwich, Conn., 1961. 176 pp., illus. $9.50.

A reprint of a rare 1864 catalog of firearms, military goods, uniforms, etc. An extensive source of information for Civil War collectors.

Sears, Roebuck & Co. Catalogue No. 117, J.J. Schroeder, ed. A reprint of the 1908 work. Gun Digest Publ., Northfield, Ill., 1969. 1,184 pp., profusely illus., paper covers. $3.95.

This reprint of a famous catalog brings to all arms collectors a treasured replica of the collectibles and prices of yesteryear.

The Sharps Rifle, by W. O. Smith. Morrow, N.Y.C., 1943, reprinted 1965. 138 pp., illus. $8.50.

Study of America's first successful breech-loader patented 1848, with information on its history, development, and operation.

Shosankenshu, by H. L. Joly. Holland Press, London, 1963. Unpaginated. $12.50.

List of Japanese artists' names and kakihan found on sword furniture by the late European authority. Completed in 1919, previously unpubl., this is a facsimile of Joly's MS. and line drawings. Lists nearly 3,000 names.

Shotgun Shells: Identification, Manufacturers and Checklist for Collectors, by F.H. Steward. B. and P. Associates, St. Louis, Mo., 1969. 101 pp., illus., paper covers. $4.95.

Historical data for the collector.

Single Shot Rifles, by Frank de Haas. The Gun Digest Assn., Chicago, Ill., 1968. 288 pp. within decorated paper wrappers, profusely illus. $7.95.

A comprehensive analysis of over 55 significant single shot rifles and actions, replete with mechanical details. Biographies of the inventors, history, pertinent dates and design commentary included.

Single-Shot Rifles, by James J. Grant. Wm. Morrow & Co., N.Y.C., 4th printing 1964. 385 pp., illus. $8.50.

A detailed study of these rifles by a noted collector.

Small Arms, by Frederick Wilkinson, Hawthorne Books, Inc., New York, 1966. 256 pp., illus. $4.95.

A history of small firearms, techniques of the gunsmith, equipment used by combatants, sportsmen and hunters.

Small Arms and Ammunition in the United States Service, 1776-1865, by B.R. Lewis. Smithsonian Inst., Washington, D.C., 1968. 338 pp. plus 52 plates. $10.00.

2nd printing of a distinguished work for historians and collectors. A limited number of deluxe, signed and numbered copies (1st reprinting 1960) are available in full leather and gilt top at $25.

Small Arms Makers, by Robert Gardner. Bonanza Books, N.Y., 1963. 378 pp., illus. with marks and touches in line. $5.95.

A massive directory of makers of firearms, edged weapons, crossbows and polearms, with over 13,000 entries. A useful reference.

Smith and Wesson 1857-1945, by Robert J. Neal and Roy J. Jenks. A. S. Barnes and Co., Inc., N.Y.C., 1966. 500 pp., illus. with over 300 photos and 90 radiographs. $25.00.

A long-needed book, especially for knowledgeable enthusiasts and collectors. Covers an investigation of the series of handguns produced by the Smith and Wesson Company.

The Soldier's Manual, by J. H. Nesmith. (First publ. in Philadelphia in 1824.) Geo. Shumway, York, Pa., 1963. 108 pp., frontis, and 11 color plates. $4.95.

Facsimile reproduction of an important early American militia drill manual, covering exercises with musket, pistol, sword, and artillery. The color plates depict accurately the picturesque uniforms and accoutrements of elite militia corps of Phila. and vicinity. Intro. by Anne S. K. Brown traces the origin of the text matter and the early engravers.

Sporting Guns, by Richard Akehurst. G.P. Putnam's Sons, New York, N.Y., 1968. 120 pp., excellently illus. and with 24 pp. in full color. $5.95.

One of the noted Pleasures and Treasures series. A nostalgic tracing of the history of shooting, and of the guns and rifles used by the sportsman.

Springfield Muzzle-Loading Shoulder Arms, by C.E. Fuller. F. Bannerman Sons, N.Y.C., reprinted 1968. 176 pp., illus. $12.50.

Long-awaited reprint of an important 1930 reference work on weapons produced at Springfield Armory, 1795-1865, including ordnance reports, tables, etc., on flintlock and percussion models.

The Story of Allen and Wheelock Firearms, by H. H. Thomas. C. J. Krehbiel, Cincinnati, 1965. 125 pp., illus. $6.50.

Brief history of the Allen & Wheelock guns produced in mid-19th century, and their maker. Well illus. with descriptions of specimens.

The Story of Pope's Barrels, by Ray M. Smith. Stackpole Books, Harrisburg, Pa., 1964., 211 pp., illus. $10.00.

Detailed account of the achievements and life of Harry M. Pope, master rifle bbl. maker.

Superimposed Load Firearms 1360-1860, by D. R. Baxter. Privately printed for the author in Hong Kong, 1966. $22.00. Foreword by Keith Neal. Ltd. ed., 500 copies only.

Excellently illustrated with photographs, diagrams, figures and patent drawings. Covers over-under arms of all countries, and a list of gunmakers and inventors is included.

Sword, Lance and Bayonet, by Charles ffoulkes and E. C. Hopkinson. Arco Publishing Co., N.Y., 1967. 145 pp., well illus. in line and halftone. $7.50.

A facsimile reprint of the first attempt at a consecutive account of the arms, both general and official use, since the discarding of armor.

The Sword and Same, by Arai Hakuseki & Inaba Tsurio. C. E. Tuttle, Rutland, Vt., 1963. 235 pp., illus. $17.50.

Translation of classic Japanese treatise on the sword, circa 1700. Contains much curious sword-lore, with notes and illus. by the late H. L. Joly.

The 36 Calibers of the Colt Single Action Army, by David M. Brown. Publ. by the author at Albuquerque, N.M., 1965. 222 pp., well-illus. $9.95.

Edited by Bev Mann of *Guns Magazine*. This is an unusual approach to the many details of the Colt S.A. Army revolver. Halftone and line drawings of the same models make this of especial interest.

Thoughts on the Kentucky Rifle in its Golden Age, by Joe Kindig, Jr. George Shumway, York, Pa., 1970. A facsimile reprint of the 1960 original. 561 pp., replete with fine arms and data on many makers. $9.95.

Covers mainly the arms and their makers in the Lancaster area of Pennsylvania. An authoritative work.

Treasury of the Gun, by H. L. Peterson, Crown Publishing Co.'s reprint, N.Y.C., 1965. 252 pp. profusely illus., some in color. $7.95.

A beautiful production, presenting a new high in authoritative text. Virtually every significant type of firearm of the past 650 years is shown.

Underhammer Guns, by H. C. Logan. Stackpole Books, Harrisburg, Pa., 1964. 250 pp. illus. $10.00.

A full account of an unusual form of firearm dating back to flintlock days. Both American and foreign specimens are included.

U.S. Martial and Semi-Martial Single-Shot Pistols, by C. E. Chapel, Coward-McCann Inc., N.Y.C., 1962. 352 pp., over 150 illus. $7.50.

Describes in detail all single shot martial pistols used by the US. armed forces and by military units of the states. A definitive guide.

United States Martial Pistols and Revolvers, by Col. Arcadi Gluckman. Stackpole Books, Harrisburg, Pa., 1939; 3rd printing, 1959. 249 pp. plus appendices and 29 plates. $7.95.

The models from 1799 to 1917 are fully described and identified, including arms of secondary classification and of contract makers.

U.S. Military Firearms, 1776-1956, by Maj. Jas. E. Hicks. J. E. Hicks & Son. La Canada, Calif., 216 pp., incl. 88 pages of fine plates. $12.50.

Covering 180 years of America's hand and shoulder weapons. The most authoritative book on this subject. Packed with official data.

U.S. Sword Bayonets, 1847-1865, by R. V. Davis, Jr. Priv. prt., Pittsburgh, Pa., 1963. 36 pp., 17 pl., paper. $4.00.

Histories, production data, and good photos of U. S. military sword bayonets of Civil War era.

U.S. Weapons Development 1920-25. An abridged reprint from official sources, this Section 1 covering rifles, pistols and some miscellaneous items. Design Publ., Inc. Hyattsville, Md. [circa 1968]. 57 pp., illus., paper covers. $5.00.

Dependable material for the collector and shooter.

A Universal Military Dictionary, by Captain George Smith. The rare original book was published at London in 1779. This facsimile reprint was released in 1869 by Museum Restoration Service, Ottawa, Ontario, Can. 336 pp., 16 fold-out plates. $27.50.

A most useful reference for men of arms interest. Offered only in a numbered, limited issue of 700 copies.

Waffen: Beitrag zur Historischen Waffenkunde, by J.H. Hefner-Alteneck. Akademische Druck, Graz, Austria, 1969. 58 pp., German text plus 100 plates. $30.00.

A descriptive text complements the fine illustrations depicting armor and weapons used in Europe from the middle ages through the 17th century.

Weapons, by E. Tunis. World Publishing Co., N.Y.C., 1954. 153 pp., a large book, well-illus. $4.95.

A pictorial history of arms with complementing narrative. Coverage: from the first tied stone thrown by pre-historic man to super bombs.

Weapons of the British Soldier, by Col. H. C. B. Rogers. Seeley Service & Co., London, 1960. 259 pp., illus. in line and halftone plus full color frontis. $6.50.

The story of weapons used by the British soldier throughout the ages, and the many developments in personal arms during the course of history.

The Webley Story, by Wm. C. Dowell, Skyrac Press, Leeds, Eng. 337 pp., profusely illus. $18.00.

Detailed study of Webley pistols and revolvers, covering over 250 specimens. This important reference also gives detailed listing of English small arms cartridge patents through 1880.

The Whitney Firearms, by Claud Fuller. Standard Publications, Huntington, W. Va., 1946. 334 pp., many plates and drawings. $10.00.

An authoritative history of all Whitney arms and their maker. Highly recommended. Exclusive with Ray Riling Arms Book Co.

Winchester—The Gun That Won the West, by H. F. Williamson. Combat Forces Press, Washington, D. C., 1952. Later eds. by Barnes, N. Y. 494 pp., profusely illus. $5.95.

A scholarly and essential economic history of an honored arms company, but the early and modern arms introduced will satisfy all but the exacting collector.

The Winchester Book, by Geo. Madis. Publ. by the author, Dallas, Tex., 1961. 378 pp., illus. $15.00.

Covers the famous Winchester line in great detail, with many illus. Contains much new information for the collector.

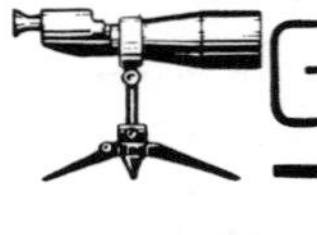

GENERAL

The Adaptable Black Bear, by J. R. Matson. Dorrance & Co., Phila., Pa., 1967. 147 pp., illus. $4.00.

Complete picture of the black bear, its adaptation to environment, habits, disposition and behavior in the wild.

Age of Great Guns, by Frank E. Comparato. Stackpole Books, Harrisburg, Pa. 1965. 386 pp. illus. $11.95.

Of cannon kings and cannoneers who forged the fire-power of artillery. A highly acclaimed work of importance to artillery enthusiasts.

Air Gun Batteries, by E. G. Wolff. Public Museum, Milwaukee, Wisc., 1964. 28 pp., illus., paperbound. 75¢.

Study of discharge mechanisms on reservoir air guns.

Air Organizations of the Third Reich, Volume I, R.J. Bender, compiler. R.J. Bender, Mountain View, Ca, 192 pp., illus., some in color. $9.95.

Concise survey of the World War II Luftwaffe organizations. Shows uniforms, weapons, identification marks and badges.

The Album of Gunfighters, by J. Marvin Hunter and Noah H. Rose, Warren Hunter, Helotes, Texas, 1965. 4th printing. 236 pp., wonderfully illus., with spectacular oldtime photos. $15.00.

For the serious gunfighter fan there is nothing to equal this factual record of the men-behind-the-star and the human targets that they faced.

American Bird Decoys, by W. J. Mackey Jr. Dutton, N.Y.C., 1965. 256 pp., illus. $10.00.

The history and fine points of decoys for all gamebird species, with much data for collectors and hunters.

Covers every article in the 1951-1960 issues of *The American Rifleman*. A valuable tool for location of material published in those years.

Americans and their Guns, compiled by Jas. B. Trefethen, ed. by Jas. E. Serven, Stackpole Books, Harrisburg, Pa., 1967. 320 pp., illus. $9.95.

The National Rifle Association of America story through nearly a century of service to the nation. More than a history—a chronical of help to novice and expert in the safe and proper use of firearms for defense and recreation, as well as a guide for the collector of arms.

America's Camping Book, by Paul Cardwell, Jr. C. Scribner's Sons, New York, N.Y. 1st ed., 1969. 591 pp., well illus., in line and halftone. $10.00.

A fine illustrated guide to camping and woodcraft, with data on equipment, techniques, emergencies and nature study.

The Anatomy of Firearms, by R. L. Wallack. Simon & Schuster, N.Y.C., 1965. 320 pp., illus. $6.95.

Guide to guns of all types, ammunition, ballistics, repairs and adjustments, and related topics.

Animals in Africa, by Peter and Philippa Scott. Clarkson N. Potter, N.Y., 1963. Profusely, magnificently illus. Unpaginated. Large format. $7.95.

The enchanting story, in words and pictures, of a journey by the authors through the National Parks of Kenya to Murchison Falls Park in Uganda. Over 180 pictures in black-and-white, 20 in full color.

Archery, by C. J. Longman and H. Walrond. Frederick Ungar Co., N.Y., 1967. 534 pp., illus. in line and halftone. $5.95.

Reproduction of a standard, important British reference work, first publ. in 1894, on the history, uses and techniques of archery.

Arco Gun Book, ed. by Larry Koller. Arco Publ. Co. Inc., N.Y.C., 1962. 397 pp., illus. $7.50.

A concise encyclopedia for arms collectors, shooters and hunters.

Armour, by Viscount Dillon. Geo. Shumway, York, Pa., 1968. 75 pp., illus., paperbound. $4.00.

Facsimile of British monographs titled *An Elizabethan Armourer's Album* and *Armour Notes.*

Armoured Fighting Vehicles, by Malcolm McGregor, Walker & Co., New York, 1967. 56 pp., illus. $15.00.

Describes 12 tanks and armored cars, representative of those used in the two World Wars. The illustrations in full-color are true scale drawn from actual models.

The Art of Archerie, by Gervase Markham. A reprint of the 1634 original, publ. in London. Geo. Shumway, York, Pa., 1968. 172 pp. $12.00.

This classic treatise, written to keep alive the art of archery in warfare, treats with the making of longbows and their use. A scholarly introduction to the new issue by S. V. Grancsay adds an enlightening historical perception.

The Art and Science of Taking to the Woods, by C.B. Colby and B. Angier, Stackpole Books, Harrisburg, Pa. 1970. 288 pp. illus. $7.95.

Illustrated camper's manual covering all types of outdoor living and transportation, for novice and expert alike.

The Art of Shooting, by C. E. Chapel. Barnes, N.Y.C., 1960. 424 pp., illus. $3.95.

A comprehensive, simplified guide to every aspect of pistol, revolver, and rifle shooting. A history of rifle development is included.

The Art of Survival, by C. Troebst. Doubleday & Co., Garden City, N.Y. 1965. 312 pp. illus. $5.95.

Narratives of devices of survival in difficult terrain or circumstances and evaluation of rescue and life-saving procedures.

The Art of the Decoy: American Bird Carvings, by Adele Earnest. Clarkson N. Potter, Inc., N.Y.C., 1966. $4.95.

The origin of a lost art explained, plus some data on the most famous carvers. Over 106 black-and-white photos, 35 line drawings and an 8-page insert in full color.

Asian Fighting Arts, by D.F. Draeger and R.W. Smith. Kodansha International Ltd., Tokyo, Japan, 2nd printing, 1969. 207 pp., well illus., in line and halftone. $10.00.

A work of monumental research, interesting to all involved in the science of fighting techniques. Covers eleven Asian skills, ranging from Chinese T'ai-chi and Burmese Bando to Japanese Jujitsu and the lethal Pentjak-silak of Indonesia.

Baron von Steuben and his Regulations, by Joseph R. Riling, Ray Riling Arms Books Co., Philadelphia, Penna., 1966. 207 pp., illus. $5.95.

A documented book on this great American Major General and the creation by him of the first official "Regulations." Includes the complete facsimile of these regulations.

Be Expert with Map and Compass, by B. Kjellstrom. Stackpole Books, Harrisburg, Pa., 1967. A reprint. 136 pp., plus practicing compass and protractor. Well illus. in line. $3.95.

Newly revised ed. of the *Orienteering Handbook*. A detailed and helpful work for the outdoorsman.

Better ways of Pathfinding, by R. S. Owendoff. Stackpole, Harrisburg, Pa., 1964. 96 pp., illus. $2.95.

Practical methods of finding one's way in unfamiliar areas, using maps, compass, and the sky.

Bring Your Own Wilderness Doctor, by Dr. E. Russel Kodet and Bradford Angier. Stackpole Books, Harrisburg, Pa., 1968. 127 pp., illus. in line drawings. $3.95.

Called the "outdoorsman's emergency manual" it offers security of knowing what to do best—in case of the worst.

A Bibliography of Military Books up to 1642, by Maurice J. D. Cockle. A new reprint of the Holland Press, London, 1965. 320 pp., illus. $15.00.

Describes the important military books from the invention of gunpowder to subject date. A standard reference.

Birds in Our Lives, ed. by A. Stefferud and A. L. Nelson. Gov't. Prtg. Office, Washington, D. C. 20402, 1966, 576 pp., 80 drawings, 372 photos. $9.00.

61 authors have contributed to this great book, the illus. by Bob Hines. A successful effort to bring any and all readers an appreciation of—and an interest in—the part birds play in their lives.

Black Powder Snapshots, by Herb Sherlock. Standard Publications, Huntington, W. Va. 50 pp., illus. $2.98.

Deluxe large volume containing 23 major Sherlock drawings and 95 punchy, marginal sketches.

The Book of the American West, ed. by Jay Monaghan. Julian Messner, New York, 1963. 608 pp., 200 illus. (many in color). $9.95.

A special chapter on frontier firearms is a feature of this massive work. 10 experts on Western hist. in as many fields of study contributed to the book. Illus. include works by the best contemporary artists.

The Book of the American Woodcock, by Wm. G. Sheldon, Ph.D. University of Mass. Press, Amherst, 1967. 227 pp., bibliography, appendices and index. $8.50.

The Bowmen of England, by D. Featherstone. C. N. Potter, Inc., N. Y., 1967. 200 pp., illus. in line and halftone. $4.50.

The English longbow—its birth, tactical use, years of victory and decline in war. For the serious student and collector.

The Boy's Book of Backyard Camping, by A.A. Macfarlan. Stackpole Books, Harrisburg, Pa. 1st ed. 1968. 160 pp., illus. in line. $4.50.

"How to use at-home space for the development of camping skills." Chapters on tents, equipment, cooking—all for out-of-doors enjoyment.

Boys in the Revolution, by Jack Coggins, Stackpole Books, Harrisburg, Pa., 1967. 96 pp., illus. $4.50.

Young Americans tell their part in the war for independence—what they did, what they wore, the gear they carried, the weapons they used, the ships they sailed on, the campaigns in which they fought.

Buxton's Guide—Foreign Firearms. John S. Herold, Greenwich, Conn., 1963. 300 pp., 745 illus. Paperbound, $2.95.

Lists modern rifles, handguns and shotguns from European and other countries, by makers, including illus., descriptions and prices.

Camper's Digest, by Cecil Coffey. Gun Digest Co., Northfield, Ill. 60093. 320 pp., paper covers, over 500 illus. $4.95.

Everything needed to be known about camping. Trails, tools, clothes, cooking, hundreds of camp grounds listed, and more.

The Camping Manual, compiled by Fred Sturges, Stackpole Books, Harrisburg, Pa., 1967. 160 pp., illus. $3.95.

An excellent refresher on the fundamentals, with a digest of the newest methods and latest advice for those who want to enjoy camping more.

Carbine Handbook, by Paul Wahl. Arco Publ. Co., N.Y.C., 1964. 80 pp., illus. Paperbound, $6.00.

A manual and guide to the U.S. Carbine, cal. .30, M1, with data on its history, operation, repair, ammunition, and shooting.

The Classic Decoy Series, Ed Zern, text; M.C. Weiller, illustrator. Winchester Press, New York, N.Y. 1969. A beautiful work picturing 24 American duck decoys in full color, printed on special paper and loose for framing. Decorated covers in slip case. Anecdotal text on each species shown. $100.00.

This deluxe collectors' work is offered in a strictly limited issue of 1000 copies, each signed by the artist and numbered.

A Colt Bibliography, by G.M. Lord. Privately produced by the author, Bothell, Wash., 1968. 32 pp., mimeographed stapled sheets. $3.00.

Lists articles, books, etc., of interest to the Colt collector, gunsmith and or historian.

Complete Book of Rifles and Shotguns, by Jack O'Connor. Harper & Bros., N.Y.C., 1961. 477 pp., illus. $6.95.

A splendid two-part book of encyclopedic coverage on every detail of rifle and shotgun.

Complete Book of Shooting, by Jack O'Connor et al. Outdoor Life—Harper & Row, N.Y.C., 1965. 385 pp., illus. $5.95.

Fundamentals of shooting with rifle, shotgun, and handgun in the hunting field and on target ranges.

Coping with Camp Cooking, by M.W. Stephens and G.S. Wells. Stackpole Books, Harrisburg, Pa. 1966. 94 pp., illus., decorated boards. $2.95.

Hints and recipes selected from the editors' writings appearing in *Camping Guide Magazine*.

Crusade for Wildlife, by J.B. Trefethen. Stackpole Books, Harrisburg, Pa., 1961. 377 pp., illus. $7.50.

History of the Boone and Crockett Club and its efforts to preserve wildlife in America, with accounts of the plight of threatened species.

Current American War Medals and Decorations, 1963-69, by E.E. Kerrigan. Medallic Publishing Co., Noroton Heights, Conn. 1st ed. 1969. Paper covers, 23 pp., illus. $3.00.

This supplement updates the author's *American War Medals and Decorations,* listing recently created awards and recipients.

The Daggers and Edged Weapons of Hitler's Germany, by Maj .J. P. Atwood. Publ. privately for the author in Berlin, Germany, 1965. 240 pp. illus. New edition, 1967. $15.00.

Lavishly illus. with many plates in full color, this is an outstanding production, easily the best information (for the collector) on the subject.

Daggers and Fighting Knives of the Western World: From the Stone Age Until 1900, by Harold L. Peterson, Walker and Co., New York, 1967. 256 pp., illus. $2.98.

The only full-scale historical and analytical work on this subject, from flint knives of the stone age to British and American naval dirks.

Decoys and Decoy Carvers of Illinols, by P.W. Parmalee and F.D. Loomis. Northern Illinois University Press, DeKalb, Ill. 1st ed., 1969, 506 pp., illus. $17.50.

A comprehensive and handsome survey, replete with photographs—many in color. The work of the makers is analyzed, with comments on Illinois duck shooting over the past century.

Design and Development of Fighting Vehicles, by R. M. Ogorkiewicz. Doubleday, N.Y.C., 1968. 208 pp. plus 174 plates. $7.95.

A review of design and engineering problems of battle tanks and other armored vehicles since World War II, with evaluations of tank design.

Die Handwaffen, by Werner Eckardt and Otto Morawietz. H. G. Schulz, Hamburg, 1957. 265 pp., 15 plates, 175 illus. $10.00.

An important work (in German) on German Service arms from their beginnings through World War II. A symposium on the subject—ancient, obsolete, semi-modern and modern.

Eat the Weeds, by B.C. Harris. Barre Publ., Barre, Mass., 1968. 223 pp., illus. $5.95.

Practical directions for collecting and drying herbs, for using edible plants and fruits as food and for medical purposes or as substitutes for cultivated vegetables.

Encyclopedia of Firearms ed. by H. L. Peterson. E. P. Dutton, N.Y.C., 1964. 367 pp., 100 pp. of illus. incl. color. $13.50.

Fine reference work on firearms, with articles by 45 top authorities covering classes of guns, manufacturers, ammunition, nomenclature, and related topics.

Encyclopedia of Modern Firearms, Vol. I, compiled and publ. by Bob Brownell, Montezuma, Iowa, 1959. 1057 pp. plus index, illus. $20.00. Dist. by the Gun Digest Co.

Massive accumulation of basic information on nearly all modern arms pertaining to "parts and assembly." Replete with arms photographs, exploded drawings, manufacturers' lists of parts, etc.

Explosives and Demolitions, U.S. Field Manual 5-25, Normount Armament Co., Forest Grove, Ore. 215 pp., illus., paperbound. $4.00.

A reprint of the Army FM dated 14 May 1959.

Fell's Guide to Guns and How to Use Them, by B.G. Wels. Frederick Fell, New York, N.Y. 1969. 173 pp., illus. in line and halftone. $4.95.

Aspects of the safe use of firearms for sportsmen, hunters and collectors.

Firearms, by H. L. Blackmore. E. P. Dutton, N.Y.C., 1964. 160 pp., well-illus., paperbound. $1.75.

Firearms history from its beginnings to recent times. Fine photographs of museum-quality arms.

Firearms, by Walter Buehr. Crowell Co., N.Y.C., 1967. 186 pp., illus. $5.95.

From gunpowder to guided missile, an illustrated history of firearms for military and sporting uses.

Firearm Silencers, by D. B. McLean. Normount Armament Co., Forest Grove, Ore., 1968. 123 pp., illus., paperbound. $4.00.

The history, design, and development of silencers for U.S. military firearms.

Firearms, Traps & Tools of the Mountain Men, by Carl P. Russell. A. A. Knopf, N.Y., 1967. 448 pp., illus. in line drawings. $12.50.

Detailed survey of fur traders' equipment in the early days of the west.

The Fireside Book of Guns, by Larry Koller. Simon & Schuster, N.Y.C., 1959. 284 pp., illus. in artistic photography and full-color plates. $12.95.

On all counts the most beautiful and colorful production of any arms book of our time, this work adequately tells the story of firearms in America—from the first explorers to today's sportsmen.

Four Studies on the History of Arms, by Arne Hoff, et al. Tojhusmuseet, Copenhagen, 1964. 145 pp., illus., paperbound $6.75.

A Danish museum publication containing in English text scholarly monographs on arms topics of historic interest.

Free for the Eating, by Bradford Angier, Stackpole Books, Harrisburg, Pa., 1966. 191 pp., illus. $4.95.

Discusses and illustrates 100 wild plants and 300 ways to use them.

More Free for the Eating, Wild Foods, by Bradford Angier, Stackpole Books, Harrisburg, Pa., 1969. 192 pp., illus. $4.95.

A sequel to *Free for the Eating,* being a nature-study cookbook with an additional 200 ways to prepare common wild plants.

The A. B. Frost Book, by Henry M. Reed. Charles E. Tuttle Co., Rutland, Vermont, 1967. 149 pp., of large format with over 70 plates, 44 in color, and many line drawings. $20.00.

A collection of the sketches, drawings and paintings by a famous outdoor artist (1851-1928). Includes his noted sporting and shooting masterpieces.

Fundamentals of Small Arms, U.S. TM9-2205. Normount Armament Co., Forest Grove, Ore. 236 pp., illus., paperbound. $3.50.

Reprint of the U.S. Army technical manual dated 7 May 1952.

Game Animals, by Leonard Lee Rue III. Harper & Row, N. Y., 1968. 655 pp., incl. appendix and index. Illus. with maps and photos. $6.50.

A concise guide to and field book of North American species.

Game and Fish Cookbook, by H. and J. Barnett. Grossman Publ., New York, N.Y. 1968, 162 pp., illus. $7.95.

Special culinary attention to fish and game, with interesting and different touches.

Game in the Kitchen, by B. Flood and W.C. Roux (eds.). Barre Publ., Barre, Mass. 1st ed., 1968, 234 pp., illus. $7.50.

A fish and game cookbook, with menus and information on preservation, cooking and serving.

Gas, Air and Spring Guns of the World, by W. H. B. Smith. Stackpole Books, Harrisburg, Pa., 1957. 279 pp., well illus. $10.00.

A detailed, well-documented history of the air and gas gun industry throughout the world. It includes ancient and modern arms, and it devotes a chapter to accurate velocity tests of modern arms.

German Infantry Weapons, ed. by D.B. McLean. Normount Armament Co., Forest Grove, Ore., 1966. 191 pp., illus., paperbound. $3.00.

World War II German weapons described and illustrated, from military intelligence research.

German Infantry Weapons of World War II, by A.J. Barker. Arco Publ. Co., New York, N.Y. 1969, 76 pp., illus. $3.50.

Historical and statistical data on all types of the subject weapons, ammunition, etc.

German Mauser Rifle, Model of 1898, by Coombes & Aney. F. Bannerman, N.Y.C., 1921. 20 pp., illus., paperbound. $1.50.

Reprint of a pamphlet describing a famous military rifle, its bayonets, ammunition, and accessories.

German Tanks of World War II, by F.M. Von Senger und Etterlin. Stackpole Books, Harrisburg, Pa., 1969. 176 pp., nearly 300 photos and drawings. Large format. $11.95.

A fully illustrated and definitive history of German armoured fighting vehicles, 1926-1945. Written in English.

German Weapons-Uniforms-Insignia 1841-1918, by Maj. J. E. Hicks. J. E. Hicks & Son, La Canada, Calif., 1958. 158 pp., illus. $6.00.

Originally published in 1937 as *Notes on German Ordnance 1841-1918,* this new edition offers the collector a wealth of information gathered from many authentic sources.

The Golden Guide to Guns, by Larry Koller. Golden Press, N.Y.C., 1966. 160 pp., illus., paperbound, pocket-size. $1.00.

Introduction to rifles, shotguns, and handguns for all uses. Profusely illus., much in color.

Gourmet Cooking for Free, by Bradford Angier. Stackpole Books, Harrisburg, Pa. 1970. 190 pp. illus. $4.95.

Cookery of large and small game, seafood and wild plants.

Great American Guns and Frontier Fighters, by Will Bryant, Grosset & Dunlap, New York, 1961. 160 pp., illus. $3.95.

Popular account of firearms in U.S. history and of the events in which they played a part.

Great Weapons of World War II, by J. Kirk and R. Young. Bonanza Books, N.Y., 1968. 348 pp., profusely illus. The latest reprint. $4.95.

Covers, in text and picture, great and powerful weapons, planes, tanks as well as small arms, miscellaneous arms and naval attack vessels.

The Gun Digest, 1944 First Annual Edition, ed. by John T. Amber. Follett Publ. Co., Chicago, Ill., 1944, 1963. 162 pp., illus., paperbound $2.95.

Reprint edition of the prized first edition of *The Gun Digest.* Many useful articles on small arms and their uses.

Gun Digest, 24th ed., 1970, ed. by John T. Amber. Gun Digest Co., Chicago, Ill., 1969, 416 pp., profusely illus. $4.95.

Known as the world's greatest gun book because of its factual, informative data for shooters, hunters, collectors, reloaders and other enthusiasts. Truly of encyclopedic importance. Decorated paper wrappers.

Gun Digest Treasury, ed. by J. T. Amber. 3rd edition, 1966. Gun Digest Co., Chicago, Ill. 416 pp., illus. Paperbound $4.95, Hardbound $7.95.

The best from 20 years of the GUN DIGEST, selected from the annual editions.

Gun Fun with Safety, by G.E. Damon. Standard Publications, Huntington, W. Va., 1947. 206 pp., well illus. $6.00.

A long out-of-print work that is still much sought. A fine general coverage of arms and ammunition, old and new, with chapters on shooting, targets, etc., with safety always upper-most.

The Gun that Made the Twenties Roar, by W.J. Helmer. Macmillan Co., N.Y. 1969. 286 pp. illus. $5.95.

Historical account of John T. Thompson and his invention, the Thompson submachine gun. Includes virtually a complete manual in detail.

Gun Trader's Guide, by Paul Wahl, Shooter's Bible, Inc., New York, 1968. 5th rev. ed. 220 pp., 8″x10″, profusely illus. Paperbound. $3.95.

Complete guide to the identification of modern firearms and giving their current market values.

The Gunfighter, Man or Myth?, by Joseph G. Rosa, Oklahoma Press, Norman, Okla., 1969. 229 pp., illus., (including weapons). $5.95.

A well-documented work on gunfights and gunfighters of the West and elsewhere. Great treat for all gunfighter buffs.

The Gunner's Bible, by Bill Riviere. Doubleday, N.Y.C., 1965. 192 pp., illus. Paperbound. $1.95.

General guide to modern sporting firearms and their accessories, for all shooters.

Gunology, by P. M. Doane. Winchester-Western, N.Y.C., 1968. 64 pp., illus., paperbound. $2.95.

A comprehensive course for professional sporting arms salesmen. Of great help to the arms man are the hundreds of questions on arms and hunting.

Guns, by Dudley Pope. Delacorte Press, N.Y.C., 1965. 256 pp., illus. $9.98.

Concise history of firearms, stressing early museum-quality weapons. Includes small arms as well as artillery, naval, and airborne types. Fine photographs, many in color.

Guns & Ammo 1970 Annual, Guns & Ammo magazine, Petersen Publ. Co., Los Angeles Ca., 1969. 378 pp. illus. Paper covers. $3.95.

Annual catalog of sporting firearms and accessories, with numerous articles for gun enthusiasts.

Guns Annual for 1971, edited by Jerome Rakusan, Publishers Development Corp., Skokie, Ill., 1970. 116 pp., well illus., decorated paper wrappers. $2.00.

An annual publication describing and illustrating firearms available in current markets, plus articles by experts in the field of collecting, shooting, ammunition, etc.

Guns Illustrated 1971, 3d ed., Gun Digest Publ., Northfield, Ill. 1970. 224 pp., Profusely illus., paper covers. $2.95.

Revised and up-dated with latest models, prices, specifications and data on handguns, rifles, shotguns, scopes, sights, etc.

Guns and Rifles of the World, by Howard L. Blackmore, The Viking Press, New York, 1965. 290 pp. 1042 halftone and line illustrations. $30.00.

One of the finest books to come out of England. Covers firearms from the handgun to air, steam, and electric guns.

Guns and Shooting, by Maj. Sir Gerald Burrard. Barnes & Co., N.Y.C., 1962. 147 pp. $1.95.

Expanded from the author's earlier *In the Gunroom,* this contains 153 often-asked questions on shotguns and rifles, with authoritative answers covering guns, ammunition, ballistics, etc.

Guns and Shooting, a Bibliography, by R. Riling. Greenberg, N.Y.C., 1951. 434 pp., illus. $20.00.

A selected listing, with pertinent comment and anecdote, of books and printed material on arms and ammunition from 1420 to 1950.

The Guns of Harpers Ferry, by S.E. Brown Jr. Virginia Book Co., Berryville, Va., 1968. 157 pp., illus. $12.50.

Catalog of all known firearms produced at the U.S. armory at Harpers Ferry, 1798-1861, with descriptions, illustrations and a history of the operations there.

Handbook on German Military Forces, a reprint of *TM-E30-451,* originating with U.S. Military Intelligence. Publ. by the Military Press, Gaithersburg, Md. 1970. 550 pp., copious illus., many in color. $14.95.

A rare restricted handbook [many destroyed] covering military systems, doctrines, SS police, home defense, etc.

Handbook on Japanese Military Forces, a reprint of *TM-E30-480,* originating with U.S. Military Intelligence. Publ. by the Military Press, Gaithersburg, Md., 1970. 550 pp., illus., 24 pp., in color. $14.95.

A rare restricted work [many destroyed] on military systems, doctrines, police, home defense. etc.

Handbook of Self-Defense for Law Enforcement Officers, by John Martone. Arco Publ. Co., New York, N.Y., 1968. 1st ed., 4th printing, 111 pp., $3.50.

A clearly-illustrated manual on offensive and defensive techniques recommended for the use of policemen.

Hatcher's Notebook, by Maj. Gen. J. S. Hatcher. Stackpole Books, Harrisburg, Pa., 1952. 2nd ed. with four new chapters, 1957. 629 pp., illus. $10.00.

A dependable source of information for gunsmiths, ballisticians, historians, hunters, and collectors.

A History of Knives, by Harold L. Peterson. Charles Scribner's Sons, N.Y.C., 1966. 64 pp., illus. $3.50.

The fine drawings of Daniel D. Feaser combine with the author's commendable text to produce an important work. From the earliest knives of prehistoric man through the evolution of the metal knife.

History of Small Arms Ammunition 1917-19. A reprint of an official U.S. Ordnance source work, *circa* 1920. Design Publ., Hyattsville, Md. Reprinted 1968. 40 pp., illus., paper covers. $5.00.

Another scarce work for the seeker of authoritative material.

A History of War and Weapons, 449 to 1660, by A. V. B. Norman and D. Pottinger. Thomas Y. Crowell Co., N.Y., 1966. 224 pp., well illus. with sketches. $6.95.

An excellent work for the scholar on the evolution of war and weapons in England. Many sketches of arms and weapons of all sorts add importance.

The History of Weapons of the American Revolution, by Geo. C. Neumann. Harper & Row, N.Y., 1967. 373 pp., fully illus. $15.00.

Collector's reference covering long arms, handguns, edged and pole weapons used in the Revolutionary War.

Home in Your Pack, by Bradford Angier, Stackpole Books, Harrisburg, Pa., 1965. 192 pp., illus. $4.50.

An outdoorsman's handbook on equipment, woodcraft, and camping techniques.

Horse Equipments and Cavalry Accoutrements 1891. A reprint of U.S. Ordnance Memoranda No. 29 by Francis Bannerman Sons, Blue Point, N.Y., 1969. 23 pp., plus 20 plates. $3.50.

U.S. army cavalry equipment described and illustrated in line.

How to Build Your Home in the Woods, by Bradford Angier, Stackpole Books, Harrisburg, Pa., 1967. 310 pp., illus. $6.00.

Detailed instructions on building cabins, shelters, etc., with natural materials. How to obtain food from nature, and how to live in the wilderness in comfort.

How to Defend Yourself, your Family, and your Home, by Geo. Hunter. David McKay, N.Y.C., 1967, 307 pp., illus. $6.95.

The only book available for the public at large that advocates their ownership of firearms—including handguns. Covers laws of self-defense, setting up home protection, and much else.

How to Live in the Woods on $10.00 a Week, by Bradford Angier, Stackpole Books, Harrisburg, Pa., 1959. 269 pp., illus. $5.00.

Modern-day homesteading explained by an expert; where to go and how to achieve freedom and comfort on today's frontiers.

Indian and Oriental Armour, by Lord Egerton of Tatton. Stackpole Books, Harrisburg, Pa., 1968. 178 pp., well illus., some in color. $14.95.

New edition of a rare work which has been a key reference for students of the subject, plus a creditable source on Oriental history.

Infantry Equipment 1875. A reprint of U.S. Ordnance Memoranda No. 19 by Francis Bannerman Sons, Blue Point, N.Y., 1969. 62 pp., plus 9 plates. $6.50.

A report covering materials, supplies, etc., to outfit troops in field and garrison.

Instinct Shooting, by Mike Jennings. Dodd, Mead & Co., N.Y.C., 1959. 157 pp., 20 line drawings, illus. $3.75.

All about Lucky McDaniel and his surprisingly successful discovery of a new aerial shooting technique, one which will let almost anyone, novices *preferred*, hit flying targets with only minutes of instruction.

Introduction to Muzzle Loading, by R. O. Ackerman. Publ. by the author, Albuquerque, N.M., 1966. 20 pp., illus. with author's sketches. $1.50.

This booklet, in paper wrappers, will be Book No. 1 of a projected series. Contains a glossary of muzzle loading terms, and is aimed at the novice.

An Introduction to Tool Marks, Firearms and the Striagraph, by J.E. Davis. Chas. C. Thomas, Springfield, Ill., 1st ed., 1958. 282 pp. $8.50.

Textbook on micro-contour analysis in criminalistics, with emphasis upon the striagraph in analysis of evidence.

Ironmaker To The Confederacy, by C. B. Dew. Yale Univ. Press, New Haven, 1966. 345 pp., illus. $10.00.

History of Joseph R. Anderson's Tredegar Iron Works in Richmond, Va., which produced weapons and military equipment essential to the Confederacy's armed forces.

Japanese Infantry Weapons, ed. by D.B. McLean. Normount Armament Co., Forest Grove, Ore., 1966. 241 pp., well illus., paperbound. $3.50.

Survey of World War II Japanese weapons, based on military intelligence research.

The Japanese Sword and Its Fittings, by members of the Japanese Sword Society of New York. Cooper Union Museum, N.Y.C., 1966. Paper covers. 26 pp. of text plus many illus. $3.50.

The authoritative text in the form of a catalog describing the illus. of items in the possession of members of the society.

Johnson Rifles and Light Machine Guns, ed. by D.B. McLean. Normount Armament Co., Forest Grove, Ore., 1968. 55 pp., illus., paperbound. $2.00.

Manual on the only recoil-operated auto-loading rifle issued to U.S. forces.

Knife Throwing as a Modern Sport, by H. K. McEvoy and C. V. Gruzanski. Charles C. Thomas, Springfield, Ill., 1965. 57 pp., illus. $4.50.

For first time, a concise, easy-to-read and complete story on this modern sport.

A Knight and His Armour, 95 pp. $3.25.
A Knight and His Castle, 108 pp., $3.25.
A Knight and His Horse, 96 pp., $3.25.
A Knight and His Weapons, 95 pp., $3.25.

A series planned for young readers, by R. E. Oakeshott. Lutterworth Press, London, 1966. All illus. Of interest to adults as well.

Lewis Automatic Machine Gun, publ. originally by Savage Arms Co., Utica, N.Y. A reprint by L.A. Funk, Puyallup, Wash., 1969. 47 pp., illus., paper covers. $1.50.

This facsimile covers the Model 1916 gun, explaining all features of operation, action, nomenclature, stripping and assembly.

Marlin Catalog of 1897. A reprint in facsimile by the Wyoming Armory, Inc., Cheyenne, Wy. 1969. 192 pp. Well illus., paper covers, $3.50.

All models are covered, cartridges, sights, engraving, accessories, reloading tools, etc.

Mexican Military Arms, The Cartridge Period, by James B. Hughes, Jr. Deep River Armory, Inc., Houston, Texas, 1967. 135 pp., photos and line drawings. $4.50.

An interesting and useful work, in imprinted wrappers, covering the period from 1866 to 1967.

Military Uniforms of the World in Color, by Preben Kannik, translated by W. Y. Carman. MacMillan Co., N.Y., N.Y., 1968. 278 pp. incl. index, 512 illus. figures in full color. $4.95.

An excellent handbook for the collector and student. The descriptive text gives good details of equipment.

The Minute Men, by J.R. Galvin. Hawthorn Books, N.Y.C., 1967. 286 pp. $6.95.

History of the colonial militia to the beginning of the Revolutionary War, including data on the battles of Lexington and Concord.

Modern ABC's of Bow and Arrow, by G. H. Gillelan. Stackpole Books, Harrisburg, Pa., 1967. 160 pp., illus. $4.95.

Survey of techniques for beginners and experts in target archery as well as bowhunting.

Modern ABC's of Guns, by R. A. Steindler. Stackpole Books, Harrisburg, Pa. 1965. 191 pp., illus. $4.95.

Concise lexicon of today's sporting firearms, their components, ammution, accessory equipment and use.

Modern Police Firearms, by Duke Roberts and A.P. Bristow. Glencoe Press, Beverly Hills, Ca., 1969. 170 pp., illus., in line and halftone. $5.95.

An informative work covering all pertinent details, with chapters on safety, ballistics, maintenance, marksmanship, chemical agents, the shotgun, plus legal and ethical aspects.

The New Way of the Wilderness, by Calvin Rutstrum. Macmillan Co., New York, N.Y. 1st ed. 1966 [4th printing]. 276 pp., illus. in line. $4.95.

An outdoorsman's manual on traveling and living in the open, with chapters on transportation, equipment, food, hunting and fishing for food.

L. D. Nimschke, Firearms Engraver, by R. L. Wilson. John J. Malloy, publisher, Teaneck, N.J., 1965. Quarto, 107 pp., profusely illus. $17.50.

Showing a wide variety of designs, initials and monograms and ever-so-many portions of collectors' arms. A thoroughly interesting work for the collector and an inspiration to the engraver.

No Second Place Winner, by Wm. H. Jordan, publ. by the author, Shreveport, La. (Box 4072), 1962. 114 pp., illus. $5.00.

Guns and gear of the peace officer, ably discussed by a U.S. Border Patrolman for over 30 years, and a first-class shooter with handgun, rifle, etc.

The Other Mr. Churchill, by Macdonald Hastings. Dodd Mead, N.Y.C., 1965. 336 pp., illus. $1.98.

Important biography of a great London gunmaker and forensic ballistics expert, who contributed much to the color and excellence of British firearms tradition.

Pageant of the Gun, by Harold L. Peterson. Doubleday & Co., Inc., Garden City, N. Y., 1967. 352 pp., profusely illus. $5.95.

A storehouse of stories on firearms, their romance and lore, their development and use through 10 centuries. A most satisfying history of firearms chronologically presented.

Paradise Below Zero, by Calvin Rutstrum. Macmillan Co., New York, N.Y. 1st ed., 1968. 244 pp., illus. in line and halftone. $5.95.

On the rewards and methods of camping and travel in Eskimo country, including check lists of provisions, tools, equipment, clothing and ways of getting about.

Picture Book of the Continental Soldier, by C.K. Wilbur. Stackpole Books, Harrisburg, Pa., 1969. 96 pp., well illus. $4.95.

A wealth of detailed material in text and fine drawings, depicting Revolutionary War weapons, accouterments, field equipment, and the routine of the soldier's life. Included are artillery, edged weapons, muskets, rifles, powder horns, etc.

Pistols, Rifles and Machine Guns, by W.G.B. Allen. English Universities Press, London, 1953. 178 pp., illus. $4.50.

A straightforward explanation of the principles that govern the operation of small arms, in simple, non-technical language.

Pocket Guide to Archery, by H.T. Sigler. Stackpole Co., Harrisburg, Pa., 1960. 96 pp., illus. $2.95.

Useful introduction to the subject, covering equipment, shooting techniques, and bow hunting of small game and deer.

Reading the Woods, by Vinson Brown. Stackpole Books, Harrisburg, Pa. 1969. 160 pp. illus. $5.95.

Clues to the past, present and future development of wooded areas by observation of signs of change, decoy, influences of water and wildlife, and the impact of man's presence.

The Records and Badges of Every Regiment and Corps in the British Army, by H.M. Chichester and Geo. Burges-Short. Fred. Muller, Ltd., London, 1970. A reprint of the 2nd ed. of 1900. 240 illus., in the text and 24 color plates. $27.50.

A magnificent facsimile with gilt top giving the history, uniforms, colors and insignia in satisfying detail of much-wanted data on subject.

The Redbook of Used Gun Values 1970, publ. by Publishers Dev. Corp., Skokie, Ill., 1969. 119 pp., illus., paper covers. $2.50.

Lists many types and modifications of rifles, shotguns and handguns, arranged by makers, with prices estimated according to condition.

Riot Control—Materiel and Techniques, by Rex Applegate. Stackpole Books, Harrisburg, Pa. 1969. 320 pp., illus. $9.95.

Originally released as *Kill or Get Killed*, later as *Crowd and Riot Control*. Designed for law officer training, plus deployment of personnel, chemicals and special equipment for best results.

Round Shot and Rammers, by H. L. Peterson. Stackpole Books, Harrisburg, Pa., 1969. 128 pp., illus. $9.95.

Artillery in America through the Civil War years, with much detail on manufacture, history, accessory equipment, and use of all types of cannon. Fine line drawings show the guns, their equipment, and the men who used them.

Second World War Combat Weapons, by Hoffschmidt & Tantum. WE, Inc., Old Greenwich, Conn., 1968. 212 pp., illus. $7.95.

German weapons, vehicles, and projectiles illustrated and described. First of a 7-vol. series.

Secret Fighting Arts of the World, by J. F. Gilbey. Tuttle, Rutland, Vt., 1963. 150 pp., illus. $3.75.

20 chapters on advanced techniques of unarmed combat, described in anecdotal form.

Shooter's Bible, No. 61, John Olson, ed. Shooter's Bible, Inc., S. Hackensack, N. J., 1970. 576 pp., illus. $3.95.

An annually-published guide to firearms, ammunition, and accessories.

Shooter's Bible Game Cook Book, by Geraldine Steindler. Follett Publ. Co., Chicago, Ill. 1965. 224 pp., illus., cloth, $6.95; paper, $3.95.

Full information on preparing game for the table, including recipes and methods of field-dressing.

Shooter's Bible Gun Trader's Guide, by Paul Wahl. Shooter's Bible, S. Hackensack, N.J., 5th edition, 1968. 220 pp., illus., paperbound. $3.95.

Revised guide to market values of modern firearms, with identification data on U.S. and imported guns.

Shooting Muzzle Loading Hand Guns, by Charles T. Haven. Guns Inc., Massachusetts, 1947. 132 pp., illus. $6.50.

A good summary of shooting methods, both contemporary and modern. Duelling with M.L. handguns is also covered.

The Shorebirds of North America, by Peter Matthiesen, ed. by Gordon Stout, with species accounts by R. S. Palmer. Viking Press, N.Y.C., 1967, 288 pp., 32 6-color plates, 10"x14", $22.50. De Luxe ltd. ed., extra bound, $50.00.

A magnificent book, probably the outstanding work on the shorebirds of the nothern western world. 32 chapters cover 59 species. The illustrations are superb.

Six-guns and Saddle Leather, by Ramon F. Adams. University of Oklahoma Press, Norman, Okla. 1969. 801 pp., $19.95.

A bibliography of books and pamphlets on Western outlaws and gunmen. A brand new revised and enlarged edition.

Sketch Book 76: The American Soldier 1775-1781, by R. Klinger and R. A. Wilder, Arlington, Va., 1967. 53 pp., illus. Paper covers. $2.50.

Sketches, notes, and patterns compiled from a study of clothing and equipment used by the American foot soldier in the Revolutionary War.

Skills for Taming the Wilds, by Bradford Angier, Stackpole Books, Harrisburg, Pa., 1967. 320 pp., illus. $6.95.

A handbook of woodcraft wisdom, by a foremost authority, showing how to obtain maximum comfort from nature.

Small Arms Lexicon and Concise Encyclopedia, by Chester Mueller and John Olson. Stoeger Arms, So. Hackensack, N.J., 1968. 312 pp., 500 illus. $14.95.

Definitions, explanations, and references on antiques, optics, ballistics, etc., from A to Z. Over 3,000 entries plus appendix.

Small Arms of the World. by W.H.B. Smith and J.E. Smith. 9th ed., 1969. Stackpole Books, Harrisburg, Pa. 786 pp., profusely illus. $17.95.

A most popular firearms classic for easy reference. Covers the small arms of 42 countries, clearly showing operational principles. A timeless volume of proven worth.

Stoeger Gun Parts Catalog, compiled and published by Stoeger Arms Corporation, South Hackensack, N.J., 1968. 416 pp., illus. $2.00.

A mail-order catalog listing over 1000 parts for pistols, rifles and shotguns, domestic and foreign. Includes gunsmith tools and accessories.

Stories of the Old Duck Hunters and Other Drivel, by Gordon MacQuarrie and compiled by Zack Taylor. Stackpole Books, Harrisburg, Pa., 1967. 223 pp., illus. $5.95.
An off-beat relaxing and enjoyable group of 19 best-remembered outdoor stories, previously publ. in magazines.

Submachine Guns Caliber .45, M3 and M3A1, U.S. FM23-41 and TM 9-1217. Normount Armament Co., Forest Grove, Ore., 1967. 141 pp., illus., paperbound. $3.00.
Reprint of two U.S. Army manuals on submachine guns.

Swords & Daggers, by Frederick Wilkinson. Hawtnorn Books, N.Y., 1968. 256 pp., well illus. $5.95.
Good general survey of edged weapons and polearms of collector interest, with 150 pp. of illustrations and descriptions of arms from Europe, Africa and the Orient.

Swords of Hitler's Third Reich, by Major J.R. Angolia, F.J. Stephens, Essex, England, 1969. Over 100 pp., well illus. $8.50.
A comprehensive work on the swords of the German Army, Navy, Air Force, SS, Police, Fire Dept., and many other government departments—plus belts, hangers, and accouterments—all described and illus.

Teaching Kids to Shoot, by Henry M. Stebbins. Stackpole Books, Harrisburg, Pa. 1966. 96 pp. illus. $2.95.
Designed for parents and leaders who want to develop safety conscious firearms-users.

Tear Gas Munitions, by T. F. Swearengen, Charles C. Thomas, Springfield, Ill., 1966. 569 pp., illus. $34.50.
An analysis of commercial (riot) gas guns, tear gas projectiles, grenades, small arms ammunition, and related tear gas devices.

Technical Dictionary for Weapon Enthusiasts, Shooters and Hunters, by Gustav Sybertz. Publ. by J. Neumann-Neudamm, 3508 Melsungen, W. Germany, 1969. 164 pp., semi-soft covers. $7.50.
A German-English and English-German dictionary for the sportsman. An excellent handy work.

Textbook of Small Arms, 1929. Reprint of an official British publ. Holland Press, London, 1961. 427 pp., illus. $12.50.
Reprint in facsimile of an official prime source on military rifles, swords, bayonets, revolvers, grenades, machine guns, cartridges, ballistics, etc.

The Thompson Gun, publ. by Numrich Arms, West Hurley, N. Y., 1967, 27 pp., illus., paper covers. $1.95.
A facsimile reprint, excellently done, of a 1923 catalog of Thompson sub-machine guns.

Thompson Submachine Guns, compiled from original manuals by the publ. Normount Armament Co., Forest Grove, Oregon, Ill., 1968. Over 230 pp., well illus., many exploded views. Paper wrappers. $4.00.
Five reprints in one book: Basic Field Manual, Cal. 45, M1928AI (U.S. Army); Cal. 45, Model 1928, (for British); Cal., 45 (U.S. Ordnance); Model MI, Cal., 45 (U.S. Ordnance) and Ultra Modern Automatic Arms (Auto-Ordnance Corp.).

The Tournament, its Periods and Phases, by R. C. Clephan. Frederick Ungar Co., N.Y., 1967. A reprint. 195 pp., illus. with contemporary pictures plus half-tones of armor and weapons used by contestants. $9.95.
A rare and eagerly-sought work, long out-of-print. A scholarly, historical and descriptive account of jousting.

Training Your Own Bird Dog, by Henry P. Davis, G.P. Putnam's Sons, New York, N.Y. New rev. ed., 1969. 168 pp., plus 10 pp. of field trial records. Illus. with photographs. $5.95.
The reappearance of a popular and practical book for the beginner starting his first bird dog—by an internationally recognized authority.

A Treatise of Artillery, by John Muller. Museum Restoration Service, Ottawa, Canada, 1965. 216 pp., plus many plates. $17.50.
A creditable reprint of a famous and excellent original work of the third ed. of 1780, printed in London. This reprint limited to 850 numbered copies. The plates should be highly useful to the artillery buff.

Uniforms, Organization and History of the Waffen SS, by R.J. Bender and H.P. Taylor. R.J. Bender, Mountain View, Cal., 1969. 160 pp., photographs and drawings. $9.95.
The first of 4 contemplated volumes on the subject, with accompanying historical text.

Use and Maintenance of the Browning "Hi-Power" Pistol, (No. 2 Mk 1 and Commercial Models), by D.B. McLean. Normount Armament Co., Forest Grove, Ore., 1966. 48 pp., illus., paperbound. $1.50.
Covers the use, maintenance, and repair of various Browning 9mm parabellum pistols.

Warriors' Weapons, by Walter Buehr. Crowell Co., N.Y.C., 1963. 186 pp., illus. $5.95.
Illustrated history of pre-gunpowder arms, from stone ax to crossbow and catapult.

Weapons of the American Revolution, and Accoutrements, by Warren Moore. Funk & Wagnalls, N.Y., 1967. 225 pp., fine illus. $10.00.
Revolutionary era shoulder arms, pistols, edged weapons, and equipment are described and shown in fine drawings and photographs, some in color.

The Weapons Merchants, by Bernt Engelmann. Crown Publ., Inc., N. Y., 1968. 224 pp., illus. $4.95.
A true account of illegal traffic in death-dealing arms by individuals and governments.

Weapons and Tactics, Hastings to Berlin, by Jac Weller, St. Martin's Press, New York, 1966. 238 pp., illus. $6.00.
Primarily on the infantry weapons of today, with basic data on those of the past.

Weapons of War, by P. E. Cleator. Crowell Co., N.Y.C., 1968. 224 pp., illus. $5.95.
A British survey of warfare from earliest times, as influenced by the weapons available for combat.

Wild Game Cookbook, ed. by L.W. "Bill" Johnson. Grosset & Dunlap, New York, N.Y. 1st ed., 1968. 160 pp., illus., paper covers. $1.95.
Recipes for the savory cooking of all sorts of large and small game, taste-tempting sauces, stuffings, etc.

Wild Game Cookbook, by L.E. Johnson. Benjamin Co., N.Y.C., 1968. 160 pp. $1.95
Recipes, sauces, and cooking hints for preparation of all types of game birds and animals.

Wild Sanctuaries . . . , by Robert Murphy. E.P. Dutton & Co., Inc., New York, N.Y., 1968, 288 pp., over 250 photographs in color and monochrome, plus 32 maps, including those of the flyways. $12.95.
Concerns America's national wildlife refuges. An all-encompassing treatise on its subject with fascinating pertinent text.

The Wild Turkey, its History and Domestication, by A. W. Schorger, Univ. of Oklahoma Press, Norman, Okla., 1966. 625 pp., illus. $10.00.
Detailed coverage of habitats, characteristics, breeding, and feeding of the American wild turkey. Bibliography.

Wilderness Cookery, by Bradford Angier. Stackpole Books, Harrisburg, Pa., 1967. 256 pp., illus. $4.95.
An excellent work, one that will be of big interest to hunters, fishermen, campers, et al.

Wildwood Wisdom, by Ellsworth Jaeger. The Macmillan Company, New York, N.Y. 1964. 491 pp. well-illus. by author. $6.95.
An authoritative work, through many editions; about all there is to know about every detail for the outdoorsman.

Williams 1968-69 Blue Book of Gun Dealing. Williams Gun Sight Co., Davison, Mich., 1968. 76 pp., illus., paperbound. $2.50.
Suggested price ranges for many models of rifles, shotguns, handguns, sights, etc., with other useful information for the gun trader.

The World of the White-Tailed Deer, by L. L. Rue III. J. B. Lippincott Co., Phila., 1967. A reprint. 137 pp., fine photos. $4.95.
An eminent naturalist-writer's account of the year-round activities of the white-tailed deer.

The World's Assault Rifles (and Automatic Carbines), by D. D. Musgrave and T. B. Nelson. T. B. N. Enterprises, Alexandria, Va., 1967. 546 pp., profusely illus. $17.50.
High velocity small-bore combat rifles are shown and described in much detail, arranged by type and nationality. A companion volume to *The World's Submachine Guns,* by Nelson and Lockhoven.

The World's Submachine Guns (and Machine Pistols), by T. B. Nelson and H. B. Lockhoven. T. B. N. Enterprises, Alexandria, Va., 1962. 739 pp., profusely illus. $15.50.
The 2nd printing (1964) of the first work with descriptive data on all significant SMGs to date, arranged by national origin. A glossary in 22 languages is included. It is a companion volume to the *The World's Assault Rifles* by Musgrave and Nelson.

You and Your Retriever, by R.W. Coykendall, Jr. Doubleday & Co., Garden City, N.Y., 1963. 155 pp., illus. $4.95.
A text on early, intermediate and advanced training of retrievers, with full information for handlers.

The Young Sportsman's Guide to Camping, by J.L. Holden. Thomas Nelson & Sons, Camden, N.J., 1962. 96 pp., illus. $2.75.
A concise and dependable guide to basic techniques of camping in comfort and safety.

The Young Sportsman's Guide to Dogs, by J.R. Falk. Thomas Nelson & Sons, Camden, N.J., 1964. 96 pp., illus. $2.75.
A creditable and concise work on the history and characteristics of 29 breeds of dogs, both working and nonsporting types.

The Young Sportsman's Guide to Target Shooting,, by Gene Seraphine. Thomas Nelson & Sons, Camden, N.J., 1964. 94 pp., illus. $2.95.
A basic introduction to marksmanship, including selection of firearms, sights, equipment, ammunition and range behavior.

Gunsmithing

Antique Firearms: Their Care, Repair and Restoration, by Ronald Lister. Crown Publ., New York, 1964. 220 pp., 66 plates, 24 fig. $2.98.
A workshop manual for collectors and gunsmiths, giving correct procedures for every step in preserving firearms.

Checkering and Carving of Gun Stocks, by Monte Kennedy. Stackpole Books, Harrisburg, Pa., 1962. 175 pp., illus. $10.00.
Rev., enlarged clothbound ed. of a much sought-after, dependable work.

Complete Guide to Gunsmithing, by C. E. Chapel. Barnes & Co., N.Y.C., 1962. 479 pp., illus. $6.95.
2nd rev. edition, known earlier as *Gun Care and Repair,* of a comprehensive book on all details of gunsmithing for the hobbyist and professional.

Firearms Blueing and Browning, by R. H. Angier. Stackpole Books, Harrisburg, Pa. 151 pp., illus. $5.00.
A useful, concise text on chemical coloring methods for the gunsmith and mechanic.

Gun Engraving Review, by E. C. Prudhomme, G. E. R. Publ. Co., Shreveport, La., 1965. 150 pp., profusely illus. (some in color.) $21.95.
Excellent examples of the gun engraver's art to serve as a guide to novice or expert. Selection of tools, techniques and a directory of engravers is given.

Gunsmith Kinks, by F.R. [Bob] Brownell. F. Brownell & Son., Montezuma, Iowa. 1st ed., 1969. 496 pp., well illus. $9.95.
A widely useful accumulation of shop kinks, short cuts, techniques and pertinent comments by practicing gunsmiths from all over the world.

Gunsmithing, by Roy F. Dunlap. Stackpole Books, Harrisburg, Pa., 714 pp., illus. $10.00.
Comprehensive work on conventional techniques, incl. recent advances in the field. Valuable to rifle owners, shooters, and practicing gunsmiths.

Gunsmithing Simplified, by H. E. Macfarland. Washington, D.C., 1950, A. S. Barnes, N.Y.C., 1959. 303 pp., illus. $6.95.
A thorough dependable concise work with many helpful short-cuts.

Gunstock Finishing and Care, by A. D. Newell. Stackpole Books, Harrisburg, Pa. A new printing, 1966. 473 pp. illus. $9.50.
Amateur's and professional's handbook on the selection, use and application of protective and decorative coatings on gun stocks.

Home Gun Care & Repair, by P. O. Ackley. Stackpole Books, Harrisburg, Pa., 1969. 191 pp., illus. $5.95.
Basic reference for safe tinkering, fixing, and converting rifles, shotguns, handguns.

Home Gunsmithing Digest, by Tommy Bish. Gun Digest Publ., Northfield, Ill., 1970, 320 pp., very well illus. within stiff decorated paper covers. $4.95.
An unusually beneficial assist for gun owners doing their own repairs, maintenance, etc. 45 chapters on tools, techniques and theories.

HOW . . . by L. Cowher, W. Hunley, and L. Johnston. NMLR Assn., Indiana, 1961. 107 pp., illus. Paper covers. $2.95.
This 1961 rev. ed., enlarged by 3 chapters and additional illustrations, covers the building of a muzzle-loading rifle, target pistol, and powder horn, and tells how to make gunflints.

How to Convert Military Rifles, by Harvey Williams, *et al.* Gun Digest Publ. Co., Northfield, Ill., 1970. 88 pp., very well illus., stiff paper covers. $1.95.
The 6th and latest ed. of a popular work formerly distributed by the author's company. Gives step-by-step instructions to convert a military rifle to a good looking and easy to handle sporter.

Introduction to Modern Gunsmithing, by H. E. MacFarland. Stackpole Books, Harrisburg, Pa., 1965. 320 pp., illus. $6.95.
Up-to-date reference for all gunsmiths on care, repair, and modification of firearms, sights, and related topics.

Lock, Stock and Barrel, by R. H. McGrory. Publ. by author at Bellmore, N.Y., 1966. Paper covers. 122 pp., illus. $3.00.

A handy and useful work for the collector or the professional with many helpful procedures shown and described on antique gun repair.

Make Muzzle Loader Accessories, by Robert H. McCrory. R. H. McCrory, Bellmore, N.Y., 1967. 28 pp., paper wrappers, illus. with sketches. $1.50.

A capably executed handbook on how to make a powder horn, capper, nipple wrench, loading block and spring vise.

Master French Gungsmith's Designs of the 17th-18th Centuries, compiled by S.V. Grancsay. Winchester Press, New York, N.Y., 1970. A brand new work of 208 pp., beautifully illus. in facsimile. Numbered, limited issue of 1000 copies. $75.00.

Magnificent ornamentation of weapons taken from a superb collection of design books, gathered by a world authority. An inspiration and a must for the gunsmith-engraver.

The Modern Gunsmith, by James V. Howe. Funk & Wagnalls, N.Y.C., 1970 reprint ed. (2 vols.). 910 pp., illus. $25.00.

Guide for amateur and professional gunsmiths on firearms design, construction, repair, etc.

The Modern Kentucky Rifle, How to Build Your Own, by R. H. McCrory. McCrory, Wantagh, N.Y., 1961. 68 pp., illus., paper bound. $3.00.

A workshop manual on how to fabricate a flintlock rifle. Also some information on pistols and percussion locks.

Professional Gunsmithing, by W. J. Howe. Stackpole Books, Harrisburg, Pa., 1968 reprinting. 526 pp., illus. $10.00.

Textbook on repair and alteration of firearms, with detailed notes on equipment and commercial gunshop operation.

Restocking a Rifle, by Alvin Linden. Stackpole Books, Harrisburg, Pa., 1969. 138 combined pp., of text. Well illus. Large format. $9.95.

A re-issue in one volume of the 3 earlier Linden instruction guides on: Stock Inletting; Shaping; Finishing of the Springfield, Enfield and Winchester M70 rifles.

handguns

Automatic Firearm Pistols, by Elmer Swanson. Wesmore Book Co., Weehawken, N.J. 1st (and only) ed. 1955. 210 pp., well illus. $15.00.

A veritable catalog exclusively on automatic handguns for collectors, with many line drawings and descriptions, plus then-market market values of each.

Automatic Pistols, by H. B. C. Pollard, WE, Old Greenwich, Conn. 1966. 110 pp., illus. $5.00.

A facsimile reprint of the scarce 1920 original. Covers historical development of military and other automatics, shooting, care, etc.

Basic Marksmanship with the Modern Handgun, by L.P. Davison, and L.A. Severson. National Police Law Enforcement Institute. n.d. 88 pp. illus. $4.00. Paper covers.

A police training handbook on fundamentals of handgun selection and use, on the firing range and in combat situations.

Book of Pistols & Revolvers, by W. H. B. Smith. Stackpole Books, Harrisburg, Pa., 1968. 758 pp., profusely illus. $14.95. Buy with Book of Rifles and both are $19.95.

Rev. and enlarged, this encyclopedic reference, first publ. in 1946, continues to be the best on its subject.

Browning Hi-Power Pistols. Normount Armament Co., Forest Grove, Ore., 1968. 48 pp., illus., paperbound. $1.50.

A handbook on all models of Browning Hi-Power pistols, covering their use, maintenance and repair.

Colt Commemorative Firearms, by R.L. Wilson. Charles Kidwell, Wichita, Kans., 1969. Unpaginated, well illus. paper covers, $5.95. In hard deluxe covers, limited issue of 1000 copies, each numbered. $10.00.

Description and fine color photographs of commemorative handguns issued by the Colt company, 1961-1969, all replicas of famous earlier models.

Combat Shooting for Police, by Paul B. Weston. Charles C. Thomas, Springfield, Ill., 1967. A reprint. 194 pp., illus. $7.50.

First publ. in 1960 this popular self-teaching manual gives basic concepts of defensive fire in every position.

The Encyclopedia of the Third Reich, Book I, by R.B. Marvin. Universal Research, Inc., Fort Lauderdale, Texas, 1969, from offset typewritten copy. 37 pp., very clear and sharp illustrations, paper covers. $4.00.

This volume considers only handguns, but is a concise collector's guide to the main types of W.W. II German pistols and revolvers.

Fired In Anger, by Robt. Elman. Doubleday, Garden City, N.Y., 1968. 416 pp., illus. with 250 photos. $7.95.

Describes and illustrates the personal handguns used by famous and infamous Americans, including soldiers, outlaws and historical figures.

Gil Hebard Guns, Gil Hebard, Knoxville, Ill. Catalog No. 19, 1969. 177 pp., illus. Paperbound, $1.00.

Outstanding sales catalog of handgunner's needs, plus excellent articles by pistol experts on sport and target shooting.

The Handbook of Handgunning, by Paul B. Weston. Crown Publ., N.Y.C., 1968. 138 pp., illus. with photos. $4.95.

"New concepts in pistol and revolver shooting," by a noted firearms instructor and writer.

Handbuch der Faustfeuerwaffen, by Gerhard Bock and W. Weigel. J. Neumann-Neudamm, Melsungen, Germany, 1968. 4th and latest ed., 724 pp., including index. Profusely illus. $21.00.

A truly encyclopedic work in German text on every aspect of handguns. Highly recommended for those who read German.

The Handgun, by Geoffrey Boothroyd. Crown Publishers, Inc., New York, N.Y., 1970. 564 pp., profusely illus., plus copious index. $19.95.

A massive and impressive work, excellently covering the subject from matchlocks to present-day automatics. Many anecdotes, much comment and pertinent data, including ammunition, etc.

Handgunner's Guide, by Chic Gaylord. Hastings House, N.Y.C., 1960. 176 pp., illus. $2.98.

From choosing a handgun to the psychology of gun-fighting, including drawing and firing for speed and accuracy.

Japanese Hand Guns, by F.E. Leithe. Borden Publ. Co., Alhambra, Calif., 1968. Unpaginated, well illus. $8.50.

Identification guide, covering models produced since the late 19th century. Brief text material gives history, descriptions, and markings.

The Luger Pistol (Pistole Parabellum), by F. A. Datig. Borden Publ. Co., Alhambra, Calif., 1962. 328 pp., well illus. $8.50.

An enlarged, rev. ed. of an important reference on the arm, its history and development from 1893 to 1945.

Lugers at Random, by Charles Kenyon, Jr. Handgun Press, Chicago, Ill. 1st ed., 1970. 416 pp., profusely illus. $15.00.

An impressive large side-opening book carrying throughout alternate facing-pages of descriptive text and clear photographs. A new boon to the Luger collector and/or shooter.

Lugers Unlimited, by F. G. Tilton, World-Wide Gun Report, Inc., Aledo, Ill., 1965. 49 pp., illus. Paper covers. $2.00.

An excellent monograph about one of the most controversial pistols since the invention of hand firearms.

The Mauser Self-Loading Pistol, by Belford & Dunlap. Borden Publ. Co., Alhambra, Calif. Over 200 pp., 300 illus., large format. $12.50.

The long-awaited book on the "Broom Handles," covering their inception in 1894 to the end of production. Complete and in detail: pocket pistols, Chinese and Spanish copies, etc.

The Modern Handgun, by Robert Hertzberg. Arco Publ. Co., New York, N.Y., 1965. 112 pp., well illus. $3.50.

Pistols and revolvers of all types are traced from their beginnings. Data on modern marksmanship included.

Modern Pistol Shooting, by P.C. Freeman. Faber & Faber, London, England, 1968. 176 pp., illus. $4.00.

How to develop accuracy with the pistol. Fine points in technique are covered, with information on competitive target shooting.

The "Parabellum" Automatic Pistol, the English version of the official DWM handbook on Luger pistols. Normount Armament Co., Forest Grove, Oregon, Ill., 1968. 42 pp., illus. Paper wrappers. $1.00.

A user's handbook, a reference work for collectors. A reprint of the original detailed instructions on use, disassembly and maintenance. Includes three folding plates.

Pistol and Revolver Guide, by George Nonte. Stoeger Arms Corp., So. Hackensack, N.J., 1967. 192 pp., well illus. Paper wrappers. $3.95.

A history of the handgun, its selection, use and care, with a glossary and trade directory.

The Pistol Shooter's Treasury, by Gil Hebard. Gil Hebard, Knoxville, Ill., 1969. 1st ed., 112 pp. illus. in halftone and full color. Color decorated paper covers. $2.50.

A gathering of the experts, by an expert—classic articles on how to shoot a handgun and prepare for competition.

Pistols, A Modern Encyclopedia, by Stebbins, Shay, & Hammond. Stackpole Co., Harrisburg, Pa., 1961. 380 pp., illus. $4.98.

Comprehensive coverage of handguns for every purpose, with material on selection, ammunition, and marksmanship.

Pistols of the World, by Claude Blair. Viking Press, N.Y.C., 1968. 206 pp., plus plates. $30.00.

Authoritive review of handguns since the 16th century, with chapters on major types, manufacture, and decoration. Fine photographic illustrations.

Report of Board on Tests of Revolvers and Automatic Pistols. From the *Annual Report* of the Chief of Ordnance, 1907. Reprinted by J.C. Tillinghast, Marlow, N.H., 1969. 34 pp., 7 plates, paper covers. $3.00.

A comparison of handguns, including Luger, Savage, Colt, Webley-Fosbery and other makes.

The Revolver, 1818-1865, by Taylerson, Andrews, & Frith. Crown Publ., N.Y.C., 1968. 360 pp., illus. $7.50.

Noted British work on early revolving arms and the principal makers, giving production data and serial numbers on many models.

The Revolver, 1865-1888, by A.W.F. Taylerson. Crown Publ., N.Y.C., 1966. 292 pp., illus. $3.49.

Detailed study of 19th-century British and U.S. revolvers, by types and makers, based on study of patent records.

Saga of the Colt Six-Shooter, and the famous men who used it, by G.E. Virgines. Frederick Fell Co., New York, N.Y., 1969. 220 pp., well illus. $7.95.

History of the Colt Single action army revolver since 1873, with much information of interest to collectors and shooters.

Sixguns by Keith, by Elmer Keith. Stackpole Co., Harrisburg, Pa., 1968 (reprint of 1961 edition.) 335 pp., illus. $12.95.

Long a popular reference on handguns, this work covers all aspects, whether for the shooter, collector or other enthusiasts.

Smith and Wesson Catalog of 1901, a reprint facsimile by The Wyoming Armory, Inc., Cheyenne, Wyo., 1969. 72 pp., well illus., paper covers. $2.25.

All models, engraving, parts and break-down lists, etc.

System Mauser, a Pictorial History of the Model 1896 Self-Loading Pistol, by J.W. Breathed, Jr., and J.J. Schroeder, Jr. Handgun Press, Chicago, Ill., 1967. 273 pp., well illus. 1st limited ed. hardbound. $12.50. Also a 2nd ed. in paper covers by Gun Digest Publ., Northfield, Ill., 1970. $4.95.

10 Shots Quick, by Daniel K. Stern. Globe Printing Co., San Jose, Calif., 1967. 153 pp., photos. $8.50.

History of Savage-made automatic pistols, models of 1903-1917, with descriptive data for shooters and collectors.

Triggernometry, by Eugene Cunningham. Caxton Printers Lt., Caldwell, Id., 1962. 441 pp. illus. $5.00.

A classic study of famous outlaws and lawmen of the West—their stature as human beings, their exploits and their skills in handling firearms—the tools of their trade.

U.S. Pistols and Revolvers Vol. 1, D.B. McLean, compiler. Normount Armament Co., Forest Grove, Ore., 1968. 2nd printing, 198 pp., well illus., paper covers. $3.50.

A useful and reliable work from authoritative sources on M1911/M1911A1 Colt pistols; M1917 S&W revolvers; M1917 and Detective Special Colt revolvers. Excellent for their use, maintenance and repair.

U.S. Test Trials 1900 Luger, by Michael Reese II. Coventry Publ. Co., Gretna, La., 1970. Illus. $7.00.

For the Luger Pistol collector.

The Webley-Fosbery Automatic Revolver. A reprint of the original undated booklet publ. by the British makers. Deep River Armory, Houston, Tex., 1968. 16 pp., illus., paper. $3.00.

An instruction manual, parts list and sales brochure on this scarce military handgun.

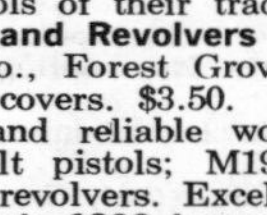

hunting

African Hunting, by Wm. C. Baldwin. Abercrombie & Fitch Library, N.Y., 1967. 451 pp., illus. $12.95.

Limited printing of a much-desired book giving vivid accounts of big game hunting exploits in Africa. First publ. in 1863.

After Wild Sheep in the Altai and Mongolia, by Prince Demidoff. Abercrombie & Fitch Library, N.Y., 1966. 324 pp., with photographs and drawings. $10.00.

Limited printing of a famous British work of 1900, on hunting big game in Asia. Long out-of-print.

American Partridge & Pheasant Shooting, by Frank Schley. Abercrombie & Fitch Library, N.Y.C., 1968. 238 pp., illus. $7.95.
Facsimile of an American sporting classic work, including detailed engravings of game birds.

The American Sportsman, by Elisha J. Lewis. Abercrombie & Fitch Library, N.Y., 1967. 510 pp., illus. $10.95.
Limited issue of a scarce classic American work on the hunting field, first publ. in 1851.

Animals of East Africa, by C.A. Spinage. Houghton Mifflin Co., Boston, Mass. 1963. 151 pp. illus. $7.50.
Foreword by Sir Julian Huxley, F.R.S., who calls this "The best collection of wild life photographs I have seen." Excellent for those planning a safari.

The Art of Hunting Big Game in North America, by Jack O'Connor. Alfred A. Knopf, N.Y., 1967. 404 pp., line drawings and photos. $8.95.
A complete book on the subject, from tracing the origin of game on this continent to the various techniques practised in the sport on different species. Rifles and cartridges discussed at length.

The Art of Wing Shooting, by W.B. Leffingwell. Abercrombie & Fitch Library, N.Y.C., 1968. 190 pp., illus. $7.95.
An outstanding treatise on shotgun marksmanship, first publ. 1894, with explicit drawings on techniques of leading the target.

Asian Jungle, African Bush, by Charles Askins. Stackpole Books, Harrisburg, Pa., 1959. 258 pp., illus. $10.00.
A where-to-go and how-to-do guide for game-rich Indo-China. The African section deals with game, the use of various arms and ammo on specific species.

The Australian Hunter, by Col. Allison with Ian Coombes. Cassell Australia Ltd., No. Melbourne, Australia, 1970. 212 pp., 58 photos., and 60 distribution maps and drawings. $7.50.
A comprehensive guide to game, equipment, hunting and photography.

Bell of Africa, by W. D. M. Bell, with foreword and introduction by Wally Taber and Col. T. Whelen. N. Spearman and Holland Press, London, 1960. 236 pp., illus. $4.75.
On elephants and the hunter, extracted from Bell's own papers, it includes an appendix on rifles and rifle shooting.

Big Game Hunting in the West, by Mike Cramond. Mitchell Press, Vancouver, B.C., Can., 1965. 164 pp., illus. $5.95.
Accounts of hunting many species of big game and predators are given plus a section on rifles, equipment, and useful tips for the field.

Big Game Shooting in Africa, ed. by Major H.C. Maydon. Seeley, Service & Co., London, n.d., 445 pp. illus. $7.50.
Vol. 14 of the Lonsdale Library, with chapters by various British writers on African big game and on hunting in various sections of Africa.

Bird Hunting Know-How, by D.M. Duffey. Van Nostrand, Princeton, N.J., 1968. 192 pp., illus. $5.95.
Game-getting techniques and sound advice on all aspects of upland bird hunting, plus data on guns and loads.

The Bobwhite Quail, its Life and Management, by Walter Rosene. Rutgers University Press, New Brunswick, N.J. 1st ed., 1969. 418 pp., photographs, maps and color plates. $20.00.
An exhaustive study of an important species which has diminished under the impact of changing agricultural and forestry practices.

Bowhunting for Deer, by H. R. Wambold. Stackpole Books, Harrisburg, Pa., 1964. 160 pp., illus. $5.95.
Useful tips on deer, their habits, anatomy, and how-when-where of hunting, plus selection and use of tackle.

A Boy and His Gun, by Edward C. Janes. A.S. Barnes & Co., New York, N.Y. 207 pp., illus., $5.00.
Introduction to rifles, shooting and hunting techniques for young shooters with practical hints on game shooting with rifle or shotgun.

Buckshot and Hounds, by C. J. Milling. A. S. Barnes, N.Y., 1967. 132 pp., illus. $4.95.
Deer-driving methods and traditions of the South and West, with present-day adaptations described.

Calling All Game, by Bert Popowski. Stackpole Books, Harrisburg, Pa., 1952, 306 pp. Illus. $4.95.
Practical methods of attracting game, from quail to moose, using artificial decoys and calls.

Charles Morgan on Retrievers, ed. by Ann Fowler and D.L. Walters. Abercrombie & Fitch, N.Y.C., 1968. 168 pp., illus. $12.50.
Based on years of success in schooling hunting dogs, this work gives full details of an expert's proven methods to guide experienced trainers.

Complete Book of Hunting, by Clyde Ormond. Harper & Bros., N.Y.C., 1962. 467 pp., well-illus. $6.95.
Part I is on game animals, Part II is on birds. Guns and ammunition, game, habitats, clothing, equipment, etc., hunters' tips are discussed.

The Complete Deer Hunt, by Joe DeFalco. Madison Publ. Co., New York, N.Y., 1970. 133 pp., well illus., in line and halftone. Stiff paper covers. $3.95.
A concise work covering field dressing, skinning, equipment and arms, methods of hunting, etc.

Crow Shooting, by Bert Popowski. A. S. Barnes and Co., N.Y.C., 1946. (4th printing 1957). 216 pp., illus. $5.00.
Practical and entertaining, telling how to locate roosts, build blinds and employ cover; the use of various decoys for shooting with rifle or shotgun.

The Deer Hunter's Bible, by Geo. Laycock. Doubleday, Garden City, N.Y., 1963. 154 pp., illus., paperbound. $1.95.
Handy summary of deer hunting lore, by an expert. Guns, loads, bowhunting, care of venison, field techniques are covered.

The Deer Hunter's Guide, by F. E. Sell. Stackpole Books, Harrisburg, Pa., 1964. 192 pp., illus. $5.00.
Western hunting lore for rifle- and bow-hunter, with data on woodcraft, trail signs, venison, and trophies, etc.

The Deer of North America, edit. by W. P. Taylor. Stackpole Books, Harrisburg, Pa., 1956. 668 pp., illus. incl. full-color plates. $12.50.
Leading authorities in all parts of the deer range have contributed their intimate studies of the animal.

Elephant Hunting in East Equatorial Africa, by Arthur H. Neumann. Abercrombie & Fitch Library, N.Y., 1966. 455 pp., illus. $12.50.
Limited ed. of a rare hunting book, first publ. in 1898 and difficult to locate. An account of 3 years' ivory hunting under Mt. Kenia . . . the Lorogi Mountains . . . and Lake Rudolph. Over 60 illus.

The End of the Game, by P. H. Beard. Viking Press, N.Y.C., 1965. 256 pp., fine illus. $12.95.
Account of recent changes in African game country and decline of the game population.

Game Bird Hunting, by F. P. Rice & J.I. Dahl. Outdoor Life—Harper & Row, N.Y.C., 1965. 190 pp., illus. $3.95.
Survey of North American game birds of all types, written by a noted scholar and a hunter of wide experience.

Game Bird Hunting in the West, by Mike Cramond. Mitchell Press, Vancouver, B.C., Can., 1967. 246 pp., illus. $5.95.
Identification and hunting methods for each species of waterfowl and upland game birds, plus a section on shotgun types, equipment, and related subjects for the hunter.

Game Shooting, by Robert Churchill (revised by Macdonald Hastings), Stackpole Books, Harrisburg, Pa., 1967. 252 pp., illus. $8.95.
A welcome reappearance of standard reference that pioneered game shooting techniques.

Good Hunting, by Jas. L. Clark, Univ. of Oklahoma Press, Norman, Okla., 1966. 242 pp., illus. $5.95.
Fifty years of collecting and preparing habitat groups for the American Museum.

The Great Arc of the Wild Sheep, by J. L. Clark. Univ. of Oklahoma Press, Norman, Okla., 1964. 247 pp., illus. $6.95.
Every classified variety of wild sheep is discussed, as found in North America, Asia & Europe. Numerous hunting stories by experts are included.

Great Game Animals of the World, by Russell B. Aitken. Winchester Press, N.Y., 1969. 192 pp. profusely illus. in monochrome and color. $22.50.
Accounts of man's pursuit of big game in all parts of the world, told in many fine pictures.

Great True Hunts, ed. by Peter Barrett. Prentice-Hall, Englewood Cliffs, N.J., 1967. 278 pp., illus. $4.95.
Big game hunting stories from *True* magazine, telling of hunting exploits of famous men around the world.

Green Hills of Africa, by Ernest Hemingway. Charles Scribner's Sons, N.Y., 1963. 295 pp. illus. $5.95.
A famous narrative of African big-game hunting, first published in 1935.

The Grizzly Bear, edited by B. D. and E. Haynes, Univ. of Oklahoma Press, Norman, Okla., 1966. 386 pp., illus. $6.95.
Collected stories about various encounters with the grizzly by mountain men, settlers, naturalists, scouts and others.

Grizzly Country, by Andy Russell. A.A. Knopf, N.Y.C., 1968. 302 pp., illus. $6.95.
Many-sided view of the grizzly bear and his world, by a noted guide, hunter and naturalist.

Guide to Safaris, by Burk H. Steizner. Charles Scribner's Sons, New York, N.Y., 1970. 178 pp., illus. $6.95.
Discussions of the different African regions, types of safari, minimal costs, etc. Highly informative for the would-be safari-goers seeking basic information.

Gun Dog, by Richard A. Wolters. E.P. Dutton, New York, N.Y., 1969. 1st ed., 11th printing. 150 pp., well illus. $5.95.
A popular manual for upland bird shooters who want to train their dogs to perfection in minimum time.

Guns & Ammo for Hunting Big Game, by Elmer Keith; John Lachuk, Ed. Petersen Publ. Co., L.A., 1965, reprinted 1967. 384 pp., illus. $4.95.
An expert on firearms and wildlife writes on hunting subjects, including guns, ammunition, and how to hunt various species of American game.

Honker, by C. S. Williams. Van Nostrand, N.Y.C., 1967. 192 pp., illus. $7.50.
A wealth of information for the hunter and conservationist, on geese exclusively — their habits, gunning techniques, ecology, etc.

How to Hunt American Game, by R.B. Vale. Stackpole Books, Harrisburg, Pa. 5th printing, 1954. 199 pp., illus. $4.00.
Wildlife habits, conservation and the encouragement of hunting. Including the author's experiences in hunting game throughout America.

How to Hunt Small American Game, by L.A. Anderson. Funk and Wagnalls, New York, N.Y., 1969. 167 pp., well illus. $5.95.
A new basic guide for the small game hunter, similar to the author's 1959 *How to Hunt Deer and Small Game.* Written for beginner and expert, covers game, guns, equipment and game habits.

How to Hunt Whitetail Deer, by L.A. Anderson. Funk & Wagnalls, N.Y.C., 1968. 116 pp., illus. $5.95.
Useful reference for deer hunters, both novice and experienced, giving basic information and valuable pointers.

A Hunter's Wanderings in Africa, by Frederick Courteney Selous. Abercrombie & Fitch Library, N.Y., 1967. 455 pp., illus. $11.95.
Limited ed. of a rare and much-sought original work of 1881. A world-famous big game hunter tells of his African exploits.

Hunting in Africa, by Frank C. Hibben, Hill and Wang, New York, N. Y., 1962. 236 pp., illus. $5.00.
18 true stories about exotic and dangerous African animals and the tracking and hunting of them.

Hunting Dog Know-How, by D. M. Duffey. Van Nostrand, Princeton, N.J., 1965. 177 pp., illus. $5.95.
Covers selection, breeds, and training of hunting dogs, problems in hunting and field trials.

Hunting Our Medium Size Game, by Clyde Ormond. Stackpole Books, Harrisburg, Pa., 1958. 219 pp., illus. $5.00.
Covers deer, whitetails and mules; black bear; antelope; coyotes; bobcats and cougar. Included are sections on equipment, use of rifles, and care of venison.

Hunting Pronghorn Antelope, by Bert Popowski. Stackpole Books, Harrisburg, Pa., 1959. 227 pp., illus. $6.50.

Hunting with Bow and Arrow, by George Laycock and Erwin Bauer. Arco Publ. Co., Inc., N.Y.C., 1966. $3.50.
A practical guide to archery as a present-day sport. Mentions equipment needed and how to select it. Illus. instructions on how to shoot with ease and accuracy.

The Imperial Collection of Audubon Animals, original text by John James Audubon and Rev. John Bachman, illus. by John James and John Woodhouse Audubon. A magnificent quarto reproduction of the rare original by Hammond, Inc., Maplewood, N.J., 1967. 307 pp., 150 animals pietured in full color. $25.00.
Each illus. accompanied by engaging text, as in the 1st ed. of 1848, including accounts of Audubon's exploring trips. A most useful work for hunters who want to know their game.

Jack O'Connor's Big Game Hunts. by Jack O'Connor. E. P. Dutton, N.Y.C., 1963. 415 pp., illus. $5.95.
26 detailed chronicles of successful trips for big game, selected from *Outdoor Life.*

Krider's Sporting Anecdotes, edited by Milnor H. Klapp. Abercrombie & Fitch Library, N.Y., 1966. 292 pp., illus. $8.00.
Limited issue of the much-wanted work on Philadelphia's renowned gunsmith, John Krider, publ. first in 1853. A rich fund of knowledge on upland shooting, dogs and match shooting, etc.

Living Off the Country, by B. Angier. Stackpole Books, Harrisburg, Pa., 1959. 241 pp., illus. $5.00.
In a simple and entertaining manner the author explains how to live off nature when emergency arises and how to stay alive in the woods.

Modern ABC's of Bird Hunting, by Dave Harbour, Stackpole Books, Harrisburg, Pa., 1966. 192 pp., illus. $4.95.

From city's edge to wilderness this gives the occasional hunter the quickest way on how to increase his bag. Covers all game birds of the U.S. or Canada.

The New Hunter's Encyclopedia, edited by Leonard Miracle and James B. Trefethen, plus specialized articles by over 60 outstanding contributors. Stackpole Books, Harrisburg, Pa. 1966. 1131 pp., profusely illus. with 2047 photos, diagrams, drawings and full-color plates. $24.95.

A massive work covering every detail of every sort of hunting in the U.S., Canada and Mexico.

Nove Secoli Di Armi Da Caccia, by L. G. Boccia. Editrice Edam, Firenze, Italy, 1967. 181 pp., illus. with many fine photos of superb museum quality in full color. $15.00.

In Italian text, a historical survey of hunting weapons of Italian origin and their makers.

On Your Own in the Wilderness, by Col. T. Whelen and B. Angier. Stackpole Books, Harrisburg, Pa., 1958. 324 pp., illus. $5.00.

Two eminent authorities give complete, accurate, and useful data on all phases of camping and travel in primitive areas.

Pocket Guide to Animal Tracks, by L.M. Henderson. Stackpole Books, Harrisburg, Pa., 1968. 57 pp., profusely illus., and bound in paper boards. $2.95.

Delightful text plus Henderson's most accurate line drawings show many signatures—paw and hoof prints, habits and characteristics, of 44 North American small and big game.

The Puma, Mysterious American Cat, by S. P. Young and E. A. Goldman, Dover Publ., N.Y., 1964. 358 pp., illus. Paper covers. $2.25.

A two-part work: the first on the history, economic status and control; the second on classifications of the races of the puma.

Ranch Life and the Hunting Trail, by Theodore Roosevelt, 1894. A fine reprint by the Winchester Press, New York, N.Y., 1969, with introduction by Kermit Roosevelt. 168 pp., and includes the Frederic Remington illustrations from the original and those added from the 1908 edition. $10.00.

The far West of the 1880s, of hunting and bags, of men and manners.

Records of North American Big Game, compiled by the Records Committee of the Boone and Crockett Club, Holt, Rinehart and Winston, N.Y.C. 3d printing of the 1964 edition. 398 pp., well illus., and with color frontis. $15.00.

The 5th issue of the famous useful series, and the largest and most complete.

The Rifle and Hound in Ceylon, by Samuel White Baker. Abercrombie & Fitch Library, N.Y., 1967. 422 pp., well illus. $12.95.

Limited printing of a classic description of elephant-hunting, deer-coursing and elk-hunting in the East. First published in the 1850s.

Rowland Ward's Records of Big Game, 13th Edition, compiled by G.A. Best. Rowland Ward Publ., Ltd., London, 1969. 38 pp., illus. $40.00.

New edition of the authoritative record of big game kills in Africa, by species.

Safari, by Elmer Keith. Safari Publ., La Jolla, Calif., 1968. 166 pp., illus. $7.95.

Guide to big game hunting in Africa, with anecdote and expert advice on hunting many species of game. Information on guns, ammunition, equipment, and planning the safari is included. Fine photographs.

Safari by Jet, through Africa and Asia, by Sister Maria del Rey, Charles Scribner's Sons, New York, N.Y., 1962. 308 pp., profusely illus., with photos. and line. $5.95.

Off-beat reading about an African-Asian grand tour, with tales of the land and the people of Tanganyika, Ceylon, the Philippines, Hong Kong, Taiwan, et al.

A Sporting chance . . . , by D. P. Mannix. E. P. Dutton & Co., N.Y., 1967. 248 pp., illus. with 50 photos. $1.98.

Unusual methods of hunting the exotic species from hounds to falcons. Inspiring reading for those desiring to get away from the commonplace.

Sporting Guns, by Richard Akehurst. G.P. Putnam's Sons, N.Y.C., 1968. 120 pp., illus. $5.95.

History of shooting and of the guns and rifles developed to meet the hunter's needs, with anecdotes of the hunting field.

The Sportsman's Companion, by Lee Wulff. Harper & Row, N.Y.C., 1968. 413 pp., illus. $11.95.

Compendium of writings by various experts on hunting and fishing for American game. A useful reference for the outdoorsman.

Sportsman's Guide to Game Animals, by Leonard Lee Rue III. Harper & Row [Outdoor Life Books], New York, N.Y. 1st ed., 2nd printing, 1969. 635 pp., illus. with photographs and maps. $6.50.

Exhaustive and capable coverage of the behavior and habits of all North American game animals.

The Standard Book of Hunting and Shooting, R.B. Stringfellow, ed. 1st ed., in 1950 by the Greystone Press, New York, N.Y. 564 pp., very well illus. $10.00.

An excellent anthology on hunting in America, giving meaningful information on all major species and on all types of guns, sights, ammunition, etc. An abridgement of the larger *Hunters Encyclopedia.*

Three Years' Hunting & Trapping in America and the Great Northwest, by J. Turner-Turner. Abercrombie & Fitch Library, N.Y.C., 1967. 182 pp., illus. $10.95.

Reprint of an 1888 account of a determined quest for valuable furs in one of the world's least hospitable regions.

Travel & Adventure in Southeast Africa, by F.C. Selous. A&F Press, N.Y.C., 1967. 522 pp., illus. $11.95.

New edition of a famous African hunting book, first published in 1893.

The Treasury of Hunting, by Larry Koller. Odyssey Press, N.Y.C., 1965. 251 pp., illus. $7.95.

Concise accounts of all types of hunting in the U.S. Excellent illustrations, many color photographs taken in various hunting fields.
ments, care of specimens in the field.

The Truth About Hunting in Today's Africa and how to go on a safari for $690.00, by G.L. Herter, Herter's, Inc., Waseca, Minn., 1970. 314 pp., well illus. $3.95.

Tells how to arrange safari costs, plus new data on weights, rifles and bullets derived from actual field tests.

The Upland Game Hunter's Bible, by Dan Holland. Doubleday, N.Y.C., 1961. 192 pp., illus. Paper covers. $1.95.

Hunter's manual on the principal species of American upland game birds and how to hunt them.

The Varmint and Crow Hunter's Bible, by Bert Popowski. Doubleday & Co., N.Y.C., 1962. 185 pp., 150 illus. Paper covers. $1.95.

Hunting and trapping techniques described by a well-known authority. Chapters on woodchucks, crows, foxes, snakes, guns, etc.

Waterfowl in the Marshes, by A.C. Becker Jr. A.S. Barnes and Co., New York, N.Y., 1969. 155 pp., photographs. $7.50.

A highly informative and practical guide to waterfowl hunting in America.

Whitetail, by George Mattis. World Publ. Co., New York, N.Y., 1969. 273 pp., including index. Illus. $6.95.

Fundamentals and fine points of compelling interest for the deer hunter.

Wild Fowl Decoys, by Joel Barber. Dover Publ., N.Y.C., 1954. 156 pp., 134 illus., paperbound. $3.50.

A fine work on making, painting, care and use of decoys in hunting, recently reprinted. Full data on design and construction.

Wildfowling, by James Andrews, et al. Seeley, Service & Co., London, n.d. 352 pp., illus. $4.50.

Articles by British sportsmen on shooting wildfowl, guns, punting, and conditions in various areas. Vol. 29 of the Lonsdale Library.

Wildfowling At A Glance, by R.W. Coykendall, Jr. Stackpole Books, Harrisburg, Pa., 1968. 94 pp., illus. $2.95.

Covers wildfowl hunting in America, including ducks, decoys, dogs, boats, and blinds.

Winchester-Western 1969-70 Hunting Guide, by E.L. Kozicky and J.B. Madson. Winchester Press, N.Y., 1969. 126 pp., illus. Paper covers. 95c.

A compendium of hunting information, seasons, licenses, prospects and best hunting areas.

Big Game and Big Game Rifles, by John Taylor. Herbert Jenkins, London, 4th printing, 1958. 215 pp. with frontis. and tables. $3.50.

Pondoro's well known and popular African work. Rifles described for all big game with data on the arm, its sights, trajectories, etc.

The Big-Game Rifle, by Jack O'Connor, Alfred A. Knopf, N.Y.C., 1951. 371 pp., plus XI pp. Well illus. $8.95.

Discusses construction, purpose and use for all types of big game as well as ammo., sights, accessories, etc.

The Book of Rifles, by W. H. B. Smith. Stackpole Books, Harrisburg, Pa., 1963 (3rd ed.). 656 pp., profusely illus. $12.50.

An encyclopedic reference work on shoulder arms, recently up-dated. Includes rifles of all types, arranged by country of origin. Buy with Book of Pistols & Revolvers and both are $19.95.

The Boy's Book of Rifles, by C. E. Chapel. Coward-McCann, N.Y.C., 1948, rev. ed., 1960. 274 pp., illus. $3.95.

For all young men of Boy Scout age at every phase of small-caliber marksmanship and safe gun handling. It tells how to qualify for NRA medals and Scout Merit Badges for Marksmanship.

Boy's Single-Shot Rifles, by Jas. J. Grant, William Morrow & Co., Inc., New York, 1967. 608 pp., illus. $10.00.

A wealth of important new material on an ever-popular subject, authoritatively presented. By the author of *Single Shot Rifles* and *More Single Shot Rifles.*

The Breech-Loading Single-Shot Match Rifle, by N. H. Roberts and K. L. Waters. D. Van Nostrand Co., Princeton, N.J., 1967. 293 pp., fine photos. $12.50.

Account of the Schuetzen rifle in America, with material on famous shooters, gunsmiths, ammunition, and related topics.

Carbines Cal. .30 M1, M1A1, M2 and M3, by D.B. McLean. Normount Armament Co., Forest Grove, Ore., 1964. 221 pp., well illus., paperbound. $3.00.

U.S. field manual reprints on these weapons, edited and reorganized.

The First Winchester, by John E. Parsons. Winchester Press, New York, N.Y., 1969. 207 pp., well illus., $8.95.

This new printing of *The Story of the 1866 Repeating Rifle* [1st publ. 1955] is revised, and additional illustrations included.

Garand Rifles MI, MIC, MID, by Donald B. McLean. Normount Armament Co., Forest Grove, Oregon, Ill., 1968. Over 160 pp., 175 illus., paper wrappers. $3.00.

Covers all facets of the arm: battlefield use, disassembly and maintenance, all details to complete lock-stock-and-barrel repair, plus variations, grenades, ammo., and accessories; plus a section on 7.62mm NATO conversions.

How to Select and Use Your Big Game Rifle, by Henry M. Stebbins. Combat Forces Press, Washington, 1952. 237 pp., illus. $6.50.

Concise valuable data on rifles, old and new—slide action, lever, semi automatic, and single shot models are covered.

Johnson Semi-Automatic Rifle, Rotary Feed Model, 1941 Instruction Manual, by the Johnson Arms Co. Design Publ., Hyattsville, Md., 1969. 72 pp. illus., paper covers. $4.00.

A reprint of the original instruction manual.

The Lee-Enfield Rifle, by E. G. B. Reynolds. Arco Publ. Co., N.Y., 1968. 224 pp., drawings and photos. $9.50.

New U.S. edition of a standard reference on models and modifications of the famous British military rifle.

Maynard Catalog of 1880, a reprint in facsimile by the Wyoming Armory, Inc., Cheyenne, Wyo., 1969. 32 pp., illus., paper covers. $2.25.

All models, sights, cartridges, targets etc.

Mister Rifleman, by Col. Townsend Whelen and Bradford Angier. Petersen Publ. Co., L.A., 1965, reprinted 1967. 377 pp., well illus. $4.95.

Autobiography of the late Col. Whelen, noted firearms authority, with supplementary material. Much on marksmanship and hunting techniques.

Notes on Sporting Rifles, by G. Burrard, E. Arnold and Co., London, England, 1953. 4th ed. rev., 183 pp., illus. $4.00.

A British book on large-bore big game rifles, particularly those for Indian and African shooting. Contains the noted "Hodsock Ballistic Tables," recomputed by O. Western.

Practical Dope on the .22, by F.C. Ness. Stackpole Books, Harrisburg, Pa. 4th printing, 1955. 313 pp., illus. $5.50.

Considerable pertinent information on 22 cal. rifles, actions, loads, plus test firing and data on their ballistics.

Principal Models of Rifles, Anon., L.E. Field, translator. Mars Equipment Corp., Lincolnwood, Ill., 1969. 14 pp., illus. in stapled paper covers. $2.00.

Translation of a Latin-American catalog listing various models of Mauser weapons.

Remarks on Rifle Guns; Fowling Pieces, The Percussion Lock and Firearms in General, by Ezekiel Baker, 1st issued 1800. A reprint of the 11th ed., by Standard Publications, Inc., Huntington, W.Va., 1946. 269 pp., plus tables, etc. $7.00.

An important work written by a famous British gunmaker, with much information on many nostalgic aspects on guns and shooting.

The Rifle Book, by Jack O'Connor. Random House (Knopf), N.Y.C., 1948. 3rd ed., 1964. 338 pp., illus. $8.95.

A definitive work, out-of-print until recently, which covers actions, design, ammunition, sights and accessories.

Rifles, a Modern Encyclopedia, by H.M. Stebbins. Book Sales, New York, N.Y. 1970. A reprint of the original of 1958. 376 pp., well illus. $4.98.

A comprehensive work covering subject for target and game. A limited number of original, deluxe and numbered full-leather bound copies at $25.00.

Rifles AR15, M16, and M16A1, 5.56 mm, by D.B. McLean. Normount Armament Co., Forest Grove, Ore., 1968. Unpaginated, illus., paper covers. $3.50.

Descriptions, specifications and operation of subject models are set forth in text and picture.

Sharps Firearms, V. 3, Pt. 3, Model 1874 Rifles, by Frank M. Sellers and DeWitt Bailey II. Frank M. Sellers, Denver, Colo., 1969. 20 pp., illus., paper covers. $7.50.

A separately printed section of a continuing comprehensive collector's reference. This current work shows and describes the known M1874 variations.

Shooter's Bible Gunsight Guide, by George Nonte. Shooter's Bible, Inc., S. Hackensack, N.J., 1968. 224 pp., illus. $3.95.

Catalog data, descriptions and comment, plus articles on all types of modern gun sights.

Shooting the Percussion Rifle, by R. O. Ackerman. Publ. by the author, Albuquerque, N.M., 1966. 19 pp., illus. in line by the author. Paper wrappers. $1.50.

This well prepared work is Book No. 2 of a projected series. This one gives basic information on the use of the muzzle-loading rifle.

Small Bore Target Shooting, by H. G. B. Fuller. Herbert Jenkins, London, 1964. 264 pp., well illus. $5.50.

Authoritative English work, covering rifle types, buying hints, ammunition, accessories, and range technique.

Sniper Rifles of Two World Wars, by W. H. Tantum IV. Museum Restoration Service, Ottawa, Can., 1967. 32 pp., illus. $1.50.

Monograph on high-accuracy rifles used by troops in World Wars I and II and in Korea. Paper wrappers.

The Sporting Rifle and Its Use in Britain, by Henry Tegner. Herbert Jenkins, London, 1962. 190 pp., illus. $4.00.

British hunting methods and equipment described by an expert, including guns, ammunition, field equipment, dogs, and stalking.

Springfield Rifles, M1903, M1903AI, M1903A3, M1903A4, compiled by the publ. Normount Armament Co., Forest Grove, Ore., 1968. Over 115 pp., illus., paper wrappers. $2.50.

Routine disassembly and maintenance to complete ordnance inspection and repair; bore sighting, trigger adjustment, accessories, etc.

Twenty-Two Caliber Varmint Rifles, by C. S. Landis. Stackpole Books, Harrisburg, Pa., 1947. 521 pp., profusely illustrated. $7.50.

A vast amount of data on the many wildcat 22's, including numerous scale drawings of cartridges and chambers.

United States Rifle, Cal. .30, Model of 1917, a reprint of an official government booklet by Normount Publ. Co., Forest Grove, Ore., 1969. 80 pp., line illus., paper covers. $2.00.

A training manual issued by the War Department in 1918. A much-wanted and useful booklet.

United States Rifle 7.62 mm, M14 and M14E2, a reprint of an official government booklet by Normount Armament Co., Forest Grove, Ore., 1968. 50 pp., illus., paper covers. $2.00.

U.S. Army Field Manual 23-8, first published in 1965.

Westley Richards Modern Sporting Rifles and Cartridges. A reprint of an original undated catalog of the British makers. Safari Outfitters, Richfield, Conn., 1968. 60 pp. illus., paper. $4.95.

Facsimile of issue, covers big game rifles and ammunition.

Winchester '73 & '76, the First Repeating Center-Fire Rifles, by D.F. Butler. Winchester Press, New York, N.Y., 1st ed., 1970. 95 pp., well and tastefully illus. in line, halftones and photos. Color frontispiece. $7.95.

A complete history of the subject arms and their then-new ammunition, plus details of their use on America's western frontiers.

American Partridge and Pheasant Shooting, Frank Schley. Abercrombie & Fitch Library, N.Y., 1967. 222 pp., illus. with detailed engravings of game birds. $7.95.

Limited printing of the rare sporting classic of 1877, considered for years the most important book available on the use of the scattergun.

The Art of Wing Shooting, by Wm. B. Leffingwell. Abercrombie & Fitch Library, N.Y., 1967. 192 pp., illus. $7.95.

Limited issue of a practical treatise on the use of the shotgun, first publ. in 1894. Contains a wealth of period anecdotes.

Automatic and Repeating Shotguns, by R. Arnold. Barnes & Co., N.Y.C., 1960. 173 pp., illus. $2.95.

Their history and development, with expert professional advice on choosing a gun for clay target shooting, game shooting, etc.

Book of the Shotgun, by Sports Illustrated eds. J.B. Lippincott Co., Phila., Pa., 1967. 90 pp., illus., $2.95.

A beginner's book on the shotgun and its use. Basic material on guns, ammunition, selection, form, and shooting.

Book of Shotgun Sports, by Sports Illustrated eds. J.B. Lippincott Co., Phila., Pa., 1967. 88 pp., illus., $2.95.

Introduction to target shooting, game shooting, and gunmanship.

Clay Pigeon Marksmanship, by Percy Stanbury and G. L. Carlisle. Herbert Jenkins, London, 1964. 216 pp., illus. $5.00.

Handbook on learning the skills, with data on guns & equipment and competition shooting at all types of clay targets; by two eminent British writers.

Field, Skeet and Trapshooting, by C. E. Chapel. Revised ed. Barnes & Co., N.Y.C., 1962. 291 pp., illus. $6.95.

A useful work on shotgun shooting, including gun types, ammo, accessories, marksmanship, etc.

Game Shooting, by Robert Churchill. (Rev. by M. Hastings.) Stackpole Books, Harrisburg, Pa., 1967. 252 pp., drawings and photos. $8.95.

A recent revision of the 1955 British treatise on modern shotguns and their use in the hunting field.

The Game Shot's Vade Mecum, by Michael Brander, A.&C. Black, London, 1st ed., 1965. 242 pp., illus., $5.00.

A British guide on the use of the shotgun in the hunting field, covers selection, marksmanship, game behavior and hunt management.

Gough Thomas's Gun Book, by G. T. Garwood. A. & C. Black, London, England, 1969. 160 pp., illus. $6.00.

Excerpts of articles on the shotgun published in Shooting Times, by a noted British authority. Wide-ranging survey of every aspect on the shotgun, its use, behavior, care, and lore.

Hartman on Skeet, by Barney Hartman. D. Van Nostrand Co., Princeton, N.J., 1967. 143 pp., illus. $8.95.

A champion shooter's explanation of Skeet shooting techniques, covering the fine points mastered by experts.

How to Shoot Straight, by Macdonald Hastings. A.S. Barnes and Co., New York, N.Y., 1970. 133 pp., illus., index ed. $5.95.

A companion volume to the author's Churchill on Game Shooting, and designed as a standard work on the modern game gun—a "teach-yourself" book.

Mastering the Shotgun, by R. A. Knight. E. P. Dutton & Co., N. Y., 1967. 123 pp. illus. with 65 drawings and photos. $4.95.

A down-to-earth commonsense guide, teaching how to hit what you aim at in the field, at skeet and at trap shooting.

The Modern Shotgun, by Maj. Sir Gerald Burrard. A. S. Barnes & Co., N.Y.C., 1961. In 2 vols., 1074 pp. Cased, $8.95.

Completely reliable and authoritative on the shotgun and its ammunition in every aspect.

Parker, America's Finest Shotgun, by P. H. Johnson. Outlet Book Co., Inc., N. Y., 1968. 260 pp., illus. $1.98.

An account of a great sporting arm—from post Civil War until 1947, when it was sold to Remington. Values, models, etc.

Shooting For Beginners, by E. N. Barclay. Percival Marshall & Co., London, 1963. 74 pp., illus. $1.75.

Concise introduction to British techniques and customs in shotgunning for game birds.

Shooting Preserve Management [The Nilo System], by E.L. Kozicky and John Madson. Winchester Press, New York., N.Y., 1969. 312 pp., photos., line drawings and diagrams. $10.00.

The new look in 13 chapters, a full account of American field shooting at Nilo Farms, the show-case of the shooting-preserve concept.

The Shot Gun, by T. D. S. & J. A. Purdey. A. & C. Black, London, Eng., 1962. 144 pp., illus. with photos and diagrams. $2.50.

Revised 3rd ed. of a well-known British work for all scattergunners by two members of the notable gunsmith family. Covers the gun and its use in the field, at traps, and for skeet.

The Shotgun Book, by Jack O'Connor. Alfred A. Knopf, N.Y., 1965. 332 pp., plus index, illus. with line and photos. $8.95.

The definitive, authoritative book with up-to-date chapters on wildfowling, upland gunning, trap and Skeet shooting. It includes practical advice on shotgun makes, models and functions, as well as data on actions, gauges, barrels, loads, chokes. pellets and ballistics.

The Shotgunner's Bible, by George Laycock. Doubleday & Co., Garden City, N.Y., 1969. 173 pp.. illus., paper covers. $1.95.

Coverage of shotguns, ammunition, marksmanship, hunting of various types of game, care and safety, etc.

The Shotgunner's Book, by Col. Charles Askins. Stackpole Books, Harrisburg, Pa., 1958. 365 pp., illus. $2.98.

Concise coverage of everything from design and manufacture to shooting form and ammunition.

Shotguns and Shooting, by E. S. McCawley Jr. Van Nostrand, N.Y.C., 1965. 146 pp., illus. $2.98.

Lucid coverage of shotgun development, various types, ammunition, and related subjects. Covers gun care, safety, and use in hunting fields or on skeet or trap ranges.

Shotguns by Keith, by E. Keith. Stackpole Books, Harrisburg, Pa., 1967. 307 pp., illus. A new edition, $7.95.

Guns and their accessories from history to ornamentation, their ammunition, and the practical use of American, English and European arms.

Skeet Shooting with D. Lee Braun, Robt. Campbell, ed. Grosset & Dunlap, N.Y., 1967. 160 pp., illus. $4.95.

Thorough instructions on the fine points of Skeet shooting.

Sure-Hit Shotgun Ways, by F. E. Sell, Stackpole Books, Harrisburg, Pa., 1967. 160 pp., illus. $5.95.

An expert with the scatter gun uncomplicates its effective use in every field, gives quick-skill methods for the sportsman.

Trapshooting with D. Lee Braun and the Remington Pros., ed. by R. Campbell. Remington Arms Co., Bridgeport, Conn., 1969. 157 pp., well illus., paper covers. $2.95.

America's masters of the scattergun give the secrets of professional marksmanship.

GLOSSARY FOR GUNNERS

Action Breech mechanism of a gun, by which it is loaded and unloaded.

Air Space Space in a loaded cartridge case not occupied by powder or bullet base.

Anvil In a primer or cartridge case, a fixed point against which the priming mixture is compressed, and thereby detonated, by the action of the firing pin.

Ball Earlier term for "bullet," and still used in some military terminology.

Ballistics Science of projectiles in motion.

Barrel The part(s) of a gun through which passes the bullet or shot, traveling from breech to muzzle.

Base Wad Compressed paper or other material inside a shotshell, varying in size and form.

Battery Cup Type of shotshell ignition form in which the cap or primer is held.

Belted Case Cartridge case with a band or belt at base, just ahead of extractor groove, and on which case (otherwise "rimless") positions in rifle chamber. See "Headspace."

Black Powder A mixture of charcoal, sulphur and saltpeter used as a propellant. Gives off much smoke when burned. See "Smokeless Powder."

Bore The inside of the barrel of a gun.

Bore Diameter In rifled arms, the diametrical measurement between tops of lands.

Breech Bolt The part of a breech that resists the rearward force of the combustion that occurs when a cartridge is fired.

BT Boat-tail, referring to the base taper given certain bullets to give them greater efficiency at long ranges.

Bullet The projectile *only*, not to be applied to the cartridge, which see. See also "Ball."

Bullet Mould Metallic device with a cavity(s) into which molten lead (or lead alloy) can be poured and allowed to harden into the projectile.

Caliber Bore or groove diameter expressed (in English) in decimals of an inch, otherwise in the metric system. Frequently compounded to indicate powder capacity of cartridge case; to show date of adoption; to show case length or to show proprietor, etc. E.g., 30-40, 30-06, 8x57mm or 375 Holland & Holland.

Cannelure Circumferential groove(s) around a bullet or cartridge case. In the latter refers to extractor groove, in lead bullets the lubrication grooves, in jacketed bullets the expansion point and/or where case is crimped.

Caplock Used of a muzzleloading gun whose ignition system employs a percussion cap, a small thimble-like metal cup containing a detonating mixture. This cup, placed on a "nipple," transmits flame to the powder charge when struck by the gun's hammer.

Cartridge A complete round of ammunition, made up, simply, of a cartridge case, primer, bullet (or shot) and powder.

Cartridge Case Commonly, the brass or copper envelope that contains powder, primer and projectile, but applicable to shotshells, too, whether of all brass (not common), paper and metal or plastic and metal.

CF Centerfire (cartridges); those ignited by means of (generally) a separate and replaceable primer.

Chamber That part of the bore, at the breech, formed to accept the cartridge.

Choke The constriction of a shotgun bore at the muzzle to various degrees, designed to control pellet charge spread at the target.

Chronograph An instrument which measures the velocity of a projectile.

Clip See "Magazine."

Cordite A nitroglycerine smokeless powder used mainly in Great Britain.

Crimp The bending inward of the case mouth perimeter, in order to grip and hold the bullet, or to keep the shot in a paper case intact.

Cylinder In a revolver, a cartridge container that rotates (generally) around an axis parallel to and below the barrel.

Die In handloading ammunition, any of a number of tools used to size bullets or cases, seat bullets, etc.

Drams Equivalent Term used to indicate that a certain charge of smokeless powder gives ballistics equal to a stated volumetric charge of black powder.

Drift The bullet's movement to right or left, away from the line of the bore, caused by bullet rotation or spin.

Drilling A three-barrel gun, popular in Europe, which usually combines smoothbore and rifled barrels.

Ejector Correctly the device(s) at the barrel breech or within the action that forcibly expels the fired case from the gun. See "Extractor."

Energy In bullets, the amount of work done, at given ranges, expressed in foot pounds.

Erosion More or less gradual wearing away of rifling by combustion gas, heat and bullet friction.

"Everlasting" Case Brass cartridge case made from heavy stock, intended for extended reloading life.

Extractor Device that removes or partially removes the fired cartridge case from the chamber. See "Ejector."

Firing Pin A part of the action, actuated by the trigger, that hits the primer and fires the cartridge.

Flintlock Used of a muzzleloading gun fired by means of a piece of flint, held in the hammer or "cock" jaws, striking against a steel "frizzen." Incandescent particles of steel scraped from the frizzen fall into a "pan" holding powder. This ignited powder flames through the "touch-hole," thus firing the main charge.

Follower A metal platform in a clip or magazine that pushes the cartridges upward at the proper angle for feeding into the chamber.

Gas Check A cup (usually copper) used on the base of a lead bullet to protect it from hot powder gases.

Gauge Unit of bore measurement in shotguns, determined by the number of solid lead round balls, of the bore diameter, obtainable from one pound of lead. E.g., 12 gauge means a bore of such size that 12 balls of that size make a pound of lead.

Gilding Metal A copper-zinc alloy used as bullet jacket material; usually 5% to 10% zinc.

Grooves Spiral cuts in a bore which cause the bullet to spin as it travels down the barrel.

Groove Diameter In rifled arms, the diametrical measurement between bottoms of grooves.

Group Number of shots fired into a target (number and range optional), usually with one sight setting.

Hammer A part of the action (in some guns) actuated by the trigger. The hammer drives the firing pin against the primer, thus igniting the cartridge powder charge.

Hang-fires Cartridges which fire as long as several seconds after firing pin strikes primer.

H.P. Hollow point, a design feature of certain bullets. See "Mushroom."

Headspace For rimmed cartridges, the distance from the face of the breechblock to the barrel seat for the forward surface of the case rim. For a rimless bottleneck cartridge, the distance from the face of the breechblock to a predetermined point on the shoulder of the chamber. For rimless straight cartridges, the distance from the face of the breechblock to the shoulder or ledge in the chamber. Belted cases headspace on the forward edge of the belt.

Lands That portion of the bore remaining after the rifling or grooves have been cut.

Leading Lead deposited on bore by bullets passing through.

Magazine Device or reservoir to hold extra cartridges, of many types and names. "Clip," once reserved for the slender metal strip from which cartridges are stripped into a magazine well, now refers to separate, detachable magazines also, as with those for autoloading pistols, many rifles and shotguns.

Matchlock An early form of firearm in which the priming charge was ignited by a cord or "match" of slow-burning material.

M.C. Metal Case, a form of bullet completely covered forward with copper or copper alloy (usually) jacket. Generally a military bullet type, and also termed "solids," and F.M.J. (full metal jacketed).

Mid-Range Usually used in connection with trajectory, referring to a point midway between muzzle and target or game.

Misfires Cartridges which do not fire when firing pin strikes primers.

MRT Mid Range Trajectory. See above.

Mushroom The capacity of certain bullets to expand on or after impact, also the term given to some soft point or hollow point bullets. See "S.P." and "H.P."

Muzzle End of barrel opposite to breech; point from which bullet or shot leaves barrel.

Muzzle-Loader Gun loaded through the front end of the bore, using loose powder and ball (or shot) or paper cartridges.

M.E. Muzzle Energy. See "Energy."

M.V. Muzzle Velocity. See "Velocity."

Nipple On muzzle-loading guns, the small metal cone at the rear of the barrel (or cylinder) through which the flame from the percussion cap passes to ignite the powder charge.

Ogive The radius of the curve of the nose of a bullet, usually expressed in calibers.

O.P.E. Open Point Expanding, a term for bullets of hollow point form made by Western Cartridge Co.

Over-bore Capacity Condition in which the volume of a cartridge case exceeds the amount of powder which can most efficiently be burned.

Pan See "Flintlock."

Paradox Smoothbore gun in which the final few inches of barrel are rifled to increase efficiency of round ball or bullet use. Also called "Explora" and "Fauneta" guns by Westley Richards.

Patching, Cloth Used to form a gas seal around the projectile (round ball or conical bullet) of a muzzle-loading gun and engage the rifling.

Pattern Of pellets from a shotgun, usually expressed as so many pellets within a 30-inch circle at 40 yards.

Percussion Cap Small metallic cup containing fulminating material that explodes when struck by gun's hammer. See "Nipple."

Pistol Said by some to derive from Pistoia, an early gun making center in Italy. Any small, concealable, short-barreled (2"-10") hand weapon, generally *not* a revolver.

Pressure The gas pressure generated in a cartridge on its being fired, usually expressed in (greatest) pounds per square inch (p.s.i.).

Primer In a centerfire cartridge, the small cup containing a detonating mixture, which is seated in a recess in the base of the case. In a rimfire, a similar mixture inside the folded rim of the case.

Proprietary Cartridge One developed and sold exclusively by one business organization.

Ramrod Rod, of wood or metal, used to force home the projectile in a muzzle-loading gun and sometimes to hold cleaning implements.

Rebated Rim Type of cartridge case rim smaller in diameter than the case is at a point just forward of the extractor groove.

Recoil The backward thrust of a gun caused by the reaction to the powder gases pushing the bullet forward.

Revolver A multi-shot handgun, using a revolving cylinder as a cartridge container.

RF Rimfire cartridges. Those containing their primer mixture in the rim, which is where they are struck by the firing pin.

Rifling Spiral grooving cut into the bore of rifles and handguns to impart spin to their bullets, thus assuring point-on flight and accuracy.

Rim The projecting edge of the base or "head" of certain cartridges.

Rook Cartridge Low powered cartridge developed in England for shooting pest birds and animals.

Shot Lead or lead-alloy spheres used as projectiles in smoothbore guns.

Shotgun A smoothbore gun using cartridges loaded with shot.

Shoulder The sloping portion of a bottleneck cartridge case that joins the body and neck.

Sizing In handloading cartridges, sizing (or resizing) brings the fired cartridge case back to the (full or partial) dimensions of the new or unfired case. Bullets are also sized.

Smokeless Powder Gunpowder which gives off almost no smoke when burned. See "Black Powder." Usually made by nitrating and otherwise chemically treating purified cotton waste.

S.P. Soft Point, a term used for bullets with partial metal jacketing, having some lead exposed at the front.

Trajectory Curved path of bullet in flight, a parabola.

Twist Angle of the rifling relative to the axis of the bore. Usually uniform, and expressed in turns or part-turns in so many inches. Less common, "progressive" or "gain" twist, usually starting at a rate at breech that becomes gradually faster.

Velocity Projectile speed, usually measured in feet per second (f.p.s.) at the muzzle and other distances such as 100 yards, 200 yards, etc.

Vent Orifice through the nipple.

Wad A disc of paper, felt, plastic or other material used in shotshells; sometimes in metallic cases, too, but not commonly today.

   a. Filler Wad—placed between the powder and card or Nitro wad to cushion the shot from the thrust of the hot powder gases, and to bring the shot to the proper height for correct crimping.

   b. Over-powder Wad—placed between powder and filler wads, sometimes called Nitro wads.

   c. Top Wad—thin card placed on top of the shot in roll crimp shells—star crimp shells do not require a top wad.

   d. Base Wad—these are permanently built into the shell at the base to hold the paper tube to the brass and give added support to the thin brass wall.

Wheel-lock Used of a muzzleloading gun fired by means of a piece of flint or pyrites, held in the hammer jaws, which is held over a serrated steel wheel. This wheel, set in motion by a tensioned spring, protrudes through the bottom of the "pan" (wherein powder has been placed) and bears against the flint. Sparks are created, as in the flintlock, and the gun is fired by a flame passing through the touch-hole.

Wildcat Cartridge designed by a private experimenter; not available as a factory-loaded round.

WCF Winchester Center Fire.

WRF Winchester Rim Fire.

Zero That sight setting which gives bullet group desired, and from which subsequent changes in sight settings will be made.

Late news! Champlin is now producing a very handsome over-under 12-gauge shotgun in de luxe grade that will sell in the $600-plus range. This will include stocks to the customer's dimensions, chokes and barrel length to order, etc. Our sample of the new Champlin double is a Skeet gun that's beautifully done—and it shoots very well indeed.

Directory of the Arms Trade

AMMUNITION (Commercial)

Alcan Shells, Inc., 3640 Seminary Rd., Alton, Ill. 62002
Amron Corp., 525 Progress Ave., Waukesha, Wis. 53186
Cascade Cartridge Inc., See Omark
Federal Cartridge Co., 2700 Foshay Tower, Minneapolis, Minn. 55402
Frontier Cartridge Co., Inc., Box 906, Grand Island, Neb. 68801
Omark-CCI, Inc., Box 856, Lewiston, Ida. 83501
Remington Arms Co., Bridgeport, Conn. 06602
Service Armament, 689 Bergen Blvd., Ridgefield, N.J. 07657
Speer-DWM, Box 896, Lewiston, Ida. 83501
Super-Vel Cartridge Co., Box 40, Shelbyville, Ind. 46176
Weatherby's, 2781 E. Firestone Blvd., South Gate, Calif. 90280
Winchester-Western, East Alton, Ill. 62024

AMMUNITION (Custom)

Ammodyne, Box 1589, Los Angeles, Calif. 90053
B&K Custom Rel. Serv., Lake 13, Farwell, Mich. 48622
Bill Ballard, 118½ Clark Ave., Billings, Mont. 59102
Jerry & Betty Bird, Box 10183, Corpus Christi, Tex. 78410
Caldwell's Loading Serv., 1314 Monroe Dr., N.E., Atlanta, Ga. 30306
Russell Campbell, 219 Leisure Dr., San Antonio, Tex. 78201
James F. Carr, White River, S. D. 57579
Cumberland Arms, 1222 Oak Dr., Manchester, Tenn. 37355
Custom Ammo & Gunsmithing, 390 S. Main, Moab, Utah 84532
E. W. Ellis Sport Shop, RFD 1, Box 139, Corinth, N.Y.
Ellwood Epps, 80 King St., Clinton, Ont., Canada
Steve Filipiak, 1270 So. Raleigh, Denver, Colo. 80219
Garrett's Sporting Goods, 195 So. Oakdale, Kankakee, Ill. 60901
R. H. Keeler, 1304 S. Oak, Port Angeles, Wash. 98362
KWT Inc., 710 Cooper-Foster Pk. Rd., Lorain, O. 44053 (tungsten bullets)
Dean Lincoln, 390 S. Main, Moab, Utah 84532
Pat B. McMillan, 4908 E. Indianola, Phoenix, Ariz. 85018
Mansfield Gunshop, Box 83, New Boston, N.H. 03070
Man-Tol Shells, Box 134, Bunnell, Fla. 32010
Moody's Reloading Serv., 2108 Broadway, Helena, Mont. 59601
Numrich Arms Corp., 203 Broadway, W. Hurley, N.Y. 12491
Robert Pomeroy, 45 Wyoming, Waterbury, Conn. 06706 (custom shells)
Sanders Cust. Gun Serv., 2358 Tyler Lane, Louisville, Ky. 40205
Shooter's Service & Dewey, Inc., Clinton Corners, N.Y. 12514
Shot Shell Components, 365 So. Moore, Lakewood, Colo. 80226
Super Vel Cartridge Corp., Shelbyville, Ind. 46176
3-D Co., Inc., Box 4411, Lincoln, Neb. 68504
James C. Tillinghast, Box 568, Marlow, N.H. 03456
Tri-Test Munitions Co., RFD 1, Box 201, Richfield, Wis. 53076
True-Blue Co., 1400 E. Palmer Ave., Glendale, Calif. 91205 (blanks)
"W" Cases, Rte. 1, Box 1018, Carnation, Wash. 98014
Walmax Inc. (See True-Blue)
Wanda Cartridge Co., P.O. Box 45901, Houston, Tex. 77045
Hugh R. Wells, Rte. 1, Box 1018, Carnation, Wash. 98014

AMMUNITION (Foreign)

Abercrombie & Fitch, Madison at 45th St., New York, N.Y. 10017
Ammodyne, Box 1859, Los Angeles, Calif. 90053 (RWS)
Canadian Ind. Ltd. (C.I.L.), Box 10, Montreal, Que., Canada
Centennial Arms Co., 3318 W. Devon Ave., Chicago, Ill. 60645 (Hirtenberg, Austrian)
Colonial Ammunition Co., Box 8511, Auckland, New Zealand
DWM, Speer Prods. Inc., Box 641, Lewiston, Ida. 83501
Gevelot of Canada, Box 1593, Saskatoon, Sask., Canada

Hudson, 52 Warren, New York, N. Y. 10007
Hy-Score Arms Co., 200 Tillary, Brooklyn, N.Y. 11201
Imperial Chemical Ind., 488 Madison Ave., N.Y., N.Y. 10022
S. E. Lazlo, 200 Tillary, Brooklyn, N.Y. 11201
NORMA-Precision, South Lansing, N.Y. 14882
Oregon Ammo Service, Box 19341, Portland, Ore. 97219
Stoeger Arms Corp., 55 Ruta Ct., So. Hackensack, N.J. 07606
James C. Tillinghast, Box 568, Marlow, N.H. 03456

ANTIQUE ARMS DEALERS

Robert Abels, 157 E. 64th St., N.Y., N.Y. 10021 (Catalog $1.00)
Ed Agramonte, 41 Riverdale Ave., Yonkers, N.Y. 10701
Antique Firearms Co., 206 Wilshire Blvd., Wilson, N.C. 27893
Armoury Inc., Rte. 25, New Preston, Conn. 06777
F. Bannerman Sons, Inc., Box 126, L.I., Blue Point, N.Y. 11715
Wm. Boggs, 1783 E. Main, Columbus, Ohio 43205
Ellwood Epps Sporting Goods, 80 King St., Clinton, Ont., Canada
Farris Muzzle Guns, 1610 Gallia St., Portsmouth, Ohio 45662
A. A. Fidd, Diamond Pt. Rd., Diamond Pt., N.Y. 12824
N. Flayderman & Co., Squash Hollow, New Milford, Conn. 06776
Herb Glass, Bullville, N.Y. 10915
Gold Rush Guns, Shop 1, 2211 Clement St., San Francisco, Cal. 94121
Gold Rush Guns, Shop 2, P.O. Box 33, Afton, Va. 22920
Goodman's for Guns, 1104 Olive St., St. Louis, Mo. 63101
Griffin's Guns & Antiques, R.R. 4, Peterboro, Ont., Canada
The Gun Shop, 6497 Pearl Rd., Cleveland, O. 44130
Heritage Firearms Co., 27 Danbury Rd., Rte. 7, Wilton, Conn. 06897
Holbrook Arms Museum, 12953 Biscayne Blvd., N. Miami, Fla. 33161
Ed Howe, 2 Main, Coopers Mills, Me. 04341
Jackson Arms, 6209 Hillcrest Ave., Dallas, Tex. 75205
Jerry's Gun Shop, 9220 Ogden Ave., Brookfield, Ill. 60513
Wm. M. Locke, 3607 Ault Pk. Rd., Cincinnati, O. 45208
John J. Malloy, Briar Ridge Rd., Danbury, Conn. 06810
Charles W. Moore, R.D. 2, Schenevus, N.Y. 12155
Museum of Historical Arms, 1038 Alton Rd., Miami Beach, Fla. 33139
National Gun Traders, Inc., Box 776, Miami, Fla. 33135
New Orleans Arms Co., Inc., 240 Chartres St., New Orleans, La. 70130
Old West Gun Room, 3509 Carlson Blvd., El Cerrito, Cal. 94804 (write for list)
Pioneer Guns, 5228 Montgomery, Norwood, O. 45212
Powell & Clements Sporting Arms, 210 E. 6th St., Cincinnati, O. 45202
Glode M. Requa, Box 35, Monsey, N.Y. 10952
Martin B. Retting Inc., 11029 Washington, Culver City, Calif. 90230
Ridge Guncraft, Inc., 234 N. Tulane Ave., Oak Ridge, Tenn. 37830
San Francisco Gun Exch., 74 Fourth, San Francisco, Calif. 94103
Santa Ana Gunroom, 1638 E. 1st St., Santa Ana, Calif. 92701
Ward & Van Valkenburg, 402-30th Ave. No., Fargo, N. Dak. 58102
M. C. Wiest, 234 N. Tulane Ave., Oak Ridge, Tenn. 37830
Yeck Antique Firearms, 579 Tecumseh, Dundee, Mich. 48131

BULLET & CASE LUBRICANTS

Alpha-Molykote, Dow Corning Corp., 45 Commerce Dr., Trumbull, Ct. 06601
Birchwood-Casey Co., Inc., 7900 Fuller Rd., Eden Prairie, Minn. 55343 (Anderol)
Bullet Pouch, Box 4285, Long Beach, Calif. 90804 (Mirror-Lube)
Chopie Tool & Die Co., 531 Copeland, La Crosse, Wis. 54601 (Black-Solve)
Cooper-Woodward, Box 972, Riverside, Cal. 92502 (Perfect Lube)
Green Bay Bullets, 233 N. Ashland, Green Bay, Wis. 54303 (EZE-Size case lube)
Herter's, Inc., Waseca, Minn. 56903 (Perfect Lubricant)
Javelina Rifle Supply, Box 337, San Bernardino, Cal. 92402 (Alox beeswax)
Jet-Aer Corp. 100 Sixth Ave., Paterson, N.J. 07524
Lenz Prod. Co., Box 1226, Sta. C, Canton, O. 44708 (Clenzoil)
Lyman Gun Sight Corp., Middlefield, Conn. 06455 (Size-Ezy)

Micro Shooter's Supply, Box 213, Las Cruces, N. Mex. 88001 (Micro-Lube)
Nutec, Box 1187, Wilmington, Del. 19899 (Dry-Lube)
Pacific Gunsight Co., Box 4495, Lincoln, Neb. 68504
Phelps Rel. Inc., Box 4004, E. Orange, N.J. 07019
RCBS, Inc., Box 1919, Oroville, Calif. 95965
SAECO Rel. Inc., 726 Hopmeadow St., Simsbury, Conn. 06070
Scientific Lubricants Co., 3753 Lawrence Ave., Chicago, Ill. 60625
Shooters Accessory Supply (SAS), Box 250, N. Bend, Ore. 97459
Sports Distr. Co., Rte. 1, Rapid City, S.D. 57701 (Reloader No. 7)

CHOKE DEVICES & RECOIL ABSORBERS

A & W Engineering, 6520 Rampart St., Houston, Tex. 77027 (shotgun diverter)
Arms Ingenuity Corp., Box 1, Weatogue, Conn. 06089 (Jet-Away)
Contra-Jet, 7920 49th Ave. So., Seattle, Wash. 98118
Dahl's Gun Shop, Rt. 2, Billings, Mont. 59101
Edwards Recoil Reducer, 269 Herbert St., Alton, Ill. 62002
Emsco Chokes, 101 Second Ave., S.E., Waseca, Minn. 56093
Herter's, Inc., Waseca, Minn. 56093. (Vari-Choke)
Lyman Gun Sight Co., Middlefield, Conn. 60455 (Cutts Comp.)
C. R. Pedersen & Son, Ludington, Mich. 49431 (Sha-Cul Brake)
Pendleton Dekickers, 1200 S. W. Hailey Ave., Pendleton, Ore. 97801
Poly-Choke Co., Inc., Box 296, Hartford, Conn. 06101
St. Louis Precision Products, 902 Michigan Ave., St. Louis, Mich. 48880 (Gun-Tamer)

CHRONOGRAPHS AND PRESSURE TOOLS

A & W Eng., 6520 Rampart St., Houston, Tex. 77027 (press. tool)
Avtron, 10409 Meech Ave., Cleveland, Ohio, 44105
B-Square Co., Box 11281, Ft. Worth, Tex. 76110
Chronograph Specialists, P.O. Box 132, Stanton, Calif. 90680
Herter's, Waseca, Minn. 56093
ITCC, 2879 Cinnabar, Phoenix, Ariz. 85028
Micro-Sight Co., 242 Harbor Blvd., Belmont, Calif. 94002 (Techsonic)
Oehler Research, P.O. Box 9135, Austin, Tex. 78756
York-Cantrell, 30241 Rosebriar, St. Clair Shores, Mich. 48082 (press. tool)

CLEANING & REFINISHING SUPPLIES

ADSCO, Box 191, Ft. Kent, Me. 04743 (stock finish)
Ed Agramonte, 41 Riverdale Ave., Yonkers, N.Y. 10701 (Ed's cold blue)
Allied Products Co., 734 N. Leavitt, Chicago, Ill. 60612 (Cor-O-Dex)
Ammodyne, Box 1589, Los Angeles, Cal. 90053 (Gun Kote)
Backus Co., 411 W. Water St., Smethport, Pa. 16749 (field gun-cleaner)
Birchwood-Casey Chem. Co., 7900 Fuller Rd., Eden Prairie, Minn. 55343 (Anderol, etc.)
Bisonite Co., Inc., Box 84, Buffalo, N.Y. 14217
Jim Brobst, 299 Poplar St., Hamburg, Pa. 19526 (J-B Compound)
Geo. Brothers, Great Barrington, Mass. 01230 (G-B Linspeed Oil)
Browning Arms, Rt. 4, Box 624-B, Arnold, Mo. 63010
Bullet Pouch, Box 4285, Long each, Cal. 90804 (Mirror Lube)
Burnishine Prod. Co., 8140 N. Ridgeway, Skokie, Ill. 60076 (Stock Glaze)
C&R Distr. Corp., 449 E. 21st So., Salt Lake City, Utah 84115
Cherry Corners Gun Shop, Rte. 1, Lodi, Ohio 44254 (buffing compound)
Chopie Tool & Die Co., 531 Copeland, La Crosse, Wis. 54601 (Black-Solve)
Clenzoil Co., Box 1226, Sta. C, Canton, O. 44708
Corrosion Reaction Consultants, Inc., Dresher, Pa. 19025 (Mask)
Custom Industries, 18900 Detroit Ave., Lakewood, O. 44107
Dex-Kleen, Box 509 Des Moines, Ia. 50302 (gun wipers)
Dri-Slide, Inc., Industrial Park, Fremont, Mich. 49412
Dry Film Gun Coatings, 1521—43rd St., W. Palm Beach, Fla. 33407
Electromation Comp. Corp., 11 Lincoln St., Copiague, N.Y. 11726 (ultrasonic cleaning tank)
F & J Derusting Co., Inc., 247 Westcott Dr., Rahway, N.J. 07065
Forty-Five Ranch Enterpr., Box 1080, Miami, Okla. 74354
Frye Industs., 1318 N. Broadway, Santa Maria, Cal. 93454
Fur Fame Bait Co., Route 1, Lindsay, O. 43442 (U.S. Bbl. Blue)
Gun-All Products, Box 244, Dowagiac, Mich. 49047
Percy Harms Corp., 7349 N. Hamlin, Skokie, Ill. 60076
Frank C. Hoppe Div., P.O. Box 97, Parkesburg, Pa. 19365
Hunting World, 247 E. 50th St., N.Y., N.Y. 10022 (P-H Safari Kit)
Jet-Aer Corp., 100 Sixth Ave., Paterson, N.J. 07524 (blues & oils)
Knox Laboratories, 2335 S. Michigan Ave., Chicago, Ill. 60616
LPS Res. Labs. Inc., 2050 Cotner Ave., Los Angeles, Calif. 90025
Carl Lampert Co., 2639 So. 31st St., Milwaukee, Wis. 53215 (gun bags)
LEM Gun Spec., Box 31, College Park, Ga. 30337 (Lewis Lead Remover)
Liquid Wrench, Box 10628, Charlotte, N.C. 28201 (pen. oil)
Lynx-Line Gun Products, Box 3985, Detroit, Mich. 48227
Marble Arms Co., 1120 Superior, Gladstone, Mich. 49837
Micro Sight Co., 242 Harbor Blvd., Belmont, Ca. 94002 (bedding)
Mill Run Prod., 1360 W. 9th, Cleveland, O. 44113 (Brite-Bore Kits)
Mint Luster Cleaners, 1102 N. Division, Appleton, Wis. 54911
Mistic Metal Mover, Inc., R.R. 2, P.O. Box 336, Princeton, Ill. 61356
Mitchell Chemical Co., Wampus Lane, Milford, Conn. (Gun Guard)
New Method Mfg. Co., Box 175, Bradford, Pa. 16701 (gun blue)
Numrich Arms Co., West Hurley, N.Y. 12491 (44-40 gun blue)
Nutec, Box 1187, Wilmington, Del. 19899 (Dry-Lube)
Outers Laboratories, Onalaska, Wis. 54650 (Gunslick kits)
R.E.I., 101 Wolpers, Park Forest, Ill. 60466 (whale oil lube)
Radiator Spec. Co., Charlotte, N.C. 28201 (liquid wrench)
Realist Inc., N. 93 W. 16288 Megal Dr., Menomonee Falls, Wis. 53051

Reardon Prod., 323 N. Main St., Roanoke, Ill. 61561 (Dry-Lube)
Riel & Fuller, 423 Woodrow Ave., Dunkirk, N.Y. 14048 (anti-rust oil)
Rig Products Co., Box 279, Oregon, Ill. 61061 (Rig Grease)
Rocket Chemical Co., Inc., 5390 Napa St., San Diego, Calif. 92110 (WD-40)
Rusteprufe Labs., Box 333, Sparta, Wis. 54656
Seatex Corp., 6400 Westpark Dr., Houston, Tex. 77027
Service Armament, 689 Bergen Blvd., Ridgefield, N. J. 07657 (Parker-Hale)
Sheldon's Inc., Box 508, Antigo, Wis. 54409 (shotgun brushes)
Shooter's Serv. & Dewey (SS&D), Clinton Corners, N.Y. 12514
Silicote Corp., Box 359, Oshkosh, Wis. 54901 (Silicone cloths)
Silver Dollar Guns, 7 Balsam St., Keene, N.H. 03431 (silicone oil)
A. D. Soucy, Box 191, Ft. Kent, Me. 04743 (stock finish)
Southeastern Coatings, Inc., (SECOA), Bldg. 132, P.B.I. Airport, W. Palm Beach, Fla. 33406
Sportsmen's Labs., Inc., Box 732, Anoka, Minn. 55303 (Gun Life lube)
Sun Ray Chemicals, 371-30th Ave., San Francisco, Calif. 94121
Taylor & Robbins, Box 164, Rixford, Pa. 16745 (Throat Saver)
C. S. Van Gorden, 120 Tenth Ave., Eau Claire, Wis. 54701 (Instant Blue)
WD-40 Co., 5390 Napa St., San Diego, Ca. 92110
W&W Mfg. Co., Box 365, Belton, Mo. 64012 (shotgun cleaner)
Webber Gage Division, 12900 Triskett Rd., Cleveland, O. 44111 (Luger oil)
West Coast Secoa, Inc., 3915 U.S. Hwy. 98 So., Lakeland, Fla. 33803
Williams Gun Sight, 7389 Lapeer Rd., Davison, Mich. 48423 (finish kit)
Winslow Arms Co., P.O. Box 578, Osprey, Fla. 33595 (refinishing kit)
Woodstream Corp., P.O. Box 327, Lititz, Pa. 17543 (Mask)

COMPONENTS—BULLETS, POWDER, PRIMERS

Accuracy Bullet Co., 2443 41st St., San Francisco, Calif. 94116 (Perfecast bullets)
Alcan, 3640 Seminary Rd., Alton, Ill. 62002
Bahler Die Shop, Box 386, Florence, Ore. 97439 (17 cal. bull.)
Lee Baker, Box 65786, Los Angeles, Calif. 90000 (17 cal. bull.)
Joe J. Balickie, 409 Rose Lane, Raleigh, N.C. 27607
Ballistic Research Industries, 116 N. Main, Sebastopol, Cal. 95472 (12 ga. Sabot bullets)
Barnes Bullets Inc., 318 Rosevale Rd., Grand Junction, Colo. 81501
Bitterroot Bullet Co., Box 412, Lewiston, Ida. 83501
Centrix, 2116 N. 10th Ave., Tucson, Ariz. 85705
Clerke Recreation Prods., Inc., 2060 Broadway, Santa Monica, Ca. 90404 (Lapua bullets)
Curry Bullet Co., 4504 E. Washington Blvd., Los Angeles, Calif. 90022
Division Lead, 7742 W. 61 Pl., Summit, Ill. 60502
DuPont, Explosives Dept., Wilmington, Del. 19898
Forty Five Ranch Enterprises, Box 1080, Miami, Okla. 74354
Godfrey Reloading Supply, P.O. Box 12, Alton, Ill. 62004
G. J. Godwin, 455 Fox Lane, Orange Park, Fla. 32073 (case bullets)
Green Bay Bullets, 233 No. Ashland, Green Bay, Wis. 54303 (lead)
Frank A. Hemsted, Box 281, Sunland, Calif. 91040
Hercules Powder Co., 910 Market St., Wilmington, Del. 19899
Herter's, Waseca, Minn. 56093
Hi-Precision Co., Box 121, Orange City, Ia. 51041
B. E. Hodgdon, Inc., 7710 W. 50th Hwy., Shawnee Mission, Kans. 66202
Hornady Mfg. Co., Box 1848, Grand Island, Neb. 68801
N. E. House Co., Middletown Rd., E. Hampton, Conn. 06424
Jurras Munition Corp., Box 163, Shelbyville, Ind. 46176
L. L. F. Die Shop, 1281 Highway 99 North, Eugene, Ore. 97402
Lee's Precision Bullets, P.O. Box 65768, Los Angeles, Ca. 90065 (17 cal.)
Lyman Gun Sight Corp., Middlefield, Conn. 06455
Markell, Inc., 4115 Judah St., San Francisco, Calif. 94112
Meyer Bros., Wabasha, Minn. 55981 (shotgun slugs)
Miller Trading Co., 20 S. Front St., Wilmington, N.C. 28401
Norma-Precision, So. Lansing, N.Y. 14882
Northridge Bullet Co., P.O. Box 1208, Vista, Ca. 92083
Nosler Bullets, P.O. Box 25347, Portland, Ore. 97225
Oregon Ammo Service, Box 19341, Portland, Ore. 97219
Robert Pomeroy, 45 Wyoming Ave., Waterbury, Conn. 06706
Rainbow Prod., P.O. Box 75, Wishram, Wash. 98673 (bullets)
Remington-Peters, Bridgeport, Conn. 06602
S. W. M. Bullet Co., 1122 S. Cherry St., Port Angeles, Wash. 98362 (17 cal.)
Sanderson's, 724 W. Edgewater, Portage, Wis. 53901 (cork wad)
Sierra Bullets Inc., 421 No. Altadena Dr., Pasadena, Ca. 91107
Sisk Bullet Co., Box 398, Iowa Park, Tex. 76367
Speedy Bullets, Box 1262, Lincoln, Neb. 68501
Speer Products Inc., Box 896, Lewiston, Ida. 83501
C. H. Stocking, Hutchinson, Minn. 55350 (17 cal. bullet jackets)
Sullivan Arms Corp., 5204 E. 25th, Indianapolis, Ind. 46218
Super-Vel Cartr. Corp., 129 E. Franklin St., Shelbyville, Ind. 46176
Taylor Bullets, P.O. Box 21254, San Antonio, Tex. 78221
True-Blue Co., 1400 E. Palmer Ave., Glendale, Calif. 91205 (blanks)
James C. Tillinghast, Box 568, Marlow, N.H. 03456
Vitt & Boos, Sugarloaf Dr., Wilton, Conn. 06897
Walker Machine Tool, 4804 Pinewood Rd., Louisville, Ky. 40218
Walmax, Inc., 1400 E. Palmer Ave., Glendale, Calif. 91205 (blanks)
Williams Custom Guns, Rt. 3, Box 809, Cleveland, Tex. 77327 (17 cal.)
Winchester-Western, New Haven, Conn. 06504
F. Wood, Box 386, Florence, Ore. 97439 (17 cal.)
Xelex Ltd., Hawksbury, Ont., Canada (powder)
Zero Bullet Co., 7254 Farnum, Inkster, Mich. 48141